Birds of Mississippi

Birds of

University Press of Mississippi / Jackson

WILLIAM H. TURCOTTE

AND

DAVID L. WATTS

Mississippi

FOREWORD BY CHANDLER S. ROBBINS

Mississippi Department of Wildlife, Fisheries and Parks

02 01 00 99 4 3 2 1

The paper in this book meets the guidelines for permanence and durability of the Committee on Production Guidelines for Book Longevity of the Council on Library Resources.

Library of Congress Cataloging-in-Publication Data

Turcotte, W. H. (William H.)
Birds of Mississippi / by William H. Turcotte, David L. Watts; foreword by Chandler S. Robbins.
p. cm.
Includes bibliographical references (p.) and index.
ISBN 1-57806-110-5 (cloth : alk. paper)
1. Birds—Mississippi. I. Title.
QL684.M7T87 1999
598'.09762—dc21 98-26339
CIP

British Library Cataloging-in-Publication Data available

Photograph and illustration credits:

The Center for American History, The University of Texas at Austin, Prints and Photographs Collection, CN 00151, p. 5
Library of Congress (photograph by Dorothea Lange), p. 17
Mississippi Department of Archives and History, pp. 2, 3, 4, 6, 16, 17, 18, 23, 259, 290
Mississippi Museum of Natural Science, pp. 9, 106
Mississippi State University Archives, p. 19
U.S. Fish and Wildlife Service (photograph by Fred Broerman), p. 153
Sterling G. Clawson, p. 125
Lula Coffey, Jr., p. 10
Jane Everett, p. 81
Joe Lee, p. 188
William Y. Quisenberry, p. 312
Nell A. Sheldon, p. 8
W. H. Turcotte, pp. 23, 24, 25, 51, 53, 85, 98, 101, 171, 187, 197, 222, 230, 251, 272, 309, 370, 390
Lovett E. Williams, Jr., pp. 243, 245, 246

All other photographs are courtesy of the Mississippi Department of Wildlife, Fisheries and Parks.

Contents

Foreword

The Magnolia State now has its very own bird book. This labor of love was decades in the making by a native son, amateur turned professional, who has spent his whole life with the birds.

Centrally located in the Mid-South, with its feet in the saltwater of the Gulf of Mexico, Mississippi is strategically located to attract great hordes of migrants as they wing their way to and from the tropics. Mississippi also claims pelagic birds in the Gulf, and more than its share of vagrants from the West.

In the mid-1960s when I was looking for a bird expert to organize the fledgling Breeding Bird Survey in Mississippi, Bill Turcotte was my logical choice. He not only knew the birds of the state very well, he also knew who the experienced observers were in all parts of the state. He graciously agreed to serve in that capacity, and he continued to coordinate the Mississippi coverage for 15 years.

Drawing on his long experience, Bill has put his personal touch into many of the species accounts. He has probably found nests of more species in Mississippi than anyone else alive, and writes with authority about the birds and their habits. Not restricted by a fixed format, he gives special emphasis to historic accounts of endangered, threatened, and game species, drawing on his own experience with the Game and Fish Commission and the records in their files.

I especially enjoyed reading, with nostalgia, the chapter on the history of ornithology in Mississippi. Many of the pioneers in Mississippi ornithology were personal friends of mine—not Bartram and Audubon, of course, but pioneers of the 20th Century. My colleague Tom Burleigh always spoke with excitement of his years on the Mississippi coast. M. G. Vaiden, with whom I carried on a lively correspondence for years, built up an enviable collection of eggs of Mississippi birds in addition to his skin collection. Ben and Lula Coffey frequently left their Coffey Grounds in Memphis to explore their nearby homeland in Mississippi, often specializing on night birds. And it was my colleague Jake Valentine who initiated the work on Mississippi Sandhill Cranes.

It is a foregone conclusion that state bird books will be out of date before they are published—especially when they include distribution maps and cite extreme dates of arrival and departure. More importantly, this publication will stimulate further investigation by revealing gaps in knowledge. Up-to-date information on distribution, habitat use, and population trends is essential for protection and intelligent management of the landscape. This book sets the stage for conservation of bird life in Mississippi in the 21st Century.

Chandler S. Robbins
Biological Resources Division, U.S. Geological Survey

Preface

This book is about birds, people who like to study birds, and places where birds are found. It was begun more than 20 years ago. I started writing the species accounts, beginning with the owls and landbirds in checklist order. I knew then that most of the birds in addition to the state list would be coastal records of pelagics, waterbirds, shorebirds, and western species. Since 1962, the state checklist has grown from 317 to 390 species. Most, but not all, of these additional species have been coastal records.

During this period, there has been an ever increasing number of active and competent birders, ranging from feeder-watchers to amateur experts in field identification to professional ornithologists in academe. At the same time, there has been a proliferation of bird books and magazines. The main catalyst for stimulating interest in birds has been the availability of well-illustrated, pocket-sized field guides.

The Mississippi Ornithological Society (MOS), which was organized in 1955, and six National Audubon Society chapters organized around a core of MOS members have accelerated interest in birds in Mississippi. Published notes and records by members in *Audubon Field Notes, American Birds, MOS Newsletter,* and *The Mississippi Kite* (an MOS periodical) document most recent additions to the state bird list. Members have participated in June breeding bird surveys, winter eagle count surveys, and the more recent Neotropical bird migration study conducted in early May.

Popular interest in bird feeding has grown to proportions never anticipated. Many birds new to Mississippi have appeared first at feeders, particularly five species of western hummingbirds captured and identified by bird banders. Also, interest in providing housing for birds around homes and on bluebird trails is widespread.

Advances in color photography and audio and video recording seem almost unbelievable. These technologies are used widely by birders to confirm identification of new birds. The availability of good binoculars and spotting telescopes has advanced field identification of birds to a level of high proficiency among many amateur birders. With modern means of communication and transportation, birding has few boundaries.

My interest in birds started in Magee when I was about seven years old. I remember seeing a small, yellow bird in a neighbor's yard and found it dead the next day. I later discovered a "rain crow" sitting on a nest on an oak limb overhanging a path, and I watched it until the young were hatched. My older brother brought home some "snowbirds" shot with his new rifle. My father took me dove shooting and showed me my first Pileated Woodpecker. He called it an "Indian hen."

My family moved to Clinton in 1923, where I attended grammar school. In 1930, Edgar and George Anderson and I started collecting bird eggs. At times, we walked out in the country to visit Ben Whitfield, who had an egg collection in addition to his collection of gems and minerals. He gave us a blow pipe, made egg drills for us in his shop, gave us some data blanks, and showed us how to make a scientific collection.

At this stage, I confess we were learning about birds in hand with the aid of neighborhood boys, our slingshots, and air rifles. We progressed to collecting eggs of Eastern Wood-Pewee, Blue-gray Gnatcatcher, Painted Bunting, Blue Grosbeak, and Yellow-breasted Chat, until George and Edgar's mother clamped down on their wanderings, forcing us to divide our egg collection.

When I was 13, two older friends, Allen McEarly and Pettigrew Warren, gave me a set of Chester A. Reed landbird and waterbird pocket guidebooks. They introduced me to finding hawk, owl, and vulture nests by walking along creek swamps. During my high school years, I roamed the woods and fields around Clinton collecting sets of eggs, a few bird skins, and some specimens, which I mounted. In my senior year, Thomas Whitfield, George Anderson, and I journeyed in a stripped-down Model-T Ford to collect eggs of herons and Anhingas at several colonies in the Delta. I had obtained state and federal scientific collecting permits at age 15. During this time, I became acquainted with Ben B. Coffey Jr. and Frances A. Cook through our common interest in birds. They encouraged my interest and urged my participation in field trips in later years.

I am grateful to my parents, who never discouraged my early interest in birds, although my mother often fretted over the possibility of my falling out of trees or getting bitten by a snake. I *did* have some falls and close calls with snakes.

My lifetime career in wildlife conservation began after my sophomore year in college. I was offered summer employment as a taxidermist and as a field collection trainer on the Mississippi Game and Fish Commission–sponsored Plant and Animal Survey Project, the forerunner of the Mississippi Museum of Natural Science (MMNS). In the late 1930s, this work provided opportunities to travel on collecting trips and to meet and associate with people interested in wildlife and birds. During this time and later, I met Andrew Allison, Albert F. Ganier, Ben and Lula Coffey Jr., Merritt G. Vaiden, R. L. Caylor, John Frazier, R. M. Freeman, and Aldo Leopold on one of his visits to Mississippi. There were other early wildlife conservationists who gave me support and encouragement, especially Frances A. Cook and W. Felder Dearman. I am thankful for their support and guidance, which led to a career in wildlife management with the Mississippi Game and Fish Commission.

Birds have been an avocation for me. I have enjoyed my association with members of the MOS. I have never known a more compatible group with common interests. Their contributions to our knowledge of state birds is evident throughout this book. I thank all of them for their support and use of notes and records.

The collections and literature at the MMNS were made accessible throughout the preparation of this book. I especially thank Libby Hartfield and her staff for many courtesies and much help, and Erskine Gandy, former director of the MMNS, for his encouragement and use of his seasonal occurrence and distribution charts. To Mary Stevens, librarian, for obtaining reference material and word processing the bibliography—thanks. Also, Will McDearman and Bob Jones assisted with their knowledge of nomenclature.

Critical review of the species accounts by Jake Valentine Jr., Tom Imhof, and Marvin Davis resulted in needed additions, deletions, corrections, and much improvement in readability. I am indebted to their contributions.

Without David L. Watts, editor of *Mississippi Outdoors* magazine, the manuscript would be a tome gathering dust in my personal archives. He has been editor-in-chief, liaison for word processing, coauthor, and final polisher from the computer to completed manuscript. Thanks, "Sir David." I am grateful to Pauline Davis, Carla Evans, Billie Ellison, Jean Caraway, Nora Chapman, and Cheryl Phillips for typing and word processing through numerous revisions; Dorothy Brown Turcotte and Bill Pitts for their help in generating the many maps and charts; copyeditor Lisa DiDonato and production editor Anne Stascavage for preparing the manuscript for publication; and artist Sam Beibers for the beautiful drawings of birds used at the beginnings of chapters and throughout the species accounts.

I was encouraged to start writing this book by Erskine Gandy and Billy Joe Cross, former executive director of the Mississippi Game and Fish Commission. I began with interest and support from them and succeeding administrations. After my retirement from active service in 1979, the Department of Wildlife, Fisheries and Parks continued to support this project. I am particularly grateful to Bill Quisenberry, administrative assistant, who has been reliable and steadfast in supporting me. It is my hope that this book will be a contribution to our Wildlife Heritage Program.

It would be heresy not to credit the forerunners of the wildlife conservation movement that began in the early 1920s. Some, but not all, are credited in the following chapters. I would like to mention here the three brave and far sighted souls who personally borrowed money to fund and start Mississippi's wildlife conservation program, which was enacted by the legislature in 1932. They were Judge W. E. McIntyre Sr. of Brandon, Ben Stevens of Richton, and W. G. McGill of New Albany.

Finally, to all new and potential birders who read this: You will never find a more rewarding avocation during your lifetime than birding. And a final salute to my venerable 1940-model Smith-Corona, which remains steadfast, dust bunnies and all, and invulnerable to later technology.

William H. Turcotte
Richland, Mississippi

The History of Ornithology in Mississippi

Mississippi is at the geographic center of the Gulf South. It is bordered on the west by the Mississippi and Pearl Rivers, on the north by Tennessee, on the east by Alabama, and on the south by the Gulf of Mexico and Louisiana. Mississippi's central location in the Gulf area made it a stopping-off place for pioneer naturalists and explorers in their quests to open western frontiers for American colonists. Very little information is available from early French and Spanish explorations that details their encounters with and observations of wildlife in what would become Mississippi. Until about 1699, when the first white settlements appeared along the Mississippi Coast and other sections of the Gulf Coast, the state was unexplored wilderness. A dearth of information exists about birdlife found along the coast, in the Natchez District, and other inland areas. This condition persisted until about the time of William Bartram, one of America's earliest pioneer naturalist-explorers. His innate curiosity and diverse interest in plants, birds, early pioneer white settlements, and Indian communities contributed valuable information about the southern region's flora and fauna.

William Bartram (Doren 1928), a naturalist-explorer of the late colonial and early American period, traveled by boat and on horseback through the Carolinas, Georgia, and Florida (1765–1766) in search of new plant species. His later travels continued across Georgia and Alabama to Mobile (1775–1777). Bartram then went by boat from Mobile, past Dauphin Island, and on to Pearl Island in Louisiana. During his trip, he became ill and blinded by an eye infection, and he made no mention of his passage through waters off the Mississippi Coast. Bartram went across Lake Ponchartrain and Lake Maurepas, up the Amite River to Bayou Manchac, then traveled overland to the Mississippi River. From here, he went upriver to the White Bluffs of Natchez in August 1777. There he abandoned plans for traveling farther southwestward because of a persistent eye disorder.

On his return voyage through Mississippi waters, Bartram described the crossing in only two sentences without mention of birds or the coastal environment. Although a hiking trail in the DeSoto National Forest bears Bartram's name, he never set foot on the Mississippi Coast. William Bartram's discoveries and writings made him famous. Through his correspondence, he introduced Thomas Jefferson to Alexander Wilson and probably encouraged or enabled Wilson to later visit Natchez and Louisiana.

Sir William Dunbar of Natchez (1930), born of Scottish nobility, was a contemporary of Bartram. He studied as a

Above: Alexander Wilson on Horseback–Old Natchez Trace

Sir William Dunbar of the Natchez District was a scientist, inventor, and explorer. Around 1800, he helped open the door to the study of ornithology in Mississippi.

naturalist at King's College at Aberdeen. He came to Mississippi in 1773 from Pennsylvania and became well known as a scientist, inventor, and explorer of what later would be called the Louisiana Purchase. Through his connections and correspondence with Thomas Jefferson and a liaison with the secretary of the army, Dunbar helped with surveys and plans for the Louisiana Purchase in 1803. His scientific writings reflect broad interests in botany, geology, and astronomy—knowledge that he used in surveying and defining land boundaries and the geography of the region.

Dunbar's writings about wildlife and the surrounding virgin habitat no doubt invited the attention of pioneer American ornithologist Alexander Wilson. Wilson visited Dunbar's home, The Forest, nine miles south of Natchez, where he wrote an account of Carolina Parakeets attracted by the calls of his pet parakeet. Wilson traveled the length of the Natchez Trace and recorded the presence of parakeets at Bayou Pierre while carrying his pet bird on horseback. Leaving Natchez, Wilson spent parts of May and June of 1810 in Louisiana and made mention of Louisiana birds in his classic *American Ornithology* (1832). Dunbar lived during the heyday of colonial and territorial rule and died in 1810. He helped open the door for the study of birds in Mississippi.

Settlement in the Mississippi Territory outside of the Natchez District was underway before the War of 1812. Military roads along the Natchez Trace and elsewhere were improved or opened. Within a generation, the territory had become the states of Mississippi and Alabama. During the

It was at "The Forest," the home of William Dunbar near Natchez, that noted American ornithologist Alexander Wilson recorded Carolina Parakeets in 1810.

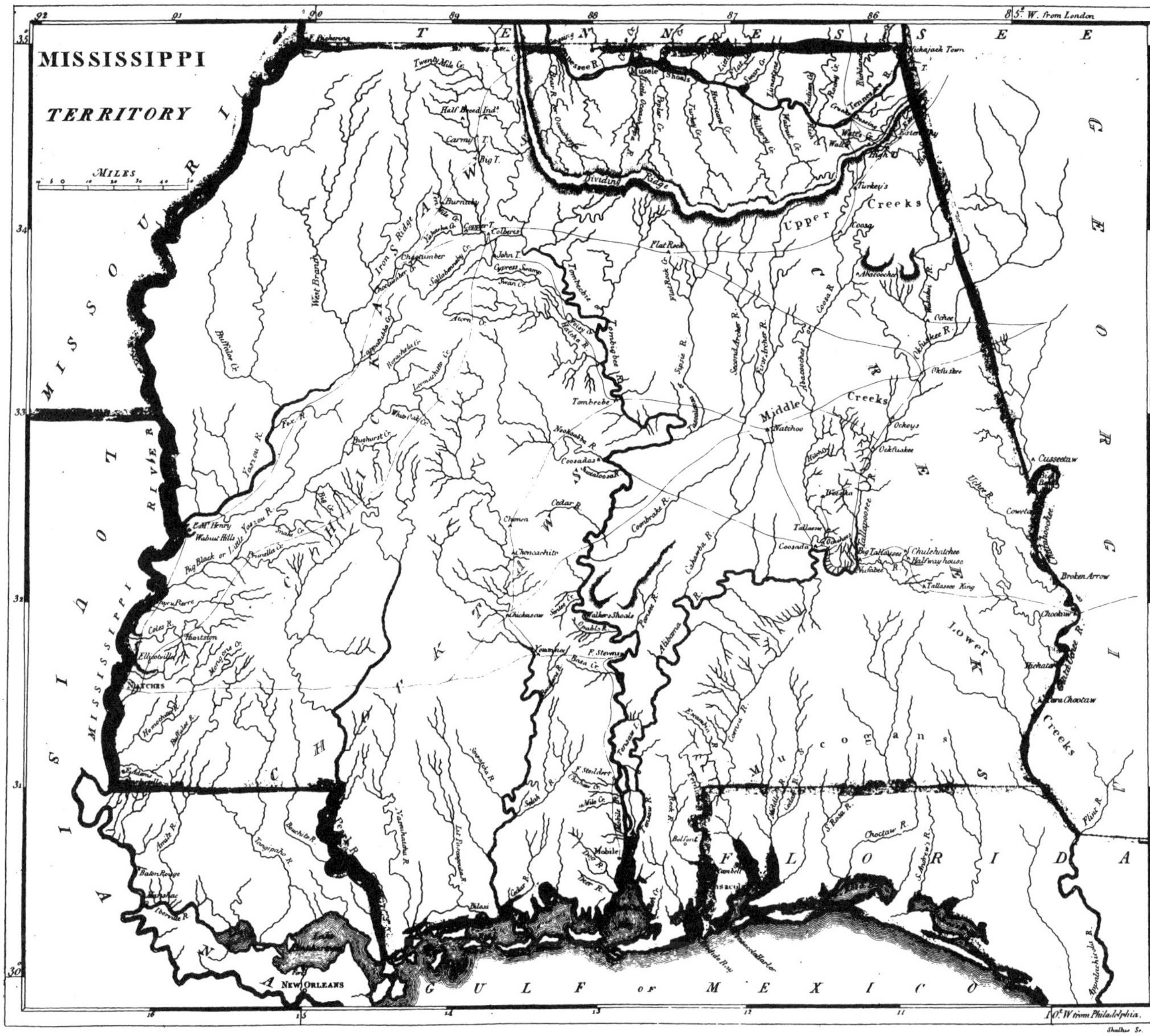

At the time of early settlement before Mississippi became a state in 1817, the Mississippi Territory encompassed what is now the states of Alabama and Mississippi.

administration of Andrew Jackson, the displacement of Native American tribes from their lands was forced through, which led to rapid settlement of the interior outside the Natchez District. The Creeks, Chickasaws, and Choctaws lost most of their lands under treaties forcing them to relocate west of the Mississippi River. Some Choctaws were rewarded and allowed to keep a portion of their land, provided they observed the white man's law.

After Mississippi became a state in 1817, two-thirds of the interior lands were opened for sale by land offices. Settlers from Georgia, the Carolinas, and the Appalachian region began claiming lands for subsistence farms. Soon, communities were formed bringing in artisans, professionals, lawyers, and businessmen, a few of whom had an interest in science and made valuable observations on the local flora and fauna. By 1830 Mississippi's statehood was well established.

The famous artist-naturalist John James Audubon eclipsed Alexander Wilson during the tumultuous times of the Mississippi Territory and early statehood. He contributed the first real literature based on scientific knowledge of American birds. His artistic skill, indomitable frontier spirit, and tenacity of purpose in painting and publishing his *Birds of America* brought him fame as the greatest frontier naturalist of his time.

Audubon traveled extensively and seldom stayed long in one place. He went on expeditions to Labrador and into Yellowstone country, exploring new frontiers in ornithology. Between expeditions, he returned to the Natchez District and his beloved Bayou Sara country in Louisiana's

John James Audubon visited Natchez and Woodville to tutor and teach violin and dance. During his stay at St. Francisville, Louisiana, and in the Natchez District, and later during his travels in the Yazoo Delta, the famous frontier artist and naturalist wrote about and drew many of the bird species he saw.

West Feliciana Parish, about 90 miles south of Natchez. Near St. Francisville, at the lower end of the Loess Bluff, he found a diversity of environments in upland and swampland habitats for observing and studying birds. While he resided at Oakley plantation, the society and atmosphere allowed Audubon the leisure time to paint many of the birds found in his folio of American birds and to write of birdlife for his *Ornithological Biography.*

Audubon's activities also extended to Natchez and Woodville in Wilkinson County. His writings on Mississippi birds are limited to the Natchez area, where he described seeing a White-headed Eagle pursuing a Fish Hawk at the waterfront. He also mentioned the Pewee Flycatcher, Mockingbird, the "Pride of China" trees, vultures along the streets, and Carrion Crows feeding at a refuse dump below the bluff. At the time, Natchez had a population of about 3000 people with mail deliveries three times a week. Audubon's visits to Natchez and Woodville were mainly social, for tutoring, or for business purposes. On one occasion he saw Indians selling Wild Turkeys and venison on the streets of Natchez.

On another expedition, Audubon described a visit to the mouth of the Yazoo River and False River above Vicksburg. He later visited the Coldwater River basin where he described a panther hunt by frontier settlers. Audubon, like Wilson, went by boat from Louisiana to Mobile but left no records of birds along the Mississippi Coast.

Eventually Audubon went to England to find an engraver for his drawings, and he journeyed to Scotland and France seeking subscriptions for the double-elephant folio of his drawings made from 1827–1838. He attained fame as an American frontiersman and artist-naturalist, captivating European audiences by his physical appearance and stamina. His last trip to Louisiana in 1837 was a boat trip from New Orleans along the Louisiana and Texas Coasts to Galveston. He died in 1851 at age 66, leaving a legacy of priceless bird artistry that was far ahead of his time.

Audubon's journals record in detail the hardships and joys experienced on journeys into wilderness areas during frontier times. He set the stage for further study and achievement in ornithology. Soon to follow were other ornithologists, including Nuttall, Brewer, Baird, Coues, Ridgeway, and others whose scientific discoveries and writings during the next half century contributed greatly to our knowledge of North American birds.

Gideon Lincecum (Rowland 1907) was a pioneer settler and founder of the city of Columbus. He was born in April 1793 and reared on the western frontier in the woods of Georgia. His parents were illiterate, and he learned Indian ways while growing up in the woods with Muskogee children as playmates. He learned their language, and at age 13, he had seven months of reading, writing, and arithmetic in a one-room school before the family moved westward. At age 15, he left the family farm to work as a clerk in a community store for several years. He gained a contract to sell books from a store that was left by the owner, who had returned to North Carolina for a year. He read avidly from books on natural history and medicine. When the owner returned, he was given a selection of books as a reward.

After volunteering and serving for several months in the War of 1812, he married. Much later he moved with his father's family and his young wife to Tuscaloosa, traversing unexplored wilderness and living off wild game, fish, nuts, and fruits as they moved from one camp to the next.

After a stay in Tuscaloosa, Lincecum left with his father and brothers, blazing a wagon train party of 36 people through uncharted wilderness. He settled on the Tombigbee River near the site of what is now Columbus. After setting up camp, Lincecum built a cabin with a dirt chimney while the party was living off the abundant fish and wildlife. He cut down about six acres of canebrakes for a corn field that would be needed to supply bread for the party after stores obtained from Indians were exhausted. The cane was cut down during the winter and left in place until the river backwater receded the following spring. After the mat of canes dried, it was burned in early May and rows of corn were planted with sharpened sticks in the rich soil and ashes. All the cultivation required was to knock down the green cane shoots several times, and the corn made a 300-bushel crop.

Dr. Gideon Lincecum was the founder of the city of Columbus, Mississippi, and was one of the founders of the state of Texas. Dr. Lincecum was a frontier explorer, settler, self-taught naturalist, and practitioner of botanical medicine. His autobiography contains much about the history of the time before white settlement in the South and the Southwest.

The settlement prospered, and Lincecum bought on credit a flatboat load of goods from a trader and opened a store at the site of present-day Columbus, selling goods to incoming settlers and trading products with Indians. The store business prospered. With his brothers he continued to hunt, explore, and fish in the swamps of the Tombigbee bottomlands, where waterfowl were found in abundance during the winter.

Lincecum was a keen observer of wildlife with what he described as his "discriminating powers," earned from his experience observing and living off the area's bountiful resources. While hunting waterfowl with his brother to supply the 36 people in the settlement, he aptly described swans, geese, and ducks.

"One was large, white, with black and brown spots on him, big as a brant [blue-morph Snow Goose]—pretty crown, bill narrow, red—too fishy for food duck [Red-breasted Merganser]." The other "was no larger than a Wild Pigeon, colors a little more brilliant, but the form, markings, male and female, precisely like a Mallard, the two curled, green feathers in the tail—everything the same." Was this a far northern breeding form of the Mallard with the same fate as the Eskimo Curlew, because it was too tame for guns? (I remember that my older brother kept miniature Mallards [English Callers] and raised them for live decoys. When training them, they were so tame they wallowed all over him and would get into crates by themselves to go to swimming water. This was in the late 1920s, when live decoys were legal for hunting ducks.)

Lincecum reported arrival of waterfowl "about the last of November in great variety—River Geese [Canadas], a few swans tarried several days, brants [blue-morph Snows], Snow Geese, sea geese [?], ducks of many types [divers], Mallards, 2 species of teal, and a black duck [Black Duck]." All are remarkably accurate descriptions.

While his business at Columbus prospered, he built a substantial home and housing for the stores of goods. The legislature appointed him to name county offices, appoint officers, and lease building lots. He appointed and organized a county court system. The sale of lots raised enough money to begin building schools in the growing community.

He moved to a river bend in Choctaw country, set up a business with an Indian partner, and built a substantial home and trading post where he learned the language, customs, and history of the Choctaw Nation. The Choctaws reserved for him the sole rights to hunting and fishing on a private reserve.

After four years of dealing in Indian trade in the settlement, he had a heart attack while hunting waterfowl. He was disabled over a period of seven years. His business partner was murdered, the store plundered, records destroyed, and he became destitute. While disabled, he had prepared himself to practice medicine by reviewing his medical library.

From 1832 to 1835, with his health restored, he was successful in the practice of medicine (Lincecum 1874a). He continued to hunt and fish in the Tombigbee bottomlands and adjacent western prairie lands. In 1832, he visited and later described a vast nesting colony of Passenger Pigeons, extending 15 miles along the virgin bottomland forest and up to two miles wide along the Tombigbee River north of Columbus. He also described passing beneath a vast roost of the pigeons extending over an area of about 50 square miles of mature upland forest. Lincecum (1874b) published an article about the Passenger Pigeon roost and nesting colony. It was written shortly before his death on November 28, 1873.

The wilderness travels of Lincecum were published in 1874 as personal memoirs written the year before his death. He also organized an extensive exploring trip over much of Texas, traveling on horseback in a small party. He continued exploring Texas frontier lands, traveling alone on horseback and living off the land for another year before settling down in Houston in 1848, where he lived until his death.

John Wesley Monette (Riley 1906), a physician and historian, lived in Washington in Adams County from 1821 until his death in 1851. He was born in Virginia in 1803 and educated at Chilicothe Ohio Academy, where he became proficient in natural science, literature, and the classics. In 1821 he began to study medicine under the direction of his physician father. He then obtained a medical degree at Transylvania University, Lexington, Kentucky. He began the practice of medicine in 1825 in Washington, where be became noted for applying and enforcing quarantine for yellow fever victims in the Natchez area, which proved to be highly successful. He accumulated and maintained a large personal library and spent much of his spare time writing on various medical subjects and other matters. In 1833 he began to write on the history and physical geography of the Mississippi Valley based on his knowledge of the Ohio region and the Lower Mississippi Valley region. His work on the Mississippi Valley history prior to and after the Louisiana Purchase was published by Harpers in 1846.

Monette's later unpublished, handwritten manuscripts on the geography of the Mississippi Valley are now in Clements Library at the University of Michigan. An appendix copied by Riley (1906) from the barely legible, yellowed manuscripts summarizes the scope and contents of Monette's books on physical geography. Monette's treatment of subject matter by river regions was unique for his time. Books 3 and 4 are particularly interesting for descriptions of the Yazoo River system, including the tributary streams, connecting bayous, and the oxbow lakes of the Delta. Monette described and related original alluvial soils and forest types in the Delta to natural seasonal flooding and elevations along stream bank levees, swamp ridges, wetter sites, and swamps. He described the original canebrakes along the stream levees as "dense undergrowth which is an infallible index to the best cotton land." His descriptions of virgin ecosystems, the topsoil (12–14 inches), canebrakes, and indigenous bottomland and upland forests are unique. He described the exploitation for cultivation of crops in the Delta and along the Loess Bluff and predicted the reclamation of most Delta land for agriculture by use of levees and interior drainage, much as exists today.

John Wesley Monette was a Natchez-area physician, historian, and geographer. In addition to medical subjects, he wrote about the flora and fauna of the Yazoo Basin and the bordering Loess Bluff.

In Book 4, Monette described the indigenous upland and lowland growths, listing and describing those species uncommon in other regions. Undergrowth and vines were also described. His description of canebrakes is interesting in that the underlying soils were deep and fertile, but highly erodible following cultivation of several crops. He described the height of giant cane (25–30 feet), its size and extent of growth, and the burning of a deadened canebrake "resembling a military engagement with musquetry." The virgin pine forests of southern Mississippi were described as a seemingly endless monotony that provided solitude for anyone traveling through them.

In Book 5, entitled *Zoology or Natural History of Birds and Animals,* lists and descriptions of mammals, amphibians, reptiles, and birds are included with detailed accounts of species deemed worthy of special notice.

Monette lists over 150 species of birds by common and scientific names. He deemed 20 species of landbirds and waterbirds worthy of "special notice," some of which he described from personal experience. The list contains many obsolete common and scientific names, and it reflects the lack of knowledge of many species on the western frontier. The omission of herons, gulls, terns, many shorebirds, and common landbirds shows his lack of knowledge and experience in the field identification of birds. On the other hand, 20 accounts of species reflect some personal observations worth mentioning. His account of the Ivory-billed Woodpecker describes the haunts, behavior, and feeding habits that must have resulted from sightings and first-hand knowledge, including his dissection of a specimen and the description of its musculature, tongue, and skeleton.

Monette quoted Wilson's account of the Wild (Passenger) Pigeon on its breeding grounds, but added a description of communal roosts, areas used by the birds while on feeding forays, with birds traveling 70–80 miles daily, then returning for the night. When neighboring food supplies became exhausted, the feeding flocks moved their roosts to another food source. His account of robins roosting in large numbers in canebrakes is interesting. I found no reference to grackles and blackbirds roosting in canebrakes with robins. There are historical and folkloric references to blackbird roosts in cane thickets, and "blackbird thrashing" with sticks and lights was practiced. The roosting of blackbirds in canebrakes may have helped to maintain them. Even today blackbirds are drawn to roost in thickets of bamboo in urban areas.

A. J. Brown (1964), a historian of the period 1834–1894, described blackbird roosts in "reed-cane brakes" of Newton County at the time of frontier settlement. He described a number of "reed-brakes" fed by one or more springs feeding a valley that became overgrown with reed-cane differing from that growing in the swamps. "They were very boggy places, covered with reed. . . . This invited the blackbirds to roost, and after the lapse of centuries, perhaps, this stream is filled up by these bird deposits, and becomes a dangerous quagmire, until after it is ditched, then it becomes a thing of beauty and profit—the most fruitful sources of corn in the county."

Nineteenth-century historians and geographers like Lincecum, Monette, and Brown should be appreciated for preserving many facts about the appearance of indigenous ecosystems, early settlements, conflict, reconstruction, exploitation, and development of natural and human resources. The activities of humans continue to define nature at the expense of wildlife. If we are to save endangered and threatened wildlife, even our songbirds, concerted actions must be taken to save habitat and the diverse ecosystems necessary for their life support. We will save a vital part of our natural heritage and ourselves only by actions to preserve and restore them for future generations.

After a turbulent start at statehood and a change of governors from George Poindexter to Walter Leake, the legislature held its first session in Jackson in 1822. By 1830, railroads were being constructed. The cotton economy had seen good and bad times. Divisive politics between plantation slaveholders and a majority of interior hill-country settlers continued until 1840. Plantation owners dominated the political scene, and controversy over the slavery issue continued until secession and the outbreak of the Civil War in 1861. The first capitol building, now known as the Old Capitol, was completed in 1841. Education for elementary and secondary schools lacked public support. Many private academies and small colleges were supported by religious groups. The legislature chartered The University of Mississippi in 1844, and it opened at Oxford in 1848. Mississippi remained a frontier area until late in the nineteenth century. However, cultural and scientific elements were present in the old Natchez District and were emerging in other parts of the state.

Bird literature was almost absent until 1854 when the legislature ordered the *Report on Agriculture and Geology of Mississippi.* State Geologist Benjamin Wailes (1854) included as a part of his report a list of 89 bird species found in the state, including some coastal birds.

The Civil War brought devastation to Mississippi and chaos to its agrarian economy. The political and economic turmoil lasted through Reconstruction and well into the twentieth century. A comprehensive railroad system was developed around the turn of the century, enabling the exploitation of the state's virgin timber resources. Numerous sawmills, cottonseed oil and textile mills, and railroads provided employment closely tied to agriculture. A system of tenant farming, or sharecropping, with its attendant soil erosion and depletion, led to exploitation of human resources. The cutover pinelands became blackened stump forests, purposely burned over for open range grazing by sheep or cattle. Deer, turkeys, and other game animals were almost depleted. Hardwood stands were mostly high graded for sawmills and firewood. Wildfire control was absent and large-scale fires were a way of life until conservation measures became necessary during the Great Depression.

Into this post-Reconstruction era came Andrew Allison, the first Mississippi ornithologist of distinction. Born in New Orleans, he attended Tulane University (1894–1900), obtaining a master's degree. Allison worked as a bacteriological analyst at the New Orleans waterworks and taught school in Louisiana and at Gloster and Ellisville in Mississippi. After his marriage in Ellisville in 1910, he was called to foreign mission service in China. He became an ordained minister in 1935 and returned to China, where he was imprisoned by the Japanese and repatriated in 1943. He again went to China and was taken prisoner by the Chinese Communists. Returning to Mississippi in 1949, Allison and his wife retired at Ellisville. Ben B. Coffey Jr. of Memphis (1961b) wrote an account of Allison's life work and compiled a list of his published writings on birds.

Allison studied the birdlife of Louisiana and published lists and bird notes in *Auk,* the journal of the American Ornithologists' Union. After visits to Hancock and Tishomingo Counties from 1899 to 1907, he published bird notes in *Auk,* listing the species he observed. He provided the first state records for the Sprague's Pipit and Swainson's Warbler, and the first comprehensive reports and lists of the winter birds of Hancock County and the summer birds of Tishomingo County. Allison also was an accomplished field botanist. While in China, he collected a series of bird skins and made excellent drawings of southern China birds. He was a charter member and one of three honorary life

A bacteriologist, teacher, and missionary to China, the Rev. Andrew Allison was also a noted botanist. He became Mississippi's first ornithologist of distinction around the turn of the 20th century.

members of the Mississippi Ornithological Society, which was organized in 1955. He died on June 6, 1960, at age 81.

Andrew Allison, H. H. Kopman, and George E. Beyer collaborated in publishing lists of Louisiana birds, and by 1915 the Louisiana state bird list contained 315 species (Lowery 1974). Allison's work, along with the completion of direct railroad connections to the Gulf Coast, may have encouraged out-of-state birders to come to Mississippi.

Charles Stockard (1904, 1905) collected eggs and published notes and nesting records of birds on Mississippi's Gulf Coast, in southwestern Mississippi, and in Lowndes County. He also documented nesting records of Royal Terns and Sandwich Terns on the barrier islands and Clapper Rails and Tricolored Herons on the Mississippi Coast.

Albert F. Ganier (1902, 1963) studied and photographed Mississippi Kites nesting in the Vicksburg area from 1901 to 1902 (Bent 1937, 167:64–65). He supplied the National Museum in Washington with excellent photographs of three nests and a wing-tipped adult. Ganier, self-taught through a lifetime of studying plants and birds, was a founder and curator of the Tennessee Ornithological Society. He was a charter and honorary life member of the Mississippi Ornithological Society. He contributed notes for the *MOS Newsletter* and an original drawing of nesting kites for a frontispiece in *The Mississippi Kite* (1973), the official bulletin of the MOS.

Julian D. Corrington (1922) listed 96 species of winter birds he observed near Biloxi from January 13 to March 31 and December 23 to 31, 1921. His article described in detail the environmental and social conditions on the coastal mainland, offshore and barrier islands of Mississippi Sound, the Pascagoula River swamp, and neighboring water and marsh areas. Habitats were listed under nine categories. The bird list included notes and records by Andrew Allison and H. H. Kopman on 16 species not observed by Corrington, further illustrating the influence of Allison and Kopman on other birders.

Corrington described historic landmarks on the coast and transportation facilities including the completed Gulf and Ship Island, Louisville and Nashville railroads, the electric interurban railway, and "shell roads in good condition." Tourist accommodations (Great Southern Hotel with golf links and fishing piers "crossing over a good-sized saltwater marsh") and the hospitality of the people were described. The only industries reported were seafood canning and export. He made three 80-mile auto trips to the Pascagoula River swamp, which he described as a vast primeval forest flooded with water "good enough to drink." His travels through the swamp forest were by dugout canoe. Two doubtful sightings of Ivory-billed Woodpeckers in the swamp are lacking in descriptive field marks and dates. The calls of a distant bird are described and were thought to be those of the Ivory-billed Woodpecker.

Local residents reported Sandhill Cranes, and Corrington listed them as a hypothetical species of the region. Apparently, however, he discounted the information after seeing numerous Great Blue Herons. He did not search the pine barrens and crane meadows in Jackson County. His reference is the first published report of Sandhill Cranes in Mississippi.

Frances A. Cook, a pioneer conservationist and scientist, was a native of Crystal Springs. She was better known by friends and coworkers as Miss Fannye. After obtaining a bachelor's degree from Mississippi State College for Women, she taught history and English literature in Mississippi at West Point and Louisville, and in Panama and Wyoming (Gandy 1965a). She attended the University of Colorado and George Washington University, completing work (except the thesis) toward a master's degree. She studied ornithology at Colorado and spent a year in Washington, D.C., as a tax auditor while studying at night and working at the Smithsonian Institution doing research and preparing specimens.

In 1926, after making valuable acquaintances with Smithsonian and Bureau of Biological Survey scientists in Washington, Miss Cook returned to Mississippi to promote wildlife conservation. Her campaign began in 1926 and continued largely at her own expense. She attended fairs, set up exhibits, made speeches at schools and clubs, and

Frances A. (Fannye) Cook was a wildlife conservationist, research assistant, and founder and director of the Museum of Natural Science from 1935 to 1958. With help from charter members, she organized the Mississippi Ornithological Society in 1955.

organized the Mississippi Association for the Conservation of Wildlife. As executive secretary of the group, she obtained support from early conservation-minded citizens including R. W. Harned, W. F. Bond, J. W. Tucker, Wiley P. Harris, Judge W. E. McIntire Sr., Ben Stevens, David Atwood, Judge Clarence E. Morgan Sr., and R. D. (Bob) Morrow. Conservation legislation introduced in 1928 was supported by the American Legion and state garden clubs, but failed to pass. An improved bill, modeled after game laws of Pennsylvania, created the Mississippi Game and Fish Commission in 1932 under the administration of Governor Mike Conner.

Miss Cook was appointed by the Game and Fish Commission as research assistant to the director. In 1935 she planned, and the commission sponsored, a state Plant and Animal Survey Project, which was a Works Progress Administration (WPA) activity. Miss Cook was leader of the project from 1935 to 1941. Museum workers and field collectors were trained under her supervision. Some of the field collectors of museum specimens and bird skins were Henry Owens, R. M. Freeman, Homer L. Tackett, B. A. Bloodsworth, H. C. Robinson, C. D. Turnipseed, Winston Nolan, James Batson, and W. D. Lewis.

The project established 18 collecting units at community colleges and one in Jackson, which became the basis for a permanent state museum that opened on January 3, 1939. Miss Cook served as museum director for 26 years until her retirement in 1958. She was instrumental in organizing the Mississippi Ornithological Society, which began on April 30, 1955, and served for two years as its first president. Her publications include many articles and bulletins about wildlife in Mississippi, including the 123-page bulletin *Game Birds of Mississippi* (1945a).

Organization of the Mississippi Ornithological Society, publication of its *MOS Newsletter,* and annual spring and fall meetings and field trips encouraged participation by many active birders. The MOS soon developed over 100 active members.

As a memorial to Miss Cook's conservation service, the Mississippi Legislature passed a resolution commending her life work and recommending the state wildlife museum be

From 1935 to 1941, the Works Progress Administration Plant and Animal Survey employed field collectors to collect and prepare specimens for use in museums.

This 1938 exhibit, depicting plants and animals collected through the WPA Plant and Animal Survey, was housed in the Old Asylum Building in Jackson, the forerunner of the Museum of Natural Science.

named in her honor. The Game and Fish Commission named the Mississippi Museum of Natural Science the Fannye A. Cook Memorial. Miss Cook died on April 30, 1964.

Winchester Jenkins (1933) deserves mention as an early wildlife conservationist. He was a self-taught woodsman, expert turkey hunter, dog trainer, and author of a popular paperback, *Wildlife in Mississippi.* An early game warden in Adams County from 1926 to 1932, he advocated fire control, game law enforcement, habitat improvements, and the restocking of forest game. Jenkins was a strong supporter of the conservation movement and the newly established Mississippi Game and Fish Commission.

The late Ben B. Coffey Jr. and his wife, Lula, were indefatigable birders over the Mid-south and beyond beginning about 1928. Their contributions to the ornithology of the region and to Mississippi are phenomenal. The Coffeys' publications in his *Mid-South Bird Notes* (Jackson 1981a), the Tennessee Ornithological Society journal *The Migrant, MOS Newsletter,* and *The Mississippi Kite* reflect only partially their contributions and interests.

Ben Coffey Jr. was a longtime Boy Scout leader in Memphis. He came from Nashville with ties to Mississippi through his parents. His father was from Lafayette County and his mother was from Iuka. In Nashville, Albert F. Ganier had been Coffey's mentor, and in January 1930, a small group formed the Memphis Chapter of the Tennessee Ornithological Society with Ben as its first president. Ben and Lula

Ben B. and Lula Coffey Jr. of Memphis, Tennessee, spent much of their lifetimes banding birds, recording bird songs, and studying the occurrence and distribution of birds in Mississippi and adjacent states.

Coffey's field work in Mississippi included banding herons in the northern Delta, and participation in numerous annual Christmas Bird Counts and breeding bird surveys. They took their annual vacations to Mexico to study birds. They enlisted scouts to help band over 15,000 herons and 1500 Anhingas in the Delta (1941a) and over 106,000 Chimney Swifts near Memphis. Some of the scouts retained exceptional interest in birds, and many other birders were influenced by their field work.

Long-term distributional studies by the Coffeys of the Whip-poor-will, Eastern Phoebe, Cliff Swallow, and Barn Swallow documented range extensions and previously unknown breeding localities for these species. Their work on the Sprague's Pipit and Smith's Longspur demonstrated habitat preferences, food habits, and state records of these little known, winter-resident birds in Mississippi. Ben compiled the first preliminary checklist of Mississippi birds based on his field work, published records, and correspondence (1936). He contributed the first state breeding records for the Cliff Swallow in Tishomingo County, and the only state nesting record of the Double-crested Cormorant in Tunica County (1952).

In 1964, Coffey began recording bird songs, with emphasis on wrens and goatsuckers, that were later produced on records. Trips were made to Mexico and Central and South America to record Neotropical birds. His recordings were used frequently with slide programs at bird club meetings, where he often claimed equal time to play his tapes and emphasize the importance of identifying bird songs.

Ben and Lula Coffey Jr. are charter and associate life members of the Mississippi Ornithological Society. They have contributed knowledge and birding experience for their own enjoyment and at their own expense. They never forget their birding friends or fail to share their knowledge and interest. Not much more could be said of a professional.

Merritt G. Vaiden began studying, collecting specimens, and reporting bird records in Bolivar County about 1928. He collected over 3500 bird skins that later were given to The University of Mississippi's Department of Biological Sciences. Vaiden trained his wife and young men in the Rosedale area to prepare bird skins and help with field collecting and finding birds. His young protégés Alan Feduccia, Billy Smith-Vaniz, Sammy Ray, Edgar Grissom, and Sammie Danna Jr. were encouraged by Vaiden to further their scientific education and interest in birds.

Vaiden's collection and published records in *Auk* and *The Migrant* include some of Mississippi's first state specimen records. Many were identified as subspecies with the assistance of Alexander Wetmore, John Aldrich, and Allen Duvall at the Smithsonian. Vaiden's particular interest in nomenclature accounted for the only specimen record of the Western Wood-Pewee. He was a loner, a self-taught man who sought out experts with access to type specimens for comparison with his collections. He consulted and corresponded frequently with George H. Lowery Jr. at the Louisiana State University Museum of Zoology. The Vaiden collection is truly an invaluable contribution to ornithology in Mississippi.

Benjamin A. Warriner contributed bird notes and records from the Corinth area from 1933 to 1962. Most of his articles were published in *The Migrant.* Warriner conducted some annual Christmas counts in the Corinth area from 1933 to 1938. He recorded the first state nesting records of Horned Larks in Alcorn County (1935, 1945) and the first nesting of Dickcissels. He also recorded the first state sight record of the Limpkin near Corinth (1962) and an early sight record of the Tree Sparrow (1936).

Thomas D. Burleigh (1945) studied birdlife and collected 350 species and subspecies of birds in Mississippi's three coastal counties from September 1935 to September 1943. Burleigh's work is valuable in summarizing the early history of ornithological activity on the Mississippi Coast. His descriptions of the coastal flora and associated avifauna are valuable for reference and comparison with present and future changes in the coastal environment.

Burleigh was probably the last of our "shotgun ornithologists," one who collected a series of specimens to verify unusual species or occurrences. Burleigh's collecting activities centered around Gulfport, Biloxi, Deer Island, and the barrier islands in Mississippi Sound. Evidently he overlooked or failed to visit some of the more productive birding places in the Pascagoula River marsh and the Hancock County beaches and marshlands.

Burleigh's bibliography (1945) is a useful summary of early coastal birding activity. His specimens documenting the first state records were deposited in the collections of the Fish and Wildlife Service and the Louisiana State University Museum of Zoology. George H. Lowery Jr. collaborated in the initial publication of Burleigh's work as LSU Museum of Zoology Occasional Papers No. 20, 1944.

H. M. Stevenson furnished seasonal notes and conducted a Christmas bird census while living at Oxford from 1943 to 1945. He published notes on the birds of northern Mississippi (1945).

B. E. Gandy succeeded Fannye A. Cook as director of the Mississippi Museum of Natural Science in Jackson. Gandy assumed the responsibilities of bird curator for the museum's collections and its depository for MOS members' collections, photographs, and sight records. He compiled and published the Museum bulletin, *Catalog of Mississippi Bird Records, Vol. 1* (Gandy and Turcotte 1970). He compiled a list of seasonal occurrence records of Mississippi birds (1963) and published *A Preliminary Check List of the Vertebrates of Mississippi* (1969). As museum director, Gandy assisted in planning and designing the display areas and habitat groups for a new museum building. Gandy contributed notes and articles for the *MOS Newsletter* and helped compile and distribute MOS field checklists. He served the MOS as treasurer-secretary from 1961 through 1975. He contributed the first state specimen records for the Black Rail and Evening Grosbeak and assisted in collecting Mississippi's first Say's Phoebe. Gandy was an early participant and organizer of the Jackson Christmas Bird Count. He retired in 1987.

Charter members of the MOS were catalysts for stimulating interest in documenting coastal birds. These members include John Frazier, R. L. Caylor, Ben B. Coffey Jr., Mr. and Mrs. Mayo Tolman, J. L. Dorn, and T. J. Hatrel. Frazier and Dr. Caylor (1936) brought some of their students from Mississippi Southern and Delta State, respectively, to the coast and elsewhere on field trips to study birds and marine life. The Tolmans were active birders from Nicholson in Pearl River County where Amy B. Tolman observed and reported the first Black-headed Grosbeak, later collected for a specimen record. Also, she contributed a sight record of a Harris' Hawk, and the first locality record of a Lapland Longspur and Vermilion Flycatcher.

MOS charter members St. Clair Thompson and John H. Phares recorded Magnificent Frigatebirds blown inland to Hinds County, and the communal roosting of Long-eared Owls in Copiah County. Thompson discovered the first nesting colony of White Ibises by aerial reconnaissance and visited the area with Hal Moore. He spotted ibises among the several thousand Little Blue Herons and Cattle Egrets nesting at Carter Lake in Warren County. White Ibis nests, eggs, and young were confirmed with photographs by Moore (1988) and Turcotte (1975b). John Phares also served two terms as MOS president (1959–1961).

Henry D. Haberyan and Ethyl Floyd were active Gulfport bird banders and consecutive MOS presidents. Their banding activities on the coast extended from the late 1950s to the early 1960s. Floyd continued banding birds until the mid-1970s. Both were influential in promoting amateur coastal birding (Turcotte 1962a). Ethyl Floyd initiated a column about coastal birding in the Gulfport newspaper. She succeeded in getting the Harrison County Board of Supervisors to set aside a protected beachfront for nesting Least Terns. The project, known as Nest in Peace, is continued by the Mississippi Coast Audubon Society (Toups 1976; Peterson 1984). Haberyan and Floyd recorded the first record of the Black-throated Gray Warbler on the coast and contributed additional records for the Gray Kingbird, Yellow Rail, and numerous notes and records published in the *MOS Newsletter.*

Birding interest and activities were accelerated on the coast and elsewhere in the state when it became known that pesticides were polluting the coastal environment and causing mortality among Brown Pelicans, Ospreys, and Southern Bald Eagles. Also, during the early 1960s there was a surge of interest statewide in feeding birds that coincided with the invasion of Evening Grosbeaks across Mississippi.

Wildlife biologists Sterling G. Clawson and Lovett E. Williams Jr. were active birders on the coast during 1960–1962. They made numerous collecting trips on the mainland and barrier islands. Clawson lived in Bay St. Louis, while Williams, a member of the Coast Guard, was stationed at New Orleans and Galveston. They provided numerous first state specimen records and first nesting records (Williams 1962b; Williams and Clawson 1963). Clawson was killed by lightning while visiting a Common Tern nest at the Pascagoula River estuary (Turcotte 1963a).

Clawson and Williams banded numerous Royal Terns and Sandwich Terns on Petit Bois Island and an adjacent spoil island. Williams returned in July 1964 to band and colormark over 3000 Royal and Sandwich Terns with Bob Skinner, Mac Myers, and Gulf Islands National Wildlife Refuge Manager Jerry Blackard. Williams compiled the 1961 Bayou Caddy–Pass Christian Christmas Bird Count (123 species).

In 1963, Jacob M. Valentine Jr., a Bureau of Sport Fisheries and Wildlife biologist, began studying the Sandhill Cranes in Jackson County. As the work progressed, state Game and Fish Commission Biologists Robert E. Noble, Lon Strong Jr., and Bill Quisenberry participated within guidelines of a federal aid Pittman-Robertson project. The work led to egg collecting and propagation of a captive flock of Mississippi Sandhill Cranes at the Patuxent Wildlife Research Center in Laurel, Maryland. The study determined that the resident, nonmigratory cranes were endangered as a result of unfavorable timber management, encroaching commercial and residential development, and highway construction (Valentine and Noble 1970). The Mississippi birds were scientifically described by John Aldrich (1972) as a subspecies, leading to protection under the Endangered Species Act and eventual establishment of the Mississippi Sandhill Crane National Wildlife Refuge. The first land acquisition to protect the cranes consisted of 1709 acres purchased by The Nature Conservancy in 1974. In 1989, the U.S. Fish and Wildlife Service purchased additional lands, bringing total refuge lands to 19,273 acres.

The Mississippi Kite, the MOS periodical, was first published in 1965, resumed in 1972, and continues through 26 volumes in 1996. This bulletin and the *MOS Newsletter* furnish a medium for exchanging observations and field notes, publication of articles on birds, and records of seasonal distribution and occurrence. As MOS membership increases, field observations increase, along with participation in Christmas Bird Counts and June breeding bird surveys, and articles published in *American Birds.*

Birding activities increased dramatically in the 1970s. Mississippi was a fertile field for older and newer, more active birders. Under the leadership of Evelyn Tackett and Dudley Peeler, the first National Audubon Society chapter was organized in Jackson on November 16, 1971, followed by chapters at Natchez, Hattiesburg, the Gulf Coast, Starkville, and Greenville. These Audubon chapters have encouraged local participation in field trips, special projects, Christmas counts, June breeding bird surveys, and midwinter eagle counts.

Many first state bird records were published in *The Mississippi Kite* and *American Birds* in the years after 1975. Serious amateurs have played a major role in contributing to our knowledge of Mississippi's avifauna. Some professionally trained students of ornithology have conducted research projects under the direction of Dr. Jerome A. Jackson and Dr. George A. Hurst at Mississippi State University. These studies include a Ph.D. dissertation comparing birdlife of the barrier islands and the mainland by Wayne C. Weber (1983), a master's thesis on nesting ecology of Least Terns by Martha B. Hays (1980), and studies by Jerome A. Jackson and Bette J. S. Jackson on colonial waterbirds and endangered species (Jackson 1976b, 1988, 1989; Jackson et al. 1979; Jackson and Jackson 1985).

Other graduate students who contributed numerous field observations, articles in *The Mississippi Kite,* or first state bird records include Malcolm F. Hodges Jr. (Sooty Shearwater and Bronzed Cowbird), Martha B. Hays (first nesting of Snowy Plover, and a Bridled Tern on the mainland), Randy C. Warren (nesting of Red Crossbill and American Goldfinch), Wayne C. Weber (Brant on Ship Island and first nesting of Black-necked Stilt and Gray Kingbird), C. D. Mackler (first Cave Swallow), and C. Dwight Cooley (Band-tailed Pigeon). Other recent major contributions of first state bird or first state nesting records on the Gulf Coast have been made by Judith A. Toups, J. M. McGee, John Izral, Lydia Schultz, Larry and Terrie Gates, Dalton S. King, and J. L. Spence. Visiting birders Mac Myers, Paul Sunby, E. A. McIlhenny, and others have furnished first state bird or first state nesting records for the coast.

The melding of professional studies on the coast and amateur and semiprofessional birders' intensive field observations and records resulted in publication of the first comprehensive book, *Birds and Birding on the Mississippi Coast* (Toups and Jackson 1987). The book lists 357 species of birds in Hancock, Harrison, and Jackson Counties. It identifies the best birding places with descriptions of habitat and accompanying "how to find" maps, and it contains seasonal occurrence bar graphs, and a chapter on Mississippi Coast birding history. Detailed in the work are descriptions of offshore islands with listings of their peculiar avifauna and a month-by-month calendar of what, when, and where to look for birds along the coast.

Dr. Jerome A. Jackson has served as editor of *The Mississippi Kite* since 1975. His many publications on birds are national in scope. He has worked with others on recovery plans for the endangered Red-cockaded Woodpecker and has surveyed the southeastern states and part of Cuba to determine the status of the Ivory-billed Woodpecker. (Apparently vanished from the Southeast, the woodpecker is possibly extant in remote parts of Cuba.)

Judith A. Toups has been the Gulf Coast's most active and consistent birder. Since 1976 she has written a weekly newspaper column about birds and birding. She has compiled the southern Hancock County Christmas Bird Count, hosted and guided numerous field trips, and conducted bird study seminars. With the Mississippi Gulf Coast Audubon Society, she has helped maintain the beachfront Least Tern nesting colony. Her published articles in the MOS periodical and notes in *American Birds* are numerous.

Larry and Terrie Fairley Gates have been active birders in the Hattiesburg area and on the Gulf Coast. Larry has compiled the Jackson County Christmas Bird Count since 1973. It usually leads the central southern region with 150 species or more. He and others have furnished first state records for the Black-whiskered Vireo, Sulphur-bellied Flycatcher, Black-capped Vireo (by Toups and Gates), and Lark Bunting on the Mississippi Coast. On the productive Hattiesburg sewage lagoons, he furnished the first state inland record for the King Eider, the first state Red-necked Grebe record (Gates and Moore 1978), the first inland Bridled Tern record, and numerous other first locality records. Larry Gates has compiled the Pinewood Audubon Society's Christmas Bird Count for the Hattiesburg area. Dan Carroll and Glen Oussett (Hodges 1988), recorded the first sight record of the Ash-throated Flycatcher at Waveland in Hancock County. Richard Moore, Terrie Fairley, and Pedro Rodriguez recorded an October Tree Sparrow arrival in the Hattiesburg area (1980).

Much of the birding activity in Mississippi occurs around population centers, large reservoirs, along the Mississippi River and oxbow lakes, and not surprisingly, at backyard feeding stations. City sewage lagoons attract a variety of shorebirds and waterfowl during migration and some interesting landbirds to the surrounding habitat. Birders seek areas with more diversified habitat, knowing it supports a greater variety of species. The four flood control reservoirs in northern Mississippi, especially Grenada and Sardis, have furnished many first state sight and locality records.

W. Marvin Davis has compiled the Sardis and Grenada Christmas Bird Counts since 1975. Davis has been an acute and active birder for 46 years, 26 years in northern Mississippi. His birding activity has caused Memphis and local birdwatchers to come to the reservoirs. Davis alone has added first state bird records for the Western Grebe, Little Gull, Black-legged Kittiwake, and Black-headed Gull. He and Gene Knight added the first Mountain Plover photo record (1989).

Grenada Reservoir had the first Mountain Bluebird recorded by R. L. Whittington on a Christmas Bird Count (1980). Gene Knight, an Oxford birder, reported the first state occurrence of the Lazuli Bunting at a feeder in Oxford and the first inland records of a Ruff and Northern Goshawk at Sardis Reservoir. First locality records for the Laughing Gull, Franklin's Gull, Red-throated Loon, Rough-legged Hawk, Ferruginous Hawk, and Red Phalarope were recorded by Davis. He is a past president of MOS and has been the editor of the *MOS Newsletter* since 1990.

Noxubee National Wildlife Refuge and the Starkville area have been hotbeds for ornithology since about 1970. Burton S. Webster (Jackson 1981b), manager of the refuge for 25 years, was an outspoken conservation leader and a principal organizer of the Oktibbeha Audubon Society. A longtime MOS member, he contributed a first locality photo record for the Roseate Spoonbill and a first state photo record of the Fulvous Whistling-Duck.

Webster organized a cooperative effort by MOS members to maintain the Brooksville heron rookery, which was located in a bald prairie thicket on private land and was the site of one of the first state Cattle Egret nestings. He organized a drive that stopped illegal killing of Northern Harriers during initial construction of the Golden Triangle Regional Airport. A trained forester, he supported diversified land use and forest management practices for wildlife. Webster welcomed, hosted, and guided many bird group visitors at the refuge. He served one term as MOS president and frequently contributed records and notes for the *MOS Newsletter.*

Noxubee Refuge and the Starkville area contain a large diversity of habitats, including bottomland hardwoods, flatwoods, pine-hardwood uplands, large lakes, black prairies, extensive agricultural holdings, Mississippi State University forest and agriculture experimental properties, the MSU campus, and the Starkville residential area. Starkville birders have added numerous first locality records and first state records. These include the first Snow Bunting, first breeding record for the House Finch (Jackson et al. 1986), the first inland breeding of the American Coot (Jackson and Watson 1983), and first state nesting records of the Red Crossbill (Warren et al. 1977) and Scissor-tailed Flycatcher (Jackson and Werschkul 1977).

Birding activities in the Mississippi Yazoo Delta have centered around Greenville and Yazoo National Wildlife Refuge. G. E. Alexander Jr. is one of the principal organizers of the Greenville Audubon Society and a frequent contributor of bird notes and records to *The Mississippi Kite* and *MOS Newsletter.* He served as MOS president from 1975 to 1976. He recorded the first state record of the Cinnamon Teal at Yazoo Refuge and the first locality records of the

Vermilion Flycatcher in Washington County. John Fulton recorded the first state sighting of four Ross' Geese among Snow Geese on Yazoo Refuge (1987) and reported the first state record of the Black-bellied Whistling-Duck.

Nona Herbert, an active birding enthusiast at Shaw with over 25 years experience, sighted the state's first Trumpeter Swan in Bolivar County (Herbert and Simons 1991). Her discovery was confirmed by Don Simons and W. Marvin Davis, who put the news on the verbal hotline. Numerous local and out-of-state observers came to see the Trumpeter from January 15 through February 10, 1990, when it left the area. Herbert served a term as president of MOS from 1981 to 1982.

Areas around Vicksburg affording fine birding opportunities include the Loess Bluff, the lower portion of the Delta with its bordering batture forest and sand fields, and the oxbow lakes along the mainline Mississippi River levee. Eagle Lake, Chotard and Albermarle Lakes, borrow pits, and the mainline levee system are favorite places to see Mississippi Kites, Warbling Vireos, Painted Buntings, Wild Turkey, and herds of white-tailed deer. Larger lakes, catfish ponds, and agricultural lands attract numerous barren-ground birds, waterfowl, and shorebirds on rainpools or during seasonal flooding of low-lying lands. The 65,000-acre Delta National Forest near Rolling Fork is contiguous bottomland forest with small lakes bordered by cypress and tupelo. The area supports a variety of game animals and nongame species. The extensive Loess Bluff forest north of Bovina supports a great diversity of summer resident birds.

Lewis Cashman (Moore 1989) and the late Hal Moore were instrumental in organizing the Vicksburg Birders and have compiled the Vicksburg Christmas Bird Count. The Vicksburg group conducts annual hawk counts organized by John Battalio (1987) along the Loess Bluff and within the Vicksburg National Military Park. Cashman served two terms as MOS president (from 1972 to 1974), with Hal and Anna Moore hosted meetings of the MOS, and conducted field trips to the Tensas National Wildlife Refuge in Louisiana and to the well-known Bovina birding area favored by Jackson Audubon Society members.

The Natchez Audubon Society is another group with immediate access to places visited by John James Audubon. The Homochitto River bottomlands, large agricultural tracts adjacent to the Mississippi River, extensive Loess Bluff forest uplands, the Natchez Trace Parkway, and the Homochitto National Forest are easily accessible from Natchez. Historic sites from precolonial and antebellum times invite visitors to Emerald Mound, Old Natchez Indian Village State Park, and the plantation homes of the Old Natchez District and the territorial period.

Mr. and Mrs. Orrick Metcalf and Dr. Clifford Tillman were early MOS members who helped develop interest in birding at Natchez. In April 1964, they were hosts for an enjoyable MOS spring meeting held at The Parsonage that included a field trip. The Natchez Audubon Society was formed around a small group of Natchez "early birders." Annual Christmas Bird Counts in the Natchez area have been conducted since 1966. Earlier counts in 1955 and 1956 were made by Ben and Lula Coffey Jr., Alice Smith, and R. Demett Smith Jr., who spotted the first state Black-throated Gray Warbler at the country club. Beverly Aldridge and Ralph Shields were compilers of the Natchez bird counts.

The new St. Catherine's Creek National Wildlife Refuge below Natchez and bordering the Mississippi River is being acquired and developed by the U.S. Fish and Wildlife Service. The refuge is expected to contain 20,000 acres. The location is ideal for attracting large numbers of wintering waterfowl, migratory shorebirds, and waterbirds. When included in the refuge, bordering Loess Bluff lands will provide greater access by the public to view an array of resident and summer-resident birds. This new refuge should increase local interest in birds and boost tourism to the Natchez area.

The Ross Barnett Reservoir, completed and partly impounded in the fall of 1963, has greatly accelerated birding in the Jackson area. The development of the Pearl River Waterfowl Refuge and Wildlife Management Area provides for public use and access above Mississippi 43. There are numerous other interesting areas and access points for public recreational use around the reservoir. The waterfowl refuge attracts many waterfowl species each winter. The reservoir area has provided many first locality records in the Jackson area.

The Jackson Audubon Society was organized in 1971 by Evelyn Tackett, Dudley Peeler, and others. Christmas Bird Counts and field trips to neighboring areas have been organized and conducted every year since 1971. Members have furnished state records of the Say's Phoebe, nesting of the White-breasted Nuthatch and American Redstart, the first specimen record of the Evening Grosbeak, and the second state sight record of the Western Grebe. Numerous first locality sight records have been reported, including the Vaux's Swift, Oldsquaw, Lesser Black-backed Gull, Tundra Swan, Greater Scaup, Marsh Wren, Common Moorhen, and Franklin's Gull. Members have conducted various breeding bird surveys, and regular winter eagle counts on Ross Barnett Reservoir.

More than 50 species of birds have been added to the Mississippi list from 1975 to 1990. That is an astounding record furnished by the relatively few birders in the Magnolia State. Mississippi is still a fertile field for new discoveries and additions to the ever-growing state bird list.

Wildlife Conservation and Management

We think of wildlife conservation as a relatively new concept. For thousands of years wildlife populations have both flourished and declined as a result of man's use of the land. American Indians raised corn, pumpkins, maize, beans, and peas in communal farms and family gardens. They systematically burned grasslands to maintain open prairies for buffalo. They harvested animals needed for food and used fruits, nuts, and other products of the forest to meet their needs for food, clothing, and shelter. Indians grew gourds for storage containers and even erected martin gourd poles. By living off the land and taking only for their needs, they sustained the yield and diversity of plants and animals, thereby protecting naturally fertile, unabused soil and water resources.

Prior to European exploration, the Indian population of what is now Mississippi consisted of about 30,000 Natchez, Choctaws, and Chickasaws scattered in small villages. Most of the state lay in what now would be regarded as virgin wilderness when European settlers arrived around 1700. The French explorer d'Iberville reported seeing hundreds of buffalo during his travels along the coast. Early European hunters filled their boats with buffalo, deer, and other game around Bay St. Louis. An English historian described "an abundance of buffalo, deer, turkey, duck, and fish," and the soil seemed "exceedingly fertile." Natural resources appeared to be inexhaustible to these early pioneers.

By the late eighteenth century an influx of settlers had overcome the Natchez Indians in the Old Natchez District. Settlers began in-migrations to form wilderness settlements. An agricultural economy developed around Natchez, where crops of tobacco and cotton were grown on the fertile soil. Statehood in 1817 and the continuing in-roads into Indian lands brought an influx of settlers who relied on subsistence farming and cotton as a cash crop.

From a statewide perspective, early settlers made few alterations to the landscape. They improved habitat for some wildlife species by small-patch farming, creating forest openings, and using controlled burns of pinelands to improve livestock grazing. New ecotones were created by these practices that reverted plant succession. Similarly, forest game resources were exploited for food and commercial sale, using every available means to take them. The agrarian economy, based largely on cotton and corn, prospered, and communities formed that brought in artisans and professionals. In the decade before the Civil War, levees were built and virgin hardwoods were cleared for crops along

Above: Bobwhite Quail

Pierre le Moyne d'Iberville was a Canadian-French explorer and founder of Louisiana. He established the first Mississippi settlement at Biloxi around 1700.

the main stream courses in the Mississippi-Yazoo Delta. Wildlife, including bear, deer, Wild Turkeys, and an abundance of fish, remained in large, inaccessible parts of the Delta.

After the Civil War, there was a new influx of settlers, and as the population increased, vast changes to the landscape occurred. By the turn of the twentieth century, one-third of the original Delta bottomland hardwood forest had been cleared for agriculture. The commercial value of various hardwoods and pines in southern forests was recognized when the forest resources in the eastern and northern forests of the United States became exhausted. In the latter part of the eighteenth century, wealthy opportunists bought up large acreages of forest lands and, with the help of the railroads, opened up the vast acreages of Mississippi forest land for exploitation.

By 1900, Mississippi was a leading timber exporting state. The "cut out and get out" policy adopted by many loggers left millions of acres here bare and subject to erosion, later to be further degraded by wildfire and uncontrolled grazing practices. Lumber operators had little regard for wildlife, and loggers and market hunters systematically killed off forest game. The forest resources that had covered 95 percent of the state in 1800 were practically gone

This was a typical hunting camp scene in 1897. During this period when most of the original timberlands were logged, deer and black bear were almost extirpated.

This was what an original stand of loblolly pines looked like before clear-cutting began in the early 1900s.

by 1930. Small farm ownership, the tenant or sharecropping system, and the irregular use of fire in farming areas were favorable for small game animals, but abusive to valuable topsoil. Destructive practices of hunting game and non-game species were recognized by the United States Congress when the Lacey Act was passed in 1909 to stop the killing of herons and egrets for their colorful and showy plumes. The Migratory Bird Treaty Act, passed by Congress in 1918, was an agreement between Great Britain and the United States for the protection and management of migratory birds, which was extended to Mexico by a 1936 treaty. These important acts were effective in requiring individual states to extend protection to their resident wildlife resources.

In Mississippi, market hunting of small game, waterfowl, and the commercial sale of game fish, remained a problem until the late 1930s. In the early 1920s when migratory game bird hunting regulations became effective, the state legislature passed Mississippi's first comprehensive game laws. The 1922 regular session of the legislature enacted statutes recognizing federal migratory bird treaty regulations and provided statutory definitions and open seasons for game, furbearing animals, and fish. Regulatory authority was extended to county boards of supervisors with provisions for law enforcement, fines, penalties, and the issuance of hunting and fishing licenses by counties. In 1926 the legislature strengthened county authority to regulate and enforce game laws and to employ county game wardens to be paid from county license sales special funds.

Sawmills with their millponds and power generators supplied needed electricity for company-owned mill towns. Most were abandoned by the late 1920s.

Log trains such as this one hauled logs from clear-cuts to nearby sawmills on temporary railroad tracks called "dummy lines."

From about 1900 until the late 1920s, logging of pinelands left little behind except a blackened stump forest. These bare grounds were often abused through the setting of wildfires and open range grazing of sheep and cattle.

These early efforts to protect wildlife and enforce game laws were not effective statewide. A few informed and farsighted Mississippians were concerned about the depletion of forest game and the continuing abuse of forest lands. Also, they were dissatisfied with the lack of game law enforcement in most counties. The Mississippi Association for the Conservation of Wildlife was organized with the intent of securing passage of legislation establishing a state game department for the protection and management of wildlife resources. Legislation introduced in 1928 failed to pass after it had been weakened by amendments, and the association withdrew support.

A bill to create the Mississippi Game and Fish Commission and establish a Game and Fish Protection Fund was introduced and passed by the 1932 regular session of the legislature. During the Great Depression, no funds were appropriated for operations. Governor Mike Conner signed the bill and appointed Ben M. Stevens of Richton, W. E. McIntyre Sr. of Brandon, and W. G. McGill of New Albany as the first commissioners. Given office space in the New Capitol, they borrowed $1500 from a Jackson bank on a signature loan and bought furnishings and supplies. After spending the $1500, they bounced a $5 check made out to Daniel Boone to close the checking account.

The newly formed commission organized their efforts around administration and law enforcement, restoration

The state Game and Fish Commission began functioning on July 1, 1932, thanks to a bill signed by Gov. Mike Conner.

W. E. McIntyre Sr. was the first chairman of the state Game and Fish Commission. He authored the first manual of instructions on legal procedure and related subjects for newly appointed game wardens in 1932.

and restocking, and education and public relations. Hunter Kimball was employed as the first director of conservation and a secretary-bookkeeper was hired on August 3, 1932. Miss Frances A. (Fannye) Cook was employed as research assistant on September 7. A full-time bookkeeper, W. F. Dearman, was employed on September 23. License sales enabled the employment of part-time game wardens for the next hunting seasons at a salary of $50 per month and $40 for car expenses.

With administration and law enforcement under way, the commission used its regulatory authority to close several counties to deer and turkey hunting and to control commercial fishing in some areas. The commission contracted for the removal of nongame gross fish from some Delta lakes. They set up game fish rescue operations to transplant fish from drying up borrow pits and shallow lakes. Plans were completed in 1933 for deer, turkey, fox, and raccoon purchases, and operations began the following year.

Protection refuges were established. These operations demonstrated that conservation required concerted action to improve conditions for wildlife. These early commissioners also realized that effective wildlife conservation begins with public education, which brings about public cooperation and acceptance of state and local game laws.

Aldo Leopold (1929) made a game survey of Mississippi in 1928. His findings about game animals were:

> Wild Turkeys are steadily decreasing. They have been cleaned out of upland ranges, and there is barely a seed stock left in the larger swamps. Deer are in like case, but the declination of the remaining stock is more complete. By and large small game conditions are fair and big game bad. The present game supply is so far the result of accident rather than design. There is no state game department and only the beginnings of a conservation movement, no refuge system, and little law enforcement. There is one offset to all these defects, a widespread and intense popular interest in game and hunting. In this respect Mississippi excels any other state so far surveyed.

In his lifetime, Leopold was recognized as the father of modern wildlife management. Today, he is better known as a pioneer ecologist and for his writings and essays in *A Sand County Almanac,* his foremost work. His 1929 game survey report played a role in shaping the future of Mississippi's wildlife restoration program.

Some of the main problems of game law enforcement in the years before the Great Depression were illegal market hunting, trapping, commercial fishing, and sale of game fish. Fur was in great demand and brought high prices in the 1920s and 1930s. Raccoons, foxes, and mink were depleted, while river otters and beavers were almost exterminated. Commercial fishing was widespread and bootlegging of game

Subsistence farming was a way of life for early settlers. Family and tenant farming created and maintained almost ideal habitat for Bobwhite Quail and other small game. Mechanization of agriculture has resulted in abandonment or consolidation of family farms to improved pasture, timber, or intensive row crops that are less productive for many wildlife species.

fish was common. Automobiles made it possible to operate a quail trapping and bootlegging ring in some southern counties. In northern Mississippi another market hunting operation existed selling wild ducks and game fish. Federal game agents and a few selected state game wardens worked undercover to stop marketing of game and furbearing animals, but it remained a problem for law enforcement for many years.

The commission conducted an early game survey by requiring game wardens to report locations of deer, Wild Turkey, beavers, and habitat suitable for protection refuges or needing restocking. The national economic recovery program provided impetus and federal money for conservation projects. One such program sponsored by the commission was a WPA statewide Plant and Animal Survey Project. Headquartered in Jackson with branches at state colleges, the survey used relief and nonrelief workers to gather collections and prepare museum specimens. Exhibits were prepared that formed the beginning of the Museum of Natural Science, which opened in the winter of 1939. WPA lake construction projects sponsored and completed by the commission were Bogue Homa Lake in Jones County, Lake Dockery in Hinds County, and Pelahatchie Lake in Rankin County. After its completion, Dixie Springs Lake in Pike County was taken over by the commission for management and operation. Joint Federal and State Park Commission project lakes built were Legion Park Lake in Winston County, Clarke Lake in Clarke County, Holmes County Lake in Holmes County, Spring Lake in Marshall County, Tishomingo Lake in Tishomingo County, Tombigbee Lake in Lee County, and Leroy Percy Park Lake in Washington County.

The commission purchased a 1934-model truck with an enclosed body for portable wildlife exhibits and a movie projector, screen, and auxiliary generator. A 30-minute film on the commission's early projects was produced and widely shown with the traveling exhibits. Educational materials and exhibits were provided along with live wild animals for many local fairs and the annual state fair in Jackson.

During the agency's first four years, a foundation was laid for another public relations demonstration. Under Governor Hugh White's administration, Si Corley, director of conservation, purchased and released 80,000 Mexican Bobwhite Quail and several hundred deer imported from Mexico. The quail were distributed statewide and released

Game wardens working undercover seized these live-trapped quail from a large illegal operation in southern Mississippi in the 1930s. Operations such as this one supplied game to markets as far away as Chicago.

In the late 1930s, this truck was outfitted with an electric power generator, movie projection equipment, and portable exhibits in an effort to take the conservation message and the work of the Game and Fish Commission to the people.

in pairs by game wardens with as much local fanfare and publicity as possible. The quail releases served little purpose, since an adequate breeding stock of native birds existed. However, the Mexican quail were never forgotten by a generation of quail hunters who attributed successful hunts or failures to those "Mexican birds." Today, game managers scoff at the idea of stocking quail. But during these early days, quail releases earned public support for future deer and Wild Turkey restocking programs. The commission never ventured into the expensive and wasteful game farm business, a practice that should be remembered.

When deer and Wild Turkey were found in short supply or even absent in suitable habitat, restocking took on major importance. The earlier protection refuge program was enlarged. Since deer and Wild Turkey were not available in Mississippi for restocking, the first purchases of deer were made in North Carolina. They came from the Pisgah National Forest, which was already experiencing overpopulation problems. The first release of 36 North Carolina deer was made in the Holly Springs National Forest. Subsequently, in the late 1930s, deer were imported from Mexico and held temporarily at the Jackson Zoo for distribution at selected locations and refuges.

Beavers were live trapped in Amite County by several local trappers using Bailey live traps supplied by the commission. Trappers were paid $15 for each beaver caught and released, since these animals were much in demand by landowners.

The only source of wild-strain turkeys was pen-raised, game farm birds. The best available wild-strain birds came from David C. Atwood of Kosciusko for $25 each. These were semiwild turkeys from hen nests situated in an open, high-fenced enclosure. The eggs of wild-strain birds were hatched by chicken hens. Later, poults were transferred to a brood domestic turkey hen in the enclosure. When poults were half grown, the hen and brood were allowed to range freely into adjacent fields and woods with other semiwild turkeys. These birds remained where they were raised and periodically were fed corn in the woods. The adult birds were wild enough that they had to be caught with baited pole and net traps. The supply was limited, but over a period of several years, adult birds survived after release in the wild, but were never known to reproduce successfully. Most of the Atwood turkeys kept under observation died from attrition and predation. A survey completed in 1941 investigated 576 individual releases of 2743 semiwild and pen-raised, wild-strain turkeys (Cook 1945a). Most of the turkey releases were failures, the survey showed. It was noted that most other successful releases or admixtures were in areas with some breeding stock of native Wild Turkeys. The study evaluated potential habitat for stocking and recommended that future restocking projects use only live-trapped, native Wild Turkeys. W. F. Dearman negotiated the purchase of most of the imported quail and deer from Mexico, and purchases of turkeys within the state.

In the early 1930s, the federal government activated plans to purchase cut-over forest lands for national forests. The state had passed enabling legislation in 1926 for Congress and the federal government to purchase land for migratory bird refuges and national forest reserves. Thousands of acres of land already had reverted to state ownership for nonpayment of taxes. In 1933, the boundary for the Homochitto National Forest was approved, followed by the Biloxi, Leaf River, Holly Springs, and Bienville National Forest units. The Delta Forest unit followed in 1935. In March 1934, the Coordination of Wildlife Conservation Act was passed, authorizing the secretary of agriculture and the secretary of commerce to cooperate with federal and state agencies in wildlife conservation and rehabilitation projects. This act made acquisition, development, and improvement of land and water areas possible in state parks, national forests, land utilization (LU) and resettlement projects, and migratory bird refuges. The Civilian Conservation Corps (CCC) and the WPA became involved in work on submarginal lands in state parks, national forests, and jointly built lakes and other construction projects.

The Federal Aid in Wildlife Restoration Act (Pittman-Robertson Act) diverted federal excise taxes on sporting arms and ammunition to the states on the basis of land area and hunting license sales. These funds were made available in annual apportionments on a three-to-one matching basis for use on approved projects such as wildlife coordination, land acquisition, development or maintenance, research, surveys, and investigation projects.

By 1940, the commission's refuge program contained some 40 refuges for deer and Wild Turkeys, encompassing more than 250,000 acres (Mississippi Game and Fish Commission 1978). The Leaf River Refuge, established in 1939, was one of the first federal aid development projects on 33,000 acres of national forest land in Perry County. This area was initially stocked with about 200 Mexican deer in an enclosed 1300-acre "deer pasture." Later, it became a major source for live-trapped deer and Wild Turkeys for restocking in other parts of the state, and it became one of the first wildlife management areas opened for public hunting.

The first federal aid research project was approved and work started in May 1940. The commission transplanted 173 beavers from the Amite River between 1935 and 1937. A survey of all streams was made to evaluate the success of the plantings. Some 49 beaver colonies from plantings prior to 1940 were found to contain 467 individuals (Cook 1945b). Native beaver colonies in the Tallahatchie, Big Black, Tombigbee, and Amite River watersheds contained 257 animals. Beaver colonies were found in 42 counties, and the total estimated population of transplanted and native beavers was 1094. The largest concentrations were native colonies in Lauderdale, Kemper, and Amite Counties.

A statewide survey was conducted from October 1941 to June 30, 1942, to determine the distribution and estimated population of Wild Turkeys, and to identify suitable habitat for restocking. The total estimated population of Wild Turkeys was 4757 birds in 41 counties.

In October 1940, the federal aid live-trapping program, known as Mississippi Project 6-D, was initiated. An experienced beaver trapper and two assistants live trapped and transplanted 212 native beavers from nuisance colonies in Lauderdale, Webster, and Amite Counties to establish beaver colonies in 74 of the 82 counties. Also the project workers transplanted live-trapped deer and Wild Turkeys from the Ran Batson private game preserve at Hillsdale in Pearl River County. Releases of these deer and the first live-trapped, native Wild Turkeys were made on the Leaf River Refuge in Perry County and the H. B. Cole Refuge in Leake County in 1940 and 1941.

During the period 1940–41, some 212 beavers were trapped and transplanted from native colonies in Amite, Lauderdale, and Kemper Counties in an effort to establish beavers in 74 of the 82 counties.

Deer trapping and transplanting from state refuges was begun in 1945 and continued through the 1950s. Deer were restocked in all 82 counties. In 1970, all counties had open deer-hunting seasons.

W. F. Dearman succeeded Si Corley as director of conservation in 1939. During World War II the commission was forced to curtail some programs and activities. However, the commission initiated a coastal muskrat restoration project and established the Bienville Refuge in Scott County, the University Refuge in Stone and Jackson Counties, and the Upper Sardis Refuge in Lafayette County.

R. M. Freeman was director of conservation during the administrations of governors Tom Bailey and Fielding Wright. The legislature empowered the commission to regulate and enforce stream pollution laws, but municipalities were exempted. Pollution control regulations were promulgated, adopted, and enforced by the commission. In 1946, additional federal aid refuges were established in Calhoun and Jasper Counties, and deer trapping was begun on the Leaf River Refuge. A public relations department was established, and an educational film library was started in 1946. In July 1947, publication of a formal monthly magazine, *Mississippi Game and Fish,* was begun. The commission initiated a fox-quail relationship study, and a Yazoo Basin Wildlife Resources Survey project to inventory and map forest cover and wildlife resources was begun. The game division and fisheries division were organized and staffed with wildlife and fisheries biologists. In 1948, the Choctaw Refuge was established and stocked with deer and Wild Turkeys. A farm game habitat improvement program was initiated with distribution of perennial lespedeza bicolor plants. Boys' Conservation Schools were begun to teach wildlife conservation and management at summer camps in state parks.

Freeman placed emphasis on law enforcement training by holding game warden schools for several years at Roosevelt State Park. The number of supervisory wardens was increased, and law enforcement was organized into smaller districts to improve efficiency. Efforts were successful at breaking up the last vestiges of illegal commercial fishing, market hunting, and selling of game fish. Undercover operations, followed up by organized raids to remove illegal nets and fish traps, were particularly successful on Lake Washington and on Muddy Bayou connecting Eagle Lake and Steele Bayou in Warren County. Many convictions and illegal net and wire-trap seizures resulted from these operations.

During World War II, the commission accumulated a surplus of about $500,000 in the Game and Fish Protection Fund and unobligated Pittman-Robertson apportionments. In 1949, the commission purchased the Hugh L. White Wildlife Management Area in Marion County (7500 acres) for $49,500. The Copiah County Wildlife Management Area (6500 acres) was purchased with existing improvements and a short-term timber reservation. The hardwood was repurchased after pines of a specified diameter were removed. Total cost of land, timber, and improvements was about $115,000. Both areas were fenced, developed for small game, and stocked with deer and Wild Turkeys.

Sardis Waterfowl Refuge was established in 1948 under a license agreement with the U.S. Army Corps of Engineers. The area was intensively developed with upland plantings of corn and winter grains. Subimpoundments, called "duck-motels," were built below the reservoir flood pool, planted in millet, and reflooded by pumping and runoff waters to attract and hold ducks in the 1800-acre refuge. The developments were extended to adjacent lands open for hunting. A decoy flock of Canada Geese attracted and held about 150 wild Canadas during the refuge's first year of operation. The goose flock continued to increase to as high as 5000 wintering birds. The Sardis Waterfowl Refuge still supports wintering waterfowl and Mississippi's largest flock of wintering Canada Geese.

In the late 1940s and early 1950s, a waterfowl biologist was employed and a statewide survey was conducted to identify key waterfowl areas suitable for acquisition and development. The survey identified many strategic areas in the Delta. Reconnaissance appraisals were made for land acquisition on four large areas. At the time, most of the land was in bottomland hardwoods and considered submarginal for agriculture. Land acquisition in the Delta gained no public interest or support. For the next two decades, most of the wetlands were cleared and sheared off for intensive, subsidized agriculture, encouraged by federal flood control and channelization projects.

In 1950, the Adams County Refuge was established and later restocked with deer and wild-trapped turkeys. Fish population studies on the flood control reservoirs were begun, and a commercial fish removal and shad control program was initiated on Moon Lake in Coahoma County. An intensive quail research and management program was begun on the Copiah County Wildlife Management Area.

From its inception, the Game and Fish Commission had never depended on appropriations from the general fund, instead operating entirely on revenues from license sales and matching federal aid funds for approved projects. This was soon to change. In the 1950 regular session, a bill was introduced and passed that limited the commission's expenditures to 75 percent of revenues during the next biennial period. This in effect was enough to hamstring existing operations.

Toward the end of the biennial period, the commission decided to furnish jeeps to its game wardens. Most officers were using outdated personal vehicles that did not enable them to patrol many areas where violations were known to occur. Governor Fielding Wright and a representative from the attorney general's office concurred at a meeting with the chairman and representatives of the commission that the purchase of equipment was permissible. The commission then bought a fleet of 82 modified jeeps. Toward the end of the biennial period, an audit determined that the commission had violated statutory limitations on expenditures. The commission was then reorganized and required to prepare and operate under a budget approved by the legislature.

In 1952, the commission initiated a program to provide managed and controlled public hunting areas. A number

State game wardens had little effective transportation for carrying out their responsibilities until the agency purchased modified Jeeps in the early 1950s.

of state refuges were nearing carrying capacity, since deer and Wild Turkeys were increasing in sufficient numbers to begin a restocking program. Already, problems had erupted with hunters encroaching around refuge boundaries, since the refuges were mostly on national forest or corporate timberlands. The U.S. Forest Service agreed to the management area program under existing cooperative agreements. The large timberland owners responded similarly.

The success of the program, however, hinged on the many individual, small landowners. Without the cooperation of these thousands of individual owners, a successful wildlife management area program would not come together. Although it took much time and effort to explain and sell the program, most landowners cooperated and signed agreements. A documentary film was produced and shown widely, explaining the intent and purpose of management areas,

This fine buck was taken on the first day of the first open deer season on the Leaf River Wildlife Management Area in Perry County.

Often called a "piney woods tom," this Eastern Wild Turkey was harvested on the Red Creek Wildlife Management Area during the spring season in 1957.

emphasizing Wild Turkey and deer restoration and management. It helped sell the program. Within a decade, 1.25 million acres were placed under the wildlife management area program, later expanded to 1.5 million acres.

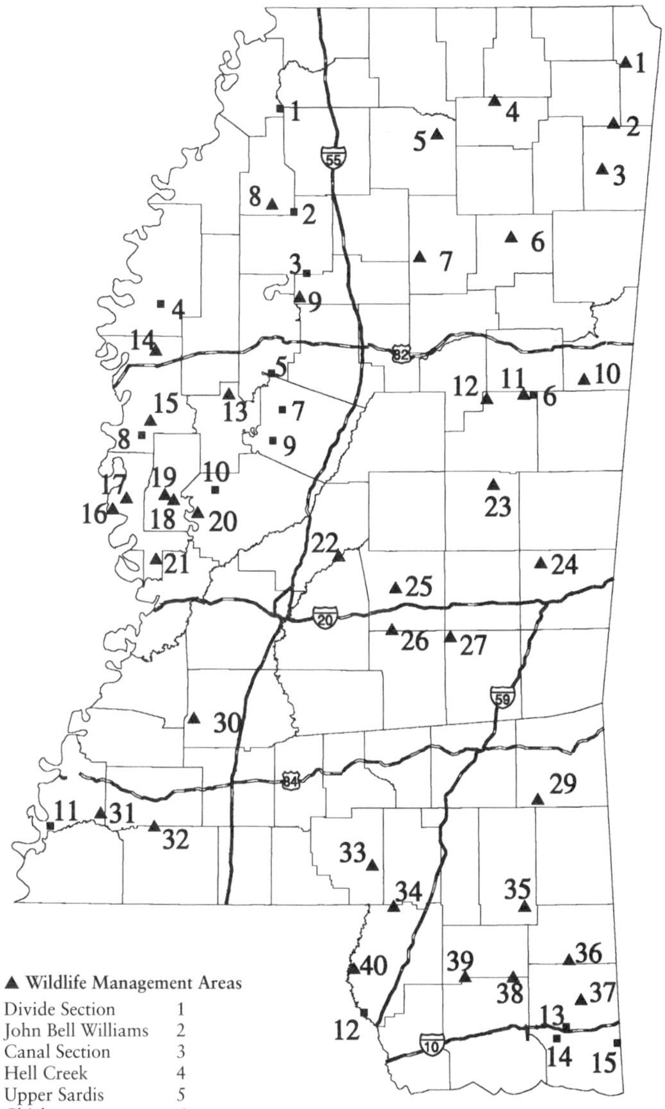

▲ Wildlife Management Areas

Divide Section	1
John Bell Williams	2
Canal Section	3
Hell Creek	4
Upper Sardis	5
Chickasaw	6
Calhoun County	7
O'Keefe	8
Malmaison	9
Black Prairie	10
John W. Starr Memorial Forest	11
Choctaw	12
Sky Lake	13
Stoneville	14
Leroy Percy	15
Shipland	16
Anderson-Tully	17
Sunflower	18
Twin Oaks	19
Lake George	20
Mahannah	21
Pearl River	22
Nanih Waiya	23
Okatibbee	24
Bienville	25
Caney Creek	26
Tallahala	27
Chickasawhay	29
Copiah County	30
Sandy Creek	31
Caston Creek	32
Marion County	33
Wolf River	34
Leaf River	35
Pascagoula River	36
Ward Bayou	37
Red Creek	38
Little Biloxi	39
Old River	40

■ National Wildlife Refuges

Tallahatchie	1
Tallahatchie	2
Tallahatchie	3
Dahomey	4
Mathews Brake	5
Noxubee	6
Morgan Brake	7
Yazoo	8
Hillside	9
Panther Swamp	10
St. Catherine Creek	11
Bogue Chitto	12
Sandhill Crane	13
Gulf Island	14
Grand Bay	15

Mississippi's State Wildlife Management Areas and National Wildlife Refuges.

Wildlife biologists and area managers worked together to establish and enlarge public hunting areas. Biologist L. P. Heard, left, and former Copiah County Wildlife Area Manager Ed Givens managed this area for Bobwhite Quail and small game hunting. A host of songbird species benefit from the game management techniques applied to public wildlife management areas.

The Federal Aid to Fisheries (Dingell-Johnson Act), became effective, and Lake Mary Crawford was constructed during 1951 and 1952. The commission initiated a deer research study in the same period to determine the reproductive characteristics of Mississippi's deer herd, which was expanding rapidly. The deer stocking program was nearing completion, and refuge areas were approaching carrying capacity. During the 1950s, about 1300 deer were transplanted to most counties without breeding stock.

In 1954, the live trapping of Wild Turkeys with cannon-projected nets was begun on the Leaf River Refuge. Live trapping was expanded, and turkey releases were made on other refuges and management areas. Flock-size releases of birds were made at previously planned and scheduled locations in counties closed to hunting or on private lands where protection by landowners was certain. Trapping operations later were expanded to Adams County Refuge; Friars Point Refuge owned by John McKee; private lands owned by Fred Anderson in Amite County; and on Bucatunna, Chickasawhay, and Red Creek Management Areas. The success of deer and Wild Turkey restocking operations exceeded all expectations. The program coincided with protection and regeneration of forest lands and better public support and cooperation of landowners.

The 1950s also was a period of gradual deterioration and loss of farm habitat suitable for game. More intensive, mechanized, large-scale, clean farming operations and expanded acreage in improved pastureland were not favorable for small game. Insidious losses of bottomland hardwoods, channelization of stream courses, flood control projects, and the use of long-lasting insecticides combined to cause irreplaceable losses of wetlands, fish, and wildlife on a massive scale in the Delta.

The commission renewed a construction program for public fishing lakes in 1956. During the administrations of Governors J. P. Coleman and Paul B. Johnson Jr. the following state-owned lakes were built: Columbia, Lauderdale (Tom Bailey), Mike Conner, Walthall, Jasper, Monroe, Perry, Jefferson Davis, Lowndes, and Smith County.

In the 1950s and 1960s, we saw an alarming change in land utilization in Mississippi. Alligators were disappearing. The resident colony of Sandhill Cranes in Jackson County was threatened by development. Brown Pelicans disappeared on the northern Gulf Coast. Resident southern Bald Eagles were gone from along the Mississippi River, and nesting Ospreys on the coast almost vanished. The Red-cockaded Woodpecker was disappearing due to U.S. Forest Service policy of cutting and removing all residual, "overmature" pines on national forests.

The decade of the 1960s brought a new generation of hunters and fishers. Fishing license sales increased with the completion of five flood control reservoirs, Ross Barnett Reservoir, and state-owned or operated lakes. Rapidly expanding deer herds, increased waterfowl hunting opportunities, and public hunting areas helped increase license sales. The commission initiated electronic data processing and license handling procedures. Field personnel were furnished uniforms along with radio-equipped and upgraded transportation. Warden training schools were begun with required attendance at the Law Enforcement Officer's Training Academy near Whitfield. The Pearl River Waterfowl Refuge and Management Area and the Sunflower, Indian Bayou, and Leflore County greentree waterfowl projects were completed. A fisheries laboratory and work station was built on Ross Barnett Reservoir. A boat launching ramp program was begun, and sea-run striped bass were stocked in reservoirs. In 1970, the Malmaison Wildlife Management Area in Grenada and Leflore Counties was acquired.

Large pumps such as these on the Sunflower Wildlife Management Area in Delta National Forest near Rolling Fork were used annually to flood "greentree reservoirs" to benefit wintering waterfowl and for public hunting.

Personnel with the state Game and Fish Commission brought these nonmigratory "giant" Canada Geese from a refuge in the upper Midwest for this first release of geese on the Pearl River Waterfowl Area north of Jackson.

Following World War II, large areas of bottomland forests and associated wetlands were cleared for soybean farming and catfish production.

In 1964, the statewide deer harvest was 14,820. In 1970, it had more than doubled to 31,578. Overpopulation and deterioration of deer herds in the Delta were occurring on some hunting club lands. The state's first experimental anterless deer hunting season was held on Catfish Point in Bolivar County during the 1961–1962 season. By the end of the decade, anterless deer hunting was becoming widely accepted as a necessary deer management practice.

The Southeastern Cooperative Wildlife Disease Study, working with state wildlife biologists and hunting clubs, rendered valuable assistance in identifying parasite and disease problems associated with high deer and turkey populations in the Delta. Directed by Dr. Frank Hayes and a field staff of veterinary technicians from the University of Georgia, these studies were helpful in demonstrating to sport hunters that endemic disease and parasites act to control high densities of game animals. The studies helped convince hunters that it is better to harvest surplus animals when they approach carrying capacity.

Rachel Carson's 1962 book, *Silent Spring*, aroused widespread concern about environmental pollution. In general, the 1960s was a time of awakening and realization of the consequences of unrestrained use and abuse of insecticides, wetland drainage, clearing on a massive scale for intensive agriculture, and almost complete destruction of natural lakes and streams supporting fish and wildlife resources. The effects of DDT and other chlorinated hydrocarbon insecticides became obvious after predatory and fish-eating birds began experiencing reproduction failures. The loss of sport fishing in Delta streams and lakes became self-evident. Also, it became evident that deer herds should be managed to prevent crop depredations and overbrowsing of their natural food supplies.

In 1970, 82 counties were open to deer hunting. Primitive firearms hunting in special seasons and special archery seasons allowed more hunting opportunities and brought in additional license sales. In 1971, the Okatibbee Waterfowl and Upland Game Management Area was established. A Wood Duck nest box program and utilization study was continued on waterfowl areas. In 1972, the legal harvest of Wild Turkeys reached 5691 gobblers in the 60 counties open for hunting.

National concern about endangered species brought passage of the Endangered Species Act of 1969. In 1972, the commission organized and convened a Committee on Rare and Endangered Species composed of scientists from universities and representatives of state and federal agencies knowledgeable about each group of vertebrate animals. The committee compiled a *Preliminary List of Rare and Threatened Vertebrates of Mississippi*, published by the commission in January 1975. The commission supported and had introduced in the 1974 legislature a model act for the protection and management of nongame species and endangered vertebrates. This law, after passage and signature by Governor William L. Waller, became effective July 1, 1974. On April 8, 1975, the commission adopted regulations that set up an official state list of endangered and threatened vertebrate species.

In 1973, the Lyman Fisheries Station was transferred to the commission for operation and production of game fish. A chemical analysis annex to the fisheries laboratory was completed. A Delta Lakes Pesticide Study was begun. An American alligator restocking project restocked 1066 Louisiana alligators in 60 counties in 1973. The new Mississippi Museum of Natural Science building was dedicated on November 9, 1973. A hunter safety program was under way, and state game wardens were designated as conservation officers.

In 1974, a sea-run striped bass culture from Ross Barnett Reservoir stock was begun in experimental rearing ponds

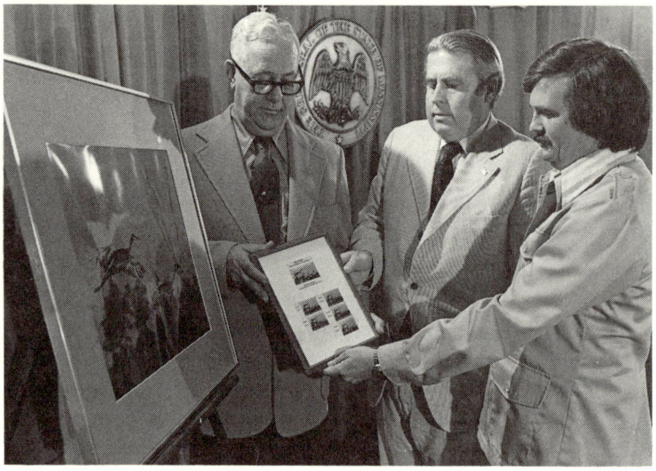

Author William H. Turcotte, left, looked on as photographer Joe Lee of Jackson, right, presented a framed print of Mississippi Sandhill Cranes to Gov. William Waller. Lee's picture was used for the first endangered species stamp produced by the Game and Fish Commission.

built on the reservoir. A public boat-launching ramp program was accelerated. On the Malmaison Wildlife Management Area, a Canada Goose flock was established. The alligator stocking program was continued, and an additional 1115 Louisiana alligators were released in 58 counties.

Also in 1974, following about two years of meetings and consultations, a representative of The Nature Conservancy, Dave Morine, and Bill Quisenberry, a biologist representing the commission, convinced key members of the legislature that a Mississippi Heritage Program should be launched. Legislation was introduced and passed in 1974, creating a state Wildlife Heritage Committee. The committee was the brainchild of Avery Wood, director of conservation, and Morine, who wanted a heritage program to identify Mississippi's unique natural areas and a program that would lead to acquisitions by purchase, gift, or other methods. Above all, Morine's hope for a project and acquisition of a unique area like the Pascagoula River hardwood tract in Jackson County challenged everyone connected with the program.

Avery Wood and state representative Charles Deaton of Greenwood had succeeded in getting some $700,000 of the Game and Fish Commission's "frozen fund" monies appropriated for use by the committee, monies that could be used to match federal aid funds to buy land. With matching federal funds, the committee had about $3 million available for land purchases, but the amount was inadequate for purchasing the extensive Pascagoula River lands. Preliminary contacts with the family owners of the land were not encouraging. They were already negotiating a possible sale or transfer of stock with another company and seemed adamant and unwilling to consider dealing with the state.

The committee was made up of Charles Deaton, Jim Neal, and Tommy Gollott, all from the House of Representatives, and three state senators, Donald Strider, Ray Montgomery, and "Son" Rhodes. The three appointees of Governor Waller to the committee were John Vaught, Bill Allen, and Bruce Brady. The first meeting of the committee, held at the Game and Fish Commission conference room in the old Robert E. Lee Hotel, was exploratory in nature with little understanding of specific objectives. Later, it developed that one family-member stockholder, Graham Wisner, was interested in helping The Nature Conservancy and the committee acquire the Pascagoula hardwood land and preserve it as an ecosystem for the citizens of Mississippi. When negotiations for the stock transfer failed and a major timber company withdrew plans to buy the land, the door opened for possible acquisition by the state.

After a lot of soul-searching and indecision by the participants, a meeting was arranged by Avery Wood for committee members, Governor Waller, important state officials, representatives of the Game and Fish Commission, and other state agencies to try and gain public support for the Pascagoula swamp project. Dave Morine and Graham Wisner made their presentations at the meeting. Governor Waller agreed to a proposal by Morine to draft a resolution instructing the Game and Fish Commission and the Wildlife Heritage Committee to explore the possibility of purchasing the 42,000 acres for the state.

These actions of the committee, and those following, make for the most intriguing story of salesmanship, political activism, and land purchase negotiations imaginable (Schueler 1980). Avery Wood got agency employees Bill Quisenberry and Melvin Tingle to produce a film on the Pascagoula tract. Quisenberry used it in promotional talks on at least 450 speaking engagements from November 1974 to May 1976, obtaining widespread public support from civic and special interest groups across the state. As a member of the Wildlife Heritage Committee, chairman of the House Game and Fish Committee, and member of the House Appropriations Committee, Charles Deaton introduced House Bill 914 to purchase the Pascagoula lands. The bill passed on a final vote of 52 to zero on March 19, 1975, authorizing funding of $15 million for the purchase.

In the following months, land purchase negotiations between The Nature Conservancy and the Pascagoula Hardwood Company continued. Finally, the Conservancy purchased 32,000 acres of the property, the company reserving some of the bordering pinelands from the sale. In turn, the state bought land with funds from the sale of $13.5 million in general obligation bonds. The deed was transferred ceremoniously to the committee for the state by The Nature Conservancy on September 26, 1978. The Conservancy later purchased an additional 3000 acres for the committee with

$2.5 million appropriated by the legislature. With the help of Dave Morine, the Wildlife Heritage Committee purchased the 808-acre McIntyre Scatters annex to the Malmaison Wildlife Management Area, 3682 acres in Issaquena County for the Shipland Wildlife Management Area, and 14,000 acres in the Old River Wildlife Management Area in Pearl River County. The 1000-acre Clark Creek Natural Area was acquired by charitable gift from International Paper Company and purchase of an additional, smaller acreage. The Dunn's Falls Natural Area in Newton County also was acquired by the committee. The work of the Wildlife Heritage Committee was terminated on July 1, 1978, by legislation transferring its functions and responsibilities for the Mississippi Heritage Program to the Game and Fish Commission. The program continues to function and pursue the heritage goals of identification and inventory, protection by acquisition or other means, and stewardship of Mississippi's native floral and faunal ecosystems.

The Game and Fish Commission's projects and programs were not interrupted during the process of buying land. Lake Bill Waller (200 acres) was constructed in Marion County in 1975 and opened for public fishing in 1977. The Caney Creek Wildlife Management Area was established in Scott County, and a Cooperative Wildlife Research Agreement with Mississippi State University was signed and initiated in 1975.

In 1976, the deer harvest in 82 counties was 43,608 legal deer. The Wild Turkey kill exceeded 8300 birds in the spring and fall seasons in 71 open counties. The commission issued and sold 31,000 of its first waterfowl hunting stamps, and hosted the thirtieth annual conference of the Southeastern Association of Fish and Wildlife Agencies in Jackson, with an attendance of 1200. A lower Pascagoula River fisheries and water quality survey was begun. Over two million game fish were produced at the Lyman Fisheries Station and stocked in public waters. The alligator stocking project was continued, and 777 Louisiana alligators were released in 24 counties.

The restocking program of the Eastern Wild Turkey was successful across Mississippi, thanks in part to available natural habitat, the efforts of the Department of Wildlife, Fisheries and Parks, successful law enforcement, and the cooperation of local landowners and hunters.

A fisheries and water quality survey on the lower Pearl River was initiated in 1977. The commission's game management operations in the field were organized into six districts with a program designed to provide technical assistance to landowners and hunting clubs to manage deer herds and other wildlife. Smallmouth bass were stocked in Bull Mountain Creek.

The 1979 regular session of the legislature reorganized the Game and Fish Commission. Renamed the Department of Wildlife Conservation, it incorporated the former Marine Resources Council, the Marine Conservation Commission, and the Boating Safety Commission, each of which had previously operated as separate state agencies.

In the 1980s, administrative supervision and accounting practices were improved. Data processing equipment was upgraded, and personal computers were made available to improve speed and quality of communications and issuance of licenses.

The public relations department obtained word processing and typesetting equipment, enabling the typesetting of brochures, publications, and the bimonthly magazine, *Mississippi Outdoors*. The magazine began using four-color illustrations in September 1986 and had attained a circulation of about 120,000 by 1991. Weekly educational television programs were initiated by the department using film and videotape equipment, and began with the cooperation of Mississippi Educational Television in 1990. These half-hour programs are shown twice weekly on the ETV network.

The game division added a nuisance predator control program designed primarily to relocate nuisance alligators, mainly in the three coastal counties, until legal harvest methods could be established. Upland game management was expanded to the Divide Cut Wildlife Management Area, lands acquired by the U.S. Army Corps of Engineers for the Tennessee-Tombigbee Waterway. The Caney Creek Wildlife Management Area annexed 15,000 acres on Bienville National Forest in Smith County. A long-term cooperative research study of the Wild Turkey is now being conducted by graduate students of Mississippi State University. The study is designed to monitor reproduction success related to weather conditions and other environmental factors that in the long term can be used to regulate legal harvest.

The freshwater fisheries management program has improved with innovative stocking of Florida bass, hybrid striped bass, and walleye. The Florida bass lives longer, attains larger size, and has been used exclusively for restocking in state-owned lakes and public waters. Hybrid striped bass, propagated and used for stocking in reservoirs, also are known to be reproducing successfully in river systems. A native walleye stocking program with the University of Mississippi is being carried out on Bull Mountain and Luxapalila Creeks. A fisheries field office and laboratory at Lake Monroe is helping improve the fish management program in northeast Mississippi. A headquarters building for equipment storage and maintenance is in use on Ross Barnett Reservoir by personnel working on construction of public boat launching ramps. A portable barge and pile driver has been readied for use in building fishing piers on public lakes.

The Wallop-Breaux Act, passed by Congress October 1, 1985, provided for increased federal funding for fisheries research and management, enabling the department to expand its research and development capabilities. A four-man research team of two biologists and two technicians is employed on short-term fish management problems. Recent improvements include: construction of six hatchery ponds and a water supply well on Ross Barnett Reservoir; replacement of drain culverts on Lakes Waller, Claude Bennett, Mike Conner, and Oktibbeha County; fish shelters; sand beaches; graveled spawning beds; and ramps and other facilities for the handicapped. The department has taken responsibility for management of Kemper County Lake (652 acres) and Neshoba Legion Lake (225 acres). Buildings, ramps, picnic areas, and other facilities are being provided.

The cooperative research program with state universities has furnished information needed to manage various fish species, including freshwater drum, striped bass, largemouth bass, walleye, and crappie. Study and experience have led to a recent reduction of the daily limit on crappie and a minimum size limit that should result in a better catch of large crappie. Continuing angler surveys will evaluate the success of new fish management practices.

The duties and powers of the Marine Resources Council and the Marine Conservation Commission were transferred and consolidated within the Department of Wildlife Conservation's Bureau of Marine Resources on July 1, 1979. At the time, there were 47 marine resources employees. Bureau personnel manage the commercial and recreational fisheries and associated wetlands so important to continuing fisheries production, and a variety of other species of wildlife along the 370 miles of Mississippi tidelands. The functions of the bureau require law enforcement to protect resources and insure boating safety and rescue operations. Bureau personnel have the responsibility of guarding against pollution and destructive encroachments upon the estuaries, tidewater marshes, and prime water bottoms for shellfish. Coastal zone management is needed to insure continued productivity of all marine resources. This cannot be done without researching, planning, identifying, and utilizing improvements to offset losses to the estuarine environment.

Industrial, commercial, port, transportation, and in some instances, housing and recreational developments have severely altered marshlands and estuarine resources. As the diversity of wildlife habitats and marine life resources diminishes, so does the quality of life in the coastal zone and its attractiveness to tourists and all Mississippians. Fortunately, barrier and offshore islands have escaped development. The Gulf Islands National Seashore, about 20,000 acres of coastal savannas in the Mississippi Sandhill Crane National Wildlife Refuge, have been acquired, and other savanna and tidewater lands are under consideration for acquisition and management. Other strategic areas should be considered for preservation. There are many possibilities of improvements for wildlife species on lands already altered by dredge fills or by marshland ditching. Attention should be given to preserving and maintaining even small marsh areas before they are destroyed and used for other purposes.

The Game and Fish Commission began operations in 1932 with three commissioners and five employees. As soon as hunting and fishing license monies were available, law enforcement and the beginning of a wildlife conservation program were organized. Hunters, fishers, and outdoor recreationists have willingly supported programs for protecting, increasing, and managing our outdoor heritage with their excise taxes, permits, user fees, and licenses. The general public and Mississippi's economy have derived and enjoyed great benefits from its attention to conservation. It should be remembered that conservation is dependent on wise *utilization* of natural and wildlife resources. This requires continuing conservation education and resource management, since few among us are born conservationists.

A few people would deny others the enjoyment and use of wildlife resources. Some species of wild animals can sustain harvestable surpluses. Therefore hunting, fishing, and trapping, when allowed for the ultimate benefit of a species, should be permitted. The importance of our natural heritage cannot be overestimated. It must be nurtured by all Mississippians for future generations to enjoy.

Birds and the Environment

The occurrence and distribution of birds is largely determined by patterns of land use, which are always changing to some degree. These changes affect the seasonal occurrence and abundance of birds and other wildlife. Mississippi has a diversity of soils and plant life, and an abundance of wildlife habitat. The humid subtropical climate with four distinct seasons, adequate rainfall, and mild winters attracts large numbers of summer-resident, breeding birds and winter residents. Lying directly above the geographic center of the Gulf of Mexico and north of the Yucatan Peninsula, Mississippi is in the main passageway of transgulf migrants.

Physical Characteristics

Mississippi has 44 miles of coastline. Latitudes range from 30°13' on the coast to 35° at the Tennessee border. Longitude extremes from Alabama on the east to the Mississippi River on the west are 88°07' and 91°41'. The surface area is 47,716 square miles, which includes 450 square miles of inland water. Elevations range from sea level to the 806-foot Woodall Mountain in Tishomingo County. The five major drainage systems are the Tombigbee, Pascagoula, Pearl, Big Black, and Yazoo Rivers. All empty into the Gulf of Mexico either directly or through the Mississippi River.

The state is generally divided into three soil regions: the river flood plain, loess belt (windblown alluvium), and the coastal plain. The interior coastal plain reaches its limit in Tishomingo County, where it joins a unique section, the oldest geologic formation in Mississippi. Exposed rocks formed during the Devonian and Mississippian Periods are characteristic of this small, unique section of northeastern Mississippi. The remainder of the state was once covered by an extension of the Gulf of Mexico, which began to recede in the early Cretaceous Period, leaving sedimentary deposits with low topographic elevations forming the coastal plain and sloping gently toward the Gulf of Mexico.

Mississippi is further divided into soil resource areas with distinct physical characteristics. They are: (1) Mississippi-Yazoo Delta; (2) brown loam (thick loess bluff); (3) thin loess; (4) upper coastal plain; (5) blacklands (northeast and central prairie); (6) interior flatwoods; (7) lower coastal plain; and (8) coastal flatwoods. These soil resource areas are discussed individually below.

Above: Robin

Major physiographic regions of Mississsippi.

Mississippi-Yazoo Delta

The Delta is comprised of alluvial soil deposits of the Mississippi and Yazoo Rivers and their tributary streams. It is bordered on the east by the Loess Bluff (brown loam) belt and on the west by meanders of the Mississippi River. That portion lying above Vicksburg is protected by the mainline levee and a backwater levee system along the Yazoo River. The batture lands and associated levees, bendways, and oxbow lakes are highly productive for timber, livestock, fish, and wildlife. The fertile, generally level land of the Delta protected by the levee system (except for the Delta National Forest, timber company holdings, refuges, and other isolated tracts) is devoted to intensive agriculture. The remaining hardwood bottomlands support higher forest wildlife populations than any other area in the state. The Delta also has the majority of waterfowl habitat.

Brown Loam

Developed from windblown soil particles, this region has some of the state's most highly productive soils. The brown loam soil is generally over four feet thick. It is highly erodible and over much of the area the terrain is too steep for cultivation. The brown loam belt has a diverse and highly valuable association of hardwoods and mixed forest types. Much of the area consists of steep hills and narrow valleys devoted to timber production. Where the terrain permits, the land is used for row crops and pasture. This area supports a great variety of wildlife and a diversity of vegetative types. The southern part of the loess belt extends from the western border of Tennessee below Memphis, bordering the Delta on the east to Vicksburg. Below Vicksburg it borders the Mississippi River bottomlands to the northern boundary of Louisiana.

Thin Loess

This is a belt of silty soils overlying various kinds of coastal plain soils and is generally less than four feet thick. Soils are highly eroded and fertility is generally low. Much of this area is forested in stands of pine, upland hardwoods, mixed pine and hardwoods, and hardwood bottomlands. The thin loess is a transitional belt of mixed soils lying between the brown loam on the west and coastal plain on the east. The terrain is generally rolling land devoted to timber, pasture, and row crops on the better soils and stream bottoms. Wildlife production is low or high depending on land use, soil quality, and types of vegetation.

Upper Coastal Plain

This land area includes the greater part of northeast and east-central Mississippi. The soils are made up of sand, clays, slab rock, and some gravel deposits of coastal plain origin. Many soil types have developed from these materials. The topography varies from level to steep. The soils are acidic and low in fertility. Steep and rolling lands are better suited for trees than row crops. Farms are mainly small and large tracts of forest land are found throughout the upper coastal plain.

Blacklands

The Northeast Prairie and Central Prairie are separate blackland areas. The larger one, called the black belt, extends from the southern boundary of Alcorn County, where it is bordered by the upper coastal plain and the interior flatwoods on the west into Kemper County, where it continues into Alabama. The Central Prairie region extends from Madison County across parts of Rankin, Scott, Smith, Newton, Jasper, Clarke, and Wayne Counties, terminating at the Alabama state boundary. Black belt soils are high in lime, tend toward heavy clay textures, and are well suited to pasture, forage, and hay crops.

The topography is level to gentle relief. Bottomlands in this area are highly productive. General features of this region are suitable to fields, large pasturelands, and meadows.

Interior Flatwoods

This belt of flatwoods extends across northeastern Mississippi from the Tennessee boundary south and southeast, bordering the Pontotoc Ridge and the Northeast Prairie to Kemper County, where it continues into Alabama. The soils are generally poorly drained and low in productivity. Most of the area is suitable for production of pines, and forest acreage is abundant.

Lower Coastal Plain

This soil resource area is one of the largest and occupies the southern and southeastern part of the state. The many kinds of soil are generally low in fertility and support natural stands of pines and mixed pine and hardwoods. The topography varies from level to steep with large areas of gently sloping land suitable for crops and pasture. Much of this area is devoted to timber production. The pine forests are generally low in wildlife population density, although at some stages of forest management quail and turkey production may be good.

Coastal Flatwoods

This area borders Mississippi Sound and includes the barrier islands about 12 miles offshore. The land is flat to gently sloping, largely covered in longleaf or slash pines, and near the coastline has numerous marshlands and savannas. The soils are acidic and fertility is very low. The principal use of underdeveloped areas is timber production. Along the coastline, beaches, and marshes along estuaries and bays, live oak groves and hammocks add a great diversity of habitats attractive to large numbers of migrant and winter-resident birds. Forest game animal production is generally low due to low soil fertility and human disturbances.

Coastal flatwoods with their savannas, hammocks, cheniers, fresh and salt marshes, beaches, and open water areas are havens for migrants and many kinds of wintering and breeding birds not found elsewhere in the state.

Forested Lands

Forests dominate the Mississippi landscape even after generations of land clearing and development. Over half of the 30,250,140 acres total land area (about 55 percent) are forested lands. The state continues to lose forest wildlife habitat to urban and industrial development, highways, and dredge and fill operations. A substantial amount of forest land is converted to intensive farming, aquaculture, and monocultural tree farming, which has reduced the value for birds and other wildlife.

Forest Types

Bottomland hardwoods, upland hardwoods, mixed pine and hardwoods, longleaf-slash pines, and loblolly-shortleaf pines are the major forest types.

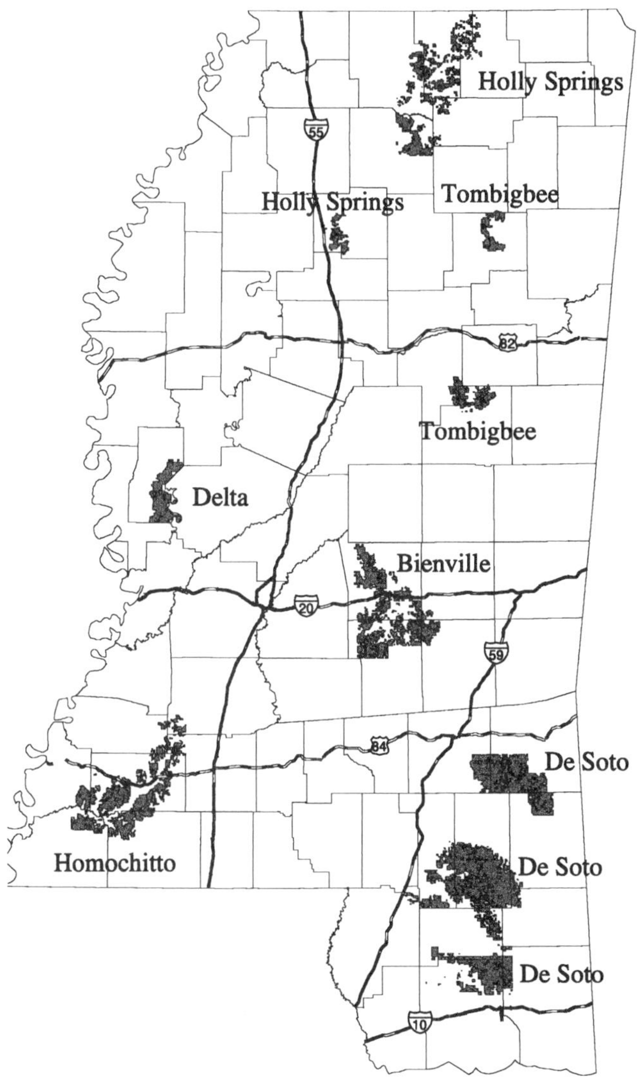

National Forests in Mississsippi.

Bottomland hardwood forests have more than half the stand in oak, sweet gum, tupelo, cypress, and common associates including cottonwood, sycamore, willow, ash, elm, hackberry, and maple. Bottomland forests are in the Yazoo-Mississippi alluvial plain and along the flood plains of other waterways throughout the state. In association with scattered open lands, old oxbows, and other wetland types, bottomlands are the most productive wildlife habitat. It is the type of wildlife habitat most affected by land clearing, drainage, and conversion to other uses. About 3.6 million acres (11.9 percent) remain in the state.

Upland hardwoods (oak, hickory) make up about 4.3 million acres (14.2 percent) of forest types. Common associates are sweet gum, yellow poplar, elm, ash, and maple. On rich upland soils such as the deep loess hills, this type is productive for wildlife and contains a large diversity of trees such as oaks, sweet gum, yellow poplar, beech, magnolias, linden, black walnut, black locust, and scattered pines along ridgetops. On poor soils of north-central and northeastern counties, due to mismanagement, this type is generally not productive, and the poorer soils are better suited to pine forests.

Mixed pine and hardwood (pine-oak) forests are more than 50 percent oaks and other hardwoods with 25 percent or more southern pines. Associates include sweet gum, hickory, and yellow poplar. These are commonly found in the upper coastal plain and adjacent to the loess hills area, where they intersperse stands of loblolly-shortleaf pines. The mixed stands of pine and hardwood result from changes in land use associated with human activities. This forest type makes up about 3.4 million acres (11.2 percent) of forest types.

Longleaf-slash pine, totaling about 1.3 million acres (4.3 percent), occurs mainly on the sandy soils of the lower coastal plain. This forest type has 50 percent or more of the stand in longleaf and slash pines with common associates being oaks, sweet gum, and other pines. Longleaf pine occurs on the drier sites such as deep sands. Slash pines, being less fire resistant, occur naturally on the wetter soils, such as the poorly drained coastal savanna lands of the coastal terrace and on the barrier islands. With fire control and recent planting and harvesting practices, slash pine has invaded sites formerly dominated by longleaf pines. The poorer, usually drier soils with which this type is associated are generally less productive wildlife habitat. With wildlife management practices, open pine forests can be made more productive for deer, Wild Turkeys, and quail by the use of controlled burning. Clear-cutting and the following burning and replanting can benefit quail, some nongame birds, and other wildlife during early stages of growth, but soon become unproductive when dense pine plantations develop. This forest type mixed with pond cypress and wet-site hardwood growths dominates the lower parts of the coastal counties and will invade the open savannas in the absence of regular fires. The Mississippi Sandhill Crane and some overwintering Sandhill Cranes from northern states occupy the savanna lands of lower Jackson County, which are critical habitat for the resident crane population.

Bottomland hardwoods and associated wetlands of the 65,000-acre Delta National Forest in Mississippi's lower Delta support a great diversity of birds and other wildlife species.

Shortleaf-loblolly pines occupy about 4.7 million acres (14 percent) of forest types. This type has more than 50 percent shortleaf and loblolly in association with other southern pines, oak, hickory, and sweet gum. Loblolly pine is usually dominant, prefers moister sites, and grows faster, making up most of the pine timber volume harvested in the state. Conversion of hardwoods to pine and the establishment of pine plantations following clear-cutting has had an overall negative effect on wildlife in many parts of the upper coastal plain, where this is the dominant forest type. This forest type occupies most of the land area north of the lower coastal plain.

Agricultural Lands

Approximately 12.3 million acres (about 37 percent) in Mississippi are devoted to crops and pasture. Since the end of World War II, there has been a great increase in the average size of farms, a drastic reduction in the number of farms, and a decrease in the total acreage in cropland. Mechanization of agricultural operations has led to consolidation of land ownership, the abandonment of family farms, changing to pasture or timber production, and the movement of people from rural areas to towns and cities to find employment. Mississippi farmers have always relied on cotton as the major cash crop. Since 1950, soybean production has increased at a rate exceeding national averages. There has been large-scale clearing of land in bottomland hardwoods

Most catfish farms are flooded year-round. When drawn down to low levels, a variety of waterfowl, herons, shorebirds, and other species are attracted to feeding opportunities on the muddy bottoms of individual ponds.

once considered marginal for row crop production. The increased demand for soybeans, widespread land clearing, and subsequent production has resulted in a loss of valuable wetlands and bottomland hardwoods critical for forest wildlife and waterfowl. Recently, following a decline in world prices for soybeans, catfish farming and rice and wheat production have replaced soybeans on some of the marginal lands. These changes in land use, especially in the Delta, have favored barren-ground and open-country birds, migrating shorebirds, fish-eating birds utilizing catfish ponds, and ducks, geese, and swans under extreme backwater flooding of low-lying farm lands. Subtle changes in land use values, together with the restricted use of pesticides, establishment of refuges and wildlife management areas, improved water quality standards, and rules for protection of wildlife and wetlands are beginning to enhance wildlife values on these farm lands.

Land diverted from row crops to improved pasture, hay, and grain sorghum has increased more than three-fold since 1950. Beef cattle production in some ways has enhanced populations of birds such as starlings, blackbirds, Cattle Egrets, and some that feed on sod and flying insects or other invertebrates.

Other Open Lands

Urban areas, industrial developments, highways, power lines and other rights-of-way, and water areas occupy about 1.1 million acres (3.6 percent) of land area in Mississippi.

There are 11 river basins and five major river systems. The Mississippi River drains the Delta and headwaters of the Yazoo River. Big Black River empties into the Mississippi at Grand Gulf. The Tombigbee, Pearl, and Pascagoula Rivers empty into the Gulf of Mexico. Stream reservoirs are important habitat for birds and other wildlife. The four flood control reservoirs in northern Mississippi are important for recreation and wildlife. The Tennessee-Tombigbee Waterway in the northeastern counties and the impoundments above the locks are providing new kinds of habitat for wildlife and water-related recreation. Ross Barnett Reservoir on Pearl River above Jackson, built for water supply, recreation, and shoreline development, has enhanced the diversity of wintering and summer-resident waterbirds. The Okatibbee flood control reservoir on the headwaters of the Chickasawhay River above Meridian has also diversified and increased wildlife and water-based recreation opportunities. There are numerous smaller reservoirs, state-owned public lakes, private lakes, small ponds, and sewage lagoons scattered throughout the state. All of these smaller water areas contribute variety to bird and animal populations. Old meanders of stream courses and the oxbow lakes along the Mississippi River and their associated wetlands are important for wintering waterfowl. Moon, Beulah, Ferguson, Bolivar, Washington, and Eagle Lakes are some of the larger natural lakes along the Mississippi River.

Power lines and railroad rights-of-way are important for providing diversity and edge effect. The modern highway system with concrete bridges and box culverts has accelerated southward expansion of the breeding ranges of several bird species including Barn and Cliff Swallows and Eastern Phoebes that nest under bridges or in box culverts. Fish Crows utilize highway corridors, roadside parks, and other developed recreation areas, feeding on road kills or refuse. Red-tailed Hawks utilize interstate highways during the winter months, perching on bordering trees or power lines and hunting for rodents along the rights-of-way. Rock Doves also utilize highway bridges and trestle crossings for nesting and roosting.

Urban areas provide a large diversity of habitats for wildlife. Areas such as parks, airports, residential areas, idle or undeveloped vacant space, industrial sites, and even graveled roofs of buildings are utilized by birds. Industrial sites along the coast have some of the most attractive habitats for shorebirds and migrants, but access to these areas may be restricted. Sewage lagoons and their adjacent borders attract migrant shorebirds and rarities such as phalaropes, scoters, and western grebes. On the coast, Least Terns have nested on gravel roofs and nighthawks, Killdeers, American Kestrels, and House Finches have adapted to nest on downtown buildings in Jackson. Fish Crows, Ring-billed Gulls, and Rock Doves frequent shopping malls and fast-food establishments. More than 30 species of resident and migratory landbirds can be found nesting in residential parts of cities. A nonmigratory Canada Goose flock frequents the highly developed shorelines of Ross Barnett Reservoir and parts of the Jackson metropolitan area. Land-fills are

Large inland reservoirs used for flood control, water supply, and recreation have created new kinds of wetlands that attract more kinds of wildlife by providing open water, shorelines, mud flats, and freshwater marshes.

frequented by scavengers such as crows, gulls, and vultures. The spillways below reservoirs are the best locations for finding rare species of wintering gulls. The highly developed coast has produced the largest number of new species of birds on the state list. Airports have yielded most of the state records for Sprague's Pipit and Smith's Longspur. Even Wild Turkeys are known to occur in metropolitan Jackson, and Mississippi Kites nest regularly in parts of Jackson. Blackbirds, unfortunately, have adapted to roosting in large numbers in towns and cities, usually in residential areas and particularly in the Delta.

After World War II, vast changes in land use have occurred in Mississippi. Overall, these changes have been beneficial to the economy of the state, and the result is a greater diversity of wildlife species. Total populations of some species have increased, while others have declined as a result of habitat loss or alteration. Some Neotropical birds are declining due to loss of breeding habitat. Waterfowl populations, except the Wood Duck, have declined for the same reason. Fish-eating birds suffered declines due to long-lived pesticides in their food chain, but are recovering. Bobwhite populations are reduced, while Wild Turkeys have expanded in range and numbers as a result of restocking with wild-trapped birds. A number of western and exotic species have invaded and become resident breeders or appear likely to become so. These include the Cattle Egret, Shiny Cowbird, the introduced House Finch, and western birds such as the Bronzed Cowbird, Scissor-tailed Flycatcher, and White-tailed Kite. Hopefully, the recovery programs for endangered, threatened, and nongame species including the Red-cockaded Woodpecker, Bald Eagle, Mississippi Sandhill Crane, and others will insure their preservation. Wildlife heritage programs in place that identify unique or critical habitats for plants and wildlife should result in their preservation by acquisition or by other measures.

Finding Birds

Finding birds, better known as birding or bird-watching, has really caught on across most of the United States. According to a recent survey by the U.S. Fish and Wildlife Service, 76 million American's have enjoyed nonconsumptive activities such as observing, feeding, or photographing birds and other wildlife. Almost 4.9 million participants, or about 42 percent of the population, enjoyed nonconsumptive recreation such as bird-watching in Alabama, Kentucky, Mississippi, and Tennessee. During 1991, they spent $889 million on birding expenses in these four states. Birding, it seems, is big business where you find it.

Birding is best done in a small group, and parties of one to three are better than larger groups. Birding can be done very effectively from an automobile, using it as a blind. Frequent stops made in different habitat types where birds are encountered is the usual procedure. When wary birds such as waterfowl, shorebirds, hawks, and distant birds are seen, it is best to view them by using the car as a blind and a support for binoculars and spotting scopes.

The best time for observing birds during the breeding season is usually from daylight (or just before) until about 10 A.M., when they become less active. Dusk is a rewarding time to see and hear waterbirds and flycatchers that call or sing before roosting. Owls, goatsuckers, night-herons, some wintering sparrows, American Woodcocks, waterfowl, Northern Bobwhites, and others are active at dusk and call or sing before nightfall.

In winter, birds may be active throughout the day and getting an early start is not as important. On warm winter days some birds become less active at midday or under weather conditions such as gusting rain and high wind. The presence of a Sharp-shinned Hawk or Cooper's Hawk will cause small birds to hide and remain inactive for 20 minutes or more.

When possible, birding trips should be planned so the sun is behind the observer. Birds in silhouette or backlighted are hard to identify. Bird walks in the morning should proceed westward. Seeing all field marks in good light is necessary to identify some birds, unless they can be identified by song.

While in the field, keep to paths and make frequent stops for looking and listening. Follow through by careful viewing with binoculars until each bird is identified by field marks, behavior, and habitat preference. It may help to sit and wait for birds to appear at a food supply, such as a fruiting mulberry tree, or a watering place used for drinking and bathing. Some birds seen will escape identification even by expert birders.

Weather conditions can affect bird-watching, especially strong wind and heavy rain. Fog, light rain, and drizzle generally do not affect bird activity, but make distant birds harder to identify. During high winds, birds stay in heavier cover and show themselves only briefly. On windy days, birds find shelter on the leeward side of dense cover and shorelines.

When daytime temperatures remain below freezing, bird activity increases in Mississippi. During extremely cold weather, with heavy snowfall and icy conditions in the northern United States and southern Canada, expect an influx of birds such as Purple Finches, Fox Sparrows, Horned Larks, Lapland Longspurs, Pine Siskins, Evening Grosbeaks, Bald Eagles, and waterfowl.

Sometimes tropical storms push pelagic birds ashore and inland. In late summer and fall, hurricanes along the coast may cause unusual concentrations of migrants and western species to appear. Strong cold fronts during spring and fall migrations can cause fallouts of migrants along the coast and at places inland. These fallouts enhance birding opportunities.

With experience, birders learn to associate different birds with their habitats. If birders expect to find a variety of birds on a field trip, it is important to cover a variety of habitats, particularly near wetlands and open water. Proximity to salt water affords even greater habitat diversity. Habitats containing the greatest diversity are along the coastline, where open water converges with beaches; dunes; saltwater, brackish, and freshwater marshes; hammocks; savannas; mixed pine and hardwoods with well-developed shrub layers; and areas altered or disturbed by industrial or residential development.

Bottomlands with mixed stands of hardwoods and evergreens, associated wetlands, and open water have a larger variety of birds than other inland sites. Bottomlands are enhanced by the presence of wildlife refuges, reservoirs, and other man-made alterations that create diversity.

Upland hardwoods with scattered stands of pines or other evergreens such as those found in the Loess Bluff with its rugged, deep ravines and fertile soils have abundant birdlife, especially Neotropical migratory birds in spring and summer. Fewer birds occur in dominant pine stands of the coastal plain. Pinelands of the lower coastal plain, however, afford a diversity of birdlife with species such as Red-cockaded Woodpecker, Brown-headed Nuthatch, Bachman's Sparrow, Prairie Warbler, Pine Warbler, and Mississippi Sandhill Crane. Look for winter residents such as the Short-billed Marsh Wren, Palm Warbler, Yellow-rumped Warbler, Tree Swallow, and Sharp-tailed Sparrow.

Diverse birdlife occurs in the Yazoo Delta, where most of the land is in intensive agriculture. Barren-ground and short-grass birds such as Horned Larks, Lapland Longspurs, meadowlarks, resident and migrant shorebirds, waterfowl, blackbirds, robins, sparrows, and starlings utilize large expanses of open fields dotted with pockets of open water. Numerous catfish farms and rice-growing operations in the Delta have a variety of birdlife including wintering waterfowl.

The Mississippi River and adjacent land beside the levees afford unique birding opportunities. In spring and summer, batture lands between the main levees with their sandbars, open parklike sand fields, scattered brushy areas, open cottonwood groves, willow thickets, borrow pits, old river runs, and large tracts of bottomland hardwoods provide interesting places to see birds and other wildlife. Access to these lands is limited, but public-access fishing camps, lands, or parks are available, and other areas can be entered by asking the landowner's permission.

Segments of the main levees are open for travel either as public roads or as subject to control by local levee boards. These land and water areas are likely places to see numbers of Mississippi Kites, Warbling Vireos, Painted Buntings, Indigo Buntings, Dickcissels, Wild Turkeys, inland Least Terns, Red-headed Woodpeckers, Baltimore Orioles, Orchard Orioles, and many others. In late summer and fall Wood Storks, White Pelicans, herons, swallows, shorebirds, and other migrant birds occur periodically in large numbers.

Another part of the state unique for its birdlife is Tishomingo County. Summer-resident breeding populations of Scarlet Tanagers, Ovenbirds, Eastern Phoebes, Whip-poor-wills, and American Goldfinches occur regularly. Tishomingo State Park is the best locality for finding most of these species, and White-breasted Nuthatches are also fairly common there. The first known breeding colonies of Cliff Swallows were found under bridges and large box culverts along Highway 25 near Pickwick Lake.

Intensive farming practices in the Mississippi Delta leave little room for protective cover needed by wildlife. Agricultural activities favor barren ground and open country birds. Wetter sites attract and hold wintering waterfowl and migrant shorebirds.

Old oxbow lakes and associated wetlands found amid bottomland hardwoods are some of Mississippi's most productive bird habitats.

The northeastern and central black belts have some of the more interesting places for finding birds. For reasons unknown, the black belts have attracted western birds such as Scissor-tailed Flycatchers breeding in Lee and Newton Counties, a wintering Ash-throated Flycatcher, and one record of Townsend Solitaire in Newton County. Near Starkville, Red Crossbills breeding on Noxubee National Wildlife Refuge, a Yellow Wagtail on a sewage lagoon, and a Snow Bunting on the Mississippi State University campus are unique sightings, and their discovery was probably due to the activity of several keen birders.

Lark Sparrows and Horned Larks are probable resident breeding birds in the black belts meriting further study. Wintering Northern Harrier and Short-eared Owl roost fields have been discovered, and more observations of these species are needed. Communal roosts of the Long-eared Owl are likely in cedar thickets of the northeastern black belt. Further study is needed on short-grass and barren-ground birds such as longspurs and some sparrows.

The Tennessee-Tombigbee Waterway has created aquatic habitats and new birding opportunities in northeastern counties. Noxubee National Wildlife Refuge and Bienville National Forest in the black belts have the largest and most accessible concentrations of the Red-cockaded Woodpecker. Both areas have management programs for this endangered cavity nester.

The three coastal counties offer the widest range of opportunities for birding in this descending order: Jackson, Hancock, and Harrison. Unique opportunities on the Mississippi Coast for finding birds can be found in *Birds and Birding on the Mississippi Coast* (Toups and Jackson 1987), available at most local bookstores. This book treats most of the more than 357 bird species recorded on the coast. It has seasonal distribution and occurrence records and charts, best birding areas with detailed locality maps, and treatment of 357 species accounts. The book also has two chapters devoted to "birding by the calendar" (what and where to find by months) and a "big day" birding outline for finding more than 50 percent of coastal avifauna. A chapter is also devoted to birding the barrier islands and for pelagic species.

In Jackson County, the best-known areas for birding are: Bayou Casotte–Greenwood Island Industrial area, the swamps and marshes on the lower Pascagoula and Escatawpa Rivers, the Pascagoula estuary and industrial area landfills (known as Pascagoula flats), the Mississippi Sandhill Crane National Wildlife Refuge, the Gautier area including Shepard State Park and Graveline Bayou, and Bellefontaine Beach–Davis Bayou including the Gulf Islands National Seashore grounds. Petit Bois, Anderson Spoil Island, Ship Island, and Horn Island, part of the Gulf Islands National Seashore, offer good year-round birding.

The 26 miles of Harrison County beaches are noted for nesting Least Terns and Black Skimmers, rare gulls, and numerous shorebirds and waterbirds. Inland areas such as parks, live oak groves, marinas, small marshes, stream borders, and open pinelands afford birding opportunities. Lyman Fish Hatchery off U.S. Highway 49 is noted for its fall and winter visitors. Often, hurricanes and storms propel birds inland and account for many shorebird and pelagic bird records in late summer and fall. Spring and fall storms or cold fronts precipitate migrants along shorelines and bring some western birds to the coastal zone.

Hancock County is known for casual western bird visitors, a diversity of species and habitat, and rural environments affording easygoing birding at numerous sites along secondary roads. Large expanses of open pasture, pinelands, and clear-cuts are havens for wintering raptors, including the resident, breeding White-tailed Kite, and numerous sparrows. The Logtown-Pearlington areas border the Pearl River and include part of the NASA buffer zone. Here old home sites, massive live oaks, openings, and pinelands harbor summer residents and spring and fall migrant landbirds.

The Port Bienville Industrial Park west of Waveland is a large complex of open land with scattered industrial plants and roads with bordering freshwater ponds, brushy thickets, scattered pines, and marshy bayous. This area, along with most of the Ansley Marsh–Bayou Caddy areas, are "migrant traps" for western strays and other species at times during the spring and fall. The Ansley and Bayou Caddy areas have extensive salt and brackish marshlands, cheniers, hammocks, and open pasture not easily accessible except by boat.

The beachfront from Bay St. Louis to Bayou Caddy and at Buccaneer State Park are best for herons, gulls, terns, Brown Pelicans, and shorebirds. Offshore ducks, grebes, scoters, and occasional rarities follow storms or strong northerly winds. Buccaneer Park has boardwalks over marshes that harbor several species of rails. Live oaks, brush, and pine areas are havens for incoming migrants, fall arrivals, and winter residents.

Brackish and freshwater ponds adjacent to the L & N Railroad between Clermont Harbor and Lakeshore are interesting for herons, ibises, rails, gallinules, Marsh Wrens, ducks, and occasional shorebirds. In Waveland, the sewage lagoon and Jackson marsh often highlight any coast birding trip. The lagoon is bordered by mixed woodlands and attracts a great diversity of landbirds and waterbirds, particularly during migration when it becomes a migrant trap for warblers and occasional rarities.

Jackson marsh in Waveland is a freshwater swamp bordered by cypress and mixed woods and has open water with emergent aquatic vegetation. From November to March, expect to see surface-feeding ducks, Wood Ducks, gallinules, and landbird migrants in spring and fall. Herons and egrets sometimes use bordering thickets for roosting.

Reservoirs

Reservoirs built for flood control, water supply, and recreation by government agencies are good locations to find a variety of birds. Of the four flood control lakes in north-central Mississippi, Sardis and Grenada are the largest and afford the best birding. With more flood storage capacity and draw-downs to conservation pool level, large reservoirs have more exposed mud flats attractive to shore- and waterbirds. Exposed shorelines are revegetated during draw-down. When reflooded, waterfowl food plants and grasses become available to ducks and geese.

Sardis Waterfowl Refuge has a winter flock of several thousand Canada Geese and other geese and ducks. Grenada Waterfowl Refuge on Big Creek is on the upper end of the Grenada Reservoir and accessible from U.S. Highway 8. Sardis, Enid, and Grenada Lakes have state parks on adjacent lands.

The spillways below Sardis and Grenada Lakes are noted for rare gulls. Other bird rarities recorded on the reservoirs include Mountain Bluebird (Grenada damsite); Mountain Plover (Grenada mud flat); Prairie Falcon (Enid, Cossar State Park); Brant, Trumpeter Swan, Sandhill Crane, Northern Goshawk (Sardis Refuge); and Western Grebe, Red-throated Loon, and Pacific Loon (Sardis Lake). In winter, the exposed lands below the flood pools of these reservoirs and bordering uplands harbor many kinds of landbirds.

Built for water supply, recreation, and shoreline development, Ross Barnett Reservoir on Pearl River north of Jackson has approximately 33,000 acres of water and wetlands. It has enhanced birding in the Jackson area for gulls, terns, waterfowl, waterbirds, shorebirds, and landbirds from numerous access places along the Natchez Trace Parkway, Highway 43, and Pearl River Waterfowl Refuge. Christmas Bird Counts in the reservoir area have recorded over 125 species overall and some 111 species on individual count days.

Okatibbee Lake near Meridian is the smallest of the flood-control impoundments. Upper parts of the lake are managed for wildlife. It is attractive for numerous waterfowl, including Tundra Swans that appeared one winter and fed in a nearby rye grass pasture. After a successful eagle hacking program on the lake in 1992 in which 16 Bald Eagles were fledged, wintering Bald Eagles are regular visitors.

Public Fishing Lakes, State Parks, and Wildlife Management Areas

Numerous state-owned and -leased fishing lakes managed by the Department of Wildlife, Fisheries and Parks are located in state parks or on land acquired for their construc-

Lotus, water lily, Southern wild rice, cattail and other emergent aquatic plants provide nesting and brood habitat for gallinules, rails, and Least Bitterns. They also serve as feeding and resting areas for ducks and other waterfowl. Lotus provides ideal food and brood-rearing habitat for Wood Ducks.

tion for public fishing and recreation. Most have facilities for access and use. Many provide opportunities for seeing migrant shorebirds, waterbirds, and landbirds in diverse habitats. Although each lake differs, most have some bordering mixed pine and hardwoods or bottomland hardwoods.

Many state parks commemorate historical events, contain battlegrounds and archaeological sites, and provide public use facilities. At times these parklands with their camping areas and nature trails become migrant traps and are good places to find resident and migratory birds. Birding parties will find the scenic parks convenient for use as headquarters while birding in the park and surrounding areas.

The Vicksburg Military Park is a good place to view landbirds and migrants. It is one of the best spots in the state to watch annual Broad-winged Hawk migrations in September and early October along bluffs overlooking the Mississippi River.

The Natchez Trace Parkway extends from Tishomingo County to Natchez. Nearly completed, the Parkway has numerous nature areas for birding along its 310-mile length with many points of historical interest, all well interpreted.

National wildlife refuges and state wildlife management areas are operated to provide public recreation. Some refuges and management areas provide controlled public access for birding, hunting for upland game, and other outdoor recreational opportunities. Six national forests encompass more than a million acres and offer opportunities for finding diverse bird species. To help birders and others, the approximate boundaries of national forests and wildlife refuges, scenic and military parks, and state wildlife management areas are shown on official state highway maps.

Mississippi has numerous state wildlife management areas and federal national wildlife refuges operated to provide public recreation. Some provide controlled access for birding, hunting, and other outdoor opportunities. Many areas are good sites to visit and see species such as these Eastern Wild Turkeys.

Fish Farms, Sewage Lagoons, and Airports

Catfish farming is a thriving industry in the Delta. Leveed ponds are flooded almost year-round and attract waterfowl, herons, and even shorebirds when drawn down to low levels (Hodges 1989). Nearby rice farming makes fish farms more attractive for ducks and migrating shorebirds when adjacent fields have pockets of open water after heavy rains.

Canada Geese have begun using fish pond levees as feeding and resting areas. Cormorants are frequent visitors during winter and are considered a nuisance by farmers when they appear in large numbers. Access to catfish ponds is privately controlled, but some are visible from nearby public roads or levees. One should secure permission from landowners before entering private roads.

Sewage treatment lagoons have become migrant traps for ducks, grebes, gulls, swallows, terns, and shorebirds. Most lagoons are situated in bottomlands where surrounding habitats are attractive to migrating landbirds, probably because of the seasonal abundance of emerging aquatic insects. Some lagoons have areas with emergent aquatic plants that become havens for gallinules and other marsh birds.

The Waveland lagoon and large lagoons at Hattiesburg are outstanding for new first inland and first state bird records. Lagoons at Canton, Grenada, Kosciusko, and Starkville have had first locality or first state bird records for the Eared Grebe, Surf Scoter, Northern Phalarope, and Yellow Wagtail, respectively.

Airports and turf farms provide habitat attractive to Horned Larks, Sprague's Pipit, Lapland Longspur, Smith's Longspur, and numerous shorebirds. Most state records for Sprague's Pipit and Smith's Longspur are from airports. Baird's, Upland, and Buff-breasted Sandpipers and American Golden Plovers are most likely to appear on airports and turf farms after heavy rains and at peak migration periods. The turf farm at the former airport along Highway 7 south of Oxford is noted for 22 species of shorebirds recorded by Gene Knight (Davis 1992).

For more information on finding individual birds, consult the species accounts and accompanying distribution charts and maps.

Birding Ethics

Bird-watching is a popular and enjoyable pastime for millions of people across America. For it to be enjoyable, however, birders should observe certain rules of conduct. Birding is akin to southern "rednecking" in which a group of people with common and diverse interests enjoy simple outdoor pleasures, dress comfortably, eat common food, and enjoy each other's company in a common style.

Sometimes called "yellowhammer," the Northern Flicker faces serious competition with the European Starling for available nesting cavities.

For safety, convenience, and respect for the feelings, privacy, and property rights of others while birding, here are important rules of conduct:

1. Observe all traffic safety rules. Avoid sudden stops. Park only on road shoulders or parking bays. Walk on road shoulders and stay off public roads. Drive with the traffic flow, avoiding slowdowns to observe birds.
2. Ask permission before entering private property. Use primitive roads only during dry weather to avoid getting stuck. Do not block roads. Leave all gates as you found them. Thank the landowners.
3. Use public areas or private lands where owners knowingly allow birding, such as timberlands owned by corporations or national forests.
4. Avoid conflict on public and private lands during legal hunting seasons. Hunters pay for leases and hunting privileges, so respect their rights. Hunting clubs and public hunting areas have special rules or regulations that require compliance.
5. Follow instructions of party leaders. Avoid loud talk and boisterous conduct. Share equipment, experience, and knowledge with others, especially beginners and young people.
6. When rare birds are sighted, take care to approach without disturbing the species while keeping it in view so others may see it. Report the location of rare bird sightings only with the consent of the property owner and the person making the discovery. Visit only with permission.
7. Plan ahead on field trips for convenience and rest stops for party participants.
8. Leave no litter, only footprints.
9. In urban and suburban areas, do not stop in driveways or peer around homesites with binoculars without first making your presence and intentions known to the owners.
10. Avoid excessive or prolonged playing of owl or other call tapes to attract territorial birds. It can be annoying to others and harmful to birds near their nests.
11. View bird nests carefully when discovered. Trampling and repeated visits around nests may cause abandonment.
12. Be courteous and respectful of others and project a good image of bird-watchers.

Field Identification and Behavior of Birds

The first step in learning to identify birds in the field is motivation. In the study of birds, most beginners are familiar with Northern Cardinals, Blue Jays, woodpeckers, crows, and other common birds. Motivation and interest in learning more about birds can be aroused by finding a new kind of bird in the backyard or at a bird feeder and identifying it with a bird book.

Someone may have given you a pair of binoculars and you began to see birds in a way you never thought possible. Or, maybe you have visited a waterfowl refuge and seen numbers of different kinds of ducks, geese, and wading birds or a Bald Eagle. You may have participated in a field trip with emphasis on seeing and identifying birds, or by association with a friend with a serious interest in birds. Every serious bird student or bird-watcher can recall events and people that led them to becoming proficient in the field study and identification of birds.

The ability to recognize and identify birds in the field should be the main objective of the bird student. Recognizing birds can become an art with practice, experience, and continued interest. The beginning bird student will need equipment, field guides, and other materials, as well as to learn and follow certain procedures used to identify birds in the field.

Equipment

Optical Equipment

The first investment in birding equipment should be good-quality, 7 x 35 binoculars with center focus and coated optics. The "7" indicates magnification, with the image appearing seven times closer to the viewer. The "35" is the size of the objective lens in millimeters.

Most binoculars have an adjustable right eyepiece that compensates for differences between the eyes of viewers. To make this adjustment, focus on a subject with the left eye, then without changing the center focus, adjust the right eyepiece into sharp focus. Finally, adjust the binocular to the distance between the eyes that brings the two fields together.

Standard binoculars are regular models, not those with wide-field or wide-angle objective lenses or other specially built models. Wide-field binoculars pass more light through the binocular, giving greater brightness and less glare, but with an increase in size and weight. Factory coating of lenses and prisms increases relative brightness by 50 percent, a feature of most good-quality models and more than worth the additional cost. With proper care, binoculars last a long time and should be purchased and considered as a long-term investment.

Many newer binoculars have rubberlike coatings that protect exterior parts from wear. Other models serve special purposes, such as 6 x 30 for close viewing and greater brightness in woods. The 7 x 50 models work well in the dim light of early morning or late evening and in shadows. Magnifying powers above 9x are difficult to hold steady and are bulky to carry. Comfortable, wide neck straps should be worn with binoculars while in use to prevent dropping.

First-time binocular users need to practice locating and focusing quickly on stationary objects. With moving subjects, keep the eyes on the subject while raising the binocular. This will soon become a habit, making bird finding and tracking easier.

Well-known models of binoculars used by birders are Bausch and Lomb, Bushnell, and Swift. Used and factory reconditioned binoculars can be purchased at reasonable cost from reputable dealers. Foreign-made models of excellent quality are also available, and some are very expensive. They should be purchased from reputable vendors that can guarantee repair services.

For watching and identifying shorebirds, waterfowl, seabirds, waders, raptors, sparrows, and other open-country landbirds, a spotting telescope is particularly useful. Careful viewing of distant birds is possible with a telescope and tripod, an essential equipment item. Tripods should be extendable to a comfortable eye level. Car window and car top, short-legged tripods are available and useful for roadside viewing. A gunstock or shoulder mount is practical for following a moving bird and easy to carry while walking.

The 60-mm model spotting telescope with a lens that zooms from 15x to 60x is desirable and practical for long-term use. The "zoom-scope" has fingertip focus adjustment at the lowest magnification setting to find a bird, center it in the field of view, and then zoom-up the bird for a close view.

Some scopes come with separate, interchangeable lenses at extra cost with magnifications of 15x, 20x, 40x, and 60x. Since higher magnifications are used less often, the 20x might be the best choice when buying a scope. Bausch and Lomb, Bushnell, and Swift spotting scopes are popular with birders. Foreign-made telescopes are also available, but cost more. Most domestic dealers can provide repair service on the makes mentioned above.

Field Guides

This book is not designed for use as a field guide. The serious bird student should carry one or more of the popular field guides. These contain color plates of artists' drawings of each species, range and distribution maps, sonograms or song descriptions, line drawings, bird topography drawings, and definitions that help identify birds in the field. These guides come in pocket-sized paperback or hardback editions. Eventually, they will become worn from constant use and filled with marginal notes and records.

Roger Tory Peterson's *A Field Guide to the Birds of the Eastern United States* is by far the best single guide for beginning bird students in this area. His *A Field Guide to the Birds of Texas* is a step beyond and includes most western birds occurring in Mississippi as casual or accidental visitors. Peterson's guides use arrows to show diagnostic field marks and their variations for each species.

My description of the Peterson guides is not meant to belittle other excellent field guides that include most or all North American birds. One is *Birds of North America: A Guide to Field Identification* by Chandler S. Robbins, Bertel Bruun, and Herbert S. Zim, and illustrated by Arthur Singer. This guide includes range maps opposite the illustration and a description of each species, as well as sonograms of many of the birds' songs. A more recent (1987) guide, *Field Guide to the Birds of North America* is published by the National Geographic Society. Both of these North American field guides are recommended for more advanced studies and for identifying birds occurring in other regions of the continental United States and Canada.

Daily Field Checklist

This checklist is a list of the birds found in a state or region. *The Birds of Mississippi* (1991) checklist is published by the Mississippi Ornithological Society's Records Committee and is updated periodically. The list has occurrence codes opposite accidentals and casual visitors, with symbols identifying species that breed in Mississippi.

The list is pocket-sized and contains spaces to check off species seen or heard, and for recording dates, weather, locality, names of observers, and totals. Each completed copy properly filled out serves as a permanent record. Checklists are available by writing the Mississippi Ornithological Society, Mississippi State University, PO Drawer EM, Mississippi State, MS 39762. Copies can be made for personal use.

Local or regional checklists are also available. Some national wildlife refuges have local lists at their headquarters. The U.S. Army Corps of Engineers has published a checklist for Sardis Lake. The Gulf Coast Audubon Society sells a checklist of birds of the three coastal counties. Annotated lists of Gulf Coast birds with maps and best birding area descriptions by Burleigh (1945, now out of print) and by Toups and Jackson (1987) are recommended for studying coastal birds.

Pocket Notebook

A durable, pocket-sized, loose-leaf notebook is essential for recording field notes. When rare or unusual birds are sighted, it is important to make notes, drawings, or sketches of the species showing field marks. Try to obtain an identifiable photograph for publication to substantiate the record. Some observers carry index cards for use in making notes in the field on each species, storing them in a card file.

Recording Equipment

A portable, transistor-type, battery-powered tape recorder is useful on field trips to bring territorial singing birds into closer view. This is particularly helpful during the breeding season for calling up singing males with prerecorded songs on cassette tapes. Many singing males of summer-resident species will respond to song tapes and show defensive behavior such as vibrating wings or producing alarm calls and territorial songs. Care should be taken not to prolong these demonstrations.

Dual-cassette recorders can be used for playback of prerecorded bird songs, for duplicating and extending the length of recorded songs, or making a series of different bird songs on one cassette for use in the field. Tape recordings of owls are useful in attracting attention of some winter birds, bringing them closer for viewing. Birds that seldom sing during the winter months, such as the Winter Wren, Hermit Thrush, and Fox Sparrow, will respond to prerecorded songs at appropriate times in early morning or evening and sing or make territorial alarm calls.

The variety of responses to prerecorded songs and territorial behavior is amazing and almost unbelievable. I have called up courting woodcock males that "hiccupped" and "beeped" while standing within two feet of my toes and a spring male Ruby-crowned Kinglet that chattered and sang while sitting on my microphone in the parabolic reflector.

Bird Song Recording Equipment

Like photography, recording bird and animal sounds is a specialized pursuit by individuals, and usually requires expensive equipment for best results. Basic equipment for recording quality bird songs is available in cassette or reel-to-reel recorders. This includes a parabolic reflector rigged with a sensitive microphone at the focal point, headphones, and electrical cords with jacks to fit the recorder.

For most recording, the reel-type portable recorder is best, but they cost more. Cassette recorders can be used for original recordings provided they have headphone, remote microphone, and auxiliary input-output fittings.

Some microphones preamplify the output to the recorder. Battery-powered preamplifiers can be attached to recorders. Low cost, battery-powered equalizers also amplify microphone signals to the recorder. Preamplifiers allow the recorder to use a lower recording level and thereby eliminate some of the noise level obtained with higher settings.

The offshore barrier islands are good places to see a variety of warblers, vireos, flycatchers, tanagers, and other birds during the spring and fall migrations.

Recording bird songs can be useful, rewarding, and at times frustrating. Patience and know-how as to when, where, and what you are recording are prerequisites. It is often necessary, though difficult, to find quiet places without the background noise of chain saws, motorboats, aircraft, or distant 18-wheelers. Leaf noise, wind, and rain can make recording impossible. As a general rule, recording songbirds is best accomplished at dawn and in early morning. At other times opportunities vary, so take advantage of them when they occur.

Be sure to identify the bird song while recording. It is easy to mistake an unfamiliar bird song without positively identifying the singing bird. Make notes on time, place, habitat, and behavior, and enter species name, date, and locality at the end of the tape or on the reel box or label supplied with the cassette holder. Properly identified bird song recordings can be used to substantiate records of species such as Eastern and Western Wood-Pewees, Eastern and Western Meadowlarks, and *Empidonax* flycatchers, since voice is the main or only criteria in field identification.

In tropical jungles, it is difficult to observe some songbirds. Prerecorded song tapes are used to bring them up for closer viewing. By recording and playing back songs of some tropical birds previously unknown to scientists, new species have been discovered and identified. Records and tapes of bird songs are valuable aids in learning to identify birds by their distinctive calls and songs. (See the "Song and Call Notes" section below for information about where to obtain such recordings.)

Identifying Birds

There are many ways to identify birds in the field besides matching form, color patterns, and descriptions with pictures in a field guide. Birds in the field often are seen moving through foliage, in shadow, or backlighting that obscures color and distinctive field marks. Subtle differences such as song, call notes, size, posture, flocking and feeding habits, and behavior patterns such as tail-wagging or head-bobbing furnish clues for identification.

Other clues are learned with practice and experience. These include knowledge of the seasonal occurrences and distribution of birds, and knowing their habitat preferences such as marsh, shoreline, deciduous forest, or open fields. When used in combination with posture, tail length, or size and shape of the head, silhouettes help identify "wire-sitters" such as bluebirds, starlings, and shrikes.

Birds in flight can be identified overhead by their outlines, silhouettes, and wing or tail shape. Flight patterns and wingbeats will help identify some woodpeckers, meadowlarks, and goldfinches that have alternating or undulating flight. Locomotion, such as walking, climbing, hopping, diving, wading, and pouncing is a source of identification clues. Behavior such as scratching with one foot at a time (Brown Thrasher) or with both feet (Fox Sparrow and Eastern Towhee) helps in identification.

Feeding patterns help identify certain species. Does the bird hop and jump around with spread wings while feeding in shallow water like the Snowy Egret or the Reddish Egret? Does it run along the ground and spread its wings to flush grasshoppers like the Northern Mockingbird and Brown Thrasher? Does it run a short distance, pause with bill slightly elevated while staring downward looking for movement of an insect or worm like an American Robin? Is the bird always nervously flitting about while feeding like the Ruby-crowned Kinglet? Or is it a flycatcher that darts from a perch to snap up a flying insect? Does it actively pursue and catch flying insects within a deciduous forest canopy and spread its wings and tail while perched like an American Redstart?

By noticing a bird's behavior patterns, size, shape, and posture and associating them with habitat, along with a knowledge of seasonal occurrence and distribution, many kinds of birds can be recognized by species or by family group. The general color pattern, distinctive field markings, call or song, and other physical features can confirm identification. Lacking one or more critical field characteristics such as call or song notes, bill length, or the presence or shape of an eye ring can make identification uncertain. Field identification of some immature jaegers, gulls, and terns in immature or changing plumage, and some warblers in immature fall plumage, is confusing and sometimes impossible.

Song and Call Notes

The songs and calls of most songbirds and many other birds are distinctive. Songs and calls are used by birds for communication and territorial definition or defense. Recognizing birds by their songs is difficult, but it is necessary if a birder is to be proficient in finding and identifying birds. Most beginning bird students have not trained their ears to hear natural sounds and distinguish bird songs. *Good hearing* and *listening* are valuable aids for identifying birds. Experienced birders rely on hearing to recognize most of the birds they record on a field trip.

Carefully listening to records or tape cassettes of bird songs is helpful, but most learning is acquired from actual sounds in the field. Repeated listening to bird voices eventually will lead to instant recognition. The following learning procedures are recommended.

First, refer to species accounts in the field guides. They will contain phonetic renderings of birds' songs expressed as words, syllables, and phrases or by descriptive words such as buzzing, flutelike, piping, low, short, or kingfisher-like rattle. Words or symbols cannot accurately describe a bird's song or its variations. Yet, typical bird songs are distinctive enough to be recognized by an experienced birder.

Many bird songs can be remembered by word association such as "chuck-will's-widow," or by "pee-ah-wee" for the Eastern Wood-Pewee. Word association is not possible for bird songs like the Winter Wren or Baltimore Oriole. Their songs are long (Winter Wren) or highly variable (Baltimore Oriole) but unique, and are best remembered by descriptive words.

Recording bird songs and using them for playback in the field will help commit them to memory. *A Field Guide to Bird Songs* (1990) contains about 450 recordings of 300 species of eastern birds and is designed to accompany Peterson's *A Field Guide to the Birds of the Eastern United States*. The selections are necessarily short. Records and cassettes can be obtained from the Cornell Laboratory of Natural Sounds, 159 Sapsucker Woods Road, Ithaca, NY 14850.

Available from the same source are *Bird Sounds* by the National Geographic Society (1983), a four-disk album with sounds from 174 species, and *Songs of the Warblers of North America* (1985) by Donald J. Borror and William W. H. Gunn in a two-cassette or three-disc album. The second contains recordings of 57 North American warbler species arranged in a checklist order. It contains regional examples of songs of the same species to show intraspecific variations. A key to warbler song identification accompanies the data on the recordings. Song descriptions and phonetic interpretations are given for each species. Sonograms, or voice prints, showing regional song variations for each species are included. Information in the accompanying brochure is the best available source for recognition of warbler songs and for learning to read and interpret sonograms by comparing them with accompanying sound selections and song descriptions.

Warbler songs are some of the most difficult to learn and remember without the aid of recordings or an experienced observer. Also available is a two-cassette collection,

A Guide to Mississippi Bird Songs (Mississippi Department of Wildlife, Fisheries and Parks 1985) containing calls and songs of 115 species known to occur in Mississippi. The recordings are identified by a narrator and accompanying brochure. Each 60-minute cassette is made intentionally long, so that each selection includes song variations and encourages learning by repetition. The album can be obtained by writing the Mississippi Wildlife Heritage Program, PO Box 451, Jackson, MS 39205-0451.

Some bird voices are beyond hearing range and silent to millions of bird listeners. For some people over 60, it is difficult or impossible to hear songs in the upper frequency range without the amplification of hearing aids or stereo devices that lower the pitch by reducing the frequency range to normal hearing perception. Unfortunately, hearing aids often do not allow the user to judge distance and direction of incoming sounds.

Newer stereo listening devices allow users to judge distance and direction of high frequency sounds. Incoming sounds are picked up by tiny microphones in or above the ears and routed through a processor that returns lower-pitched sounds to small earphones without affecting normal hearing.

Advanced Guides for Field Identification

In addition to field identification guides, other sources of useful information are available to advanced birders. Bird populations are always changing in numbers and distribution and with the changing seasons. To keep in step with advances in field identification methods, the following guides are useful and at times essential for identifying birds in all plumage and their nests and eggs: *Birds' Nests: A Field Guide* (Headstrom 1949), *North American Bird Eggs* (Reed 1965), *Gulls: A Guide to Identification* (Grant 1982), *A Field Guide to Hawks of North America* (Clark and Wheeler 1987), *Hawks in Flight: The Flight Identification of North American Migrant Raptors* (Dunne and Sibley 1988), *Wildfowl: An Identification Guide to the Ducks, Geese, and Swans of the World* (Madge and Burn 1987), *A Field Guide to Advanced Birding* (Kaufman 1990), and *Shorebirds: An Identification Guide* (Marchant et al. 1991).

Field Observation and Study of Behavior

Recognizing birds in the field by size, form, color patterns, and song soon becomes routine for avid birders. They begin to pursue other birding interests and challenges—and there is always something new and interesting to see and learn about birds. Even commonplace birds reveal secrets when their behavior is watched and studied carefully. These observations on behavior may point to interspecific or intraspecific behavior and competition for a place in a particular environment.

The waters of Mississippi Sound and the adjacent Gulf of Mexico winter large numbers of diving ducks each year.

Behavior is what a bird does to take care of itself, how it relates to other living organisms, and how it reproduces and survives. Some behavior patterns are *innate* or instinctive. Others are learned by *imprinting* early in life by receiving and following signals from adults. *Adaptive behavior* is a result of experience, habit, or trial and error.

Some birds seem to learn by unique experiences, such as the wing-tipped Blue Jay that survived in our yard by climbing a fence and a bush to get to a tree limb. Later it learned to hop and claw its way up a tree trunk to the first limb, then glide down to a nearby feeder. It survived the ordeal of a broken wing tip and eventually regained full flight. Outlined below are other types of bird behavior.

Care of body parts, especially the feathers, is essential for bird survival. As nestlings, birds begin to peck and *preen* themselves as feathers emerge. They also learn to scratch in response to irritations, but more importantly for care of the head and neck plumage, which cannot be reached with the bill. Preening continues throughout the bird's life, and is done daily during brief or extended rest periods.

Most birds *bathe*, even waterbirds. Landbirds bathe by immersing the head, neck, and part of the wings in shallow water, at the same time splashing water as they withdraw the head and beat the water with the wings to wet the back and underparts. Waterfowl and waders immerse their heads and necks and quickly withdraw them to throw water on their backs. At the same time they raise the wings to splash water under them, ruffle feathers, and then rub the head along the sides and flanks. Birds such as swallows and swifts skim along the water's surface to drink and to wet their plumage, or they bathe in falling rain. Hummingbirds bathe in the troughs of leaves wet with dew or rain. Bathing helps keep a bird's plumage in order and conforming to body shape. At times, bathing is done to clean feathers. A flock of Wood Ducks feeding on soybeans and corn in a muddy field was seen to fly immediately to a nearby river to bathe and remove streamers of corn leaves from their muddy feet. Other common birds like chickadees and titmice bathe in wet foliage after light showers, in the spray from a lawn sprinkler, or in a "mister" now available at nature shops.

Dusting is a form of maintenance behavior. It is helpful in controlling ectoparasites. Gallinaceous birds only dust and do not bathe, while some species like the Brown Thrasher both bathe and dust. Birds wallow out a hollow depression while scratching and pecking until the soil is loose. While sitting in the dust, the bird shakes and beats its wings to raise dust into the feathers, eventually shaking the dust out of the feathers.

Anting is a rarely seen behavior. A bird will approach an ant bed, catch and crush an ant to release formic acid, then work it among the feathers. Some birds, like Northern Mockingbirds, Loggerhead Shrikes, and Brown Thrashers I have watched, lie down among ants with wings and tail spread while going through the same motions and seeming to enjoy the performance. The purpose of anting is unknown, but presumably it helps control feather mites.

Sunning is a practice that birds appear to enjoy. All birds react at times to warm sunlight by raising the feathers and spreading wings and tail. This is a response by birds to warmth that airs or dries the feathers. Often, vultures are seen perched with wings spread facing the sun. Anhingas and cormorants sun themselves in a similar manner after swimming. Anhingas must dry their feathers after feeding in water, since their feathers are not water resistant.

Oiling the bill and feathers is a necessary behavior for many but not all birds. Glands at the dorsal base of the tail feathers secrete an oily, waxy substance from a nipple-like structure surrounded by small feathers that act like bristles and spread the oil when stimulated. Birds oil their bills, then smear the substance over the feathers by rubbing with the head and bill. The oil gland is large in most birds but may be absent or rudimentary in some others, apparently according to their environmental needs. The gland is larger on waterfowl and other birds that remain in water, as it is essential for their survival to keep their feathers water repellent.

Roosting behavior varies widely and seasonally among species and is interesting to observe. Blackbirds, starlings, and robins use common winter roosts where they congregate in groups of thousands or millions at sites covered by thickets of pines, cedars, canes, or thick deciduous growths. Crows usually locate winter roosts in thick pine stands. Woodpeckers, wrens, chickadees, and titmice roost in cavities or niches in protected places. In extremely cold weather, bluebirds, and Carolina and Winter Wrens share common roosting cavities.

Vultures and cormorants have common roosts. Vultures roost in tall trees in isolated parts of swamps. Cormorants congregate on winter roosts in cypress swamps or trees and snags over or near large bodies of water. Great Blue Herons have winter roosts in cypress-tupelo swamps. Other herons and Wood Storks have been seen roosting in cypress–button bush swamps along the Mississippi River in their postbreeding season, wandering period. Large numbers of Cattle Egrets have congregated to roost in a water privet thicket in an oxbow lake in Marion County near the Pearl River. When the birds settled to roost, the thicket looked like a mound of white.

Cedar Waxwings have roosted in flocks of 10 to 30 birds for 13 years on the same lowest red oak limb over our driveway in Richland. They have come intermittently in late January and February. They go to roost early, usually near sunset. The flock settles as close together as possible among the brown leaves that persist through the winter. When disturbed before dark, the flock does not return the same night, but returns later.

Roosting individual birds sometimes exhibit interesting diversion behavior. A Carolina Chickadee that roosted regularly in the open end of a large pipe supporting grapevines always delayed its entrance until no one was near. A pet crow I raised roosted in the top of an apple tree pruned to bunch the upper limbs. Before going to roost on the same limb, the crow would bring attention to itself while preening and calling. Toward nightfall, it would fly back and forth in the tops of nearby pines, then before dark it would sail down to a lower limb of the apple tree and hop upward to the protection of limb clusters around the same roosting limb it used every night. The protective limbs insured that the crow's worst enemy, the Great Horned Owl, would not be able to reach it without warning. This diversion tactic in dim light helped to prevent discovery of the roost site by a watchful predator.

On its wintering grounds, the American Woodcock spends daylight hours in woodland thickets. At dusk, it flies out to feed and roost in open pastureland with sparse ground cover bordering wetlands. Woodcocks congregate in fields where many can be netted and banded with the aid of strong sealed-beam lights.

Nocturnal birds roost during the day. Goatsuckers roost on the ground or horizontally on a limb, wire, or post. Short-eared Owls use common winter roosting places in tall-grass fields. Long-eared Owls find common roosts on wintering grounds in thickets of pine and cedar.

The Northern Harrier has winter roosts scattered over large broomsedge fields. They approach their roosts from a wide area near sunset, sometimes in numbers of 100 or more. Northern Bobwhites roost side by side in a circle with heads pointed outward so they can scatter if disturbed. They often rise in a tight group and fly directly to the roost at dusk to avoid detection by ground predators. The roosting behaviors of the birds described above are seldom encountered in the field, though I have seen all of them one or more times.

Birds engage in *play* at an early age as chicks in a brood or as nestlings. Play begins as gentle pecking that may become antagonistic. Playing helps develop social order in birds that have large broods, like waterfowl. Game birds and other species that have precocial young engage in play by chasing and fleeing to escape pecking by others in the brood. Waterfowl broods engage in chasing, fleeing, diving, and pecking that form the beginning of dominance and social order in the family flock.

Social behavior involves activities that protect birds as individuals or groups to survive and reproduce successfully in their environment. The study of social behavior is an interesting and rewarding part of birding. Birds must successfully locate and defend a territory with habitat that meets their requirements for food, shelter, and reproduction. Defining a territory and defending it requires aggression against invaders of like species.

Defense behavior includes threat displays and ruses such as songs and distress calls, "freezing" (remaining motionless) or fleeing to escape predators, and distraction displays. Threat and appeasement are tactics birds use to defend a food supply and maintain territorial dominance. Song and calls are used to define territorial boundaries. Threat displays such as ruffling feathers and feinting attacks are used along boundaries to dispel invaders. Threats avoid actual fighting, but if an intruder persists, even the gentle bluebird will attack and fight to the finish. Appeasement displays by hunching down with the head low, facing away from the defender, or standing still show submission and help avoid serious conflict.

Mockingbirds engage in a "face-off" dance used for territorial defense and courtship ritual. Two birds face each other while raising wings, side-stepping, staring at each other, and moving about to repeat the performance.

Close observation of a singing male Hooded Warbler reveals that he has singing perches and moves from one to another to advertise his territorial boundaries. Red-winged Blackbirds sharply define and defend their territories by frequent songs and flashing their red shoulder patches.

A pair of Eastern Bluebirds will define and defend about two acres of territory. If there is an adjacent occupied territory, the two males will define the boundaries by song, threat, chasing, or fighting and eventually respect each other's territory, insuring an adequate food supply for raising young.

Some colonial nesting birds defend territories that are only pecking distance apart from the other nests. They are defended by threat displays and actual fighting. While defending young, some birds will attack predators or intruders. I can attest to this because I have been struck repeatedly on the head by an irate Brown Thrasher while I was at its nest. Another pecked my hand several times when I tried to count young in its nest.

Small birds engage in displays by *mobbing* predators. Hawks, owls, and rat snakes often are mobbed by jays, crows, and other small birds while they give loud alarm signals. Flocks of starlings will sometimes engage hawks in flight, harassing them by wheeling around in unison, as if in play.

Other birds often use *distraction displays* to draw attention from their nests and young. A sitting Killdeer will leave her open nest on the ground, run a considerable distance away, then call to attract attention to herself and away from the camouflaged eggs. If incubation is advanced, the bird will feign a broken wing while spreading its rufous tail to draw attention from the nest.

The Wild Turkey hen with newly hatched young will sometimes not flee, allowing an intruder to approach closely while the young scatter and "freeze" in the ground cover. The young birds flatten themselves, permitting their camouflage colors to protect them while hiding. Northern Bobwhites react similarly when they have downy young. Goatsuckers depend on their camouflage colors for protection, but when flushed off the nest or young, they put on the broken-wing act.

Nesting birds are very secretive. Often, they will leave the nest vicinity so as not to call attention to eggs or young. When disturbed on its ground nest, the Kentucky Warbler will flee quickly, giving the impression of a running mouse to draw attention from the nest location. Most birds are cautious not to reveal the location of the nest and will not approach it when they know they are being watched. The Eastern Meadowlark will alight away from its nest on the ground and approach it stealthily to avoid detection.

Known as "redbird," the Cardinal is one of Mississippi's most common statewide permanent residents. It is a favorite with many backyard bird-watchers.

Some birds are most vulnerable from the time of hatching until leaving the nest. Altricial young remain in the nest as fledglings until they are able to fly or move about. Some passerines leave the nest and continue development before they are able to fly. Precocial young, eyes open and covered with down, leave the nest soon after hatching. They are capable of locomotion and are able to feed themselves. Most are protectively colored and remain under care of the adults in family groups or mixed créches guarded by one or more adults. Time in the nest varies from about 10 days for some ground-nesting passerines, like the Worm-eating Warbler, to several months for the Bald Eagle.

The care and feeding of young in the nest is always interesting to watch. Doves feed their young on "pigeon milk," partly digested seeds mixed with glandular secretions in the crop. Herons and other fish-eating birds feed their young on fish regurgitated from the stomach. Least Terns feed small fish directly to their young. Altricial birds instinctively gape minutes after hatching and soon begin begging actions followed by vocalizations in response to vibrations or calls made by adults approaching the nest. Young woodpeckers, hatched naked and blind, respond to noise and blockage of light as the adult enters the nest hole. (The response to light and darkness was proven to my satisfaction when I saw a juvenile Red-bellied Woodpecker, only days from the nest, fly directly from a feeder to a camera flash and alight above the camera on the photographer's scalp.)

A pair of Northern Mockingbirds with a nest at our back window became oblivious to our watching and photographing during the whole nesting cycle. We saw that the eggs were abandoned for hours at a time on very warm days. However, the young were covered by an adult as soon as rain began and were shaded from the hot sun at times during the day. Both adults fed the nestlings and, although they were busy finding food, they spent time with the young at the nest, giving attention to each one as if some kind of bonding was happening.

I have observed that Blue Jays are equally attentive to their nests and young. Some passerines communicate with each other while one is incubating. I discovered that an Eastern Wood-Pewee on the nest would answer each time its mate sang with a call note the same as their young make after fledging. The answering call was short, faint, and directly following its mate so the two calls were barely separable. I have noted similar acts by Olive-backed Thrushes and Western Meadowlarks.

Nesting birds are mainly concerned with intraspecific competition. Most birds require a certain type of nesting habitat or microhabitat. The Worm-eating Warbler nests exclusively on hillsides and utilizes certain plants associated with its habitat in nest construction. The Swainson's Warbler nests near the ground in canebrakes, sawbriers, or thickets. The Red-eyed Vireo nests at any height in saplings or trees, while the White-eyed Vireo nests near the ground in understory bushes. These birds may compete to some extent for food supplies, but all have distinct feeding habits, so there is little interspecific competition within their nesting territories. Bluebirds, shrikes, and mockingbirds compete for insects during their nesting season in the same or overlapping territories. They may chase and harass one another without displacing the other competing occupants of their breeding territory.

Courtship and *mating* behaviors vary according to species. Most birds are monogamous during the reproduction cycle. Some are obviously promiscuous such as the Brown-headed Cowbird. During the egg-laying season, a female cowbird often will have four or five males in pursuit as she looks for another bird's nest in which to lay an egg. Other birds are polygamous, with males mating with more than one female or females mating with one or more males. The Wild Turkey gobbler mates with a harem of hens and abandons all of them to hatch and raise the young without his assistance.

Mating displays help start and complete the reproductive cycle. These displays include visual performances such as leaping and dancing (cranes), strutting, foot-stomping, wing-spreading, ruffling feathers, inflating air sacs with accompanying auditory signals (grouse and turkeys), or mutual ritual displays between the sexes such as bowing, fawning, and billing or bill-clacking (albatross).

Many birds display unique courtship plumages such as nuptial plumes (egrets). Others develop bright colors on facial skin, gular pouches, ruffs, crests, or legs. The American Woodcock male performs a solo display on his "singing ground" accompanied by the well-known "sky dance."

Collective displays by two or more promiscuous males in a "lek" or arena are exemplified by several species of grouse and by the unique, different-colored males of the Ruff. Courtship displays promote pair bonding in monogamous species. Pair bonding is sometimes accompanied by chase and pursuit between sexes, dummy nest-building by males or "dump-nesting" by females, and by courtship feeding of the female by the male during the nesting cycle. Courtship and mating performances rarely are seen. Often, they are overlooked or misunderstood by casual birders who fail to recognize and appreciate these acts.

Flocking is a form of behavior for many birds. Most birds are gregarious to some degree after the breeding season. Nesting seabirds, ibises, herons, Anhingas, Wood Storks, and swallows gather in colonies. Nests are placed close together in a territory that meets the birds' needs for food, isolation from disturbance, and habitat suitable for nests.

Breeding colonies may be composed of more than one species with similar or different feeding habits. Colonial nesting birds tend to congregate or remain in flocks after the breeding season while feeding, resting, or roosting, often in company with other species. Grackles and other icterids form breeding colonies and tend to gather in feeding and roosting flocks throughout the year.

Geese, swans, ducks, and cranes gather and migrate in family groups to congregate in feeding flocks on their wintering grounds. After pairing and returning to breeding grounds, they select individual breeding territories. Common landbirds associate in feeding flocks outside the breeding season. Cardinals, towhees, Brown Thrashers, and White-throated Sparrows are seen in loose flocks in winter. Pine Warblers, kinglets, Chipping Sparrows, Brown-headed Nuthatches, Brown Creepers, Carolina Chickadees, Tufted Titmice, Dark-eyed Juncos, and Downy Woodpeckers associate in foraging flocks in winter.

Associations of birds with differing food habits probably help minimize the danger of attack by predators through "safety in numbers." Hordes of Common Grackles, Red-winged Blackbirds, Brown-headed Cowbirds, and other blackbirds scour the countryside in all directions from common roosts. Foraging flocks always appear to be finding food and seem almost invulnerable to attack by predators.

There are interesting interspecific relationships between feeding flocks of birds. Bonaparte's Gulls follow Horned Grebes feeding in flocks to catch small fish forced to the surface or steal fish from the grebes as they pop to the surface. Feeding frenzies of large rafts of Double-crested Cormorants are joined by White Pelicans, gulls, and terns. American Wigeons, unlike most surface-feeding ducks, prefer stems and leaves of aquatic plants and often follow feeding American Coots and Redheads to steal plant food as the coots and ducks surface. Bald Eagles attack Ospreys, and frigatebirds attack fish-eating birds, forcing them to drop or disgorge food. Gulls and Fish Crows are noted for stealing eggs or young of colonial nesting birds.

Although blackbird roosts are a nuisance around human dwellings, the hordes of birds may render valuable help by controlling noxious weeds and insects over a wide territory. During an outbreak of forest tent caterpillars in the lower Yazoo Delta in 1990 and 1991, Common Grackles were the only birds seen feeding on the larvae, pupae in cocoons, and adults of this insect that defoliated about 50 percent of the trees on Delta National Forest. The situation was being surveyed by air and on the ground by the U.S. Forest Service in anticipation of a possible damage-control program the following year. Fortunately, damage control by widespread spraying was unnecessary.

While driving through vast stretches of farmland in the Texas Panhandle, I noticed hundreds of Cliff Swallows rising from the pavement and road shoulders and milling around in the air. I made the remark that I had never seen a road-killed swallow and about that time one hit the car. As we

The Clark Creek Natural Area in Wilkinson County west of Woodville is an excellent upland hardwood site to see and hear a variety of resident and migratory songbirds during the year.

reduced speed I noticed some large grasshoppers on the pavement and untold numbers of small ones. The swallows were feeding on them. At a local business, I asked the manager if there was a plague of grasshoppers. He said farmers in the area were watching the situation, and some were starting to prepare for spraying programs.

Colonial nesting and flocking behavior of the Passenger Pigeon led to its wholesale destruction on its breeding grounds well before food sources were exhausted (see Passenger Pigeon species account). The flocking habit of foraging Carolina Parakeets also contributed to their demise. A flock would not desert a trapped or injured member, allowing the entire flock to be taken for whatever reason. Large flocks of blackbirds, starlings, cormorants, and other birds sometimes become nuisances or cause property damage. Control measures are, and should continue to be, regulated to prevent any wholesale destruction without evaluating the benefits of the targeted species to the ecosystem.

Behavior, whether driven by instinct, adaptation to environmental stress, or a grand design for survival, is a fascinating study for birders. Some will "graduate" from other birding pursuits and learn to look closely at the complex relationships between birds and the habitats that maintain them. Survival is the first law of the universe, and studying behavior can be the key that opens the door to understanding.

Migration

The study of birds would be far less interesting and enjoyable without the seasonal variations in their diversity and numbers due to migration. Twice a year, untold numbers of migratory birds respond to inner urgings and external stimuli that cause them to embark on incredible journeys. Unseen forces impel them to leave their breeding grounds and fly to warmer places or find sources of food in other locales that they need to survive. Large and strong-winged birds join many smaller species of landbirds to repeat an even more remarkable spectacle, the spring migration and return to the places where they hatched. What triggers these marvelous flights of millions upon millions of migrating birds? What forces guide their way with the accuracy and timing that never cease to amaze us?

Bird migration is a fascinating study. Millions of records have been kept by ornithologists and bird banders on this subject. Complete books and countless articles on their annual journeys have been written, but no one can explain the exact nature of all of these processes. Perhaps, it is just as well that parts of this mystery remain unsolved; we can simply enjoy its visible manifestations each spring and fall.

Most waterfowl, gulls, terns, and shorebirds migrate either by night or day. Hawks, eagles, vultures, falcons, crows, hummingbirds, swifts, and swallows migrate by day. Nearly all passerines (except swifts and swallows) migrate mainly at night. Night migration affords protection from predatory birds and allows time during daylight hours for resting and feeding to regain energy and resume migration.

There are visible and audible signs of nocturnal and daytime bird migrations. Most everyone at some time or another has seen or heard geese flying overhead during the night or day. Radar has been used effectively to detect and measure height, ground speed, and direction of travel of migrating birds. Airplanes have been used to follow the path of migrating Whooping Cranes. The call notes of shorebirds and the fainter chip notes of small landbirds can sometimes be heard when they fly beneath low cloud cover. By using a 60-power spotting telescope focused on the full moon, a team of observers in one night can plainly see the silhouettes of birds crossing the moon's face. The number of birds, direction of travel, and frequency of passage can be recorded, noting the times of increase, peak time of passage, and waning of passage. Even the smallest landbirds are visible under ideal conditions as they move across the moon's face, more slowly than one would suspect.

Landbirds often are attracted to airports, where ceilometers are used to measure cloud ceilings. Sometimes birds encountering the lights projected by these instruments in bad weather are attracted to them, flying around and through the beam and striking nearby buildings, or settling on the ground. Tall television towers reaching upward of 2000 feet have lights that attract birds during adverse weather. Sometimes thousands of migrating birds attracted by these lights are killed by striking guy wires around the towers. I have seen over 500 birds killed around one tower in a bad night. At other times, I have seen groups of one or more species of migrating fall warblers clustered in trees around television towers in early morning when there was no inclement weather to cause them to drop down. Apparently they were attracted by the lights and chose to land around the tower.

Another manifestation of migration occurs on stormy, rainy nights when migrants mistake paved roads for waterways, or drop down to shallow, flooded fields. I have seen grebes and Ring-billed Gulls that landed on roads during rainstorms at night. I know of one instance where a Common Loon landed in a flooded soybean field at night and could not get airborne. It was found in a small pool and died soon afterward. Daytime migrants are sometimes forced down by storm systems with very heavy rainfall. Once in Issaquena County after a passing rainstorm had flooded a newly leveled field, I counted over 70 Golden Plovers and numerous Ring-billed Gulls standing in or flying over the shallow water left by the passing storm. Some of the birds were just beginning to leave the field and others left while I watched them.

More noticeable evidence of migration is the sight of numerous robins in clusters along roadways in the spring migration movement. They appear to move northward in waves. I have noted this on several occasions by seeing Hermit Thrushes on the ground at the edge of woods bordering roads. To me, this indicated a migration in progress. I have experienced and observed migrational movements of woodcocks in late January and early February by finding concentrations

During the period October 1–2, 1965, more than 500 migrating birds struck the WLBT television tower in rural Hinds County. Of the 222 specimens picked up, 39 species were identified, including 19 species of warblers.

while hunting them in cover where they ordinarily did not occur. At other times, I have heard unusual numbers of woodcocks make singing flights over areas where they ordinarily should not be found.

Mississippi lies at the lower end of what biologists refer to as the Mississippi Flyway, a large corridor of the central portion of the United States and southern Canada by which vast numbers of transient and wintering birds move southward. Some species in passage go to more southern wintering grounds across the Gulf of Mexico or follow a land route along the northern Gulf Coast to Mexico and beyond.

There are four broadly defined migration routes, or flyways, that birds use in passage to and from their breeding territories. These are the Atlantic, Mississippi, Central, and Pacific Flyways. A minor flyway used by some waterfowl and a few landbirds extends eastward along the Great Lakes to the Atlantic Ocean and southward. Within the larger flyways, there are well-defined corridors or routes where segments of populations may converge at staging areas before final departure for wintering grounds in one or more flyways or destinations farther south.

This is true particularly for segments of the waterfowl population. The return migration to breeding areas in the upper Midwest and portions of Canada may follow the same or different corridors or flyways in some species. Staging areas for the northward migration seem to be of less importance for most species, but may have greater significance in others like the Sandhill Cranes' staging grounds on the Platte River in Nebraska. There, a major segment of the population gathers to roost, perform courtship displays, and feed in the extensive surrounding grain fields before going to northern breeding grounds.

There are segments of populations of some species that are nonmigratory like the resident Mississippi and Florida Sandhill Cranes. Others, such as some Canada Goose flocks, have been conditioned to become nonmigratory, or "captive" flocks, and have been short-stopped on northern refuges by feeding programs so they no longer return to ancestral wintering grounds farther south.

Some species like the Wood Stork and southern Bald Eagle migrate northward in summer after their late winter nesting period. White Pelicans that breed on western and northwestern lakes regularly migrate eastward to winter along the Atlantic and Gulf Coasts. Herons are noted for wandering beyond their normal breeding territories after their nesting cycle. Some species of boreal forest birds do not migrate beyond the southern borders of their winter range in the northern tier of states unless a shortage of food supplies occurs. Then we may see invasions or irruptions of Evening Grosbeaks, Pine Siskins, Red Crossbills, or even a few occurrences of the Northern Goshawk or Snowy Owl far south of their normal wintering range.

Survival is the main reason that birds migrate. Most bird species migrate as short a distance as possible to find food and to escape intolerable weather conditions, where finding food becomes impossible. "The inhospitality of each region—breeding and wintering area—at different times of the year dictate the seasonal movements to and from the region" (Bellrose 1976). Shorebirds and waterfowl that nest on Arctic tundra in the short summer there find space and teeming life on which to raise their young. Food sources soon are unobtainable when waters freeze over. Breeding shorebirds in the Arctic are noted for early spring departure or passage to breeding grounds and late summer or early fall migration southward to wintering areas.

Aside from the necessity to escape intolerable weather conditions and to find food sources, there are internal factors that prepare birds to migrate long distances. External and internal factors work together and trigger the urge to migrate. One main factor is photoperiodism—the relative lengths of day and night as they affect the growth of an organism. This sets an internal clock governing the release of hormones by the pituitary gland, which controls an internal, annual clock. The clock must then run through an annual cycle before it can be reset. The clock is started as light increases, and it runs through spring migration, courtship and mating, breeding and rearing young, molting, and accumulating and storing energy for return migration. Only then is the internal clock reset to trigger a return migration and escape often impending, intolerable conditions.

Horn Island, a wilderness area maintained by the U.S. Department of Interior's Gulf Islands National Seashore, is located south of Ocean Springs in Mississippi Sound. Each year many bird-watchers visit the island to see a variety of colorful birds.

During and after the molting period, migratory birds accumulate and store large amounts of body fat. Only then are they disposed to migrate. Fat reserves gathered on the breeding grounds are used to supply needed energy for long distance flights. Fat is the most efficient form of body tissue storage per unit of weight. Some shorebirds begin their long migrations when they are exceedingly fat. Fat is stored internally and in layers underneath the skin and along the underside of feather tracts. I have collected museum specimens of dowitchers and Upland Sandpipers that were so heavily layered in body fat in late summer that I was almost unable to remove all of it while I prepared study skins. These birds were well prepared for a long trip southward.

How high and how long can birds fly? The answer is different for different species. Waterfowl have been observed migrating at 20,000 feet and as low as only several feet above the ocean, a path followed by most sea ducks. Waterfowl are capable of long, continuous flights over hostile environments. Snow Geese are known to make nonstop flights from their staging area on the lower part of James Bay to the Louisiana marshes, a distance of some 1600 miles. Most birds traveling at night fly below 5000 feet, most frequently between 1500 and 3000 feet.

The presence or absence of cloud cover can influence the altitude at which birds migrate. They migrate over or under layered clouds and sometime between layers. Migrants of the same species tend to fly higher at night than during the day, and some are known to migrate higher over land than water.

The rate at which birds travel during migration varies among species. Most passerine birds fly at ground speeds of 20 to 25 miles per hour. Larger and stronger birds attain much higher rates of travel overland. Ducks, geese, shorebirds, hawks, falcons, and swifts are capable of ground speed flights averaging 50 miles per hour. A means of measuring speed is to record the time it takes for birds to return to their nest after moving and releasing them a known distance.

A question often asked is "*How* do birds migrate?" Giving an answer is not so simple, since different species follow different rules. Researchers have shown by large-scale banding that ducks and geese have an ability to return to the wintering and breeding areas used in previous years. They return using the same migration corridors, and the same stopover and staging grounds used in previous years. Their ability to navigate and find the same breeding grounds is uncanny. Waterfowl and some shorebirds migrate in flocks diurnally. In formations at night they communicate by calls. Observers have discovered that ducks and geese use the terrain below them in navigating cross-country. Bellrose (1976) observed that hundreds of waterfowl migrating diurnally abruptly change course to follow rivers before finally homing in on their particular destination. There seems to be little doubt that immatures in a flock learn from landscape clues on their first migration flights led by adults that have used the landmarks previously. The same is probably true for other migratory birds, although they also use other clues to navigate. This has been proven by holding back immature birds until all of their species had migrated. They still found their wintering grounds without great difficulty.

The southwesterly slant of the Appalachian Mountains also seems to guide migrants from the eastern United States toward Mississippi. Annually in late September, the spectacle of Broad-winged Hawks migrating southwesterly in flocks across our state can be observed. These birds travel in flocks during midday hours, spiraling upward on thermals or updrafts along mountain slopes to ridge tops, then set their wings to sail along in the direction of their migration southward into Mexico. The sight of hundreds of migrating Broad-wings is an unforgettable experience that shows how these birds utilize the terrain and prevailing weather conditions to find their wintering grounds.

Landscape clues alone, however, insufficiently explain how birds navigate. Experiments have demonstrated that birds use celestial navigation to guide their direction by day and at night. Their internal guidance mechanism enables them to adjust their direction by reference to the position of the sun or to constellations at night (Bellrose 1976). Under clear skies, birds have little difficulty in finding their way using landscape and celestial cues.

There is also evidence to support the fact that some, if not all, birds are able to use the earth's magnetic field for navigation when other cues are unavailable. This may be the missing link enabling them to navigate between or even through cloud layers without other directional cues. Field observations have shown that various species of birds rely on different navigational cues to varying degrees, some relying more on landscape and others not at all.

Prevailing strong winds also provide navigational hints. It is logical that migrants fleeing advancing cold weather in the fall would move southward with the wind and advance northward in the spring with warm fronts and prevailing southerly breezes. Cold fronts in spring prevent or delay northward migration. So, small landbirds move northward ahead of weather warm enough to meet their need for insect and other food supplies.

By whatever means of navigation, migratory birds are able to find their breeding territories and their wintering grounds. Many return to their exact summer homes where they hatched or lived earlier in the year. No doubt this homing ability merges to some degree with prior familiarity of the landscape on the path to their home range.

Researchers use mist nets to catch a variety of songbird species for banding and data gathering. For many years, Ethel Floyd netted and banded birds such as this Hooded Warbler and other spring migrants at various locations along the Mississippi Coast.

Generally, the fall migration of small landbirds proceeds at a slower rate than in spring. The opposite may occur during late fall migrations of ducks and geese when they pass from breeding areas to wintering grounds in a short series of mass migrations. These flights are triggered by the passage of a cold weather front.

In the spring, migrants begin their northward movement at the onset of warm fronts and proceed until the onset of a cold front, which will slow or stop their movement. Unusual weather conditions with prevailing high winds can deflect birds from their usual routes and carry them beyond normal geographical limits. High westerly winds sometimes push western species into Mississippi. The hurricanes along the Gulf Coast sometimes force gulls, terns, and other seabirds inland, and these high winds can cause fall migrants to concentrate in large numbers in our coastal areas.

During spring migration, cold fronts bring inclement weather and sometimes precipitate waves of incoming migrants. At such times, it is possible to observe concentrations of hundreds of small landbirds including transient warblers, thrushes, vireos, orioles, tanagers, grosbeaks, and buntings. Such fall-outs of returning migrants can occur at any place inland, but are more pronounced along the coastline when birds make their first landfall after crossing the Gulf of Mexico. At these times, the barrier islands and coastline teem with incoming migrants that may remain for a day or more.

When incoming birds encounter strong northerly winds before reaching land, they often are nearly exhausted and require time to rest and recuperate before continuing northward. During these days, it is possible to observe a great number and variety of species such as five or six kinds of warblers in a single large tree or bush. They may appear to be very tame and allow close observation. When transgulf migrants encounter good weather conditions, they usually fly farther inland before settling down to land and are more dispersed and less noticeable.

Sometimes migrating birds encounter sudden, unseasonable weather conditions such as freezing and snowfall or very high winds that can result in disaster. Fog blankets sometimes can cause landbirds to overshoot their wintering grounds along the Gulf Coast, which causes them to perish in the open sea. This occurred in October 1972 along the Alabama, Mississippi, and Louisiana Coasts when thousands of Blue Jays were drowned and washed ashore on the barrier islands (Gunter 1972, 1975). Others that survived this disaster were seen migrating westward in large numbers across the barrier islands toward Louisiana. Transgulf spring migrants encountering strong wind and cold, stormy weather arrive in an exhausted condition, some even perishing in the open sea. This is especially true of small landbirds that cross the Gulf of Mexico after leaving the Yucatan Peninsula, where most of them depart for their northbound flight. Man-made structures such as tall, lighted buildings; lighthouses; or televisions towers attract low-flying birds at night beneath insurmountable cloud layers. Birds have become blinded by these lights and flown into the structures, killing themselves. Along the Mississippi Coast, small warblers have been attracted by street lights or lighted, low buildings and been killed by flying into these structures. Hurricanes frequently force fall migrants to stall out along the coast, and sometimes cause mortalities to both resident and migrating birds. Sometimes seabirds are blown far inland on hurricane winds, forced down on highways mistaken at night for water, and killed by passing automobiles (Phares 1970).

An interesting aspect of bird migration is the tendency of individuals of some species to wander far from their normal range. Herons, Wood Storks, ibises, Roseate Spoonbills, and some landbirds are noted for their postbreeding season appearances as casual late summer and early fall visitors far away from their breeding territories. During the fall migration, continental air currents shift frontal systems eastward, sometimes driven by high, northwesterly winds. Under these exceptional weather conditions, western species migrating south are deflected from their usual route and appear in our area as casual fall visitors.

By studying weather maps and frontal movements it is sometimes possible to anticipate precipitations of spring migrants. The best time frame for anticipating waves of incoming migrants is usually during the last two weeks of April. Transient species, as well as our summer residents still in passage father north, will be migrating. By studying weather patterns, it is possible to be on the coast at the right time and experience one of the unforgettable precipitations of birds making their first landfall in almost unbelievable numbers. It may be possible in one day to see most of the warblers, vireos, thrushes, tanagers, grosbeaks, and buntings that occur in the eastern United States in large numbers.

Birders in the field can hardly fail to note daily the regularity of the spring arrival and passage of migrating birds. The Purple Martin is one of the earliest to arrive in Mississippi from its wintering grounds in Brazil. They arrive in numbers when most wintering robins, grackles, and other winter residents begin departing. Waves of early migrants soon follow, with warblers, vireos, shorebirds, and night-herons arriving by early April. The northward migration continues through April with the arrival of most summer residents and the passage of others. The late migration of transient species continues to about mid-May or sometimes later. By then, most of our winter-resident species have departed. Some, like the White-throated Sparrow, Yellow-rumped Warbler, and Ruby-crowned Kinglet, are in full breeding plumage or in full song before they leave.

The sequence of spring migration is interesting to observe and follow from late January, when the first Purple Martin scouts arrive on the coast. By the end of March all females martins will have arrived and occupied housing provided for them. By the end of the hunting season, Mallards, Wood Ducks, and Northern Shovellers will be paired. Resident Wood Ducks will be looking for housing or nest cavities. Resident bluebirds will be establishing territories while others are in passage. Numbers of robins begin their northward movements that continue through February. Roadsides, lawns, pastures, and fallow fields contain numbers of this species. When the red maples show tinges of bloom and winged elms turn pinkish brown, the American Woodcock begins his courtship "sky dance," while others in passage follow just below the freezing line toward northern breeding areas. Their passage ends by late February, as our resident birds are incubating eggs.

By mid-March, migrating gulls are noticeable around large bodies of water and even small lakes, or flying in flocks overland where they are not ordinarily seen. Flocks of Golden Plovers in passage can be found on newly plowed large fields, open pastures, or airports. Northern Bald Eagles and Red-tailed Hawks are leaving for northern breeding territories. The earliest landbird arrivals begin to appear on the coast: Ruby-throated Hummingbirds, Parula Warblers, Black-and-white Warblers, Blue-gray Gnatcatchers, and Barn Swallows. By the end of March, a host of other land-

Shallow sloughs, lakes, and swamps with available water are excellent over-wintering areas in many parts of Mississippi for mallards, wood ducks, gadwall, and other shallow water "dabbling" ducks.

birds and shorebirds are in passage or have arrived here as summer residents. These include the Yellow-throated Vireo, White-eyed Vireo, Hooded Warbler, Louisiana Waterthrush, Chimney Swift, and most summer-resident Barn Swallows and Rough-winged Swallows. Shorebirds are also noticeable in passage over inland parts of the state, including Greater Yellowlegs and Lesser Yellowlegs and most of the other sandpipers and plovers that nest farther north. Their passage continues through most of April and into early May.

By April, it is apparent that spring songbirds have timed their arrivals as food supplies become available. The early arriving swallows find flying insects already emerging, especially around bodies of water. Red buckeye already is blooming as hummingbirds arrive in force. Early arriving landbirds get here just as the trees are budding and leafing out, about the same time as the leaf-eating larvae of many insects are hatching. The winter rains and warming earth have brought the larvae of sod insects and earthworms to the surface, where passing robins, woodcocks, starlings, and blackbirds feed. Cedar Waxwings appear in large flocks in towns and cities to feed on the last privet and pyracantha berries or to consume the petals of pear, flowering crabapple, and peach, even behaving like flycatchers at times by taking flying insects on warm days.

April brings the remainder of our summer-resident species and passage of many transients on their way to more northern breeding territories. Also, it signals the departure of most winter residents, but not before many of them are singing in full breeding plumage. Purple Finches, goldfinches, Pine Siskins, Ruby-crowned Kinglets, White-throated Sparrows, White-crowned Sparrows, and occasionally Song Sparrows can be heard in full song before departure. Other summer-resident warblers, vireos, tanagers, orioles, buntings, and grosbeaks are in passage or have arrived during April.

Toward the end of April and in early May, transient thrushes, warblers, and cuckoos arrive or pass through Mississippi. Late March and early April bring passage of the Whip-poor-will, and if one is active in the woods at daybreak, their calls can be heard before our Chuck-will's-widow begins calling. April brings the passage or return of Broad-winged Hawks and Mississippi Kites. Late in April or early May is the time of passage for Bobolinks and Dickcissels, visible in large fields of oats, wheat, rye grass, and vetch, where they feed on ripening seeds and emerging insects. Late-migrating Bank and Cliff Swallows can be seen feeding over these fields when Bobolinks are in migration.

I never cease to marvel and wonder about the mysteries of bird migration, and look forward each spring and fall to the return of familiar songs and sights of birds. Perhaps this next season will bring along that "once-in-a-lifetime" casual or accidental bird visitor.

Attracting Birds

Interest in attracting birds has become widespread in recent years. Many Americans find pleasure in feeding songbirds, landscaping yards and gardens, and providing nest boxes and watering places for birds. Yard and garden stores offer unlimited supplies of bird seeds, custom-built nest boxes, a wide selection of bird feeders, and landscaping plants and services to make homesites attractive and useful for birds.

Bird Feeders

Bird feeding requires a few simple feeding trays and other devices for holding food. Most seed-eating birds respond to food on covered feeding trays and on open ground. Feeders should be placed in view of windows and preferably near some kind of escape cover. Containers for holding beef suet, corn bread, and other food mixtures are easy to make using one-half-inch wire mesh or nylon netting. A simple feeder can be made by boring holes in a section of wood or a dead tree limb and stuffing a mixture of peanut butter and other bird foods into the holes. Some birds, like the Eastern Towhee, Mourning Dove, Fox Sparrow, and White-throated Sparrow, prefer to feed on the ground near shrubbery.

Hummingbird and oriole feeders are available at many hardware and specialty stores, or suitable substitutes can be made using small wide-mouthed jars or vials with a wire twisted around the neck and bent for hanging on a convenient tree limb. The rims should be painted with red lacquer as an attractant. One part granulated sugar to four parts water is the preferred nectar mixture. Feeders should be changed and cleaned frequently.

Sunflower seeds are preferred by most birds. The black variety grown for its oil content is cheaper and available in large quantities from seed and feed stores. Bird seed mixtures contain some sunflower seeds, millet, milo maize, wheat, and cracked corn. Mixtures are preferred by ground feeding birds such as sparrows, doves, blackbirds, towhees, juncos, and finches. Beef suet is utilized during cold weather by many woodpeckers, titmice, chickadees, Blue Jays, and other birds. Peanut butter mixed with oatmeal, mixed bird seeds, cornmeal, and some kitchen fat will be used by most feeder birds. Suet and peanut butter mixes are "hot" foods needed by birds in cold weather or when they are feeding young, and should be used accordingly. Corn bread is a favorite food of woodpeckers and Blue Jays.

Placement of bird foods should be regulated to prevent spoilage and waste. It is better to put out food in the evening

Above: Waxwing

after grackles and Brown-headed Cowbirds have gone to roost. This permits cardinals and other seedeaters to feed before nightfall and early the next morning before blackbirds return from roosting. By watching the feeders during the day, seed replacements can be made to attract the more desirable birds.

Hummingbirds arrive in mid- to late March, and by mid-April there is a flurry of hummingbird activity at feeders from new arrivals and those in passage northward. By early May, resident hummingbird populations begin nesting, and there is a hiatus from local feeders, since nesting hummingbirds stay close to their nests and remain less visible. In July and August many young-of-the-year hummingbirds appear at feeders, and nectar utilization at feeders peaks. Females and immatures greatly outnumber adult males.

In September, adult male hummingbirds begin migrating southward, and by October few remain here. Females and immatures may stay in small numbers until mid-October, but usually all will be gone with the first cold weather. Any hummingbird seen in Mississippi after October 15 is likely to be a western species that occurs rarely in late fall, usually the Rufous Hummingbird. Contrary to popular belief, it is not harmful to leave hummingbird feeders out as long as they are used. These birds will migrate only when they have the urge to leave and seldom later than the earliest frost in October.

Water

Bird baths and watering places are effective attractants to birds. Baths are used throughout the year, especially during summer and fall. The bath can be as simple as a shallow pan on the ground filled with an inch of water. Preferably, the bath should be located near feeders and on an elevated stand. A four-foot length of concrete or ceramic tile set in the ground with the enlarged end up makes a suitable pedestal for supporting a large, galvanized, garbage-can lid. A heavy weight wired to the lid handle and hung inside the tile will hold it in place. Bird baths should be cleaned and refilled regularly.

Birds are attracted to running or dripping water for drinking and bathing. Running water will attract migrating warblers and other small landbirds not ordinarily seen at bird baths. Bird baths can be purchased with built-in connections to a convenient water source. Plastic tubing and fittings for drip irrigation can be rigged to a water supply for dripping water into a bird bath. Landscaped pools with shallow basins for drinking and bathing can be designed and built with simulated waterfalls over rocks and concrete. Submersible pumps are used to recirculate water from the pool to a fountain or to cascade over rocks to the bath basins and back to the pool. Landscaping with native shrubs, ferns, and other plants will make the pool area more attractive.

In hot, dry weather some birds are attracted to mist sprayers and rotating lawn sprinklers. When spray water falls on overhanging limbs of leafy plants, birds will sometimes bathe in the dripping water. Apparently this kind of "leaf-bathing" occurs after brief rain showers when standing water is scarce for bathing. I have observed the Tufted Titmouse, Carolina Chickadee, and Northern Cardinal bathing where water fell on limbs of a crepe myrtle tree overhanging my garden fence. Also, a Ruby-throated Hummingbird bathed in the troughs of strawberry leaves and drank droplets of water from pine needles during the same time and later preened on the garden fence. By providing a water supply at all times, birds will find and use it. Observing behaviors such as drinking, bathing, and preening adds pleasure to feeder-watching.

Nests

More than 20 species of birds will use nest boxes or other structures. Each bird's special needs or requirements must be met for best utilization.

Purple Martins have become dependent on artificial housing, and the only way to attract them is to provide boxes with multiple compartments or gourds on poles in open surroundings, preferably at upward of 10 to 15 feet. They prefer to nest in colonies of 10 or more pairs. For best nesting results, at least two 12-compartment houses or 20 martin gourds should be erected and spaced apart on separate but nearby poles. Commercially available martin houses usually come with telescoping poles or with collapsing bases so they can be lowered for cleaning.

Martin gourd poles can be made easily by using one 14-foot piece of treated 2 x 4 wired to an eight-foot metal or treated wood post set in concrete. Crossarms made of three-quarter-inch PVC pipe, drilled and fastened to the pole at varying heights, will support gourds suspended on coat-hanger wire from holes spaced and drilled through the crossarms.

Another alternative is to use a 12-foot metal pipe fitted over a metal fence post set in the ground as above. Next, using PVC pipe, cut a length with a cap or coupling on one end fitted into the metal pipe for 12 inches or more. Cement a T-connector on the top end. Using the same diameter pipe, cut two or more riser pipes for additional Ts with three-quarter-inch reducers to receive supporting lengths of pipe for holding two or three gourds each. Drill and space holes on the arms for the gourds. Finally, cement a short length of riser pipe in the top T and cap the top end. Drill one-quarter-inch holes in the bottom of the gourds for drainage and through the neck for support wires. The two-and-one-quarter-inch entrance hole should be made two to three inches above the bottom of the gourd. It is best to drill and clean out the gourds and wire all of them before placement on the supports.

Housing for Purple Martins should be placed 50 feet or more from trees or buildings with as much open space as possible around the poles. When martins are nesting and feeding young in Mississippi, prevailing winds are mostly from the south. They make hundreds of take-offs and landings into the wind daily. While feeding young, they usually carry away a fecal pellet with each visit to the nest and drop it about 100 feet away, usually toward the southeast or southwest. Some Purple Martins fall out of nests or fledge too early. (If they fly far enough to alight in a tree when thrown into the air, they will probably survive.) Nest mortality is compensated for by the number of eggs laid and successfully hatched and by renesting.

Eastern Bluebird populations have made a remarkable recovery after many years of decline. The recovery has been made possible by the popular and increasing interest and participation in providing nest boxes and "bluebird trails." These trails are located where individuals erect and maintain houses along roads through rural areas.

Like Purple Martins, bluebirds have become dependent on man-made boxes because of the scarcity of natural cavities once numerous in now cut-over forests. Also natural cavities in wooden posts that often provided natural or woodpecker excavated cavities for bluebirds became outmoded with the use of metal fence posts.

Bluebirds will use nest boxes placed in open areas maintained by cultivation or mowing. During the nesting season, bluebirds are territorial and a pair will defend about two acres of suitable habitat. They feed from elevated perches, pouncing on insects and other invertebrates. While foraging, they utilize posts, fences, utility wires, eaves of buildings, tree branches, and scattered low trees or bushes for perches. Bluebirds are competitors with robins, mockingbirds, Loggerhead Shrikes, and Brown Thrashers for insects. Shrikes and mockingbirds are aggressive toward bluebirds in their nesting territories, but bluebirds are capable of avoiding attempts to drive them away.

Bluebird nest boxes are available at most lawn and garden stores. They are easy to make using cypress or western cedar and rust resistant nails or screws. Dimensions for building boxes and the entrance holes will be found under the bluebird species account. Boxes should be spaced about 200 feet apart. Several boxes should be erected in each territory to allow for choice by a pair of bluebirds or possible occupancy by the Carolina Chickadee or Tufted Titmouse. Renesting by bluebirds occurs after the first brood fledges.

Bluebird nest boxes require adequate ventilation of about one-half inch on two sides beneath the roof. Drilling holes in the bottom or sawing off corners of the bottom piece when it is an inset design allows for drainage. The use of PVC pipe sections for making bluebird boxes is *not recommended.* In my experience, such boxes get too hot inside for second and third broods and can result in nest failure.

Nest boxes should be inspected to observe brood success and to remove used nests. Wasp nests should be sprayed and removed. House Sparrows will occupy bluebird boxes, and they are persistent in rebuilding when their nests are destroyed. Continued removal of nests will eventually discourage them.

The Carolina Chickadee is an early nester, and many of these birds are sitting on eggs or feeding young around April 1. Chickadees will utilize bluebird boxes placed on fence lines or on posts. Nest box dimensions can be the same as for bluebirds. A one-inch-wide entrance hole will discourage larger birds. Boxes should be ready for occupancy by mid-February when these birds begin selecting territories.

Like the chickadee, the Tufted Titmouse utilizes boxes built and placed for bluebirds. Bluebird nest boxes placed on the trunks of trees at a height of six to 10 feet are more likely to be occupied by the Tufted Titmouse.

The Great Crested Flycatcher is a common, statewide summer resident of woodlands and suburbs. It arrives in May and nests in tree cavities or abandoned woodpecker holes. Nest boxes or martin gourds with a two-inch entrance hole placed eight to 10 feet or higher on a tree trunk or post near trees will encourage this attractive and noisy flycatcher to nest.

Another flycatcher, the Eastern Phoebe, nests under bridges, in large box culverts under roads, on protected ledges or other supports around buildings, and under or on rock ledges. Phoebes can be invited to nest on covered porches or under the eaves of buildings by providing a six-inch-wide shelf about the same distance below the ceiling or roof overhang.

Barn Swallows build cup-shaped nests placed under bridges, in box culverts, under open porches, or under the eaves or projections of buildings affording protection from rain. Barn Swallows can be invited to nest under open porches by nailing a strip of crown molding about six inches below the ceiling for nest support. Nesting swallows are interesting to watch, but they can be messy and will require extra housecleaning. If you have them and don't want them, remove all nest supports.

Woodpeckers build their own nest cavities in dead trees, limbs, or stumps. They can be encouraged to nest by allowing dead or dying trees to remain in place. The top limbs of willow, sweet gum, and chinaberry trees have a tendency to die and are favorite places for Red-bellied Woodpecker nests. Dead pines are utilized by Red-headed Woodpeckers and Northern Flickers. Flickers will occasionally use nest boxes erected for Wood Ducks or a box with a three-inch entrance hole and a depth of 10 to 12 inches. A layer of coarse sawdust or wood shavings should be placed in the box. Other woodpeckers seldom use man-made nest boxes.

Screech Owls will nest in Wood Duck nest boxes or boxes with a three-inch entrance hole. The Barn Owl also will occupy a box with a six-inch entrance hole eight inches above the bottom. The floor should be 18 x 24 inches with an overall box height of 14 inches. The box can be placed in a barn loft, a vacant silo, a dark area of a vacant building, or 10 to 12 feet high on the trunk of a large tree in a wooded area or on a substantial supporting post. A two-inch layer of wood shavings should be added before the box is erected.

Carolina Wrens build a bulky nest of leaves and straw that is arched over with a side entrance. They will nest in protected places in outbuildings, covered patios, open garages, or on top of masonry piers under houses. The nest is usually placed in some type of container such as a basket, a large open can, or even an old hat or large flowerpot. Carolina Wrens seldom nest in man-made nest boxes.

The Bewick's Wren is a rare summer resident in northern Mississippi. In the western part of its range, it nests in natural tree or rock cavities and will use nest boxes. It also will nest in protected places around buildings. Anyone in Mississippi fortunate enough to have a breeding pair of Bewick's Wrens should encourage them by providing nest structures under protected parts of homes and outbuildings.

Nests of Bewick's Wrens I have seen were open, cup-shaped nests on or inside buildings with the exception of a nest built in a tree cavity. One nest was constructed in a metal water pitcher hung on a nail under the eaves of an outbuilding. Two others were in a coffee can on a board beneath the eaves of an open garage shed. One nest in an open garage was built on top of a toy doll lying on a shelf with the doll's legs and arms extended and supporting the nest (found in Oxford by Aubrey Seay; MMNS). The Carolina and Bewick's Wrens roost inside protective cavities, often in flowerpots, building crevices, or roost boxes or gourds placed on building walls.

The Prothonotary Warbler, a fairly common summer resident, usually nests along stream courses, old river lakes, or sloughs and deciduous upland forests with deep ravines and branchheads. The nest usually is built in a natural cavity in a dead stump or tree. This warbler also will nest in man-made boxes or gourds with an entrance the same size as for bluebirds. Nest boxes placed within the breeding territories of this warbler have a good chance for occupancy.

Wood Ducks and Hooded Mergansers have the same nest box requirements. The box should be made of cypress or treated wood for long life. Floor dimensions should be at least 12 x 14 inches. Height of the front is 22 inches and back 26 inches with the front entrance hole four inches in diameter and 16 inches above the floor. One side of the box should be sawed across at an angle 12 to 14 inches above floor level. The top part requires two hinges and a screen door fastener to allow inspection and removal of wasp nests, bees, and unwanted nests of other animals.

To erect, a 10-foot, four-inch diameter treated post is set in concrete in a three-foot deep hole. At the time of erection, attach a treated 2 x 4 timber to the back of the box extending at least 24 inches below the bottom. The box is then ready for placement on top of the post with the 2 x 4 securely nailed to the post. Finally, attach a predator guard to the post 24 inches beneath the box floor. Make the guard from sheet metal to form a cone about 14 inches wide at the bottom and to fit tightly around the post where it is nailed in place. The guard is necessary to repel mammalian predators and reptiles, especially rat snakes.

Wood Ducks and Hooded Mergansers will sometimes nest considerable distances from water. For best nesting results, however, the boxes should be placed around shorelines of lakes, bayous, or streams above high-water levels. It is not necessary to erect boxes over water. Easy access for observation and maintenance is more important. Only a stepladder is required to check boxes when they are placed along shorelines. A six-inch layer of hardwood sawdust or fine wood shavings should be added to new boxes. Old nests should be removed as soon as broods fledge so that second nestings can occur.

Boxes should be inspected, cleaned out, and readied for occupancy by late January or earlier if possible. After utilization of first-time boxes, multiples of boxes can be erected at the same locations. Wood Ducks readily use boxes placed several feet apart on platforms made with dimension lumber and two or more posts for support. For more information about Wood Ducks and Hooded Mergansers, refer to the species accounts.

Canada Geese will utilize artificial nest platforms erected above high-water level in secluded parts of large lakes, reservoirs, and marshes. People living along shorelines of large reservoirs and lakes with captive flocks of nonmigratory geese may want to experiment with platform nest structures.

Canada Geese have utilized two types of raised platform nests. A No. 3 galvanized washtub with drain holes in the bottom erected on a substantial platform or post and filled with sawdust topped with straw is one kind. The other is a four-foot platform on posts with straw added. An old tire can be used to hold the straw. Some goose managers have added a "gander-lander" or extension of one side of the platform for use by the male while he guards the incubating female and the nest.

Captive-flock Canada Geese, which are found around large reservoirs and national wildlife refuges, are wild birds but will become surprisingly tame when they are not being hunted. Feeding them should be avoided or at least carefully regulated. They can create a nuisance with their droppings or cause damage by eating grasses where flocks or family groups of birds congregate.

The House Finch, an introduced species from the western United States, is a common winter resident that utilizes bird feeders statewide. The first confirmed nesting records were at Starkville and Jackson (Jackson et al. 1986; Turcotte and Hutto 1991). This newcomer builds a cup-shaped nest of weed stems lined with grasses. The seven nests I have examined in Jackson were either in welded wire covers over fluorescent lights in an open parking garage or in Boston ferns hanging on a porch.

This species seems destined to become a glorified House Sparrow as it continues to increase in numbers and expand its breeding range in the eastern states. Unlike most birds, it does not clean its nest of the fecal pellets of nestlings. Dried, fresh droppings accumulate an inch or more around the nest rim. Nests I have examined were infested with mites. Because of these filthy nests, House Finch nesting should not be encouraged around homes or other buildings.

Landscaping for Birds

Interest in landscaping for birds has increased in recent years along with feeding birds and providing proper housing to attract them. Nurseries and landscaping services now can provide a diversity of cultivated plants, ornamental shrubs, and native plants and seeds useful in making yards and other properties more attractive.

All plants and birds serve some useful purpose. Some also have undesirable traits or habits. Nature provides a sequence of plant growth that eventually will occupy vacant ground caused by death or disturbance of plant growth. Some seeds, tubers, or roots already are present in what only appears as bare ground.

Birds play an important role in distributing seeds of berries and fruiting plants that furnish part of birds' food supplies. Acorns are carried by jays and woodpeckers to be dropped on the ground or stored. The seeds of berries and fruits eaten by some birds pass through their digestive tracts and are distributed where they perch or roost.

A study of plants and their identification is important in understanding plant succession and utilization of their products by birds and other animals. Natural succession begins with annual growth from seeds, tubers, rhizomes, and roots of perennials already in the soil. If this succession is not interrupted by cultivation, grazing, mowing, burning, or other disturbances, other pioneering plants like pines, sweet gum, willow, and broomsedge will invade and become dominant by crowding or shading out competing growths. As pioneer plants eventually die out, they are replaced by oaks, hickories, beech, and other deciduous, climax forest trees.

Many of our native trees, shrubs, vines, and herbaceous plants have ornamental value and provide food, shelter, and nesting places for birds. Cultivars that attract birds also are available and useful as ornamentals. Here are some of the more useful trees, shrubs, vines, and plants for attracting birds.

Southern magnolia *(Magnolia grandiflora)*. Resting and roosting cover.

Wild black cherry *(Prunus serotina)*. Fruit eaten by many birds. Tree harbors tent caterpillars eaten by cuckoos.

Mulberry *(Morus rubra)*. A cultivar is preferred to native tree. Plant two or more for pollination and fruiting. Edible fruit highly attractive to birds.

Hackberry or sugarberry *(Celtis laevigata)*. Robins and other birds relish fruit.

Southern red oak *(Quercus rubra)*. A large shade tree, retains leaves through February on lower limbs and on young trees. Favored for roosting by wintering waxwings. Acorns highly preferred by jays, woodpeckers, and blackbirds.

Water oak *(Quercus nigra)*. Popular shade and nest tree for jays and robins. Acorns used by jays, woodpeckers, and other birds.

Willow oak *(Quercus phellos)*. Shade tree with small leaves and acorns requiring low maintenance. Acorns used by many birds.

Live oak *(Quercus virginiana)*. Young trees favored by mockingbirds for nesting. Larger trees may invite roosting by unwanted House Sparrows or winter flocks of robins and blackbirds. Pruning of older trees should eliminate problems with this evergreen oak.

Sycamore *(Platanus occidentalis)*. Shade tree sheds bark in June and large leaves in early fall. Seeds are shed in late winter. Seeds eaten by goldfinches and siskins, and leaf down is used by hummingbirds for nest-building. Drooping limbs invite nesting Baltimore Orioles.

American elm *(Ulmus americana)* and winged elm *(Ulmus alat)*. Shade trees bear early spring seeds eaten by cardinals, Purple Finches, White-throated Sparrows, and goldfinches. Preferred nest tree for orioles and kingbirds.

Loblolly pine *(Pinus taeda)*, longleaf pine *(Pinus palustris)*, and shortleaf pine *(Pinus echinata)*. Seeds from cones fall in November and are eaten by many birds, including doves, quails, nuthatches, and sparrows. Nest tree for doves, tanagers, robins, Pine Warblers, and Chipping Sparrows. Dead limbs, trunks, and stumps used by woodpeckers, nuthatches, and other birds for nest cavities.

Sweet gum *(Styraciflua liquidamber)*. Goldfinches and Pine Siskins eat the winged seeds in winter. Favorite nest tree of Mississippi Kite along stream courses and bottomlands. Has tendency to die back on top, affording dead limbs for woodpecker nest cavities.

Black gum *(Nyssa sylvatica)*. Blue black fruit eaten by many birds. Foliage shows red in fall.

Black willow *(Salix nigra)*. This tree seeds around shorelines. If left to grow, it tends to die back and affords woodpeckers and other hole-nesting birds places to build nests. Highly favored nest tree for Red-bellied and Red-headed Woodpeckers.

Red cedar *(Juniperus virginiana)*. A columnar ornamental providing shelter for resting and roosting. Berries are eaten by waxwings, starling, mockingbirds, thrashers, and other birds during winter. Chickadees, titmice, and other birds use bark shreds for nest material. Small cedars are favored nest sites for thrashers, mockingbirds, and towhees.

Crepe myrtle *(Lagerstroemia indica)*. An ornamental. When used as specimen or border, will form small tree used by birds for perching.

Apple *(Malus domestica)*, pear *(Pyrus spp.)*, plum *(Prunus spp.)*, and peach *(Prunus persica)*. Fruit-bearing cultivars. Select hardy and disease-resistant varieties producing edible fruit favored by birds. Ornamental and fruit-bearing types provide nest sites and perches when planted along fence rows or borders. Cedar Waxwings and House Finches eat petals from trees.

Mayhaw *(Crataegus aestivalis)*. Native, small trees producing small fruit eaten by many birds. Highly favored for making jelly.

Redhaw *(Crataegus marshallii)*. Red fruit eaten by birds. Affords nest sites preferred by thrashers and mockingbirds.

Parsleyhaw *(Crataegus coccinea)*. Small red fruit persists in fall and is eaten by many birds.

Swamp dogwood *(Cornus stricta)*. A small native tree producing white fruit in October that persists through winter. Highly favored by most birds including fall transients and winter residents.

Hollies *(evergreen and deciduous Ilex spp.)*. Red fruit persists through winter and is eaten by many birds. The native deciduous holly holds fruit until late winter. Evergreen varieties are favored nest sites for mockingbirds and thrashers. Yaupon and firebush or pyracantha *(Ilex spp.)* bear red berries consumed in late winter by waxwings, mockingbirds, and other birds.

Beauty berry *(Callicarpa americana)*. Called "French mulberry," this deciduous native shrub grows to a height of six feet. Bears purple berries in clusters along branches in summer. Fruits are eaten by songbirds.

Wax myrtle or bayberry *(Myrica cerifera)*. Large semievergreen native shrub containing wax-coated seeds that persist on branches during winter and are consumed by some birds. Foliage has pleasant fragrance. Seeds are used to make scented candles. Best use is for hedgerow or border.

Japanese privet *(Ligustrum japonica)*. Forms hedges or thickets. Black fruit clusters persist through winter or until eaten in late winter by Cedar Waxwings, Purple Finches, or other birds. Needs control by removing unwanted seedlings as they appear.

Red buckeye *(Aesculus pavia)*. Native large woodland shrub or small tree with red, tubular flowers in early spring, attractive to arriving hummingbirds. Grows well in sun or partial shade.

Spicebush *(Lindera benzoin)*. Deciduous shrub on swamp ridges and common in Loess Bluff. Leaves have spicy fragrance. Red berries eaten by birds in late summer and fall. Small yellow flowers appear in early spring. Host plant for spicebush butterfly; caterpillars of this species eat the leaves.

Blackberry *(Rubus spp.)*. Fruits eaten by many birds from late April to early July. Propagates by seed and sprouts from roots. Provides nest sites highly favored by cardinals, mockingbirds, thrashers, Field Sparrows, and other birds. Canes bear fruit on second-year growth.

Highbush and rabbiteye blueberries *(Vaccinium spp.)*. Cultivars grown in rows for fresh berries or for making jams and jellies. Attractive in flower. Several varieties provide more than enough to supply needs for home use and birds.

Service berry *(Amelanchier arborea)*. Small native tree bearing white flowers in early spring. Large, red-to-purple berries are used for jams and jellies. Highly attractive to songbirds. Cultivars available from nurseries.

Elderberry *(Sambucus canadensis)*. Hardy, native perennial. Large white flower clusters on terminal stalks produce purple berries relished by songbirds in summer. Volunteers and grows readily along fence rows and waste places.

Sparkleberry or winter huckleberry *(Vaccinium arboreum)*. Large shrub bearing edible, black, gritty berries. Foliage turns red in fall. Fruit eaten by winter birds.

Mock-orange or English dogwood *(Prunus caroliniana)*. Large, white, profuse flowers appear in early spring on curving branches and sprouts. Brown Thrashers, cardinals, and towhees use for nesting after flowering period.

Bridal wreath *(Spirea prunifolia)*. Small, white, compact flowers appear in early spring on curving branches and sprouts. Will form large bush or hedgerow useful as screen or fence. Good nesting and escape cover. Red and yellow fall color.

Turk's turban *(Clerodendrum indicum)*. Bears small red flowers until frost. Attractive to hummingbirds. Prune dead growth for annual regrowth from winter-hardy rootstock.

Muscadine *(Vitis spp.)*. Cultivated varieties on wire trellis or arbor provide good nest sites for mockingbirds and thrashers. With drip irrigation, annual fertilizing, and pruning, self-fertile and pistillate cultivars produce abundant berries favored by cardinals, orioles, jays, woodpeckers, and others. Several vines properly maintained produce enough fruit for home use and birds. Noble, Welder, and Scuppernong cultivars make good combinations.

Trumpet creeper *(Campsis radicans)*. A vigorous, hardy, ornamental cultivar of a native vine. Bears clusters of orange red, trumpet-shaped flowers larger than native vine. Attractive to hummingbirds and orioles. Orioles split flowers at base to secure nectar. Plant in full sun on substantial trellis, or best, train vine on single post to form umbrella shape. Needs dormant pruning to remove dead wood and encourage annual growth that bears flower clusters May through summer. Favored nest site for mockingbirds.

Poison ivy *(Toxicodendron radicans)* and Virginia creeper *(Parathenocissus quinquefolia)*. Native vines form ground cover or climb to treetops if allowed. Poison ivy is noxious to some people. Both vines produce berries after several years. Tree climbers reach large size, and berries are attractive for birds and squirrels.

Pepper vine or buckvine *(Ampolopsis arborea)*. A vigorous native vine bearing shiny, black berries in summer. Volunteers and grows readily along fencerows and waste places where bird droppings have spread seeds.

Rattan vine or supplejack *(Berchemia scandens).* Vigorous tree-climber forms branch clusters where exposed to sunlight. Cluster of black berries eaten by birds. Provides nest sites for shrikes, thrashers, and mockingbirds.

Japanese honeysuckle *(Lonicera japonica).* Vigorous climber and forms ground cover. Black berries eaten by most birds in fall and early winter. Forms support for bird nests along fence rows and thickets. Nectar attractive to hummingbirds. Needs control by removing unwanted seedlings.

Cypress vine *(Ipomoea quamoclit).* A hardy annual vine with star-shaped, red or white, tubular flowers that attract hummingbirds. Reseeds and grows vigorously to cover fences or trellises. Blooms until frost. Can be used as ground cover in open beds.

Hyacinth runner bean *(Phaseolus coccineus).* Hardy annual vine bearing foot-long spikes of pink flowers. Purple seed pods resemble lima bean pods. Ornamental vine attractive to hummingbirds and butterflies.

Woodbine or coral honeysuckle *(Lonicera sempervirens).* Native woodland, perennial vine that doesn't spread like Japanese honeysuckle. Nectar of red, tubular flowers attracts orioles and hummingbirds over long blooming period. Plant in sun or partial shade.

Cleome or spider flower *(Cleome houtteana).* Pink blossoms open in late evening light and attract hummingbirds and sphinx moths. Hardy, old-fashioned annual is four to five feet tall.

Coral bean *(Erythrina herbacea).* Native perennial, several feet tall, bears long spikes of red flowers. Attracts hummingbirds.

Texas sage *(Salvia coccinea)* and pineapple sage *(Salvia elegans).* Both attract hummingbirds to red, tubular flowers. *Salvia elegans* can be overwintered as perennial when brought inside as potted plant.

Pokeweed *(Phytolaca americana).* Purple berries on tall, herbaceous stalks from perennial rootstock attractive to bluebirds, robins, mockingbirds, and other songbirds. Volunteers along fence rows from seed spread in bird droppings. Fruits from mid-July through September.

Russian olive *(Elaeagnus pungeus).* An evergreen, vigorous, and hardy shrub or small tree. Fruit eaten by birds in early spring, especially Cedar Waxwings. Several types of cultivars available from nurseries for hedgerows, large shrubbery, or wildlife areas.

Oregon grape *(Mahonia bealei).* An evergreen used for specimen plantings, early spring panicles of yellow flowers are followed by clusters of blue fruit with purple juice. Grows to five or six feet in height; has caney shoots. Used by mockingbirds, thrashers, and other birds.

All plants are beneficial in some respect, since they form the basis for food chains that support all animals. Many other native and naturalized herbaceous plants and grasses afford food and cover needs of songbirds. Common garden weeds and grasses produce prodigious numbers of seeds. Native weeds and grasses provide nesting and winter cover, prevent erosion, and their residues enrich and aerate the soil. Wild legumes add nitrogen to the soil. Many birds feed on insects such as grasshoppers, crickets, and beetles hosted by wild plants and cultivars, and cicadas that spend part of their life cycle underground.

Open space maintained by cultivation, mowing, burning, or other disturbances is important for birds. Many birds depend on open grasslands and the early stages of plant succession. Regular lawn mowing and annual mowing of hay fields favor bluebirds, robins, shrikes, mockingbirds, thrashers, meadowlarks, and swallows that feed on sod and flying insects, their larvae, or other invertebrates. Later stages of plant succession bring perennial growths in open areas that provide cover, food, and nest sites for many birds. Open spaces that remain undisturbed are eventually reclaimed by trees, shrubs, and vines. A diversity of all stages of plant growth will support more species of birds on any land area as large as a city lot or larger. Water, even small ponds and poorly drained marshy places, will invite herons, kingfishers, Swamp and Song Sparrows, or shorebirds. All species have a knack for finding and using wetlands.

Birds are interesting, colorfully attractive creatures that are highly mobile and more visible than other animals. By encouraging them around our homes, we get the opportunity to observe and study their behavior at our leisure, which is rewarding and raises more questions than provides answers. Feeding birds and supplying water will attract more and different species for close observation through the seasons. By providing nest boxes and nest sites, we can watch and enjoy their reproductive cycles, which include arrival, territorial definition and defense, songs and calls, nest-building, egg laying and incubation, feeding and fledging young, and departure. By landscaping and manipulating native plant growth, we make our homes more attractive and productive for ourselves, birds, and other wildlife.

Attracting birds can become addictive and create problems, frustrations, surprises, a lot of extra work, and extra expense for limited budgets. Grackles and cowbirds, as well as goldfinches, Evening Grosbeaks, Pine Siskins, and House Finches appearing in large flocks soon become worrisome and expensive if feeding is unregulated. Starling pairs that take over martin gourds may cause frustration when they break off vegetable transplants in nearby gardens. Cars parked under shade trees can become spotted with bird droppings. Bird baths need frequent cleaning and fresh water. Feeding birds tends to become both a regular habit and a never-ending chore. Nest boxes need monitoring and old nests must be removed. Occasionally nest boxes and gourds need replacing.

The Carolina Chickadee is a common backyard bird across Mississippi. It is readily attracted to bird feeding stations and man-made nesting structures.

Numbers of birds at feeding stations attract predators such as the wintering Sharp-shinned Hawk that feeds mainly on small birds. Nest boxes and bird nests with young invite rat snakes, animals that can climb almost anywhere. Sometimes feeder birds take alarm and fly into glass doors and windows, usually glancing off, but occasionally being killed by the impact. Nest mortality caused by ants, inclement weather, or predation is likely. Injured or sick birds will appear and remain at feeders, and it is always best to leave them alone.

Landscape plantings for ornamental and home use are themselves rewarding, but require pruning and other maintenance. The scope of planning and work involved in attracting birds should not exceed the enjoyment it provides.

Organizations, Societies, and Bird Clubs

Around the turn of the century there was little general interest in birds. There were a few individuals with more than casual interest in Mississippi birdlife, and they were motivated primarily by collecting specimens of birds and eggs for identification or establishing new state records or lists of species.

Andrew Allison (1899, 1900), a pioneer collector, published lists and notes on birds of Hancock and Tishomingo Counties. His publications probably led Charles Stockard (1904, 1905) to make egg collections and publish notes on birds breeding in Mississippi. J. D. Corrington (1922), also influenced by Allison's work, published notes and records of winter birds in the region of Biloxi.

Albert F. Ganier (1902), a lifelong student of birds and founder of the Tennessee Ornithological Society, studied and photographed nesting Mississippi Kites while living at Vicksburg in 1901 and 1902. Merritt G. Vaiden, a resident of Rosedale in Bolivar County, made an extensive collection of over 3500 bird skins and influenced a number of young protégés to continue advanced studies of birds. These pioneers and others to follow influenced or assisted in the organization of ornithological interests, societies, and bird clubs.

The Mississippi Association for the Conservation of Wildlife was organized between 1926 and 1927 for the sole purpose of securing passage of laws establishing a state agency for the conservation and management of wildlife resources. Frances A. Cook was the principal organizer and secretary. With the support of private citizens and conservation-minded civic organizations, legislation was passed creating the Mississippi Game and Fish Commission in 1932. The association soon disbanded.

The commission employed Cook as research assistant and in 1935 initiated a WPA-sponsored statewide Plant and Animal Survey Project. Under Cook's direction, collections of plants and animals were made and educational exhibits were prepared. The project terminated in 1940, forming the basis for the Mississippi Museum of Natural Science, which opened officially on January 3, 1939, at Congress and Pearl Streets in Jackson. It was later moved to its present location on North Jefferson Street.

As director of the museum, Cook organized, encouraged, and participated in bird study activities and field trips, and the museum became a focal point for local and statewide birding activities before and following World War II. Field trips were planned and conducted by local birders and visiting groups. Bird record collections have been encouraged by museum directors.

The Museum of Natural Science has been the main depository for specimens, photographs, and notes substantiating state bird records. The museum library maintains bird record files and publications on Mississippi ornithology. Dioramas of native wildlife including endangered species, interpretive exhibits, aquariums with native fish, and periodic educational programs are featured. Native trees, shrubs, and vines are used in landscaping the foyer and grounds.

In the past 40 years, popular interest in birds has increased remarkably. This interest has been broadened by the publication of several field guides to bird identification, video broadcasts on birds and other wildlife, magazines featuring popular articles about birds, and the availability of good birding equipment including binoculars, spotting telescopes, and bird song tapes.

The decline in populations of hawks, eagles, falcons, pelicans, ospreys, and other fish-eating birds, due to widespread use of insecticides and loss of wetlands, bottomland hardwoods, and other wildlife habitat, stirred public reactions and concern for endangered and threatened species. Attracting birds by use of feeders, bird baths, nest boxes, and landscape plantings has accelerated due to the availability of bird seeds, bird feeders, and custom-built bird houses. This widespread interest in birds led to the formation of bird clubs and societies with special interests in birds.

The Mississippi Ornithological Society (MOS) was organized in 1955 with 22 charter members. Frances A. Cook was the principal organizer with other active birders and ornithologists including Andrew Allison, R. L. Caylor, Ben B. Coffey Jr., Lula Coffey, J. L. Dorn, John Frazier, Albert F. Ganier, T. J. Hatrel, John H. Phares, St. Clair Thompson, Mayo and Amy Tolman, and W. H. Turcotte. The society was organized to encourage research in ornithology and greater appreciation and protection of native birds.

Anyone with a serious interest in birds should affiliate with the MOS. Statewide spring and fall meetings are held annually at different locations favorable for bird study. The meetings provide opportunities for beginning birders, regardless of age or professional status, to learn more about finding birds and field identification from other members. Novice birders are welcomed.

The quarterly *MOS Newsletter* keeps members informed on meetings, events, and items about birds. The MOS bulletin, *The Mississippi Kite,* is released in one or more issues throughout the year and contains articles and records on seasonal distribution and occurrence. Twenty-seven volumes have been published since 1965.

The weekend gatherings of MOS members provide social events, business meetings, and field trips for identifying and listing birds. (On one field trip to the coast on November 1–2, 1985, following the passage of Hurricane Juan, members identified and listed 175 species of birds.) Membership information is available from the Mississippi Museum of Natural Science, 111 North Jefferson Street, Jackson, MS 39202-2897, or the Department of Biological Science, Mississippi State University, Mississippi State, MS 39762. Annual dues are $10 for individuals, which includes the cost for publications.

The National Audubon Society was founded in 1902. The society acquires and maintains wildlife sanctuaries and actively supports conservation agencies and other groups concerned with the protection of birds, other wildlife, and natural areas. Members are entitled to affiliate with any one of many local chapters that hold monthly meetings, sponsor educational programs, and conduct field trips for study and recreation. The society can be reached at 950 Third Avenue, New York, NY 10022.

Audubon chapter members participate in Christmas Bird Counts, June breeding bird surveys, winter eagle counts, and contribute notes on the seasonal occurrence and distribution of birds. Membership includes subscription to *Audubon,* a bimonthly magazine. The Audubon Society also publishes *Field Notes* (formerly *American Birds*), a magazine devoted to seasonal bird records and environmental concerns. Subscription to *Field Notes* is optional, but it is a valuable aid that should be on every serious birder's subscription list. It is published five times yearly and includes the Christmas Bird Count issue, articles on birds, and seasonal summaries of birdlife in the United States and Canada.

Mississippi has seven Audubon chapters (1997). These chapters are located in Jackson, Greenville, Starkville, Natchez, Meridian, Hattiesburg, and on the Gulf Coast. The Vicksburg Birders (not an affiliate of Audubon) are also active in the Vicksburg area and neighboring Louisiana. The groups participate in Christmas Bird Counts, fall hawk migration counts, and contribute notes and seasonal bird records.

The American Birding Association (ABA), founded in 1969, promotes birding as a hobby and sport. The association had over 14,000 members in 1994. Competition among ABA members is encouraged with emphasis on finding, identifying, and listing species (North American, state, and local lists; life lists; big day; birding marathon participation; etc.). Some members may assist with planning or conducting bird-finding trips in their region of expertise as a service to other members.

American Birding Association members support public education and appreciation of birds and their contributions to the environment. The ABA contributes improved methods and information on finding birds, field identification, and population studies of birds. ABA's magazine, *Birding,* is published bimonthly and a checklist of North American birds is published irregularly. Their address is: American Birding Association, PO Box 6599, Colorado Springs, CO 80934.

The American Ornithologists' Union (AOU), founded in 1883, has over 5000 members (Gruber 1987). The membership includes ornithologists, conservationists, game managers, bird banders, educators, students, zoologists,

The Northern Mockingbird, Mississippi's state bird, can be found nesting in shrubs and foliage in many urban and rural areas. The mockingbird is an excellent mimic of other species and often can be heard singing at night.

and people with an avocational interest in birds. The AOU irregularly updates bird nomenclature and classification and publishes the official *Check-list of North American Birds.* A quarterly journal, *Auk,* contains scientific papers on birds, and monographs are published periodically. National meetings at different locations are held annually, and various committees handle publications, awards, and local arrangements or responsibilities.

The Wilson Ornithological Society (WOS), founded in 1888, is named after Alexander Wilson (1766–1813). Its approximately 1600 members are professional ornithologists, biologists, and hobbyists with special interest in birds. Library affiliates, researchers, and magazine publishers are provided exchange services from over 4100 volumes and a large number of reprints from the WOS library. Prizes are awarded for best student papers and best papers published in their quarterly publication, *The Wilson Bulletin.* Annual WOS meetings are composed of the presentation of scientific papers and field trips. The society also offers research grants. Their headquarters address is: Museum of Zoology, University of Michigan, Ann Arbor, MI 48109.

The Cooper Ornithological Society (COS), founded in 1893, has about 2000 members affiliated with the American Ornithologists' Union and the Wilson Ornithological Society. COS is a professional society of ornithologists, students, and others interested in birds. An annual conference is held at different locations. *Condor* is the official quarterly publication. The headquarters address is: PO Box 2168, Columbus, OH 43221.

Cornell University's Laboratory of Ornithology was founded in 1956 and has over 10,000 members. Located at 159 Sapsucker Woods Road, Ithaca, NY 14850, the lab acts as an educational link between professional ornithologists and the public, and promotes the study and cultural appreciation of birds. A public bird sanctuary is maintained with research facilities, and home-study courses and seminars are offered for studies in the biology of birds.

The Laboratory of Ornithology's Library of Natural Sounds contains extensive collections of taped bird sounds. It operates a recording studio and produces tape albums and furnishes recorded bird songs available by order. The laboratory conducts a nest record program to gather data on the breeding biology of all species of birds and maintains a colonial bird register to assess the status of waterbird nesting colonies. The *Living Bird,* a popular magazine, is published quarterly.

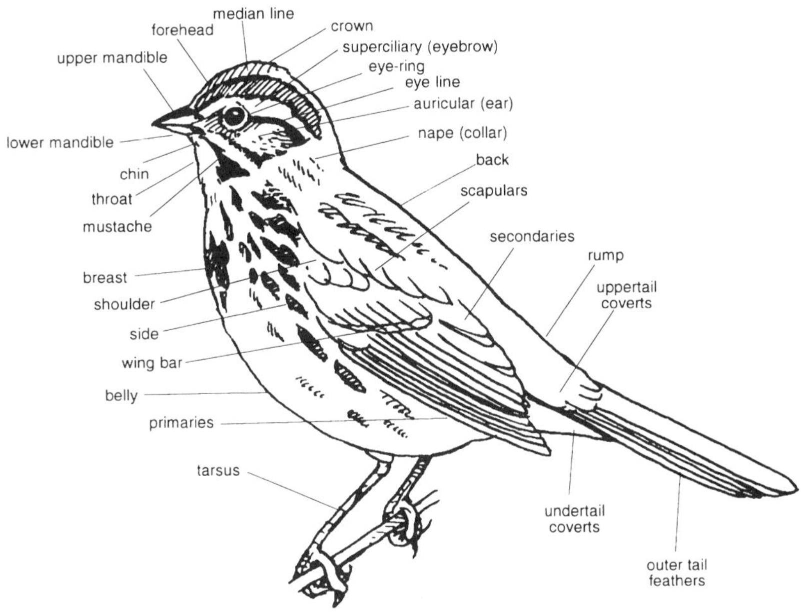

The Species Accounts

The first sighting of a rare or improbable bird new to our state list is always noteworthy of publication. Birds do not know state boundaries or read range maps in bird books. Errant individuals and unusual weather conditions will bring new species that fly where books say they should not be, a fact that consistently makes bird-watching interesting.

Some rare or unusual birds may be instantly recognized by their distinctive markings. Others defy field identification even when conditions are ideal for the observer. The acumen, experience, and practiced eye of the observer are then crucial, since positive identification may hinge upon one or more field marks or characteristics. Prominent field marks critical to identification for the species are italicized in the text.

The following accounts include 380 species that have occurred in Mississippi. Species names and taxonomic sequence are those of the *American Ornithologists' Union Check-list of North American Birds, 6th edition* (1983) as amended in the Fortieth Supplement (*Auk*, July 1995). The accounts include species of record accepted and published by the Mississippi Ornithological Society (MOS) and records of additional species subject to acceptance and addition to the checklist by the MOS Records Committee. Accounts of the Ivory-billed Woodpecker, presumed extinct in its former range in the United States, and the extinct Carolina Parakeet and Passenger Pigeon are included, but range maps have been omitted.

Brackets enclosing a species' common name indicate five or less acceptable records on file and that additional documentation by photograph or specimen is needed. Citations for historical reference are included for many first-occurrence, breeding records, and for observation of rare, accidental, or casual species.

The Bird Life of the Gulf Coast Region of Mississippi (Burleigh 1945) and *Birds and Birding on the Mississippi Coast* (Toups and Jackson 1987) are sources frequently used to document first-occurrence and other records on coastal birdlife. *The Mississippi Kite* and *MOS Newsletter,* publications of the MOS since 1955, and *Field Notes* (formerly *American Birds*), published by the National Audubon Society, are sources for first-occurrence records, breeding records, and seasonal occurrence, abundance, and distribution information. The bird skin, egg, and photograph collections; seasonal occurrence and distribution charts; and MOS Records Committee files at the Mississippi Museum of Natural Science (MMNS) in Jackson were used for reference and citation. Specimen and photographic records at the Department of Biology at Mississippi State University (MSU) in Starkville also are cited.

In the text, seasons are: spring (migration period) March, April, and May; summer (summer residents) June and July; fall (migration period) August, September, October, and November; and winter (winter residents) December, January, and February.

Abundance is relative to season and amount of suitable habitat for the species. The terms used here are *abundant, common, fairly common, uncommon, rare, casual,* and *accidental.* Abundant, common, fairly common, and uncommon species occur annually in very large, moderately large, relatively smaller, and much smaller numbers, respectively. Rare species occur in very small numbers annually or nearly every year. Casual species have less than 10 occurrence records on the MOS state list. Accidentals are species not expected to occur here and for which there are only one to five state records. In the text, they have brackets around the common name.

Though common in specific suitable habitat, some species are not easy to find because of shyness or seclusion in dense understory. The Swainson's Warbler, a common summer resident in stream bottoms with dense understory and cane thickets, is difficult to see but can be located by its song, though it sings infrequently. The Bachman's Sparrow is almost impossible to locate in winter because it is silent, retiring, and difficult to flush, yet locally common in open pine woods as a winter resident.

The bar graph accompanying each species account indicates by the width of the bar the chance of discovery of that species in suitable habitat. The wider the bar, the greater the abundance or conspicuousness of the species. The smallest of the bars indicates rareness (annual occurrence in low numbers, inconspicuousness, and also arrival and departure extremes). Accidental, casual, extremely rare, and out-of-season occurrences are indicated by dots or a dotted line. Observations of species in this category should be reported to the MMNS and documented with written details or photographs.

A bar graph accompanying each species having one or more breeding records (confirmed by photograph, egg collection, or sighting of actual breeding supported by written details) indicates weekly the month(s) in which breeding has been noted. Breeding records from the MMNS egg collection, card files, and published records are indicated separately from the W. H. Turcotte (WHT) egg collection, photographs, and published breeding records.

My wife, Dorothy Brown Turcotte, and I researched the maps, and she did most of the work of plotting the species' records under my supervision. The reduced county outline maps show location of records by numbers in the county or counties. The number (1) is a specimen or photographic record; (2) is a confirmed sighting; (3) a confirmed breeding record; and (4) an unconfirmed sight record. Although many more records confirmed by specimen, photograph, or sightings are available, only one entry per county is shown, except for breeding records, where more than one entry may be shown. The bases for breeding records on the maps include photographs, published sight records, egg collection, or juvenile specimens or photographs.

As noted above, the accompanying maps show breeding localities indicated by the number (3) in the county of occurrence. For species known to breed locally and erratically in Mississippi (e.g., Lark Sparrow, Dickcissel, Horned Lark) and those that have peripheral breeding ranges in the state (e.g., Ovenbird, Eastern Phoebe, Scarlet Tanager, Whip-poor-will, American Goldfinch), dotted lines are used to delineate approximate breeding limits. Birds breeding only along the Gulf Coast are indicated by the number (3) in the county of record. Arrows on the range maps show spring and fall migration routes through Mississippi for regular migrants, transients, and others that breed further north. The letters **C, L, S, A,** stand for distribution or breeding as *Coastal, Local, Statewide, or Accidental.*

The following species accounts are written in narrative style and include many personal experiences and observations. Some sightings were made in other states. Out-of-state references to breeding habitat and behavior are included for species not breeding in Mississippi. Place names are cited where these might invite birders to visit and share similar experiences.

Some species accounts are lengthy, especially the game birds and waterfowl, in the hope that hunters and birders will find the accounts useful and be better informed on management, utilization, and identification of game birds.

Loons (Gaviiformes)

Loons are admirably adapted for swimming and are powerful fliers when airborne. They are open-water birds, sitting low in the water and usually diving to escape notice. They raise the body forward and above the surface when diving, but they can submerge gradually. They are capable of staying submerged for long periods of time.

Loons are as large as small geese. Their necks are thicker than grebes, and they have sharp, daggerlike bills. Their toes have flattened edges and very flat nails. The body is long, and their strong legs are thin laterally and attached far to the rear, giving a powerful thrust to their large, fully webbed feet. This provides more efficient forward propulsion in water, but makes for awkward walking on land.

On land, a loon can only push forward on its belly, since it cannot stand erect. Sometimes during rainstorms they land on wet pavement or flooded fields too shallow for them to take flight. On water, they paddle on the surface to get airborne. In flight, they hold their head lower than the body, giving them a hunch-backed appearance. Their wingbeats are fast and continuous.

Loons come ashore only to nest on shorelines in Alaska, Canada, and the northern United States. They lay two, sometimes three, olive brown, black-spotted eggs. They feed on fish and other aquatic animals, including insects.

Of the four loon species occurring in North America, three have been recorded in Mississippi. These birds are migrants during spring and fall, and are winter residents along our coastal waters. The Common Loon appears regularly during migration on some of our larger inland lakes and reservoirs.

Above: Common Loon

Gaviidae (Loons)

Red-throated Loon *Gavia stellata*

This species has been seen, identified, and photographed on the Mississippi Gulf Coast. The first sighting of a Red-throated Loon at Biloxi on February 6, 1960, was reported by B. M. Myers (1960; James 1960), and the bird's distinctive field marks were described. Lovett E. Williams Jr. reported birds at Gulfport on November 28 and December 17, 1960 (Turcotte 1960c). W. Marvin Davis (1971a) recorded the fourth bird at Gulfport on December 7, 1969, at a distance of 10 to 15 yards. One summer sight record of a single Red-throated Loon in winter plumage was made in waters off Ship Island in Harrison County in June 1977 by Wayne C. Weber (1978b). Records show this loon occurred as a rare winter resident on larger inland waters.

About the size of a Mallard, the Red-throated Loon is considerably smaller than the Common Loon. In winter, the back is light gray with small, white spots, and the *bill is light colored and held in a distinct, upturned manner.* In breeding plumage, the head is gray with white stripes extending up the back of the neck to the head, and it has a triangular, red throat patch. This species breeds in the Arctic and winters mainly along the northern Pacific and Atlantic Coasts.

[Pacific Loon] *Gavia pacifica*

This accidental winter visitor from the far north usually winters on the Pacific Coast. The first sight record was by Larry Gates and Steve Peterson (Imhof 1980) on March 15, 1980, at the Davis Bayou area in Jackson County. Robert Chapel saw another bird on December 21, 1980, at the Pascagoula River marsh in Jackson County, the second and only other occurrence of this species on the Mississippi Gulf Coast (Jackson 1981c).

The Pacific Loon (formerly Arctic Loon) is smaller than a Common Loon and about the same size as the Red-throated Loon. The bill is *thin and straight,* neither distinctly upturned like the Red-throated Loon's nor stout like the larger Common Loon. In winter plumage, this species is identified by the *straight* bill, slimmer size compared to the Common Loon, and darker and more contrasting appearance than the Red-throated Loon. The white throat of winter birds is bordered by a *narrow dark line* extending from the eye to

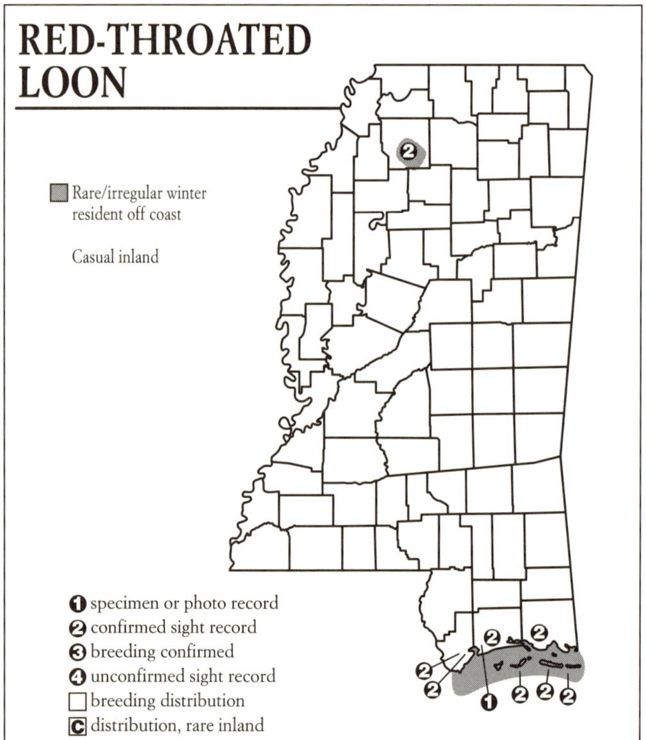

	JAN	FEB	MAR	APR	MAY	JUN	JUL	AUG	SEP	OCT	NOV	DEC
OCCURRENCE	oooo	oooo	oooo	10 oo		14 o					28 o	oooo
MUSEUM*												
WHT*												

*Breeding confirmed by egg, sight, or photographic record.

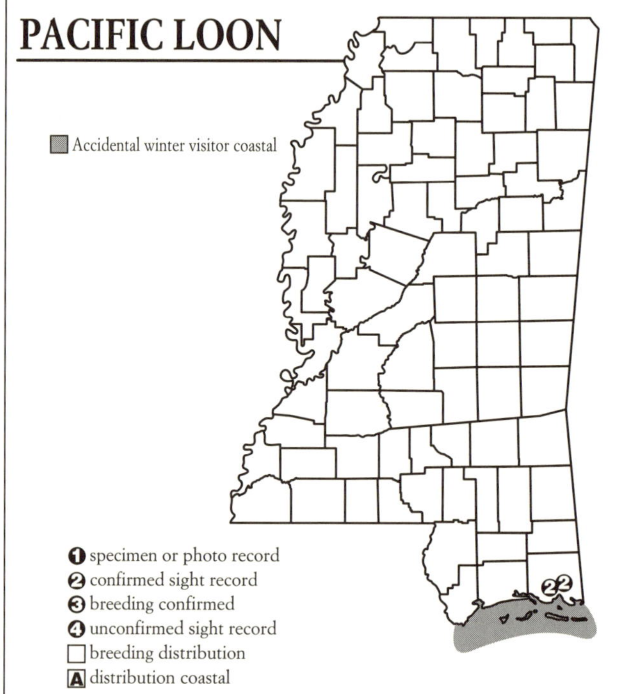

	JAN	FEB	MAR	APR	MAY	JUN	JUL	AUG	SEP	OCT	NOV	DEC
OCCURRENCE			15 o									21 o
MUSEUM*												
WHT*												

*Breeding confirmed by egg, sight, or photographic record.

the back of the nape. The crown and nape are paler gray than the back. Some individuals have a thin row of spots at the chin and throat line in winter plumage.

Breeding adults have a gray head and *gray nape.* The throat has a purplish patch bordered by parallel stripes and checkered spots across the throat at the chin line. The dark back is checkered with white, and the sides are uniformly dark.

This species nests on lakes in the Arctic tundra regions of central Canada and Alaska.

Common Loon *Gavia immer*

The Common Loon is a regular, fairly common, fall and early winter migrant on large inland lakes and reservoirs. On the Mississippi Gulf Coast it is a regular, common, and sometimes abundant winter resident on offshore waters and large bays. Fall arrivals appear early in November. Most migrants have passed through inland areas to winter on coastal waters during January, February, and March.

Spring migration begins in March when these birds attain breeding plumage and continues until May. Occasional nonbreeders may be seen in coastal waters in summer, but few remain after mid-May. The spring migration of Common Loons occurs with only occasional birds seen on inland lakes and reservoirs.

In winter, the Common Loon is white below with dark gray upperparts. The stout, long, straight, sharply pointed bill is held horizontally. In spring, the back is black, extensively cross-banded with white. The sides are black, finely covered with white dots. The head and neck are glossy black, except for a black-streaked, white neck collar and small throat patch.

At times, loons may resemble immature cormorants and mergansers. Cormorants on the water hold their hooked bills at an upward angle, have longer tails, hold their neck and head high, and are never completely white underneath. Mergansers have more slender bills and noticeable crests (except the male Common Merganser), and hold the head, neck, and body horizontal in flight.

Common Loon (winter)

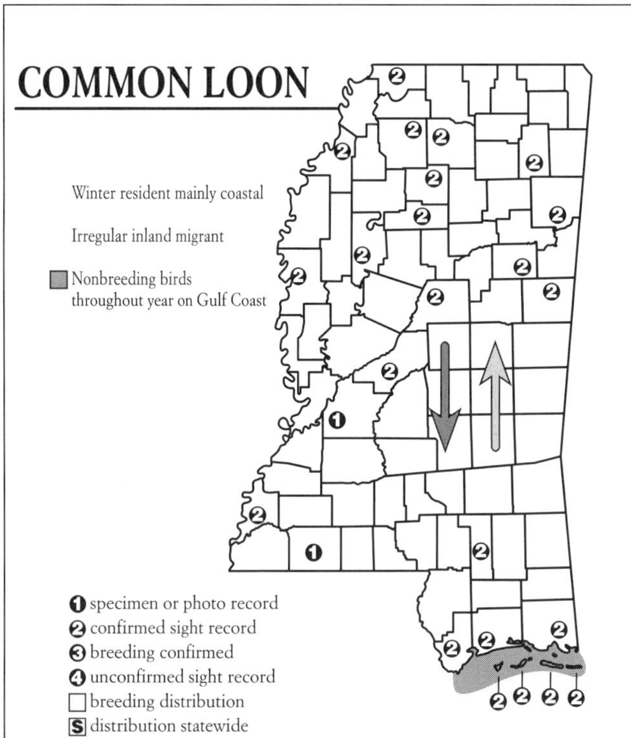

	JAN	FEB	MAR	APR	MAY	JUN	JUL	AUG	SEP	OCT	NOV	DEC
OCCURRENCE												
MUSEUM*												
WHT*												

*Breeding confirmed by egg, sight, or photographic record.

The Common Loon nests on the shores of wild, northern lakes where it lays two olive brown, black-spotted eggs on a mass of grasses and other debris arranged in a slight depression. During courtship on the breeding grounds, their weird, laughing calls are heard frequently, especially at night. In winter, loons are silent birds. During spring migration, the wild, yodeling call is heard rarely.

I was fortunate enough to hear the call of a migrating Common Loon on only one occasion, when a bird was circling low over the Ross Barnett Reservoir. It called just before landing. "Crazy as a loon" is an expression derived from the quavering, laughterlike calls it gives on the breeding grounds.

The Yellow-billed Loon, *G. adamsii,* is similar to the Common Loon in size and general appearance, except for its yellow bill with an upward slant and a distinct dark patch behind the eye in winter plumage. This species breeds on rivers and lakes of Arctic tundra, where it replaces the Common Loon. One sight record, by Martha Waldron and four other observers, of a bird seen feeding with cormorants on February 19, 1995, on Noxubee National Wildlife Refuge in Noxubee County is on file at the MMNS. All details were described as seen through binoculars and a telescope. Waldron had previously seen the Yellow-billed Loon in Alaska.

Grebes (Podicipediformes)

Grebes are ducklike, diving birds closely related to loons, although they differ anatomically from loons and ducks. Grebes have little more than a tuft of tail feathers. The neck is held upright with the pointed bill held horizontally. Grebes have a remarkable ability to submerge in water. They compress their puffy feathers to decrease water displacement and sink gradually into the water instead of diving headfirst like most divers.

I have never seen a grebe take flight from water. They escape by diving and swimming underwater, only to reappear at a distance with just their head above water. Grebes require a considerable run along the water's surface to gain flight. Once airborne on rapidly beating wings, they are capable of long, sustained flight during their night migrations.

Once while driving at night in a rainstorm on U.S. 61 in Claiborne County, I saw a bird on the wet pavement. I stopped, backed up, and found a Pied-billed Grebe. It was not injured, so I threw it into the air. It became airborne immediately.

Five species of grebes have occurred in Mississippi, including the common, permanent-resident Pied-billed Grebe. The Horned Grebe is a common winter resident along the Gulf Coast, and a few nonbreeders have remained in coastal waters through the spring and summer. Elsewhere on inland waters, the Horned Grebe occurs as a spring and fall transient or casual winter resident.

The Eared Grebe occurs casually as a winter visitor on the coast and sometimes as a transient visitor there. On inland waters, it has been a casual, transient visitor. Red-necked and Western Grebes are rarely seen as casual fall or early spring visitors in Mississippi. These species breed in northern midwestern and western states and into Canada. They winter mostly along coastlines. The Western Grebe is a rare straggler east of the Mississippi River.

Above: Pied-billed Grebe

Podicipedidae (Grebes)

Pied-billed Grebe *Podilymbus podiceps*

Known locally as "di-dapper," "dab-chick," and "hell-diver," this small grebe is a fairly common, permanent resident that breeds locally on freshwater lakes and marshlands. With the influx of wintering populations from mid-November until late March, this species is common on inland water areas and coastal marshes. It nests statewide in suitable habitat bordering shorelines.

The nest is made of dead and decaying vegetation, filamentous algae, and submerged aquatic plants to form a floating platform barely above the water. The four to six eggs are bluish white and soon become a nest-stained olive brown. The eggs are covered with nest material during the egg-laying and incubation periods whenever the birds leave the nest.

Nesting begins in late April and May, and the young are in downy or juvenile plumage until late July. Five egg collection records extend from April 22 to May 14. Sight records of young extend from May 19 to July 19.

The Pied-billed Grebe is seldom seen in flight or on land.

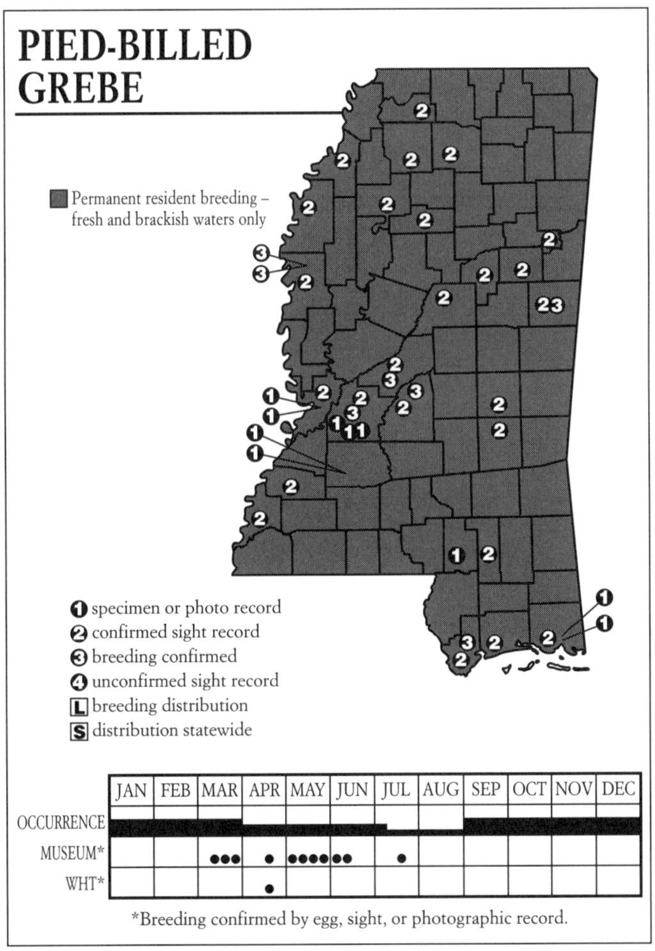

In breeding plumage, the adult is drab brown overall with a black chin and throat; pale belly; buffy white rear; a thick, chickenlike bill with a black ring; and a yellowish eye ring. In winter, the overall plumage is more brownish, and black is absent on the chin, throat, and bill. Downy chicks are mostly white on the underparts and heavily striped lengthwise with black on the upperparts, head, and sides of the neck, with a small patch of red behind the eye. Juveniles retain the head and neck streaking until late summer.

These birds are shy and usually are seen singly or scattered in groups of two or three, or occasionally more. They may nest individually or in small colonies in favorable nesting habitat. The first three nests I found on April 29, 1940, were grouped together around water reeds and clumps of sawgrass and button bushes in Mann Lake, a shallow cypress swamp in Washington County southwest of Lake Washington. The nests contained one set of six eggs and two sets of three eggs.

The downy chicks take to the water immediately after the brood hatches. They often ride on the backs of the adults, but they are perfectly adapted for swimming and diving soon after hatching.

By compressing the feathers, this grebe is able to sink its body beneath the water surface and swim about with only its head above water. It can slowly sink in the water without leaving a ripple and reappear a considerable distance away with only the head above water.

This grebe subsists on small fish, frogs, tadpoles, aquatic insects, and invertebrate organisms. The cuckoolike calls are heard during courtship. At other times, it seems to be entirely voiceless.

Horned Grebe *Podiceps auritus*

The Horned Grebe derives its name from golden feather tufts adorning the black head, which extend backward and upward behind the red eyes of adults in breeding plumage. The neck and sides of breeding birds are a rich, chestnut brown. The upperparts are blackish and underparts are white.

In winter garb, the head is black above the eye line, extending thinly down the nape and back of the neck, and merging with the blackish upperparts. The auriculars, cheeks, chin, and throat are white. The sides are dusky and the underparts are mostly white. The bill of this species is straight, thicker than the Eared Grebe's, and slightly decurved at the tip of the upper mandible. White secondaries show in flight and when the grebe is preening. Some individuals show a pale spot between the eye and bill. The crown is flattened on winter Horned Grebes and noticeably higher on Eared Grebes.

This grebe winters on coastal saltwater areas. It is a common winter resident along the Mississippi Coast where it

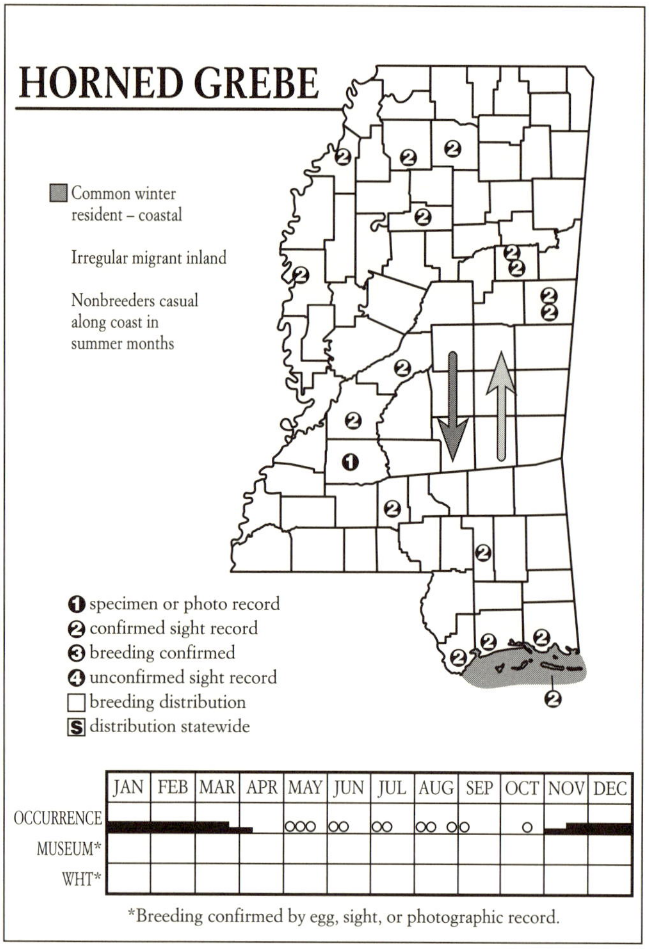

is often seen feeding in large flocks. Horned Grebes frequent bays and offshore islands, as well as open waters of Mississippi Sound. I have watched feeding flocks at Gulfport harbor. They were diving continuously, pitching well forward and downward and returning to the surface only to swallow small fish. Gulls and terns milled above the feeding grebes and occasionally retrieved or caught small fish from the water's surface among the foraging grebes.

On larger inland lakes and reservoirs, this grebe occurs at intervals during winter, and in spring and fall migrations. Extreme arrival and departure dates are August 31 at the Hattiesburg sewage lagoons, a bird observed by Larry Gates in partial breeding plumage, and on May 8 at Ocean Springs, a bird in breeding plumage seen by Judith Toups. A few coastal records of nonbreeding individuals of this species extend through June, July, and August.

Flocks totaling 50 to 250 birds or more have been counted by Marvin Davis on Sardis Lake and by observers on other inland waters. This species breeds over wide areas of western Canada, Alaska, and northern prairie states. It winters in coastal waters of the Pacific and Atlantic Oceans and the Gulf of Mexico. The nesting and food habits are similar to other grebes.

Red-necked Grebe *Podiceps grisegena*

This large eastern grebe has a long, thick, tapered, yellowish bill about the length of the head. In winter plumage, the head of the adult is blackish above the level of the eyes, with a grayish nape and neck. An *inverted white crescent* on the chin and sides of the face curves upward behind the eye. The upperparts are gray. In breeding plumage, the neck is rufous red. The head is black capped with a small crest and white on the chin and sides of the face below the eyes. Its eyes are dark brown. Immatures are mostly gray on the head, neck, and body, distinguished by their large size; long neck; and long, thick, tapered, yellowish bill.

The Red-necked Grebe breeds on shallow lakes from northern Minnesota and parts of the northwestern states into southern Canada and most of Alaska. It winters along the Pacific Coast of Alaska southward to southern California and on the Atlantic Coast to southern Florida. It occurs on the Great Lakes and on inland waters of northeastern states during migration, but winters mainly on salt waters of the Atlantic and Pacific Coasts.

The first Mississippi record of this species was made at the Hattiesburg sewage lagoons by Larry Gates and Richard

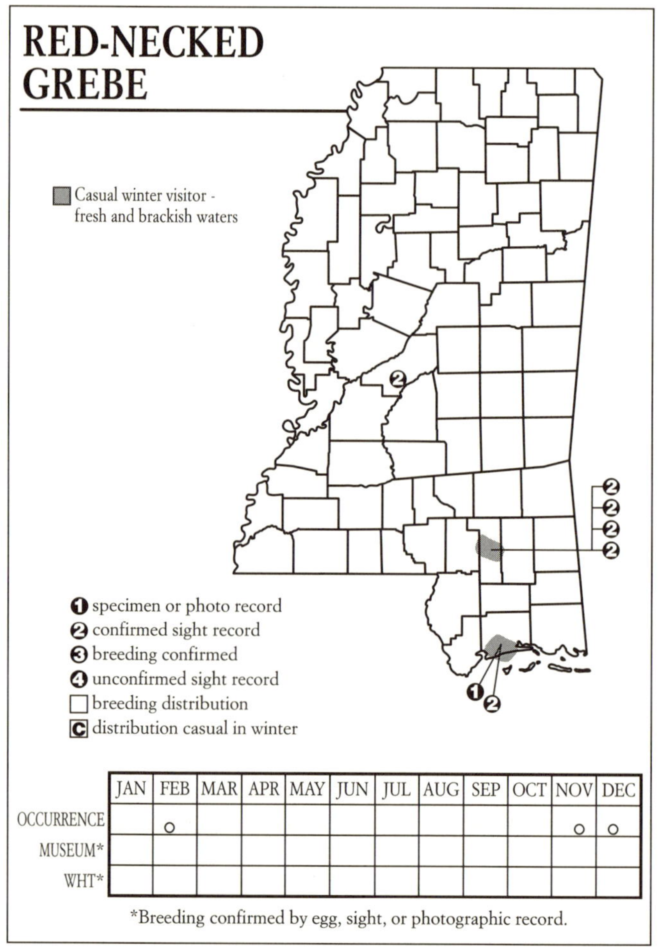

Moore (Gates and Moore 1978) between December 9 and 12, 1978. Later, the sighting was confirmed by Judith Toups and Bob Wood. All field marks were noted and described. A member of this species appeared at the same location and was observed by Richard Moore, Larry Gates, and Terrie Fairley on November 23, 1979 (Jackson and Schardien 1980a). Another sighting of one by Terrie Fairley occurred on December 23, 1979, and a third sight record by Fairley and David Hamilton was made on February 16, 1980. One coastal record was a Red-necked Grebe photographed by Robert Hare at Broadwater Marina in mid-December 1983 (Toups and Jackson 1987).

Eared Grebe *Podiceps nigricollis*

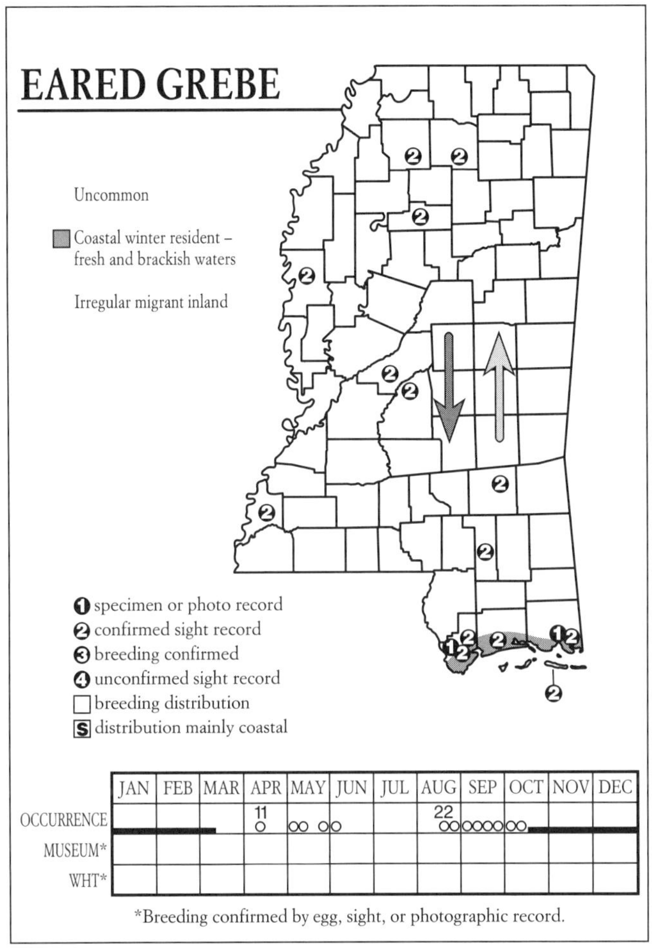

The adult in breeding plumage has a peaked, blackish head with golden plumelike feathers fanning out behind its red eyes. The thin neck and upperparts are dusky black, and the sides and flanks rusty with mostly white underparts. In winter, the head is slightly peaked and blackish with a whitish inverted crescent extending from the chin beneath and upward behind the ear. The back is dusky black, and the neck and sides are dusky.

This is a common species in the western prairie and plains states, where it breeds northward into southern Canada and west to the Pacific Coast. It winters into northern Mexico and the southern part of its breeding range, along the Pacific coastline and along the Gulf Coast casually to the Florida Panhandle. It is an uncommon winter resident on inland waters in northern Mississippi.

In winter plumage, this species resembles the more common winter-resident Horned Grebe. The Eared Grebe has a thinner, longer bill, which is angled upward at the end of the lower mandible. In winter, the throat and sides of the throat are duskier than the Horned Grebe, which has a white throat. In winter plumage, a whitish spot behind the eye of the Eared Grebe contrasts sharply with its dusky head and dingy throat. Observers should carefully note these differences in field marks before identifying the two species in winter plumage. In breeding plumage, the Horned Grebe has a chestnut-colored neck compared to the Eared Grebe's black neck. This species may occur more commonly than present state records indicate.

The Eared Grebe nests in colonies and builds a floating nest of vegetable matter. Colony nests are sometimes closely spaced together in open areas in shallow marshes. At times, individual nests are placed in or under concealing vegetation. The five to nine bluish white eggs are always nest stained a drab olive or brown.

Extreme dates of arrival and departure for this species are August 22 and June 5. The first state collection record was a bird taken by Lovett E. Williams Jr. (1962a) on March 11, 1962, at Pascagoula Marsh. An adult in full breeding plumage was observed on the Hattiesburg sewage lagoons on June 1 and 2, 1979, by Larry Gates and Terrie Fairley. As many as 59 Eared Grebes were counted at this area on March 1, 1980, by Terrie Fairley and David Hamilton (Jackson and Schardien 1980a). Fifty-five were seen there on December 18, 1980, by the same observers (Jackson 1981c).

[Western Grebe] *Aechmophorus occidentalis*

There are few Mississippi records for this accidental western visitor. The first occurrence was recorded by W. Marvin Davis on January 29, 1965, at Grenada Lake (James 1965). A second sight record on December 2, 1972, at the Mississippi Highway 43 crossing on Ross Barnett Reservoir was made by Frances Wills Jr. and Christine Berry (Turcotte 1972c). For comparison, this bird was among Ruddy Ducks, several Canvasbacks, and at least four Horned Grebes. It was observed closely and at leisure with all distinctive field marks noted including the yellow bill.

Other confirmed sight records of one bird at the Hattiesburg sewage lagoons by Richard Moore, Pedro Rodriguez, Larry Gates, and Terrie Fairley occurred on September 15, 16,

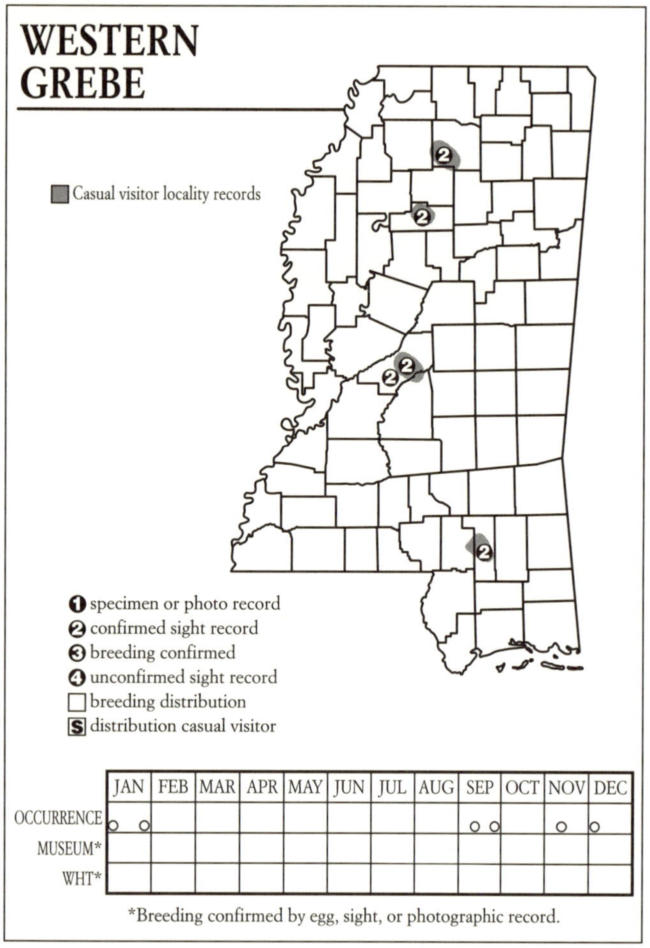

24, and 26, 1979, and one on November 11, 1979, by Terrie Fairley at the same location (Jackson and Schardien 1980a). Four records of single birds seen on Sardis Lake near the dam occurred on January 3, 10, 24, and November 8, 1976.

The Western Grebe breeds on open water, reed-bordered marshes of midwestern prairies, and rivers of the western states. The species is gregarious on the breeding grounds. It winters along the Pacific Coast from northwestern Washington to Mexico's Baja Peninsula, on reservoirs of New Mexico and western Texas, and along the coastal waters of southwestern Texas.

The field marks of this grebe are unmistakable: the long, straight, pointed yellow bill; long, swanlike neck with white throat, chin, cheeks, and underparts; and slate gray crown narrowing down the back of the neck to slaty upperparts. The sides and flanks are dusky. The very similar Clark's Grebe, *A. clarkii,* has more white extending from the upper mandible over and behind the eyes. Dark-phase birds are pale, slaty gray from the bill extending in a line slightly beneath the eye. The eyes of this grebe are large and strikingly red. The neck is carried high and nearly straight. Feathered juveniles are similar to adults.

These nesting Cattle Egrets were part of a large heronry that contained an estimated 10,000 nesting birds. Nesting in the same freshwater marsh were Pied-bill Grebes, Little Blue Herons, and Moorhens.

I have observed and photographed dark-phase birds on Lake Andes National Wildlife Refuge in South Dakota. I was fortunate to tape record the double-noted, high-pitched calls of adults and young, and simultaneously tape record the spectacular "walking on water" courtship dance of another pair. With their bodies raised in an erect stance, necks arched, and bills at a slight upward angle, they sprint side by side for a considerable distance across the water's surface. The refuge manager told me that it was rather unusual to see the courtship performance when young birds were nearly grown. I have seen these birds in numbers on the Bear River marshes bordering Great Salt Lake in Utah, in Yellowstone National Park in Wyoming, and on Lostwood National Wildlife Refuge in North Dakota.

Albatrosses, Shearwaters, and Petrels (Procellariiformes)

Members of this order are wanderers of the open oceans, coming to land only to breed and raise their young. They are entirely dependent on the open seas for their existence. These birds spend the remainder of their lives on and over the high seas searching for food or resting and roosting on water or on floating weeds or debris.

Birds of this order have tubular nostrils and palmate feet. Petrels have tubular nostrils on top of the bill separated by a partition not visible behind a single opening. The shearwater's nostrils are on top of the bill and show two distinct openings. Albatrosses have tubular nostrils separated on each side of the culmen.

Most petrels and shearwaters nest in burrows or rock crevices and lay a single, white egg. Albatrosses breed in open colonies on remote islands and instinctively return to their natal breeding grounds.

Birders have little chance of seeing birds of this order without having access to the blue waters, waves, and swells of the open seas. Only by being on the Gulf Coast during tropical storms will these birds be seen along the Mississippi coastline. Such was the case when a Yellow-nosed Albatross appeared along the Louisiana coastline and was photographed by Joseph C. Kennedy and James McDaniel west of Holly Beach in Cameron Parish (Lowery 1974). Records of two species of shearwaters and the one species of petrel on the Mississippi coastline occurred during tropical storms.

Above: Sooty Shearwater

Procellariidae (Shearwaters)

[Sooty Shearwater] *Puffinus griseus*

The Sooty Shearwater is totally dark above and below, except for whitish median underwing coverts. The bill is also dark. It is the only dark-bellied shearwater likely to be seen along the northern Gulf Coast.

A first sighting of the Sooty Shearwater occurred on September 2, 1985, along the Ocean Springs beach in Jackson County. A few hours after Hurricane Elena made landfall, Malcolm F. Hodges Jr. saw a single bird riding updrafts in strong wind (Hodges 1986). All field identification marks were observed including the hooked bill and raised nostrils. Stiff-winged flight with short gliding was also described. Hodges Jr. had previously seen many shearwaters migrating along the California Coast.

Other sightings have occurred along the northern Gulf of Mexico from April through September from Texas to Florida, including this first Procellariidae record in Mississippi. A second anomalous winter sight record occurred on the count week of the southern Hancock County Christmas Bird Count conducted on December 29, 1988, and reported by Judith A. Toups (Imhof 1989).

SOOTY SHEARWATER

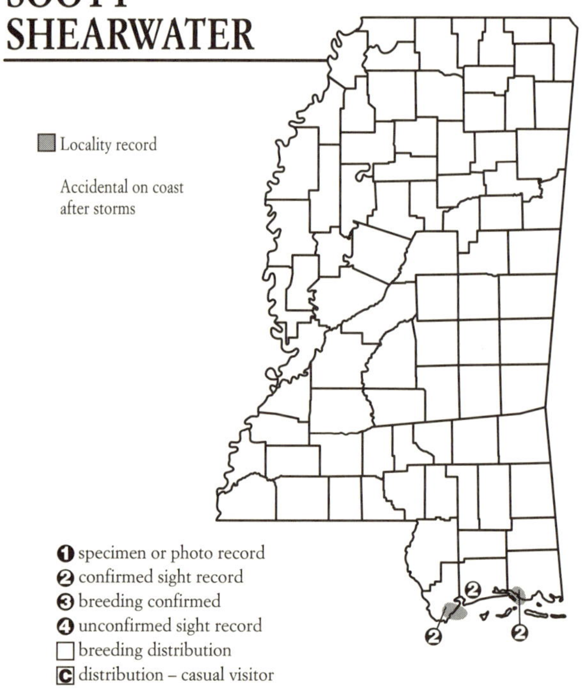

	JAN	FEB	MAR	APR	MAY	JUN	JUL	AUG	SEP	OCT	NOV	DEC
OCCURRENCE			22 ○						2 ○			27 ○
MUSEUM*												
WHT*												

*Breeding confirmed by egg, sight, or photographic record.

[Audubon's Shearwater] *Puffinus lherminieri*

Audubon's Shearwater has a cigar-shaped body, dark brown upperparts, and mostly white underparts except for its dark brown undertail coverts and brown patches on the sides of the breast to the shoulder. The long tail and narrow wings are brown. The primaries are dark on the underside with large, inner white patches bordered equally by brown on the leading and trailing edges of the wings.

The flight of this small shearwater is low over water while feeding. Wingbeats are shallow and rapid, alternating with stiff-winged glides. The bill is small in proportion to the size of its head when compared with larger shearwaters.

This casual, pelagic wanderer breeds on Caribbean islands and stays far out in the open Atlantic and blue waters of the Gulf of Mexico. It does not frequent shorelines except to breed or when forced inland by stormy weather.

Lovett E. Williams Jr. called attention to the dearth of information on pelagic birds in the northern Gulf while he was stationed at Galveston, Texas, with the U. S. Coast Guard. While aboard the Coast Guard cutter *Gentian,* he rode out Hurricane Carla in the Gulf 100 miles from shore. In the process, he collected several specimens of Noddy and Bridled

AUDUBON'S SHEARWATER

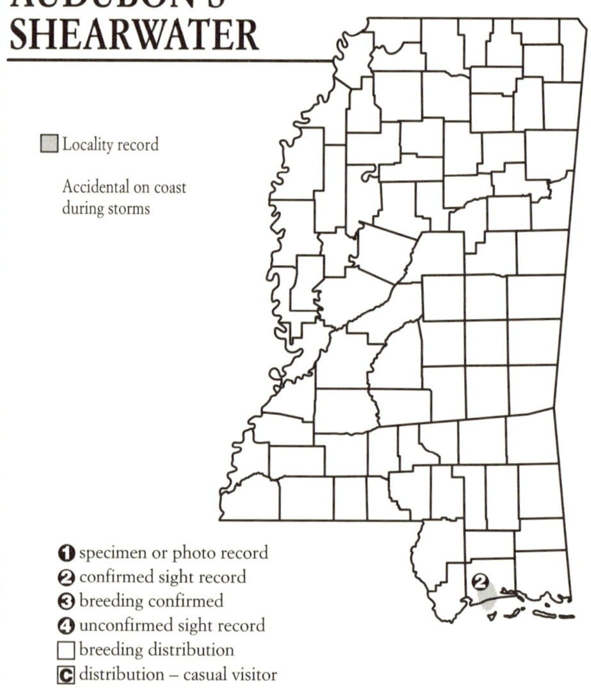

	JAN	FEB	MAR	APR	MAY	JUN	JUL	AUG	SEP	OCT	NOV	DEC
OCCURRENCE								9 ●				
MUSEUM*												
WHT*												

*Breeding confirmed by egg, sight, or photographic record.

Terns, and saw Sooty Terns and unidentified shearwaters. Upon returning to shore two days after Carla went inland, he wrote on September 15, 1961: "By all odds, the Bridled Tern was the most frequently observed species at sea during the hurricane. I will be surprised not to hear of an outbreak of Bridled Tern records for the Northern Gulf following the hurricane. Upon returning to Galveston two days after Carla, I saw a Bridled Tern in Galveston Bay" (Turcotte 1961d).

Williams' assessment of the effects of the hurricane was accurate. Lowery Jr. (1974) wrote that the first Bridled Tern record for Louisiana occurred on September 16, 1961, at Holly Beach in Cameron Parish. The second Louisiana record of the Brown Noddy occurred on the same date and locality where dead specimens of each tern were collected by Keith A. Arnold and Edward T. Armstrong, following Hurricane Carla. A Sooty Tern was also sighted at Holly Beach on September 15, 1961. An astounding 14 carcasses of the Audubon Shearwater were recovered from Cameron Parish beaches on September 15 and 16, 1961. Thirteen were preserved as specimens in the Louisiana State University Museum of Zoology.

The first Mississippi sighting of Audubon's Shearwater was recorded at Long Beach Harbor in Harrison County, on August 9, 1988 (Hodges 1988). Judith A. Toups, Terence Schiefer, and Malcolm F. Hodges Jr. observed and described field marks of a single bird flying low over the water. Although the sighting was over in less than a minute, the bird was seen through binoculars and telescopes. The three observers had previous experience observing other species of shearwaters. The sighting was made during strong southerly winds from tropical storm Beryl as it made landfall at New Orleans.

Hydrobatidae (Petrels)

[Wilson's Storm-Petrel] *Oceanites oceanicus*

"Mother Carey's chickens," as these birds have been called by ocean voyagers, travel the wide oceans, where they are perfectly at home. They skim across the water surface with fluttering wingbeats, sometimes feeding in the troughs of swells while avoiding being swamped by waves.

In June 1945, while returning to New York after World War II, I saw Wilson's Storm-Petrels far from land from the deck of the Liberty Ship *Marine Robin*. These birds were feeding on invisible matter floating on the water's surface. On another pelagic boat trip, I saw one or two of these petrels flitting by and feeding along the dividing line between salt and fresh water off the Alabama Coast southeast of Dauphin Island. This halocline mixing and upwelling of saline and fresh water caused a line of drift to form on

WILSON'S STORM-PETREL

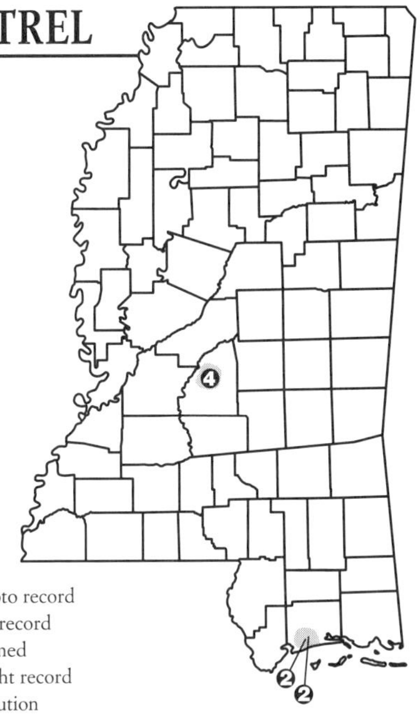

	JAN	FEB	MAR	APR	MAY	JUN	JUL	AUG	SEP	OCT	NOV	DEC
OCCURRENCE								15 ○		29 ○		
MUSEUM*												
WHT*												

*Breeding confirmed by egg, sight, or photographic record.

the surface, and several pelagic terns and this petrel were feeding on nutrients brought to the surface. A few Bridled Terns were seen feeding along the surface or resting on bits of debris floating on the relatively calm water.

One recent sight record of Wilson's Storm-Petrel occurred on August 15, 1985, at Gulfport in Harrison County. Dalton S. King, Judith A. Toups, and Malcolm F. Hodges Jr. sighted this swallow-sized bird feeding in the troughs of waves spawned by tropical storm Danny, which was crossing the Louisiana Coast (King et al. 1985b). A second sighting of this petrel was reported by King, Toups, and Hodges Jr. on October 29, 1985, along the Gulfport beach during strong southerly winds from Hurricane Juan, which was hovering off the Louisiana Coast. Both sight records for this petrel are supported by all pertinent details.

A third sight record with questionable details as to species, but unquestionably an inland occurrence record of a petrel, occurred on July 25, 1970, at Pelahatchie Lake in Rankin County. Six birds were reported seen by E. B. Hoover (1971) and described as Purple Martin–sized, dark with a white rump patch, and skimming over the water's surface like nighthawks. The details of the tail were not noticed or described by Hoover, and he later reported them as Leach's

Visitors to the Mississippi Gulf Coast discover a variety of gulls all along the sand beaches. Often, tourists throw bits of food into the air to be snapped up by the hungry birds.

Storm-Petrels. That identification is questionable because the forked tail of the Wilson's and the rounded tail of the Leach's are distinguishing field marks of each bird. However, Hoover's observation is worthy of reporting here as the only inland sighting of petrels in Mississippi. On July 22 and 23, 1970, prior to this sighting, the center of Hurricane Becky passed Montgomery, Alabama, and a strong eastward airflow followed passage of the storm. It seems likely that the hypothetical species occurrence would have been Wilson's Storm-Petrels blown inland by the hurricane in the Gulf.

Identifying field marks for the Wilson's Storm-Petrel are overall brownish black plumage with a pale, brownish wing patch; a U-shaped white patch around the rump extending onto the flanks and tail coverts; a roundish tail; and short, rounded wings. The feet have yellow webs and trail slightly beyond the tip of the tail.

Wilson's Storm-Petrels are common on the open seas of the Gulf and Atlantic Coasts from May to early fall. They return to the Antarctic to nest in the crevices of rocky coasts and islands. They lay one elongate, oval, white egg. The birds are voiceless, except on the breeding territories when they return at night and make their hooting sounds. These petrels will follow boats and can be enticed by distributing oily food substances that float.

Pelicans and Allies (Pelicaniformes)

Tropic birds, pelicans, boobies, cormorants, anhingas, and gannets belong to this order. Tropic birds, boobies, and gannets are pelagic, meaning that they spend their lives at sea. Ordinarily, they do not come to land except to reproduce. Birds in this group have webbed toes. In all other web-footed birds, the hind toe is free.

Pelicans and cormorants inhabit shorelines of the seas or inland lakes. Anhingas inhabit freshwater swamps and lakes. Since members of this order are aquatic, they feed chiefly on fish, crustaceans, and other aquatic organisms. All are expert swimmers and divers.

The tropic birds rarely visit waters of the Gulf of Mexico. They are birds of the tropical oceans, and their occurrence on the northern Gulf Coast is only accidental. Boobies also are more or less accidental pelagic visitors, and there are few Mississippi occurrence records of them. Observers on waters near the barrier islands of Mississippi Sound should be on the lookout for boobies in the summer months after tropical storms. Gannets are coldwater seabirds, and occur in winter in the open waters of the Gulf beyond the barrier islands.

Above: Pelican

Northern Gannet

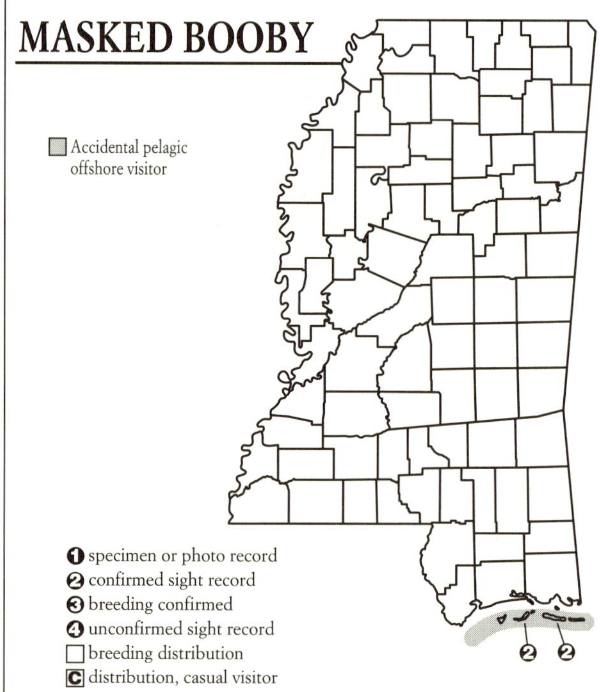

	JAN	FEB	MAR	APR	MAY	JUN	JUL	AUG	SEP	OCT	NOV	DEC
OCCURRENCE							6 ○		17-23 ○○			
MUSEUM*												
WHT*												

*Breeding confirmed by egg, sight, or photographic record.

Sulidae (Boobies and Gannets)

Boobies and gannets live on the seas and are close relatives of pelicans. These goose-sized birds have long, pointed bills, wings, and tails, which give them a "pointed at both ends" appearance.

Boobies nest on tropical sea islands and range northward after the breeding season. Gannets are slightly larger than boobies. They nest on sea cliffs of the North Atlantic and winter offshore in the Atlantic and southward to the Gulf of Mexico. They catch fish by plunging from heights of up to 50 feet or more.

[Masked Booby] *Sula dactylatra*

This tropical seabird, formerly called the Blue-faced Booby, occurs over the open waters of the Gulf of Mexico and rarely comes inland. Two sightings have occurred on the Mississippi Coast. The first, recorded by Judith Toups and Gerry Morgan, was of five birds at Biloxi on September 23, 1978 (Jackson and Cooley 1978). The second sighting of one immature, described with supporting details, was recorded by C. Dwight Cooley, Jerome A. Jackson, and Donald K. Cavin offshore at Horn Island on July 6, 1979 (Cooley et al. 1979a).

Adult plumage is similar to the Northern Gannet, but is readily identified by the yellow bill (yellowish on immature), black on the entire trailing edge of wings, black tail, and a large amount of black skin on the face and chin. The remainder of the head and body plumage is white. Immatures have a dark brownish head, tail, and upperparts, with white patches on the upper back and rump. Wing coverts are mostly whitish, and underwings and belly are mostly white.

Boobies hunt and dive for fish from great heights and descend below the water surface in pursuit of fish. These birds nest in colonies on deserted tropical islands. The nest is a shallow scrape to which nest material is sometimes added.

The eggs are bluish white and coated with a chalky white, soft substance that becomes stained during incubation. Usually only one young is reared. Frigatebirds prey on the small, unguarded young of boobies and often attack the adults, forcing them to disgorge fish from their gullets. After the nesting season, these birds wander the open Gulf of Mexico and the Pacific Ocean north to about 30° latitude.

Northern Gannet *Sula bassanus*

This coldwater, goose-sized bird breeds in the North Atlantic and is a fairly regular winter visitor to the open waters of the Gulf of Mexico offshore from the islands bordering Mississippi Sound. Thomas D. Burleigh (1945) did not find Northern Gannets on the coast during his eight years of bird study. More recently, Lovett E. Williams Jr. (1962c) and Sterling G. Clawson collected four specimens on February 12, 1961, in waters south of Horn and Ship Islands.

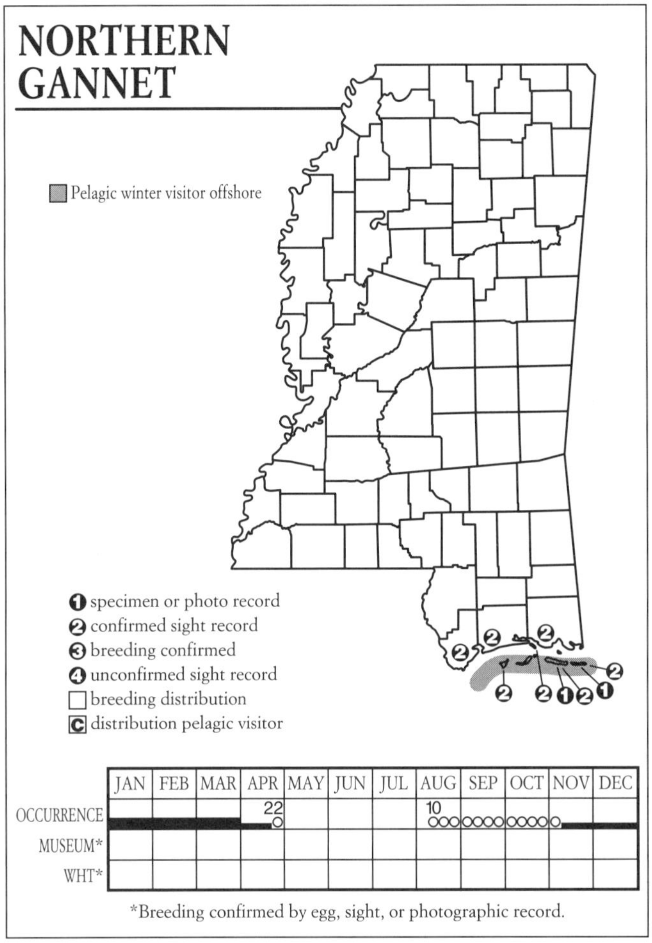

Northern Gannets also have been recorded in Mississippi Sound and offshore in the Gulf waters around the coastal islands. Up to several hundred birds have been seen in feeding flocks on one boat trip.

Although there are few reported sightings of these birds, they occur in Mississippi coastal waters from late December to mid-March. There is an anomalous June record of one bird in Mississippi found by Gordon Gunter and W. David Burke (Gunter and Burke 1977).

Adult gannets are white with black wing tips. The large, pointed bill, long, white, pointed tail, and cigar-shaped body give it a double-ended look in flight. Immatures are brownish gray flecked with white. Subadults have a mottled, black-and-white appearance above, with black on the tips and trailing edges of the wings. Searching for fish, gannets wheel and circle over the water with their bill pointed downward, then dive into the water. Their flight is strong and stiff with alternate wing flapping and gliding.

The Northern Gannet nests in large colonies on rocky cliff ledges of the North Atlantic Coasts around the Gulf of St. Lawrence, Iceland, and the British Isles. The large nests are built of seaweeds and flotsam. The single egg is bluish white and covered with a dingy, chalky deposit.

Pelecanidae (Pelicans)

American White Pelican
Pelecanus erythrorhynchos

With a wingspan of nine feet, this is one of the largest American birds. The body and head are all white, and the primaries and half of the secondary wing feathers are black. The huge, yellow, flattened bill and pouch give this bird an ungainly but dignified appearance. In breeding plumage, both sexes develop a flat, horny growth on top of the bill and pale yellow plumes on the crest and breast.

White Pelicans winter regularly in small numbers on the waters of Mississippi Sound and occasionally on inland reservoirs. They also occur as spring and fall migrants on the Mississippi Coast, and not uncommonly, a few nonbreeders may summer there. The most attractive areas for pelicans are the shallow waters and spoil areas around the mouth of the Pascagoula River and the shoreline westward to Ocean Springs.

From late March through May flocks of migrating White Pelicans appear and may linger for several days on large inland lakes, reservoirs, catfish farms, or flooded fields in

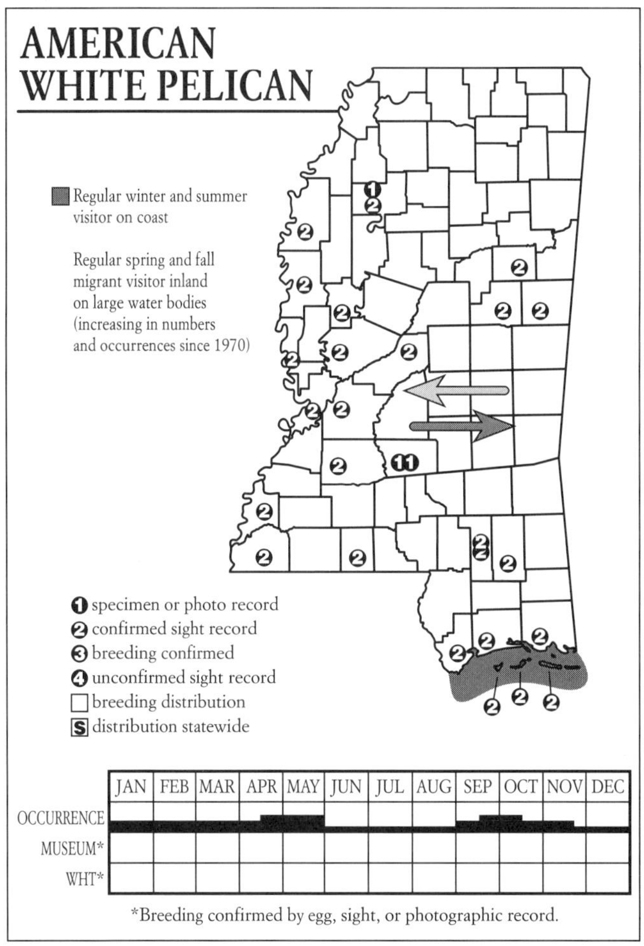

river bottoms. These are birds that have wintered along the Gulf of Mexico or South Atlantic Coasts and are returning to breeding grounds in the western states and western Canada.

Since Ross Barnett Reservoir was flooded in the mid-1960s, White Pelicans have occurred in flocks numbering more than 500 almost every year during April or early May. On several occasions, soaring flocks have been seen and reported over Jackson and its vicinity. On one occasion while working in my yard in West Jackson, I heard a swishing sound and looked up to see about 40 of these majestic birds in single file flying westward, just above the treetops. In early fall they sometimes occur as migrants on oxbow lakes along the Mississippi River.

White Pelicans sit high on the water and feed in groups, surrounding fish and scooping them into their pouches. They fly in single file or in long, wavy lines, flapping several times, then gliding for short distances. Flocks often soar in circles at great heights.

The American White Pelican nests in colonies on islands of remote inland lakes in western Canada and the western states. An isolated breeding colony is located on South Island at Laguna Madre in southern Texas. Nests are depressions in the ground or in small mounds of dirt and debris scraped together from the immediate vicinity. Two chalky white eggs are the usual clutch.

Brown Pelican *Pelecanus occidentalis*

The Brown Pelican was once a common sight on the Mississippi Gulf Coast. From late August through the winter months until late February, hardly a pier or piling along the beach was without its quota of pelicans. While breeding in colonies on the Chandeleurs and other Louisiana islands in spring and summer, only a few nonbreeders occurred in Mississippi Sound.

Until the mid-1950s, Brown Pelicans were common along our coast, diving after fish, sitting on piers, buoys, pilings, or sandspits, and in the breeding colony on North Island (Cook 1956). In the late 1950s, the birds disappeared suddenly and frighteningly from the coast. A few dead birds were found in 1956. The Christmas Bird Counts at New Orleans and Cameron Parish areas of Louisiana in 1958 recorded no Brown Pelicans.

On June 7 and 8, 1958, a party of MOS members and guests visited the Brown Pelican breeding colony on North Island, lying west of the Chandeleur chain. Here's what we found:

> Brown Pelicans were nesting by the thousands, mainly in mangrove bushes on the western side of North Island. Many of the young had left the nest and wandered about in small groups. Nests contained eggs or young pelicans of all ages. . . . A visit to the Chandeleur Islands is a rewarding experience to those who love the outdoors, the solitude of broad expanses of water, marsh, sand and shells and with bird life *unaffected by the activities of man* [emphasis added]. Most everyone can benefit from the experience of wilderness and build "a state of awareness to the land's collective functioning," as was Aldo Leopold's definition of culture. Life processes can be observed from their beginning in the sea where minerals, air, water, and sunlight are utilized through a chain of life that produces plankton to feed the menhaden and other marine life on which water birds feed. Gulls and Man-o'-war Birds scavenge or prey on the pelicans and other water birds for food to draw out the chain of life still farther. An awareness of these complex life relationships can lead to rich experiences in Nature's world of the outdoors. (Turcotte 1958d)

I did not know then that persistent pesticides in the pelican's food chain were already having an effect on them. The breeding colony seemed to be thriving. I recall noting a few dead young pelicans and some soft-shelled or dehydrated pelican eggs on this visit to North Island, but I attached no significance to my observations.

George H. Lowery Jr. (1974) reported that other observers visiting the North Island pelican colony found only 200 pairs nesting on April 20, 1960; 150 nests on June 6, 1961; and six adults but no nests on June 6, 7, and 8, 1962. Observers on the Mississippi Coast noticed the almost complete absence of Brown Pelicans after the winter of 1958 (Turcotte 1965a). Since 1962, the original native stock of Brown Pelicans has not nested in Louisiana. Reports indicate that the species had completely disappeared from Louisiana by 1963.

Chemical contamination of this pelican's food chain with chlorinated hydrocarbon pesticides was the probable cause of their disappearance from waters along the northern Gulf Coast. Millions of acres of land were treated with DDT, Endrin, and other long-lived chlorinated hydrocarbon pesticides to control insect pests. These chemicals become attached to soil particles, and silt runoff containing these poisons empties into nearby streams. As water-borne silt, they are carried to larger tributaries and eventually empty into the sea.

Small animal life in lakes and streams easily accumulate small amounts of these chemical poisons in their tissues with each intake of food. In turn, the more numerous plankton and smaller fish are eaten by larger predatory fish. Soon the concentration of poison in the tissues is magnified and stored in the fat of these fish until a lethal amount accumulates. Death is not always immediate for the victim carrying sublethal amounts of these poisons.

Pelicans that fed almost exclusively on pesticide-contaminated fish gradually accumulated the poisons and stored them in their fatty tissue. During periods of stress, such as a storm or other inclement weather, fatty

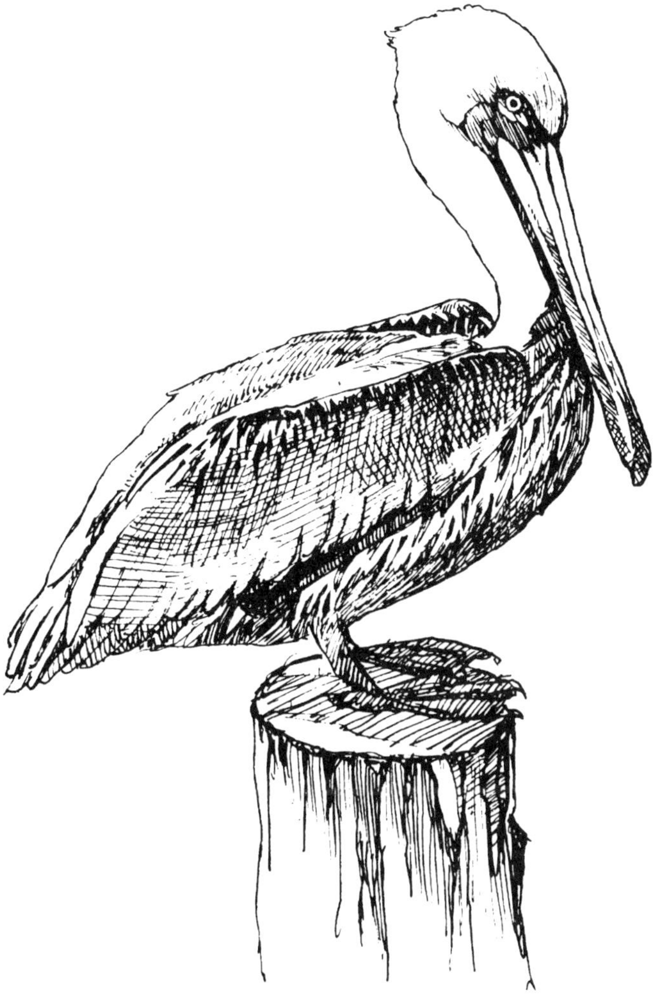

Brown Pelican on Piling

tissues were resorbed along with the lethal amounts of poisons. Pelicans managing to survive through stress periods suffered reproduction failures, very often laying thin-shelled, soft-shelled, or pesticide-contaminated eggs that broke or could not hatch. Unfortunately, the die-off of Brown Pelicans along the northern Gulf Coast was not documented by chemical analyses of eggs or tissues while it was occurring. However, a similar occurrence off the California coastline was well documented by researchers. Their studies showed direct and indirect Brown Pelican mortality as well as reproductive failures due to thin-shelled eggs caused by ingestion of chlorinated hydrocarbons.

Pesticide use in agriculture was not the only contributing cause of the pelican die-off on the Gulf Coast. In the 1950s, massive fish kills occurred along the lower Mississippi River. After these extensive fish kills, authorities finally identified the lethal agent as Endrin in the early 1960s. Its source had been a plant near Memphis that manufactured this pesticide and had dumped pesticide wastes that eventually seeped into the river. The fact that North Island supported the last breeding colony of Brown Pelicans in Louisiana was presumably because it was farthest away from this source of poisons coming down the Mississippi and Atchafalaya Rivers.

Restocking with immature birds from Florida was begun in 1968. After initial failures, breeding populations now have been re-established in Barataria Bay, Louisiana, and on North Island. Louisiana officials report that both colonies are producing some 1000 birds annually.

Brown Pelicans now are uncommon, regular visitors on the Mississippi Coast and more sightings are being reported each year. For years the Brown Pelican was on the U.S. Department of Interior's list of endangered species. Recently, however, the bird was removed from this ranking and listed as threatened on the East Coast and along the Gulf Coast to the Alabama-Mississippi line. From this point westward, though, the Brown Pelican is still considered endangered.

The Brown Pelican has a wingspan of more than six feet. The adults are dark, grayish brown on the wings and body. The head, front, and back of the neck are white in winter. In spring breeding plumage, the front and back of the neck are a rich mahogany brown with white remaining on the front portions of the head and neck. In all plumages, adults have a tinge of yellow on the crown and a small crest on the back of the head. Immatures are dull brown on their head and upperparts, and whitish underneath. These pelicans have dark gray bills and throat pouches.

Brown Pelicans feed entirely on fish by plunging after them, often from a height of up to 30 feet. They hunt schools of small fish, largely menhaden and other species of little

These downy young Brown Pelicans were photographed in their nest among black mangroves on North Island, Louisiana, on June 7, 1958.

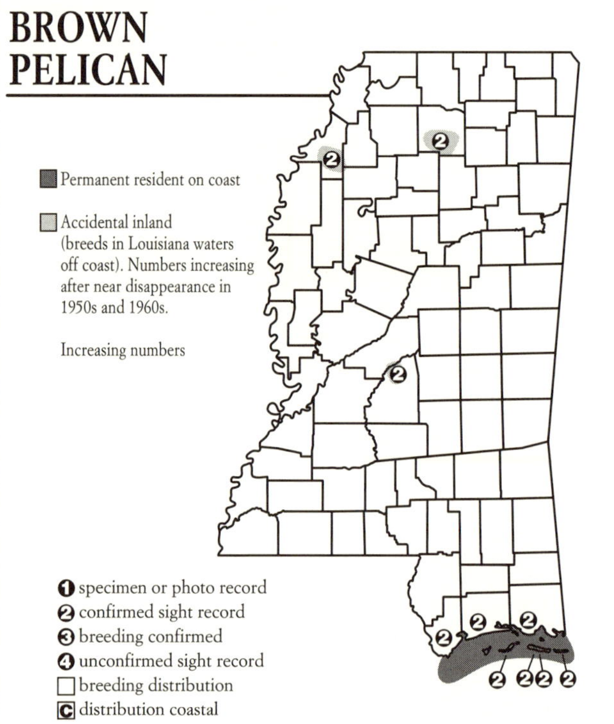

	JAN	FEB	MAR	APR	MAY	JUN	JUL	AUG	SEP	OCT	NOV	DEC
OCCURRENCE												
MUSEUM*												
WHT*												

*Breeding confirmed by egg, sight, or photographic record.

commercial value. Diving into a school of fish with a large splash, they almost disappear from sight, scooping the fish in their great pouch. White Pelicans feed in groups, surrounding schools of fish and feeding on them by dipping their heads underwater.

Brown Pelicans breed in colonies on coastal islands. Nests may be placed in black mangrove bushes or other vegetation and on shell banks. Sometimes they are arranged on bare ground or shell dunes. The nest is a flattened platform of sticks, grass, and weeds when placed in bushes, or a flattened pile of the same materials on the ground. The two or three chalky white eggs soon become nest stained. When the young hatch, they are naked and a brownish purple color, but soon become covered with white down.

Adults feed the young on regurgitated, partially digested fish. The young feed by placing their bills in the adult's open pouch. Before the young are fully feathered, they leave the nest and wander around the colony, begging noisily for food. When approached, they make a hissing noise and vigorously snap their bills at intruders approaching too close. The adults are voiceless except for an occasional low grunt.

The height of the nesting season on North Island used to be the first few weeks of June. At that time, flightless young of all ages, as well as eggs and young in the nest, could be seen. At the peak of the nesting season, it was not uncommon to see hundreds of Magnificent Frigatebirds over the North Island colony. Thousands roosted on the mangrove bushes on a nearby island and probably were scrounging fish from the pelicans.

Although the Brown Pelican normally is confined to the coastal zone, inland records have occurred in several states. W. M. Davis saw a single adult above the Sardis Lake dam on December 7, 1982. Another adult, seen by several observers, appeared on Pelahatchie Bay of Ross Barnett Reservoir north of Jackson and remained several days.

Phalacrocoracidae (Cormorants)

Great Cormorant *Phalacrocorax carbo*

This species is a casual visitor to the Gulf Coast. It is larger than the Double-crested Cormorant and has a longer and larger bill. The gular pouch is *yellow* with a *wide, white border.* Immatures have brownish upperparts, a *white* belly and *brown-streaked* neck, breast, and flanks. Birds in second-year plumage resemble adults, but the plumage is more

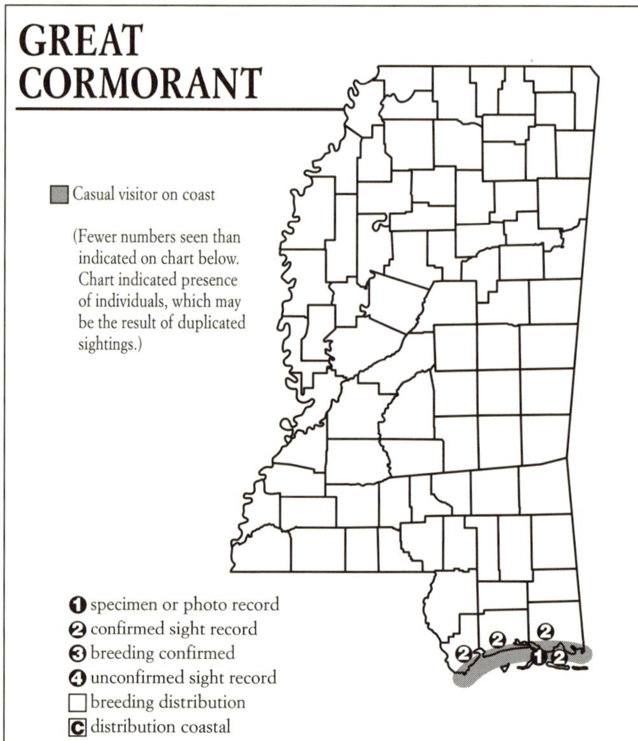

	JAN	FEB	MAR	APR	MAY	JUN	JUL	AUG	SEP	OCT	NOV	DEC
OCCURRENCE	oooo	oooo	oooo	10 o					8 oooo	oooo	oooo	oooo
MUSEUM*												
WHT*												

*Breeding confirmed by egg, sight, or photographic record.

brownish. These birds are strictly coastal and nest on sea cliffs of the North Atlantic. They are accidental inland and casual visitors on the Atlantic Coast to Florida.

There are four occurrence records in Mississippi for the species. Judith Toups and Larry Gates sighted one immature on November 1, 1978, and reported their observation at Bellefontaine Point as lacking in all supporting details (Jackson and Cooley 1978). Linda Austin, James Spence, Harriet Wessel, and Martha Powell (Austin et al. 1984) described another immature sighting on September 8, 1984, at the same locality in Jackson County with all supporting details and a photograph. Brown Pelicans and Double-crested Cormorants were nearby for comparison. Another sighting, reported by Judith Toups, was an immature bird at Biloxi on April 10, 1984 (Hodges and Jackson 1984). J. A. Jackson (1986) found and photographed a first-year plumaged Great Cormorant on the East Pascagoula River above Ingalls Shipyard on February 26, 1986.

Double-crested Cormorant
Phalacrocorax auritus

My first encounter with cormorants came in March 1934. Fannye A. Cook, then a research assistant with the newly formed Mississippi Game and Fish Commission, called me for assistance in removing and preserving fish from the stomachs of 20 or more of these birds. Following that, I prepared study skins of a few specimens. I worked for parts of three days and nights for what was to a schoolboy the handsome sum of $2 per day.

The birds' stomachs contained largely shad and nongame rough fish. As I recall, the cormorants came from Delta oxbow lakes and were collected by game wardens to determine what the birds ate. Double-crested Cormorants were in disfavor with fishers because of their fish-eating habits. From what we now know, those waters supported an abundance of nongame fish, and the removal of the surplus poundage of shad by cormorants and other fish-eating birds probably served both sport and commercial fishing interests.

The Double-crested Cormorant is a common and sometimes abundant winter resident in coastal waters. In migration, it is common on large rivers, inland lakes, and reservoirs. It is an uncommon winter resident in small flocks on larger reservoirs and lakes. The fall arrival begins in late September, and spring departure occurs during March and April. Extremes of arrival and departure dates on the Gulf Coast are September 21 and May 10.

The Double-crested Cormorant is a goose-sized bird with a slender, hook-tipped bill, long tail, and long neck. Adults are black with green iridescence. Immatures are light brown, tan, or whitish on the neck and breast, and the upperparts and belly are darker.

Double-crested Cormorant

These birds feed on fish by swimming and diving from the surface. They sit upright on limbs, buoys, or pilings and often spread their wings for drying. In flight and on the water, cormorants hold the head tilted upward. They fly in wedge-shaped or line formations like geese, but they are silent, and their wingbeats are more rapid. They often fly close to the water's surface.

The Double-crested Cormorant nests in colonies on lakes and along seacoasts in the northern states and Canada. Their nest of weeds and sticks is placed on horizontal limbs of trees or bushes or on the ground on islands. The three or four eggs are bluish white with chalky deposits, almost obscuring the ground color. The young hatch naked and are soon covered with black down until they are feathered.

Ben B. Coffey Jr. (1952) recorded the only known nesting record for this species in Mississippi. A tall cypress tree supporting large nests was found by him on December 30, 1951, in a slough connected to Beaverdam Lake about one mile west of Clayton in Tunica County. When the site was revisited by Coffey Jr. and R. Demmett Smith Jr. on May 18, 1952, the tree contained 45 nests, 12 with cormorant nestlings, with the remainder being Great Blue Heron nests.

During the 1930s and 1940s, cormorants were much more numerous transients in the Delta lakes and on the

DOUBLE-CRESTED CORMORANT

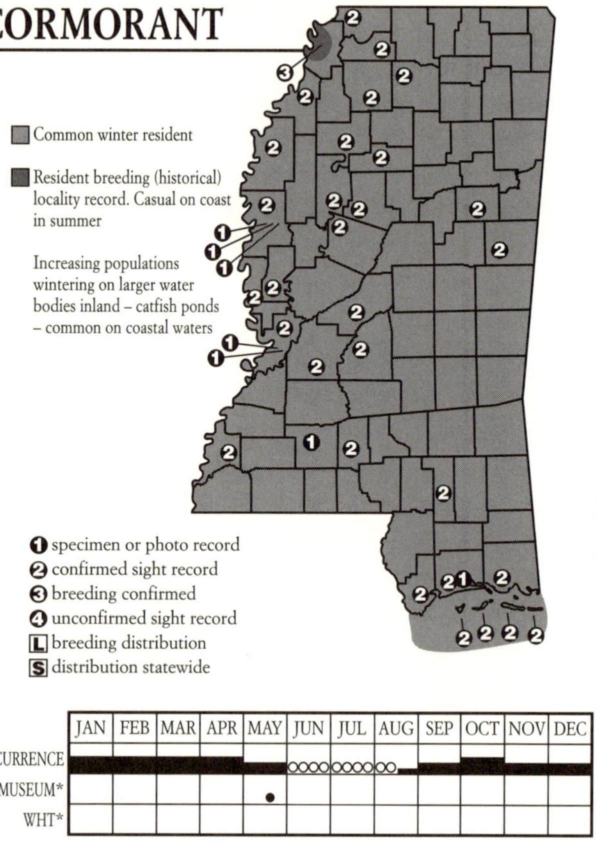

*Breeding confirmed by egg, sight, or photographic record.

Mississippi River. After the 1950s, they suffered an apparent decline in numbers, probably due to the use and effect of chlorinated hydrocarbon pesticides. Some indications of an increasing population of these birds have been noticed in recent years. Several large flocks and roosts have been noted in winter with as many as 200 or more birds on lakes in Leflore County, and in dead timber areas and open water on Ross Barnett Reservoir above Jackson.

They occur on catfish ponds in the Yazoo Delta where they sometimes congregate in large numbers on the levees. Their droppings in the water on these commercial fish farms may cause problems. The effect of their preying on catfish and possibly transporting fish diseases is relatively unknown and needs further study.

[Olivaceous Cormorant]
Phalacrocorax olivaceus

This cormorant is strictly coastal. Its breeding range is along the Pacific Coast and along the southern Gulf of Mexico to coastal Texas and Cameron Parish, Louisiana. It is a permanent resident within this breeding range, and wanderers have occurred along the eastern Louisiana Coast.

Known also as the Mexican or Neotropic Cormorant, this bird appeared on our state bird list only recently. It seemed inevitable that it would occur here as a straggler. Eventually, it may extend eastward, since no climatic barriers exist that would prevent expansion of its range.

The first sight record of this species was on August 4, 1979, at Bellefontaine Beach in Jackson County. Toups and Hodges Jr. (1980) observed and photographed an immature Olivaceous Cormorant with a Royal Tern for size comparison. Supporting details were noted. A second sight record by Robert Chapel and Terry Fairley occurred on December 20, 1980, at the same location (Jackson 1981c).

This species is noticeably *smaller* than the Double-crested Cormorant, but is otherwise similar. Comparative features of this species are a smaller, less orange, dull-colored throat pouch with a pale feather border extending to a point behind the eye. In breeding plumage, the border around the throat patch becomes white. Immatures are browner than adults, particularly on underparts, and smaller than immature Double-crested Cormorants, but otherwise they are similar. This species breeds regularly in colonies in Cameron Parish, Louisiana. It nests in trees or bushes near or in open water.

OLIVACEOUS CORMORANT

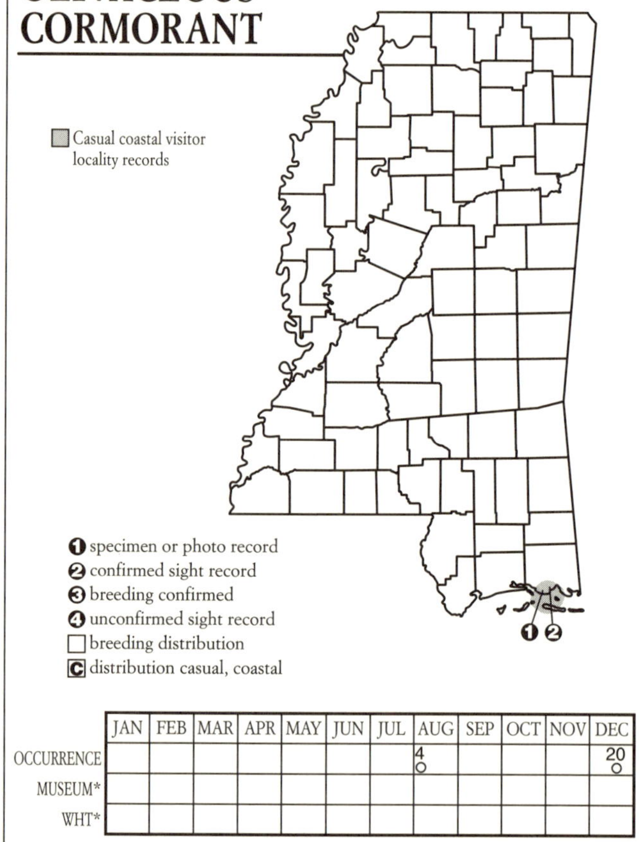

*Breeding confirmed by egg, sight, or photographic record.

Anhingidae (Darters)

Anhinga *Anhinga anhinga*

The "water turkey" or "snake bird," as the Anhinga is commonly known, is a locally common, breeding summer resident in some remote inland cypress and willow swamps. It is a rare winter resident. Anhingas return in March and April and begin nesting soon after arrival. Departure is usually complete by the end of October.

Anhingas, or "darters," are interesting to watch while swimming, flying, and soaring, or perched on some snag with wings spread to dry in the sum. They are similar to cormorants, but have slender bodies with thin, long necks and tails, and a slender, sharp, pointed bill. They can swim with the body submerged, and their food is mostly fish and other aquatic organisms caught while swimming underwater.

The male Anhinga is mostly black except for silvery white patches on the wings and streaks on the back. The long tail is tipped with buffy white. In nuptial plumage, a few short plumes develop on the back of the neck and sides of the head.

The female and young are brown on the head, neck, and on the upper breast above a sharply defined demarcation where the brown joins black underparts. Otherwise, they are similar to the male. The young are hatched naked, but are soon covered with thick, buff-colored down. They are strange-looking creatures sitting in the nest with their mouths open, throat pouches distended and vibrating rapidly as they pant in the heat of the day.

Anhingas usually nest together with herons, ibises, and other wading birds. Their colonies are located in swamp lakes grown up in cypress, willow, tupelo gum, button bush, swamp privet, and water elm. The nest is roughly made of sticks, twigs, and leaves. Green twigs and leaves usually are in the nest during incubation. The four or five pale blue eggs are covered with a soft, white, chalky deposit and soon become nest stained. Nests are placed over water on the limb of a cypress or in a willow, water elm, swamp privet, or button bush.

My first experience with heron colonies was on April 29 and 30, 1934. George Anderson, Thomas Whitfield, and I located two colonies in Holmes County by watching herons in flight and talking to local people during a Model-T Ford trip to the Delta. The first colony was in a cypress–button bush brake a few miles southeast of Cruger. We found Anhingas nesting with Snowy Egrets, Great Egrets, and Little Blue Herons.

The next day, after camping on the bank of a large, horseshoe cypress-tupelo brake at Good Hope in Holmes County, we waded out to a large heronry containing many nests of Little Blue Herons, Great Egrets, Anhingas, Yellow-crowned Night-Herons, and several Black-crowned Night-Herons. We collected sets of eggs of all these species except the Snowy Egret and Black-crowned Night-Heron. These we did not positively distinguish from the numerous Little Blue Heron and Yellow-crowned Night-Heron nests.

The water and wading bird colonies, once commonplace sights in the Yazoo Delta, began to disappear in the late 1950s. The widespread application of persistent agricultural insecticides, along with draining, clearing, and conversion of wetlands to crop or pasture, combined to reduce aquatic food supplies needed to sustain these colonies.

Now, it is uncommon to see Anhingas, Great Egrets, Snowy Egrets, and Little Blue Herons in the Delta during early summer. A few Anhingas still breed in swamps along the lower Big Black River, lower Bayou Pierre Creek, and along the Mississippi River bottomlands south of Vicksburg.

On June 23, 1971, Robert E. Noble found upwards of 500 Anhinga nests with young at a cypress swamp in Jefferson County (Turcotte 1971a). Inaccessible at times because of backwater, this breeding site was in a remote area near Cole's Creek along the Mississippi River. Much of the timber here has since been cleared and the land converted to agriculture.

A few Anhingas shared a nesting site with Cattle Egrets until 1977 on the Yazoo National Wildlife Refuge in Washington County. A small colony has nested with Great Blue

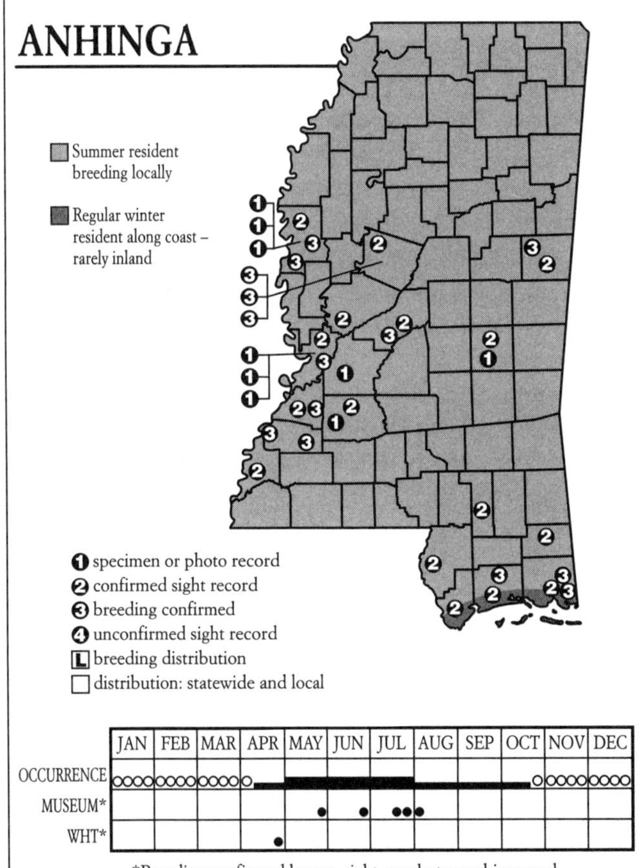

*Breeding confirmed by egg, sight, or photographic record.

Herons, Little Blue Herons, and Cattle Egrets in a cypress-tupelo brake on the Pearl River Waterfowl Refuge in Madison County for several years. Anhingas nesting with Cattle Egrets and other herons were documented with photographs of nests and young in Harrison County, July 3–6, 1986 (Toups and Hodges 1986).

Fregatidae (Frigatebirds)

Magnificent Frigatebird *Fregata magnificens*

MAGNIFICENT FRIGATEBIRD

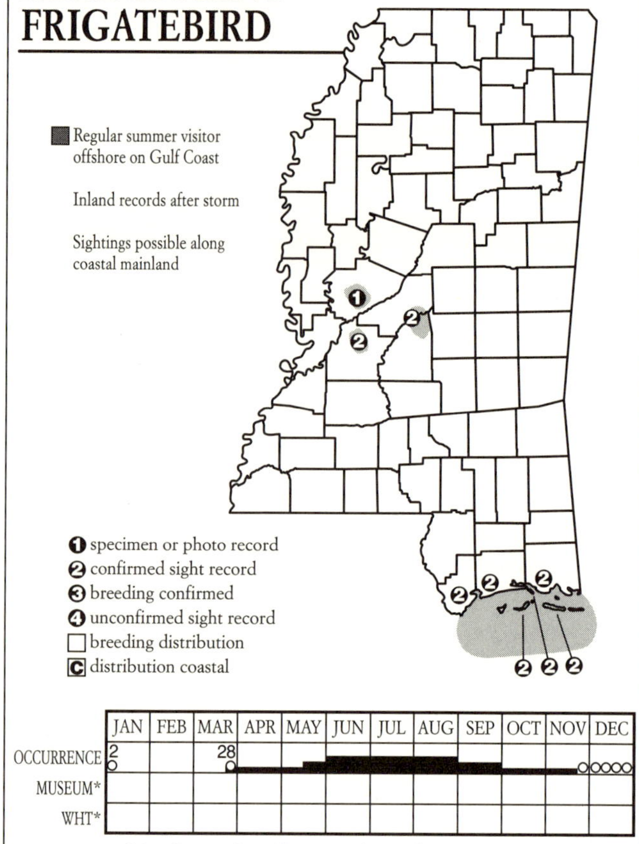

*Breeding confirmed by egg, sight, or photographic record.

The Magnificent Frigatebird was once called the Man-o'-war Bird, acquiring the name from its habit of robbing other seabirds of their young or their catch of fish. These long-winged, fork-tailed, tropical seabirds are regular summer visitors around the offshore islands in Mississippi Sound. They are instantly recognized by their nearly eight-foot wingspan; long, deeply forked tail; slender, hook-tipped bill; and black appearance.

This frigatebird measures about 40 inches in length. The tail is about 18 inches long, with the fork depth more than 10 inches. For its size, this bird is extremely light, weighing only four pounds or less. Despite its large size and awkward appearance on land, it is as graceful and agile as a swallow in the air, and can soar effortlessly to great heights.

The adult male is *black* with a green iridescence and an inflatable orange throat pouch. The female is similar to the male, but has a white breast. Immatures less than a year old have a white head and extensive *white* on the underparts. Young are hatched naked and are brooded until after they are covered with white down.

Normally, they do not land on water, but deftly seize their food from the surface, or catch it in midair after forcing another seabird to drop or disgorge its catch of fish. They nest in large colonies on tropical sea islands, building a platform nest of sticks in low bushes and other vegetation, or sometimes arranging their nest on the ground. A single white egg is laid. During the breeding period the male inflates a red gular pouch to an enormous size as part of the courtship ritual.

After the breeding season, thousands of frigatebirds gather around North Island in Louisiana where they spend most of the summer. The mangrove bushes are used for resting and roosting. When the birds on the island are approached, they take wing and mill around in the air.

In the early 1950s, when a large colony of Brown Pelicans was actively nesting on North Island, literally thousands of Man-o'-wars could be seen each year from May to September. Apparently, they fed on fish scrounged from pelicans, gulls, and terns concentrated around the Chandeleur Island chain.

Recorded dates of usual occurrence in Mississippi extend from March 28 to October 13. On June 29, 1957, a frigatebird was killed near Satartia in Yazoo County, two days following Hurricane Audrey (Turcotte 1957b). Another inland sighting of four birds by John H. Phares and St. Clair Thompson was made near Utica in Hinds County on September 19, 1957, the day following passage of another tropical storm (Phares and Thompson 1958). A few early winter records in December and early January have been reported in coastal counties.

Storks, Ibises, Herons, and Allies (Ciconiiformes)

The birds of this order are long-necked, long-legged, wading birds with short tails; long, rounded wings; and long, straight, or decurved bills. Usually they feed on aquatic animals including fish, crustaceans, small reptiles, frogs, insects, and sometimes small rodents.

Large breeding colonies or rookeries are often located over water in trees, bushes, or other aquatic vegetation. The birds sometimes travel long distances to and from their feeding grounds. Most species build platform nests of sticks or reeds, though not always in large colonies. They are noted for their postbreeding season wanderings over large areas of the country.

Above: Great Blue Heron

Ardeidae (Bitterns and Herons)

American Bittern *Botaurus lentiginosus*

There is no reason for an observer to be confused in identifying our only two species of bitterns. The great difference in size immediately separates them. The American Bittern more closely resembles immature night-herons in size and coloration. It is beautifully colored, presenting an overall rich, tawny brown appearance, which at close range is a mixture of shades of buff, tan, tannish brown, yellowish brown, gray, and black. The breast is prominently streaked, and the throat is buffy white bordered by a black stripe along the sides of the neck. The black mark on the neck, blackish outer wings and greenish yellow, sharply pointed bill carried upward are distinctive marks setting it apart from immature night-herons.

The habits and habitat preferences are similar to the Least Bittern, although the American Bittern exposes itself more often. During spring migration, it frequents flooded, wooded swamps; wet fields of grass and weeds; and brushy edges of wooded ponds and lakes.

The American Bittern is a shy and solitary bird, and its slow, deliberate movements give it a solemn look. During one spring migration, Ed Givens and I flushed seven bitterns from briers and brushy edges of a small woodland pond on the Copiah County Wildlife Management Area west of Hazlehurst.

This bittern breeds in marshes of the northern states to the Arctic Circle and locally in Florida, Texas, and the Atlantic coastal states north of Georgia. There are no known breeding records of the American Bittern in Mississippi. Its nest is a platform structure of dead marsh vegetation placed a few inches above water or on ground level in cattails, rushes, or marsh grasses. The nest is usually well concealed by surrounding growth. The four to six distinctively colored eggs vary from olive buff to buffy brown.

The young are fed by regurgitation, similar to other members of the heron family. Frogs, fish, small reptiles, rodents, crustaceans, and large insects are this bittern's principal food items.

It is a regular and fairly common spring migrant and an uncommon winter resident in Mississippi coastal marshes. Inland, it is a casual winter resident. In late February, migrants returning from the West Indies begin their northward passage, which peaks in late March and early April. Fall migrants appear in October, mainly on the Gulf Coast. There is one anomalous sight record on July 24, 1960, at Bayou Caddy in Hancock County by Sterling G. Clawson (Gandy and Turcotte 1970).

A common colloquial name for the American Bittern is "stargazer," because of its habit of freezing with its bill pointed skyward. On its northern breeding grounds, it is called "thunder-pumper," because of its weird, low call notes resembling a wooden water pump in operation. The call is verbally described by the late Roger T. Peterson as *oong-ka-choonk,* the middle syllable being louder at a distance and resembling a stake being driven into the ground by a wooden mallet, hence another common name, "stake-driver."

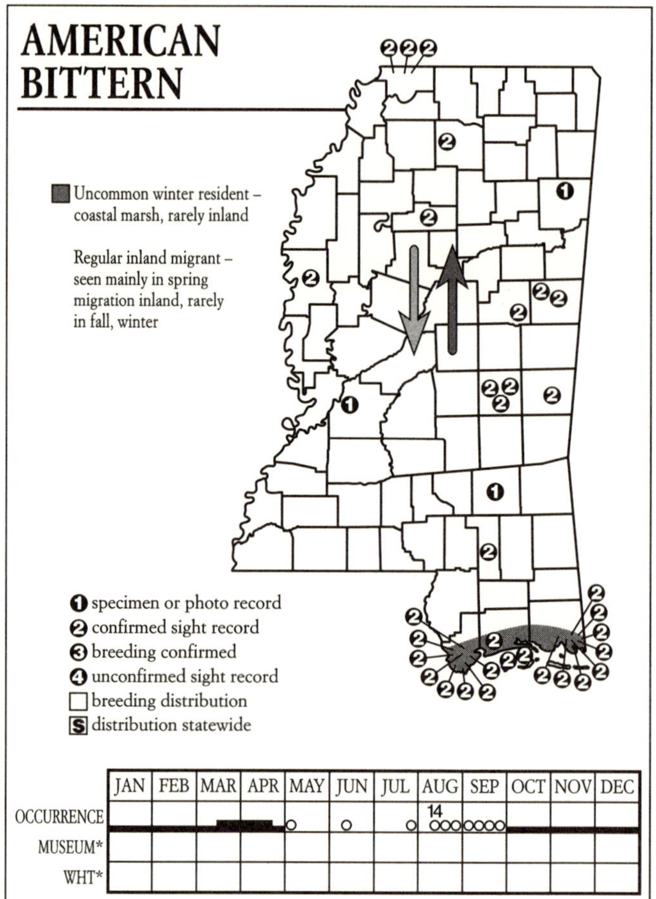

*Breeding confirmed by egg, sight, or photographic record.

Least Bittern *Ixobrychus exilis*

Bitterns differ from other herons in their habitat requirements and secretive behavior. They live and breed in marshes, where tall reeds and grasses afford protective cover and concealment for their flat, platform nests suspended among reeds, cattails, or stalks of other marsh plants. The ability to freeze upright and remain almost motionless with their bill pointed skyward is instinctive. They seem to know that with this posture, the vertical streaking and protective coloration blends perfectly with the upright marsh vegetation. When detected, they turn slowly to face an observer so as to keep the streaked underparts in view.

This trim little member of the heron family is easily identified by its small size, black crown and back, large patches

LEAST BITTERN

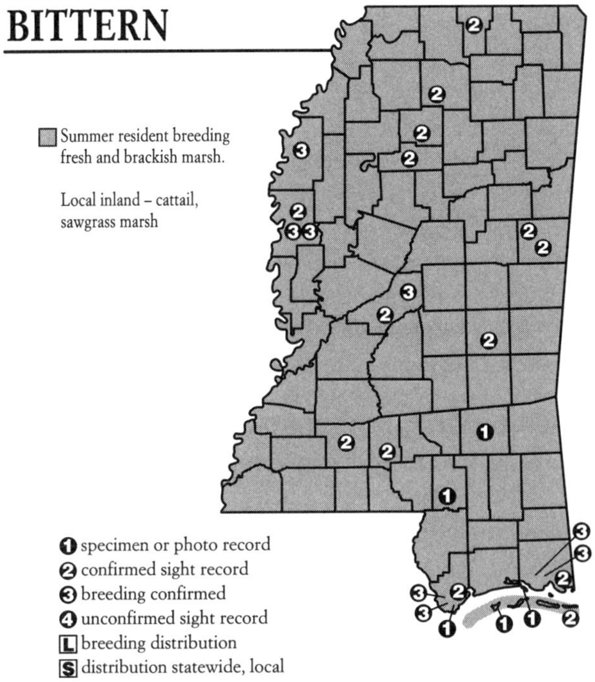

	JAN	FEB	MAR	APR	MAY	JUN	JUL	AUG	SEP	OCT	NOV	DEC
OCCURRENCE			13							23	12	31
MUSEUM*				29								
WHT*												

*Breeding confirmed by egg, sight, or photographic record.

of buff on the chestnut-colored wings, and chestnut on the sides of the head and neck. The underparts are largely white. This bittern should not be confused with the Green Heron, which has dark wings and underparts.

The Least Bittern is a summer resident in Mississippi. It is a common breeding bird on the coast, where it nests in salt, brackish, and freshwater marshes. Inland, it is rarely found because of the limited distribution of cattail and tall grass marshes in which it lives and nests.

Spring arrival begins around mid-March, but most migrants appear in April. Because of its furtive habits, this diminutive member of the heron family is seldom seen inland during migration. It moves under cover of darkness, remaining in dense marsh cover during the day, where it is adept at alighting and climbing among dense marsh vegetation.

These shy birds are hard to find without bogging through mud and marsh vegetation. They flush close at hand and allow only a brief glimpse of weak and wobbly flight before dropping down out of sight. A casual observer is even less likely to recognize the three or four soft, low, cuckoolike calls repeated at infrequent intervals from the marsh depths.

I have found nests of the Least Bittern in marsh plants near the mouth of the Pearl River in Hancock County. The first I found on April 29, 1940, were in sawgrass and cattails bordering open water in Mann Lake, a shallow cypress-bordered willow and button bush swamp west of Lake Washington in Washington County. The two nests were small platforms of sawgrass and cattail woven to the supporting vegetation, about two feet over water and barely large enough to hold four bluish white eggs. Nearby were three floating nests with eggs of the Pied-billed Grebe. (It was here in the marsh at the deepest part of the open water that I stepped off into an alligator den hole and went down in water over my head.) Five sets of three to five eggs in the MMNS were taken between April 29 and May 29, 1940.

M. G. Vaiden (1943) found 14 Least Bittern nests in 1938 in small willows over water in Bolivar County. A successful nesting in Lafayette County was noted on July 23, 1985, where five immatures were seen by W. M. Davis and other observers.

There is one December 31 winter record and very few fall records for the Least Bittern in Mississippi. These bitterns depart in late September and October. One sighting of the dark-phase bird (formerly known as Cory's Least Bittern) came on June 23, 1962, at Pascagoula in Jackson County by Lovett E. Williams Jr., Sterling G. Clawson, and H. D. Haberyan.

Great Blue Heron *Ardea herodias*

This species has a statewide distribution and is a permanent resident, breeding locally in small colonies high on the outer limbs of tall trees in remote bottomlands. It is the largest of the North American herons, standing about four feet tall with neck outstretched and having a six-foot wingspan. It is easily recognized by the blue-gray on its wings and over most of the body. It has a white head and neck, and a large, yellow bill.

While feeding in shallow water, it often stands motionless, either with neck erect or hunched down between the shoulders. In flight, the folded neck and arched wings with slow wingbeats mark it as a heron and distinguish it from the Sandhill Crane. The call of the Great Blue Heron is a low, harsh series of croaks described as *frahnk, frahnk, frahnk.*

Usually, four bluish green eggs are laid by Great Blue Herons with incubation lasting 28 days. When first hatched, the young are feeble and covered with long, whitish and grayish plumes. The feathers develop rapidly, but the down persists on the crown and rump area until the young are nearly grown. The bird's principal food is fish, but frogs, tadpoles, salamanders, lizards, small snakes, crayfish, mice, insects, and small birds are eaten.

The Great Blue Heron is solitary in its habits except during the breeding period. It frequently feeds at farm ponds

Great Blue Heron

as well as larger bodies of water. It is not uncommon to see this heron during the winter months when northern populations augment our resident population. Especially large numbers gather on the large reservoirs of northern and central Mississippi during fall and winter draw-downs.

When nesting, Great Blues and their young are very noisy birds. The young keep up a continuous chant while adults are around or approaching with food. The adults make various croaking sounds, some even resembling the hooting of an owl. These calls are apparently associated with the activity of feeding nestlings. I spent several hours at a small colony on the Pearl River waterfowl refuge in Madison County with David Watts and recorded the various sounds of birds nesting in cypress trees. A few pairs of Anhingas and some Yellow-crowned Night-Herons were nesting in nearby willows and tupelo gum trees.

Ben B. Coffey Jr. (1952) described a breeding colony of Great Blue Herons nesting in a tall cypress tree with Double-crested Cormorants at Beaverdam Lake in Tunica County on May 18, 1952 (see account of Double-crested Cormorant). Homer L. Tackett and I found a colony of a dozen or more active nests with eggs at Mann Lake in Washington County near Lake Jackson on April 29, 1940 (Gandy and Turcotte 1970). I succeeded in talking Homer into climbing the tall cypress tree and moving onto the outer limbs to collect two sets of four eggs for the Natural Science Museum collection. The eggs were fresh, and the large, platform nests were made entirely of long sticks and placed well out on horizontal limbs. This heronry was over shallow water where a colony of Anhingas, Common Egrets, Green Herons, and Little Blue Herons were beginning to nest in nearby willows, button bushes, and water elms.

An isolated, small colony of Great Blue Herons nested in the top of a tall pine in early April at the edge of a swamp on the east fork of the Amite River in Amite County. I observed this colony with H. Champ Clark while hunting turkeys on Longleaf Farm, a privately owned timber, cattle, and hunting preserve. The seven nests contained eggs as evidenced by several freshly broken shells found under the tree. These nests were not associated with other heron species and were not located over water.

On February 9, 1991, I went with David L. Watts to perhaps the largest Great Blue Heron rookery I have seen. Watts first observed the birds on February 2 carrying nesting materials to their nests. Located on an old slough within the Pearl River Waterfowl Area in Madison County adjacent to Ross Barnett Reservoir and the Pearl River, the rookery contained what turned out to be about 125 nesting Great Blues. At about midmorning on February 16, after overnight temperatures approached 19°F, Watts saw at least four pairs of birds copulating on their nests. Among those birds observed, the shortest duration for copulation was 13 seconds and the longest was 16 seconds.

Watts continued to monitor nesting and mating activities through mid-March. He observed initially that the Great Blues were quick to spook, leave their nest, and fly around the rookery for a brief time before returning and perching. According to his field notes, "We stood there as quietly and as still as possible in several spots watching them. And I came away impressed with their vigilance and

GREAT BLUE HERON

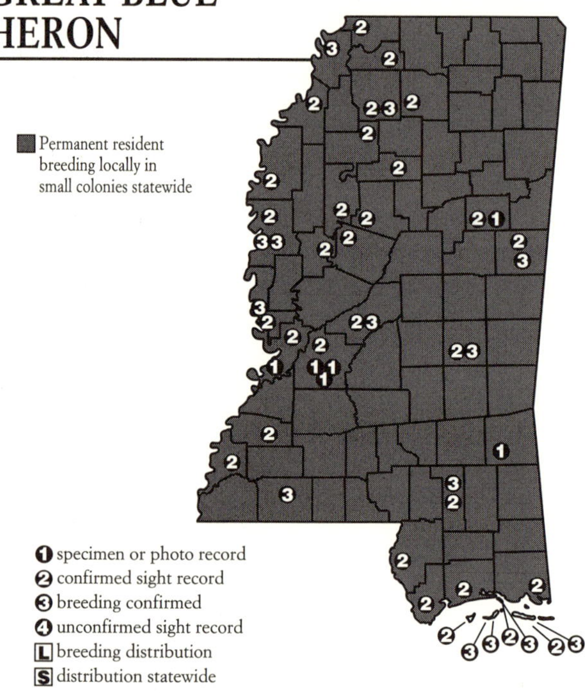

	JAN	FEB	MAR	APR	MAY	JUN	JUL	AUG	SEP	OCT	NOV	DEC
OCCURRENCE	█	█	█	█	█	█	█	█	█	█	█	█
MUSEUM*			•	••	•	•	••					
WHT*												

*Breeding confirmed by egg, sight, or photographic record.

their keen eyesight. We would simply shift from one foot to another . . . and the birds would spook and get up from their perches, fly and circle several times overhead, then settle down on another perch nearby." As nesting progressed, the birds became somewhat more tolerant of intrusions and were less apt to leave their nests when disturbed. Those that did spook returned to their nest duties much quicker than they had several weeks before.

Watts reported on March 16 that the entire Great Blue Heron rookery had been vacated. Not one nesting heron remained. Subsequent visits to the rookery revealed that the birds never returned that nesting season. It is believed that smoke and burning operations on nearby levees and fields in a newly impounded waterfowl area had caused the birds to abandon nesting activities. These management activities were conducted to knock back plant succession to stimulate the annual growth of seed-bearing waterfowl plants.

Great Egret *Casmerodius albus*

This large, slender heron is snowy white with a yellow bill and black feet and legs. In the breeding season, the Great Egret has long, straight plumes on the back trailing beyond the end of the tail. The long neck and legs give it a slender look, and although it has a much lighter build, is almost equal in stature to the Great Blue Heron.

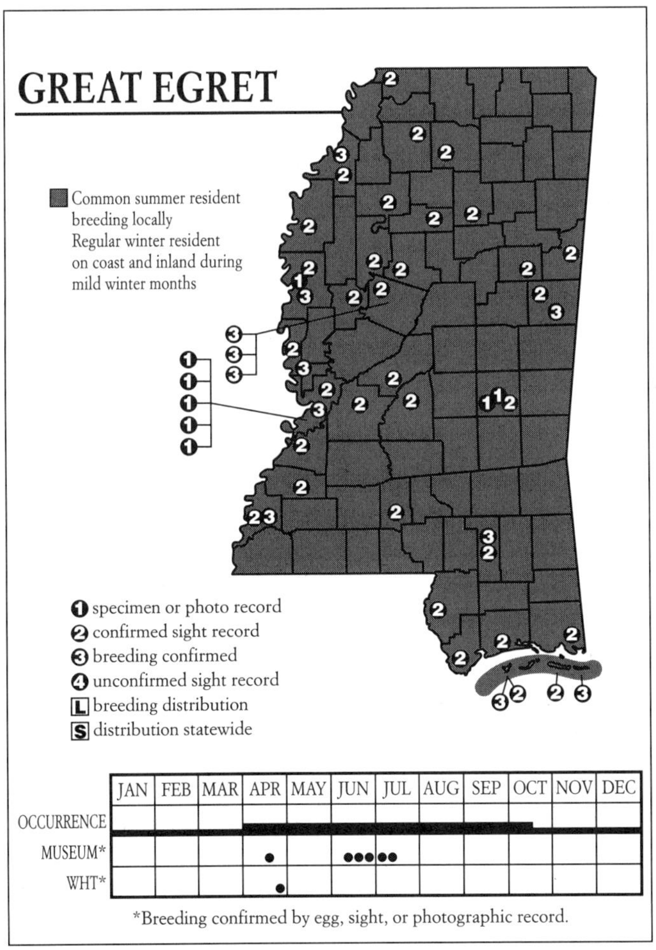

*Breeding confirmed by egg, sight, or photographic record.

The combination of black legs and feet and large, yellow bill separate it from the four other white herons. The Cattle Egret has a yellow bill and the immatures have dark feet and legs, but their stocky appearance and thicker, shorter necks readily identify them. The Snowy Egret has *yellow toes*. The immature and mostly white Little Blue Heron has greenish yellow legs and feet. The all white "great white heron" color phase of the Great Blue Heron has yellow legs and occurs mostly in southern Florida. It is unlikely to occur in Mississippi, although one sight record at Bay St. Louis occurred on July 4, 1945 (Greene 1946).

The Great Egret, formerly called the Common or American Egret, is a common, summer-resident, breeding bird. It breeds locally in colonies with Cattle Egrets, Little Blues, and other herons, but only rarely are more than several breeding pairs found in a heronry. Breeding colonies of Great Egrets were fairly common in cypress–button bush swamps of the Yazoo Delta until the late 1940s, but none have been recorded in recent years.

A large, stick-platform nest is made in bushes or on a horizontal tree limb, and usually four bluish green eggs are laid. Nesting occurs from late April through June. Post-breeding season wanderers are moderately common statewide in late summer and early fall. On the Gulf Coast, this egret occurs regularly as a resident during mild winters and irregularly in winter on inland waters.

Snowy Egret *Egretta thula*

This lovely, snow white heron has a shaggy crest and lacy, recurved plumes on its back and neck, which are displayed in courtship. The Snowy Egret is readily identified by the snow white plumage; thin, black bill with a patch of bare, yellow skin at the base; and black legs with *yellow toes*. It is slim and very active and about half the size of the Great Egret. It is almost the same size as the immature Little Blue Heron, which is white, except for dark-tipped primaries, with greenish yellow legs. The stockier Cattle Egret is similar in size, but has a yellow or pinkish orange bill.

The Snowy Egret was once a fairly common, summer-resident, breeding bird nesting in colonies with Great Egrets and Little Blue Herons in the Yazoo Delta. Except in migration and during postnuptial wanderings, the Snowy Egret is now an uncommon species on inland water areas. On the Mississippi Gulf Coast, it appears regularly as a spring and summer resident and also occurs irregularly as a late fall and winter resident during mild winters. It is absent or rare in the interior of the state from November through March.

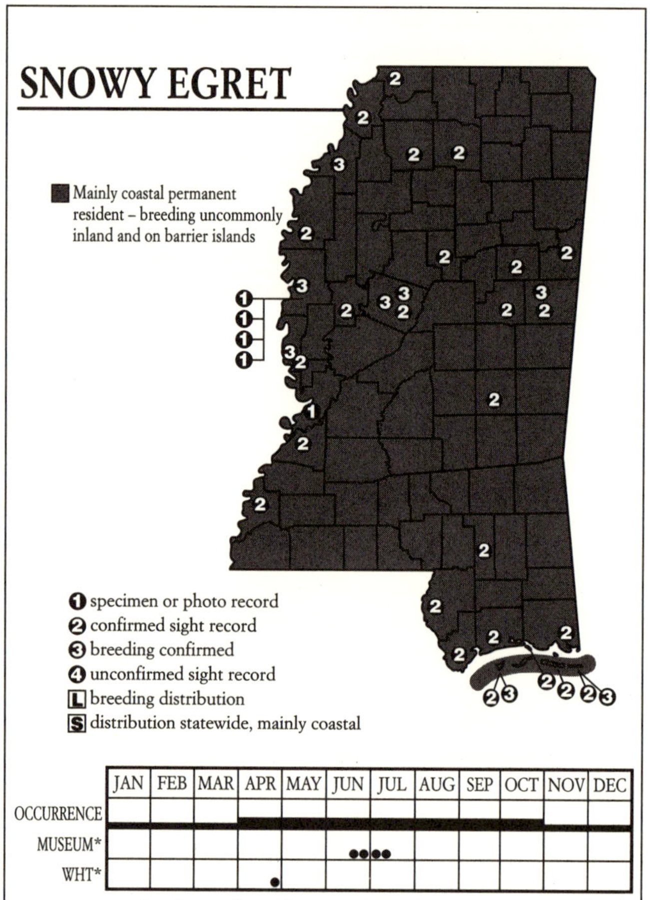

*Breeding confirmed by egg, sight, or photographic record.

Snowy Egrets with flightless young were found nesting with Tricolored Herons on the western end of Petit Bois Island by Henry D. Haberyan on June 30, 1962, and May 27, 1963 (Gandy and Turcotte 1970). On those dates, young of both species were banded. I found numerous nests and eggs of this species on April 29, 1934, in a cypress–button bush brake near Cruger in Holmes County, where Little Blue Herons, Great Egrets, and Anhingas were nesting. R. L. Caylor (1936) described heronries containing Snowy Egret nests and young at Mann Lake in Washington County where Ben B. Coffey Jr. (1941b) banded 102 nestlings. He noted that a few Snowy Egrets nested with Little Blues at Moon Lake in Coahoma County, on June 1, 1941.

Little Blue Heron *Egretta caerulea*

The adults of this medium-sized heron are dark, slaty blue with a dark maroon head and neck, and dark bluish green legs. The bill is bluish with a black tip. Immatures are white with dull, greenish legs and a bluish bill with a dark tip. Immatures are white with dusky wing tips and dark bill and feet. When they are changing to adult plumage, they are a mixture of white and slaty blue called "calico." Most birds have changed to full adult plumage in their first winter, but a few of the calico birds are seen during spring.

The Little Blue Heron is a common, statewide summer resident. Although a few occasionally overwinter on inland areas and regularly on the coast, the majority leave by late October to winter across the Gulf of Mexico. The return migration begins around mid-March with the herons going immediately to their nesting grounds.

Little Blues prefer to nest in cypress-tupelo swamps. Button bush, water elm, black willow, and water privet are usually selected for building their stick-platform nests. Sometimes as many as a dozen or more nests will be placed in a single tree or bush. Little Blues nest in heronries with Cattle Egrets, but the Cattle Egret nests later than Little Blues. This exotic egret competes for living space and nest material and greatly outnumbers Little Blue Herons.

In late June and July adults and the white immatures disperse from heronries, and postbreeding wanderers may appear at inland lakes or ponds. On the Gulf Coast, the population of Little Blue Herons increases at this time.

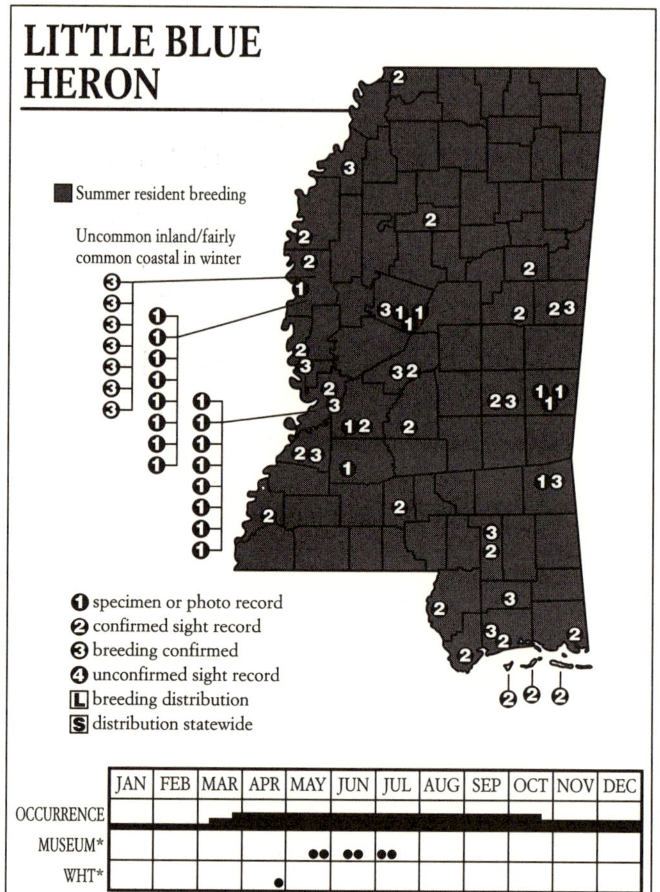

*Breeding confirmed by egg, sight, or photographic record.

Tricolored Heron *Egretta tricolor*

Formerly called Louisiana Heron, this species is a breeding bird of marshes on the offshore islands of Mississippi Sound. Thomas D. Burleigh (1945) recorded that Arthur M. Howell found a colony of about 100 pairs nesting on Petit Bois Island in 1913. A small colony of Tricolored Herons with flightless young was found nesting on the western part of Petit Bois Island by Henry D. Haberyan on June 30, 1962, and May 27, 1963 (Gandy and Turcotte 1970). Joe Jacobs (pers. comm.) reported another small nesting colony on a marshy portion of Cat Island. This species nests commonly in mangrove thickets on North Island and other localities in Louisiana coastal waters (Gandy and Turcotte 1970).

The Tricolored Heron is strictly a coastal resident during the breeding season. In summer after the breeding season, many wander northward and appear as irregular visitors on waters in the interior parts of Mississippi until late October. On the Mississippi Gulf Coast, this heron is a winter resident of open, shallow marshes and shorelines in varying abundance from year to year.

Dark upperparts, white rump, and sharply defined white belly of this slender-necked heron are distinctive field marks. Immature birds show much reddish brown on the wings, head, and neck.

Reddish Egret *Egretta rufescens*

This egret is a regular but uncommon visitor to the shallow water beaches along the Gulf Coast from May to December, especially on the barrier islands of Mississippi Sound, where it occurs in small numbers but is not known to nest.

On June 7, 1958, while visiting the Brown Pelican colony on North Island with a party of MOS observers, H. A. J. Evans and I identified a small breeding colony. We saw two adults feeding two young in a nest in tall, black mangrove bushes a short distance from the pelican nesting site. This was the first Louisiana breeding record for the Reddish Egret (Lowery 1974). Since that date, further breeding has been confirmed by photographs, and a small breeding population has occurred regularly in that area of Louisiana.

The adult Reddish Egret is larger and lighter, grayer than the Little Blue Heron that it resembles. The Little Blue has a dark maroon head and neck, while the Reddish

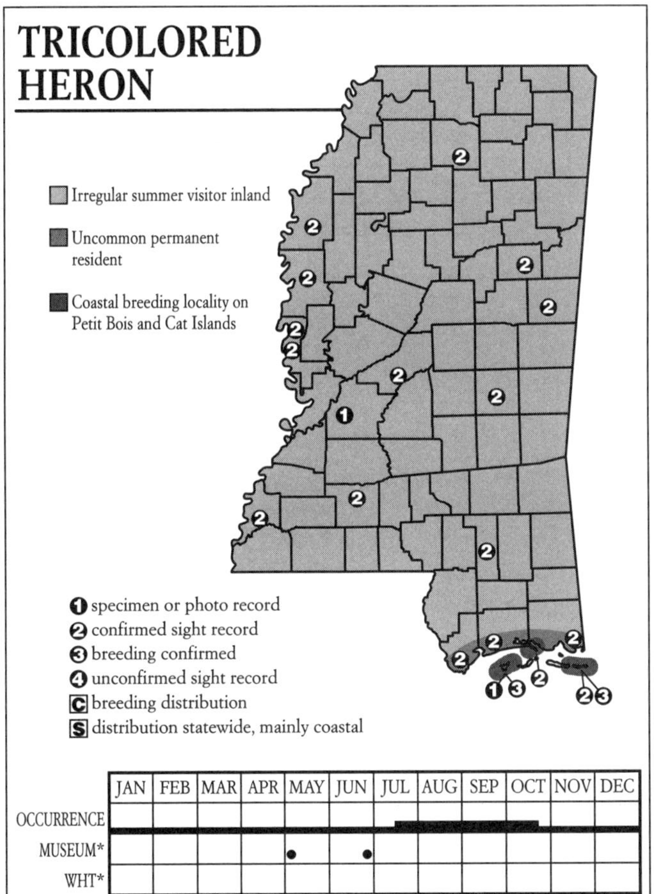

*Breeding confirmed by egg, sight, or photographic record.

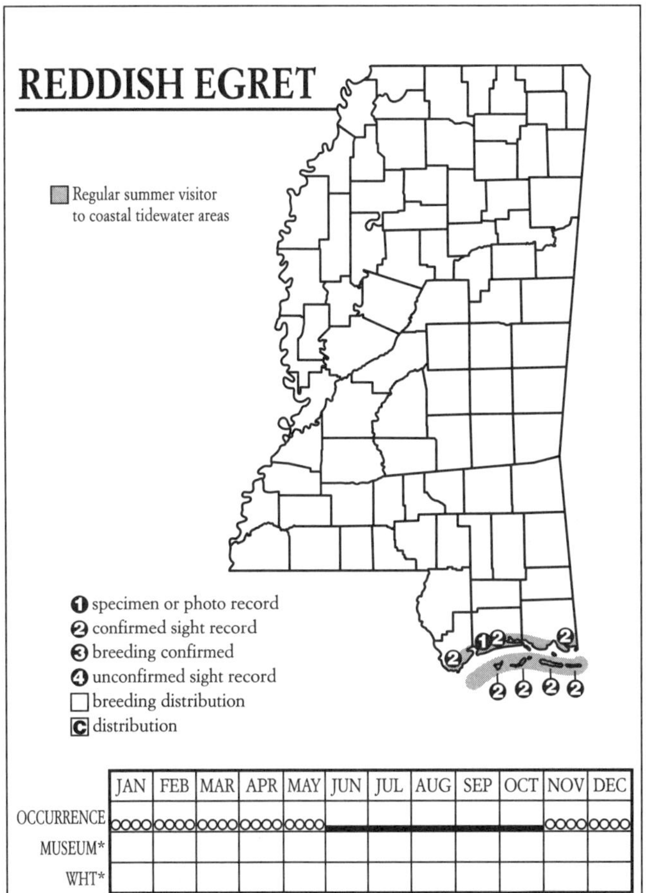

*Breeding confirmed by egg, sight, or photographic record.

Egret's is reddish tan. The best field mark for distinguishing between the two species is the bill color of the adults: *flesh colored* to the base in the Reddish Egret, *bluish* to the base in the Little Blue Heron. Both species have black-tipped bills.

The head and neck of the Reddish Egret appear shaggy, and it frequents shallow, tidewater shores, and salt marshes. The Reddish Egret can be recognized at a distance by its feeding habits. It is very active, running, hopping, and arching the wings in a manner peculiar to this egret known as "canopy" feeding.

Immature birds have black bills and dark, greenish black legs. A rare, white phase is identified by the black-tipped, flesh-colored bill that separates it from the Great Egret, which has a yellow bill. Four North Island sightings of white-phase birds (Valentine, pers. comm.) and one Louisiana collection by Allan Ensminger have been recorded. The dark feet and legs readily separate it from the Snowy Egret, with its yellow feet.

There are no known inland records for the Reddish Egret. Records on the Mississippi Coast and offshore islands extend from May 11 to December 14. The first state records of this egret were specimens taken by Thomas D. Burleigh (1945) at Deer Island on August 6, 1938, at Gulfport on September 29, 1939, and on July 10, 1940.

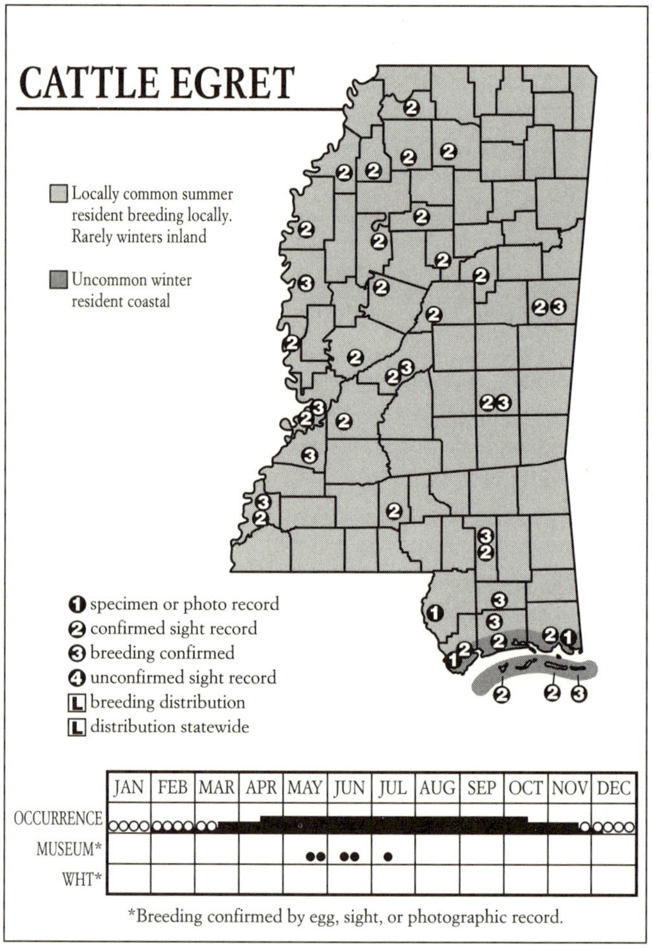

Cattle Egret *Bubulcus ibis*

This interloper has invaded our state and is increasing its numbers annually. Now, in summer it is a common sight flying to and from its heronries and in its association with cattle grazing in pastures.

Cattle Egrets and a few Anhingas and Little Blue Herons comprised this large breeding colony at an old oxbow lake of Leaf River in Forrest County on May 12, 1988.

The Cattle Egret first spread naturally to South America from Africa and then up the West Indies to Florida, where it started nesting. It spread rapidly, appearing in Texas and Louisiana in 1955. By 1958 it was breeding in Texas and Louisiana. Since then its rapid increase and dispersal along the coastal states and inland areas has been spectacular.

The Cattle Egret appeared in southern Florida in 1942. I saw them in pastures with cattle at Clewiston, Florida, near the lower end of Okeechobee Lake in July 1954. The first record of their appearance in Mississippi was reported by Amy Tolman (1959) near Kiln in Hancock County on April 3, 1959. Lovett E. Williams Jr. observed two Cattle Egrets in a pasture east of Pascagoula in Jackson County on May 29, 1960, and collected one, an adult female, for the first state specimen (Gandy and Turcotte 1970). In 1961 and 1962, it occurred in the three counties bordering the Gulf Coast and also in Pearl River County.

This species was first recorded nesting in May 1967, on Yazoo National Wildlife Refuge in Washington County by Earl Cunningham (Turcotte 1968a). By late summer of that year, he reported an estimated 4000 Cattle Egrets and young in the colony. In May 1968, Burton S. Webster (Jackson 1981b) reported numerous Cattle Egrets nesting with Little Blue Herons near Brooksville in Noxubee County. In photographing a Cattle Egret at a nest containing eggs, he established the first photographic nest record for this species.

In the past decade, numerous heronries have been reported from many parts of Mississippi. One of the largest sighted is on the Pearl River Waterfowl Refuge on Ross Barnett Reservoir above Jackson. In June 1993, David L. Watts with the Department of Wildlife, Fisheries and Parks conservatively estimated 5000 breeding pairs in the heronry, where he was banding nestling birds. The species is a locally common, breeding summer resident, and in spring and fall migration it appears regularly throughout Mississippi.

This small, white heron is similar in appearance and size to the immature Little Blue Heron, but the Cattle Egret is stockier and its posture more erect. It has a puffy throat and jowls and is thicker necked than the Snowy Egret and immature Little Blue Heron. Immatures and winter adults are mostly white. In the breeding season, adults have buffy patches of feathers on the crown, lower neck, and back. The bill is yellow, but for a short period in the adults, it turns reddish yellow in spring, then pinkish orange at nesting time. Immatures have blackish legs. The bills of chicks are black with yellow tips. The bills turn yellow as the young mature.

The symbiotic relationship between this heron and grazing animals affords a ready means of identification. It is generally seen in pastures with livestock, where the bird feeds on insects stirred up by grazing animals. Flies and other insects are also taken from their bodies. Cattle Egrets often can be seen alighting on the backs of cattle or catching horseflies at their shanks. The egrets now seem to exert a calming influence on livestock. Other herons also frequent pastures, but the behavior of the Cattle Egret feeding around the feet and head of grazing cattle is a good first clue to its identity.

In Mississippi, this species has nested in heronries with Little Blue Herons, Yellow-crowned Night-Herons, Great Egrets, Anhingas, and White Ibises. In most of the known heronries, Cattle Egrets far outnumber other herons. The nesting sites can be located by watching the direction of flight in late evening as feeding birds return to roost. Nests of Cattle Egrets are stick platforms placed in bushes or trees in a swamp, or sometimes in an upland thicket. The four or five bluish eggs are laid in May or June.

The spring migration of this species begins in late March and continues through April. Fall migration occurs in October, but late stragglers may be seen through November or December. A few of these birds regularly winter in the Gulf Coast region, but most of the population leaves for warmer regions farther south. There are a few northern Mississippi winter records from December to February.

Green Heron *Butorides virescens*

The Green Heron has a dark crown with a shaggy crest. The chestnut neck has a white stripe down the front. The back, wings, and underparts are dark greenish blue and gray. It is about the same size as a crow and appears dark at a distance. Immatures have lighter underparts and streaked necks.

The flight somewhat resembles that of a crow, but the deep beat of the arched wings readily identifies it as a heron. It is found frequently on ponds and small streams, as well as on large bodies of fresh and salt water. The legs of this small heron are shorter than those of larger herons. They are orange during the breeding season and greenish yellow at other times. When alarmed, the bird erects its crest, stretches its neck to full length, bobs its tail, and usually takes flight with a loud *skee-ow.* Local names for the Green Heron are "shite-poke," "fly-up-the-creek," and "Indian hen."

It is mostly a solitary bird, more often nesting in single pairs, although several pairs may nest near each other. The nest is a slight platform of twigs placed on a limb high in a bush, sapling, or tree. The nest usually is concealed from below by leafy vegetation and often located in a thicket near water.

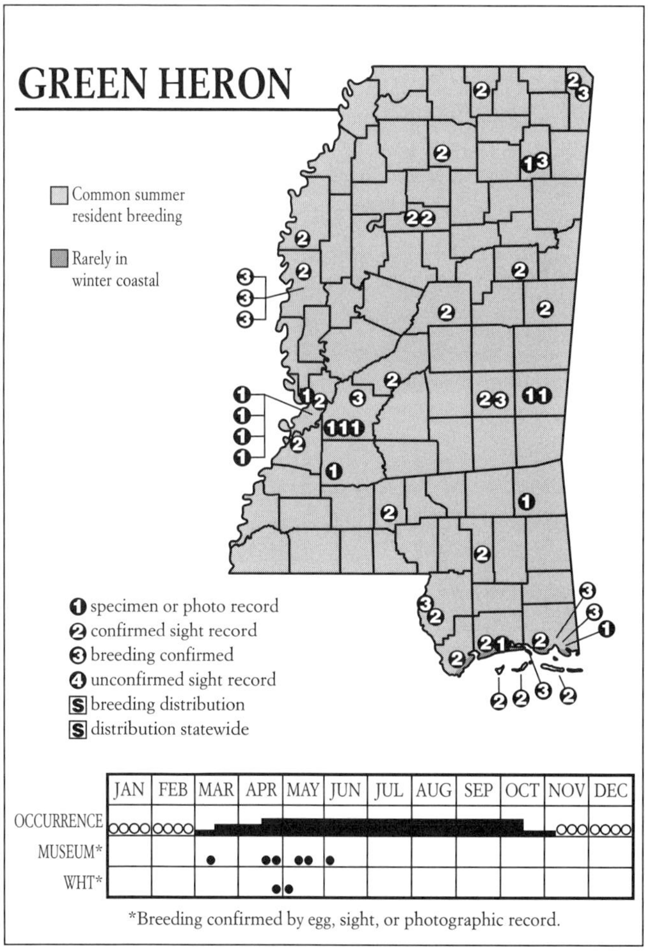

*Breeding confirmed by egg, sight, or photographic record.

Four or five bluish green eggs are laid usually from late April through May. Egg record dates extend from April 22 to June 3.

The Green Heron is widely distributed throughout Mississippi as a common breeding bird. Spring arrival begins in late March, and by early April this species can be found throughout the state. By mid-November, most Green Herons have migrated across the Gulf of Mexico. A few winter inland and along the Gulf Coast.

Black-crowned Night-Heron
Nycticorax nycticorax

The night-herons are stockier with shorter, thicker bills and shorter legs than most herons. The thick-necked, big-headed, and hunch-backed posture readily separates them from other herons. At close range, the large eyes are noticeable. They spend the day at roost and, except during the breeding season, are seen or heard as they fly overhead at dusk or night enroute to their feeding grounds. When young are being fed at the nest, night-herons are more active during the day.

The Black-crowned Night-Heron is a fairly common spring and fall migrant and rare summer resident in the coastal counties. It is a rare transient elsewhere in Mississippi. It winters rarely in the vicinity of the coastal marshes.

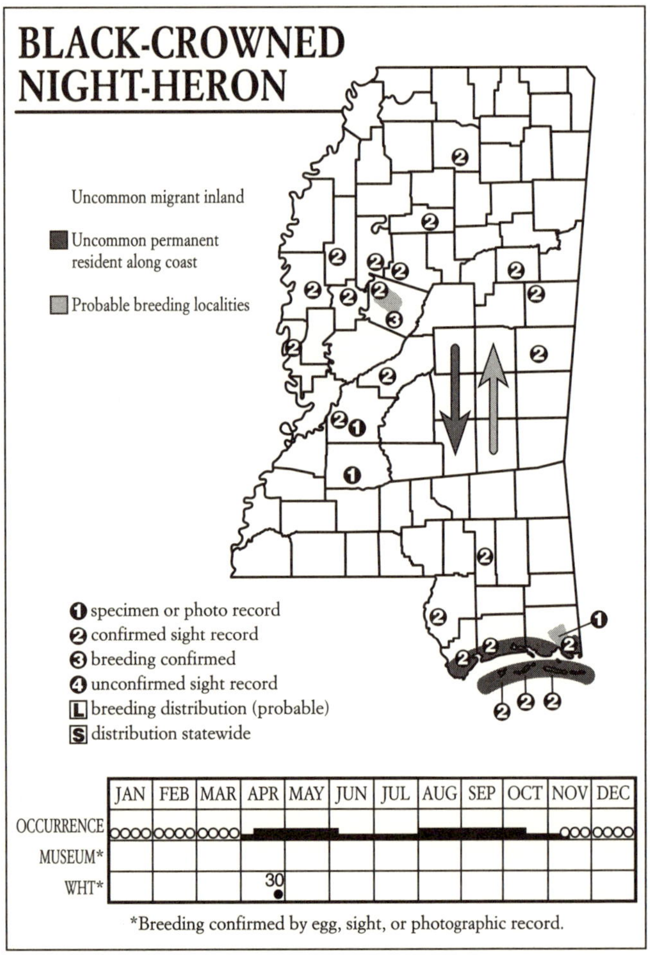

Charles R. Stockard (1905) recorded this species nesting in flooded bottomland on the spreading limbs of a water oak tree in Lowndes County. Several pairs nested in the tree each year. Egg record dates extended from March 21 to May 11 in 1895 and 1897. On April 30, 1934, I observed several pairs near nests with eggs in a colony with Yellow-crowned Night-Herons at Horseshoe Brake near Good Hope in Holmes County. M. G. Vaiden (1953a) recorded a colony of about 15 birds on May 23, 1953, in Bolivar County.

Further study is needed to determine the breeding status of this species on the Gulf Coast and in Mississippi's interior. The inland breeding range in the United States is mostly farther north than Mississippi. Apparently, it is replaced in Mississippi as a breeding bird by the more common Yellow-crowned Night-Heron.

The adult Black-Crowned Night-Heron has white underparts, a black back, black on top of the head, and gray wings. In nuptial plumage, several long, white plumes extend from the black crown. Its legs are pinkish and shorter than the Yellow-crowned Night-Herons. The short, thick bill is black, and the eyes are red. Immatures are brownish, heavily streaked below, and coarsely spotted with white on the wings and back. Immature Black-crowned Night-Herons differ from young Yellow-crowned Night-Herons by having larger, coarser spotting, more brownish coloration (rather than slaty brown), and shorter legs that reveal in flight *only the toes* extending beyond the end of the tail.

The call of the Black-crowned Night-Heron is a single, loud *quawk,* lower in pitch than the Yellow-crowned. The calls of both species are most frequently heard at night while the birds are in flight.

Yellow-crowned Night-Heron
Nycticorax violaceus

The adult is clear gray on the body with shades of light and dark gray on the wings and back, giving the bird's back a streaked appearance. The head and throat are black except for the yellowish white crown and prominent white cheeks bordered by black. A stocky gray body and black and white face are distinctive field marks. Immatures are *slaty brown,* and the wings and back are more finely speckled with white than the immature Black-crowned Night-Heron. In flight, *the feet and part of the legs* extend beyond the end of the tail.

The Yellow-crowned Night-Heron is a locally common summer resident breeding in small colonies of its own or with other herons. Breeding sites are usually in cypress-tupelo swamps, although oaks and other bottomland hardwoods are sometimes used.

Nests are substantial stick platforms placed on tree limbs at a greater height than most herons with the exception of

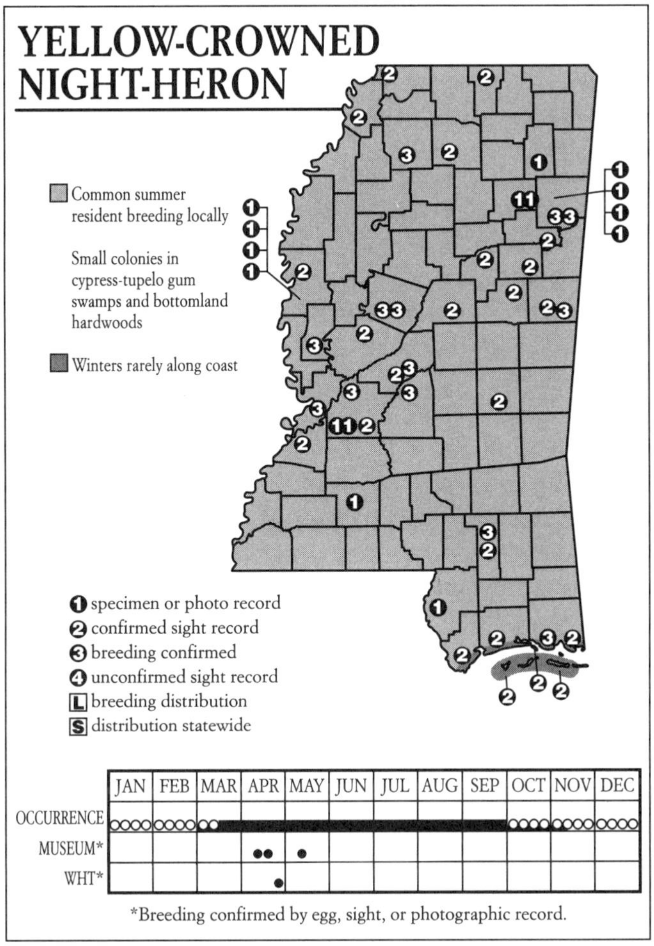

the Great Blue. At most of the breeding colonies I have visited, the nests were on the lower or middle limbs of cypress or tupelo trees, and the birds were nesting with other herons. One colony of about eight pairs nested on Noxubee National Wildlife Refuge near Starkville in large overcup oak trees bordering a cypress–tupelo gum brake. These nests contained young on May 13, 1967 (Turcotte 1967a). Egg record dates extend from April 12 to 29. The four or five blue green eggs are unmarked. A nest near Sardis Dam fledged three young by July 14, 1990 (Schiefer 1991).

The Yellow-crowned Night-Heron is the night-heron usually observed in Mississippi. It arrives around mid-March, and its departure is almost complete by late September. On the Gulf Coast, the fall departure is mostly complete by late October. Winter residents are rare on the Gulf Coast and casual in the interior parts of the state.

This heron prefers bottomlands subject to overflow, shallow cypress and tupelo swamp lakes, and lower-lying hardwood swamps. Yellow-crowned Night-Herons are commonly seen around the edge of backwater during spring floods and on wet, crayfish-laden bottomlands often used for marginal crops or pasture. Crayfish, crabs, frogs, tadpoles, small reptiles, snails, and small fish are main foods, with crayfish preferred.

Threskiornithidae (Ibises and Spoonbills)

White Ibis *Eudocimus albus*

The White Ibis is a graceful, all white bird except for its black wing tips, which show in flight. The face and legs are bright coral red, and the long, decurved bill is pinkish. Flights numbering a hundred or more birds are not uncommon during their westerly spring migration along the Gulf Coast or from their nesting colonies as they go to or from feeding grounds. They travel in long, wavy lines, alternately flying and sailing over treetops, water, or marsh.

These medium-sized waders are common migrants along the Mississippi Coast in late March and April as they wing their way westward to breeding grounds in Louisiana. They prefer to nest near coastal marshes or in wooded inland swamps. In southern Louisiana, the White Ibis is a permanent resident of the coastal marshes. In Mississippi, it is mostly a summer visitor to our inland swamps and lakes. Immature birds in dark plumage are more commonly seen as post-breeding season wanderers, and they remain until early fall.

In recent years, only one colony has been found where White Ibises were nesting. Prior to 1975, St. Clair Thompson and others reported seeing flocks of adults as they crossed Big Black River swamp on Mississippi 27 and east of Vicksburg from May through July. In May 1975 Thompson located a large heronry in Big Black River swamp in Warren County, a few miles north of the highway. The heronry contained several thousand nesting Cattle Egrets, a few Little Blue Herons, and Anhingas. The heronry was located at one end of a shallow, cypress-bordered oxbow lake.

On May 25, 1975, we paddled among the button bush, water privet, and water elms to where the egrets, herons, and Anhingas nested. We saw several pairs of White Ibises, and a flock of about 20 more flew into a more distant area. Three White Ibis nests were in small cypress trees border-

These White Ibis nestlings were found in a breeding colony of about 200 birds nesting with Cattle Egrets, Little Blue Herons, and Anhingas at Carter Lake in southern Warren County on July 6, 1975.

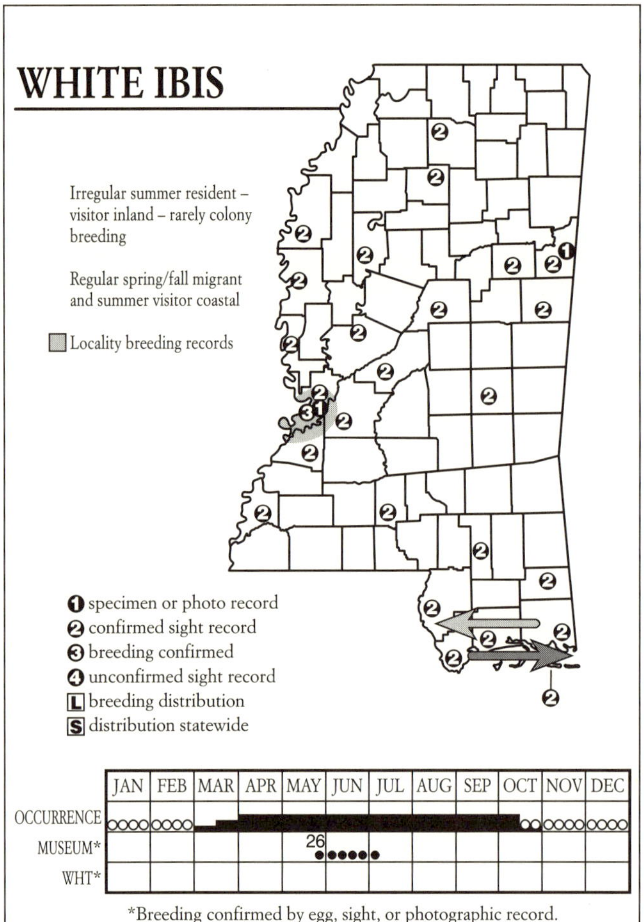

*Breeding confirmed by egg, sight, or photographic record.

ing the lake shoreline, which was flooded by backwaters from Big Black River. They contained one, two, and three eggs, respectively. The nests were platforms of sticks and leaves lined with green leaves. The eggs were a light buff or olive buff ground color, beautifully blotched with light and dark shades of brown.

On July 6, 1975, Charles Crowther, St. Clair Thompson, and I returned and found about 200 White Ibises nesting in the colony with hatchlings and free climbers (Turcotte 1975b). The nests containing young were more substantial structures and some had Spanish moss for lining. All nests contained two to three eggs or young. Photographs were taken of eggs and young in different stages of development to confirm the breeding record. The late Hal Moore (1988) and the late Louis Cashman visited this rookery on June 21, July 5, and July 15, 1975, and photographed nests with eggs and young.

The heronry was at the same location and contained nesting White Ibises in the 1976 breeding season. The next year, the colony apparently moved to a cypress swamp a few miles upstream. It was not found until September 1977, when it contained a large roosting concentration of birds. During the 1978 breeding season, the colony contained at least 10,000 adults and young of Cattle Egrets, Little Blue Herons, and a few nests containing the young of Yellow-crowned Night-Herons and Anhingas. A few adult White Ibises were present, but nesting was not confirmed.

Occurrence records are from March 3 to January 3. By early fall most have departed, but a few remain in coastal marshes until extreme cold weather. Mississippi winter sightings were made on coastal Christmas Bird Counts. Two are from Jackson County on January 3, 1976, one on December 18, 1976 (21 sighted), and two seen in Hancock County on December 29, 1976.

The immature White Ibis is dark brown on its wings and back with a blackish tail, white rump and belly. The head and neck are dark brown and finely streaked with white. The long, decurved beak is blackish toward the tip and pinkish at the base and on the bare face. Downy young are first black and turn dark gray as they grow larger. The bill is blackish, marked with two orange-colored encircling stripes near the base and tip of each mandible.

The White Ibis feeds on crayfish, snails, aquatic and terrestrial insects, small reptiles and amphibians, small fish, and occasionally small mammals.

Glossy Ibis *Plegadis falcinellus*

The first occurrence of a *Plegadis* in Mississippi was reported by Ben B. Coffey Jr. (1936). He saw one at Lake View in Desoto County, on May 15 and 21, 1932. Thomas D. Burleigh (1945) saw four flying low overhead at Gulfport in Harrison County on September 28, 1940, and two more in a flock of White Ibises at the same location the following day. Ben B. Coffey Jr. and George Peyton Jr. reported another *Plegadis* at Lake View on April 13, 1957 (Newman 1957). Sterling G. Clawson collected the first known Mississippi specimen of the Glossy Ibis at Lakeshore on May 4, 1962 (Williams and Clawson 1963). The specimen was identified at the U.S. National Museum and is in the MMNS (Gandy 1962c).

Mrs. E. C. Bowers Jr. saw six *Plegadis* at a flooded pasture on the Pearl River Waterfowl Refuge in Madison County on March 30 and 31, 1965 (Turcotte 1965c). I observed and photographed four on April 1, 1965, at the same location. Burton S. Webster reported a "few Glossy Ibis in the cypress sloughs" on Noxubee National Wildlife Refuge on September 10, 1972. Tom J. Gary (Jackson 1976a) observed and photographed two *Plegadis* species at the captive goose enclosure on Malmaison Wildlife Management Area in Grenada County in February 1976. Judy and Jay Toups saw one Glossy Ibis at Waveland in Hancock County on August 30, 1976 (Jackson and Weber 1976).

These records indicate that the *Plegadis* are erratic, casual spring and early fall visitors to coastal and inland areas of our state. Because Mississippi is in the geographic range of both *Plegadis,* the occurrence of either the Glossy

GLOSSY IBIS

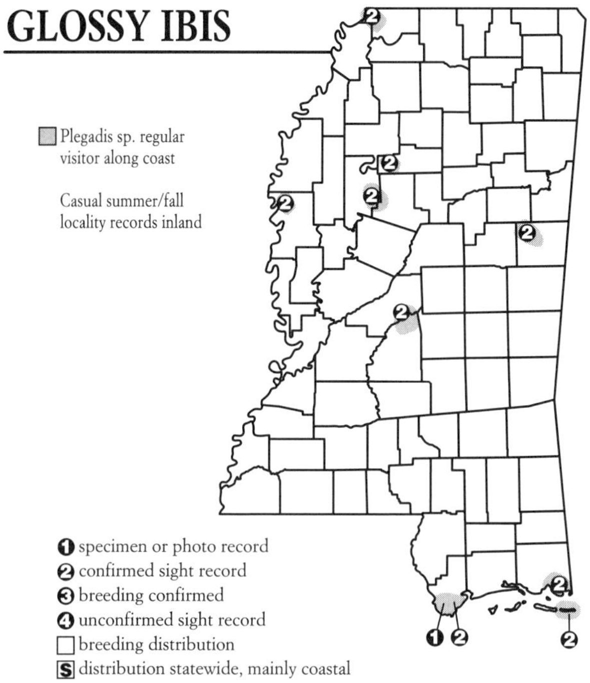

	JAN	FEB	MAR	APR	MAY	JUN	JUL	AUG	SEP	OCT	NOV	DEC
OCCURRENCE	oo		o o	oo	o	o	o	o	oo	ooo	ooo	o o
MUSEUM*												
WHT*												

*Breeding confirmed by egg, sight, or photographic record.

or White-faced Ibis is possible. Under most field conditions, the two species are indistinguishable except during the breeding season. The White-faced Ibis adult can be reliably identified in close view only by the *red eyes* and white line of feathers extending *behind* the eye.

The two *Plegadis* differ very slightly, and their breeding ranges overlap in southern Louisiana. During the breeding season, the adult Glossy Ibis has dark gray skin on the bare face and *brown* eyes. The breeding adult White-faced Ibis has bare, reddish brown skin on the face, red eyes, and a line of white feathers around the face behind the eye and extending under the chin.

To further confuse identification even during the breeding season, some Glossy Ibises have a narrow border of light blue or whitish skin bordering their facial feathers. Also, the White-faced Ibis is without the white face when not breeding. Both species are very similar in general appearance. At a distance they appear almost black. Close up they are mostly reddish chestnut brown with iridescent purple and green backs and wings.

The Glossy Ibis frequents wet pastures around bays, estuaries, marshes, and coastal islands. It breeds in Florida and north along the Atlantic Coast to New Jersey. Lowery Jr. (1974) lists them as scarce breeding birds in the Mississippi River Delta below New Orleans and on islands in Barataria Bay.

In southern Louisiana the White-faced Ibis is a permanent-resident breeding bird in the Delta below New Orleans and westward where it inhabits marshlands and rice fields. The White-faced is abundant in southwestern Louisiana. These dark ibises build similar nests of sticks, reeds, and rushes placed in low bushes or reeds in marshes over water. Both species lay three or four eggs, which are bluish green.

White-faced Ibis *Plegadis chihi*

A juvenile specimen, identified by Roxie L. Layborne of the U.S. Fish and Wildlife Service, was collected by Sterling G. Clawson on September 17, 1960, at Claiborne in Hancock County, two days after Hurricane Ethel. This record was reported by Williams Jr. and Clawson (1963), and the specimen is in the MMNS.

This ibis, an abundant permanent resident of the marshes and rice fields of southern Louisiana, rarely strays far from the eastward limit of its normal range near the mouth of the Mississippi River. Its breeding range includes California, south into Mexico, north to Oregon, Idaho, Nevada, and Utah. The win-

WHITE-FACED IBIS

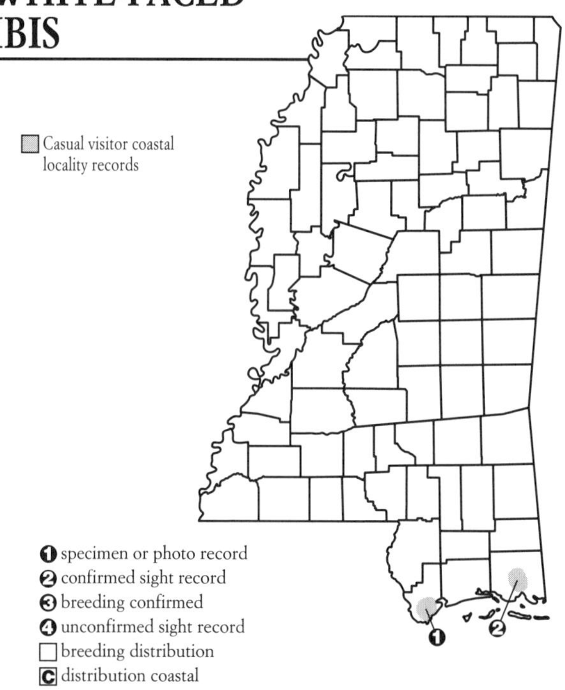

	JAN	FEB	MAR	APR	MAY	JUN	JUL	AUG	SEP	OCT	NOV	DEC
OCCURRENCE		ooo	o	Plegadis sp. all year on MS coast					17 o		13-18 oo	
MUSEUM*												
WHT*												

*Breeding confirmed by egg, sight, or photographic record.

ter range includes coastal Louisiana and Texas, the southwestern United States to California, and south to Argentina and Chile.

The relative abundance and distribution of the two *Plegadis* species in Mississippi remains uncertain, because the identification of nonbreeding and immature dark ibises is difficult. Distinctive field marks for this species are described under the Glossy Ibis.

Roseate Spoonbill *Ajaia ajaja*

A sighting of the Roseate Spoonbill in Mississippi is a rare and special occasion. Its occurrence as a casual summer and fall visitor has been documented by one identifiable photograph. Burton S. Webster photographed in color four Roseate Spoonbills with a flock of Wood Storks on Bluff Lake on Noxubee National Wildlife Refuge in August 1967 (Turcotte 1968b). They were first seen on June 20, 1967. One had acquired a pink plumage, and the others were whitish immatures.

Longstreet Minor (pers. comm.) described in detail seven Roseate Spoonbills seen in pink plumage on September 5, 1959, at Round Lake located between Claiborne County, Mississippi, and Tensas Parish, Louisiana. Minor and a friend saw the spoonbills while touring Togo Island Hunting Club. Later, John H. Phares and B. E. Gandy made a trip to confirm this bird's presence, but could not get to Round Lake.

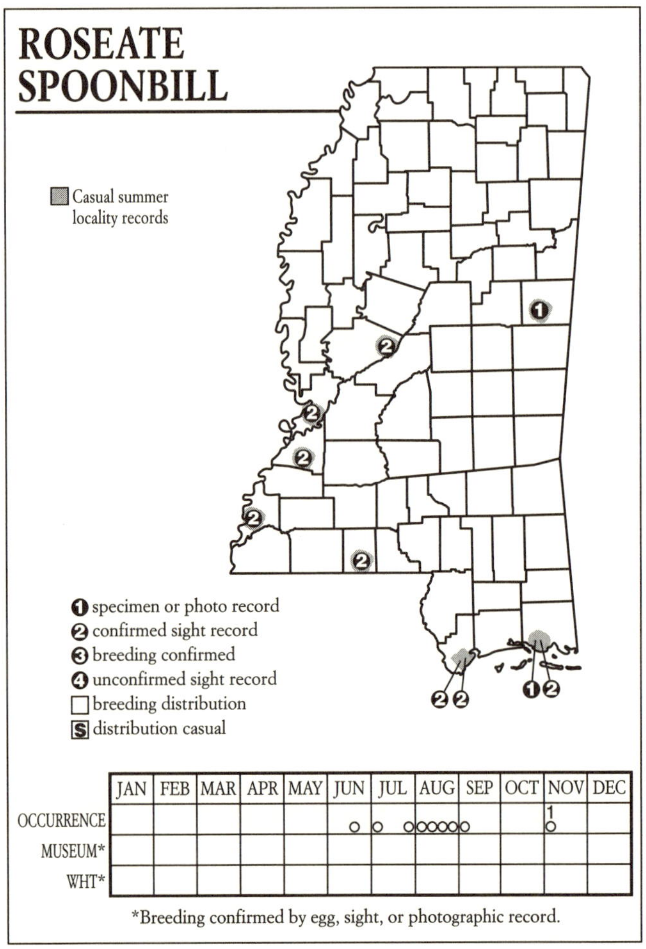

Douglas E. Hassel (pers. comm.) saw and photographed a single pink spoonbill on October 30, 1976, on Rhodes Bayou near Beardsley Lake at Moss Point in Jackson County. This bird was perched in a dead tree when photographed. It had been associating with numerous immature White Ibises feeding in adjacent marshes. Although the photo by Hassel did not show sufficient details, he believed it was a Roseate Spoonbill. Recent sightings indicate this species may be increasing in numbers.

The Roseate Spoonbill, a common breeding bird in southern Florida, is called "pink" or "pink curlew." Populations of the birds were decimated toward the end of the last century by plume hunters. They were killed at nesting and roosting sites, and by 1890 they had become almost extinct in Florida and on the southern Texas Coast. The species made a remarkable recovery after plume hunters ceased operations. They now breed locally in mangroves, cypresses, or low bushes in southern Florida, southern Texas, and southwestern Louisiana, where they are resident.

In Louisiana, breeding colonies are found on Rabbit Island in Sabine Lake and on Lacassine National Wildlife Refuge. Except on rare occasions, birds from this colony do not migrate outside of the two southwestern Louisiana parishes of Cameron and Vermilion. Most spoonbills do not leave Louisiana in winter, and many die during hard freezes (Valentine, pers. comm.). They nest with herons, Olivaceous Cormorants, and Anhingas. The two or three dull, greenish white eggs are blotched with brown and laid in a platform nest of sticks and leaves.

The Roseate Spoonbill adult is pink and white with blood red marks on its pink wings, breast, and lower belly. The tail is orange. The spoonlike bill and naked head are grayish green. The legs and feet are red. Immatures are white or faintly pink with yellow legs and bill. The pink on immatures intensifies with age.

These birds frequent shallow saltwater and brackish marshes. They occur only rarely on inland areas along mud flats and shallow water shorelines. They feed mainly on small marine life by swinging the spatulate bill rapidly from side to side. They often travel in company with ibises and Wood Storks. In flight they extend their neck and legs, and alternately flap their wings and glide.

Ciconiidae (Storks)

Wood Stork *Mycteria americana*

The Wood Stork, formerly named Wood Ibis, is almost as tall as the Great Blue Heron and has a heavier body. It is commonly known as "gourdhead" or "flinthead" because

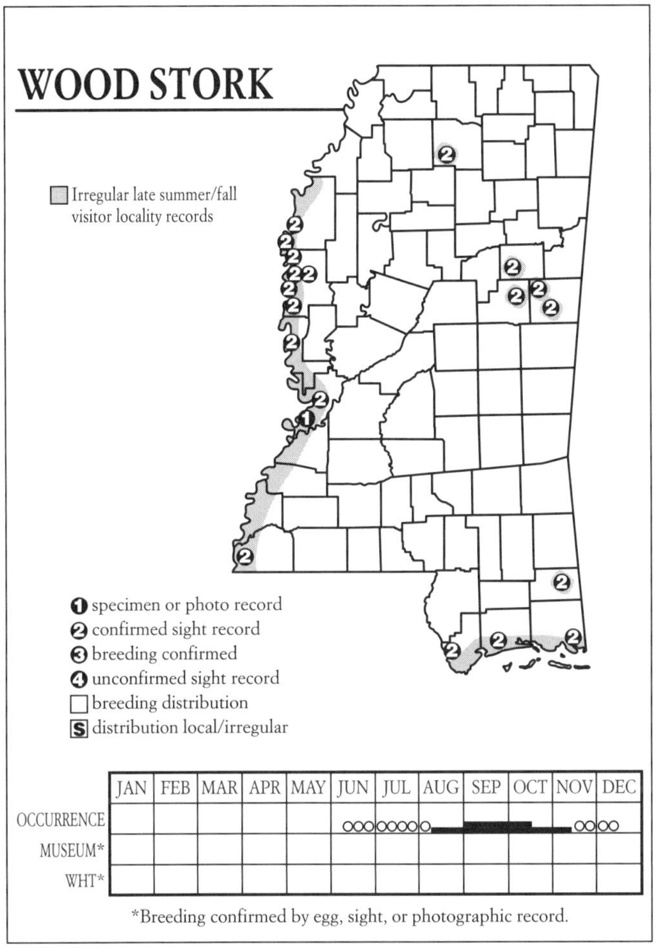

of the unfeathered head and long, thick, decurved bill. At rest, the body appears mostly white. In flight, the glossy black tail and black flight feathers show prominently. White inner wing linings contrast sharply with the large amount of black in the wings. The head, neck, and bill are blackish. Immatures are dingier, having a paler head and neck and a yellowish bill.

Storks are long-legged, long-necked birds with long bills. They walk with a precise and stately gait and fly with their neck and legs fully extended. The wingbeats are powerful, slow, and deliberate. At rest, these birds have a solemn appearance. They occur in temperate and tropical regions and have a worldwide distribution. The well-known European Stork often builds nests on housetops and chimneys. The Wood Stork is the only North American stork species. It is a wary bird and takes flight readily when approached.

The Wood Stork alternately flaps its wings and sails, often soaring to great heights in much the same manner as the White Pelican. It forages for food in borrow pits along levees, in river bottom lakes and sloughs, and along shallow shorelines of freshwater marshes or marginal wetlands that are drying up. The Wood Stork feeds on fish, crayfish, small reptiles, and amphibians by stirring up the bottom mud and catching the prey as it surfaces. It perches in the tall trees of river swamps.

These large birds are irregular late summer visitors to wooded swamps and shallow water areas along the Mississippi River. They seem to know when water levels are right for making aquatic foods available. At these times, they may become common locally and remain until available foods are exhausted. Sometimes flocks of several hundred or more storks gather to feed and roost in company with other wading birds.

On July 24, 1960, I encountered several hundred Wood Storks feeding along nearly dry borrow pits west of the main Mississippi River levee below Mayersville in Issaquena County. Late that evening, I saw them going to roost at a shallow lake near the upper end of Albemarle Lake. It was an unusual treat to watch large numbers of them as they flapped and sailed into the nearby roost along with hundreds of the Little Blue Herons and Great Egrets.

The Wood Stork breeds over a wide range in Central America, South America, and Mexico. In the United States, it breeds in central and southern Florida in cypress and mangrove swamps. The nests are made of sticks lined with leaves and contain from two to four chalky white eggs. Nesting occurs early in the year. After the breeding season, northward wanderers are found mainly in the Gulf states. There is no breeding record in Mississippi.

During late summer, Wood Storks wander widely around the Southeast. They can be found in bottomland hardwood areas in the Delta, along the Mississippi River, and in other parts of Mississippi.

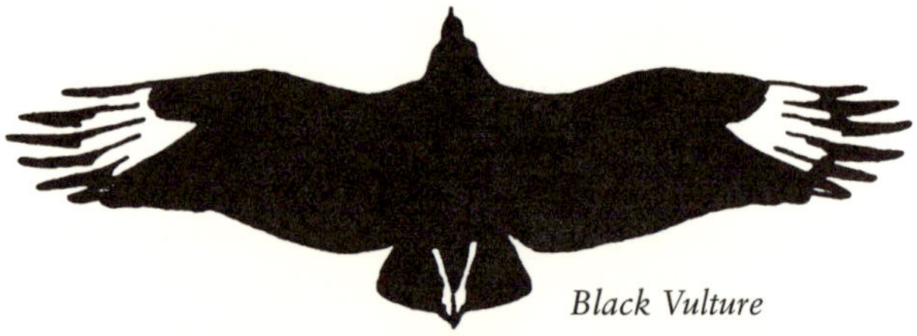

Black Vulture

Turkey Vulture

Cathartidae (Vultures)

Vultures are valuable as scavengers of dead animals, which they locate mainly by sight. When a carcass is found, others quickly congregate until only bones are left. Black Vultures are more gregarious off the roost than Turkey Vultures. As many as a hundred or more may congregate to feed on a large animal.

Black Vultures have been known to attack newborn or sick animals. This usually happens where large numbers of the birds concentrate at roosts near livestock areas. Some people who find vultures feeding on dead newborn animals or livestock believe that vultures killed them. In the absence of proof, the animals may have been stillborn or dead from other causes. In primitive areas without sanitary facilities, vultures provide a useful service by disposing of carrion and garbage that otherwise would pollute the environment. At one time, vultures were suspected of spreading anthrax. However, scientists have not found that vultures or their droppings spread that disease.

Some livestock producers have attempted to control vulture numbers. Large net-wire and pole traps, which the birds enter through funnel openings, have been baited with carcasses. Trapped birds have been clubbed and left in the trap for bait. Such practices have seldom been justifiable. Now, however, vultures are protected by state and federal laws.

Our two vultures, commonly called "buzzards," are thought to be the same species by most people. The Black Vulture, or "carrion-crow," is a common species throughout the state except in the Yazoo Delta, where it seldom occurs beyond the bordering Loess Bluff hills. This species is not migratory and tends to remain in favored localities and common roosting places. The Black Vulture is mostly dull black except for the white undersides of the wing tips. In flight, the wings are broad and extended flat. In level flight, it alternately flaps and sails laboriously, and soars easily only when riding a thermal or updraft.

Our other species, the Turkey Vulture, has longer, narrower wings and is brownish black. In flight, the wings are carried at an upward angle and appear slightly swept back at the tips. The undersides of the primary and secondary wing feathers and tail are silvery gray. The tail is long and slightly rounded and extends well beyond the feet. With a little practice these two vultures can be distinguished in flight at any distance.

Black Vulture *Coragyps atratus*

I think I am as qualified as any Mississippian as an expert on the nesting and other habits of Black Vultures. From 1933 through 1941, I found and collected 27 sets of eggs of these birds, under federal and state scientific collecting permits. Some of the eggs were traded to other collectors for eggs of foreign species, a practice legal at the time with appropriate state and federal permits. Other nests contained young birds or were left undisturbed.

During the Depression years, Black Vulture eggs were worth $1.25 each in exchange with other collectors. Collecting and exchanging them enabled me to add foreign species to my scientific collection, which is now at the MMNS.

During my high school and college years in Clinton and at Mississippi College, there was a large vulture roost in Bogue Chitto creek swamp about four miles north of town. The roost was in a grove of towering sycamore trees in a remote bend of the creek. I visited it many times.

The limbs of the trees were whitewashed, and the acrid smell of ammonia from droppings on the ground was noticeable, somewhat like the smell of a poultry yard. However, there was no smell of putrefaction. The ground usually had scattered feathers beneath the roost. Most of the nests and eggs I found were within two miles of this roost. Other

In April 1939 north of Clinton, these downy young Black Vultures were photographed near their nest site located under the trunk of a large oak.

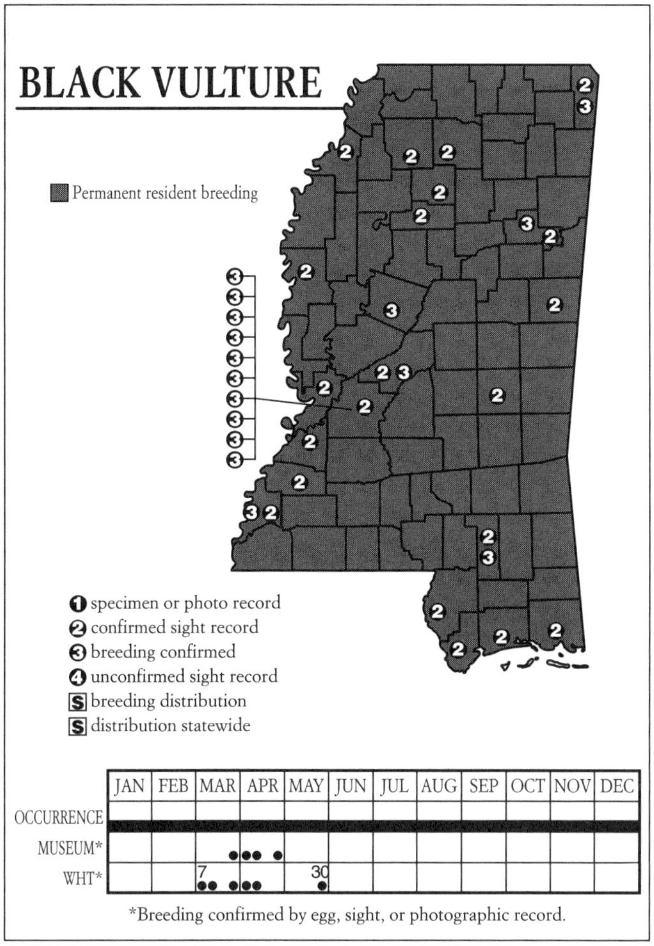

nests were found within walking distance in creek swamps or large patches of woods south and southwest of Clinton.

I would combine hunting for vulture and Red-shouldered Hawk nests, since both usually nest in bottomland hardwoods and breeding activities occur at about the same time. I also would rap on hollow trees to locate Barred Owl nests, and I would watch for Great Horned Owls nesting.

Vultures form pair bonds by late February. (I once found two frozen Black Vulture eggs on February 10.) In February, it is not unusual to observe the mating flight of Black Vultures as one or more males pursue a female in a flapping, erratic flight hardly above treetop level. Such flights are visible for only a few minutes and would not be recognized as mating flights by casual observers.

After pair bonds are formed and before nesting occurs, Black Vultures select and remain around a nest site before egg laying begins. Droppings, a few feathers, and signs of nest scraping can be found at or near the site. Sometimes these birds will flush from the nest location before eggs are laid.

At first, there is no sign of a nest other than scratchings or droppings. Eggs are laid on bare ground, leaves, and dead wood chips. During incubation, a shallow depression may be formed from surrounding debris.

The large, greenish white eggs are variously blotched with chocolate or reddish brown color. Some may be heavily marked, while others may be almost white. However, they are always marked around the larger end. Two eggs are laid, and rarely will there be only one or three. Most of the sets of two eggs I have found had a noticeable difference in shape, one being more pointed at the smaller end.

Nest locations are usually under a fallen tree or treetop, in or beside a log, stump, or rotted hollow of a large tree. Such places become overgrown with briars, brush, vines, or canes, affording a thicket or concealment. In creek swamps, the higher ridges formed by stream banks or along the second bottom of the flood plain are preferred nesting sites. The same locations may be used in successive years. Sites can be highly variable. Sometimes isolated, abandoned barns or buildings are selected for nesting, or the eggs may be deposited on the ground in a canebrake or vine-tangled thicket.

Except for bare, black heads, young vultures are covered with a creamy buff-colored down. After feathers appear, the down feathers become whiter and gradually wear off. When first hatched, they are awkward and almost helpless. They are fed by regurgitation from the adults. While small, the young insert their bills and feed on partly digested food in the gullet of the adult. At first the young are listless, but when they become older they hiss, posture, and retreat when disturbed, often emptying their stomach contents. This may serve as a defensive mechanism against intruders smelling the offensive offal.

As the undertakers of nature's bird realm, Black Vultures put on an impressive performance when a large group gathers for the last rites of a large animal. The strongly hooked beak is used to tear into the carcass at vital spots. But if the hide is tough, the birds wait until decomposition makes entry possible. Black vultures tear and pull on the carcass, push, hop, and shove to get a share of the meal. They leap and flop their wings and sometimes appear to be doing a ritual dance as they bow, scrape, and pull while devouring their meal.

A good friend, David C. Atwood, who lived west of Kosciusko, was a keen observer and lover of wildlife. Although not blessed with much formal education, he accumulated a wealth of knowledge from his observations in the woods while hunting, trapping, or fishing. He loved to dance and often invited hundreds of people for dances and other entertainment at his private fishing lake and lodge.

"Mr. Dave" performed what he called his "buzzard dance." He would climb atop a table or desk, fold both hands behind his back, extend his neck forward in a hunched-over position, and begin a foot-shuffling jig that went faster and faster until he raised and flapped his arms while jumping to the floor. I saw him perform this act several times after he was more than 70 years old.

Dave Atwood kept many wild animals as pets and could mimic many wildlife sounds. He raised and sold many wild-strain turkeys from eggs he originally obtained from his woods. Although his wild-strain turkeys were not as successful as wild-trapped birds, they survived as adults better than other pen-reared birds.

Turkey Vulture *Cathartes aura*

The Turkey Vulture, with a greater wingspan than the Black Vulture, is the essence of graceful flight with its slightly upward tilted (called dihedral) wings. While riding updrafts and thermals, it seldom flaps the wings and often teeters from side to side.

The secondary and primary wing feathers show silvery gray underneath in contrast to the black forward linings of the wings. The underside of the long, slightly rounded tail also is silvery gray. In contrast, the Black Vulture is totally black except for the gray and white wing tips, and the tail is short and square at the end.

The general appearance of the Turkey Vulture at close range is dark brownish black. The Turkey Vulture's head is red with a white beak, except in the immature, which has a black head and beak. The toes of both vultures have talons not suited for attacking or grasping prey. Their bare legs and feet are strong and admirably suited for perching or roosting. The bare legs and feet of the Turkey Vulture are red on the adult, black on the immature, and dirty white on the Black Vulture.

In Mississippi, the nesting habits of the Turkey Vulture are similar to the Black Vulture. Records and nests that I have inspected indicate that nests are built about one month later than those of the Black Vulture.

Egg laying usually starts in April. Two nests with fresh eggs that I found in early April were almost unapproachable from the ground. One, beside a large tree stump, was surrounded by tall, thick blackberry canes and vines on a swamp ridge. The other nest, on a creek bank between two fallen logs and tangles of large dead limbs, was approachable only by climbing over the logs. The vultures had to alight on the logs and jump down to the nest or crawl under a tunnel of thick vegetation. An intruder would not have found this nest unless the bird had flushed, and Turkey Vultures do not flush readily while incubating.

The eggs of Turkey Vultures are slightly smaller than the Black Vulture's and more elliptical. Ground color is creamy white, and the eggs are heavily blotched with shades from dark brown to reddish brown. They are deposited on the ground, but may have finely shredded wood punk or other debris added around them as incubation advances.

I found a nest 20 feet up in the large hollow of a white oak tree where a main branch broke from the trunk. Both birds were seen at this site, which was within a large tract of upland hardwoods in rough hills near a creek bed. Unfortunately, I could not examine this nest.

Henry L. Owens found and collected a set of two eggs on April 30, 1941, in Tishomingo County. The nest was in a cave under a rock cliff and incubation was advanced. These birds commonly use canyon or rock cliffs, caves, and crevices for nest sites throughout their extensive range.

Turkey Vultures are migratory in the northern part of their breeding range. In the Deep South states, they are permanent residents. Large numbers winter in Florida and the Gulf states and return to breeding areas in February and March. In early February 1983, my wife and I saw a roost of about 1500 birds at sunrise alongside the levee of Lake Okeechobee near Clewiston, Florida. Most of these birds had flown down from roost trees and were sunning with outstretched wings in the early light. This awesome sight extended for several hundred yards along the top of the levee. Vulture roosts like this one are nuisances when they utilize nearby microwave or other towers. They have been known to roost on public buildings in the older parts of Miami.

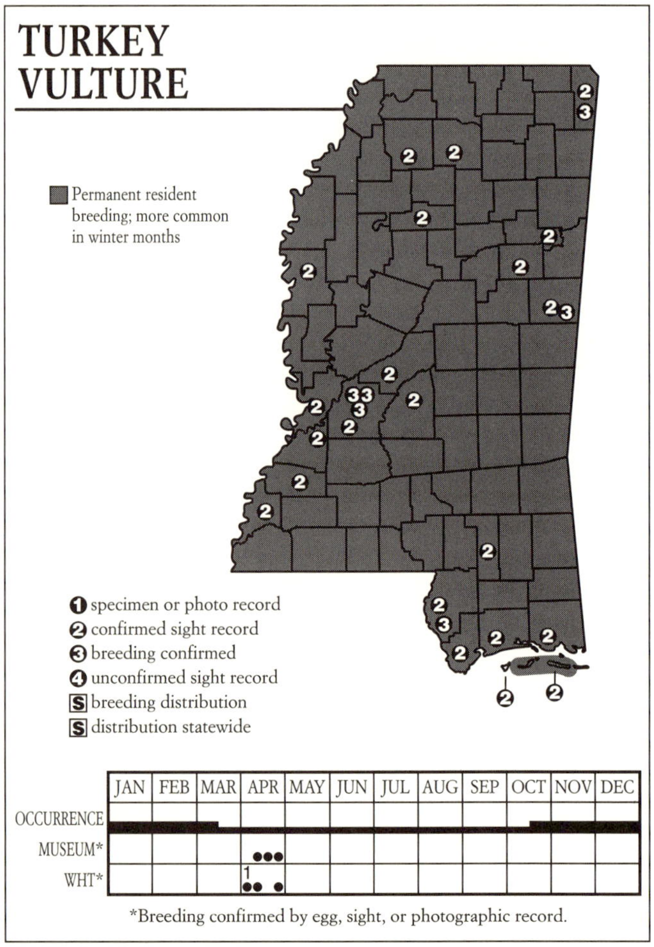

*Breeding confirmed by egg, sight, or photographic record.

It has been said that the Turkey Vulture leads a life that no one envies. It flies just above gunshot range, with no one wasting expensive shotgun shells or ever wanting to eat it. However, one cannot help but marvel at his graceful and seemingly endless, aimless flight and ability to travel over beautiful country to seek out environments that meet its needs. Death always meets the Turkey Vulture's food requirements, and few begrudge its daily meals except its blacker relative, the "carrion-crow," or Black Vulture. Eons of time have produced and maintained this remarkable, adaptable, common, and widespread scavenger.

Swans, Geese, and Ducks (Anseriformes)

Waterfowl are divided into seven subfamilies. Swans (Cygninae) are long-necked, large, white birds that feed on submerged plants by dipping the head underwater and by browsing on shoreline grasses and sprouts. They fly in lines or V-formations.

Geese (Anserinae) have plump bodies, short legs, long necks, and strong, round-tipped bills. They feed on grasses, grain seeds, sprouts, and some aquatic vegetation. Geese are strong flyers with deep wingbeats, and they fly in V-formations or in wavy lines. The sexes are similar in appearance.

Ducks are divided into five subfamilies. Whistling Ducks (Dendrocygninae), formerly called Tree Ducks, have long legs and necks. While standing, they resemble geese. In flight, the legs extend beyond the tail, and when landing the neck and legs are extended downward. These ducks are nocturnal feeders on corn, rice, and other seeds. The sexes are alike in appearance, and the calls are shrill whistles.

Surface-feeding or puddle ducks (Anatinae) dabble and tip up while feeding in shallow water areas. They rise almost vertically when taking flight. Males and females have different plumages. Males are more colorful in fall and winter, but assume a duller eclipse plumage in summer before molting to basic plumage. Both sexes have rectangular, usually more colorful patches on the trailing edges of the wings. Surface-feeding ducks have distinctive calls. Most will respond to decoys and expert calling, but they soon learn to become "decoy and call shy." Surface-feeding ducks make up the major part of ducks harvested in the Mississippi Flyway.

Diving ducks (Aythyinae) can be separated as bay ducks and sea ducks. Most divers harvested in the Mississippi Flyway are bay ducks. Bay and sea ducks winter mainly along coastal bays and estuaries. They dive and swim underwater for food and eat more animal foods than most surface-feeders. Diving ducks differ from surface-feeding ducks by having fleshy, flattened lobes on the hind toes. When taking flight, they paddle along the water surface to gain speed before becoming airborne. The calls of most divers are coarse croaking sounds not easily recognized.

Sea ducks are heavy-bodied birds that winter along coastlines and sometimes occur in large flocks or rafts on open water. They are expert divers and feed largely on molluscs. This subfamily includes eiders, scoters, and Harlequin and Oldsquaw Ducks.

Mergansers (Mergini) are fish-eating, diving ducks with long, narrow bills serrated on the sides. The wingbeats are

Above: Shovelers tipping

fluttery and faster than most puddle ducks. In flight, the extended neck is held in line with the body. All three North American mergansers have crests (except the male Common Merganser) and rectangular white wing patches visible at rest and in flight. They have coarse quack calls.

The stiff-tailed ducks (Oxyurini) have thick necks and short, stocky bodies. The tail feathers are stiff and spiny and usually carried at an upturned angle or are sometimes fanned and held in a vertical position. The legs are set farther back on the body than most ducks. Only two species, the Ruddy and Masked Ducks, occur in North America. The Masked Duck is regular in winter in southern Texas and a casual winter visitor into southwestern Louisiana. There is no record of its occurrence in Mississippi.

These Tundra Swans were photographed adjacent to Okatibbee Lake in Lauderdale County. The birds spent nearly two weeks roosting locally and feeding in nearby rye grass fields during the day.

The waterfowl population is a precious natural resource. Millions of ducks, geese, and swans from breeding grounds extending into the Arctic travel the four continental flyways to wintering grounds as far as northern South America. A great expenditure of money and effort is devoted to waterfowl research, protection, and management, but some populations are declining due to loss of wetlands on northern breeding grounds and southern wintering areas. Swan and goose populations now fare better than the prairie pothole-nesting ducks because of better protection, controlled harvest, and extensive state and federal refuge systems. Habitat loss from drainage and clearing of bottomlands and destruction of glacial potholes and marshes on the breeding grounds is a more serious problem than the regulated annual harvest of birds taken by hunters.

Waterfowl identification is an art developed by training and experience. The practiced eyes of the best duck hunters can identify waterfowl by species far beyond shooting range by characteristic flight patterns, wingbeats, body shape, size, calls, silhouette, color patterns, and posture on the water or by special features and marks on the wings and body. A well-trained biologist can determine sex and identify any species by characteristic wing marks.

Good hunters separate waterfowl by the seven subfamilies at a glance, then by knowing all the characteristic features, they can sort out the particular species under observation. Years of experience observing or hunting waterfowl make instant recognition possible. Federal and state laws require hunters to identify species in the bag before completing a daily limit.

Dendrocygninae (Whistling-Ducks)

Fulvous Whistling-Duck *Dendrocygna bicolor*

Until recently, the two members of this subfamily were called Tree Ducks. However, this is a misnomer since this species does not ordinarily frequent trees. It nests in marsh vegetation and on rice-field contour levees and rarely, if ever, uses a tree cavity. The Black-bellied Whistling-Duck nests in tree cavities and readily accepts nest boxes. The breeding ranges of the two species overlap in southern Texas and Mexico. The name "whistling-duck" is now the accepted common name applied to both species. It alludes to the squealing, whistle-like calls common to both. "Mexican squealer" is another widely used local name for the Fulvous Whistling-Duck. Its call is a shrill double-note whistle.

This long-necked and long-legged whistling-duck looks more like a goose than a duck. The legs are bluish, the head and underparts are tawny, and the back and wings are dark. A noticeable white line extends along its flanks and contrasts with its dark wings. A U-shaped white patch at the base of the tail and the strong, slow, gooselike flight are distinctive. The flat crown gives this bird an odd profile. White streaks on the neck are not always visible.

In flight, the wing tips appear rounded, and the feet and legs extend well beyond the end of their short tail. When alighting, this duck extends its feet and neck downward in the manner of a goose.

The Fulvous Whistling-Duck is a casual spring and fall visitor in Mississippi. The first state record reported by Webster was a specimen trapped, photographed, and banded at Bluff Lake on the Noxubee National Wildlife Refuge on February 26, 1965 (Gandy and Turcotte 1970). A second record, at the Pearl River Waterfowl Refuge in Madison County, was made on November 26, 1969, when John H. Phares and I observed a flock of about 30 birds in shallow water by a goose enclosure near a flooded millet field. A photo taken of these Fulvous Whistling-Ducks in flight showed at least 30 individuals (Gandy and Turcotte 1970). They remained on the refuge until about February 26, 1970. George Chandler (pers. comm.), Richard Dent, and Gene Stokes saw three birds of this species in flight near a flooded wheat field at Steele Bayou in Issaquena County, on May 26, 1973. Three were seen flying at Lakeshore in Hancock County on October 29, 1978 (Toups and Jackson 1987).

The Fulvous Whistling-Duck has a unique distribution. It breeds locally in Florida, Louisiana, Texas, California, and throughout Mexico. The same species occurs in South America, Africa, Burma, and India. Although separated by vast distances and differences of terrain and water, it maintains virtually the same size and plumage throughout its range. In North America, the species breeds mostly in Mexico, with smaller populations breeding in marshes and rice fields of southwestern Louisiana and Texas. In California, nesting occurs almost exclusively in dense marsh vegetation.

The bowl-shaped nest is made of surrounding grasses and marsh vegetation, usually only a few inches above water level. The eggs are white to buff. Clutch sizes average from nine to 13 or more. Dump-nesting occurs, when more than one female uses a single nest, and nests containing 30 or more eggs have been found.

The Fulvous Whistling-Duck is noted for nocturnal feeding in rice and corn fields, important grain foods when available. Natural foods consist of grass seeds and the seeds and parts of aquatic plants. Most of these birds winter in Mexico. They usually arrive along the coasts of Louisiana and Texas in late April, nest in May and June, and depart from breeding grounds in September and early October. Erratic fall wanderings account for most inland records from the Mississippi Valley and along the Atlantic Coast.

FULVOUS WHISTLING-DUCK

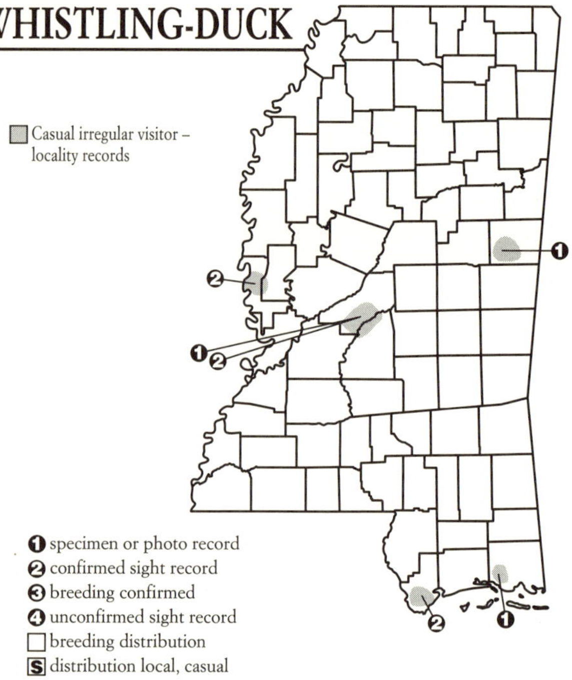

	JAN	FEB	MAR	APR	MAY	JUN	JUL	AUG	SEP	OCT	NOV	DEC
OCCURRENCE		o		o	o o					27 o	ooo	o
MUSEUM*												
WHT*												

*Breeding confirmed by egg, sight, or photographic record.

[Black-bellied Whistling-Duck]
Dendrocygna autumnalis

This species of Mexican origin is extending its breeding range eastward along the Texas Gulf Coast. The range extension reached eastward to the Welder Wildlife Research Station near Sinton, Texas, by 1972. They are common on the Santa Ana National Wildlife Refuge in the Lower Rio Grande Valley. I have seen them in numbers on water tanks or ponds on the King Ranch near Kingsville, Texas. I found adults with broods of small young on tidal ponds on the Kennedy Ranch south of Sarita, Texas.

The Louisiana Wildlife and Fisheries Commission has released these birds on the Rockefeller Wildlife Refuge in Cameron Parish where they have nested successfully in the rice-growing region. Hundreds are seen in autumn on Lacassine National Wildlife Refuge.

This handsome duck nests in tree cavities and artificial nest boxes designed and placed for their use. The large size, long legs, and feet extending beyond the tail in flight give it an unducklike appearance.

The legs and bill are red. The face, with its white eye ring, and the throat are gray. The lower neck, back, and breast are tawny brown. The belly, rump, tail, primaries, and secondaries are black. Wing coverts are mostly white, and the underwings are black. Large white wing patches and black underparts are distinctive field marks.

This species has been bred in captivity for its attractiveness, and captive birds become tame and gentle. The origin of Black-bellied Whistling-Ducks outside their normal breeding range is uncertain because of escapes from captivity.

One occurrence record of two Black-bellied Whistling-Ducks in Mississippi has been reported and documented by photographs (Hodges 1985). John Fulton, Tim Wilkins, Anita Bowman, and John Fleming found the two birds on the Yazoo National Wildlife Refuge between May 8 and 10, 1985. This refuge is adjacent to rice farms and catfish ponds in Washington and adjacent counties.

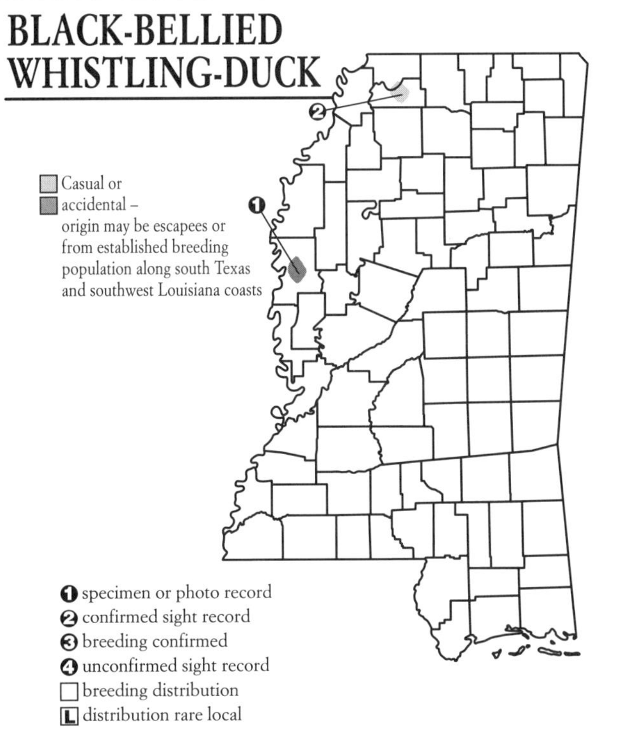

	JAN	FEB	MAR	APR	MAY	JUN	JUL	AUG	SEP	OCT	NOV	DEC
OCCURRENCE					8-10 ○ ○	20-25						
MUSEUM*												
WHT*												

*Breeding confirmed by egg, sight, or photographic record.

Cygninae (Swans)

Tundra Swan *Cygnus columbianus*

This large, all white swan flies with its long neck outstretched. Swans are unmistakable in the field since all other white, long-necked birds of similar size and appearance have conspicuous black marks in flight.

It is an uncommon winter visitor to some larger bodies of water in the Yazoo Delta and flood control reservoirs in Mississippi. The earliest specimen record in the MMNS, substantiated by the head and feet only, is that of a bird killed at McComb Lake in Pike County on January 11, 1946 (Turcotte and Gandy 1970). Recent sight records of this species indicate it is now a regular winter visitor.

In January and early February 1990, following heavy rains that flooded low-lying fields in northern Delta counties, Tundra Swans appeared in record numbers. They were seen mostly on flooded soybean fields in Tunica, Panola, Leflore, and Bolivar Counties.

A family group of two adults and four nearly all white immatures spent several weeks on an upland rye grass pasture near Okatibbee Lake in Lauderdale County. The birds appeared daily for more than two weeks between January 10 and 25, 1990. The larger adult stayed a day or two, left the remaining five, returned to remain a day, and then left the area. These swans presumably roosted on the lake. They returned each morning, fed on rye grass, and preened and watered on a small pond. They were seen by numerous observers from local roads on both sides of the field.

Lewis W. Bays and I saw a color photograph displayed at Cliff Marter's bait shop of a Tundra Swan shot by a hunter near Graysport Crossing on Grenada Lake prior to 1968. A flock of nine was seen January 8, 1968, by Ken Babcock on Enid Lake in Yalobusha County while conducting aerial midwinter waterfowl surveys. Probably the same flock of

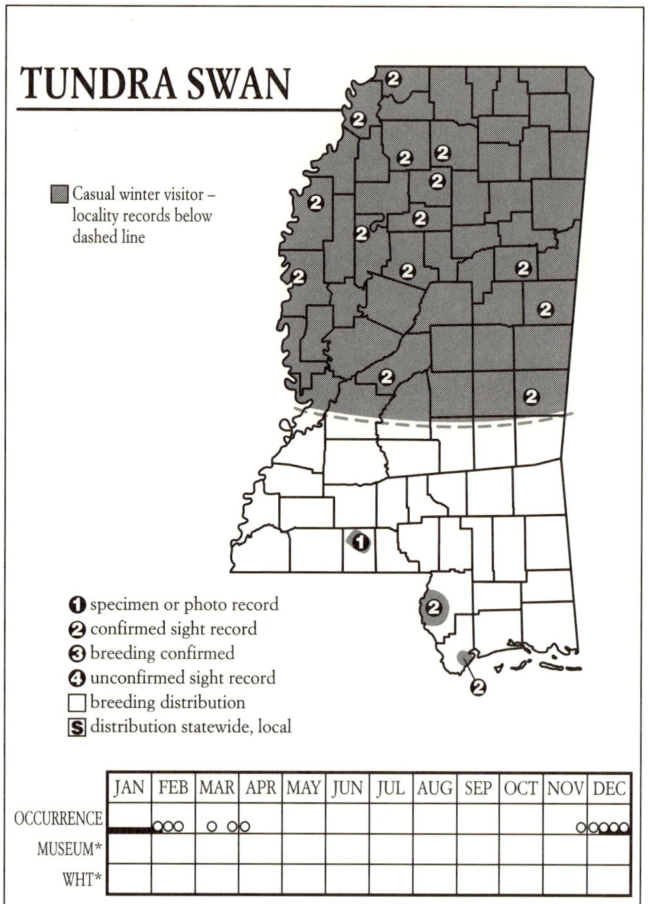

*Breeding confirmed by egg, sight, or photographic record.

nine appeared on an impoundment at the Sardis Waterfowl Refuge in Lafayette County on January 22, 1968. They remained for several days, mingling with Canada Geese and ducks.

W. Marvin Davis (1971a) saw a Tundra Swan on Sardis Waterfowl Refuge on March 14, 1970. An immature was seen and reported on this area by Refuge Manager R. L. Rodgers seven to 10 days later. On December 17, 1972, W. Marvin Davis observed another at Sardis Lake.

Conservation Officer T. C. Thornton reported five swans in flooded soybean fields four miles west of Tunica in Tunica County, on December 31, 1974. They had been seen several times previously and were among flocks of Mallards. Forty Tundra Swans were seen and photographed by Richard Wells on a flooded field in Grenada County in December 1984 while on an aerial waterfowl survey.

The Tundra Swan has a black bill with a small yellow spot in front of the eye. The spot is not always present in adult birds and is visible only at close range. Immatures are light grayish brown with a pink, dusky tipped bill. The Mute Swan, introduced from Europe, has established breeding populations locally along the Atlantic Coast from Long Island to New Jersey. This species has an orange bill with a prominent black knob and carries its neck in an S-curve with the bill pointed downward. The Tundra Swan carries its neck straight and holds the bill level while swimming.

Tundra Swans breed in Arctic and sub-Arctic regions in Alaska and Canada and winter in the United States on the Atlantic Coast around Chesapeake Bay and southward along the Virginia and North Carolina Coasts. A population winters along the northern Pacific Coast, in marshes back of San Francisco Bay, and on inland marshes of Oregon, Utah, Nevada, and California. The eastern wintering population uses a migration corridor through the Great Lakes region across Wisconsin, Minnesota, Michigan, and Ohio.

[Trumpeter Swan] *Cygnus buccinator*

The Trumpeter Swan, once near extinction, is now recovering but considered rare over most of its former range. Through most of the nineteenth century, swans were killed for their down, feathers, and meat. Their skins were bought and sold commercially. Indians took the young and adults on the breeding grounds for food and clothing. As the birds became scarce, they were prized as trophies by some hunters.

Trumpeters survived the onslaught only on remote breeding grounds in Alaska and northwestern Canada. In recent years, these birds have recovered under protection and through reintroduction in parts of their former breeding range in Canada and the midwestern and western states.

Currently, Trumpeter Swans breed in Alaska along the river deltas on the Gulf of Alaska and in inland river valleys and basins. Alberta and Saskatchewan also have small breeding populations. Yellowstone National Park in Wyoming, Red Rocks National Wildlife Refuge in Montana, and the Yellowstone-Centennial Valley have the major breeding populations in the contiguous United States (Bellrose 1976).

Breeding populations of Trumpeter Swans from Alaska winter along the Pacific Coast from Alaska to the mouth of the Columbia River and on a few inland waters of British Columbia and Washington. Breeding populations from Alberta and Saskatchewan winter mainly in the Red Rock Lakes region and the Henrys Fork of the Snake River near Island Park in Idaho (Banko 1960). The Yellowstone Park breeding population winters in the park or in nearby areas. Wintering is made possible by warm springs in the mountain valleys where swans can find open waters even at subzero temperatures.

I was fortunate to observe Trumpeter Swans with cygnets on Red Rocks National Wildlife Refuge on July 25, 1984, and on a river near the western entrance to Yellowstone National Park the next day. Both parents were with the young, and I was able to obtain good photographs. The pair on the river in Yellowstone was visible from the road and easily approached at an observation point and parking area.

TRUMPETER SWAN

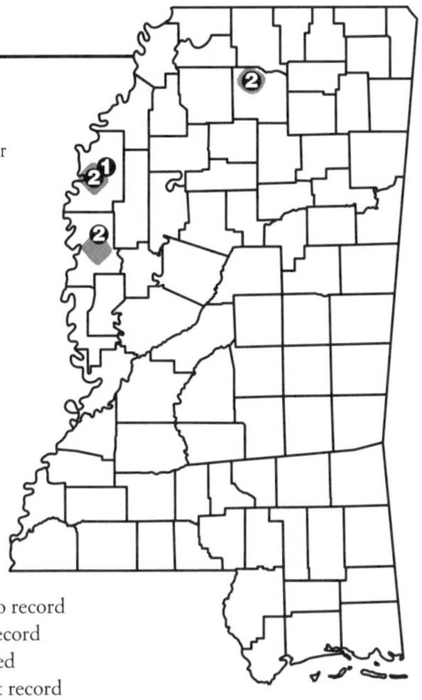

■ Accidental winter visitor locality record

❶ specimen or photo record
❷ confirmed sight record
❸ breeding confirmed
❹ unconfirmed sight record
☐ breeding distribution
🅰 distribution local

	JAN	FEB	MAR	APR	MAY	JUN	JUL	AUG	SEP	OCT	NOV	DEC
OCCURRENCE	oooo	oo										oo
MUSEUM*												
WHT*												

*Breeding confirmed by egg, sight, or photographic record.

The Trumpeter Swan is not easily identified in the field. Adults have a large, sloping, black bill with narrow, pinkish streaking on the mandibles extending from the jawline. The forehead slopes in a straight line with the bill, reminiscent of the Canvasback profile. The black facial skin forms a broad point at the eye. The facial skin bordering the forehead feathers forms a distinctive V-shape. The neck is usually held straight with a backward kink at the base when the bird is at rest.

Calls of the Trumpeter and Tundra Swans are distinctively different. The Trumpeter's call is likened to single or double notes played on a French horn and louder than the high-pitched, triple-noted, melodious, quavering calls of the Tundra Swan, which remind one of Snow Geese.

Immature Trumpeter Swans retain their gray plumage until the following spring. Immature Tundras appear much whiter by midwinter. Because swans usually associate in family groups, the degree of white on immatures can be a clue to their identification in winter.

Identification of the Trumpeter Swan is infallible only by dissection of the breastbone. The windpipe makes a vertical loop over a bony hump absent in the Tundra Swan. Measurement of the top of the bill of adult Trumpeters usually exceeds two inches in length. Tundra Swans usually have a top-of-the-bill length under two inches. Both species are all white in adult plumage, but sometimes are stained rusty around the head and neck by feeding in waters that contain ferric acid. Swans fly with their necks fully outstretched, and when swimming the neck is held erect.

Trumpeter Swan recovery from near extinction in Canada and the contiguous United States came about through rigid protection on wildlife refuges and national parks. The discovery of a large breeding population of some 3000 Trumpeters in the 1960s in Alaska removed all doubt that the species was no longer endangered.

More recent efforts to establish breeding populations in parts of their known former breeding range have been successful on refuges. Transplants of birds from Red Rock Lakes in Montana have established small breeding populations on the following National Wildlife Refuges: Malheur (Oregon), Lacreek (South Dakota), Ruby Lake (Nevada), and Turnbull (Washington). Other Trumpeter releases were made at Delta, Manitoba, and in Minnesota. There are no historical records of this species occurring in Mississippi, although it probably once migrated here in winter and wintered westward along the northern Gulf Coast.

On January 9, 1990, J. C. and Nona Herbert visited a neighbor's flooded field near Shaw and saw two wild swans, which were assumed to be Tundras since a flock of 14 had appeared earlier in December in nearby fields. However, one bird appeared noticeably larger when seen again on January 10.

On January 13, Nona participated in an eagle count around Lake Chicot in Arkansas, led by Don Simons, a park naturalist. On January 14, after following her home to see the two swans, Simons identified the larger swan in close view as a Trumpeter Swan, the first historical record of this bird in Mississippi. Its companion was a Tundra Swan.

Early the following morning Nona and J. C. Herbert observed both birds from a gravel road at a distance of about 100 feet. All details were seen and described with comparisons noted between the two swans by Nona Herbert (Herbert and Simons 1991). She called W. Marvin Davis at Oxford to verify her identification and to notify regional birders of the rare occurrence. Davis verified the identification of the Trumpeter on January 15.

A local reporter wrote an account of the rare event published January 17, 1990, in *The Clarion-Ledger.* This brought in an influx of local people and birders from adjacent states. The unpaved road where the birds could be seen was so heavily rutted by visitors who had been alerted on the "verbal hotline" that it subsequently was upgraded by Bolivar County supervisors.

The Herberts kept the two swans under observation until last seen on February 10, 1990. In her detailed style after numerous observations, Nona described and compared the obvious differences in call notes, posture, preening (that would "put Gypsy Rose Lee to shame" as she described it), murmuring, walking, feeding, and flight. The swans fed on winter grass and beans that had sprouted through field stubble in a new, shallow, flooded catfish pond. Before leaving the area, they became wilder and more retiring from view.

The second occurrence of an immature Trumpeter Swan within two years was at Sardis Waterfowl Refuge in Lafayette County. A swan was first seen by Refuge Manager Vic Theobald, where it had remained since the third week in December 1991. It was seen by five observers during the Christmas Bird Court on December 21 and tentatively identified as a Tundra Swan. On December 30, in close comparison to Canada Geese, it was identified by Thomas Heatley and Marvin Davis. Identification was confirmed by Jeff Wilson, and Gene Knight on January 13 with a telescope (Davis, pers. comm.). Much grayness on the head, neck, and body and distance from nostrils to the tip of the longer bill were noted.

Anserinae (Geese)

Greater White-fronted Goose *Anser albifrons*

GREATER WHITE-FRONTED GOOSE

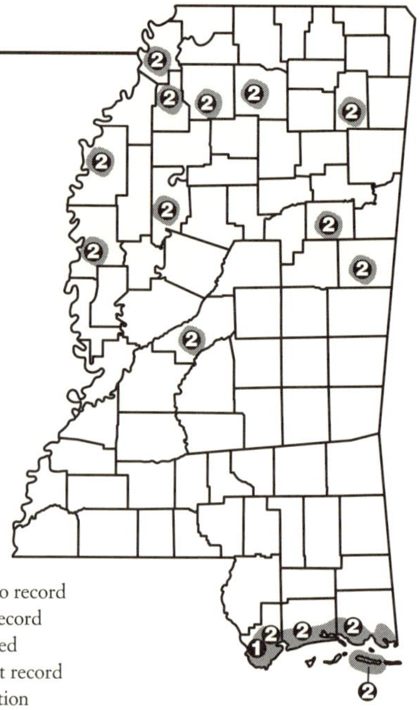

Uncommon migrant - winter visitor locality records

❶ specimen or photo record
❷ confirmed sight record
❸ breeding confirmed
❹ unconfirmed sight record
□ breeding distribution
S distribution statewide, local

	JAN	FEB	MAR	APR	MAY	JUN	JUL	AUG	SEP	OCT	NOV	DEC
OCCURRENCE	oooo	oooo	oooo							ooo	oooo	oooo
MUSEUM*												
WHT*												

*Breeding confirmed by egg, sight, or photographic record.

This gray brown goose is known commonly as "speckle belly." The species derives its name from the white face of the adult, which contrasts sharply with the brown head and neck. The light gray underparts of the adults are blotched with irregular black marks. Adults have a pinkish bill and either orange or yellow legs. Immature birds are dusky with yellow legs and bill. The immatures resemble the young of the blue-morph Snow Goose, formerly treated as a separate species known as the Blue Goose. The immature White-front is best distinguished from the young blue morph of the Snow Goose by the yellow bill and legs. Immature Blue Geese have dark bluish legs and blackish bills.

The White-fronted Goose is common on its wintering grounds west of the Mississippi River. In Mississippi, it occurs as a casual spring and fall migrant and a rare winter resident.

The first state record was a sighting of a bird at Lakeshore in Hancock County by Lovett E. Williams Jr. and Sterling G. Clawson on January 15, 1961 (Turcotte 1961g). The second record is a specimen taken by Lovett E. Williams Jr. (1962d) on December 23, 1961, near Heron Bay in Hancock County. Burton S. Webster reported an overwintering flock of 23 to 29 birds that arrived on Noxubee National Wildlife Refuge during the last week in November 1963 and departed the second week in February 1964.

A single bird was seen at Tupelo in Lee County on December 21, 1964, by Dean Crabbs and Laura J. Bowers. Winter flocks of five birds on January 8, 1970, and 12 birds on January 2, 1972, were present on Noxubee Refuge. A flock of four White-fronts was recorded by Edward and Virginia Alexander Jr. on Yazoo National Wildlife Refuge during the Seventy-third Christmas Bird Count on December 31, 1972. Stephen Peterson observed 27 geese in a flock on the same refuge during the Christmas Bird Count on January 4, 1976. At Sardis Waterfowl Refuge, W. Marvin Davis observed two geese on November 24, 1973. On the Pearl River Waterfowl Refuge in Madison County, two White-fronts remained from March 13 to 19, 1968.

Edward Alexander Jr. reported two birds at Yazoo National Wildlife Refuge from October 29 to November 4, 1972, the earliest arrival date for this species. A late occurrence record is March 21, 1971, when one bird was seen and recorded by Robert Lilly near Morgan City in Leflore County. Extreme dates of occurrence recorded by Gene Knight at Sardis Waterfowl Refuge in Lafayette County are September 23 and March 24.

The White-fronted Goose breeds on the Arctic tundra of central and western Canada and northern Alaska. The principal wintering ground for the midcontinent population is the coastal marshes, rice, and grain fields of southwestern Louisiana and Texas, and on the East Coast and interior of Mexico. In the Pacific Flyway, the largest concentration winters in the Central Valley of California and along the western coast of Mexico.

Snow Goose *Chen caerulescens*

The common name is thought to refer to the remote, snowy regions of the Arctic where this species breeds. There are two color phases of the Snow Goose, the white phase and blue phase. The white phase is white except for black wing tips. The young are duskier than adults, but much paler than blue-phase immatures. Adults of the blue color phase have blue gray bodies and a white head and neck. Blue-phase immatures are dusky on the head and body with lighter colored wings. Adults of both color phases have pink bills and legs. Immatures of both have dark feet and bills. Adults often have rusty stains on the head.

The Snow Goose winters in all four waterfowl flyways. In the Atlantic Flyway, the wintering grounds of the "greater" Snow Goose extend along the coastlines of New Jersey, Maryland, Virginia, and North Carolina. The Mississippi and Central Flyway wintering grounds extend along the coastal plains in Louisiana and Texas. The blue phase winters in southeastern Louisiana and the white phase predominantly in southwestern Louisiana and Texas.

In recent years there has been more intermingling of the white and blue phases of the midcontinent population. The trend is toward a more uniform distribution of the two color phases in the Central and Mississippi Flyways. Also, there is a very pronounced tendency for a large proportion of these birds to spend the early part of the winter in the upper portions of these flyways. The Pacific Flyway population winters largely in the Central and Imperial Valleys of California, with smaller numbers northward in Puget Sound and scattered locations in the southwestern states and into Mexico.

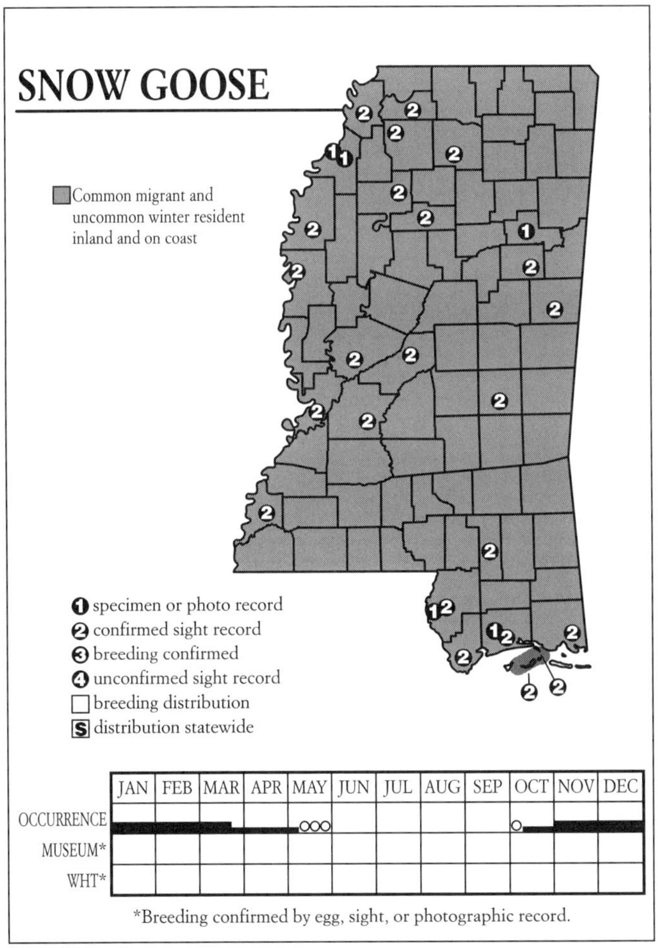

Snow Geese fly in undulating, V-shaped or irregular, wavy masses. They are known as "wavies" because of their peculiar flight. Flocks of up to 100 or more birds travel together over long distances by day and night. They breed in the Arctic regions of North America and northeastern Siberia.

The eastern Arctic breeding population, which furnishes most of the midcontinent wintering birds, gathers in great numbers at the end of James Bay, where blue-morph birds predominate in this staging area. White-morph birds stage along the southwestern coast of James Bay. The populations merge in migration corridors through the Midwest with stopovers there and in the Great Plains states before arriving in the coastal marshes of Louisiana and Texas.

Snow Geese feed on the roots, tubers, and tender shoots of terrestrial aquatic plants. Increasingly, they are interrupting or terminating their fall flights on refuges in the upper Mississippi Valley to feed on plantings of grain, green browse crops, and waste grains from adjacent agricultural lands. In coastal Louisiana and Texas, pasture grasses and rice fields are utilized.

The fall passage of Snow Geese in Mississippi may begin in late September, but the main flights occur after the first week in October until early November. The northward migration begins in late March and continues until late May. In the fall migration, Snow Geese weakened by their long journey (mostly immatures) often will be seen in pastures or fields where they may stay for a short time before continuing southward. Other flocks occasionally remain inland on state or federal refuge areas until late winter.

[Ross' Goose] *Chen rossii*

Ross' Goose is a miniature version mainly of the white morph of the Snow Goose. It breeds in northwestern Canada on islands and tundra of the high Arctic and winters primarily in California. A smaller population breeds locally northwest of Hudson Bay and winters locally in southwestern Louisiana and Texas, where it mingles with Snow Geese.

As in the Snow Goose, a blue-morph Ross' Goose occurs. Ross' Goose is about the size of a Mallard, having a shorter neck, more rounded head, and flying with faster wingbeats than the Snow Goose. The bill of Ross' Goose is stubby and lacks the "grinning patch" of the Snow Goose. A warty protuberance at the base of the bill is a characteristic absent in the Snow Goose.

ROSS' GOOSE

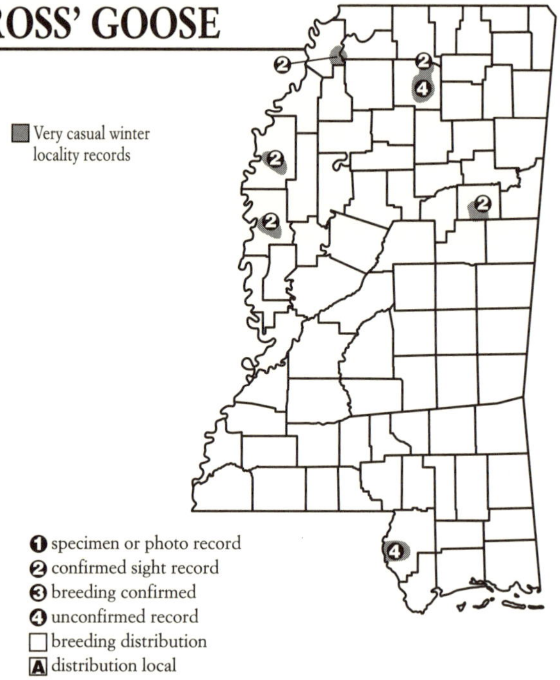

	JAN	FEB	MAR	APR	MAY	JUN	JUL	AUG	SEP	OCT	NOV	DEC
OCCURRENCE	oo	ooooo	30 ooooo								oo	
MUSEUM*												
WHT*												

*Breeding confirmed by egg, sight, or photographic record.

The eastern population sometimes hybridizes with the blue morph of the Snow Goose. The resulting hybrid is an intermediate that adds confusion to the field identification of this species. Hybridization also occurs with the western population of the white morph of the Snow Goose.

The white-phase Ross' Goose is all white except for black primaries. The bill is pink except at the bluish or greenish warty base. Unlike the Snow Goose, the white head is seldom rust stained.

A mounted specimen of Ross' Goose reported to B. E. Gandy by George H. Lowery Jr. (who also sent a photograph of the specimen alongside a Snow Goose and a White-fronted Goose for comparison) appears to substantiate a southern Mississippi record. This specimen was reportedly taken by a Louisiana resident. Two photographs of the goose were taken in a taxidermy shop in Louisiana, but the details, unfortunately, of the locality in Mississippi and when it was taken were not furnished.

A recent sighting of a Ross' Goose on February 16, 1986, by Fulton (1987; Jackson 1986) occurred on the Yazoo National Wildlife Refuge in Washington County. The sighting and written details substantiate the first state record for Mississippi. Additional sightings of Ross' Goose occurred from January 28 to March 3, 1990, in Tunica County. On January 27, 1990, W. Marvin Davis (pers. comm.) observed a flock of about 4000 Snow Geese northeast of Prichard and south of Highway 304. Davis reported the goose flock to Jeff Wilson of Memphis, who tentatively identified two Ross' Geese among the Snow Geese on January 28 and three on February 3. Davis and Gene Knight returned on February 4 and found the goose flock had moved southwestward from Prichard and numbered from 18,000 to 20,000 birds, including at least 40 White-fronted Geese and 150 Canada Geese. Among almost 1000 Snow Geese carefully viewed, four Ross' Geese were identified by Davis and Knight. The next weekend in February, Gene and Shannon Knight saw 30 to 40 Ross' Geese and Jeff Wilson observed the same numbers about that time. On February 25, Ben and Lula Coffey Jr. and other Memphis observers obtained good views of Ross' Goose. Jeff Wilson, and Judy and Dick Burkepile of Oxford last sighted 11 Ross' Geese with a flock of about 3500 Snow Geese on March 30, 1990.

[Brant] *Branta bernicla*

This small, dark, stockily built goose breeds in the high tundra regions of Canada and Alaska and winters along the Atlantic and Pacific Coasts. The eastern population (once named *B. b. hrota*) winters regularly on the Atlantic Coast as far south as North Carolina.

The first confirmed record of its occurrence in Mississippi is a sighting of an adult bird by Weber (1979a) on the east spit of East Ship Island in Harrison County on July 1, 1978. This bird was feeding along a shallow pond edge and was observed with a telescope. All field marks were observed and noted. The bird flew well, but was observed to have a limp while walking. Because Brants are not ordinarily raised as captive birds, this individual probably had been injured and was unable to migrate north.

On November 19, 1991, refuge manager Vic Theobald observed a Brant among the smaller race of Canada Geese on Sardis Waterfowl Refuge in Lafayette County. The bird was recognized by the black neck from the head onto the breast, a white neck mark, and silvery white sides and rear of the body. Identification was confirmed the same day by Gene and Shannon Knight. The bird was seen by others in December and January. Photographs on file at the MMNS by Theobald, W. Marvin Davis, and Jeff R. Wilson on January 19 confirmed this first inland record.

The eastern population has a *black head, neck,* and *breast.* Triangular white patches on the sides of the throat beneath the head, formed by three radiating white stripes and enclosed by a white stripe at the rear, *do not* meet at the front of the neck as in the western subspecies. The wings and

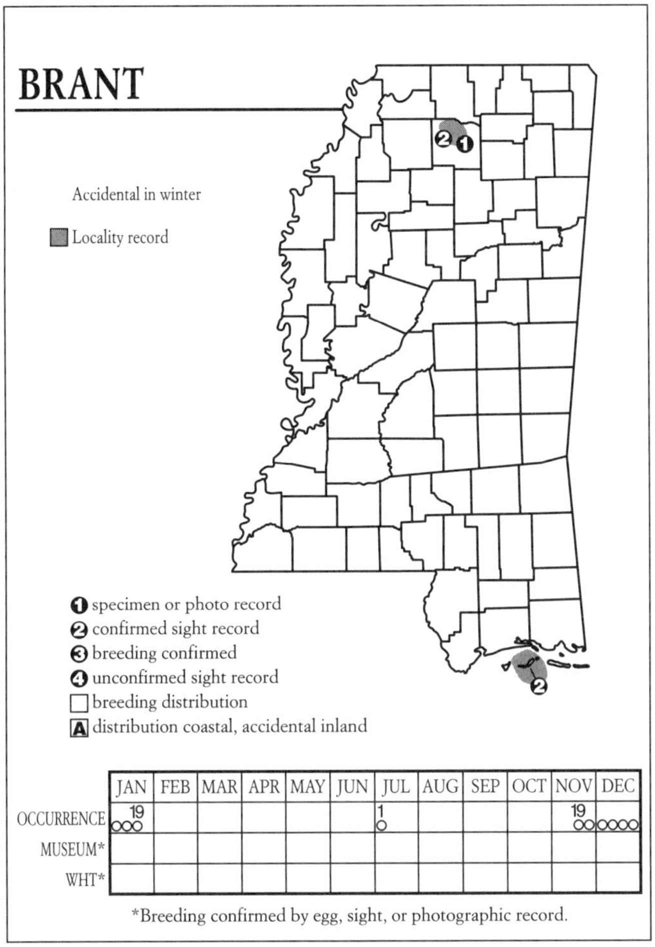

back are blackish in adults and brownish with light edgings to the secondaries and wing coverts in immatures, which may lack the white throat patches. The pale breast and sides of the eastern race are markedly different from the dark-bellied western population (formerly called the Black Brant). Tail coverts are all white and mostly obscure the black tail. Legs, feet, and bill are black.

Brant are mostly sea geese. They fly close to the water in strung-out lines with quick strokes of their long, pointed wings and with their short necks extended. They tip to feed on coastal aquatic plants in bays and estuaries. There are several Alabama and Louisiana records reported by Lowery Jr. (1974) and Imhof. The casual occurrence of Brant on the Gulf Coast during winter months and on the offshore islands, coastal bays, and estuary areas is probable.

Canada Goose *Branta canadensis*

The Canada Goose is a gray brown, plump-bodied, and long-necked bird with black feet, legs, and bill. The head and neck are black except for wide, white cheek patches that meet under the chin. Canadas travel in flocks of V-shaped wedges or wavy lines.

"Canadian honkers" were regular winter residents along the mud flats and sandbars of the Mississippi River until the late 1940s. The establishment of state and federal waterfowl refuges with extensive development and winter feeding operations in the upper portion of the Mississippi Flyway has short-stopped most of the Canada Goose population. Only one flock of several thousand birds regularly winters in Mississippi on the Upper Sardis Wildlife Management Area on Sardis Reservoir.

Small flocks are regular winter visitors to Noxubee and Yazoo National Wildlife Refuges, which also have small, "captive" or nonmigratory breeding flocks of penned or free-flying birds. The state-owned Malmaison Wildlife Management Area in western Grenada County and Sardis Waterfowl Refuge on Sardis Reservoir also have had small, captive breeding flocks. Another captive flock on the Pearl River Waterfowl Refuge on Ross Barnett Reservoir is expanding each year. Fifty to 75 young have been raised in each of several recent years by this nonmigratory flock.

Fall flights of Canadas appear on Sardis Reservoir in late October. The first contingent of about 200 birds is part of the Tennessee Valley population of an interior race of geese that breeds in the muskeg bogs extending eastward from

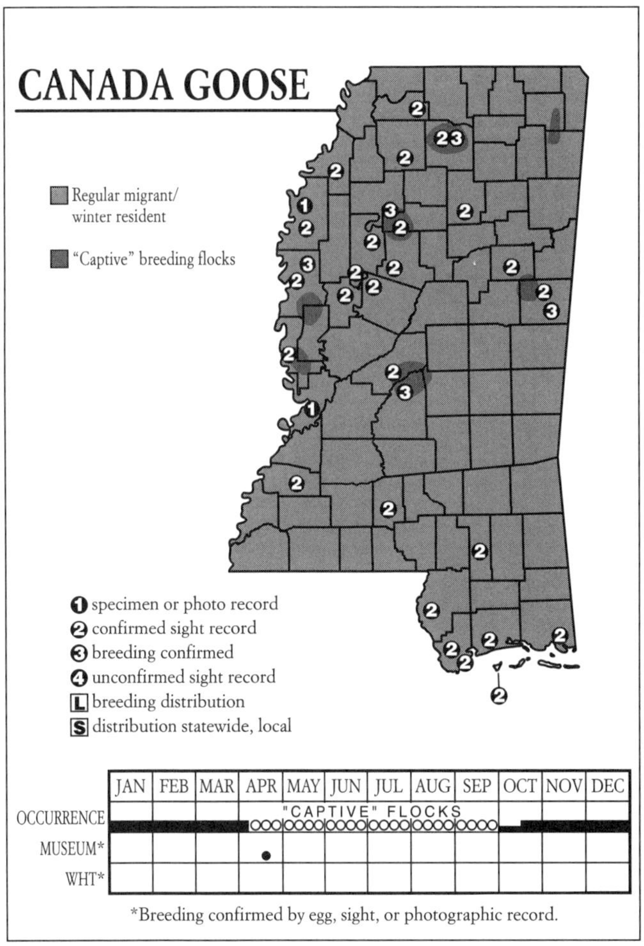

the eastern coast of St. James Bay. The larger contingent of the Sardis Lake goose flock is composed of the "giant race" of Canadas. Arrival of these large geese extends over a longer period through November, with the population usually peaking in late December. This giant Canada population on Sardis Reservoir comes from the Great Lakes region and the Midwest. Important staging areas during migration are in refuges in Ontario, Michigan, Ohio, and Tennessee. Small groups of up to 50 small geese, presumably the mallard-sized Richardson's Goose *(B. c. hutchinsi)*, regularly visit Sardis Refuge. These diminutive Canadas remain apart from the larger birds.

The vast breeding range of the Canada Goose extends across the northern United States to northern Alaska and Canada. There are 11 recognized subspecies differing greatly in size and slightly in color. The differences in subspecies are primarily due to ecological or geographical isolation on their breeding grounds. The larger races of geese have calls that are longer and lower in pitch, and the smaller races have yelping or cackling, high-pitched calls. The different geographical populations have discrete migration corridors and wintering grounds. Some populations mingle together on staging and wintering areas.

The management of the Atlantic, Mississippi, and Central Flyway Canada Goose flocks during the past several decades has met with spectacular results. Goose populations have increased in all three flyways due to the many carefully managed refuges under state and federal control. These refuges maintain wintering habitat to provide an adequate food supply for birds. A carefully regulated and controlled harvest insures that adequate numbers of mature birds in good breeding condition are carried over each year to return to their nesting grounds.

Canada Geese nest in a great diversity of situations, but usually close to water. They nest in marshes, abandoned nests of large birds, muskeg, and on islands, tundra, cliffs, man-made platforms, haystacks, and ditch banks or dikes. Their nest is situated to provide the incubating bird with an open view.

The nest is a scrape to which vegetation from the surrounding area is added to form a rim. Down plucked from the breast is added for lining as the eggs are laid. Clutch sizes range from four to seven creamy white eggs. The female incubates her eggs and broods her young, while the male stands guard nearby. Both parents escort their young when they are ready to leave the nest.

RUDDY SHELDUCK

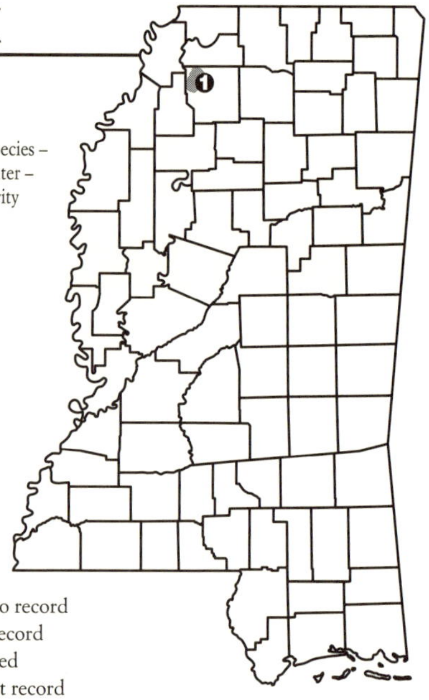

Accidental Eurasian species – specimen taken by hunter – no signs of prior captivity

■ Locality record

❶ specimen or photo record
❷ confirmed sight record
❸ breeding confirmed
❹ unconfirmed sight record
□ breeding distribution
[A] distribution statewide

	JAN	FEB	MAR	APR	MAY	JUN	JUL	AUG	SEP	OCT	NOV	DEC
OCCURRENCE	8 ○											
MUSEUM*												
WHT*												

*Breeding confirmed by egg, sight, or photographic record.

[Ruddy Shelduck] *Tadorna ferruginea*

This Afro-Eurasian species is kept in zoos and private waterfowl collections. It is large and somewhat gooselike, distinguished by orange chestnut plumage, pale head, small blackish bill, black tail, and black wing feathers with a green speculum. The male has a narrow neck ring absent on the female, which has a nearly white head. In flight, the conspicuous white wing coverts are also diagnostic. The calls are gooselike, described as *ah-onk*.

A male Ruddy Shelduck shot on January 8, 1989, by James Simmerman on Nelson Creek in Panola County about four miles above Sardis Lake dam was identified by Paul Lago, confirmed and reported by Davis (1990). This specimen showed no signs of captivity, was healthy, and apparently living in a feral state when shot over decoys after circling twice. It is the first state record for the species. Photographs taken of the specimen before mounting are deposited in the MMNS and the Department of Biological Sciences at MSU.

The Ruddy Shelduck has been recorded casually in Greenland, and several occurrences have been reported in the interior of North America.

Anatinae (Ducks)

Wood Duck *Aix sponsa*

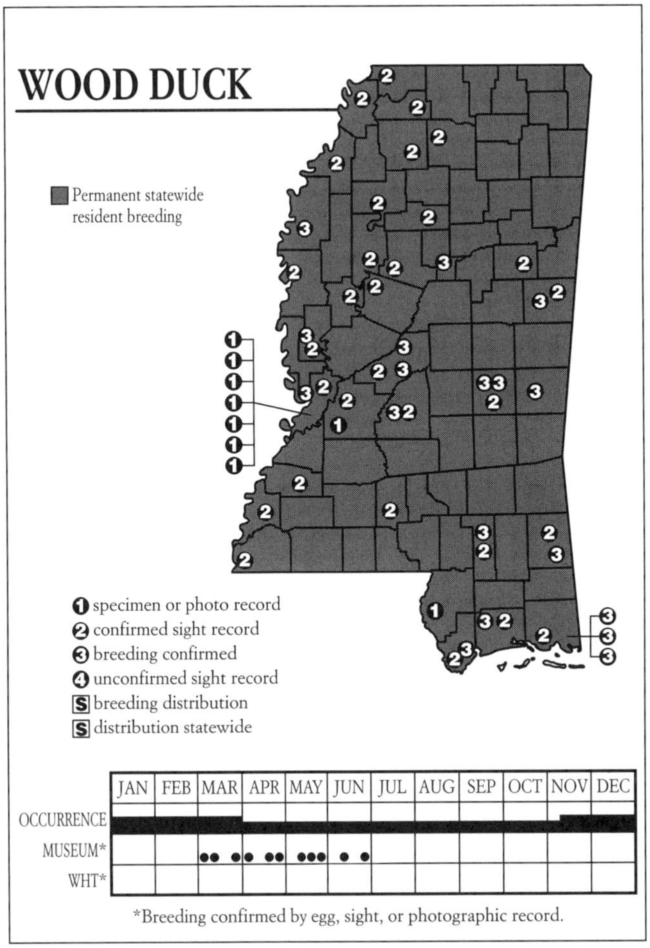

Mrs. William W. Waller was instrumental in supporting the introduction and passage of a 1974 law that designated this beautiful duck as the official state waterfowl. The first state duck stamp issued in 1975 featured a color photograph of the Wood Duck taken by the late Dr. Carroll J. Perkins of Starkville. To me, the "woodie," also known as "squealer" and "summer duck," is the most beautiful of North American wildfowl.

The drake has the sides of its crested head marked with lustrous, metallic shades of burgundy and green. The top of the head is iridescent green. The back is arrayed in green, purple, and bronze. These colors vary with changes in light intensity and direction or by the bird's movements.

Adult and immature males have *two distinctive white prongs* extending upward from the white chin and throat. The bill of the adult male is black on the tip and ridge, white on the side, red at the base, with a narrow, yellow border next to the feathers. Two prominent white stripes extend above and behind the red eye to the back of the crest. The gold sides are vermiculated with fine, black lines and bordered on the upward side by black-and-white-tipped feathers, which appear as a white line against the darker upperparts. The breast is dark burgundy with white flocking, bordered by the white belly and wide white and black stripes separating the gold sides below the point of the wing. The flanks are also burgundy red with narrow, tawny and black, plumelike feathers bordering and overhanging the dorsal side of the flank feathers. At a distance in flight, the spread wings appear dark above and below. A close view reveals steel blue secondaries bordered with white.

The female "woodie," although more colorful than hens of most other dabblers, is drab brown and gray on the head and body, with iridescent greenish gloss on the crest and back. The belly, chin, throat, and undertail coverts are white. A distinctive *tear-drop-shaped, white patch surrounds the brown eye* and extends backward to the crest. Immature males resemble adult females but display white face marks suggestive of the adult male. Immature females may or may not have white eye rings. In eclipse plumage, males resemble female but have much more white on the throat, and they retain the red iris and red base of the bill.

The widespread and successful use of predator-proof Wood Duck nest boxes on state and federal waterfowl management areas has resulted in complete utilization of the boxes and increased brood production.

Wood Ducks are recognized in flight by the short neck; long, dark, square tail; and a white belly contrasting sharply with dark wings and tail. The bill is carried pointing downward at a sharp angle. The head is held above the level of the back and is often moved from side to side. The female often calls on the water and in flight with a loud *wee-e-e-e-t*. The male has a barely audible call like the high-pitched, whining *tweee, tweee* of a goldfinch.

Wood Ducks are resident breeding birds found statewide. The resident population is supplemented by large numbers of wintering birds that arrive from northern areas by early November. These ducks are inhabitants of rivers, creeks, floodplains, lakes, or sloughs, wooded and shrub swamps, and beaver ponds. Except when nesting, they usually occur in small flocks.

Their flight is moderately fast. On feeding and roosting flights, they travel swiftly, directly, and well above gun range. In timber, they are remarkably agile, twisting and turning their way through tree trunks and branches. They are usually "acorn fat," respond to calls and decoys, and have exceptionally good eyesight. They are clever, wary, and quick to avoid danger.

Hunting Wood Ducks is best in the backwaters of flooded bottomland hardwoods with an abundance of acorns in shallow water areas. The "stump" or "pass" shooter takes them without use of decoys by selecting suitable terrain used as regular passageways. The "roost shooter" is an abominable violator, despised by law-abiding hunters and wildlife conservation officers, who resorts to shooting birds flying into communal roosts at the edge of night. Roost shooting after sunset is unlawful and results in a wanton waste of birds that cannot be retrieved after dark. Wood Ducks are highly regarded as table fare.

Wood Ducks feed on a variety of vegetation and seeds of aquatic plants. A small portion of their diet consists of small animals that live in the aquatic environment. Wild fruits, including grape, mulberry, and swamp privet are consumed when available. However, acorns are this duck's important food. They seek acorns in flooded oak flats or along the banks of streams or sloughs bordered by oaks. Water, willow, and Nuttall oak acorns are swallowed whole. I once found a dozen of the large, striped Nuttall oak acorns in the gullet of a Wood Duck killed on Delta National Forest. Others commonly held five or six acorns.

A large feeding flight of woodies is a fascinating sight. On Twelvemile Lake, an oxbow lake in Yazoo County, I once watched a late afternoon flight of several hundred birds come in during the open duck season to a bordering ridge to feed on willow and water oak acorns. As I stood beside a stump at the water's edge, a small flock landed in open water and swam to the bank. Other flocks followed, and soon the air above was filled with flocks that spiraled downward to land at the same spot. They moved rapidly to the lake shore and up the bank to the ridge top, until the ground was covered with birds scrambling and flying over each other as they fed. Other incoming birds began to land and feed in the trees. The ducks on the ground began to leave first and as they left, those in the trees followed. The entire feeding flight lasted only about 10 minutes.

Wood Ducks also feed on agricultural crops, especially corn and soybeans. I saw a late afternoon flight just west of Holly Bluff in Yazoo County at a soybean and corn field adjacent to Big Sunflower River. Homer L. Tackett and I were driving toward Holly Bluff when we saw a flock of woodies land on a pocket of water in a harvested bean field adjoining a harvested corn field. In the distance, we saw other flocks approaching in a continuous stream. They landed on the water and within a few minutes several hundred were on the ground feeding in a "skirmish line."

They moved into the corn field and as the line of birds advanced those left behind would fly ahead of the line. Within about 10 minutes, small flocks began leaving the field, and eventually all flew to the Big Sunflower River. As they left, some birds still had streamers of corn leaves stuck to their muddy feet. After about five minutes on the river, they began to leave in small flocks. All of them flew in the direction from which they had come.

In late winter, communal roosting occurs. Roosting flights begin after sunset and hundreds or even thousands of woodies may return to a common roosting site. Remote wooded or shrub swamps and large beaver ponds with an abundance of thick brush are preferred roosting areas.

Pairing begins in late fall and continues through winter. The male usually follows the hen in flight. Females begin searching for natural tree cavities by late January with nesting beginning in early February. Broods begin hatching in late March and early April. Peak nesting occurs around mid-April. Nest starts and renesting continue into June.

The nest consists of litter in the cavity arranged into a cup. As egg laying progresses, down is added to the nest to form a thick covering for the eggs. The litter or down covering is moved aside while eggs are being laid and during incubation. Eggs are covered over before the adult leaves the nest.

Twelve to 15 white eggs are laid, but several females may lay in one nest, a practice called "dump-nesting." These dump-nests may contain 30 or more eggs and may be incubated successfully by one or rarely two hens. Sometimes dump-nests are not incubated.

Predator-proof wood or metal nest boxes are accepted readily by woodies. Many of these structures have been placed on state and federal refuges and management areas. When properly installed near suitable brood habitat, utilization has been highly successful.

In a protected wood box utilization study conducted by Lon Strong Jr., 1747 box occupancies of 2475 boxes available to Wood Ducks (68 percent) hatched broods. Strong Jr. found that Hooded Mergansers utilized some artificial nest boxes at most of the localities studied in Mississippi during the 1969–1971 nesting seasons (Strong 1972).

The female broods her young for about 24 hours after hatching. At a signal call from the hen, the ducklings leave the nest cavity. They jump or climb to the entrance, and jump out onto the ground or water below without injury. The hen then leads them in single file to the nearest brood habitat.

This important game bird responds well to management. Populations once near depletion are now capable of supporting regular limited harvests. In recent years, hunters have been allowed two woodies in the daily bag limit. With continued management and concern for the protection of essential bottomland hardwood habitat, the Wood Duck is capable of maintaining huntable populations.

Green-winged Teal *Anas crecca*

The Green-winged Teal is the smallest of the surface-feeding ducks. Its pigeon-sized appearance is conspicuous when compared to other surface-feeding ducks seen at the same time. Green-wings fly in compact, close-order flocks with fast wingbeats, twisting and turning in unison, alternately flashing their white bellies and dark upperparts. The flashing white underparts distinguish flocks of Green-wings from the Blue-winged Teal, which has a brown belly. Also, Green-wings occur in larger flocks than other teals.

In good view, the drake has a cinnamon brown head and a prominent green eye stripe. The breast is pinkish brown with small, black speckles. The sides, flanks, and back are vermiculated gray with a *vertical white stripe in front of the wing*. The metallic green speculum is edged with black on the sides, and white or buff stripes border the forward and hind edges. The outer undertail coverts are buffy and contrast sharply with the dark tail and central black undertail coverts. The bill is black and the feet and legs are gray. Females are mottled brown and difficult to distinguish from the female Blue-wing on the water. In flight, the hen Green-wing shows a light belly and dark wings with a green speculum. The slightly larger female Blue-winged Teal has a dark belly, shows a patch of chalky blue on the forward edge of the wing, and has a larger bill.

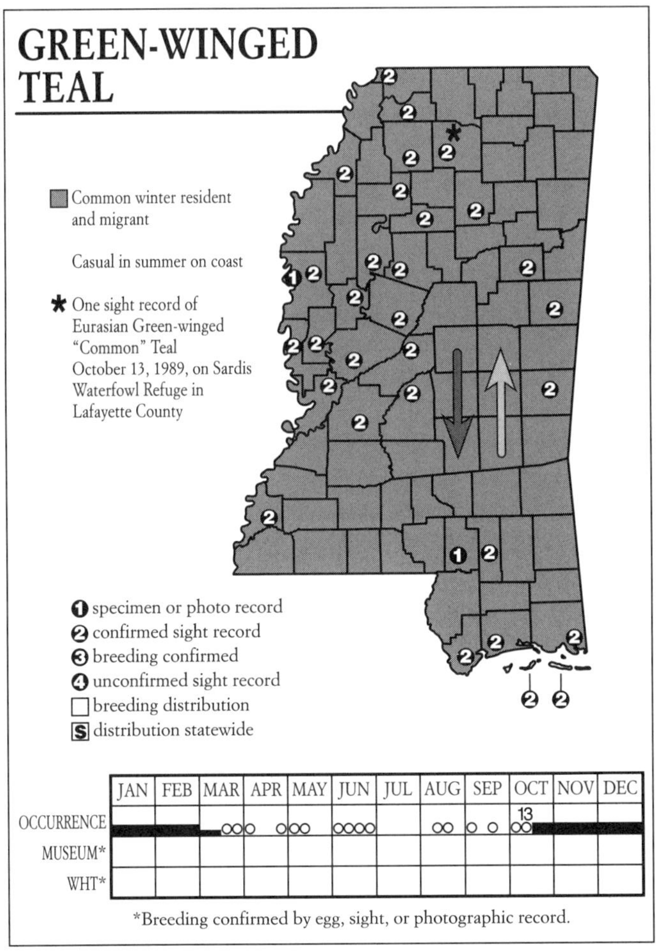

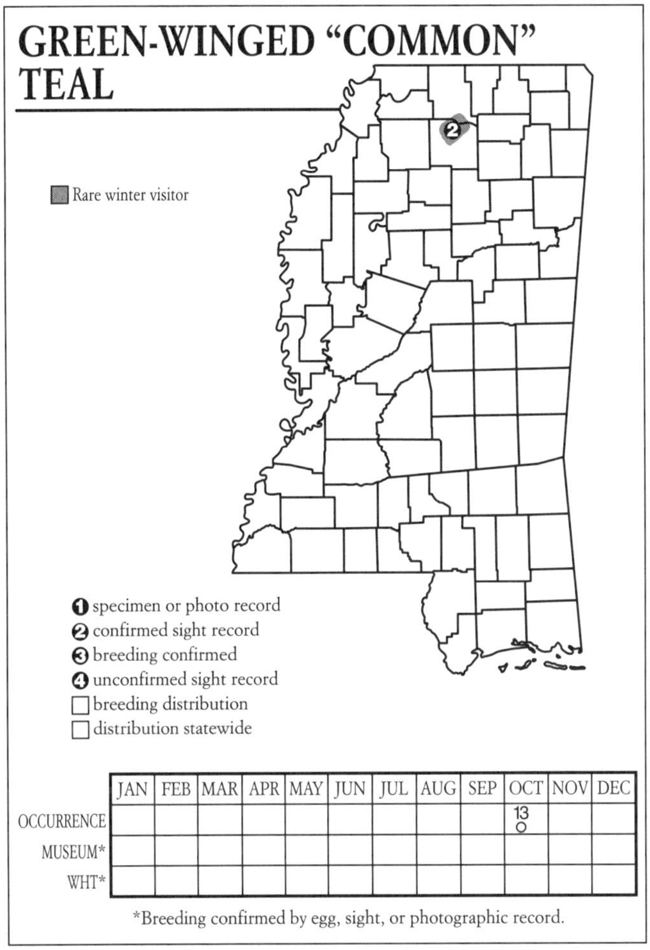

The Eurasian Green-winged Common Teal (subspecies *nimia*) and *A. crecca* were formerly considered separate species. The Eurasian male *lacks the vertical white bar* in front of the wing and has a *white stripe along the scapulars*. Females are indistinguishable from American Green-winged females. Eurasian Green-wings are rare visitors to Alaska and along the East and West Coasts. Inland occurrences may be escapes from captivity. The first state record in Mississippi was a Eurasian male seen October 13, 1989, at Sardis Waterfowl Refuge in Lafayette County by Gene Knight and Vic Theobald (Schiefer 1990).

The Green-winged Teal is a fairly common, statewide migrant and winter resident. It arrives early in September and remains until April or May. Most of the early fall flights pass through on their way to coastal marshes. The largest segment of the Mississippi Flyway population winters in the rice fields and coastal marshes of Louisiana and Texas, and the warmer regions of Mexico, Central America, and South America.

This duck is winter hardy, however, and enough birds remain on inland and coastal waterfowl areas during the duck season to afford Mississippi hunters a significant harvest. The species ranks fifth among dabbling ducks bagged by state hunters in recent years. Green-wings comprise a very small percentage of the special September teal season harvest allowed in recent years. This special season gives hunters a chance to hunt Blue-winged Teal during their early fall southward flight, which occurs long before the regular duck season opens in Mississippi.

American Black Duck *Anas rubripes*

The Black Duck is a regular winter resident of Mississippi, occurring only in small numbers and often seen among flocks of Mallards. In the Atlantic Flyway, the American Black Duck is the most abundant dabbling duck, especially in marshes along the Atlantic Coast.

The breeding range of this duck extends across the northern tier of states west to the Mississippi River and in Canada north to the tundra through Ontario and northeastern Manitoba. Migration corridors and wintering areas extend across the lower Great Lakes region to the Atlantic Coast from the Canadian border to central Florida.

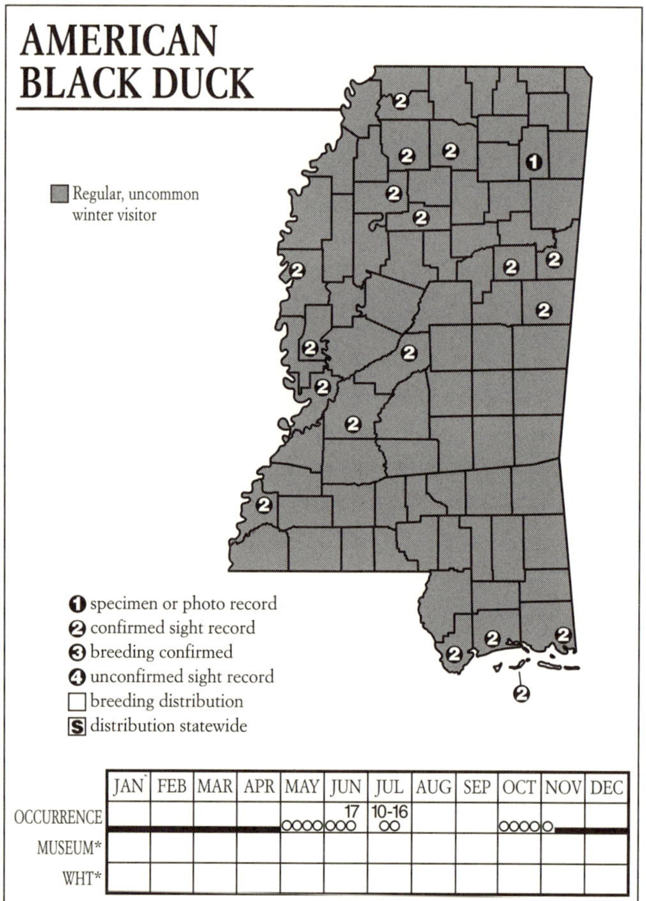

*Breeding confirmed by egg, sight, or photographic record.

Most of the eastern population winters between Long Island and North Carolina. The principal winter range in the interior states extends along the lower Great Lakes marshes and the larger river valleys of Ohio, Indiana, Michigan, and Illinois, south into the Tennessee River Valley. Only small numbers of American Black Ducks winter in the marshes along the northern Gulf Coast. They are most often seen on the lakes, reservoirs, flooded river bottoms, and soybean fields in the northern half of our state.

The sexes of the American Black Duck look similar. Sex can be determined by the bill. The drake has a bright yellow bill, and that of the female is olive green mottled with black. This duck can be identified in flight at a distance by its sooty brown body, which contrasts sharply with white underwings. Both sexes have a *purple* speculum bordered in black, and sometimes they have a faint white line on the back margin.

On the Mississippi Gulf Coast, this species is easily confused with the Mottled Duck. The latter has a much paler head, yellower bill, and a more pronounced white bar behind its *blue green* speculum. The Mallard hen has a *blue* speculum broadly bordered with two white stripes and is much lighter colored than the American Black Duck and Mottled Ducks.

American Black Ducks are wary birds and do not decoy or respond to the calls of hunters as readily as Mallards. They feed on the vegetation and seeds of many wild terrestrial and aquatic plants and cultivated grain crops. Molluscs, snails, amphibians, crustaceans, and insects make up much of its winter food. As a result, they usually do not taste as good as Mallards, which feed mainly on grain and mast crops or plant seeds.

In the last few years, the Black Duck has declined in population, causing concern among wildlife scientists. Although biologists admit that the decline in Black Duck numbers is not well understood, they do know that disturbance and loss of habitat from certain human activities are part of the problem. Many prime nesting and wintering grounds have been lost or are declining in quality.

Mallard–Black Duck hybrids are not uncommon. These hybrids have the general appearance of "black ducks" with dark body feathers, and drakes lack the white neck collar of the Mallard. Because these species readily interbreed, the result could be a loss of the pure genetic Black Duck strain. No one is sure if this interbreeding can be prevented. Some wildlife officials say that current levels of Black Duck harvest are not the major factor affecting this duck's population decline. However, in recent years the harvest of the Black Duck has been severely restricted.

Mottled Duck *Anas fulvigula*

This species is now a fairly common, permanent resident of our coastal marshes, where it is the only duck that breeds in appreciable numbers. Resembling the female Mallard and the American Black Duck, the Mottled Duck has a paler head, a *blue green* instead of *purple* speculum, and a broad, white bar on the back edge of the speculum. In contrast, the Black Duck has only a trace and sometimes no white on the back edge of wing. The female Mallard has two white wing bars and white outer-tail feathers, while the Mottled and Black Ducks have *no white* in the tail and much darker bodies.

Thomas D. Burleigh did not record the Mottled Duck during his observation and collecting activities on the Mississippi Gulf Coast between 1935 and 1943. He noted that American Black Ducks occurred frequently from November to late March on streams, bayous, and shallow salt waters of Mississippi Sound.

Sterling G. Clawson and Lovett E. Williams Jr. found the Mottled Duck fairly common in the marshes around Bayou Caddy in Hancock County, recording the first sighting there on July 9, 1960. They observed them at several other marshes in the county during July and August. In September 1960, flocks of six, five, and 23 were sighted near Lake Borgne at Clairborne, and two specimens were taken by Williams Jr. on September 9 (Gandy and Turcotte 1970). Three of these ducks were seen again on September 12.

Clawson and Williams Jr. searched for and observed Mottled Ducks in Hancock County marshes near Clairborne, Lakeshore, and Ansley in 1961 and 1962. A single abandoned fresh egg was found on a mud lump in a brackish marsh east of Clairborne on April 22, 1962. Subsequently on July 1, 1962, they flushed a female Mottled Duck from a nest containing seven eggs. A photograph was taken of the nest of marsh grasses and sedges lined with down. Later, after the nest was abandoned, the eggs were taken and deposited in the MMNS (Gandy and Turcotte 1970).

This nest and eggs of the Mottled Duck was discovered in a marsh near Lakeshore in Hancock County on March 7, 1962.

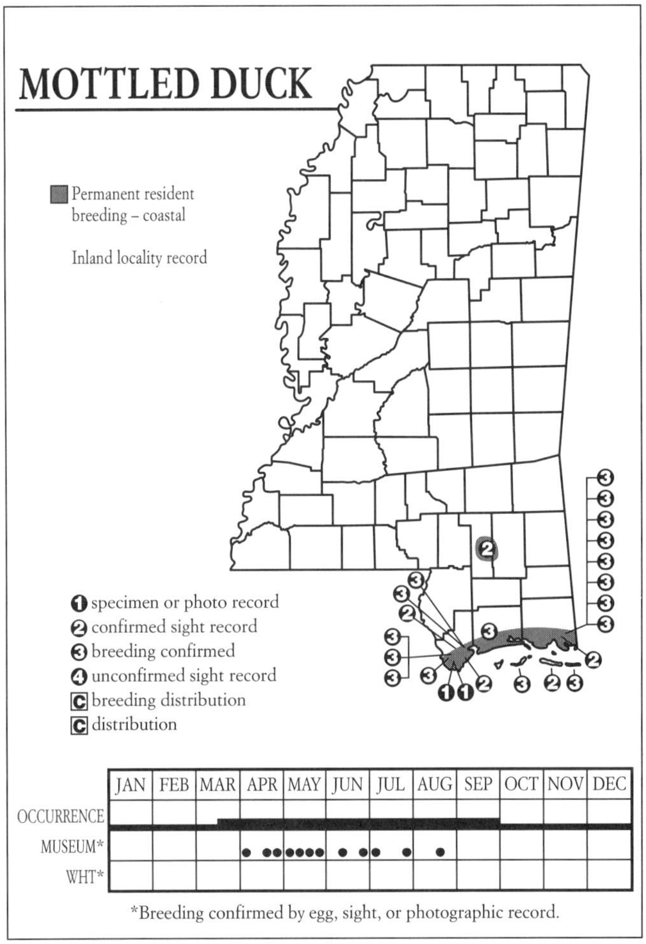

When reporting these breeding records, Williams Jr. observed, "The residents at Ansley, Clairborne, and Lakeshore are familiar with the 'French duck' and claim to see a few downy young each summer." A later breeding record was reported by George Chandler when, on August 16, 1971, during an alligator survey, he saw a female and four young about two-thirds grown that were spotlighted at Ansley marsh in Hancock County.

Courtney T. and Olga P. Hackney flushed a female from another nest on a marsh island at the western side of Bay St. Louis in Hancock County on April 4, 1975. On April 25, this nest contained only shell fragments. The species probably nests in other marsh areas around the Pascagoula River estuary, where it occurs regularly on shallow water ponds and bayous. A party of MOS observers saw several pairs at a shallow pond on the Pascagoula flats between the East and West Pascagoula Rivers in Jackson County on April 22, 1978.

The Mottled Duck feeds largely on animal matter and seeds of aquatic plants. Insects, snails, fish, crustaceans, and other invertebrates constitute over half the bird's diet. The seeds of wild millet, rice, bulrushes, pondweeds, and other aquatics make up the remainder of its food.

Mallard *Anas platyrhynchos*

This best-known, most abundant, and widespread member of the subfamily Anatinae, the dabbling or surface-feeding ducks, is a common, statewide winter resident. By far the most commonly hunted waterfowl species in the state, Mallards are the mainstay of the dedicated Mississippi duck hunter's sport. They outnumber all other ducks harvested in the Mississippi Flyway. Domes-ticated Mallards are commonly seen in parks and poultry yards. Wild Mallards occasionally nest in Mississippi, but nearly all the wintering population return to the main breeding grounds on northern prairies, marshes, and parklands.

The male is unmistakable with a dark purplish brown breast; narrow white collar; iridescent green head; white tail with black, curled, central feathers; yellowish bill; and orange or red feet and legs. The body is mostly gray. The violet blue speculum, bordered front and back by a pronounced white stripe, is distinctive in all plumages. The female Mallard is straw brown, streaked, and mottled with dark brown. The bill is dark with patches of orange. The white outer-tail feathers are splotched with brown and the underwings are white. The violet blue, white-bordered speculum is distinctive in flight.

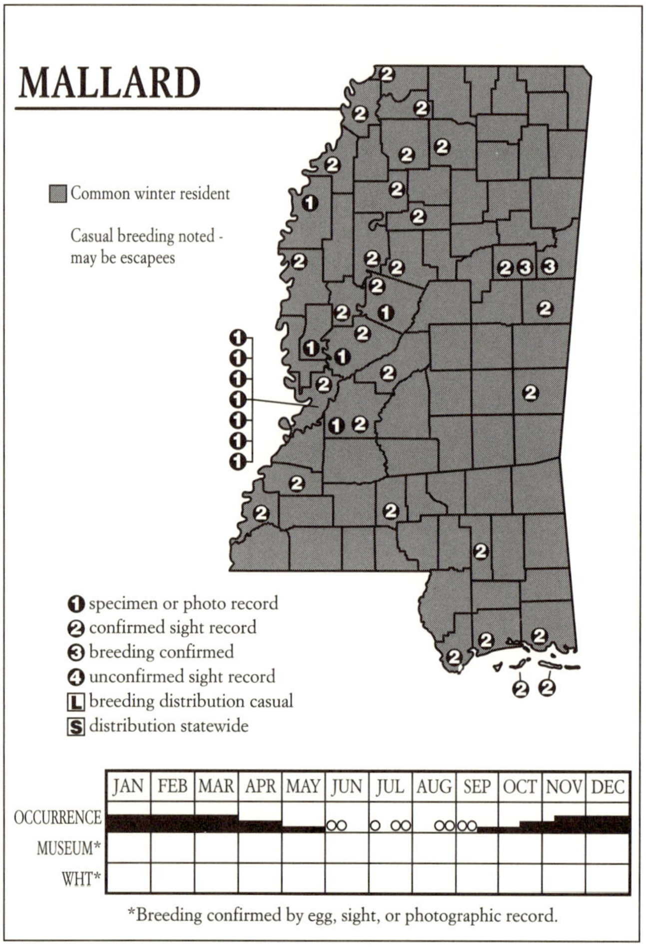

Mallard drakes are commonly known as "greenheads," and the hens are called "suzies" by hunters. Mallards respond well to decoys and duck calls. The species is highly adaptable to a variety of wintering habitats, and they utilize a larger variety of natural and agricultural food crops than any other duck.

In northern areas, they feed in wheat, barley, and corn fields. In the South, rice, soybeans, and sorghum grains are favored. Mallards frequent flooded bottomland hardwoods and are often found on wooded lakes and sloughs as well as marshes, ponds, and pockets of water standing over agricultural crops. Acorns are a prime attraction when flooding makes them available. The seeds of grasses, various sedges, smartweeds, and the seeds, leaves, and stems of many submerged and emergent aquatic plants are utilized.

Depending on weather and water conditions, Mallards usually appear gradually, and populations begin increasing through November and December, with a peak buildup in January. The largest populations occur when rivers and creeks overflow their banks and flood adjacent bottomland timber and agricultural crop lands. When those conditions exist after heavy winter rains, and prolonged subfreezing temperatures occur simultaneously in the northern states, we can expect an influx of Mallards. They are reluctant to leave abundant food supplies farther north until snow and ice conditions force them to move south.

One of the management practices on public and private waterfowl areas is the construction of "duck-motels" and "green-tree reservoirs." Sections of bottomlands and hardwoods, when leveed and flooded by diversion or water pumped during late fall and winter, are especially attractive to Mallards and Wood Ducks. These reservoirs provide resting and feeding places on state and federal refuges and controlled hunting on private and public hunting areas.

Northern Pintail *Anas acuta*

The Northern Pintail, or "sprig" as many hunters know it, is a slender-bodied duck with a long, slim neck. The male is white-breasted with a chocolate brown head and conspicuous white stripe on the sides of the neck and head. The upperparts and sides are vermiculated with gray, and the white flanks contrast with the black upper- and undertail coverts. Two long, needle-pointed, central tail feathers are about one-fourth the tail's total length. The bills of both sexes are blue gray, black along the central ridge in the male, and blotched with black in the female.

The hen is mottled brown with an elongated, wedge-shaped tail. The long, narrow wings are centered on long, slim bodies. The male's speculum is metallic green brown, bordered black with white on the hind edge, and a tawny brown stripe at the forward edge. The hen's speculum is

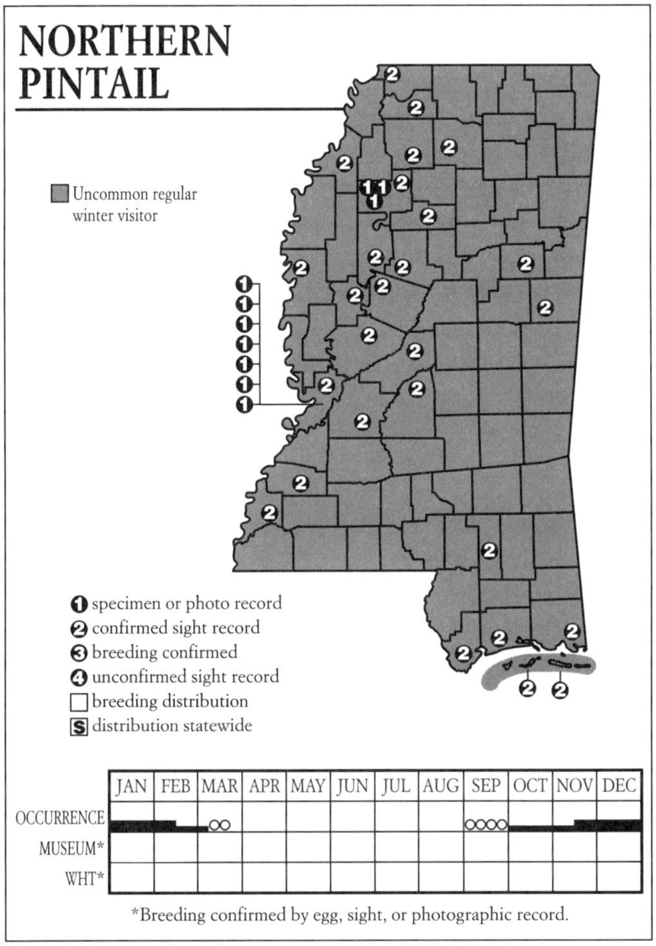

dull brown or greenish bronze, bordered on the hind edge with a white stripe. Both sexes have gray feet and legs. The flight of the Northern Pintail is swift and impressive.

This elegant duck is an early fall migrant and uncommon, late winter resident in Mississippi. Most of the early fall pintails in the Mississippi and Central Flyways fly on to Louisiana and Texas coastal marshes and wintering grounds in Mexico, while those farther west move into inland valleys of California. Even under favorable conditions, only small numbers of pintails overwinter in Mississippi on the reservoirs, Mississippi River areas, waterfowl refuges, and rice and soybean fields.

When late winter rains overflow river banks and flood low-lying soybean fields, pintails are likely to be present. They seem to prefer open water and flooded agricultural fields. They are suspicious and wary of hunters, who find them more difficult to work over decoys. A circling and whistling flock, high above the decoys and beyond gun range, is often the only reward these shy ducks afford the hunter.

Pintails are abundant in the Central and Pacific Flyways and common in the Mississippi and Atlantic Flyways. In most years, they constitute less than one or two percent of the total ducks harvested in Mississippi. Their breeding range extends to the Arctic regions of Alaska and Canada. In the United States, most of the pintail's breeding range is in the northern Great Plains, with smaller numbers nesting in marshes and river valleys of the western states.

Blue-winged Teal *Anas discors*

Blue-wings are common late summer and early fall migrants. They are abundant during the spring migration throughout Mississippi. A few individuals may overwinter on the Mississippi Gulf Coast.

The adult male Blue-winged Teal is easily recognized by the large, white crescent on the dark head and face, and white flank patch contrasting with its black tail. Both sexes have a pale blue patch on the forewing.

The female and immatures can be distinguished from immatures and female Green-winged Teal by the pale blue patch on the forewing. The wings of immature and female Green-wings are dark, except for a small green speculum. Females and juvenile males of the Cinnamon Teal and Blue-winged Teal are almost identical and cannot be separated reliably in the field. Both have similar pale blue wing patches. The female Northern Shoveler also has a pale blue patch on the forewing and is similar in color to the Blue-wing female and immature. The large, spoon-shaped bill and larger size of the Northern Shoveler identifies it in any plumage.

During the spring of 1963, St. Clair Thompson, left, and Jack Akins trapped and banded Blue-winged Teal on the Grenada Waterfowl Area.

The migratory behavior of the Blue-winged Teal differs markedly from other ducks. Large fall concentrations seldom occur on staging areas or breeding grounds. Their migration corridors are poorly defined. Most migrate southward well ahead of severe cold, and they are among the last ducks to return to spring breeding territories. They are widespread during migration and may occur in small flocks on small ponds, rain-filled ditches, borrow pits, or small pockets of standing water in fields.

The peak of spring passage through Mississippi occurs from about mid-March to mid-April, with the northward movement complete by mid-May. Nearly all Blue-wings are paired during spring migration and are easily identified by the dark-headed male with a crescent-shaped patch in front of the eye and a white flank patch.

Blue-wings winter farther south and in larger numbers than any other duck in North America. Most migrate to northern South America, and substantial numbers winter in Mexico and Central America. In recent years, Louisiana has recorded significant numbers wintering along the coastal marshes.

Because of the late date of the main duck season and early passage of these ducks, most Mississippi hunters never had a legal opportunity to hunt Blue-winged Teal. After several years of experiment and evaluation in the mid-1970s, federal regulations permitted state wildlife departments the option of selecting a special early teal season of not more than nine consecutive days in September. This special season provides additional recreation and opportunity for hunters to bag a limit of these sporty and tasty ducks.

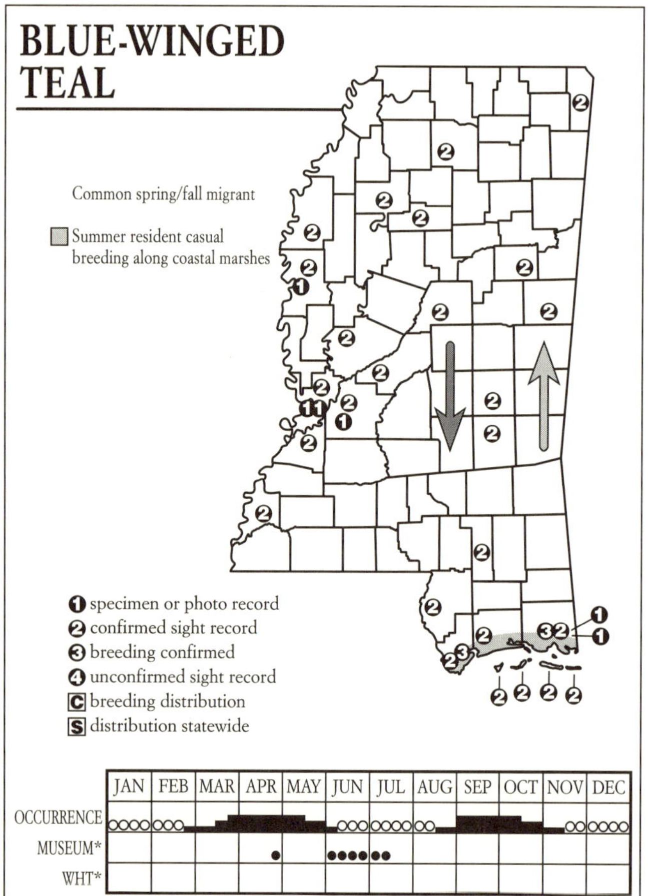

*Breeding confirmed by egg, sight, or photographic record.

Blue-wings begin arriving in Mississippi usually by the last week in August. The main flights arrive in September, and the special nine-day season usually is set to open on or after the second weekend of the month.

This species has been breeding regularly in the Louisiana marshes and rarely at scattered locations in Alabama. Recent observations on the Mississippi Coast by Wayne C. Weber, Judy Toups, and Robert P. Russell indicate casual breeding. They saw several Blue-wings at the Pascagoula River marsh in Jackson County throughout June 1977, with a maximum of 12 seen on June 19. Weber and Russell saw four birds in the same locality on July 30, 1977. On July 9, 1979, Judith A. Toups (Toups and Donaldson 1979) recorded an adult with six half-grown young at the Pascagoula River marsh. In April, 1984, a female and three young were observed at the Waveland Lagoon in Hancock County. These sightings confirmed breeding records for the Blue-winged Teal on the Mississippi Gulf Coast.

[Cinnamon Teal] *Anas cyanoptera*

This small duck, the western counterpart of the Blue-winged Teal, is found in similar habitats and is common within its main breeding range west of the Rocky Mountains. The duck's winter range is largely in Mexico and Central America. A few of these teals winter in coastal and southwest Texas and rarely in southwestern Louisiana. The species is casual east of the Mississippi River and is a recent addition to our state bird list.

Few Mississippi sight records of Cinnamon Teal have been reported. Ginger and G. E. Alexander Jr. (1973) observed and carefully studied an adult male and female in a small, shallow pond on September 23, 1973, at the Yazoo National Wildlife Refuge in Washington County. Another pair was observed by the Alexanders on February 25, 1978, at close range on the same pond. The male was in full plumage, and the female was indistinguishable from the female Blue-winged Teal present at the same time, but she never left the male's side. This pair was seen on several other occasions at close range until March 11, 1978. The observation was confirmed by a photograph taken March 1, 1978.

A male and two females were seen on December 1 and 19, 1979, at a roadside ditch on Bayou Cassotte in Hancock County (Jackson and Schardien 1980a). On April 6, 1995, Dale Adams, an area manager with the Department of Wild-

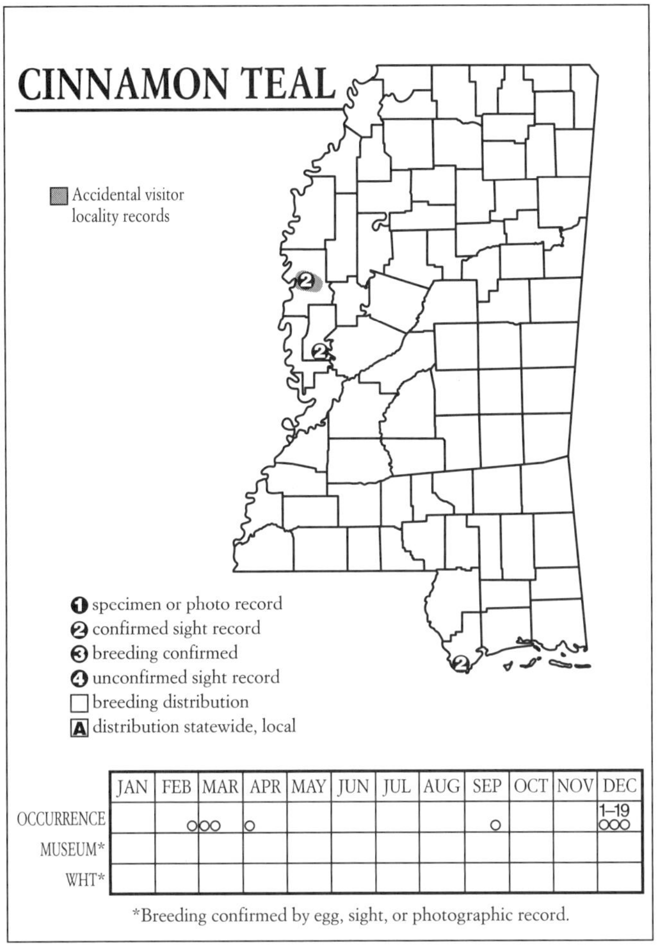

life, Fisheries and Parks, observed a single adult male on the beaver pond just north of the 706 road that extends through Delta National Forest. Any hunter who takes a Cinnamon Teal should freeze it and deliver the whole specimen to the MMNS for preservation as a specimen record.

The adult Cinnamon Teal drake in breeding plumage is cinnamon red on the head and body. The front part of the wing has a chalky blue patch bordered by a white stripe in front of the green speculum. The back, tail, rump, and uppertail coverts are brown. The undertail coverts and the bill are black. The feet and legs are yellow. Females and immatures are not distinguishable in the field from female and immature Blue-wings, though they can be recognized in the field by association with the colorful adult male.

Northern Shoveler *Anas clypeata*

Duck hunters regard the Northern Shoveler as a poor second to other dabblers. Because of its reputation as a bad-tasting duck, experienced hunters who happen to bag one will sometimes give it to an unsuspecting novice hunter or a neighbor. Hunters give the shoveler a variety of local names such as "spoonbill" or "smiling mallard" because of the large, spoon-shaped bill with its large "grinning patch" and superficial resemblance to the esteemed Mallard.

Shovelers in any plumage are easily recognized by the flat-headed profile and large spatulate bill, which is longer than the head and carried downward at an angle of 30° or more in flight or at rest. The drake in breeding plumage is a handsome bird with a black bill, dark green head, a white breast with chestnut belly and sides, and white on the flanks, tail, and sides of the back. The tail is white with opposing black on the upper- and undertail coverts. The wings have a bright, pale blue patch on the forewing bordered by a wide, white stripe forward of the wide, brilliant green speculum. Feet and legs are orange or reddish orange in both sexes. The female is drab, mottled brown with a whitish tail and resembles the hen Mallard, except for her smaller size, bluish gray wing patches, and the large bill.

Shovelers arrive in late September and October and remain as common winter residents throughout the state until April and early May. They appear to be most numerous in early spring when pair bonds are being formed and the hens are paired with or courted by one or more colorful drakes. At this time, courtship flights occur with one or more males in pursuit of the hen. The humpbacked appearance of these

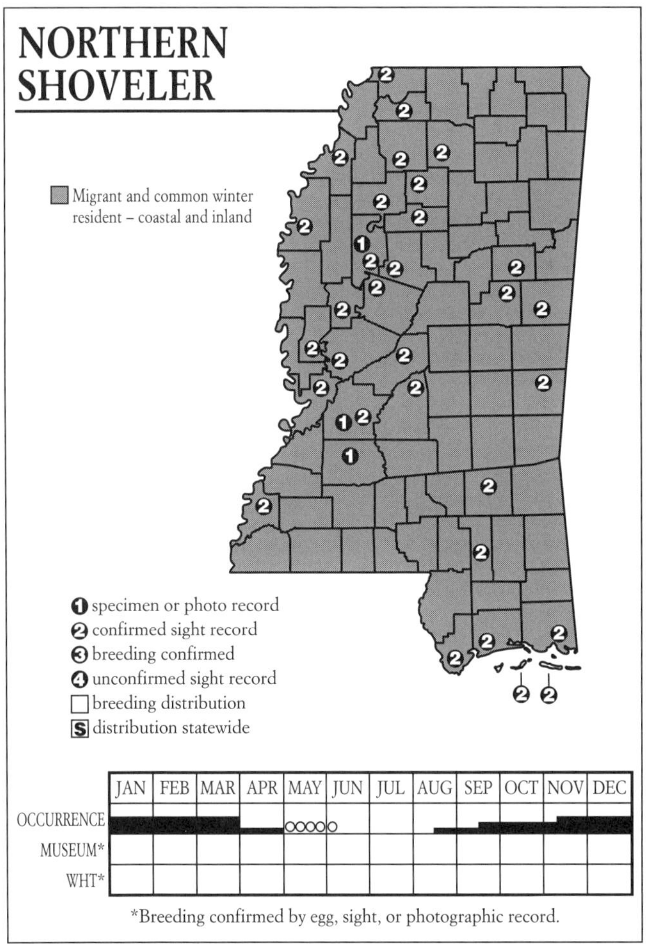

birds in flight is distinctive. Their courtship display while swimming low in the water and skimming the surface with their spoonlike bills is distinctive.

The Northern Shoveler is a dabbling duck and frequents the same habitat as other shallow-water ducks that tip up to feed. Their food consists of aquatic animals, more so than other puddle ducks, which accounts for their unsavory flesh. Shovelers skim the surface of the water with their oversize bills and strain out minute animal foods, or paddle through the water and mud of shallow ponds and shorelines for aquatic insects, snails, and other molluscs, small crustaceans, and the seeds and fleshy parts of aquatic plants.

Their call is similar to a weak-voiced Mallard hen. It consists of several short quacks, each progressively weaker and squeakier, with some low, clucking sounds.

Gadwall *Anas strepera*

After Mallards and Wood Ducks, the Gadwall, or "gray duck," ranks third in the number of puddle ducks harvested by Mississippi hunters. For tastiness, I rate the Wood Duck first, followed by the Mallard, Pintail, and Gadwall. Tastiness, however, depends upon condition of the bird and what they have been eating, as well as the expertise of the cook.

While on the water, the male Gadwall appears drab gray on the body and grayish brown on the head. The upper- and undertail coverts are jet black and provide the best field mark for identification. The female is mottled brown above with a *white speculum* that usually is visible while swimming. In flight, *both* sexes show a prominent *white speculum* on the hind edge of the wing and a reddish brown patch forward, a sharply defined white breast and belly, yellow feet, and ash brown in the spread tail feathers. The bill of the male is black, and the female's is dusky yellow and dotted with black on the lower margin.

The Gadwall ordinarily does not congregate or travel in large flocks. In recent years, it has become one of the more common dabblers in Mississippi from late October until early May. While feeding, Gadwalls mix with Mallards, pintails, wigeons, and Ring-necked Ducks. Its preferred winter habitat is shallow-water shorelines with submerged aquatic plants and filamentous algae. I have noticed the Gadwall often frequenting the edges of open water lakes, sloughs, and swamps fringed by willows with an abundance of standing or submerged dead timber.

The breeding grounds of this duck are largely in mixed prairies of the Dakotas, Montana, and the prairie provinces and parklands of Canada. Gadwalls also breed in the intermountain valleys and marshes of the western states. Isolated breeding locations extend eastward across the northern tier of states down to Virginia and North Carolina.

A large segment of the population winters in marshes

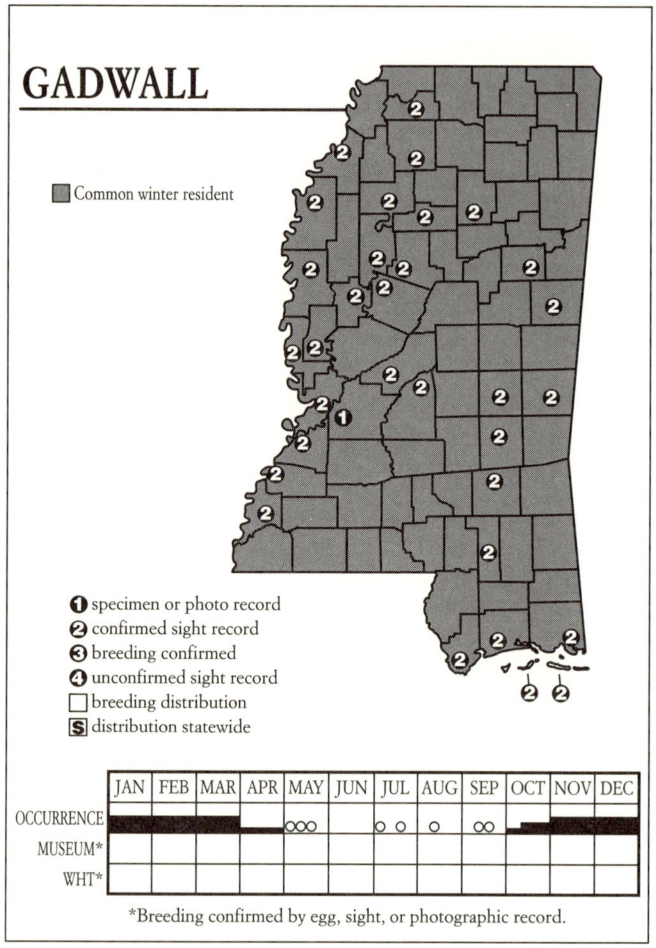

fringing the Gulf of Mexico from Mobile Bay westward through Louisiana, Texas, Mexico, and Yucatan. Smaller numbers winter on the East Coast. Out West, wintering areas are located in the interior of California and along the Pacific Coast and interior part of Mexico.

[Eurasian Wigeon] *Anas penelope*

The drake Eurasian Wigeon has a *buff or cream-colored (not white) forehead and crown* and a *brown head*. The vinaceous breast is sharply defined at the point where the folded wings meet the *gray sides* and *gray back*.

Both the Eurasian and American Wigeons can be recognized in flight by the large, white shoulder patches on their upperwings. The axillars of the Eurasian Wigeon are grayish, not white, as on the American Wigeon. The female Eurasian Wigeon has rufous coloring on the head and neck, but some gray-phase females can be distinguished only by the gray axillaries.

This species occurs regularly on the Atlantic and Pacific Coasts, but rarely inland. A male sighted on a pond in the Pascagoula River marsh on December 16, 1978, by Larry Gates (1979) is the first coastal record for Mississippi. Other

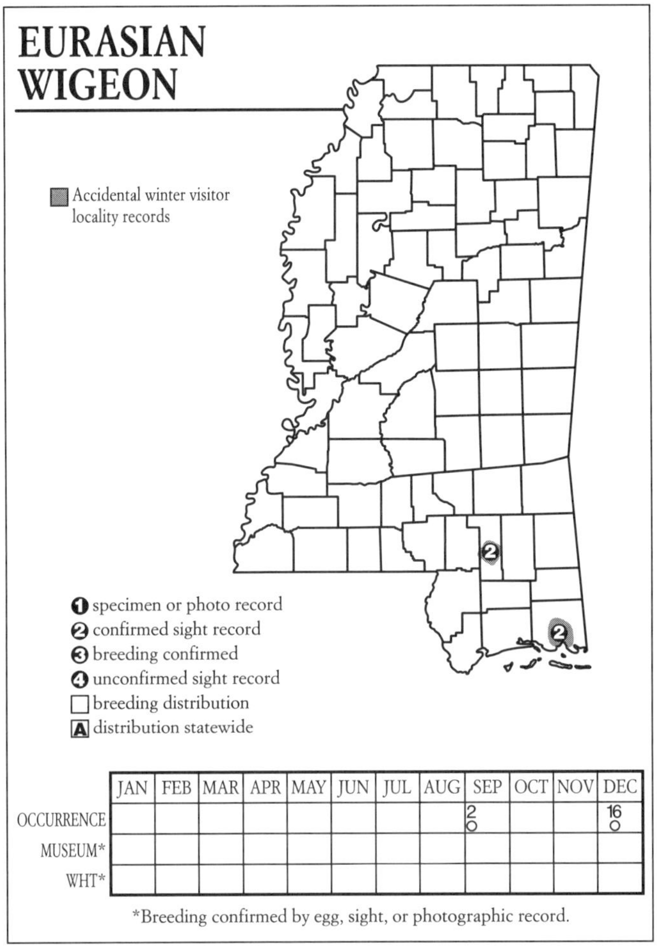

Gulf Coast records from Florida to Louisiana have been reported. Two pairs of Eurasian Wigeons were identified at the Hattiesburg sewage lagoons on September 2, 1980, by Terrie Fairley and David Hamilton (Jackson 1981c). Wigeon flocks should be observed carefully for probable occurrence of this species or hybrids. A bird seen by J. A. Toups and A. Duchein on the Jackson County Christmas Bird Count on December 16, 1978, was either a Eurasian or possibly a Eurasian-American hybrid (Weber 1979d).

American Wigeon *Anas americana*

The American Wigeon, a surface-feeding duck, is a common, statewide migrant and winter resident. The drake is known for its three distinctive, piping, whistling notes—*whee, whee, whew*—given at frequent intervals. The middle note is higher and the last note lower. The Northern Pintail has similar whistles, but briefer and more evenly pitched. The call of the female wigeon is a guttural *kaow, kaow.*

The drake wigeon is recognized by a broad white patch on its forewing bordered by a black stripe in front of its black speculum, which is tinged with a small amount of metallic green on the forward edge. The white crown is distinctive and gives this duck its name, "baldpate." A green band through the eye extends to the rear of its head and neck, which are buffy and streaked with black. The back and sides are pinkish brown mixed with black. The breast is plain pinkish brown. The white flanks contrast sharply with the black tail and tail coverts. Both sexes show an elliptical white belly in flight. The feet and legs are gray, and the wigeon's bill in all plumages is short, bluish, and tipped with black.

The female has a buffy head and neck streaked with black that appears gray at a distance. Her breast, sides, and back are reddish brown. The forepart of the wing is gray bordered by a white stripe forward of the black speculum, which is sometimes lightly tinged with green. Immature hens and drakes resemble the adult female.

American Wigeons fly in tight flocks without semblance of a V-formation. During the hunting season, they become "decoy shy." When attracted by decoys, wigeons are noted for circling high over decoys, making repeated feints again and again until the hunter becomes exasperated by this neck-twisting behavior.

The "baldpate" has also acquired the local name of "poacher," stemming from its habit of associating with coots and diving ducks and stealing bits of aquatic vegetation

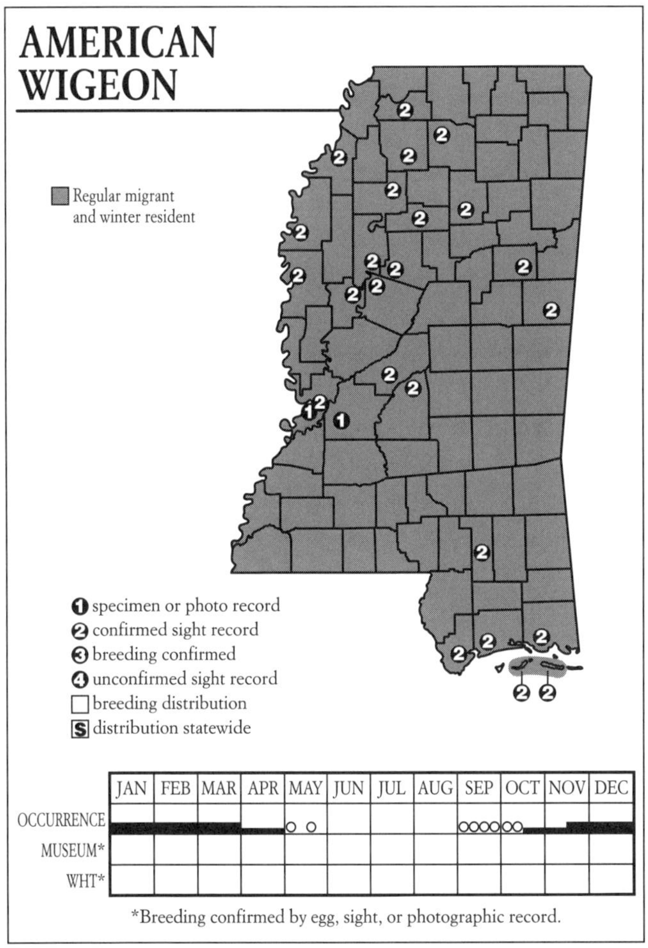

brought to the surface. Wigeons prefer to eat leaves and stems of aquatic plants and browse upon green grasses and clovers. The birds also mix with Mallards and other surface-feeders to feed upon waste grain in fields.

The American Wigeon breeds in the prairies, marshes, and parklands of northwestern North America. The breeding range extends to the coastal and inland tundra of northern Alaska and western Canada. The extensive winter range includes interior river valleys in Washington, Oregon, and California; marshes and tidal flats on the Atlantic Coast; and the coastal marshlands of Louisiana, Texas, and Mexico. Most wintering populations in the Mississippi Valley stay in southeastern Louisiana, eastern Arkansas, and western Tennessee. In Mississippi, flights of this species show up in October with peak numbers in December. Look for wigeons to depart from April to early May.

Aythyinae (Pochards and Allies)

Canvasback *Aythya valisineria*

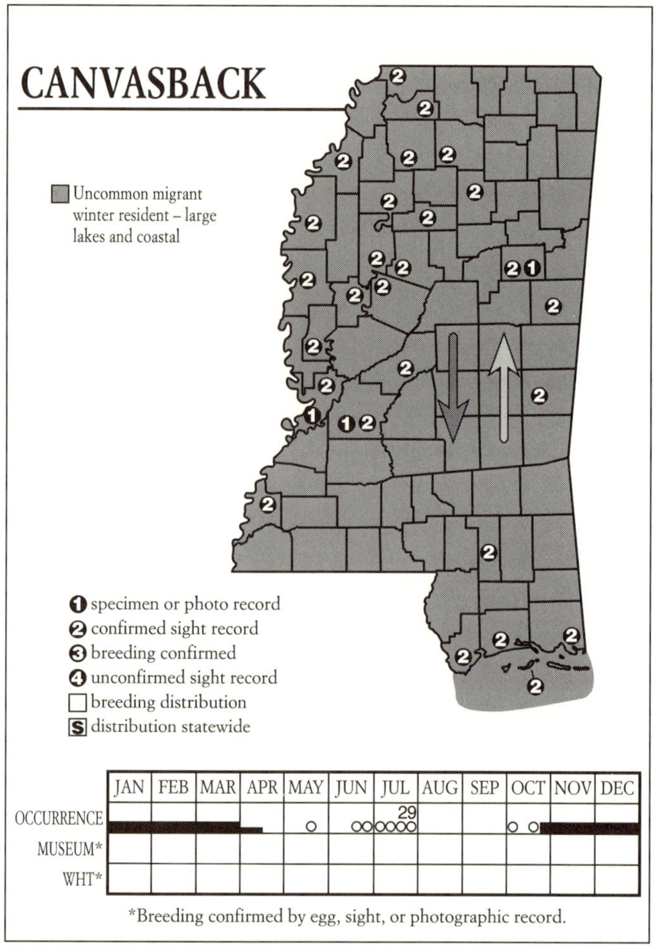

No other diving duck is more easily identifiable than the Canvasback. Their distinctive field mark is the wedge-shaped profile of the head, which slants gradually upward from the tip of the black bill to the crown. The rusty red head, white back and sides of the drake in nuptial plumage contrast sharply with its black breast and tail. In winter, the female is dull gray over most of her body and light brown on the head and neck, shading to darker brown on the breast and back.

"Cans" are the largest of the diving ducks and are prized by hunters because of their size, good taste, and the usual difficulties experienced in bagging them. In recent years, this highly esteemed duck has declined in numbers due partly to habitat destruction. Now, only one is permitted in the daily hunter bag.

Canvasbacks arrive in Mississippi during the last of October and usually depart by late April. They are regular late fall and winter residents on large inland lakes and reservoirs, usually in small rafts, but sometimes more than a thousand are seen on lakes. Concentrations also frequent the bays and estuaries along the Mississippi Gulf Coast.

A large part of Atlantic Flyway Canvasbacks spend the winter on Chesapeake Bay and in the sounds and large coastal rivers of Virginia and North Carolina. Their favored foods are pondweeds, wigeon grass, wild celery, delta duck potato, eelgrass, small shellfish, molluscs, snails, and insect larvae.

I have observed Canvasbacks on Ross Barnett Reservoir consistently rafting offshore in the same places each year with scaups and Ruddy Ducks. When feeding, Canvasbacks would tend to move inshore, where submerged and emergent aquatic plants occur in abundance. Windrows of uneaten portions of submerged plants were visible along the shoreline where these ducks fed.

Cans fly in wedge-shaped flocks or lines when traveling over long distances. The large expanse of white on their back, belly, and inner half of the wing, along with their rapid, deep wingbeats identify this species in flight.

Redhead *Aythya americana*

Redheads are deep divers and frequent deeper lakes, rivers, coastal estuaries, and open seas. They feed on aquatic plants, fish, shellfish, and molluscs. Their wing patches are generally dull gray or white and lack the iridescence of the speculums of puddle ducks.

When taking flight, most divers patter in a running fashion along the water to get airborne. Their wings are smaller in proportion to body size and weight, and their wingbeats are more rapid than those of puddle ducks. They sit low in the water and often congregate in large rafts on open water. They are clumsier on land than most dabbling ducks because their large feet and strong legs are set closer to the tail than dabblers, but they are better equipped for diving and swimming underwater.

The Redhead is an uncommon winter resident on our inland lakes. On the Mississippi Gulf Coast, it is common at times around the barrier islands in Mississippi Sound, and large rafts winter in Louisiana waters off the Chandeleur Islands. These ducks frequently associate with scaups and other diving ducks.

The Redhead drake has a large, round, rufous red head and upper neck; black lower neck and breast; vermiculated dark gray back and sides; white belly; and black tail and tail converts. The bill is blue gray with a black tip. At a distance on the water, the Redhead shows a sharp, upward angle between its blue bill and forehead when compared with the gently sloping profile of the Canvasback, which has a black bill. The back and sides of the Redhead drake are dark gray, while the adult male Canvasback has a white back.

The female Redhead has a rounded head, a plain bluish bill, a poorly defined whitish patch at the base of the bill with an abrupt angle between the forehead and bill. The hen is browner than the female Canvasback and lacks the prominent, white ring on the bill and white eye ring and cheek patch of the female Ring-necked Duck. In flight, the Redhead shows a broad, light gray band across the top of the dark gray wing. Scaups have white wing stripes.

Extreme dates of occurrence are October 16 and June 5. On April 27, 1962, a museum specimen was collected by Sterling G. Clawson at Lakeshore in Hancock County. This diving duck has been observed most frequently on inland waters during November, late February, and March.

Ring-necked Duck *Aythya collaris*

The Ring-necked Duck frequents open inland, wooded lakes and ponds, and feeds in water usually less than six feet deep. Seeds and vegetative parts of aquatic plants make up most of the winter food, but clams, snails, and insects are eaten in smaller quantities. Ring-necks travel in small flocks and fly in open formations with fast wingbeats. They dart and wheel about more like teals than diving ducks. The main flights appear in mid-November and some overwinter here. Spring departure begins in February and continues through March.

The drake Ring-necked Duck, commonly called "blackjack," is easily recognized at a distance by the black on the back, head, and breast, and a prominent *white inverted V-notch* at the point where the wing separates the black of the breast and the gray sides. The blue gray bill is black at the tip with two white rings, one across the top and one bordering the base. A faint chestnut collar around the neck and dull gray wing stripes are identifying field marks.

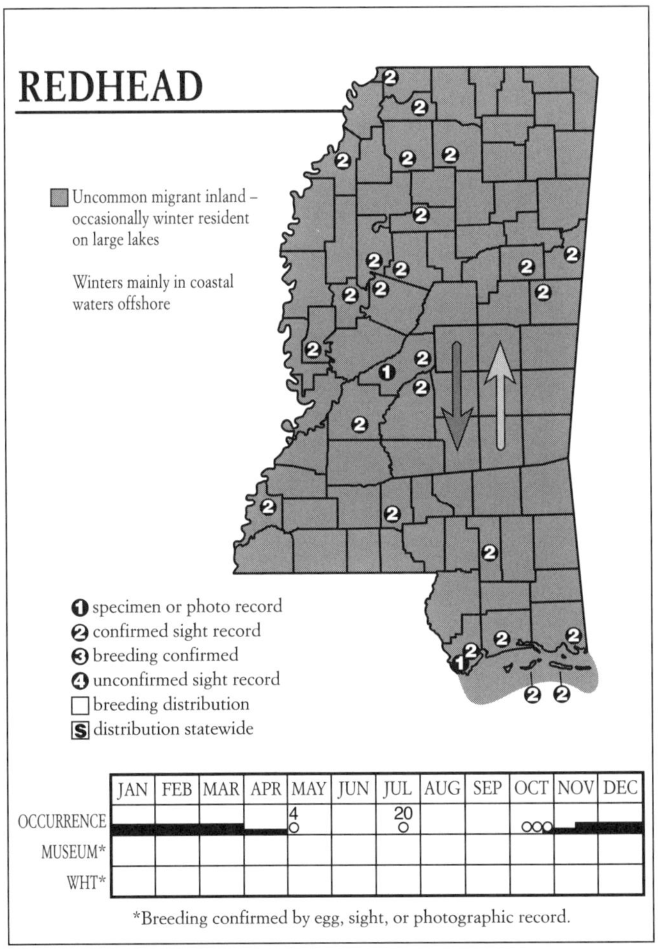

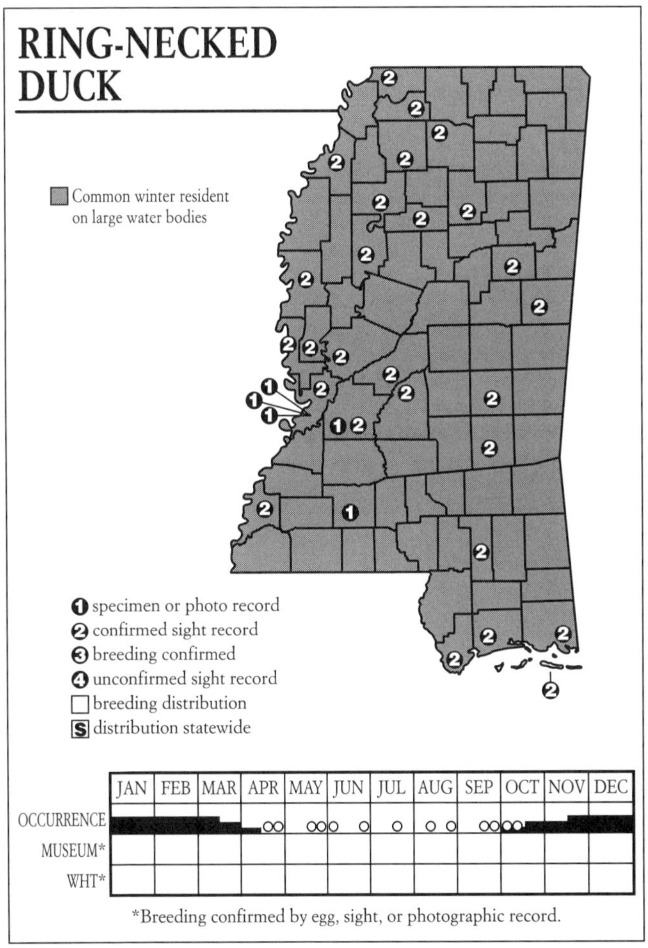

The female is dull brown and duskier on the crown and back, having *one* white ring across the top of the blue bill, a *white eye ring,* and an indistinct, light area around the bill that blends into the darker-colored head. Female scaups have a well-defined white patch bordering a solid blue bill. Female Redheads and female Ring-necks look much alike. The Redhead female is larger, lacks the white bill ring, and its face marks show little contrast. The drake Ring-neck has a slight, erectable crest that shows when the bird is alarmed or in courtship display. When raised, the crest gives the head a triangular shape.

Diving ducks make up about four percent of the average annual waterfowl harvest in Mississippi. The Ring-necked Duck affords inland hunters more hunting opportunity than any other diver. In coastal counties, the Lesser Scaup is harvested in greater numbers, and the harvest of Ring-necks is not significant. These birds decoy readily and often land without circling. They are generally fat during the hunting season and rate well on flavor as table food compared with some other divers.

Greater Scaup *Aythya marila*

This species is uncommon on coastal waters and rare on large, inland waters in Mississippi. Only one specimen is in the MMNS, a female taken by C. D. Turnipseed at Gulfport on May 24, 1940 (Gandy and Turcotte 1970).

Wing collection surveys made by the U.S. Fish and Wildlife Service and reported by M. F. Sorenson and S. M. Carney (1972) record a total of only 190 Greater Scaups taken by Mississippi hunters during open seasons from 1961 through 1970. Over the same period, the wings of 3457 Lesser Scaups were collected and voluntarily returned by Mississippi hunters. A total of 162 Greater Scaup wings came from the three coastal counties and the remainder from the Yazoo Delta counties. Sight records are scarce for this species, presumably because of difficulty in distinguishing it from the Lesser Scaup in the field.

In good light, the Greater Scaup drake shows a greenish gloss on the head. The head of the male Lesser Scaup has a purplish sheen. These colors vary with light incidence, and identification by head color alone is difficult or impossible. When both are seen together, size comparison is helpful, but this difference is slight.

The wings of the two scaups are different. An observer must wait for birds on the water to show the white wing stripes or see them in flight. The wing stripes of Lesser Scaups extend no more than half the length of the wing, whereas on the Greater Scaup the white stripes extend almost to the tip. Lesser Scaups often use marshes and ponds. The Greater Scaup prefers large, open bodies of water and apparently frequents salt water more often than the Lesser Scaup.

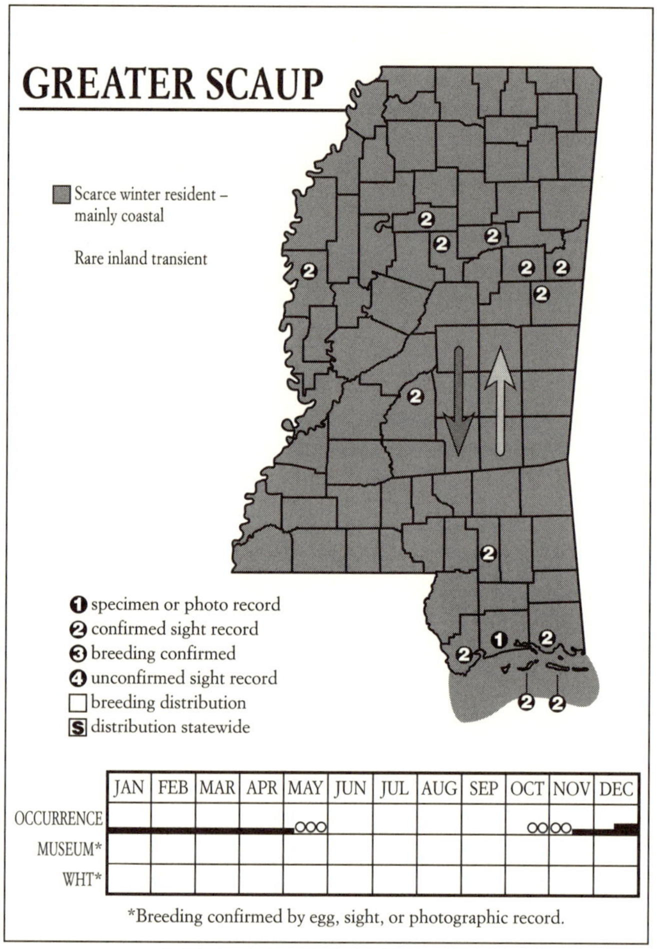

Commonly called "bluebills," males and females have solid blue bills with black nails. Except for differences of the white wing stripe, the two species appear almost identical in the field. Both have dark heads, black breast and tail, dark wings with white bands, white bellies, and salt-and-pepper backs and sides. In bright light on the water and at a distance, the back and sides appear almost pure white.

Lesser Scaup *Aythya affinis*

The Lesser Scaup, also known as "bluebill," is Mississippi's most abundant diving duck. It is a common, statewide, fall and winter resident arriving in numbers in early November. Even though most depart by early April, some flocks remain until late May. Single nonbreeders, probably crippled birds, may be seen on large bodies of water throughout the year. Lesser Scaups winter in rafts along the Mississippi coastline and on larger, open water, inland lakes. In late winter and early spring, small flocks commonly occur on smaller lakes, ponds, and sewage lagoons.

The Lesser Scaup is about the same size and color as the Ring-necked Duck. The distinctions between Lesser and Greater Scaups are mentioned in the preceding account.

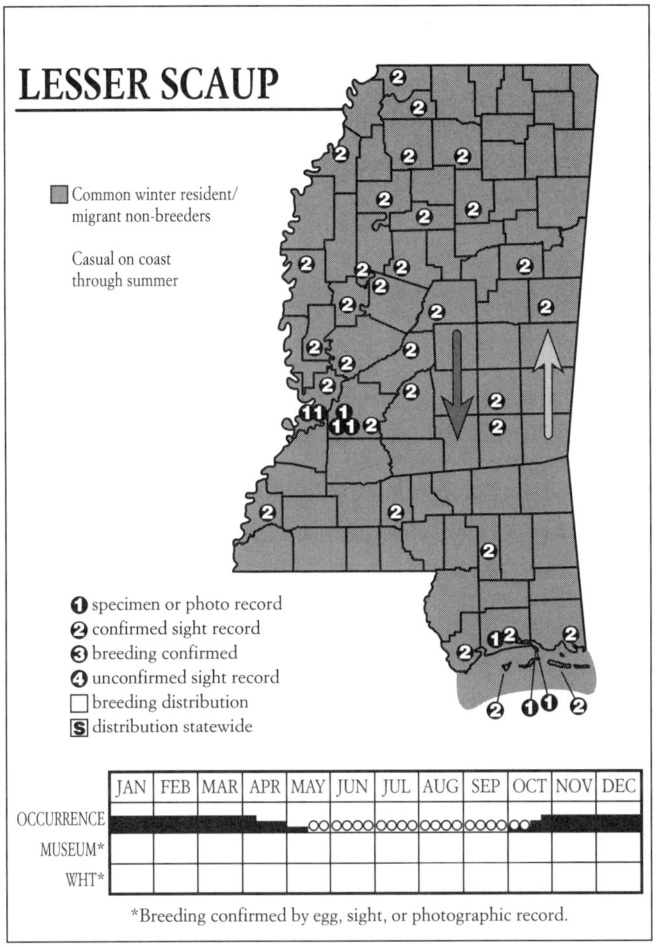

The scaups lack the white ring that Ring-necked Ducks have around the tip of their bill. The Ring-neck has a black back, and the scaups have a vermiculated gray back and sides that appear almost white.

Male scaups lack the prominent, white, inverted V-notch between the black breast, gray sides, and black back and wings of the drake Ring-neck. Female scaups have a distinct, white patch on the face. Female Ring-necked Ducks have narrow, white eye rings and the whitish area at the base of the bill is not sharply outlined, but blends gradually into the dark cheeks. Otherwise, female scaups and Ring-necks resemble each other in body coloration. In flight, male and female Ring-necked Ducks show gray wing stripes, whereas those of scaups are distinctly white.

[King Eider] *Somateria spectabilis*

The first specimen of this large sea duck was taken at Pascagoula in Jackson County on December 17, 1960, by L. M. Brister. He shot the bird while duck hunting and returned a wing in a collection envelope furnished by the annual Waterfowl Harvest Survey conducted by the U.S. Fish and Wildlife Service. Sam Carney, who conducted the harvest survey, referred some of the duck wings to the bird laboratory at the Patuxent Wildlife Research Center in Laurel, Maryland. Among them was the King Eider wing identified by Roxie C. Laybourne and Thomas D. Burleigh. The specimen now is in the duck-wing survey collection of the Fish and Wildlife Service at Patuxent (Gandy 1962d).

The only other King Eider record is a sighting of an immature male in Forrest County at the Hattiesburg sewage lagoons by Larry Gates (1975a) on November 10, 1974. This bird was with Lesser Scaups and American Coots. It was studied carefully through a telescope. A rough sketch with notes on identifying field marks and two identifiable photographs were forwarded to the Museum of Natural Science in Jackson to substantiate this sight record. To establish acceptable records of rare bird sightings, such careful procedures are recommended. In addition, field notes and sketches made by two other competent observers (without reference to field guide descriptions) make a new or rare state bird record more acceptable.

The King Eider has a short, stocky appearance and a sloping, heavily shielded, orange bill. The black back and white foreparts identify the adult male. Immature males in fall and winter plumage appear grayish brown with

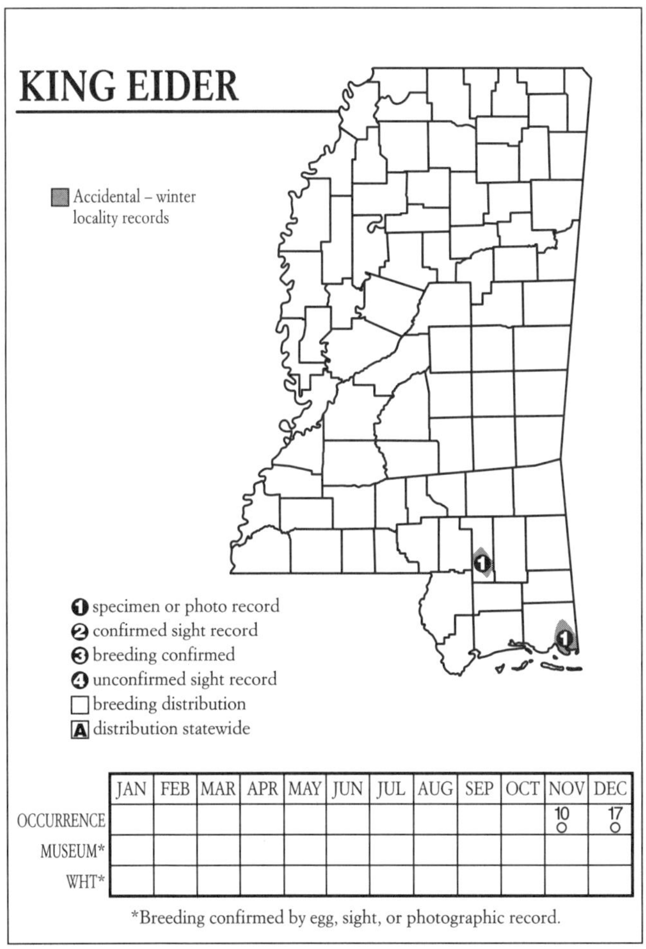

paler breasts and dusky brown heads. The females are tannish brown with darker brown, crescent-shaped marks on the body feathers, presenting an overall rich brown appearance.

The range of the King Eider is circumpolar. It breeds near shorelines of the Arctic coasts in Alaska and Canada. The winter range is as far north as the seas remain open and free of ice. King Eiders visit the Great Lakes and are casual visitors elsewhere on inland waters of the United States. Small numbers winter irregularly along Atlantic coastal states southward to Virginia and along the Northern Pacific coasts of Washington and Oregon.

Oldsquaw *Clangula hyemalis*

The first state specimen of this sea duck was collected by Fannye A. Cook on Lake Concordia in Bolivar County on January 21, 1925 (Gandy and Turcotte 1970). Burleigh (1945) collected three specimens and reported two sight records of Oldsquaws on the Mississippi Coast from 1936 to 1942. The species was considered by Burleigh to be "at least of casual occurrence on the Gulf Coast during the late winter and spring months."

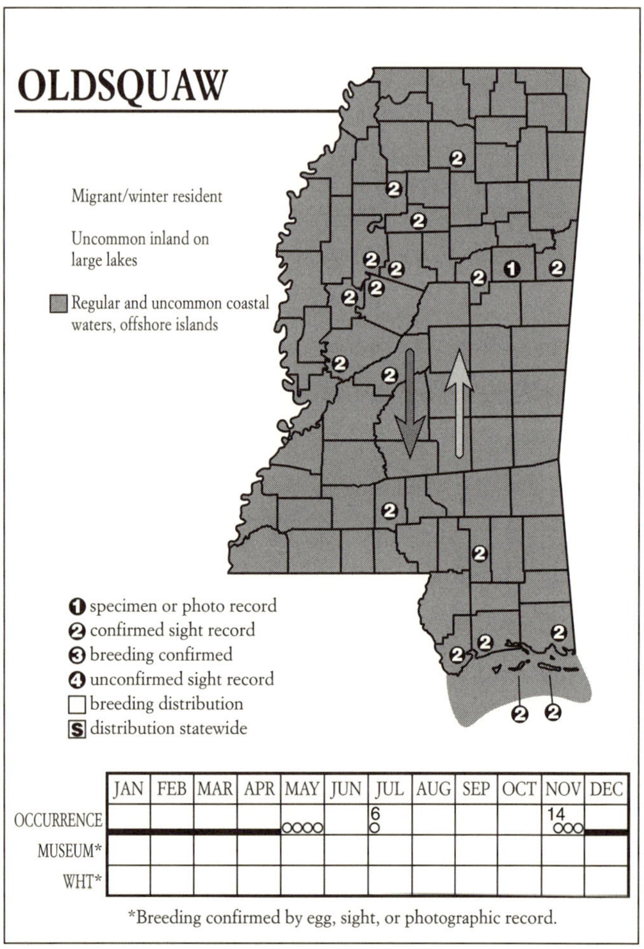

Since the late 1950s, the Oldsquaw has appeared regularly in small numbers in coastal bays and waters of Mississippi Sound. Carney and Sorenson reported 27 Oldsquaws taken by hunters in Jackson County during the 1961–1970 wing collection surveys conducted by the U.S. Fish and Wildlife Service.

This duck is erratic in midwinter on deeper waters of inland lakes and reservoirs. It has appeared on Ross Barnett Reservoir almost annually since 1973. Occurrence records extend from November 14 (a sighting by Larry Gates on the Hattiesburg sewage lagoons) to July 6 (an anomalous sight record at Gulfport reported by H. D. Haberyan). Most state records extend from late December to early April.

The Oldsquaw prefers a marine environment, and most of the worldwide population winters along northern seacoasts. Sizeable numbers also winter on the Great Lakes. Only a few of these birds winter as far south as the northern Gulf Coast, where it is an uncommon to rare winter and spring visitor. This duck has a circumpolar distribution and breeds on tundra lakes of the northern Arctic.

In winter, the male Oldsquaw is boldly marked with black and white. The two long, distinctive, needle-pointed tail plumes, white head with a dark face patch, and predominantly white body with dark brown or blackish breast, wings, and hindback identify the winter male. In spring and early summer plumage, the male is black brown except for a white face patch and white belly, sides, flanks, and undertail coverts.

The female in winter has slightly elongated tail feathers and is gray brown on the upperparts. Her head and neck are white, except for a blackish crown and cheek spots. A gray brown band separates the white neck from the white breast and belly of the winter female. In spring and summer, the female becomes noticeably darker on the head, neck, chest, and upperparts of the body.

The male Oldsquaw is said to be one of the most garrulous of ducks. On the several occasions that I have seen them in Mississippi, they were always quiet. The call is described as a melodious whistling.

Black Scoter *Melanitta nigra*

Scoters are large, heavy sea ducks found primarily in coastal and offshore waters, sometimes far out at sea. Occasionally, one or more of the three species occur on large inland bodies of water in Mississippi. The males are nearly all black and females mostly black brown. The black or black-and-white, cootlike appearance has given them colloquial names associated with their coloration and head shape such as "skunk-head," "bald-headed coot," or "black coot."

Scoters are remarkable divers and can remain underwater for a minute or more. They fly in irregular formations

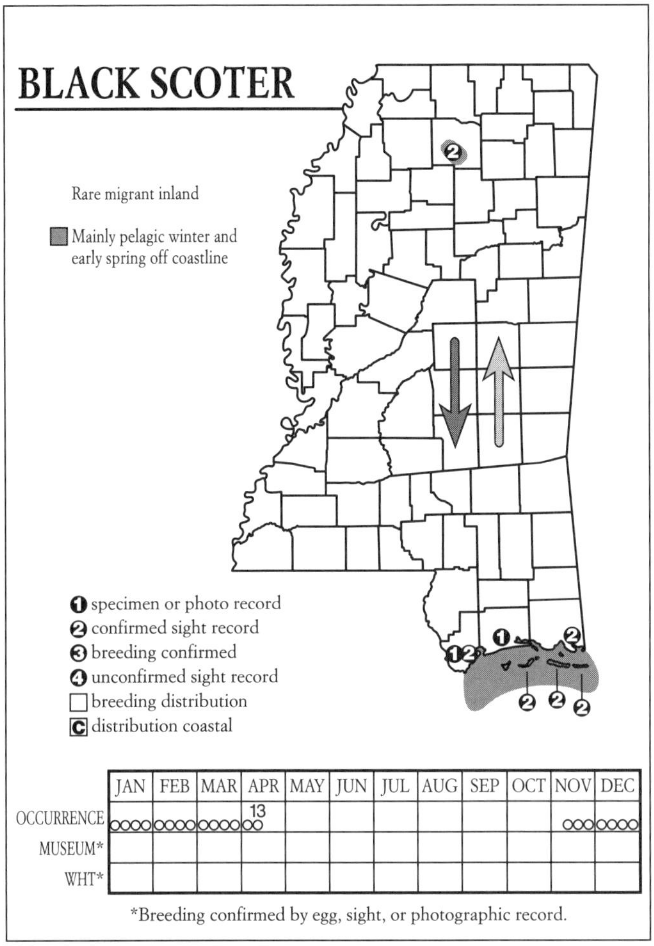

of wavering lines often low over the water. They feed largely on molluscs and crustaceans, but insects, fish, and plant parts are also eaten in smaller amounts.

This species was known as the American or Common Scoter until recently. The present common name is more appropriate because both male and female have entirely black bills and plumage, with the female appearing sooty black with a gray face in good light. The prominent, orange yellow protuberance on the black bill of the male and the black legs and feet are distinctive field marks separating this species from other scoters (see the two following accounts).

The Black Scoter is a rare and irregular state visitor. The first state sight record is a distant, though recognizable, photograph of three females (or immature males) on Sardis Lake by W. Marvin Davis (Weber 1977). The birds were present from early November until December 22, 1976, when last observed and reported on the Seventy-seventh Christmas Bird Count. A second record, by Wayne C. Weber, is of a sighting of two immature males and six females at the eastern end of Ship Island on March 10, 1977 (Weber and Jackson 1977b). Detailed notes are on record at MSU for this sighting.

More recent sightings reported by Judith A. Toups and Jerome A. Jackson in coastal waters suggest that Black Scoters may be overlooked by most observers because they tend to raft offshore with other common divers (Toups and Jackson 1987). Rafts of up to 175 of these birds have been recorded near Petit Bois and Ship Islands.

Surf Scoter *Melanitta perspicillata*

This is the most common sea duck and the one most likely to occur on coastal waters of Mississippi. It is a late fall and winter visitor on the Mississippi Gulf Coast and a casual visitor on inland lakes and reservoirs.

The black male Surf Scoter has a wedge-shaped, thick-based, multicolored bill. It has a round black spot near the base, bordered by white with red along the ridge, orange at the base of the bill, and yellow at the tip. The female and immatures are blackish brown and have dark gray bills with a darker spot at the base. Indistinct white patches are on the cheeks beneath and behind the eye. The adult male has two distinct white patches on the top and back of the head. The wings of both the Black and Surf Scoters are black. The feet and legs of the male Surf Scoter are reddish orange, and those of females and immatures are yellow to rusty brown.

The first inland Mississippi record for the Surf Scoter

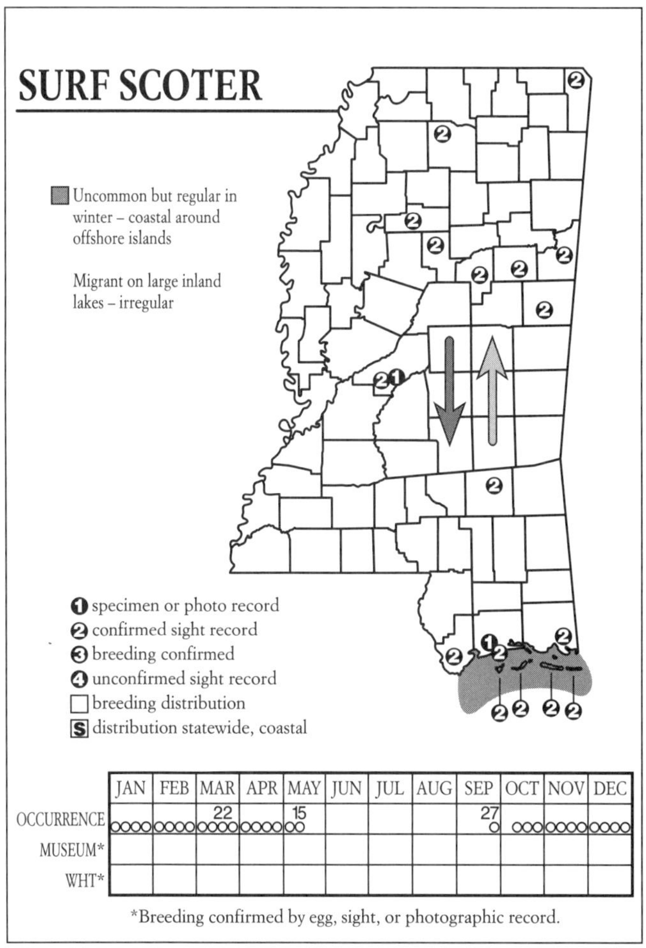

was a group of five seen and identified on January 2, 1967, near Ross Barnett Reservoir dam in Madison County, by Frances Wills Jr. and Christine Berry (Turcotte 1967b). I saw and photographed a single bird at the same place the following day. John H. Phares and I carefully studied and identified two birds again on January 10, 1967.

The second inland record substantiated by recognizable photographs was a single female seen from early November until December 22, 1976, at Sardis Lake by W. Marvin Davis (Weber 1977). A third inland record at Noxubee National Wildlife Refuge was two females or immatures seen by Wayne C. Weber, who studied them carefully and recorded detailed field notes.

Additional occurrence records on the Mississippi Coast are of three male and two female Surf Scoters seen at Horn Island in Jackson County on May 15, 1977, by Donald M. Bradburn. Jacob M. Valentine Jr. and Jerry Blackard counted two flocks of 58 of these scoters during an aerial survey off Petit Bois and Horn Islands on March 22, 1965 (Toups and Jackson 1987). Surf Scoters have appeared annually in recent years on the coast, indicating they are regular, but uncommon to rare, winter visitors.

In Mississippi, these ducks are rarely shot by hunters. Carney and Sorenson (duck-wing collection surveys 1961–1970) recorded a total of 20 Surf Scoters killed by Jackson County hunters. No hunters returned scoter wings from other counties during the survey period. Scoters are not highly regarded as table fare because of their oily flavor. They are hunted for sport in the United States mainly along northern seacoasts.

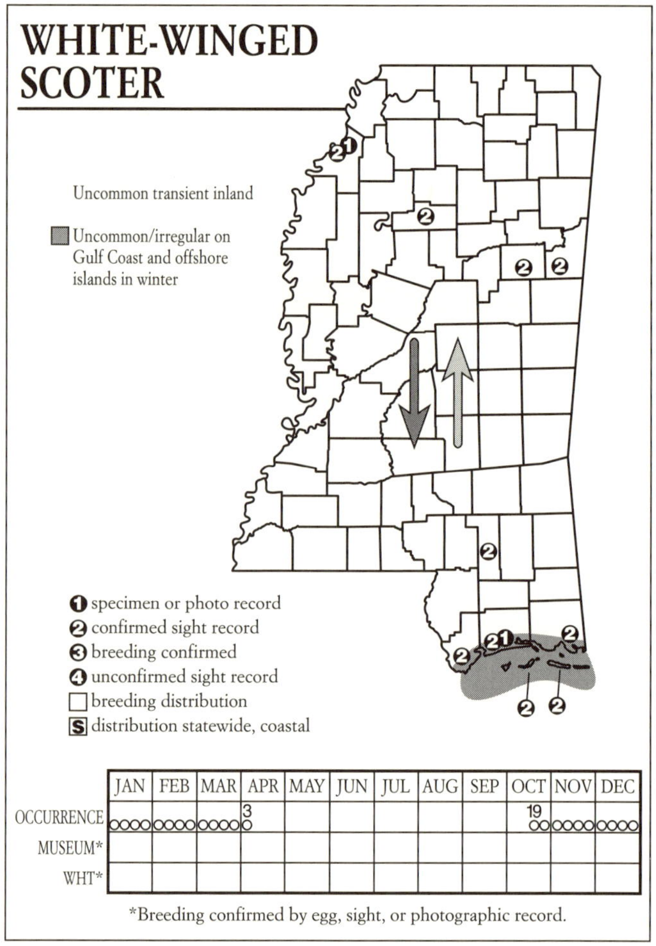

White-winged Scoter *Melanitta fusca*

The White-winged Scoter is the largest of the three species of scoters and is easiest to identify in all plumages by its white speculum on the black wing, which shows well in flight or on the water when the wings are raised. The other two scoters have all black wings.

The adult male is mostly black with blackish brown sides, a white speculum, and a white dash around and curving upward behind the eye. Female and immatures are brownish black with whitish patches behind and in front of the eye. The bill of the male is orange with a black knob at the base. This knob is less prominent on the dark bills of females and immatures. Both males and females have pinkish legs.

The first of four state records for this casual winter visitor is a mounted specimen in the private collection of T. C. Hicks of Shelby (Gandy and Turcotte 1970). The bird had been shot in the wing and was taken dead from a fish net on December 6, 1960, from De Soto Lake in Coahoma County. The second record is a sighting of 12 birds by Jacob M. Valentine Jr. and Sidney A. Woodson off the western end of Horn Island in Jackson County on January 22, 1977. Judy Toups reported the third sight record, a single female at Gulfport on April 1, 1977. Larry Gates (Weber and Jackson 1978) reported the fourth state record, a single bird seen at the Hattiesburg sewage lagoons on November 30, 1977. This species can be expected to occur almost annually on the coast in fall and winter, but in smaller numbers than the other two species. Extreme dates of occurence are October 19 and April 3.

Common Goldeneye *Bucephala clangula*

The Common Goldeneye is a large, chunky, diving duck with a puffy, round head and short neck. The head of the male appears black at a distance with an oval white patch between the eye and the bill. The neck, breast, and belly are white. The back and tail are black, except for a large, elongated white patch along the edge of the back and wings when the bird is resting.

In flight, large white patches show at the base of the wing. On close examination the head of the drake has a greenish sheen. The female and immatures have round, brown heads; white neck collars; and dappled gray bodies. The feet and legs are yellowish orange in both sexes. The eyes are a bright amber.

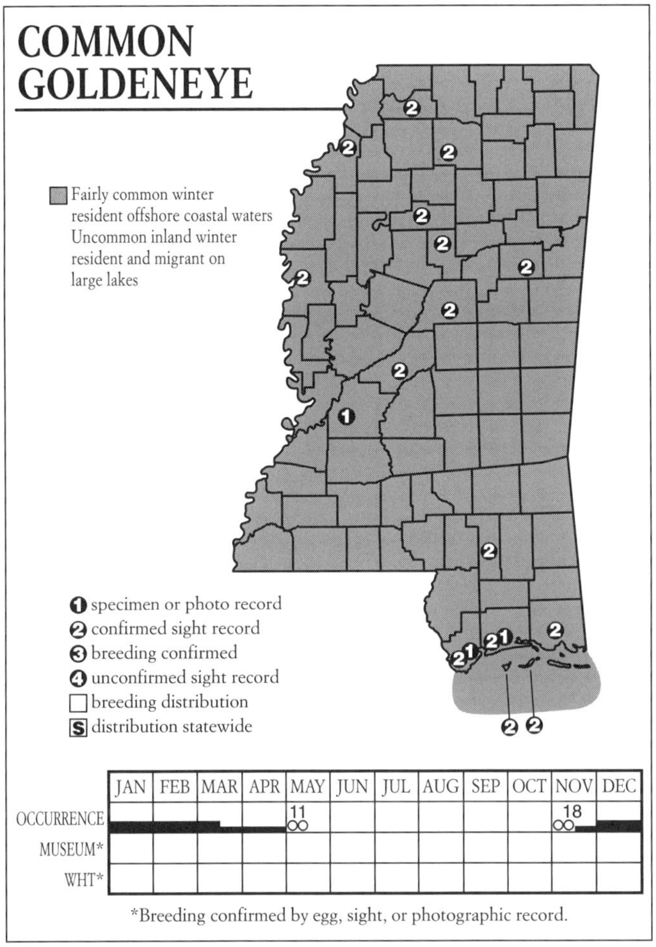

Goldeneyes are late to arrive and early to depart. Extreme dates of occurrence recorded for Mississippi are November 18 and May 11. They usually are seen in pairs or small flocks, mainly on large inland lakes and reservoirs, and on coastal bays and waters of Mississippi Sound. They never occur in large numbers in Mississippi, but appear regularly from December through February at favored locations on large inland lakes. They are more common along the Mississippi Coast on waters of Mississippi Sound.

The Common Goldeneye, or "whistler," flies in small, compact formations. Their flight is fast with rapid and deep wingbeats. In flight they have a blocky appearance due to their short, thick necks and chunky bodies. The rapid wingbeats create a resonant, whistling sound audible at a distance.

Goldeneyes nest in the boreal forest regions. They nest in natural tree cavities and nest boxes. Most of the population winter in northern states and the waters off the Atlantic and Pacific Coasts.

Bufflehead *Bucephala albeola*

This small diver vies with the Ruddy Duck and Green-winged Teal for being the smallest of our ducks. It is black and white like the Goldeneye, but the drake can be distinguished by its small size. It has a white, wedge-shaped patch below and behind the eye and across the top of its puffy head. The female is grayish black with a diagnostic elliptical white spot behind the eye. Up close, the head of the male shows green and purple gloss.

Buffleheads commonly occur in pairs or flocks of less than 10. They fly with rapid wingbeats and are among the fastest flying waterfowl. The black wings of the male in flight show broad white patches. The dusky wings of the female have a small white patch on the secondaries near the body, which is often visible on birds at rest. Like other divers, Buffleheads sit low in the water. They are diving continuously while feeding, and it is usually difficult to see all of a flock on the water at the same time.

The Bufflehead or "butterball" occurs regularly in small numbers on the larger inland lakes and the waters of Mississippi Sound mainly from November through March. Of all the diving ducks, this handsome little duck is my favorite to watch. Nearly every winter since the Ross Barnett Reservoir near Jackson was flooded in 1965, I have observed pairs and small groups on the Pearl River Waterfowl Refuge.

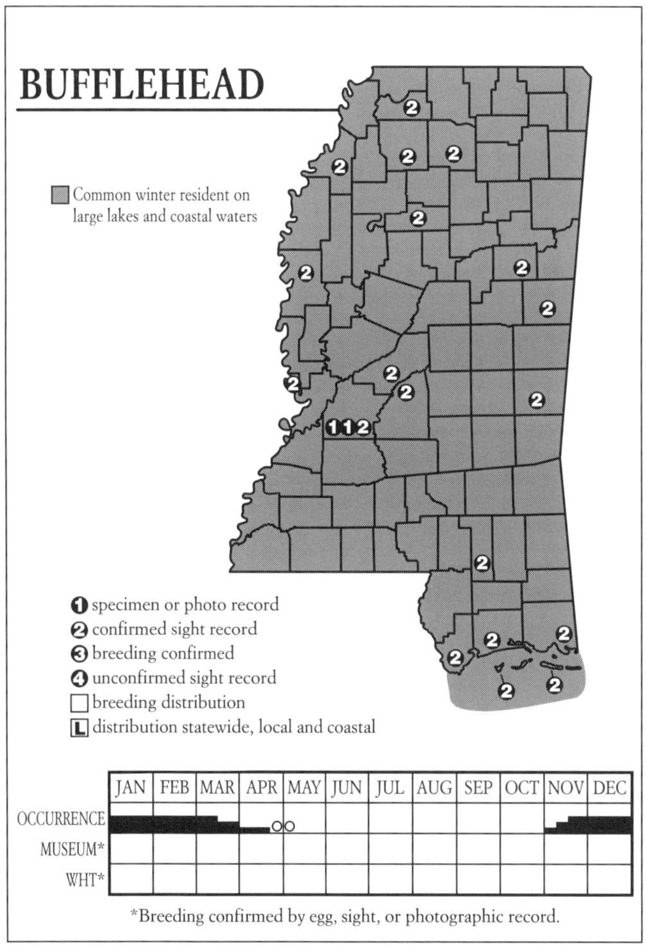

Mergini (Mergansers)

Hooded Merganser *Lophodytes cucullatus*

The subfamily tribe Mergini, the fish-eating ducks, includes our three mergansers. They have slender bills *hooked* at the tip with *sharp* serrations on the side. They feed mostly on small fish, but also take crayfish, frogs, tadpoles, crabs, shrimp, shellfish, aquatic insects, and some seeds or parts of aquatic plants. They catch food by diving and swimming underwater.

To take flight, they scamper over the water like other diving ducks. Their flight is low and fast over water and their *rapid* wingbeats describe *very shallow arcs* at the tips. They sit low in the water with the tail awash. All except the male Common Merganser have prominent crests.

The male Hooded Merganser is a pretty duck, black and white except for tawny brown flanks and sides finely vermiculated with vertical black lines. The head and neck are black except for a triangular white patch extending behind the yellow eye and surrounded by black. The breast and belly are white with *two* vertical black bars ahead of the wing. The black wings have a prominent white patch, and the secondaries and tertials are prominently striped with black and white crossed by black bars across the white. The feet are dull yellow.

Adult females and immatures are similar with the young having smaller crests. They are gray on the head, neck, breast, sides, and flanks and brownish black on the back, rump, and tail. The loose, tawny brown crest, dark head, orange yellow bill, and smaller size distinguish the female and immatures from the other two mergansers. Their calls are low, unmusical, croaking notes.

The Hooded Merganser prefers wooded lakes, sloughs, and streams, where it often associates with Wood Ducks.

Hooded Merganser

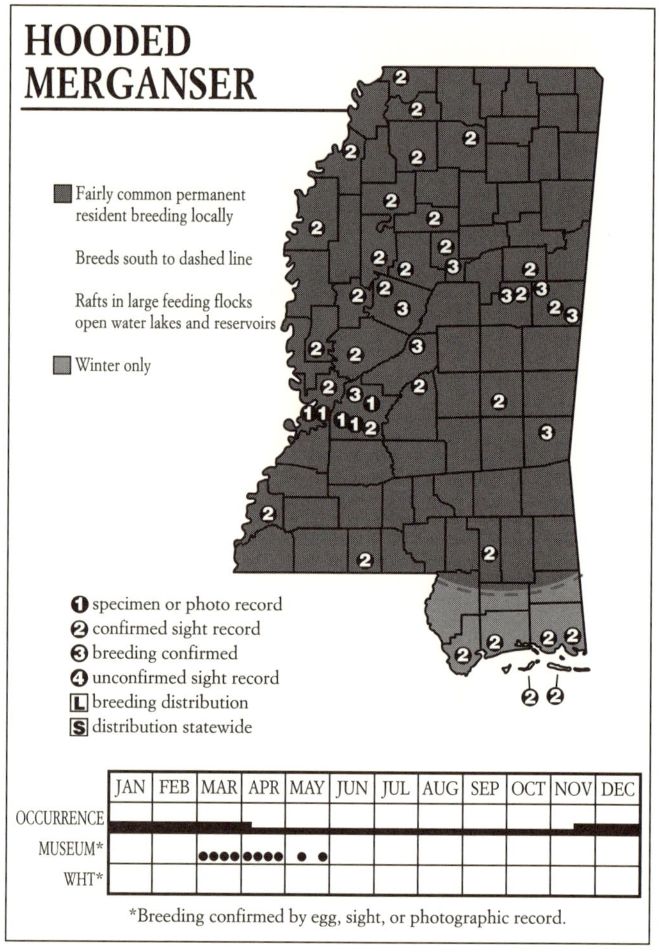

In winter, it may feed in large rafts on open water lakes. Usually it is seen in pairs or small groups in secluded parts of swamps. It is the size and shape of the Wood Duck in flight, but the rapid wingbeats describe short arcs at the tips and distinguish the "hoodie" from the "woodie." Also, it flies with the neck extended and the head held slightly below the plane of a horizontal line through the neck and body.

Hooded Mergansers are winter residents and locally common, permanent-resident breeding birds in northern Mississippi. They nest in natural tree cavities in swamps and commonly use artificial nest boxes. Lon Strong Jr. (1972) found 45 nests of the Hooded Merganser in nest boxes in wooded swamps in Lowndes, Madison, and Montgomery Counties. Nineteen nest starts were observed as early as March 16. Nests contained from eight to 13 or more ivory white eggs, and seven contained from one to four Wood Duck eggs.

I observed a brood of half-grown young captured May 8, 1960, on a street in Jackson and penned overnight by Thomas E. Kennedy (Turcotte 1960b). One died in the cage, and I picked up the other four and released them on a small minnow pond. They fed ravenously on large tadpoles and crayfish. All attained flight and left the pond on May 24.

Common Merganser *Mergus merganser*

This species, formerly known as the American Merganser, is one of three races found around the world in the Northern Hemisphere. It is an irregular, casual, winter visitor, and there are few occurrence records in Mississippi. Most of the Mississippi Flyway population winters north of Arkansas and Tennessee on deeper inland waters. It seldom reaches the central Gulf states. It is so winter hardy that it remains on icy northern waters as long as it finds open water.

The Common Merganser breeds in northern forest and mountainous regions of Canada, Alaska, and the northern United States. It prefers to nest in tree cavities, but will nest in a wide variety of places near water. It has nested in holes or on the ledges of cliffs or stream banks, among rock boulders, in vacant buildings, on the open ground of islands, or under thick bushes.

The male Common Merganser is a large, long-bodied duck about the size of a Mallard. The head is greenish black without a crest. The lower neck, breast, sides, and flanks are white tinged with pink. Adult males have brown eyes. Females and immatures have brown eyes circled by yellow. The back and tail are black in the male.

This duck's wings are largely white on the inner halves and black on the outer parts. Females and immatures have white underparts and silvery gray sides, flanks, and undertail coverts. The back, tail, and front half of the wings are gray. The secondaries are white on the trailing edge, bordered by black at the front and sides. The head is red brown and crested at the back with a *sharply defined* contrast between the rufous neck and whitish throat, where it joins the back and breast. The white throat patch is *distinctly* margined by the red feathers of the head and neck. Females and immatures closely resemble their Red-breasted Merganser counterparts, whose whitish throat and neck marks blend indistinctly with the red.

Coastal and inland records for this casual winter visitor extend from December 19 through January 15.

Red-breasted Merganser *Mergus serrator*

This merganser is common or at times abundant as a winter resident of Mississippi Sound and the bays and estuaries on the Mississippi Gulf Coast from early December through April. A few individuals remain there throughout the summer (Jackson and Schardien 1980b). On large inland waters,

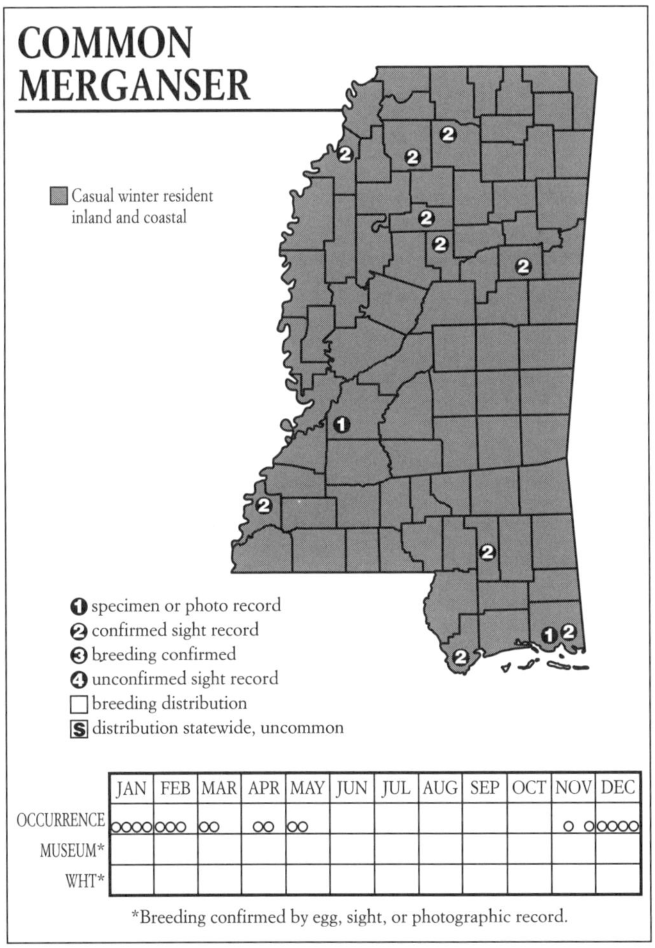

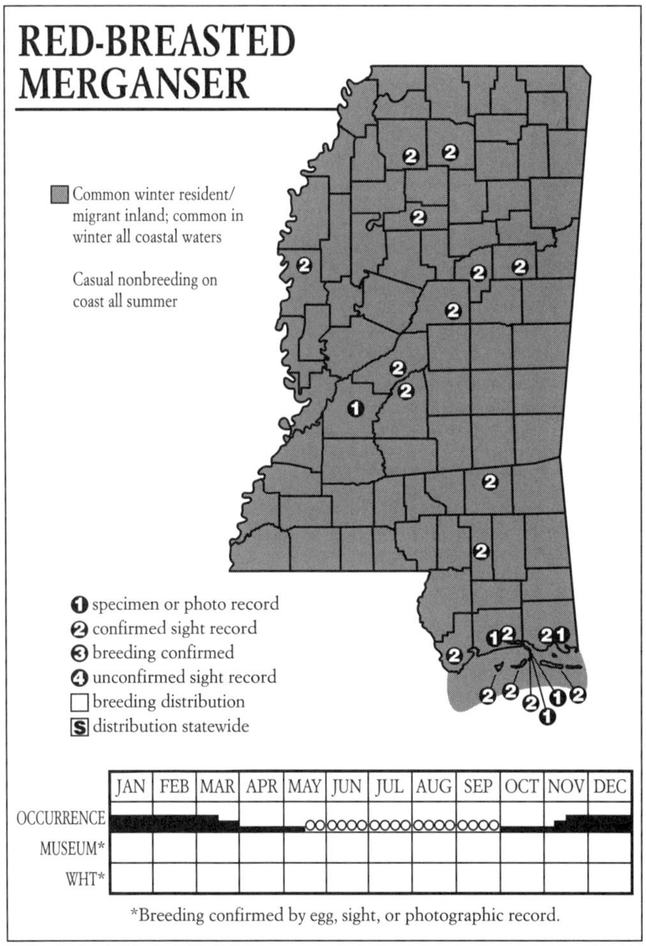

it occurs regularly in low numbers from December through March. In migration and occasionally during the early winter, it is locally common on the larger reservoirs and oxbows along the Mississippi River.

The male Red-breasted Merganser is easily identified by the conspicuous crest; black head with green gloss; and wide, white collar separating the rusty breast and head. The sides and flanks are white with vertical black lines that appear gray from a distance. At times, the sides and white underparts are deeply stained with rusty brown.

Females and immatures closely resemble Common Mergansers. The two species can best be distinguished by observing the white of the throat and neck of the Red-breasted, which merges *indistinctly* with the reddish brown head. Those of the Common Merganser female and immature are *sharply defined* against the reddish brown head and neck.

This species breeds generally farther north than the Common Merganser. Their breeding ranges overlap in the southern parts, but the Red-breasted Merganser alone breeds north into the Arctic tundra regions. Unlike the Common Merganser, it does not nest in tree cavities, but on the ground where the nest is concealed by vegetation, shrubbery, driftwood, or boulders. The olive buff eggs number eight to 10 in a clutch. Their nests are lined profusely with down and usually located near water of a lake or marsh.

Oxyurini (Stiff-tailed Ducks)

Ruddy Duck *Oxyura jamaicensis*

The Ruddy Duck is one of six species of the subfamily tribe Oxyurini, the stiff-tailed ducks that are found mostly in tropical waters or in the southern parts of the world. The Masked Duck, the only other species found in North America besides the Ruddy, occurs casually along the southwestern Louisiana and Texas Coasts.

These small, stocky ducks differ from other diving ducks in several ways. The tail feathers are very stiff and spiny. The male often erects the tail at a 45° angle while sitting on the water. During courtship, the tail may be fanned and raised to a higher, vertical position. The legs are placed so far back on the body that it is difficult for these birds to walk. Their necks are short and thick. The nail at the tip of the bill is sharply hooked.

The Ruddy Duck is easily recognized at a distance by the elevated tail. The male in winter has a blackish cap, white cheeks, and an unpatterned brownish gray body. The female is similar to the winter male, but with dingier cheeks bisected by a dark line.

In breeding plumage, the back, neck, sides, and breast of the male become rich, reddish brown, and the bill changes

Ruddy Duck ♂ Winter

from gray black to bright blue. The plumage changes occur gradually. Some males can be observed in changing or nuptial plumage from February through April. Immatures resemble females. Juvenile males develop the white cheek patches in late December and January.

"Ruddies" have dull brown, short, oval-rounded wings. Their fast, shallow wingbeats and relatively large body give

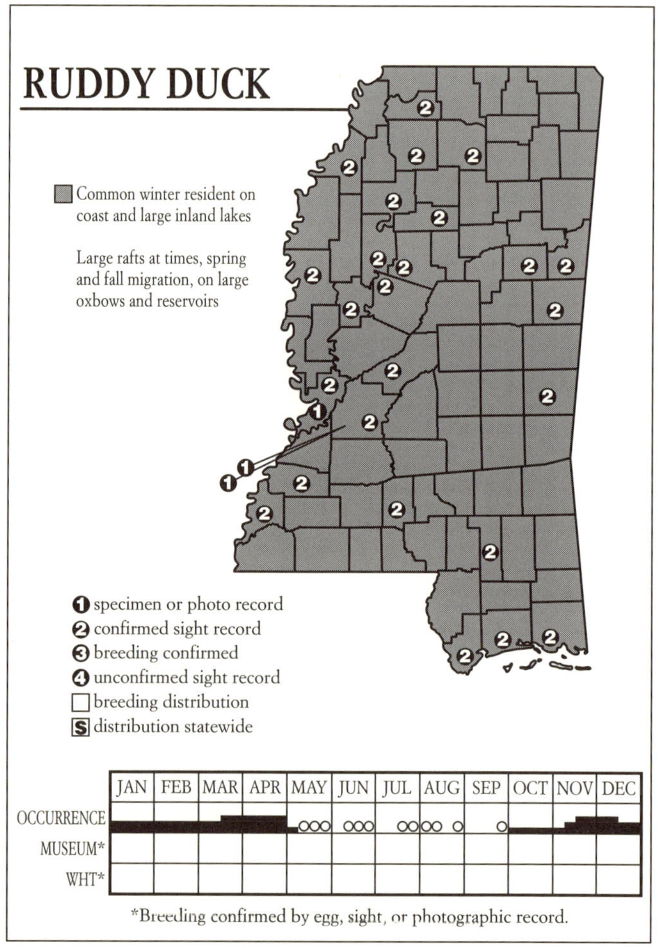

their flight a buzzy or bumblebee-like appearance. They fly in small compact flocks, usually skimming low over the water. They swim away or dive to escape close observation.

Hunters have little regard for ruddies. They usually sit in rafts on open, fairly deep water. The numbers taken by hunters in Mississippi are insignificant, probably because of their habits, small size, and unsightly appearance after being dressed—it is virtually impossible to clean one without tearing off the skin.

The Ruddy Duck is a common migrant and winter resident on reservoirs, oxbow lakes, ponds, and sewage lagoons. It is less common in waters along the Mississippi Gulf Coast than on interior lakes and reservoirs. The first arrivals appear in early October, and they increase in numbers from late December to March. Departure is mostly complete by late April, but a few remain until mid-May.

Large concentrations of several thousand birds appear on the oxbow lakes along the Mississippi. Rafts of up to 5000 birds have been sighted on Lake Washington and Moon Lake on Christmas Bird Counts and during the northward migration in February and March.

Ruddy Ducks breed in northern and prairie marshes and build a woven nest of marsh vegetation. Their nest may be attached to emergent aquatic plants or built up from the bottom and above the water surface. Down is added as incubation advances. The white eggs have a granular surface and are exceptionally large for the bird's size. The hen ruddy is noted for parasitizing the nests of other waterfowl and also for "dump-nesting," the practice whereby several females deposit their eggs in the same nest, often without incubation. The Ruddy Duck is not known to breed in Mississippi.

Kites, Eagles, Hawks, Falcons, and Allies (Falconiformes)

This order contains three families: Accipitridae, the hawks and kites; the subfamily Pandioninae, the fish hawk or osprey; and Falconidae, the caracaras and falcons. These large, carrion-eating or predatory birds are endowed with powerful flight, and are fully capable of soaring, diving, or darting to find or seize their prey. All have very keen eyesight. Most have long, sharp claws for seizing prey.

Falcons and eagles have been tamed and used for hunting since the dawn of history, and falconry is still considered a sport of kings and princes. At times in recorded history even the vultures have been regarded with respect or reverence.

Some 20 species of hawks, and falcons have been recorded in Mississippi. Ten species have confirmed breeding records on the MOS state bird list. Four western or northern species of hawks occur rarely or as accidentals. The Crested Caracara has been documented here and has been listed as an accidental, meaning that there are less than five records of its occurrence. Four sightings of the Northern Goshawk have been reported in Mississippi.

In Mississippi, this order includes the Osprey or "fish hawk," three species of kites, the Northern Harrier, two eagles, three accipiter or short-winged hawks, and the broad-winged hawks or buteos. The Osprey, almost the size of an eagle, has highly specialized feet and claws suitable for grasping a fish while plunging feet first into water. Kites have long wings and tails, much like overgrown swallows, and are exceptionally graceful fliers. Kites inhabit stream bottoms and nest in tall trees. Accipiters have short, rounded wings and long tails. They are woodland species, often called "darters" because of their rapid wingbeats and maneuverability while pursuing small birds through trees and brush. In contrast, the Northern Harrier flies low over sedge fields, open grasslands or marshes, and often hovers while leisurely hunting rodents.

The broad-winged hawks have wings suitable for soaring and gliding. Usually they can be seen on a high perch from which they glide and pounce on small rodents. With the exception of eagles, buteos are our most numerous and widespread hawks.

Hawks are notorious wanderers and most species migrate from their breeding range. Fall migrations of hawks, particularly broad-wings, are spectacular sights. In migration, hawks follow the updrafts along mountain ridges or along higher terrain bordering stream valleys where thermals build up. Hundreds or even thousands have been seen over a period of a few hours riding these warm air currents to considerable heights, then gliding southward to soar again on the next uplift.

Located about 13 miles south of Ocean Springs in Mississippi Sound, Horn Island is a mecca for wild birds. During the spring and fall migrations, the island is one of the best places to see transient hawks and Peregrine Falcons. Ospreys have nested on the island for years. Beginning in 1988, the Department of Wildlife, Fisheries and Parks worked for several years with the Interior Department's National Park Service on Horn Island in hacking and releasing into the wild some 44 Bald Eagles.

Broad-winged Hawk migrations often follow high ridges bordering the Big Black River and converge at the Loess Bluff, which leads southwesterly toward Vicksburg and down the Mississippi River. These movements mainly occur in late September and early October on sunny days when thermals and updrafts rise. After passage of a cold front, northwesterly winds striking hills or ridges can produce what is called a "ridge lift," a column of rising air that often propels hawks to heights of several hundred feet, sometimes enabling them to migrate hundreds of miles.

The value of hawks and other predatory birds is neither understood nor fully appreciated by most people, including many hunters. Few are able to recognize the different species in the field, and fewer know much about their feeding habits. Many assume that all hawks are destructive of game birds and animals.

Predatory birds and animals serve us best by controlling surplus populations of animals that are either economic pests or likely to become pests without controls. Red-tailed Hawks feed mostly on the hispic cotton rat, a small animal harmful to food crops and one which destroys the eggs of ground-nesting birds.

The numbers of wild rats, mice, and shrews on a single acre of Bobwhite Quail habitat would astound most quail hunters. These rodents compete directly for quail foods. A hunter might see a Cooper's Hawk or Sharp-shinned Hawk in pursuit of a bird and assume all hawks are predators of quail, seldom reasoning that quail would not "freeze" and hold to a point by a dog unless this tactic had been imprinted on quail over countless generations by encounters with predatory birds.

Accipitridae (Kites, Eagles, Hawks, and Allies)

Osprey *Pandion haliaetus*

The Osprey is mainly a local, breeding summer resident on the offshore islands and estuaries of the Mississippi Gulf Coast. It has nested on or near reservoirs or large lakes in several places, but only two recent nests were observed and reported during active stages.

One nest was observed with three large and feathered fledglings on September 29, 1971, by former state conservation officer Harold Kelly at Lake Lamar Bruce, a state-owned lake in Lee County near Saltillo north of Tupelo. The adults frequented this lake during two nesting seasons. The large nest, about four feet across, was in a live beech tree in a ravine near a beaver pond separated from the lake's upper end. The Ospreys built and used the nest in 1970 and 1971, abandoning it the following year.

I once saw an inactive nest in a remote cypress brake northwest of Cary near the Issaquena and Sharkey County line. I was with a party of dove hunters and local landowners on September 3, 1972, when I saw this nest in a tall cypress. It was as large as an eagle nest. The landowner had seen the birds at the nest, but thought they were large hawks. This nest was near Steele Bayou, several oxbow lakes along the Mississippi River, catfish ponds, and rice fields.

The successful nesting of a pair of Ospreys on his property in northern Rankin County was reported to me by Charles M. Wright on July 10, 1974. The nest, in a tall pine, produced three young that stayed near the site until mid-June. This was the third year of nesting. The first nest was abandoned after lightning killed the nest tree, and the birds moved onto his property. I saw Ospreys regularly on the upper reservoir during and after the time of these reports, but I failed to see the second nest.

Thomas D. Burleigh (1945) observed Ospreys nesting commonly on Horn, Ship, and Cat Islands from 1935 to 1943, but did not find any nesting on Deer Island at Biloxi or on the mainland. In the early 1940s, a colony of five or more pairs nested around a tidal estuary on the East Pascagoula River immediately above the mouth of the Escatawpa River. I observed these active nests while driving north along Mississippi 63 from Moss Point. At that time, two nests were visible east of the highway along the Escatawpa River. All of these nests were in dead or living cypress trees. Ava Tabor (1958), Sidney Gauthreaux, and others observed two active nests from Mississippi 63 at the Escatawpa River location on June 21, 1958. One nest held two young birds with an adult.

In the 1960s, there were only two records of Ospreys nesting on the Gulf Coast. Henry D. Haberyan (1963b) observed two pairs with occupied nests on Horn Island on May 23, 1963, and a party of MOS members found and recorded one pair nesting on this island on May 11, 1968.

Sterling G. Clawson and Lovett E. Williams Jr. (1962) made numerous boat trips to islands in Mississippi Sound to collect specimens from early 1960 to August 1962. Their collection records and published notes on observations in MOS newsletters contain no references to nesting Ospreys on the islands or mainland during that period.

Ospreys on the Mississippi Gulf Coast, as elsewhere throughout most of their range in the eastern United States, experienced a serious decline in numbers in the late 1950s and 1960s. Breeding populations on the coast and barrier islands have slowly recovered since the late 1960s, and by May 1979 numerous pairs of Ospreys were nesting on Horn, Ship, and Round Islands in Mississippi Sound.

On an aerial survey on April 15, 1979, Jerome A. Jackson and C. Dwight Cooley found active nests, three on Round Island, 10 on Horn Island, six on East Ship Island, and 15 along the Escatawpa River bottomlands on the mainland (Jackson and Schardien 1979). In May 1978 on a boat tour up the East Pascagoula River, I counted seven active nests above and below the Interstate 10 bridge. Inland sight records have increased steadily throughout Mississippi since the late 1970s.

The decline of Osprey populations along the Mississippi Gulf Coast was concurrent with the decline and disappearance of resident breeding Brown Pelicans. No evidence of the effects of pesticide contamination on Osprey reproduction was discovered during the same period, other than declining numbers.

The Osprey builds a massive nest of sticks, driftwood, shoreline flotsam of all kinds, dried grasses, fish net, nylon rope, seaweed, wings and feathers of dead birds, dry animal

Osprey

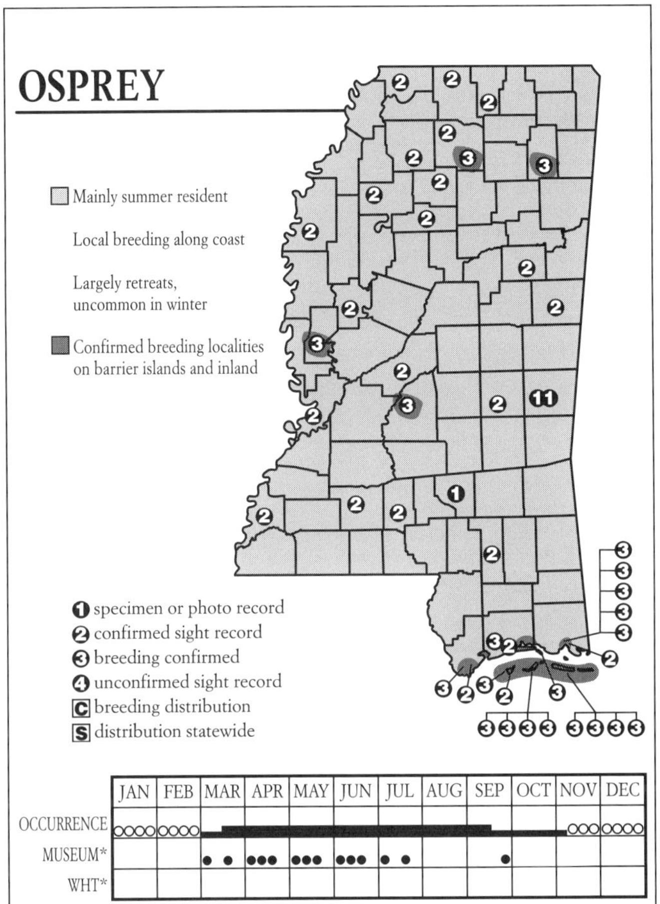

*Breeding confirmed by egg, sight, or photographic record.

bones, green twigs of trees, and almost any kind of available trash. The four eggs are laid in a nest lined with softer material. The eggs vary in ground color from almost white to cinnamon, and are heavily blotched and spotted with shades of dark brown to drab or reddish brown, often obscuring the ground color. Eggs are incubated as deposited, and the last young to hatch is often at a disadvantage when the adults fail to find enough food. The weakest may die or be forced from the nest by siblings. On coastal islands, nests are usually in the tallest pine tree. Along rivers and estuaries, nests are placed mostly in the tops of tall cypress trees.

Ospreys and their eggs have a "musky," pungent odor, peculiar to this bird. The smell is not unpleasant or "fishy" and is retained for years afterward in stored museum specimens of these birds.

Distinctive field marks for this large, fish-eating bird are the long crooked wings, white belly, and *white wing linings with a black wrist patch*. The upperparts are dark blackish brown. The head is mostly white with a *black cheek patch* extending across the front of the head. The sharp, hooked bill is black, and the iris is yellow. Adult females have a necklace of brown, tear-shaped spotting across the upper breast, which is mostly absent on the male. The dark tail is banded with a wider black terminal band. The tarsi and toes are a light, almost sky blue color. Immatures are similar to adults, but have lighter upperparts due to pale buff edging of the feathers on wings and back.

The food is almost exclusively live fish that the Osprey locates by flying and hovering on its long wings. It then dives on bent wings folded upon impact with the water, feet extended to grasp the prey below the water surface. After shaking itself, the bird rises easily and carries the fish head first to the nest or nearest perch to feed its young or eat the catch. Bald Eagles and Magnificent Frigatebirds frequently harass Ospreys and steal from adults and young in the nest.

Ospreys are adaptable birds, and will tolerate humans to a surprising degree where they are protected. On shorelines and beaches, they sometimes nest on piers, pilings, artificial platforms, utility poles, and piles of driftwood near dwellings where they are disturbed only when strange people are around. On remote islands, Ospreys often nest on the ground where large predators are few or absent, but they prefer to place nests on a prominence or projection near water.

Ospreys are watchful birds, and one or both adults remain at or near the nest while hatching and rearing young. They are noisy whenever humans approach the nest and usually take to the air when a nest is disturbed. When approached at the nest, the birds begin a musical whistling cackle and upon leaving and circling around they continue to scream and call in shrieking, staccato *ick, ick, ick* notes and frenzied screams.

When hatched, young Ospreys are unlike other hawks. They are covered in drab-colored down with darker spottings and marks, which camouflage them until feathers develop. The young assume a frozen, flattened position with neck outstretched when threatened in the nest by a potential enemy.

Most Ospreys seen inland are migrants or late summer wanderers. Migrating birds are seen inland mostly during March and April and again in fall until late November. They winter regularly along the coast and occasionally on inland areas. Most Ospreys in passage winter farther south and return around mid-March when there is a pronounced arrival and northward movement.

American Swallow-tailed Kite
Elanoides forficatus

No other large landbird closely resembles this uncommon summer resident, which breeds locally along the lower Pascagoula and Pearl River systems. Seen in flight, the *deeply forked, black tail* and sharply defined black and white plumage readily identify this hawk. It is somewhat gregarious and remains near its nesting territory during the breeding season.

To see these beautiful birds, one must search for them. The large expanse of swampland on the lower Pascagoula River below Mississippi Highway 26 affords the best opportunity. This requires a boat trip from one of the several landings. Several pairs of Swallow-tailed Kites occur there regularly and may be seen from the river and connecting oxbow lakes, river bridges, or from the meandering channels of the Pascagoula marsh.

These birds arrive in late March and April, but are most active and more easily seen during May or June. The lower Pearl River above Pearlington and U. S. Highway 90 is another site favored by Swallow-tails during the nesting season. A boat trip up the Pearl River to Honey Island swamp is a most likely place to view them.

Swallow-tailed Kites catch and eat most of their food in flight. Their diet consists of large insects, frogs, lizards, and small snakes or young birds. Most of their feeding is done over the river swamps and open fields near their nest territory.

The nest is built of sticks and usually contains Spanish moss. The eggs are white or cream colored and heavily marked with dark brown and reddish brown. Usually two or three eggs are laid.

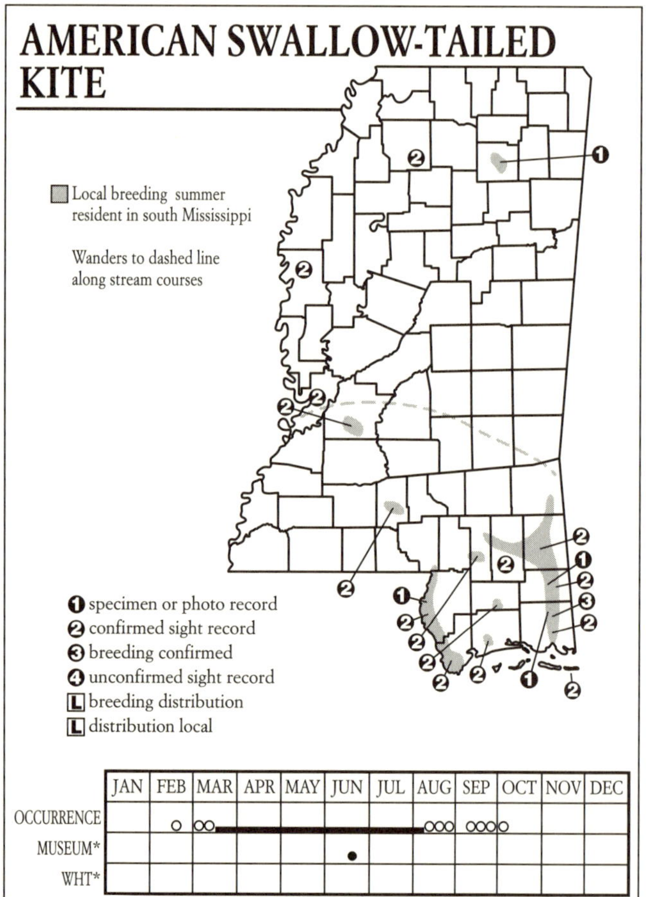

*Breeding confirmed by egg, sight, or photographic record.

Only one substantiated nest record for Mississippi has been reported. A nest containing young was found by Leron Vickery on Bluff Creek near Vancleave on June 20, 1982. The nest, made of sticks and Spanish moss in the top of an 85-foot slash pine, was photographed by Bridget Russel and recorded by Rev. John A. Izral (1982).

Immature Swallow-tails resemble adults, but the tail is shorter and white tipped. These kites are such masters of flight that seeing them diving, sailing, and soaring over treetops leaves one in awe. Several kites often hunt together in the same territory. After nesting, wanderers are seen along river swamps well beyond their breeding places (Coffey 1951; Gandy and Turcotte 1970). Most birds depart from breeding grounds by early August.

White-tailed Kite *Elanus leucurus*

Formerly named Black-shouldered Kite, this bird is a newcomer of record to Mississippi. The occurrence of two adults in Hancock County at Port Bienville Industrial Park near Pearlington was first noted and reported by Judith Toups and Evelyn Johnson on October 27, 1982 (Toups et al. 1985b). The two birds remained in the area through the winter.

Credit for the discovery of this species in Hancock County and subsequent documentation of the first breeding records belongs to Judith Toups and Evelyn Johnson. Toups is known as a most enthusiastic and accomplished birder, whose field observations and bird conservation work on the Mississippi Gulf Coast deserves recognition here.

On January 6, 1983, a second pair of adults was found about four miles north of the Port Bienville site. Both pairs were observed at regular intervals each month until February 26, 1983, when Toups found the nest of the second pair with one adult bird sitting. One or both adults were seen by Toups and others on six visits to the nest site between March 7 and April 1. On April 4 and 5, both kites were seen on or near the nest. One or both carried material to the nest and apparently caught food nearby, bringing and tearing it up in the nest as if feeding young. No movement of young in this nest was observed.

On April 10 while both adults were nearby, this nest was examined by Jerome A. Jackson, Betty Schardien, and Toups. They found no evidence of brooding or young. On April 17 Jackson climbed the nest tree and found two eggs in the nest. This pair remained at the nest site until last seen on April 21, 1983. The nesting produced no young.

On August 10, 1983, Toups and Mickey Baker found two immature kites perched together on a wire at the Port Bienville Park. These young birds were presumably raised by the adult pair earlier seen in this area, but the nesting site was not seen.

WHITE-TAILED KITE

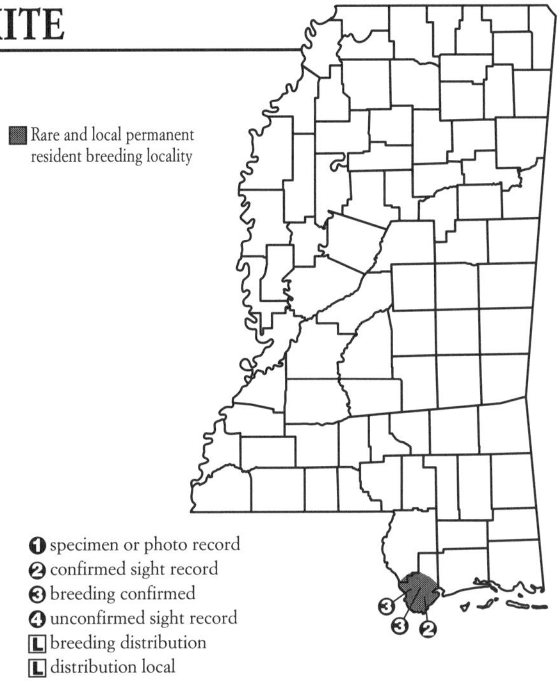

	JAN	FEB	MAR	APR	MAY	JUN	JUL	AUG	SEP	OCT	NOV	DEC
OCCURRENCE	○○○○	○○○○	○○○○	○○○○	○○○○	○○	○○○○	○○	○○○○	○○○○	○○○○	○○○○
MUSEUM*		●	●		●			●●●				
WHT*												

*Breeding confirmed by egg, sight, or photographic record.

Adult pairs were observed at Port Bienville Park and nearby locations from October 23 to March 8, 1984, by Toups and others. On March 10, she observed two adults at a nest about two miles northeast of Port Bienville Park. This nesting pair was seen regularly through March and April of 1984. On May 16, the nest was approached by Wayne C. Weber, Wendy Weber, and Toups. Three fully grown young were found sitting on the edge of the nest. This documented the first successful nesting of this species in Mississippi.

The White-tailed Kite is similar in size to the Mississippi Kite. White underparts, mostly white tail, black on the upper leading edges of the inner wings, and a small black patch underneath the wings distinguish it from the Mississippi Kite. Juveniles are streaked with rufous on the head and underparts. The tail is light gray without spotting or marks. The black leading edges of the inner wings from above and small patches of black below are present at all ages.

The range of this species in the last century extended from California to southern Texas and to South Carolina and southern Florida. Eastern populations disappeared, but western populations have shown recent increases and extensions of their breeding range.

The habitat occupied by these birds in Hancock County is coastal plain with open pine and savannah lands interspersed by fresh- and brackish water ponds and marshes and live oak hammocks. The breeding territories have been mostly open sites containing small live oaks left following clear-cutting and replanting with pine. Nests were located in these oaks.

Eggs laid by this kite number from three to five. They are white and usually profusely marked or blotched with shades of brown. The nest is a substantial, deeply cupped structure of twigs and leaves lined with grasses, weed stems, moss, and other soft materials.

Mississippi Kite *Ictinia mississippiensis*

If I had been permitted to choose our state bird, I would have selected the Mississippi Kite. It is the shoulder patch emblem of the Mississippi Ornithological Society, which has named its official bulletin *The Mississippi Kite.*

A summer-resident species, this hawk of graceful flight arrives in late March on the coast and remains until late September. It is common along the batture lands of the Mississippi River below Memphis and can be found breeding locally along our rivers and streams emptying into the Gulf of Mexico and into the Mississippi River. Cottonwood groves between the main levees of the Mississippi River are its preferred nesting places, but this species may nest in deciduous hardwoods of the Loess Bluff bordering the Yazoo Delta and the Mississippi River.

I have seen adults wheeling and coursing over these areas on numerous occasions. The open grass fields formed on old Mississippi River sandbars and adjacent levee systems are preferred feeding sites.

Mississippi Kites eat large insects, mainly cicadas, dragonflies, and grasshoppers. Outbreaks of prodigious numbers of these insects occur in the batture lands of the Mississippi River. After these insects emerge in early summer, I have seen every weed and bush laden with shed cicada skins. Swarms of dragonflies also emerge from the watery basins and borrow pits along the levees. Grasshoppers and crickets are at times innumerable.

Mississippi Kite

Summer resident Mississippi Kites nest in tall sweetgum and cottonwood trees in the batture lands along the Mississippi River levee. Along this mainline levee and nearby sandfields, the birds feed on a variety of flying insects.

I have watched flocks of 50 or more of these kites wheeling through the air and feeding in flight on swarms of dragonflies. Flying insects are caught in the talons, transferred to the beak, and eaten in flight. Cicadas or grasshoppers plucked from tree limbs or ground vegetation also are eaten on the wing.

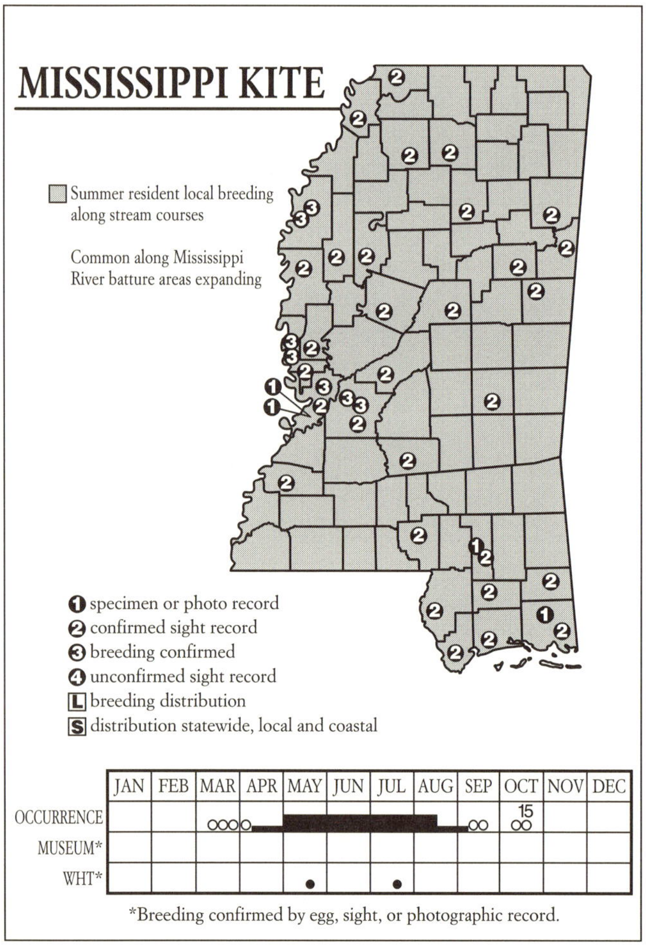

Mississippi Kites prefer to nest in tall cottonwood and sweet gum trees (Ganier 1902, 1973). I saw one nest on an outer branch of a tall wild pecan tree on the bank of Lake Chotard in Issaquena County. Another nest containing one large young on July 14, 1960, was in a cottonwood alongside the main levee near Fitler in Issaquena County. These kites have nested at several wooded locations within the city limits of Jackson.

The nest is a small platform of twigs and sticks with a few leaves nestled around the eggs. One or two white eggs are laid. Nesting occurs in late May and June. Nests are usually placed in the terminal fork of a sweet gum or cottonwood tree. Loose colonies of several pairs sometimes nest in cottonwood groves in the batture areas and along the Mississippi River levees. Nests remain visible through the winter and are sometimes rebuilt and used the next season (Ganier 1963).

A pearl gray head; slate gray upperparts; light gray underparts; long pointed wings with black tips and white secondaries; and a long, slightly notched, black tail identify the adult. The outer edges of the primaries are sometimes edged with chestnut brown. The iris of the adult is red. Young birds are heavily spotted and streaked with brown and have yellow irises. First-year adults have pale bands on the tail and dark brownish wings and upperparts similar to the juvenile.

The Mississippi Kite is gregarious during the summer months and flocks of 50 to 100 can be seen coursing or circling while feeding or playing. The winter range is in South America. In recent years, populations of this kite have increased remarkably well.

Bald Eagle *Haliaeetus leucocephalus*

A dark brown body, completely white head and tail, massive yellow bill, and yellow eyes readily identify the adult Bald Eagle. Full adult plumage is attained when the bird is four or five years old. Immatures are mostly dark, including the bill, and in flight may be confused with the immature Golden Eagle, which has sharply defined white patches at the base of the primary wing feathers, and white undertail bordered with a well-defined, dark terminal band. The underwings of immature Bald Eagles show blotchy white patterns, and the light and dark pattern under the tail is not sharply defined. The legs of Golden Eagles are feathered to the toes, while the tarsi of Bald Eagles are bare.

Bald Eagles soar with occasional wingbeats on flat wings, which extend from seven to eight feet. Turkey Vultures soar with upswept wings that readily distinguish them from immature Bald Eagles.

The Bald Eagle is our national emblem. On the $1 bill, it appears on the great seal behind a shield holding arrows and an olive branch in each talon. It symbolizes freedom and the power to protect and hold the peace. The spread eagle is also on many of our coins, emblems, and patriotic posters. It appears on Mississippi's state seal and rests above the dome of the State Capitol facing southward.

It is no secret that the Bald Eagle has declined in numbers in the eastern portion of its range due to human encroachments, shooting, and chemical contamination of its natural food supplies. Pesticides such as DDT, Endrin, and other insecticides persisting over long periods of time in the food chain of fish, which is this eagle's main diet, have caused reproductive failure leading to its decline. This failure was due to sublethal accumulations of chlorinated hydrocarbons, which disrupted the calcium metabolism of the Bald Eagle (along with the Brown Pelican, and other fish-eating birds). This caused them to lay weak or soft-shelled eggs that were unable to withstand incubation. Ingestion of lead pellets from dead or crippled waterfowl also causes mortality through lead poisoning. The sale of these long-lived environmental contaminants has been restricted or banned for agricultural use.

Recovery of Bald Eagle populations is progressing. The U.S. Fish and Wildlife Service says that Bald Eagle populations in all states except those in the Southwest are strong enough to reclassify the bird from endangered to threatened. The announcement was made in June 1994 by Service Director Mollie Beattie at Blackwater National Wildlife Refuge in Maryland. The Bald Eagle is common in Alaska and is migratory over its range in North America. Central and southern Florida have good local breeding populations.

In 1963, the National Audubon Society and others surveyed the lower 48 states and located only 417 active Bald Eagle nests. Since 1990, the U.S. Fish and Wildlife Service has recorded more than 3000 occupied territories, and in 1993, 4016 were identified. In 1984, there were 13 states with no known nesting Bald Eagles. In 1992, only three states had none. Alaska has an estimated healthy population of Bald Eagles numbering upwards of 50,000.

Thomas D. Burleigh (1945) found an active Bald Eagle nest on Ship Island on April 10, 1940. Burleigh reported that the nest contained small young and that both parent birds were apparently disturbed by his presence. Later, successful breeding populations of Bald Eagles in Mississippi were wiped out during the 1950s. All known nesting locations were unoccupied in the decade after 1960.

Prior to their disappearance, Bald Eagles nested along the Mississippi River near oxbow lakes, in the lower Yazoo Delta along lower Steele Bayou, near the mouth of Big Black River in Warren County, and on coastal estuaries and offshore islands. Single pairs have nested on Noxubee National Wildlife Refuge in Noxubee County and on the Yazoo National Wildlife Refuge in Washington County.

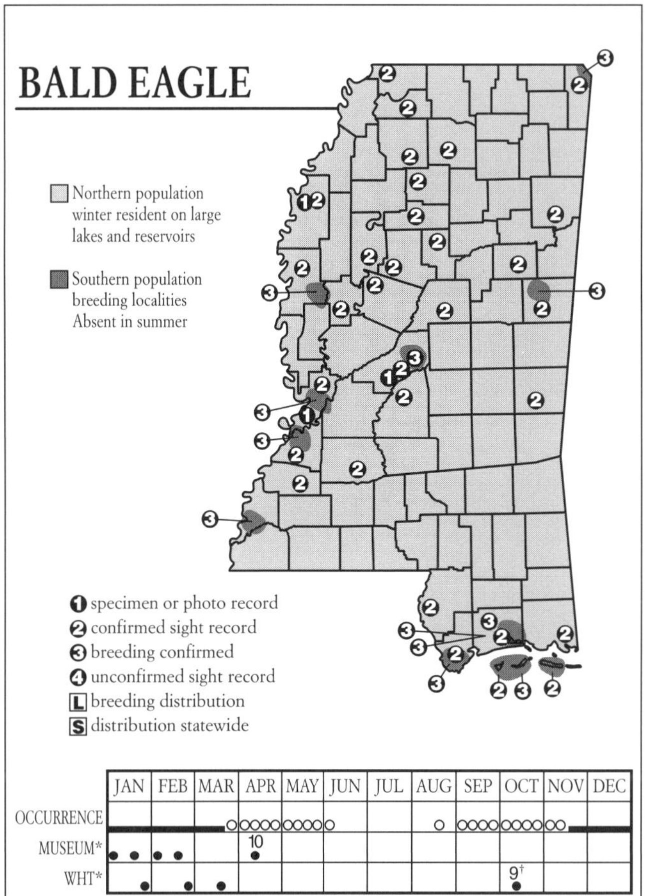

*Breeding confirmed by egg, sight, or photographic record.
†Adult on nest

From early November until March, Bald Eagles occur regularly on reservoirs and lakes, along large rivers, and on the Gulf Coast. Eagles arrive in larger numbers when prolonged below-freezing weather exists in northern states. During periods when most open water freezes, larger than usual incursions occur along the southern edge of the freeze line.

These weather conditions prevailed when most of Ross Barnett Reservoir was frozen over during late December 1983. Observers on the Jackson Christmas Bird Count saw a record number of 18 Bald Eagles on the lake. At one period on the count day, eight birds were seen soaring and engaging in courtship flights over the lake. A pair of eagles would swoop together, clasp talons in midair, and free-fall before releasing their hold. These antics were repeated until the birds drifted beyond view over shoreline treetops.

In Mississippi at least three breeding pairs are known to have raised young successfully in recent years. One pair built a large nest in a living pine at the edge of the river marsh bordering the Biloxi River in the early 1970s and fledged one or more young (Turcotte 1975c). After a marsh fire burned the nest, the pair later hatched and fledged young at a less exposed, nearby location.

In early 1984 another pair built and occupied a nest, but raised no young, at a site near Eagle Lake in Issaquena County. Nestings in later years at this site have fledged numerous young birds. This nest was in a tall dead cypress tree near the main levee of the Mississippi River. A storm later caused the adult birds to abandon this nest and build another nearby. The pair have since raised several young from this new nest.

In 1992, David L. Watts discovered an active Bald Eagle nest in a tall pine on the shoreline at Bay Springs Lake on the Tennessee-Tombigbee Waterway in Tishomingo County. Both adults were seen at the nest. Located on an inlet of the lake, the nest has produced several young. Each year, the inlet is closed to protect the birds from intrusions by boaters.

Bald Eagle nesting in Mississippi begins in late December, after the birds build a large nest of sticks lined with grass, moss, and soft material. Nests are enlarged and reused for years. Usually they are placed 40 feet or higher in large trees. Cypress and pine trees are preferred, but other Mississippi nests have been built in wild pecan, oak, and sycamore trees in the Yazoo Delta.

Two white, nearly oval eggs are usually laid. They are deeply covered with nest material when not being incubated. Incubation lasts about five weeks, and the young, which initially are covered with a smokey brown down, require about eight weeks of care and feeding in the nest before fledging. Both adults assist in incubation, brooding, and feeding the young eaglets.

Southern eagles migrate northward during June, July, and August, a fact confirmed by Charles L. Broley. He banded over 800 eagles from nests in Florida from 1936 to 1946. Most band recoveries came from points north of Florida, and one-third of them as far away as a thousand miles.

Bald Eagles spend much time perching on trees or snags around water, and can be located by scanning the area with binoculars or a telescope. Their food consists largely of fish, which they grab with their talons after a gliding approach, hardly touching the water. They also feed on carrion, especially dead or dying fish that drift to the shore. Bald Eagles watch for and chase Ospreys catching and carrying fish. The Osprey will usually drop a fish to avoid being attacked, and the eagle will retrieve it in midair or on the ground or water. Waterfowl, mammals, and birds found in aquatic environments attract eagles. On several occasions, I have watched a foraging Bald Eagle flush ducks and coots, evidently looking for dead or injured waterfowl.

Under the federal Endangered Species Act, Bald Eagles are classified as threatened species in the lower 48 states. All eagles are strictly protected by federal and state laws. Concerted efforts are being undertaken to restore breeding populations to unoccupied former nesting sites. Eggs taken from active eagle nests or from captive birds are hatched in captivity. The young eaglets are then banded and "hacked," an ancient falconry method involving raising and feeding the birds in cages on a raised platform with almost no human contact.

The Mississippi Department of Wildlife, Fisheries and Parks cooperated with the National Park Service at the Gulf Islands National Seashore in Jackson County in a hacking effort to return Bald Eagles to their native range along the Gulf Coast and barrier islands. Begun in December 1988, this project was the first nongame and endangered management project to receive funds from the income tax check-off program, a project of the Mississippi Wildlife Heritage Program. Approximately 44 Bald Eagles were released back into the wild. Also, during this project, at a site farther west along the coast mainland, another 17 bald eagles were hacked and released.

In February 1992, the U.S. Army Corps of Engineers became active in helping restore this eagle to its traditional southern nesting grounds. The Department of Wildlife, Fisheries and Parks; the George M. Sutton Avian Research Center; the National Wild Turkey Foundation; and numerous small cooperators assisted the Corps in hacking and releasing 46 immature Bald Eagles in northeastern Mississippi.

Fifteen birds were placed in a hacking tower on Okatibbee Lake north of Meridian. Since then, several banded immature eagles have been seen for several years on the lake during the winter. Additional eagles were placed in hacking towers at two sites along the Tennessee-Tombigbee Waterway. Sixteen eagles were hacked at a site on Bay Springs Lake about 20 miles south of Iuka in Tishomingo County. Another 15 immature Bald Eagles were hacked at Pool B near Lock B north of Amory. Scientists hope that the immature birds that grew to flight stage and fledged in these areas will return in four or five years as adults to nest and help perpetuate the tradition of America's national symbol.

Northern Harrier *Circus cyaneus*

This long-tailed hawk with a *prominent white rump patch* and owl-like facial discs is a regular winter resident. Formerly named Marsh Hawk, the harrier is often called "rabbit hawk" locally. Some females and immatures begin arriving in late August. Males arrive in late fall or winter months. A late departure date is May 17 at Grenada Lake (Davis and Knight, pers. comm.)

These hawks frequent open fields and wetlands and either perch low or on the ground. Harriers fly low to the ground, tilting, sailing, and hovering on upraised wings as they search methodically over open lands for small rodents, large insects, and other small prey, including at times small

Northern Harrier

landbirds. A large number of regurgitated pellets that I have examined contained fur and bones of cotton rats, harvest mice, or shrews. Others contained feathers and bones of ground-dwelling birds such as meadowlarks or sparrows and the remains of large grasshoppers.

They are communal roosters on the ground in broomsedge, tall grass, or marsh grass. Dozens or even hundreds have been seen roosting in large broomsedge fields where they congregate at dusk (Jackson et al. 1972). The small nestlike opening made in tall grass usually contains pellets of bones, hair, or feathers, as the same roosts are used by the birds over extended periods during the winter.

The adult female harrier is dark brown above, white below, and heavily streaked with brown to the flanks. Immatures resemble adult females, but are washed with cinnamon brown below and a lighter brown edging of feathers on the back. Adult males have light gray upperparts, black wing tips, and are mostly white below and washed and streaked lightly with pinkish brown. The long tail is distinctly banded above and below, and the white rump patch is very noticeable in flight on immatures and adults.

Fred Broerman with the U.S. Fish and Wildlife Service photographed downy young Northern Harriers in their nest on May 28, 1997, in Quitman County, the first state nest record.

NORTHERN HARRIER

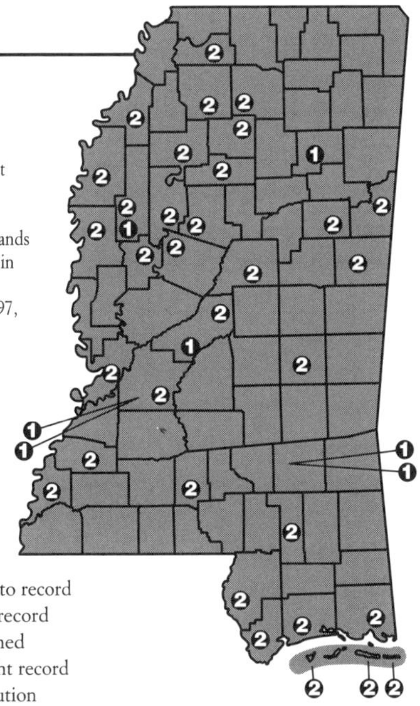

Fairly common fall and winter resident

Breeding probable in north Mississippi wetlands
Recent nesting record in north Delta county of Quitman, late May 1997, nest and five young
Photographed by Fred Broerman: MOS Newsletter 42,2

❶ specimen or photo record
❷ confirmed sight record
❸ breeding confirmed
❹ unconfirmed sight record
L breeding distribution
S distribution statewide

	JAN	FEB	MAR	APR	MAY	JUN	JUL	AUG	SEP	OCT	NOV	DEC
OCCURRENCE					13 o	5-19 ooo		oo oo	oo			
MUSEUM*					●●							
WHT*												

*Breeding confirmed by egg, sight, or photographic record.

Northern Harriers nest on the ground in marshes and prairie grasslands, preferably near wetlands, in the western and northern states and Canada. Four to seven dull white eggs are laid in a nest of grasses, marsh vegetation, and sticks.

Sharp-shinned Hawk *Accipiter striatus*

Three accipiters occur in North America, the Sharp-shinned Hawk, the Cooper's Hawk, and the larger Northern Goshawk, a bird that rarely ranges this far south in winter. Accipiters prey mostly on small birds. They have long, barred, rounded tails, except the Sharp-shinned, which has a *square* tail, slightly notched when folded. Sharp-shinned and Cooper's Hawks have short, rounded wings, and slim bodies. Both are commonly called "blue darters." They are fierce and bold in pursuit of small birds and are not easily disturbed while plucking and eating their prey.

The adult male Sharp-shinned Hawk is bluish gray above, with black on top and back of the head. The long tail is narrowly tipped with white and has four dark bands. Underparts are white and boldly barred in rusty red. Undertail coverts are white. The larger female adult is

Sharp-shinned Hawk

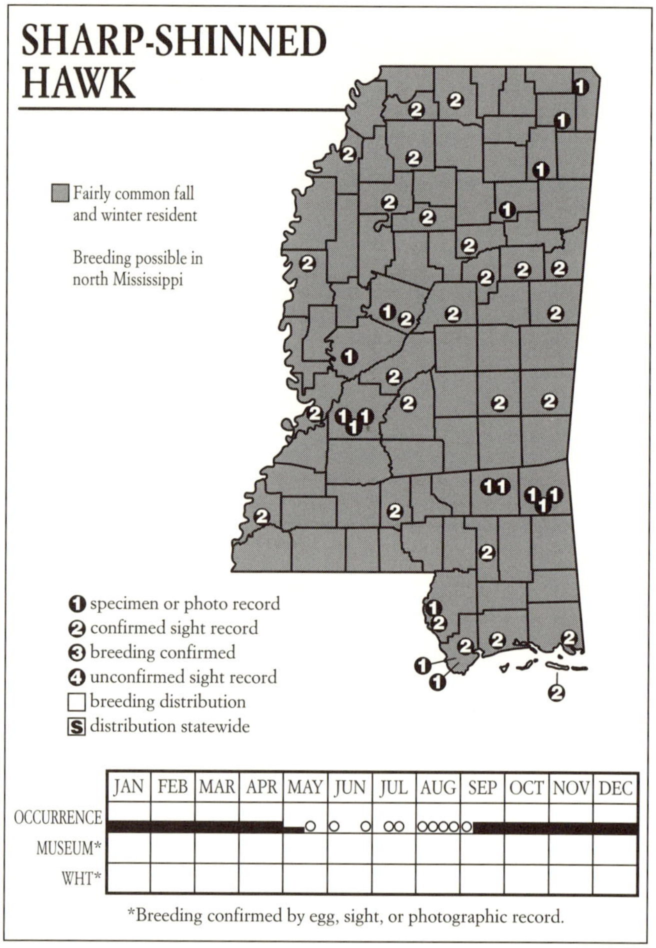

similar. Immatures of both sexes have mostly white underparts with bold, brownish streaking on the breast and sides.

Sharp-shins are fall and winter residents in Mississippi. They arrive in late September and October and depart by late April. There is no record of their nesting here, but a female specimen collected on July 10, 1939, by H. L. Owen at Blue Springs in Tishomingo County indicated breeding may occur in northern Mississippi. A few nesting records have been reported in northern Louisiana and Alabama.

This species and the Cooper's Hawk underwent a serious population decline following the heavy use of insecticides after World War II. Being at the top of the food chain and feeding almost exclusively on smaller, mostly insect-eating birds, the accipiters accumulated toxic chlorinated hydrocarbon residues that caused reproduction failure. As a result, very few of these birds were seen during the decades of the 1960s and 1970s. In recent years the Sharp-shinned Hawk has recovered and now occurs commonly as a winter resident. The Cooper's Hawk is uncommon and seldom found in Mississippi during the breeding season.

The Sharp-shinned Hawk strikes small birds with little warning. On several occasions, I have watched Sharp-shins attack or pursue small birds. Once, as I watched a flock of juncos at a small clearing in the woods, this hawk darted in view and swooped through the opening and passed out of view. The juncos vanished from sight in a nearby grassy opening. Although I saw them disappear in the grass as the hawk approached, I could not flush one of the dozen or more hiding birds. Small birds seem to know instinctively that their best escape from being caught is to take cover and stay motionless until danger is past. Escaping by flight alone would be a deadly mistake with a Sharp-shinned Hawk in pursuit.

This hawk species is often attracted to bird feeders to the dismay of backyard feeder-watchers. For two winters, I have seen Sharp-shins attack, catch, and eat birds using our feeders. On one occasion, a female Sharp-shin caught a male Brown-headed Cowbird, plucked it on the limb of an oak tree, and remained there until all of it was eaten. Afterward, she caught a male Purple Martin and carried it to the same limb and ate it, not more than 20 feet above my head. She seemed oblivious to my presence. On other occasions, this hawk made futile passes at birds. For long periods after each attack, birds stayed hidden from sight. Although a Red-tailed Hawk sat or flew regularly along a nearby field and fence row, the birds ignored its presence and continued feeding.

The Sharp-shinned Hawk builds a large nest of twigs lined with leaves and finer materials, usually high in a coniferous tree in a large wooded area. The four or five eggs are dull white and heavily marked with shades of brown. They are considered to be the most beautifully marked of all hawk eggs.

Cooper's Hawk *Accipiter cooperii*

This larger species is almost identical to the Sharp-shinned Hawk in color and marks except for size, and the fact that the Cooper's Hawk has a *rounded* instead of square tail. The size of the smaller male Cooper's Hawk overlaps the size of large specimens of female Sharp-shins, so that the two species cannot be distinguished by size alone. Seen in flight or at rest, the *rounded* or *graduated ends of the tail feathers* are the only useful field marks separating this species from the *square-tailed* Sharp-shinned Hawk.

The Cooper's Hawk was once widespread but was never a common permanent resident in Mississippi. It still occurs sparingly as a breeding species, but is observed mostly during fall and winter as a winter resident. Probably most sightings of this hawk occur in September and October during fall migration and in April during spring migration.

Unlike other hawk species, the Cooper's Hawk population has not recovered from a serious decline during the 1960s and 1970s, when its numbers plummeted to near extinction. From then to 1985, I positively identified Cooper's Hawks on only four occasions. Two adults were possible breeding birds.

The first Cooper's Hawk I saw was carrying a small bird and being pursued by a male Red-winged Blackbird in southwest Hinds County in June. A second sighting came in late May when a large adult Cooper's Hawk flew across a road through open woods in Copiah County. Another adult was seen in Madison County on a Christmas Bird Count. The fourth record was in the Loess Bluff hills of Warren County, where in early April I found a dead adult on a logging road. It had been shot and left hanging on a bush, apparently by a turkey hunter.

In earlier times, most rural families kept chickens in yards or let them range free about their property. In those days, "big blue darters" boldly raided chicken yards and stained the reputations of all large hawks as chicken thieves. Consequently, hawks were shot indiscriminately, and many people often carried rifles to shoot hawks perched along roadsides.

Thankfully, times have changed. Now, most chickens are housed for mass production, and few hawk depredations occur. Cooper's Hawks and all other hawks are beneficial as natural predators in controlling excess numbers of harmful species. They eat injured, weak, and diseased birds and small animals. All hawks are protected by state and federal laws.

Two experiences I had while quail hunting persist in my memory and illustrate the audacity and tenacity of this hawk while pursuing its prey. After my pointer dog trailed some birds along a stream bank and came to a point at a large blackberry thicket, I could hear the excited chattering of bobwhites in the briers as I approached. Circling around the patch I could see part of the covey moving among the canes as a Cooper's Hawk stalked them. I stood and watched, and although the hawk saw me, it flew off only after I approached within 20 feet. I did not shoot at the hawk or the quail that pitched across the stream into a thicket of honeysuckle vines.

Another time, a covey flushed wild in an open field and scattered toward me. A Cooper's Hawk darted from a tree

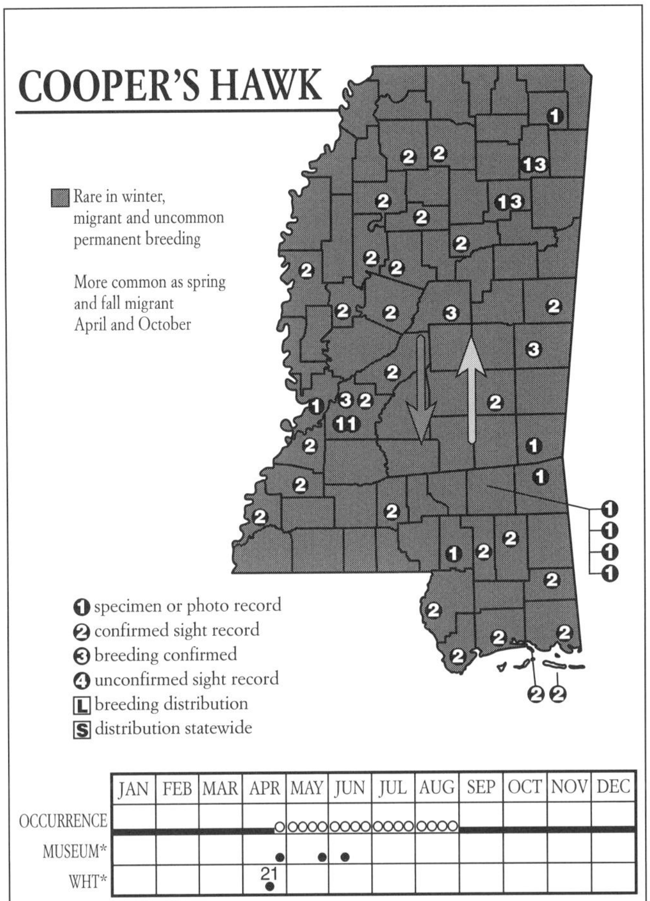

*Breeding confirmed by egg, sight, or photographic record.

along a fence row and singled out one bird that came my way. I watched as the quail sailed into a plum thicket with the hawk close behind. I went directly to the spot where they came down and found the hawk stunned on the ground from impact with the plum bushes. I left it to recover.

The few confirmed breeding records for the Cooper's Hawk all precede World War II. The earliest is a nest with four fresh eggs that I collected on April 21, 1934, in open woods southeast of Clinton in Hinds County. This nest was made of dead oak twigs lined with a small amount of bark and a few green leaves. It was in the topmost fork of a large willow oak tree.

Later nest and egg records in the MMNS are from Chickasaw County (May 25, 1939), Attala County (April 29, 1940), and Lee County (April 28, 1941), where Eugene Patton collected five fresh eggs from a nest of sticks lined with bark about 50 feet high in a tall pine.

The eggs of the Cooper's Hawk are bluish white when fresh, but soon become nest stained. Occasionally, the eggs have a sprinkling of small, pale reddish brown spots. The usual clutch is four or five eggs. Young are in the nest in late May and June, a time when smaller birds and their young are most vulnerable and abundant.

[Northern Goshawk] *Accipiter gentilis*

This large and fierce accipiter is a resident of mixed hardwoods and evergreens of northern forests, seldom wintering farther south. There are a few Mississippi sightings of individual birds and only one specimen record.

The Northern Goshawk is a casual late fall and winter visitor to the northern Gulf states and Florida. It is larger than the female Cooper's Hawk. Field marks of the adult are whitish, finely barred and streaked underparts, fluffy white undertail coverts, blackish crown and cheeks, and a broad white stripe over the eye. The long, banded tail and long, rounded wings identify it as an accipiter. The bird's back is grayer than the Cooper's Hawk, reminiscent of the adult male Northern Harrier. Immature Northern Goshawks have dark brown upperparts. Underparts are heavily streaked with dark brown, especially on the flanks. A *pale stripe over the eye* and *wavy or zigzag tail banding* separate the immature Northern Goshawk, which is usually larger, from the immature Cooper's Hawk.

Periodically, this hawk irrupts in numbers, and some move southward below their normal winter range above and along the northern states. Normally they feed on small birds, waterfowl, and small mammals. They are apt to appear where large concentrations of waterfowl and smaller birds are present in very cold winters.

Accounts and sightings of two or more individual birds seen by Vic Theobald and Gene Knight (MMNS) are noteworthy for the historical record. On January 3, 1986, at Sardis Waterfowl Refuge, Gene Knight and David Elmendorf saw and agreed in identifying a hawk overhead and flying directly toward them as an immature Northern Goshawk. They noted the bird's brown topsides, heavily streaked underparts, barred tail, shape, and size. Earlier and afterward (no dates), Theobald had seen a large hawk in dead trees on the refuge that flew into wooded growth before it was identified. Elmendorf had prior knowledge of the hawk in northern areas.

On January 31, 1984, Refuge Manager Vic Theobald picked up an injured hawk on a road leading to Sardis Lake several miles from the refuge. This bird was caged and fed for a month and a half, then released. Afterwards, upon consulting a field guide, he and Area Supervisor Benny Herring agreed it was an adult Northern Goshawk. Unfortunately, it was not photographed or reported for positive identification before release.

Terrie Gates and Robert Chapel observed a Northern Goshawk at the Hattiesburg sewage lagoons during the annual Christmas Bird Count on December 31, 1983 (Imhof 1984). Details of this sight record were submitted by Robert Chapel who had prior experience with the bird in northern Illinois. The hawk, seen as it flew over an open area, was an adult bird with good coloration and all marks were noted, including the conspicuous fluffy white undertail coverts (Gates, pers. comm.).

NORTHERN GOSHAWK

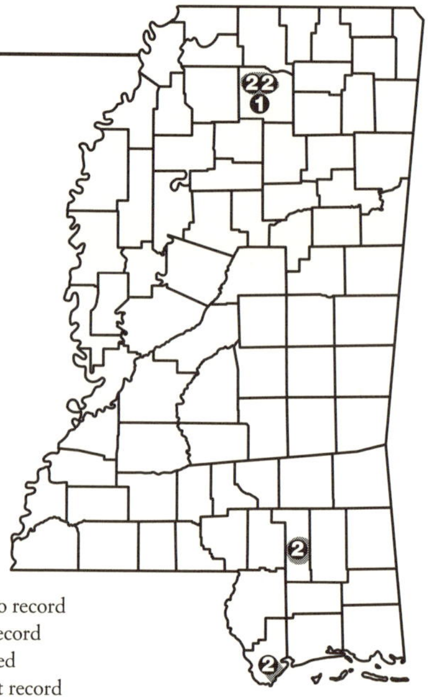

Casual winter visitor rare and irregular locality records

❶ specimen or photo record
❷ confirmed sight record
❸ breeding confirmed
❹ unconfirmed sight record
☐ breeding distribution
L distribution statewide

	JAN	FEB	MAR	APR	MAY	JUN	JUL	AUG	SEP	OCT	NOV	DEC
OCCURRENCE	3 31									25		31
MUSEUM*												
WHT*												

*Breeding confirmed by egg, sight, or photographic record.

Another adult Northern Goshawk sighting by Judith A. Toups and Gerry Morgan occurred over a freshwater pond at Clermont Harbor in Hancock County. The bird was seen in flight and most field marks were noted and described. The bird was in view of both observers using binoculars for about 20 seconds. At the same time, it was compared in size with a pursuing Sharp-shinned Hawk at a height where size, plumage coloring, tail shape and marks, wing shape, flight style, and head marks could be seen and noted before it escaped into cover. An unusual number of hawks had been seen, including 10 Sharp-shinned Hawks, one Cooper's Hawk, four unidentified accipiters, 20 Red-tails, one Red-shouldered Hawk, and two Northern Harriers. Strong northwest winds and a frontal movement were favorable for hawk migration and the concentration of hawks. This first Mississippi sight record occurred on October 25, 1983 (MMNS).

One state specimen record documents the occurrence of this hawk, a female in the MMNS in Jackson. The bird was first found southwest of Oxford by Judy Burkepile as it crossed the road in front of her car with an injured wing on March 10, 1993. It was captured the following morning by Keith Meals, Marvin Davis, and Burkepile. The hawk was emaciated and had a fractured humerus. A lead slug was imbedded in wing tissue. Reparative surgery was attempted by a veterinarian, but the hawk never recovered from the anesthesia.

[Harris' Hawk] *Parabuteo unicinctus*

This is one of the prettiest of all hawks. The head, body, and upperparts are chocolate brown, except for the chestnut shoulder patches, wing linings, and feathers covering the thighs. The long tail is white at the base (white encircles the tail) with a broad black band narrowly tipped with white. The legs and cere (the fleshy area at base of bill) are bright yellow. Immature birds resemble the Red-shouldered Hawk, but are darker above and have more white at the base and tip of the tail. They are heavily streaked below with rufous shoulders and wing linings. Thigh feathers are barred with rufous. The tail is narrowly banded with a wider, white terminal band.

This hawk inhabits the mesquite brushlands and semiarid woodlands of southwestern Texas, southern New Mexico, and parts of the Sonoran Desert in Arizona. Its range extends into northern Mexico, where it is moderately common in open, arid brush country.

The Harris' Hawk is included on Mississippi's state bird list on the basis of a collected specimen taken between Bayou Sara, Louisiana, and Natchez by John James Audubon. The specimen was described and named by him and the following account was published in the *Proceedings of the Academy of Natural Sciences of Philadelphia:* "At a stated meeting, September 1, 1846, Vice-President Morton in the chair, a specimen in skin of *Buteo unicinctus* (*Falco harrisii,* Aud.) from the vicinity of Natchez, Mississippi from Dr. J. C. Jenkins of Natchez was announced."

A second sight record near Picayune in Pearl River County on May 11, 1943, was reported by letter to the MMNS. Additional sightings in the same locality occurred on July 9 and 15, 1943. At the time, much of the county was open, cut-over pinelands with open range grazing. Pines and scrub oaks were scattered among the stumps of cut-over virgin pines. These sightings were made and reported by Amy Tolman, a competent observer who lived near Picayune.

A sighting with photographs of a Harris' Hawk occurred near Pascagoula in Jackson County on December 6, 1988. The sighting was made and reported by C. Delmas and Dave Ruple (Muth 1989).

HARRIS' HAWK

Accidental sight record; only one photograph record

❶ specimen or photo record
❷ confirmed sight record
❸ breeding confirmed
❹ unconfirmed record
☐ breeding distribution
A distribution statewide

	JAN	FEB	MAR	APR	MAY	JUN	JUL	AUG	SEP	OCT	NOV	DEC
OCCURRENCE					11 ○		9 15 ○ ○					6 ○
MUSEUM*												
WHT*												

*Breeding confirmed by egg, sight, or photographic record.

Red-shouldered Hawk *Buteo lineatus*

The male Red-shouldered Hawk is dark brown above, evenly barred with reddish on white, with vertical, narrow black streaks on the breast. The belly and undertail coverts are white. Broad, red shoulder patches extend about one-fourth the length of the folded wings. The tail is black with four to six *narrow* white bands. When soaring overhead against a bright sky, translucent "windows" at the base of the outer primary wing feathers are distinctive.

The female is orange red on the breast, but otherwise is similar to the male. Immatures are mostly brown above and white below with heavy dark brown streaks on the breast and sides. The tail is banded like the adults.

The Red-shouldered Hawk frequents moist woodlands and open fields along stream bottoms. Like other buteos, this species locates prey while perching and captures it by gliding and pouncing on the victim. Its food consists of small rodents, crayfish, small reptiles, amphibians, large insects, and occasionally small birds. It is a beneficial species, seldom straying far from bottomland hardwood swamps.

Throughout its wide range, it is fairly common, although in recent years it has declined in numbers. In Mississippi, it occurs statewide as a permanent resident.

Red-shouldered Hawks engage in soaring and courtship flights during the mating and nesting season, when their

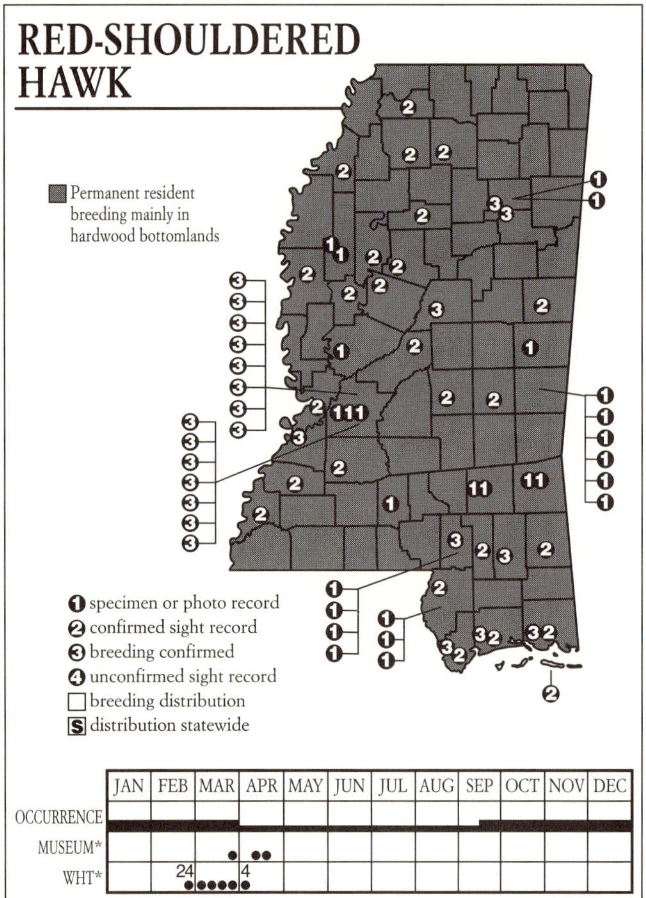

*Breeding confirmed by egg, sight, or photographic record.

piercing calls are most noticeable. Their mating flights are spectacular, with the male pursuing a female while diving, soaring, chasing, and screaming. Blue Jays often imitate the calls of this hawk.

Nesting begins in late February and most egg laying occurs in early March. The nest is a large structure of sticks, twigs, and bark, usually containing some Spanish moss. During incubation, some green leaves are added to the nest lining and down feathers are usually visible on the edges. Nests are placed in a tree fork, usually 30 to 50 feet aboveground in oak, sweet gum, cypress, and other tall trees.

The eggs number from two to four. They are bluish white when fresh and variously blotched with dark brown to reddish brown. The first egg laid is most heavily marked. Subsequent eggs in a set vary from lightly marked to sometimes almost unmarked. Downy young are in the nest after mid-April when trees are in full foliage.

Broad-winged Hawk *Buteo platypterus*

This species is a summer resident in the eastern United States and Canada. About the size of a crow, it can be recognized by white underwings showing black tips, and the wide tailbanding in the adult having white bands *about equal* to the three or four wide black bands. Immatures have white underwings; brown-streaked white underparts; and the tail appears longer with narrower, dark tail bands more numerous than in the adult, which obscure the lighter bands. The adults have white underparts heavily barred with dark reddish brown. Upperparts are dark slate brown.

While at rest, this hawk has a chunky appearance. In flight, the breadth of the wings at the body is about half the total length. A specimen in hand shows three notched outer primary wing feathers compared to four or more found on the Red-shouldered Hawk.

The high-pitched call is similar to that of the Eastern Wood-Pewee, only more hawklike in volume with a higher inflection at first and diminishing at the end: *p-weeeeeee*. I have heard Blue Jays mimic the Broad-wing call so perfectly that I could not detect a difference until I saw the imitator. The call can be imitated by whistling with the lower lip curled back over the bottom teeth.

Broad-wings arrive around April 1 and depart in September and early October. Spring arrivals appear gradually and are seen in noticeable numbers until mid-April when the northward passage slows. The main southward migration begins in early September and diminishes in early October.

In fall, these hawks migrate in a southwesterly direction across Mississippi (westerly on the coast) and through Louisiana and Texas. They usually are seen traveling in upward spiralling flocks called "kettles," then sailing beyond sight on set wings.

During one day of observation, migrating fall flocks may contain several thousand birds in passage. I have seen two Broad-wing flock migrations. The first, at the Vicksburg National Military Park, had 114 birds in flocks of 73, 34, and seven birds only minutes apart. The second observation at Richland in Rankin County occurred on September 11, 1985, when I saw a spiral of hawks and counted 100 of the lowest birds. I estimated as many birds higher as they moved out of sight when another spiraling flock of more than 100 appeared and passed from view.

Several similar fall flights have been reported to me by other observers during September. A passage of more than a thousand birds was reported by two observers west of Kosciusko on the Big Black River in Attala County at 10:30 A.M. (Turcotte 1971c). A short while later, a man called from Flora to report similar flocks in passage along the same river in Madison County. A few days later, I learned about the passage of "thousands" of hawks over the Brownsville community in Hinds County, at about noon on the same day of the earlier reports. Vicksburg bird-watchers also reported migrating hawks over the city and the Vicksburg National Military Park (Battalio 1987).

Broad-winged Hawks nest locally in Mississippi. Preferred nesting sites are deciduous upland forests and groves on rugged terrain, where hardwoods are dominant. They occur as summer residents and nest sparingly along the length of the Loess Bluff region extending from Wilkinson County along the Mississippi River north to Vicksburg and around the Yazoo Delta to Memphis. These highly eroded hills and deep ravines are mostly covered in hardwoods, with pines dominant only on the highest ridgetops. Similar terrain with dominant hardwood forests and groves is found locally elsewhere in central and northern Mississippi where this species nests. A confirmed photo record from June 30 to July 7, 1986, of a nest and fledgling young near Logtown in Hancock County was reported (Hodges and Toups 1986).

The nest of the Broad-winged Hawk is usually in the fork of a tall hardwood tree, but sometimes in a pine. The nest is shabbily constructed of sticks, twigs, bark, and moss, with green leafy twigs added during incubation.

Two eggs are usually laid, but occasionally there are three or four. They appear greenish white and variously spotted or blotched with brown. There are only two records confirmed by egg collection: May 10, 1940, by B. Hamberlin at Phoenix in Yazoo County (two fresh eggs with a nest in a beech tree); and May 29, 1940, by W. D. Lewis (two eggs with incubation advanced). The nest of sticks and bark was in a tree fork in Pearl River County.

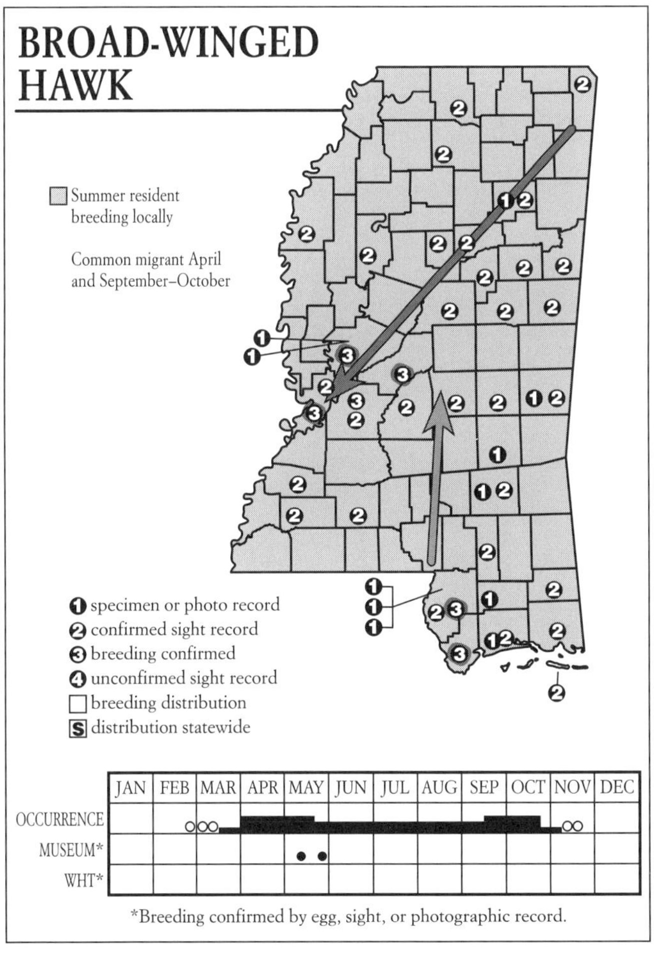

I have never found an active nest, but I located one in Warren County under construction in a beech tree with adult birds present. I observed an adult carrying nest material in Madison County, and I found an abandoned nest where a pair had been seen carrying nest material and food in Hinds County.

This gentle and beneficial hawk is tamer than most birds of prey. Its food is mainly large insects, lizards, small reptiles, mice, and, I suspect, chipmunks. These small rodents are common along the Loess Bluff where the Broad-winged Hawk is fairly common in summer.

Swainson's Hawk *Buteo swainsoni*

The Swainson's Hawk is common on the plains and deserts of western states, but rarely occurs east of the Mississippi River. It may migrate through and escape notice among migrating flocks of Broad-winged Hawks. Two collection records by Vaiden (1952b) substantiate the occurrence of this species in Mississippi. Two female specimens were taken by him about nine miles south of Rosedale in Bolivar County on September 27 and October 19, 1952.

This hawk is similar in size to the Red-tailed Hawk, but has longer and more pointed wings. It flies with wings tilted slightly upward and teeters in flight like the Turkey Vulture. A dark band across the breast is *sharply defined* against the white or pale buff belly and wing linings. Distinctive field marks for the adult light-color phase are the *sharp contrast* between the wing linings and dark, barred flight feathers. A dark phase, with dark brown above and below, shows little contrast between the flight feathers and wing linings. An intermediate, red color phase is dark brown above and below, with the belly and thighs conspicuously barred reddish except for white undertail coverts.

Immatures are dark above with a prominent eyebrow line and dark moustache lines extending and widening beneath the eyes to form dark patches on the sides of the breast. Their underparts are buffy and heavily streaked with dark brown that becomes patches on the sides. The thighs are lightly barred with rufous.

On its home range, the Swainson's Hawk can be seen soaring or perching on posts in open country, where it is usually found. It is sometimes surprisingly tame. In southwestern Montana near the Red Rock National Wildlife Refuge, two of these hawks sat on fence posts along a ranch road and allowed themselves to be photographed at close range from our car window. When disturbed, they flew a short distance ahead or behind our car and alighted on another post. These birds seemed to be

SWAINSON'S HAWK

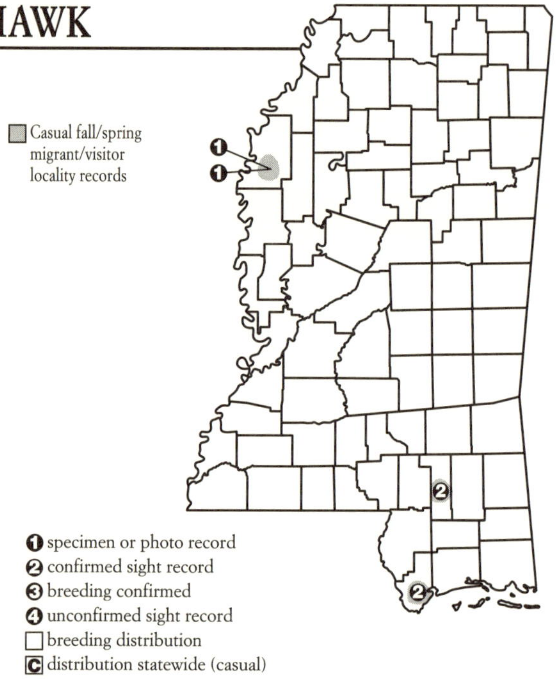

	JAN	FEB	MAR	APR	MAY	JUN	JUL	AUG	SEP	OCT	NOV	DEC
OCCURRENCE		27 o	oooo				oo		oo	oo	o	31 o
MUSEUM*												
WHT*												

*Breeding confirmed by egg, sight, or photographic record.

absorbed with trying to catch the numerous ground squirrels we saw along the fences and roadsides in June 1984.

Sightings of this hawk in Mississippi are most likely to occur in September and October during Broad-winged Hawk migrations. Like the Broad-wing, this species migrates and winters mainly in South America. It can be expected to occur again in late March or April on the return migration. Some of these hawks have been observed wintering regularly in Florida, so it is likely that this species is being overlooked during migration in Mississippi.

Recent sight records in southern Mississippi indicate this species may also occur as a casual winter visitor. One occurrence was on December 31, 1979, a bird observed by Larry Gates on the Hancock County Christmas Bird Count (Toups 1980b). A second late winter sighting of one dark-phase individual at Pearlington in Hancock County was reported from February 27 to March 8, 1984, by Judith Toups, Mickey Baker, Gerry Morgan, and Evelyn Johnson (Hodges and Jackson 1984). Sightings of two birds were made at Clermont Harbor in Hancock County on October 30, 1984, by Judith Toups and Morgan (Hodges and Jackson 1984). At Hattiesburg in Forrest County, Richard Moore and Pedro Rodriguez observed one bird on March 21, 1982 (Jackson 1982).

Red-tailed Hawk *Buteo jamaicensis*

Buteos have broad wings and tails, and are noted for their soaring abilities. Red-tailed Hawks breed locally in the central and northern parts of Mississippi and probably to the coast. From mid-November to late March, large numbers of Red-tails appear in the Gulf states from their northern breeding territories as far away as British Columbia and Alaska. In winter, this hawk is abundant statewide and is frequently seen along roadsides, especially the interstate highways, where it becomes exceedingly tame and oblivious to busy traffic.

Most Red-tailed Hawks in adult plumage can be identified by the broad tail narrowly banded at the tip with a reddish upper surface, which is visible as the bird soars and wheels aloft. It is the largest of the common buteos. Immatures are dark brown above and mostly white below, except for a band of dark brown feathers across the belly that is also present on adults. The tail of immatures is brown streaked with narrow, darker brown banding on the upperside.

Wintering individuals of this species show a wide degree of color variation, largely because of geographical differences over their wide range. Geographical races, or subspecies, together with melanistic or dark-phased individuals that occur in all races of Red-tailed Hawks, make field identification by subspecies difficult and confusing.

The Harlan's Hawk, once regarded as a species but now a Red-tail subspecies, breeds in Alaska and British Columbia. Melanism is common in the *harlani* race, and dark-phase individuals are seen regularly overwintering in Mississippi. This subspecies has a tail that is mostly white toward the base. Red is mostly absent in their tail or occurs only in patches or streaks with banding or mottling of black, brown, and white. As these characteristics are hard to see, it is difficult to confirm identification in the field without a good view through a telescope. I always stop to view and admire an all black individual of this color phase. In the light color phase, individual Harlan's Hawks are identified by the tail marks described above.

Red-tails use the perch, glide, and pounce method of

Red-tailed Hawk

capturing their food, which consists of cotton rats, rice rats, harvest mice, and other small rodents inhabiting open grasslands and brushy or weedy openings. Occasionally they will hover momentarily before pouncing. I saw this on one occasion while riding in a car with John Phares on the Copiah County Wildlife Management Area. As we turned from the public road onto an area road, a Red-tail dove, then hovered momentarily and lit on the ground in an open field about 50 feet to our left. We stopped the car opposite the hawk as it flew away. Upon checking the spot where the bird went down, we found the complete skin of a large cotton rat. The hawk had captured, skinned, and eaten its prey, and flown away in less than a minute.

This species nests in most of Mississippi, but there are confirmed records only from central and northern counties. On March 31, 1939, near Okolona in Chickasaw County, H. L. Owens collected a set of two eggs now in the MMNS. I found nests on two successive years in the same wooded area adjacent to idle land and cultivated fields near Brownsville in Hinds County. The first nest was about 30 feet high in a pine tree growing among other tall pines in gullied land adjacent to a wooded pasture. This nest held downy young in late May. The following year a second nest was found about 200 yards from the first. It was in a tall pine 40 feet aboveground. The nest held feathered fledglings in early June.

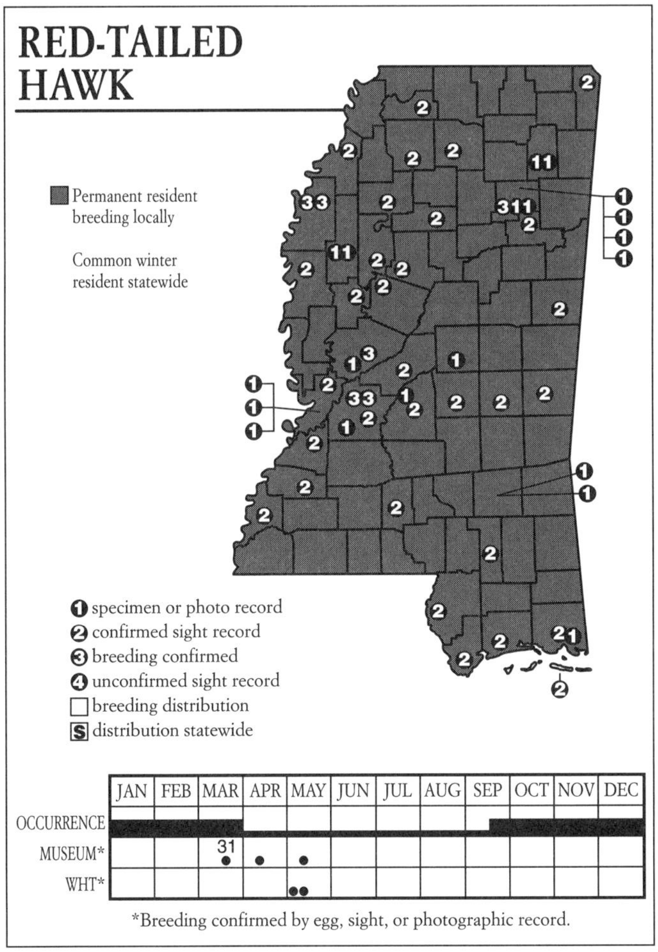

Another nest I observed with adults present was in a tall hardwood on the edge of the Loess Bluff between Satartia and Yazoo City in Yazoo County. Another nest under construction on March 21 was in hardwoods bordering a pasture adjacent to the Natchez Trace Parkway in Claiborne County. From the Trace, I watched adults carry material to the nest in a large white oak tree. Sight records of adult pairs on the coast in Hancock County and in Pearl River County in late May and early June indicate nesting yet to be confirmed.

The nest of the Red-tailed Hawk is a large platform of sticks, twigs, leaves, and moss placed in a tree fork or large limb crotch in tall trees of woodlands adjacent to open lands. Eggs number two or three and are bluish white variously marked with shades of brown to reddish brown.

This large, common hawk is helpful in controlling populations of harmful rodents that compete with birds for wild seeds and waste grain seeds. In times past, large numbers of Red-tailed Hawks were shot by hunters because of the bird's large size and relative tameness. Hunters should think twice before pulling the trigger on one of these wild benefactors, now protected by state and federal laws.

[Ferruginous Hawk] *Buteo regalis*

On the afternoon of December 28, 1986, my wife, Dorothy, and I had a "close encounter" with a bird of this species. We were on the Jackson Christmas Bird Count, covering a segment of Madison County along Mississippi Highway 43. Just after we had turned onto a primitive dead-end road and crossed a wooden bridge, a hawk sailed from a grove of tall trees, and swooped down directly in front of our car. It then spiraled and soared to about 200 feet above us. I managed to get out of the car and view it with binoculars until it soared out of sight over the tall trees behind us.

The hawk was *rusty red* on the back, the *tail was not banded but white at the base* and *pale rusty without marks or band.* Overhead, the wings and tail were nearly all pale or white, except for dark edging on the primaries and secondaries. The hawk had *rufous edgings* on the *white wing linings, rufous on the sides and legs,* which formed a V-*shape* and widened out along the edgings of the wing linings to the wrists. This bird was as large as a Red-tailed Hawk, but appeared to have *longer wings.* I have seen hundreds of Red-tails in many adult and immature plumage variations, but none resembling this hawk. The *italicized* parts of the above description are distinctive field marks for the light-phase adult *regalis.* Unfortunately, we could not relocate the bird for a better view.

FERRUGINOUS HAWK

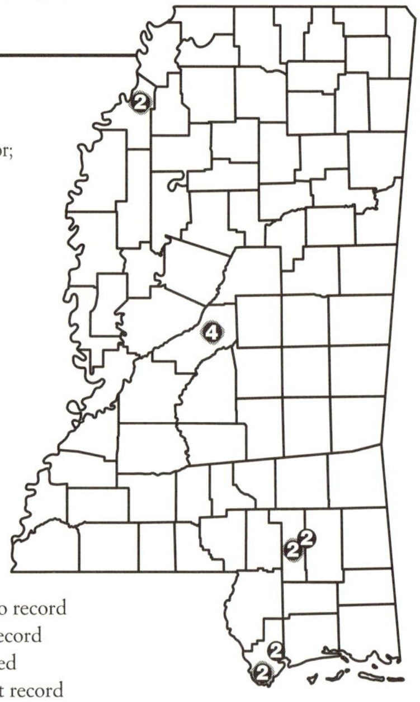

■ Accidental winter visitor; locality records

❶ specimen or photo record
❷ confirmed sight record
❸ breeding confirmed
❹ unconfirmed sight record
□ breeding distribution
🅰 distribution statewide

	JAN	FEB	MAR	APR	MAY	JUN	JUL	AUG	SEP	OCT	NOV	DEC
OCCURRENCE	3 ○											8 27 ○○○
MUSEUM*												
WHT*												

*Breeding confirmed by egg, sight, or photographic record.

The Ferruginous Hawk is common on the Great Plains, and its range extends west to the Pacific Coast and western provinces of Canada. The Ferruginous Hawk normally winters in the southwestern states to western Texas and into northern parts of Mexico, but is rare or uncommon in winter east of the Great Plains to the Mississippi River and casual farther eastward. Lowery Jr. (1974) listed seven Louisiana sight records extending from November 1 to March 8.

The Ferruginous Hawk has a dark phase with underparts of the adult a dark rusty brown. Dark brown wing linings contrast sharply with the pale underside of the tail. Upperparts are uniformly dark except for the white or pale rusty unbanded, unmarked tail.

On January 3, 1965, Sharon and Marvin Davis (Coffey and Coffey 1965) of Oxford reported the first Mississippi sight record of a light-phase Ferruginous Hawk. The carefully studied observation was made on the Moon Lake (Lula) Christmas Bird Count.

Two other sight records, one in southern Hancock County by Robert Chapel (Hamilton 1981) on December 27, 1980, and one immature on December 8 and 27, 1979, at Hattiesburg by Terrie Fairly have been reported (Jackson and Schardien 1980a).

Rough-legged Hawk *Buteo lagopus*

This large buteo prefers open country. It is a rare or casual winter visitor to the Gulf states and most parts of the Southeast. In winter, it rarely occurs with any regularity farther south than Tennessee and northern Arkansas.

This hawk is best identified in the field by a combination of field marks and behavior patterns. Like the Northern Harrier, it prefers to hunt over open country. It often *hovers,* but does not fly with upswept wings and lacks the white rump patch of the Northern Harrier, but instead its tail is white with a wide black band at the tip. It has the body shape of a buteo with a longer tail and slightly longer wings, but is not nearly as thin bodied and slim tailed as the Northern Harrier. It perches lower than the Red-tailed Hawk and is often seen on posts, stumps, or on the ground.

Prominent field marks on the *light phase* are a long *white* tail with broad *black terminal band* or bands, a *dark belly band,* and *dark wrist patches* that contrast with the paler head and base of the primaries. Seen from above, the white tail and small *white patches* at the base of the primary wing feathers contrast with the darker upperparts. A dark phase of the Rough-legged Hawk is best recognized by the dark

ROUGH-LEGGED HAWK

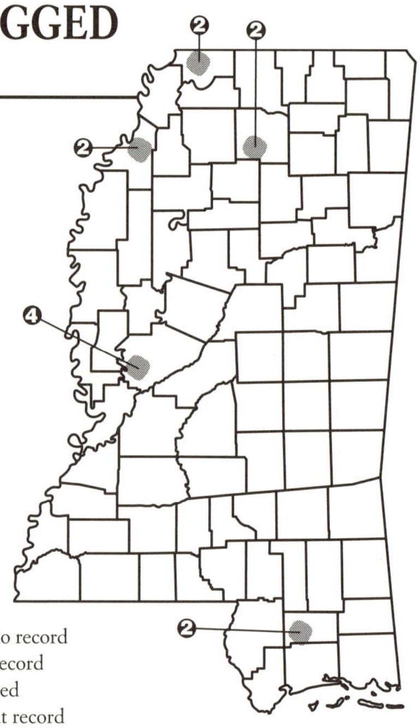

■ Casual, sight record localities

❶ specimen or photo record
❷ confirmed sight record
❸ breeding confirmed
❹ unconfirmed sight record
□ breeding distribution
🅰 distribution statewide

	JAN	FEB	MAR	APR	MAY	JUN	JUL	AUG	SEP	OCT	NOV	DEC
OCCURRENCE	2 15 ○ ○	17 ○		5 22 ○ ○								31 ○○
MUSEUM*												
WHT*												

*Breeding confirmed by egg, sight, or photographic record.

wing linings that contrast sharply with the underside of the flight feathers and by the white tail with terminal black band or bands. Immatures and females have a brownish terminal band on the white tail. The legs are *feathered to the toes.*

Coffey Jr. (1953) reported the first record of a Rough-legged Hawk supported by substantiating details and multiple observers. This sighting was made on April 5, 1953, about four miles west of Walls in Desoto County. The hawk, a light-phase individual, was perched on a pole at 40 yards. Following the bird as it flew away, the observers noted that it was joined by a Red-tailed Hawk.

Pursuit by Coffey's party turned up another Rough-legged Hawk, both in view with a Red-tail nearby for comparison by the five observers. Publication of this sight record with detailed descriptions made by Coffey Jr. met the requirements for adding this species to the state bird list. An earlier sight record mentioned by Coffey Jr. in the Walls area by W. Whittemore and Simpson is mentioned, but no supporting details were added. No earlier historical records for this hawk have been located.

Occurrence records since the above confirmed sighting of Rough-legs in Mississippi are one at Moon Lake in Coahoma County by Harry Wilcox (Coffey 1956b) on January 2, 1956; a light phase at Sardis Lake by W. Marvin Davis (Jackson and Weber 1977) on January 15, 1977; one light phase on Sardis Lake during the Christmas Bird Count on December 31, 1977, by W. Marvin Davis (Weber 1977); one light phase at Wiggins in Stone County on April 22, 1978, by Larry Gates (Imhof 1978); and two seen by W. Marvin Davis at Sardis Lake on February 17, 1985.

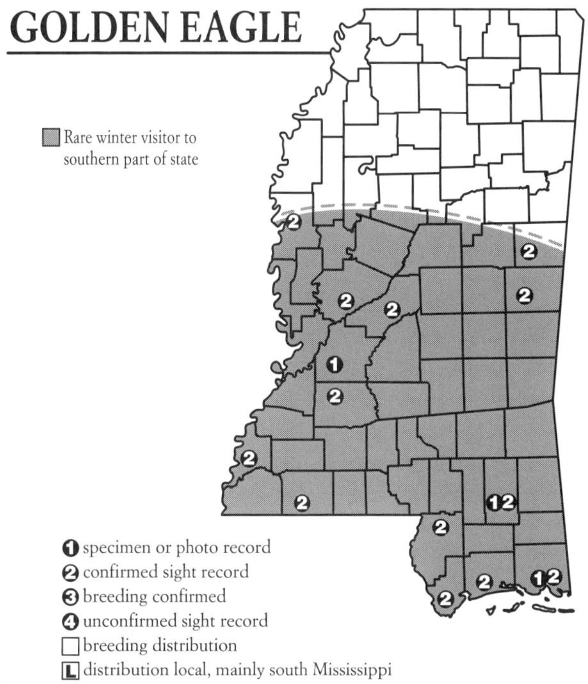

	JAN	FEB	MAR	APR	MAY	JUN	JUL	AUG	SEP	OCT	NOV	DEC
OCCURRENCE	oooo	oooo									oooo	oooo
MUSEUM*												
WHT*												

*Breeding confirmed by egg, sight, or photographic record.

Golden Eagle *Aquila chrysaetos*

This majestic bird soars with a seven-foot wingspan and glides on *flat* wings with occasional beats. The large size of the Golden Eagle separates it from dark-phase buteos. The adult has a dark brown body and a *golden wash* behind the neck. The wings are dark brown above and below. The tail is banded indistinctly at the base and broadly at the end. The bill and eyes are dark brown.

In overhead flight, the spread wings are *uniformly dark* on the adult. Immatures are easier to separate from immature Bald Eagles than the adults because immature Golden Eagles have a *white patch in the wings* at the base of the primaries, and a *white tail* with a *broad brownish black terminal band.* Immature Bald Eagles have a *blotchy white underwing and tail,* not sharply defined as on immature Golden Eagles. Otherwise, immatures resemble the adults, and both have *legs feathered to the toes.*

Golden Eagles are occasional winter visitors to Mississippi. They migrate here from their breeding territories in the western and northern regions of North America to the Arctic, where they inhabit open mountains, foothills, open country, and the Great Plains. They nest on the face of cliffs in canyons or mesas, in high mountains and occasionally in trees.

Their nest, or aerie, is composed of large sticks and coarse material with a lining of softer grasses, weeds, bark, and other dried vegetation. One to three white or cream-colored eggs spotted or blotched with various shades of brown may be found in a nest. An average of two eggs are laid.

Incubation of Golden Eagle eggs takes about 43 to 45 days. Eaglets are covered in yellowish white down when hatched. For about four weeks after hatching, they have a thick, white covering of down. For the next four weeks, feathers grow and nearly obscure the down covering. During the final three or four weeks, the feathered fledglings spend time stretching their wings, preening, and eating. Juveniles remain with their parents in the nesting territory until they acquire the tactics for surviving on their own.

This eagle is a capable predator, but not averse to eating carcasses of dead wild and domestic animals. Its food consists mostly of mammals including cottontail and jack rabbits, marmots, prairie dogs, ground squirrels, and other small rodents. Some birds are eaten, and other mammals are sometimes captured. These include small deer fawns, lambs of domestic and mountain sheep, kids of goats and pronghorn, and even foxes or other animals caught in traps.

In the past, occasional depredations or suspected killing of domestic animals by Golden Eagles has led to attempts at wholesale slaughter by shooting from airplanes, poisoning animal carcasses, and trapping. Popular misconceptions have obscured the beneficial traits in controlling populations of prairie dogs, rabbits, marmots, ground squirrels, rats, and other rodents that compete directly for the forage of domestic livestock.

In Mississippi, wintering Golden Eagles occur regularly in small numbers from October through March, but often escape notice because they are usually in heavily timbered or wide open lands far from human settlements. They move and soar at great heights. At rest they are not easily observed in remote areas.

In the early 1950s, one or more Golden Eagles visited the Leaf River Wildlife Refuge in Perry County each winter for several years. At that time, deer and Wild Turkey numbers were very high. In winter, deer and turkeys fed daily in large openings planted in winter wheat and crimson clover and no doubt attracted these birds to the 1300-acre fenced "deer pasture."

The area manager, Quinton Breland, recounted an observation of an encounter between a Golden Eagle and a large flock of Wild Turkeys. While baiting deer traps with yellow corn, he noticed a sizable flock of turkeys on the opposite side of a food patch. A low-flying eagle made a pass at the turkey flock and missed. The turkeys scattered but did not fly. The eagle wheeled around and landed among the scattered turkeys in the open field. The birds stood erect around the eagle, which made several futile darts at them before flying away. Breland said the turkeys seemed to show no fear of the eagle on the ground and easily dodged it.

At times, Breland set traps on the refuge for bobcats, foxes, and skunks. He caught a skunk in one trap, killed it, reset the trap, and left the carcass near the trap. The trap next caught a Turkey Vulture. After resetting the trap he caught a Golden Eagle that I brought unharmed to the Livingston Park Zoo in Jackson.

After building a large cage, he continued to set baited traps, and for several winters, he captured alive five or six more Golden Eagles. They were not injured and all were released after being caged and fed until the deer and turkey live-trapping ended in late February.

Using binoculars I have seen and identified soaring Golden Eagles, all of them in southern Mississippi below Hattiesburg. I saw one at rest in a tree and later in flight on the Leaf River Refuge. H. Champ Clark reported a Golden Eagle in Amite County on the Fred Anderson property. The bird remained for several weeks and fed on trapped animal carcasses and road kills. Two specimens in the MMNS were taken November 20, 1937 (no locality), and on January 13, 1940, near Vancleave in Jackson County.

Once in late winter, I responded to a telephone call and captured an immature that had landed in a pasture near Byram in Hinds County. This bird was emaciated and unable to fly. It proved to be blind in one eye and easily approached and covered. Afterward, I delivered the bird to the Jackson Zoo.

I have watched Golden Eagles on their home territories in western Texas, the Colorado mountains, the badlands and eroded plains of Utah, and the Grand Canyon of Arizona. I saw a lofty aerie on a cliff face at Ramsey Canyon in southeastern Arizona and an occupied nest atop a high mesa in western Texas. Seeing them in the vast, open spaces of the West leaves one in awe of the prowess and freedom these birds seem to possess and enjoy.

Falconidae (Caracaras and Falcons)

[Crested Caracara] *Polyborus plancus*

This bird, with its vulturelike habits, was formerly called Audubon's Caracara. Its breeding range in North America is limited to central and southern Florida, southwestern Louisiana, and parts of southwestern Texas. It is local and rare throughout its range, and populations are diminishing and threatened. In the Southwest, it is sometimes called "Mexican eagle" or "Mexican buzzard."

In Florida, caracaras inhabit open prairie ranchlands among cabbage palms, where they usually nest. In Louisiana on a large ranch at Sun Cove in Cameron Parish, one or more pairs have nested in clumps of Cherokee rose. According to George H. Lowery Jr., this ranch has protected these birds for years. But the small population has been limited to one or two pairs and a few young, and has not shown signs of expansion. There are a few inland Louisiana records, mostly in the southern parts of the state, occurring every month of the year.

In the coastal counties of southern Texas and in the mesquite and brush country of southwestern Texas west of Kingsville, caracaras are found on large ranchlands where they nest in low trees. They are hard to find during the nesting season because they remain near the nest and spend much time on the ground concealed by brush. I have observed these birds perched by the roadside on posts and in cabbage palms on Florida ranchlands. While driving along the highways between Kingsville and McAllen in Kleberg and Kennedy Counties in Texas, I have seen them sitting in the dead tops of mesquite trees.

CRESTED CARACARA

Accidental

■ Late winter sightings

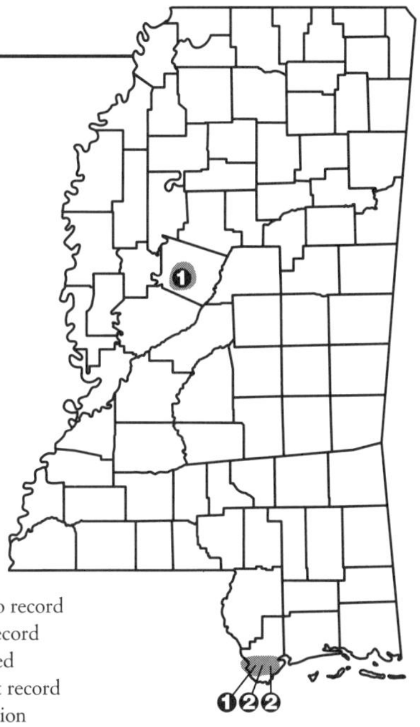

❶ specimen or photo record
❷ confirmed sight record
❸ breeding confirmed
❹ unconfirmed sight record
□ breeding distribution
🅰 distribution statewide

	JAN	FEB	MAR	APR	MAY	JUN	JUL	AUG	SEP	OCT	NOV	DEC
OCCURRENCE			13 •	14 •								
MUSEUM*												
WHT*												

*Breeding confirmed by egg, sight, or photographic record.

Caracaras build large nests in palms, large cacti, yucca, oak, hackberry, and sometimes on cliffs. Their nest is coarsely but strongly made of twigs, weeds, and other debris. Preferred sites are usually in or near clumps of trees providing an open view of the surrounding prairie country.

The eggs are ovate, white to buffy ground color, and usually heavily marked with scrawls and blotches of various shades of brown. When first hatched, the young are covered with cinnamon-colored down with darker, rich brown on top of the head, large brown oval spots on the shoulders, and smaller ones on the tail and thighs. The young in the nest are fed mostly on captured prey, even turtles that are brought to the nest, torn apart by the adult, and fed to the nestlings. Adult caracaras feed on carrion, but are capable predators on a large variety of reptiles, mammals, fish, frogs, and vulnerable young of some birds.

They are not great wanderers and under ordinary circumstances do not range very far from their home territories. With birds capable of strong flight like this species, exceptions occur.

A notable example is the occurrence of a Crested Caracara on the Hillside National Wildlife Refuge in Holmes County, on March 13, 1981. While flying a waterfowl survey on the refuge, Sidney A. Woodson and Sarah M. McClellan (1981) saw a caracara fly and alight in a large oak tree bordering fields and water impoundments. Woodson, then an agent and pilot with the U.S. Fish and Wildlife Service, had seen caracaras previously in Florida and recognized it as an unusual occurrence in Mississippi.

All field marks were observed, including the dark crested crown, dark belly, whitish tail with dark terminal band, white neck down to shoulders, white outer wing patches, and even the long, yellow legs and pinkish red, bare face. After six or eight passes as close as 50 feet, an identifiable color photograph was taken. On March 14, the bird was seen and photographed again as it flew. This bird was not seen after March 14, although attempts were made to locate it in the same area. Photographs are on file at MSU and the MMNS. A coastal sight record on April 14, 1982, by Ren Lohoefener (Jackson 1982) occurred near Waveland in Hancock County.

In overhead flight, the longish, white tail with terminal black band; thick, long, whitish neck down to the shoulders; and whitish patches in the dark wings swept back from the wrist will distinguish the caracara from the vultures. The Crested Caracara is the northern species of this subfamily that ranges southward into Cuba and Central America. The South American caracara ranges southward into Argentina.

American Kestrel *Falco sparverius*

The American Kestrel is the only *small* hawk with a *rufous tail and back*. In flight, it resembles an oversized swallow. The wings of the male are blue gray with dark gray on the primaries and secondaries. Females are rufous on the back, wings, and tail, which are narrowly barred with black. Both sexes have double black stripes on a white face and a blue gray crown with a rufous center patch.

The male has pinkish white underparts flecked with rounded black dots. The female has mostly white underparts lightly streaked with rufous. Undertail coverts are white. Immatures resemble adults, but have more streaked underparts.

Called "sparrow hawk," the American Kestrel is the smallest and most common of our falcons. It is seen often along roadsides perched on a wire or post in an erect posture and occasionally lifting its tail. While hunting, it often hovers before pouncing on its prey of large insects, small rodents, small reptiles, frogs, and occasionally small birds. Usually this bird prefers hunting from a high perch, scanning the ground for insects, then sailing down to pounce on prey in the manner of shrikes and bluebirds.

Open countryside is the preferred habitat of this gentle and lively bird, but it has also adapted to inner-city life,

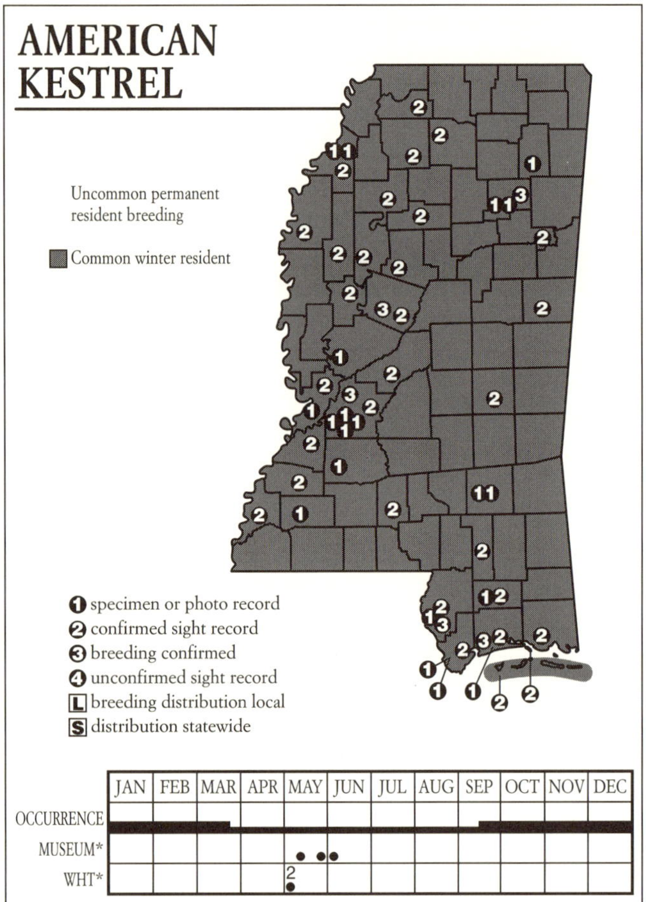

*Breeding confirmed by egg, sight, or photographic record.

where it sometimes nests or roosts on roofs or in crevices of tall buildings. In the country, it is usually found along the woods bordering open fields and usually nests in cavities or abandoned holes of the Northern Flicker or Pileated Woodpecker in lofty snags and stumps.

Both kestrel nests I have seen were in dead trees, one a pine and the other a tall oak. On May 2, 1940, I found one nest, a flicker hole in a dead pine on an idle field border in Holmes County about 20 feet aboveground. It contained five eggs, and the set was collected for a museum specimen record. They were creamy white, blotched and smeared with reddish brown that almost obscured the ground color.

The other nest was in a Pileated Woodpecker hole in the terminal snag of a lone dead oak in an open pasture near Brownsville in Hinds County in late May. It contained at least three fledglings peering out of the nest hole and almost ready to leave the nest.

Other nesting records for this species are May 24, 1939, of four eggs in a dead tree stump nine miles south of Okalona in Chickasaw County by H. L. Owens. On May 9, 1940, four eggs were seen in a flicker hole in a dead tree by W. D. Lewis in Pearl River County.

The American Kestrel is one of a group of small falcons found around the world in temperate and tropical zones. They are similar in habits and appearance and will be encountered and recognized by their traits in many countries. Such was the case when I returned to England on a group tour to my World War II bomb-group base near Cambridge.

One of the first British birds I saw was their kestrel hovering over an open field. It appeared to be one-and-one-half times the size of the male of our species. I saw others during our bus tours and while touring for birds with an English farm couple, Frank and Maud Pepper. The kestrels we saw were all hovering in the air while heading into the prevailing wind.

The American Kestrel ranges over most of North and South America and breeds in the temperate zones of both continents. It breeds north to the tree line in Canada and Alaska and to the Gulf states, though sparingly in the southern part of the breeding range. In the eastern and southern states, populations have been declining.

In Mississippi, this species is an uncommon, permanent-resident breeding bird. In fall and winter, it is common statewide due to the influx of overwintering northern birds. In Mississippi's coastal counties, it occurs sparingly as a spring and summer resident and has nested on a downtown building in Gulfport. It is common along the Mississippi Coast and the barrier islands in fall and winter until about March, when most wintering birds depart.

The call notes or songs of the American Kestrel are not frequently heard during the winter when the birds are most common in Mississippi. Since these birds nest sparingly here, and are more vocal on their home nesting territory, it is usually a territorial bird that will be heard calling.

These birds are vocal during courtship and nesting. Their calls are rather high, double notes suggested by *kil'ly-kil'ly-kil'ly,* with the apostrophes indicating very brief pauses. Calls resemble the staccato song of the Northern Flicker, but the flicker's calls are not double noted.

Merlin *Falco columbarius*

This little falcon, slightly larger than the American Kestrel and formerly known as the Pigeon Hawk, is an uncommon, irregular winter resident in Mississippi. However, it occurs regularly in winter along the Mississippi coastline and on the islands of Mississippi Sound. Inland, it is sparsely distributed in winter and seldom encountered. Except on the coastline and offshore islands, it is seldom seen during spring and fall migration.

Arrivals begin early in September and continue through October. Most of the birds depart by late March and early April. Extreme dates of arrival and departure are August 22 and May 10.

The Merlin breeds mainly in the evergreen forests of

Canada and Alaska and sparingly in the northern states and in western mountains south to Oregon and Colorado. It winters in the Gulf states, the Caribbean Islands, in northern South America and Central America, and rarely to the southern limits of its breeding range. This species is sparsely distributed throughout the wintering range in the United States.

I have seen this bird on only two or three occasions. It is not highly visible like the American Kestrel. The Merlin prefers open country and low perches and concealment, and usually flies near the ground while hunting and pursuing the small birds that make up the main portion of its diet. It also eats insects and small rodents. During migration, it is found around marshes and coastlines, where it often hunts for shorebirds.

The male is gray blue above with long, pointed wings and a broadly banded gray tail. The slightly larger female and immatures are dark brown above with broadly banded, brown tails. The underparts of both sexes and immatures are buff colored and boldly streaked with brown. A prominent black moustache mark extends beneath the eye bordering the white throat. The general appearance at rest and in flight is like a small version of the Peregrine Falcon.

In the coniferous forests, taller trees are preferred for nesting, but Merlins sometimes nest on the ground, on prominences, or on cliffs. Four or five creamy white eggs variously spotted or blotched with shades of brown are laid in an abandoned hawk or crow nest or one built by the birds. Cliff or ground nests are little more than a hollow with some added material around it. In some places, these birds have adapted to nesting on buildings in parts of their circumpolar range.

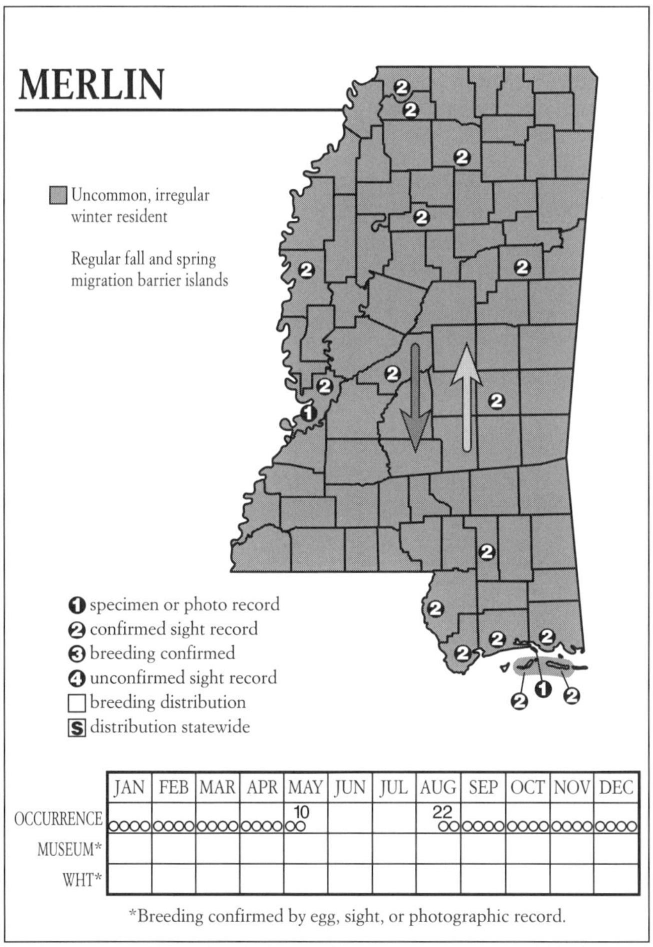

The last bird I mounted while working for the wildlife museum project in 1940 was a beautiful female Merlin. It is still on display at the MMNS and is one of only two specimens in the collection. It was taken by C. D. Turnipseed on Deer Island in Harrison County on May 2, 1940. The other specimen record was a female collected by H. G. Lynn on Diamond Island in Warren County. Thomas Burleigh collected three specimens from Harrison County, one at Saucier on October 15, 1936, one on Deer Island on September 11, 1937, and one at Cat Island on September 21, 1939.

Peregrine Falcon *Falco peregrinus*

Commonly called the "duck hawk," this falcon is about the size of a Common Crow. The common name is a misnomer since this falcon is not very selective of birds, which make up its principal diet. Although it does kill and eat ducks, the few taken by this rare and endangered species would probably not equal the number of cripples shot and not retrieved by hunters on one morning of the hunting season. As a duck hunter, I would gladly forfeit a daily bag limit of ducks for the chance to see this magnificent falcon display its skill at taking one duck on the wing.

This falcon varies in plumage coloring in the different regions where it breeds. Most of the birds seen along coastlines in the eastern and Gulf states are from tundra regions of the far north. Adults have underparts of dark gray, a black crown, and a triangular wedge extending along the throat and part of the nape. The breast is pale pinkish buff, and the underparts and leggings are heavily streaked and barred. The falcon's long tail is barred gray with a terminal dark band. Its long pointed wings and crow size, along with its black "helmet," long tail, and swift flight are distinctive field characteristics. Immatures are dark brown above and heavily streaked below.

I have read and used the word "peregrine" many times and have seen the word "peregrinations." Only recently I consulted the dictionary to learn that peregrine used as an adjective means "having a tendency to wander as a pilgrim or foreigner" and to peregrinate means "to travel." This falcon then is aptly named. It is a cosmopolitan, migratory species, well armed and capable of rapid and easy transit to all points north and south, wandering at will to find and take its sustenance.

Peregrine Falcon

In North America, these birds breed north to the tree line and beyond, then migrate as far as South America. They spend much of the time in migration along shorelines. By following the migrations and landfalls of other birds, they seek and find an abundance of other birds. All birds up to their size are vulnerable to their outstanding talent for pursuing and capturing prey species.

The Peregrine Falcon in level flight has been clocked at 175 miles per hour, and few other birds except some swifts can evade or outfly it. In a power dive exceeding 200 miles per hour, this falcon can strike a victim from above, deal a stunning blow with large feet and talons, and then retrieve the victim in midair.

Along with pelicans, Ospreys, and the Bald Eagle, the Peregrine Falcon underwent a serious decline, especially in breeding populations of the eastern United States. Populations of these birds have always been sparse, and they were almost totally eliminated by chlorinated hydrocarbon insecticides permeating their food chain. As a result of the decline, this falcon was placed on the federal list of endangered species. However, thanks to public and private reintroduction and recovery efforts, the Peregrine Falcon is becoming more common. Currently in the United States and Canada, there are almost 1600 nesting pairs, well above the recovery goal of 631 pairs. The U.S. Fish and Wildlife Service expects soon to delist the Peregrine Falcon from the federal Endangered Species List.

Peregrine Falcons appear and winter regularly in small numbers on Horn, East Ship, and Cat Islands, and coastal marshes and bays along our coastline. On inland lakes and reservoirs and along the Mississippi River, they are rare winter visitors, but regular, uncommon migrants. Migration periods during April to mid-May and in September and October on the Mississippi coastline and barrier islands afford the best opportunities for finding this falcon. Gulls, terns, shorebirds, and waterfowl concentrate on points and sandspits on the islands. Peregrine Falcons are attracted to such concentrations of other birds and in such places the falcons are most likely to appear. On several visits to Horn Island, I have seen single Peregrines in passage along the shoreline or perched in snag trees along the western end of the island.

PEREGRINE FALCON

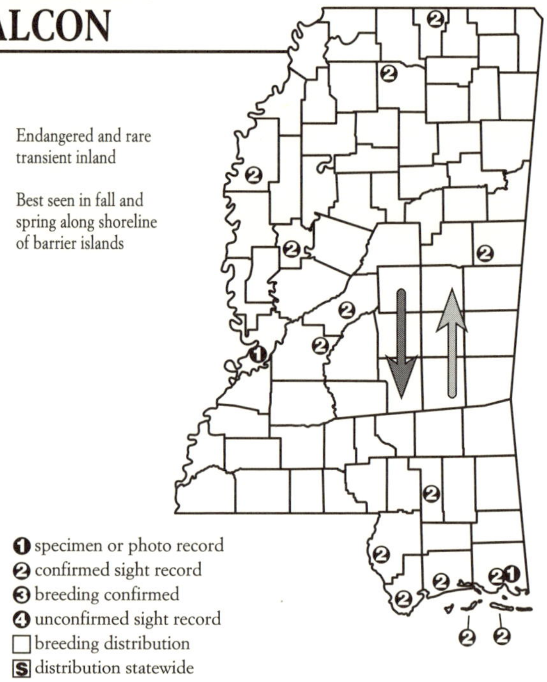

	JAN	FEB	MAR	APR	MAY	JUN	JUL	AUG	SEP	OCT	NOV	DEC
OCCURRENCE	oooo	oooo	oooo	oooo	oooo	2 o	o	o	oooo	oooo	oooo	oooo
MUSEUM*												
WHT*												

*Breeding confirmed by egg, sight, or photographic record.

One of the most stirring sightings I remember was on the Mississippi River below Greenville at the end of World War II. I was in a small cabin boat with my brother and his young son, and we had pulled up to land on the Arkansas side. While the boat was tied to a willow, I walked up to the point of a bluff, and from there I saw a Peregrine Falcon in the air on the Mississippi side. A lone Great Egret appeared flying low downstream, and the falcon made a power dive and swoop at the heron before again climbing aloft to make another swoop. But the falcon did not touch the hapless bird. On the third pass, the heron conceded to the apparent play and indulged the falcon by taking to the water and drifting downstream. The falcon rose and disappeared from sight upriver.

The Peregrine Falcon nests on rocky cliff ledges, occasionally in abandoned nests of hawks or eagles, in hollows of tall trees, and sometimes on ledges of tall buildings in the heart of big cities. Their lofty aeries are little more than a shallow scrape, which receive the three to five eggs scrawled and marked with various shades of brown that almost obscure the cream or pinkish ground color. The aerie is the scene of much courtship activity and aerial gymnastics while the adults mate, hatch, and rear their young.

Restoration of eastern Peregrine Falcon populations is underway. Attempts to reestablish breeding pairs at historical aeries along the eastern seaboard and in New England have been successful and are continuing. The restoration project is centered at Cornell University in Ithaca, New York. There, captive rearing produces fledglings for hacking on tower platforms in cooperation with state and federal agencies and supported by falconers and privately funded agencies. In the western mountain states and on Pacific islands, local nesting sites are protected and monitored. Hopefully, these efforts will continue to succeed.

Thomas D. Burleigh studied and collected birds on the Mississippi Coast and coastal islands from 1935 to 1943. On frequent trips to Deer Island and less frequent visits to outer barrier islands, he noted single wintering Peregrine Falcons. On October 7, 1941, he observed three birds on Deer Island at Biloxi. Mid-October is about the peak time for arrival of winter residents and passage of migrants going farther south.

[Prairie Falcon] *Falco mexicanus*

The Prairie Falcon is about the size of the Peregrine Falcon. It is *pale brown* above with pale buff, heavily streaked, and spotted underparts. The streaked crown is bordered by a light line extending above the eye. A *narrow* moustache mark extending below the eye is separated from the *dark auricular region* by a *broad light area. Black axillaries* and dark underwing coverts are distinctive for all ages.

Prairie Falcons inhabit open country of western prairies and plains and occasionally woods. There are records of its occurrence in Arkansas, Tennessee, and Alabama.

The first Prairie Falcon record in Mississippi was on December 7, 1991, on the southern shoreline of Enid Lake in Yalobusha County (Davis et al. 1992). The bird was seen in flight and identified by its black axillars by Gene

PRAIRIE FALCON

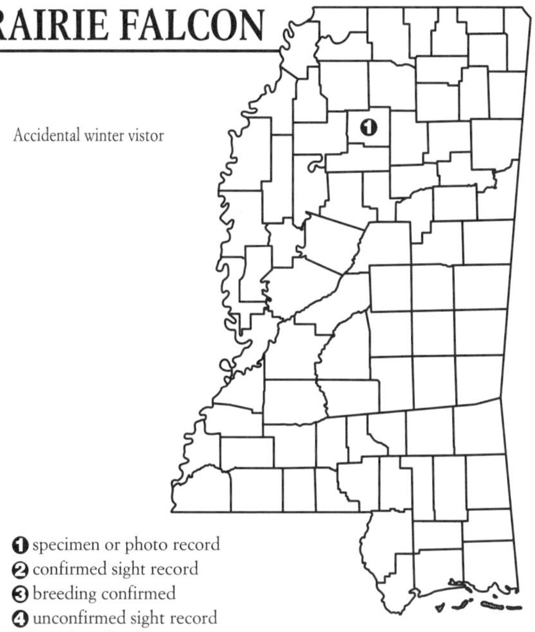

1 specimen or photo record
2 confirmed sight record
3 breeding confirmed
4 unconfirmed sight record
□ breeding distribution
□ distribution: statewide and local

	JAN	FEB	MAR	APR	MAY	JUN	JUL	AUG	SEP	OCT	NOV	DEC
OCCURRENCE	●●●● 30											7 ●●●●
MUSEUM*												
WHT*												

*Breeding confirmed by egg, sight, or photographic record.

and Shannon Knight and Robert Briscoe. It was seen by multiple observers at a nearby location in Cossar State Park, where it appeared regularly in late afternoon to perch in one of several sweet gum trees. Identifiable photographs were made on January 1, 1992, and deposited for record at the MMNS and MSU. Other sight records were made on December 15 and 30 and January 3, 5, and 30, 1992.

Gallinaceous Birds (Galliformes)

This order contains the fowl-like birds and includes many domesticated species. The most important and most utilized are the domesticated chickens that were developed from jungle fowl. Turkeys were first domesticated by the Aztecs and later taken to Europe, where our domesticated strains developed.

This order contains mainly nonmigratory and ground-dwelling species. Most are highly regarded as game birds. All have heavy bodies; stout, short bills with decurved upper mandibles; short, rounded wings; and rather long legs. Most species are capable only of short bursts of flight. All feed on seeds and other plant parts, insects, and occasionally other organisms.

These birds have a worldwide distribution. Species adaptations enable them to live under wide ranges of climate and topography and in habitat from the Arctic to the tropics, but limit their ability to live in other regions. Birds of this order nest on the ground, with the exception of a few, such as the chachalaca, an arboreal species.

There are four families of gallinaceous birds: Cracidae (chachalacas), Meleagrididae (turkeys), Tetraonidae (grouses), and Odontophorinae (quails, partridges, and pheasants). There have been many attempts to introduce exotic game birds, such as pheasants, chukars, and migratory quail *(Coturnix),* into Mississippi. None have been successful. Only three species of exotic game birds have successfully adapted and become common in the United States. These are the Ring-necked Pheasant, in northern, midwestern, and western regions; the Gray Partridge, in open agricultural lands of southern Canada and northern border states; and the Chukar, successfully established in arid, rocky regions of western states.

In this order, the males of most species are more colorful than the duller females. Some males engage in elaborate courtship displays of dancing, strutting, spreading and puffing the feathers, inflating air sacs, drumming with wings, and vocalizing courtship sounds such as crowing, gobbling, and expelling air.

Only two species of native game birds occur in Mississippi: the eastern form of the Wild Turkey and the Northern Bobwhite. Both are superb game birds, *nonpareil* in every sense of the word.

Above: Wild Turkey

Meleagrididae (Turkeys)

Wild Turkey *Meleagris gallopavo*

A Wild Turkey is a member of this species raised only in its natural habitat *by a wild hen.* Regardless of its ancestry, any other is simply a "turkey," incapable of surviving for long in a state of wildness and *reproducing* in the wild. These statements have proven factual and are needed to dispel popular misconceptions about the stocking of artificially raised or pen-reared, wild-strain turkeys (Cook 1945a).

Wild Turkeys trapped by the use of cannon-projected nets and released to suitable habitats in flock-sized numbers have been used to restore huntable populations of this game bird throughout their former range in most Mississippi counties and in other states (Commer 1987). Restoration by stocking Wild Turkeys in depleted ranges has been one of the most outstanding and valuable contributions of game management in this century (Hewitt 1967). Earlier stocking attempts using expensive, pen-reared birds were worthless in establishing viable wild populations.

There were no Wild Turkeys in Delta National Forest before restocking with 65 wild-trapped birds from Coahoma County in the late 1950s. This hunter bagged a fine gobbler during the first open spring season.

Almost without exception, the releases of wild-trapped turkeys have been successful. The restoration and management of this fine game bird is discussed further in the chapter on conservation and management.

The Wild Turkey is one of my favorite species, both as a game bird and as a magnificent survivor in borderline wilderness. It lives in the open forest, but is surprisingly adaptable to a wide variety of habitats if given some degree of protection from overhunting.

Forest openings and edges are important for successful reproduction of the species. Turkey poults need open areas that afford quantities of insects, seeds, and small fruits, and areas that can provide nesting sites with concealment preferred by the hen. A fair degree of remoteness from human disturbances is an important factor for their survival. Escape and roosting cover is also important, and a range of several thousand acres or more of contiguous, diverse habitat is necessary to support viable, huntable numbers of these birds.

The Wild Turkey is the largest North American game bird. The adult gobbler or "tom" weighs 18 to 20 pounds. Young gobblers or "jakes" weigh about 10 to 14 pounds. The hens weigh six to eight pounds.

There are five races of turkeys: the *osceola* found in Florida; our eastern form; the Merriam's or western mountain species; the Rio Grande form native to southern Texas and northern Mexico; and the brilliantly colored Ocellated Turkey of southern Mexico and the Yucatan Peninsula. The eastern and Florida races have brown terminal bands on the tail of the gobblers and hens. These feathers are white on the Rio Grande or Mexican form. Domestic turkeys retain the white outer coloring of the Mexican form from which they originated.

In the breeding of domestic turkeys, several color variations or strains have been developed. These are white, rusty red, and smoke gray. These color variants, or mutations, occur rarely and naturally in our native wild populations. Occasionally all white, all red, red-and-white, and smokey gray birds appear in wild flocks. White or smoke gray variants are more common. The red phase is very rare. The red-and-white variation occurs more often than red. One of the latter was shot and photographed by a hunter in east-central Mississippi. These variants in Wild Turkeys are not admixtures with domestic turkeys. White wild hens that survive as adults have been known to rear broods of poults successfully over periods of several years.

The eastern form of the Wild Turkey gobbler has iridescent bronze body feathers tipped with black. On the hens these feathers are tipped with brown. The rump feathers, tail, and undertail coverts have transverse bands edged with chestnut brown at the tips. The secondary coverts are bronze tipped with black. The primaries are white, barred, and

WILD TURKEY

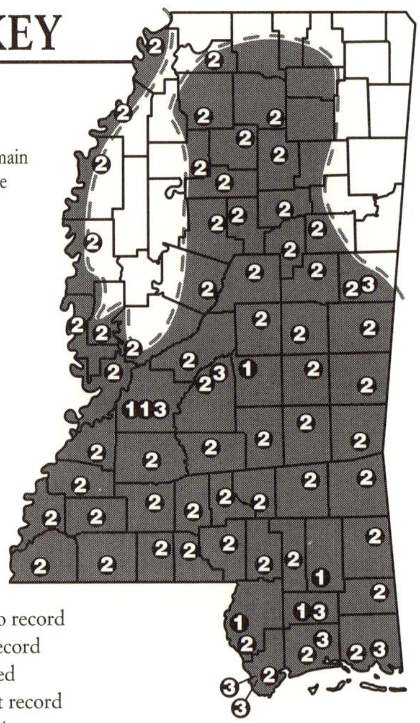

■ Permanent resident to main occupied breeding range shown by dashed line

❶ specimen or photo record
❷ confirmed sight record
❸ breeding confirmed
❹ unconfirmed sight record
🄻 breeding distribution
🅂 distribution statewide, local

	JAN	FEB	MAR	APR	MAY	JUN	JUL	AUG	SEP	OCT	NOV	DEC
OCCURRENCE	■	■	■	■	■	■	■	■	■	■	■	■
MUSEUM*				•	•		•	•				
WHT*				15 • •	3 •							

*Breeding confirmed by egg, sight, or photographic record.

reticulated with black. The reddish legs are long and strong with recurved spurs inside the legs and above the feet of the gobbler. The head is bare except for a few modified feathers resembling hair.

The adult gobbler, one-year-old jakes, and some hens have a beard at the breastbone, a round tuft of modified feathers 10 to 12 inches long in the adult. The gobbler's head has an extendable caruncle at the foot of the upper mandible. Skin on the bare head is wrinkled and mostly white with pink, white, red, purple, and blue coloring that varies with sexual activity and excitement in the adult male. The throat and sides of the neck are covered by wattles with a dewlap under the neck that swells and turns crimson during courtship display and excitement.

The hens are similar to males, but more protectively colored and with less iridescence on the body feathers. The hen lacks the long caruncle and extensive wattling of the male. The adult gobbler has a thick, spongy, air-filled mass under the skin of the breast that serves as protection in fighting or assists with feather erection in courtship display while strutting.

Immature gobblers and hens resemble adults. The central pair of tail feathers in young males is slightly longer than those of adult males, which have tail feathers of equal length when fanned. The primaries of juveniles have sharp points with less barring than adults. Up to about 18 months of age, juveniles can be aged by the rate of molting of eight of the 10 primary feathers.

Wild Turkeys are polygamous and have a well-defined social order. Dominant males reserve for themselves a harem of hens in a prescribed territory. Subdominant males may follow or associate with a dominant male, or stay with other gobblers, but the dominant gobbler usually mates with the hens. Young males forego breeding until they attain dominance as adults. There is a distinct pecking order at all times among adult males, adult hens, immatures, and even poults. These devices insure that dominant and stronger survival traits are passed to succeeding generations.

Prior to the breeding season, Wild Turkeys tend to gather in large flocks of both sexes. As the nesting season approaches, hens scatter to individual nesting sites, and a dominant male patrols a territory to display and mate with hens. Juvenile males usually remain in small groups or with subdominant males.

Nesting and egg laying begins in late March and April, and by mid-May poults begin hatching. From 10 to 12 or more smooth, creamy white eggs, finely sprinkled with reddish brown dots are laid in a slight scrape and covered with leaves or other debris until incubation starts. The poult brood hatches in about 28 days.

The hen alone raises the poults and accompanies them until they are fully grown and incorporated into fall flocks. The poults are capable of flight to roost at two weeks of age and thereafter are less vulnerable to ground predators. Without constant care by the hen for protection from predators and the elements, few poults would survive the harsh realities of their environment. On the other hand, the Wild Turkey continues to be wild and survive *because* of predators and other realities learned by experience and passed on by the hen to her offspring.

Wild Turkeys subsist on a great variety of plant and animal foods. These include grass and weed seeds; wild fruits and berries; leaves, buds, and green shoots of grasses and other plants; rhizomes; tubers; large insects (mostly grasshoppers); and miscellaneous invertebrates. Beech and pine mast, wild pecans, acorns, dogwood, black gum, wild grape, hackberries, poison ivy berries, dewberries, blackberries, blueberries, spicebush, and magnolia seeds are important seasonal foods. The leaves of grasses such as oats, wheat, rye grass, and clover are important winter foods. Seeds of carpet grass, panic grass, paspalums, and other native grasses and plants are stripped and eaten avidly.

Turkeys scratch for roots, tubers, and rhizomes of certain sedges, legumes, and grasses. The rhizomes of giant cane are important winter foods in bottomlands, and dense cane thickets afford excellent escape and protection cover. Insects are important food for poults, particularly grasshoppers and crickets from open areas.

Diseases and internal parasites are endemic to our native Wild Turkey populations, and are of concern when bird numbers reach a high density. Blackhead, a disease caused by a protozoan parasite, and coccidiosis can cause insidious, largely unseen mortality when turkey populations exceed normal capacity levels. The disease organisms build in proportion to the population density on a given area, and density-related exposure to the disease organisms increases and spills over to succeeding poult generations, resulting in reproduction failures. Some individuals in turkey flocks become resistant carriers that perpetuate the disease cycle. Occasional sightings of sick adult turkeys occur as these diseases run their course, but poult mortality can easily escape notice.

In past years, turkey flocks on the hunting club lands in Washington, Bolivar, and Coahoma Counties along the Mississippi River experienced extremely high population densities followed by disease mortality of adult turkeys. Poor reproduction followed. In some instances, inadequate harvest of only gobblers during spring gobbler-only hunting seasons has allowed turkeys to increase to an epidemic disease level.

The introduction of fall either-sex hunting seasons increased the legal harvest of these surplus turkeys. This helped control the spread of disease by reducing population density. Extreme fluctuations in turkey numbers were controlled by increasing the annual harvest. This was accomplished through a better understanding of the disease problems, and by the cooperation of the hunting clubs involved.

I have been fortunate to spend many rewarding hours observing and photographing turkeys from deer-trap blinds on state wildlife management areas. I have enjoyed many spring days calling, tape recording, and hunting turkeys. I called up and watched gobblers on several occasions and finally killed one in Attala County. I learned that killing a fine gobbler is an anticlimax to the emotional experience of spring turkey hunting.

Many qualities describe this fine game bird. It has keen eyesight and an ability to detect slight movement. It has a good sense of hearing and ability to know exactly where a hunter is calling from. Finally, it has an ability to silently and slowly approach, and usually discover, the hunter awaiting in ambush.

Wild Turkeys have a great variety of communication calls. The gobble is the territorial claim and advertisement notice of the adult male, and occasionally it is imitated by the year-old jakes. Strutting gobblers puff the feathers, fan the tail, lower and vibrate the wings, pat their feet on the ground, and expel air to make sounds called "droning." The alarm note is a sharp *putt*.

Hens announce their presence with calls known as "yelps" by hunters, interpreted as a series of resonant *younk-younk-younk* calls. These are easily imitated by use of various calling devices such as a cedar box, slate, or rubber mouth diaphragm. Hunters use imitations of various "lost calls" to entice turkeys from scattered flocks, or by the "mating call" of the hen to entice a gobbler from the roost.

Some experienced turkey hunters are very knowledgeable and adept in using these devices to call up and kill adult gobblers during the spring gobbler season or fall hunting seasons in open areas. However, the ability to call turkeys is not all of the skill and sport of turkey hunting. There are many other tricks and bits of lore about turkey hunting that are needed for success, the most important being patience, the ability to remain motionless, and prior experience along with a lot of luck and loss of sleep.

Odontophorinae (Quails)

Northern Bobwhite *Colinus virginianus*

This hardy and well-loved game bird of the South has few equals among the many species in this family, which has an almost cosmopolitan distribution. Known locally as "quail," "partridge," or simply "bobwhite," it has been and remains as our most popular game bird. Total populations and hunting opportunities have declined over large areas of Mississippi due to vast changes in land use, practices that have rendered much former quail habitat unsuitable. Yet, Northern Bobwhites hold their own where essential food and cover conditions meet their requirements. June breeding bird surveys reveal that bobwhites have been among the top three most commonly seen and heard birds in rural areas, with the exception of most parts of the Yazoo Delta.

Northern Bobwhites have been among the most intensively studied and managed game birds. Land use and management are the keys to abundance or near total absence of their numbers. Highly mechanized, monocultural farming and forest management practices, largely on short rotations excluding the use of controlled burning, are not conducive to providing suitable habitat conditions for sustained production of this species.

Quail thrive best under conditions conflicting with intensive land management for crops, pasture, and wood production. The abandonment of small farms and their consolidation for pulpwood and timber production in upland sections of Mississippi have favored production of deer and Wild Turkeys. The extensive draining of bottomland forests and subsequent clearing for intensive agriculture on Delta lands has left little room for quail habitat. A review of recent history will help anyone understand and put into perspective the vast changes affecting the land, our people, and Northern Bobwhites.

After 1900, Mississippi's remaining virgin timber was cut over. The human population was largely rural, and most engaged in family subsistence farming. Cotton, corn, and livestock were the main cash or subsistence crops, and owners and tenants raised most of their other foods.

Family farms were small. They broke the landscape into diverse patterns of small fields, patches, small pastures, woodlots, fencerows, and idle land. Clean farming was not the rule except where crops were growing. When crops were gathered, their residues were left in the field. Farm animals were turned onto fields after crops were harvested or allowed to roam free. Cropland, idle land, woodlots, and former timberlands were indiscriminately burned over in late winter months.

Over large areas of southern Mississippi, sheep, cattle, and hogs grazing on open range was a common practice, and remaining woods and virgin stump forests were regularly burned over to promote an annual growth of vegetation. These conditions continued well after the depression of the 1930s, until the arrival of the present age of mechanization and intensive land use for maximum production with minimum human labor.

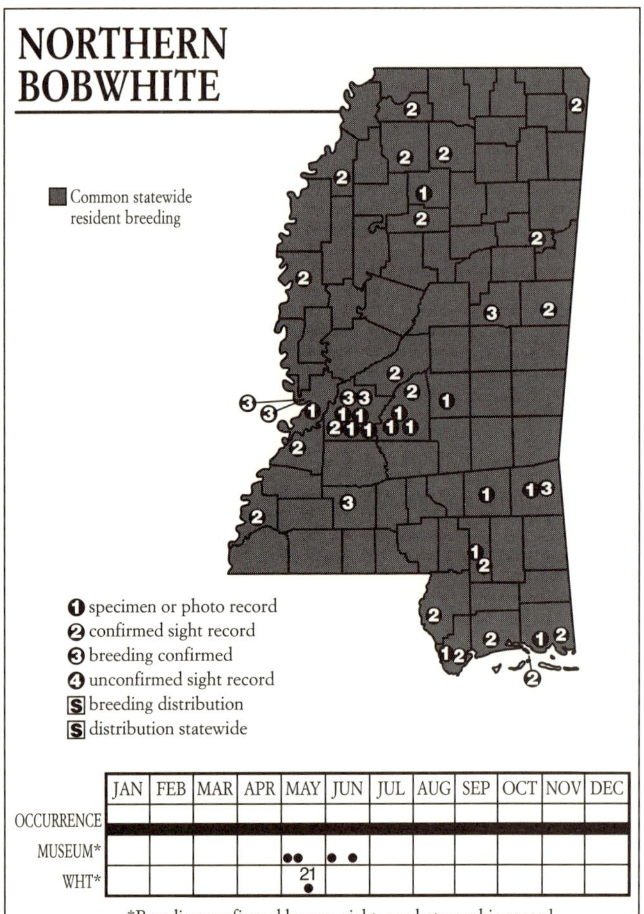

*Breeding confirmed by egg, sight, or photographic record.

Present and future young generations of quail hunters should have a better understanding of the living conditions outlined above, which were primitive and harsh by today's standards, but nevertheless provided nearly ideal food, cover, and habitat for the Northern Bobwhite. An abundance of quail was produced, and hunting was open and free as a matter of custom and tradition. A quail hunter with a good dog could easily find 10 or more coveys in a day and kill a limit of 10 or 12 birds daily, amounting to two or three hundred in a season. I know because I was one of them during my late teen and college years in the decades of the 1930s and 1940s.

Land can be developed and intensively managed for quail hunting, but it is expensive and impractical except for the very wealthy. The few remaining quail hunting plantations today are in northern Florida, southern Georgia, and South Carolina. Quail management on a statewide basis usually cannot be justified economically or put into practice by a government agency without ownership of the land.

A knowledge of plants and plant succession, the population dynamics of quail, their food and cover requirements, and practices that can be used to develop, manage, or manipulate land use for optimum quail habitat are necessary to manage land for quail hunting. Add to this ownership of considerable acres of contiguous land; money for labor, equipment, and materials; and the necessary use of fire for regular controlled burning, and you could have a quail hunting plantation. At best, you could perhaps expect an annual harvest of one quail per acre without using supplemental pen-raised birds.

Quail need adequate winter plant foods well distributed over the normal winter covey range of 20 to 30 acres. They require well-distributed travel lanes, escape, and roosting cover. For brood production, annual growths of native grasses, legumes, and weeds provide "bugging" areas for young broods and offer protection from predators and weather. Supplementary annual food patch plantings of small grains and legumes are enhancements usually provided for optimum benefits.

The best conditions needed by quail must be provided by annual manipulation and management to include seasonal and selective use of controlled burning in patches, since fire is the cheapest and best tool for quail management. However, the overuse of fire can be detrimental and result in dense growths of unproductive broomsedge. Controlled summer grazing can help control broomsedge following a burn, but even this will temporarily reduce perennial native legumes. It will however, encourage the spread and growth of common lespedeza, an important annual quail food.

Wild legumes such as partridge peas, milk peas, beggarweeds, perennial and annual lespedezas, and wild beans provide the bulk of winter foods needed by quail. These are supplemented by grass, weed, and mast or tree seeds such as pine, acorns, and sweet gum. Parts of green plants and a few insects supplement the winter diet of the Northern Bobwhite. Summer foods are more varied and include seeds, small fruits, and insects.

Since quail are ground dwellers, they are subject to numerous terrestrial and winged predators and competitors for locally available foods. Numerous wild rodents compete for foods, and some, like the cotton rat, will destroy quail nests. Skunks, opossums, foxes, coyotes, bobcats, and some predatory birds exact a toll of eggs, young, and adults, but do not seriously limit quail production. Add to this the toll taken by extreme weather, hunting, and accidents, and the annual turnover of quail numbers is approximately 70 percent, if a population is hunted for food and sport. A legal harvest by hunters of 50 percent of the fall population is possible without affecting the next year's crop of birds.

Quail lay an average of 14 eggs. Extremes of summer rainfall and temperature largely determine the success of annual brood production. Too much rain reduces nesting success and brood survival. Excessively high ground temperatures affect egg hatching while reducing insect foods for broods. These environmental stresses lower the annual production by reducing the average brood size. Years with well-distributed summer rainfall and few temperature extremes result in larger fall populations of Northern Bobwhites.

This discussion may seem somewhat superfluous in a bird book, but I consider it important to a proper understanding of this valuable game bird. My observations are based upon a lifetime of hunting, wildlife management study, and practical experience, supplemented with the sheer enjoyment of seeing, hearing, and learning the habits and behavior of the Northern Bobwhite.

Our quail is a plump, short-tailed bird that weighs about four ounces. Its upperparts are mottled shades of gray, brown, and buff. The primaries are dark gray with rufous on the wing coverts. Underparts are white and barred with black on the belly and broadly streaked with reddish brown on the sides. The male has a conspicuous white throat and eye line with black bordering the white on the head and neck. On the female, the throat and eye line are buffy, and the head and neck border is brown. The breast is reddish brown and blends to blackish bordering the throat. The legs are long and well muscled. Both sexes have a small, erectable crest.

The song of the male is a *bob-bob-white,* a loud ascending whistle loudest on the last syllable. Another call, the caterwaul or crowing call, is heard infrequently. I have often induced a calling male to caterwaul by imitating the *bob-white* call followed by the *whoikee* answer call. The other calls are the covey call or scatter call, *whoiloyhee,* and the excitement or alarm call, which consists of rapid "chipperings." Calling males are easily decoyed by whistling a combination of the calls. Bobwhites are quiet birds after the nesting and brood rearing seasons. Covey calls can be heard at daybreak or at sundown when coveys become scattered during the day.

Bobwhites usually roost on the ground in rough cover, preferably broomsedge fields, weed and briar tangles, and honeysuckle tangles or thickets. Occasionally they are found roosting in honeysuckle-covered bushes in thickets. On the ground, they roost in a tight circle with tails in and heads outside the circle. Favored roosting sites may be used repeatedly by the same covey through the winter months as indicated by roost dropping piles scattered over a small area. Some coveys have a roost strategy that avoids detection by nighttime predators. I have seen a covey of 15 or more birds rise at dusk and fly in a tight group before dropping down to a roost site, all without leaving a scent trail for a ground predator to follow.

The Northern Bobwhite begins nesting in late May. The nest is placed in a slight depression and made of grasses slightly or completely arched over and concealed by surrounding vegetation. Quail nests are difficult to find, and most are located accidentally. Nine to 20 or more sharply pointed, white eggs are laid, after which both the male and female incubate the clutch.

The male is solicitous of the female on or off the nest during the nesting and brood-rearing periods. Renesting follows nest failure until a brood is produced. Brood hatching peaks occur in the early parts of July, August, and September. However, I have found active quail nests with eggs as late as early October. Males will sometimes raise broods when the hen is lost and have been known to adopt and raise young from other broods.

Quail chicks are precocious and leave the nest as soon as all the brood has hatched. They are covered with brown and buff downy feathers. When a downy brood is discovered, upon signal by the adults, the brood scatters and "freezes" in the ground cover. They are almost impossible to discover once they have scattered and flattened themselves on the ground in cover. Within two weeks the broods are able to fly short distances, and they mature as "squealers" in about three months.

In early autumn, a "fall shuffle" or movement of complete broods occurs. I have seen this in progress on several occasions as nearly mature coveys were moving like a swarm

Because of its high reproductive capacity and innate survival instincts, the Northern Bobwhite Quail is a capable survivor.

of bees to find and establish a winter range. I have seen broods of squealers on housetops and in yards in Clinton and on the old Central High School grounds in downtown Jackson. This fall shuffle insures redistribution and survival of breeding stock to suitable wintering habitat. Further redistribution to suitable brood production habitat will occur during the pair bonding and mating periods, when survivors break up from coveys in April or early May.

Quail in a hunter's bag can be aged by examining their primary wing coverts. Young of the year will have brown and tan flockings on the primary coverts. Adult birds have a solid, dark gray. When used on a large sample of quail wing examinations from a hunter's bag, this technique will indicate the large, annual population turnover of this species and the degree of success of annual reproduction.

It has been well demonstrated that fall and winter hunting seasons do not deplete populations of this game bird below the level needed for a breeding stock during the upcoming season. Because of its high reproductive capacity and innate survival instincts, the Northern Bobwhite is a capable survivor. There is also a law of diminishing returns, which is discouraging for hunters in late winter. This is evident when coveys take to heavy cover in swamps, or become wilder and hold to point less readily for hunting dogs. Also, there is always much land closed to quail hunting where whole coveys survive the winter.

Stocking of pen-reared quail and pheasants was once thought by bird hunters to be a panacea for reduced numbers of quail in an area. Nearly all states have abandoned game bird hatchery programs since they are enormously expensive, wasteful, and unnecessary. The same applies to the introduction here of exotic game bird species. In our region, the Northern Bobwhite and the Wild Turkey meet our needs as capably as our use of the land permits.

Cranes, Rails, and Allies (Gruiformes)

The families belonging to this order are: Gruidae (cranes), Aramidae (limpkins), and Rallidae (rails, gallinules, and coots). These marsh-dwelling birds have short tails, rounded wings, and long legs. Most are shy and retiring, and their calls are loud and distinctive. They are active in early morning and late afternoon, or at night. All have downy, precocious young.

Cranes are tall, long-legged, and stately birds. They have heavy bodies and fly with the neck extended. Cranes nest on the ground and lay two eggs. Limpkins are medium-sized birds with long legs, a long neck, and a long, slightly decurved, thin bill. Rails and gallinules have long legs and toes, laterally compressed bodies, and short necks. Their downy chicks are mostly black. Coots have ducklike bodies and chickenlike bills. The toes of coots have flattened lobes. Their downy young also are black with reddish orange on the head, bill, and shoulders.

Above: Sandhill Crane

Rallidae (Rails, Gallinules, and Coots)

Yellow Rail *Coturnicops noveboracensis*

Mississippi records for this rail are few. Although it may be a fairly common winter resident on the marshes and grassy meadows of southern Mississippi, few observers have ever really looked for Yellow Rails.

Two specimens in the MMNS were taken in Wilkinson and Lamar Counties. The specimen records occurred on January 7, 1937, a male taken at Centerville, and January 26, 1940, a female in the Lumberton area by James Batson. Henry D. Haberyan (1961) photographed a live specimen taken by a bird dog near Gautier on February 9, 1961. Another specimen was taken by him in the same area. He commented that "these rails are rather numerous in this area during the winter, and I hope to do some banding of them." Haberyan later told me he used bird dogs to locate Yellow Rails.

Valentine Jr. (1971) and Lawrence Walkinshaw observed two of these rails near Fontainebleau, one on April 28, 1970, and the other on April 25, 1971. These observations occurred while searches were being made for nests of the Mississippi Sandhill Crane on savanna grasslands.

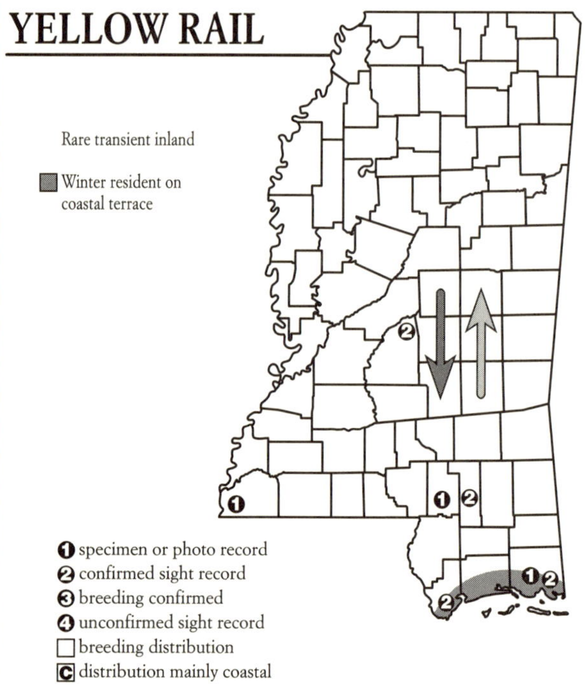

	JAN	FEB	MAR	APR	MAY	JUN	JUL	AUG	SEP	OCT	NOV	DEC
OCCURRENCE	oooo	oooo	oooo	28 oooo						23 oo	oooo	oooo
MUSEUM*												
WHT*												

*Breeding confirmed by egg, sight, or photographic record.

More recent sight records of single Yellow Rails have been recorded on December 15, 1979, at Bellefontaine Beach in Jackson County by Terrie Fairley; on November 11, 1980, at Bay St. Louis by Ren Lohoefener; and on April 17, 1982, on the Pascagoula River marsh in Jackson County by Judith A. Toups. Toups and others found Yellow Rails at a rice field in Hancock County from October through November 1989. Extreme dates of occurrence are October 23 and April 28.

Very little is known about the population status and winter range of these rails. Their secretive habits, small size, and preference for dense cover make them almost impossible to observe. To learn more about wintering habitat preference, special techniques are required.

The wet, open savanna grasslands of the coastal terrace probably harbor many Yellow Rails. Lowery Jr. reported marsh buggies and rotary mowers were effective in flushing them. All-terrain vehicles equipped with flushing bars, tape recordings of Yellow Rail calls, and bird dogs are methods that researchers may use effectively to learn more about them.

The Yellow Rail, about the size of a week-old chicken, is tawny yellow on the upperparts with wide, black stripes cross-barred with white at the tips of the feathers. The cheeks, throat, and eye stripe are yellowish buff. In flight the wings show a square, white patch on the secondaries. The yellowish brown breast is lightly barred with darker brown. The sides and flanks have broad gray and white bars. The short chickenlike bill is yellow.

This species breeds very locally in the southern provinces of Canada and in the parts of northern states bordering Canada. The calls of this rail are like the rhythmic clicking together of two pebbles. I heard these *tic-tic, tic-tic, tic-tic-tic* calls in a grassy meadow bordering a marsh on Agassiz National Wildlife Refuge in Minnesota while watching Sedge Wrens. I played a prerecorded tape of the Yellow Rail, and a bird responded with similar calls, but it stayed hidden in the ground cover.

Black Rail *Laterallus jamaicensis*

All I have seen of this tiny rail is the solitary specimen in the MMNS in Jackson. That bird, a migrant found on March 26, 1954, on Capitol Street in Jackson, was picked up by an unknown person and taken to the museum for identification.

The Black Rail is a mysterious bird, and little is known about its breeding distribution. It is very rare and local on interior freshwater marshes and meadowlands. It breeds locally along the Atlantic Coast and west to central California, north to the southern shorelines of the Great Lakes, and very locally along the Gulf Coast and in the West Indies.

Because of its small size, secretive nocturnal habits, and widespread but very local distribution, it is a difficult bird to find. Most sightings of the bird are accidental. Following are sight records for the Black Rail in Mississippi. On October 25, 1962, Henry D. Haberyan recorded one bird seen at Gulfport near the marine aquarium (Gandy and Turcotte 1970). Ren Lohoefenor saw three on November 7, one on November 11, and one on December 2, 1980, at Bay St. Louis (Jackson 1981c). Judith A. Toups and Evelyn Johnson observed one on November 20, 1980, at Buccaneer State Park in Hancock County (Jackson 1981c).

This species has been known to nest in salt- and freshwater marshes, in meadowlands, and in grain fields. The woven nest, about the size of a meadowlark's nest, is suspended in a surrounding clump of vegetation. Eight to 11 eggs speckled with reddish brown over a creamy white ground color are laid in the nest.

The Black Rail is blackish overall with small white fleckings on the wings and back, and narrow, white barring on the sides and flanks. The nape is dark chestnut brown and the *black bill* is diagnostic.

The call of the male is a series of *kik-kik-kik* notes. The cuckoolike calls of the female are *kik-kee-doo'*. These birds call mainly at night. Tape recordings of Black Rail calls played late at night can sometimes help locate Black Rails in marshy areas, where they have been known to nest or occur as fall and winter residents.

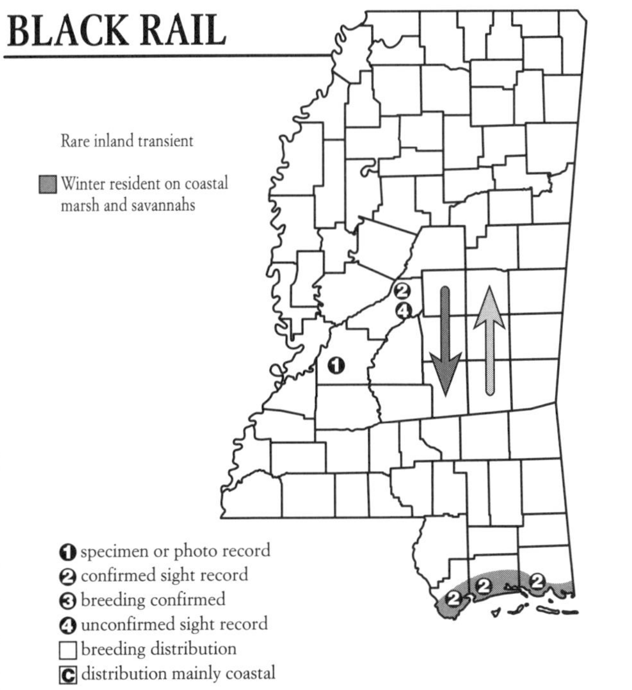

	JAN	FEB	MAR	APR	MAY	JUN	JUL	AUG	SEP	OCT	NOV	DEC
OCCURRENCE	oooo	oooo	oooo	12 oo		14 o				7 oooo	oooo	oooo
MUSEUM*												
WHT*												

*Breeding confirmed by egg, sight, or photographic record.

Clapper Rail *Rallus longirostris*

Clapper Rails are saltwater and brackish marsh dwellers. The subspecies along the shores of the Atlantic and Gulf Coasts is the same size as the King Rail. Distinguishing the two species in the field where their ranges overlap can be difficult.

The Clapper Rail has gray cheeks compared to rusty cheeks on the King Rail. Generally, the Clapper Rail is more grayish on the throat, breast, and wing coverts. These and other marks are paler, giving an overall grayer or duller appearance than the more colorful King Rail. The two species are the largest of our rails and are the size of half-grown chickens. Distinctions between this species and the King Rail are described further under the following account.

The Clapper Rail is a common, permanent-resident breeding bird of the saltwater marshes on the Gulf Coast. It can be seen best at dusk and early morning and when the tide is out. At these times, it often feeds along the exposed, muddy edges of drains, ditches, and bayous. At other times, it stays well hidden in marsh grasses.

These rails call mostly during crepuscular light and at night. The calls are similar to the King Rail, but longer in duration, especially the monotone clicking calls, *tek-tek-tek,* repeated continuously for long periods.

Fiddler crabs are a main food item of Clapper Rails. They also eat shrimp, snails, marine molluscs, insects, small fish and reptiles, and aquatic plant seeds.

This rail suspends a platform nest above normal tidewater level in protective marsh vegetation. The nest is made of marsh grasses and vegetation. Usually eight to 12 eggs are laid during April and May. They are buff colored and irregularly spotted with brown and gray.

Many of our coastal marshes have been altered by ditching and filling with dredge spoil for industrial developments, private recreational boating, and fishing camps. These developments alter the marsh ecology and lower the productivity for many wildlife species dependent upon marshland. Development encourages invasion by more terrestrial forms of life, including human disturbances. The Mottled Duck, Clapper Rail, Marsh Wren, Seaside Sparrow, and muskrat are permanent-resident marsh dwellers on the coast. They and many other animals are adversely affected when marshlands are drained and altered.

It is remarkable that marsh birds can ever survive the fury of wind and surging waters of tropical hurricanes. When Hurricane Juan hovered off the Louisiana Coast and then turned eastward to a landfall in Alabama, it left a

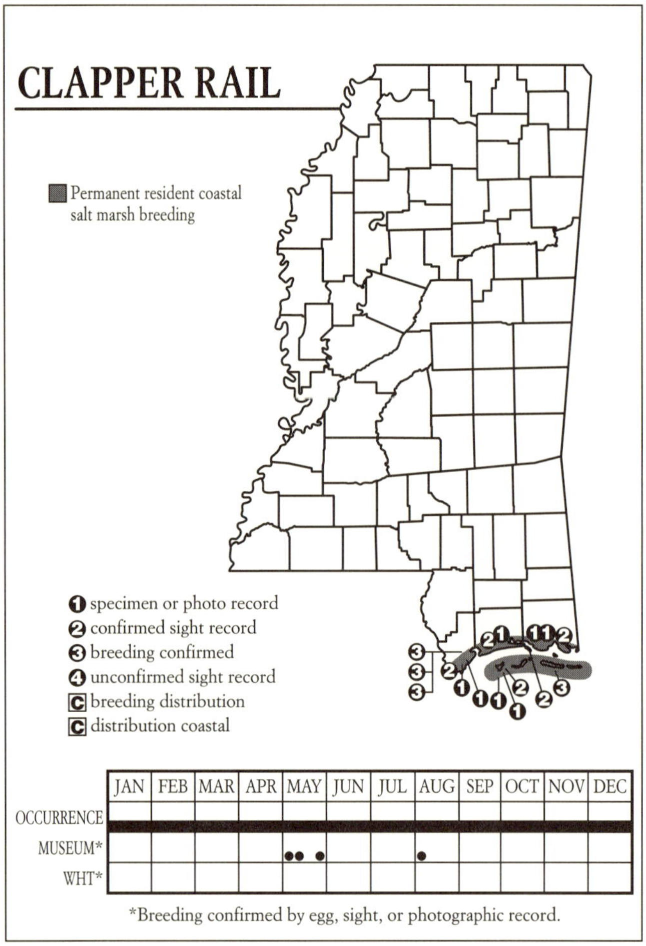

*Breeding confirmed by egg, sight, or photographic record.

toll of destruction (and mixed blessings for bird watchers) on the Hancock County coastline. The most apparent victims among bird life were Clapper Rails.

In her weekly newspaper column, Judith Toups described the passage of Juan and its effect:

> On October 28, 1985, Hurricane Juan was there to the southwest. It must have inundated the Chandeleurs and other islands off the Louisiana Coast. On the 28th marsh grasses started washing onto our coastal beaches. It carried with it raccoons, muskrats, nutrias, among others, and hundreds of Clapper Rails or "marsh hens" that dwell in the salt marshes along the Atlantic and Gulf Coasts.
>
> On October 29, Mal and I drove as far as we could go along South Beach Boulevard in Bay St. Louis. The sight was not to be believed—and one we will not forget. Clapper Rails were scampering by the hundreds in the tangled grass. Many of them, disoriented and traumatized, were running across the road. They were being killed by cars and were dying from trauma. The same scene was taking place in Pass Christian and other places.
>
> In the wind and rising water, we walked a short section of road and counted about 450 Clapper Rails, still alive, in about 400 feet of grass-obscured beach. They had nowhere to go. All of our marshland was by then underwater, too.

On November 2, following the passage of Juan, members of the MOS participated in a previously scheduled field trip in Hancock County. One hundred seventy-five species of birds were counted during the day. The list included accidental, rare, and many western species and unprecedented numbers of fall migrants delayed in passage by the storm. A better demonstration of the effects of a tropical storm on migration, unusual movements, and mortality can hardly be found on record.

King Rail *Rallus elegans*

As a boy in Clinton, my first encounter with the "marsh hen" or King Rail was on May 1, 1932. After climbing a water oak below the dam of Lake Wilson to collect a set of Green Heron eggs, I was resting on my back in the warm sun by the ditch, surrounded by broomsedge and clumps of blackberries. I heard a ticking sound, then a scolding call. When I turned on my side, there was a King Rail eyeing me from a distance of four or five feet. We stared at each other until it casually moved into a marshy place out of sight. Lake Wilson eventually was drained and is now residential and commercial property.

The King Rail is about the size of a half-grown chicken. It has a long, slightly decurved, slender bill, and *rusty cheeks,* neck, breast, and wing coverts. The upperparts are streaked and mottled with olive, buff, and dark brown. The sides, flanks, and undertail coverts are broadly barred with black. The head is dark brownish black on the crown and face with a partial eye ring and pale stripe between the eye and bill. The long legs and toes are reddish. The chin and throat are white.

The King Rail winters along the South Atlantic and Gulf Coasts and on inland marshes in the Gulf states. The breeding range extends westward to the Great Plains and north into

King Rail

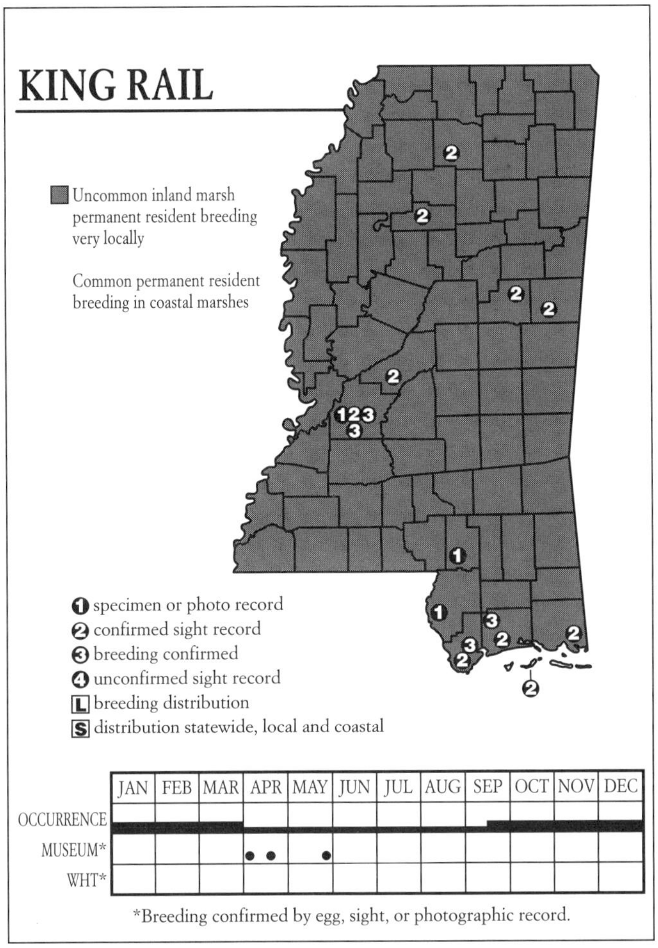

the northern tier of states. King Rails migrate from northern parts of the breeding range and winter commonly along the Atlantic Coast and the Gulf Coast to southwestern Texas. This rail breeds mainly in freshwater marshes, but also nests with Clapper Rails in saltwater coastal marshes. Young with adults were recorded at the Lyman Fish Hatchery on April 4, 1962 (Haberyan 1962b). The two are listed as separate species, but may hybridize where coastal breeding territories overlap. The Clapper Rail is strictly confined to coastal salt marshes.

Rails have short, rounded wings, and are reluctant but capable fliers. They escape detection during long flights across country by migrating at night and hiding themselves in daylight hours.

Foods of the King Rail are crustaceans, frogs and their tadpoles, large terrestrial and aquatic insects, snails, small fishes, and the seeds of some marsh plants.

The King Rail has a loud, raucous call beginning with coarse *pup-pup-pup* calls followed by clamorous, metallic-sounding single notes descending in volume and frequency, much like a silver coin sounds when settling to a stop after being dropped on a hard, metallic surface. The *pup-pup-pup* call notes are lower in pitch and not as continuous and evenly spaced as the *tek-tek-tek* calls of the Clapper Rail.

This rail builds a loosely woven platform nest supported and concealed in grass clumps or stems of marsh plants above water. As many as 12 creamy buff eggs spotted and blotched with brown and lavender are laid in a clutch. Nesting occurs in Mississippi from late March to early June. Dependent young will be seen until mid-July.

A sudden, loud noise such as slamming a car door will sometimes start rails to calling. Playing a prerecorded tape at dusk, dawn, and at night is the best way to get responsive calls and detect the presence of this rail. On one occasion in May 1980 while with our English friends, Arthur and Eileen Jenkins, I called Clapper, King, and Sora Rails out of a small Pascagoula River marsh into simultaneous view by playing tapes of their calls.

Virginia Rail *Rallus limicola*

The Virginia Rail is about the *size of a meadowlark*. With the exception of having *bluish gray cheeks*, the adult is almost a color replica of the King Rail. The Virginia Rail's colors are more intense, especially on the underparts and wing coverts. The wing coverts are a richer chestnut color. The legs are also redder. Juveniles are blackish brown above

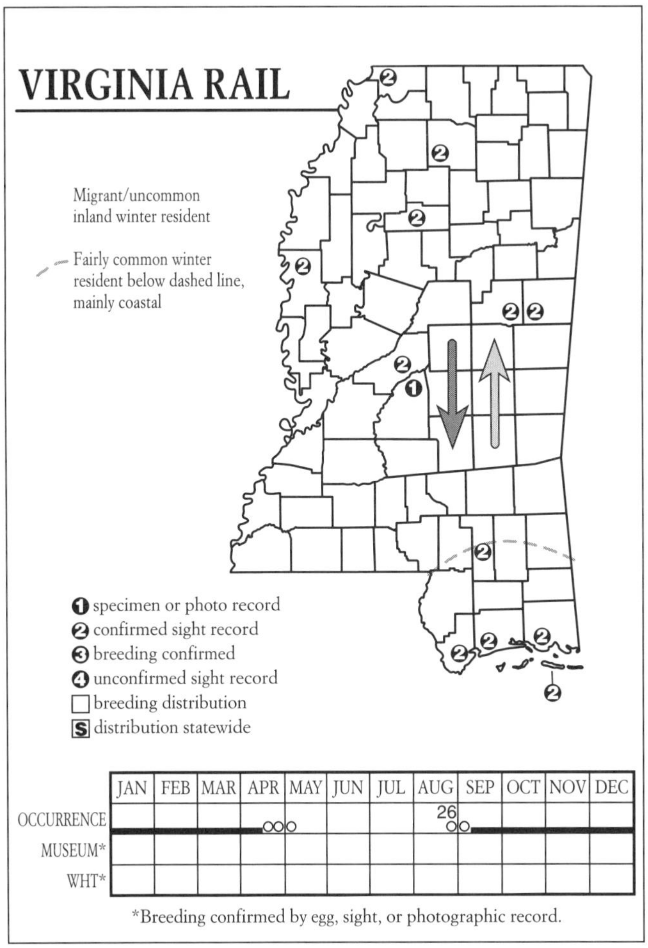

and mottled gray and black on the underparts with chestnut wing coverts. The bill is long and slightly decurved like the King Rail and Clapper Rail.

This rail is secretive and difficult to see as it darts like a rat or mouse through concealing vegetation. It is easily recognized by the distinctive *kidick-kidick-kidick* call and a loud, double-noted whinny descending in volume and frequency similar to the King Rail. There are other call variations, but a combination of those described here will identify this species. Rail voices are distinctive enough to identify each species. Prerecorded tapes of rail calls are very helpful in learning these distinctions and in locating and studying these birds in the field.

Virginia Rails are common fall and winter residents on the Gulf Coast, but uncommon on inland wetlands and marshes at this time of year. In northern Mississippi, they are casual winter residents. Breeding records have occurred in northern Alabama and in Louisiana, where adults have been seen with downy broods. This species may breed casually in Mississippi, but it has not been recorded. The breeding range is extensive over most marshes and wetlands of the interior states and north into southern Canada. It winters mainly in the southern Pacific, Atlantic, and Gulf coastal states.

This rail builds its suspended nest above water in clumps of vegetation in freshwater marshes. The eight to 12 creamy white eggs are speckled with shades of reddish brown.

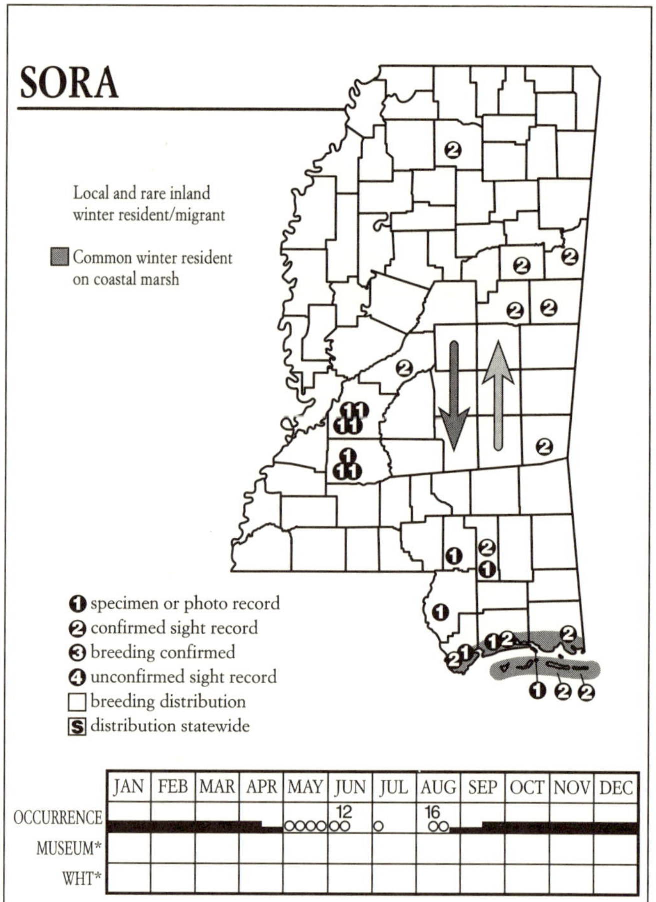

*Breeding confirmed by egg, sight, or photographic record.

Sora *Porzana carolina*

A small rail the size of a meadowlark, the Sora is a fairly common transient and uncommon winter resident on inland freshwater wetlands. It is a common winter resident on the Gulf Coast. It arrives in September and departs in April or early May. The bird's vast breeding range extends to freshwater marshes of the Canadian provinces and northern states, but excludes most southeastern states. It is the most common of the rails in the United States, wintering on the Gulf Coast and along the southern Atlantic and Pacific coastal marshes.

The Sora has a thick, *short, yellow bill,* a *black* or *blackish face,* and *white undertail coverts,* which are distinct from other small rails. It is gray on the cheeks and sides of the throat with a *black patch* in the center part on adults, but absent on immatures. The sides are barred gray and white. Upperparts are brownish olive, widely streaked with black, and narrowly streaked with white.

Sora calls are distinctive. When disturbed, the froglike, sharp, *keek* call, usually followed by a *tseet* call, can be heard. Winter calls are usually the high *kerwee.* A long, loud whinny starting high and gradually descending in volume and frequency of notes also identifies this rail.

I have found that rails are difficult to locate by their calls, and in most instances, it is even harder to tape record their calls. Except for recording the Clapper Rail's continuous clicking calls, I have had mostly bad luck. One never knows exactly when the bird will call or where the bird is located. By the time I have gotten the birds located and set a proper recording level, they have either quit calling or moved away—and then another bird called from behind in the marsh. At best, I usually get only part of their calls. They are amusing but frustrating birds to study and record, unless you live nearby and catch them when everything is just right.

Purple Gallinule *Porphyrula martinica*

It is hard to imagine a more colorful bird than the Purple Gallinule. The head, neck, and underparts are purple, shading to blue on the sides. The upperparts are greenish bronze and brownish. Long, *bright yellow* legs and extra long toes adapt it for walking and climbing among emergent aquatic vegetation. The bill is red tipped with yellow and set against a *pale blue* frontal shield. Undertail coverts are *white* beneath the short tail, which is carried at an upward angle and with frequent jerky motions. Juveniles are drab brown on the upperparts, buffy brown on the head and underparts, and white on the undertail coverts. The yellowish brown bill, greenish wing feathers, dark olive legs and feet, and *absence* of white streaking on the flanks distinguish juveniles from those of the similar-sized Common Moorhen.

Our two gallinules are classified as migratory game birds for which there is a fall hunting season. Except on the Gulf Coast, these birds are highly migratory, and most of them leave inland areas by early fall. Few licensed hunters on inland parts of the state have ever seen a gallinule, and most hunters would not care to hunt them. Also, most Mississippi hunters do not care to hunt more visible and numerous American Coots. The impact of our hunting seasons on gallinules, coots, and their cousins, the secretive rails, is negligible.

Purple Gallinules breed mainly on coastal brackish and freshwater marshes amid an abundance of emergent aquatic plants and shallow water shoreline areas. American lotus, white waterlily, cattail, sawgrass clumps, fallen dead timber covered with aquatic growths, and large amounts of submerged and floating aquatic plants provide the feeding and nesting habitat preferred by gallinules. Shallow oxbow lakes and the edges of larger lakes and permanent water reservoirs best meet this bird's habitat requirements. Flood control reservoirs with drastic summer draw-downs do not favor these birds, however.

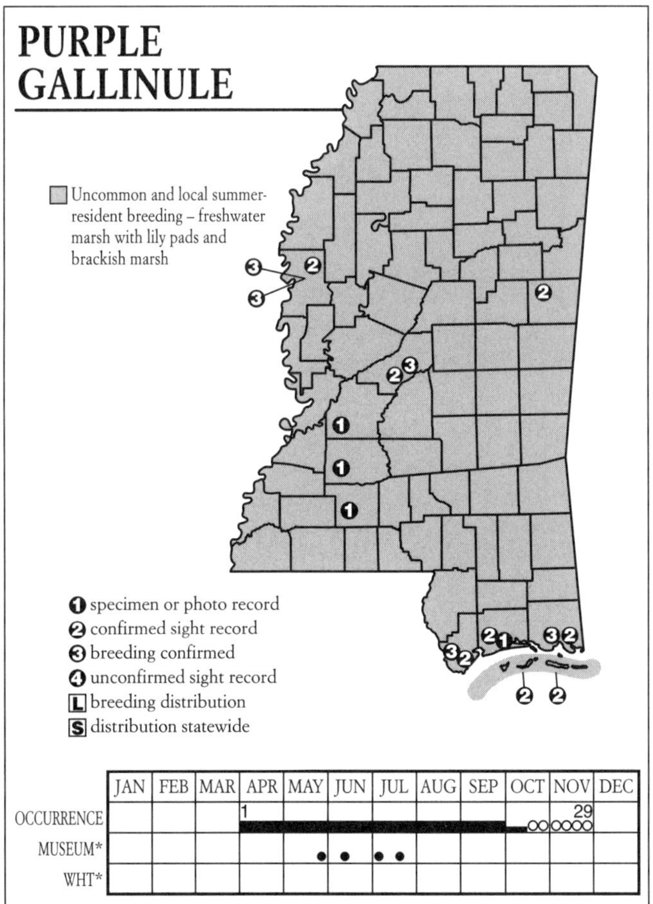

*Breeding confirmed by egg, sight, or photographic record.

Gallinules are shy birds, but they are active during daylight and can be observed by patiently watching as they cross openings in the marsh. When disturbed, they go into hiding quickly. They are reluctant fliers, but I have seen them take to the air to cross open water. In flight, their long, dangling, yellow legs are conspicuous.

On the nesting territory, they respond to tape recordings of their calls. I have called both gallinules to within a few feet of the shoreline of Deer Lake on the Yazoo National Wildlife Refuge. On the Pearl River Waterfowl Refuge in Madison County, I have seen Purple Gallinules respond and fly out of the marsh vegetation toward me while I played a tape of their call.

The Purple Gallinule has a variety of calls and call notes. The distinctive call notes I have heard are like the sound made by knocking two large pebbles together, fast at first then slowing, followed by high, froglike, squeaky single notes. A louder, cackling call is usually accompanied by the pebble-clicking call notes at the beginning or ending.

Purple Gallinules attach their platform nests of woven leaves of cattail or other marsh plants to reed stalks one to two feet above water. They sometimes build nests on floating masses of vegetation surrounded by deep water. They prefer sites surrounded by or over deep water so that a boat is usually needed to search for nests concealed in tall marsh growths.

Usually six to eight eggs are laid. They are pale buff, speckled thinly overall with chestnut brown. The downy young are black with grayish white on the throat and forepart of the head. Their bill is red with a yellow tip.

Purple Gallinules are fairly common breeding birds in the Yazoo Delta on oxbow lakes and open water marshes affording suitable habitat. Elsewhere on upland parts of Mississippi, they are mostly absent or seen casually during migration. They are less common than moorhens on coastal freshwater and brackish marshes. They breed locally in freshwater ponds and along stream courses near the coast. They are fairly common, summer-resident, breeding birds on the upper reaches of Ross Barnett Reservoir in Madison and Rankin Counties where cattails, lotus, water lilies, sawgrass, and other aquatics afford abundant food and cover. These birds are somewhat colonial nesters. While searching for nests in sawgrass and cattails, five nests with eggs were found in less than an acre of marsh on the reservoir.

Common Moorhen *Gallinula chloropus*

Until recently, this bird was called Common Gallinule or Florida Gallinule. The name change to Common Moorhen was made to match the names of its Eurasian and African counterparts.

These birds breed over a wide range from the eastern United States to the Great Plains, and from southern Canada

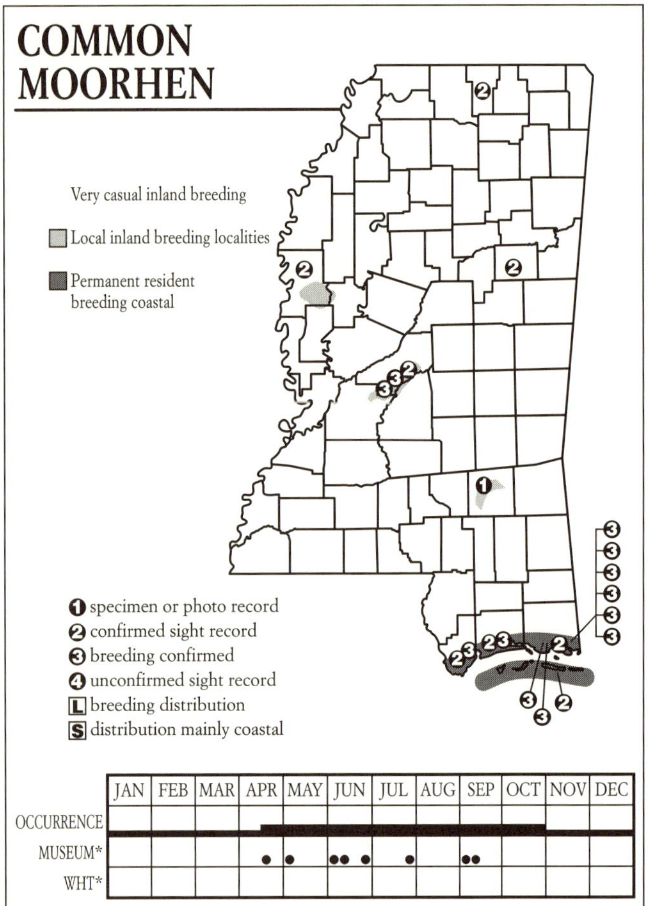

*Breeding confirmed by egg, sight, or photographic record.

to Argentina. They also breed in freshwater marshes of the southwestern states. Moorhens winter in marshes along the Gulf Coast and rarely inland. They are migratory from the more northern parts of their breeding range.

Moorhens nest commonly in marshes of our coastal counties and occur very locally as summer residents on freshwater marshes in Mississippi. Two sightings of juvenile broods have been reported in Madison County on the Pearl River Wildlife Management Area. Frances Wills Jr., Ruth Downey, and Evelyn Tackett saw a brood of four on August 30, 1986. A party of MOS observers saw a separate brood of juveniles on October 18, 1986. Moorhens are common summer residents on Deer Lake in Yazoo National Wildlife Refuge in Washington County. Gene and Shannon Knight saw an adult with three chicks on August 23, 1986, near Graysport on Grenada Lake.

The adults have slate gray underparts with a *thin, white streak* along the sides and flanks. The head is black with a *red* frontal shield and a red bill with yellow tip. Outer undertail coverts are white, the inner ones black. The feet and legs are greenish yellow. Juveniles are paler and brownish above and can be distinguished from juvenile coots and Purple Gallinules by the whitish throat and the *white lateral line* on the sides. In winter, the frontal shield of adults and young is brown. The bill is brown and tipped with yellow. At a glance these birds can be mistaken for coots.

The behavior of Moorhens is similar to coots and ducks. They tend to swim and feed along the edges of aquatic vegetation, and when disturbed, they seek cover. They are good swimmers but move jerkily through the water, moving their head back and forth. When walking, they flick their tail and show the white underneath. In courtship display, the male spreads and lowers his wings while fanning his tail and displaying the white outer and black inner undertail coverts.

Like the Purple Gallinule, the Common Moorhen builds a platform nest of cattails and marsh plants concealed at or near the water's edge. Eggs are buffy, speckled and blotched with chestnut, and number from eight to 12.

American Coot *Fulica americana*

The "mud hen," sometimes called "poule d'eau," is slate gray with a shiny, white, chickenlike bill. Undertail coverts are white on the outside and divided by black inner coverts. A white margin on the secondaries shows in flight or when wings are extended. The large feet have flat lobes and sharp claws. The body is ducklike and about the size of a small duck.

Coots feed along the water's edge by dabbling and sometimes diving. They often feed on green grasses and seeds and parts of aquatic and terrestrial plants along shorelines. They are highly gregarious during fall and winter months, and congregate while feeding or resting. At dusk they fly toward open water and roost there in rafts. They often feed in company with dabbling ducks along shorelines. While swimming or walking, they bob their heads back and forth.

In Mississippi, the American Coot is a common fall and winter resident arriving in October and departing in April or early May. A few nest on the Gulf Coast, but rarely inland. Although summer sight records of coots are not uncommon, most of these sightings are probably nonbreeders.

Jerome A. Jackson and J. Ray Watson (1983) found an adult with three half-grown young on May 28, 1983, at Bluff Lake at Noxubee National Wildlife Refuge in Noxubee County. Joe McGee (Hodges 1985) recorded adults with young on Ross Barnett Reservoir in Madison County on August 21 and September 9, 1985. Judith A. Toups, Dalton King, and Malcolm F. Hodges Jr. (Hodges and Jackson 1984) observed two adults with one or two young on the Pascagoula River marsh in Jackson County, August 7–18, 1984. Toups (Hodges 1985) recorded 20 adults with many immatures at Jackson Marsh in Hancock County on July 26, 1985. An adult with one downy young was seen by Hodges Jr. (1985) on August 5, 1985, on the Pascagoula River marsh.

Coots have a variety of calls. Low, ducklike *kuk, kuk-kuk, kuk* calls are heard most commonly. Loud, cackling choruses

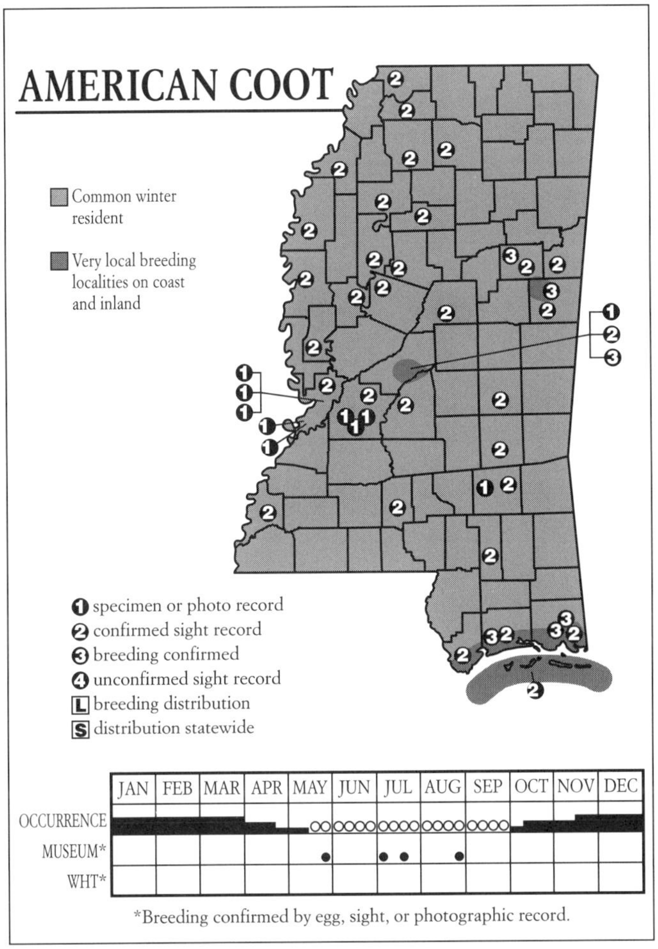

of shrill, double-noted *kew-rack, kew-rack'* calls mixed with the softer *kuk-kuk* calls are heard when these birds are actively feeding and moving about in early morning.

Coots build nest platforms of cattails and marsh grasses over water, supported by plant stems or reeds, usually well hidden, but sometimes in open situations. The eight to 14 or more buff-colored eggs are evenly sprinkled with small blackish spots. The downy young are brownish black. They have red bills and reddish orange, curly, hairlike feathers on the head and shoulders. Juveniles are lighter than adults, especially on underparts with pale edgings on the feathers.

Aramidae (Limpkins)

[Limpkin] *Aramus guarauna*

Statements about bird ranges do not always hold true. All birds capable of flight can be forced to wander by storms or unusual weather disturbances, not to mention depletion or expansion of available food sources and habitat. For whatever reason, previously unknown bird species continue to occur in our state, and new species are added to our list of Mississippi birds.

One occurrence in Mississippi of the Limpkin, or "crying bird," has been substantiated by a photograph. These birds were once common and tame until they were hunted almost to extinction. Their populations since have increased under protection. Now, they are locally common in the freshwater swamps and marshlands, along stream courses of central and southern Florida, and in the Florida Panhandle to near Tallahassee.

I first saw Limpkins in timbered parts of the Florida Everglades along the Old Tamiami Trail highway. Later, I saw them and recorded their wailing cries along a boat channel at Clewiston, and at Wakulla Springs south of Tallahassee where they are fairly common. The large apple snail is locally abundant along Florida's spring-fed rivers, streams, and wooded swamps. Limpkins feed on these large molluscs by probing the bottom to locate them. The birds then take the snails to the shoreline or a log where the Limpkin uses its curved bill to remove the mollusc from its shell.

Warriner (1962) recorded the first Mississippi sighting of three Limpkins on May 2 and 3, 1956, at Waukomis Lake just east of Corinth. On May 2, the three birds flushed and flew and alighted in trees. On the following day at the same site about sunset, a single Limpkin called and flushed at 50 feet.

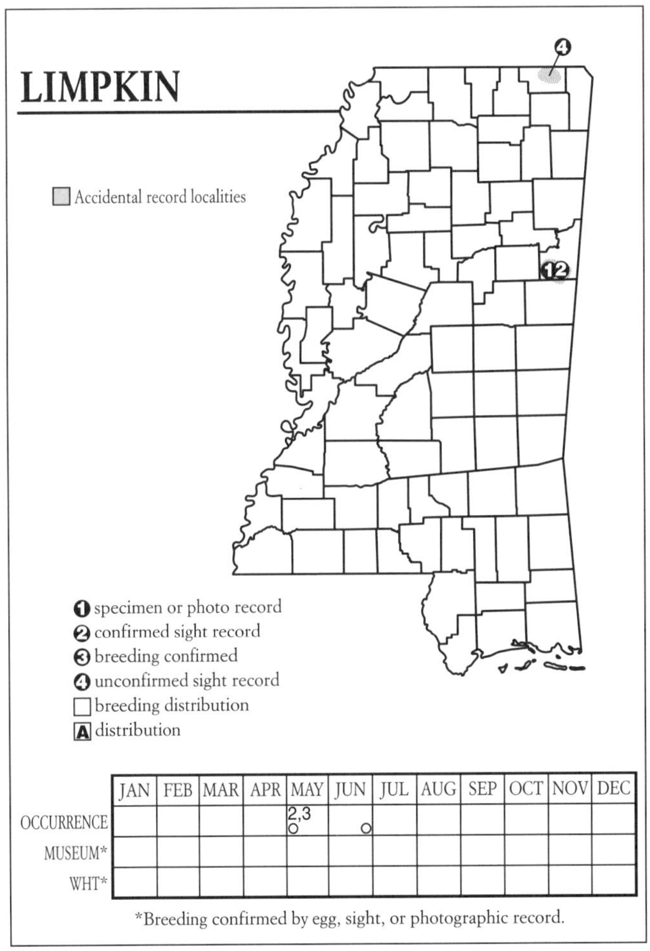

In the summer of 1972, a party of Jackson Audubon Society canoeists including Steve Peterson and Dudley Peeler saw a Limpkin along a vegetated shoreline of the Tombigbee River near Columbus. Color 8-mm movies were being taken on the canoe trip. The Limpkin was in plain view of several observers, and a short strip of film was made by Dudley Peeler showing all details including the *decurved bill;* long legs; streaked, long neck; and *dark brown body color* with *tear-shaped, white spots on the sides and back.* The bird moved slowly out of sight into concealing cover. I saw this film with the scene repeated several times, and it was unmistakably a Limpkin.

Unlike rails, Limpkins are at times quite visible while actively feeding or calling. They frequently call from bushes or even tall trees along shorelines. The Limpkin calls are loud, mournful cries somewhat like the male peafowl. They can be described as *kree-owww, kree-oww,* sometimes repeated incessantly at night, less frequently in daylight. They flush with long legs dangling, but they are strong fliers with legs extended behind and necks outstretched in level flight.

Limpkins build a platform nest of marsh vegetation woven into and supported by concealing vegetation. Their nests are sometimes built in or on supporting vine tangles, sawgrass, or grass tussocks on logs or isolated shorelines. Five to eight buff-colored eggs splotched with shades of drab brown complete a clutch. The downy young are covered in soft, cinnamon and snuff-colored down with whitish down around the throat and pale brown on the underparts.

The Limpkin should not be confused with *brown-backed,* immature ibises, which have similar decurved bills and body sizes. Immature night-herons have brown bodies streaked and spotted on the back with white and *straight,* sharp-pointed bills. The curved bill, brown body color, streaked neck, and white spots on the sides and back of the Limpkin are its distinctive field marks.

Mississippi Sandhill Crane

Gruidae (Cranes)

Stately is the best way to describe this family of large, long-legged, long-necked birds with long, heavy bills. They stand erect, and their elongated tertials droop over their rump like a bustle. In flight, the neck and legs are fully extended. They are noted for loud calls and frenzied courtship rituals with leaps and dancing.

Some 17 species of cranes are found worldwide on all continents except South America and Antarctica. Only Sandhill Cranes occur locally east of the Mississippi River. The Whooping Crane winters along the Texas Gulf Coast at Aransas National Wildlife Refuge, and a few winter in New Mexico. A Eurasian species, the Common Crane, is a rare vagrant to the Great Plains, western Canada, and Alaska.

Except for immatures, all cranes have bare, usually red, facial or crown skin. A Demoiselle Crane lived on the Mississippi Sandhill Crane National Wildlife Refuge at Gautier until 1989, its origin unknown (Valentine, pers. comm.) Two escaped birds of the exotic Crowned Crane (Hodges 1987) were seen and photographed on September 8, 1987, at ponds near Kiln in Hancock County. The Mississippi Sandhill Crane, a subspecies, is endemic to Jackson County.

Mississippi Sandhill Crane
Grus canadensis pulla

Two migrant races of Sandhill Crane have been found in Mississippi, the Greater *(G. c. tabida)* and the Lesser *(G. c. canadensis)* found in Alaska and Canada. Migrant cranes in small flocks have been seen on the Mississippi Sandhill Crane National Wildlife Refuge (Valentine, pers. comm.). These birds have been presumed to be Greater Sandhill Cranes, as is a similar small group that winters in Baldwin County, Alabama.

I observed a mixed flock of cranes on the refuge on January 30, 1985. A group of 15 birds, much lighter gray overall and presumed to be Greaters, remained separate from 13 banded and released Mississippi Sandhill Cranes in the same field. I had been in a blind with David L. Watts observing and recording calls from 7 A.M. to 1:30 P.M. The Mississippi birds were distinctly different in appearance. Overall, they were darker, especially on the head and neck. The Mississippi birds could be distinguished at a glance from the migrant birds by their darker plumage and the noticeable contrast between their white cheeks and darker neck and ear patches.

Migrant cranes have occurred elsewhere in Mississippi. A flock of 65 Sandhill Cranes of unknown origin was observed at the NASA Test Site in Hancock County by Ren Lohoefener on February 22, 1980 (Jackson 1981c). Inland records of single migrants were reported near Hollandale from December 30, 1971, to January 14, 1972, by E. J. Ganier Jr. (Turcotte 1972a) and at Sardis Waterfowl Refuge on November 2, 1976, by Rab Rodgers and Richard Wells. Another record of a juvenile occurred near Fitler in Issaquena County (Turcotte 1972a). John Kerr reported seeing the bird with a drooping wing in a pasture on January 10. It was found dead on January 12 by Henry Bobbs Jr. It wore a numbered, plastic leg band, which later proved it was a Lesser Sandhill Crane banded in Alaska by Cheryl Boise (1979).

Mississippi Sandhill Crane

Mississippi Sandhill Cranes nest in pond cypress and wet meadows of coastal savannas in Jackson County.

The Mississippi Sandhill Crane is similar in size to the common Great Blue Heron. Both stand about four feet tall. The crane's body, however, is more robust and stately in appearance. Cranes fly with the neck extended. All herons fly with their neck folded back to the shoulders. Tertiary feathers of the crane are long and curve downward to droop over the rump and tail like a bustle. The red, bald crown of the adult crane is distinctive.

The Mississippi Sandhill Crane nests on the ground in marshy savannas or around the edges of pond cypress swamps. Occasionally, nests have been located in open pine plantations grown on former savannas. The nest site is always in an opening covered with grasses, sedges and water-tolerant plants. Nesting and egg-laying begin in late March. The peak hatching period is from about May 1 to May 20.

The nest is made of grass, sedges, and other surrounding vegetation. Among 93 nest sites, 43 (46 percent) were dry at initial visits, 17 (18 percent) were moist (water on surface), and 33 (36 percent) were wet (Valentine 1984). As the savannas dry out later in the season, some nests may have no water surrounding them. Renesting may occur following an earlier nest and egg loss.

Incubation lasts 28 to 31 days, but 30 days is normal. Two large, buff-colored eggs, variously splotched with rich brown, are usually laid. The downy chicks hatch a day apart and remain one or two days in the nest until led away by the adults. Both adults tend the young until the next spring.

The Mississippi Sandhill Crane feeds on a variety of plant and animal foods. Seeds, fruit, leaves, grasses, and the roots of marsh and bog plants are eaten regularly. Insects, other invertebrates, and small vertebrates are also important foods. Crops including corn, millet, chufa, and winter grains are used readily by these birds.

The Mississippi Sandhill Crane is a nonmigratory, endangered subspecies endemic to Jackson County, Mississippi. The current range is within an area from the Pascagoula River to the Jackson County line on the west and from Simmons Bayou to about four miles north of Vancleave on the north. As of December 1994, the total estimated population of native and captive-reared, banded birds was 115, of which 20 percent or less were from wild-hatched chicks. From 1989 through 1994, approximately 30 captive-reared birds were released each year.

Mississippi Sandhill Cranes are an endangered subspecies endemic to Jackson County.

The Mississippi Sandhill Crane has an interesting history. It was unknown to ornithologists until reported by Aldo Leopold (1929). While conducting a game survey of Mississippi and interviewing local residents, Leopold recorded the presence of a small flock of these birds between Fontainebleau and Vancleave and west of the Pascagoula River. This sparsely settled area was largely composed of cut and burned-over pine barrens and open savannas of the coastal terrace.

A few, scattered, small farms on hammocks and higher elevations lay within the cranes' territory. Local residents on small landholdings and the larger landowners who ranged sheep and cattle knew of the cranes. They understood little about the cranes' breeding habits, because few people bothered to explore the poorly drained, widely dispersed pond cypress bogs where cranes nested and reared their young. Only a few riders running cattle on the open range knew about the birds' breeding habits.

Most resident landowners never harmed the birds. They tolerated and even admired their presence when small flocks invaded harvested corn fields and fenced pastures. Occasional sniping was known to occur, but the wary cranes survived because of their relative isolation on larger landholdings. The extreme poverty of the soils made most of the land unsuitable for farming, which allowed savannas and open pine lands to remain idle.

I learned of the Sandhill Cranes in Jackson County in 1936, when as a student I worked with Frances A. Cook, leader of the statewide Plant and Animal Survey Project, a forerunner of the MMNS. Miss Cook had Leopold's report and arranged a trip to the crane area in 1937. Because of my growing interest in birds, she let me accompany her. At the Hilda fire tower we met a local resident who knew the location of a crane nest. This guide led us along a CCC road to Ben Williams Pond. We flushed a pair of the cranes, but found only an unoccupied nest of the previous season. Thus began a long and continuing involvement to study, inventory, protect, and manage this disjunct, remnant population of Sandhill Cranes.

In the late 1930s, R. M. Freeman, the unit supervisor of the Plant and Animal Survey Project, was assigned by Miss Cook to conduct a survey of the Fontainebleau crane roosting and resting areas. Cranes were observed in the Paige Bayou marsh and an area near Vancleave known as Freeman's Farms. Freeman's observations accounted for 20 or more birds using the Fontainebleau area, but it was known that all the cranes were not using the same winter roosts, and the counts were inconclusive.

E. A. McIlhenny (1938), a prominent Louisiana wildlife enthusiast and early wildlife conservationist, learned about the Mississippi cranes. With the help of H. P. Flateau, manager of Fontainebleau Farms, and some farmworkers, McIlhenny

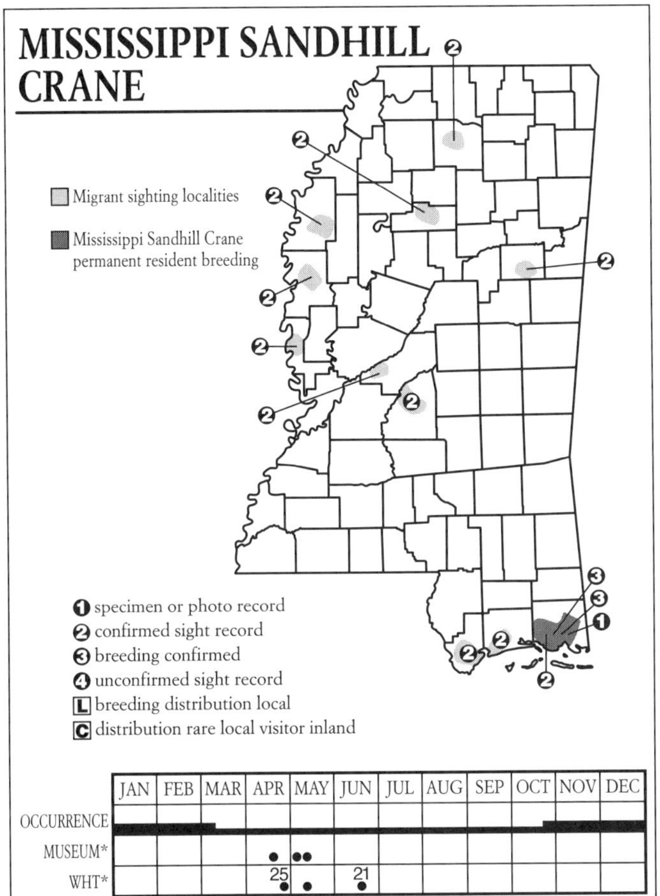

*Breeding confirmed by egg, sight, or photographic record.

located and described the crane colony and his observations on 13 nests with eggs and young for a scientific journal.

He also reported the presence of a crane group north and northeast of Ocean Springs, separate from the Fontainebleau flock. John King, a local resident and Fontainebleau Farms employee, told Walkinshaw (1949) that he had resided in the area for 40 years and had observed cranes there since 1898. McIlhenny took at least two young birds to his estate at Avery Island, Louisiana, where they were raised and photographed as juveniles. His article included a picture of a crane nest with eggs, the two juveniles, and an adult crane.

On April 25, 1939, I visited the crane area and found an abandoned crane nest with one egg about three miles north of Fontainebleau. On May 9, 1941, Freeman and I visited H. P. Flateau at his home on old U.S. 90. Flateau, dressed in a white linen suit, elaborated on McIlhenny's visits and described the Bear Pond nesting area. One of his employees told about finding nests and watching cranes dance on the "sheep pasture," an open space on the southern side of Bear Pond.

We walked from Mississippi 57 along a cypress brake that opened out into Bear Pond. After passing the open sheep pasture, we searched Bear Pond and flushed a crane from a nest containing two eggs, one cracked and one addled. The spoiled eggs were not taken, but nest and egg data were recorded for the museum egg collection.

Later that day, we searched the Ben Williams Pond nesting area. We found a large, fresh nest with crane feathers on it. Adults were not present, and we had started to leave the nest when I decided to return and search for young around the nest. We found two small young motionless and hiding in a clump of lizard tail about a yard from the nest. The chicks were returned to the nest and photographed.

Following World War II, St. Regis Paper Company acquired land and timber rights on large acreages in the area. Although some company employees and the local forester in charge were aware of the cranes and were concerned about protecting them, later habitat alterations were detrimental to the cranes. Several access roads and fire lanes were constructed. With heavy equipment available, the company soon began ditching out shallow drains through some nesting ponds. Parallel ditches were plowed through open savanna grassland (crane meadows), and slash pines were planted on the ridges. Thousands of acres of crane meadows necessary for the cranes' survival were essentially made unsuitable for nesting.

The improved drainage allowed the wetter nesting swamps to grow up in dense brush and vine tangles, reducing crane nesting and feeding habitat. Pine plantations were established where they never grew before. These practices and other human encroachments seriously degraded breeding habitat and threatened extirpation of the cranes. Firebreaks and fire control protecting the pine plantations allowed some of the best nesting areas such as Bear Pond to become dense forest. The open range policy became unlawful in 1958 and eliminated most of the burning practices that formerly maintained open wet prairie grasslands.

The completion of four-lane U.S. 90 and postwar industrial development at Pascagoula increased tourist and commuter traffic. Commercial encroachment formed a strip city along the edges of the cranes' territory and threatened their isolation. Housing developments spread north of Gautier, Ocean Springs, and around Fontainebleau, engulfing parts of the wet prairie and bordering crane breeding areas. Increased human activities and random shooting of cranes combined with natural mortalities to threaten the continued survival of the Mississippi Sandhill Cranes.

Dr. Lawrence Walkinshaw, an international authority on world cranes, visited Jackson County in 1940 and described their nesting habitat (1949). After a later visit, he expressed concern about human activities, random crane shootings, and other encroachments (1960).

In 1961, the Mississippi Game and Fish Commission, other wildlife managers, and conservationists were seriously concerned about the impact of the proposed Interstate

10 crossing that would bisect the Sandhill Crane nesting territory in Jackson County (Turcotte 1961f). At a public hearing in Pascagoula, the Mississippi Highway Department proposed routing I-10 through the Fontainebleau crane area with interchanges at Mississippi 57 and the Vancleave-Gautier Road. The hearing was attended mostly by proponents of the highway plans.

I attended the meeting and stated briefly that construction would bisect the Sandhill Cranes' breeding territories between Brown's Trail and Ben Williams Pond and would invite encroachments around the interchanges. I also stated that a trestle-type bridge across the Pascagoula marsh was preferable to another dredge fill crossing that would further alter and damage productive marshlands.

At that time there were no state or federal laws protecting the habitat of threatened wildlife species. The Mississippi crane colony was thought to be a disjunct population of the nonmigratory Florida Sandhill Crane, which was not considered endangered. The proposed construction in Jackson County was scheduled for completion by about 1969.

In the late 1950s, there was national concern about the decline of eastern populations of the Bald Eagle, Osprey, and Peregrine Falcon. A similar decline in Brown Pelicans was noticed along the northern Gulf Coast. A massive die-off and complete extirpation of Brown Pelicans along the Louisiana and Mississippi Coasts may have resulted from the cumulative effects of poisoning in the food chain by the use and abuse of chlorinated hydrocarbon pesticides. Chronic leaking of pesticides from a manufacturing plant near Memphis may have been the major cause of the catastrophe. Regardless, environmental and endangered species protection had become recognized as a nationwide problem.

In 1963, the Bureau of Sport Fisheries and Wildlife began an investigation of the probable effects of the I-10 crossing through the Sandhill Crane breeding territory in Jackson County. Jacob M. Valentine Jr., a wildlife management biologist, was assigned to study the breeding biology, life history, feeding habits, range, and environmental conditions of the cranes. During this research, the Bureau of Sport Fisheries and Wildlife and the Game and Fish Commission entered into an agreement permitting not more than six eggs annually to be taken from crane nests for transfer to the Patuxent Wildlife Research Center in Laurel, Maryland (Turcotte 1971d). Here, hatching and propagation would take place to establish a "captive" breeding flock of cranes.

As the study progressed, state wildlife biologists Robert E. Noble and Lon Strong Jr. studied the breeding biology and population under a part-time Pittman-Robertson project (Noble 1967). Later Valentine Jr. and Noble (1970) published "A Colony of Sandhill Cranes in Mississippi" in *The Journal of Wildlife Management*. The study delineated feeding and nesting habitats and estimated the total crane population at 38 to 40 birds. Pine plantations, drainage, an interstate highway, and increasing housing developments were listed as endangering crane survival.

Wildlife management biologists Jacob M. Valentine Jr., left, and Robert E. Noble collaborated in a study of the Mississippi Sandhill Crane in Jackson County.

The establishment of state, federal, or private refuges was recommended if the crane colony was to survive. Valentine Jr. and Noble also suggested that the Mississippi crane should be considered a distinct ecotype or subspecies. The study concluded that "the present land use, planned highway construction, and impending residential developments are destroying the habitats essential to the cranes."

The Mississippi and Florida Sandhill Cranes were listed as rare in the 1968 Federal List of Endangered Fish and Wildlife. In 1971, the Mississippi Game and Fish Commission approved the establishment of the Mississippi Sandhill Crane National Wildlife Refuge.

John Aldrich (1972) described the Mississippi Sandhill Crane as a new subspecies after studying seven live captive birds at Patuxent raised from eggs collected in Mississippi. The subspecies designated as *Grus canadensis pulla* was based on its dark color (darker than all other sandhill cranes) and size differences. The Mississippi Sandhill Crane was listed as endangered in the United States List of Endangered Fish and Wildlife on June 4, 1973 (Turcotte 1974b).

Following this action, the U.S. Fish and Wildlife Service established the Mississippi Sandhill Crane National Wildlife Refuge. The initial acquisition of 1709 acres was made by The Nature Conservancy in 1974, with the U.S. Fish and Wildlife Service purchasing these lands in 1975. Subsequent purchases, including 6029 acres from St. Regis Paper Company, were acquired by the Fish and Wildlife Service, bringing total refuge lands to 19,273 acres in 1989.

During the progress of crane research over 25 years, 139 crane nests were studied. The captive breeding flock, established at Patuxent Wildlife Research Center, contained 33 adult Mississippi cranes in 1988. In 1981, the first release of nine captive-raised juvenile cranes was made. Releases have been made each year since. In 1989, 29 juveniles were freed into the refuge. At the end of 1989, 56 were known to be alive from a total of 96 released to date (refuge files).

While land acquisition for the crane refuge progressed and I-10 was being constructed, the National Wildlife Federation and its Mississippi affiliate questioned the effect of highway construction on critical habitat of the endangered Mississippi cranes. Together they filed federal court action against the U.S. Department of Transportation and others.

On June 26, 1975, a hearing was held at Biloxi in U.S. District Court, Judge Walter Nixon presiding. Jacob M. Valentine Jr. testified on behalf of the plaintiff. Nixon's ruling on August 4, 1975, said that construction of I-10 should not threaten the existence of Mississippi cranes.

An appeal was filed to the U.S. Fifth Circuit Court of Appeals in New Orleans on August 24, 1975. On December 9, 1975, the court enjoined the highway agencies from work on the disputed Vancleave-Gautier interchange and excluded borrow pits adjacent to the highway. The court agreed that loss of land due to construction would not endanger the cranes, but that private development, or indirect causes, was the major danger to the birds. Borrow pits would destroy or damage critical habitat. The court deferred to the U.S. Department of Interior to determine the conditions under which the interchange could be built without endangering the cranes.

The Mississippi Highway Department brought the case to the U.S. Supreme Court, and the court refused to review the appellate court's ruling. This was an important test of provisions of Section 7 of the Endangered Species Act of 1973, which provides protection for critical habitat and extends protection to ecotypes or subspecies of populations considered endangered. At the time of the trial, the U.S. Fish and Wildlife Service entered an emergency order effective June 25, 1975, declaring 100,000 acres in the Mississippi crane range as critical habitat. The final rulemaking on August 8, 1977, designated about 26,000 acres as critical habitat for the Mississippi Sandhill Crane.

Acquisition of critical habitat around the contested Vancleave-Gautier interchange was authorized and funded by Congress. About 1900 acres were acquired around the interchange and along the Vancleave-Gautier Road while construction proceeded to complete the interchange. The Mississippi Highway Department bridged the Pascagoula Marsh with minimal damage and used dredge spoil for landfill above the level of marshlands.

The Mississippi Sandhill Crane Recovery Plan (Valentine 1984) was devised by a recovery team "to prevent the extinction of the Mississippi Sandhill Crane in the short term and to reclassify the crane from endangered to threatened status in the long term." By preserving, protecting, and enhancing the crane environment in Jackson County, the minimum population goal of the plan is at least 30 pairs and 40 nonbreeding cranes, and at least 30 active nests per season over a period of five years.

Development and management practices on the crane refuge are approaching recovery plan objectives. A headquarters office, interpretation center, and maintenance work buildings are completed. Access to refuge lands is restricted and permission is required on all parts of the refuge. Land acquisition is nearly completed except for about 600 acres of nesting and feeding habitat. Five hundred acres of roosting marsh in the Paige Bayou area were acquired. Ten agricultural crop units have been established and numerous ponds created or enlarged.

Releases of captive-reared cranes are monitored. Radiotracking of released cranes is a continuing program. Pairing and nesting between native and pen-reared birds has begun. Some predator control has been done. Techniques for detecting inviable eggs in crane nests by flotation and replacement with viable eggs from Patuxent have been used successfully.

Yearly nest and roost surveys are conducted, and population counts are made twice each year. Hand clearing, bulldozing, and controlled burning of pine plantations have restored savanna nesting sites. New techniques are being used at Patuxent to prevent human imprinting on released cranes.

A 250-acre wastewater treatment facility in the Ocean Springs Unit is under easement to the Fish and Wildlife Service. Treated wastewater is sprayed over grassland, and excess water is collected in several ponds used by cranes as feeding and roosting sites. Nesting was confirmed in 1991. The grasslands are used as loafing and feeding sites by the birds. Ten or more drinking, nesting, and roosting ponds have been created by bulldozing and diking or by raising culverts and roadbeds. Some have control structures to hold or retard water runoff.

A debt of gratitude is owed to the people living in the crane area. Their mode of living on and off the land has benefited the cranes. The regular use of fire kept savanna grasslands open for grazing, creating and maintaining a symbiotic relationship benefiting both cranes and people. The loud, unforgettable calls, the musical duetting, and courtship dance rituals of cranes on the wet meadows of Jackson County are a heritage worthy of preservation.

Shorebirds and Allies (Charadriiformes)

This large order includes the shorebirds, gulls, terns, auks, and their allies. Although they may differ widely in habits, most frequent the sea and shorelines and flock together in large numbers. They have long, pointed wings and a similar shape, with the legs set at the center of the body.

Many species of this order breed in the far north and produce downy, precocious young that develop rapidly during the relatively short breeding seasons. Most species have dense feathers or downy plumage suitable for aquatic habitats. Many lay eggs that are large in proportion to their body size and pointed at one end.

No less than 70 species of this order have been found to occur in Mississippi. At inland areas, relatively few species are known to breed, and usually occur only for short periods in passage to or from northern breeding grounds. On the Gulf Coast, observers are fortunate to have shoreline beaches and more suitable habitat for supporting large numbers of these birds. Many of these species are known to occur almost year-round in our coastal areas. In some months, they occur there in large numbers and afford opportunities for observers to differentiate between similar species of shorebirds, gulls, and terns.

The shorebirds will challenge serious birders as well as casual observers in field identification. They can be difficult to differentiate because of similarities in appearance among the species and variations among immature individuals and those in basic and breeding plumages.

Above: Lesser Yellowlegs

Semipalmated Plover

Charadriidae (Plovers)

Plovers are wading birds with large eyes, and thick, relatively short, stubby, pigeonlike bills. They are mostly white underneath with bold markings of black, brown, and shades of gray on the upperparts. Dark head, facial, neck, belly, and breast patterns contrast sharply with bordering white marks. Compared to sandpipers, their bodies are more compact with thick necks. When seen in profile and in flight, they resemble gulls.

Eight plover species occur in Mississippi. Only three are permanent residents known to breed here: the Killdeer (common statewide), the Snowy Plover (found on Gulf Coast beaches and the barrier islands), and the Wilson's Plover (summer-resident breeder on the Gulf Coast). The American Golden-Plover occurs mainly in late February to early April enroute to far northern breeding grounds. Black-bellied Plovers occur commonly on the Gulf Coast as winter residents, sparingly in summer, and rarely inland during migration or wanderings.

The other two belted or "ringed" plovers—the Semipalmated and Piping—occur mainly on coastal beaches and tidal flats as spring and fall migrants. The Piping Plover occurs regularly in winter on some coastal beaches. During summer, both species may occur rarely on the coast. The Mountain Plover is an accidental late fall visitor.

Black-bellied Plover *Pluvialis squatarola*

Black-bellied Plovers are common along our coastal beaches and mud flats from late summer until early June. A few nonbreeders remain on the coast through summer. Many in breeding plumage can be seen until early May before departure to Arctic tundra nesting grounds. The species is circumpolar in distribution.

These birds migrate primarily along coastlines or widely dispersed inland areas during the spring migration. Migrants occur inland more regularly during fall migration from late August to late November, usually seen as individuals or in small groups on shorelines of large bodies of water.

About 12 inches long, this species is large compared to other plovers occurring in Mississippi. In basic, *nonbreeding* plumage, adults and immatures are brownish gray above and mostly gray-looking, stocky birds with a hunch-backed appearance and pigeonlike bill. In flight and in all plumages, the distinctive field marks are white uppertail coverts and barred white tail, *black axillary feathers* at the wing pits, and a bold white stripe on the upper surface of the wings.

In the strikingly black-and-white alternate plumage, frequently attained before leaving coastal wintering grounds, a prominent white band extends from the bill across the forehead, around the crown above the eyes, and down the sides of the breast. The face, throat, breast, belly, flanks, and axillars are black.

The *undertail coverts are white* in *all* plumages. The upperparts are pale, speckled gray. The lighter parts of the speckled crown are slightly tinged with yellow.

This plover has three plaintive, whistled call notes *whee'-oo-eee'*, with a lower emphasis on the middle note.

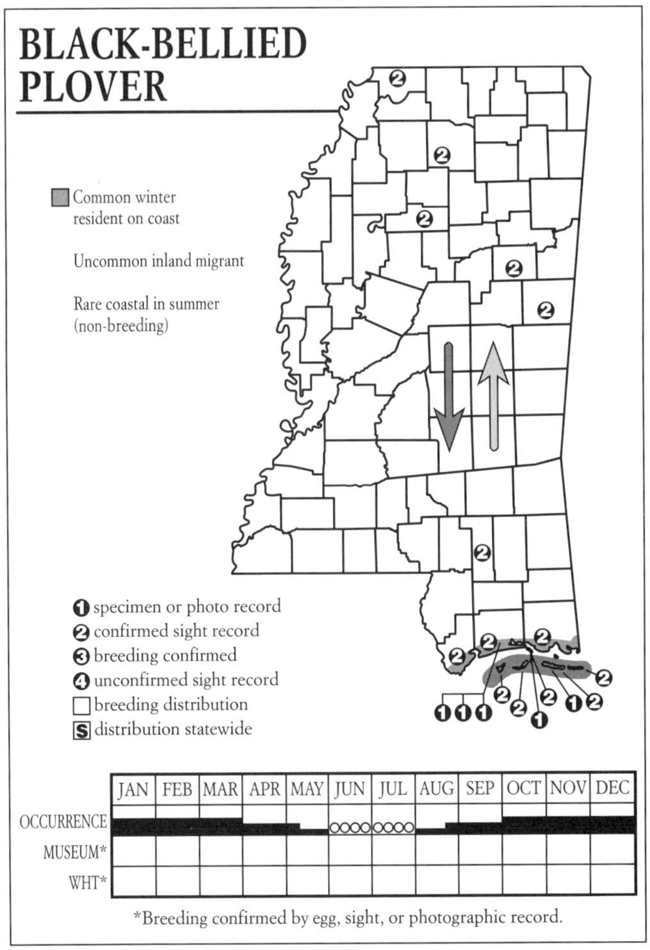

American Golden-Plover *Pluvialis dominica*

Formerly known as the Lesser Golden-Plover, this species is a regular spring transient found at certain open places along the coast and at opportune times in large, open fields; wetlands; and plowed fields primarily during March and April. The spring migration in North America is mainly through the Mississippi Valley to northern breeding grounds. In fall, most of these birds move to staging areas in Labrador and along the North Atlantic Coast, then fly across the ocean to Brazil. Some fall migrants return along the spring route.

In the Yazoo Delta, I have seen flocks of up to 80 or more in passage during March and early April on newly plowed or fallow, harvested soybean and cotton fields; open pastures with flooded areas; and in open wetlands adjacent to catfish ponds. Immediately following rainstorms along a frontal movement, these migrants seem to congregate and remain at temporary rainwater pools and flooded areas.

In migration, this plover is nearly always in basic plumage. Occasional birds that rarely winter on the coast are in winter dress. This species is slightly smaller than the Black-bellied Plover, or about the size of a Killdeer. In basic plumage, it is darker, smaller in size, and has a much smaller bill than the Black-bellied Plover.

In flight, the all dark upperparts, *absence* of white upperwing stripes, grayish white underwings, and *gray* axillars are its other distinctive field marks. In full alternate plumage, the American Golden-Plover is *all black* below in both sexes with *no black* axillars. The black upperparts are speckled gold and white. A wide band of white encircles the forehead and crown above the black face and extends along the neck to the sides of the upper breast.

The Pacific Golden-Plover *(P. fulva)* breeds in western Alaska. Golden-plovers are circumpolar and winter from southern Eurasia and the United States, southern Asia, Australia, to the Argentine pampas.

Snowy Plover *Charadrius alexandrinus*

This pale, compact, little bird lives and breeds on sand dunes and beaches of the barrier islands and on the broad expanse of bare beaches on the mainland. It is a rare, endangered, breeding permanent resident.

Very pale above and white below, these Gulf Coast birds

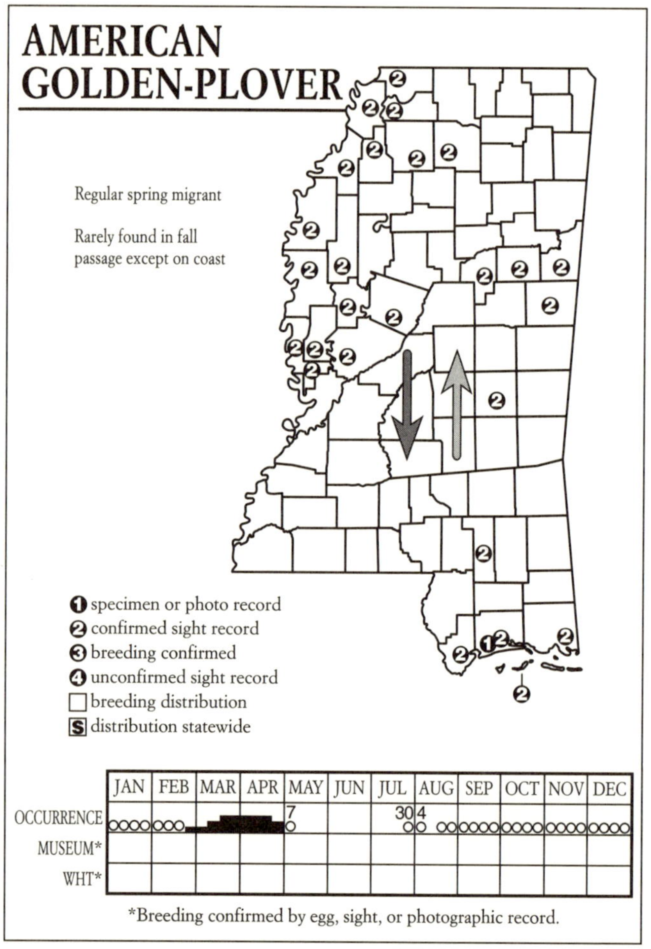

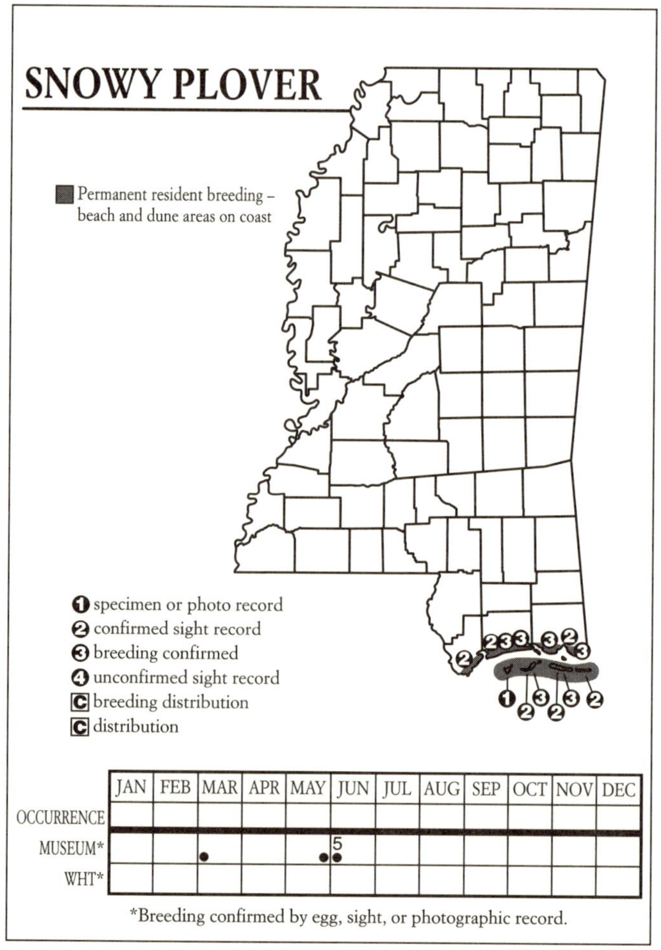

resemble the Piping Plover, but the Snowy Plover has dark or blackish legs, a thinner bill, and a dark patch behind the eye. The legs of the Piping Plover are distinctively orange colored, duller in winter dress. In flight, look for the dark, central uppertail (rump patch feathers are white on the Piping Plover). In juvenile plumage, the backs of banded plovers have a scaly appearance but otherwise resemble adults.

Inland breeding populations of the Snowy Plover occur in Texas, western Oklahoma, western Kansas, and other western states. This species is distributed along the Gulf Coast beaches from southwestern Texas to southern Florida, where its populations and habitat are declining due to shoreline development and intensive human use and disturbance. All North American populations are considered threatened or endangered because of continuing habitat loss.

The nest of this species is a shallow scrape close to open shoreline in or near clumps of concealing, low vegetation. The outside perimeter of the nest is usually ornamented by a scattering of shell bits or other debris that blends the nest into the surroundings. The three or four eggs are pale buff, evenly spotted with large black and brown dots.

A nest with three eggs was found and photographed on the mainland beach at Mississippi City on May 3, 1978 (Hays 1978). The nest contained two pipped eggs and one downy young near the nest on June 5. Nesting and young have been documented by observers on Horn, Ship, and Cat Islands.

WILSON'S PLOVER

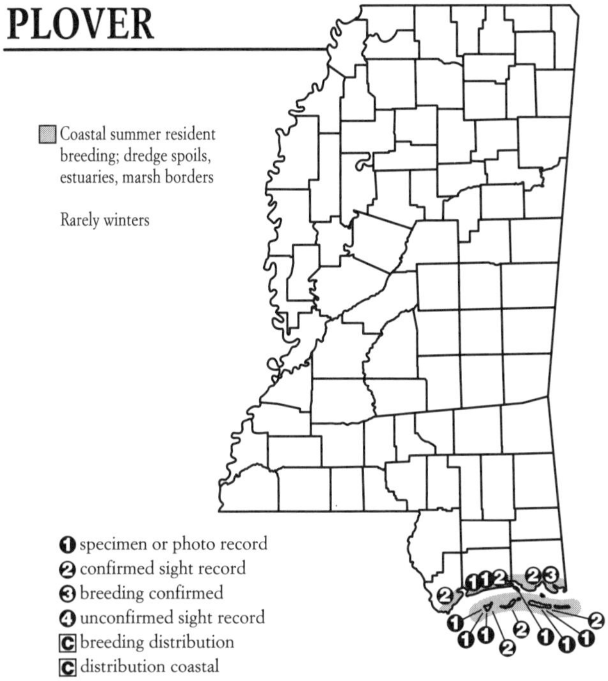

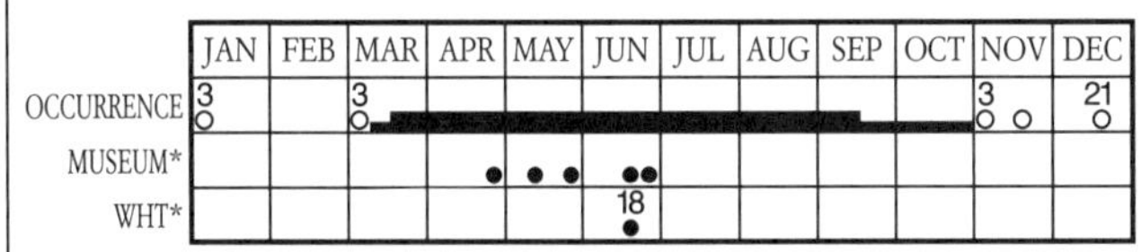

*Breeding confirmed by egg, sight, or photographic record.

Wilson's Plover *Charadrius wilsonia*

The Wilson's Plover is an uncommon, regular, breeding summer resident of the mud flats and adjacent higher dunes or spoil areas above tidal action. Here it nests. These birds frequent such places in the Pascagoula River estuary and on the inland side of offshore islands.

Elsewhere on the coast, they are absent or scarce because of disturbances along coastal beaches. This plover is usually seen as singles, in small groups, or as nesting pairs, never abundant anywhere on the coastal beaches, mud flats, or seashore. It occurs inland on intertidal zones of river estuaries.

Once called Thick-billed Plover, this "belted" species has a long, black, *thick bill;* a broad, uninterrupted breast band; dark upperparts; grayish pink legs; and is larger than the also belted Semipalmated Plover, which has orange or yellow legs and dark upperparts.

I found and photographed one Wilson's Plover nest with four eggs on June 18, 1961 (Gandy and Turcotte 1970) on a recent dredge fill adjacent to U.S. 90 near the East Pascagoula River bridge. The bare spoil area had a large colony of nesting Black Skimmers, Least Terns, and several pairs of Gull-billed Terns, all with eggs or young.

While photographing these colonial birds, I noticed a Wilson's Plover skulking about in a shallow depression draining into the tidal marsh. Its nest had four olive buff, heavily marked eggs camouflaged by matching bits of shell and debris scattered around the nest hollow and under the eggs. The eggs were collected to substantiate the nest record. Other earlier sight records of nesting on offshore islands by Burleigh (1945) and a nest with three eggs found by Lovett E. Williams Jr. on May 27, 1961, on the mainland in Jackson County further substantiate breeding (Gandy and Turcotte 1970).

The Wilson's Plover arrives on the coast in March and departs by late October or early November. There are two anomalous December 21 and January 3 records for the Gulf Coast. Extreme arrival and departure dates are March 3 and November 3.

Semipalmated Plover *Charadrius semipalmatus*

Birders usually shorten this plover's common name to "semipalm." During passage along our coastline, it is usually the most common of the smaller, banded plovers.

Consider this banded, far north migrant as a pint-sized edition of a quart-sized killdeer with only *one complete* breast band. This plover is *dark brown* above with *orange*

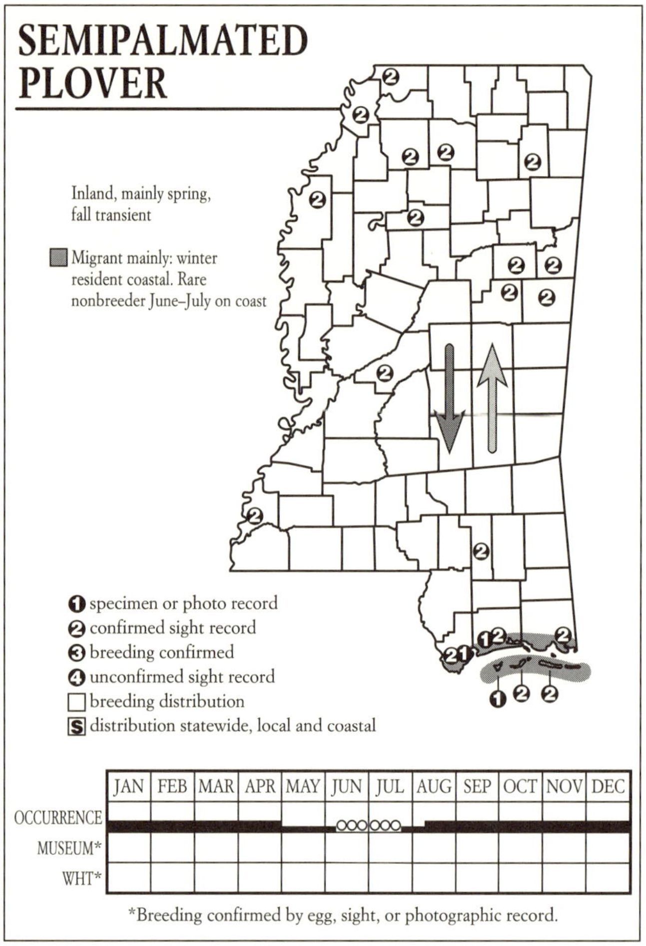

or yellow legs. The small bill is *orange* with a black tip (all dark in winter). The Semipalmated Plover has mud-colored upperparts compared to the pale, dry sand coloring of the Piping Plover.

The similarly dark Wilson's Plover has a larger, longer bill and flesh-colored legs. The dark tail of the semipalmated is white on the tip and outer feather edges. Its inner and middle toes have basal webs, hence the specific name that separates it from the similar Ringed Plover of Greenland and the Old World. The Ringed Plover has no webbing between the toes and breeds on Arctic islands of the far north in North America.

This plover is common on the beaches and tidal mud flats along the Gulf Coast from March to mid-May and from late July to November. In the winter, it is regular in small numbers on the tidal mud flats around the Pascagoula River, but scarcer on the beaches. A few nonbreeders remain on coastal areas through the summer. It occurs along shorelines of inland waters during its late summer and fall passage to wintering grounds that extend as far south as Patagonia.

This plover can be seen in spring passage as it makes its way to breeding grounds on shorelines and islands in the Arctic of North America. These birds have one of the longer migration routes of our shorebirds, equaled or exceeded only by the Red Knot, Sanderling, American Golden-Plover, Hudsonian Godwit, and White-rumped Sandpiper.

Piping Plover *Charadrius melodus*

The Piping Plover is another of our five banded or belted species, all of which have distinctive dark and white patterns or bands on the head, neck, and upper breast. It occurs as a fairly common migrant and winter visitor on coastal beaches. It is uncommon on inland shorelines as a fall migrant. Most of these birds depart in May. A few occur rarely during June and July on the Mississippi Coast.

This species is on the federal and state lists of endangered species. It breeds on deserted sand and gravel shorelines of glaciated northern lakes to southern Canada and sparingly along major river courses of the northern Great Plains and the northeastern Atlantic Coast. Extralimital nesting also has occurred in southeastern Colorado and the Oklahoma Panhandle. Like the Snowy Plover, its populations are declining over large parts of the breeding range because of encroaching development and human disturbances on its restricted and specialized nesting habitats.

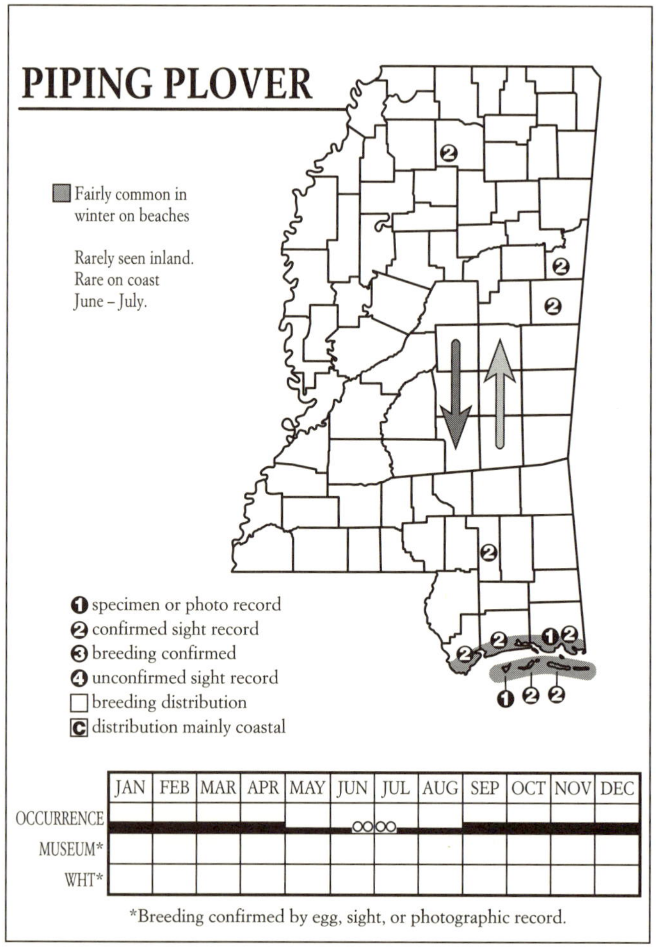

Piping Plovers have pallid upperparts the color of dry sand. While feeding along beaches, their short forward movements make them noticeable. When they stop suddenly, they seem to disappear into the sand.

I noticed this phenomenon near Lakeshore in Hancock County while watching a bird on the beachfront on November 2, 1985. When it started feeding at the water's edge, I noted another peculiar habit. Each time it stopped at the edge of gentle waves lapping the shallow shoreline, it would extend one foot forward and stand perfectly still, the extended foot resting on the wet sand. I could not detect any movement, but as water formed around the foot, it would pick up small particles of food, presumably marine crustaceans, insects, or other animals.

On June 18, 1985, at a glaciated lake shore on the Lostwood National Wildlife Refuge in North Dakota, I watched and taped the plaintive, double-noted whistle calls of a pair of these plovers. The birds were nesting on a sand and gravel bar extending from the shoreline. The call notes sounded to me like *peet'-low,* with the first note higher. We did not try to approach the nest site that had been located by refuge personnel prior to our visit.

Comparative field marks of this species and the Snowy Plover are discussed under a preceding account. The yellowish or orange legs and a black-tipped, orange bill on breeding adults are distinctive field marks for Piping Plovers. The bill of the Piping Plover is short, and the Snowy Plover has a noticeably long, attenuated bill and blackish or grayish legs.

The Piping Plover's nest is a hollow on sand spits or bars and usually lined with small pebbles. The pale clay-colored eggs are sparsely speckled with small dots.

Killdeer *Charadrius vociferus*

Since I found my first "killdee" nest on May 4, 1931, on top of a newly planted row in a corn field, this bird and its nesting behavior have intrigued me. I was impressed by the open nest depression with bits of debris around the four large, darkly blotched eggs fitting neatly together with their pointed ends downward. The adult's actions, feigning injury to draw my attention away from the nest by dropping and twisting the spread wings and fanning the rufous, black-banded tail, was a new experience for me.

This plover is well known statewide as a permanent-resident breeding bird on open farmland and other open spaces having almost barren ground. It is more commonly seen in fall and winter congregating in loose flocks of a hundred or more scattered over wet pasturelands. On the Gulf Coast, it is abundant after the breeding season, mingling with other shorebirds on mud flats, beaches, and shorelines. Killdeers also commonly occur on golf courses, airports, well-maintained cemeteries, and newly plowed, planted,

Killdeer will nest in a variety of open habitats. This bird chose to build its nest at the Grenada airport.

or harvested fields with little or no ground cover. Our resident population is supplemented by northern birds wintering in the Gulf states.

The Killdeer is known by its noisy calls, bowing and bobbing actions, and a habit of running along the ground in short spurts with frequent stops, much like robins feeding on a lawn. Their distinctive calls, *kill-deeah, dee-dee-dee* and softer warbling song notes, readily identify them day or night, sight unseen. They are good "watch dogs" in pastures and take flight readily when disturbed by intruders while repeating their loud calls.

In early spring and through the nesting season, courtship or nuptial flight songs announce the presence of a breeding pair. The male ascends a hundred feet or more to perform aerial peregrinations that may cover a wide area, all the time calling incessantly before returning to a favored nesting site. As incubation progresses, the male remains relatively well away from the nest, but relieves the incubating female for short periods in the morning and afternoon.

In early April 1987, I noticed a pair of Killdeers regularly on the idle rows of my garden in Richland. On April 10, on one of the rows I found their nest depression containing two black and brown spotted eggs with an ochre ground color. A set of four eggs was laid, and incubation had begun by April 14. I watched the incubation process to completion and noted some interesting behavior patterns of the nesting birds.

KILLDEER

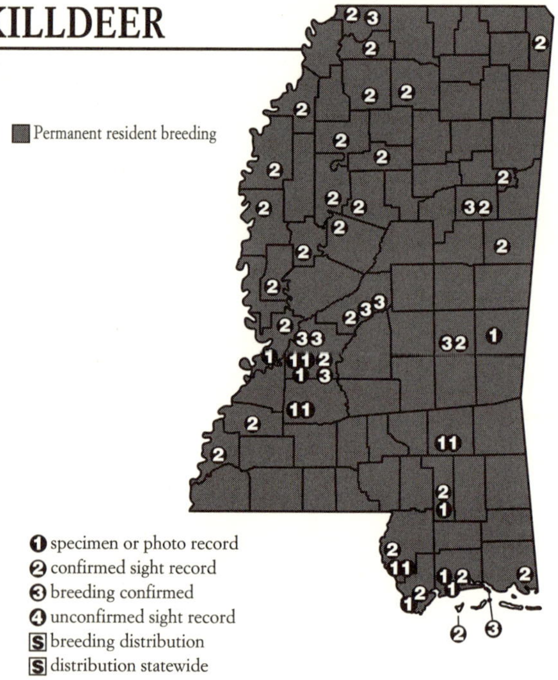

	JAN	FEB	MAR	APR	MAY	JUN	JUL	AUG	SEP	OCT	NOV	DEC
OCCURRENCE	▬	▬	▬	▬	▬	▬	▬	▬	▬	▬	▬	▬
MUSEUM*			●	● ●	●		●					
WHT*			17 ●	●	4 ●							

*Breeding confirmed by egg, sight, or photographic record.

During early incubation, the sitting bird left the nest before I approached the garden gate and ran between rows to one corner, then called loudly before flying off, all before I reached the garden gate. Initially, the bird would not return until I was out of sight. As incubation progressed, the sitting bird always left the nest as I approached the gate, and went to the corner of the garden to remain there a while. When I worked or sat to rest, she would return and resume incubation.

During midmorning and midafternoon, the male would fly in from a nearby pasture. He always called once or twice as he crossed over the street in front of the house and circled before landing in a corner of the garden. The male would call after landing to attract attention, but never approached the nest while I was present in the garden.

Toward the end of incubation, the sitting bird tolerated my presence in the garden and soon returned to the nest to resume incubating. Once as I sat on the garden stool with the bird on the nest, I watched her preen and turn the eggs. As I was looking directly at her she suddenly left the nest, moved away to her corner, and began to call as a Fish Crow flew directly over the nest. The bird had noticed the crow approaching and left the nest long before it came over so as not to reveal the nest location.

During the last days of incubation, I saw the male relieve the female on the nest. After his usual approach to the area, he watched me for several minutes while I sat still. He gradually moved down the last rows to a point directly behind my view of the sitting bird. He would walk across each row and slowly approach the nest. The exchange occurred quickly at the nest, and the relieved bird went to the usual corner, called briefly, then flew from the garden. On May 10, I found half an egg shell in the garden. The nest was empty and apparently produced a brood of spindly legged young.

Killdeers have a preference for nesting on gravel and frequently nest on road shoulders and sometimes on flat graveled roofs. The downy, precocial chicks remain in the nest until all eggs hatch. Young have marks similar to adults, but with only *one* dark band across the breast. Adults are easily distinguished by the *two* black bands across the white breast; the longish, tawny tail with terminal black band tipped with a white, orange tawny rump patch; and prominent white stripes on the upperwings when spread or in flight.

The Killdeer feeds almost entirely on grubs, worms, and insects. It breeds in most parts of southern Canada and the United States. It migrates from the northern parts of the breeding range to winter in the southern states and southward.

[Mountain Plover] *Charadrius montanus*

The first occurrence of a new bird species and its documentation for addition to a state list is always a blessed event for the fortunate birders finding and identifying it. A Mountain Plover appeared on the exposed bottom of Grenada Lake near the northern dam abutment on December 17, 1988, where it was discovered, identified, and photographed by W. Marvin Davis and Gene Knight (1989). The bird was rather tame and approachable on the exposed mud flats, where it remained until January 10, 1989. About 20 more observers saw the bird. Excellent photographs were obtained and filed at the MMNS and at MSU.

The Mountain Plover breeds on dry uplands, semidesert, and short-grass prairie regions mainly east of the Rocky Mountains. It normally migrates and winters westward to California and northern Mexico, occurring in small flocks on cactus deserts, high plain habitat, and dirt fields, often far from water.

In alternate plumage, the Mountain Plover is drab brown above with *unbanded* white underparts; a white forehead, face and eyebrow; black lores; and a black frontal crown bar. The sides of the neck and breast are buffy. In basic plumage, the buffy tinge is more extensive on the breast, the black lores and frontal bar are absent, and the

MOUNTAIN PLOVER

Accidental locality record

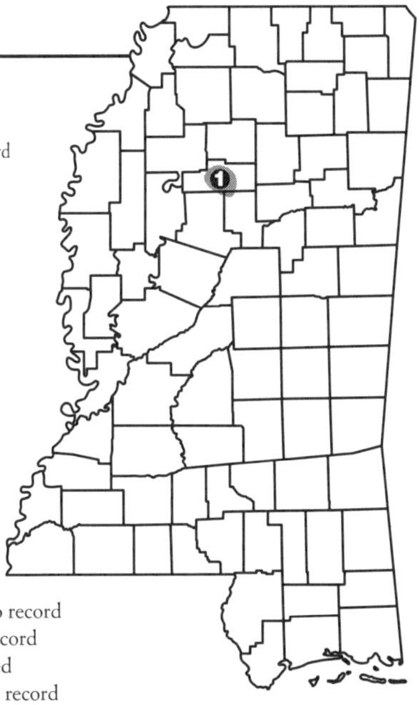

❶ specimen or photo record
❷ confirmed sight record
❸ breeding confirmed
❹ unconfirmed sight record
☐ breeding distribution
Ⓐ distribution statewide

	JAN	FEB	MAR	APR	MAY	JUN	JUL	AUG	SEP	OCT	NOV	DEC
OCCURRENCE	10 oo											17 ooo
MUSEUM*												
WHT*												

*Breeding confirmed by egg, sight, or photographic record.

white facial pattern is not distinct. In flight, the underwings are white. A thin, white stripe borders the brown of the upperwings, and the rounded, spread tail shows a narrow white border. The feet and legs are pale, not blackish.

The Mountain Plover has occurred as an accidental visitor in Arkansas, Alabama, Georgia, Florida, and Virginia.

Oystercatcher

Haematopodidae (Oystercatchers)

There are six species of these large, plump shorebirds worldwide. One species, the American Oystercatcher, occurs along the Atlantic and Gulf Coasts and casually on southern California seashores. The Black Oystercatcher, *Haematopus bachmani,* ranges along the Pacific Coast on rocky islands and shores from the Aleutians into Baja California.

Oystercatchers feed on shellfish and marine organisms, opening their shells with the large, red or orange, laterally flattened, chisel-like bills. Sexes are alike in appearance.

American Oystercatcher *Haematopus palliatus*

A half-century has elapsed since my first experience with a pair of these birds on Freemason Island, an outer shell island off the Chandeleur chain in Louisiana waters south of Biloxi.

On May 26, 1938, a party of WPA workers under the direction of Frances A. Cook made a two-day collecting trip on a Coast Guard cutter to the Chandeleurs. After passing the large Brown Pelican rookery on North Island, the party went on to Freemason Island. It was there that I saw a pair of oystercatchers.

On Freemason Island, most of my time was spent collecting eggs of Black Skimmer, Laughing Gull, and Royal, Caspian, and Sandwich terns for the museum project under federal and Louisiana permits. R. M. Freeman took a museum specimen of this bird on another part of the island that day.

The pair of American Oystercatchers I saw may have been nesting or with young. They moved about excitedly and were very noisy with their loud *pick pick pick* and *bhweep bhweep* calls. On an earlier visit to the Chandeleurs and on several later visits, I saw no oystercatchers.

This large, chunky shorebird occurs on tidal mud flats and remote seashores of the Atlantic, southern California, and Gulf Coast. It rarely occurs on the mainland and barrier islands of Mississippi Sound.

Burleigh (1945) found and collected the first specimen on Deer Island on September 21, 1941. After many years it was next recorded on Horn Island where three birds were seen on May 15, 1976. In 1977 it was recorded by Larry J. Gates and Steven W. Peterson on the mainland during the Jackson County Christmas Bird Count on December 17, 1977 (Weber 1978a).

Another oystercatcher was reportedly seen by Arthur V. Hays and George Thatcher on Cat Island. Subsequently, these birds were seen by other observers at Gautier in Jackson County on March 25, 1979, and in February 1985 and January 1986 at Waveland in Hancock County, where two were seen.

Sightings occurred in Harrison County during passage of Hurricane Juan from October 28 to 29, 1985. Toups and Jackson (1987) observed that the Hancock County occurrences of oystercatchers were during strong northern winds that exposed large tidal flats. Hurricane Juan probably accounted for the Harrison County appearance of these visitors. Weather conditions no doubt caused their appearance, but these records would not be in print without the presence of avid, local birders.

The picturesque sand dunes and beaches found on offshore islands provide resting and feeding areas for many coastal shorebirds and water birds.

AMERICAN OYSTERCATCHER

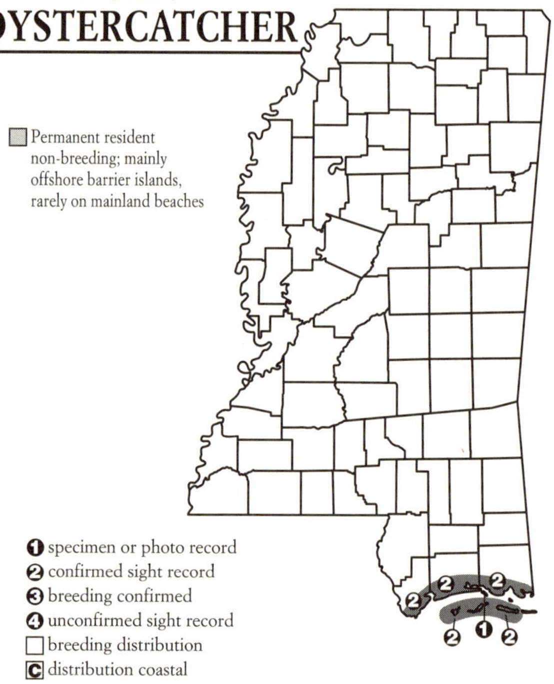

	JAN	FEB	MAR	APR	MAY	JUN	JUL	AUG	SEP	OCT	NOV	DEC
OCCURRENCE	oooo	oooo	oooo	oooo	oooo	oooo		25 oo	oo	oooo	oooo	oooo
MUSEUM*												
WHT*												

*Breeding confirmed by egg, sight, or photographic record.

A long, stout, laterally compressed *red bill,* black head and neck, dark back, white underparts, and white patches on wings and rump are this bird's distinctive field marks. The legs are a pale flesh color. Immatures are browner above, while their upper mandible and outer half of the bill are dark. The bill is used as a chisel to pry open shellfish and crabs, or to probe on beaches and mud flats for marine organisms, extracting them in a manner resembling the use of tongs or forceps.

The American Oystercatcher nests on remote parts of islands and mainland seashores. Their nest is a hollow in sand or shell fragments. The two or three brownish buff eggs are spotted with irregular black, brown, and subdued lavender marks.

Breeding on the Mississippi mainland or islands has not been reported. These birds prefer to nest near exposed oyster and shell reefs. In Mississippi Sound and on offshore islands, reefs and oyster beds often are not exposed at low tide. Breeding is possible but unlikely on the mainland because of shoreline disturbances and developments.

The Wood Duck is one of the world's most beautiful ducks. In Mississippi it ranks second to the mallard in the hunter's bag. Enforcement of hunting regulations and habitat management by private landowners and the Department of Wildlife, Fisheries and Parks has helped keep the population of this species strong.

The Eastern Wild Turkey is one of the most popular game birds in Mississippi. Through the years, sportsmen, hunting clubs, and landowners have worked with the Department of Wildlife, Fisheries and Parks to trap turkeys in areas with high population densities and release them in other suitable habitat areas.

The widespread placement of nest boxes by wildlife agency personnel and the establishment of "bluebird trails" have helped bring the Eastern Bluebird back from perilously low numbers. Author William H. Turcotte inspects a nest of young that hatched in an artificial nesting structure on his property in Richland.

Researchers at the University of Southern Mississippi capture, band, and release passerine birds on Horn Island during the spring migration. Research has shown that many songbird species are declining at alarming rates. To combat this downturn, Partners in Flight was formed in the early 1990s. This international group of biologists, bird-watchers, and researchers hopes to better understand what factors are contributing to the declines among birds such as the Purple Martin that breeds in North America and winters in Central and South America.

The Carolina Chickadee is one of many species that will nest in man-made nesting structures. The bird is very tolerant of humans and feeds on a variety of insects and seeds. This nest with young, temporarily removed from the nest box, is lined with cotton and fibers from nearby plants.

The coastal pine savannas and adjacent habitat are some of Mississippi's richest areas for a diversity of songbird species. These pristine sites are also the feeding and breeding grounds for the Mississippi Sandhill Crane and many species of gulls, terns, shorebirds, and marsh and wading birds.

The population of the Brown Pelican, a permanent resident bird along the Mississippi Gulf Coast, has rebounded within the past 15 years. This recovery came about in part due to a ban on the manufacture and use of DDT in this country in the early 1970s. Researchers discovered that large water and predatory birds were picking up harmful traces of the pesticide and other chlorinated hydrocarbons through their food chain.

For a long time Mississippi has been a traditional wintering area for the Canada Goose. Today, thanks in part to habitat management, sensible harvest strategies, and reintroduction programs, the bird is nesting and bringing up young in many areas of Mississippi.

American Avocet

Recurvirostridae (Stilts and Avocets)

These birds are sleek and graceful waders. They have long, spindly legs; necks longer than most sandpipers; and long, slender bills. Stilts have straight, needle-like bills. Avocets have thin, upturned bills that are usually longer on the males. Two species of this family occur in North America. Both occur in Mississippi, mainly on Gulf Coast tidal marshlands, but occasionally inland during migration or during postbreeding season wandering. The Black-necked Stilt is a locally common, permanent-resident breeding bird on the Pascagoula River tidal marshlands.

Black-necked Stilt *Himantopus mexicanus*

The male Black-necked Stilt is black above, except the white tail and rump, and entirely white below. Its grotesquely long legs are red or pink. Females have brownish upperparts. Stilts with young are very noisy birds near their nest. Adults chatter their *kip-kip-kip* calls to advertise their presence and draw attention from nests and young.

Black-necked Stilts are locally common, breeding permanent residents on dredge spoil areas of the Pascagoula River marsh below U.S. 90 in Jackson County. These spoil or dredge-filled areas border and drain into tidal flats and marshlands. Such open areas with low vegetative cover provide the nesting environment that stilts require.

Breeding on the Pascagoula flats was first noted by Weber (Weber et al. 1978). Two nests with broken eggshells collected at the site and a nearby stilt carcass were found on June 6, 1977. Another active nest was found by Nell Powers and others on July 22, 1977, near the earlier nest. Eight or more adults were calling and diving, and the female was seen incubating.

Two partly grown juveniles were found on a large pond in the area on August 14 and again on August 22. Also present were seven nearly grown young. Two young with brownish feather edging remained until September 18, 1977. Three downy young and 10 juveniles were seen by observers in the Pascagoula estuary in 1985 and 1986.

Lovett E. Williams Jr. collected the first Mississippi immature specimen of this species on September 24, 1960, at the Bayou Casotte industrial area in Jackson County (Gandy and Turcotte 1970). On the same date, Williams Jr. and Sterling G. Clawson found seven stilts on this dredge-filled area, Mississippi's first sight record (Turcotte 1961e).

The Black-necked Stilt is now a locally common permanent resident along the coast, although usually scarce in winter. On inland areas, it is a migrant, and few sightings have been recorded. Two stilts were recorded by Tom Gary on the Malmaison Wildlife Management Area in Grenada County on May 26, 1976. One at Kosciusko on April 11, 1978, was reported by James A. Sanders. Three birds were

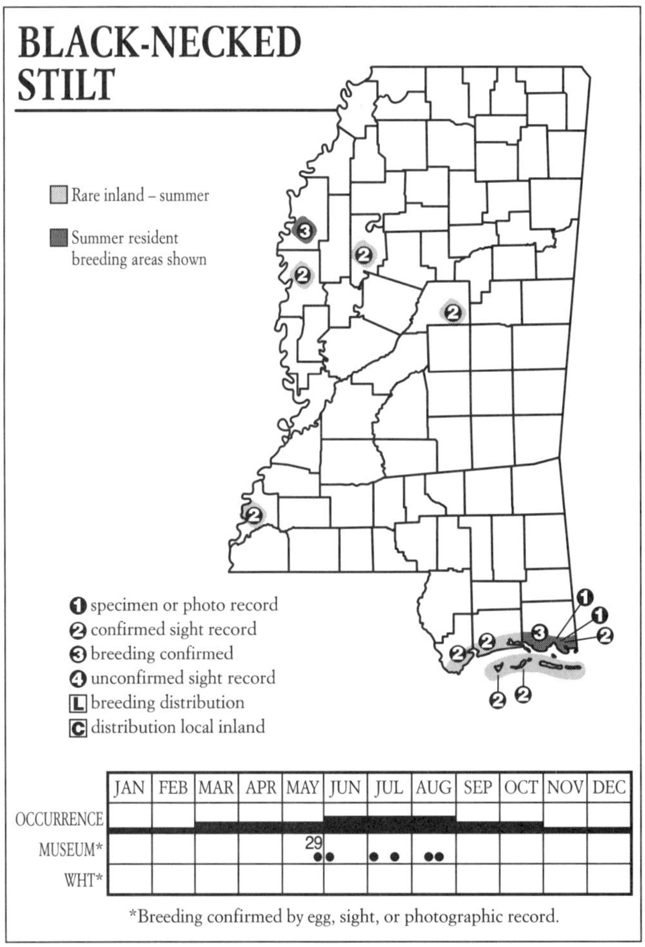

sighted at Yazoo National Wildlife Refuge in Washington County on March 28, 1985, and one bird on April 15, 1985, was seen by Tim Wilkins and Lucian Newton.

On the coast, stilts occur in greatest numbers at nest sites and late summer staging areas around the Pascagoula River estuary. Outside the breeding period, stilts may occur at suitable locations on the coast.

The stilt nest is a collection of grass and debris lining a depression and partially concealed in grasses of open dunes or meadows near marshes or bordering lakes. The Black-necked Stilt was found nesting and with young near Shaw in Bolivar County from June 14 to July 27, 1990, by Nona and J. C. Herbert and others (Purrington 1990). An active nest destroyed by mowing was found near a drained catfish pond. Later in the same area and in bordering rice fields, an adult with four young and another adult with one young were seen.

Stilts breed locally in southern Florida, along the Atlantic seashore, the northern Gulf Coast, and in wet meadows and marshlands of western and Great Plains states. They winter sparsely along the Gulf Coast, in parts of southern Florida, and mainly south of the United States.

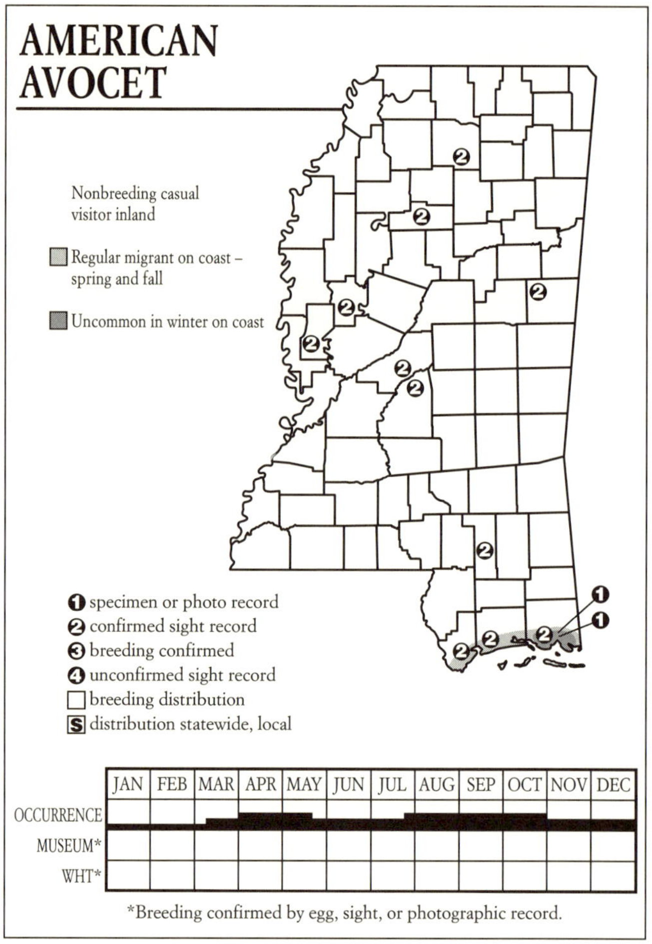

American Avocet *Recurvirostra americana*

Avocets are graceful, nonbreeding, resident waders with slender, upturned bills. They are regular visitors on the Mississippi Coast, more common in late summer and early fall and less common in winter.

The dredge-spoil areas and collecting pools at Pascagoula River marsh are used by this species and other shorebirds as a staging area during migration periods. On other coastal beaches, mud flats, and shorelines, small numbers may occur throughout the year. Inland sightings are uncommon and occur mainly during migration in summer (as early as July 9 at Grenada Lake) and early fall.

The first state record for this bird was at the Pascagoula River marsh when a specimen was collected on January 22, 1961, by Lovett E. Williams Jr. (Gandy and Turcotte 1970). Avocets have been recorded inland on large lakes and reservoirs, sewage lagoons, and catfish ponds.

American Avocets breed mainly in the western and midwestern states and rarely on the coast of Texas. Populations have been increasing along the Gulf Coast. At the Pascagoula marsh, flocks numbering over 400 have been observed in fall migration. As many as 90 have been seen in December, and more than 50 during the spring migration.

The striking black-and-white pattern on the wings and back, upturned black bill, bluish legs, and all white body are unmistakable field marks. In alternate plumage, the pinkish rust head and neck also are unmistakable. In basic plumage the head and neck are gray. Immatures have a cinnamon wash on the neck and head. Feeding avocets move their bills through the water from side to side as if they were sweeping the bottom.

Avocets breed in loose colonies at shallow lake shores, grassy marshes, and pools. Their nest is a hollow on the ground lined with grasses and other plants. The three or four greenish buff eggs are boldly spotted and scrawled with brown and black.

Like the Black-necked Stilt, avocets are noisy birds when disturbed around their breeding site. Their sharp *wheet-wheet-wheet* calls are continuous when nests or young are nearby.

Scolopacidae (Sandpipers and Allies)

Greater Yellowlegs *Tringa melanoleuca*

Size and call notes separate the Greater and Lesser Yellowlegs. Greaters are usually seen in fewer numbers in migration and on the Mississippi Coast, where both species regularly winter.

These tall and slender, gray sandpipers have yellow or yellowish orange legs; a *checkered* black, gray, and white back; and in flight show a *white rump* with *dark* upper-

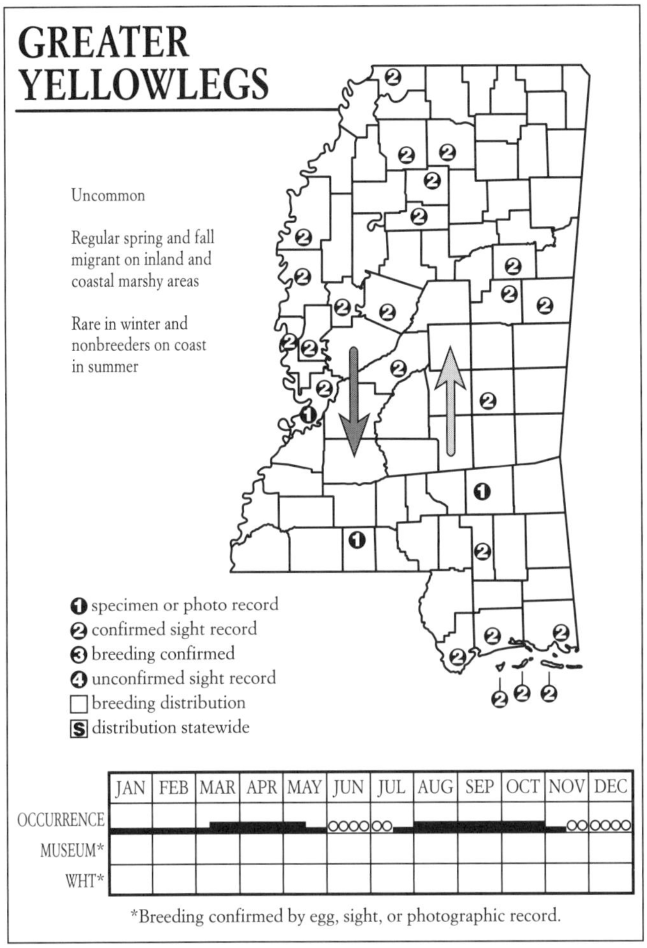

wings without white stripes. When the two species are seen together, Lesser Yellowlegs appear about two-thirds the size of the Greater Yellowlegs. The finer distinctions between the two species require close observation. The Greater Yellowlegs has a *longer* and stouter, *barely upturned* bill and *thicker* leg joints. The Lesser has a thin, *straight* bill, and slenderer legs. However, these two distinctions are not reliable for field identification.

The call notes of the two species are distinctive and should be memorized. The Greater has a penetrating three-note, descending, whistle: *wheu-wheu-wheu.* The Lesser's call is a softer one or two-note whistled *tew* or *tew-tew* without the loud ringing quality of the Greater's. These tall, slim sandpipers are readily separated from others by *yellow* legs, dark upperparts *without* white wing stripes, and *white rump.*

Both species of yellowlegs are migrant, nonbreeding inhabitants of our open marshes, mud flats, and shorelines of streams and ponds. They are commonly seen inland from late February to May migrating in small, loose flocks to northern tundra and boreal forest nesting grounds. Fall migrants begin their return in July and are commonly seen inland and on the Gulf Coast until November. In mild winters, the two species are fairly common to rare along the coast at favored locations such as mud flats and shallow ponds of the Pascagoula River marshlands.

The Greater Yellowlegs is uncommon or rare on the coast in winter and usually is found only at a few favorite locations in open marshland and mud flats. Both species are mostly absent from Mississippi in summer months, but records of nonbreeding individuals of both species extend throughout the summer on the coast.

These birds breed mainly on tundra near shorelines of streams or lakes in northern Canada and Alaska. The nest is only a scrape to receive the four buff-colored eggs blotched with shades of brown, black, and purplish brown. The Lesser Yellowlegs prefers to breed in open boreal woods and selects a dry location near a pond or open marsh for its nest.

Lesser Yellowlegs *Tringa flavipes*

The Lesser Yellowlegs is a common spring migrant through Mississippi in March and April, returning from northern breeding grounds from July to November. During migration it is common inland, and on the Mississippi Coast it is sometimes abundant. It is fairly common at favored spots

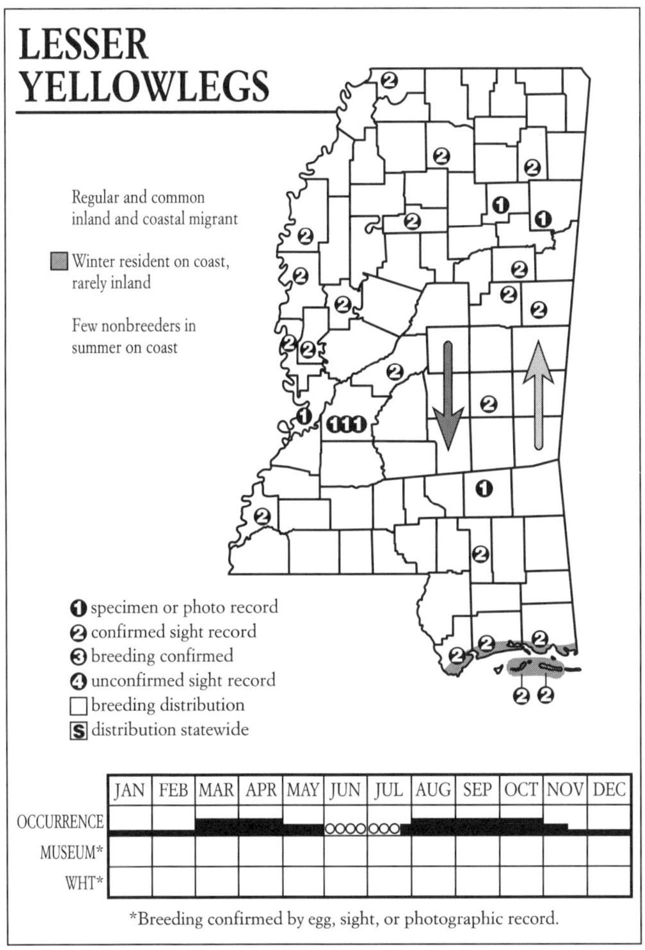

along the coast during most winters. Some nonbreeders remain at marshland mud flats through June and July.

Field marks and call notes are described in the preceding account. Overall smaller size; smaller, straight bill; and shriller, shorter call notes distinguish the Lesser from the otherwise similar Greater Yellowlegs.

This shorebird breeds over a wider range, generally farther north in tundra and south into open boreal woodlands. Nests and eggs are similar to those of the Greater Yellowlegs.

Solitary Sandpiper *Tringa solitaria*

SOLITARY SANDPIPER

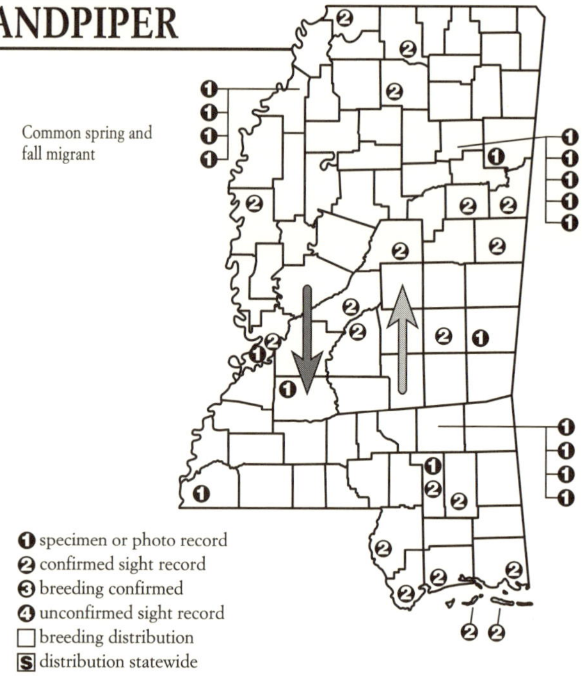

	JAN	FEB	MAR	APR	MAY	JUN	JUL	AUG	SEP	OCT	NOV	DEC
OCCURRENCE		23 ○				3 ○	16 ○			19 ○		
MUSEUM*												
WHT*												

*Breeding confirmed by egg, sight, or photographic record.

Larger than most sandpipers and smaller than the Lesser Yellowlegs, this trim and graceful little wader is one of the prettiest of all the shorebirds in its activities on the ground and in its bounding, swallowlike flight. When alighting, the bird often keeps its wings raised high and slowly folds them.

Slim bodied like the yellowlegs, it also bobs its head. The Solitary Sandpiper's dark brown back and wing coverts wear a soft sheen and evenly spaced, rounded, buff spots. The dark rump; dark, central tail feathers; white outer tail feathers barred with black; prominent white eye ring; and olive green legs distinguish the Solitary Sandpiper from the Lesser Yellowlegs.

The throat, breast, and sides are heavily streaked with blackish brown. The belly is white and underwings are dark. Nearly always alone, the Solitary Sandpiper is frequently true to its name in migration. Its movements are more deliberate than most sandpipers. It stands still longer, nodding, preening, and occasionally bowing gracefully to allow close observation. This species is also less suspicious and more reluctant to take flight while being observed.

The Solitary Sandpiper is a spring migrant from late February to June. It returns from its northern breeding grounds during late July to mid-October, enroute to wintering grounds mostly in the West Indies and South America. It winters rarely along the northern Gulf Coast, where it usually avoids beaches. This sandpiper prefers the shallow, muddy edges of ponds, marshes, drainage and roadside ditches, and even small temporary rainpools in open pastures and grassy fields.

Its nesting habits are unique among our shorebirds. In the northern boreal forest and muskeg, the Solitary Sandpiper deposits its four greenish or buff, heavily spotted eggs in an abandoned bird nest in a tree or low bush. It prefers the used nests of robins, Rusty Blackbirds, grackles, and waxwings located near ponds.

The nesting habits were unknown until 1903, when a northern settler discovered eggs in a robin's nest after seeing a Solitary Sandpiper fly into a tamarack tree containing the nest. The observer, Evan Thomson, was clearing trees in the muskeg near his cabin and collected eggs for Walter Raine, who later confirmed and published the records of this and two other nests (Bent 1927–1929). Additional nest records by scientists have confirmed the tree-nesting habits of this sandpiper.

The calls of the Solitary Sandpiper are a shrill *peet* and in flight a series of *weet-weet-weet* notes, higher than calls of the Spotted Sandpiper with which it might be mistaken.

Willet *Catoptrophorus semipalmatus*

The Willet and the American Woodcock are the only species in the Sandpiper family known to breed in Mississippi. Most sandpipers nest in sub-Arctic regions or on northern prairies, marshes, and shorelines and are transients, winter residents, or occasional, nonbreeding summer residents.

Willets are permanent residents on the Mississippi Coast where they nest around marshes on barrier islands and on the Pascagoula River marsh. On inland areas, Willets are migrants in passage to and from northern breeding grounds.

At rest, the Willet is a large, plump, grayish, rather nondescript shorebird. When it arises, its striking black-and-white patterns on the wings and strong, direct flight identify this shorebird. A common sight on our coastal beaches, the

Willet is usually single or in loose flocks with other shorebirds. Sometimes larger aggregations occur along beaches when the birds are resting or actively feeding.

Willets nest in loose colonies on dry areas bordering marshes on the offshore islands. On the mainland, they are known to nest on the edges of spoil areas in the Pascagoula River estuary. Willets are easily alarmed when a nest is approached and do not adapt to nesting at sites where human disturbances frequently occur.

My first experience with nesting Willets was at North Island, Louisiana, on May 13, 1938 (Gandy and Turcotte 1970). I saw a small colony of less than 10 birds with nests and eggs scattered among low bushes and prickly pear cactus. The ground cover was sparse grasses growing in dry muck and shells back from the marshy shoreline. I found three nests lined with grass, each containing four heavily blotched, olive buff eggs in shallow hollows in the shells. One nest was concealed in a clump of grass. The nests were in an area of four or five acres, bordered by shell ridges and marshlands.

Willets are noisy birds around their nests. Their incessant *kip, kip, kip* calls and constant circling, diving, and other displays to distract intruders can be irritating at times.

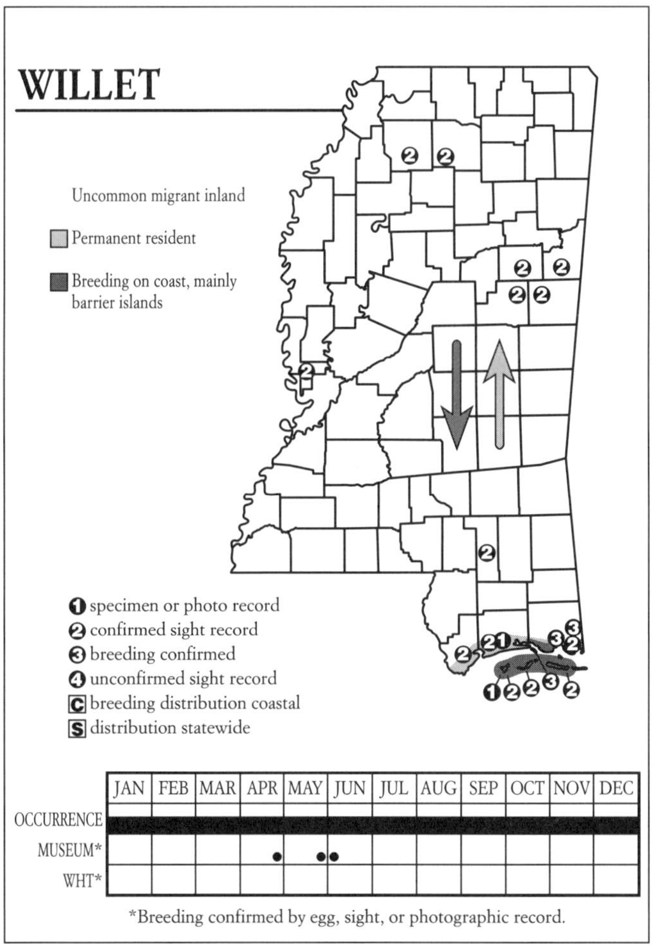

The normal call after taking flight sounds like *whee'-we-we.* On the breeding grounds, their flight song is a whistled *pill-will-willet.* I have heard it on trips to our offshore islands, in the short-grass high plains at Lostwood National Wildlife Refuge in North Dakota, and at a marsh on the mainland east of Bayou Casotte in Jackson County.

Eastern Willets breed along the shorelines of the Atlantic Coast north to New England and along coastlines of the Gulf states to northern Mexico. Western birds breed on inland marshes, wet meadows, and shorelines, wintering mainly along the Pacific Coast of California and Mexico.

On long stretches of beach along the Mississippi Coast, the Willet is seen commonly in company with smaller sandpipers, plovers, gulls, terns, and Black Skimmers resting on the sand or feeding along the tideline. Populations of these birds on the coast are enhanced during the fall migration.

In basic plumage, the Willet is uniformly gray above and whitish below. In alternate plumage, it is heavily mottled above, on the breast, and the sides. Juveniles have the feathers of the upperparts edged with light buff, giving them a scaly appearance. In basic plumage, the Hudsonian Godwit closely resembles the Willet in size and coloration at rest and in flight. The wing patterns of black and white are less contrasting on the Hudsonian Godwit, which is much darker above and below and has a wide, black terminal tail band. The *slightly upturned bills* of the godwits identify them. On the coast, a closer observation of what is presumed to be Willets might turn up more records of the Hudsonian Godwit, which usually migrates farther west in the spring and farther east in fall.

Spotted Sandpiper *Actitis macularia*

This singular little water sprite is a widely distributed and fairly common migrant, uncommon to rare in winter, and usually absent in midsummer, except for nonbreeding individuals that sometimes remain. This species has a wide breeding range across the central United States to northern Canada and Alaska.

In alternate plumage, it is white below with evenly spaced *round spots.* Upperparts are olive brown barred with black. White outer feathers of the dark tail are distinctly banded with black. The yellow bill has a dark tip. Legs and feet are yellowish. In *basic* and *juvenile* plumage, the Spotted Sandpiper lacks the spotting below, but has olive brown above with contrasting barring on the wing coverts. Look for its dark bill, a white line over the eye, and an inverted white V-shape at the point of the wing bordered by dusky on sides of the breast. The legs are greenish olive in basic plumage.

The usual flight of the Spotted Sandpiper is diagnostic. The wingbeats are rapid, shallow, and kept below horizontal before gliding to a landing on cupped, downward tilted

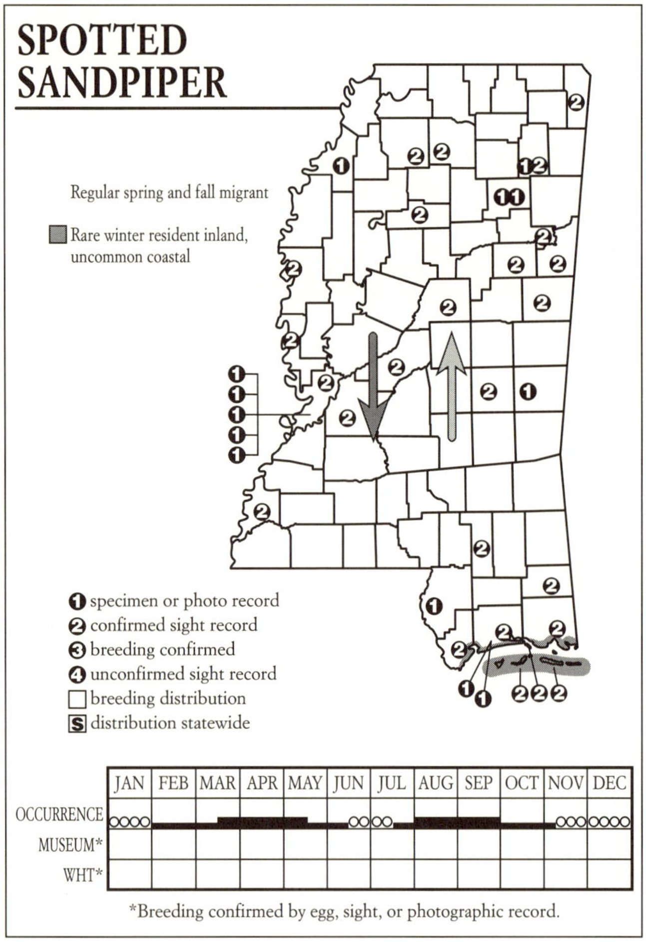

wings. On the ground the body is held on a horizontal plane. It constantly bobs its head and teeters its tail up and down.

Spotted Sandpipers prefer sheltered or wooded edges of streams, lakes, ponds, and marshes. In migration, they are likely to appear at sewage lagoons or open water. They have a peculiar habit of resting on stones, logs, or other objects along shorelines, tilting their body downward, bobbing the head, and tipping the tail up and down. On the Mississippi Coast, they prefer edges of shallow, marshy ponds and lagoons, but also occur on the beaches, especially during migration.

There is no evidence of Spotted Sandpipers' breeding in Mississippi, but it is possible in northern or northeastern parts of the state. Investigations along the Tennessee River and the Tennessee-Tombigbee Waterway might produce a first Mississippi breeding record.

The nest is a hollow lined with grass, moss, or weeds, and usually concealed or sheltered by grass, weeds, logs, or overhanging rocks or logs near a stream side, shore, or wet meadow. The three or four grayish buff eggs are speckled and spotted with blackish brown.

Shrill *peet-weet* call notes are lower than those of the Solitary Sandpiper. In flight, the call is a series of *peet-weet-weet-weet-weet* notes.

Upland Sandpiper *Bartramia longicauda*

Pleasant memories remain of my experiences of seeing these birds or hearing their melodious calls at night while they flew high overhead during brief spring and summer migrations. They are like Bobolinks in spring passage: Now you see or hear them, soon you don't. In late summer, mainly August, they are heard calling overhead at night on their long trek to the pampas in South America.

My first encounter with these birds was in Coahoma County on August 8, 1941. Henry L. Owens and I were on a museum collecting trip, and we found a flock of about 20 in a large alfalfa field. After futile attempts to sneak within gunshot, our efforts seemed doomed until the flock settled near a turn-row. We decided to try and drive the car up to them. Surprisingly, they showed no fear of our vehicle, and we managed to collect six museum specimens. At the time these birds were called "upland plovers" because of their preference for open fields, prairies, pastures, and ploverlike habits. Yet, they were classed as sandpipers and originally called the Bartramian Sandpiper.

I was surprised at how fat these six Upland Sandpipers were as we made them into museum study skins. They were

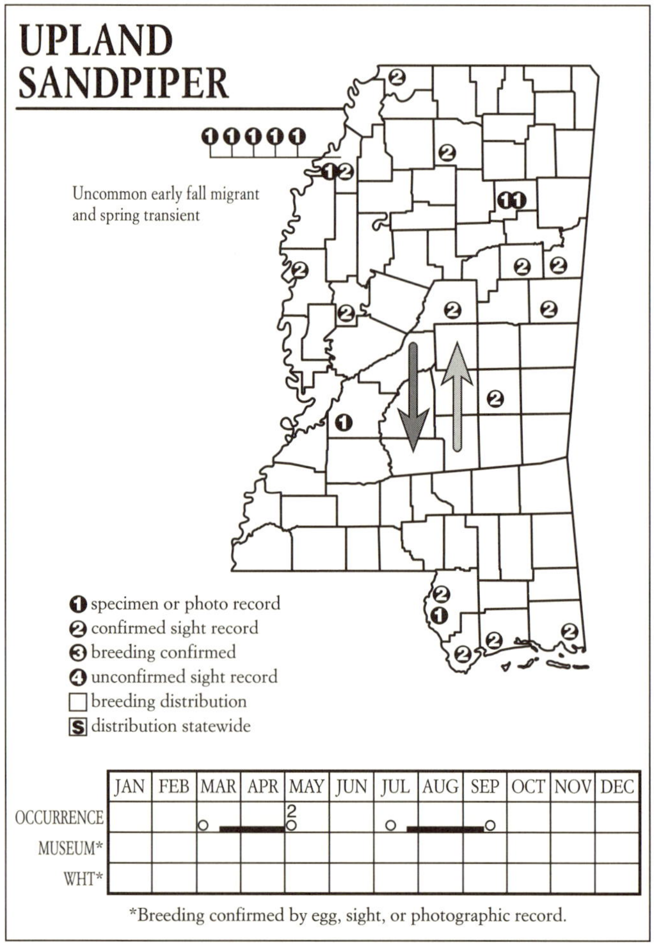

plump birds, and their fat clusters would literally roll from the skin and body. Feather tracts beneath the skin had to be scraped free of fat, which required considerable care not to tear the skin. We used a homemade tool for this, a table knife cut off with a row of sewing needles soldered to the end of the blade. The birds were certainly well prepared for their long flight to South American wintering grounds.

Most Upland Sandpiper records have occurred in the Yazoo Delta, Jackson Prairie, and Black Prairie regions with a few sightings on the coast. Individuals or small groups seen were on beaches, mud flats, open pastures, and cultivated fields.

I have seen these birds in passage only in the Yazoo Delta, where they seem to prefer brief stops in short-grass pastures. Such places are rare now. On March 29, 1963, I saw a flock of 16 amid 22 American Golden-Plovers in a pasture two miles south of Louise (Turcotte 1963b).

Upland Sandpipers have brown upperparts. Their back and wing covert feathers are mottled with black, brown, and buff. Juveniles are browner on the back, and the feathers have buff, scaly edges. The neck and breast are buffy and streaked with brown. The crown and outer wings are darker than other parts of the plumage.

In silhouette, the small dovelike head with large button eyes, short bill, and long neck, wings, tail, and legs give this ploverlike bird a unique look. Taken together with its habit of perching atop posts in its grassland breeding haunts, this large sandpiper is unmistakable. I remember seeing one sitting on a pole at sunrise in a North Dakota pasture. I stopped the car, backed along the road shoulder, and saw the bird's silhouette against the face of the sun between two distant, dark trees and a red sky. In late July 1984, we saw more of these birds perched on fence posts as we drove past Montana and South Dakota wheat fields that had been harvested and plowed under. These birds were scarce in wheat country, where they once occurred in great numbers before the prairies were cultivated.

I have heard older rural people talk about "flying mares" passing over unseen at night. The rolling, musical whistled calls of the Upland Sandpiper can be likened to the distant neighing of a horse. The night calls of these or other shorebird migrants, unseen as they pass over at considerable altitude, are probably responsible for the folklore. The migration periods occur mainly from March 15 to April 30 and during August.

The Upland Sandpiper nest is a hollow scoop lined with grasses in a grass tuft or concealed in grass fields. The four eggs are more ovate than most sandpipers. The buff ground color is evenly spotted and blotched with shades of brown and black. The breeding grounds are northern prairies and plains of midwestern states and Canada, with few breeding in the eastern United States.

Whimbrel *Numenius phaeopus*

The Whimbrel, formerly called the Hudsonian Curlew, was common in migration along the Atlantic Coast for much of the last century. During their short migration periods, Whimbrels and Eskimo Curlews (the latter once in prodigious numbers) were shot for food and market.

Eskimo Curlews traveling in fall flocks were exceedingly tame and vulnerable to gunners on the East Coast. On their return migration across the western plains, they were shot in great numbers. Extravagant killing of these birds almost led to the extinction of the Eskimo Curlew.

Whimbrels survived the gunning pressure in larger numbers because they migrated in smaller flocks, were wilder, and more wary of decoys and hunters. The Long-billed Curlew, then a fairly common transient on the Atlantic Coast, now occurs only rarely as a winter resident along the southeastern Atlantic Coast. Its breeding range is restricted to the western plains, prairies, and wet and dry uplands. The Whimbrel breeds on open, Arctic tundra, and its range is circumpolar.

The North American subspecies, *N. p. hudsonicus*, follows the migration route of the Lesser Golden-Plover down the

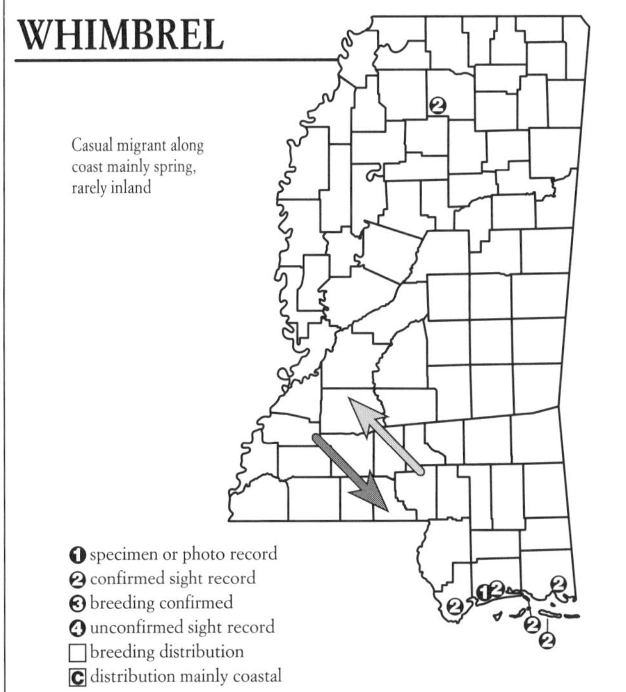

	JAN	FEB	MAR	APR	MAY	JUN	JUL	AUG	SEP	OCT	NOV	DEC
OCCURRENCE			31			7		12			11	
MUSEUM*												
WHT*												

*Breeding confirmed by egg, sight, or photographic record.

Atlantic Coast in fall and through the Mississippi Valley and western prairies and plains in spring. The spring and fall migrations occur mainly west of Mississippi in spring and farther east in fall.

The Whimbrel has occurred on the coast in all counties and on Deer, Horn, and West Ship Islands, where it is an uncommon to rare spring and fall transient. Extreme dates of occurrence on the coast are March 31 to June 7 and August 12 to November 11. These birds surely overfly interior parts of Mississippi, but have gone unnoticed, probably because their distinctive calls go unheard or unrecognized.

They are rare fall migrants, more commonly seen during brief spring stopovers. The one inland record is a single bird seen and photographed May 1, 1988, on a turf farm in Lafayette County by Gene and Shannon Knight and Vic Theobald (Hodges 1988). The Whimbrel occurs along coastal beaches, on tidal mud flats, and tidal pools with grassy or marshy edges. They feed on fiddler crabs and other marine organisms, insects, and small fruits or berries.

The Whimbrel is grayer above than the Long-billed Curlew. The decurved bill, about three to four inches long, is half the length of the Long-billed Curlew, which has twice the body bulk of the Whimbrel. The streaked whitish underparts, boldly striped crown, and dark eye line of this species are also distinctive.

LONG-BILLED CURLEW

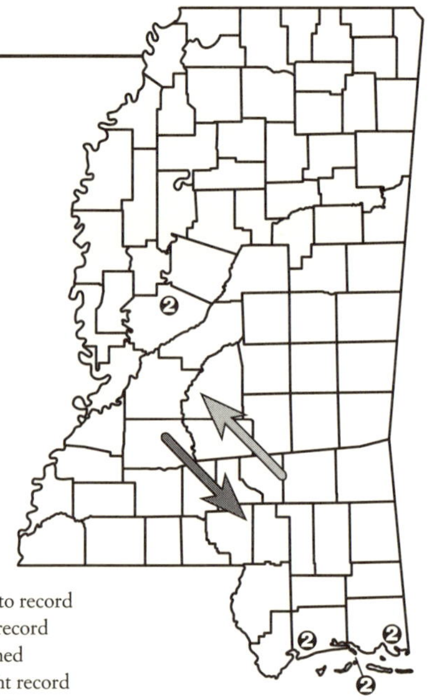

Coastal

Rare, irregular spring and fall transient, accidental inland

❶ specimen or photo record
❷ confirmed sight record
❸ breeding confirmed
❹ unconfirmed sight record
☐ breeding distribution
[C] distribution local

	JAN	FEB	MAR	APR	MAY	JUN	JUL	AUG	SEP	OCT	NOV	DEC
OCCURRENCE	5 oooo	ooooo	oooo	ooooo	ooo		o	ooo	ooooo	oooo	oooo	oooo
MUSEUM*												
WHT*												

*Breeding confirmed by egg, sight, or photographic record.

Long-billed Curlew *Numenius americanus*

Largest of our shorebirds, the Long-billed Curlew with its eight- to nine-inch-long bill; dark, cinnamon brown upperparts; and cinnamon buff underparts is unmistakable. About 24 inches long, it is larger than the Marbled Godwit and easily recognized by the long, scythe-shaped, *downcurved* bill. In flight, the bright *cinnamon underwing linings* are distinctive.

Although once a fairly common migrant and winter resident on the South Atlantic Coast, this curlew now occurs mainly on the prairies, plains, and dry uplands of the western states. It nests on both wet and dry uplands near lakes, marshes, wet meadows, and ranchlands of the high plains and western mountain states.

The winter range extends from southwestern Louisiana along the Texas coastline and interior of southern Texas south to Guatemala. In Mississippi, it has been sighted once in the interior. It is a rare and irregular transient on the Mississippi Coast along tidewater areas, grasslands, or beaches. One individual wintered on the beach in Gulfport between 1977 and 1978, a notable exception (Toups and Jackson 1987).

I have observed Long-billed Curlews along the Texas Coast on croplands, tidal flats, beaches, and salt marshes in July and August as they arrived from northern breeding grounds. In Kingsville, Texas, they were common on school yards and open, grassy places, seemingly oblivious to automobile traffic around them.

On June 22, 1985, on the Blackfeet Indian Reservation north of Browning, Montana, I found several breeding pairs of Long-billed Curlews and tape recorded their calls. It was an interesting experience on these high plains and open grasslands. With the mountains of Glacier National Park as a distant background, my wife, Dorothy, and I explored parts of the reservation before we saw a pair of curlews on a distant hill.

The roadsides were tightly fenced with no access. While we stopped to watch the birds, several cars passed and the occupants eyed us curiously. Another car stopped and asked if we were lost and if they could help. I told the Blackfeet Indian driver we were looking for a place to record the calls of curlews.

He told us to go over several hills and look for them in a broad, wet meadow. As soon as we stopped we sighted several pairs and the nearest pair started making alarm calls while I was setting up the equipment. One bird, presumably the male, came closer and continued making loud *cur-lee'* calls interspersed with trilling *klee-klee-klee* notes.

After circling overhead several times, it landed not far away. I succeeded in getting good recordings of this bird and the others calling in the background.

As I was carrying equipment to the car, a uniformed Indian agent drove up behind us to inquire about our presence on the reservation. She was courteous to us, but after our stay in Browning and trips over the reservation, we realized the Blackfeet owned this land, and it was private property. We should have known better. However, we never left the road right-of-way, did no harm, and left only footprints.

[Hudsonian Godwit] *Limosa haemastica*

This migratory counterpart (not generic) of the permanent-resident Willet is a casual spring and fall transient on the Mississippi Coast. Two birds were photographed at Pascagoula marsh on May 13 and 14, 1978 (Donaldson 1978). An immature was photographed and seen by many at Gulfport Harbor on October 31 and November 1, 1985 (Hodges 1985) after passage of Hurricane Juan.

Because of their similar appearance to the common Willet, Hudsonian Godwits can easily escape notice during spring and fall migrations. The godwit is slightly smaller with a long, *slightly upturned,* basally flesh-colored bill. The *black tail band, white* uppertail and tail coverts, and *black* underwing linings confirm identification. In alternate plumage, the male is ruddy below and finely barred. The female is duller. Adults in fall have gray backs and pale gray underparts. Juveniles are more buffy below, and the buff feather edges make the upperparts appear scaly.

Hudsonian Godwits nest in the high Arctic, and their breeding range is not well known. They winter in South America and migrate north in spring, passing from western Louisiana and the Texas Coast through the Great Plains. The fall migration occurs primarily along the East Coast.

Large migrating spring waders should be observed carefully in April and May for possible inland and coastal appearances of this species. Flooded rice fields, catfish farms, and shorelines of large water bodies or flooded fields are likely places for this uncommon transient to appear.

Marbled Godwit *Limosa fedoa*

Tawny brown, buffy, and cinnamon are the distinctive colorations best describing the Marbled Godwit. It breeds on the northern Great Plains and winters in northern South

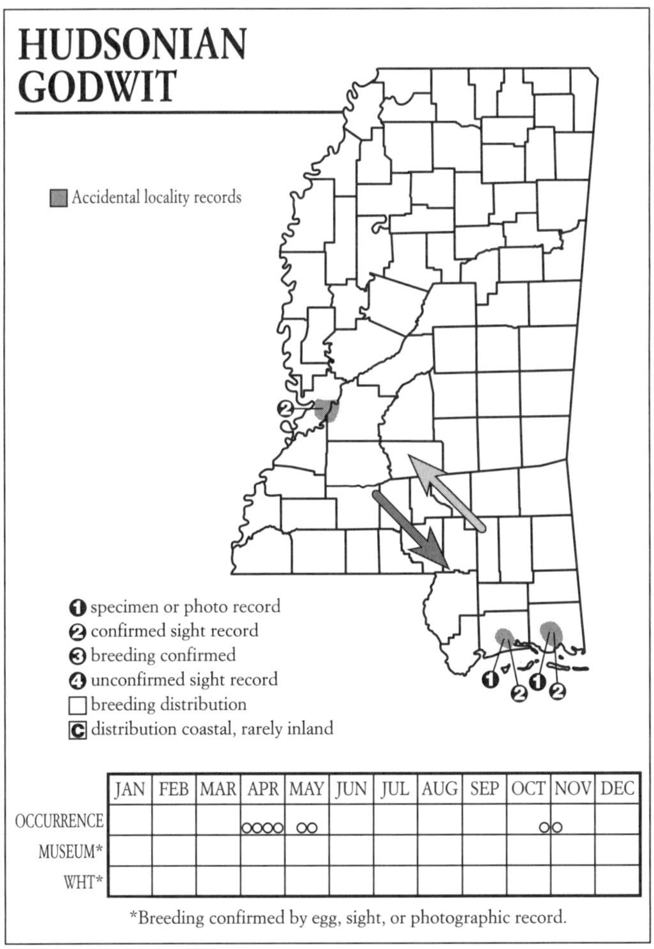

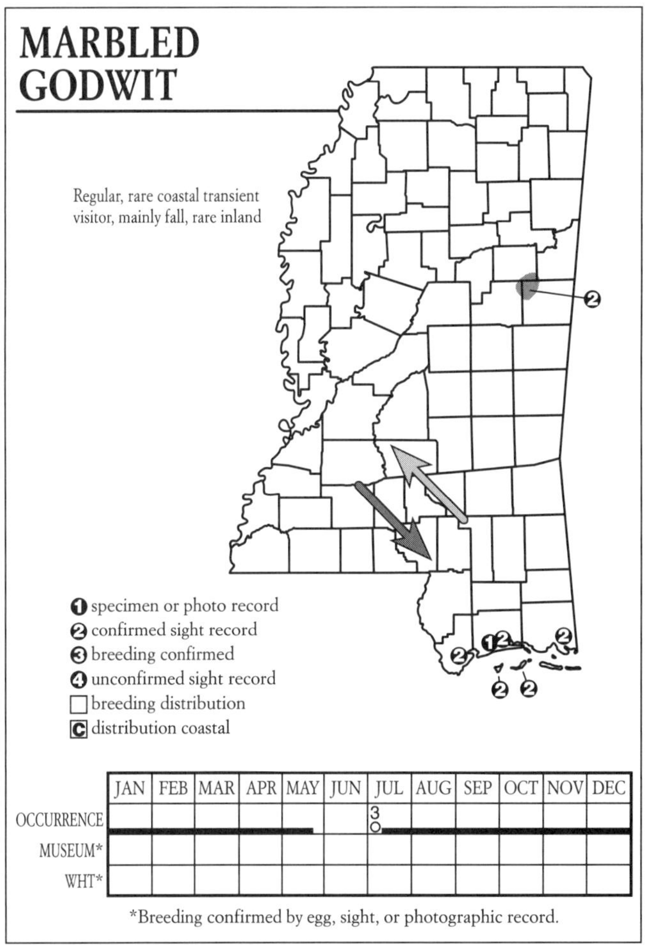

America and the southern United States. On the Mississippi Coast, it is a regular, uncommon fall migrant, rare spring transient, and casual winter visitor.

Its similarities in size and general coloration to the Long-billed Curlew are striking when these large shorebirds are compared. The long *upturned* bill of the Marbled Godwit readily separates it from the curlew, which has a long, downcurved bill. Both species have cinnamon wing linings. The Marbled Godwit in flight and at rest shows light cinnamon on primary and secondary wing feathers. I have seen migrant Marbled Godwits on the Pascagoula River marsh on one occasion.

On July 22 and 23, 1984, flocks of these birds were feeding with other shorebirds on the shallow pools of the Bear River marshes near Brigham City, Utah, and in June 1985, breeding pairs were seen in northwestern Minnesota, near the Red Lake Indian Reservation, where two startled Marbled Godwits flew from a roadside ditch to a field edge. The nearer bird started calling and flew over and around our car several times before alighting. Loud cries aloft and on the ground were almost continuous. The strident *kerwhit, whit, whit-whit* alarm calls of the Godwit and the demonstrative distraction displays in flight overhead were impressive. On June 19, 1985, at the Lostwood National Wildlife Refuge in North Dakota, breeding pairs near glaciated lake shores were equally disturbed and noisy. Earlier sightings of these birds in feeding flocks showed no tendency toward alarm.

Ruddy Turnstone *Arenaria interpres*

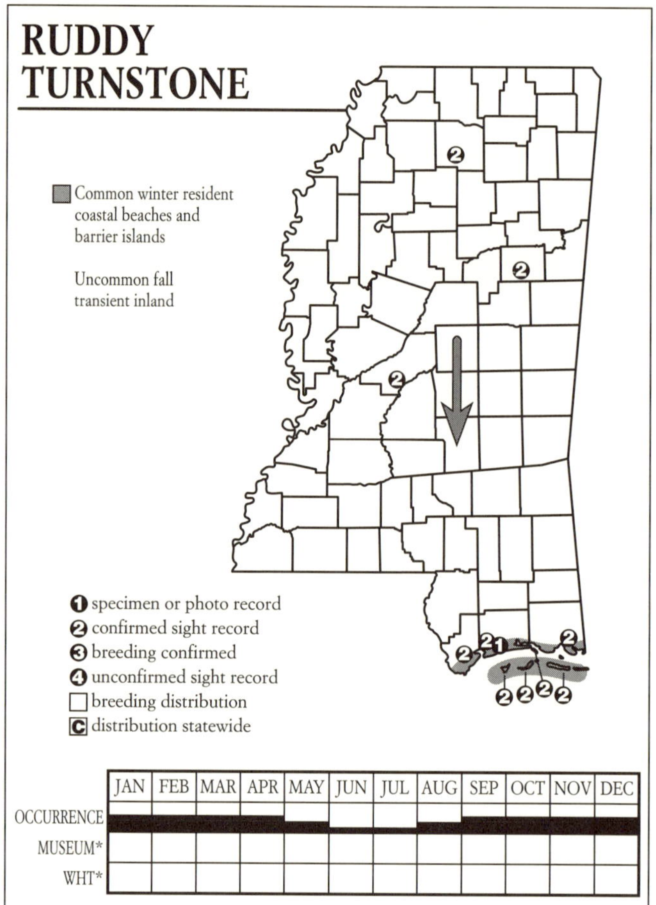

*Breeding confirmed by egg, sight, or photographic record.

This stocky shorebird with variegated marks and orange legs is easy to identify in alternate plumage. It strongly resembles the plovers in habits and general appearance and sometimes associates with them. Their practice of probing and turning over shells, stones, and shoreline debris to feed upon marine organisms is quite distinctive. The strong, sharp bill is used to probe and pry into mollusc shells. It is sometimes predatory on the eggs of nesting birds.

A ruddy back and harlequin face and bib distinguish this bird in its uniquely patterned alternate plumage. Russet, black, and white upperparts present an even more striking look when the bird is at rest and in flight. Immaculate white underparts contrast sharply with the black breast and ruddy sides. In basic plumage, orange legs and the basic bib pattern are retained. Juvenile and winter birds are brownish gray above, and the facial patterns are obscured. The guttural *tuck-a-tuck-a-tuck* calls are distinctive.

The Ruddy Turnstone is common on barrier islands and beaches along the Mississippi Coast. It is present during spring and fall migration, through the winter months until late May, and absent or rare until August. Beaches, breakwaters, pebbled bars, shell banks, and emergent, barnacle-covered vegetable matter at tidewater are favorite haunts. Turnstones are rarely seen inland and migrate mostly along seashores. They are circumpolar in distribution and nest on coastal tundra of the Arctic and sub-Arctic. They winter along the coastal United States and in the Southern Hemisphere.

I have watched these birds in late May disturbing the nesting colony of Least Terns on the Harrison County beach in front of Beauvoir. Fortunately for the terns, the turnstones leave for northern breeding grounds before nesting is well advanced.

Red Knot *Calidris canutus*

The Red Knot is a large, chunky, beach-dwelling sandpiper with short, greenish legs and a short bill. The breeding adult is dappled gray and brown on the upperparts. The breast and face are pale robin red. The short, typical sandpiper bill and the *absence* of a white streak on the back distinguish the Red Knot from similar Long-billed and Short-billed Dowitchers. In basic plumage, the Red Knot has a dumpy look, scaly gray upperparts, a pale rump patch, greenish legs, and the short sandpiper bill.

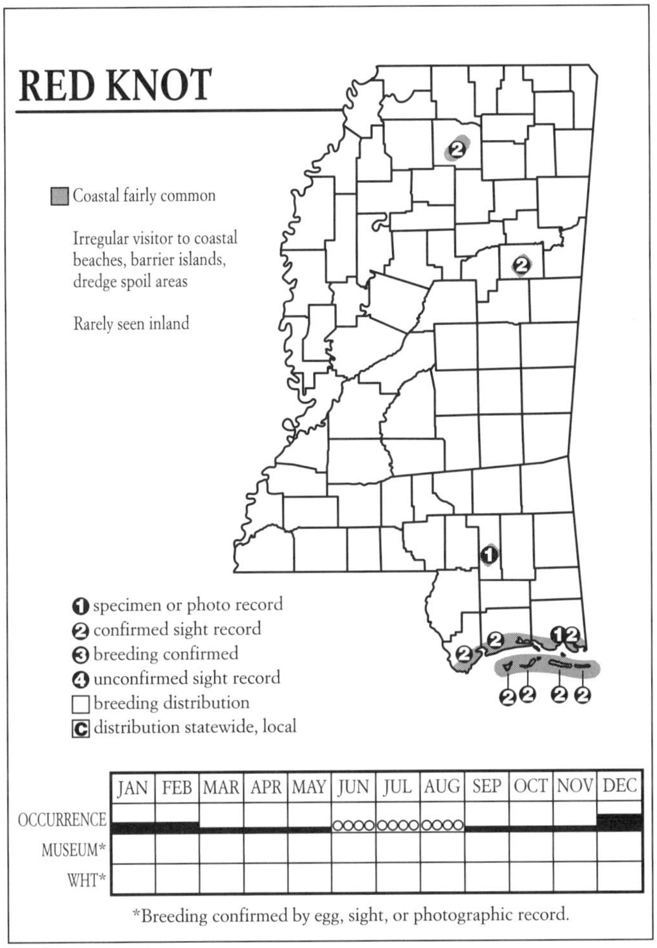

The breeding range of the Red Knot was long unknown. We now know that it nests on Arctic, dry tundra uplands. The nest is a shallow scrape lined with dry moss and other plant materials. The incubating bird sits tightly on the nest. Nests are widely scattered over remote areas, making them hard to locate. The nesting birds are seldom seen near their nest, although they may be in feeding flocks around nearby marshes or ponds. They begin nesting before all snow melts and start their southward migration in July.

Knots winter along the Atlantic and Gulf seashores of the United States and along South American coastlines to Argentina, Patagonia, and Chile. In the eastern United States, the spring northward migration is strictly along the Atlantic Coast.

Red Knots are seldom seen inland in Mississippi. Two interior records were from fall migration, a single bird seen September 13, 1979, at Hattiesburg by Larry Gates and Terrie Fairley (Jackson and Schardien 1980a) and six seen on Oktibbeha County Lake from August 29 to September 7, 1980, by Douglas McNair (Jackson 1981c). The Hattiesburg sighting occurred following the eastward passage of Hurricane Frederick.

On the Mississippi Coast, the Red Knot is an uncommon winter visitor and in migration may be fairly common along beaches in flocks of 20 or more birds. The tidal flats, islands, and diked spoil-collecting ponds of the Pascagoula River marshes are also frequently used during migration. Red Knots in alternate or basic plumage may be seen during spring migration, and early fall migrants may be in basic or alternate plumage. On the Gulf Coast, they are frequently seen with Black-bellied Plovers and dowitchers along beaches and offshore islands.

Red Knots feed like other sandpipers, probing the sand beaches and tidal flats for molluscs, crustaceans, and marine insect larvae. They also feed on the seeds of some plants. The soft, mellow call, *qua-whoit,* can be imitated by whistling the notes.

Sanderling *Calidris alba*

Sanderlings are cosmopolitan wanderers of the outer beaches and range along the seashores of all the continents. They nest on the tundra regions and Arctic islands and winter along the shorelines of the United States and South America to Argentina and Chile.

On the Mississippi Coast, they are ubiquitous residents along mainland sand beaches and offshore barrier islands.

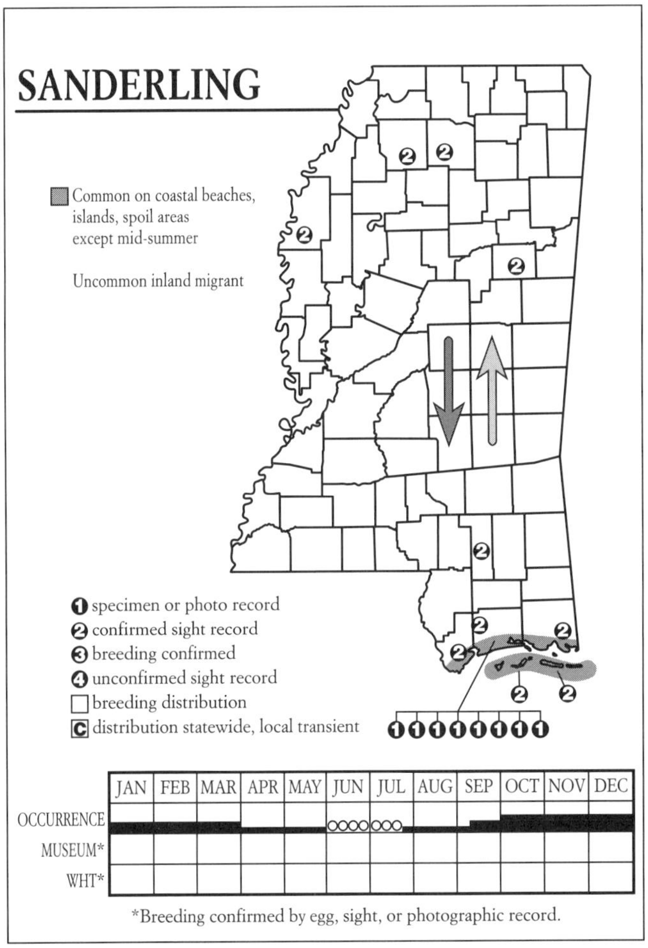

Occasionally during migration, they occur on interior reservoirs and lake shores. These "beach bums" subsist on marine organisms on the ocean shores and are absent from the Mississippi Coast only during their June and July breeding season.

At times in winter and in migration, Sanderlings may be found in flocks of 20 to 100 or more along mainland beaches. They mingle with plovers and other shorebirds while resting. They are forever on the move while feeding, following the ebb and flow of waves and tide to catch small crustaceans, molluscs, insect larvae, and other marine forms. A gathering of shorebirds at rest on Gulf Coast beaches is almost certain to include a few Sanderlings.

The Sanderling is slightly larger than other sandpipers or "peeps" and has a plumper look. On their short legs, Sanderlings *move incredibly fast,* chasing receding waves to hunt for food on the wet sand. This trait alone helps identify them. Their black legs and bill; white underparts; *pale gray* upperparts; and prominent, white wing stripe with a black shoulder patch are distinctive field marks. The upperparts become *rusty,* and the head, back, and sides of the breast change to bright rust in alternate plumage. In basic plumage, it is the *palest* of the small *Calidris* peeps. The call of the Sanderling is a sharp, short *kip* or a series of these distinctive notes.

Coastal records extend throughout the year. Inland sightings of Sanderlings have been recorded from Forrest, Oktibbeha, Panola, and Lafayette Counties. I observed them once on Ross Barnett Reservoir feeding on mud flats with unusual numbers of Dunlins and Common Snipe after a fall water draw-down.

Semipalmated Sandpiper *Calidris pusilla*

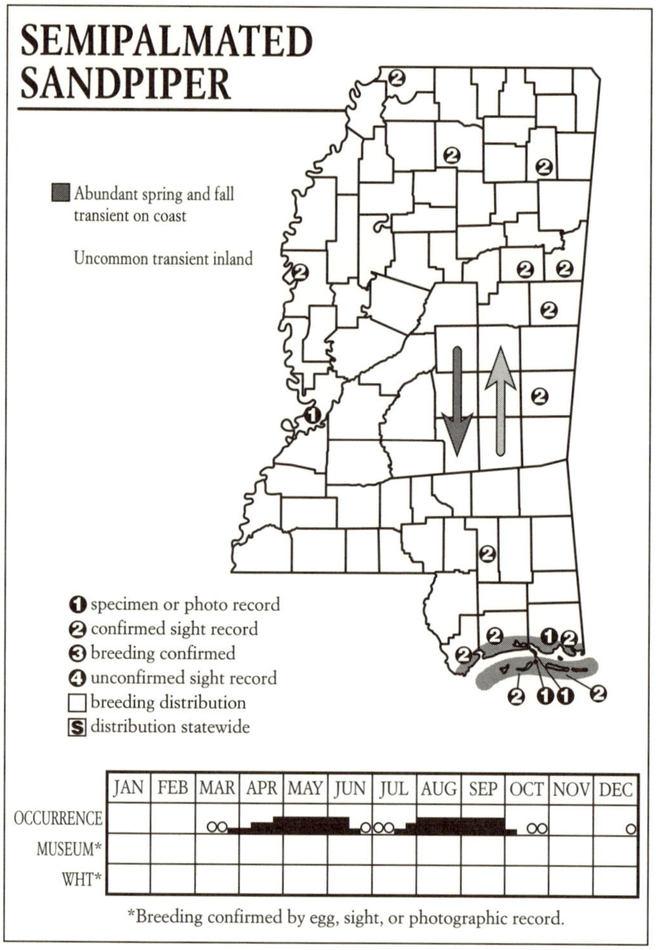

The "semipalm" is a transient that moves to and from its Arctic breeding grounds and wintering places, which are mainly in South America. On the Mississippi Coast, it is sometimes an abundant migrant in late spring (May) and early fall (August through September). During this same time period, the more common Least Sandpiper and Western Sandpiper require an observer to use caution before making a positive field identification. Also at this time, it is a widespread migrant in the interior and is likely to appear on exposed wet mud flats.

Many of these sparrow-sized "peeps" will be in confusing changing plumages. Close-up scrutiny for comparative field marks and separation by species is often difficult. Overlapping bill sizes occur due to age, sex, and individual variations, especially during fall migration. It is better to call them peeps under doubtful circumstances than to fool yourself with wrong thinking.

A few nonbreeding birds, or early migrants, occur on the Gulf Coast through the summer. Winter sight records should be presumed as sightings of Western Sandpiper until proven otherwise.

The Semipalmated Sandpiper has partial webbing of the anterior toes, black or greenish black legs, and a straight, attenuated bill, which is shorter than the width of the head. The Western Sandpiper has a bill longer than its head width, thicker at the base, and a slight droop at the tip. This species frequently feeds in water nearly to its belly. Least Sandpipers have a longish, *thin* bill, *greenish* or yellowish green *legs,* and are *reddish brown* on the upperparts and breast (brighter in alternate plumage). The Least Sandpiper is smaller than most sparrows. The Semipalmated Sandpiper is *grayer* than the rusty-backed Least and Western Sandpipers. The Western Sandpiper in alternate plumage shows *reddish brown* at the base of the scapulars, on the crown, face, and auriculars. In fall the Semipalmated is almost inseparable from the Western Sandpiper.

The calls of these three sandpipers are distinctive. The Least has a high raspy *bree-eep.* The Semipalmated call is a low, single, soft, *chet* not much lower in pitch than the Least Sandpiper. The Western Sandpiper's call note is a thin, high *cheep,* different than the low, soft note of the Semipalmated Sandpiper.

A knowledge of time and place when peeps occur as migrants or visitors, their call notes, and the unique field marks of each species are essential before one can readily identify them. Peeps are the ultimate challenge to birders trying to identify them without all available clues.

Western Sandpiper *Calidris mauri*

The Western Sandpiper and its very similar counterpart, the Semipalmated Sandpiper, are described in the preceding account. Although similar in appearance, their calls, breeding ranges, and migration habits differ. Bill shape, foot structure, and alternate plumage colorations are other distinctions, and these differences mark them as separate species. The breeding and winter ranges overlap somewhat. The Semipalmated breeds along the northern coasts of Alaska and Canada to the Atlantic, and winters mainly south of the United States. The Western Sandpiper breeds mainly in Alaska and winters along the coastlines of the United States and northern South America.

On the Mississippi Coast, the Western Sandpiper frequents beaches and wetlands, occurring in great abundance on tidal flats and other shoreline edges during migration. Migration peaks occur in March and August, when thousands of Western Sandpipers may be seen at staging areas on the coast before moving north or south. They are common winter residents and at times locally abundant under favorable weather conditions and other variables. On inland areas during migration, the Western Sandpiper is more common than the Semipalmated Sandpiper. In winter, it is rarely found far inland.

Least Sandpiper *Calidris minutilla*

As the name implies, this is the smallest of our sandpipers. Hardly the size of most sparrows, it is also the brownest on the back and breast of all the "peeps." The short, thin bill and yellow legs and feet set it apart from other *Calidris* members.

This species is noted for a remarkable behavior characteristic of its group. They feed in loose flocks with quick movements, scampering about *picking* and probing wet sand beaches or mud flats for food in continuous movements, literally straining the area with their sensitive bills. When a feeding flock is approached, the birds take flight in unison to settle down farther up the sand or wheel about in perfect formation to circle over water and land behind and beyond an onlooker.

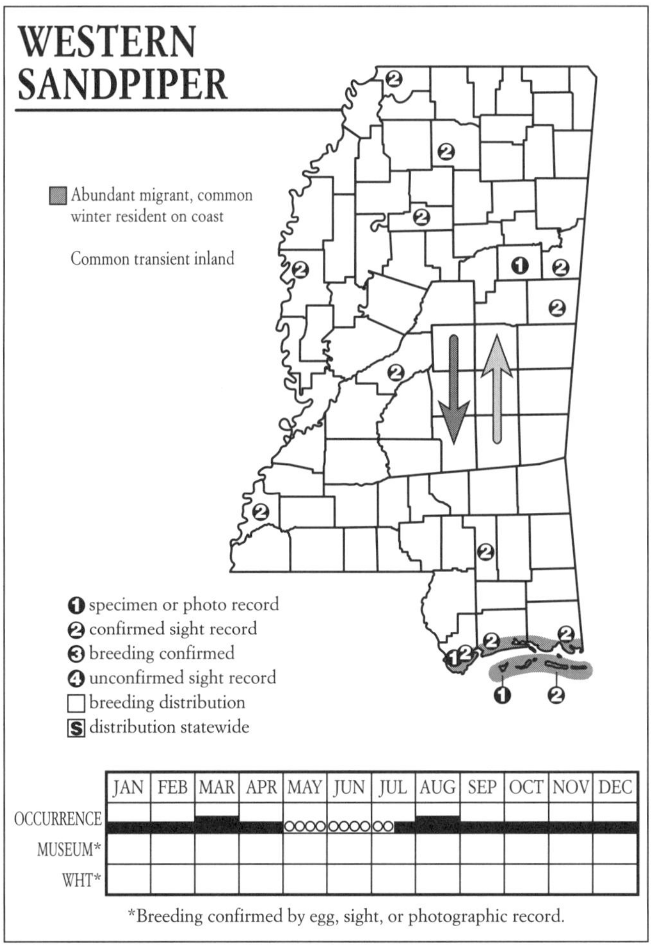

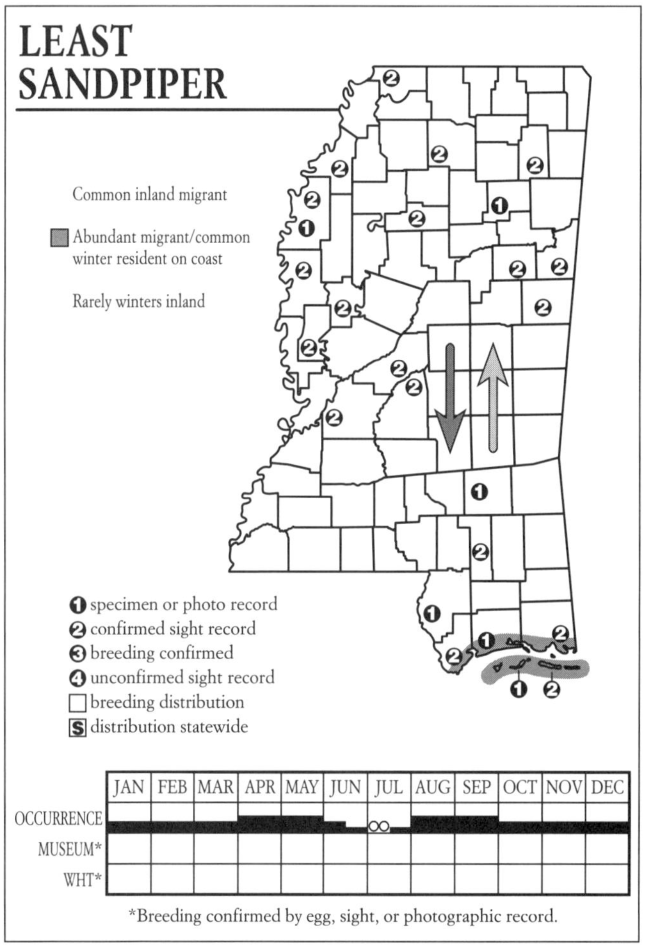

Hundreds of these birds can fly in compact flocks wheeling and turning together, with wings almost touching another bird. Each bird's reflexes are in tune with every other one in the flock. How each bird achieves such perfection in formation flight, especially the rear echelon, which must describe a wider arc at faster speeds, is cause for wonder. Nature must have endowed these birds with flight senses that other bird species never gained or have lost.

The Least Sandpiper is the most common sandpiper in the peep group in migration through inland parts of Mississippi. On the coast it is abundant during migration peaks and common to abundant during winter. It is mostly absent from May to mid-July, although a few remain on the coast throughout the breeding season.

Shoreline habitats such as grassy shallows, tidal beaches, or mud flats, and especially the wet edges just above the waterline, are the favorite haunts of Least Sandpipers. They have less affinity for feeding in the water and prefer to feed near the water's edge.

These sandpipers breed across a wide band of northern Canada and Alaska to the Arctic. They winter on shorelines of the southern United States southward to Brazil. They are uncommon, irregular winter residents on inland parts of the Gulf and southern Atlantic states. The thin, high-pitched *bree-eep* call notes are distinctive and should be learned as a valuable part of field identification.

White-rumped Sandpiper *Calidris fuscicollis*

Largest of the "peeps," the White-rumped Sandpiper is the easiest to identify. It is helpful to know that it occurs mainly as a spring transient and rarely in fall. In spring it migrates through the interior. It follows an eastward course in fall mainly along and across the Atlantic Ocean, much like the American Golden-Plover. It is fairly common on beaches, but prefers tidal mud flats on the Mis-sissippi Coast.

Spring migration occurs from March 22 to June 23. On inland areas during spring passage, it is most likely seen from mid-May to early June. Fall migrants are casual on inland and coastal areas from July 15 to September 5.

In flight, the conspicuous white rump, long wings extending beyond the tail, and larger, grayer, streaked sides are field marks to confirm sightings. In alternate plumage, streaking on the sides shows below the wings to the flanks, and these birds have a rustier appearance. The high, squeaky call note is a goldfinchlike *cheet*.

The White-rumped Sandpiper's longer wings carry it on the longest migrations of any peep. It nests around freshwater ponds and wet swales above the Arctic Circle away from seashores. The three or four gray-colored eggs are dotted with dark brown and lilac marks. The wintering range is southern South America to Cape Horn and the Straits of Magellan.

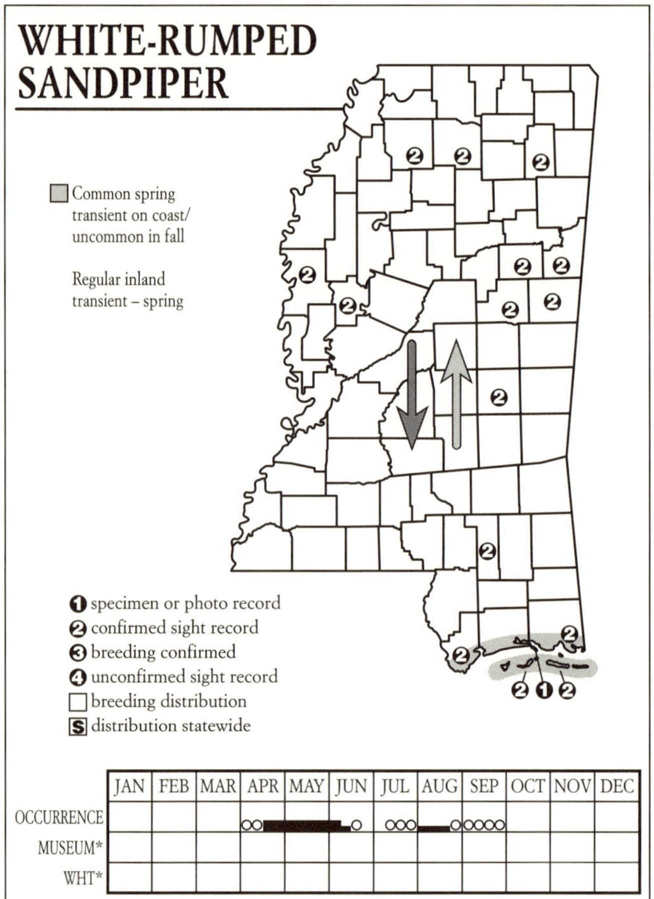

*Breeding confirmed by egg, sight, or photographic record.

Baird's Sandpiper *Calidris bairdii*

The first state record for this rare "peep" is a specimen taken by Vaiden (1939) in Bolivar County on October 14, 1937. The second is a male taken by Burleigh (1945) at Lyman in Harrison County on November 10, 1942. Among the few inland sight records are one at Hattiesburg, on September 11, 1983, by Larry and Terrie Gates (Schardien and Jackson 1983), and another at Sardis dam on May 11, 1985, by Marvin Davis and Gene Knight (Hodges 1985). Schiefer and Hodges Jr. (1987) and others made multiple sightings on Oktibbeha County Lake from September 27 to November 8, 1986. A high count of 23 birds was on September 28, 1986.

On the Mississippi Coast, the Baird's Sandpiper is a rare, irregular spring migrant and a regular, rare, fall transient. Records extend from March 22 to May 4 and from July 20 to September 18. Inland records occurred on May 11 and from September 11 to November 10, later than the coast. It has been seen on coastal beaches in spring, and most fall sight records have occurred on Pascagoula River marshlands.

Since May 1978, Judith A. Toups, Larry Gates, and others have recorded three spring and six fall sightings on

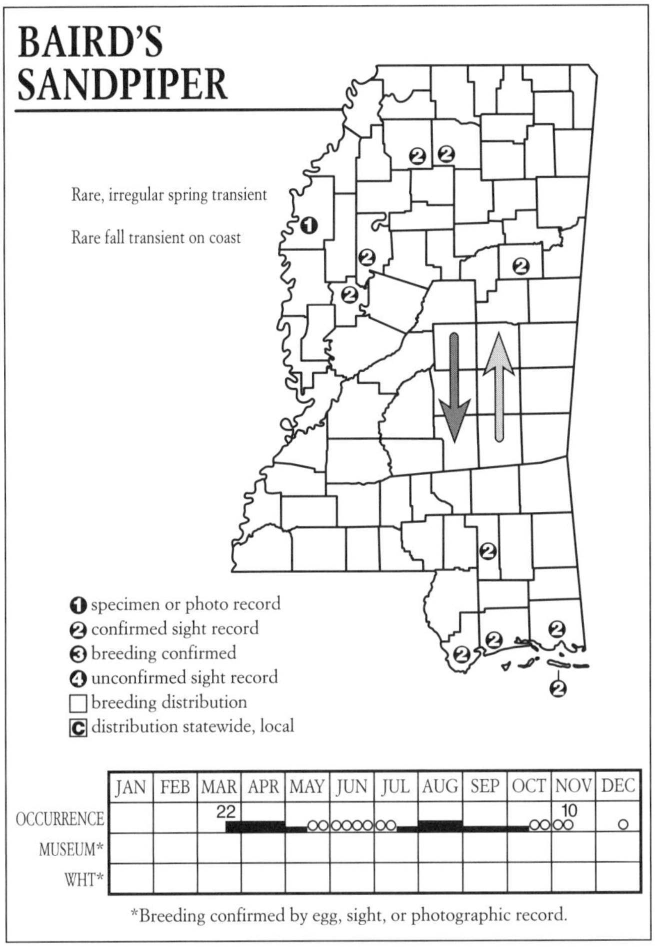

the Mississippi Coast of individual birds or groups of from two to five. This species may occur during spring and fall passage on the coast more commonly than records indicate. To determine this would require careful viewing with a telescope at the multitude of small migrating sandpipers using the beaches and tidal flats.

Baird's Sandpiper is most like the White-rumped Sandpiper in size and shape. The wings extend one-half inch beyond the tail, giving it a long, pointed appearance. The upperparts are brown with buffy edging, giving the back a scaly look. The breast is faintly streaked with *brownish buff* across the breast. The *absence* of a white rump patch separates this species from the White-rumped Sandpiper. The larger Pectoral Sandpiper and the Sanderling in alternate plumage have similar appearances.

Like the Pectoral Sandpiper, Baird's is often quite tame in migration. It prefers grassy shorelines, rainpools, mud flats, lake shores, and the upperparts of beaches, where it feeds by picking. The Pectoral Sandpiper has *greenish* legs, and the Sanderling displays its identity by its hyperactive movements and shorter wings.

Baird's Sandpipers nest on dry tundra of Arctic North America and eastern Siberia. They migrate across the western states and interior of the United States, but rarely east of the Mississippi River. They winter in southern South America to both coasts.

Pectoral Sandpiper *Calidris melanotos*

The Pectoral is the *largest* sandpiper of the *Calidris* group and the *brownest,* with the possible exception of the Least Sandpiper. Both have yellow or greenish yellow legs, but the Pectoral Sandpiper is more than a half-size larger, or almost 10 inches in length. The larger size, dark brown, *heavily streaked throat and breast ending abruptly in sharp contrast* with the white underparts are distinctive field marks. The Pectoral has a longer neck than most smaller "peeps." The dark brown feathers on the back are whitish on the outer edges and give a *striped look* to the back.

The Pectoral Sandpiper in migration prefers mud flats of tidal and freshwater marshlands, rain pools in open fields, and ponds or lakes with muddy, grassy edges. It migrates north in small flocks in late March and early April. On the Mississippi Coast, it is fairly common in spring and fall while staging at suitable sites around marshy shorelines. It is a regular transient inland and on the coast.

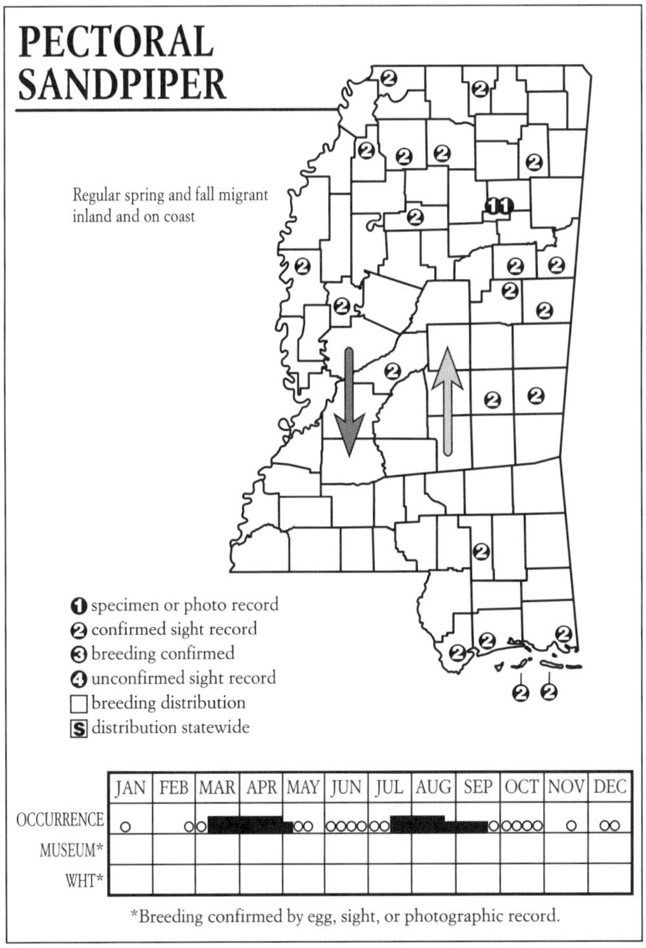

A few coastal records extend into summer and early winter, but most fall migrants depart by early October for South America. The Pectoral Sandpiper breeds on Arctic tundra, nesting on dry, upland grassy sites, which afford concealment for the eggs.

The double-noted, mellow, whistled call, *preep-preep,* is usually heard when these birds take flight in the zigzag fashion of the Common Snipe. On the breeding grounds, the male Pectoral Sandpiper has a song flight and courtship display. The low, booming calls are made while inflating a throat sac with air, and the throat and breast are distended. This display and the calls are made in flight and on the ground while performing before a female.

[Purple Sandpiper] *Calidris maritima*

This chunky sandpiper has *short yellow legs, slate gray* head and upperparts, *white eye ring,* and white belly in basic plumage. It normally winters on rocky shores and jetties of northern Atlantic provinces and states, and is accidental on the coasts of Texas, Louisiana, and Mississippi.

The alternate plumage is much browner and heavily streaked above, on the breast, and on the sides to the flanks.

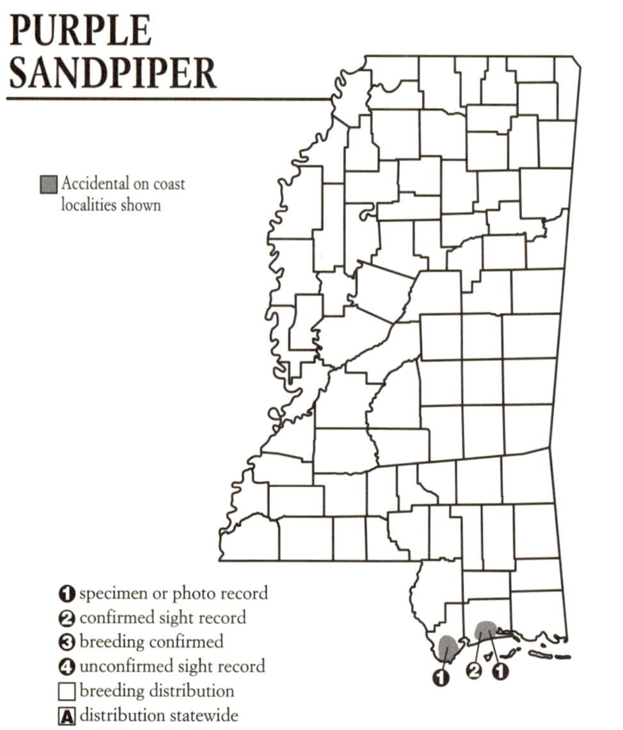

	JAN	FEB	MAR	APR	MAY	JUN	JUL	AUG	SEP	OCT	NOV	DEC
OCCURRENCE	19 ○			10-20 ○○							11-12 ○ 28 ○	2 ○○○○
MUSEUM*												
WHT*												

*Breeding confirmed by egg, sight, or photographic record.

The longish, dark bill is *slightly downcurved toward the tip* and *yellowish at the base.* The winter Dunlin is similar in size and appearance to the Purple Sandpiper, but it has *black legs.* The soft *twit* or *weet-wit* call notes are infrequent and usually heard when the bird takes flight.

This hardy species winters farther north along the Atlantic Coast than other shorebirds. It breeds on Arctic islands of northeastern Canada and in southern Greenland, while wintering commonly southward along the Atlantic Coast. Here, it mingles with Sanderlings and Ruddy Turnstones.

The first Mississippi sight record was a single bird seen feeding at the waterline among rocks by Sunby (1986) at the Pass Christian Harbor in Harrison County on January 19, 1985.

A second record for the Purple Sandpiper was one photographed by Judith A. Toups at the Scotland Catfish Ponds near Kiln in Hancock County on November 11 and 12, 1987 (Hodges 1987). It was first seen by Mickey Baker and was identified by Toups. This sandpiper was out of the natural element with which it is usually associated. It was on a freshwater shoreline bordered by reedy vegetation with no rocks present other than the crushed gravel of a roadbed.

A third sight record occurred from April 10 to 20, 1988, at Gulfport Harbor, a single bird observed and reported by Harry E. Slack on April 10 and confirmed by a photograph by Judith A. Toups and others (Hodges 1988). This bird was feeding along the waterline bordering a concrete walkway and was photographed on rocks with a Ruddy Turnstone.

Dunlin *Calidris alpina*

The Dunlin, formerly Red-backed Sandpiper, is an abundant fall and winter resident on Gulf Coast beaches and tidal mud flats. It is noted inland along shorelines during migration. On the coast, it occurs in flocks or mixed with other shorebirds from September through May. During migration, it far outnumbers other sandpipers. A few nonbreeders occur on the coast from June through August.

The Dunlin is slightly larger than the more active and common Sanderling. A descriptive term for recognizing the Dunlin is "droop-snoot." Its bill is longer and stouter than the Sanderling's, thickened near the base, and decurved near the tip. It has a hunched appearance while feeding and a shorter, thicker neck. Basic plumage is plain gray above and whitish below with a dash of plain gray and faint streaking on the breast. Before spring departure, Dunlins develop alternate plumage like no other sandpiper. The back, nape, and crown are patterned *reddish brown.* Underparts are whitish and finely streaked with a conspicuous, black patch on the belly.

Dunlins breed along Arctic coastlines and are circumpolar in distribution. They winter along the Atlantic, Gulf, and Pacific Coasts and southward along the coasts of Mexico.

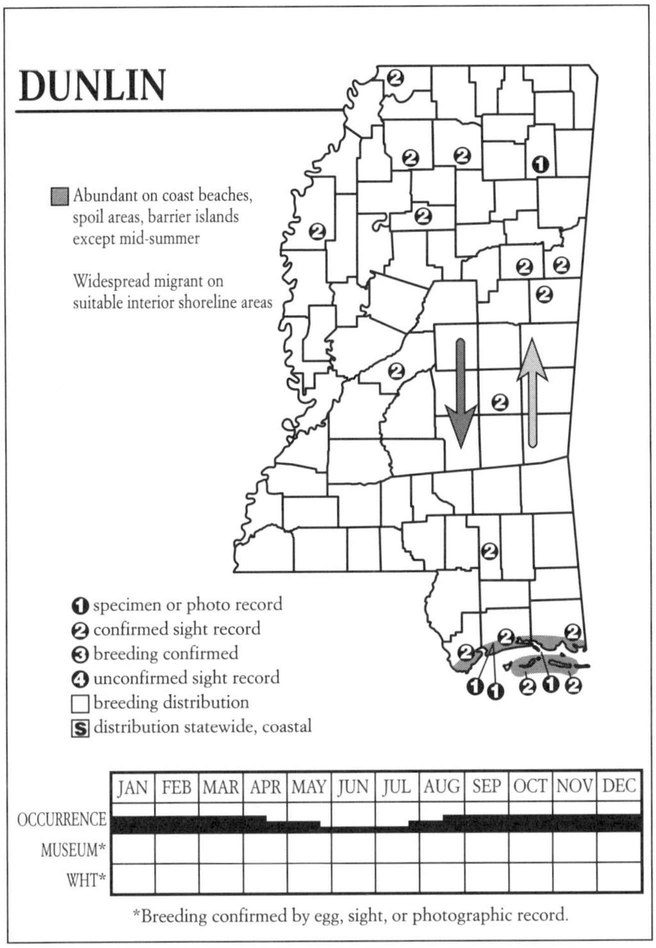

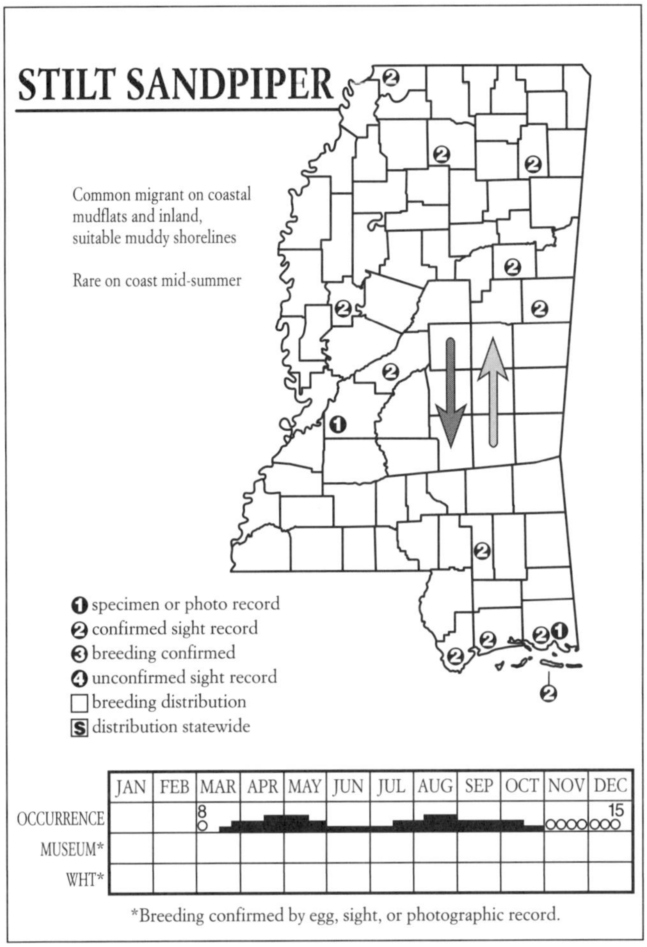

Stilt Sandpiper *Calidris himantopus*

Stilt Sandpipers are easy to identify in alternate plumage. The *heavily cross-barred underparts; rusty stripes* on the sides of the head; long, greenish legs; and a prominent white stripe over the eye are identification marks.

In basic plumage, they bear a close resemblance to yellowlegs, but are grayer above with whiter underparts. Unlike the yellowlegs' straight bill, the Stilt Sandpiper's is de-curved, noticeably tapered, and slightly drooping at the tip. A prominent white line over the eye, greenish legs, and different feeding styles also separate these two sandpipers.

The "stilts" feed like dowitchers, making quick, stabbing, sweeping motions as they probe bottom muds for food. In flight, the clear, white rump patch and dark trailing edges of the wings help to confirm identity of winter plumaged birds of this species.

I have found these sandpipers several times on the spoil disposal ponds and tidewater flats of the Pascagoula River marsh below U.S. 90. They always were seen with dowitchers probing for food on the mud bottom or resting on the muddy shoreline.

Stilt Sandpipers begin to arrive on the coast the second week in March from wintering grounds in southern South America. They are common on tidal mud flats along the Pascagoula marshes during peak times of spring and early fall passage in April and August. Occasionally, a few may linger on the coast through June and July. Extreme dates of arrival and departure are March 8 and December 15 on the Mississippi Coast. The breeding range is on the Arctic tundra.

Migration occurs mainly through the Mississippi Valley and westward through the Great Plains. Expect these birds to occur as spring and fall migrants through Mississippi on wet boggy grasslands, marshy edges, and muddy shallows of lakes.

Buff-breasted Sandpiper *Tryngites subruficollis*

This little sandpiper is unique and unmistakable. Its clear buffy face and underparts; light brown upperparts with the feathers broadly edged buffy; the erect, long-necked posture; and yellowish legs give it a distinctive look, somewhat like the much larger Upland Sandpiper.

Its habits in migration are different from most sandpipers. It prefers short-grass habitats such as airports, open, closely grazed pastures, wet or upland prairies, dune areas of open beaches, open sandbars found along the Mississippi River, and similar places where Upland Sandpipers and Lesser Golden-Plovers usually occur. On the coast they sometimes are found on open beaches, where they frequent the higher, drier parts.

These migrants are irregular and uncommon to rare in migration to or from northern breeding grounds in the northwestern Arctic. They winter in Argentina and parts of Uruguay. Their migration route is mainly through the central United States.

Burleigh (1945) recorded the first sighting and specimen for Mississippi, a female taken on Deer Island on September 6, 1940. Vaiden (1960) reported the first inland records and collected eight specimens from two flocks of Buff-breasted Sandpipers totaling 42 birds in Bolivar County from August 29 to September 17, 1960.

Haberyan (1963a) observed three birds on the Pascagoula River flats in Jackson County, one of which he netted and banded on August 25, 1962. Recent sightings of individuals and flocks of up to 17 birds have occurred on the coast from March 23 to May 11, on June 6, and from August 11 to October 29.

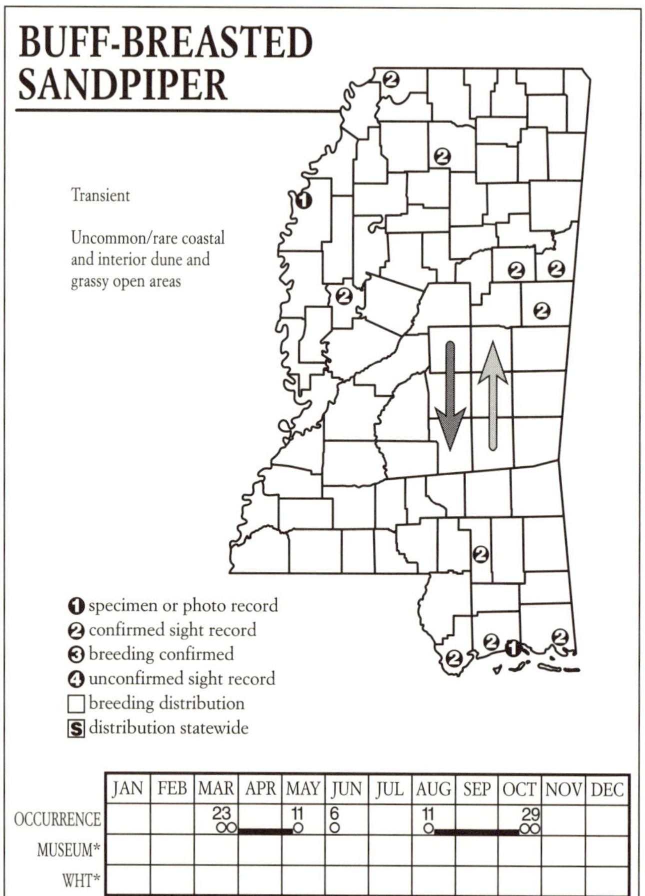

*Breeding confirmed by egg, sight, or photographic record.

Inland, this sandpiper has been recorded only in fall. Marvin Davis reported 80 birds at Sardis Reservoir on September 4, 1980, seven on August 29, and 21 on September 6 (Jackson 1981c). Other inland records were in September 1980 at Noxubee National Wildlife Refuge, Oktibbeha County Lake, and on the Hattiesburg sewage lagoons in Forrest County.

My first sighting of this species, an individual against a backdrop of Sanderlings and Dunlins at the water's edge, occurred at the beach opposite the Small Craft Harbor in Gulfport. It stood erect and apart from other shorebirds on the dry sand. The plain, buffy breast, plumpish body, pigeonlike head, and long neck were in stark contrast to the white sand and lighter-colored and more active shorebirds beyond it. I was able to photograph the bird in good light as it stayed quietly on the beach.

[Ruff] *Philomachus pugnax*

Unexpected birds are expertly identified by birders who happen to appear simultaneously, and a new species is added to the growing list of local, state, or North American bird records. Such is the case of a shorebird wanderer, the Ruff, that appeared at the Pascagoula River marsh on August 1, 1982.

"Gestalt" is a name for recognition characteristics that together add up to a distinctive whole pattern of behavior including biological, physiological, and psychological phenomena. Instant recognition of birds in the field is learned from broad experience with not only a single species, but with all or many species with similar but different traits.

Toups and Roemer (1982) found a Ruff feeding among Greater Yellowlegs and Lesser Yellowlegs on a mud flat in one of the spoil disposal ponds on the Pascagoula River marsh on August 1, 1982. Differences in plumage color and pattern, posture, behavior, feeding habits, and a stockier neck and pectoral area set it apart from the similar yellowlegs. If this Ruff had been in the unlikely alternate plumage with neck *ruff* and *ear tufts* of white, red, black, or barred feathers, it would be unmistakable. In basic plumage, this Ruff had a thickened appearance in the neck and pectoral region, overall brownish appearance, white chin area, creamy white underparts, a light brown throat and bib, and characteristic *oval white spots* on the sides of the tail. These features, compared with those of the yellowlegs, were noted together with the erect, horizontal body posture of the Ruff and its deliberate feeding posture and actions without the head bobbing characteristic of the yellowlegs. These attributes were noted by two observers using telescopes in favorable light for more than an hour of studying and comparing details with other shorebirds.

The Ruff is an Old World wanderer occurring mainly in the

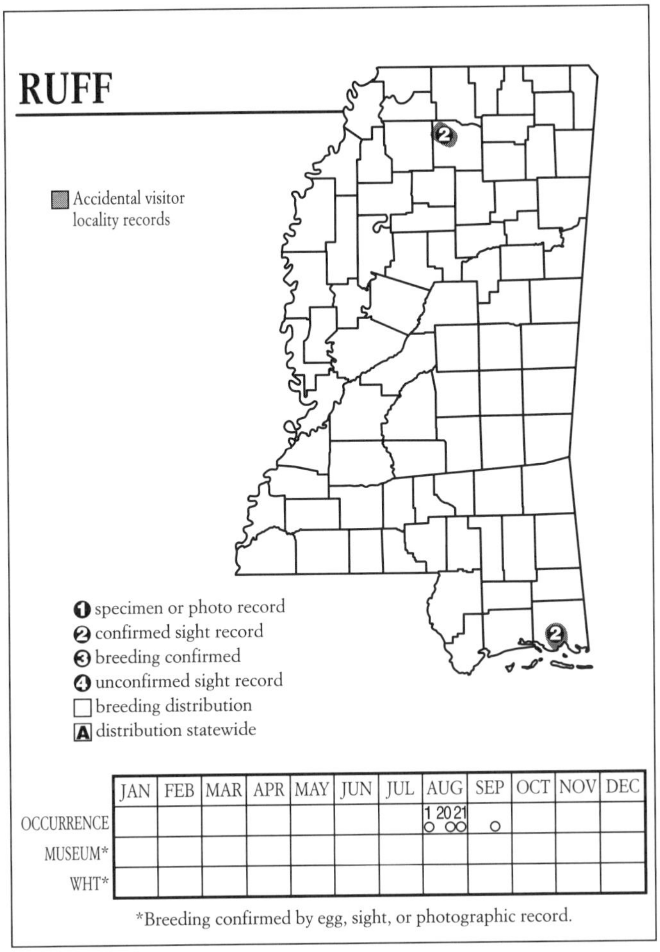

fall (rarely in spring) along northeastern Atlantic and Pacific Coasts. Frequency of sightings in the southeastern states has increased in recent years. Judith Toups, Martha Powell, and Malcolm Hodges Jr. reported a second Ruff at Bayou Cassotte in Jackson County, on August 20, 1988 (Hodges 1988).

There is only one inland record of the Ruff. Gene and Shannon Knight and Vic Theobald identified with written descriptions all details of an individual at a shallow backwater along Clear Creek Road at Sardis Lake in Lafayette County on August 21, 1989. The bird was with Lesser Yellowlegs and Killdeers. It was seen with a telescope and binoculars as close as 75 feet. Low, guttural, single *krook* call notes were heard several times.

Short-billed Dowitcher *Limnodromus griseus*

The two species of dowitchers occurring in Mississippi differ more in habitat preference and call notes than in bill length or other visible characteristics. The Short-billed Dowitcher prefers tidewater marshes and beaches on Gulf coastlines. Although the Long-billed Dowitcher shares similar tidewater mud flats, it seldom occurs on coastal beaches where the Short-billed is commonly found.

In alternate plumage, the Short-billed Dowitcher has a rusty red breast, *spotted* rather than barred on the sides, and *whitish underparts.* The Long-billed Dowitcher is barred on the sides of its reddish breast, sides, and flanks. The *reddish underside* extends to the front of the belly. The Short-billed Dowitcher's barred tail has *whiter* bars, while the Long-billed has *blacker* bars on the white tail. A white rump patch extends far up the back between the wings on both birds.

In basic plumage, the two dowitchers are almost alike and call notes are best used to distinguish them. The Short-billed arrives earlier than the Long-billed in this area and departs later. Although it is common during peak migrations on the coast, the Long-billed is less commonly seen in late spring and in July to mid-August. A few nonbreeders of both species remain on the Mississippi Coast through the summer. Both dowitchers winter mainly along coastlines in the southern United States and southward.

To further complicate field identification of dowitchers, there are three recognized subspecies of the Short-billed Dowitcher. *Limnodromus griseus hendersoni* is the subspecies most commonly found in this area. The other subspecies, *L. g. caurinus* and *L. g. griseus,* migrate and winter mainly along the Pacific and Atlantic Coasts, respectively.

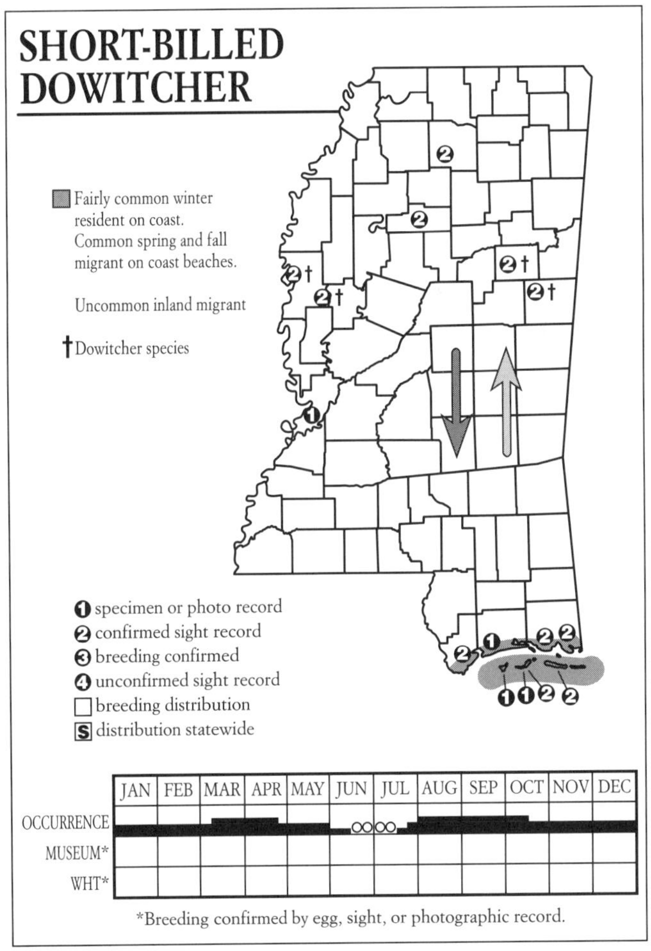

Limnodromus griseus hendersoni breeds in western and central Canada and migrates from the central plains eastward in the United States. Field identification of both dowitchers is sometimes difficult or impossible for many observers without careful study and reference to field guides. When in doubt, it is better to consult all field guides and literature on the subject. Then, if call notes are not decisive, just call the birds "dowitcher species."

The Short-billed Dowitcher has a mellow, low, alarm call, *tu-tu-tu,* which is similar to that of the yellowlegs. The alarm calls of the Long-billed are a rapid series of high, thin *keek* notes in either single-, two-, or three-note sequences.

My first encounter with dowitchers was on July 14, 1937, at Lake Dockery in Hinds County when I collected a specimen of the Long-billed Dowitcher out of a flock of five. The specimen was in alternate plumage and was placed in the MMNS.

Dowitchers differ from Common Snipe in preferring more open habitat and having little tendency to "freeze" when approached, like the snipe. Dowitchers feed with quick, stabbing motions of their long, slender bills while probing the bottom muds for animal organisms. They rest on open shorelines, standing on one foot with the bill resting on the back between the wings. They often associate with other shorebirds along the coastlines.

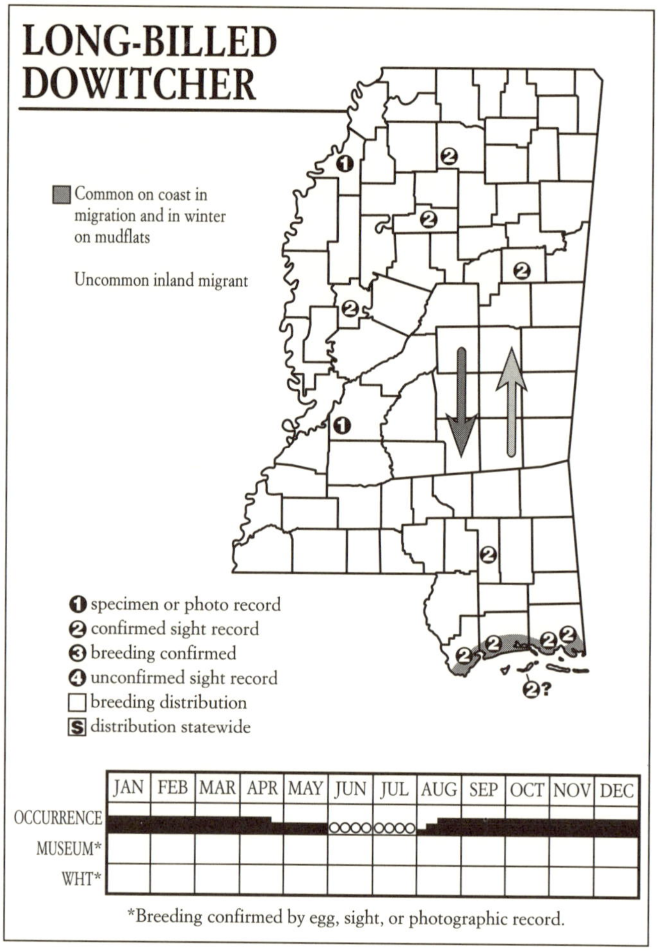

*Breeding confirmed by egg, sight, or photographic record.

Long-billed Dowitcher *Limnodromus scolopaceus*

Both dowitchers occurring in Mississippi have extremely long bills. On occasions during spring migration peaks, it is possible to see both species together and sort out the ones with three-inch bills. Then one can compare and verify the differences in alternate plumage described in the preceding account. At such times the voice differences can be analyzed and learned.

On the Mississippi Coast, the best opportunity for seeing dowitchers is at spoil disposal ponds and other marshland edges known as the Pascagoula flats south of U. S. 90 along the road leading to Ingalls Shipyard. Access to this area is sometimes restricted by heavy traffic or local construction.

I always visit this place while in Jackson County. There are other good shorebird viewing areas on the coast, but this has been the best for many kinds of shorebirds, and especially for finding dowitchers during most seasons. Unfortunately, industrial development is discouraging access and once attractive habitats are changed or destroyed.

In identifying the Long-billed Dowitcher in breeding plumage, look for a *dark tail* with *narrow* white or reddish barring, *heavy spotting on neck and breast, bars on sides,* and *entirely reddish* underparts. The bills of some birds will be twice the head length and exceedingly long.

The Long-billed Dowitcher breeds in northern Siberia, and across northern Alaska and northwest Canada. It migrates through the western and midwestern states to winter along the coasts of the southern states and coasts and interior parts of Mexico into Central America.

Common Snipe *Gallinago gallinago*

The Common Snipe, or "jacksnipe," is the only shorebird other than the American Woodcock that is legal game for hunting under the Migratory Bird Treaty Act. It is locally abundant in migration and as a winter resident from mid-October to mid-April. It frequents lake shores, marshes, wet meadowlands, bogs, or any small, conveniently flooded grassy area or ditch.

It has a knack for finding and hiding in even the smallest of boggy, wetland sites, where it blends with cover and usually escapes detection until accidentally flushed. The explosive flight; the rasping, *scape* alarm calls; zigzag movements on pointy wings; and orange banding on the short tail are certain recognition characteristics. This bird was called Wilson's Snipe in older field guides.

The Common Snipe is brownish and stocky with short, greenish legs and a long bill. Underparts are mostly white with distinct barring on the sides. The head, neck, breast, and back are alternately barred dark and rusty orange with white tips. Prominent, buff-colored stripes on the dark back are especially noticeable in flight.

The Common Snipe breeds over a wide range around marshland and bogs of our northern states and most of Canada and Alaska. The nest, like that of most shorebirds, is made of grass, leaves, or other plant materials. The usual four eggs and nest are naturally camouflaged and concealed by matching colors of the eggs, all blending with the surroundings. The nest may be in wet or dry sites, such as a grass tussock growing in a bog or on drier ground near a stream, marshy edge, or bog.

In Mississippi, the Common Snipe is not a popular game bird. Most hunters are reluctant to walk around in wet fields or marshland to hunt. Although at times they can offer some good concentrations to hunt, snipe often escape notice. As a boy, I hunted and killed a few of these birds by sneaking along lake shores and in boggy cropland and pastures. They were not very tasty for eating when compared with the plentiful supplies of Northern Bobwhite.

On its breeding grounds, the Common Snipe has a spectacular song flight. It ascends, circles, and descends while making low, winnowing sounds with its beating wings and spread outer-tail feathers. I have never seen this courtship behavior on the breeding grounds. However, on March 19, 1972, I observed a similar flight behavior by one of these birds. I was watching 10 Common Snipe resting and feeding among weed stems on the edge of a wet depression in a field beside the Satartia–Holly Bluff road. While watching the snipe with binoculars from the car, several snipe began chasing each other, and one bird was particularly aggressive, forcing the other two to take flight.

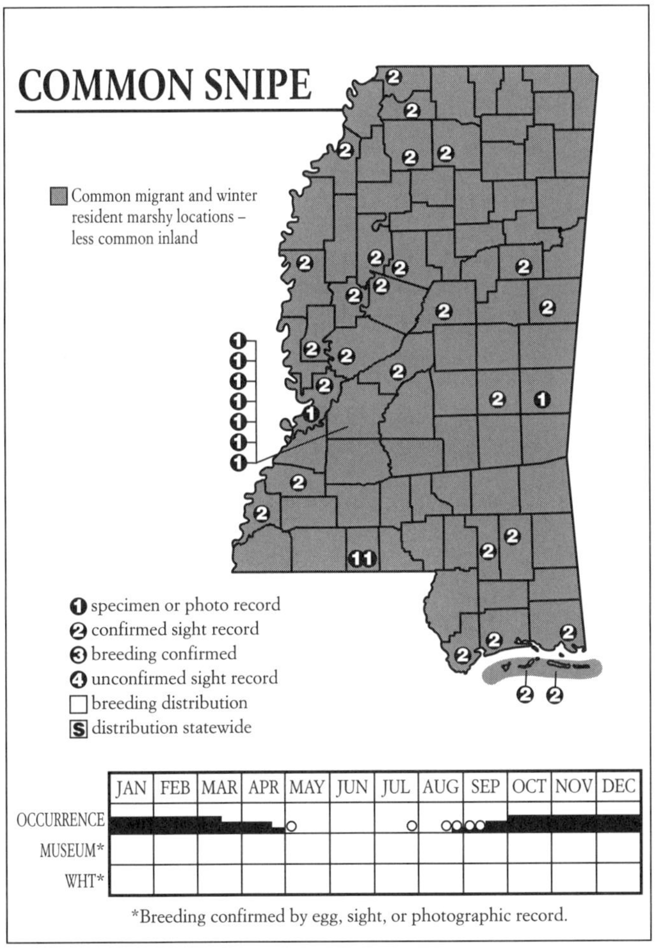

The aggressor then made an elliptical flight to about 100 feet into the air, and while returning downward, made strange, grating, chuckling sounds entirely different than the usual *scape* calls heard when these birds flush. When the snipe landed, it lowered its wings, fanned its tail, and strutted before once again repeating the flight performance. The actions of this bird appeared to be a territorial defense display rather than courtship behavior. The time of this episode was sunset when I noted that an American Golden-Plover had alighted in the field.

American Woodcock *Scolopax minor*

The American Woodcock is unique among shorebirds and, in my opinion, the most interesting. It is solitary and secretive by day, active in crepuscular light, and nocturnal in feeding and roosting. It frequents dense cover in thickets, briers, or brush heaps of moist woodlands by day. At twilight it seeks out open, marginal, wet pastureland or open ground of second-growth bottoms and uplands. There, it feeds and sleeps in the open at night before returning to thick woodland haunts at daybreak. While in migration and during courtship periods in late winter, it is very active at night and at times congregates in great numbers on nightly staging grounds.

In late January and February, resident breeding birds carry on spectacular courtship and song flight displays in the twilight of dusk and dawn. They usually nest on brushy uplands near bottomlands or the headwaters of upland streams in hill country.

The American Woodcock has been called by such names as "timberdoodle," "bogsucker," "woodsnipe," "swamp partridge," and "becasse," the last given by French-speaking people of southern Louisiana and the Gulf Coast. These colloquial names are descriptive of the habitat and habits associated with this bird and its long beak. I have spent more hours over the past 20 years in late January and February observing, tape recording, photographing, hunting, and helping to locate and band American Woodcock than any other outdoor activity.

Following World War II, I had observed the courtship antics of singing males on several of our state game management areas. In late winter, when the winged elm and red

Game birds such as the American Woodcock and Northern Bobwhite Quail are a favorite with biologist Benny Herring of Kilmichael. Woodcock inhabit wetland thickets along stream courses, especially near beaver ponds, springheads, and bayheads.

maple bloom and show pinkish brown or red color, I would watch and listen for birds making song flights after sundown. In the dim light before darkness, the male woodcock flies to his "singing ground." Upon his arrival, the light intensity was measurable on the lower scale of a light meter.

The site of a singing ground may be a small opening such as a log road, fence or power line right-of-way, a recently burned or cleared area, or a natural opening in brushy uplands, usually in the second-growth bottom along stream courses or near beaver ponds, bayheads, or spring seeps in uplands. As soon as the male descends for courtship display, he begins the nasal, nighthawklike *bzeep* call notes interspersed with a low, barely audible *tuk-oo* or *hic-cup* preceding each *peenting* call.

While on the ground, the bird's short neck is extended fully during the calling with the bill resting slightly downward. The bill is opened with each *peent.* The song flight or "sky dance" begins when the bird rises, first making a whistling sound with the wings. While ascending in a wide, counter-clockwise spiral, the flight song begins with soft twitterings. At its zenith of about 200 to 300 feet, while in butterfly-like flight, the twitterings become soft warblings.

The zigzag downward flight is punctuated by staccato *chip* notes as the bird descends to the ground, usually at or near his takeoff point. On moonlit nights, the song flights continue until dark or longer. Usually at least four or five will be made. If a female woodcock approaches, the male takes off in pursuit. On two occasions, copulation occurred after a female descended nearby, and the male flew immediately to her. A spotlight on singing males and females did not deter their actions.

The response of singing male woodcocks to a playback of their recorded calls is sometimes unbelievable. On several occasions, I took friends with me while recording or photographing woodcocks. The first occasion was with a visiting birder from Ohio. After visiting a colony of Red-cockaded Woodpeckers on the Natchez Trace in Madison County to watch these birds go to roost, I suggested we try watching the courtship display of a woodcock on the Pearl River Waterfowl Refuge.

I had located the singing ground the day before and recorded the time and light meter reading when the male flew down to the display ground on a road. We arrived at the spot and set up my recording equipment. Looking at my watch and light meter, I told my birding friend exactly when the woodcock would arrive. As it dropped down about 30 feet from us, I recorded its calls, and we watched it make several song flights. Then I played back the recording, and the bird walked toward us and stood about six feet away while I taped his *hic-cup* and *peent* calls. At other times, I have seen these birds become very agitated, make froglike croaking sounds, and approach within two feet of where I was standing playing back call notes.

On another occasion in Rankin County, with the aid of wildlife biologists Wendell Neal and Benny Herring, I made color movies of a singing male. We set up a 16-mm movie camera with a sealed-beam light bar. When the male woodcock flew in and made his first aerial flight, I put the tape player where the bird had taken flight and started a playback. The bird landed and went toward the recorder.

During the bird's second flight song, I moved the tape player under the camera tripod and switched on the bar lights as soon as he landed. We filmed the bird calling and walking toward the camera, and it finally walked under the legs of the tripod. The bird was netted and banded while I filmed its capture and release. We later filmed other night scenes of netting and banding of woodcocks on night feeding and roosting areas to complete a 10-minute movie.

The American Woodcock is a stocky, gray brown bird, about the size of a Northern Bobwhite or slightly larger, with buffy face and underparts, and a broadly barred crown. The bill is extremely long, and the wings and tail are short

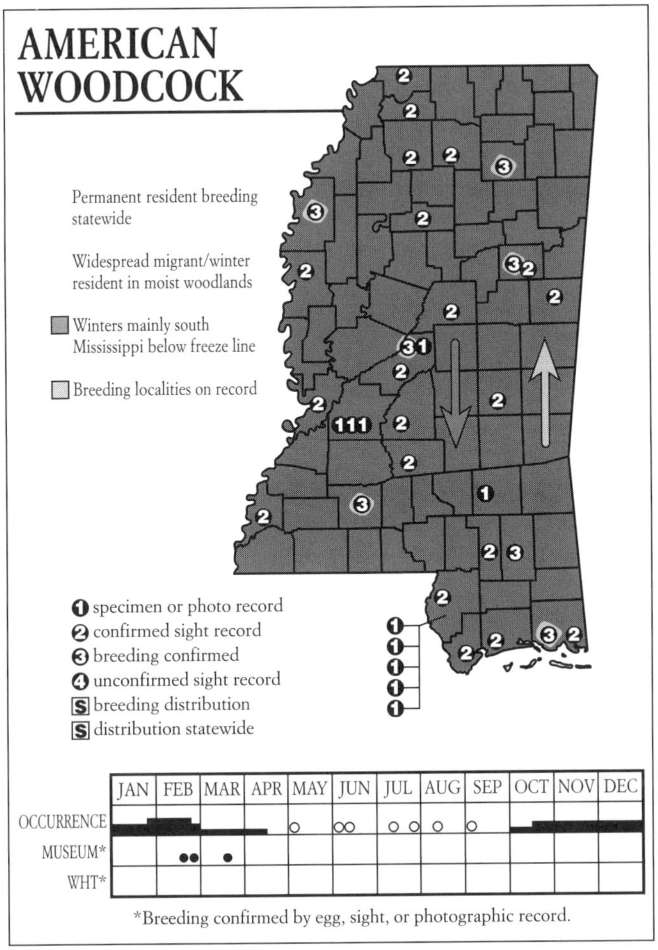

and rounded. The bird's large, bulging eyes are set high and far back on its large head. The ears are set forward and beneath the eyes. The upperparts are colored to perfectly blend with leafy ground cover.

The breeding range extends eastward from the Great Plains and northward to the lower portions of the Canadian provinces. In the Gulf states, the range extends from the coastal terrace of eastern Texas to the coasts of Georgia and extreme northern Florida. In Mississippi, it is a common fall migrant after late October and a fairly common, widely dispersed resident through milder winters. In late January and February, when northward migrations begin from wintering grounds in southern Louisiana, large waves or concentrations of these birds may appear and remain locally.

Concentrations of migrants have been detected by hunters and biologists while netting and banding woodcocks on roosting and feeding fields on successive nights. Permanent-resident breeding populations that remain may begin courtship activity in late December and January. Most nesting activity occurs in February or early March.

A woodcock nest is exceedingly hard to find. The birds sit tight on the eggs, and most nests are located by hunters or forest workers after accidentally flushing the sitting bird.

I have seen only two active nests, one near Flora in Madison County on February 22, 1971, that contained four eggs. The nest was among dead goldenrod stems in a young thicket of black locust sprouts at the edge of an open field near a small creek swamp. The other nest was found in early March on the Leaf River Refuge in Perry County by Phil Goodrum, a U.S. Fish and Wildlife Service biologist. This nest was on a grass tussock among cypress knees and sphagnum moss at the outer fringe of a bayhead in brushy hills. When first located, the nest held four eggs. When I was shown the nest a day or so later, the female flushed nearby, and the nest held four newly hatched young.

S. E. Moreton recorded finding a female with four young near Brookhaven in Lincoln County on February 25, 1958 (Turcotte 1958a). Nests with four eggs each were found in Oktibbeha County on February 25, 1972 (Hurst 1972) and in Bolivar County on March 3, 1961 (Coleman 1961). Noble (1971) reported three apparent flying juveniles seen by David Hayden on May 1, 1971, while searching for Sandhill Crane nests in a savanna five miles north of Ocean Springs in Jackson County.

Wilson's Phalarope

Phalaropodinae (Phalaropes)

These small, elegant, sandpiper-like shorebirds differ from other sandpipers in several ways. Females are more colorful and larger than males, they initiate courtship, and do not incubate eggs or care for chicks. Both sexes are equally at home while feeding at the shoreline, on open water, or at sea.

Phalaropes' soft, tight plumage makes them water resistant and buoyant. They swim like spinning tops *with partly lobed feet* that stir up minute marine organisms, which they pick out with needle-shaped bills. Two pelagic species are circumpolar and breed on the tundra of Arctic, sub-Arctic, or boreal regions.

The Wilson's Phalarope breeds around shallow prairie lakes and marshlands of southwestern Canada and midwestern and western states. Phalaropes frequent freshwater and saltwater marshes and grassy shorelines during migration. They winter mainly at sea, though their winter range is not well known. The Wilson's Phalarope is more inclined to shorelines. It winters primarily in South America and casually to the northern Gulf Coast.

Wilson's Phalarope *Phalaropus tricolor*

This dainty and rather tame little shorebird is the one of our three phalaropes most likely to occur in Mississippi. It nests inland on northern and western prairie ponds and marshy sloughs. In migration, it occurs on grassy shorelines of lakes, ponds, sewage lagoons, large reservoirs, and brackish or saltwater marshes.

It migrates mainly through western states and the Great Plains. In Mississippi, it occurs as an uncommon inland fall migrant from mid-August to late-September. On the coast, it is fairly common in fall migration, occurring locally on offshore islands and tidewater marshes. In spring migration during late April and May, it rarely occurs inland and usually is found in smaller numbers on the Gulf Coast. It has occurred rarely on the Mississippi Coast in summer and as an accidental winter visitor in January.

In basic plumage, the Wilson's Phalarope resembles the Stilt Sandpiper and Lesser Yellowlegs in that it is *gray* above and has *no wing stripes.* The Stilt Sandpiper has greenish legs, while the Wilson's Phalarope has creamy yellow or straw-colored legs. The Lesser Yellowlegs has barring on the breast, sides, and tail. This phalarope has no barring, is immaculate white below, and is uniformly light gray on the upperparts with no wing stripes.

The black, needle-shaped bill is longer than the head. The Red-necked Phalarope has a shorter bill, thicker and sometimes yellowish at the base in fall. In alternate plumage, the more colorful female is pale gray on the head and nape. The gray back has two lengthwise chestnut stripes, the upper one blending with a dark chestnut "phalarope patch" on the sides of the neck. The face and chin are white with a broad black stripe extending to and blending

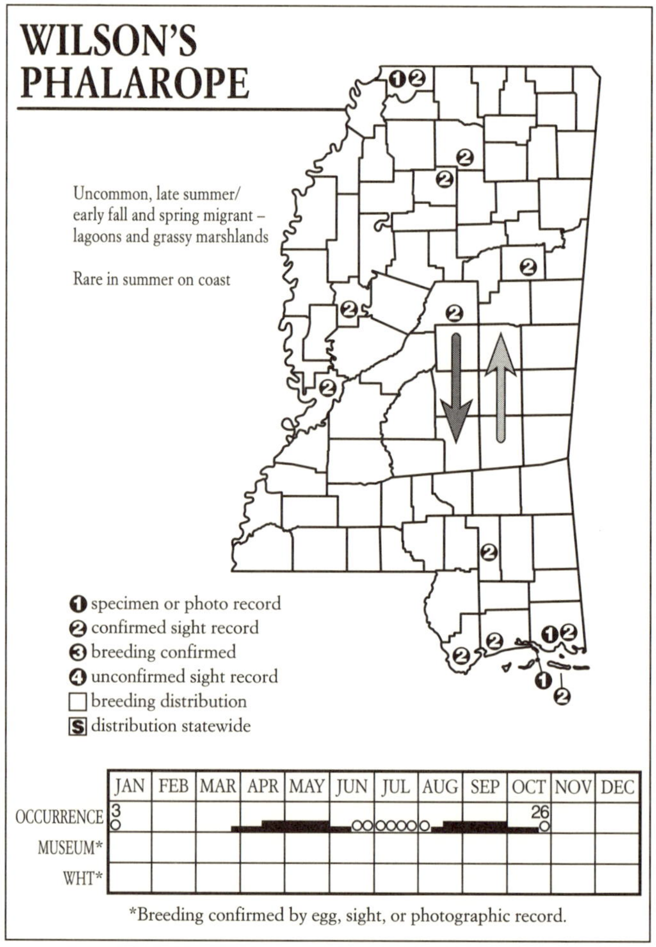

into chestnut and cinnamon on the neck and upper breast. The wings are gray above *without stripes* and blending in to darker gray on the outer secondaries and primaries. Males are much duller with only a slight wash of cinnamon on the sides of the neck and back and a small, white spot on the back of the head.

My first encounter with these birds was at Agassiz National Wildlife Refuge in northwestern Minnesota on June 15, 1985. They were feeding in a shallow rainpool with other shorebirds. On the Lostwood National Wildlife Refuge in North Dakota on June 19, I observed and photographed them in a small, grassy slough. They were very tame and busily feeding in the water and muddy shallows, dabbling after invisible foods among emergent aquatic plants. They allowed a close approach without alarm and only swam or flitted across the narrow slough when approached. We studied them at leisure, listening to their low, barely audible, gallinule-like calls.

Red-necked Phalarope *Phalaropus lobatus*

RED-NECKED PHALAROPE

Rare transient. Winters at sea.

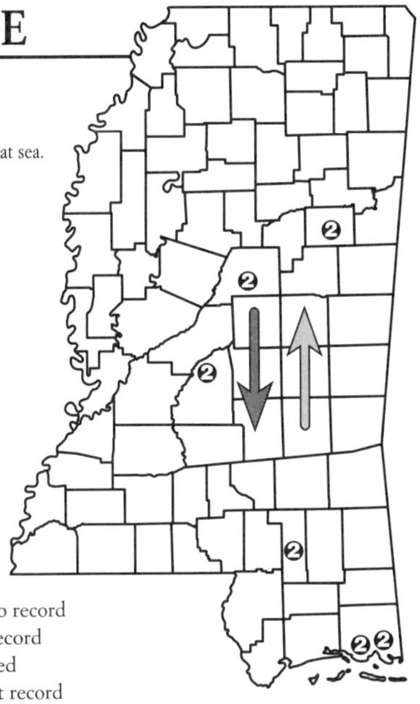

❶ specimen or photo record
❷ confirmed sight record
❸ breeding confirmed
❹ unconfirmed sight record
☐ breeding distribution
[S] distribution statewide

	JAN	FEB	MAR	APR	MAY	JUN	JUL	AUG	SEP	OCT	NOV	DEC
OCCURRENCE				26 ○	20 ○○○	6-7 ○			5 21 ○○○○			
MUSEUM*												
WHT*												

*Breeding confirmed by egg, sight, or photographic record.

This mainly pelagic species was formerly named Northern Phalarope. The first two state records occurred inland and almost simultaneously. Sanders (1976) reported the first sighting of an individual on the Kosciusko sewage lagoons after detailed studies and observations with Ray Weeks. The very tame bird was in basic plumage and allowed close study with a telescope on September 11, 12, and 13, 1976.

A second record of this bird by Gates (1976) occurred at the Hattiesburg sewage lagoons on September 21, 1976. This bird, in basic plumage, was carefully studied in good light with a telescope, and all details were noted in the company of Terrie Fairley.

The first record on the coast with all supporting details was a sighting of an individual by Judith A. Toups, Kim R. Eckert, and Robert P. Russell on September 10, 1977, at the Pascagoula River marsh in Jackson County (Weber and Jackson 1978). Three additional fall sightings (September 5–11), two spring sightings (April 26–May 20), and a June 6–7, 1978, sighting confirmed by a photograph by Peter Donaldson have occurred on the Mississippi Coast (Toups et al. 1979).

This species is more common than the Red Phalarope and occurs more frequently inland. The Red-necked Phalarope breeds on the tundra of northern boreal regions and is circumpolar in distribution. It winters at sea to the Southern Hemisphere. In migration, it occurs mainly on lakes, ponds, bays, seashores, tidewater pools, and estuary marshes.

In basic plumage this species can be identified by a dark patch through the eye, thinner bill, *strongly streaked back*, and whirligig feeding behavior (spinning around while feeding on water). The *dark crown*, dark patch through the eye, and strongly *streaked back* are distinctive field marks. The other two species of phalaropes have plain gray unstreaked backs in basic plumage.

In full alternate plumage, the brightly colored female has a gray head, a white chin and eye ring, and a dark gray back with buff stripes along the sides. A chestnut patch on the *front and sides* of the neck is distinctive on the female. The male in breeding plumage is browner and duller, but otherwise similar. The thin bill is intermediate in length, shorter than the Wilson's Phalarope, and thinner than the Red Phalarope.

[Red Phalarope] *Phalaropus fulicaria*

My first and only experience with this rare transient lasted only a few fleeting moments. I was standing on the stern of the Gulf Coast Research Laboratory vessel, *Hermes*, with other MOS members. Returning from a field trip to Freemason Island, Louisiana, on June 1, 1957, we were in Chandeleur Sound with no land in sight when I saw two Red Phalaropes in alternate plumage not more than 30 yards to my right. I watched them with binoculars showing their brick red underparts and white faces as they bobbed high on the shallow waves until they disappeared from sight into the waves and wake of our boat. I knew immediately that I had seen phalaropes, and they had to be the Red Phalarope.

The first state record of this species was on October 9, 1977, by Gates and Runzo (1978) at Hattiesburg in Forrest County. The bird appeared on a sewage lagoon pond following a heavy rain. It was in basic plumage, and the following field marks were noted after close-up observation and study: relative fearlessness; white below; uniformly gray back; a darker line marking the back edge of the folded wing; no streaking on the back; a gray stripe on back of the neck diverging and forming a Y-shape on the top, back portion of the head, giving the head a bald look; a distinct "phalarope mark" through the eye; and a bill shorter than the head and thicker at the base with a slight yellow coloring at the base.

The first coastal record of a Red Phalarope was made in Mississippi Sound about eight kilometers south of Biloxi on September 30, 1978, by C. Dwight Cooley (Purrington 1979).

A second inland record for this species, substantiated by a closeup photograph showing all details, occurred between

Sand spits, spoil banks, and beach areas along the Gulf Coast are favorite gathering places for shorebirds such as these Willets.

October 12 and 15, 1980. Richard Moore, Terrie Fairley, David Hamilton, and Pedro Rodriguez observed this individual on the Hattiesburg sewage lagoons over a period of four days (Moore et al. 1981). Another record of a single Red Phalarope was recorded by Larry and Terrie Gates at the Hattiesburg sewage lagoons on September 21 and 22, 1983 (Schardien and Jackson 1983). It is ironic that more inland sightings have been made of this rare, pelagic species than on the coast.

The first northern Mississippi record, a single bird in basic plumage, was seen on October 13, 1984, on a flooded bottomland field in Panola County and reported by Davis (1985).

There are no state coastal or inland spring records for this species. The return migration to northern breeding grounds apparently follows routes across the open sea. Lowery Jr. (1974) did not report spring records for Louisiana. This phalarope is known to winter far out on the open Gulf off the coast of the Florida Panhandle and southern Alabama.

The field marks of the Red Phalarope in basic plumage are mentioned above. In alternate plumage, the female has chestnut red underparts, a black crown, and a white face. The breeding male is smaller and duller with similar marks. Both adults in alternate and basic plumages have shorter and thicker bills than other phalaropes. Bills are yellow with a black tip in breeding adults and dark in winter adults and juveniles.

RED PHALAROPE

Rare transient. Winters open sea.

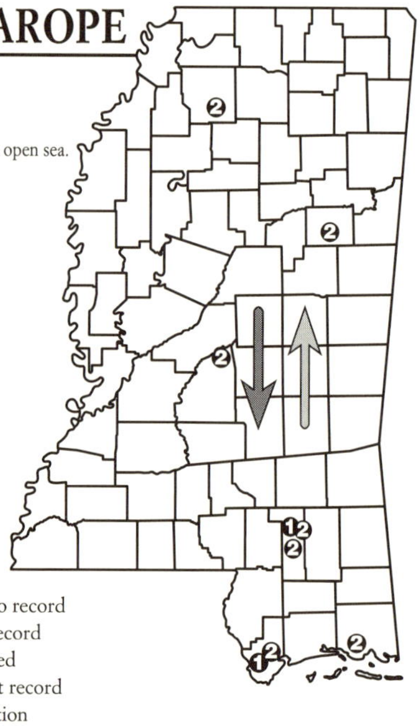

❶ specimen or photo record
❷ confirmed sight record
❸ breeding confirmed
❹ unconfirmed sight record
☐ breeding distribution
🄰 distribution statewide

	JAN	FEB	MAR	APR	MAY	JUN	JUL	AUG	SEP	OCT	NOV	DEC
OCCURRENCE									21 ∞	18 ∞		
MUSEUM*												
WHT*												

*Breeding confirmed by egg, sight, or photographic record.

Laughing Gulls

Laridae (Jaegers, Gulls, Terns, and Skimmers Account)

This large family includes four subfamilies: Stercorariinae (jaegers and skuas), Larinae (gulls), Sterninae (terns), and Rynchopinae (skimmers). Twenty-seven species, including two jaegers, 15 gulls, 12 terns, and one skimmer species, have been recorded on coastal or inland waters of Mississippi.

The birds in this family have long, pointed wings and are capable of superb flight. The bend of the wing is carried upward and forward in "gull-winged" flight. They have stout bills suited to the manner of feeding. Jaegers, skuas, and gulls have hooked bills used for killing or tearing food. Terns and skimmers have straight, pointed bills used in diving or skimming the water to capture food.

Most species in this family are either highly pelagic or frequent seashores. Some frequent inland lake shores and marshes during migration and breeding. One gull species, six terns, and the Black Skimmer breed on the Mississippi mainland or on the barrier islands.

Parasitic Jaeger

Stercorariinae (Jaegers and Skuas)

Jaegers and skuas are piratical, oceanic birds that come inland only to nest on Arctic tundra. They are strong fliers with wings more pointed at the tips than the gulls. They have strongly hooked beaks, and prey on gulls, terns, and other waterbirds and shorebirds, robbing nests of eggs and young. These species chase gulls and terns, forcing them to disgorge food. They rest and roost on the open ocean.

Jaegers and skuas vary greatly in plumage with dark, light, and intermediate color phases. Both have wedge-shaped tails. The tails of adult jaegers have two elongated central tail feathers, which are longer than the lateral ones. The relative size and shape of the tail points help in identification.

Skuas have slightly wedge-shaped tails but do not have elongated central tail feathers. Skuas are large, about the size of Herring Gulls, with wider wings that are less pointed at the tips than the jaegers. Their large, stocky size; dark brown color; rusty underparts; and *conspicuous, white wing patches* on the primaries identify skuas. All members of this subfamily show a flash of white in the primaries of their otherwise dark wings.

[Pomarine Jaeger] *Stercorarius pomarinus*

The word jaeger ('ya-ger) is derived from the German word *jager,* meaning "hunter." In World War II, our bomber crews encountered Jagers, fighter pursuit squadrons of Messerschmidt 109s, FW 190s, or twin-engine ME-210s, lobbing salvos of rockets at bomb group formations from the rear, or finishing off lone stragglers with 20-mm cannon fire.

Jaegers, relentless in their pursuit of feeding gulls and terns, will attack a hapless bird until it drops or disgorges its prey. Also, they prey upon the eggs and young of nesting

POMARINE JAEGER

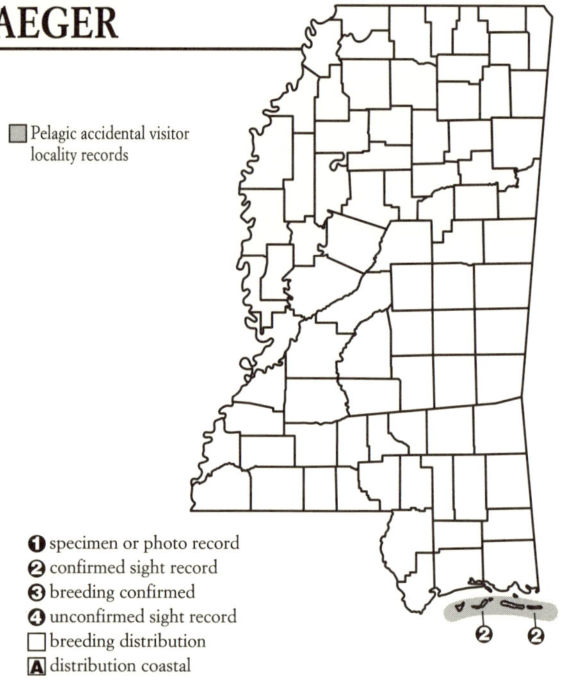

	JAN	FEB	MAR	APR	MAY	JUN	JUL	AUG	SEP	OCT	NOV	DEC
OCCURRENCE							16 ○				10 ○	
MUSEUM*												
WHT*												

*Breeding confirmed by egg, sight, or photographic record.

birds. The three species of jaegers, circumpolar in distribution, breed on Arctic tundra and spend the fall and winter on the open oceans and southward along our coasts to southern South America.

Pomarine and Long-tailed Jaegers occur only as accidental visitors to the open waters of the Gulf of Mexico. The Parasitic Jaeger winters in offshore waters of the Gulf of Mexico. It occurs annually on waters of Mississippi Sound but seldom appears near the mainland except when driven by storms. The occurrence and distribution of jaegers in these waters is poorly known and needs further study by offshore birders.

The plumage of jaegers is varied and occurs in three color morphs: dark, intermediate, and light. All three show white at the base of the primaries in all plumages. White quills of the dark primary wing feathers produce this effect. The Pomarine Jaeger has the greatest white showing and is the largest of the three, almost as large as the Herring Gull.

The elongated, *twisted,* central tail feathers of adults are quite noticeable. They twist from normal horizontal to a vertical plane and are *rounded* at the ends. The Parasitic Jaeger, the size of the Laughing Gull, has a bill half the size of the Pomarine, and the central tail feathers are *pointed* and extend to slightly more than three inches. The wings have less white in the primaries than the Pomarine. The Long-tailed Jaeger has the central tail streamers extending *six* to *nine inches* on breeding adults. Identification of immatures without the identifying tail features is extremely difficult under most field conditions. The extent of *white on more than five* of the outer primary wing feathers *should be* diagnostic for the Pomarine Jaeger.

On the basis of current records, the Pomarine Jaeger occurs as an accidental on the Mississippi Coast. The Long-tailed Jaeger has not been identified on the Mississippi Coast, but probably occurs in open Gulf waters in migration or winter periods. A specimen collected on April 24, 1965, reported by Lowery Jr. (1974) confirmed the appearance of the Long-tailed Jaeger in Louisiana waters.

Identification of immature jaegers is difficult and risky even with field guides and reference material at hand. Unless *all* field marks can be observed and noted, a doubtful jaeger sighting should be recorded simply as *Stercorarius.*

Lovett E. Williams Jr. and others observed two subadult Pomarine Jaegers on July 16, 1964, about five miles from the Ship Island Lighthouse (Stewart 1964). Another sight record of two birds observed by Thomas A. Imhof (Toups and Jackson 1987) occurred on November 10, 1974, in Mississippi waters just west of the Alabama-Mississippi line. Both records were made by observers with prior experience in sighting or collecting specimens of jaegers in offshore waters.

All three species of jaegers nest on the tundra of Arctic shores and islands. The nest is shallow; sparsely lined with moss, leaves, or grasses; and usually found in marshy places or nearby on dry rocky tundra. Usually two eggs are laid. They are greenish brown, ovate in shape, and marked with various shades of black and brown blotches. On the breeding grounds they prey upon eggs and young of birds, lemmings, and large insects, or feed on refuse or offal.

Parasitic Jaeger *Stercorarius parasiticus*

The first Mississippi specimen of a Parasitic Jaeger was taken by Williams Jr. (1962c) near Horn Island on February 26, 1961. On February 24, 1962, Williams Jr. and Clawson (1963) observed five Parasitic Jaegers attacking terns going to roost on spoil banks offshore from Pascagoula. Two light-phase immature females were collected. These two specimens and one collected earlier by Williams Jr. are deposited in the MMNS.

In 1961 and 1962, Williams Jr. and Clawson spent considerable time on the Mississippi Coast observing and collecting pelagic birds and later banding and color-marking nesting gulls and terns. They made frequent trips offshore to observe and collect specimens of seabirds. While on Coast Guard vessels, Williams Jr. observed Wilson's Storm Petrel, Audubon's Shearwater, Brown Booby, Masked Booby, Brown Noddy, and Bridled and Sooty Terns in offshore Texas waters (Turcotte 1961d). In the summer of 1961, he recorded no less than 30 Parasitic and Pomarine Jaegers within 20 miles of shore off the Texas and Louisiana shorelines. His observations and experiences in Texas waters emphasized the need for further study of pelagic birds along the coast.

Since 1970 jaeger sightings have increased due to a greater number of experienced observers visiting mainland shores and barrier islands of Mississippi Sound. Sightings of jaegers can be expected during storms offshore. Along mainland vantage points, six or more sight records have occurred (Toups and Hodges 1985).

Since 1974 the Parasitic Jaeger has been seen annually from August to May 6, either on Mississippi Sound or along shorelines of the three coastal counties. Mainland sightings have occurred in inclement weather and also in weather not associated with offshore storms. Field marks of the Parasitic Jaeger are described in the preceding species account of the Pomarine Jaeger.

PARASITIC JAEGER

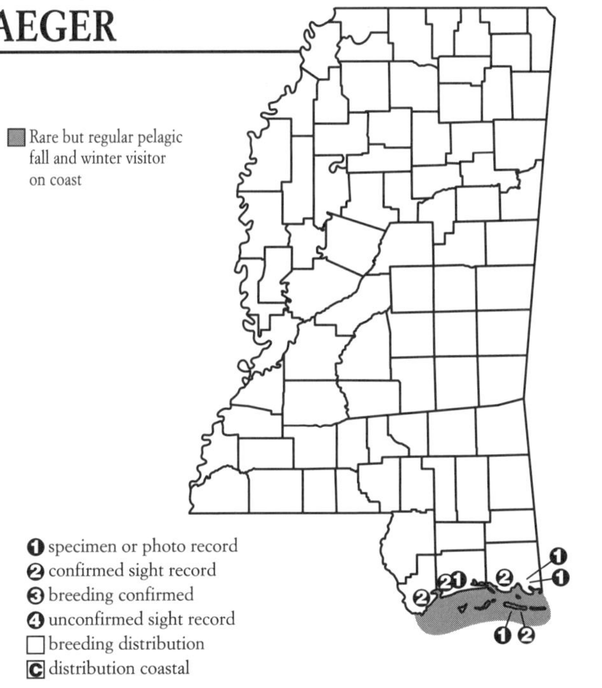

	JAN	FEB	MAR	APR	MAY	JUN	JUL	AUG	SEP	OCT	NOV	DEC
OCCURRENCE	oooo	oooo	oooo	oooo	6 o			26 o	oooo	oooo	oooo	oooo
MUSEUM*												
WHT*												

*Breeding confirmed by egg, sight, or photographic record.

Laughing Gull

Larinae (Gulls)

Gulls are often called "seagulls," but many species nest inland on northern lake shores and marshes. They are omnivorous scavengers and feed upon the water for marine organisms, plant and animal life, garbage, and carrion. Gulls are distributed worldwide. Their flight is superb on long wings, which are wider and less pointed than terns.

Gulls have longer legs and more robust bodies than terns. Their feet are webbed, and their bills are slightly hooked. Some species have distinctive bill markings or color spots. They are good swimmers, but usually do not hover and dive for prey like terns. Gulls have rounded or square tails, rarely notched or wedge shaped.

Most tern species have forked tails and long, pointed bills. Gulls nest in isolated colonies along seashores, on remote islands, sea cliffs, and inland marshes or lake shores. They usually build substantial nests of grasses, seaweed, or flotsam, and lay two or three gray, greenish, or brownish eggs, variously spotted or scrawled with shades of brown and black.

Only one species, the Laughing Gull, is known to breed on the Mississippi Coast. Twelve species have occurred in Mississippi. Gulls require two, three, or four years to attain their first full breeding plumage. Identification of immatures in various stages of plumage development is a special challenge—and sometimes impossible—for most birders.

Laughing Gull *Larus atricilla*

This small, *hooded,* coastal gull is an abundant permanent resident on the coast and occasionally occurs inland on large water bodies. Sometimes following the passage of tropical hurricanes, this species has been forced inland in numbers into parts of southern Mississippi along with other gulls, terns, and skimmers.

This coastal gull has occurred in northern Mississippi mainly in spring from April 15 to May 15 (Davis 1986b).

This nest and eggs of the Laughing Gull were photographed along the Mississippi coast.

Davis reported nine spring sightings of one to three individuals at Sardis and Enid reservoirs. An anomalous record on January 29, 1983, occurred at Grenada Reservoir, where two were sighted by Davis among a flock of Ring-billed and Bonaparte's Gulls resting on the water. These sightings occurred in five of eight years of observation.

Three years are required for the Laughing Gull to attain adult breeding plumage with the black hood. The adult has dark, slate gray wings that blend with its black outer primaries. In alternate plumage, the underparts, neck below the hood, and tail are white. The bill and mouth are carmine red in summer. Winter adults and immatures have *black* or *blackish* bills. The head of the adult changes to white in winter with a wash of light gray extending behind the eye and on the nape.

First-winter birds have dark heads and sides, a white rump, and a dark, complete, subterminal tail band. Second-winter birds have a gray wash on the sides of the breast and on the nape to the back. Juveniles are browner on the head and body than first-winter birds. Laughing Gulls in all plumages have a white border on the trailing edge of their wings.

Laughing Gulls nest in large colonies on the Chandeleur Islands and mud lumps around the mouth of the Mississippi River in Louisiana. The Chandeleurs are about 30 miles due south of Biloxi. These islands are made up of sand and shells, and contain marshes, mangrove thickets, mud flats, dunes, beaches, and higher ground vegetated with grasses, vines, groundsel bush, and other woody growth.

On May 26, 1938, I visited Freemason Island in Chandeleur Sound and found a large colony of these gulls nesting in prickly pear clumps and under bushes. The nests were poorly constructed of grass, twigs, and trashy materials, and contained mostly fresh eggs in sets of two or three. Most were greenish gray or olive marked with brown and black spots. Several sets of eggs were taken for the MMNS.

In 1961, John Walther, refuge manager at Gulf Islands National Wildlife Refuge, reported to Lovett E. Williams Jr. a large colony of Laughing Gulls and terns nesting on Petit Bois Island. On June 24, Sterling G. Clawson, Robert W. Skinner, and Williams Jr. visited the western end of the island and found the birds nesting over 50 acres that contained approximately 3000 pairs with eggs and young.

Return visits to band young gulls and terns were made on June 30 and July 18. Several eggs were collected on June 30 and deposited in the MMNS to authenticate a first state breeding record for this bird. Henry D. Haberyan and John Walther accompanied Williams Jr. and Clawson on the June 30 visit. On the last visit on July 18, flying ju-

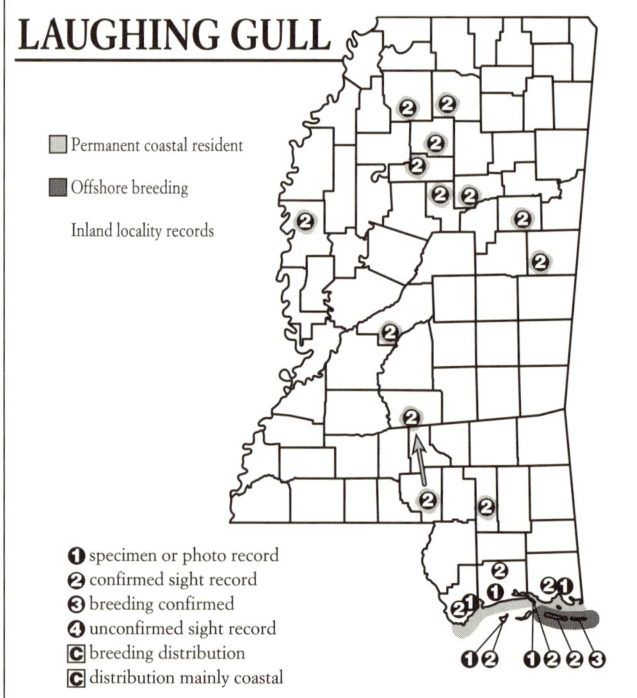

	JAN	FEB	MAR	APR	MAY	JUN	JUL	AUG	SEP	OCT	NOV	DEC
OCCURRENCE	■	■	■	■	■	■	■	■	■	■	■	■
MUSEUM*						24 ●	18 ●					
WHT*												

*Breeding confirmed by egg, sight, or photographic record.

veniles and many nests with fresh eggs were found. Sporadic nesting of Laughing Gulls on Petit Bois and Horn Islands was recorded by Portnoy (1977) between 1962 and 1968. Recent nesting on Mississippi barrier islands has not been confirmed.

Laughing Gulls are common along the beaches, bays, and barrier islands of Mississippi Sound. They follow fishing boats in the sound and often congregate in large flocks. Along beaches they usually respond to feeding and can be observed close at hand or with other species of gulls for comparison. During the summer, numbers diminish along the mainland while nesting is in progress offshore.

The loud call gives this gull its name, a series of staccato *ha-ha-ha-ha* notes followed by louder, longer, ascending-descending *haah-haah-haah* calls. The feeding calls are lower, chuckling *ha-ha* notes. Laughing Gulls are quick to prey on unprotected eggs of terns and other seabirds. For this reason, it is unwise to disturb colonial nesting birds while nests contain eggs or small young.

Franklin's Gull *Larus pipixcan*

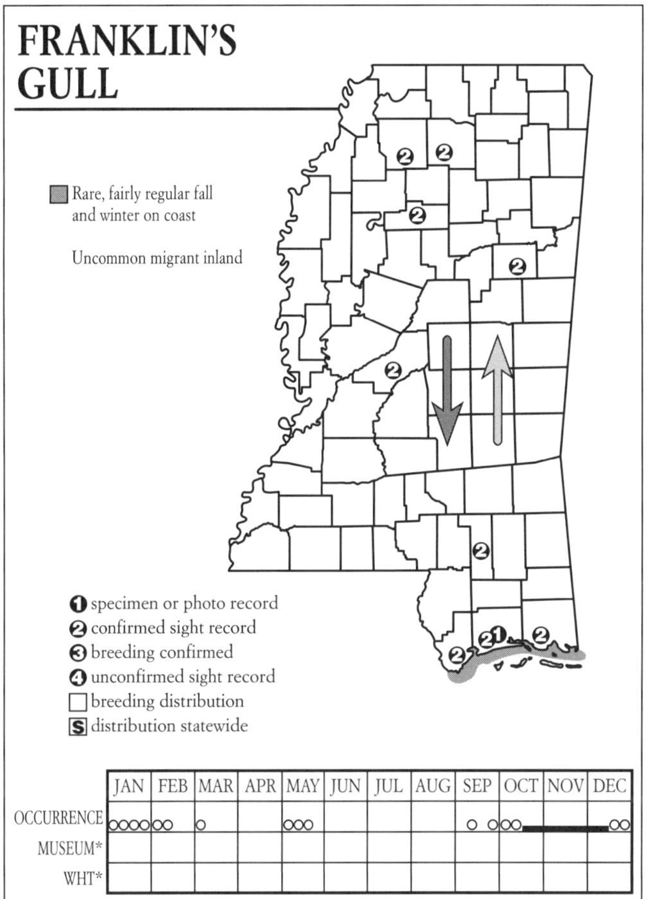

*Breeding confirmed by egg, sight, or photographic record.

At first glance, this two-year gull is similar to our common Laughing Gull, especially in basic plumage. Both species are hooded in alternate plumage. The Franklin's Gull is noticeably petite and has a *much smaller head and bill.* The distinctive difference in breeding adults is a *white band* separating the gray upperwing from the *black primaries.* In basic plumage, the Franklin's Gull is best distinguished by the smaller head and bill, *darker cheeks,* and *more extensive hooded effect* than the winter Laughing Gull.

Immature Franklin's Gulls are so nearly like first-winter Laughing Gulls that only close, direct comparison of head and bill size may disclose the difference. First-winter Franklin's Gulls have white heads and whiter tails than Laughing Gulls. The outermost tail feathers of the first-winter Franklin's are *all white* or very faintly marked gray or black on the inner web at the tip of the tail. On the first-winter Laughing Gull, the black tail band extends *across* the tip of the outermost feathers.

This gull breeds on northern prairie marshes and migrates southward mainly across the Great Plains and Texas Coast. It is a common breeding gull of prairie farmlands of the middle United States and northward. A large colony of these gulls was seen nesting on marshes of the Agassiz National Wildlife Refuge, Minnesota, on June 14 and 15, 1985. For miles around the refuge, they were feeding over open fields and following the plows behind tractors, feeding on insects and invertebrates.

We stopped at one field to photograph and admire these beautiful and graceful "prairie doves" as they followed behind the plows at every turn around the field. The nearby nesting colony on the refuge was inaccessible for a closer view. As we watched countless numbers of birds coming and going to and from their nests, we heard their distinctive cries from the nesting grounds, located among reeds in the shallow parts of impounded wetlands.

The Franklin's Gull is a regular but uncommon migrant inland and on the coast from mid-October to late December. It has occurred on the coast and inland from May 4 to May 27. The first state specimen record of the Franklin's Gull was a juvenile taken at Gulfport harbor on December 24, 1961, by Lovett E. Williams Jr. (Gandy and Turcotte 1970). Early winter records occurred on November 27, 1972, at Sardis Lake by W. M. Davis, and December 31, 1976, at Hattiesburg by Larry Gates and John Izral (Weber 1977). February 11 and May 11 sightings on the Gulf Coast are exceptional dates. Two adults in alternate plumage were seen on the lake below Sardis Dam, Panola County on May 4 and 5, 1983, by Davis (1986b).

Franklin's Gulls winter south of the United States and rarely winter on the Gulf Coast. Hodges Jr. and Toups (1981) observed a flock of 22 adults in basic plumage at Bay St. Louis on November 10, 1980. An adult in alternate plumage was seen by Downey et al. (1981) on December 19 and 20, 1981, on Ross Barnett Reservoir among several hundred Bonaparte's and other gulls. The bird's head was black with a white eye ring and cherry red bill. Distinguishing white bands separating the gray from the black on the wings and other details were noted.

[Little Gull] *Larus minutus*

The Little Gull has been recorded on Sardis and Grenada Lakes in Panola and Grenada Counties. The first Mississippi sight record occurred on March 15, 1970, at the Lower Lake below Sardis Lake dam. This adult bird was collected by W. Marvin Davis with Y. J. McGaha on March 16 and is in the Vaiden Collection at the University of Mississippi (Davis 1971b). The first and two later sightings by Davis (1976), an adult on January 3 and 4 and an immature on February 5, 1978, occurred at the same location. A fourth record by Davis was on the Grenada Lake outlet channel on January 7, 1984. A fifth sighting by Davis and Gene Knight (Muth 1985) was on the Grenada Christmas Bird Count on December 19, 1984, at the same location. The latter two sightings were single birds in first-winter plumage. These records were made while Little Gulls were mingling with Bonaparte's Gulls. Single adults were seen at Grenada Lake by Gene Knight on January 15 and February 15 and 16, 1991, and confirmed by a photograph taken by Jeffrey Wilson on February 16.

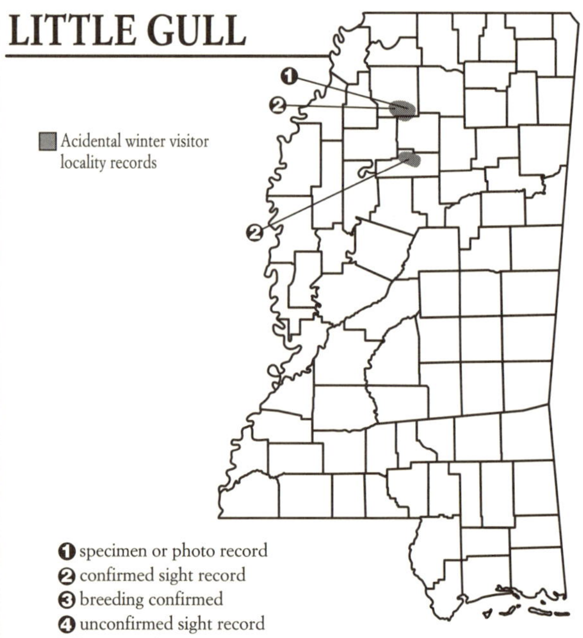

❶ specimen or photo record
❷ confirmed sight record
❸ breeding confirmed
❹ unconfirmed sight record
☐ breeding distribution
[A] distribution local, usually with Bonaparte's

	JAN	FEB	MAR	APR	MAY	JUN	JUL	AUG	SEP	OCT	NOV	DEC
OCCURRENCE	o	o	o									o
MUSEUM*												
WHT*												

*Breeding confirmed by egg, sight, or photographic record.

This two-year gull is the smallest of our gulls and distinguishable by size when seen in association with Bonaparte's Gull. In winter dress, adults have dark underwings, white tail and underparts, gray mantle, a neat *dark cap* (absent on Bonaparte's), and *rounded wings*. First-winter birds have black M-shaped marks from the mantle to the outer primaries, a white tail with narrow black band, white underparts, and the neat dark cap. The dusky cap is the most easily discernable field mark for adults and immatures in basic plumage. In alternate plumage, adults have a black hood, an indistinct eye ring, dark red bill, red legs, and a pink tinge on the breast.

The Little Gull is an Old World species and has been recorded nesting on the Great Lakes. It is an uncommon but regular migrant and winter visitor to the Great Lakes and along the East Coast. It is casual elsewhere in the United States and usually occurs in association with the Bonaparte's Gull.

[Common Black-headed Gull] *Larus ridibundus*

This gull, slightly larger than the Bonaparte's Gull with which it is often seen, has a dark *red bill,* red legs, *brown* hood, and *blackish undersides of the primaries* in summer alternate plumage. First-winter birds have a yellowish ochre, *black-tipped bill; dusky undersides* of the primaries; and are noticeably larger when seen with Bonaparte's Gulls. In basic plumage, adults and immatures have white heads, black ear spots, white outer primaries, and a gray mantle. The mantle of the Bonaparte's Gull is a bit darker gray than this species.

The first two Mississippi sight records of the Black-headed Gull were made by W. Marvin Davis at Grenada Lake on December 20, 1972, and on January 9, 1986. The first sighting occurred during the Grenada Lake Christmas Bird Count (Davis 1973). One adult and an immature identified by Davis were seen later that day by Lula and Ben B. Coffey Jr. who concurred in the identification. The second sighting by Davis was a single adult observed for about four minutes over the Grenada Lake outlet channel among about 70 Bonaparte's Gulls (Davis 1986a). Judith A. Toups identified a Black-headed Gull at the Grenada Lake dam in January 1987 for a third state record at that location.

Another locality record on January 12, 1991, on Pickwick Lake in Tishomingo County was a single bird sighted by Jeffrey R. Wilson among several hundred Bonaparte's Gulls and confirmed by Gene Knight, who was able to discern the dark outer one-third of the underwing, a trait differentiating the Black-headed from the Bonaparte's Gull (Davis et al. 1991).

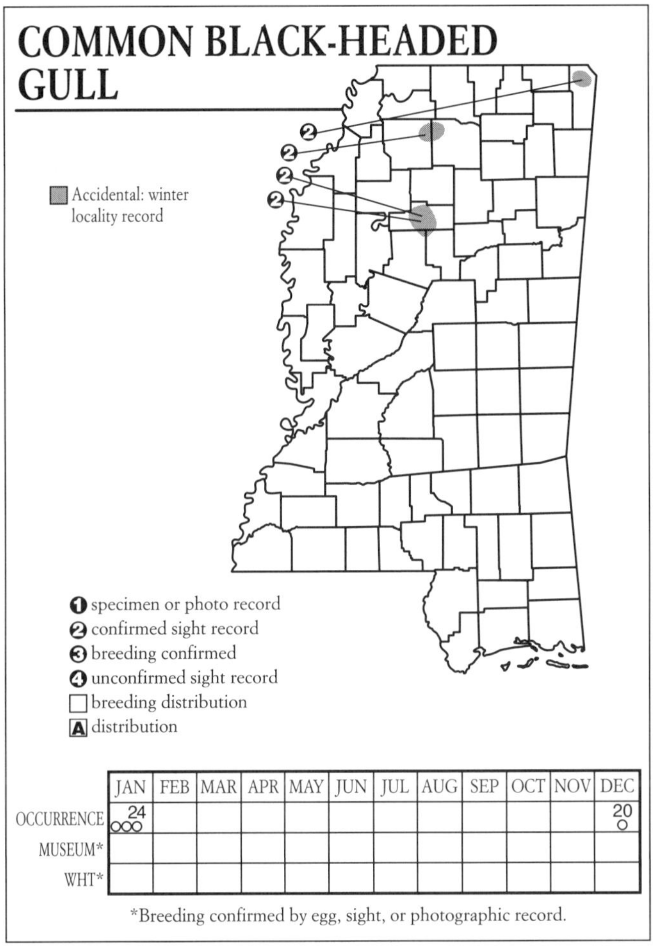

A third locality record of an adult Black-headed Gull at the outlet channel of Sardis Lake dam was confirmed by a photograph by W. Marvin Davis on January 18, 1991. The bird was seen again by Gene Knight on January 24 at the same location (Davis et al. 1991).

The Black-headed Gull is native to Eurasia and Iceland. In recent years, it has appeared increasingly along the northeastern Atlantic Coast. It is a casual winter visitor in the interior of the United States. It has been a casual breeding gull in Newfoundland. This rare, small gull usually occurs here from early December to late March in association with the more common Bonaparte's Gull.

Bonaparte's Gull *Larus philadelphia*

Bonaparte's Gull is the smallest and easiest to recognize of our three common, migrant, and winter-resident gulls. It is almost like a tern in flight, buoyant and with bill pointed downward. The winter adult has a gray mantle, white tail and underparts, red legs, black bill, and white head with roundish *black ear spots*. The underwings are white with black tips.

In flight the upperside of the wing shows a wide, white wedge from the wrist to the black tips of the primaries. First-winter birds have a narrow, black tail band, a black ear spot, a dark brown bar at the leading edge and a dark band at the trailing edge of the wings. In flight, the outer primaries show a black-and-white pattern bordering the gray on top of the wing.

It should be noted that the dark ear spot alone is not diagnostic for this species. The Black-headed Gull, Little Gull, and Black-legged Kittiwake in basic plumage have similar spots. Careful attention should be given to all plumage details when viewing our small gulls in basic plumage. The rarer species often accompany Bonaparte's Gulls.

This species is a regular, common migrant and winter resident on the coast from mid-October to late May. It is a regular migrant on large inland lakes and reservoirs. During most winters, it is not uncommon to find Bonaparte's Gulls on inland reservoirs and at their outlet channels. On the beaches, bays, estuaries, and offshore waters of Mississippi Sound, they are common in winter. They usually depart in basic plumage. Adults in alternate plumage with the black hood are rarely seen in this area.

These gulls nest in north-central Canada and Alaska on marsh and muskeg. Their chattering calls are somewhat like those of terns. I have watched and listened to them while a

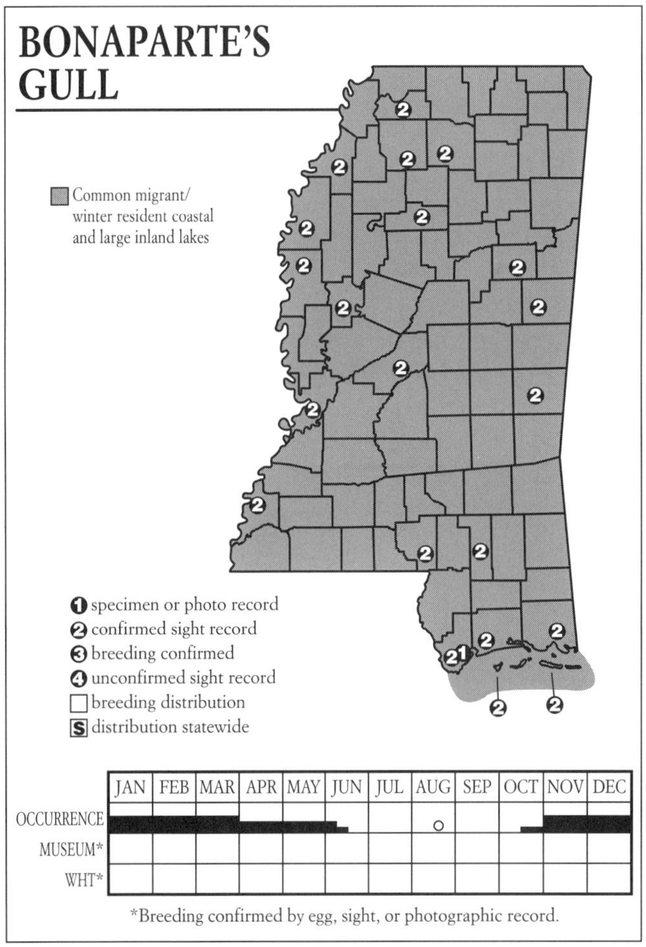

flock was feeding at Gulfport Harbor. At the same time, 30 or more Horned Grebes were feeding on a school of small fish. A dozen or more gulls hovered around and above the feeding grebes when they surfaced, and fed on fish that surfaced or were stolen from a grebe. Other gulls sat on the water or swam around among the feeding grebes, which spent more time underwater than on the surface. This species also feeds on small fishes by diving headlong into the water after hovering in flight over its prey. It sometimes completely submerges during the plunge in pursuit of its prey.

Ring-billed Gull *Larus delawarensis*

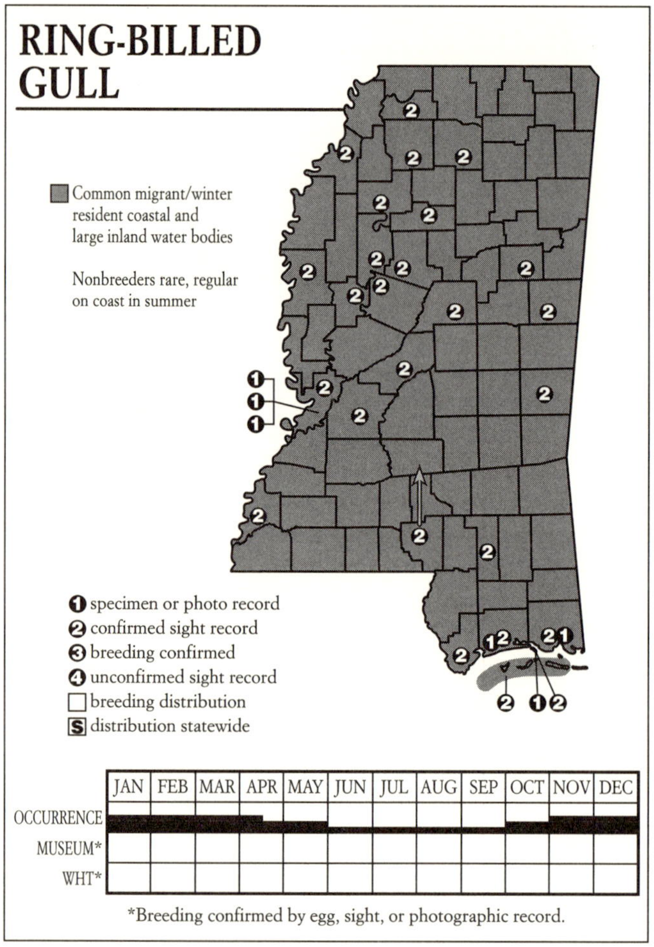

This species is the most common of our winter-resident gulls from October to May on inland lakes, rivers, and reservoirs. At times in winter, it may be fairly common to uncommon on inland waters. On the coast in fall and winter, it is regularly common to abundant. A ubiquitous species on the coast, the Ring-billed Gull gathers in flocks on beaches, piers, and vacant areas with other gulls and shorebirds. It frequents commercial areas, parking lots, and dumps to feed on refuse or handouts. Nonbreeding birds are regular but rare on the coast through the summer.

After mid-March, I have observed migrations of Ring-billed Gulls when they suddenly appeared in numbers on inland waters where they seldom occur in winter. Usually their stay is short lived, and they move northward after several days. I also have seen them forced down by heavy spring rainstorms and concentrated on flooded fields in the Yazoo Delta. On March 19, 1960, at Eagle Lake in Warren County, several thousand or more were concentrated and feeding on shad. High wave action and muddy water entering the lake caused the shad to surface, and the gulls were busy across the lake gorging themselves.

The winter-resident, third-year Ring-billed Gull is easy to identify in its full adult plumage. The head, underparts, and tail are white. The stout, yellow bill has a subterminal black ring, and the feet and legs are greenish yellow. The mantle and upperwings are pearl gray with black primaries tipped with two white spots. The trailing edges of the wings are white.

The winter adult Ring-billed Gull is similar to the alternate plumaged adult bird, but may have flecks of gray and brown on the head and nape. Second-winter birds have a broader, dark bill ring; a narrow black tail band; and more black on the primaries but are otherwise similar to the adult. The first-winter bird has a gray mantle, blackish brown primaries, brown wings, a fairly well-defined subterminal tail band, and a semblance of a ring on the end of the bill. It is mottled gray on the head and neck, and has white underparts.

Immature Ring-bills are much lighter in all plumages than the larger and darker immature Herring Gulls. In flight, the Ring-bill also is more ternlike and buoyant. The gray or flesh-colored legs of immature Ring-billed Gulls are not distinctive.

Ring-billed Gulls breed over a wide range in the northern United States. Their breeding range extends from southern Oregon into Idaho, Utah, North Dakota, northern Minnesota, locally on the Great Lakes, then northward in Canadian maritime provinces, and central and prairie provinces. They nest in colonies on remote islands, around prairie marshes, and on lake shores. Often on the coast, they nest on rocky shores or cliffs. They usually lay three gray or olive, heavily blotched eggs in a nest made on the ground of twigs, grass, leaves, rubbish, and feathers.

[California Gull] *Larus californicus*

This four-year gull is less variable in plumage than the Herring Gull and similar large gulls. The adult has a *dark gray* mantle and white head heavily streaked with brown in its basic plumage. The legs are grayish green, and the bill is yellow with *red* and *black* spotting. It has a rounder head and smaller bill than the Herring Gull. *Dark eyes* and a *darker mantle* separate this gull from the smaller, yellow-eyed Ring-billed Gull.

CALIFORNIA GULL

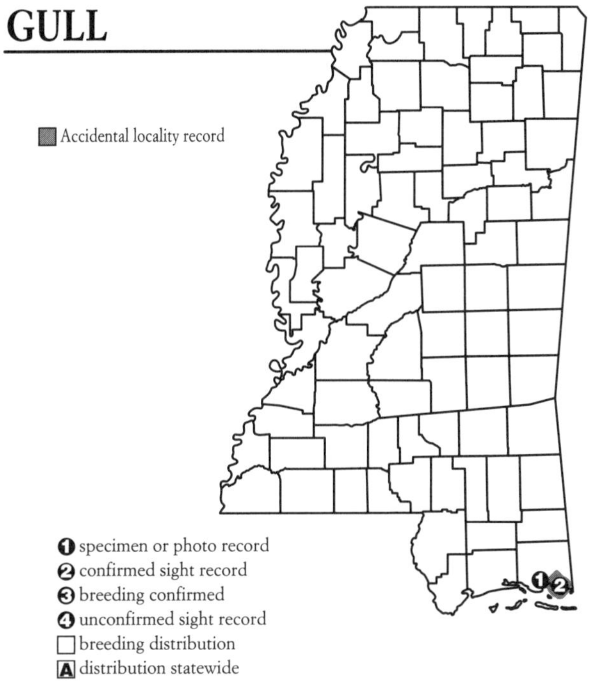

	JAN	FEB	MAR	APR	MAY	JUN	JUL	AUG	SEP	OCT	NOV	DEC
OCCURRENCE												19 ○
MUSEUM*												
WHT*												

*Breeding confirmed by egg, sight, or photographic record.

Adult California Gulls have black wing tips with outer, nondistinctive white spots. A third-year California Gull is like an adult, except its bill is heavily smudged black and yellow toward the base. Second-winter birds have gray backs, brown wings, grayish legs, and yellow, black-tipped bills. First-winter birds are overall brown with a two-toned yellow and black bill.

In flight the trailing outer primaries and secondaries show two dark bars along the wing. The very dark overall appearance is similar to the first-winter Herring Gull, but the shorter bill and round head of the California help set it apart.

Larry and Terrie Gates identified and photographed a first-winter California Gull on the annual Jackson County Christmas Bird Count on December 19, 1987 (Gates 1987). Complete notes and details were furnished with a color photo to substantiate this first Mississippi record, which was published in *American Birds*.

Herring Gull *Larus argentatus*

The Herring Gull is mainly an interior migrant and winters regularly on the larger lakes and reservoirs in smaller numbers than the Ring-billed and Bonaparte's Gulls. On the coast, it is common in winter and easily recognized by its large size. The adult in fourth-year alternate plumage generally resembles the adult Ring-billed Gull, but has a large yellow bill with a *red spot* on the lower mandible and *flesh-colored legs.*

The first-year immature is overall dusky brown with a dark bill and dark eyes. Second-winter birds have gray backs; brownish wings; a yellowish, black-tipped bill; and pale eyes. Third-winter birds have a black smudge on the yellow bill, a broadly banded white tail, and brown smudging on the body. Winter adults have brownish smudges around the head, neck, and upper breast. Individuals in all plumages can be highly variable, but all have pink or flesh-colored legs. Immatures always outnumber birds in full adult plumage.

Herring Gulls depart by mid-April or early May, though a few nonbreeding birds remain on the coast in summer. Return migration begins in early October. In the northern United States and Canada, where they breed in large colonies on islands or remote places, their numbers are increasing. The breeding range is expanding southward along the East Coast. Herring Gulls winter on both coasts, on the Great Lakes, and wherever there is open water southward into the Gulf of Mexico. The species is circumpolar in distribution.

HERRING GULL

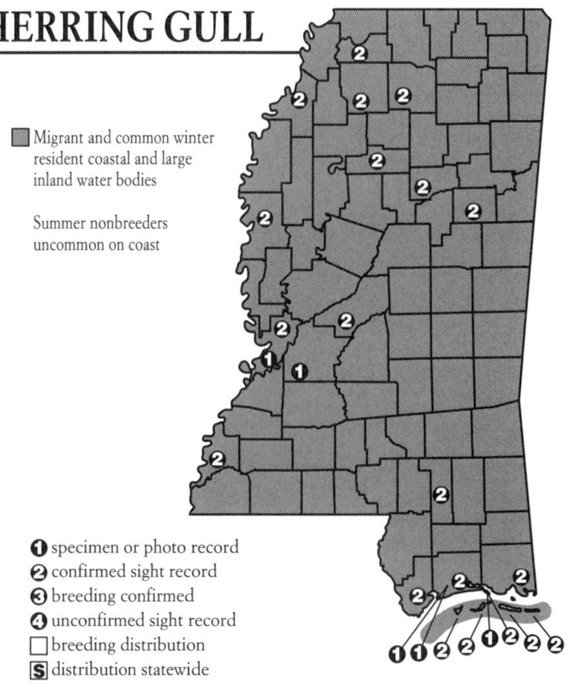

	JAN	FEB	MAR	APR	MAY	JUN	JUL	AUG	SEP	OCT	NOV	DEC
OCCURRENCE												
MUSEUM*												
WHT*												

*Breeding confirmed by egg, sight, or photographic record.

These gulls are scavengers around ports and large cities, where they frequent dumps and landfills or follow garbage scows. They render a valuable service by removing dead fish and other refuse thrown from fishing boats. Like most large gulls, this species preys on the eggs and young of other colonial nesting birds near their breeding colonies. It is fully capable of catching its own food and feeds voraciously on schooling fish, which it picks from the water. Occasionally it plunges into the water to catch its food.

[Thayer's Gull] *Larus thayeri*

This gull was formerly considered a variant or subspecies of the Herring Gull. It breeds farther north in the Arctic and winters along the California Coast and northward to peninsular Alaska. It has been reported in the interior and eastern United States as a casual visitor. The Thayer's Gull is extremely difficult to identify, mainly because it takes four years to reach maturity.

Judith A. Toups and Gerry Morgan identified a Thayer's Gull in first-winter plumage at Pass Christian on February 5, 1988 (Hodges 1988). The bird was under observation with binoculars and telescopes for 10 to 15 minutes before it took flight and was not seen again. The bird was with a group of gulls among which were first-year Herring Gulls for direct comparison. All field marks of the Thayer's Gull were noted and compared with the Herring Gulls present. Comparative details noticed eliminated the improbable and similar Iceland Gull and the easier identified Glaucous Gull previously recorded on the coast. Both observers are experienced "gullers" and live on the coast, but neither had prior experience with the Thayer's Gull. Unfortunately, the bird flew before they could take a photograph.

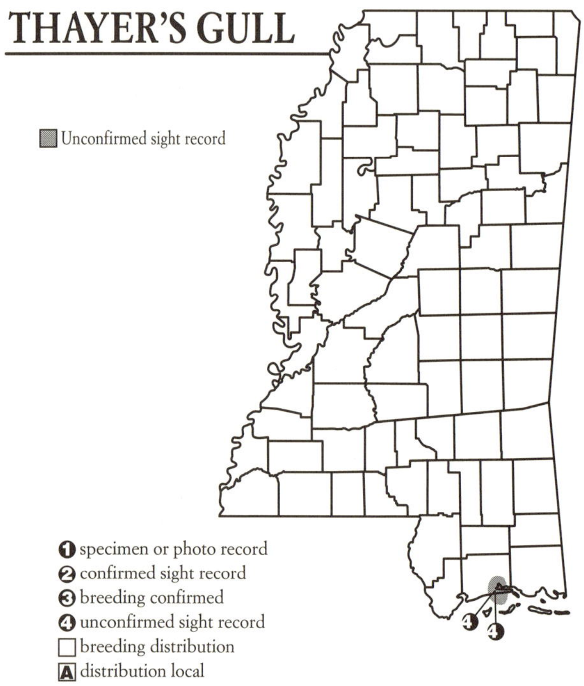

	JAN	FEB	MAR	APR	MAY	JUN	JUL	AUG	SEP	OCT	NOV	DEC
OCCURRENCE		5 O										
MUSEUM*												
WHT*												

*Breeding confirmed by egg, sight, or photographic record.

Toups supplied details (MMNS) including distinctive marks compared with the common Herring Gull in the same age class. The Thayer's Gull had an entirely black bill that was smaller, more slender, shorter in length, slightly curved on the upper mandible, and not pinkish toward the base. The bird had a medium brown back rather evenly patterned with a checkered appearance. Contrast between the primaries and the rest of the wing was minimal, and the secondaries lacked the contrast seen on the Herring Gull. In flight, the underwings were silver on the inner primaries, and a blackish subterminal tail band was indistinctly seen.

Second-year Thayer's Gulls have a gray mantle, a more contrasting tail band, and dark eyes. Adults have dark eyes, and darker legs than similar gulls. Upperparts are dark gray. Underwing primaries are pale gray, while the outer ones are narrowly edged with black at the tips.

Lesser Black-backed Gull *Larus fuscus*

The Lesser Black-backed Gull is a European species that occurs regularly along the East Coast as an uncommon to casual visitor. On our coast, it has occurred as an accidental winter visitor.

First noted on March 2, 1983, and photographed on the Gulfport beach by Mickey Baker, Marianne Towell, and Judith A. Toups, the adult in basic plumage remained in the area until March 31, 1983, and was seen almost daily (Toups 1985). Apparently this bird returned on November 12, 1983, and remained in the same vicinity until March 27, 1984. It returned again on October 25 and was observed repeatedly until March 18, 1985.

Many observers, including myself, were first introduced to this bird while it remained on the beach. Another sighting and photograph record was made by Toups (1985) of a second-winter immature in the same general location on January 30, 1985.

Records for this species along the Gulf Coasts of Alabama, Louisiana, and Texas have occurred regularly, but its appearance is still regarded as casual. Recurrent records, however, are anticipated.

Two inland records for the Lesser Black-backed Gull have been reported. An adult was seen at the Lower Lake below

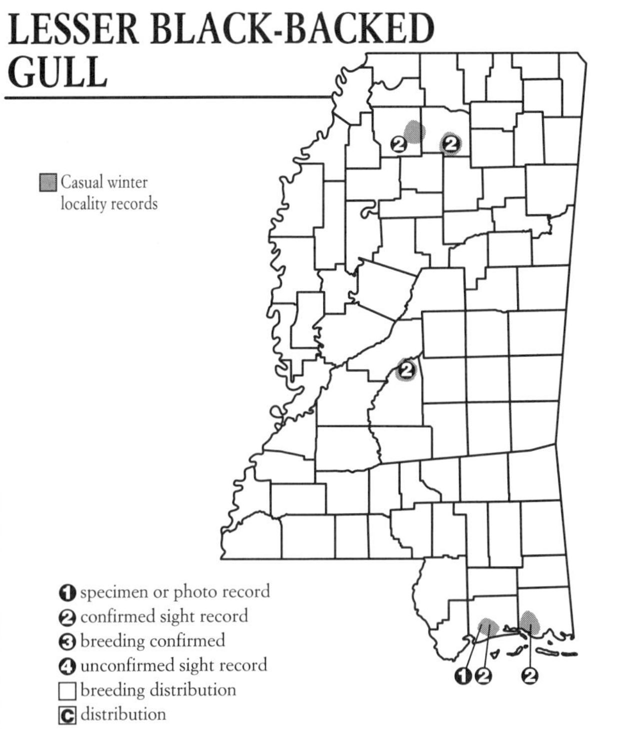

	JAN	FEB	MAR	APR	MAY	JUN	JUL	AUG	SEP	OCT	NOV	DEC
OCCURRENCE	oooo	oooo	oooo 27						ooo	25 o	ooooo	oooo
MUSEUM*												
WHT*												

*Breeding confirmed by egg, sight, or photographic record.

Sardis Lake dam in Panola County on December 22, 1983, by W. Marvin Davis (Hodges and Jackson 1984). An immature was identified during the Jackson Christmas Bird Count by Malcolm F. Hodges Jr. and Steve and Carole Peterson at Ross Barnett Reservoir (Peterson and Turcotte 1990).

The adult Lesser Black-backed Gull is similar to the Great Black-backed, but much smaller. It has *yellow,* not flesh-colored legs. This four-year gull is on average slightly smaller than the Herring Gull. First-winter birds, much like first-winter Herring Gulls, are not easily separated. The first-winter Lesser Black-backed has a paler head and underparts.

The upperparts show more contrasting dark and light on the feathers and between the light colored rump and back. The primaries and wing coverts are darker than on first-winter Herring Gulls. Second-winter birds are separable by the *dark gray back* and some may have yellow legs. Third-winter birds usually have yellow legs, some brown on the wings, and a dark smudge on the bill.

Several races or subspecies of this gull exist. The form regularly occurring in North America, *L. f. graellsi,* breeds in Iceland, the British Isles and Faroes, and on the French and Spanish Coasts. Other races occur in Scandinavia and Siberia.

[Glaucous Gull] *Larus hyperboreus*

The large size and light color of this unusual winter visitor should catch the eye of gull-watchers. Adults in alternate plumage are larger than a Herring Gull; chalky white; with pale gray mantle and *wings;* and *plain, white,* or frosty gray *primaries.* The large bill is yellow with a red spot. Feet and legs are pink in all plumages. In its first-winter plumage, this gull is buffy, tan, or almost white, with a flesh-colored bill and a smudge of black on the tip. The *translucent tips of the white primaries* are distinctive in the first-winter plumage and all others.

Second-winter birds are pale or whitish overall with a black smudge on the bill. Third-winter birds retain the dark bill smudge, but lack the pale gray mantle and wings of the adult. In winter, the head of the adult Glaucous Gull is lightly streaked with brown. At times seasonal plumage changes and variation among individuals of other gull species make differentiation of three- and four-year gulls difficult. Identification of the Glaucous Gull is easier in all ages.

There are only four Mississippi records of the Glaucous Gull, all from the coast. A sighting by Burleigh (1945) at Gulfport on December 22, 1941, is the first published record. Lovett E. Williams Jr. and Sterling G. Clawson substantiated

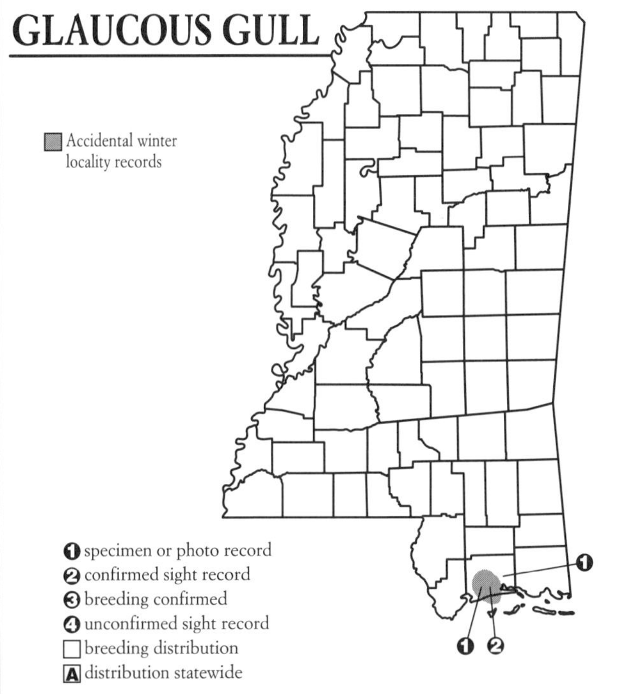

	JAN	FEB	MAR	APR	MAY	JUN	JUL	AUG	SEP	OCT	NOV	DEC
OCCURRENCE	14 oo		23 o							31 o		22 o
MUSEUM*												
WHT*												

*Breeding confirmed by egg, sight, or photographic record.

the second state record by a specimen collected on January 14, 1961, at the Pascagoula River marsh area (Turcotte 1961b). Haberyan (1961) observed an all white individual at Gulfport on March 23, 1961. With three immature Herring Gulls, it was larger in size and had a flesh-colored bill with black tip. A fourth record by Judith A. Toups and Joe W. Taylor was at Gulfport, a second-winter individual seen and photographed January 3–6, 1985 (Hodges 1985).

The Glaucous Gull has a circumpolar distribution and breeds on coastal shores and cliffs in the Arctic. It winters on the Great Lakes, along coastlines of northern states, and casually to the northern Gulf Coast. It is highly predatory on the eggs and young of birds, including other gull species.

[Great Black-backed Gull] *Larus marinus*

In adult breeding dress this large and handsome gull is snowy white on the head, body, and tail, with black upperparts, pale eyes, pink legs, and a large yellow bill with a red spot. First-winter birds have a lighter color on the head and body than the Herring Gull. In flight, the rump and tail show mostly white with a subterminal, black tail band. The head, dark bill, and body size are larger than the immature Herring Gull. The back and wings have a patterned look with pale edging on the feathers. Second-winter birds have pale eyes, a yellow bill with dark tip, and black back. The wings and tail are similar to its first-winter plumage. During the bird's third winter, the plumage is like the adult, except for a black smudge on the bill and brown instead of black on the wings. In winter, the white headed gulls of this and other species may be streaked or smudged dusky on the head and neck.

GREAT BLACK-BACKED GULL

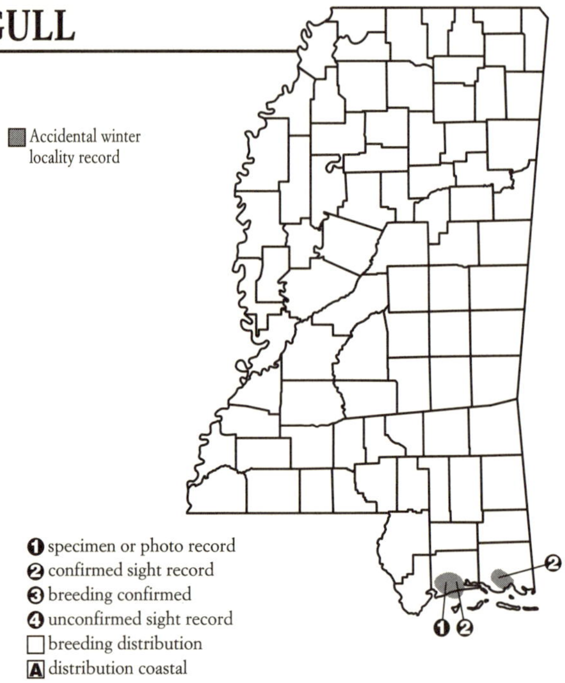

	JAN	FEB	MAR	APR	MAY	JUN	JUL	AUG	SEP	OCT	NOV	DEC
OCCURRENCE			15-19 o		8 o							17 o
MUSEUM*												
WHT*												

*Breeding confirmed by egg, sight, or photographic record.

The Great Black-backed Gull breeds along the coasts of the North Atlantic Ocean and is extending its breeding range along the Great Lakes. It is a casual winter visitor to the Florida Coast and along the Gulf Coast into Texas.

The first Mississippi record for this species was an immature in second-winter plumage identified and photographed on March 15, 1983, in Biloxi (Covington et al. 1985). The bird remained along the same beach through March 19, 1983, and was seen by numerous observers.

A second record of two immatures at Biloxi, on May 8, 1984, and a third individual seen in flight at Bellefontaine Beach in Jackson County on December 17, 1984 (Gates and Gates 1985) indicate that this gull can be expected to occur occasionally along the Gulf Coast.

These gulls are highly predatory on colonial nesting seabirds. They take eggs and young at every opportunity. Otherwise, they are omnivorous feeders on sea life, garbage, and carrion.

Black-legged Kittiwake *Rissa tridactyla*

The Black-legged Kittiwake, a gull of the open ocean, breeds on the shores and island cliffs of the Arctic, and along the Atlantic to the "bird rocks" of the Gulf of St. Lawrence. It winters at sea along the Atlantic and Pacific Coasts, rarely occurring inland during migration. It is a rare or casual winter visitor to the northern Gulf Coast.

The common name is derived from the raucous calls that suggest its name, *kitti-waak* or *kaka-week*. The specific name denotes the lack of a hind toe or its presence only in rudimentary form. The breeding adult has a small, light yellow bill and black legs. The head, underparts, and tail are white. The back and upperwings are frosty gray. Wing tips are black and form a sharply defined triangle bordering the gray of the wings. Its flight is graceful and buoyant.

Immatures have a dark ear spot, a dark collar across the nape, and wide, dark bars across the inner wings forming a wide W-shape with the black primaries. The slightly notched tail has a terminal black band. Winter adults have a smudge of gray on the nape.

The kittiwake is larger than the Bonaparte's Gull and smaller than the Ring-billed Gull. This intermediate size between the two more common gulls with which the kittiwake associates is useful for identification, along with its distinctive half-collar and wing pattern.

BLACK-LEGGED KITTIWAKE

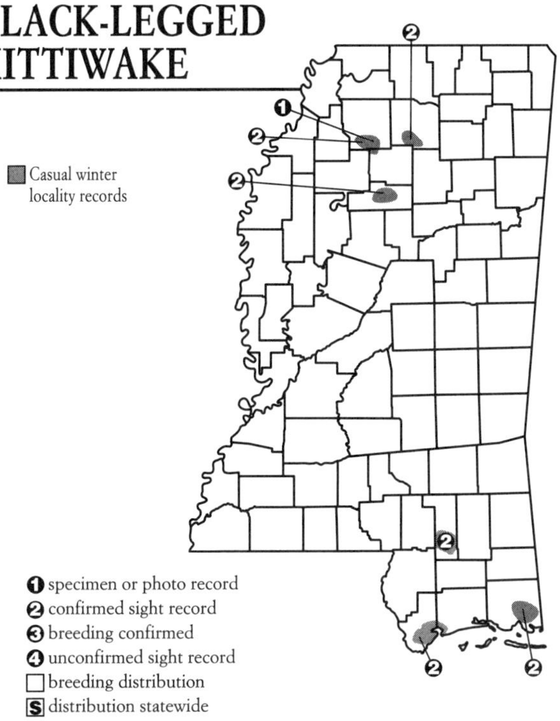

	JAN	FEB	MAR	APR	MAY	JUN	JUL	AUG	SEP	OCT	NOV	DEC
OCCURRENCE	o o	oo	21 o							28 o	o o	oooo
MUSEUM*												
WHT*												

*Breeding confirmed by egg, sight, or photographic record.

On northern breeding grounds, kittiwakes nest on vertical cliff ledges in large colonies with other seabirds such as auks, murres, and gannets. Their nest is compactly made of seaweed, grass, and moss. The eggs, like those of most gulls, are gray or buffy and heavily marked with shades of brown.

The first inland Mississippi sight record of two immature birds by W. Marvin Davis occurred near the Grenada Lake dam on December 4, 1967. A second record and the first state specimen, an immature bird observed by Davis (1970) at the Lower Lake below the Sardis Lake dam, was collected on February 10, 1969, by Davis in company with Y. J. McGaha. This bird was seen first by Davis on January 25 and several times afterward until the specimen was taken. Later sightings by Davis (1986a) of an immature on January 4 and 5, 1976, and an adult on December 28, 1983, occurred at the same site. Another sighting on Sardis Lake by Gene Knight and Vic Theobald occurred on December 12, 1990 (Schiefer 1991).

There are four sight records for this species on the coast, all immatures. The first, by R. F. Andrle, D. M. Lay, and others, occurred on October 28, 1961, about one mile offshore from Ocean Springs in Jackson County (Imhof 1962). A second sighting in Mississippi Sound about three miles southeast of the mouth of the Pascagoula River was made by Lovett E. Williams Jr., Sterling G. Clawson, and Henry D. Haberyan on March 21, 1962 (Williams 1962a).

On December 19, 1977, a sight record was made by Larry Gates and Steve Peterson at Bay St. Louis. The fourth record occurred on November 10, 1983, at Bellefontaine Beach in Jackson County, an individual seen by Judith A. Toups and Mickey Baker (Purrington 1984).

[Sabine's Gull] *Xema sabini*

The first Mississippi sight record for this gull was that reported by Lovett E. Williams Jr. (1965). On July 14, 1964, one immature was observed by Williams Jr., Bob Skinner, Mac Myers, and Jerry Blackard on Mississippi Sound about three miles west-northwest of the Ship Island Lighthouse. For several days their party was engaged in banding and color-marking Royal and Sandwich terns on offshore islands.

A second sighting, confirmed by identifiable photographs, was recorded by Malcolm F. Hodges Jr., Judith A. Toups, and Terence Schiefer at Clermont Harbor in Hancock County

SABINE'S GULL

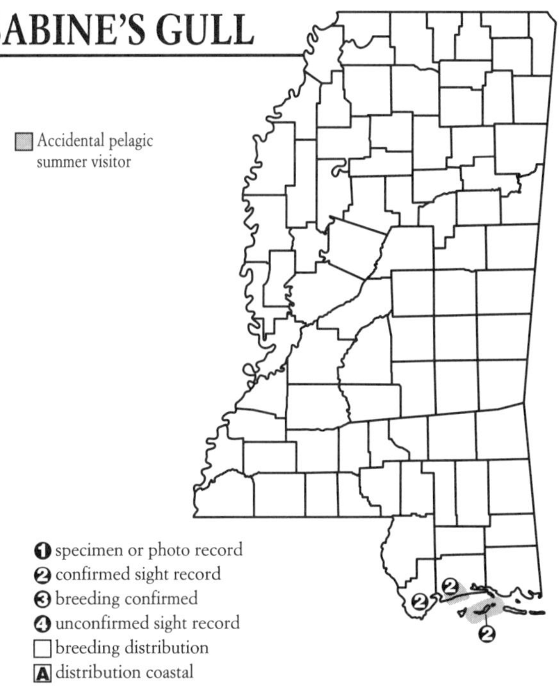

	JAN	FEB	MAR	APR	MAY	JUN	JUL	AUG	SEP	OCT	NOV	DEC
OCCURRENCE							14 o	9 o	24 o			
MUSEUM*												
WHT*												

*Breeding confirmed by egg, sight, or photographic record.

In many places along the Gulf Coast, abandoned piers and pilings are good spots to view the Laughing Gull and a variety of other species.

on August 9, 1988 (Hodges 1988). This bird was on the beach resting with other birds ahead of tropical storm Beryl, which was moving shoreward west of New Orleans. The bird was an immature in first-summer plumage. Records exist for this species occurring in Alabama, Louisiana, and Texas along the Gulf Coasts and on reservoirs in Arkansas.

This oceanic gull breeds in the Arctic and is circumpolar in distribution. It winters mainly at sea in the Southern Hemisphere. It migrates offshore along the East and West Coasts and very rarely inland. The breeding adult has a dark gray hood, black bill with yellow tip, black legs, and *forked white tail.*

In flight and in all plumages, the wings show a striking pattern of obtuse triangles: black on the outer primaries, white on the inner primaries and secondaries, and gray on the secondary coverts and mantle. Immatures are more grayish brown on the back than adults and have a black terminal tail band.

Least Tern

Sterninae (Terns)

The terns, called "sea-swallows," are strong and graceful in flight, more streamlined than gulls, and usually fly with their pointed bill downward. They have shorter legs and narrower and more pointed wings than gulls.

Most terns have forked or notched tails. They feed largely on fish, hovering before diving into the water to capture their prey. The sexes of terns are alike, and most species in alternate plumage have black caps.

Most terns are predominantly white with light gray upperparts. Some have dark wings and underparts. In winter, the black-capped terns replace the black on the forehead with white or gray. Twelve species of terns have been recorded in Mississippi.

Gull-billed Tern *Sterna nilotica*

This summer-resident tern is strictly coastal, although there is one recent inland record in Lowndes County (Schiefer and Hodges 1990), a single bird feeding over flooded fields on July 16, 1989. On the Mississippi Coast, it is an uncommon summer resident and breeds on the mainland in small colonies with Least Terns. It has nested with other terns on a spoil island near the western end of Petit Bois Island in Mississippi Sound.

After the nesting season, Gull-billed Terns in adult and immature plumages can be found in mixed flocks along beaches, bays, and estuaries of the three coastal counties. They arrive in late March and April and usually depart by early September. Several winter records, however, have been reported. Extremes of arrival and departure are March 27 and September 5.

This tern has a stout, black bill. The adult in alternate plumage is snowy white below, *pale* gray above, and has a black crown and nape. The feet and legs are black, and the tail is moderately forked. It is stockier than terns of similar size, and the wings are slightly broader. Immatures and winter adults have mostly white crowns with fine dark streaks. Juveniles have pale edgings on feathers of their upperparts and resemble small gulls. It is one of our four large terns, similar in size to the Sandwich Tern and smaller than Royal and Caspian Terns.

Size differences are important in learning to identify terns to a species, but they are not distinctive except for the smallest species, the Least Tern. Among the small tern group are the light- and dark-winged species and those of medium size between the Least Tern and the large tern group.

Gull-billed Terns have a preference for salt marshes and beaches. They often feed over open areas such as airports and marshes and take insects on the wing. Nesting on beach dunes with other terns, their two or three eggs are deposited in a scrape in bare sand or shells. They are grayish or greenish buff color and heavily marked with shades of brown and lilac. The downy young are a creamy buff color spotted or mottled with black on the head and back, shading to almost white on their underside.

Burleigh (1945) did not record Gull-billed Terns during his eight years of active study and collecting on the Mississippi Coast. The first state specimens, three birds taken on Horn Island on June 5 and 26, 1941, by Winston Nolan, are deposited in the MMNS (Gandy and Turcotte 1970). Burleigh believed these terns occurred only on offshore islands.

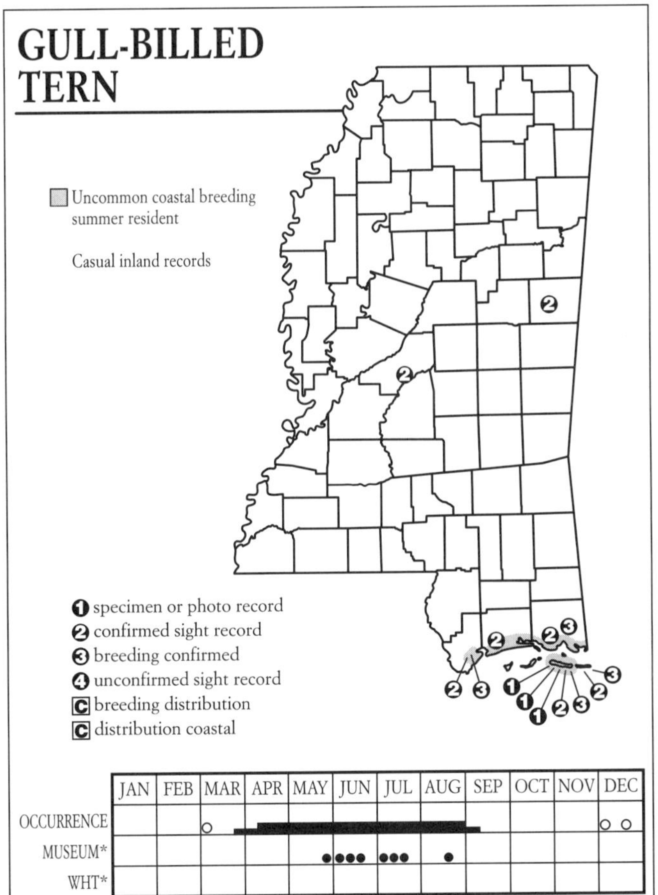

*Breeding confirmed by egg, sight, or photographic record.

Rev. J. L. Dorn reported that Gull-billed Terns apparently were nesting among a colony of Least Terns and Black Skimmers on a bare spoil area west of the East Pascagoula River bridge in June 1955. I visited this colony that month and made color movies of adults, nests, and young of Least Terns, Black Skimmers, and adult Gull-billed Terns. Presumably the Gull-billed Terns had young present, but this was not confirmed. The several pairs of adult birds dove repeatedly and were quite agitated, as were the Least Terns and skimmers. On May 5, 1956, John Phares and I visited the colony and found Least Terns nesting with Black Skimmers and several pairs of Gull-billed Terns present, but we found no nests.

Lovett E. Williams Jr. and Sterling G. Clawson recorded the first mainland nesting records. At least two pairs nested with Least Terns on Bayou Casotte in Jackson County (Williams and Clawson 1960). Egg shells were found on May 29 and July 2, 1960, at the site. Nesting was later confirmed by collection of a set of two eggs at Bayou Casotte on June 4, 1962, by Williams Jr. and Clawson (Williams 1962b).

Since these records were established, this tern has been found nesting with other terns and Black Skimmers on spoil islands in Mississippi Sound and at various locations on the Pascagoula River channel spoil. As many as 31 nests in a colony on the spoil were found on June 14, 1983, and 32 juveniles, 38 adults, and eight downy young were found there by Judith A. Toups and others on July 17, 1983 (Schardien and Jackson 1983).

These observations and other experiences indicate a good potential for development of nesting sites for Least, Gull-billed, and Common Terns, and Black Skimmers on the dredge spoil and dune areas between the East and West Pascagoula River channels. Because weeds and bushy vegetation soon cover bare areas, annual maintenance of carefully selected sites of several acres that expose bare, sandy areas for nesting would be a highly desirable nongame project. Other potential sites on the mainland could also be developed for Gull-billed Tern nesting.

Caspian Tern *Sterna caspia*

The Caspian Tern is the largest member of this subfamily. It is cosmopolitan in distribution, and in North America it breeds from the Gulf Coast to the Arctic. Unlike the Royal Tern, it breeds inland on large lakes, marshes, and islands.

The upperparts of the Caspian Tern are pearl gray, and the underparts are white. In the breeding season, the top of the head is black and *crested*. In winter, the head is streaked or dusky on the forepart, never white. The stout bill is red, not orange. The Caspian Tern is larger than the slimmer Royal Tern and approaches the size of a Herring Gull. The tail is less forked than the Royal Tern, and the Caspian Tern has much more black on the underside of its primaries. The feet and legs of all four large terns are black.

This species is a fairly common permanent resident on the Mississippi Coast and nested on Petit Bois Island in 1967 and 1968 (Portnoy 1977). It is fairly common as a breeding bird on the Chandeleurs and other Louisiana islands. I found them nesting with Royal and Sandwich Terns on Freemason Island on May 26, 1938. The nests were shallow scrapes in the bare sand or shells. There were one or two eggs in each set, with gray ground color, uniformly marked with brown and lilac, and less pointed than those of variously marked Royal Tern eggs. Several sets of eggs were taken for museum specimens. Nesting in Mississippi was not confirmed until 1967.

Coastal waters, large lakes, bays, beaches, islands, and estuaries are the habitats of this species. During migration, this tern is uncommon inland and occurs mainly on lakes or reservoirs. Inland sight records extend from March 21 to June 20, and from July 16 to October 5. An anomalous inland record at the outlet channel below Grenada Lake was one bird seen by W. Marvin Davis (pers. comm.) on December 15, 1991.

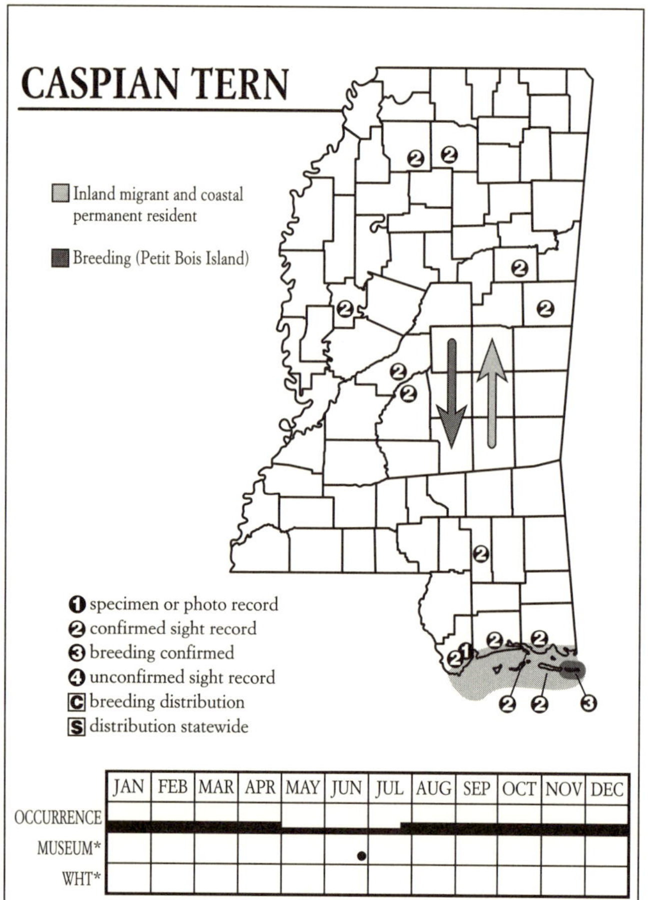

*Breeding confirmed by egg, sight, or photographic record.

Royal Tern *Sterna maxima*

The Royal Tern is a regular, common, permanent resident on the mainland beaches and offshore islands of the Mississippi Coast. It breeds in large colonies on the Chandeleur Islands in Louisiana waters and has nested in small numbers on Horn Island. In 1962 Lovett E. Williams Jr. (1962b) reported that about 500 pairs were nesting on Petit Bois Island on June 24 and 30. Over 300 young were banded by him and Sterling G. Clawson on two visits. The colony held 2500 Sandwich Tern nests, and more than 1400 of the young were banded.

In July 1964, the tern colony moved to a dredge spoil area called Walnut Island. Two addled eggs were taken to substantiate the first nesting record for Mississippi. The eggs were deposited in the MMNS.

Williams Jr., Bob Skinner, Mac Myers, and Jerry Blackard (then refuge manager of Gulf Islands National Seashore Refuge) visited the tern colony on the spoil island along the ship channel on July 13, 1964 (Turcotte 1965b). The colony had grown since the earlier visit. In recent years Royal and Sandwich Terns have continued nesting on this spoil island off the western tip of Petit Bois. (It is also named Anderson Island after Walter Anderson, an artist who spent much of his productive time on nearby Horn Island.)

Both Royal and Sandwich Terns are coastal species. Inland records for both are rare and usually follow strong coastal storms. With the passage inland of Hurricane Camille from the Mississippi Coast on August 17, 1969, large numbers of seabirds were brought inland as far north as Simpson County. On the fourth day following the storm, Phares (1970) found considerable numbers of gulls, terns, and Black Skimmers killed by cars on Highway 13 between Columbia and Simpson County. About all that remained were the wings of these birds that apparently were forced down at night. They must have sought refuge on the wet pavement that probably appeared as water to them. Five Black Skimmers and a Laughing Gull were seen on a stock pond, but no dead landbirds were noted.

Gates and Fairley (1979) reported the unusual appearance of 14 Royal Terns at the Hattiesburg sewage lagoons on September 13, 1979, following the passage of Hurricane Frederick.

The Royal Tern is highly colonial and nests with Sandwich Terns and Black Skimmers in dense colonies on remote islands. It has not been found nesting on the mainland. Bare sand or shell beaches and dunes are its preferred nesting sites.

Royal Terns usually lay only a single egg in a slight hollow. The eggs are whiter and more pointed than those of the Caspian Tern. They are variously and distinctly spotted so that no two eggs appear alike. The

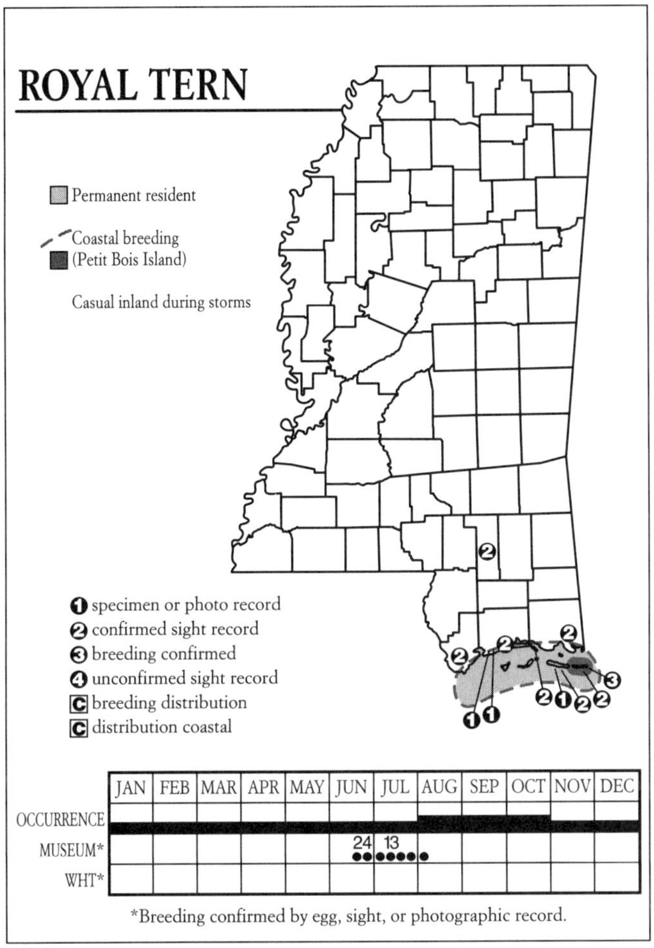

newly hatched, downy young are also variously colored and soon group together in bands with other young terns.

Colonies of hundreds of these birds have nested on Petit Bois Island and nearby spoil banks with thousands of the more common Sandwich Terns. Small colonies also have nested on Horn Island. When Royal and Sandwich Terns are nesting together, the marked differences in size and bill are readily apparent.

Royal Terns usually have an orange bill while the Caspian Tern's heavier bill is red or reddish orange. Bill color is not always distinctive. The Caspian Tern has notched or indented central tail feathers. The Royal Tern has a forked tail with the outer feathers about three inches longer than the central feathers.

The Royal Tern is slimmer and slightly smaller than the Caspian Tern and larger than the easily distinguished Sandwich Tern. The Royal Tern has a black cap only during a brief part of the nesting season. The white forehead develops during the latter part of the breeding period and is apparent during most of the year. The Caspian Tern has a dusky or streaked forehead after breeding and never shows white like the Royal Tern. Also, note the darker underside of the primaries of the Caspian Tern.

Sandwich Tern *Sterna sandvicensis*

The Sandwich Tern, formerly Cabot's Tern, is strictly a coastal species. It is a regular summer resident on the Mississippi Coast and nests in large colonies on barrier islands. On the mainland, it is common on beaches and all islands after the breeding season.

Spring arrivals begin appearing in late March, and most depart by mid-October. A few records on the coast extend to late December. An estimated 2500 pairs of Sandwich Terns have nested on the spoil banks off the western end of Petit Bois Island (Williams 1962b).

Smaller numbers have nested on other shell islands, especially on North Island and Freemason Island, Louisiana, where I have found them nesting abundantly with Royal and Caspian Terns and Black Skimmers. On May 26, 1938, I collected sets of eggs on the shell ridges. On June 7 and 8, 1957, I made another trip to North Island to the Brown Pelican rookery and to Freemason Island to tern and gull colonies. Members of the Mississippi and Louisiana ornithological societies were on this boat trip. Numerous "bands" or créches of Sandwich and Royal Tern downy young were seen and photographed. Young birds herded together along the shell ridges bordering the beach, near large nesting colonies of Laughing Gulls and Black Skimmers. Sandwich Tern nests were shallow depressions in the shells and contained only one or rarely two creamy white eggs boldly marked with black, brown, and lavender spots.

This nesting colony of Sandwich Terns was photographed on July 14, 1965, on spoil banks near Pascagoula in Jackson County.

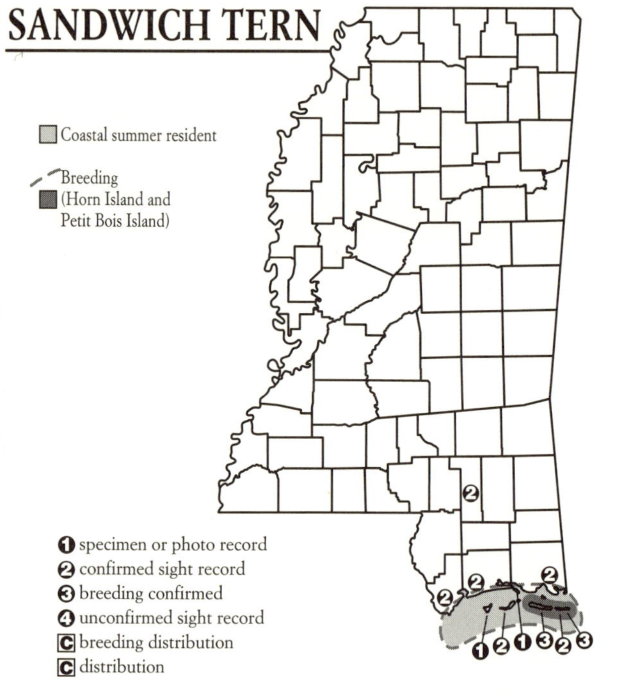

	JAN	FEB	MAR	APR	MAY	JUN	JUL	AUG	SEP	OCT	NOV	DEC
OCCURRENCE			17								24 ∞	15-30 ∞
MUSEUM*						24 ●●	13 ●●●●	4 ●				
WHT*												

*Breeding confirmed by egg, sight, or photographic record.

The Sandwich Tern is grouped with the large terns. It is considerably smaller than the Royal Tern and larger and slimmer than the Gull-billed Tern. The adult has a distinctive long and slender black bill *with a yellow tip,* the only tern marked in this manner. In alternate plumage, adults are light gray above and have a black cap and crest, soon replaced in basic plumage by a white forehead, black-streaked crown, and grayer tail. The white tail is deeply forked, but comparatively short. Juveniles have black bills and are darker above than adults with blackish V-shaped marks on the tail and scapulars. In flight, the tips of the primaries show some black.

Burleigh (1945) described this species as less common than other terns on the Mississippi Coast. Other earlier writers described it as a casual breeder along the northern Gulf Coast. Apparently, around the turn of the century breeding colonies were depleted. The Sandwich Tern breeding population along the coast has increased considerably in recent years along with the Royal Tern, with which it prefers to keep company in nesting areas.

[Roseate Tern] *Sterna dougallii*

Four species of the smaller terns occurring in Mississippi have gray mantles, which distinguish them from the small, dark terns. They have whitish underparts, forked white or pale gray tails, and black caps. The four species are: Least Tern, the regular summer resident; Forster's Tern, a regular, common winter resident and probable local breeder on our coastal marshes; Common Tern, an uncommon local and coastal summer resident; and Roseate Tern, a recent, accidental visitor to the Mississippi Gulf Coast.

Roseate Terns are maritime birds and seldom come ashore except to nest. They breed at widely scattered locations along the Atlantic seaboard from Nova Scotia to the Dry Tortugas west of the Florida Keys, usually nesting with other tern species.

Breeding adults of this species are difficult to separate from the similar Common and Forster's Terns. The distinctive field marks on the Roseate Tern are the deeply forked, *all white tail,* which is much longer than the folded wings; *absence of black* on the underside of the wings; a *mostly black bill;* and a variable amount of red at the base of the bill.

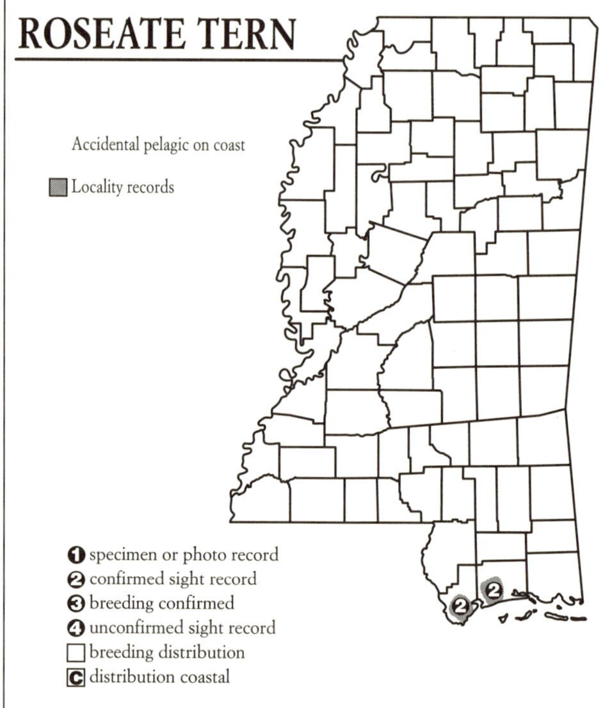

	JAN	FEB	MAR	APR	MAY	JUN	JUL	AUG	SEP	OCT	NOV	DEC
OCCURRENCE			∞									
MUSEUM*												
WHT*												

*Breeding confirmed by egg, sight, or photographic record.

The juvenile has a scaly look on the mantle and is barred black on the lower back. Its bill and legs are black, and the cap is brownish black, extending back from the bill. In the second summer, immature terns have a *white forehead,* and the legs and feet are bright orange like the breeding adult. The tails of first-year birds are shorter than those of breeding adults.

In basic plumage, the Roseate Tern is most likely seen in the company of Forster's Terns, which have a white crown and a *black mask* through the eyes and auriculars. Forster's Terns have gray on the *inner* edges of the tail and white only on the outer-tail feathers.

The black mask of the Roseate Tern in basic plumage extends *across the nape* to form a partial black or dusky cap behind the white forepart of the crown. At rest, the all white tail of the Roseate extends well past the wing tips. Its wings are shorter, and the wingbeats are faster than the Forster's Tern. Identifying this species among numerous Forster's can be difficult. Distinctive field marks should be compared with the Forster's Tern and carefully noted before reporting this accidental species. The Roseate Tern has been recorded on the Mississippi Coast at only two locations by Judith A. Toups and others.

Three Roseate Terns were seen at Gulfport on March 11 and 15, 1976, and another at Waveland on March 11, 1977 (Toups et al. 1987). No inland records have been reported.

Spoil banks along the coast have been favored nesting sites for Common Terns.

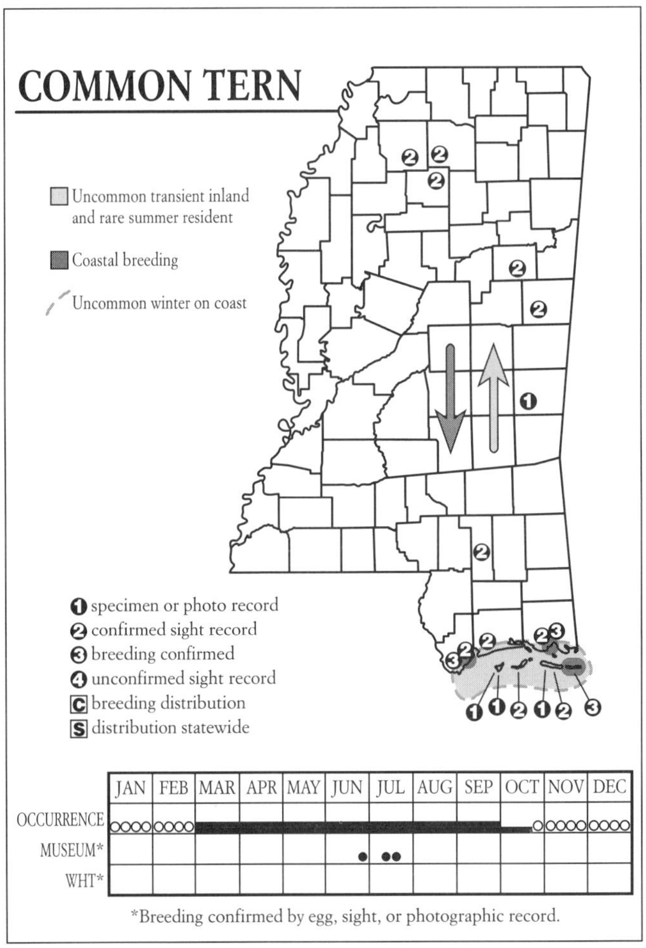

Common Tern *Sterna hirundo*

The Common Tern in alternate plumage has a red bill with a black tip, a black cap and nape, orange red feet and legs, medium gray mantle, pearl gray underparts, white undertail coverts, and a deeply forked tail. Juveniles are brownish above and white below, with a dark bill and yellowish at the base.

All Common Terns in basic plumage have a *dark bar on the shoulders,* a white forehead, and blackish crown and nape. The wing tips extend to the end of the tail or slightly beyond. Breeding adults usually show a *dark wedge* on the upperwing near the end.

This tern has a wide breeding range along the Atlantic Coast and in the interior. It nests in large colonies on beaches and islands along lakes, bays, and estuaries in the northern tier of states and lower Canadian provinces. The nest of the Common Tern is only a hollow in the sand, and two or three gray or buffy, blotched and spotted eggs are laid.

On the Mississippi Coast, it is an uncommon, breeding summer resident. It was first discovered nesting on the Pascagoula River estuary by Lovett E. Williams Jr., Sterling G. Clawson, and Henry D. Haberyan on July 14, 1962 (Williams 1962b). Nesting was also confirmed on the spoil banks of Anderson Island off the western tip of Petit Bois

This adult Common Tern incubates eggs on its nest at a spoil bank near Pascagoula on July 15, 1965.

Island (Jackson 1979) and at Delisle on Bay St. Louis in Hancock County (Toups and Jackson 1987). Williams Jr. confirmed the first Common Tern nest record with several photographs of the nest, eggs, and adults at the nest in the middle of a nesting colony of other terns and Black Skimmers. (Clawson was killed by a lightning strike on August 4, 1962, near the colonial nesting bird colony [Turcotte 1963a].)

On inland waters, the Common Tern is a spring and fall migrant only, mostly recorded in May on lakes and reservoirs and in fall from early August to late November. Six birds were seen by Jerome A. Jackson (1976a) at Bluff Lake in Noxubee County on May 25, 1976, and 35 Common Terns were seen on Sardis Lake by W. Marvin Davis (pers. comm.) on May 10, 1988. On the coast, it has been recorded in all months, but is mostly absent from November through February. It occurs as a summer resident in all coastal counties. It is more common on beaches in August and September.

Forster's Tern *Sterna forsteri*

Although yet to be found nesting on any marshlands of the Mississippi Coast, the Forster's Tern is a common year-round resident. In nearby Louisiana marshes, it nests in colonies or small groups. It has been found nesting in Mobile County, Alabama. Further study is needed to determine this bird's breeding status on our marshlands.

The Forster's Tern has a widely scattered breeding distribution on freshwater and salt marshes. It builds a substantial nest of marsh plants in marshes of the northern Gulf states and some Atlantic seaboard states. Along the Great Lakes, the Forster's Tern nests locally. In midwestern prairie states and Canadian provinces, it is a common breeder in large colonies, and also nests across the northern mountain states to the Pacific where there are suitable marshes. It usually lays three eggs, which are buffy or olivaceous and variously spotted with brown and lilac.

On lakes and reservoirs of Mississippi, the Forster's Tern is a fairly common spring and fall migrant. It is not uncommon to find these terns wintering on lakes and reservoirs. They have occurred at Sardis Lake during 12 months from 1983 to 1991 (Davis, pers. comm.). On the Mississippi Coast, it becomes abundant in the fall with the arrival of young-of-the-year and migrants from northern breeding areas. Beaches and marshes around river estuaries are favorite wintering areas. This bird is the most common of the smaller terns wintering on the Gulf Coast and inland waters.

Forster's Tern is similar to the Common Tern in general appearance. A combination of field marks is used to identify it in the several plumages. The breeding adult Forster's Tern has *orange* legs and feet with orange on the base of the bill. The outer primaries are *lighter than the remainder of the wing*. The tail is *gray* on the margins of the *inner* tail feathers. The Common Tern has *red* legs and feet, pale gray underparts, *dark* outer primaries, and gray margins on the *outer*-tail feathers. Both species have deeply forked tails.

In winter, the Forster's Tern has a *black mask* extending through the eye and the ear, whereas the Common Tern has a black mask extending *across* the back of the head

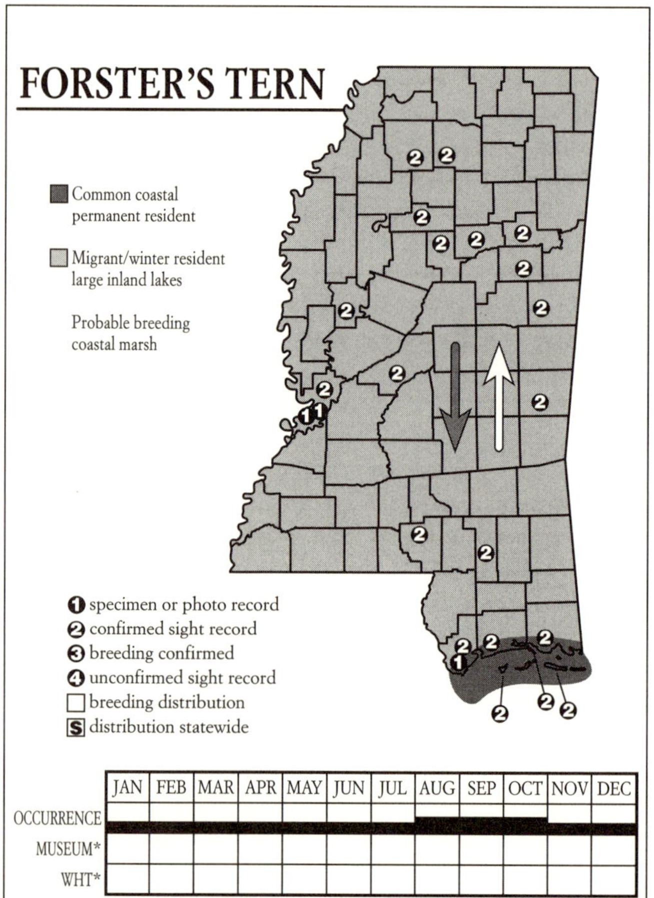

*Breeding confirmed by egg, sight, or photographic record.

and nape. The immature Forster's Tern lacks the dark leading edge of the wings of the immature Common Tern, and the outer primaries of the Forster's Tern are frosty instead of dusky. In winter, adults and immatures of both species have blackish bills.

Least Tern *Sterna antillarum*

From early April until late September, this little "sea-swallow" is abundant along Gulf Coast beaches, bays, and estuaries. Smallest of the North American terns, the Least Tern arrives from wintering grounds, builds in numbers quickly, nests, raises its young on beaches or bare sandy places, then departs as suddenly as it came. In flight, it is the essence of grace, buoyant and swift. At rest, its dainty plumage, joyful behavior, and courtship antics are a pleasure to behold.

The breeding adult has a black cap and nape; white forehead; orange yellow legs; and a yellow, dark-tipped beak. The upperparts are gray and underparts are immaculate white. In flight, the outer primaries form a noticeable, tapering black wedge. The tail is deeply forked and rather short. First-summer birds have dark bills and legs, a dusky patch behind the eyes extending around the nape, dark shoulder bars, and dusky primaries. Juveniles have scaly, pinkish buff upperparts, a dusky crown, a dark smudge behind the eye, and dusky shoulder bars and primaries.

Least Terns (formerly the Little Tern) nest in scattered large and small colonies on barrier islands, coastal beaches, and spoil areas in the Pascagoula River marsh. On the coast, they have nested on the U.S. Navy base at Gulfport, at Keesler Air Force Base in Biloxi, and even on the gravel roofs of shopping centers.

Eggs are placed on bare shells, sand, and other coarse material with some shell bits or debris placed around the shallow nest scrape. Usually only two eggs are laid, sometimes three, but rarely four. They are the color of beach sand, variously spotted and blotched with dark brown and purplish brown or lavender.

The downy young are colored to match wet or dry sand. They are plain white below and white or buff above, either plain, streaked or blotched on the head, wings, and back. Two basic color variations of chicks were noted by Jackson (1976b) in a study of Least Terns on the beach at Gulfport. They may be tan or white above, with infinite individual variations in marks, as found among Royal Tern chicks and eggs, though not as pronounced. The protective coloration of Least Tern chicks and their tendency to hide or remain motionless in available cover helps them to escape predators. Variable coloration aids parents in recognizing chicks when they wander and bunch in créches.

The Mississippi Coast has 28 miles of broad, man-made, sand beaches extending from Bay St. Louis to Biloxi. Periodic maintenance and replacement of sand by dredge fill is required. Before construction, Least Terns, Black Skimmers, and some shorebirds were nesting along the natural shoreline paralleling the seawall and U.S. 90. After construction, the long artificial beach was considered a primary tourist attraction, and it was constantly graded, raked, and groomed. By 1972, the nesting colonies of terns, skimmers, and shorebirds had almost vanished or were periodically scraped away by maintenance equipment (Peterson 1984).

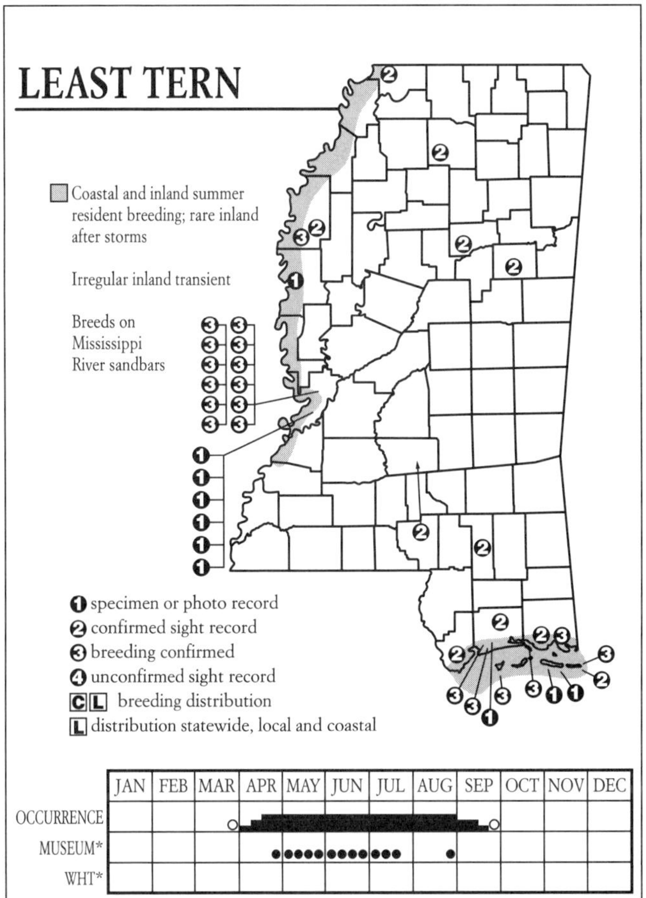

*Breeding confirmed by egg, sight, or photographic record.

Prior to 1974, Ethel Floyd, past-president of the MOS and a Gulfport resident, noticed a few Least Terns trying to nest on a local beach. Knowing that past nesting attempts had been frustrated by maintenance or disturbance, she contacted the Harrison County Board of Supervisors about protecting the birds. They were benignly amused by the request, but took no action.

The following spring she noticed the terns were back at the same site, time, and location. Enlisting aid and support of the MOS and past-president Marjorie Cleveland of Gulfport, they contacted Arlan Robinson, then a member of the Board of Supervisors. With his support, the Board agreed to leave a one-mile stretch of beach east of Beauvoir undisturbed for the 1974 nesting season. It was a modestly successful season.

The following season, protection signs were placed on the beach in spite of verbal outcries and ridicule from some citizens and commercial enterprises. Opposing views were exchanged in the local daily newspaper. About 350 pairs of terns nested on the Gulfport beach and approximately 1000 pairs nested on the Longbeach–Pass Christian beach in 1975. Subsequent protection of the bird colonies has been supported by the Mississippi Coast Audubon Society (MCAS), the Boards of Supervisors, and most of the local citizens, who now regard the bird colonies as assets.

Judith A. Toups and other members of MCAS have marked nests, and encouraged further protection, management, research, and development of the colonies. Toups, a prime mover of the tern colony project with other members, has described in detail the history of the efforts to restore this tern to the Mississippi Coast (Toups 1976).

An increasing human population, commercial and industrial development, and dredging and filling of marshes for highways, industrial, and recreational use have altered and diminished much of the natural wildlife habitat on the Mississippi Coast. Nevertheless, the coast retains a great diversity of wildlife habitat. Unfortunately, many of the best areas are unknown or inaccessible at times to most birders without local guidance. The Gulf Islands National Seashore in Ocean Springs, the Mississippi Sandhill Crane National Wildlife Refuge at Gautier, and a recent guidebook to birds and birding on the Mississippi Coast (Toups and Jackson 1987) are recommended sources of information.

The Least Tern ranges inland and breeds in colonies on sandbars of large rivers in Mississippi, Louisiana, Texas, and on the Mississippi River and its tributaries. Inland populations are declining. Alterations of river courses for flood control, navigation, and irrigation have diminished and altered formerly available nesting and foraging habitat.

In the Midwest, impounded waters used for irrigation have reduced water flows, allowing rapid vegetative encroachment to claim formerly open sandbars. Along the Mississippi River, the cutting off of river bends has reduced sandbar formation and encouraged revegetation on the bendways.

The Least Tern occurs as a transient in small numbers on inland waters (notably Sardis Lake) from spring (earliest May 9) through summer (June to September 4). An exceptional record was one bird seen March 31, 1991, by W. Marvin Davis and Gilbert Beaver near Walls in Desoto County with gulls at a wet place in fields (Muth 1991).

The extensive use of insecticides following World War II probably played a major role in reducing inland populations of the Least Tern and other birds. Before, Least Terns nested in small colonies on sandbars above and below Vicksburg in Warren County. Twelve sets of fresh eggs taken on June 1, 1937, and May 23, 1938, confirm nesting at the two Warren County locations (Gandy and Turcotte 1970).

A study of Mississippi River sandbars to substantiate and quantify the current nesting of the Least Tern is needed. Currently, these birds are seen during summer in Bolivar County opposite Great River Road State Park. On June 22, 1988, 10 adults and eight recently hatched chicks were seen at this location by Terence Schiefer (Hodges 1988). Hal Moore recorded another nesting colony of 25 to 60 adults with nests, eggs, and young present from June 3 to July 23, 1988, on a Mississippi River sandbar near the indefinite boundary between Warren County and Madison Parish, Louisiana (Hodges 1988).

On the coast, nesting records extend from May 7 (first egg) to August 25, the estimated time of last fledgling observed by J. A. Jackson in the study cited above. The breeding biology of Least Terns in the Gulfport colony has been the subject of a study conducted by M. B. Hays (1980).

[Bridled Tern] *Sterna anaethetus*

Bridled Terns are common on their nesting grounds in the Bahamas and the West Indies. In summer, they occur offshore in the Gulf of Mexico and the Atlantic Ocean, mainly following the Gulf Stream to North Carolina's

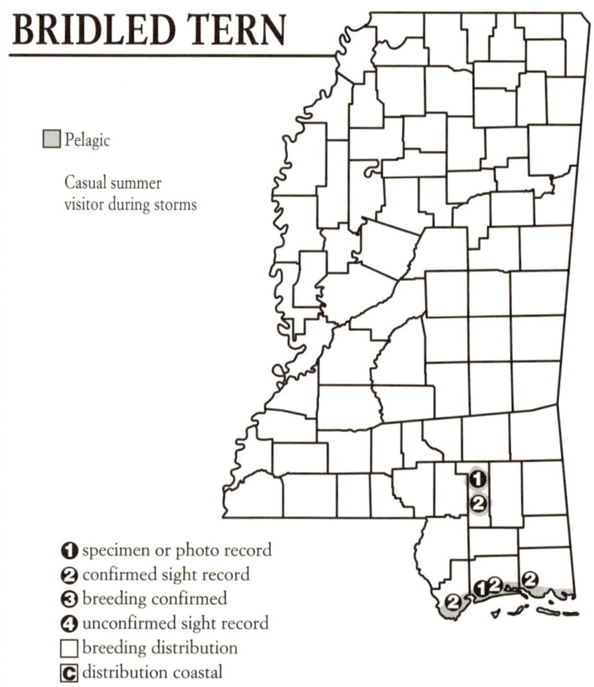

	JAN	FEB	MAR	APR	MAY	JUN	JUL	AUG	SEP	OCT	NOV	DEC
OCCURRENCE					26 ○				2 13 ○○	29 ○		
MUSEUM*												
WHT*												

*Breeding confirmed by egg, sight, or photographic record.

Cape Hatteras. Like the Sooty Tern, this species is pelagic on tropical seas and comes inland only when driven by tropical storms.

Mostly dark above and with white underparts, the adult Bridled Tern is slightly smaller than the Sooty Tern, which it resembles. The Bridled Tern has a *white collar* behind the black crown and the white forehead extends above and *behind* the eye. The *gray* back extends to the central feathers of the white-edged, forked tail. Feet and legs are black. The upperparts of the wings are gray brown. Juveniles resemble the adult but are overall more grayish and with pale mottling on the upperparts.

Although the remains of a Bridled Tern were found on the coast at Gulfport on May 26, 1979 (Hays 1979), the first coastal sightings occurred when seven were found along the beach between Gulfport and Ocean Springs during Hurricane Elena on September 2, 1985 (Toups et al. 1985a). During Hurricane Juan on October 29, 1985, nine more of these terns were sighted in Harrison County on or near the beach, and one was photographed.

The only inland records for the Bridled Tern occurred at the Hattiesburg sewage lagoons on September 13, 1979, and September 2, 1985, following passage of Hurricanes Elena and Frederick (Gates and Fairley 1979). A single bird was seen at close range, and an identifiable photograph was made September 13 of a bird in flight. Fourteen Royal Terns and three Sandwich Terns were recorded at this location on the same date. An adult and one immature were sighted by Larry and Terrie Gates concurrent with the above-mentioned coastal sightings on September 2, 1985 (Hodges 1985).

My first and only encounter with Bridled Terns was in the Gulf of Mexico on a pelagic birding trip about 40 miles southeast of Dauphin Island. The late John Thompson and I were with a small group of birders when several Bridled Terns were seen sitting on floating debris and occasionally feeding along the water's surface. Only one other species of bird was seen in this area. One, or possibly two, Wilson's Storm-Petrels were seen feeding on invisible marine life while flitting over the surface.

Sooty Tern *Sterna fuscata*

Sooty Terns are mainly pelagic over tropical waters and come to land only to nest or when blown inland by storms. Large numbers nest on the desolate Dry Tortugas west of the Florida Keys. Small nesting colonies have been recorded on the Chandeleur Islands of Louisiana south of Biloxi and on some offshore Texas islands. These terns usually are seen in flight over the open sea, where they feed on small fish and other marine life by plucking them from the water surface, not by diving.

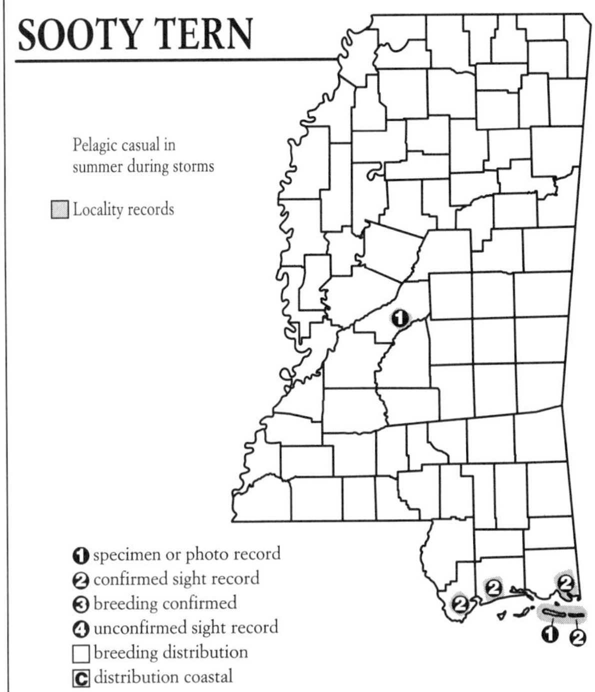

	JAN	FEB	MAR	APR	MAY	JUN	JUL	AUG	SEP	OCT	NOV	DEC
OCCURRENCE						17 o	11 ooo	oooo	oooo	oooo 29		
MUSEUM*												
WHT*												

*Breeding confirmed by egg, sight, or photographic record.

The Sooty Tern is recognized by blackish upperparts, deeply forked tail with white edges, white forehead and underparts, and a black bill and legs. Juveniles are sooty brown overall with whitish flecking on the upperparts, pale underwings and pale whitish on the lower belly and tail coverts.

This species has been recorded in the three coastal counties. All occurrences were associated with southerly storm winds or tropical hurricanes and were within a period from July 11 to October 29. The first coastal record was a dead bird found on June 17, 1956 (Newman 1956). A first mainland sighting at Bay St. Louis was on August 1, 1974 (Toups and Jackson 1987).

Subsequently, sightings by others have occurred on Horn Island on October 14, 1978 (Jackson et al. 1978), at Gulfport in Harrison County on August 15, 1985, and in Jackson County on July 11, 1979, 19 were sighted during Hurricane Bob. Five sightings along the mainland occurred during Hurricanes Danny and Juan in 1985 (King et al. 1985a). Oddly, the first collected specimen from Canton in Madison County was a bird found dead on September 20, 1957, by Roy Stephens after inland passage of Hurricane Ester (Gandy and Turcotte 1970). The specimen is in the MMNS. An inland sighting of three birds occurred on September 13, 1979, following Hurricane Frederick at Hattiesburg in Forrest County.

Sooty Terns lay only one egg in a slight scrape on dunes under a bush or near some grass or object. The eggs have a whitish or buff ground color, variously spotted with dark shades of brown. After nesting, these terns wander the tropical seas.

Black Tern *Chlidonias niger*

The Black Tern is a fairly common summer visitor to the Mississippi Coast on barrier islands, beaches, and marshes. In late summer and in passage from their northern breeding grounds, these terns are common and concentrate on beaches and islands until early October.

Black Terns nest in marshes of the Canadian provinces and northern United States. They migrate mainly through the Mississippi Valley. In spring passage, they occur on the coast from late March or early April and on inland lakes and reservoirs from mid-April to June. Inland passage from breeding grounds to staging grounds along the coast occurs from mid-July to October. The wintering grounds are in southern South America.

The breeding adult is *all black* on the head and body, except for *white* undertail coverts. The back, wings, and tail are dark gray above. In flight, the underwings show *uniform light gray.* The tail is shorter than most terns of similar size and *slightly forked.* Juveniles and winter adults are all white below with *dark gray* upperparts and tail, and a dark crown and ear patch extending from the crown. In flight, the sides of the breast show a dark smudge or bar.

Adults in late summer molt have patchy, irregular black-and-white plumage. Although considerably smaller in size, single nonbreeding Black Terns in basic plumage occur in midsummer on the Gulf Coast and can be mistaken for the adult Sooty Tern. However, the adult Sooty Tern is much darker above, all white below, and lacks the dark smudge extending to the sides of the breast of juvenile and adult Black Terns in basic plumage.

[Brown Noddy] *Anous stolidus*

This pelagic bird ranges widely over tropical oceans, where it breeds in colonies on islands. Unlike most terns, the Brown Noddy builds a nest in trees or bushes, usually laying a single egg. Large numbers breed with Sooty Terns on the Dry

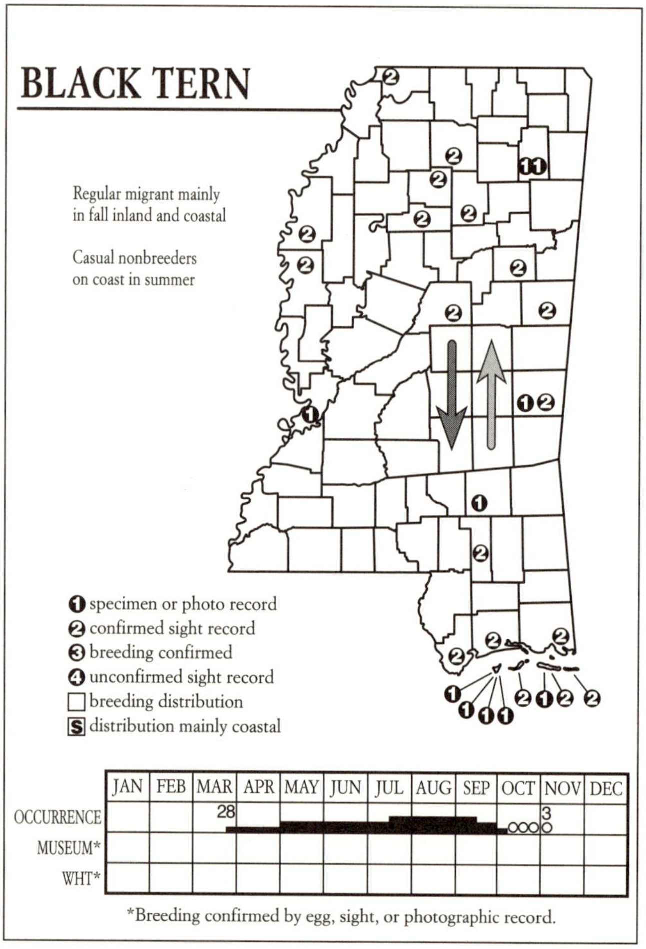

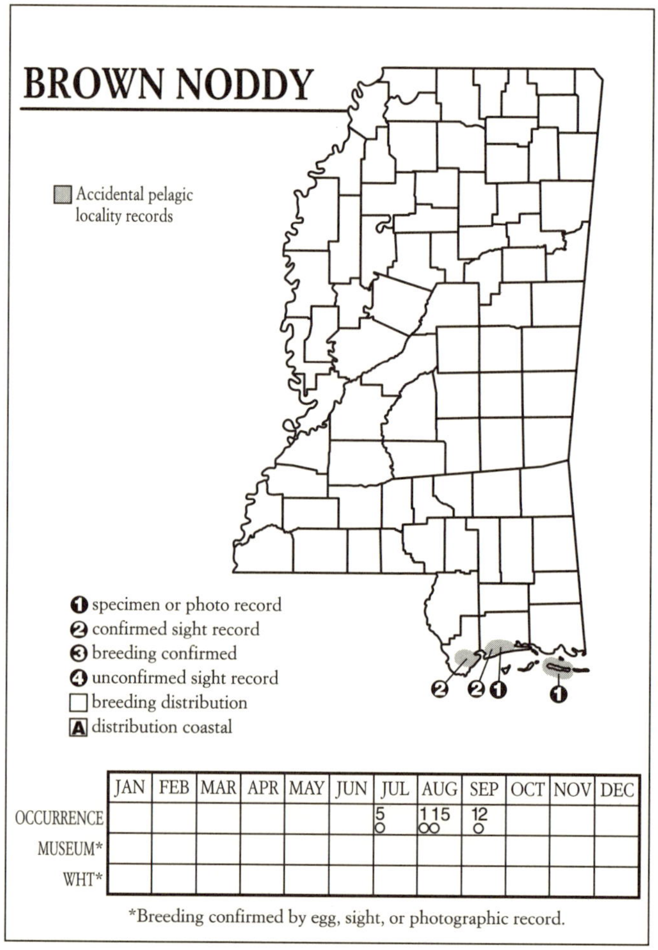

Tortugas off the western coast of the Florida Keys. Along the Atlantic Coast north to Cape Hatteras, and along the northern Gulf Coast, occurrences of Brown Noddies are related to tropical storms or hurricanes moving toward land.

The Brown Noddy derives its name from habitual head-bobbing in courtship and feeding rituals during nest construction and incubation. The female stays with the nest, and the male brings her food. The overall *dusky brown body* coloration; *whitish cap;* and a *long, wedge-shaped tail* with a small V-notch at the end are the key field identification marks for noddies. Other terns with dark bodies have noticeably forked tails.

The first Mississippi record for the Brown Noddy is a specimen in the MMNS found dead in Gulfport on September 20, 1961, by Dr. Maurice F. Baker following passage of Hurricane Carla (Clawson 1961). Three were seen by Judith A. Toups at Clermont Harbor on August 1, 1974, the first sight record for this species. A tropical storm was in progress at the time. A second dead specimen was found on Horn Island on July 5, 1979 (Jackson and Cooley 1980). Another sight record was of a grounded bird during Hurricane Danny at Gulfport on August 15, 1985 (King 1985). All Brown Noddy sightings on the Gulf Coast have been related to tropical storms.

Frequently Black Skimmers, their nests, and young, are found on sand and shell dunes in Mississippi Sound.

Rynchopinae (Skimmers)

Black Skimmer *Rynchops niger*

The Black Skimmer is a common permanent resident on the Mississippi Coast. On rare occasions, it has occurred inland during passing hurricanes. It breeds in colonies on the barrier islands, where it nests on beaches and on dredge spoil areas of the Pascagoula River estuary. It usually nests near colonies of Least, Sandwich, Royal, or Caspian Terns, and Laughing Gulls. On our mainland estuaries and beaches, it has nested with Least and Gull-billed Terns.

The Black Skimmer nest is a shallow scrape in the sand or shells. The four or five eggs are creamy white and boldly blotched, splashed, and spotted with blackish brown, gray, and lavender to match the shells, sand, and other surrounding debris. Colonies of 200 or more pairs have been found on coastal islands and beaches in May, June, and July.

The adult Black Skimmer in alternate plumage is black on the crown and upperparts. In flight its long, narrow wings show white outer margins on the secondaries. The face, outer-tail feathers, and underparts are white. The primary and secondary wing feathers are dusky on the underside. Underwing coverts are white. At rest, the red feet and legs; large black-tipped, bright red bill with a *longer lower mandible;* black upperparts; and white lower parts are distinctive.

Skimmers at rest along shorelines usually are seen in

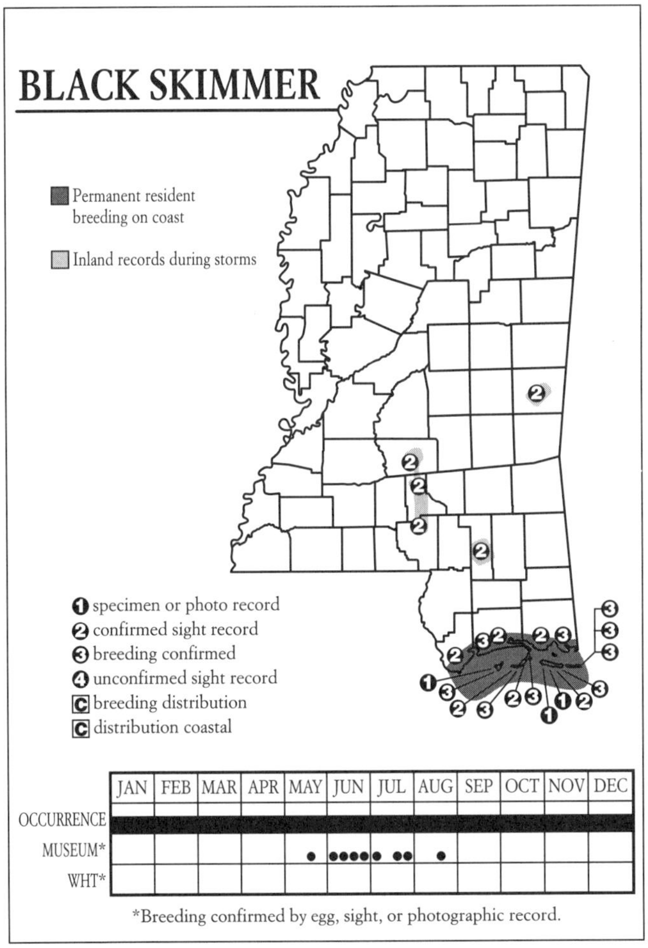

The advance and recession of the tide along the Gulf Coast creates a myriad of tidal pools where many species of shore and wading birds can be seen feeding.

sizeable flocks with their long silhouettes facing windward. They frequently associate with gulls, terns, and shorebirds while resting at favorite sites along the beach from Biloxi to Pass Christian. When flushed, a flock of skimmers takes off simultaneously, rising, wheeling, and turning in unison before descending to alight on another part of the beach.

The Black Skimmer in basic adult plumage shows a whitish collar separating the crown from black upperparts. Juveniles are mottled brownish on the crown and back. They have smaller bills than adults.

The Black Skimmer feeds mostly at night when it is fully capable of skimming the water of bays, bayous, and narrow, shallow inlets far into the upperparts of marshes to obtain its food supplies. Often it prefers to feed along the shallows of tidal shorelines and mud flats.

Black Skimmers are known by several local names along the Mississippi Coast. Fishermen use the name "seadog," which is derived from the low, barking calls made by these birds. Another local term is "scissor-bill," or "shearwater," a name derived from its unusual feeding habit. Skimmers are unrelated to oceanic shearwaters.

The downy young of Black Skimmer are the color of damp beach sand with dusky spots on the head and back and white underparts. While small, they remain together in the nest scrape. When alarmed they have the peculiar protection device of quickly digging themselves downward into loose sand, flattening the body and remaining motionless to escape detection.

Pigeons and Doves (Columbiformes)

These birds are nearly worldwide in distribution in tropical and temperate regions. They have small heads relative to their plump bodies and walk with a head-bobbing gait on short legs. They have fan-shaped or pointed tails and long, pointed wings. They are strong, fast flyers and prized as game birds. They feed mostly on wild seeds, grains, and fruits.

Some species in this family nest in loose colonies. Most build platform nests and lay two white eggs. The young are fed by regurgitation with a mixture of partly digested food and "pigeon milk" from glands in the crops of adults. The young develop quickly in the nest and are able to fly at an early age.

Females have duller plumage than males. The immatures have paler feather tips and lack the colorful neck markings of the adults. Pigeons and doves give cooing calls.

Above: Mourning Dove

Columbidae (Pigeons and Doves)

Rock Dove *Columba livia*

The domesticated pigeon or Rock Dove is familiar to city dwellers in most of the world. It was introduced from Europe and now occurs in a semiwild state in the United States, Canada, and Mexico. In the feral state, it lives in cities, where it nests on building ledges and under bridges. In the countryside, it adapts to nesting in lofts or on roofs of farm buildings and under bridges and overpasses of highways and railroads. It has adapted to feeding on spilled grain from rail cars as well as on grain fields, and on grains spilled or wasted around farms, feed lots, and storage bins. In cities and parks, Rock Doves often survive on handouts from people.

The Rock Dove has been domesticated for several thousand years and has been bred selectively into numerous colors, shapes, and sizes. Many are raised for speed, endurance, and homing instincts for racing and carrying messages by pigeon fanciers.

The original Rock Dove was mostly slate gray with iridescent patches on the sides of the neck, a white rump patch, dark terminal tail band, and two black bars across the secondaries. Most feral Rock Doves (except white forms) still retain all or some of these marks.

Rock Doves raise multiple broods over a long reproductive season. Even though only two white eggs are laid for a clutch, successive broods allow a high reproductive rate.

Feral pigeons often become nuisances in parks and cities when they become too numerous. Their constant cooing and their droppings become a problem when they congregate to nest on buildings in large numbers. Control measures such as trapping are often used by city officials to remove surplus birds. In Mississippi, this species is a breeding permanent resident in cities, towns, countryside farms, interstate highway bridges, and overpasses.

[Band-tailed Pigeon] *Columba fasciata*

This bird of the western states is larger than a Rock Dove. It breeds locally on the lower slopes of the Rocky Mountains in oak and pine forests and westward to the Pacific Coast. It winters in Mexico, California, Arizona, and New Mexico. It is a noted wanderer, however, and has occurred in Alabama, Tennessee, Louisiana, and Florida.

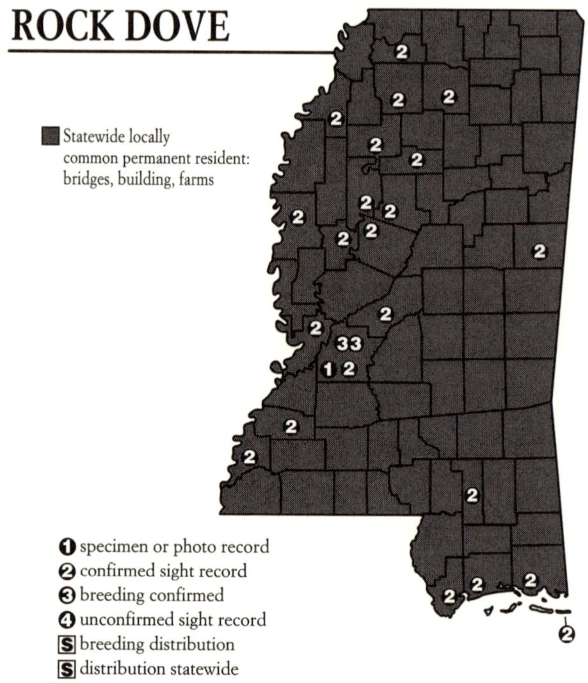

	JAN	FEB	MAR	APR	MAY	JUN	JUL	AUG	SEP	OCT	NOV	DEC
OCCURRENCE												
MUSEUM*												
WHT*							12 18 ●●					

*Breeding confirmed by egg, sight, or photographic record.

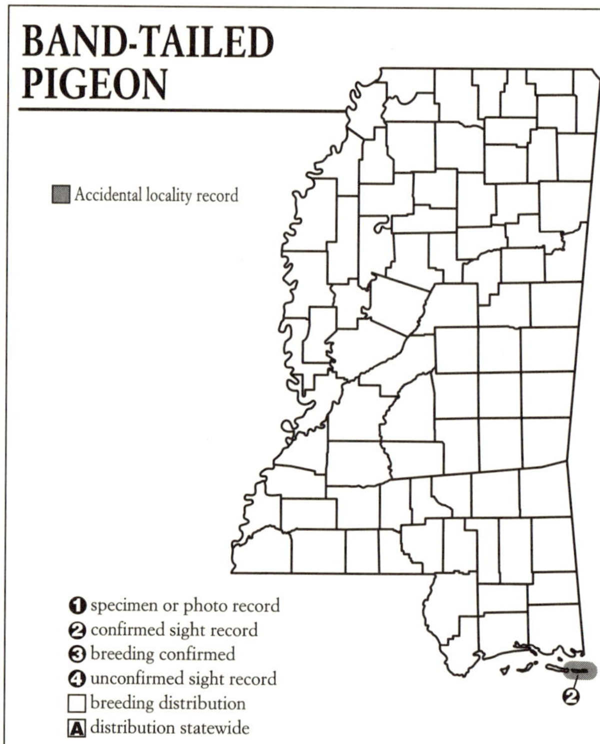

	JAN	FEB	MAR	APR	MAY	JUN	JUL	AUG	SEP	OCT	NOV	DEC
OCCURRENCE												2 ○
MUSEUM*												
WHT*												

*Breeding confirmed by egg, sight, or photographic record.

We have only one substantiated sight record for Mississippi, a single bird seen on December 2, 1978, by Cooley et al. (1979b) on Petit Bois Island in Jackson County. While camping on the island, a party of observers saw the Band-tailed Pigeon approach the only trees near the camp and circle several times. It attempted to alight in a pine within 30 feet of the observers, who viewed it in good light over a period of at least five minutes. Distinctive field marks were noted and described.

A broad, gray tip on a fan-shaped tail, large size, and a white, crescent-shaped band across the back of the neck identify this species. The yellow bill with a dark tip also should be noted. The head and breast are purplish with iridescence on the back of the neck behind the narrow, white neck band. Feet and legs are yellow. The wings and the remainder of the body are similar in color to the Mourning Dove. The large size, distinctly banded tail, and somewhat erratic, side-to-side, zigzag movements, and swift flight are noticeably different from Rock Doves.

The calls of Band-tailed Pigeons resemble the hootings of an owl and the calls of domestic pigeons. Unlike most doves and pigeons, this species rarely lays more than one egg, which is placed in a platform nest, usually in scrubby trees.

WHITE-WINGED DOVE

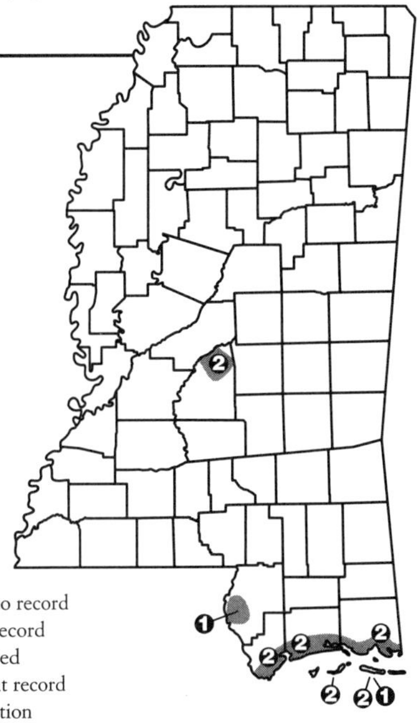

■ Uncommon visitor locality records fall & winter, mainly coastal

❶ specimen or photo record
❷ confirmed sight record
❸ breeding confirmed
❹ unconfirmed sight record
□ breeding distribution
Ⓒ distribution mainly coastal

	JAN	FEB	MAR	APR	MAY	JUN	JUL	AUG	SEP	OCT	NOV	DEC
OCCURRENCE	oooo	oooo	oooo	oooo	30 oooo					3 oooo	oooo	oooo
MUSEUM*												
WHT*												

*Breeding confirmed by egg, sight, or photographic record.

White-winged Dove *Zenaida asiatica*

The White-winged Dove is commonly found as a breeding bird in the Rio Grande Valley of Texas, New Mexico, and other southwestern border states. In the valley, large numbers invade the irrigated croplands, affording local hunters a short open season. They nest in large colonies along the border, in Mexico, and Central America. Citrus groves, mesquite thickets, riparian woodlands, and saguaro-paloverde deserts are favored nesting sites.

This species is slightly larger in body size than the Mourning Dove. It has uniformly gray upper and lower parts, white primary and secondary coverts, and some white on the tips of the secondaries. At rest, the *large patches* on the wings identify it. The fan-shaped, *rounded* tail has *white tips* on the outer feathers. A narrow, black bar below the auriculars separates an iridescent patch on the sides of the neck. The feet and legs are red.

The White-winged Dove is an uncommon fall and winter visitor to the coastal counties, but rarely occurs farther inland. Among the thousands of Mourning Doves taken by Mississippi hunters, only one interior record has been reported of a White-winged Dove being taken, a bird killed by Joseph Spiers at Carriere in Pearl River County on October 3, 1957 (Gandy and Turcotte 1970).

This dove occurs on the Gulf Coast in October, November, and December regularly in low numbers, usually sightings of single birds. One flock of six was seen on October 9, 1984, at Bellefontaine Beach in Jackson County. There are recent records of the White-winged Dove in the three coastal counties from October 9 to May 30.

Mourning Dove *Zenaida macroura*

This migratory bird is common over its breeding range, in all of the United States and parts of southern Canada and Mexico. The Mourning Dove is a popular game bird, except in some northern states where it is considered a songbird. In the Southeast and Southwest, it is highly regarded as game and is hunted over planted or harvested grain fields and around watering places. Hunting these birds has had little impact on the population other than removing part of an annual surplus, leaving more than enough breeders for next year's population.

Although these and most other doves usually lay only two eggs at a setting, Mourning Doves usually raise multiple broods. As many as four or five nestings in one season by a single pair have been noted. The reproduction cycle from egg to fledging of young takes little more than three weeks. A few doves in the Southeast and Southwest begin nesting in late February, and some nesting continues into September. David Watts of the Department of Wildlife, Fisheries and Parks banded two Mourning Dove nestlings on March 24, 1993, in a nest in B. E. Gandy's front yard in Brandon. The birds fledged the next day. Backdating from the fledging day means that nesting and courtship took place in February.

The Mourning Dove builds a flimsy platform nest, usually on a tree or shrub limb or occasionally on the ground in protective cover. Pecan groves and peach orchards are preferred nesting sites. Pines and oaks with spreading branches in open pastures or woodland borders are frequently used for nesting.

In the Yazoo Delta, where suitable nesting places are sparse and widely separated, nesting occurs mainly along ditches and bayous, where the water locust is the preferred nest tree. Pecan groves in the Delta support numerous nesting pairs and ornamental or shade trees in towns are commonly used by nesting birds.

The young in the nest are fed by both adults on partially digested seeds and pigeon milk produced by glands in the dove's crop. The regurgitated food is then pumped into the throat of nestlings until they fledge. The adults then immediately start another nesting cycle.

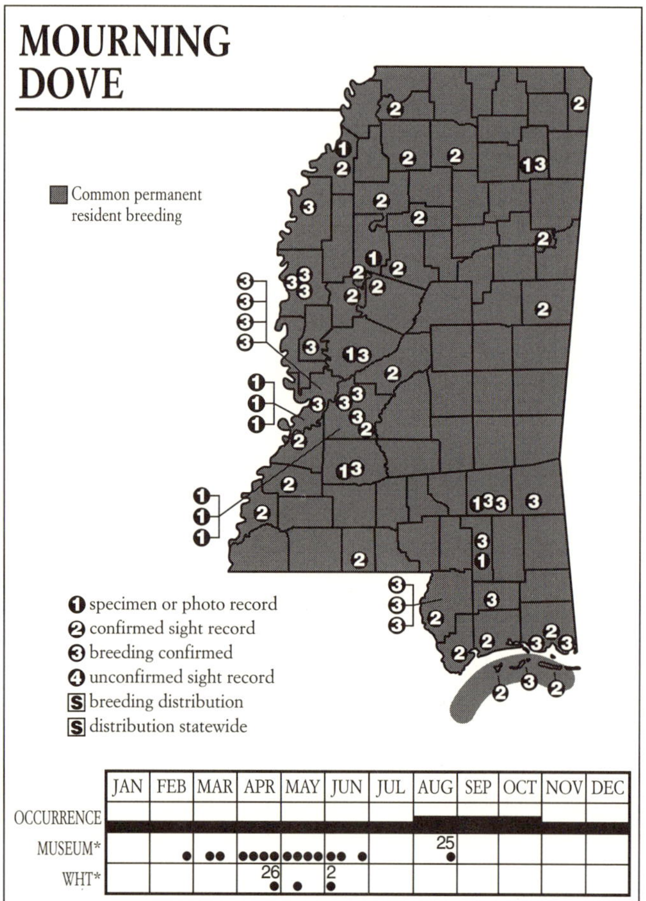

*Breeding confirmed by egg, sight, or photographic record.

Young doves leaving the nest have light-colored edging on the primary wing coverts. These are molted in sequence from the inside outward as juveniles develop adult plumage. Examination of dove wings in hunters' bags has shown that 70 percent or more of doves harvested in the early part of open seasons are young of the year. Federal migratory game bird regulations establish seasons and bag limits annually, usually with options for individual states to select a season or split seasons within an overall established framework.

Dove hunting is a popular sport in early fall when organized dove shoots usually are held on newly planted or harvested grain fields. These early hunts are widely dispersed, and not always successful. After two or three early season hunts on concentrations of mostly young-of-the-year birds, the law of diminishing returns sets in, and dove hunting tapers off for the remainder of the season for most hunters.

The Mourning Dove is easily recognized by its plump yet slim body; short legs; small, bobbing head; long, pointed wings; and long tail feathers tapering to a point with white outer tips showing in flight. Adults have black spots on the upperwing and a pink wash on the buffy underparts. Juveniles have heavy spotting and a scaly appearance on the wings. Females are duller than males. Adults have a patch of iridescence on the sides of the neck and a small black spot below the auriculars. The bird's general appearance is mostly gray above and buffy on the undersides.

The cooing calls of the Mourning Dove start with a double note *oowoo'* followed by the mournful *ooo-oo-oo*. Singing males are especially active in the early morning hours of the breeding season.

[Passenger Pigeon] *Ectopistes migratorius*

The Passenger Pigeon is extinct, and perhaps the very name implies that Passenger Pigeons were destined for passage from the planet. We need to remember the often-told stories of their mass slaughter and extermination by market hunters at immense breeding colonies. This unlimited killing was aided by apathy and carelessness, an expanding human population, and technology. The last Passenger Pigeon, named Martha, died on September 1, 1914, as a captive in the Cincinnati Zoological Park. On that date, the species joined ranks with the Dodo, a large flightless pigeon once inhabiting islands off the coast of Madagascar. Dodos were exterminated for food by early explorers who killed them with clubs. No trace of Dodos remains today other than drawings made by travelers.

Before this country was settled, vast regions of the eastern United States were covered with hardwood forests. Passenger Pigeons, estimated in the billions by early explorers, ranged over the forest, feeding on the mast of beech,

The Passenger Pigeon, immortalized in Alexander Wilson's *American Ornithology,* was once a common sight across Mississippi. The bird became extinct in 1914.

oaks, and native chestnuts. Huge flocks of birds in passage to and from feeding grounds and communal roosts darkened the sky.

They were known to break large limbs off trees by their sheer weight on roosts, which could cover 40 square miles or more, their droppings covering the ground to a depth of several inches. Natural predators including wolves, foxes, bobcats, hawks, owls, and even vultures could not penetrate or decimate their immense numbers on roosts and at breeding colonies.

Early settlers took Passenger Pigeons for food with traps, nets, and guns, but this had little effect because the flocks were highly mobile. They moved on when food supplies were exhausted, a strategy similar to that used today by insects such as cicadas and grasshoppers. The birds overwhelmed their natural predators either by their great numbers or mobility, enabling them to exploit all available food sources.

The Passenger Pigeon became vulnerable only when advancing civilization brought railroads and the telegraph within easy reach of breeding colonies (Blockstein and Tordoff 1985). In 1871, one colony in Wisconsin covered *850 square miles* and contained an estimated *135 million* birds. Such large concentrations, when accessible to eastern markets by telegraph and a network of available railroads, were marked for extinction by professional pigeon hunters.

Every conceivable method was used to decimate the breeding birds and ship them in barrels and carloads to big city markets for human consumption. In the 1890s deforestation and exploitation had their final effects on the birds, and the last wild specimens were taken in Wisconsin and Ohio. The last sight records of Passenger Pigeons are debatable.

Gideon Lincecum (1874b) visited and explored a breeding colony of Passenger Pigeons in April and early May of 1832. It occurred north of Columbus along 15 miles of Tombigbee River bottomland in virgin timber that was up to two miles wide. Five excursions were made during the breeding cycle. Nest-building, egg laying, young in the nest, and fledging of the young were described.

Lincecum (1874b) described the nests and nest-building period:

> They made their nests of small dry twigs, bits of sticks, dry leaves and all kind of trash found on the ground, and by the time they had completed their work, the entire bottom looked black and clear of litter as if it had been swept with a broom, not a leaf nor a stick was left, and to judge from the appearance of the scanty nests, the birds didn't have half enough.
>
> Through all the before mentioned 30 square miles of that densely timbered bottom, from as high as one's head on horseback on the saplings, to the topmost limbs on the tallest trees, not a vacant spot where a nest could be crowded in, was to be found anywhere.

Egg laying commenced synchronously and only one egg per nest was found on a later visit. During the incubation period,

> the foliage of the trees had not yet unfolded but the packed and muffled up appearance of their tops made the swamp dark as midsummer. On the large horizontal prongs of the big trees, were long rows of nests, closely jammed side by side, and in all the forks, on projecting knots and many more unlikely places nests were found. Many on the saplings were frequently found so low that sitting on horseback one could peep into them; and finding but one egg in each, we surmised that they were not done laying. . . . Three days after we went again, but there were no more eggs, one a piece was all that was deposited at that nesting place.

Lincecum described the enormous activity and noise of feeding the young on later visits. Then, the adults suddenly abandoned the fledglings in the nests for two days when all of the young left simultaneously. Two days later great numbers of the young pigeons were on adjacent prairies of the Chickasaw and Choctaw Nations feeding on the fields of wild strawberries. The Indians were killing them with sticks for food. Four days later all were gone. The adults presumably moved northward to new feeding grounds and were followed by the young as soon as the strawberries were consumed. Lincecum confirmed the presence and departure of the young pigeons from the strawberry fields on two hunting trips to the prairie to shoot pigeons and night-hunt for deer.

Although the Passenger Pigeon once occurred and even nested in Mississippi, there is little evidence. Imhof (1976) records it in Alabama in large flocks up to 1881 and last seen in 1890. Only a few place names such as Pigeon Roost Creek and a marker on the Natchez Trace remind us of the birds' former presence. Ample evidence of the Passenger Pigeon can be found in literature, and many museum specimens and exhibits remain to document its passage to extinction.

The reproductive potential of the Passenger Pigeon was very low compared to the Mourning Dove and Bobwhite Quail. The dove commonly lays two eggs and produces multiple broods each season. Quail lay 10 or more eggs and renest until a brood is hatched. But the Passenger Pigeon laid only one egg, and laying and hatching in the colonies were highly synchronous. Although the pigeons would renest, the pressures of feeding young in large colonies constricted the breeding period. The ability of both adults to produce pigeon milk while feeding young twice a day was abetted by mobility, enabling them to range far and wide to obtain sufficient food.

The Passenger Pigeon was larger than but similar to the Mourning Dove. It had a longer tail and was bluish gray instead of brown on the back and head. The adult male was more colorful on the throat, breast, and sides. Being highly esteemed as food made the birds a candidate for early destruction. Squabs were a prized delicacy. The American bison was threatened in a similar fashion, but fortunately it has survived.

Common Ground-Dove *Columbina passerina*

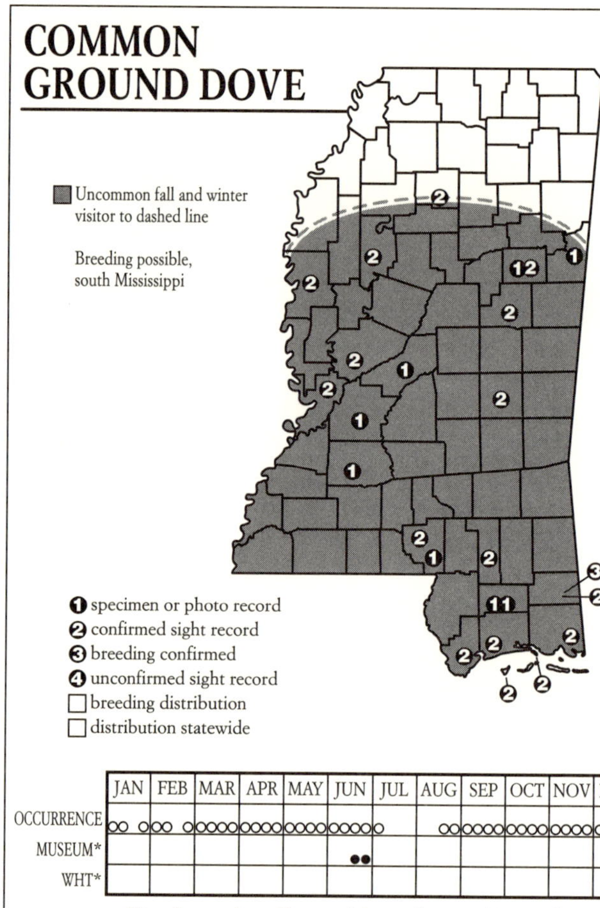

*Breeding confirmed by egg, sight, or photographic record.

This diminutive species, not much larger than a sparrow, is an uncommon fall and winter visitor along the Gulf Coast and a rare, local summer resident. Breeding has been reported in Mississippi only as late as 1995. It occurs rarely at inland areas during early fall and early winter. Vaiden (1952a) and Burleigh (1945) collected specimens in fall and winter that were identified as the western subspecies found in southern Texas and Mexico. Most state records are from the three coastal counties.

The Common Ground-Dove can be recognized by its small size, pinkish gray underparts, rufous red primaries and wing linings, and short, black tail with white-tipped outer feathers. It has yellow legs and feet, nods its head, and often raises the tail when walking. Most sight records are of single birds, for it is seldom seen in flocks.

These birds can easily escape notice. They spend most of their time on the ground and are reluctant to flush. They usually are found in open country on croplands and weedy field edges, and along protected beach edges and roadsides. Ground-Doves breed in Alabama and in Louisiana, so they probably will nest in some coastal counties and possibly in the Yazoo Delta.

I have seen single birds in Yazoo County on April 19 and June 3, 1960, and on two other occasions in early September in the same area, an indication that these birds may breed locally. Johnson and Phares (1959) reported a single bird on October 7, 1959, near Lawrence in Newton County.

The first nesting record in George County was a pair that fledged two young between June 18 and 28, 1995. The nest was in a greenhouse and seen by Lucy Jacobson and multiple observers (Purrington 1995). Chita Cassibry photographed one of the adult birds on the nest.

Ground-Doves build a small platform nest usually on the ground or in low bushes. Two white or creamy white eggs make a setting. The call is a soft, ascending *wooo-ah*.

Typical Parrots (Psittaciformes)

Members of the parrot family and their allies are native to the southern hemisphere in tropical and temperate zones. Mexican species occur as far north as the Texas and Arizona border. Several species from northern Mexico occur rarely, or annually, along the lower Rio Grande Valley into Texas and occasionally into southeastern Arizona. The only endemic species of birds in this order, the Carolina Parakeet, is extinct.

Any parrot, parakeet, or Cockatiel seen in Mississippi is almost certain to be an escape. I have investigated reports of unusual birds that proved to be Budgerigars (parakeets) or Cockatiels. A Monk Parakeet appeared in our garden once, and while it sat eating on an ear of corn, my wife Dorothy captured and throttled it without being bitten. It wore an aluminum band and later was taken to the Jackson Zoological Park.

A dozen or more parrot or parakeet species are being propagated in aviaries. Several kinds of the parakeets have become naturalized, mainly in Florida, around large cities and suburbs, along the East Coast, and in the Los Angeles area. The Monk Parakeet is established in Tampa and other Florida cities where it builds huge, communal nests of sticks on utility poles, in palms, and other trees.

Parrots are colorful, short-necked, noisy, and they have stout, hooked beaks. They are long-lived and require constant attention and special care as pets in captivity. Outside of their cages, they can bite and be destructive, and sometimes their screechings can be unbearable nuisances.

Above: Carolina Parakeet

Psittacidae (Typical Parrots)

[Carolina Parakeet] *Conuropsis carolinensis*

Once endemic to the Southeast, the Carolina Parakeet is extinct. The last known record of this small parakeet was in 1920 in Florida. In most of its former range, it was on the verge of extinction by the 1800s due to activities of early settlers.

These birds were shot for food and the millinery trade. They also were netted and sold as pets. They were regarded as pests because they ate many kinds of fruits and raided farmers' corn fields. The birds were highly vulnerable, because when one was shot or crippled the flock would not leave the wounded member. Large numbers were shot in that manner.

There are no verifiable Mississippi records of the Carolina Parakeet, other than sightings by travelers during the early 1800s (McKinley 1981). Hahn (1963) lists only two museum specimens from Mississippi; both have incomplete records and questionable origins. Undoubtedly these birds were present in Mississippi at Natchez and along Bayou Pierre in Claiborne County, where they were seen and reported by Alexander Wilson (1811).

The Carolina Parakeet ranged widely and traveled in large flocks. It fed on a large variety of wild fruits, seeds, nuts, acorns, and cultivated orchard fruits and grain crops. Favorite wild plant foods were cocklebur and thistle seeds in their milky stage of development.

The head and short neck of the adult parakeet were yellow with red bordering the bill and extending across the forehead to a line under the eye. The remainder of the bird was bright green, except for yellow or orange edging at the bend of the wings.

Cuckoos and Allies (Cuculiformes)

The cuckoos and their relatives, the roadrunners and anis, are long-tailed birds with two toes directed forward and two directed to the rear. In the Eastern Hemisphere, the members of this family are parasitic in their nesting habits. They build no nests, but instead deposit their eggs in the nests of other, usually smaller, birds. The victimized bird then assumes the responsibility for raising the cuckoo's young, often at the expense of losing its own eggs or young. American cuckoos raise their own young and are notorious for building frail platform nests.

Some anis have communal nesting habits and share a common nest, incubation of the eggs, and raising of the young. Roadrunners are large cuckoos that are mostly terrestrial in their habits. They have not occurred in Mississippi, but are extending their range eastward from northwestern Louisiana and southwestern Arkansas.

Above: Yellow-billed Cuckoo

Cuculidae (Cuckoos and Allies)

Black-billed Cuckoo *Coccyzus erythropthalmus*

This species is a spring and fall transient throughout our state. It is a rather scarce migrant in the spring from late April to early June. Fall records extend from late August to mid-October. There are no published breeding records for this bird in Mississippi.

Both mandibles of this bird's bill are uniformly black, and the adults have red eyelids. The tail feathers are dark gray on the underside with grayish white tips bordered inwardly with dusky coloring. The white tips on the tail feathers are much smaller than the white tips on the tail feathers of the Yellow-billed Cuckoo. The inner webs of the primary wing feathers are brownish instead of the rufous color of the Yellow-billed Cuckoo.

The song is a series of rhythmic, guttural notes in groups of three, four, or five. The song is similar to that of the Yellow-billed Cuckoo, but does not get slower near the end.

Yellow-billed Cuckoo *Coccyzus americanus*

The Yellow-billed Cuckoo is a slender, long-tailed bird about the size of a Mourning Dove. This species, along with the Black-billed Cuckoo, is commonly known as "rain-crow." They are slow and deliberate in their movements and often perch motionless for several minutes at a time. The song of the Yellow-billed Cuckoo is a long series of guttural *cowk, cowk* notes uttered rapidly and slowing down to *ceow-ceow* notes toward the end. The call is a prolonged, single, deep *ceowk* note.

Its underparts are pure white and upperparts are olive brown. The feathers of the long tail are graduated in length with the outer feathers being shorter than the inner ones. Tail feathers are black underneath and broadly tipped with white. When spread, primary wing feathers show a large amount of bright rufous. The lower mandible is yellow, and the upper is black.

This cuckoo arrives in late March through early May. It is a common, summer-resident, breeding bird throughout Mississippi, except on the barrier islands. Its departure begins in August and continues until late October.

The nest of this species is a frail, flat platform of twigs, catkins, and leaves usually placed on the horizontal branch

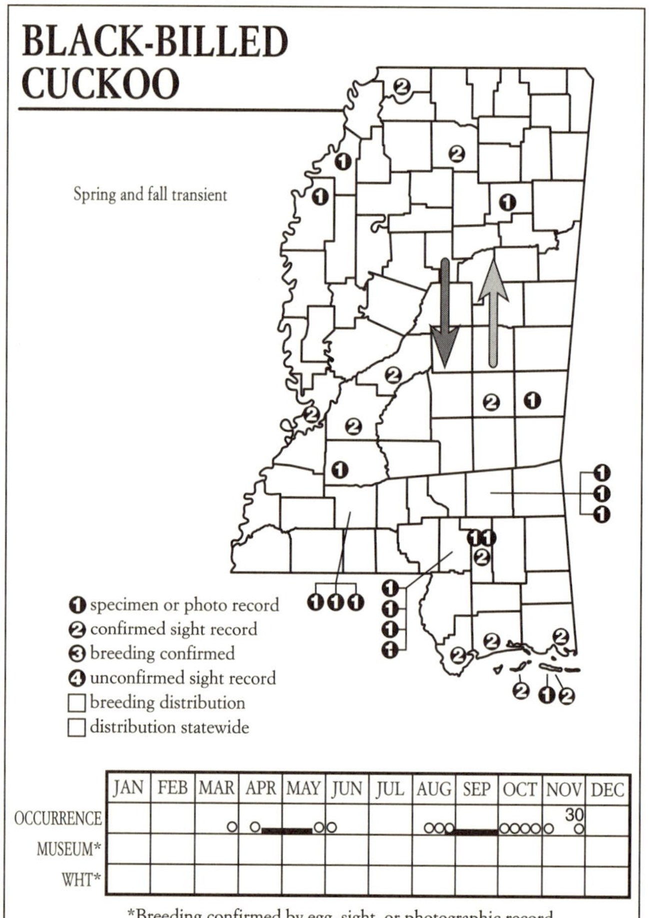

*Breeding confirmed by egg, sight, or photographic record.

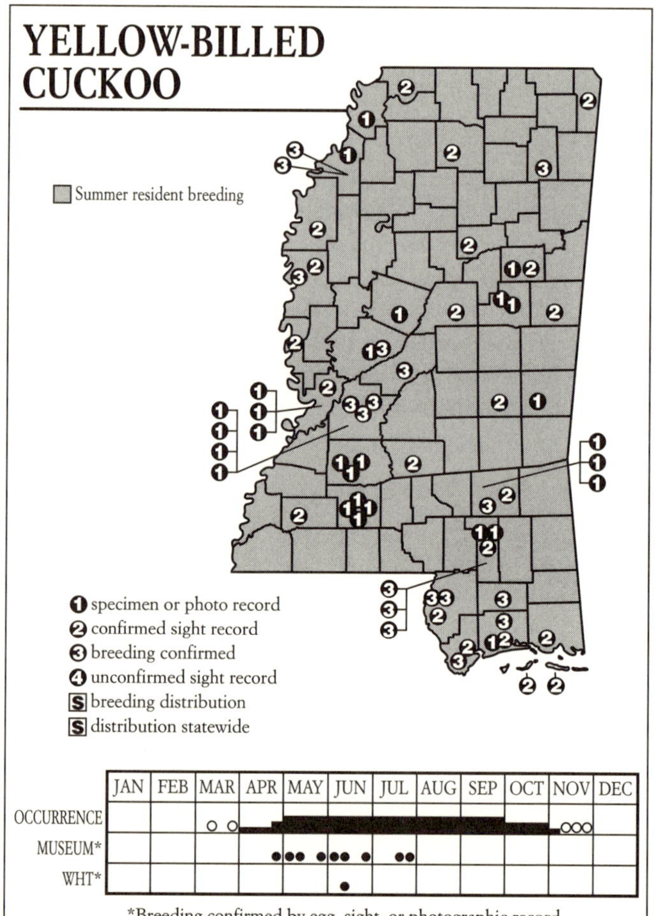

*Breeding confirmed by egg, sight, or photographic record.

of a tree or large shrub from eight to 20 feet or more aboveground. Three to five bluish green eggs make up a clutch. Nesting occurs mostly in May, June, and July.

The cuckoos eat mostly insects and sometimes small fruits. They are great destroyers of caterpillars and are highly beneficial birds to man.

Groove-billed Ani *Crotophaga sulcirostris*

Occurrence of the Groove-billed Ani in Mississippi is substantiated by two collected specimens. James Batson took one near Lumberton in Lamar County on October 5, 1940. This female specimen is in the MMNS in Jackson. The other specimen was taken by Thomas D. Burleigh at Gulfport in Harrison County on November 4, 1941. John G. McCloskey (Turcotte 1972e) reported another occurrence of anis when four appeared at his home in Pass Christian in Harrison County during the winter of 1972. They roosted in a bamboo thicket on an adjoining lot and remained until April. Three reappeared on his property during the fall of 1973.

Anis, about the same size as the Common Grackle, are solid black with some iridescence on the wings, back, and tail. The enormous, arched bill is a distinctive field mark. Parallel grooves on the sides of the upper mandible of adults characterize this species. Their flight is distinctive with alternate, labored flapping of the wings, then sailing and sidling usually for only a short distance to the nearest cover.

Anis are peculiar and unique birds that can be mistaken for the Common Grackle by a casual observer. They are found along the coast of Texas into the Rio Grande Valley, where they frequent woodlands and farm fields and are often seen feeding on insects around cattle. For some reason, a few migrate northeastward every year in the fall and appear regularly in southern Louisiana, especially below New Orleans. Lowery Jr. (1974) reported one instance of their breeding in a citrus grove in this part of Louisiana. In recent years, this ani has occurred regularly in low numbers along our coast in the fall and winter months.

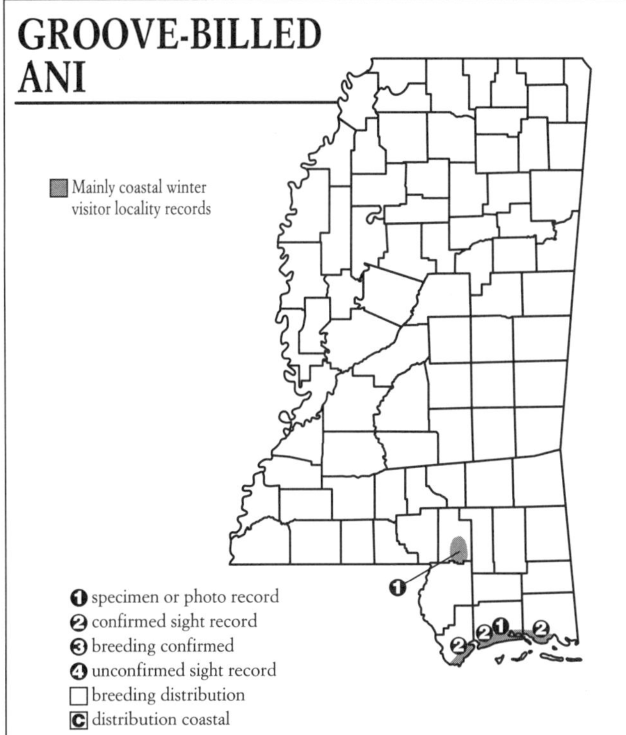

	JAN	FEB	MAR	APR	MAY	JUN	JUL	AUG	SEP	OCT	NOV	DEC
OCCURRENCE	5 o		o	o					8 o	2 oooo	oooo	oooo
MUSEUM*												
WHT*												

*Breeding confirmed by egg, sight, or photographic record.

Owls (Strigiformes)

These birds of prey are mostly nocturnal. They are easily recognized by their flat facial discs with eyes fixed in the sockets so they peer straight forward. The eyes are large and adapted for keen vision either at night or in daylight. Owls have strong, hooked bills; long, sharp claws; and long legs with the toes often feathered. Their feathers are usually soft and flexible and their flight is noiseless, enabling these birds to descend swiftly and capture prey without advanced warning.

The ears of owls are large, and their sense of hearing is very acute. They have large heads and short necks. Some species have conspicuous tufts of feathers called "horns." The sexes are alike, but the female is larger. Owls nest either in tree cavities or use the abandoned nests of crows, hawks, or squirrels. Their calls are distinctive whistles, wails, or hoots.

Above: Great Horned Owl

Tytonidae (Barn Owls)

Common Barn Owl *Tyto alba*

The Barn Owl, commonly called the "monkey-faced owl," is an uncommon permanent resident. It roosts and nests in lofts of barns, silos, abandoned buildings, and in hollow trees. It is the only owl with a white, heart-shaped facial disc.

The legs are long and have the appearance of being knock-kneed. Underparts are white or buffy and finely spotted with dark brown. Upperparts are reddish brown to yellowish buff and thinly spotted with dark brown dots. The call, a loud hissing sound much like steam escaping from a radiator, is seldom heard.

The Barn Owl is one of our most useful birds of prey. Its food consists almost entirely of rodents, among which Norway rats, rice rats, cotton rats, house mice, wood mice, field mice, and shrews are favorite items. Small birds and insects are also taken, but birds constitute only a small part of their diet.

The Barn Owl is erratic in its nesting habits. Eggs or young are likely to be found during any month of the year. The eggs are white and number from five to seven or more. They are laid at irregular intervals, and incubation begins as soon as the first egg is laid. Consequently, the young vary considerably in size. The nest consists of disgorged pellets that form a bed for the eggs and young. Hollow trees or stumps and dark recesses of bridges, abandoned buildings, barns, or silos are used for nesting.

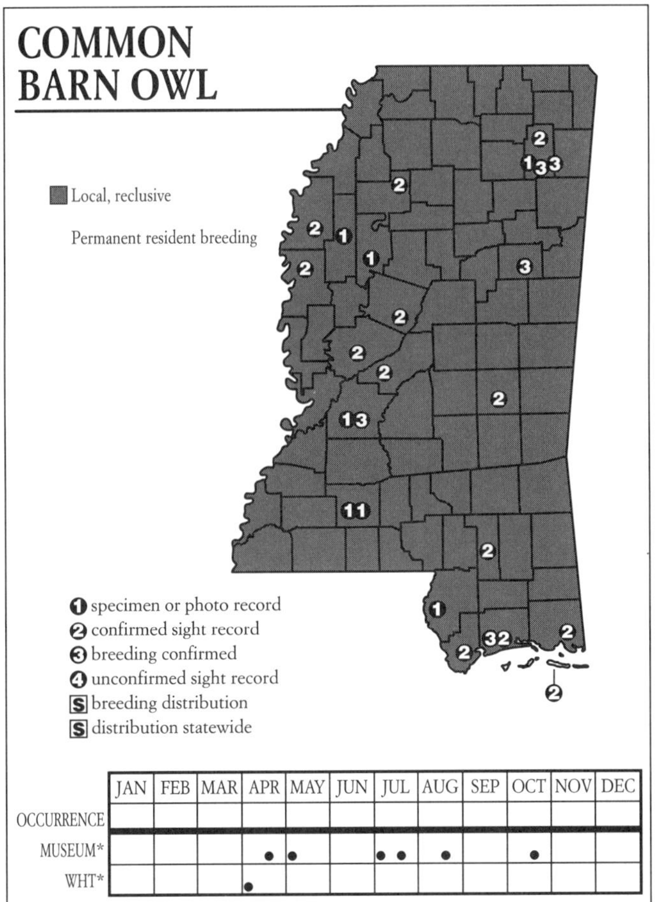

*Breeding confirmed by egg, sight, or photographic record.

This owl is distributed worldwide. It occurs in tropical and temperate areas of South America and north to southern Canada. The bird is declining in numbers in portions of the eastern and midwestern states.

Barn Owls are secretive during the day. Daytime is spent roosting in dark buildings, hollow trees, or in trees or evergreen thickets providing concealment and solitude. They hunt mostly at night and are seldom active in twilight hours. These owls prefer to hunt in open farming country, but they often are found in towns and cities where suitable nesting and roosting sites are available. They can be encouraged to use large nest boxes placed in silos, farm buildings, or on poles in or near woodlands or other quiet places.

Strigidae (Typical Owls)

Eastern Screech-Owl *Otus asio*

The Eastern Screech-Owl is a fairly common permanent resident throughout Mississippi. It is the only small owl with prominent ear tufts or "horns" occurring here. There are three color phases that appear in about equal proportions in the population. The gray and reddish brown color phases are the opposite extremes of coloration with an intermediate brown phase. In all color phases the upper and lower parts are heavily streaked lengthwise.

This owl is commonly known by its calls, a quavering whistle and a series of short, tremulous notes given in the same pitch. Its usual haunts are woodlands, orchards, and shade trees around urban residences. In daylight hours, it spends most of the time hiding in a tree cavity, a leafy brown bush, or in a dense, evergreen thicket. When approached, it is likely to assume its hiding pose—the body stretched out to the limit, its wings and feathers pressed closely to the body, and the eyes closed to slits, all to give the resemblance to the stub of a dead limb. Only when it is sure it has been discovered will it finally relax its pose and fly away.

Screech-Owls have a varied diet that includes almost every class of animal food. Its first order of food are insects such as large beetles, crickets, grasshoppers, and large moths. Next in order of preference are wood mice and field mice. Small birds are an important food item when young are being fed in the nest. In addition to insects, mammals, and birds, the Eastern Screech-Owl eats small snakes, lizards, frogs, fish, crayfish, and numerous invertebrates.

The Eastern Screech-Owl prefers to nest in woodpecker holes or natural tree cavities, but sometimes will utilize a

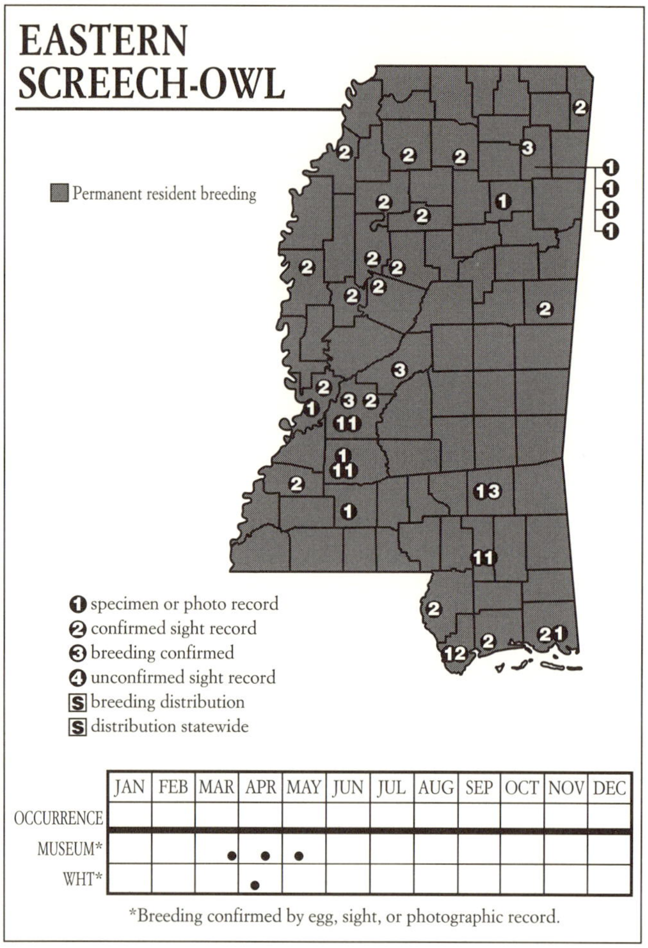

nest box. Nesting begins in late March or April. The three or five eggs are laid on wood chips or other debris at the bottom of the nest cavity. Like most owl eggs, they are white, slightly glossy, and usually oval or nearly globular in shape.

Chickadees, titmice, woodpeckers, and jays recognize the screech-owl as an enemy. When this owl is discovered in daylight, it is frequently mobbed by small birds with loud chattering and scoldings. A tape recording of the Eastern Screech-Owl's calls played during daytime usually will call up a troupe of birds. At night, these owls respond to a tape recording when played within their hearing range.

On one occasion, I played owl tapes while trying to attract and record a screech-owl. I was near a rural farmhouse on a winter night. Three screech-owls responded to the playback from trees near the house. I heard a door open and the occupant came out on the front porch, got a stick of stovewood, and started banging away on the side of the house. I decided to make a safe getaway before he brought out the shotgun.

I have discovered this owl roosting in a cedar tree or in a cluster of brown leaves. I watched their eyes following as I walked a circle around them. Imperceptibly, the owl's head would snap around so as to follow my movements when I got beyond the range of its fixed, straight-ahead vision.

Folklore has it that if you tie a knot in the corner of the bedsheet, a "scratch owl" will choke and go away at night. Needless to say, some people are superstitious about these little owls and think they are bad omens.

Great Horned Owl *Bubo virginianus*

The Great Horned Owl is the largest owl with ear tufts or "horns." It attains a length of almost two feet and is larger than any of the large hawks. The big eyes are yellow, and a prominent white collar extends across the throat. The upperparts are dark brown, and the underparts are finely barred horizontally.

The hooting calls of the Horned Owl are quite different from the well-known hooting of the Barred Owl. The sound can be likened to the deep-voiced baying of a hound dog in the distance. The call note is repeated four or five times, a low-pitched, tremulous *whoo, whoo-whoo, whoo, whoo.*

This owl is a common, widespread, breeding permanent resident in Mississippi. It frequents large, woodland tracts, and nearly every large woodland has its pair. They are fiercely possessive of their territory.

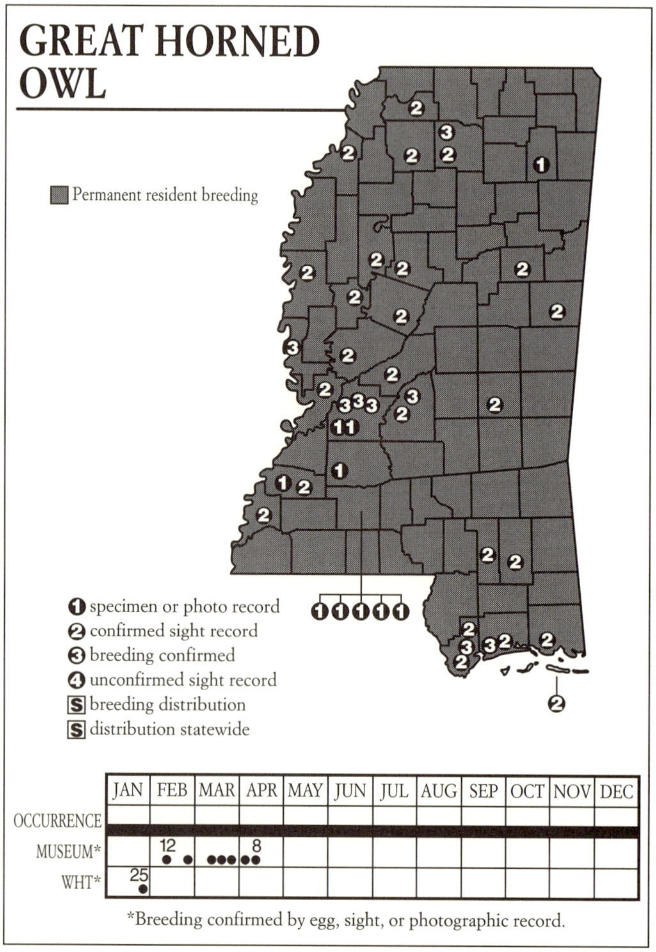

In Mississippi, the Great Horned Owl nests very early, about mid-January to February. I have found nests with small young around the first of March. This owl usually appropriates the old nest of a hawk, crow, or squirrel and lays one to three white, oval eggs. I found one nest with two eggs in the open, hollow fork of a large oak tree. All of the reoccupied nests I have examined, except one, were in squirrel, Red-shouldered Hawk, or Red-tailed Hawk nests. The other was in a Mississippi Kite nest in a tall cottonwood tree in a grove alongside the Mississippi River levee in Issaquena County.

This owl is the principal predator of skunks and crows. Nearly all that I have examined smelled strongly of skunk. Depredations upon poultry have given this owl a bad name. However, its good deeds are not often reported. It consumes great quantities of rodents, and rabbits are an important food item. A great variety of birds also may be eaten. In addition, it feeds upon snakes, frogs, fish, crayfish, and large insects.

[Snowy Owl] *Nyctea scandiaca*

This large, diurnal owl is circumpolar in distribution. It is mostly white, barred and flecked with dusky on the roundish head, body, and wings (heavier on immatures), with feathered feet and legs, and yellow eyes. It breeds on arctic tundra and retreats in winter to southern Canada and northern states, where a few may appear annually.

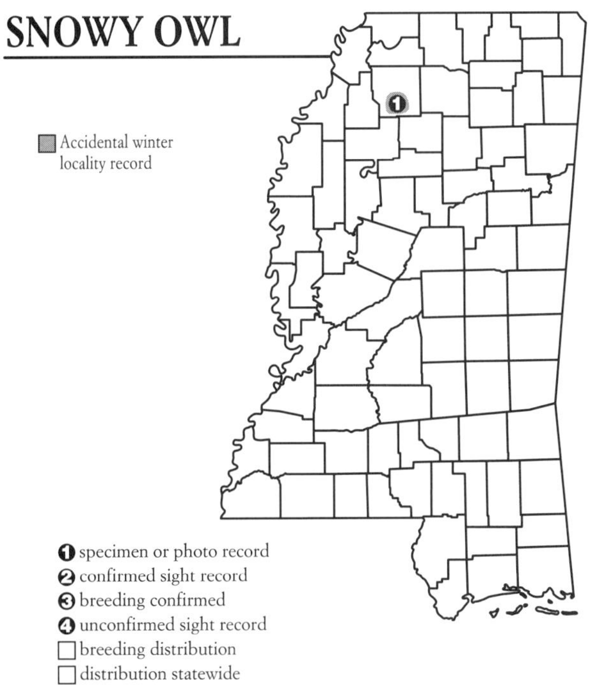

	JAN	FEB	MAR	APR	MAY	JUN	JUL	AUG	SEP	OCT	NOV	DEC
OCCURRENCE												12/19/30 ○
MUSEUM*												
WHT*												

*Breeding confirmed by egg, sight, or photographic record.

The Snowy Owl preys mostly on lemmings, and the bird's populations are related to the cyclic decline or increase of the arctic rodent population. Periodic irruptions of these owls occur when lemming populations decline, and young Snowy Owls may wander farther southward than their normal winter range.

Only one record of the Snowy Owl in Mississippi has been reported. A single specimen was shot at Como in Panola County on December 19, 1930, and examined by Coffey Jr. (1931). Three concurrent Tennessee records were reported on December 3, 22, and 31, 1930. The records were of specimens either shot or captured, then examined by Coffey Jr. and others. The Tennessee birds were taken at Reelfoot Lake, Johnson City, and Paris, Tennessee.

Burrowing Owl *Speotyto cunicularia*

The Burrowing Owl is common on the western plains and is a permanent resident in Florida, where it inhabits prairies and airports. In Mississippi, it is only a casual fall and winter visitor from about October 14 to April 11. It is long legged, somewhat diurnal in habits, and about the same size as the Eastern Screech-Owl. It is light brown, and barred and spotted below. Usually it sits on the ground, atop a fence post, or in a pile of rocks, rubble, driftwood, or debris into which it can escape or hide.

Vaiden (1939) collected the first Mississippi specimen on April 11, 1937, south of Moon Lake in Coahoma County. Sammie M. Ray collected another specimen north of Moorhead in Sunflower County, on February 21, 1940 (Vaiden 1940). Elie Ganier Jr. recorded sightings of another Burrowing Owl in Washington County from November 1959 through March 27, 1960. This owl dug burrows and formed a large mound of dirt from the holes during the time it was under observation. Ben B. Coffey Jr. reported this species in Coahoma County on December 31, 1939.

Burleigh (1945) found this owl regularly on the open island beaches in Mississippi Sound and collected three specimens on the coast from late October to mid-December. He recorded a Burrowing Owl at Deer Island on January 18. My only collection record for this species is a specimen taken on October 14, 1940. This bird was found sitting on a large pile of rocks beside U.S. 80 west of Brandon in Rankin County. Another bird was recorded at Lake Hico at Jackson in Hinds County on January 2, 1960. It was sitting on a pile of concrete rubble and was observed by Ernest and Katherine Goodpasture and others participating in a Christmas Bird Count.

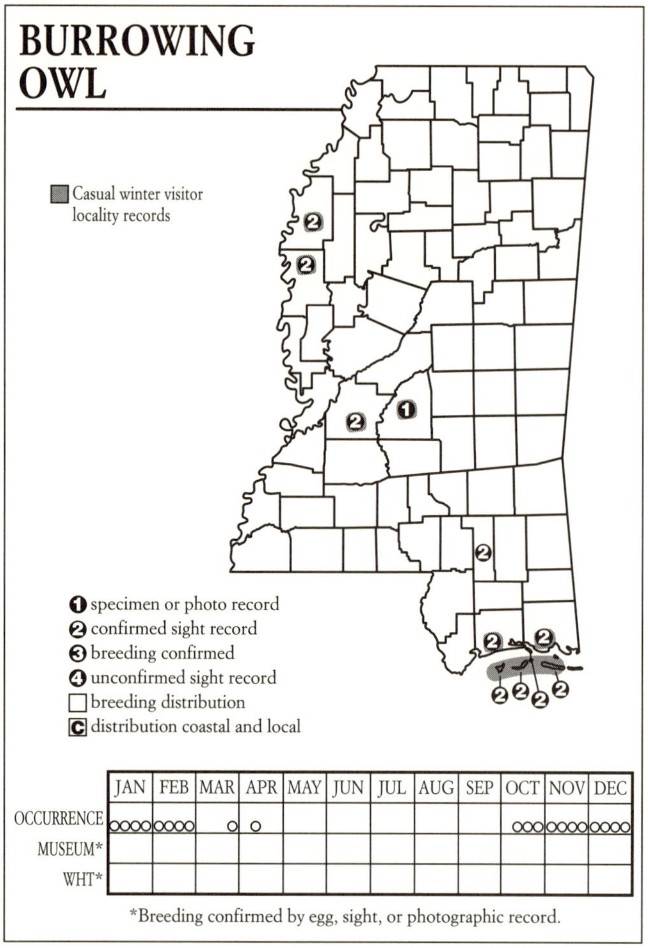

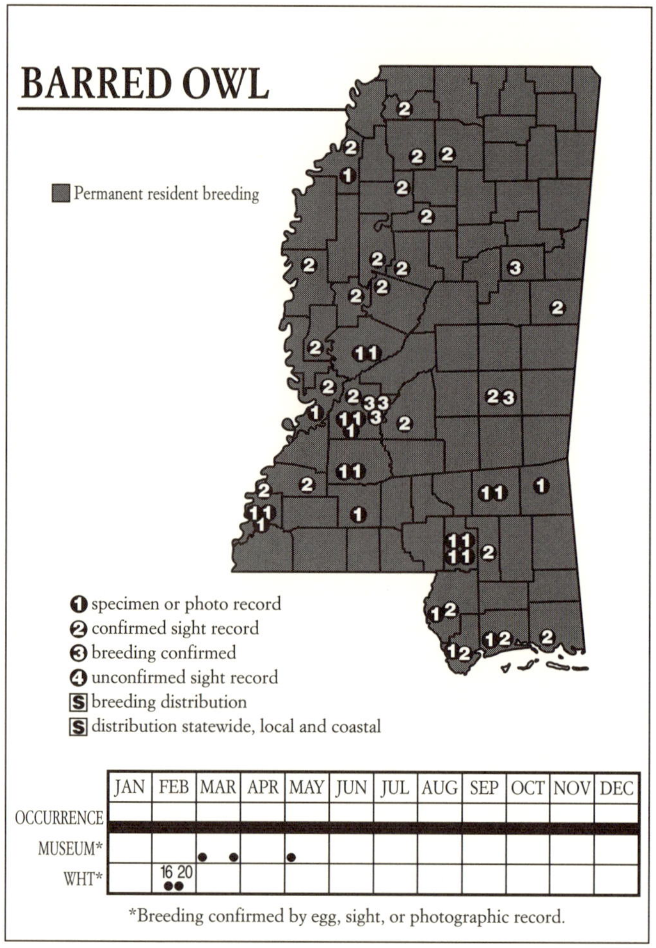

In Florida, the Burrowing Owl digs its own nest burrows, which are usually five to nine feet long and one or two feet below the ground level. The burrow is enlarged at the end to form a nest chamber and lined with dried cow dung or other debris. On the western plains these owls use the deserted burrows of prairie dogs or badgers, cleaning them out or enlarging them to suit their needs. The four to 11 eggs are white and rounded ovate in shape.

Barred Owl *Strix varia*

This large, dark brown owl is heavily barred on the head and neck, and streaked lengthwise on the belly. It has brown eyes and is without ear tufts. In Mississippi the Barred Owl and the Barn Owl are the only owls having brown eyes.

The Barred Owl is the best known and the most common owl in our state. Its favorite haunts are bottomland hardwoods, but it occurs in most stretches of woods of any size. Barred Owls are active during the day, especially when feeding young.

The Barred Owl is best known for the familiar hootings that reverberate back and forth from the depths of swampy woodlands. Sometimes several owls join together in an eerie chorus with many variations. The usual call consists of four couplets or eight notes, the last note being loudest and diminishing into a final drawl: *whoo-whoo, whoo-whoo, whoo-whoo-whoo-whoo-ah-h-h-h.*

This owl begins nesting in late January or early February. The nests I have seen were in hollows of broken-off tree trunks or in cavities of living trees. From one to four white eggs are laid at the bottom of the cavity.

The Barred Owl's food is determined mainly by availability. It cannot subdue mammals larger than a rabbit or birds larger than a meadowlark. Crayfish and fish are favored when available, but rats, mice, and other small rodents are its principal food items. Insects, small birds, snakes, frogs, and other cold-blooded animals are part of its diet.

Long-eared Owl *Asio otus*

The Long-eared Owl is a rarely seen irregular winter visitor in Mississippi. Its breeding range includes northern and mountain states and southern Canada. It looks like a miniature Great Horned Owl, but its ear tufts are placed closer together. It lacks the white throat collar, and its belly is streaked lengthwise rather than barred crosswise.

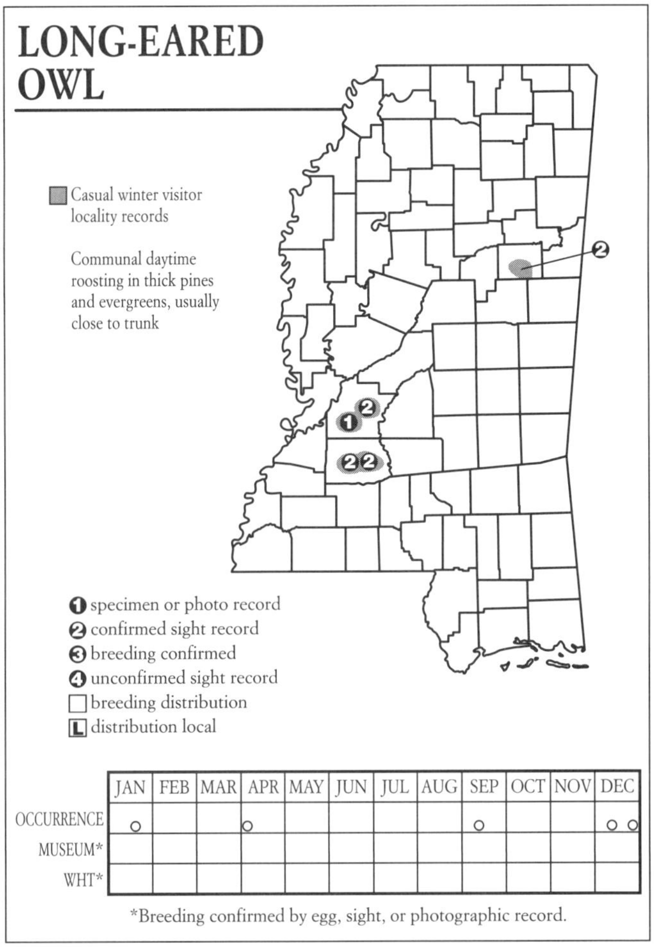

I found only seven recorded observations for this species in Mississippi and only one collection record. I collected a specimen while quail hunting on December 24, 1956, near Brownsville in Hinds County (Turcotte 1957a). I observed another one roosting in a dense cedar tree near this same location. On December 10, 1958, St. Clair Thompson and Hazel Strong saw five Long-eared Owls roosting in a pine tree amid a dense pine thicket in western Copiah County (Phares 1958).

John Phares and Robert Mills (pers. comm.) recorded eight or nine of these owls on the Copiah County Wildlife Management Area on January 18, 1968. These birds were flushed from a dense thicket of planted pine trees surrounded by open fields and broomsedge. Afterward, Phares and I revisited the plantation and flushed about six owls. Pellets found under the owl roosting places contained mostly bones and hair of shrews and harvest mice.

A Long-eared Owl was seen by Ren Lohoefener on September 10, 1978, near Starkville (Weber 1979c). From one to six Long-eared Owls were seen November 22 and 23, 1986, by Jim McCafferty, Gene Knight, and others in Lafayette County (Jackson and Hodges 1986). Another one was seen at Grenada Lake dam on December 19 and 29, 1990, by Gene Knight and Tom Heatley (Schiefer 1991).

The Long-eared Owl is probably a more frequent winter visitor to Mississippi than these records indicate. The fact that they use communal roosts, and that eight or nine owls found each other and were roosting in the same thicket, indicates that they may be more numerous and may simply escape detection because of their retiring habits in daytime.

Short-eared Owl *Asio flammeus*

The Short-eared Owl is a rarely seen, irregular northern visitor appearing in Mississippi only during fall and winter. It is found in open country and around sloughs, rice fields, and marshes.

The plumage of this owl is a soft, tawny brown streaked lengthwise on the head, back, and underparts with dark brown. Part of its facial disc bordering the yellow eyes is black. In flight, it shows large, buffy patches on the upperside of the wing and black patches on the underside of the bend in the wings. The flight is floppy and irregular, somewhat mothlike.

These owls often feed at dusk or in daytime. I have seen them on three occasions, all at the same location near Fitler in Issaquena County. The first observation was January 3,

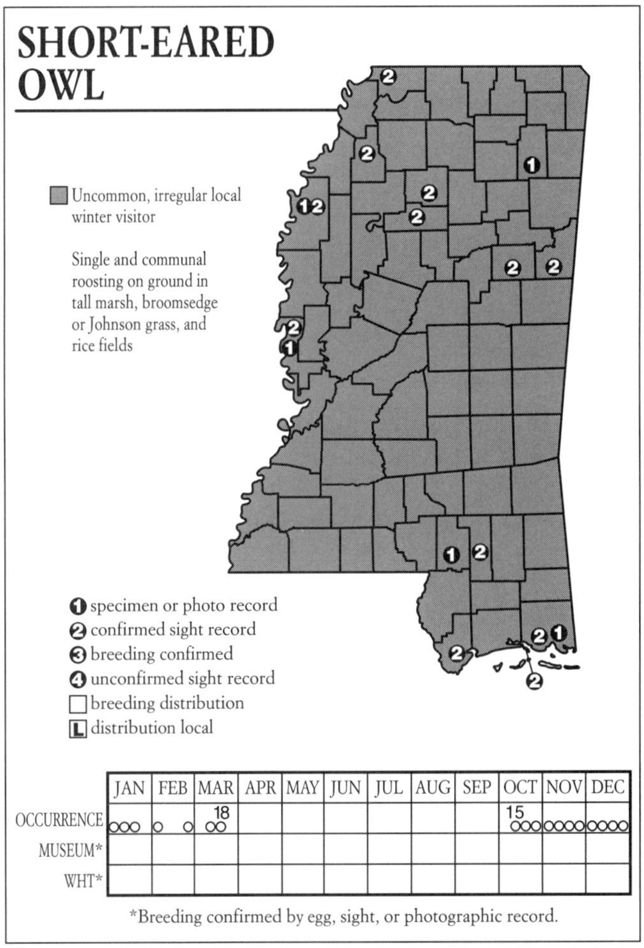

1964, when seven birds were flushed from their roosts on the ground in a 30-acre Johnson grass field (Turcotte 1964). Large acreages had been cleared and planted to cottonwood plantations. Two owls were seen late in the afternoon flying low over the fields near the roost. In walking over the same area on February 28, 1964, 12 were flushed from roosts. Again on March 10, eight were flushed from the same area. Examination of a large number of regurgitated pellets found at the roosting places showed that cotton rats made up most of these birds' diet.

Burleigh (1945) reported only one record for this species between 1935 and 1943 in the Gulf Coast region, a sighting in an open salt marsh on Deer Island on November 23, 1937. L. E. Williams Jr. and S. G. Clawson reported one sighting at Bayou Caddy and Heron Bay in Hancock County, on January 15, 1961. A specimen in the MMNS was taken October 15, 1940, near Mississippi Sound at Pascagoula in Jackson County by Winston Nolan. Two other museum specimens were taken on December 9, 1939, near Lumberton in Lamar County by James Batson and on December 29, 1939, near Tupelo in Lee County by Eugene Patton.

Vaiden (1953b) found Short-eared Owls in flocks numbering up to 50 wintering in burned-over or dried-out rice fields in Bolivar County. He collected three specimens near Perthshire on November 9 and 10, 1952. An earlier specimen was taken by Vaiden near Rosedale on March 18, 1940. Ben B. Coffey Jr. recorded sightings on December 29, 1940, and on January 12, 1941, in Coahoma County at Moon Lake.

NORTHERN SAW-WHET OWL

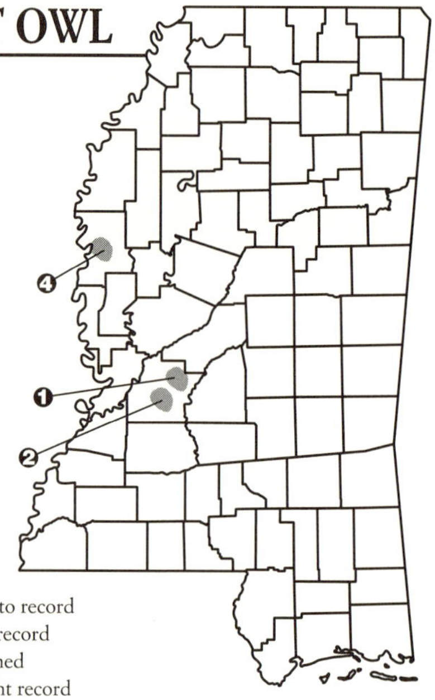

Acidental winter locality records

❶ specimen or photo record
❷ confirmed sight record
❸ breeding confirmed
❹ unconfirmed sight record
☐ breeding distribution
[L] distribution local

	JAN	FEB	MAR	APR	MAY	JUN	JUL	AUG	SEP	OCT	NOV	DEC
OCCURRENCE				o				o			o	
MUSEUM*												
WHT*												

*Breeding confirmed by egg, sight, or photographic record.

[Northern Saw-whet Owl] *Aegolius acadicus*

This is the smallest owl that has occurred in Mississippi. There are only two definite records with one sighting of two birds in Washington County.

Following is an account of the first record as written by Peterson (1975):

> At approximately 12:30 on April 16, 1974, I was at my parents' home when we heard the mobbing calls of several Blue Jays. I investigated and found the Jays clustered around a hedge of Ligustrum at the eastern end of the house. Searching the hedge, I literally came face to face with an adult Saw-whet Owl. The owl was typical in all field marks with rounded, earless head, dark brown in color, and facial discs streaked with white. The dark brown upperparts were irregularly spotted with white. Breast and belly were white with rufous streaks running full length. Eyes were yellow. The owl was approximately seven inches long, noticeably smaller than an Eastern Screech-Owl.
>
> The owl's behavior was typical of the Saw-whet. It was extremely tame, allowing a very close approach. The lens of a camera two feet away did not bother it in the least, nor did the constant stream of observers. The owl remained on its perch in the Ligustrum for approximately seven hours until nightfall when it left. It was not seen again.

On November 12, 1976, another Saw-whet Owl was found injured in the middle of Dixon Road in west Jackson after being hit by a car. This bird was picked up by Mr. and Mrs. Fatheree and kept by them until November 15. They gave it to me for the MMNS. It did not recover from its head injury and was made into a study skin for the museum collection.

This little northern owl seldom winters as far south as the Gulf states. Lowery Jr. (1974) lists only two occurrence records for Louisiana, and Imhof (1976) records only one record for Alabama. This species nests in woodpecker holes or tree cavities. The breeding range is mostly in evergreens of northern states and Canada and the higher mountains south into Tennessee and northern Missouri.

Goatsuckers and Allies (Caprimulgiformes)

Members of this family are grayish or brownish birds with long wings and long tails. They have a small bill and a large mouth with an exceptionally large gape. The mouth has long, stiff bristles on each side for capturing flying insects. The feet are small and weak and are used only for perching.

Goatsuckers have large eyes and are mostly nocturnal or crepuscular in their habits. These birds usually remain quiet during daylight hours as they perch horizontally on the ground or lengthwise on a tree limb. They are protectively colored to match their surroundings so they can escape detection while resting. Their silent, mothlike flight and large eyes adapt them for catching nocturnal insects.

These birds usually deposit their two eggs directly on the ground or leaf litter. The birds and their eggs are protectively colored with soft grays and browns. Their common names interpret nighttime calls such as *poor-will, whip-poor-will,* and *chuck-will's-widow,* or reflect some distinctive habits.

The name "goatsucker" was derived from folklore and superstition. Rural people were accustomed to seeing these birds feeding on flying insects among goat herds at dusk. After noticing the exceptionally large mouth on these birds, people believed they were capable of sucking the teats of large animals and stealing the milk.

Strangely, some goatsuckers are capable of periods of torpidity or hibernation during cold weather. It has been proven that the western Poor-will sometimes hibernates in rock crevices of canyons.

Above: Common Nighthawk

Caprimulgidae (Goatsuckers and Allies)

Common Nighthawk *Chordeiles minor*

The Common Nighthawk is a common, breeding summer resident throughout Mississippi. It arrives from wintering grounds in South America in early April and remains until late October. Being less nocturnal than its relatives, the Chuck-will's-widow and Whip-poor-will, the Nighthawk is seen most often in the open air while feeding on flying insects late in the afternoon. "Bullbat" is a commonly used local name for this bird.

During courtship, the male makes a spectacular aerial display, diving earthward and then suddenly zooming up sharply. Air rushing through the flight feathers makes a booming sound similar to the bellow of a bull, the probable derivation of the name "bullbat." The distinctive call note usually heard is a nasal *peent* or *pee-auk*.

The Common Nighthawk has long, pointed wings extending beyond the tip of the tail when the bird is at rest. The male's throat is white and the female's is buff colored.

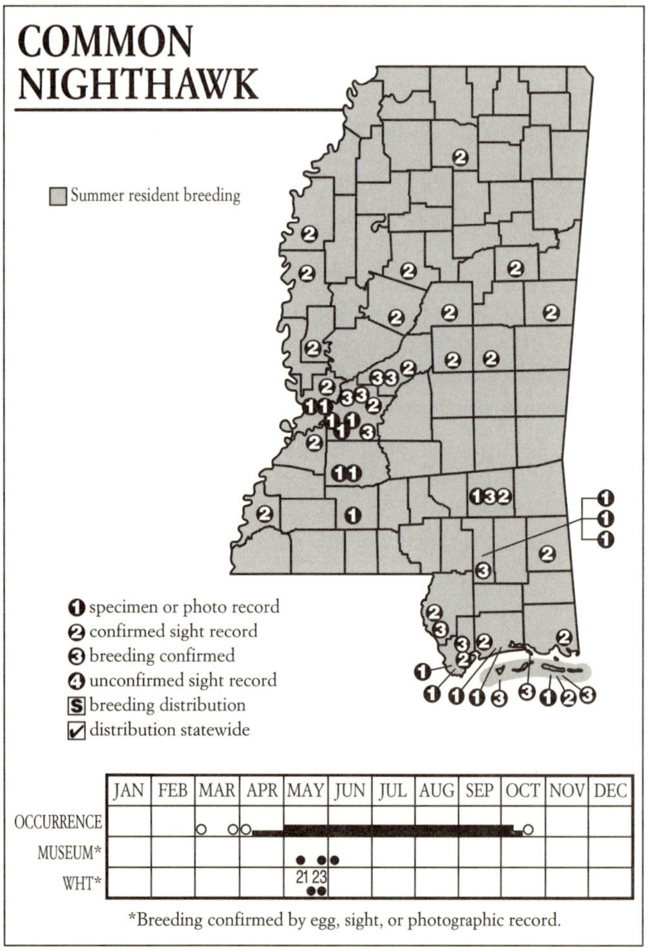

The tail is slightly forked instead of rounded as in the goatsuckers of the two following accounts. The tail and breast are barred in gray and white, and a broad, white patch extends about midway across the primaries.

Nighthawks nest in open country, but they are found often in cities where they rest during the day and nest on the gravel roofs of buildings. The two eggs are deposited on bare ground or on a gravel roof. The eggs are buff colored, and heavily blotched with black, gray, and brown.

Freeman (1961) reported seeing 60 Nighthawks in a migrating flock on September 27, 1961, near Vaiden in Carroll County. In Sharkey County on August 25, 1959, I saw at least 75 in a moving, loose flock, at 200 to 300 feet over Delta National Forest. Vaiden (1952a) reported migrating flocks of Nighthawks on September 7, 1947, and October 2, 1949, in Bolivar County.

Chuck-will's-widow *Caprimulgus carolinensis*

The Chuck-will's-widow is the largest of the three goatsucker species in the United States. It is often confused with the Whip-poor-will, which is much smaller and has entirely different call notes. The call of the latter is a *whip-poor-will'* with accent on the last syllable. The call of this species is *chuck-wills'-wid'ow* with accent on the second and third syllables. The *chuck* is sometimes inaudible except at close range. The call or alarm notes, not frequently heard, are harsh, low, chucking sounds much like the voice of a frog.

The Chuck-will's-widow is a common summer resident throughout the state. It arrives around mid-April and soon begins calling. It remains here until early fall, but calling

The Chuck-will's-widow and its nest are often impossible to spot on the forest floor. This nest and eggs of the bird was photographed near Clinton on May 4, 1946.

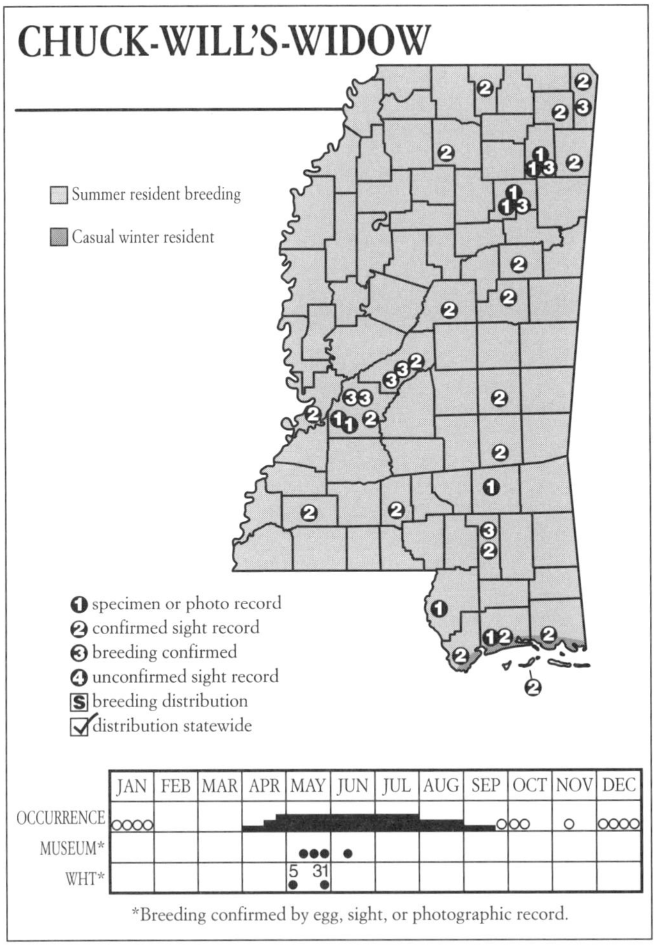

ceases during late summer. By late September, most of these birds have left for their wintering grounds in Central America and South America. Rarely in mild winters a few birds remain along the Gulf Coast.

This species is common in woodlands, where it usually spends the day perched on the ground. It perches lengthwise when alighting on a tree limb. The bird's large size and buff-colored throat distinguish it from the Whip-poor-will. The male has white on the inner webs of the outer-tail feathers and a narrow, white line below the throat extending across the breast. The female has pale buff marks where those in the male are white.

In May or June nesting occurs on the ground, where the female deposits two eggs on leaf litter. The eggs have a creamy ground color and are beautifully marked with shades of brown and lavender. When flushed from the nest, the parent bird makes low croaklike calls, and performs a broken-wing act to lure intruders from the nest.

Whip-poor-will *Caprimulgus vociferus*

The Whip-poor-will is a regular spring and fall transient through the southern and central parts of Mississippi. The northward passage of migrants occurs in late March and April. It is a summer resident only in the higher elevations of the northeastern hill counties.

This species has been heard calling as far south as Kemper, Winston, Attala, and Montgomery Counties during the breeding season (Coffey 1970, 1971; Coffey and Coffey 1971). It can be found regularly farther north in the state, where it occurs along high ridges. There are few records of its occurrence during the period of its southward return to the wintering grounds. Fall and winter records of the few overwintering birds on the coast extend from September 9 to January 29 (Toups and Jackson 1987).

The Whip-poor-will is about half the size of the Chuck-will's-widow. Its call notes are described in the preceding account. The Whip-poor-will has a black throat, and the white marks on the male are more prominent than those on the Chuck-will's-widow. The white marks of the male are replaced by buff coloring on the female.

The two white eggs are blotched and mottled with shades of gray and brown. They are deposited on dead leaves on the ground in the woods. Breeding was documented by a photograph of a downy chick in a nest found June 22, 1992, in Oktibbeha County taken by David McEwen (Muth 1992).

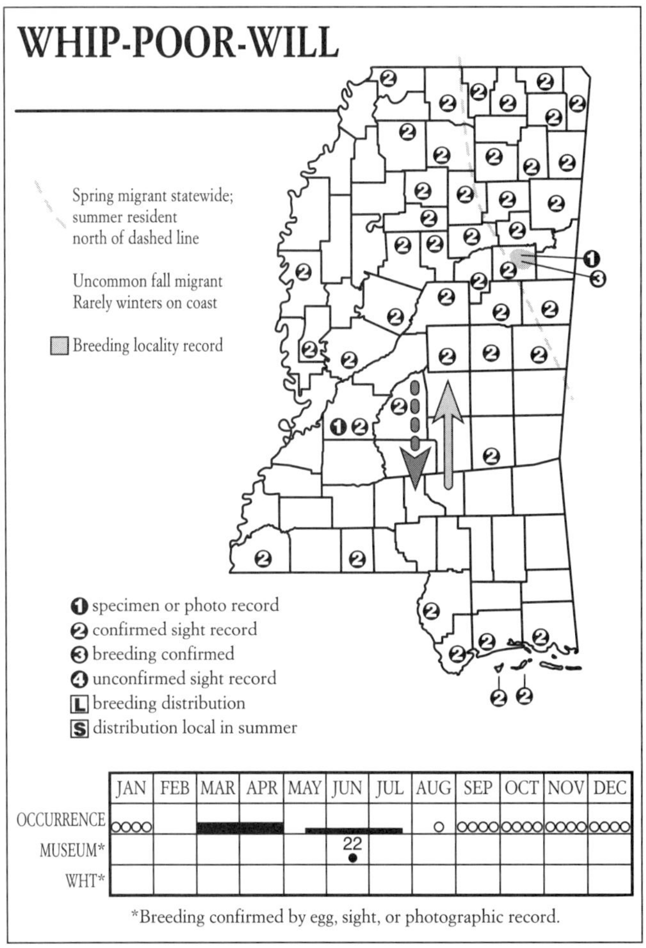

Swifts (Apodiformes)

Swifts are distributed worldwide. They are fast flyers on bowed wings with streamlined, cigar-shaped bodies. They have flattened skulls and mouths with wide gapes for feeding on flying insects. Active during daylight hours, swifts spend most of their time aloft. The sexes are similar. Their four toes, used mainly for clinging, point forward.

The Chimney Swift and the smaller Vaux's Swift have square, short tails with protruding sharp spines at the end that are used for support in clinging to vertical surfaces. Four larger western species have notched or deeply forked tails and a more swallowlike appearance.

Above: Chimney Swift

Apodidae (Swifts)

Chimney Swift *Chaetura pelagica*

The "chimney sweep," as this bird is commonly called, is a common, breeding summer resident. It winters in eastern Peru at the headwaters of the Amazon River, and it almost invariably arrives here the third week in March and remains until late October.

The Chimney Swift has long, narrow, bladelike wings; a large mouth; and weak feet. It is brownish black, although the throat is lighter gray when not darkened by soot. The call notes are a loud, rapid twittering given almost continuously while the bird is in courtship flight and when congregating to roost. In flight, it appears to be almost without a tail. The tail is stiff and bristled at the tip for support while at rest in a vertical position.

Chimney Swifts are abundant migrants in the fall, when they gather in large flocks to roost in a favorite, large chimney. Roosts in large chimneys have been known to contain several thousand birds. Birds gather in late afternoon to circle and wheel around in the sky before descending into the chimney for the night.

The Chimney Swift nests almost exclusively in chimneys, but it sometimes nests inside buildings or cisterns. The nest is made of twigs broken off by the birds in flight. These are cemented together with saliva and glued to the side of the chimney or other structure to form a strong hammocklike cup. Three or four white eggs laid in May or early June constitute the usual clutch. The young are very noisy and make loud begging calls while being fed in the nest.

[Vaux's Swift] *Chaetura vauxi*

A possible sighting of this far western species in Mississippi was reported by Haberyan (1962a) when he observed a swift he believed to be a Vaux's. Haberyan discovered the lone bird at dusk over the Pascagoula River marsh on November 29, 1961. Since Chimney Swifts have nearly always departed for wintering grounds after the first week of November, this sighting was probably a Vaux's Swift. Records for this species in Louisiana have been recorded between November and March 3 (Lowery 1974).

A second record of a swift occurred on December 31, 1983, in Rankin County at Ross Barnett Reservoir. The

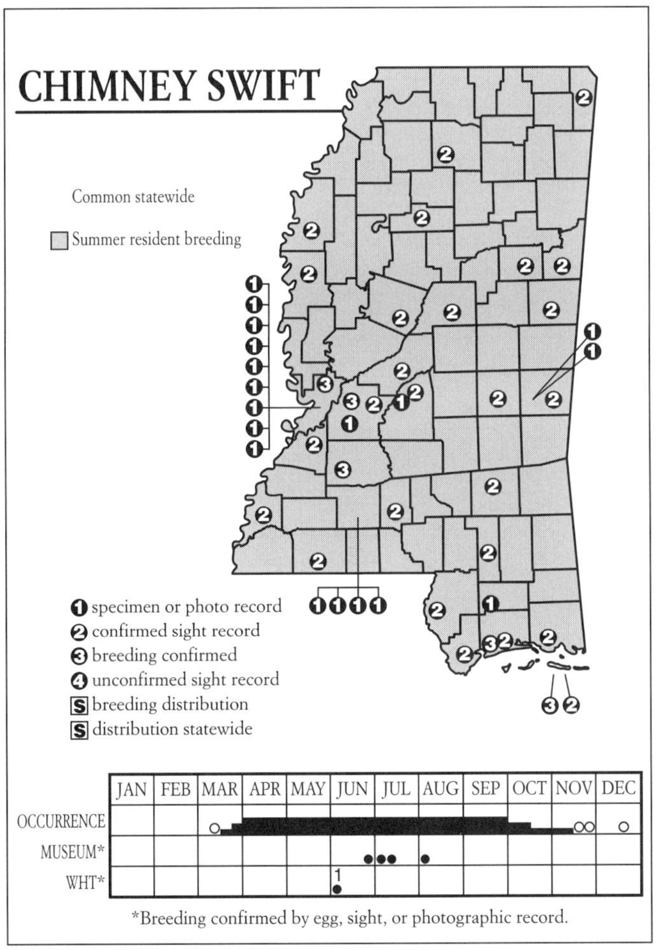

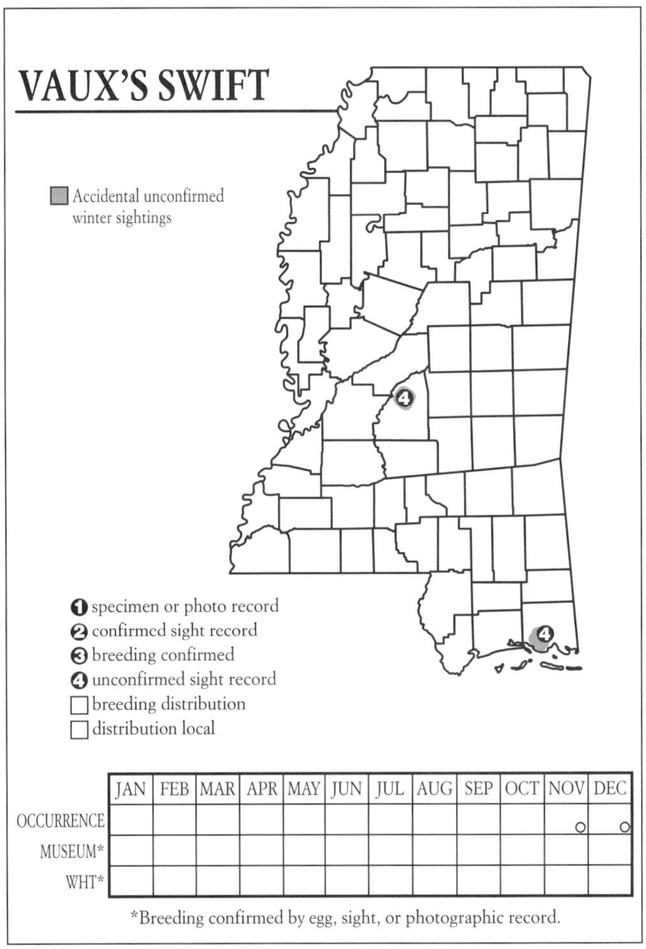

sighting was made by Bob Lewis on the Jackson Christmas Bird Count. It was probably a Vaux's Swift (Imhof 1984). This swift is the one most likely to occur after the first week in November along the Mississippi Coast, or as an early arrival in late February and early March.

Unlike the Chimney Swift, in an unsoiled condition the Vaux's Swift is paler below and on the rump patch. Its flight is continuous without much soaring. It is the *smallest* of North American swifts, about one-half inch shorter than the Chimney Swift. Any swift seen after the first week of November or earlier than March 10 should be observed carefully. Look for the lighter throat, underparts, and rump patch; a smaller size than Chimney Swift; continuous flight with little soaring; and weaker twitterings.

Ruby-throated Hummingbird

Trochilidae (Hummingbirds)

Hummingbirds are the smallest of all birds. Their wings are narrow, stiff, and bladelike and move so rapidly they become almost invisible. They can hover in flight and fly backward. Their plumage is highly iridescent. The metallic colors of hummingbirds are refracted light from the peculiar feather structure, not pigment. The males have gorgets, or jewel-like chins, and throat feathers. Females are mostly greenish above and whitish below, most lacking gorget feathers. Young birds resemble females, and field identification is often difficult or impossible. The bills of hummingbirds are long, slender, and adapted for feeding in tubular flowers. For their size, these birds require enormous amounts of energy.

The Ruby-throated Hummingbird is the only species that breeds east of the Mississippi River. It is rare in the Gulf states from October to March. The Rufous Hummingbird is a casual but regular visitor to Mississippi in fall and winter. Usually it is detected at feeders by its brownish coloration. Other western species can be expected to occur sparingly as spring migrants or casual fall and winter visitors, especially along the coast.

Along with using hummingbird feeders, homeowners are planting shrubs and flowers to attract and hold "hummers" during migration periods and through the winter. Using feeders to attract hummingbirds led Nancy Newfield of Metairie, Louisiana, into banding them. She soon found that western species were more than accidentals, some even returned in following years.

Bob and Martha Sargent began attracting and banding hummers near Birmingham in 1987 when they banded their first Rufous Hummingbird. Inspired, they used a drop-door trap with a feeder inside to catch and band wintering birds at other locations. This led to their forming the Hummer/Bird Study Group, which in 1995 and 1996 involved more than 1000 observers in the southeastern states reporting overwintering birds for capture, identification, and banding. The Sargents and banders on the Mississippi Coast, Bennet Carver and partner Doris Hope, make an effort to band as many hummers as possible from November to March. Results have been astounding as the following accounts of western hummers will show. Most have been confirmed by banding records of birds reported by feeder-watchers.

Western hummingbirds are acclimated to withstand colder weather, and they survive our milder winters in the Gulf states. It is only a matter of time before two more western species, the Magnificent and Blue-throated Hummingbirds, appear on our state bird list. Other western or even tropical hummers are possible.

WHITE-EARED HUMMINGBIRD

Accidental vagrant in winter

❶ banding record
❷ confirmed sight record
❸ breeding confirmed
❹ unconfirmed sight record
☐ breeding distribution
🄰 distribution statewide

	JAN	FEB	MAR	APR	MAY	JUN	JUL	AUG	SEP	OCT	NOV	DEC
OCCURRENCE	o										o	oooo
MUSEUM*												
WHT*												

*Breeding confirmed by egg, sight, or photographic record.

[White-eared Hummingbird]
Hylocharis leucotis

An incredible first record of this Mexican species on the Mississippi Coast and the southeastern states east of Texas occurred in November 1995. A single female appeared at the feeder of Sybil Hall at Gulfport. After reading about reporting wintering hummers in a news article, she called Gulfport bird bander Bennet Carver on December 29, 1995. She described a bird having a *white head stripe* and about the size of a Ruby-throated Hummingbird. Carver and banding partner Doris Hope banded the bird by 10:30 A.M. that same day. The following week, more than 100 people came to see the Mexican visitor, which was last seen on January 4, 1996.

The adult male has a purple chin and crown patch and shiny emerald gorget. Both sexes have metallic green backsides, prominent *white eye stripes,* and *black ear patch.* Underparts are gray washed with green on the male and green spottings on the chin, throat, breast, and flanks of the female. Males and females have short bills dark toward the tip and pinkish on the base. The male has a dark, square tail, green on the topside when folded. The female has a rounded tail with white tips.

Thanks to a small host of dedicated overwinter feeder-watchers, western hummers found and liked southern hospitality. And thanks to a few dedicated and persistent banders, the western hummers are blanketing the South to Georgia and the Carolinas and enlightening the birding community about overwintering hummingbirds. Mississippi has nine hummer species on its state list, seven of them added since 1988.

Buff-bellied Hummingbird
Amazilia yucatanensis

This Mexican hummingbird is a fairly common resident along the lower Rio Grande River. It has appeared as a casual winter visitor along the Texas and Louisiana Coasts.

The first Mississippi record, confirmed by a photograph and multiple observers, was at Bay St. Louis in Hancock County from November 26 to 30, 1987. The bird was seen first by Lydia Schultz (1988) in her yard feeding on a Mexican cigar plant. A second sight record by multiple observers at the same location occurred on December 29, 1988, on the Christmas Bird Count in southern Hancock County (Muth 1989).

Other coastal records are one at Biloxi in Harrison County on December 21, 1992, banded by Robert R.

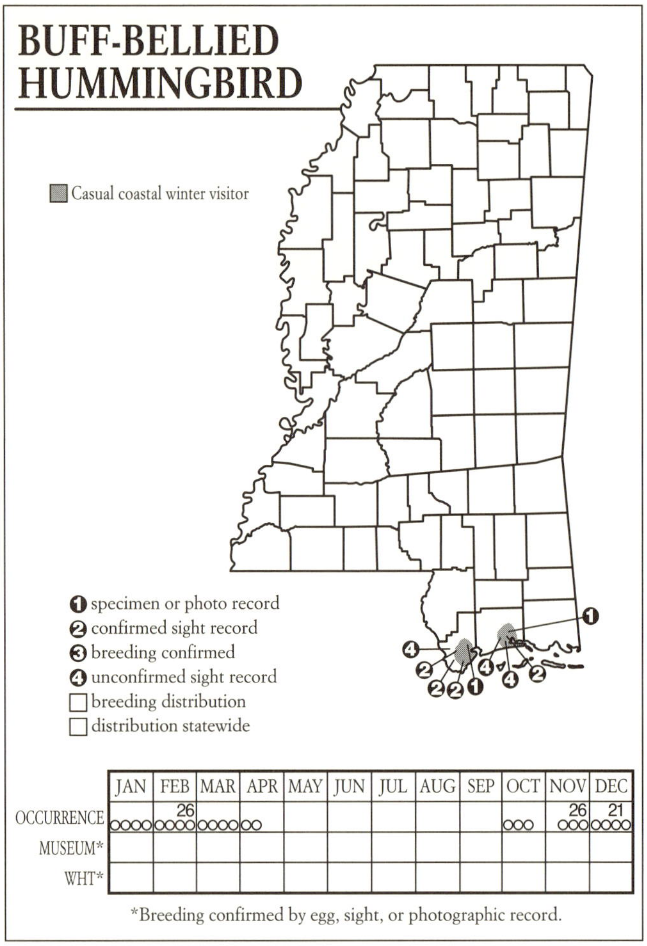

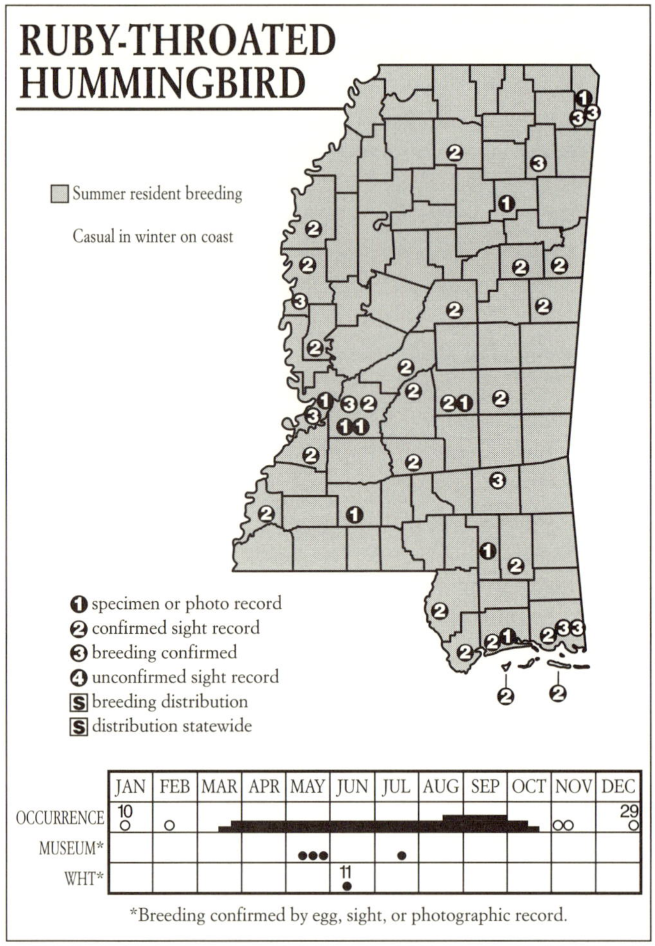

Sargent; one on December 28, 1992, in Hancock County on the Christmas Bird Count (Imhof 1993); and one overwintering late record bird in the yard of Lydia Schultz in Hancock County seen by Ken Hackman and others on February 26, 1993. At least three Buff-bellied Hummingbirds occurred along the Mississippi Coast during the winter of 1995–1996 (Stedman 1996).

The Buff-bellied Hummingbird is larger than the Ruby-throated, Black-chinned, and Rufous Hummingbirds. The long *pinkish orange, dark-tipped bill; green breast and throat;* green head and upperparts; *buff belly;* and chestnut brown tail are identifying field marks. The sexes are alike. Call notes are squeaky, higher, and noticeably different than the three species mentioned above.

Ruby-throated Hummingbird
Archilochus colubris

The Ruby-throated Hummingbird is a common, breeding summer resident throughout Mississippi. It returns from the wintering grounds in March and remains until late October. Adult males depart the breeding grounds earlier than females and immatures.

The male Ruby-throat has a solid, metallic green back; a black, noticeably forked tail; and a glowing, ruby red throat. The female is bright, shining green above with a white throat and underparts. Young birds resemble the female, and both have rounded, white-tipped tails. The adult male's red gorget appears to be black when the light source is from the "wrong" angle.

The Ruby-throat is a woodland bird that frequently visits gardens. It is especially attracted to red and blue flowers. Its food consists of nectar, spiders, aphids, and other small insects. The voice is a rapid, squeaky chipping accompanied in flight by the humming sound of its wings. The male in courtship display flight above a female swings back and forth like a pendulum in an arc of 40 feet or more, humming with each swing through the air.

Nesting begins in late May and continues through June. The nest is made of soft plant down formed in the shape of a small cup. It is ornamented on the outside with lichens and held together with cobwebs. The nest resembles a growth or knot and is usually saddled on a small, horizontal limb, often over an opening or water. The female lays two tiny, elongated, white eggs about the same diameter as a pencil.

Hummingbird feeders are widely popular with people who enjoy watching garden birds; and these small, active hummingbirds are certainly entertaining to watch. They are surprisingly aggressive, and one or more will try to dominate each feeder. Sugar water made with one part sugar and four parts water (no honey or coloring) seems to be an appropriate mixture. Garden plantings of the trumpet creeper vine, the feathery leaved cypress vine, red salvia, red buckeye, woodbine or red honeysuckle, and any red tubular annual or perennial flowering plants will attract hummingbirds.

Black-chinned Hummingbird *Archilochus alexandri*

The adult male Black-chinned Hummingbird is metallic green on the crown and upperparts. The throat is black with a *violet band* bordering the lower edge of the black throat. Underparts are white or whitish with the sides and flanks greenish gray.

Females and immatures are practically indistinguishable from female and immature male Ruby-throats. Winter hummingbirds of the genus *Archilochus* are likely to be of this species and should be observed carefully.

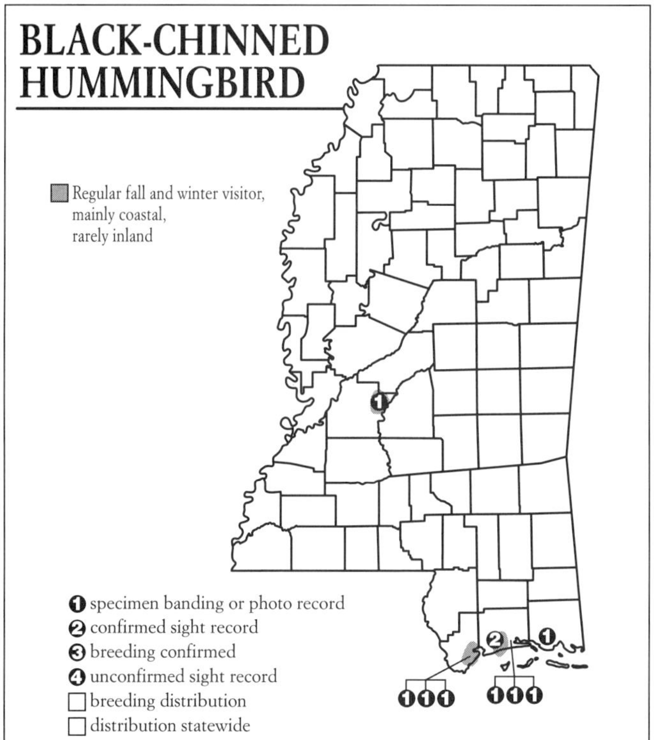

	JAN	FEB	MAR	APR	MAY	JUN	JUL	AUG	SEP	OCT	NOV	DEC
OCCURRENCE	OOOO	26 OOOO							O		8-9 26 O O	OOOO
MUSEUM*												
WHT*												

*Breeding confirmed by egg, sight, or photographic record.

The Black-chinned is the western counterpart of the Ruby-throat. It is common in low mountains and lowlands on the Pacific Coast and eastward to the Great Plains and central Texas. It is a rare but regular fall and winter visitor to the southeastern Gulf states.

The first confirmed Mississippi record is an immature male at the feeder of Lydia Schultz in Hancock County on November 26 and 27, 1987 (Hodges 1987). The identification was confirmed by hummingbird expert Nancy Newfield of Metairie, Louisiana, who mist-netted, banded, and photographed the bird. A single violet gorget feather on the lower throat was removed, photographed, and preserved for confirmation of the identification.

Afterward, numerous observers at the same location saw this bird along with several Ruby-throats and a new state species that also appeared from November 26 to 30, 1987, the Buff-bellied Hummingbird. The second state record, a sighting by Judith Toups and others, occurred on November 8 and 9, 1988, at Gulfport (Hodges 1988). The first inland record was a Black-chinned banded by Robert R. Sargent at Jackson in Hinds County on February 26, 1993.

Black-chinned Hummingbirds occurred on the coast on January 13 and 14, 1994, at Ocean Springs and Long Beach, and on September 23 and December 3 at Gulfport and Diamondhead. Seven were banded on the coast by Bennet Carver during the winter of 1995–1996 along with four Ruby-throats. The records indicate that Black-chinned Hummingbirds are regular visitors to the Mississippi Coast.

[Anna's Hummingbird] *Calypte anna*

The Anna's Hummingbird is abundant along the Pacific Coast states in lowlands, deserts, and mountains and in southern Arizona. It winters throughout its breeding range.

The male Anna's has a rose red head, throat, and neck and a black tail. Adult females have flecks of red on the throat. Males and females have grayish underparts daubed with green. Females and immatures have white-tipped tails. Adults and immatures have metallic green upperparts.

Immature males may have some red on the *crown* and throat. Juveniles may have streaks but no red on the throat, and are greenish on the backside. Otherwise, they resemble females. Immatures can be confused with the smaller Black-chinned Hummingbird.

Mississippi's first Anna's Hummingbird was recorded in Hancock County from mid-December until late January 1995 and seen by Judith Toups, Lydia Schultz, Terence Schiefer, Robert Sargent, and others. The first inland and second coastal Mississippi records were at Starkville from November 27 to December 30, 1995, banded by Robert and Martha Sargent, and in Harrison County on December 19, 1995, banded by Bennet Carver (Stedman 1996).

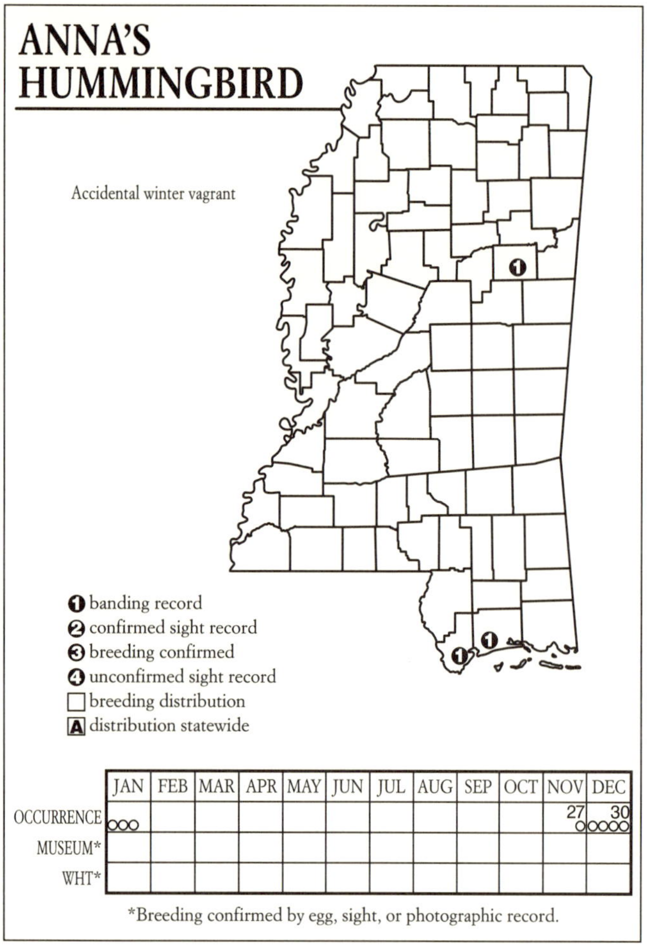

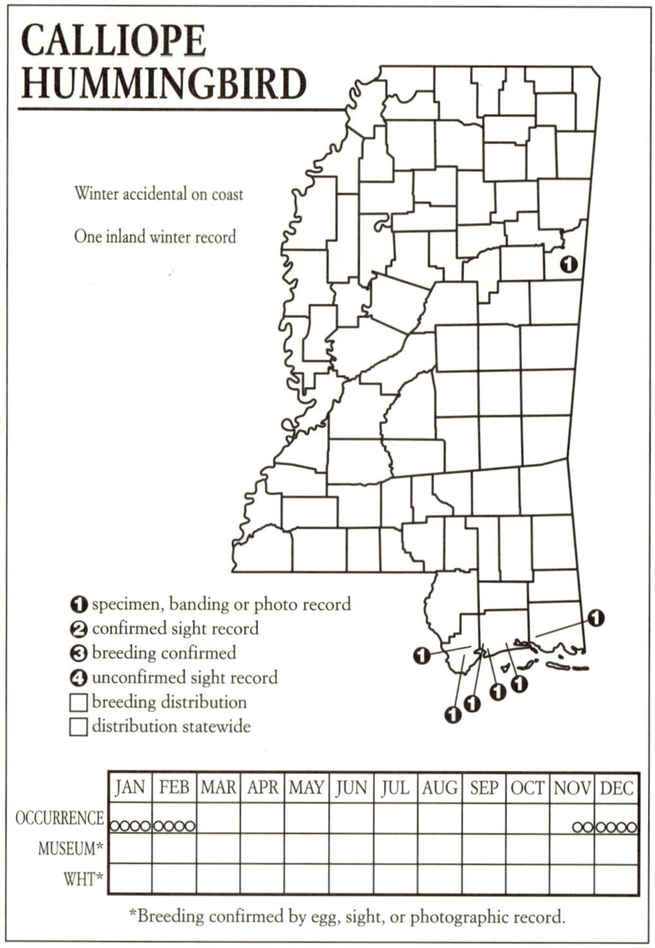

Calliope Hummingbird *Stellula calliope*

The Calliope Hummingbird, smallest of North American species, is common in western mountains and canyons. The male has a streaked, V-shaped, reddish purple gorget against a white background. These feathers form a bib and can be distended. The shorter tail, short bill, smaller size, green upperparts, white underparts, and greenish sides identify the adult male. The female is green above, has underparts and flanks tinged pale rufous, and the throat is streaked or lightly spotted. Females and immatures are smaller, slimmer, and shorter tailed than Allen's and Rufous Hummingbirds. At rest, the wings of Calliopes extend beyond the tail.

I saw a Calliope feeding on small, yellow flowers of a low shrub at Ramsey Canyon in southeastern Arizona. Its feeding behavior was slow and deliberate, much like a large bumblebee as it moved from flower to flower, pausing at times as if clinging like a bee at each blossom.

The Calliope is casual along the Gulf Coast. The first Mississippi record was netted and banded on January 3, 1992, at Diamondhead in Harrison County by Robert Sargent. This bird was seen by numerous observers at the home of Doris Hope, whose yard was planted to attract hummers. It remained until the weekend of February 26.

Additional banding records in the three coastal counties are: January 31, 1994, at Ocean Springs; December 26, 1994, at Diamondhead; January 30, 1995, at Gulfport; January 31, 1995, at Diamondhead; and November through January 6, 1996, in Hancock County.

The first inland record of the Calliope Hummingbird was at Columbus in Lowndes County. This bird remained through the winter of 1994–1995 and was seen by multiple observers and banded by Robert Sargent.

This hummer's name is said to derive from Kalliope, the Greek muse of elegance and poetry. I had guessed the name alluded to the elegant, erectile, irregular-length gorget feathers, which are like the pipes of the steam whistle calliope we associate with steamboats, carnivals, and circus parades.

[Broad-tailed Hummingbird] *Selasphorus platycercus*

Occurrence of the Broad-tailed Hummingbird was confirmed by a second-year male captured and banded by Robert R. Sargent at Carriere in Pearl River County on January 14,

BROAD-TAILED HUMMINGBIRD

Non-breeding casual visitor inland

Casual in winter on coast

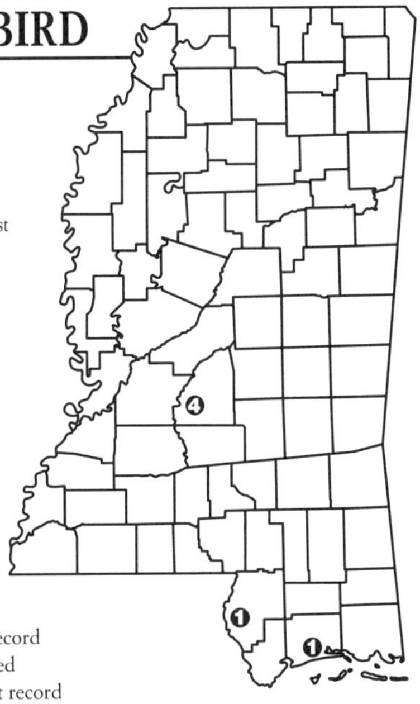

❶ banding record
❷ confirmed sight record
❸ breeding confirmed
❹ unconfirmed sight record
□ breeding distribution
🄲 distribution local

	JAN	FEB	MAR	APR	MAY	JUN	JUL	AUG	SEP	OCT	NOV	DEC
OCCURRENCE	14 o								9-18 oo			19 o
MUSEUM*												
WHT*												

*Breeding confirmed by egg, sight, or photographic record.

1994. A second record in Harrison County was a bird captured and banded on December 19, 1995, by Bennet Carver, an associate of Sargent.

The Broad-tailed is a common species in the Rocky Mountains, bordering foothills, and mountains of the Great Basin. Their range extends southward into Mexico.

Adult males and females are metallic green above like the Ruby-throated Hummingbird. The male has a metallic, *rose-colored* gorget, and *white* breast, belly, and undertail coverts. A patch of green appears on the sides. The tail of the male is broad and rounded when fanned. Females have a wash of pale cinnamon on the sides and a speckled white throat. Their green, broad tail is rounded and the outer feathers are tipped with white. The inner portions of the outer-tail feathers show rufous when spread.

A Broad-tailed Hummingbird appeared at my home in Richland and remained from September 9 to 18, 1995. The bird was an immature male with fully developed gorget feathers along the sides of the neck and three across the lower border of the *immaculate white* chin and throat and *rose red* gorget. It was totally dominant at our feeders. Over its extended stay, it was carefully observed, reported to other birders with all details noted, and the bird was photographed for record. No other observers came to see the bird, even after being reported on the local Audubon Hot Line.

Other distinctions were noted about this bird: broad, rounded, wider tail with three outer worn and frayed tips, and more white than the adult Ruby-throat females and immatures that were present for comparison. At rest the bird's tail was wider than the Ruby-throat and square at the tip, with all white showing. The breast and belly were *silvery white* and distinctly contrasting with the *pure white* at the gorget feather line in bright sunlight.

The photos enlarged to 5 x 7 laser copies were distorted due to backlighting and red reflections from the feeder. The distortions of color made the underparts show pinkish rather than white, and the one gorget feather showing red was not distinctive enough. Although I looked carefully with binocular and scope, I was unable to see any rufous color when the tail feathers were spread, which was usually while the bird was in flight, chased by local Ruby-throats. Throughout its stay, the bird fed on small flying insects among the leaves of a nearby Southern red oak.

The bird could not be confirmed by an identifiable photograph. However, the *rose* gorget feathers were seen under all favorable light conditions and similarities to the Ruby-throated Hummingbird were apparent. I believe the bird was an early hatched Broad-tailed male. This species commonly raises two broods, one at low elevations and a second at higher elevations.

An interesting thing occurred within two days of the Broad-tailed Hummingbird departing. I had parked a car under the spreading oak limbs where the hummingbird had spent most of its time away from the feeders. After sundown, the city mosquito control truck sprayed a fine mist that enveloped the oak tree. The next morning the car top was covered with aphids, small insect larvae, predatory lacewings, and several ladybugs in a torpid state, as well as being dotted with sweet aphid secretions. To me, this was evidence that hummingbirds find abundant insects for fat, protein, and well-needed energy from the "honey dew" of the aphids' sugary secretions.

Rufous Hummingbird *Selasphorus rufus*

The Rufous Hummingbird is a common migrant in western mountains. It breeds commonly in western Oregon and Washington and in western Canada into southern Alaska. It is a regular fall and winter visitor to the Gulf states, but rarely occurs in spring.

Since the advent of hummingbird feeders and their widespread use, this species and other western *Selasphorus* hummingbirds have been recorded increasingly in the fall along the Gulf Coast. While most *Selasphorus* sightings are probably Rufous Hummingbirds, other species of the same genus are the Broad-tailed Hummingbird *(S. platycercus)* and the Allen's Hummingbird *(S. sasin)*, which are nearly impossible to differentiate if not adult males. From present data, we must suppose that most fall and winter sightings here are Rufous Hummingbirds. Many, if not most, are immatures or females that defy positive field identification and should be reported only as *Selasphorus* species.

The adult male Rufous Hummingbird is identified by a reddish brown back and sides, mainly reddish tail, green crown, and orange red gorget. Immature and adult females have reddish sides, red brown in the tail bordered by green, white-tipped outer feathers, a green crown, and green back. The white breast and belly of adult and immature females contrast with the reddish sides, flanks, and undertail coverts. Immature males have whitish throats before acquiring the reddish orange gorget. Immature males and some males in adult plumage may show green speckles on the back. Note the similarity of immature and female Rufous Hummingbirds to another *Selasphorus* species, the Allen's Hummingbird in the accompanying account.

Rufous Hummingbirds have occurred on the Mississippi Coast in all three counties and on East Ship Island

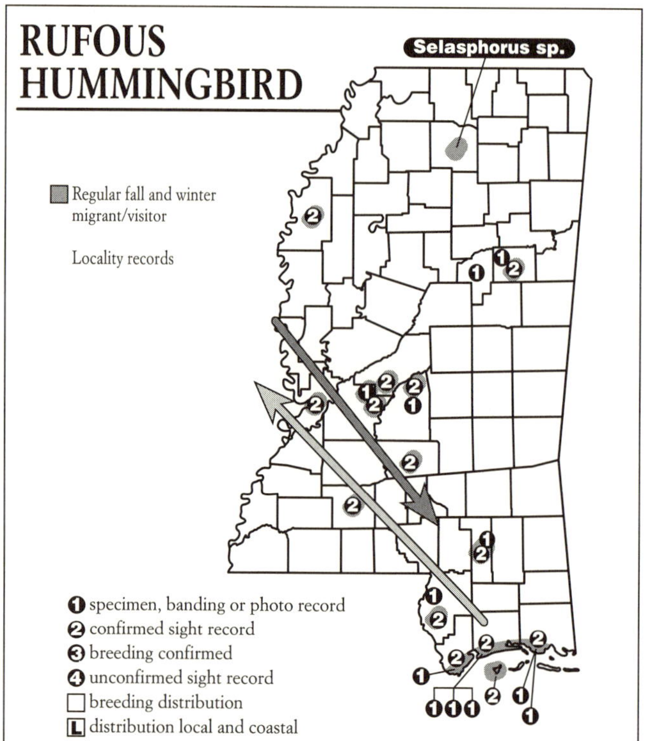

	JAN	FEB	MAR	APR	MAY	JUN	JUL	AUG	SEP	OCT	NOV	DEC
OCCURRENCE	○○○○	○○○○	26 ○○○	Selasphorus spp. August – March				○	○	○○	○○○○	○○○○
MUSEUM*												
WHT*												

*Breeding confirmed by egg, sight, or photographic record.

(Toups and Jackson 1987). Sight records of this species and other *Selasphorus* species extend from early August to mid-March. The first Mississippi specimen record of the Rufous Hummingbird was a bird observed by Dalton King at a feeder in Gulfport from December 28, 1984, until January 21, 1985, when it was found dead (Muth 1985). The specimen was deposited in the MSU collection.

Sight records of adult male Rufous Hummingbirds have been recorded at Hattiesburg by Larry and Terrie Gates (Jackson and Hodges 1986). The late John Thompson and I observed an adult male that remained at a flower garden and feeder in Jackson for about two weeks during October. At the same time, an adult male Rufous was observed at the Thompson home in Brookhaven.

Late fall occurrences have been reported of single adult male Rufous Hummingbirds seen at feeders by multiple observers in Madison and Rankin Counties and at Vicksburg. A sighting of one immature female *Selasphorus* species at Oxford on September 16 and 17, 1986, was confirmed by multiple observers (Jackson and Hodges 1986).

While observing and photographing the adult male Rufous Hummingbird in Jackson, I noticed a marked difference in its behavior compared to the Ruby-throat's. The bird was feeding from red, tubular flowers of a tall plant that reached to the eaves of a house, as well as a nearby feeder suspended on the house. Its feeding behavior was deliberate, like a sphinx moth, inserting the bill and drinking without removal. While hovering to feed, it appeared to be clinging by its bill for support.

After feeding it would fly away to other locations, invariably returning after five to 10 minutes to rest concealed in the same camellia bush. The bird rested almost motionless in a nearly torpid state until it resumed feeding. Observations of this bird were made over a period of more than two hours on a mild, sunny afternoon. The backyard garden was bordered with red and pink begonia beds, impatiens, and other fall flowers.

The *Selasphorus* hummingbirds in fall and winter are attracted to garden flowers, and well-placed feeders will hold them longer for better study, identification, and photography. The Rufous Hummingbird and possibly other western species, once attracted, might be induced by the careful use of feeders to overwinter and return the following year.

In recent years Rufous Hummingbirds have occurred in Mississippi and the Southeast in increasing numbers. There is little doubt that this is due to widespread placement of feeders during fall and winter seasons, reporting for identification, and banding. In 1993 and 1994, 12 Rufous Hummingbirds were banded inland and 12 were banded on the Mississippi Coast. In 1995 and 1996, 48 Rufous Hummingbirds were banded in Hancock, Harrison, and Jackson Counties.

[Allen's Hummingbird] *Selasphorus sasin*

Allen's Hummingbird is much like the Rufous Hummingbird. The main difference is the solid green crown and back of the Allen's male. The Allen's has narrower tail feathers than the Rufous, a minor difference. Females and immatures are separable from the Rufous only on the breeding grounds, where they migrate earlier in spring and fall in discrete California breeding territories. Males of both species have orange red gorgets.

On November 22, 1992, Robert R. Sargent netted and banded an Allen's Hummingbird at Bay St. Louis, the first state record (MMNS). Second and third state records are second-year males banded on January 13, 1994, at Pascagoula in Jackson County and January 31, 1995, at Diamondhead in Hancock County. This species is a casual vagrant along the Gulf Coast from its breeding territory mainly in western California, where it is common in brush and woodlands. Both Allen's and Rufous Hummingbirds have similar wing whistles and calls, but their courtship displays differ.

ALLEN'S HUMMINGBIRD

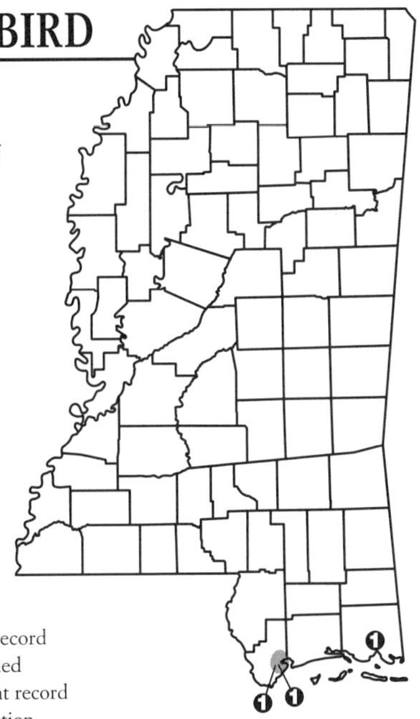

■ Casual vagrant on Gulf Coast, locality records

❶ banding record
❷ confirmed sight record
❸ breeding confirmed
❹ unconfirmed sight record
□ breeding distribution
Ⓒ distribution local

	JAN	FEB	MAR	APR	MAY	JUN	JUL	AUG	SEP	OCT	NOV	DEC
OCCURRENCE	13 31 ○ ○										22 ○	
MUSEUM*												
WHT*												

*Breeding confirmed by egg, sight, or photographic record.

Kingfishers (Coraciiformes)

Kingfishers are almost worldwide in distribution. They are solitary birds with large lancelike beaks, strong feet, and the three North American species are fish eaters. They frequent stream courses and shorelines, perching and then hovering before diving to catch fish.

The Belted and larger Ringed Kingfisher have ragged crests. The much smaller Green Kingfisher and the Ringed Kingfisher occur in southern and southwestern Texas, mainly along the Rio Grande Valley and casually farther inland. The Belted Kingfisher occurs in most of North America.

The two larger kingfisher females are more colorful than the males. The little Green Kingfisher male is more colorful than the female, and both have inconspicuous crests. The kingfishers have two toes partly joined. Their heavy bills and strong legs are used for digging long tunnels leading to their nests in sand banks or stream banks. The song of the Belted Kingfisher is a loud ratchety rattle.

Above: Belted Kingfisher

Alcedinidae (Kingfishers)

Belted Kingfisher *Ceryle alcyon*

The Belted Kingfisher is a common, breeding permanent resident over most of Mississippi. It is usually seen near water, the source of its food supply. It avoids salt water, but frequents all of our other water courses. Even the smallest pond is likely to have this visitor at one time or another.

This bird lives almost entirely on small, mostly non-game fish, but at times it eats crawfish, small frogs, turtles, snakes, large insects, and other aquatic animal life. It is adept at catching its prey by hovering over water and then diving in headlong.

The Kingfisher has a large head and bill with a prominent, irregular crest. It is mostly bright blue on the upperparts and white on the underparts. A broad, white collar almost circles the neck. On the male, a bluish gray band crosses the breast beneath the white collar. Below the gray band on the female, an additional rufous band extends across the breast along the sides. Thus, the Belted Kingfisher is one of the few birds in which the female is more colorful than the male. The call is a loud rattle usually emitted while the bird is in flight.

The Kingfisher is a familiar sight around water, where it sits on overhanging wires or limbs surveying an area of water beneath its perch. A bird usually sights its prey from a perch, then flies out, hovers momentarily, then makes a headlong plunge into the water to seize its food. It usually returns to a perch to feed.

The Kingfisher's nest is built in April or early May at the slightly elevated and enlarged end of a tunnel, which is usually dug horizontally into the side of a stream bank. Sometimes nests are built in burrows a considerable distance from water. The entrance to the tunnel is near the top of the exposed bank. From five to eight pure white eggs are laid on the bare soil at the end of the nest tunnel.

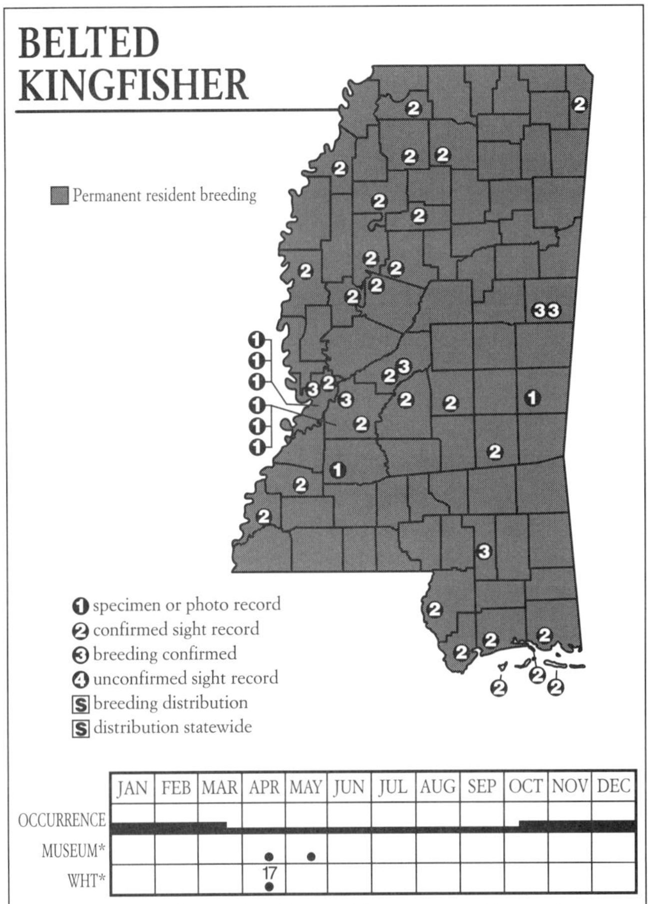

*Breeding confirmed by egg, sight, or photographic record.

During extremely cold weather when water is frozen at the surface for a week or more, the Kingfisher may withdraw to warmer parts of our state. At such times an influx of Kingfishers may appear in parts of Mississippi having open water areas.

Woodpeckers (Piciformes)

Woodpeckers are uniquely adapted for wood boring and climbing on the trunks and limbs of trees. They have strong, chisel-like bills and remarkably long, barbed, extendable tongues suitable for spearing and extracting wood-boring insects. Their tail feathers have stiff spines that act as props to assist the birds in climbing trees. The two forward and two backward-pointing toes are equipped with sharp claws. The plumage is largely black and white, and the males of most species have some red on the head. Their flight is strong and undulating.

Woodpeckers excavate holes for nesting and roosting, and all lay pure white eggs. Their abandoned roosting cavities provide homes for other cavity-nesting birds. Generally, they are early to bed and late to rise in the morning and are less active in rainy, cloudy, and inclement weather.

These birds are widely regarded as beneficial to humans because they consume millions of harmful forest insects. Woodpeckers' food consists of wood-borers, ants and other insects, and wild fruits and berries. Some species consume tree sap. Most of the common woodpeckers, except the Northern Flicker, readily use suet, peanut butter, cornbread, and other tidbits placed at bird feeders. Most members of this family have loud calls. Their drummings are distinctive for each species and serve to define and to defend their territories.

Above: Red-cockaded Woodpecker

Picidae (Woodpeckers)

Red-headed Woodpecker
Melanerpes erythrocephalus

At one time this species was common throughout Mississippi, in open country and around farmlands. Now it seems to be confined mostly to more extensive woodlands, especially bottomland hardwoods. But even there it appears to be diminishing in abundance.

The European Starling probably is responsible for the decline of the "redhead." Through aggressive, persistent harassment, starlings appropriate the nest cavities of this woodpecker, as well as the nests of Red-bellied Woodpeckers and Northern Flickers. With constant interference from the starling, Red-headed Woodpecker nests are abandoned one after another until there may be a complete nesting failure.

This is the only Mississippi woodpecker with the entire head red down to its shoulders. The back, tail, and outer wing feathers are blue black. The rest of the body and a large wing patch are white. Juveniles have a dingy brown head until the fall molt when they attain adult plumage. Sexes are alike in appearance.

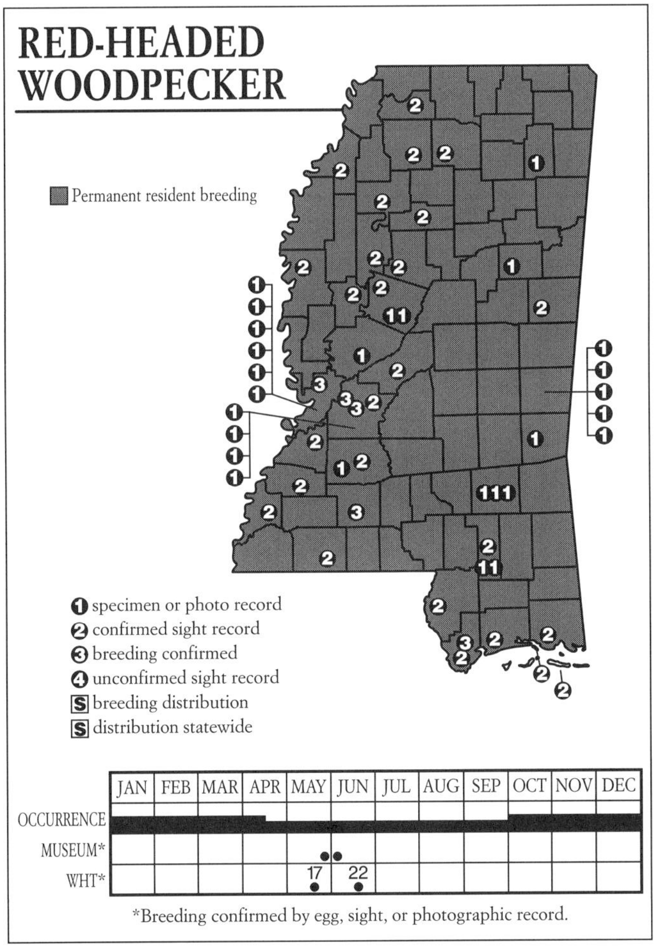

The Red-headed Woodpecker prefers open habitat for nesting, making it more vulnerable than other woodpeckers to having its nest taken by starlings. Dead timber is their preferred nesting location. The birds drill the nest cavity in a dead tree, limb, post, or stump from 10 to 70 feet or more aboveground. The four or five white eggs are laid in May on a bed of wood chips in the nest cavity.

A considerable portion of the insect food of this handsome woodpecker is obtained on the ground. It feeds extensively on ants, beetles, grasshoppers, caterpillars, and bugs. It does not feed to a great extent on wood-boring insect larvae. About 50 percent of the Red-headed Woodpecker's diet is fruit, such as cherry, mulberry, blackberry, elderberry, pokeberry, corn, and grape. Acorns are eaten in large quantities and often stored away in cracks for future use.

In winter this species often moves to wooded swamps and seldom is seen in open country. The winter population is supplemented by migrants from farther north.

The call note of the Red-headed Woodpecker is a loud *queer* or *queeah,* being much louder and higher pitched than the call of the Red-bellied Woodpecker. It also has a rolling call and drum similar to those made by other woodpeckers.

Red-bellied Woodpecker *Melanerpes carolinus*

This "zebra-backed" woodpecker with a prominent white rump patch has pale gray underparts lightly tinged with red on the extreme lower portion of the belly. The entire crown and hind neck of the male are bright, scarlet red. Only the nape of the female is red, and the forepart of the top of the head is gray. Juveniles are marked like adults, but have grayish brown heads without red marks.

This species and the Downy Woodpecker are two of our most common woodpeckers, and they can be found in almost any patch of woods in our state. The call note is a rapidly repeated, guttural *chow-chow-chow,* and they repeat rapidly a hoarse, rattling *chur-r-r-rrrr-rr.* Like most woodpeckers, the Red-bellied is a noisy bird. It responds readily to a recorded playback of its call and to an imitation of owl hootings. The male also has a seldom heard *wick-up* call very similar to the Northern Flicker.

Throughout Mississippi, the Red-bellied Woodpecker is common to abundant as a breeding permanent resident. It excavates a hole in dead wood of a tree or post from 10 to 70 feet aboveground. The four or five white eggs are laid in May on a layer of wood chips at the bottom of the nest cavity. It eats large quantities of insects, but varies its diet in winter by eating fruit, berries, acorns, and nuts. Like the Red-headed Woodpecker, it frequently stores food in bark crevices or cracks in wood.

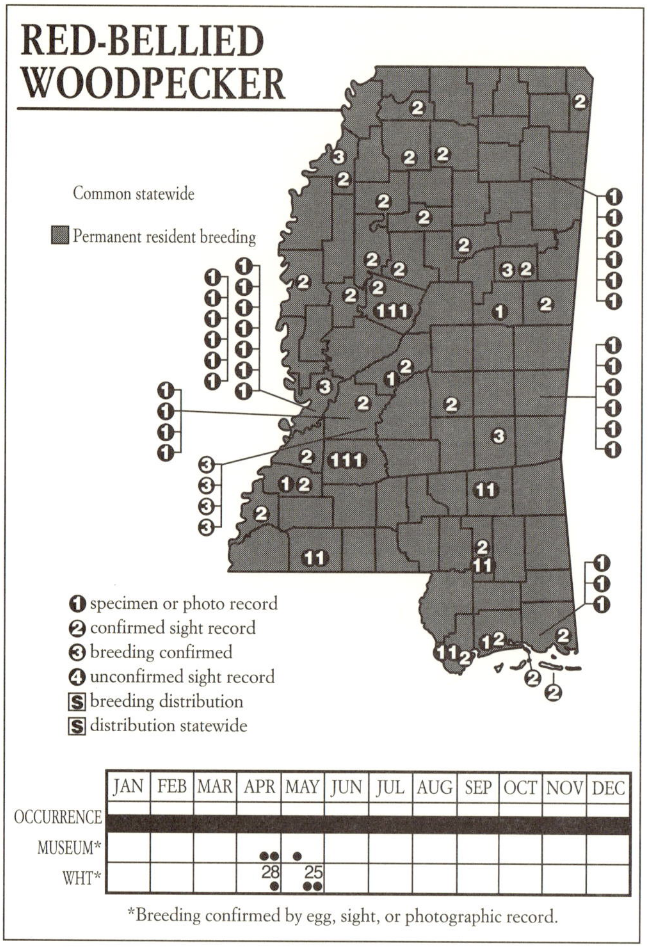

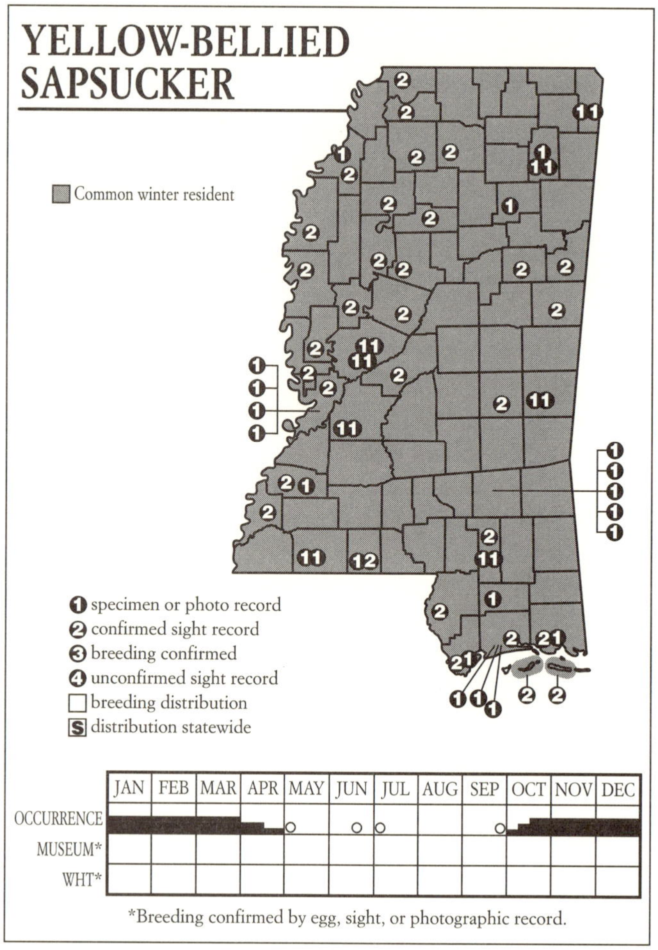

Yellow-bellied Sapsucker *Sphyrapicus varius*

Adults are identified by the combination of red patch on the forehead and a white, longitudinal patch on the wing. The male has a *red* throat patch and the female has a *white* one. This black-and-white woodpecker has a yellowish wash on the belly and is about the same size as the Hairy Woodpecker. Immatures have a brownish head and may show incomplete development of the adult's head marks. Their calls are distinctive whining or mewing notes described as *whee-ur* that slur downward at the end.

This is the only woodpecker on our state's bird list that does not nest in Mississippi. It is a common, statewide winter resident found in all wooded sections. Arrival occurs in early October and departure is almost complete by April, though sometimes a few remain until early May.

The sapsucker is usually a quiet, solitary bird. It can be overlooked because it spends much of its time clinging to the side of a tree. It drills concentric rows of holes around the limbs and trunks of trees. Sometimes trees are permanently damaged or even killed by either the sapsucker's attacks or a disease that may enter the injured parts of the tree. The sapsucker feeds on the cambium bast next to the wood, drinks heavily of the sap exuding from the holes, and eats insects attracted by the sap. Wild fruits, particularly poison ivy and holly berries, are sometimes eaten during its sojourn here during fall and winter. I have found this bird to be unusually responsive to imitations of owl hoots or screech-owl recordings.

Downy Woodpecker *Picoides pubescens*

There is little difference in appearance between Downy and Hairy Woodpeckers. Both have longitudinal white patches on the back and are spotted with black and white on the wings. Except for the size of the bill and the difference in overall size of the birds, there is little to distinguish between them.

The Downy, a black-and-white woodpecker, is the smallest and one of the common members of its family. This bird's small bill is shorter than one-half the length of its head. The outer-tail feathers are white and lightly barred with black. These tail feathers are all white in the Hairy Woodpecker. The male of both species has a small, red patch on the back of the head. The call of the Downy Woodpecker is lower in pitch and volume than the Hairy Woodpecker.

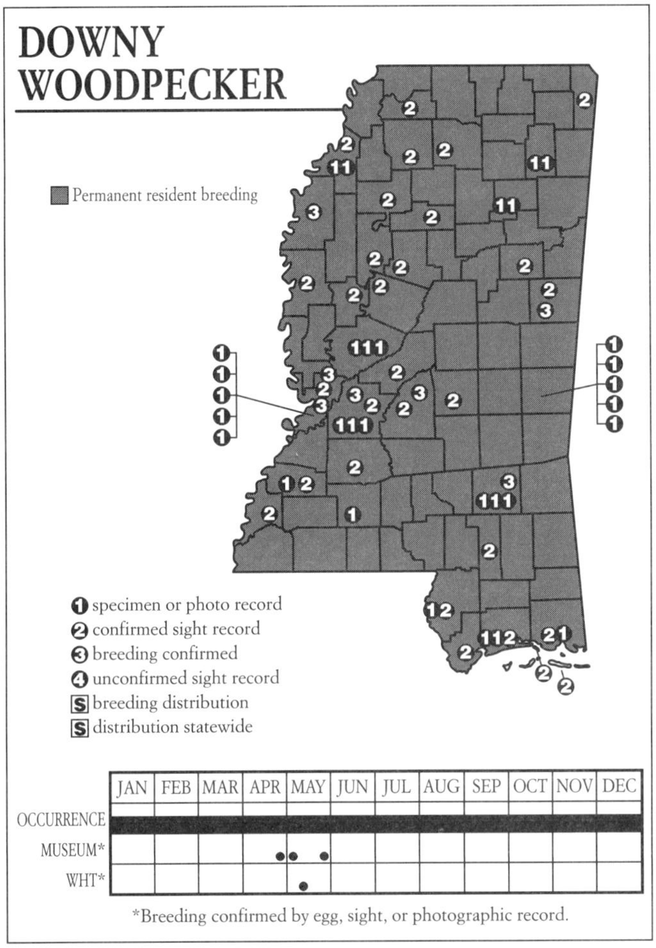

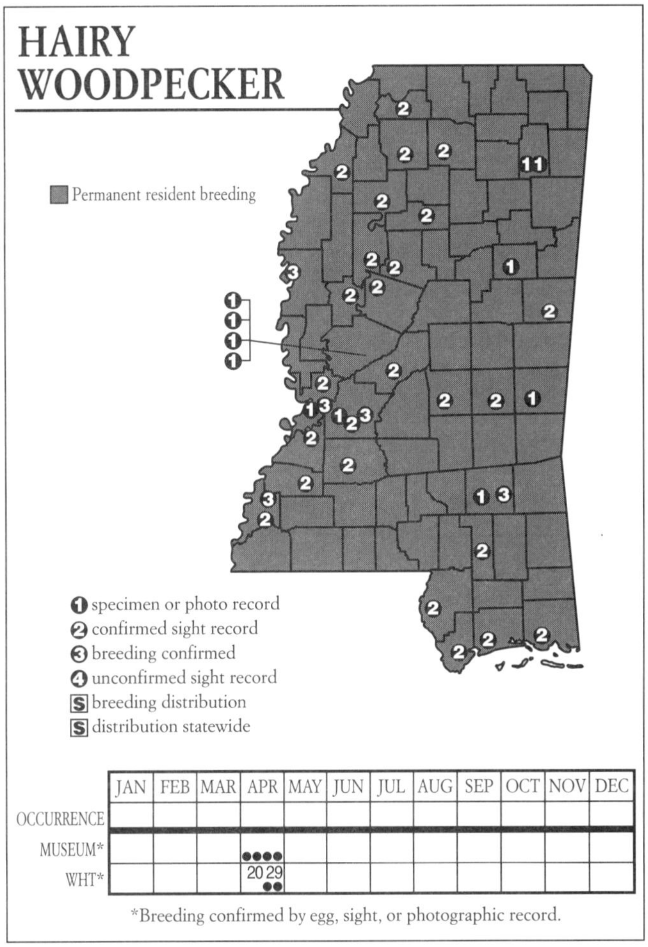

The male drums long and persistently before and during the nesting season, and its drums are longer than other woodpeckers.

Nesting occurs in a hole dug into the dead limb or stump of a hardwood tree 10 to 70 feet or more aboveground. The three or four white eggs are laid in April or early May on wood chips at the bottom of the cavity.

The food habits of the Downy Woodpecker make it one of our most useful birds. This small woodpecker spends most of its time pecking away at the bark of trees after noxious insects. Its food consists mainly of spiders and their egg cocoons, beetles and their wood-boring larvae, ants, caterpillars, other insects, and wild fruit. It is a breeding permanent resident in all sections of Mississippi.

Hairy Woodpecker *Picoides villosus*

The Downy and Hairy Woodpeckers are almost identical in appearance. Both are breeding permanent residents in all sections of Mississippi. The Hairy Woodpecker has a large bill more than half the length of its head. (The Downy's bill is noticeably small, less than one-half its head length.) Outer-tail feathers of the Hairy Woodpecker are white, and those of the Downy are lightly barred with black. The Downy Woodpecker measures only about six or seven inches in length, while the Hairy Woodpecker is about nine or 10 inches long. The males of both species show a small patch of red on the back of the head. The call note of the Hairy Woodpecker is a loud *peek* higher in pitch than the Downy's. The kingfisher-like rattling calls are louder and higher in pitch than those of the Downy.

This species is less common than the Downy Woodpecker and is shy and retiring in its habits. It is usually solitary, but sometimes joins with bands of roving chickadees, titmice, and other woodland birds outside the breeding season. It prefers to nest in a hardwood tree, where it excavates a cavity in dead wood about 10 or 12 inches deep. The three or four white eggs are deposited in late March, April, or May on wood chips. The nest of this species is difficult to find since it is usually in or near an extensive woodland.

The principal food of this woodpecker is wood-boring insect larvae. Ants, spiders, caterpillars, and other insects and their eggs are important food items. The diet is varied with fruits, seeds, acorns, and nuts, which make up about 25 percent of its food.

Red-cockaded Woodpecker *Picoides borealis*

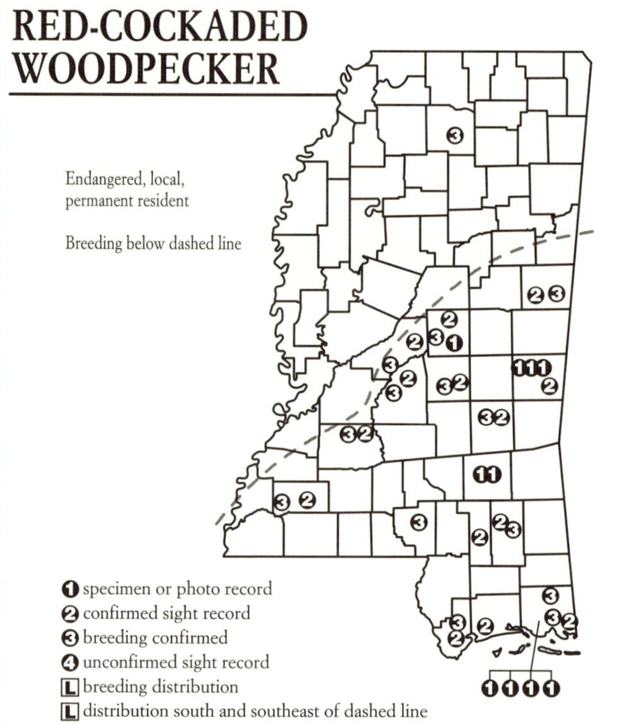

	JAN	FEB	MAR	APR	MAY	JUN	JUL	AUG	SEP	OCT	NOV	DEC
OCCURRENCE												
MUSEUM*				●●	●●●				●			
WHT*												

*Breeding confirmed by egg, sight, or photographic record.

The habitat requirements of this black-and-white woodpecker are so highly specialized that it is on the verge of extirpation in Mississippi. It is listed as an endangered species by the federal government and many states. Its decline is due to destruction of essential habitat: the open, overmature, living pine trees with little or no understory that are necessary to this species for nesting and roosting.

Red-cockaded Woodpeckers nest only in living pines that have become infected with red heart disease. Timber harvesting and planting practices in this state have removed most old pine stands, and cutting on a short rotation does not allow time for replacement of overmature trees suitable for this woodpecker's particular requirements.

The Red-cockaded Woodpecker has become very local in distribution and is now a rare permanent resident. It occurs locally in central and southern Mississippi where old, open pine stands remain. It is found at widely scattered locations on Noxubee National Wildlife Refuge near Starkville; along the Natchez Trace Parkway; on the Bienville, DeSoto, and Homochitto National Forests; and at a few other locations on state-operated wildlife management areas. But few or none are found on corporate-owned timberlands. Fortunately, some of these areas, mainly on national forests and military reservations where birds still remain, are being managed to retain old pine stands and provide for replacement trees as old ones die. Burning or herbicide injections are necessary practices to retard hardwood understory encroachment that causes family colonies or "clans" to abandon otherwise suitable habitat.

Alexander Wilson named the Red-cockaded Woodpecker after the red feathers—cockades—worn by some American soldiers on their three-cornered hats during the American Revolution.

This species is *zebra-backed* and has *large, white cheek patches.* It has a black crown and hindneck and two small spots of red feathers near the ears on the male, the "cockades" from which this bird gets its name. The call is a rasping, nasal *srip, srip* that aids in locating and identifying this bird.

The nesting and roosting habits of this woodpecker are unique. The bird drills its cavity into the dead heartwood of living pine trees from 20 to 80 feet aboveground. The cavity goes slightly up and toward the center of the tree, then downward for 12 to 14 inches.

Around the nest entrance, the birds peck numerous holes or remove the bark entirely. This causes pine gum to flow freely down the side of the tree. It forms a glaze known to discourage or repel rat snakes and other predators or competitors that might enter and destroy the nest contents, or take over the cavity for their purposes. When not used for raising a brood, nest holes are used for roosting throughout the year. As long as they are needed for nesting or roosting, the flow of pine gum is kept active by pecking new holes in the bark. The two to four eggs are deposited on a layer of wood chips. The eggs are often soiled with pine resin from the breasts of incubating birds.

This highly specialized woodpecker is gregarious and ordinarily occurs in small groups of up to six or eight individuals, which seem to keep in touch with each other by calling back and forth. Family groups remain together throughout the year. They often associate with Pine Warblers, Brown-headed Nuthatches, Eastern Bluebirds, and other small birds frequenting pine woodlands.

Red-cockaded Woodpeckers feed on wood-borers, ants, and other destructive forest insects found on or under the bark of pine trees. They continually chip off flakes of bark from pine trees while looking for bark insects. Much of their feeding is done in the tops of tall pines, especially by the females.

This species is threatened by loss of habitat, lack of proper management to prevent hardwood encroachment in mature or overmature stands, clear-cutting, regeneration of pine plantations on short rotations, and forced isolation in limited habitat suitable for survival. This bird is highly vulnerable in pinelands north of the longleaf and slash pine belt of southern Mississippi. It needs and deserves careful management to ensure its survival, especially on public lands.

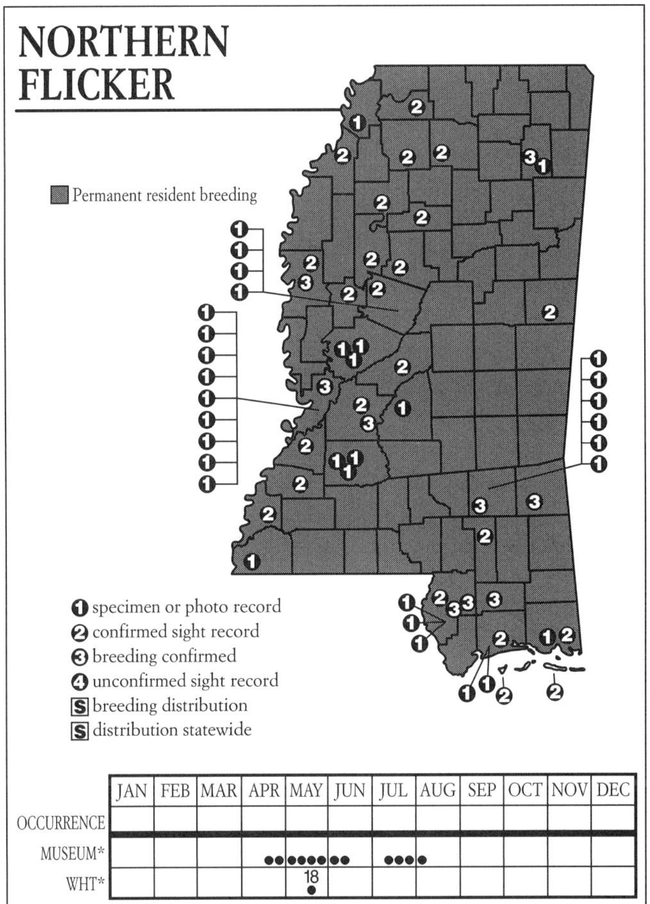

*Breeding confirmed by egg, sight, or photographic record.

Northern Flicker *Colaptes auratus*

In the eastern United States, this species is commonly called "yellowhammer." In flight, it flashes a white rump and overhead shows much yellow in its wings and tail. It has a brownish back transversely striped with black, a wide, black crescent on the breast, and a crescent of red on the back of the head. Males have black moustache marks. The breast and underparts are soft, silky, pinkish brown evenly sprinkled with black dots.

The song is a rapidly repeated *wick, wick, wick, wick*. During courtship display, or when two or more birds confront each other, they make squeaky *wick'-up, wick'up* or *flick'a, flick'-a* sounds. The name flicker comes from the sound of these call notes. Another common call note is a loud *klee'-yer*.

Flickers spend much more time on the ground than other woodpeckers. They are usually on the ground probing and searching for ants, which they consume in large quantities. Other insect foods are taken when available. During fall and winter, over half of their food is wild fruits. Poison ivy, Virginia creeper, hackberries, and other fruits, acorns, nuts, and seeds are taken in quantity.

Usually, the Northern Flicker excavates its nest cavity in a dead tree trunk or limb. In April or May, the female lays from five to seven glossy white eggs. Sometimes they resort to building nests or roost cavities in the sides of wooden buildings. I have seen two nest cavities excavated into the ground beside power poles. One of these nests was successful in producing a brood.

The European Starling is a serious competitor with the Northern Flicker for nest holes, and this pest bird will often appropriate a flicker's nest as soon as it is completed. Since the starling now occupies much of the same range as the flicker, this competition likely will continue to be serious.

Flickers will use nest boxes made of cypress or cedar wood, 6 x 6 inches inside, and 14 inches in depth below the bottom of a three-inch entrance hole. For ease of maintenance, boxes should be placed six to eight feet aboveground on substantial posts with a two-inch layer of wood shavings added before erection. One side of the box or the roof should be hinged to allow inspection and maintenance.

Pileated Woodpecker *Dryocopus pileatus*

This crow-sized woodpecker with a conspicuous red crest is commonly called "Indian hen," "lord-god," or "woodchuck." Its large size, mostly black plumage, and undulating flight with deliberate sweeping wingbeats, combine to present a spectacular appearance. The female has a black forehead and lacks the red moustache mark and full red crest of the male. The red moustache extends from the bill beneath and behind the eye. In flight, the underwings show a great deal of white.

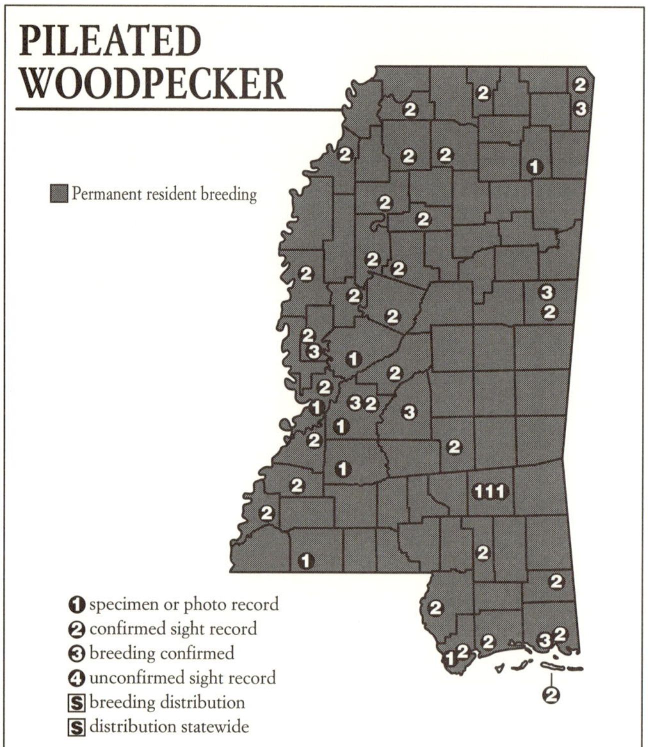

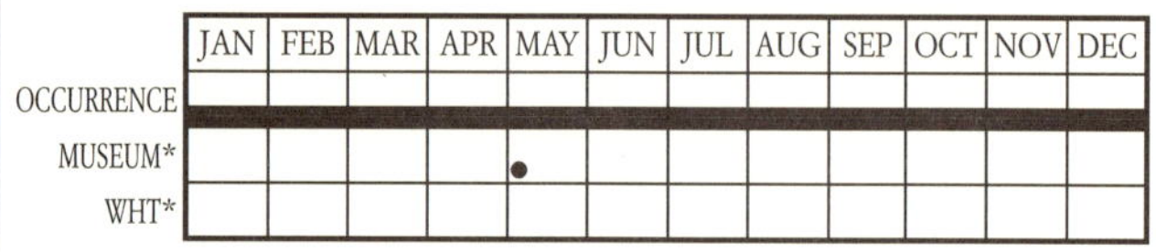

*Breeding confirmed by egg, sight, or photographic record.

The call notes are similar to those of the Northern Flicker, but are louder and sometimes much more interrupted and prolonged. The call can be described as *kuk-kuk-kukkuk—kuk-kuk,* with a rising or falling pitch. More than other woodpeckers, it seems to delight in drumming a very loud and resonant tattoo on a dead limb, especially in the early spring before nesting starts. These drummings serve the same purpose as songs and call notes of other birds. They advertise to conspecifics their intent to protect and defend a certain territory.

The Pileated Woodpecker is a fairly common, breeding permanent resident in all larger wooded portions of Mississippi. Most large patches of woods contain at least a pair of these birds. After the virgin timberlands were cut, this species adapted to living in the second growth forests and now seems to be holding its own or increasing in many parts of Mississippi.

The nest cavity of the Pileated Woodpecker is in large woodlands and is usually dug in March or April in a dead tree trunk 30 feet or more aboveground. The three to five glossy white eggs are laid on a layer of wood chips. The entrance hole is three or four inches across. The abandoned nest cavities of this species are often used by Wood Ducks for nesting.

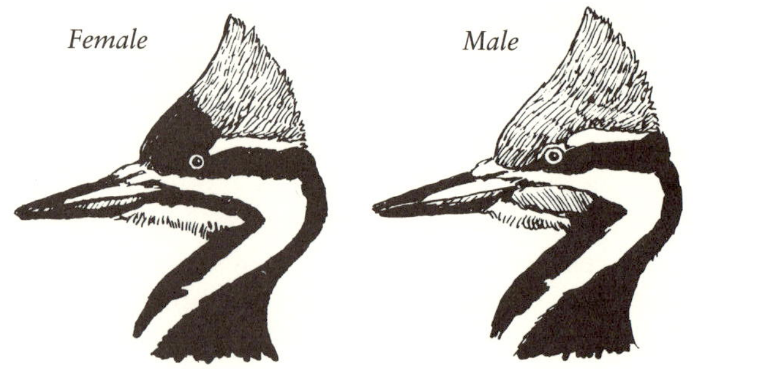

Pileated Woodpecker

Ants, termites, and wood-boring insects make up the largest portion of this woodpecker's food. Pileated Woodpeckers often feed on the ground where termites and other insects invade fallen trees, limbs, and rotten wood. Besides insects, this woodpecker consumes fruits, berries, acorns, and nuts. The large, oblong excavations and large wood chips left on the forest floor indicate its presence.

[Ivory-billed Woodpecker] *Campephilus principalis*

This largest of North American woodpeckers, if it still exists, is on the list of endangered species. The decline of the Ivory-billed Woodpecker and its probable extinction is clearly evident based on knowledge of its habits and specific habitat requirements. Its demise in Louisiana began in the 1930s and extended to December 1946, when it was last seen in the Singer Tract south of Tallulah, now the Tensas National Wildlife Refuge (Tanner 1942; Peterson 1988). Most of the remaining large timber was removed during World War II, resulting in the loss of a family group known to be present until lumbering operations began in the late 1930s. In Florida, small colonies were known to exist and were widespread until the turn of the century.

Widespread logging over the Ivory-bill's habitat combined with illicit and immoral shooting for specimens prized by collectors contributed to the loss of the remaining few birds that were vulnerable while nesting. Isolated reports of sightings and the last reported Florida specimens (usually in pairs) occurred up to 1924. Since then, reported inconclusive sightings have occurred in one or more isolated Florida swamplands. The Big Thicket National Preserve north of Beaumont in eastern Texas reportedly had the last known remnant population of Ivory-billed Woodpeckers. After about 1950, reports of sightings in the Big Thicket area subsided, and those birds are now believed to be extirpated.

The former range of the Ivory-billed Woodpecker extended from southern Illinois and Indiana to include most southeastern states to the Gulf of Mexico and westward to the Brazos River and inland to about 70 miles north of eastern Texas. In Mississippi, the probable habitat was along the major stream courses of the Pearl, Wolf, and Pascagoula Rivers; the Yazoo and Mississippi Deltas; the Tombigbee River; and lower tributaries and wider parts of the Big Black River.

Early occurrence records of this species in Mississippi in the nineteenth century were not well documented. Only six specimen records are known from Mississippi: two from Bolivar County, two from near Mississippi City in Harrison County, and two from unspecified localities taken in March and April 1883 (Hahn 1963). The disappearance of Ivory-bills over these ranges coincided with selective cutting of virgin hardwoods during early settlement. Clear-cutting of virgin pines following the Civil War and accelerated cutting between the end of the last century until about 1920 contributed to this woodpecker's demise.

There have been individual unconfirmed accounts of sightings or hearing the calls of Ivory-bills in Mississippi since 1920. However, none are acceptable for lack of proof, such as a photograph, specimen, or a detailed account by multiple observers describing *all* supporting details of bill, white wing patches, locality, head mark (whether male or female), and a description of the distinctive calls of this woodpecker.

The Ivory-billed Woodpecker has an *ivory white bill,* all white secondaries *visible in flight and at rest,* and white patches on the *forward part of the underwings* extending to the shoulders. The male has a *black forehead,* a *black chin,* and a red crest. The female (about 20 inches in length) has a *black chin* and an *all black crest.* The slightly smaller Pileated Woodpecker has a *white chin* and *black secondaries* visible in flight and at rest. The male Pileated has a *red forehead and crest* and a red moustache mark. The female has a *black forehead,* a *red* crest, a *black* moustache, and a *white chin.* Both sexes of both species have white lines above and behind the eye, the lower ones widening and extending down the sides of the neck to the wing pit.

Jackson (1988, 1989) and Sauey (*in* Jackson 1989), accompanied by Charlie Luthin, have published recent accounts of surveys in Mississippi. Jackson and Malcolm F. Hodges Jr. were playing tapes while surveying a large, isolated bottomland hardwood tract below the old run of the Yazoo River between the mouth of the Yazoo and Mississippi Rivers. Calls like the Ivory-bill's were heard but no sighting occurred. Calls they heard the next day in the area came from a Blue Jay. Both observers believe they heard an Ivory-bill calling the previous day and tried to approach it, but it was gone.

Sauey and his companion were floating Black Creek in 1978 on a survey for Ivory-bills, and at one location heard some tappings and calls described as nuthatchlike and similar to the Ivory-bill call on prerecorded tapes. No bird was seen making the calls.

John Phares and I made similar surveys in March 1977 and 1978 to investigate detailed reported sightings of Ivory-billed Woodpeckers in Yazoo and Holmes Counties along the Loess Bluff bordering Hillside National Wildlife Refuge. These surveys were planned in response to reported accidental sightings described by J. W. Robinson in a six-page letter referred to our attention and written to the regional director of the U.S. Fish and Wildlife Service.

Our initial two-day survey made March 28–29, 1977, produced negative results. We played tape recordings of Ivory-billed and Pileated Woodpecker calls. Seven Pileated Woodpeckers responded along the Loess Bluff escarpment and in the Hillside Floodway bottomland hardwoods containing large amounts of flooded living and dead timber. These woodpeckers came well within viewing range with binoculars. Other Pileated Woodpeckers were heard and not seen. The area had numerous other species of woodpeckers, especially in flooded dead timber.

Our second survey made March 14–15, 1978, brought similar results. On the second day we heard and saw two Pileated Woodpeckers along the bluff escarpment at our first stop by a willow brake at 7:30 A.M. We returned to the bluff area about 11:00 A.M. and parked at a roadside pullout overlooking the oak-bitternut hickory swamp nearest the bluff. The following was recorded in my field notes:

> I hooted up an owl that flew out of the swamp woods and lit in a cottonwood behind us. While sitting in the car, I thought I heard several calls in the direction the owl had flown. . . . I heard several nuthatchlike calls and one which sounded, I thought, like the tin horn blast of the Ivory-bill, distinct but not too close. I opened the car door after asking Phares if he heard what I heard. He said "No." I slammed the door but saw and heard no more sounds. . . . The owl began hooting and before we left, [it] flew back to the swamp with three Blue Jays behind it. Afterward, we drove along the top of the bluff with open land immediately behind the bluff's edge. I have . . . discounted all possibility of hearing an Ivory-billed Woodpecker at that time.

The Blue Jay has a great variety of call and song notes. It is noted for mimicry of Red-tailed, Red-Shouldered, and Broad-winged Hawks. I have heard jays mimic all to near perfection. Bird voices are programmed genetically with individual and regional song variations related to their environment. It is reasonable to believe that some Blue Jays are capable of almost perfect mimicry of Ivory-bill's call notes. I believe this is true of calls I have heard and seen them make.

The one instance I described was near-perfect mimicry, enough to fool my ears. Playing of the Pileated and Ivory-billed Woodpecker recordings and Barred Owl hoots could have stimulated and activated ancestral memory bits and vocal chords of that particular jay or jays. Or else the Blue Jays might mimic the White-breasted Nuthatch found in mature bottomland and upland hardwoods where the mimicry was heard. "Grail hunts" like the ones I have described often yield unexpected dividends of another sort.

The Ivory-billed Woodpecker's call is best described as a single-noted, high, nasal *kent* or *kwank* like the White-breasted Nuthatch, or a high, short, false note on a clarinet. More than one bird calling together performed chorus calls like that on the Cornell University tape recordings made by A. A. Allen and P. P. Kellogg on the Singer Tract in Louisiana in the late 1930s.

This highly specialized woodpecker apparently has been extinct since 1950, unless it still exists in Cuba. Loss of overmature, virgin bottomland hardwoods and pinelands, together with their associated food chains and environmental factors including direct and indirect human disturbances, have caused its disappearance. The question remains whether to call it an endangered species, an extinct species, or probably extinct species. The first category seems best until all hope for recovery is gone. Like the Great Auk, Carolina Parakeet, Passenger Pigeon, and Heath Hen, the Ivory-billed Woodpecker seems to have been forced to extinction by the hands of humans.

Perching Birds (Passeriformes)

This large order includes the suborder Tyranni, the Family Tyrannidae or perching birds, which includes the flycatchers. The order includes many families, subfamilies, and tribes in the following species accounts. The suborder Passeres includes the land birds called songbirds, many of which but not all are neotropical migrants.

Some of our passerines are experiencing problems on their wintering and breeding grounds due to a loss of suitable habitat and fragmentation of large woodland tracts. Cowbird parasitism and more intensive land use have caused problems with some species. Concerted conservation measures like those being planned and implemented by the international Partners In Flight coalition are designed to insure the survival of songbirds for future generations to enjoy.

Many resident passerine land birds are not threatened. Some are favored by present habitat configuration and land use changes, and certain species are adapting to habitat alteration. A few birds such as crows, doves, robins, and some finches are adapting well and becoming "citified." The ever-present mockingbird has adapted well to urban, suburban, and country life around man's residences.

Others, however, like the Northern Bobwhite and the Eastern Meadowlark have undergone population declines due to more intensive land use for crops and growing pine plantations. Permanent resident species such as the cavity-nesting Eastern Bluebird will continue to need the man-made nesting structures we provide. In return, they repay us in color, song, and interesting behavior.

Above: Eastern Wood-pewee

Tyrannidae (Flycatchers)

Olive-sided Flycatcher *Contopus borealis*

This flycatcher can be regarded only as a rare, late spring and early fall transient in Mississippi. There is only one specimen record, a male taken by Vaiden (1953a) at Black's Cypress Brake in Bolivar County on May 8, 1949, which was his fifth sight record of this species.

There are two other early sight records for this flycatcher. Amy G. Tolman recorded one in Pearl River County on September 5, and Lovett E. Williams Jr. reported one at Lakeshore in Hancock County on August 27, 1960 (Williams and Clawson 1960). Recently, as the number of observers has increased, sightings of individual birds in the fall have occurred more frequently inland and near the coast. These birds prefer tall perches on snags in open areas, particularly cut-over woodlands.

This species slightly resembles the smaller Eastern Phoebe, but it has a chunky appearance. The head and bill are large, and the dark tail is short. The throat and center of the breast are white and contrast with the dark head, back, and conspicuous dark olive sides of the breast. Two white tufts of feathers protrude behind the wings near the base of the tail.

The Olive-sided Flycatcher winters in northern South America and breeds in the coniferous forests of the northern United States and Canada. It also breeds in the eastern mountains south into eastern Tennessee and western North Carolina.

My first encounter with this species was on June 12, 1985, a quiet bird beside a northern Minnesota lake. It appeared above me on a low limb, and I recognized it by the *dark plumage, white marks,* and its *larger size* compared with other plain flycatchers. My second encounter was a noisy one at daylight on a log road in the cut-over northern woods near Jackman, Maine, on June 23, 1986. The very first bird song I heard was the *quick-three-beers* call interspersed with *pip-pip-pip* notes. Whoever devised this description of its song and call notes did not have to be imaginative. The bird actually says it so plainly you know it instantly. The rest of my morning was a pleasant experience tape recording Winter Wren and Hermit Thrush songs.

[Western Wood-Pewee] *Contopus sordidulus*

There is only one Mississippi collection record for the Western Wood-Pewee. It is a specimen taken on September 10, 1960, at Cleveland in Bolivar County by Alan Feduccia (Vaiden 1960).

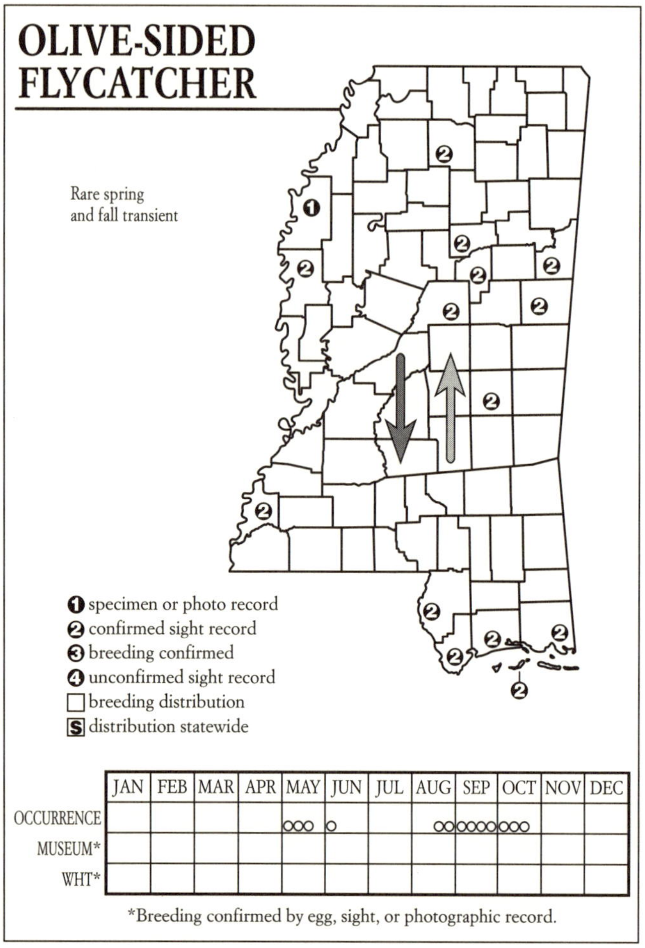

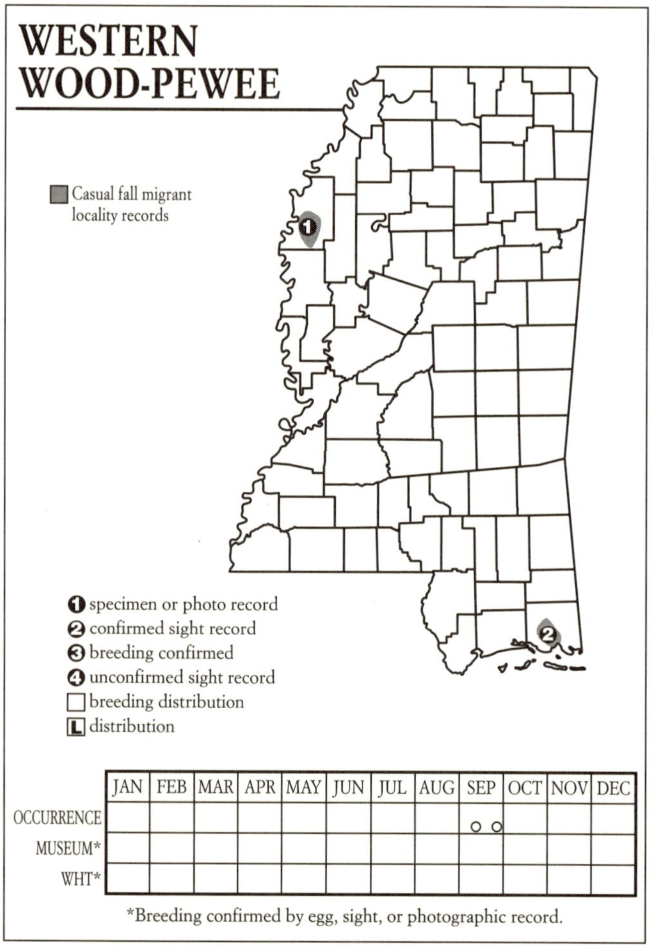

This species is inseparable in the field from the Eastern Wood-Pewee except by the song, which is more nasal, burry, and described as *peeyee* or *peeeer.* This western species is darker on the breast, sides, and underwings than the Eastern Wood-Pewee.

One sight record of a bird seen at Bellefontaine in Jackson County was identified by its call on September 30, 1978 (Weber et al. 1979). Another record is one identified by voice on July 28, 1991, seven miles south of Oxford by Gene and Shannon Knight (Schiefer 1991). These records of birds identified by call notes by multiple observers suggest that the western form of the Wood-Pewee may occur east of the Mississippi River more often than records indicate.

Eastern Wood-Pewee *Contopus virens*

The Eastern Wood-Pewee frequents dry upland woods and pine forests. It is a common, statewide, breeding summer resident. About the size of a sparrow, it has dark olive or olive gray upperparts, and grayish underparts with an olive gray wash on the sides. It has two conspicuous wing bars and lacks an eye ring. It does not wag the tail as does the Eastern Phoebe. The lower mandible is yellow, and the tail is slightly notched.

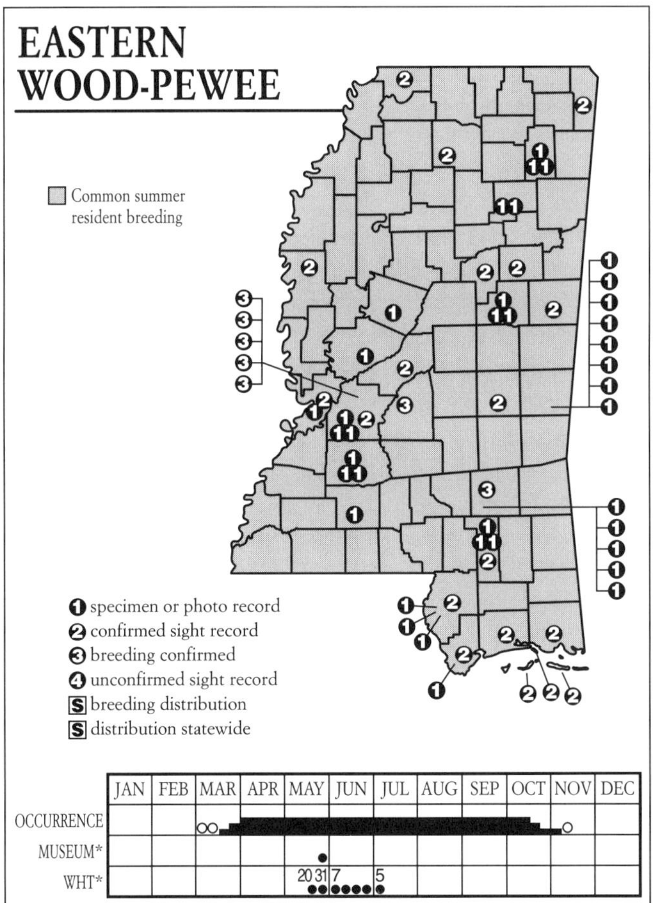

*Breeding confirmed by egg, sight, or photographic record.

It can be identified easily by its plaintive, whistled call that can be heard throughout the day during the breeding season. The song has been described as *pee-a-wee, pee-ur.* The dawn and twilight songs consist of rapid repetitions of these phrases with additional *pee-widdi* calls not usually heard during the daytime.

The Eastern Wood-Pewee arrives in late March and April from its wintering grounds in Central America and South America. It remains as a summer resident until October and has departed for its wintering grounds by mid-November.

The Eastern Wood-Pewee nests from late May to July. The nest is a beautiful compact structure in the shape of a very shallow cup made of fine grasses, mosses, and cobwebs and ornamented with lichens on the outside. It is usually saddled in the fork of a tree limb 20 to 40 feet aboveground. The two or three eggs are creamy white with a wreath of lavender and brown blotches around the large end.

This bird is common in open groves of oaks or pines, preferably on dry upland sites. The nest is difficult to find without patiently waiting and watching for an adult to visit it. I discovered that the incubating female answers the male each time he calls with the same call their fledglings make after they leave the nest. This has been a successful method for helping me locate nests.

Yellow-bellied Flycatcher *Empidonax flaviventris*

The small flycatchers of the genus *Empidonax* are difficult to identify by their field marks. In most cases, field identification should be made with caution. The five species are drab greenish or olive gray above and yellowish or light colored below. All have similar eye-ring and wing marks. All but the *Acadian and Willow Flycatchers* are spring and fall transients only. Unfortunately, those transient species are generally silent during migration. The call notes for each bird are distinctive, however, and are the best means of field identification. Each have distinct breeding behavior patterns, and they do not interbreed. The transient species are generally more numerous in the fall than during spring migration.

Based on collection records, the Yellow-bellied Flycatcher appears to be an uncommon spring migrant and of unusual occurrence in the fall. Collection records by Merrit G. Vaiden in Bolivar County extend from August 7 to September 24. Burleigh (1945) found this species to be "a regular and not uncommon fall transient on the Mississippi Coast but is only of accidental occurrence in spring." Burleigh collected 10 specimens on the Mississippi Coast in the fall from August 9 to October 13. A single spring specimen was taken on May 12. Collection records in the MMNS are specimens taken from August 25 to October 14. Two other spring collection records indicate this species is a late spring

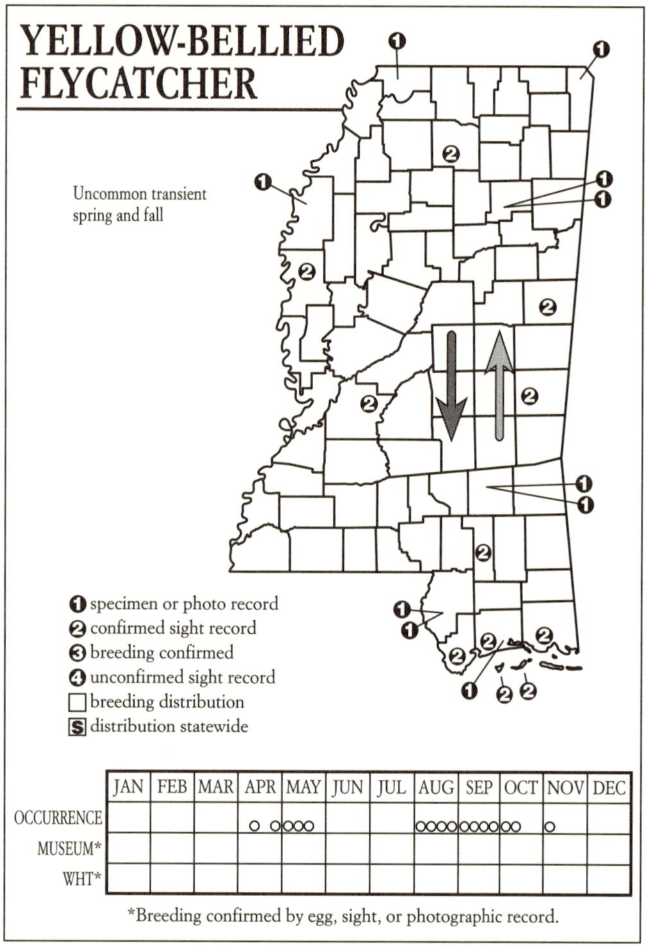

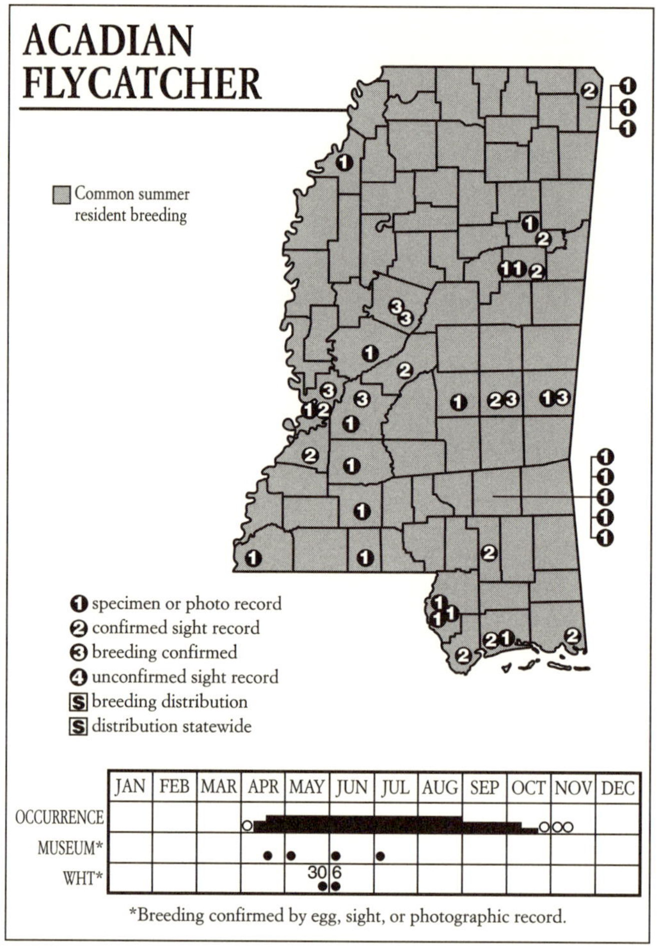

migrant. One specimen was taken by Allison (1907) on May 9, 1904, in Tishomingo County, and the other by R. Demett Smith Jr. on May 20, 1950, at Lakeview in DeSoto County.

This species has a yellow throat, eye ring, and underparts. Fall Acadian Flycatchers may look like the Yellow-bellied Flycatcher, which makes separation in the field next to impossible. Even museum specimens of these two species taken in the fall may be confusing. The call notes of this species are seldom heard here. The song is a simple, whistled *per-wee*. Its breeding range is central Canada south into the central and eastern United States.

Acadian Flycatcher *Empidonax virescens*

This small bird is a common, breeding summer resident in moist bottomlands, shady and deciduous woods, especially along streams and swamps. It is the only *Empidonax* flycatcher that *regularly* breeds in Mississippi.

Its nest is a shallow cup woven between the outer twigs of a tree limb. It is often composed entirely of Spanish moss and its black inner fibers. A marked preference is shown for building over water and the nest is usually placed from 10 to 20 feet high. It is often so thinly woven that the contents can be seen from underneath. Two or three creamy white eggs wreathed with brown spots around the large end make up a clutch.

The Acadian Flycatcher has a conspicuous light eye ring, a white throat in spring, two light wing bars, and a yellow belly. Its sides are greenish, the back grayish olive, and the sides of the breast washed with greenish yellow.

Once learned, the song, along with other field characteristics, serves to identify this species on its breeding grounds. It is an explosive *spit-chee* sometimes interspersed with twitterings as the bird moves about from one perch to another. Dawn and evening songs are prolonged, continuous twitterings combined with the day calls.

This flycatcher returns from its wintering grounds about mid-April. It remains here until mid-September before beginning its southward migration. By the end of October most Acadian Flycatchers have migrated back to wintering areas in northwestern South America.

Alder Flycatcher *Empidonax alnorum*

The Alder Flycatcher and the Willow Flycatcher were formerly considered one species—the Traill's Flycatcher. Each is now considered a valid species based on song,

ALDER FLYCATCHER

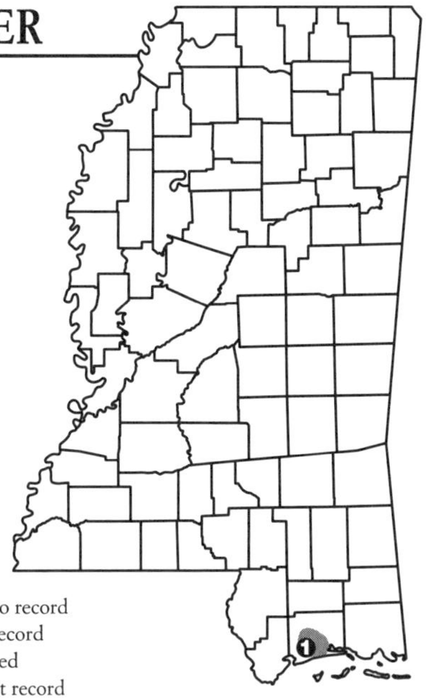

Fall migrant specimen locality records

❶ specimen or photo record
❷ confirmed sight record
❸ breeding confirmed
❹ unconfirmed sight record
☐ breeding distribution
☐ distribution statewide, local and coastal

	JAN	FEB	MAR	APR	MAY	JUN	JUL	AUG	SEP	OCT	NOV	DEC
OCCURRENCE								ooo	oooooo	oo		
MUSEUM*												
WHT*												

*Breeding confirmed by egg, sight, or photographic record.

behavioral characteristics, and differences in breeding habitat, nest construction, and range distribution.

The Willow Flycatcher has a western and southern distribution, and its song is described as *fitz-bew.* Call notes are piping *whit'* sounds. The Alder Flycatcher is northern in its distribution, breeding mainly in boreal forests. Its call note is a loud *peep,* and the song is a buzzy *fee-bee-o* or sometimes *wee-bee.* Both species have other distinctive call notes. During migration, field identification of either species is difficult, if not impossible, unless distinctive songs or call notes are heard.

The vernacular name, "Traill's Flycatcher," can best be used when specific identification of an individual cannot be made in the field. Alder and Willow Flycatchers can be confused in the field with the Least, Acadian, and Yellow-bellied Flycatchers, unless the song and call notes distinctive for each are known and heard by the observer.

[Willow Flycatcher] *Empidonax traillii*

As noted in the account of the Alder Flycatcher, the Willow Flycatcher can be identified with certainty only when the *fitz-bew* song and *whit'* calls are heard. The *peep* call notes of the almost identical Alder Flycatcher are distinctive, and the song is *fee-bee'-o.* The calls and songs of both species differ from the Yellow-bellied and Acadian Flycatchers.

Willow Flycatchers are olive brown above and whitish below, rather than olive green above and yellowish below like the Yellow-bellied and Acadian Flycatchers. Only one Mississippi specimen has been identified with certainty as *Empidonax traillii,* a bird collected on Deer Island on August 16, 1941, by Thomas Burleigh (No. 6019 in the LSU Museum of Zoology identified by J. Van Tyne).

Except on the breeding grounds when these birds are vocal, it is seldom possible to hear their songs and calls. During migration periods when they usually are silent, it is best to call them *trailli* or "Traill's Flycatcher," the vernacular name.

A first and only state breeding record for the Willow Flycatcher was discovered and reported by Gene and Shannon Knight on July 21, 1996, in Tallahatchie County, five miles south of Crowder. The nest, containing one young and a Brown-headed Cowbird, was in a small willow bordering a willow thicket along a water-filled ditch in Delta bottomland. *Whit'* calls were heard.

Supported by small, upright willow and vine stems, the nest was compactly made of small weed stems and bark,

WILLOW FLYCATCHER

Fall specimen locality record

Local, north Mississippi, breeding possible

One recent record, nest with young

❶ specimen or photo record
❷ confirmed sight record
❸ breeding confirmed
❹ unconfirmed sight record
☐ breeding distribution
☐ distribution statewide

	JAN	FEB	MAR	APR	MAY	JUN	JUL	AUG	SEP	OCT	NOV	DEC
OCCURRENCE								ooo	ooooo	o		
MUSEUM*							●●	●●				
WHT*												

*Breeding confirmed by egg, sight, or photographic record.

and lined with dried grass stems. The upper rim was bound with spider or caterpillar silk. It was distinctly different from the frail nest of the Acadian Flycatcher, which is nearly always suspended between forked twigs of a limb in the lower forest canopy.

Both adults were seen on July 27 and in August feeding both the cowbird and flycatcher fledglings out of the nest. The multiple observers were Gene Knight, Marvin Davis, and Fred Boerman. On August 10, Gene Knight found adults feeding both flying fledglings and heard the Willow Flycatcher fledgling call notes, which were different from the adults. The nest was collected and is deposited in the MMNS in Jackson.

Least Flycatcher *Empidonax minimus*

This species is the smallest of the eastern *Empidonax* flycatchers. It has a distinct white eye ring and two white wing bars. It is more grayish above and has whiter underparts than the Acadian Flycatcher. These characters, combined with a tendency to jerk the tail, are the Least Flycatcher's distinguishing field marks. The call is *che-bek'* with accent on the second syllable. The call is distinctive but seldom heard in migration.

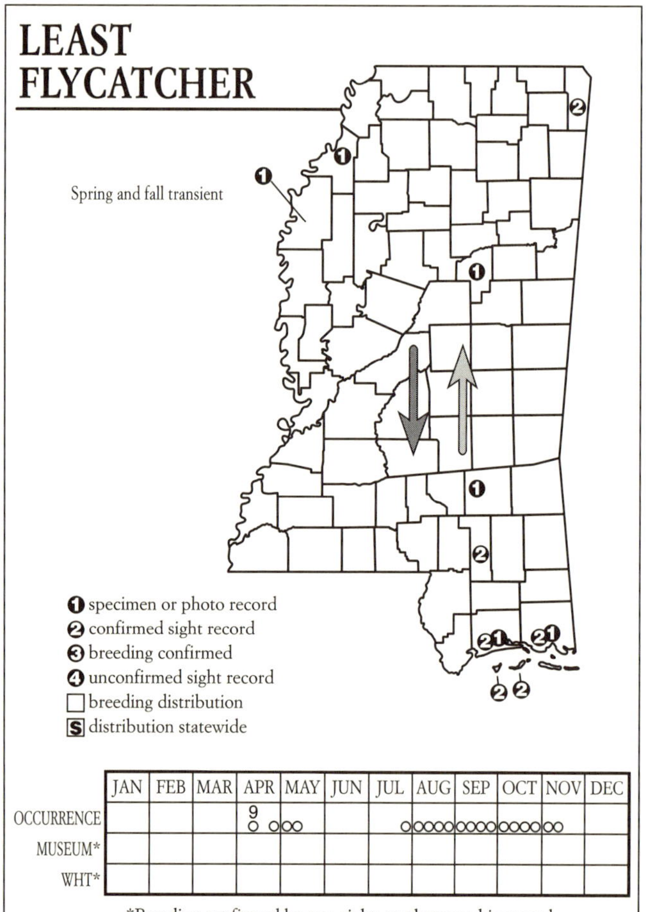

*Breeding confirmed by egg, sight, or photographic record.

Burleigh (1945) collected 29 specimens of this flycatcher on the islands in Mississippi Sound. These, combined with sight records, establish that this species is a fairly common fall migrant in that part of Mississippi. Burleigh found the Least Flycatcher occurred most frequently from late August to mid-October. His extreme dates for fall obser vations were July 31 for a specimen collected on Deer Island and November 9 for a specimen taken near Saucier in Harrison County.

Vaiden (1948) collected 16 specimens in Bolivar County. The collection dates are from April 30 to May 12 and July 29 to September 16. On the basis of these and other collection records, the Least Flycatcher is common in the fall, but rarely seen as a spring transient. It may be overlooked because it seldom calls in spring passage. A specimen I collected on May 1, 1940, near Clarksdale and one taken by R. M. Freeman near Laurel in Jones County on August 29, 1938, are in the MMNS.

Eastern Phoebe *Sayornis phoebe*

The Eastern Phoebe is dark grayish brown above with a darker head, a black bill, and pale yellowish underparts. Immature birds have buffy wing bars, which are lacking in adults. This bird's habit of wagging the tail up and down is one of the best identifying characteristics.

This species occurs commonly as a fall and winter resident throughout Mississippi, arriving in early October and departing in March or early April. It was first recorded as a breeding summer resident in Tishomingo County, where it nests under bridges or on rocky ledges along streams. I have seen it nesting at three locations in that county. One nest built on a rock ledge in the open in the middle of a stream in Tishomingo State Park containing four white eggs was found on April 28, 1957. Another nest containing young was located underneath a rock ledge overhanging a stream bank in a deep ravine. The third nest with young was attached to the wall of a large, concrete box culvert underneath a highway. The nests were composed of fine straw and mud lined with soft straw and covered on the outside with green moss.

The Eastern Phoebe is apparently extending its breeding range southward (Jackson et al. 1976). On July 19, 1974, Robert Howell and Charles Watson discovered a Phoebe nest under a bridge north of Starkville in Oktibbeha County. Another nest containing young was found on June 17, 1975, by Robert Howell and Tom Darden under a bridge five miles north of Starkville in Oktibbeha County. On July 12, 1975, Jerome A. Jackson and David Werschkul found 13 Phoebe nests at eight locations under bridges or in culverts under the Natchez Trace in Chickasaw County. At all but one of these locations, Barn Swallow

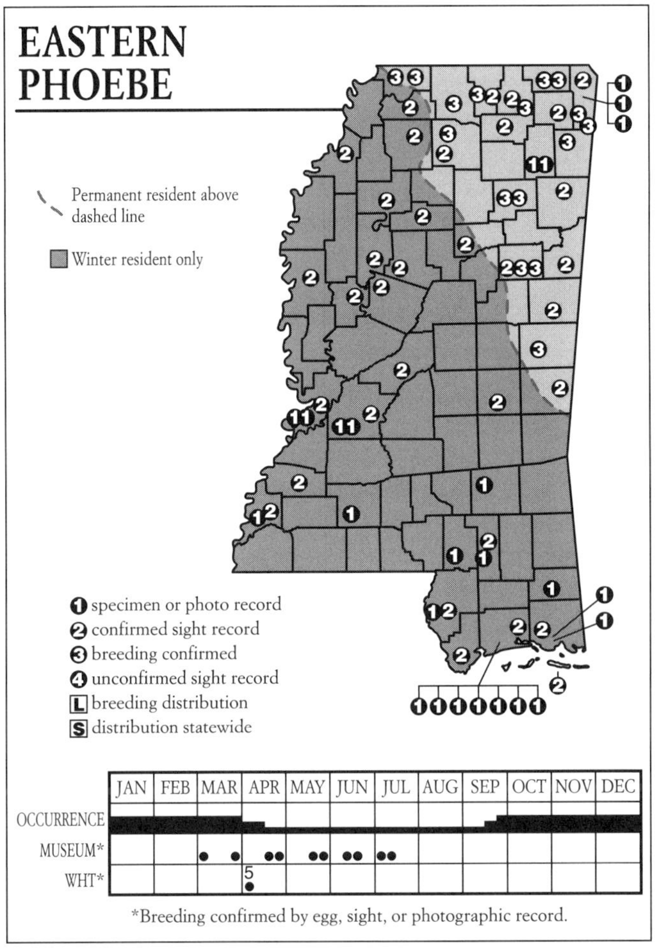

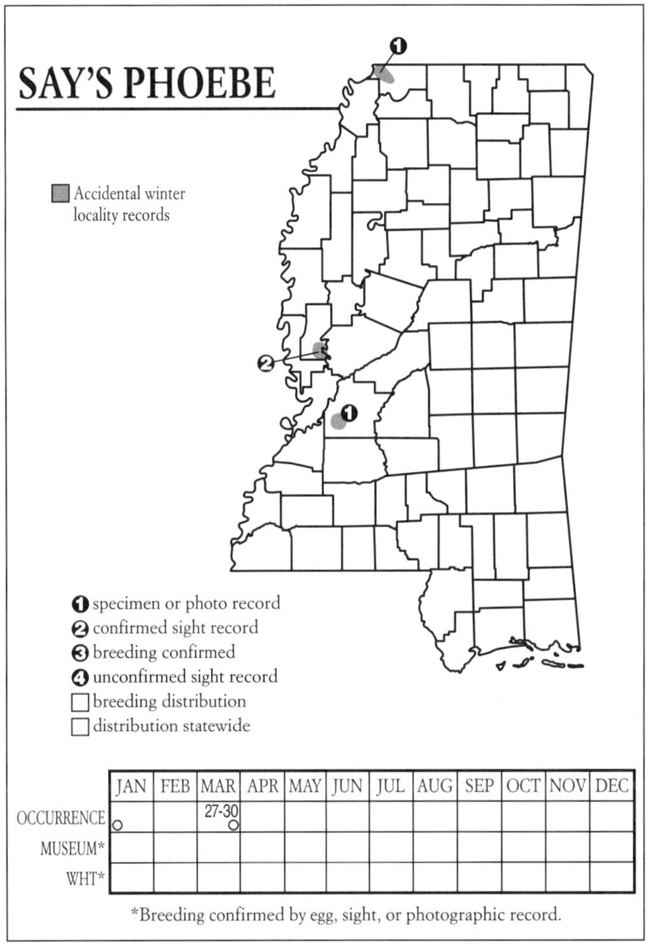

nests were present. Ben B. Coffey Jr. (1976) documents westward extensions of the breeding range to DeSoto County and southward to Kemper County. He noted breeding in all counties bordering Tennessee, and also in Panola, Yalobusha, Union, Prentiss, Itawamba, Monroe, and Chickasaw Counties.

This phoebe calls its name repeatedly in husky, unwhistled notes during the breeding season. In winter the *phee-bee* calls are heard less frequently and most often during twilight periods. The *chip* that is more frequently heard helps in locating and identifying it in winter.

The Eastern Phoebe inhabits open woods, wooded swamps, stream banks, and other areas, preferably near water. Often, it is found around farm buildings, or bridges and large road culverts, because these are sometimes used as roosting places. This species feeds on insects, but berries or other fruits are eaten when insects are scarce.

[Say's Phoebe] *Sayornis saya*

There are only one collection record and two sight records of the Say's Phoebe in Mississippi. With B. E. Gandy, I collected the first specimen of this species at the John Bell Williams Airport near Raymond in Hinds County on January 2, 1960. This bird was sighted around airport buildings as we conducted a Christmas Bird Count.

A sight record of a Say's Phoebe on March 27, 1982, was made at a concrete bridge near Blanton in Sharkey County. I saw this bird on a weed stem by a flooded slough near large catfish ponds. It was carefully studied with binoculars by the party of Jackson Audubon Chapter members I was leading on a field trip in the lower Delta. The grayish brown upperparts, darkest on the head and wings, *almost black tail, and rusty belly and undertail coverts* were unmistakable field marks. Tail-wagging was also noted.

The Say's Phoebe is a casual winter vagrant. It frequents ranch buildings and arid parts of western mountains where it prefers drier open places than its eastern relative. It is most likely to occur in Mississippi in winter around buildings or other structures in open habitats. However, an early spring record was a single photograph by Jeff W. Wilson on the Mississippi River levee west of Walls in DeSoto County on March 30, 1991 (Muth 1991).

The flat, cupped nest of this phoebe is made of compacted, soft plant materials or wool, and built on a protected ledge or crevice of a building, cliff, or rockface. Four or five white eggs are laid. I have found several nests of Say's Phoebes in southwestern Texas. Two were on ledges of buildings protected by the roof. The other was inside a small structure on posts with a roof to protect weather instruments inside.

Vermilion Flycatcher *Pyrocephalus rubinus*

The sexes of other flycatchers are essentially alike in appearance, but in this species the sexes are strikingly different. The male is a bright vermilion on the top of the head and underparts. The back, wings, tail, and a line through the eye are slaty black. Females and immatures have dusky brown upperparts, the breast is white and narrowly streaked with dusky brown, and the lower part of the belly, flanks, and undertail coverts are washed with pink on females or yellow on immatures. Both males and females have a crest. The Vermilion Flycatcher is slightly smaller than the Eastern Phoebe.

This flycatcher is a bird of the southwestern United States and Mexico. For some reason that is difficult to explain, its migration route in winter brings it northward and eastward along the northern Gulf Coast. It occurs in Mississippi as a rare fall and winter visitor. The preferred habitat of this bird is similar to the Eastern Phoebe. It is most likely to be found in the vicinity of ponds or lakes with willows or dead timber around the edges (Davis et al. 1987).

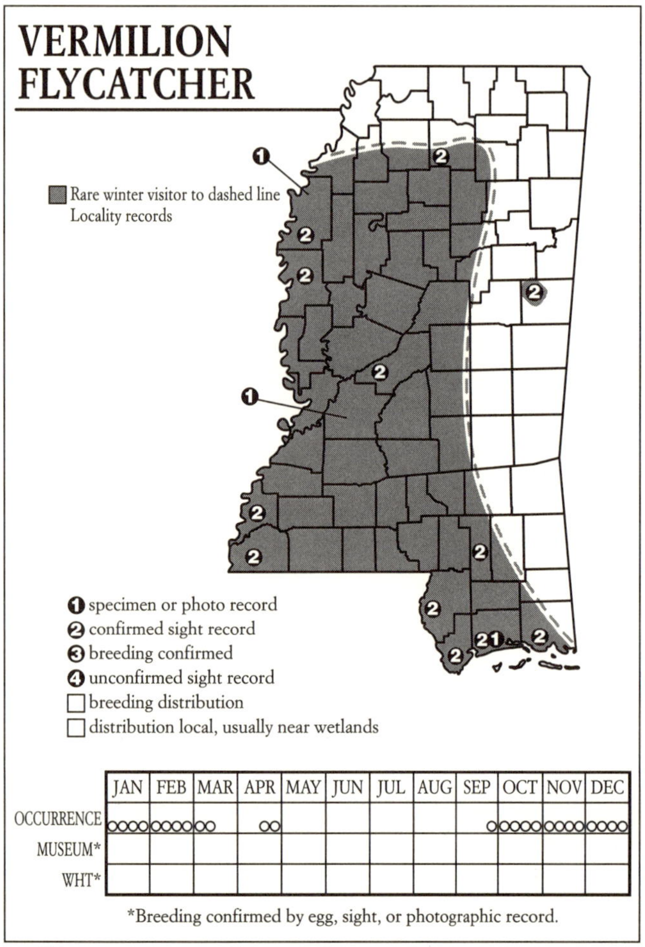

Burleigh (1945) collected the first Mississippi specimens, one male at Gulfport in December 1940, and another male at Bay St. Louis on January 17, 1942. Vaiden (1952a) collected a Bolivar County specimen on October 1, 1950. Sight records include one male and one female seen by Amy B. Tolman on February 15, 1953, east of Picayune (Phares and Tolman 1958), and one adult male at Foster Lake in Wilkinson County on December 9, 1958, by John Phares, myself, and others. On February 11, 1961, at the Lyman Fish Hatchery, Ethel B. Floyd saw two females. At the hatchery on November 17, 1962, Haberyan (1963a) collected an adult male.

On January 8, 1972, G. E. Alexander Jr. (1976) and others recorded three males and two females at Lake Jackson in Washington County. Other records from Lake Jackson were made by Alexander Jr. from October 24 to November 28, 1972, when he observed a male Vermilion Flycatcher on four or five occasions.

Other sight records on Ross Barnett Reservoir in Madison County were made by Mrs. Harold Zumalt, one male seen on January 4, 1973. From January 18 to 27, 1974, the same female or immature remained at the pecan orchard on Pearl River Waterfowl Refuge in Madison County and was seen by John H. Phares, W. H. Turcotte, Warren and Martha Garrott, and others. On October 21, 1974, two males and one female or immature were seen by Alexander Jr. on Lake Jackson. A recent sighting by Vic Theobald (Theobald and Davis 1986) of an adult male occurred on Sardis Waterfowl Refuge in Lafayette County on October 5, 1985, the northernmost Mississippi record.

[Ash-throated Flycatcher] *Myiarchus cinerascens*

This western *Myiarchus* species is an accidental late fall and winter visitor to the East. Two possible western *Myiarchus* sightings near the Mississippi Coast have been reported. One record, on file at MSU with supporting details, is a *Myiarchus* seen on December 5, 1982, in Stone County by Mary Morris (Jackson 1982). The first sight record of an Ash-throated Flycatcher is a bird at Waveland in Hancock County on November 5, 1988, by Pinewoods Audubon Society members Dan Carroll and Glen Ousset. A second sighting at the Waveland sewage lagoon was made by Judith A. Toups (pers. comm.) and others on September 25, 1990.

On February 5, 1993, Terence Schiefer and Marion Hutto (pers. comm.) found and identified an Ash-throated Fly-

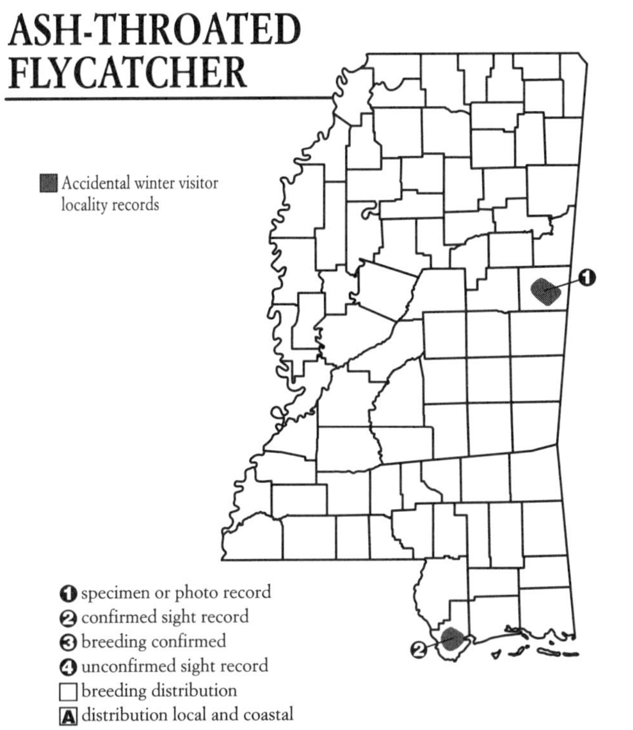

	JAN	FEB	MAR	APR	MAY	JUN	JUL	AUG	SEP	OCT	NOV	DEC
OCCURRENCE		5-6 ○							25 ○		5 ○	
MUSEUM*												
WHT*												

*Breeding confirmed by egg, sight, or photographic record.

catcher in a burned-over field north of Brooksville in Noxubee County. The following day in the same field, the bird was photographed by Jeffrey Wilson and seen by W. Marvin Davis, Gene Knight, and others, confirming the record for this species.

The Ash-throated Flycatcher is common in a wide variety of wooded, desert, and brushy habitats from central Texas to California. It is *gray brown* above with a *dark* bill, *pale gray breast and throat,* and *paler* yellow on the breast and belly than the Great Crested Flycatcher. Adult tail feathers are partly tipped with brown. Their calls are softer than the Great Crested.

For comparison purposes, the Brown-crested Flycatcher *(Myiarchus tyrannulus),* occurs in southwestern Texas along the Rio Grande Valley and in southern Arizona. It has a bushy, *brown crest;* brownish olive back; *pale gray* throat and breast; and lemon yellow underparts. The larger, longer bill is *all black.* Tail feathers show dark brown above and reddish on the inner webs when spread, but not as extensive as the Great Crested. The Brown-crested Flycatcher has occurred in Louisiana in November and January (Lowery 1974). It was formerly called Weid's Flycatcher. The species should occur eventually in Mississippi as an accidental or casual fall or winter visitor.

Great Crested Flycatcher *Myiarchus crinitus*

The Great Crested Flycatcher is a common summer resident breeding bird throughout Mississippi. It arrives in late March and April and remains until late October or early November. Extreme dates of arrival and departure are March 18 and November 2.

It has olive brown upperparts, a gray throat and breast, a yellow belly, and yellowish wing bars. The tail and primary wing feathers are reddish brown. No other eastern flycatcher has the long, rusty tail characteristic of this bird. The long feathers on the back of the head often are raised to form a crest, especially when the bird is calling.

This flycatcher prefers woodland habitat, but occurs around farms and suburban homes wherever there are trees and a suitable nesting cavity. Natural tree cavities, woodpecker holes, or bird boxes are used for nesting. In May, the nest is built of leaves, trash, and feathers to which a lining of cast-off snakeskin is added. The four to six eggs are cream colored and heavily streaked with shades of purple, brown, and lavender.

This bird is noticeable and noisy upon its arrival and during the nesting period. The call is a rapidly repeated

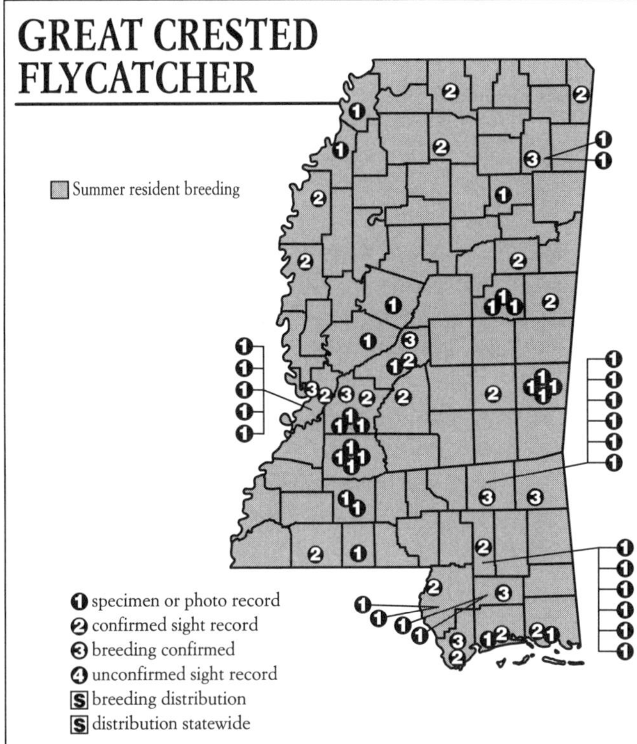

	JAN	FEB	MAR	APR	MAY	JUN	JUL	AUG	SEP	OCT	NOV	DEC
OCCURRENCE			○▬	▬	▬	▬	▬	▬	▬	▬○○○	○	
MUSEUM*					●●	●●						
WHT*						18 ●						

*Breeding confirmed by egg, sight, or photographic record.

pwet, pwet, followed by loud, harsh ascending *wheep* notes. For food the birds subsist on insects caught on the wing in typical flycatcher fashion. But some wild fruits, particularly red mulberries, sassafras, and Virginia creeper, are part of its diet. The Great Crested Flycatcher winters mainly in Central America and northern South America, and occasionally in southern Florida.

[Sulphur-bellied Flycatcher] *Myiodynastes luteiventris*

This is one of those unexpected birds, but an individual was seen and recorded by Larry and Terrie Gates at Port Bienville on the southern Hancock County Christmas Bird Count on December 31, 1978 (Hamilton 1980). Being keen birders, they documented the details with a sketch showing unmistakable field marks. This sighting is the first state record for this species.

The Sulphur-bellied Flycatcher is mainly a Mexican species and a resident of southern Arizona. My wife and I were fortunate to see one in Cave Creek Canyon at the lower edge of the Chiricahua Mountains of southeastern Arizona in June 1984. Our English friends, Frank and Maud Pepper, were with us, and while we were eating a picnic lunch, one of these birds flew down from the hardwood canopy to a perch near the ground in an opening. It remained there providing us an excellent observation. The sulphur yellow underparts with bold, black streaks; dark cheeks; streaked head and upperparts; and rusty tail and rump were distinctive.

A single record for this species in Alabama occurred September 6, 1983, on Dauphin Island. The bird was netted, banded, and photographed. It remained in the area for several days (Purrington 1983). Lowery Jr. (1974) cited an earlier sight record on Grand Isle, Louisiana, by Robert J. Newman and Edwin O. Willis on September 30, 1956.

Western Kingbird *Tyrannus verticalis*

The Western Kingbird is a casual spring and rare fall visitor from the Great Plains and the western states, where it breeds commonly. Its range includes part of the upper Mississippi Valley.

It has been recorded in Mississippi more than 20 times. Burleigh (1945) collected five specimens on the Gulf Coast in Harrison County. His dates for collecting these birds are September 25, 1936; October 3, 11, and 18, 1939, and October 12, 1940. I collected a specimen on September 8,

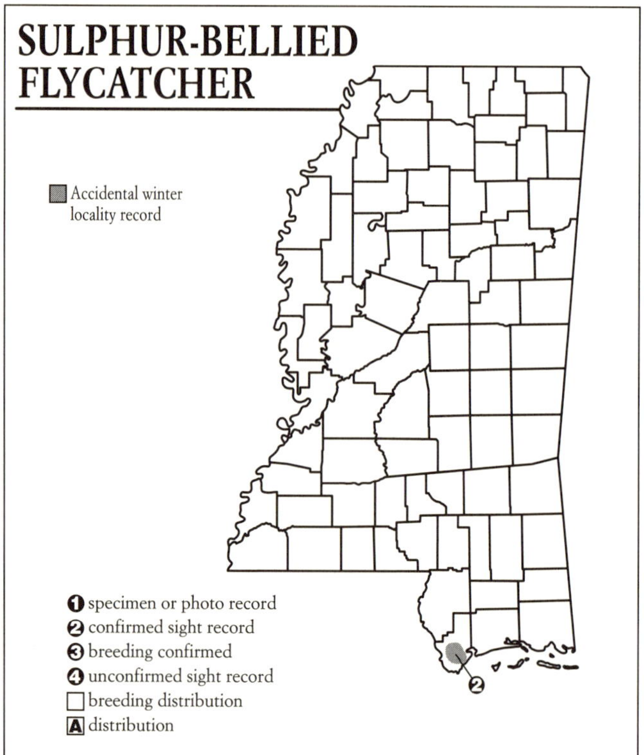

	JAN	FEB	MAR	APR	MAY	JUN	JUL	AUG	SEP	OCT	NOV	DEC
OCCURRENCE												31 o
MUSEUM*												
WHT*												

*Breeding confirmed by egg, sight, or photographic record.

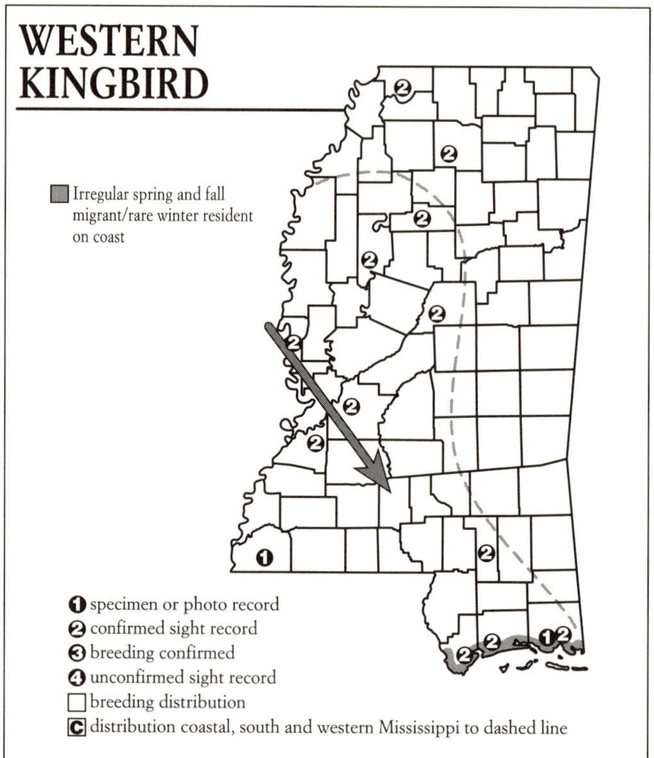

	JAN	FEB	MAR	APR	MAY	JUN	JUL	AUG	SEP	OCT	NOV	DEC
OCCURRENCE	oooo			o		oo		oooo	oooo	oooo	oooo	oooo
MUSEUM*												
WHT*												

*Breeding confirmed by egg, sight, or photographic record.

1940, in a pasture bordering the Mississippi River near Fort Adams in Wilkinson County (Gandy and Turcotte 1970). Prior to Burleigh's collection records, this species had not been reported elsewhere in Mississippi.

On September 1, 1960, I sighted a Western Kingbird near Money in Leflore County. A wintering bird that remained near the harbor in Gulfport from December 5, 1960, to January 5, 1961, was recorded by Haberyan (1961) and Lovett E. Williams Jr. I have seen the Western Kingbird on two other occasions in the fall, once in western Hinds County and the other in Attala County near Sallis. I saw a group of these birds on a power line beside Mississippi 18 in Claiborne County in late August 1984.

The Western Kingbird is approximately the same size as its eastern relative. It has a gray head with a dark mask through the eye and a darker gray back. The throat is light gray, and the belly is yellow. The *outer part of the outermost tail feathers is white,* the distinguishing field mark for identifying this species. The rest of the tail feathers are black.

Eastern Kingbird *Tyrannus tyrannus*

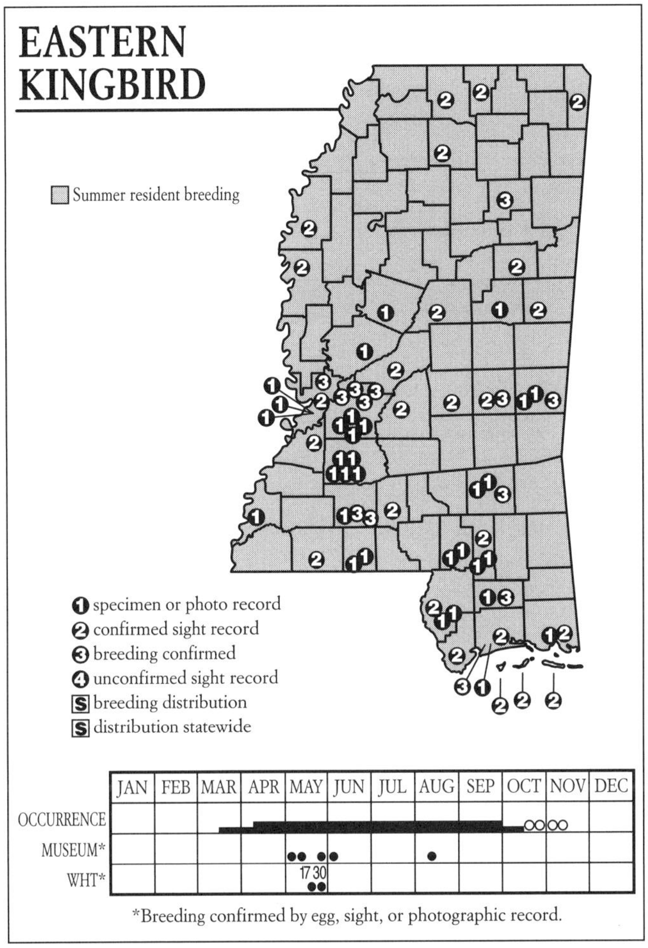

The Eastern Kingbird, or "bee martin" as it is commonly called, is a bird of open country such as field borders, fence rows, roadsides, brushy pastures, and orchards. It is a common, statewide, breeding summer resident in Mississippi, often abundant during spring and fall migration. First arrivals appear in late March, and migrations continue until early May. Fall migration begins in September and ends by late October. There are no wintering records for this species in Mississippi.

The Eastern Kingbird is a common spring and fall transient and summer resident bird across Mississippi.

Summer residents begin nesting around mid-May. The nest is usually placed on a horizontal tree limb far out from the trunk. It is placed from 10 to 30 feet aboveground and is a rather bulky structure composed of twigs, weed stalks, grass, and other coarse material. Thistle down, cotton, rags, strings, or other soft substances may line the nest, and I have found nests composed almost entirely of thistle down. Elm trees seem to be a favored location for nesting.

The eggs are among the prettiest of any North American birds. They are creamy white and beautifully marked with brown spots. Three or four eggs make up the usual clutch.

This kingbird eats flying insects, and wild fruits are taken in season. Although it eats some bees, as the name "bee martin" suggests, the numbers taken are small. Wild cherries, mulberries, sassafras, dogwood, and magnolia berries are some of its favorite wild fruits.

The Eastern Kingbird is noted for its aggressiveness toward larger birds. On its nesting grounds it rises into the air attacking and pursuing hawks, crows, even vultures. It is not unusual to see them ride on the backs of large birds, pecking and plucking at feathers until the intruder leaves.

This kingbird is black above with white underparts. The tail is black with a *white band at the tip,* a distinctive field mark. A concealed patch of orange in the crown can be seen only when the bird is excited or in hand. The call notes are a simple *tzi, tzee,* often repeated rapidly in a high-pitched, raspy chattering. The dawn song is an almost continuous rapid repetition of these call notes.

Gray Kingbird *Tyrannus dominicensis*

This species is now a fairly common summer resident, breeding along the coast of peninsular Florida and as far west as Pensacola. Breeding pairs have been found nesting at Fort Morgan and on Dauphin Island in Alabama.

In the summer of 1976, the bird was discovered breeding in Mississippi. This first nesting of Gray Kingbirds was described by Weber and Jackson (1977a) and occurred on Horn Island near the Gulf Islands National Seashore ranger station between May 20 and June 28, 1976. The nest was discovered in a slash pine about 18 feet from the ground on June 6. Fledglings were photographed near the nest on June 28, 1976, to substantiate the breeding record. Five pair were present on Horn Island in the summer of 1979 (Jackson 1979).

Earlier records for this kingbird along the Gulf Coast of Florida and Alabama show a westward expansion of range and an increase in breeding populations. As it has been discovered nesting on Horn Island, it is not unlikely that it may appear as a breeding bird on other Mississippi islands or mainland beaches.

The first published record and a specimen of this flycatcher was obtained by Clawson and Williams Jr. (1962) on Bellefontaine Beach in Jackson County on April 28, 1962. A second record was reported by Haberyan (1963b) on Horn Island on May 23, 1963. A third record was a sighting at Bellefontaine Beach on July 21, 1963 by Floyd (1964). More recent sightings were reported by Donald M. Bradburn on Horn Island in the summers of 1964, 1969, and 1974, and a single sighting on Petit Bois Island on July 13, 1974 (Weber and Jackson 1977b). There are sight records on the mainland in all coastal counties. Extreme dates of occurrence are April 13 and October 19.

The Gray Kingbird is nearly always found within sight of salt water and prefers islands or peninsulas extending into salt water. Slightly larger than the Eastern Kingbird, it is white below and dark gray on the head and back with a prominent darker mask extending through and behind the eye. It has a slightly notched, dark gray tail (without the white tip of the Eastern Kingbird), and a very large black bill.

The Gray Kingbird builds a flimsy nest of twigs with little or no lining, usually laying three pinkish eggs that are irregularly blotched and spotted with shades of rich brown. Its call is a repetition of three shrill, chattering notes with accent on the second syllable, described as *pe-cheer'-y.* This Kingbird is very noisy and, like the Eastern Kingbird, is pugnacious in vigorously pursuing and attacking larger birds while defending its domain.

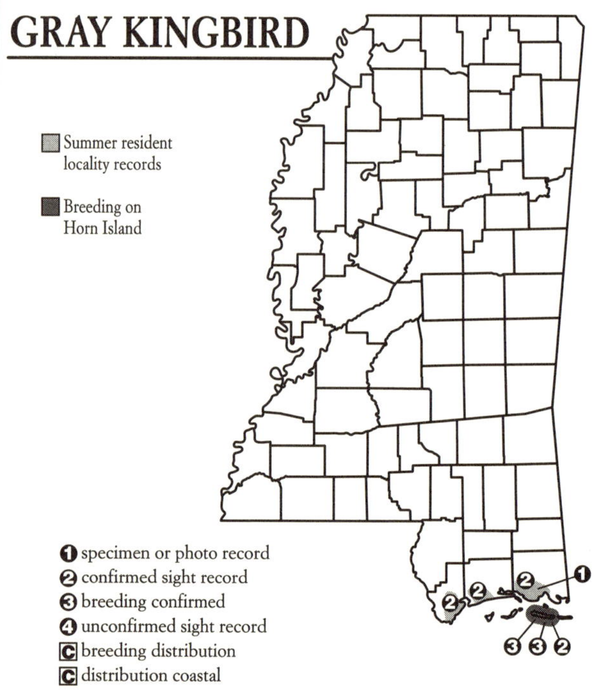

	JAN	FEB	MAR	APR	MAY	JUN	JUL	AUG	SEP	OCT	NOV	DEC
OCCURRENCE				○○○	○○○○	○○○○	○○○○	○○○○	○○	19 ○		
MUSEUM*						●	●					
WHT*												

*Breeding confirmed by egg, sight, or photographic record.

Scissor-tailed Flycatcher *Tyrannus forficatus*

I believe that this strikingly colored flycatcher is one of the most handsome birds. It is ordinarily only a spring transient and regular fall visitor and has been recorded in Mississippi fewer than a dozen times in any year. Strangely, it was reported nesting near Tupelo on July 5 and 6, 1975, by Jackson and Werschkul (1977). Located on a branch of a sweet gum tree, the nest, first discovered by Mrs. W. T. Watson, was the first known instance of the Scissor-tailed Flycatcher nesting east of the Mississippi River. This breeding record, occurring at a small pond in a heavily grazed pasture, produced a brood of three young.

On June 10, 1977, while driving west along U.S. 80 approaching Lawrence in Newton County, I saw a Scissor-tailed Flycatcher perched on a wire. After turning around, I watched the bird fly into a nearby pine where I found it brooding on a nest on a limb extending out over the highway right-of-way about 30 feet aboveground. The next morning it was still there. As I watched, the bird returned

SCISSOR-TAILED FLYCATCHER

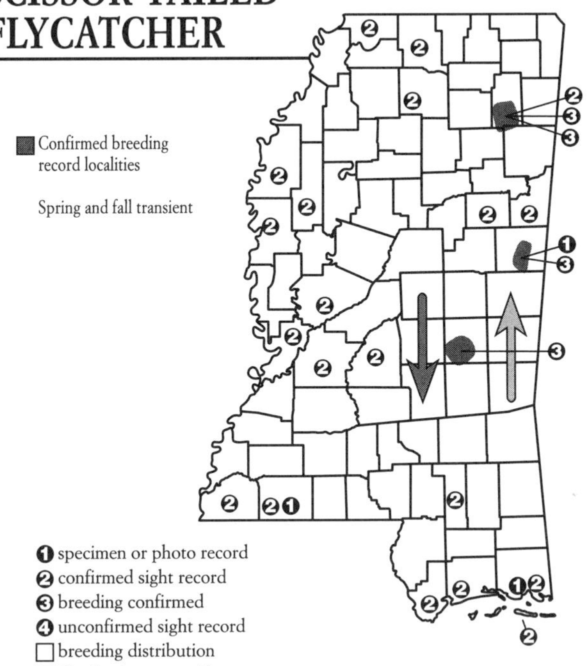

❶ specimen or photo record
❷ confirmed sight record
❸ breeding confirmed
❹ unconfirmed sight record
□ breeding distribution
□ distribution statewide

	JAN	FEB	MAR	APR	MAY	JUN	JUL	AUG	SEP	OCT	NOV	DEC
OCCURRENCE	—	3 o	ooo	oooo	oooo	oo	oo	o	oo	oooo	oooo	oo
MUSEUM*				•		••	•					
WHT*						•						

*Breeding confirmed by egg, sight, or photographic record.

once to brood on the nest before it flew out of sight. On June 21, the nest site was revisited but no Scissor-tail was seen, and the nest was apparently abandoned. At no time was more than one adult seen. This is the second known nesting locality record for Mississippi (Turcotte 1977). More recently, isolated nestings of the Scissor-tailed Flycatcher in Tennessee and Alabama have been reported.

The first substantiated sight record for this species was made on May 9, 1960, at Clermont Harbor in Hancock County by Amy B. Tolman (Gandy and Turcotte 1970). This bird was photographed the following day by Ethel Floyd. A specimen of the Scissor-tail was collected by H. Champ Clark on October 24, 1972, in Amite County. This bird is in the MMNS.

Other sightings of this flycatcher were on October 7, 1972, northeast of Rosedale in Bolivar County by Sammie Danna Jr. (1963); May 27, 1972, at Piney Woods School in Rankin County (Turcotte 1972b); September 7, 1974, on the Natchez Trace near the Leake-Attala county line by W. H. Turcotte; October 8, 1974, at Jackson in Hinds County by Ruth Downey; and on October 14, 1975, two birds were sighted at Darlove in Washington County by G. E. Alexander Jr. A bird seen by B. E. Gandy on July 17, 1993, at the Jackson Municipal Airport was hawking insects. Extreme dates of arrival and departure are March 14 and November 2.

The Scissor-tailed Flycatcher is a spectacular bird at rest and in flight. The head and body are pearl gray. Its tail feathers are pinkish, marked with black, and when fully developed the two longest ones are about nine inches long. The wings, feet, and bill are black. The sides and wing linings are brilliant salmon red.

Scissor-tails are great wanderers outside of their regular range, which extends from eastern New Mexico and southwestern Kansas east into western Arkansas and western Louisiana.

The bulky nest is usually placed at a medium height on a horizontal limb. Four to six creamy white, brown-spotted eggs are laid. Their food consists of insects caught on the wing or on the ground. Small amounts of fruit, small berries, and seeds are also eaten.

The call notes of the Scissor-tail are soft twitterings as it flies from one perch to another, and a harsh *keck* and repeated *ka-quee'-ka-quee'* notes uttered during courtship flight maneuvers and sometimes accompanied by snapping of its mandibles. Like other flycatchers, it has a dawn song described as a long series of *pup-pup-perleep* or *pup-pup-perloo* notes.

Horned Lark

Alaudidae (Larks)

Members of the lark family are barren-ground birds and are mainly terrestrial in their habits. They prefer to live on open fields, deserts, plains, prairies, or tundra. These birds are gregarious and are nearly always seen in flocks, except during the breeding season. The males ascend high into the air to sing their tinkling songs in a spectacular display flight during the breeding season. Larks are mostly brown backed and have an elongated hind claw. Paler or darker forms occur in other regions of North America.

Horned Lark *Eremophila alpestris*

The Horned Lark has a gray-and-brown streaked back, pale brown sides, and white belly. Small, black feather "horns" are not always noticeable. A broad, black stripe extends downward from the eye almost to the broad, black band across its breast. The throat and face are washed with yellow and white, and a distinct yellow stripe above the eye extends across the forehead. The greatly elongated hind claw is almost straight. In flight the Horned Lark shows a black tail with white edging on the outer feathers, which contrast with the rest of the body. Females and immatures are duller than the males.

Horned Larks are gregarious during the winter, occurring in loose flocks on open ground, but not in trees, bushes, or tall weeds. When flushed they invariably alight on the ground. These birds walk and never hop.

During the breeding season, males establish territories and defend them by fighting short aerial battles with intruders of their own species (Turcotte 1974a). Males ascend high into the air to sing in a spectacular courtship display flight that may last for several minutes. It ends with a headlong drop to the ground. Males may also sing at times on the ground. Their song is a weak, high-pitched twittering repeated frequently, usually when the bird is aloft facing into the wind and at times nearly out of sight of the ground. The call note is a *tseet* or *zu-wheet.*

Horned Larks are commonly found as permanent resident breeding birds in large open fields in the Yazoo Delta (Coffey 1940; Turcotte 1961c), in the northern and northeast hill counties (Warriner 1945), and in the northeast prairie (Coffey *in* Jackson 1981a). During periods of heavy snowfall northward, Horned Larks become more numerous below the snow line.

The Horned Lark nests on barren ground in open fields and open, overgrazed pastures, and around airports, golf courses, and turf farms. Nesting begins in March or April with renesting into May or early June. Many early nests in cultivated fields are destroyed by plowing (Feduccia 1974). The nest is a grass-lined depression in the bare ground, usually beside a tuft of vegetation, a clod, or other object. The three or four eggs are gray and heavily dotted with shades of brown that nearly obscure the ground color.

Horned Larks are locally common in larger soybean and cotton fields throughout the Yazoo Delta and in the prairie regions of northeastern Mississippi as permanent residents in open fields or at airports.

In late winter and early spring, these birds eat the early maturing seeds of plants of the mustard family found growing in large, fallow or fall-plowed fields. These plants mature about the time larks begin nesting, and I have observed them eating the tiny seeds from pods. After the seeds mature, pods split open and show the white inner surface, giving entire fields a ghostly look until plowed under. The Horned Larks and migrating Grasshopper Sparrows frequent these fields until mid-May in the Yazoo Delta. Seeds, ground insects, and tender young plant sprouts are eaten by Horned Larks.

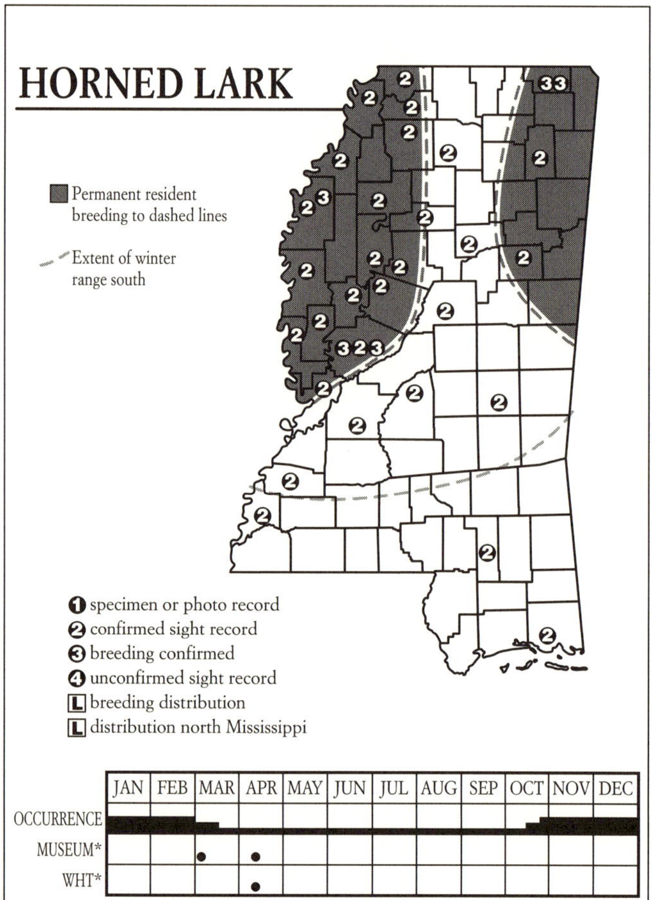

*Breeding confirmed by egg, sight, or photographic record.

Barn Swallow

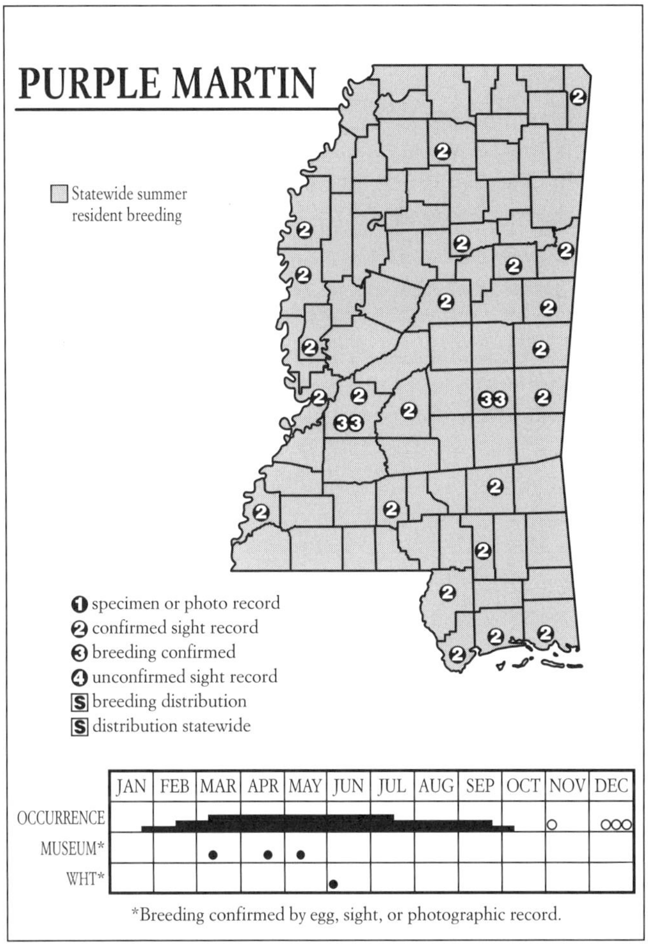

Hirundinidae (Swallows)

Birds of this family have slim, streamlined bodies with long, pointed wings and small legs and feet. They are the size of sparrows and have short, wide bills with a large gape. Swallows are strong and graceful fliers and spend much of their time flying over open land or water, feeding entirely on flying insects. Most species have notched or deeply forked tails. During migration, they travel in daylight hours. In late summer and early fall prior to migration, large flocks congregate in staging areas, usually perching on wires. Swallows build nests in places protected from rainfall.

Purple Martin *Progne subis*

The Purple Martin occurs statewide and is the largest of the swallows in Mississippi. The male is an iridescent, purplish black above and below. The tail is slightly forked. The female is similar to the male, except on the underparts, where the breast is light gray (sometimes lightly streaked) and the belly is white. Immature young and first-year males are similar to the females. First-year spring males sometimes have purplish feathers on the undersides.

As many homeowners and bird-watchers across Mississippi have discovered, gourds are a favorite nesting structure with Purple Martins.

Martins have been a favorite with humans since the Indians first hung gourds on poles encouraging them to nest about their villages. The tradition of putting up martin gourds and houses continues today. Among those erecting martin houses, there is much competition to attract the greatest number of birds.

The Purple Martin is a common to abundant summer resident, breeding in colonies throughout Mississippi. It is the first summer-resident bird to return from its winter range south of the Gulf of Mexico, arriving in late January when adult male scouts appear to occupy houses until later arrivals begin appearing in February and early March farther northward. A few birds have been seen rarely in December along the coast.

Martins are highly social birds and nest in colonies of many pairs. Multicompartmented houses or a plentiful supply of gourds will be more likely to attract and hold these birds. Nesting structures should be placed on poles in an open area 10 to 15 feet aboveground. Nest boxes should provide compartments measuring 8 x 8 x 6 inches in height. The entrance hole should be two inches in diameter and 1.5 inches from the floor.

Nesting starts about mid-April, even though most nests do not contain eggs until late April or May. The nest is composed of grass, leaves, straw, and trash. Fresh green leaves are added to the nest during the 15- to 18-day incubation period. Usually four or five white eggs are laid. The young remain in the nest four or five weeks until they are able to exit flying. It is most interesting to watch adult Purple Martins feeding their young in the nest. The nestlings often are fed dragonflies, and it is amusing to watch a young martin choke down one of these large insects.

Most young martins have left the nest by July 4. They do not return to the nest, but congregate in roosting flocks with adult birds. They remain in large congregations through August, after which their numbers gradually diminish until early September, when they have left for warmer regions farther south.

The happy gurgling songs of Purple Martins are familiar to all who provide gourds or houses for these congenial birds. Besides their joyous chirpings, the song has been interpreted through several generations of Mississippi families as *gather-up-all-the-chir'ren-and-let's-go-see-grandma-dar-r-r-ling.*

Tree Swallow *Tachycineta bicolor*

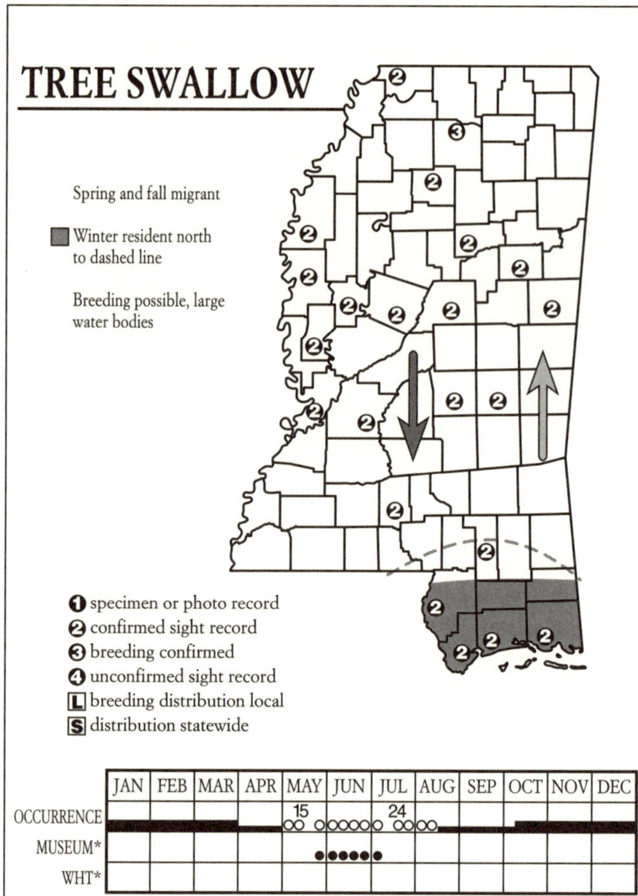

*Breeding confirmed by egg, sight, or photographic record.

The Tree Swallow is a metallic blue black or greenish black above and *white underneath* from bill to tail. No other swallow occurring in Mississippi has pure white underparts. Immatures are brownish above with a slight dusky collar on the breast and may be confused in fall and winter with the Bank Swallow or Rough-winged Swallow.

Tree Swallows are abundant in migration from March to mid-May and again from late August to November throughout the state, especially around water areas and long river valleys. In the Gulf Coast counties, the Tree Swallow occurs as a common winter resident except during extreme cold. Along the lower Mississippi River, it may occur in late fall and winter. In southern Mississippi, it subsists on wax myrtle and other berries when insects are unavailable during cold weather.

There is one confirmed breeding record for Tree Swallows in Mississippi. Davis (1995) documented the first Tree Swallow nesting over water in a dead tree snag at Hurricane Landing on the southern side of Sardis Lake in Lafayette County. Sightings of adults with young at the nest were made by Davis, Vic Theobald, and Keith Meals from May 27 through July 7, 1995. On July 7, the nest site was visited by boat. Four adults and six flying immatures soliciting food were seen. Adults were feeding a nestling in one of two nest cavities on opposite sides of the nest tree, which were 2.7 and 3.1 meters above water level. Breeding was confirmed by Davis with a photograph of adults at the nest hole feeding a nestling (photo deposited at MSU and the MMNS).

This swallow nests in tree cavities, woodpecker holes, and nest boxes. The nest is composed of straw and lined with feathers. The eggs are white and number four to six.

Lowery Jr. (1974) records this species nesting in Louisiana at Eagle Lake, which lies north of Vicksburg along the boundary between Louisiana and Mississippi. I suspect this swallow may nest in dead tree cavities along the Mississippi River. In the summer before construction began on the Grand Gulf Nuclear Power Plant, a party of fisheries biologists working on environmental impact studies told me they saw Tree Swallows nesting in willow stubs along the Mississippi River below the mouth of Big Black River in Claiborne County. At the time, no photographs or collection of specimens were made to substantiate their observations. Single-occupancy bird houses, placed on poles near or over water around the larger oxbow lakes of the Mississippi might encourage this species to nest.

Northern Rough-winged Swallow *Stelgidopteryx serripennis*

Commonly known as the "sand martin" or "gully martin," this species occurs sparingly as a breeding bird at locali-

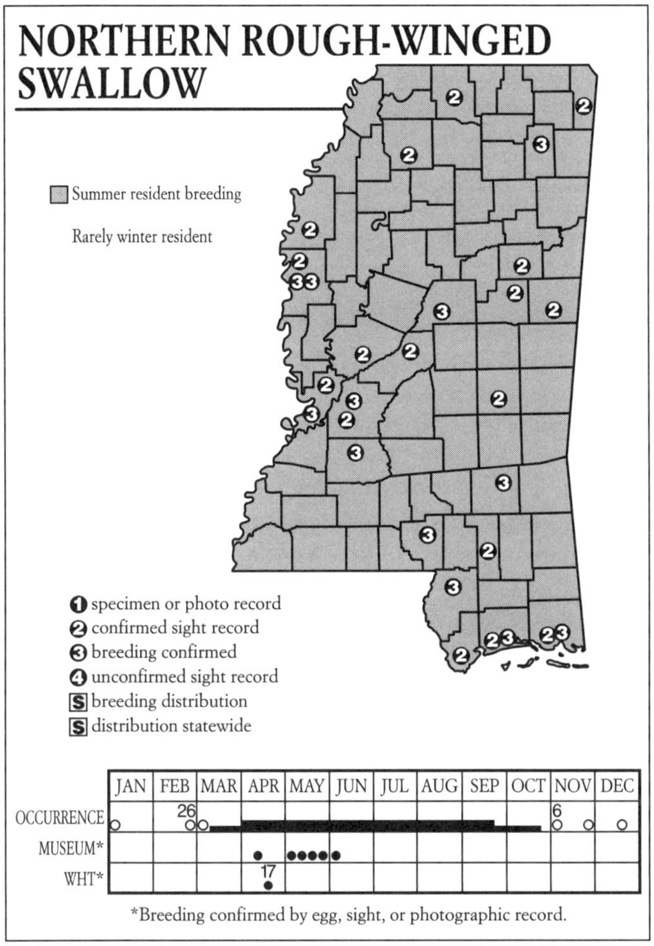

ties throughout the state where there are gullies, vertical stream banks, or roadside cuts. It has brown upperparts. The throat is dusky, and the belly is white. The flight is similar to Barn Swallows in that it is direct and at the end of each wingbeat the wings are folded back. The immature Tree Swallow and the Bank Swallow are also brown backed, but both species have clear white underparts, except for the distinct, narrow, brown breast band of the Bank Swallow.

The Rough-winged Swallow is common to abundant during fall migration until early September, when large flocks congregate over open fields, levees, and water areas, frequently perching on wires. Occasionally a few birds overwinter in southern Mississippi. The spring arrival of migrating birds begins in early March.

The Rough-winged Swallow builds a nest at the end of a tunnel dug into a bank. The nest is composed of grass, weed stems, bits of leaves, and chips of bark. From four to six elongated, glossy white eggs are laid.

This species is a solitary nester, although at times several pairs may nest at one location. Unlike the Bank Swallow, their nest tunnels are never spaced closely together in large colonies.

Bank Swallow *Riparia riparia*

This species is the *smallest* of the swallows occurring in Mississippi. It is dark brown above and white below with a *distinct, narrow, brown band across the breast.* The slightly larger Rough-winged Swallow also has brown upperparts, but lacks the well-defined breast band. The immature Tree Swallow is also brown backed, but is all white below.

The Bank Swallow occurs as a fairly common spring and fall transient. It arrives in early May enroute to northern breeding grounds and stays until late May or early June. It appears again from July through September, gradually diminishing in numbers until October.

This bird is frequently found mixed with flocks of other species of migrating swallows. There is no satisfactory evidence that the Bank Swallow breeds in the state, but it has nested along the Mississippi River bluffs above Memphis. It nests in colonies and builds its nest in tunnels burrowed into sand banks.

Stockard (1905) reported Bank Swallows nesting in railroad cuts, perpendicular cliffs on hillsides, and along the banks of the Tombigbee River in Mississippi. However, because he was from the North, he may have failed

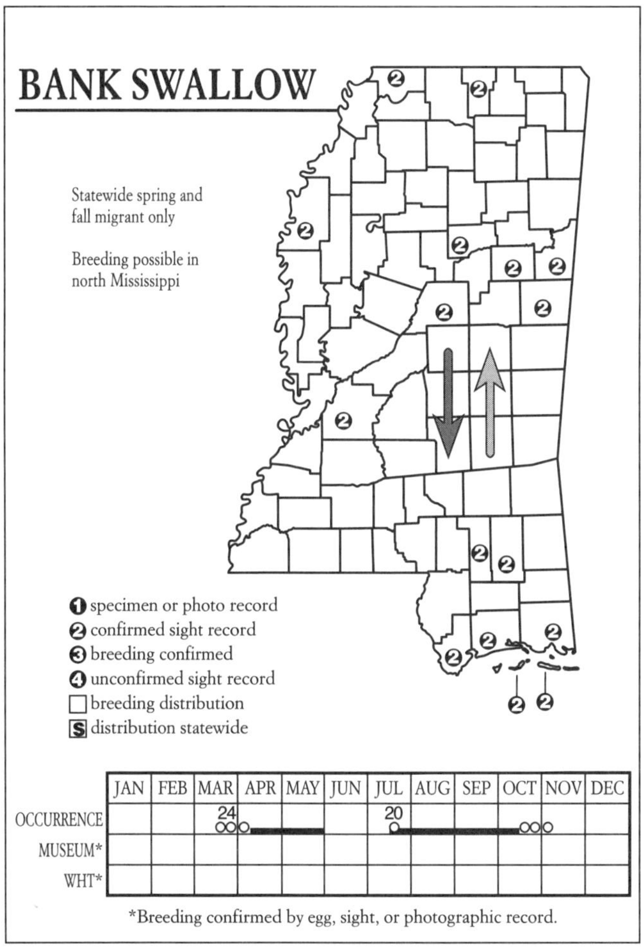

to correctly identify the birds and the nest holes he saw, confusing them with the Rough-winged Swallow, which nests throughout most of the state at similar sites.

The Bank Swallow is local and sporadic in establishing breeding territories because it prefers to nest in colonies near water and open fields in sand banks. The breeding range extends into Tennessee, northern Arkansas, and northeastern Alabama. Possible breeding along Mississippi River banks needs investigation.

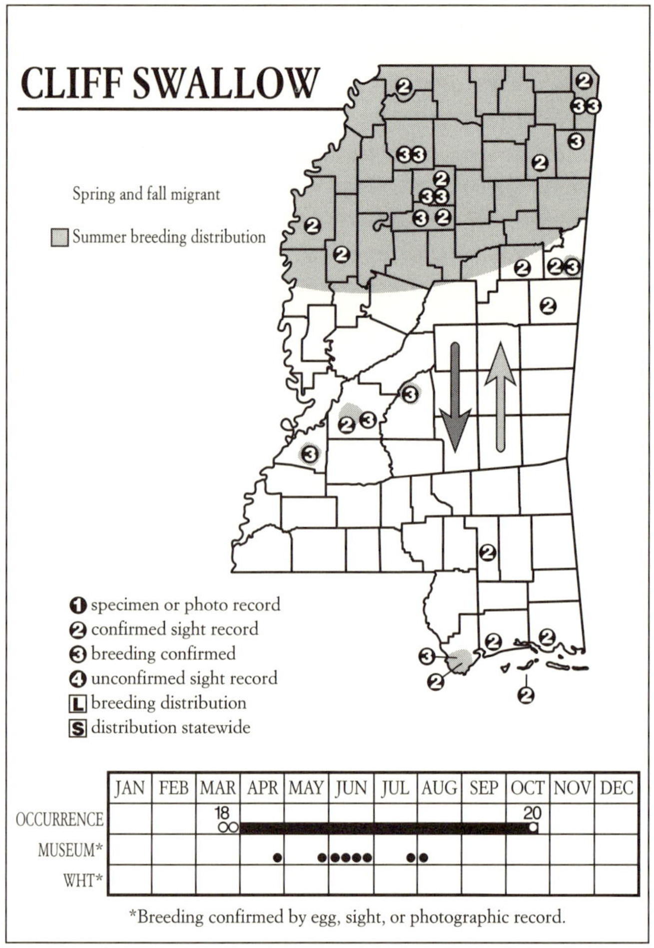

Cliff Swallow *Hirundo pyrrhonota*

In appearance, this species has a blue black crown and a white forehead. The back is blue black and lightly streaked with white. The throat and cheeks are chestnut, and the belly is light gray. The *orange rufous rump and the square tail* are distinctive field marks. Except the Cave Swallow, all other swallows occurring in Mississippi have notched or deeply forked tails. Foods of the Cliff Swallow consist almost entirely of insects caught on the wing. Berries are rarely eaten.

The Cliff Swallow most frequently is seen in Mississippi as a migrant, appearing during April, May, and early June and again from August through October, when migrating individuals or flocks move to and from the wintering grounds in South America. This species breeds sparingly in the state.

Several nesting colonies have been found under bridges or culverts north of Iuka in Tishomingo County. Three nests and several Cliff Swallows were seen by Barry Freeman and John Phares (Phares 1975) at the Bull Mountain Creek crossing on Highway 25 in Itawamba County on July 2, 1975. Frances Wills Jr. (Turcotte 1975a) found a Cliff Swallow nest at an underpass in Claiborne County along the Natchez Trace on July 27, 1975.

This gourd-shaped nest of Cliff Swallows was found within an underpass along the Natchez Trace in Hinds County on August 4, 1975.

I found another nest with Cliff Swallows in southwest Hinds County at an underpass on the Natchez Trace Parkway on August 4, 1975. This location was nearMorningstar, just north of Twelvemile Creek. Weber (1979b) found at least two pairs of Cliff Swallows nesting at the Grenada Lake Graysport Crossing Bridge on June 11, 1978.

The Cliff Swallow has extended its breeding range to the Mississippi Coast. Spence and Toups (1986) found 30 or more pairs with nests or building nests at a drawbridge spanning East Pearl River in Hancock County. The observations were made on June 10 and 13, 1986, and documented by photographs. Another small colony nesting with Barn Swallows was noted under a bridge over Pelahatchie Embayment of Ross Barnett Reservoir in Rankin County in June 1992.

In May 1993, Department of Wildlife, Fisheries and Parks employees David L. Watts and Doug Epps located several hundred nesting Cliff Swallows on the U.S. 72 bridge spanning the Tennessee-Tombigbee Waterway over the Divide Section Wildlife Management Area in Tishomingo County. The birds had built nests extending out along both sides of the bridge for a hundred feet or more and then abruptly halted, with no nests built over the open water. On the opposite side of the waterway, nests were built along the bridge in the same fashion. The birds seen were actively building and repairing nests.

Cliff Swallows nest in colonies, but individual nests may be found on the periphery of their breeding range. The nest is a gourd-shaped structure made up of mud pellets with a round opening on the side. The small nest inside the chamber is composed of straw, grass stems, and feathers. This swallow always builds nests in a place protected from rain, such as under a cliff face, concrete bridge, or in large highway culverts. Where the birds are found in large colonies, their mud nests often are attached together with separate openings to each nest.

The eggs are white and variously marked with spots or fine dots in shades of brown. Four or five eggs constitute the usual clutch.

[Cave Swallow] *Hirundo fulva*

The Cave Swallow has a square tail and buff-colored rump patch. It is distinguished from the similar-sized Cliff Swallow by the *plain buff-colored throat* and *cinnamon forehead.* Most Cliff Swallows have *pale* foreheads and some *black* on the chin and throat of adults.

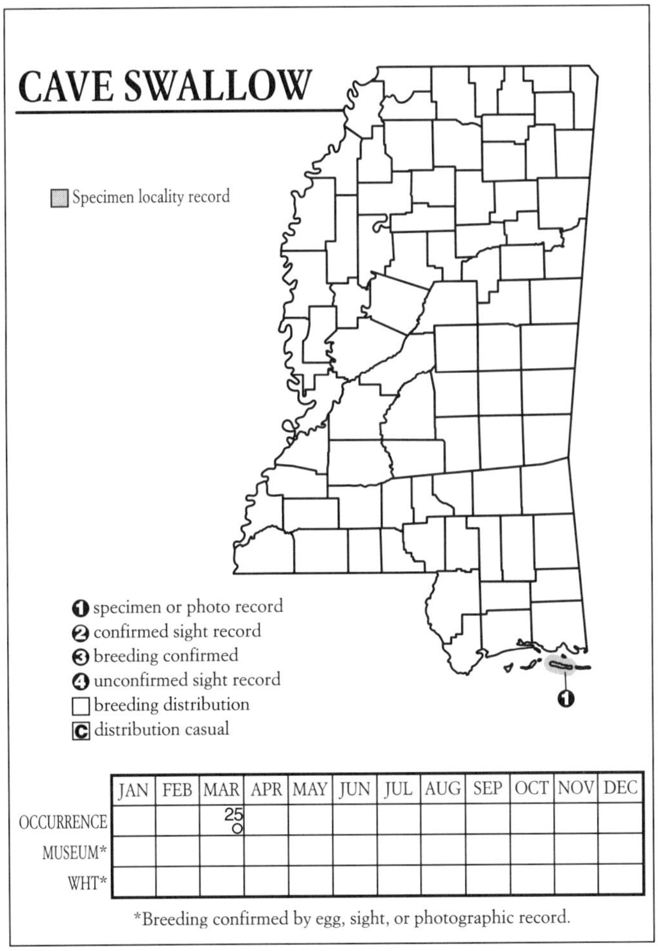

The Cave Swallow is a Central American and Caribbean species expanding its breeding range into south-central and western Texas, southeastern New Mexico, and southern Florida. It has occurred as a spring migrant in southern Florida and the Dry Tortugas. A single sight record in Alabama was made in April 1984 by Dwight Cooley and Mark Brown. The first Mississippi record was a bird found dead on Horn Island on March 25, 1986 (Mackler and Hall 1986). The specimen is at MSU.

Cave Swallows nest in limestone caves or sinks, on sides of cliffs, under bridges, and in highway culverts. I have observed colonies nesting under box culverts in the arid hill country west of the Davis Mountains in southwestern Texas.

Barn Swallow *Hirundo rustica*

This is the only swallow native to Mississippi with white spots near the margin of its deeply forked tail. The underparts are pinkish buff, the throat and forehead are rusty red, and the back is blue black. Young birds are lighter underneath and have duller coloring than adults. The flight is remarkably agile, direct, and often close to the ground with the wing tips pointing backward at the end of each forward stroke.

Along the Gulf Coast and on the coastal islands, there is a breeding population of an insular race of Barn Swallows with much paler breasts than those found farther north in the state. This coastal race has been known to breed for many years at Fort Massachusetts on Ship Island, inside warehouses at the port of Gulfport, and under bridges along the coastline. The range of this insular race extends from western Florida along the northern Gulf Coast.

There has been a noticeable southward expansion of the breeding range of the Barn Swallow (Turcotte 1961a). This extension has been made possible by the construction of concrete highway bridges and box culverts providing suitable nesting places.

Barn Swallows nest commonly to the Gulf Coast. I have found as many as 34 swallow nests in one large box culvert under the Natchez Trace Parkway in Claiborne County south of Bayou Pierre. These nests held fledglings or eggs as late as August 4.

Barn Swallows are common to abundant during migration. They arrive from South American wintering grounds in mid-March and continue migration until mid-May. Fall migration begins in August and extends through October into early November. These swallows are fairly common, summer-resident, breeding birds, nesting in coastal counties and regularly north of the longleaf pine region of southern Mississippi.

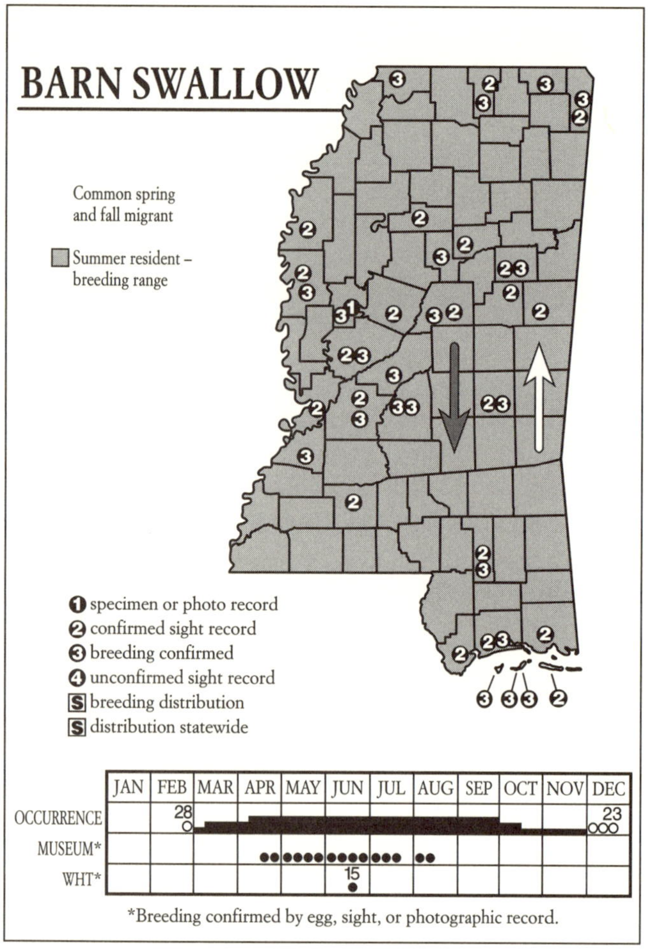

The cup-shaped nests are open on top, built of mud and grass, and lined with feathers. The four to six white eggs are marked with reddish brown spots. Nesting often occurs in colonies. This swallow prefers to nest under concrete bridges or culverts along highways, but sometimes inside buildings and porches. The nest is plastered to the side of bridge supports, walls of culverts, masonry, rafters, or other support inside buildings.

The song is a soft *kvik, kvik,* or *wit-wit.* When a nesting colony is approached, the birds become irritated and the calls are harsh *keet, keet* twitterings.

The Barn Swallow lives entirely on flying insects. I have noticed an interesting symbiotic relationship between this swallow and the organ-pipe wasp or "dirt-dauber." These birds have difficulty building nests on the smoothly finished walls of culverts under highways. The wasps usually build nests at or near the top of these culverts, and swallows use them for supporting and attaching their nests. Attached swallow nests are then reused with tier-nests built over the old nests of previous seasons. In return, the swallows probably help the wasp by consuming insects that parasitize the wasp larvae.

Corvidae (Jays and Crows)

Blue Jay *Cyanocitta cristata*

The Blue Jay is one of our most handsome birds with its blue, white, black, and gray plumage. It is full of mischief and noise, and may sometimes pilfer eggs or young from the nests of other birds. It is also beneficial in its food habits by consuming harmful insects, and carrying and planting acorns, nuts, and seeds that eventually may become trees or shrubs.

The Blue Jay has a great variety of calls besides the familiar *jay, jay.* It is so good at imitating the calls of the Red-tailed, Red-shouldered, and Broad-winged Hawks that the listener is often confused as to the real identity. It has a habit of finding and harassing hawks, owls, snakes, and other predators.

In Mississippi, this jay is abundant year-round and more numerous during the fall and winter after the arrival of northern migrants. Blue Jays migrate during the daylight hours. Northern jays migrate to the northern Gulf Coast.

An unusual event occurred along the coast from the vicinity of Mobile, Alabama, to southeastern Louisiana from October 10 to 16, 1972, when large flocks of Blue Jays appeared everywhere (Gunter 1972, 1975). They were seen migrating in a westerly direction across the islands in Mississippi Sound. Observers reported thousands of jays falling into the water, their drowned bodies washing ashore on island beaches (McGraw et al. 1973). Other jays made their way southwesterly toward Louisiana, with some seen on oil-well platforms and boats around the mouth of the Mississippi River. There were no unusual weather conditions, and no explanation could be found for their lemming-like behavior.

The Blue Jay is a bird of the woods, but it has adapted to civilization and often is found close to homes in towns. It nests from early April until June. The nest is usually in the fork of a tree trunk or limb from 10 to 40 feet or more aboveground.

Blue Jay

BLUE JAY

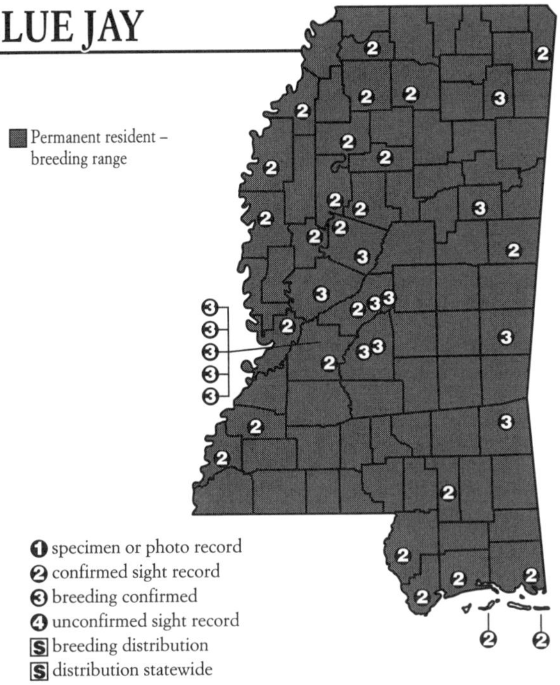

	JAN	FEB	MAR	APR	MAY	JUN	JUL	AUG	SEP	OCT	NOV	DEC
OCCURRENCE	■	■	■	■	■	■	■	■	■	■	■	■
MUSEUM*				●●●	●●	●●●						
WHT*				10 22 26 ●●●								

*Breeding confirmed by egg, sight, or photographic record.

The rather large nest is usually a platform of sticks cemented with mud that forms a cup lined with rootlets. Leaves, rags, string, paper, and dry grass are used in nest construction. Eggs number three to five in a set. They have an olive to buff ground color, rarely bluish, and are variably marked with spots and blotches of darker shades of olive and brown.

American Crow *Corvus brachyrhynchos*

The American Crow is all black in appearance, but the feathers on its upperparts have some iridescence when seen close at hand. It differs from the Fish Crow by its larger size and familiar cawing calls compared to the nasal *car* or *ca-uh* of the Fish Crow. The American Crow occurs abundantly throughout the state except on the barrier islands. Near the coast, the Fish Crow is the more common of the two birds.

Crows are wary of humans, their greatest enemies. They are shot for sport and for protection of crops, especially corn and pecans. Only when well hidden in a thicket and with the aid of a mouth or mechanical call can a crow hunter bag these birds. While feeding, a sentry is usually posted to warn of approaching danger. The danger signal is a call that sounds like *look out.*

Larger hawks and owls are the natural enemies of crows. The Great Horned Owl is probably their greatest predator. Crows often are seen harassing hawks, owls, and other large birds. They are extremely resourceful and are presumably among the most capable survivors.

Crows are disliked by many people because of their reputation for crop depredation and their habit of taking the eggs and young of other birds. Their food habits are not entirely destructive. They eat harmful insects and other invertebrates or vertebrates that are damaging to humans. The Crow eats almost any available food including refuse or carrion.

American Crows nest early, with nest construction beginning in February or early March. Nests are placed in trees or saplings from 20 to 70 feet aboveground. The nest is always in a tract of woods or a thicket, often along a water course. Conifers are preferred nesting places, but nests may be placed in any kind of tree, preferably in the uppermost fork and where thick branches or vines provide some concealment.

The nest is a bulky structure of sticks thickly and compactly lined with strips of bark, hair, or other soft materials. The bark of red cedar is often used for a lining. Eggs

AMERICAN CROW

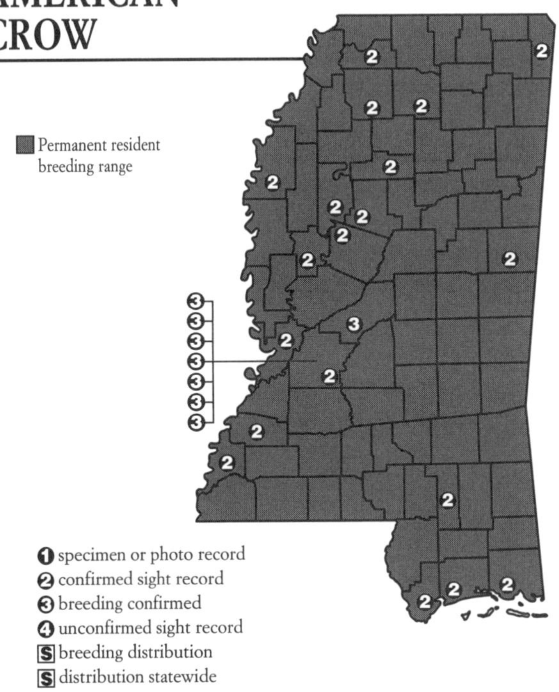

	JAN	FEB	MAR	APR	MAY	JUN	JUL	AUG	SEP	OCT	NOV	DEC
OCCURRENCE	■	■	■	■	■	■	■	■	■	■	■	■
MUSEUM*		●	●									
WHT*			2 27 ●● ●									

*Breeding confirmed by egg, sight, or photographic record.

usually are found in the nest from early March until early April. The four or five eggs are bluish green variably and heavily marked with shades of brown and gray.

Crows make interesting and amusing pets. I have raised a number of them. Young crows are attracted to bright objects and will hide them in odd places. Pet crows have a great variety of calls. They can learn to say words or even phrases such as "Hello, old crow." It is not necessary, as is often told, to split a crow's tongue for it to talk. Crows can learn to say words that are repeated often in their presence.

In spring and summer, crows are found in pairs or family groups. In the fall and winter, they form flocks and have common roosting places usually in isolated thickets of coniferous trees. However, large roosts are uncommon in Mississippi.

Fish Crow *Corvus ossifragus*

The Fish Crow is slightly smaller in size than the American Crow and is an abundant, breeding permanent resident along the Gulf Coast. In the rest of the state, they are found less commonly and mainly along larger river valleys. In northern Mississippi, they occur on the flood control reservoirs and along the Mississippi River, where they are not uncommon locally as far north as Memphis.

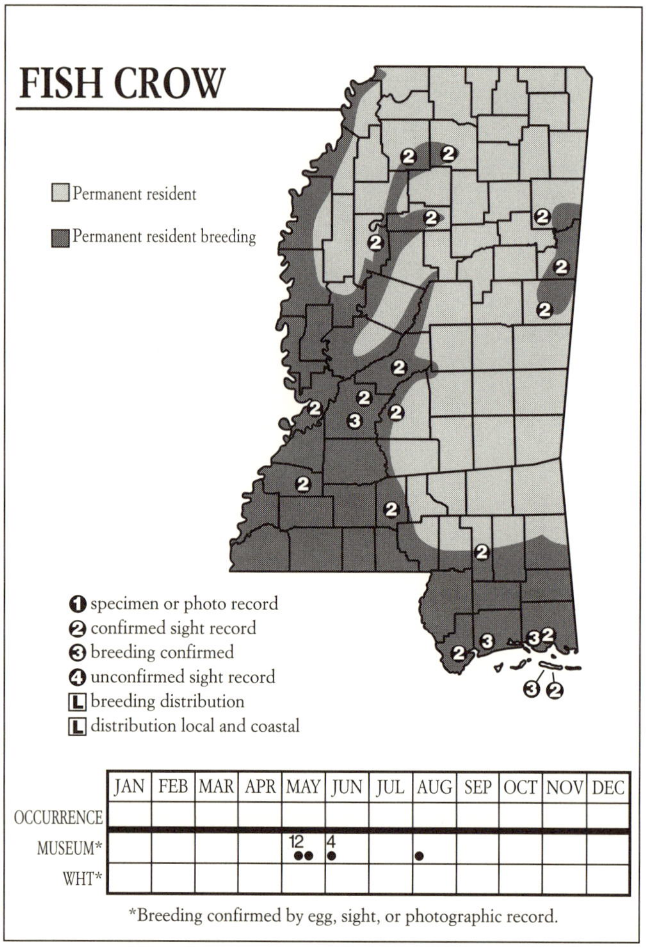

Fish Crows show a preference for water and beaches, shorelines of lakes, reservoirs, and larger streams. They also invade the river swamps and open countryside frequented by American Crows. Fish Crows are scavengers and can be found feeding on refuse at garbage dumps, around commercial and recreation areas in cities, and along highways, where they feed on the dead bodies of animals and insects killed by traffic.

The Fish Crow can be distinguished reliably in the field from the American Crow only by its call, a hoarse, nasal *car, ca* or a two-syllabled *ca-uh*. Most people recognize the familiar *caw-caw* of the American Crow, although few realize there are two distinct species of crows that do not interbreed.

There are few definite nesting reports for the Fish Crow other than on the Gulf Coast. Lovett E. Williams Jr. (1962b) and Sterling G. Clawson found seven active nests in tall pines at Pass Christian on May 12 and another in a tall pine at Bayou Casotte on June 4, 1962. These nests were not accessible, and no specimens of eggs or young were observed. Burleigh (1945) wrote that Fish Crows bred "on both the mainland and all the islands" along the Mississippi Gulf Coast.

On May 21, 1968, I observed a pair of these birds carrying sticks to build a large nest in a tall pine in a grove of trees by my yard outside Jackson, but this attempt was abandoned soon after I discovered the nest. John Phares reported Fish Crows nesting and producing young along a wooded ditch behind his home in north Jackson. I have seen the abandoned nests in deciduous trees in winter at other locations in Jackson.

I have observed Fish Crows stealing Rock Dove eggs from nests under overpasses on Interstate Highways 55 and 20 in Jackson and taking pecans from trees at the capitol. At one time they congregated on the abandoned Edwards Hotel in downtown Jackson, where they pilfered eggs from nesting Rock Doves. I have watched them along Big Black River at a heron and ibis rookery. Although I did not see them in the act of taking eggs, crow-punctured heron egg shells floated on the water under some nests. I watched a Fish Crow rob a Mourning Dove nest at my home in Richland and fly off with an egg in its mouth.

The Fish Crow is not as vulnerable to the hunter's gun as the American Crow. Crow calls do not readily attract the Fish Crow, since they are much more wary than the American Crow of attempts to decoy them in for shooting.

Tufted Titmouse

Paridae (Titmice)

These are small, usually dull-colored, short-winged, plump-bodied, and highly active birds. Paridae tend to flock and band together with other small birds when not actively nesting.

Our two representatives of this large family, the Tufted Titmouse and Carolina Chickadee, are noted for acrobatics while clinging upside down on twigs searching for insects or insect eggs. These birds have small but stout bills, which are used for cracking seeds and cleaning out or enlarging nest cavities. They are easily attracted to feeders using sunflower seeds and suet or peanut butter.

Carolina Chickadee *Parus carolinensis*

Chickadees are hardy, sociable little acrobats and year-round residents. Except when nesting, they nearly always occur in small bands with troupes of birds such as titmice, nuthatches, and Pine Warblers. In winter, I look for them with Brown Creepers, kinglets, and Yellow-rumped Warblers. Chickadees are amusing to watch while they feed, for they often hang upside down while minutely examining leaves or twigs for insects or spiders (and their eggs), their main food supply.

This bird announces its presence by repeating the well-known *chick-a-dee-dee-dee* calls. It is a gentle and confiding species, often frequenting feeding trays for handouts of crumbs, sunflower seeds, suet, or nutmeats.

The Carolina Chickadee is smaller than sparrows. It is a gray bird with a black cap, black bib, and white cheeks. Its sides are lightly washed with rusty brown.

Nesting of Carolina Chickadees begins in late February or early March with the selection of a suitable site. The male noisily proclaims a territory by singing from an elevated perch. Its spring song is quite variable from the usual calls. This bird generally enlarges or excavates the nesting cavity located in a partly decayed fence post or tree stub. The cavity is irregular in shape and varies in dimensions depending on the softness of the wood. A natural cavity, Downy Woodpecker hole, or an artificial nest box may be used for nest-building.

The nest is almost invariably begun by placing a layer of green moss at the bottom of the cavity. To this are added shreds of juniper bark or soft grasses and finer materials such as hair, carpet cleaner sweepings, fur, or feathers for the compacted nest lining. The five or six eggs are white and sprinkled with reddish brown spots. The nesting cycle is usually completed by the end of April or early May. Except for shorter tail feathers, the young resemble the adults soon after leaving the nest.

I have observed incubating adults exhibit an unusual behavior when disturbed on the nest. The incubating bird draws back its head, and then suddenly and repeatedly thrusts it forward striking the side of the cavity, emitting a hissing noise like that of a snake. This instinctive action by the adult may serve to frighten away the more timid intruders.

Chickadee and titmouse nests I have seen nearly always had a colony of small black ants at the bottom of the nest cavity by the time the young were hatching. They were not

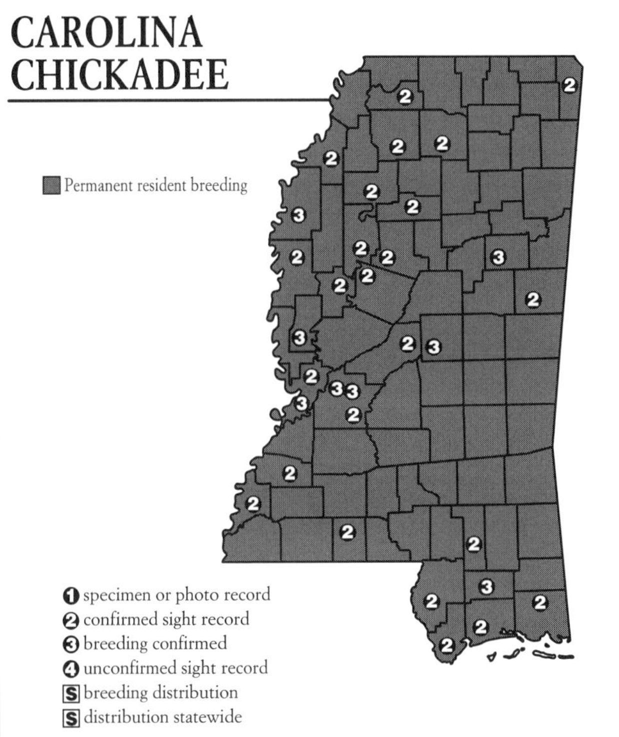

	JAN	FEB	MAR	APR	MAY	JUN	JUL	AUG	SEP	OCT	NOV	DEC
OCCURRENCE	■	■	■	■	■	■	■	■	■	■	■	■
MUSEUM*			●	● ●	●							
WHT*			14 25 ● ●	11 ●								

*Breeding confirmed by egg, sight, or photographic record.

biting or stinging ants, and I suspect there may be a symbiotic relationship. The ants perhaps utilize the protection of the cavity and the protein of the sheddings from the feather shafts; and in return, I have never seen any feather mites in any of the nests examined.

Tufted Titmouse *Parus bicolor*

This close relative of the chickadee often announces its presence by *peto, peto* calls before it can be seen. It is a breeding permanent resident, commonly found throughout the state with the possible exception of the offshore islands. However, it has been recorded on Deer Island just off the mainland from Biloxi.

The Tufted Titmouse is a somberly clad, gray-backed bird with a conspicuous gray crest and rusty flanks. There is a slight amount of black on the forehead of adults between the bill and the eye, which is absent on immatures. The breast and belly are white.

Titmice are commonly found in deciduous woods, but they sometimes invade pinelands. They often are in the company of chickadees and kinglets and appear to lead these small flocks of insect eaters as they troupe noisily together through the woods. Titmice are usually seen in pairs or family groups of not more than three to eight after the breeding season.

The Tufted Titmouse is easily attracted to backyard bird feeders and will nest in natural cavities and man-made nest boxes. A close relative of the chickadee, the Tufted Titmouse readily responds to a recording of its song.

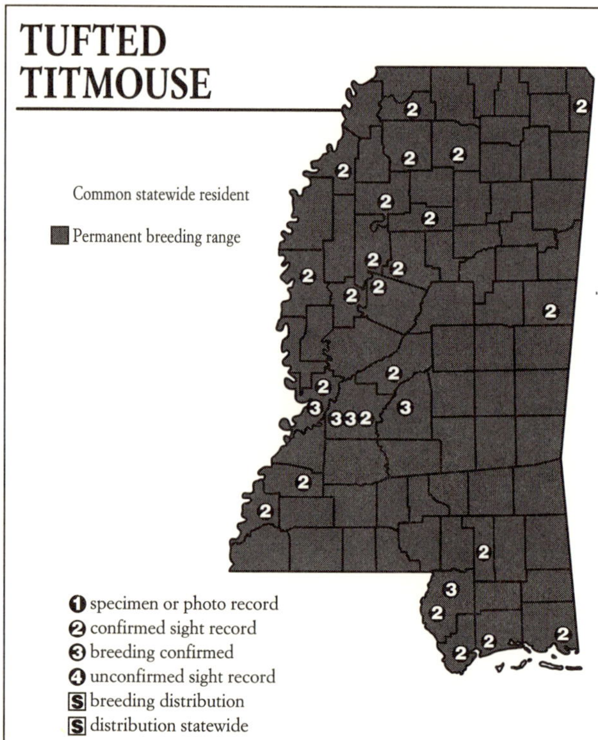

	JAN	FEB	MAR	APR	MAY	JUN	JUL	AUG	SEP	OCT	NOV	DEC
OCCURRENCE	■	■	■	■	■	■	■	■	■	■	■	■
MUSEUM*				•	• •							
WHT*												

*Breeding confirmed by egg, sight, or photographic record.

They are gentle and among the friendliest of birds and respond readily to a recording of their song. I have had them come to within a few feet of me while playing a tape recording of their calls. They responded with loud songs and several variations of their usual *peto, peto* call.

The Tufted Titmouse is agile and quick in its actions and often dangles head downward from the ends of branches or the underside of limbs in search of food. It feeds mainly on insects, but also consumes wild fruits, seeds, and acorns in quantity.

The Tufted Titmouse builds its nest in natural cavities, deserted woodpecker holes, or artificial structures. The nest is composed of leaves, green moss, fibrous bark, and lined with soft material such as hair or feathers. The five or six eggs are white or creamy white spotted evenly with reddish brown. I have had pairs nest four seasons in artificial structures placed on pine trees 12 to 15 feet aboveground in my yard. The size or depth of the structure did not seem to matter. One nest was in a gallon antifreeze container, which was first filled with leaves before the nest was finished.

Another pair raised a brood in an old, copper tea kettle that had a broken spout. A third structure, made from a four-inch terra cotta drain tile with an entrance hole pecked in the side with wood roof and bottom, was used for two successive seasons.

In April, during the spring season for hunting Wild Turkey gobblers, our woods resound at daybreak with songs of titmice, Carolina Wrens, and cardinals almost obscuring a distant turkey gobble. These songs, gobbles, and calls of early spring in the isolation of turkey woods, with new leaves and spring wildflowers blooming, make even an unsuccessful turkey hunt worth an early rising.

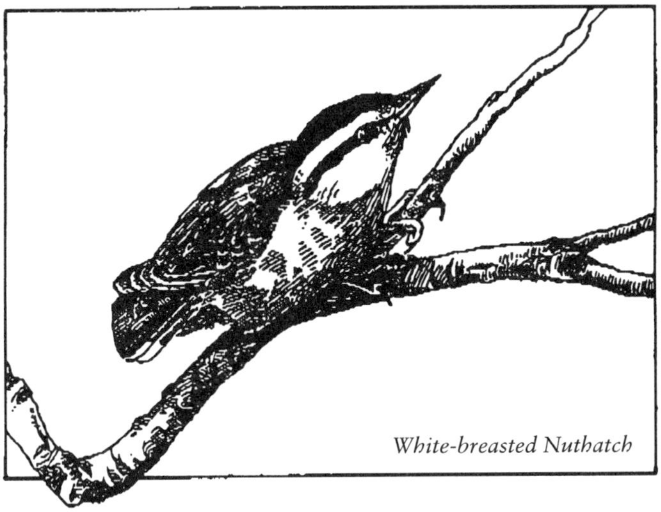

White-breasted Nuthatch

RED-BREASTED NUTHATCH

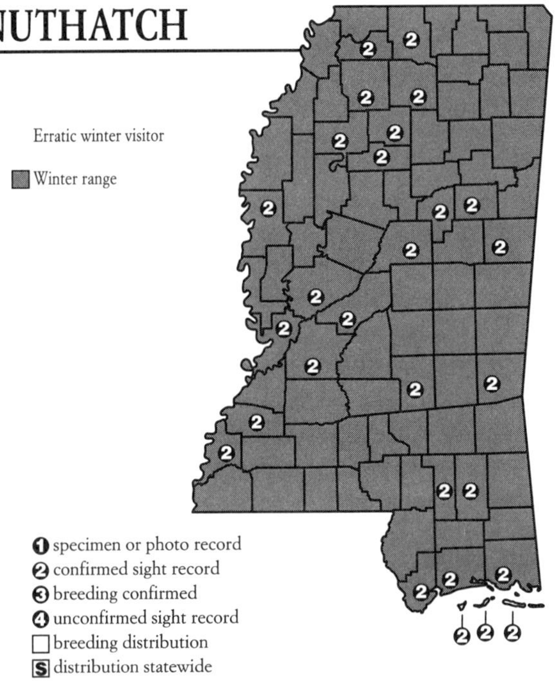

	JAN	FEB	MAR	APR	MAY	JUN	JUL	AUG	SEP	OCT	NOV	DEC
OCCURRENCE					11				3			
MUSEUM*												
WHT*												

*Breeding confirmed by egg, sight, or photographic record.

Sittidae (Nuthatches)

Nuthatches are small, active birds that spend much of their time climbing upside down on tree trunks or branches. They have straight, stout bills; short tails; and strong legs. Although they creep about on trees in woodpecker fashion, their tail is not used as a prop for support. The calls of nuthatches have a nasal quality that helps in field recognition.

Mississippi has two resident species, the White-breasted and Brown-headed Nuthatches. The Red-breasted Nuthatch is an erratic winter visitor to the state. All three species readily accept food at bird feeders. They are sociable and travel together in small, conspecific troupes or with other small birds.

Red-breasted Nuthatch *Sitta canadensis*

The Red-breasted Nuthatch is blue gray above and reddish rusty below. It has a black cap, a white line over the eye, and a broad black band through the eye. This nuthatch is intermediate in size between the other two species occurring in Mississippi, the White-breasted and Brown-headed Nuthatch.

The Red-breasted Nuthatch is an erratic winter visitor that occurs infrequently, but in some years it appears to invade the state in numbers. The winter of 1961–1962 was apparently an invasion year with records of its occurrence in various parts of the state including the coastal counties.

This bird's calls are soft twitterings and commonly described, nasal, repetitive calls resembling *enk, enk,* or the sound of a tiny, tin horn.

This nuthatch breeds in the northern United States and Canada. It has occurred in Mississippi from September to May, with most sightings during the colder months. B. E. Gandy recorded from one to three birds regularly using his feeder at Jackson in Hinds County, from November 15, 1969, through April 12, 1970. Clarence E. Morgan Jr. of Kosciusko in Attala County reported them at feeders at or near his home from October 15, 1969, through April 26, 1970. Apparently 1969–1970 was another invasion year, as they were also reported from other localities in the state. Burleigh (1945) also noted a large influx of this species in the coastal counties during the winter of 1941–1942.

White-breasted Nuthatch *Sitta carolinensis*

This nuthatch, the largest of the three nuthatches found in Mississippi, is about the size of the Tufted Titmouse. It has bluish gray upperparts, a white face, and grayish white underparts. The male has a black cap and black, beady eyes. Outer-tail feathers are edged with white. Undertail coverts and part of the lower belly are chestnut colored. The female is like the male, except the forepart of the cap is dark gray instead of black.

White-breasted Nuthatches prefer oak and pine-hardwood forests. They are locally common in northern Mississippi, uncommon in other parts, and usually scarce or absent on the coast. They show a preference for large, mature, bottomland hardwoods and oak-hickory upland hardwood types, although they sometimes frequent pines. They are permanent-resident breeding birds.

Their call notes are a hoarse, nasal *yank-yank*. The song is a series of rapid repetitions of these nasal and similar notes. This nuthatch nests in natural cavities in large-sized, living trees or woodpecker holes. Sometimes they excavate or enlarge a natural cavity. Nest material consists of leaves and strips of bark lined with finer materials such as hair, feathers, or other soft substances. The eggs are white, heavily marked with reddish brown, and number four to six in a set.

There are few breeding records for this species in Mississippi. Berry and Wills Jr. (1962) observed a pair of these birds feeding young in a natural cavity 30 feet up in a living red oak tree during the first week of April 1962 on Mayes Lake in Hinds County. The cavity entrance had been newly enlarged.

Tishomingo State Park supports a sizeable breeding population. They occur sparingly in the Yazoo Delta, usually around cypress lakes or swamps and adjacent stands of large hardwoods. In central and southern counties, they occur sparingly in hardwood bottomlands and in the uplands of the Loess Bluff bordering the Mississippi River and the Yazoo Delta. The few coastal records are mainly in fall or winter.

Brown-headed Nuthatch *Sitta pusilla*

This little nuthatch is the most abundant of the three species occurring in Mississippi. It is a permanent-resident breeding bird in pine forests, where it is frequently seen in the topmost branches, its favorite habitat. It often occurs with Pine Warblers, chickadees, and titmice.

This dwarfish, pine-loving nuthatch is found throughout the state, except in the bottomland hardwoods and batture lands of the Mississippi and Yazoo River Delta. It feeds on pine seeds extracted when the cones are open and shedding their seeds. Insects and their eggs and spiders are some other foods.

The Brown-headed Nuthatch has a gray back and grayish white underparts. The dull brown cap and a white spot on the nape of the neck are distinguishing field marks. Except when nesting, it occurs in small flocks in open pine woods where it can be located easily by its almost constant, squeaky, twittering calls, a series of rapidly repeated, high *kit, kit* or *knee-knee-knee* notes.

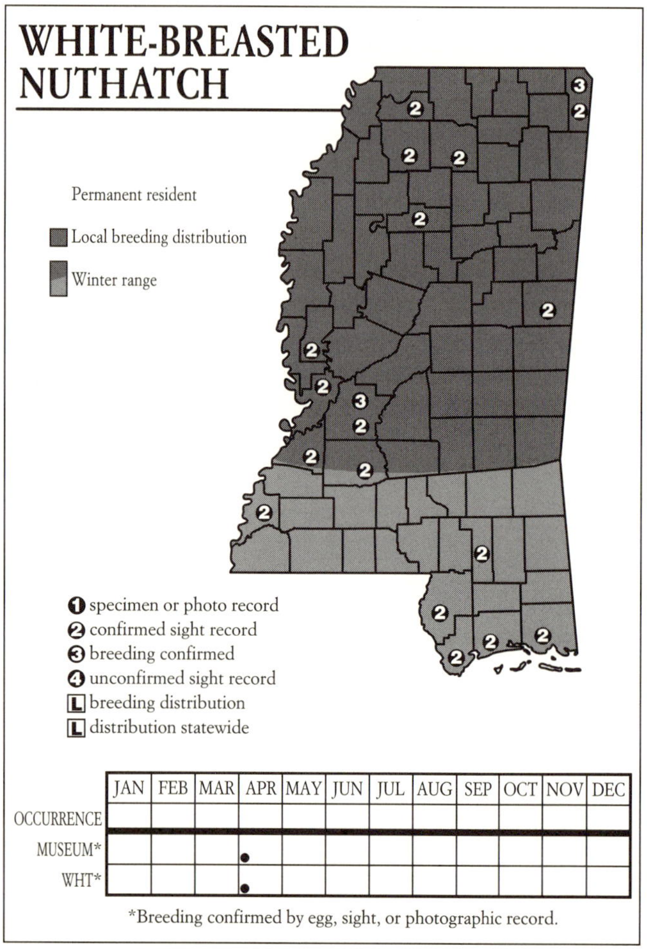

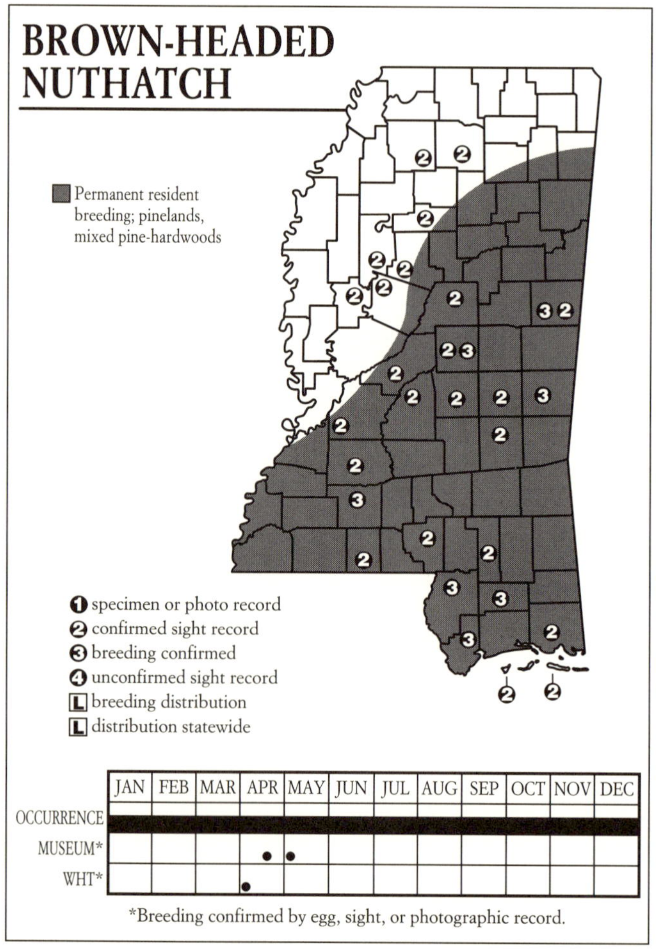

Nesting occurs in March and April. The nest is in a cavity usually excavated or enlarged by the birds. The entrance is an irregular, vertical ellipse shape. The shape of the cavity is also irregular depending upon the condition of the softer sapwood between the bark and heartwood. The cavity may be from six to nine inches or more in depth.

The nest is composed of the winged parts of pine seeds, spider cocoons, fine grasses, odd bits of soft material, moss, hair, or feathers. Dead pine snags are commonly used nesting sites, although other dead snags are used. The eggs are white, heavily spotted with reddish brown. The set is usually five to seven eggs.

Certhiidae (Creepers)

Creepers are small, slim-bodied birds with long, stiff tails and long, sharp-nailed toes for climbing trees. Their curved, sharp bill is used for extracting bark insects. The Brown Creeper is usually a solitary winter resident in Mississippi, often found with a troupe of other small, insectivorous birds. There are six creeper species worldwide.

Brown Creeper *Certhia americana*

The Brown Creeper is a fairly common, inconspicuous winter resident from early October to early April throughout Mississippi. It occurs in all types of woodlands, either singly or in small groups with other insectivorous birds such as chickadees, titmice, and kinglets.

BROWN CREEPER

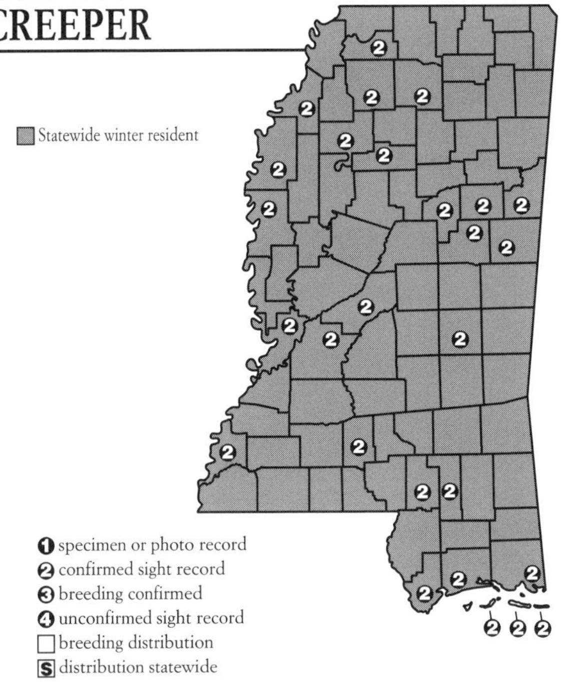

	JAN	FEB	MAR	APR	MAY	JUN	JUL	AUG	SEP	OCT	NOV	DEC
OCCURRENCE										6		
MUSEUM*												
WHT*												

*Breeding confirmed by egg, sight, or photographic record.

Brown Creepers occur in all types of woodlands along with other insect-eating birds. The slim bodied little bird busily searches the trunks of trees in a spiraling fashion from bottom to top for food items.

It is singular in its feeding habits, however, and busily searches the trunks of trees from bottom to top, feeding on insects or their eggs occurring in bark crevices. The Brown Creeper begins near the bottom of a tree trunk and ascends, sometimes spiraling or sidling around and up the trunk. Then it descends in a gliding flight to another tree where it repeats the process. It seems to be forever feeding in this manner.

The Brown Creeper is small, slim bodied, and heavily streaked with pale gray on its brownish head and upperparts. Underparts are white, and there is a distinct white eye line. The tail feathers are long and taper to points having stiff spines used for support in climbing. The beak is long, sharp, slender, and decurved. The feet are large and have sharp claws to aid in climbing.

The call note is a high pitched *seee.* The song of the Brown Creeper is rarely heard during the winter months. It typically breeds in the northern forests and high mountain regions of the eastern and western United States and southern Canada.

Long-billed Marsh Wren

Troglodytidae (Wrens)

Wrens are small, very active, brownish birds with plump bodies, slender bills, and a tail that is often cocked over their back. They usually inhabit thickets or dense, marshy areas. Wrens are noted for loud calls and scoldings that seem out of proportion to their small size.

Six species of wrens occur in Mississippi, three of which are year-round residents. The House Wren, Winter Wren, and Sedge Wren are winter residents only. The Carolina Wren is a permanent resident. The Marsh Wren is a permanent-resident breeding bird in all of our coastal marshes. It is uncommon as a transient, but in suitable habitat the Marsh Wren is an uncommon, local, winter visitor. The Bewick's Wren is an uncommon winter resident and locally rare as a breeding bird in northern Mississippi.

Carolina Wren
Thyrothorus ludovicianus

This is the largest and most common of the six species of wrens known to occur in Mississippi. Field marks are a reddish brown back, a broad white line over and behind the eye, and bright, buffy underparts. The wings, tail, and undertail coverts are barred with black. The bird has two indistinct white wing bars, and the throat is white.

Seldom seen, except when this wren is roosting on cold nights, are small white dots on the back and rump feathers, which are concealed except when fully distended. The distended feathers provide insulation and possibly camouflage. They look like cushions full of white-headed pins. I have seen pairs using common roosts, sitting close together in this distorted appearance.

In Mississippi the Carolina Wren is commonly but incorrectly called the "house wren" because it frequents places around homes, and often nests in or around buildings. It is a common permanent resident and breeds throughout the state. Thick underbrush in wooded areas is the preferred habitat of this wren, but it also frequents thick shrubbery in towns and urban areas.

The Carolina Wren is not choosy about nest locations, and it nests in a great variety of habitats. Around buildings, it may place a nest in any conceivable cavity or container or atop masonry piers under buildings. In the woods, it may build a nest on the ground, on slopes, or hidden in tree roots of overhanging stream or road banks, in cavities of stumps or logs, or in thick tangles of vines aboveground.

The nest is composed of leaves or other coarse material piled into a cavity or shaped into a loose ball and lined with any available finer materials. The entrance is usually to one side of the nest. Many of the nests I have found contained pieces of green moss. The four or five eggs are creamy white and heavily blotched with various shades of brown and lavender. Nesting extends from March to July or later, and several broods may be raised by a pair in one nesting season.

The song is loud and clear and consists of two or three syllables repeated four to six times. There are numerous variations but to me the songs most commonly heard sound

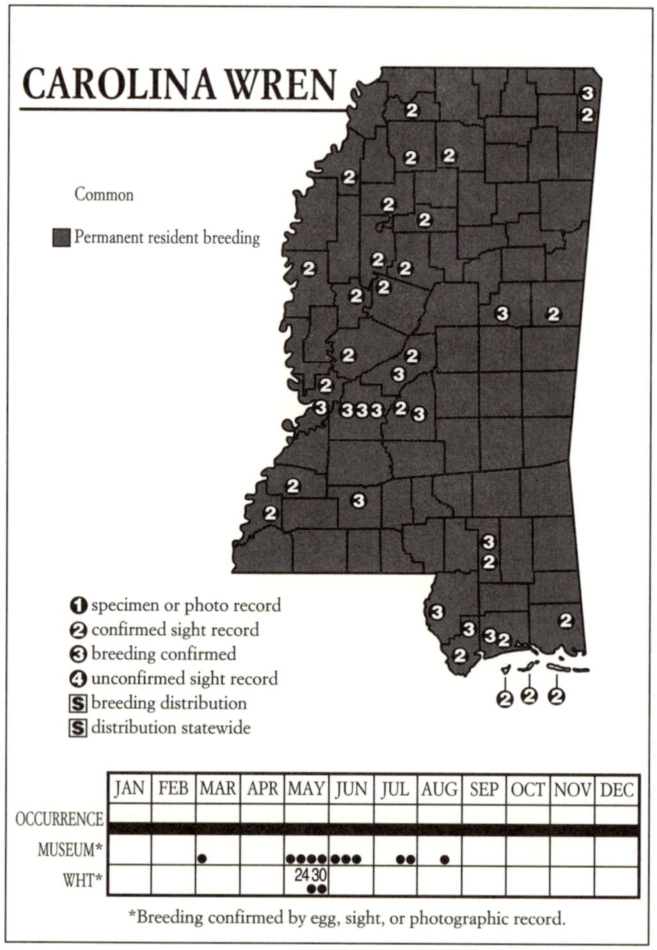

like *cha-wheet', cha-wheet'* or *cha-whee'tle, cha-whee'tle,* which is often mistaken for that of the Northern Cardinal. This wren has a large variety of rattling, monosyllabic scolding and call notes. It is one of the few birds that sings throughout the year and in all kinds of weather.

The Carolina Wren population is sometimes decimated by extreme periods of cold when temperatures plummet near zero. It soon recovers in numbers by the end of the following year. Insects and especially spiders constitute the principal food of this wren. It will visit feeders for tidbits like peanut butter, husked sunflower seed, and bread crumbs. It roosts in protected places such as flower pots, in crevices around buildings, or in a box or nest gourd hung on a porch or covered patio.

Bewick's Wren *Thryomanes bewickii*

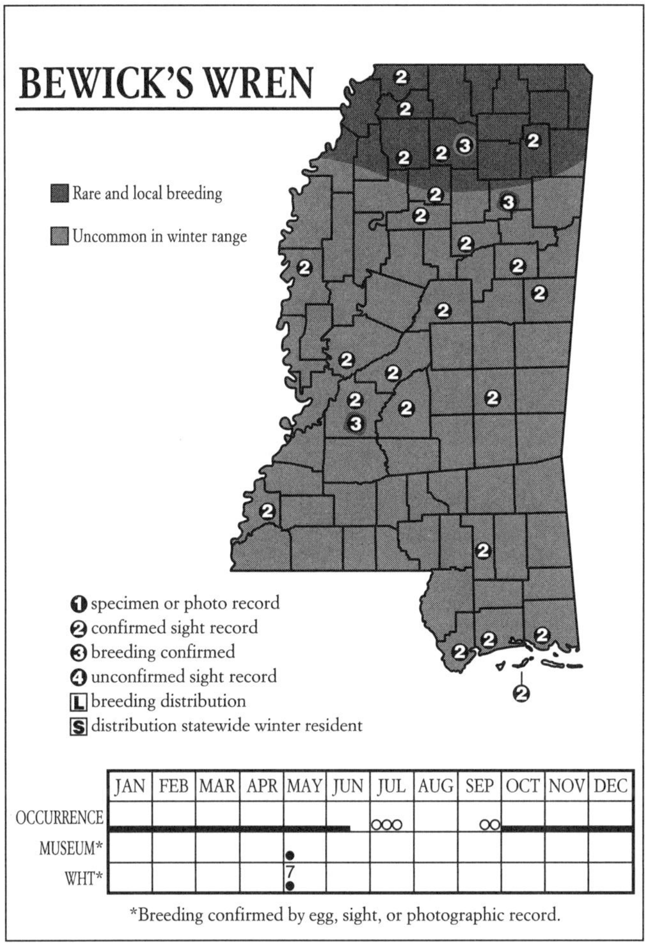

The Bewick's Wren (pronounced "buick," like the automobile) is more slender and smaller than the Carolina Wren, but slightly larger than the House Wren. Its distinctive field mark is a long, barred, rounded tail *carried erect* or at an angle to the back *and frequently wobbled from side to side.* The back and head are dark brown with a conspicuous white line over the eye. The underparts are *white,* except for the black barring on the undertail coverts. Outer-tail feathers are white, barred with black, and mostly white at the rounded corners.

The Bewick's Wren is an uncommon winter resident throughout our state. It is locally rare as a summer-resident, breeding bird in the northern hill counties and rare in the Delta. This wren prefers open countryside and seems to avoid extensive woodlands. It is more likely to be found along fence rows, thickets, underbrush, brush piles, vine tangles, woodlots and not infrequently around houses and outbuildings when nesting.

Fall and winter records for southern Mississippi extend from late September to late March. Summer records for northern and west-central Mississippi are in May and June.

Breeding records are rare. Only two sets of Bewick's Wren eggs are in the MMNS. Egg records are: Chickasaw County, four miles southwest of Okolona, May 3, 1939, four eggs collected by H. L. Owens; and Hinds County, Clinton, May 3, 1940, seven eggs collected by W. H. Turcotte (Gandy and Turcotte 1970). In addition, in the summer of 1941, I saw two nests at Clinton in Hinds County at the above location in a garage that produced two broods of six and seven young.

The Bewick's Wren nest is made of sticks and debris in a loose arrangement with an open cup lined with feathers or other soft material. Spider webs bind loose materials in place. Nests are usually in buildings or a crevice or cavity affording concealment. The three nests I have seen were built in the same one-pound coffee can resting on a board under the eave of a garage shed. The eggs are white and blotched with shades of reddish brown and lavender.

The song of the Bewick's Wren is a series of several high, thin phrases ending in a trill. It has a musical quality, bold and loud, reminiscent of the song of an Eastern Towhee. The call note is a high *chit, chit,* and the scold notes are similar to but higher pitched than the Carolina Wren. Eastern populations of this species are declining. In the West and Southwest, it is common and widespread.

House Wren *Troglodytes aedon*

In Mississippi, the House Wren occurs only as a migrant or winter resident. In northern Mississippi, it is an uncommon and irregular winter visitor. In southern Mississippi, it is a fairly common winter resident. During its winter sojourn, it stays in dense thickets or brushy openings. It arrives in late September and remains in numbers until April. The earliest arrival date for this species is September 24, and latest departure date is May 24.

The House Wren is an elusive species, often passing unnoticed except when scolding. The song, a loud, long, and bubbling musical burst in phrases rising in intensity and trailing off at the end, is seldom heard in winter.

This wren is dark brown above and grayish brown below.

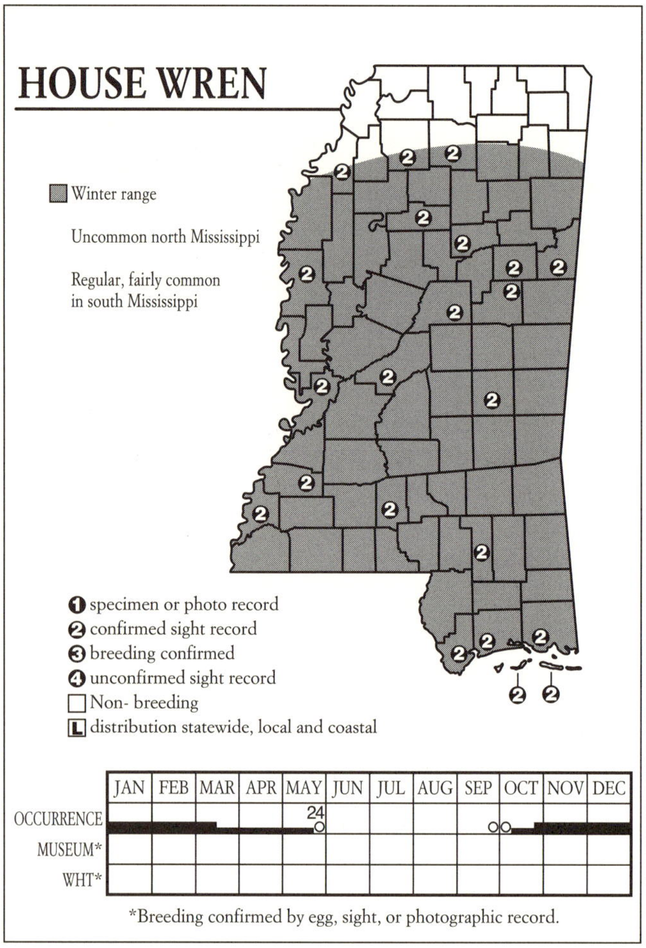

*Breeding confirmed by egg, sight, or photographic record.

It lacks distinctive head marks. It is larger than the Winter Wren and smaller than the Carolina and Bewick's Wrens. The tail is characteristically cocked over its back. Like other wrens, it is noted for its energetic actions. On its breeding grounds farther north, it is sociable and frequently nests around homes and in bird boxes. It is noted for aggressive behavior toward other birds in defending its nesting territory.

Winter Wren *Troglodytes troglodytes*

The Winter Wren is Mississippi's smallest wren, measuring about four inches in length. It is with us only in winter, arriving about mid-October and departing around mid-April. In appearance, it is the darkest of the wrens. Its short tail, about an inch long, is carried erect or at a sharp angle to the back. This wren is found in dense thickets, vine tangles, fallen trees or logs, and brush piles, where it hops about much like a small mouse.

These solitary wrens are usually difficult to see. The best views I have had of them were when I was sitting perfectly still while hunting and had them approach me. I watched one creeping among fallen logs and driftwood around a duck blind. It remained for over an hour and fed at times, dipping its bill into the duckweed-covered water, feeding upon insect or aquatic life. It showed little concern for my presence only a few feet away.

This mite of a bird bobs up and down as it creeps about. Its small size, stubby tail, barred brownish belly, heavily barred sides, and dark striped face with a faint, light line over the eye are its distinguishing field marks.

The call notes are a two-syllabled *kip-kip* given in rapid succession. The song is remarkably loud and clear for so small a bird. It consists of a long series of very high-pitched notes and trills given in rapid succession.

While squirrel hunting, I have heard the Winter Wren singing on several occasions. I once watched a bird sing from a perch on the root of a downed tree. I sat enthralled for several minutes by the song, which to me is one of the most beautiful of bird melodies. However, it seldom sings while wintering in Mississippi.

I have learned that it will respond and sing readily to a recording of its song played in early morning. I have "taped up" four individuals and had them perform at first light and on the same morning until 8:00 A.M.

The Winter Wren is a common breeder in northern hardwoods and coniferous northern and mountainous regions. This species is circumpolar in the Northern Hemisphere.

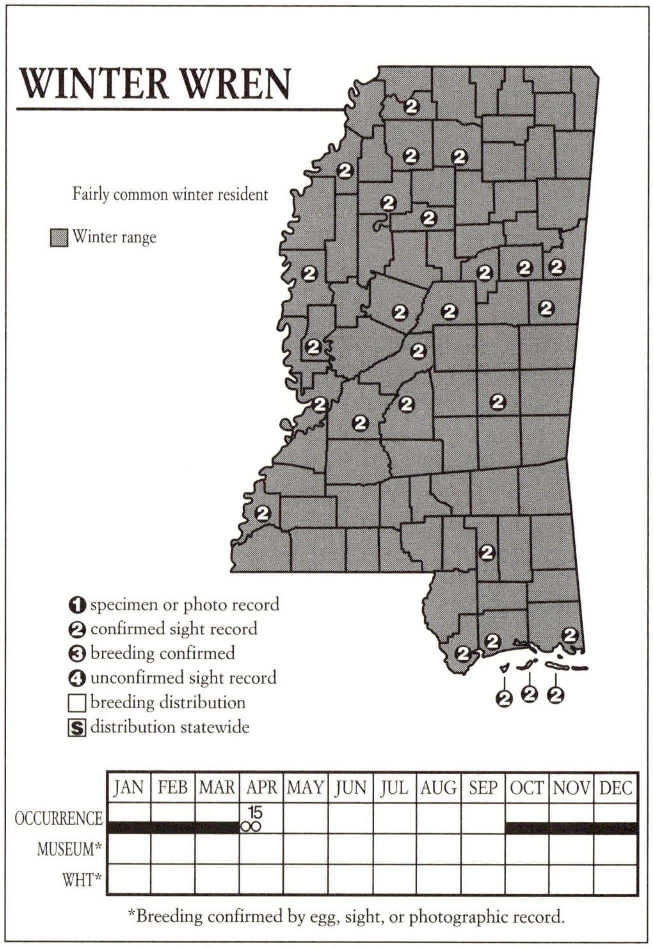

*Breeding confirmed by egg, sight, or photographic record.

Sedge Wren *Cistothorus platensis*

The Sedge Wren is a small and elusive winter visitor or migrant in northern Mississippi. In southern Mississippi, it is a regular winter resident frequently encountered in coastal flatwoods.

The Sedge Wren, formerly called the Short-billed Marsh Wren, inhabits drier, grassier areas than the Marsh Wren, which prefers tall, wet, marsh vegetation. In upland areas, the Sedge Wren prefers damp broomsedge, needlegrass, or other thick, tall grasses. Near the coast, it occurs in the grassy edges of marshes, boggy areas, or meadows in pine barrens or wherever grassy cover is two or three feet tall. The first arrivals appear in October and departure is complete in May.

The shy Sedge Wren is difficult to find and flush from its hiding places. When flushed, its flight is fluttering and labored, and the bird will shortly drop down again into hiding. This wren can be made to show itself by sucking on the back of the hand to make a squeaking noise. A prerecorded playback of song is more effective. Otherwise, fleeting glimpses are seen as this small bird skulks about in dense ground cover.

The Sedge Wren has a streaked crown and back. The bill is short and slim, and its underparts are buffy. The eye stripe is indistinct and buff colored. The tail is stubby and, like that of other wrens, is often held cocked at a sharp angle to the back.

The call is a sharp *tsip*. The scolding notes are a *chick-churr*. The song is a dry, reedy gurgling sound ending in a guttural trill.

I saw these birds and recorded their song in Minnesota on the Agassiz National Wildlife Refuge on June 15, 1985. They were common in the grassy lands bordering cattail marshes where Marsh Wrens and Yellow-headed Blackbirds were calling. One of these little fellows in full view responded to the playback of its song and entertained us for several minutes.

Marsh Wren *Cistothorus palustris*

Until recently, this species was called the Long-billed Marsh Wren. It is a locally common, permanent-resident breeding bird in the coastal marshes, but it occurs inland in marshy places only as a winter visitor or migrant. Migrants arrive in late September and depart by May.

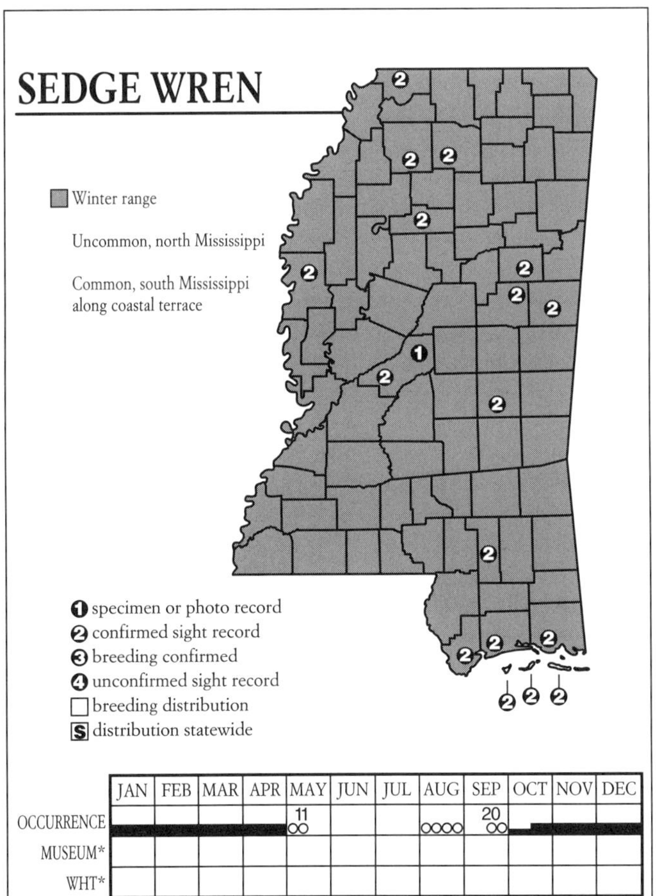

*Breeding confirmed by egg, sight, or photographic record.

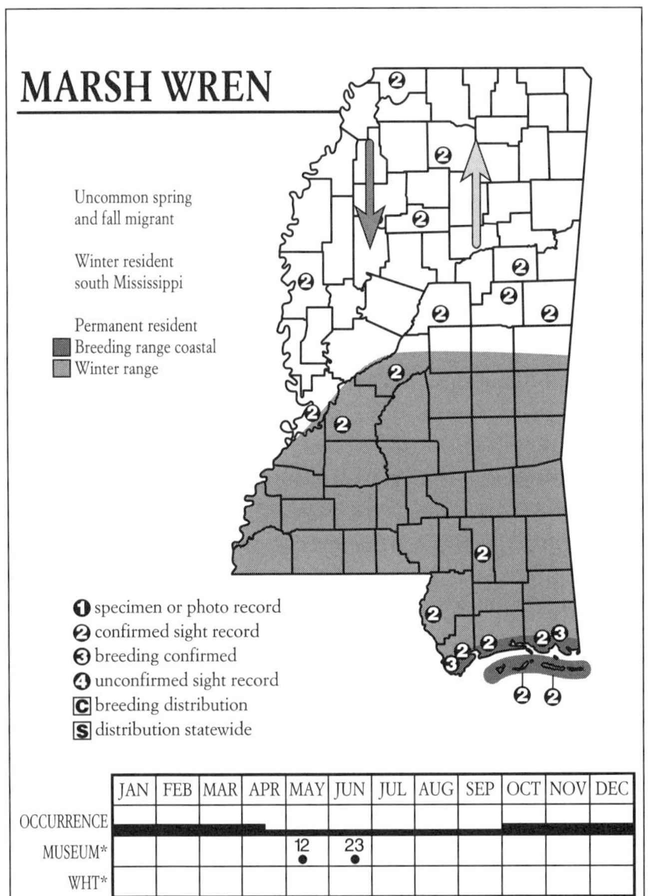

*Breeding confirmed by egg, sight, or photographic record.

The Marsh Wren frequents tall marsh vegetation. It is brown in color with *black-and-white stripes* on the back and a blackish cap. The underparts are white, and there is a prominent white line over the eye.

There are few breeding records for this wren on the Mississippi Coast. Breeding birds have been recorded in the marshes at the mouths of the Pascagoula and Pearl Rivers. Their nest is a globular structure attached to reeds or bushes and made of coarse marsh plants and grasses. The nest is lined with fine grasses and other soft materials with the entrance hole on the side. Incomplete dummy nests are built by the male, but only the active nest is completed with a lining.

The eggs are dark chocolate brown covered with darker brown spots. Three to seven eggs make a clutch. H. D. Haberyan, Lovett E. Williams Jr., and S. G. Clawson collected a set of four eggs one mile west of Pascagoula, on June 23, 1962 (Williams 1962b). These specimens are in the MMNS.

The song of the Marsh Wren is a series of musical rattling or gurgling notes of different pitches preceded by an erratic buzzing. These wrens are somewhat colonial nesters because they require tall marsh vegetation, which is usually in dispersed tracts. They may possibly nest in the few inland cattail marshes near the coast, but this remains to be discovered.

Blue-gray Gnatcatcher

Sylviinae (Old World Warblers, Kinglets, and Gnatcatchers)

Only three species of this subfamily occur in Mississippi. They are plain-colored, diminutive birds, and closely resemble wood warblers (Parulinae) in appearance. The Blue-gray Gnatcatcher is a spring and summer resident that rarely winters here, except in the coastal counties. The two kinglets are fall and winter residents only, and both have prominent wing bars.

Golden-crowned Kinglet
Regulus satrapa

The Golden-crowned Kinglet is a common winter resident throughout the state. This species and the Ruby-crowned Kinglet are among the smallest birds occurring in Mississippi. It usually *travels in small groups* and seems to prefer coniferous trees. It is frequently found in association with chickadees, titmice, Brown Creepers, nuthatches, Pine Warblers, and other small winter residents. The first arrivals appear in late September, but most early records are around mid-October. Departure is in March to about mid-April.

This kinglet is distinguished from the Ruby-crowned Kinglet by the *white line above the eye bordered above by a black stripe,* a yellow crown on the female, and the male having a golden orange stripe in the center of the yellow crown. The sexes are alike in other respects, being greenish above and grayish white below.

Their call note is an extremely high-pitched and faint *tee-tee-tee.* I have never heard this bird's song, but it is described as being less pleasing but similar to that of the Ruby-crowned Kinglet.

Kinglets appear to be in constant search of food, fluttering and flitting about searching bark, twigs, needles, or leaves for insects and their eggs or larvae. Like small fly-

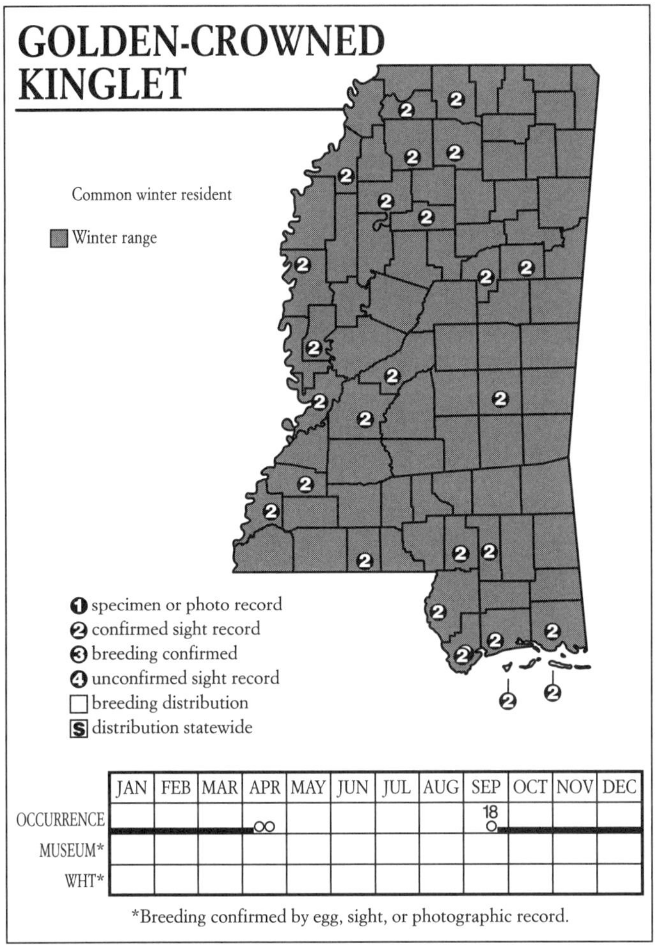

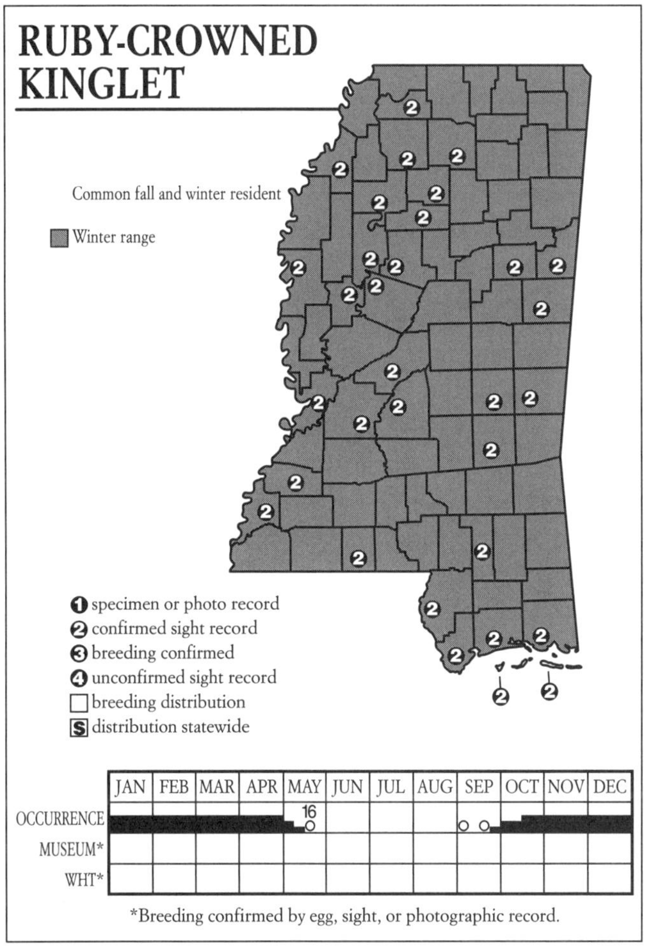

catchers, they frequently catch insects on the wing. The Ruby-crowned Kinglet is quite tame and will allow close approach. The Golden-crowned is not as easy to observe as the Ruby-crowned, as it moves faster and stays higher in trees.

The breeding range of this bird is in the conifer forests of the North and eastern and western mountains. It winters from southern Alaska and Canada south into northern Florida and Guatemala.

Ruby-crowned Kinglet *Regulus calendula*

In fall and winter, the Ruby-crowned Kinglet or "tom-tit" can be found almost anywhere in Mississippi. It is remarkably tame and commonly seen singly or in pairs, but seldom with more than three in a group. It prefers hardwoods, but can be found in all types of woodlands, especially in brushy or weedy places overgrown with vines. The Ruby-crowned Kinglet arrives in late September and remains through April or early May.

This species is greenish above and slightly grayer about the head. A white eye ring, white wing bars, flitting of the wings, and a patch of ruby red in the crown are distinctive field marks. The female does not have the red crown, which in the male is usually hidden except when alarmed.

The call note is a harsh chattering for so small a bird. Once learned, it is a clue to field identification. While the trees are leafing out in March and early April, the males begin their remarkably loud and beautiful song. It starts with a series of high-pitched squeaky notes, followed by a rapid chattering of lower notes rising in pitch, then a series of louder, more musical three-note phrases strongly accented at the end.

Some of my more delightful experiences with spring birds have been in recording the song of the Ruby-crowned Kinglet. They respond readily to a playback tape. I have had them flit to within arm's length, red crest erect, singing loudly, and very nervous and agitated. Of our winter-resident birds, only the tiny Winter Wren can match the Ruby-crowned Kinglet in charm and in performance of a wonderful song. Unfortunately, the Winter Wren seldom sings during its sojourn in Mississippi.

Blue-gray Gnatcatcher *Polioptila caerulea*

This tiny bird is bluish gray above with a white eye ring, white underparts, and a long, black tail bordered with white on the outer feathers. The male has a narrow band

BLUE-GRAY GNATCATCHER

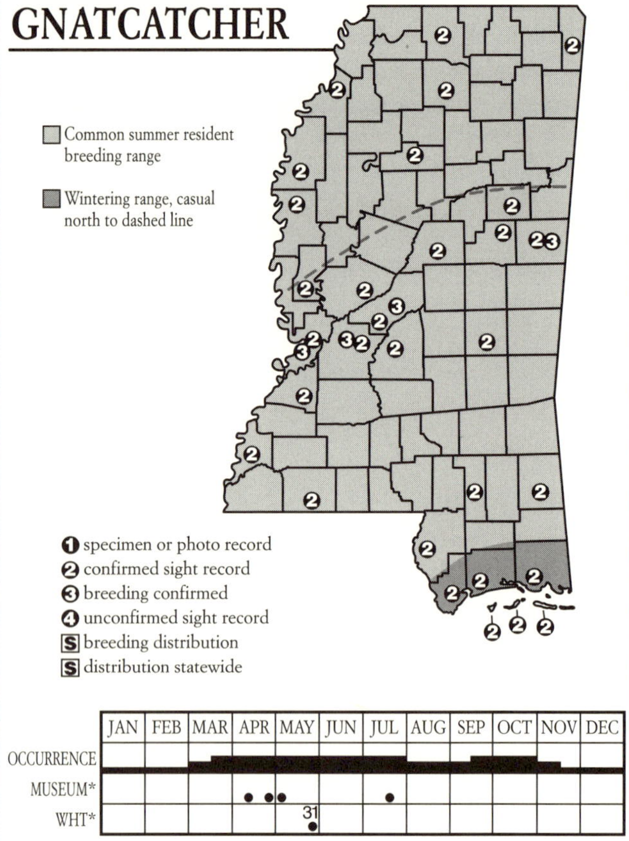

*Breeding confirmed by egg, sight, or photographic record.

of black extending from the bill above and slightly behind the eye. Except for the bluish color of the upperparts and the absence of white wing marks, it resembles a miniature mockingbird. Gnatcatchers are extremely active and constantly moving, flitting the tail while actively hopping and flying about, usually high in the trees.

The Blue-gray Gnatcatcher is a common, breeding summer resident, arriving early in March and remaining through October. There is usually a noticeable passage of these birds through the state in late March and early April.

This species begins nesting soon after its arrival, often before the trees have leafed out. The nest is a superb example of bird architecture. It is built of small weed stems and various kinds of plant down and fibers, tightly compacted and felted together to form a deep cup. It is ornamented on the outside with bits of lichens held together with spider or caterpillar silk. The nest is usually placed to resemble a knot on a horizontal limb at the fork of an upright limb.

Nests are located easily by watching the birds during nest construction or while feeding nestlings. They show no hesitancy about flying directly to their nest carrying nest material or food. I have found more nests in oak trees, but they build in elm, hackberry, box elder, sweet gum, hornbeam, and osage orange trees, usually from 20 to 50 feet aboveground.

I watched a pair of gnatcatchers working on a nearly completed nest, carrying bark stripped from dead weed stems and sycamore leaf fuzz, only to see them later disassemble the nest and use all of the materials to build at another location. Four or five pale blue eggs marked with reddish brown dots constitute a clutch.

The often repeated call notes are a high-pitched, nasal *zee*. I have heard this bird's song on only a few occasions, once by a male perched near a female incubating on the nest. The song was barely audible, very pleasing, somewhat like a vireo, and consisted of soft warblings, but is difficult to describe. Their food consists of small insects obtained from the leafy haunts of this bird.

Spring arrival dates are in mid-March. Gnatcatchers uncommonly winter in Mississippi, but there are numerous records of overwintering birds on the Gulf Coast and inland. M. G. Vaiden reported seeing and collecting one on December 22 in Bolivar County. More recent sight records occur every month of winter in the coastal counties. Other interior sightings have been reported on Christmas Bird Counts. Departure dates, indicated by museum collection and sight records and as recorded in the literature, are mostly in September and October.

The Blue-gray Gnatcatcher breeds commonly throughout our state. The breeding range extends into northern California, southern Colorado, western and central Oklahoma, and into the north-central states, east into New Jersey, and south to central Florida, the Bahamas, and Mexico. Individuals also are found north of known breeding localities after the breeding season.

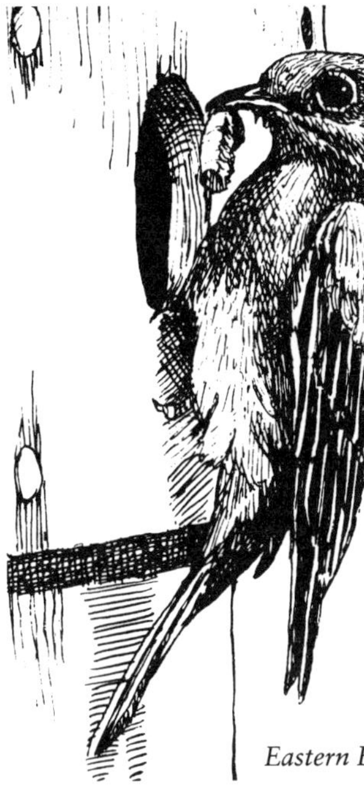

Eastern Bluebird

Turdinae (Solitaires, Thrushes, and Allies)

The true thrushes are thought of as spotted-breasted birds that inhabit shaded woods. This is generally true of most thrushes, but the American Robin and Eastern Bluebird are notable exceptions among those occurring in Mississippi. These species frequent more open places. The breasts of young robins and bluebirds are heavily spotted or speckled in juvenile plumage. Three species of thrushes—the Veery, Swainson's Thrush, and Gray-cheeked Thrush—are fairly common transients through Mississippi in April, early May, and again in September and October. The songs of the thrushes are among the most pleasing.

Eastern Bluebird *Sialia sialis*

Bluebirds are found in open places or open woods. They are particularly noticeable when perched on wires or posts along roadsides. Their hunch-backed appearance with head cocked to the side is a good identifying field mark.

The breast, throat, and sides of the neck of the male are reddish brown, the upperparts are bright azure blue, and the belly is white. The female is not as brightly colored, and juveniles have heavy speckling on the breast. All show enough blue in the upperparts to be distinctive.

The Eastern Bluebird is a fairly common, permanent resident throughout the state. Preferring open countryside, they are more numerous but less visible around homes in winter. They are particularly noticeable in early spring, when migrating waves move through or build up along cold fronts. Then they are often seen in small flocks or in company with other small birds such as Yellow-rumped and Pine Warblers.

These gentle and lovable birds are highly regarded and entirely beneficial. Their food consists mainly of insects. Wild fruits are eaten during the winter months when insects are scare.

Nesting occurs during April, May, and June. Bluebirds nest in natural tree cavities, woodpecker holes, or man-made structures. Their nest is made of fine grasses or pine needles and cupped to receive the usual four or five pale blue, or rarely, white eggs. Sometimes two broods are raised in a season. Rural mail boxes are occasionally used as nesting sites. I have also found nests in building crevices. Bluebird houses are readily accepted in rural or suburban areas, but seldom in towns or cities. Competition for nesting places is a problem.

If you want to have bluebirds, begin by providing and maintaining suitable nest boxes. They should be erected, cleaned out, and readied for occupancy in January when bluebird pairs are establishing breeding territories. Boxes should be made to exact dimensions so that starlings and most other birds will be excluded. The box should be eight to nine inches in depth, the floor five inches square, with the entrance hole 1.5 inches in diameter and six inches above

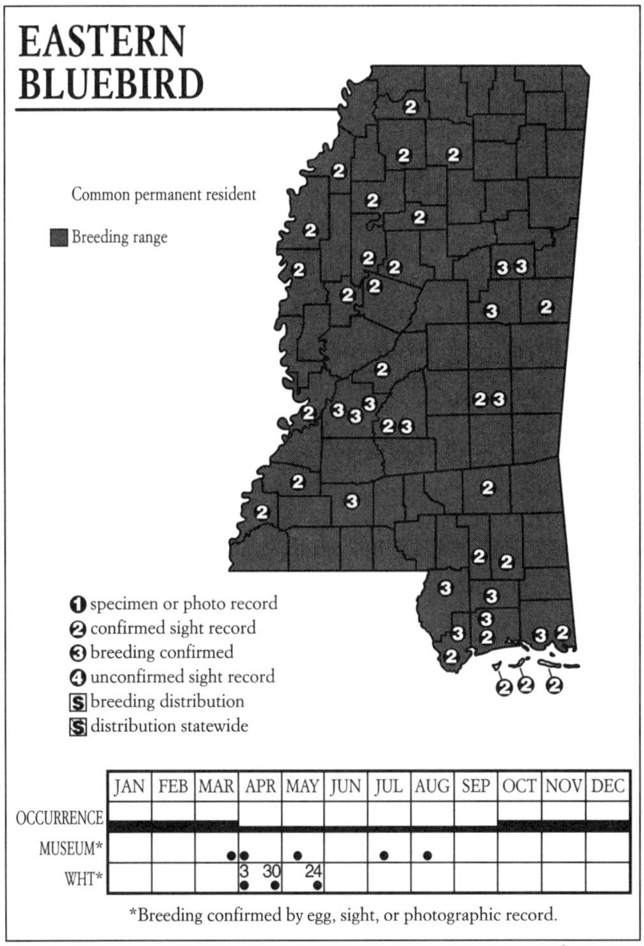

the floor. Preferably, boxes should be placed on a post or metal pipe five or six feet aboveground. Waterproof grease placed around the support will help repel ants.

The Eastern Bluebird song is a low-pitched, pleasant warbling, softly and sweetly rendered and often repeated with variations. The male sings frequently before and during the nesting season and less frequently after young are present. The call note is a soft and low two- or three-syllable *tura-lee* or *chur-wee*.

The Eastern Bluebird ranges east of the Rocky Mountains into southern Canada and south to the Gulf and into Mexico, El Salvador, and Honduras. It breeds throughout most of the northern part of its range.

Bluebirds roost in natural cavities and sometimes in boxes during very cold periods. At times a flock will roost together for added warmth in a shared cavity. I have watched single bluebirds roost in protective forks of trees.

[Mountain Bluebird] *Sialia currucoides*

This species is common throughout the mountain states west of the Great Plains and northward to Alaska. It prefers to nest in open land at elevations above 5000 feet. In winter and during migrations, it can be found in open lowlands and deserts of the West. It rarely wanders east of the Great Plains in migration or during the winter and is accidental east of the Mississippi River.

MOUNTAIN BLUEBIRD

Accidental

■ Locality photo record

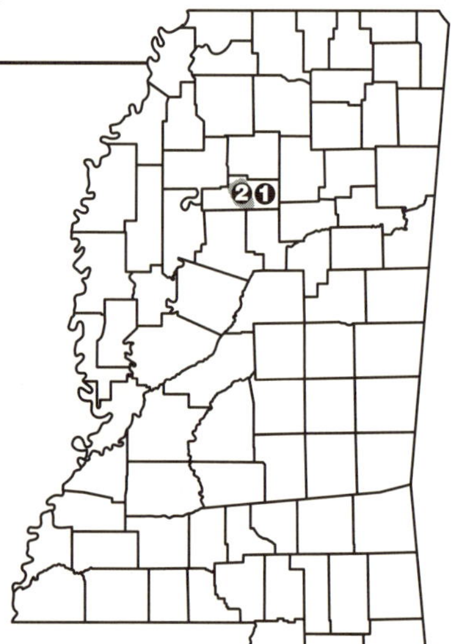

❶ specimen and photo record
❷ confirmed sight record
❸ breeding confirmed
❹ unconfirmed sight record
□ breeding distribution
🅰 distribution statewide

	JAN	FEB	MAR	APR	MAY	JUN	JUL	AUG	SEP	OCT	NOV	DEC
OCCURRENCE												26 ○
MUSEUM*												
WHT*												

*Breeding confirmed by egg, sight, or photographic record.

The male is *bright turquoise blue* above, pale blue below, and blue white on the belly and undertail coverts. The female is gray brown overall with a white belly and undertail coverts. The wings and tail feathers are tinged with blue. The folded wings have a scalloped look with paler edgings on the feathers.

The Mountain Bluebirds I have seen in western states were shyer than our familiar Eastern Bluebird. Their feeding behavior is more active and wider ranging. Insects are captured in flight, but often they *hover* before alighting to capture insect prey.

The Mountain Bluebird nests in tree cavities and man-made structures. Several bluebird box trails I saw along highways in the Rocky Mountain states had active nesting pairs, some of them feeding young. The birds I saw never sang, as they are generally silent except at dawn.

One Mississippi record of this species occurred below the Grenada Lake dam on December 26, 1978. A single male, first seen by Whittington (1980), was actively feeding in typical hovering fashion. Others on the Grenada Christmas Bird Count who saw the bird were Ben B. Coffey Jr., Alice Smith, and W. Marvin Davis. Photographs were taken to substantiate this first record. Other regional records have been reported: three in Louisiana, four in east-central Texas, and overwintering birds in Oklahoma and Missouri.

[Townsend's Solitaire] *Myadestes townsendi*

This thrush is highly migratory, occurring in western coniferous mountain slopes and canyons with rushing streams and waterfalls. It also occurs rarely in the eastern states as an accidental migrant or casual winter visitor.

Only one sight record of this species in Mississippi has been reported. On November 8, 1985, McGee (1986) identified a single bird seen under favorable conditions east of Hickory in Newton County. All field marks were seen, details described, and a comparison was made in good light with a Northern Mockingbird present during observation. McGee had seen many solitaires in western states.

Townsend's Solitaire is almost as large as a mockingbird, but more slender and gray overall with a prominent *white eye ring,* notched tail with white edging on the outer-tail feathers, and *cinnamon buff wing patches.* The bill is comparatively small and bluebirdlike. The breast is darker gray than the mockingbird. Juveniles are heavily mottled on the head, back, breast, and belly. Undertail coverts are buffy. Juveniles also have the cinnamon buff wing marks of adults.

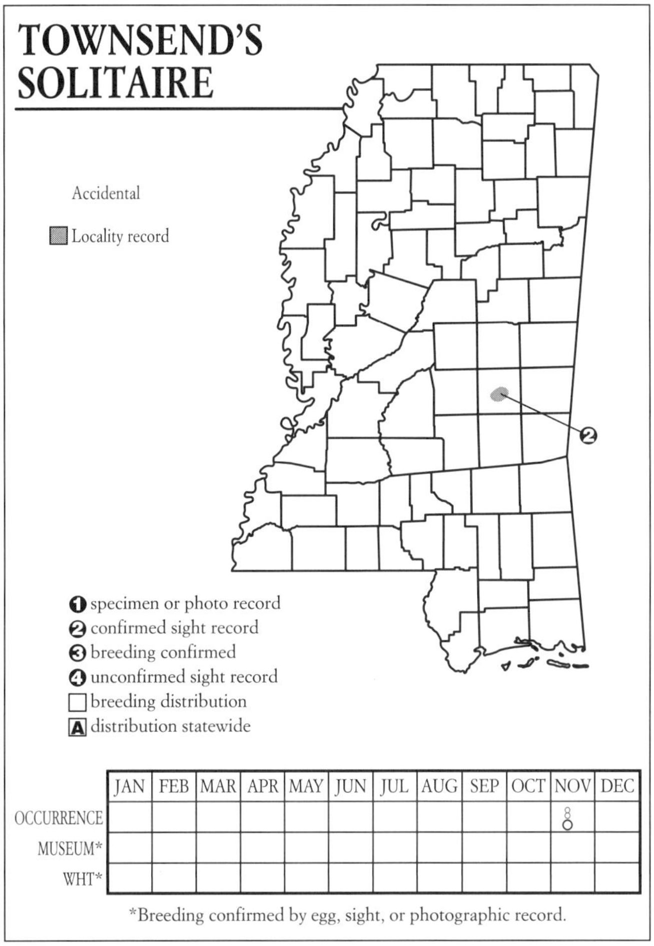

My first sighting of the Townsend's Solitaire was in ponderosa pines on the Uncompahgre National Forest near Norwood, Colorado. We were at a U.S. Forest Service work camp when a bird alighted on a dead pine branch near our tent. My first thought was "mockingbird," but the white eye ring, slender build, upright posture, and small bill identified it as a solitaire.

Later, I saw others on three visits to Telluride, Colorado, and Spearfish Canyon in the Black Hills of South Dakota. I heard the low warbling song in the canyon above Telluride, but it was almost obscured by the rushing waters of a nearby stream and waterfall. The birds were feeding from elevated perches and occasionally hawking after flying insects. Although I was able to photograph a bird at Telluride, all attempts to record the song were futile.

At Spearfish Canyon beside a mountain stream, I spent two mornings trying to record the song of a mated pair. Although I was able to record the shrill *enk* call notes, the birds never sang. However, in response to a playback, one bird sat on exposed tree roots about 10 feet away and called repeatedly for several minutes.

I also saw Townsend's Solitaires in flight at lower elevations where junipers were prevalent. They are known to have a marked preference in winter for juniper berries. Their far ranging migratory and wintering habits mark this species for possible reoccurrence in winter. Its wintertime preference for berries should be remembered when birding where red cedars are abundant.

Veery *Catharus fuscescens*

This thrush is uniformly warm brown on all its upperparts. The buffy throat has a few reddish brown spots, and its sides and belly are noticeably white without any spotting.

The Veery occurs throughout Mississippi as a fairly common spring and fall transient. It appears about the same time in spring and fall as the Gray-cheeked and Swainson's Thrush. Extreme dates of occurrence are April 13 to May 14 and August 30 to October 16. It is usually found alone in or about thickets or underbrush. The song is a series of *veeur, veeur-veer-veer* flutelike notes in phrases that suggest its name. Each phrase progresses down the scale lower than the one before.

The Veery breeds from British Columbia across Canada to Newfoundland, southward to northern Arizona, North

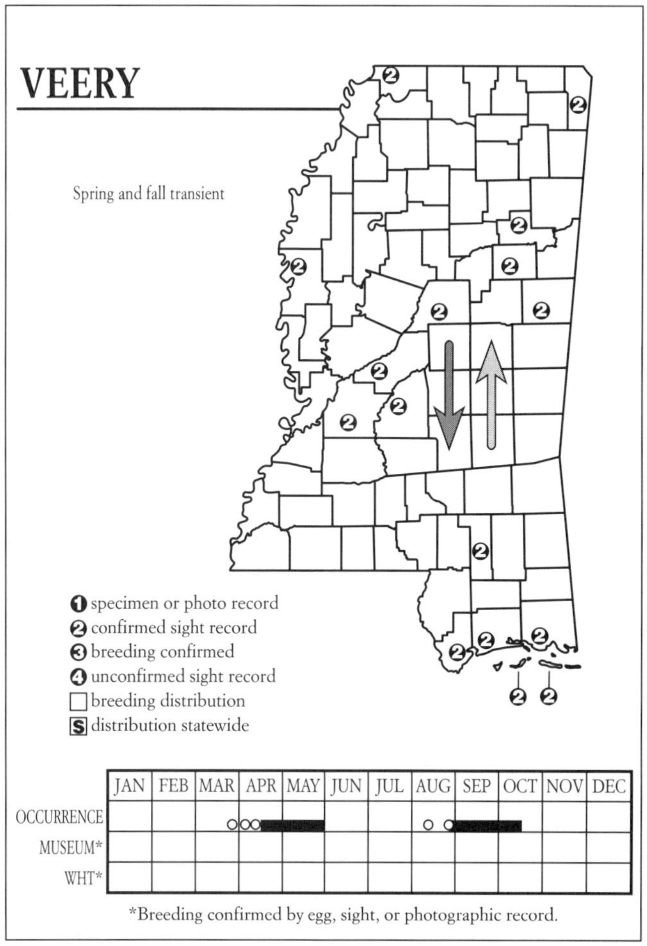

Dakota, northern Ohio, southeastern Kentucky, and in the mountains of northern Georgia. The winter range is from Colombia to southern Brazil.

I experienced the evening song and call notes of this songster on the Chippewa National Forest in Minnesota, on June 12, 1985. The songs were distinctive and lingered long in the memory after hearing it repeatedly that evening. This thrush sings occasionally during the spring migration through Mississippi.

Gray-cheeked Thrush *Catharus minimus*

This thrush occurs only as a spring and fall transient throughout Mississippi. Although less numerous, it is found in the same habitat and at about the same time as the Swainson's Thrush. Extreme dates of occurrence are April 1 to May 31 and September 12 to October 29. There are no winter records of this species in our state.

The Gray-cheeked Thrush is grayish brown on the back with a moderate amount of breast spotting. Its *gray cheeks and an indistinct eye ring* separate it from other brown thrushes. The song of the Gray-cheeked Thrush is similar to the Veery, although softer, more nasal, and rising abruptly at the end.

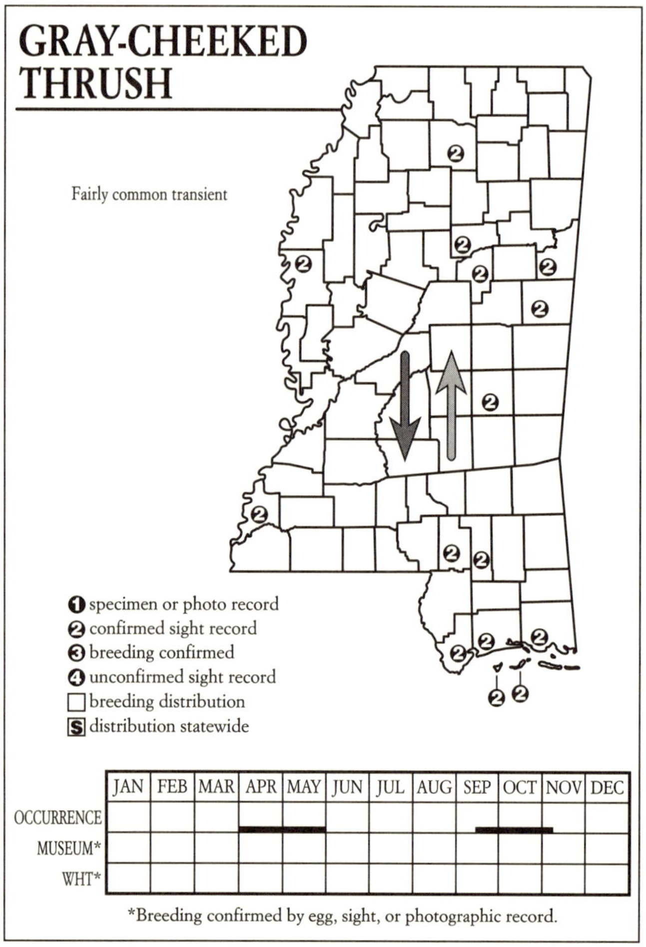

This species breeds from northern Alaska east to northern Quebec and Newfoundland and south to northeastern British Columbia, and eastward to southeastern New York and central New England. It winters in Hispaniola, Colombia, Venezuela, Ecuador, Peru, and northwestern Brazil.

Swainson's Thrush *Catharus ustulatus*

Swainson's Thrush is a fairly common spring and fall transient through Mississippi. First arrivals have been reported as early as March 27, but the main spring passage occurs from about early April to late-May. The latest (anomalous) date of spring departure is a specimen in the MMNS, a bird taken in Yazoo County by Blanche Hamberlin on June 23, 1939 (Gandy and Turcotte 1970). The fall migration occurs from mid-September to the end of October. An anomalous overwintering or early arrival date is that of two birds on February 26, 1950, in Pearl River County. The birds were spotted by Amy Tolman, a consistent and careful observer.

Like the Hermit Thrush and Gray-cheeked Thrush, this species has a dark brown or olive back and moderate breast spotting. It differs from the Hermit Thrush by

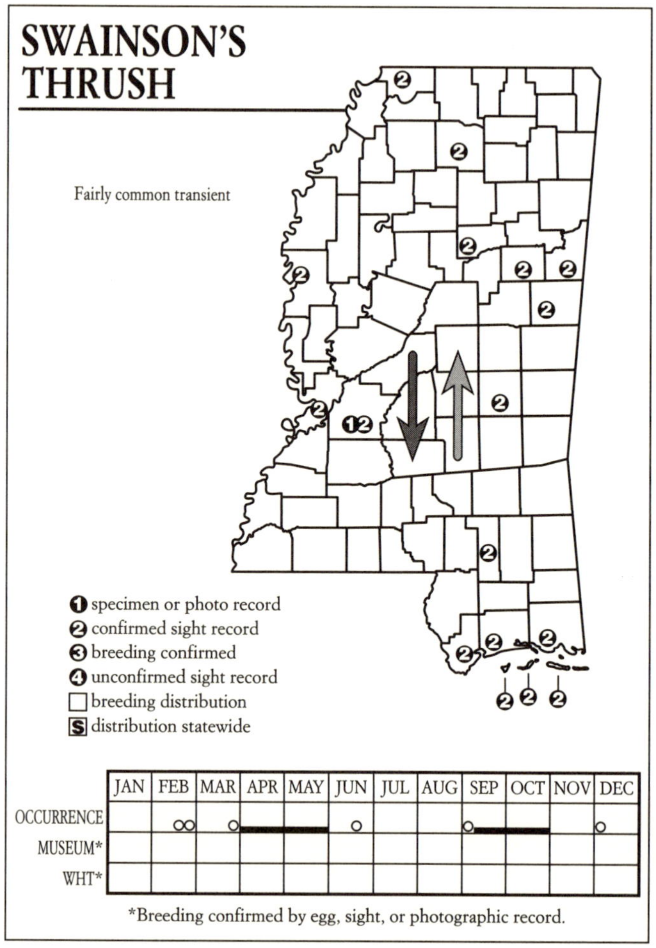

the *absence* of a reddish tail, and from the Gray-cheeked Thrush by having a *buff-colored eye ring and buff cheeks*.

Swainson's Thrush sings on spring migration, although it is usually quiet. Its song consists of a series of flutelike notes in phrases, each one rising to a higher pitch.

The breeding range of this species includes most of the forested regions of Alaska and nearly all of the Canadian Zone in Canada and Newfoundland, extending southward into northern California, Nevada, Utah, Colorado, northern Minnesota, West Virginia, and southern New England. The winter range is from southern Mexico into Peru, Bolivia, Brazil, and Argentina.

Hermit Thrush *Catharus guttatus*

This thrush is a common winter resident throughout the state, with the first arrivals appearing around mid-October. Most have departed by the end of April. The Hermit Thrush is a breeding bird in the northern and western forests. Any wintering *Catharus* species seen in Mississippi is almost certainly the Hermit Thrush.

Field marks are a grayish to olive brown head, neck, and upperparts, and a *reddish brown* tail. The foreparts of the breast are dotted with dark brown, with the sides and flanks more buffy. Underparts are white, but often appear dingy or discolored. A good field clue is the way it flits its wings while at rest and at the same time *jerking its tail upward and then gradually lowering it*. The bird often perches motionless except for the occasional tail and wing jerking.

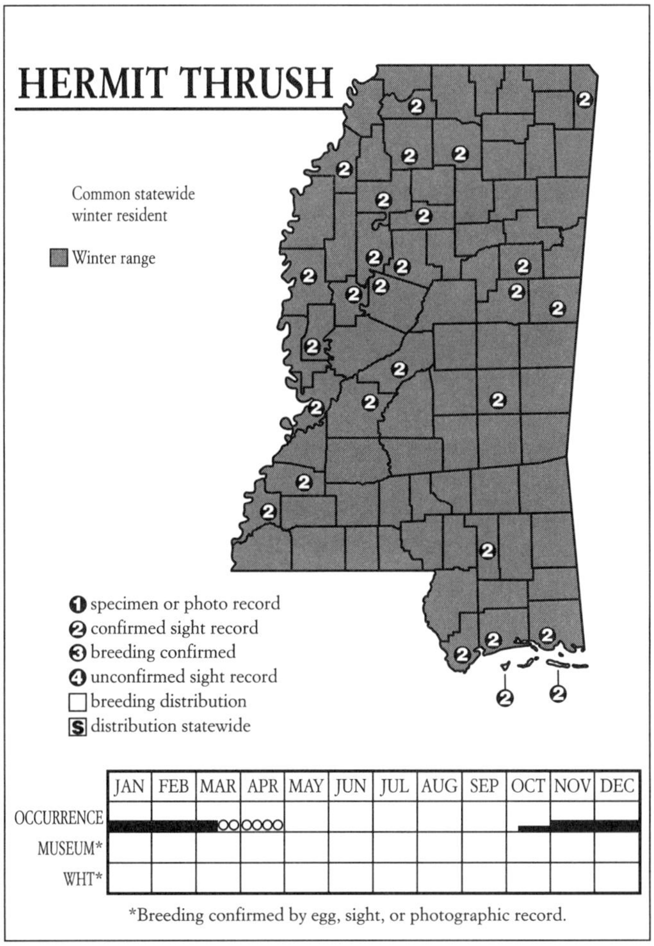

This thrush is one of the finest song birds on its breeding grounds. After vacationing in its breeding haunts, I can fully appreciate its reputation. I have heard it in song in Mississippi during the winter months only twice, once in the evening twilight and once at sunrise while duck hunting in Delta National Forest. The song was impressive, but perhaps I was not close enough to the bird, which was singing high in a tree, to fully appreciate its music. The song was similar to the Wood Thrush, but it was not as loud or rich in quality, and it did not have the varied, sweeter, longer phrases and shorter pauses of the Wood Thrush's song. The call note of the Hermit Thrush is a *chuck*, which is often heard before the bird can be seen.

After hearing and recording the Hermit Thrush on its breeding grounds in Ontario, I have a greater appreciation for its song. The song of a bird singing on a high perch had an ethereal quality with highly variable phrases, pauses, and flutelike notes over a long period, interrupted only by an Ovenbird chanting nearby.

The Hermit Thrush is solitary and seldom seen except in wooded thickets. On several occasions in early spring migration, I have seen numbers of these thrushes along roadsides or the edges of woods, often feeding on the ground. This species frequents moist and brushy places and feeds on insects and fruits during its winter sojourn in Mississippi.

Wood Thrush *Hylocichla mustelina*

The Wood Thrush is a common, statewide summer resident. It is usually found in moist, shaded hardwoods, where it prefers to live near the ground and in understory vegetation. Some birds choose to live near residential areas or in woodland parks or gardens when they find a dense understory for nesting.

The Wood Thrush is heavily marked with large, round, black spots on its white breast. The back and tail are olive brown. The rusty brown head contrasts with its upperparts. It is smaller than a robin, but larger than the brown, transient thrushes and the fall- and winter-resident Hermit Thrush.

The Wood Thrush's song is a beautiful rendition of bell or flutelike caroling. The bird is seldom seen while singing. Once in the woods bordering my lawn, I watched a performance of this songster during a sun shower in late evening. Perched in an elm tree, the bird was in full sunlight while singing in different modulations his delightful phrases of *ee-lay-o-lee* or *ay-o-lee* for several minutes. Although the Wood Thrush usually appears rather nervous, this bird seemed completely relaxed in its surroundings. Its call is a rapidly repeated *quirt*.

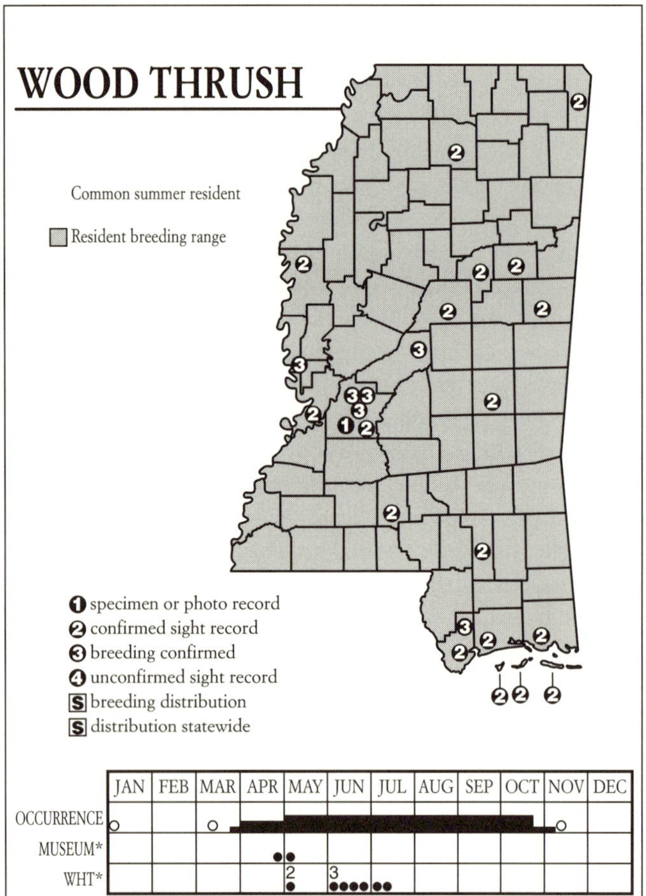

*Breeding confirmed by egg, sight, or photographic record.

Wood Thrushes usually nest from late April through June, building their nest in the understory of moist woods on branches of trees or saplings. Their nest is made of weed stems, moss, grasses, leaves, and paper compacted with a leaf mold and mud cup, and has an inner lining of fine rootlets. The three or four greenish blue eggs make up a clutch. Wood Thrush nests often have streamers of material hanging from the nest.

Wood Thrushes usually arrive in Mississippi during the last week of March. Birds are actively singing when they arrive at their nesting territories. The fall migration to wintering grounds is complete by the end of October. Foods of the Wood Thrush are insects and wild or cultivated fruits, especially red mulberries.

The Wood Thrush is one of several species of Neotropical migratory landbirds that concern biologists today. Unfortunately, this bird has experienced widespread declines in its population across the Southeast and other parts of the United States for many years, according to analysis of Breeding Bird Survey Data (Robbins et al. 1989). This decline came after approximately 10 years of stable or increasing populations for many Neotropical species.

Many researchers believe that fragmentation of large forest tracts has subjected species such as the Wood Thrush to high rates of predation and brood parasitism. In one central Illinois study at Lake Shelbyville south of Decatur, researchers discovered almost unbelievable rates of parasitism. One Wood Thrush nest contained 12 Brown-headed Cowbird eggs, and many nests contained only cowbird eggs. In a similar study in the Shawnee National Forest in Illinois, at one point researchers found 89 Wood Thrush nests that contained a total of 115 Wood Thrush eggs and 198 cowbird eggs (Sullivan 1992). The Neotropical Migratory Bird Conservation Program, better known as Partners in Flight, was formed in 1990 by the National Fish and Wildlife Foundation to better understand what's behind Neotropical migratory bird declines, to halt declines in existing populations, and to prevent declines in species with stable populations.

American Robin *Turdus migratorius*

The American Robin is best known as a fall and winter resident from October through early winter, when great numbers arrive from farther north. They seem to prefer wild fruits and insects available in wooded swamps. Robins form large roosts in bayheads, pine plantations, and thickets, often near congregations of grackles, Red-winged Blackbirds, cowbirds, and starlings.

After winter rains, when the soil begins to warm in early March and when sod insects and earthworms surface, robins are most conspicuous feeding on the ground along roadsides, in pastures, and on lawns as they migrate northward. They can be seen moving about the sod, standing stiffly erect, staring intently at the ground for any slight movement of a worm or insect. The American Robin finds earthworms by watching for their slight movements, such as when they excrete an earth pellet at the surface of a tunnel.

The back of the robin is gray brown, and the back of the head and tail are dark gray. The breast and sides are reddish orange. The lower belly and undertail coverts are white. The throat is white with dark streaks, and the bill is yellow. Juveniles have heavily spotted breasts. Females are paler in color on the upperparts and the breast. Adults and young have white eye rings.

Robins breed commonly in the northern half of the state and locally to the Gulf Coast. Most nesting occurs from mid-April to early June. Breeding occurs most commonly around residential areas, lawns, pastures, cemeteries, and parks. Shade trees are usual nesting places, but they may nest on ledges under house eaves.

The robin's nest usually is placed in a fork or on a limb of a large tree. The nest is built of loosely compacted, coarse grasses and other materials, and lined with a thick cup of mud mixed with grass. The inner lining is made of fine, soft grass. The three to five eggs are "robin's egg blue."

The American Robin's song is a loud, robust, and cheerful warbling or whistling. It can be described by the often repeated phrase *cheer-up, cheerily, cheer-ee* with numerous variations and pauses between each phrase. At times when prolonged, the songs become discordant and screechy. Singing is done mostly in the early morning and near dusk, and seldom during midday. There are numerous calls, but the one most familiar is a *plink, tuk, tuk, tuk.*

Robins breed from the northern treeline limit in Alaska and Canada and south to the northern Gulf Coast and into northern Florida. Their winter range extends casually from the extreme southern parts of the northern states southward to southern Florida and central Mexico.

The proliferation of rotary mowers since World War II has helped this species extend its breeding range southward. Thousands of acres of roadsides, lawns, golf courses, parks, and pastures maintained by frequent mowing provide the necessary sod habitat and nearby shade trees essential for breeding territories. In Mississippi, when people fenced their yards and swept them clean with a brush broom, there were few robins in the cities and towns. Since the advent of mowed lawns and pastures, robins' songs are heard commonly in spring and early summer.

AMERICAN ROBIN

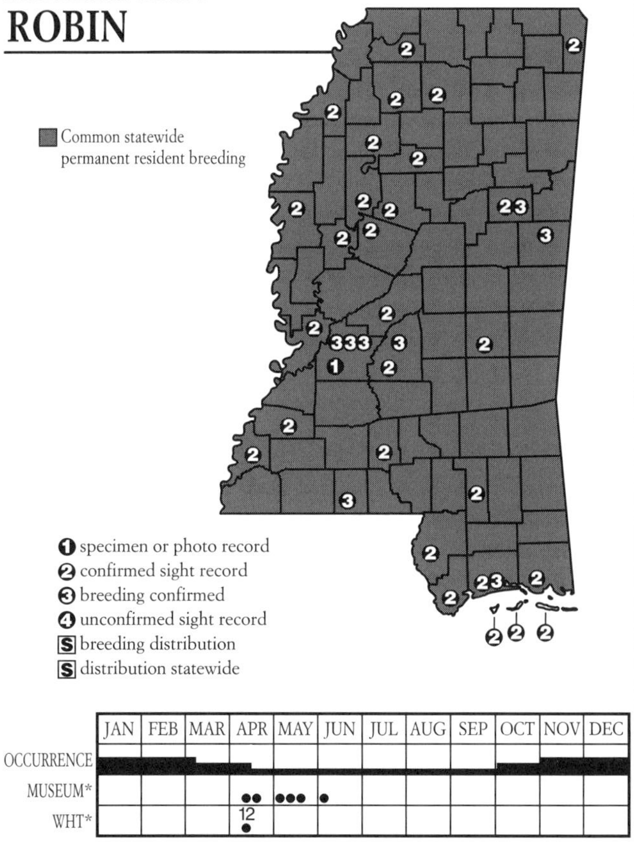

*Breeding confirmed by egg, sight, or photographic record.

Gray Catbird

Mimidae (Mockingbirds and Thrashers)

The Northern Mockingbird, Brown Thrasher, and Gray Catbird are long-tailed, slender, curve-billed, and short-winged birds. They rank high among songsters and are noted for their ability to mimic sounds and the songs of other birds.

The Northern Mockingbird is best known for its imitations. Thrashers repeat song phrases fewer times with pauses in between and with less mimicry. The Gray Catbird mimics even less and does not repeat phrases. Thickets and brushy areas are preferred habitats for these birds, although these mimic thrushes often frequent open places around wood margins and residential areas.

Gray Catbird *Dumetella carolinensis*

The Gray Catbird can best be described as "neat" in its suit of dark gray with its black eyes, black cap, blackish tail, and rusty red patch under the tail. The slate gray catbird is aptly named by reason of its mewing, catlike call notes.

Catbirds range north into the southern Canadian provinces during the breeding season and west into northern New Mexico, western Colorado, Utah, Oregon, and Washington. This species breeds in all of the Gulf and Atlantic states. It winters south into Panama and casually in the South Atlantic and Gulf states.

It is locally common as a breeding summer resident in northern Mississippi, but rare and local as a breeding bird in southern Mississippi. During migration, it is abundant in April and early May, and again in September and October. In winter, the Gray Catbird occasionally can be found retiring in thickets of our southern counties, but very rarely in the northern half of the state.

In May and early June, with the nesting season at its height, catbirds prefer dense cover, such as shrub thickets

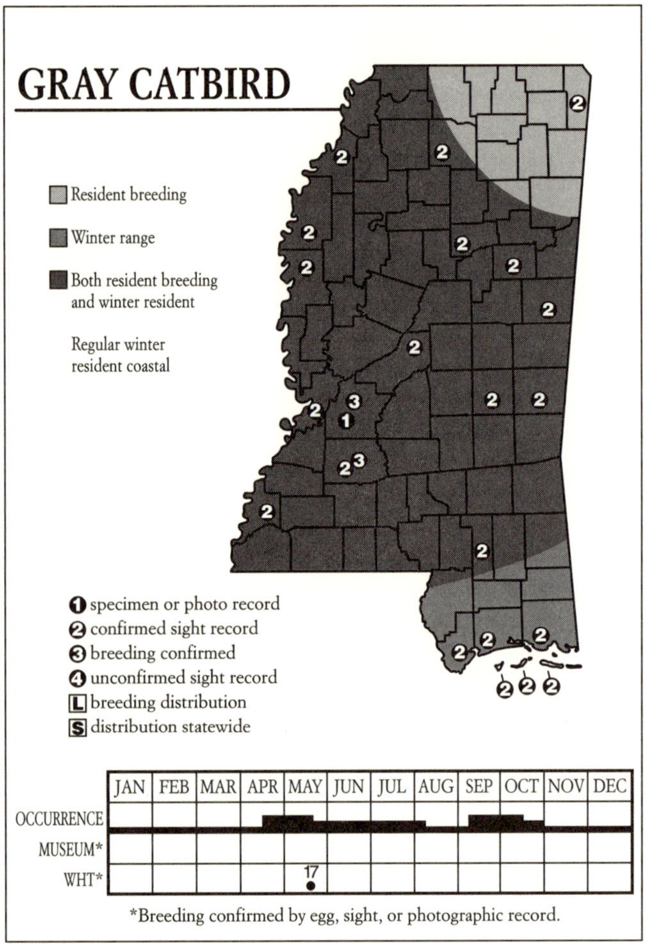

with vine tangles, for a nesting site. I have found nests near Jackson located in shrubs or shrub and vine tangles near dwellings. The nest is a bulky structure of twigs, leaves, bits of paper, bark, and grasses, and lined with rootlets or strips of bark.

The eggs are bluish green, the *greenest* of all native bird eggs. They may number three to five in a set, but usually four. I have found nests located from four to 12 feet aboveground. One nest I saw was in a shrub next to the front porch of a house.

The Gray Catbird is fond of wild fruits and berries and often visits fig and mulberry trees. Fruits and insects are the main items in its diet.

The Gray Catbird song is a prolonged series of squeaky phrases without much repetition, unlike the Brown Thrasher and Northern Mockingbird. The catbird is a poor imitator, but some individuals repeat the sounds and songs of other species. Careful listening is required to detect this mimicry, for there is little or no pause between its song phrases. Since it prefers concealment, it is best located by its squeaky song or catlike, mewing call notes. During the breeding season, it is less shy and retiring and comes close to human dwellings in towns and rural areas.

Northern Mockingbird *Mimus polyglottos*

Northern Mockingbird seems an inappropriate name for a species that the South claims as its own. This name change was made to separate this species from Central and South American forms. It is the state bird of Mississippi, Arkansas, Florida, Tennessee, and Texas. To the people of the South, it is one of the best known and most enjoyed of all songbirds. Nearly every yard, park, or neighborhood has its pair of mockingbirds.

The Northern Mockingbird is an abundant, conspicuous, statewide permanent resident. It is sedentary once a territory is established, but individuals sometimes move or migrate considerable distances. The range of this bird extends westward to northern California, and as a breeding bird its range extends northward into the southern Canadian provinces. It is not abundant in the northern parts of its breeding range and usually retreats from northern areas in winter.

The Northern Mockingbird's identifying field marks are the dark gray above and whitish below, with white in the wings and outer feathers of its long tail. The large white "window" patches under the wings show clearly in flight. At rest it is rather plain looking, showing mostly Confederate gray.

Mockingbirds are highly territorial and strongly defend their boundaries and food sources. They frequently chase robins, Cedar Waxwings, and Purple Finches away from supplies of winter fruit. Wing-flashing display may be another means of territorial defense. I have seen two or more birds square off, standing stiff legged and erect, flashing their white underwing patches, and charging back and forth in a dancing display until one or both tired or yielded.

The wing-flashing is also used to cause ground insects to flush or move. I have seen this work effectively on my lawn. When a grasshopper or other insect moves, the Northern Mockingbird pursues and usually catches it. Wing-flashing while feeding is done most frequently by adults feeding young.

Probably more than any other native bird, the mockingbird is a vehicle for spreading seeds of the fruit-bearing trees, shrubs, and vines upon which it feeds and that pass through its digestive system. I have seen seedlings of hackberry, multiflora rose, rattanvine, cedar, holly, privet, honeysuckle, wild cherry, and pokeweed along fence rows or under shrubs in my yard that could have been planted in no other way than by birds, and most likely by the Northern Mockingbirds frequently seen at these locations.

Wild fruits constitute a major part of the mockingbird's winter diet. Insects are taken when available, more so when plentiful. Damage to cultivated fruits may sometimes occur from this bird's feeding activities, but usually not in serious proportions.

NORTHERN MOCKINGBIRD

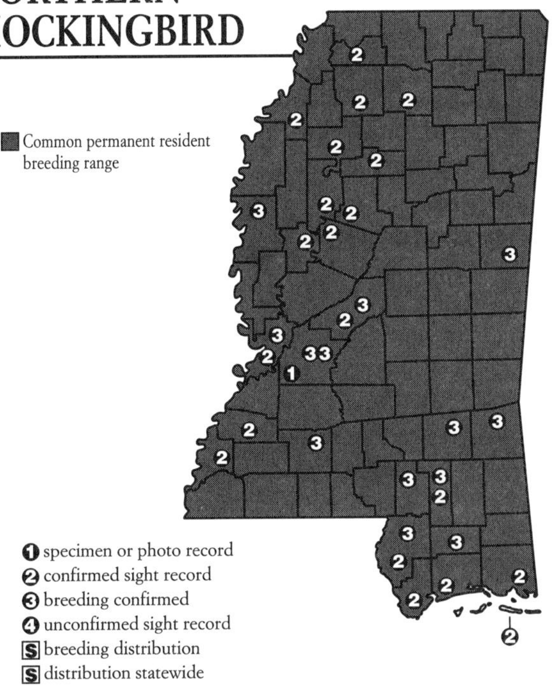

	JAN	FEB	MAR	APR	MAY	JUN	JUL	AUG	SEP	OCT	NOV	DEC
OCCURRENCE	■	■	■	■	■	■	■	■	■	■	■	■
MUSEUM*		●	●	●●●	●●●●	●●						
WHT*				14 ●	2 ●	2 ●						

*Breeding confirmed by egg, sight, or photographic record.

The typical mockingbird nest is placed three to 10 feet aboveground, often in trees, shrubs, or vines near a house. The nest is compactly made of coarse twigs, often thorny ones, and lined with grasses and rootlets. Many of the nests I have seen contained the stems and leaves of a common weed that I call "rabbit tobacco," which has silvery, woolly leaves and stems. The three to five eggs are bluish green, spotted and blotched with shades of brown. Several broods of young may be produced in a breeding season, which extends from March to June or later.

The song of the mockingbird is matchless for mimicry of the songs of other birds, as well as other sounds. I made a two-minute recording of a mockingbird that mimicked the songs of 14 other birds and additional variations of their calls. On the tape the mockingbird mimics and actually converses with a Red-eyed Vireo singing nearby, and then begins to imitate a tree cricket and a tree frog.

Almost without exception, the Northern Mockingbird sings each phrase three or more times without pausing between phrases. It sings usually from an elevated perch, and the bird will exuberantly fly up and drop down to its perch without ceasing to sing. At times it can be seen moving away from its perch and singing while it flies.

Throughout the year, mockingbirds may sing day or night, but are mostly heard during the breeding season and into early fall. This species mimics the distinctive cries of its own nestlings, and for some reason the harsh songs of the Loggerhead Shrike, which it fears. Young and adult "mockers" have a soft whisper song of their own, which is indescribably beautiful, often rendered while in concealing vegetation. They also have a harsh, scolding call suggestive of the bird's fighting temperament.

Recently, I made a recording of a Mockingbird singing at Richland. This bird in our yard, apparently an old pro, mimicked nearly every bird in our neighborhood: a total of 31 species of birds' songs, with many individual song variations, and two tree frog voices were in this bird's repertoire. I carefully listed all of them while listening to playbacks of the recording. Can anyone top this record for mimicry by a Mississippi mockingbird?

Brown Thrasher *Toxostoma rufum*

The Brown Thrasher is the state bird of Georgia. For those who like the color brown, this could be their favorite bird. It is a common, statewide, breeding permanent resident, even occurring on the barrier islands of Mississippi Sound, where it also nests.

In fall and winter, the Brown Thrasher appears to be more common. During these seasons the birds are more reclusive, retiring to vine-covered thickets, brier patches, hedgerows, and similar dense cover. It is then that they spend much time on the ground and are found in the company of towhees, White-throated Sparrows, and other ground-dwelling birds.

In early spring when plum trees blossom, the Brown Thrasher establishes its breeding territory. The male mounts a favorite high perch and begins his delightful song. Singing continues until a pair bond is formed and the nest is completed. The male then sings less frequently until another breeding cycle begins.

The thrasher's spring song almost rivals that of the mockingbird. It is a loud, continuous series of phrases repeated once or twice (seldom more) and punctuated by distinct pauses between phrases. While singing, the long tail characteristically points straight down.

The call note of the Brown Thrasher is a smacking sound like a loud kiss. Its alarm call, repeated when the bird is disturbed at the nest, sounds like *tcheeola*. The soft, purring *wheeoo* notes are heard more in the fall and winter when thrashers go to roost and at daybreak.

Although capable of mimicry, Brown Thrashers do not imitate other birds to any great extent. I made a recording of a singing male in my yard, and on that five-minute tape I could detect by careful listening the mimicry of only three birds: the Common Flicker, Chuck-will's-widow, and White-eyed Vireo.

BROWN THRASHER

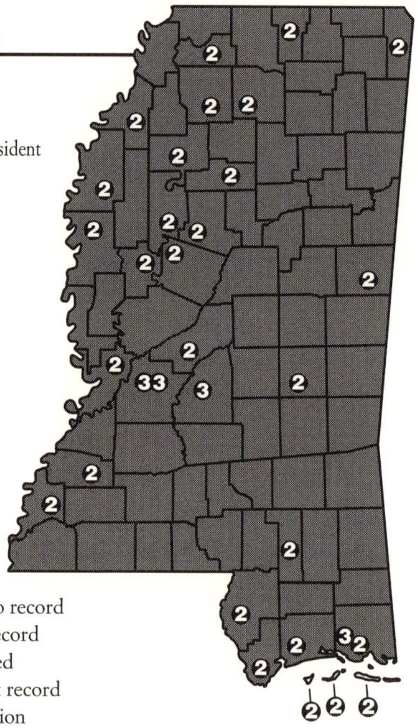

Common permanent resident

Breeding range ■

➊ specimen or photo record
➋ confirmed sight record
➌ breeding confirmed
➍ unconfirmed sight record
[S] breeding distribution
[S] distribution statewide

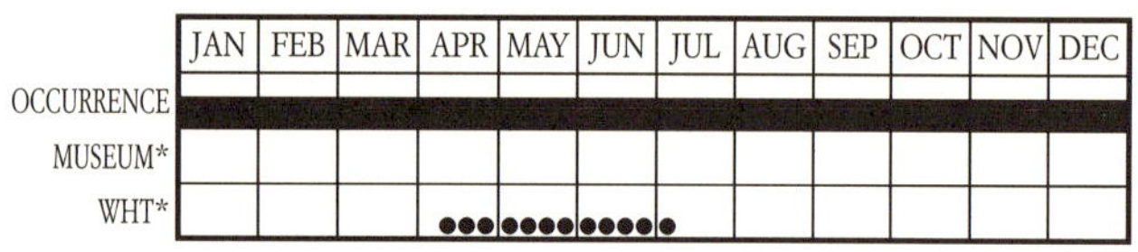

*Breeding confirmed by egg, sight, or photographic record.

This long, slim bird is a rich reddish brown on its upperparts and tail, with two prominent whitish wing bars. The underparts are yellowish buff and heavily streaked with dark brown. Its bill is long and slightly decurved, and the eyes are glaring and yellow ochre.

Thrashers do much of their feeding on the ground while walking or hopping. They use their long bill for turning over leaves or thrusting them aside. I have seen thrashers use their strong bills to hull acorns and sunflower seeds by pounding them into the ground. On several occasions, I have watched them use the mockingbird's wing-flashing technique for finding insects on the lawn. Their food is mostly insects, but they consume large quantities of wild and cultivated fruits when available.

Nesting begins in late March and may continue until late in June. The Brown Thrasher's nest is a large structure of sticks or twigs with leaves, coarse grasses, and an inner lining of rootlets. The nest is concealed in bushes, tangles of vines, and often in shrubbery near houses. Thorny trees or bushes are preferred nesting locations.

The nest is placed from three to 10 feet aboveground. Only once have I seen a nest placed on the ground, this one being at the base of a bush in a pear orchard. The three to five eggs in a clutch are pale bluish white, finely and evenly sprinkled with small, reddish brown spots.

Brown Thrashers breed northward into southern Canadian provinces, west into central Texas, east of the Rocky Mountains, and south into southern Florida and along the Gulf Coast. The winter range is north to Oklahoma and east to Maryland, but extending less regularly into the more northern states.

American Water Pipit

Motacillidae (Wagtails and Pipits)

Birds of open country, these ground-colored and ground-loving birds have long, thin, straight bills; rather long tails; and long, pointed wings. Wagtails and pipits walk rather than hop.

Two species of pipits occur in Mississippi: American and Sprague's Pipits. In winter the American Pipit is found on muddy or rocky shores; plowed fields; or bare, open ground or pastures. The Sprague's Pipit is an uncommon species found on grasslands or airports. Its outer-tail feathers are white, somewhat resembling the light-colored Vesper Sparrow in superficial appearance, but the Sprague's Pipit walks and bobs its tail differently.

CITRINE WAGTAIL

Accidental visitor

One Mississippi record

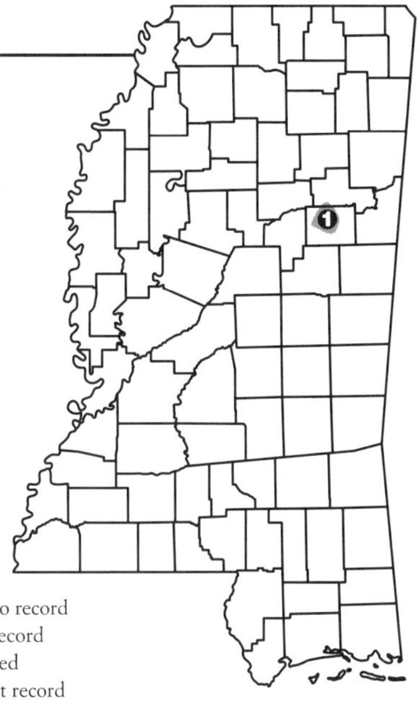

❶ specimen or photo record
❷ confirmed sight record
❸ breeding confirmed
❹ unconfirmed sight record
☐ breeding distribution
☐ distribution statewide

	JAN	FEB	MAR	APR	MAY	JUN	JUL	AUG	SEP	OCT	NOV	DEC
OCCURRENCE	31 ○											
MUSEUM*												
WHT*												

*Breeding confirmed by egg, sight, or photographic record.

[Citrine Wagtail] *Motacilla citreola*

Terence Schiefer found this "once in a lifetime" bird on January 31, 1992, at a sewage lagoon near Starkville in Oktibbeha County. It remained only until the next day, but was seen by others and a good photograph was obtained. This first eastern North America record of doubtful origin (on the basis of the photograph) appeared to be a Citrine Wagtail, a species that breeds in far eastern Europe and has never before been recorded in North America (Stedman 1992).

An Alaskan form of Yellow Wagtail, *M. flava tschutschensis,* breeds in western Alaska and occurs as a casual migrant on the California Coast. Asian and Eurasian Wagtails occur as migrants on the Aleutians and Pribilofs and rarely on western coasts of Alaska. The White Wagtail, *M. alba,* is rare to uncommon as a breeding bird of northern coastal Alaska.

The Yellow Wagtail is slender, long legged, long tailed, and olive gray above with yellow underparts and a *yellow supercilium.* The Alaskan form has a *white supercilium* and a speckled breast band. The Citrine Wagtail has yellow underparts, blue gray upperparts, and a *yellow head* and *neck* (Peterson et al. 1967). Females and juveniles are duller than males. The Yellow Wagtails intergrade where ranges overlap, so field identification is nearly always difficult.

American Pipit *Anthus rubescens*

The American Pipit is a fairly common, winter-resident bird of open country, preferring the barren ground of open plowed fields, clipped cotton fields, shorelines, and short-grass pastures. It arrives in October and may be seen as late as early May.

It frequently occurs in flocks numbering from 30 to more than 100. When flushed, the group ascends and circles in undulating flight, uttering their characteristically sharp *pit-pit* calls. They will remain in flight for long periods, usually returning to the same place or nearby.

The American Pipit is dark gray and brownish above, buff colored, and rather heavily streaked with brown below. The bill is thin and black. Their distinctive field characteristics are the outer-tail feathers that flash in flight, the

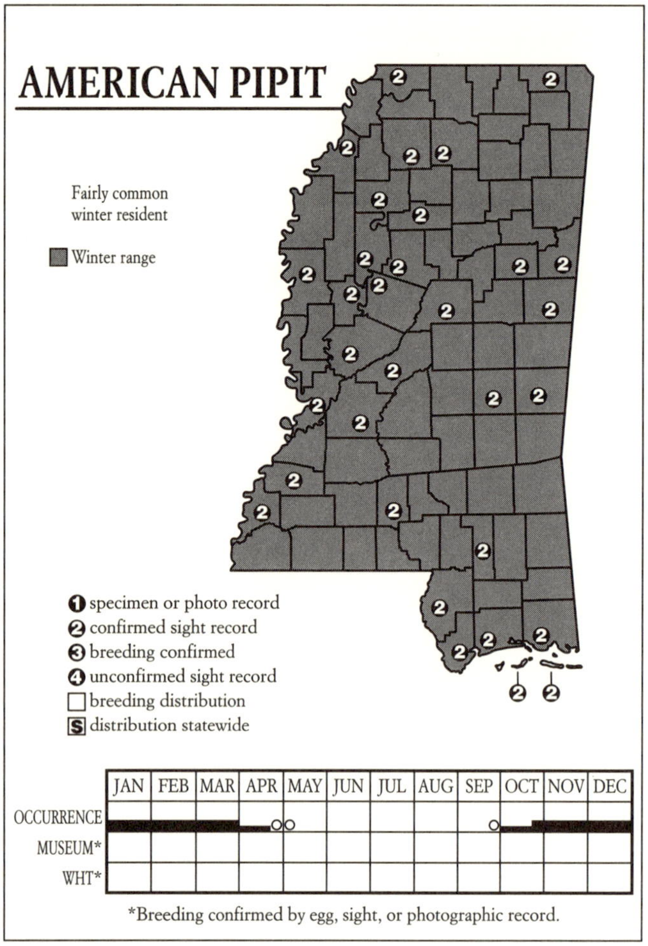

habit of circling, and the flight call notes. These birds seldom call while on the ground. They characteristically *wag their tails* up and down while walking or at rest.

The American Pipit breeds in the Arctic and alpine regions of western mountains. It winters into southern Florida and along the Gulf Coast into eastern Mexico and Guatemala.

As a boy, my first encounter with pipits was on the school ground in Clinton. The schoolyard and ball field were nearly bare of grass. One wet, winter day a flock of these birds circled and landed. They remained several days during the Christmas holidays. I knew them from a picture I had seen in the Chester A. Reed *Pocket Field Guide to Land Birds*.

More than 50 years later, I was fortunate enough to encounter and photograph one of a pair with a fledgling. While on a vacation with my wife in July 1984, we were driving in the alpine zone of Wyoming approaching Montana's Beartooth Pass when we saw a small bird carrying food descend near the roadside. I returned to the spot and found the fledgling pipit. The parent bird, in beautiful yellowish buff plumage, became very agitated. I returned to the car for my telephoto lens and camera and made a color photo of the adult sitting on a stunted evergreen bush.

Sprague's Pipit *Anthus spragueii*

Sprague's Pipit is an uncommon fall and winter visitor, occurring locally in short-grass pastures, airports, and levees. Its presence in Mississippi has been observed by only a very few people. Secretive and selective in its habits and habitat, this streaked grass dweller usually occurs alone, in pairs, or in small groups. It is heavily streaked above, and the white underparts are lightly streaked with brown on the upper breast. The two pairs of outer-tail feathers are white. The legs are yellowish, and the bird walks, never hops.

The first Mississippi record for this species was a U.S. National Museum specimen taken in an open field near Bay St. Louis in Hancock County, on January 1, 1902, by Allison (1900, 1906a). Another bird seen in the same area on February 11, 1902, was also reported by Allison. Vaiden (1953b) took two specimens in Bolivar County on January 4, 1953, and a third on January 11, when two others were found partly eaten. Later the Vaidens (Newman 1955) found this species at Perthshire in Bolivar County on October 31, 1954.

Coffey Jr. (1961a) identified this species at Sanders Field at Walls in DeSoto County on January 4, 1953, and again on

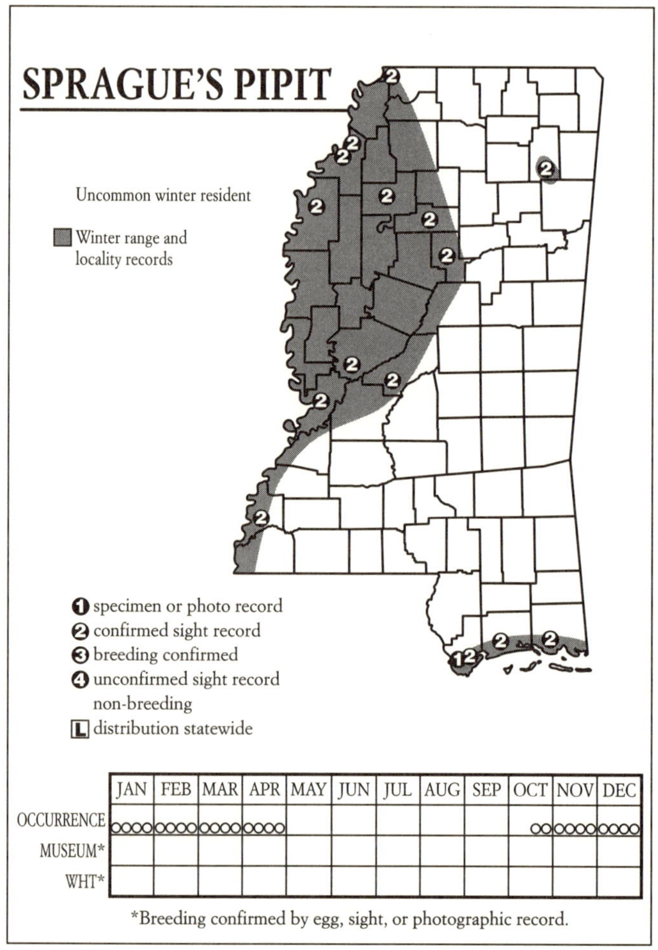

October 23, 1954 (Newman 1955). Ben and Lula Coffey Jr., R. Demett Smith Jr., and others made subsequent observation records at Walls. The extremes of occurrence there were October 23 and April 26. Ben and Lula Coffey Jr. later found the Sprague's Pipit at the Tupelo airport in Lee County, in Coahoma County between Moon Lake and Friars Point, north of Glendora in Tallahatchie County, south of Canton in Madison County, near Winona in Montgomery County, and at Bruce Campbell Airport in Madison County, Fletcher Field in Coahoma County, Vicksburg Airport in Warren County, and the Adams County Airport. W. Marvin Davis (pers. comm.) found a Sprague's Pipit at Grenada Airport on January 24, 1970. Recent Gulf Coast sightings by Judith Toups were on November 13 and 29, 1984, at Gulfport Harbor in Harrison County and Port Bienville in Hancock County (Hodges and Jackson 1984).

Ben B. Coffey Jr. (1961a), who observed this species in Mississippi more than anyone, described the bird's actions and song:

> The Sprague's Pipit gives abrupt, hoarse, high-pitched notes, usually in twos, threes, or singles. It has a very bounding flight, usually high and sometimes moving out of sight, but generally returning to drop like a Horned Lark on the same field. The flight is sometimes low, especially in late season, late in the day, or when the wind is strong; on these occasions it is usually silent.

It may be too late in the game for me to observe the Sprague's Pipit on its wintering grounds. Much walking or running over nearly barren, thin-grass, open fields or airports is required to find and flush them. I think I have seen this bird flush ahead of my dog while quail hunting. The actions described by Coffey Jr. certainly fit the bird on several of these occasions. I took it for granted that such observations were "stink-birds" (sparrows), which some dogs will point in patches of "love-grass" (*Aristida* spp.) in large open fields.

I positively encountered this bird on the Lostwood National Wildlife Refuge in North Dakota, on June 19, 1985. The refuge biologist, Robert K. Murphy, directed me to where I would find the Sprague's Pipit the next day. I was recording the song of a Grasshopper Sparrow the next morning when this pipit arose from the short-grass prairie hillside to make its aerial flight song and return nearby.

The song was incessant as long as the bird was in view. It consisted of a long series of *tzee, tzee, tzee* notes. I saw another in the alpine zone of Estes Park, Colorado. While walking across open ground to watch a marmot sitting among boulders, a Sprague's Pipit flushed and flew over and across the Continental Divide and below the horizon.

Bombycillidae (Waxwings)

Cedar Waxwing *Bombycilla cedrorum*

No other bird can match the "cedarbird" for trim, silken perfection in its blending of brown, dark blue gray, yellow, and black feathers. Dominated by a long, expressive crest and accentuated by tear-shaped, red, waxy spots on the tips of the secondaries, this elegant bird is nearly always seen in Mississippi in flocks. It is about the size of a bluebird. The back, breast, and crest of the waxwing are shades of silky brown. The wings and tail are dark blue gray. The belly and a band at the tip of the tail are lemon yellow. A velvety black mask extends from the black bill back through the eye. The chin, feet, and legs are also black.

Waxwings arrive in small numbers as early as mid-October, but they are erratic autumn visitors and usually are not common until November or December. Their numbers increase in winter and peak about the time redbud and flowering crab apple trees bloom in mid-March. Then voracious feeding flocks arrive, numbering as many as several hundred or more. They feed on fruits of berry-bearing trees and shrubs in woodlands and towns. Flocks will suddenly appear and completely strip all fruit from mistletoe, Japanese privet, pyracantha, holly, hackberry, cedar, and other wild or cultivated plants.

In spring, they will strip and eat the petals from flowering crab apple trees. Flocks sometimes remain until late

Cedar Waxwing

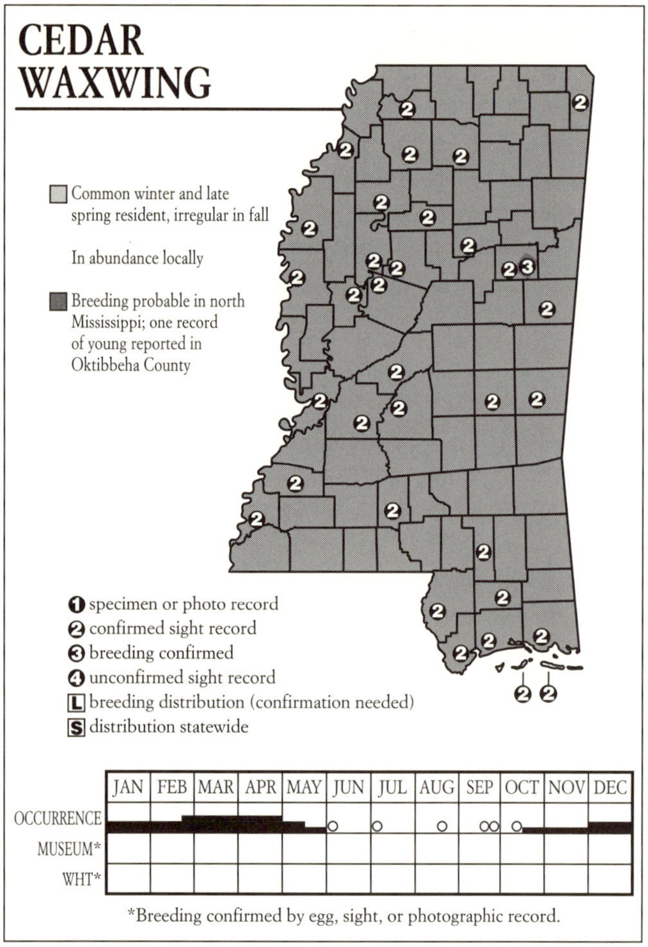

May or early June, feeding on red mulberries, a favorite fruit. Insects are also taken. I once saw a flock of waxwings near Hazlehurst feed on flying insects. They looked and behaved like flycatchers, darting out from their perches to catch insects and returning to eat. I also watched a flock of 50 or more waxwings completely strip the berries from a privet hedge in my yard, then descend and clean up all that had fallen on the ground.

On two occasions, I encountered Cedar Waxwings in flocks feeding in pine trees in Jackson. I thought this was rather strange behavior, until I examined a low pine limb and found the terminal branches covered by a large, brown, scale insect that the waxwings were eating.

The Cedar Waxwing flies in slightly undulating, compact flocks. When not actively feeding, they also rest in compact groupings, sitting very erect and motionless. They sometimes pass berries along to adjacent birds. The call note is a high-pitched, lisping monotone.

There is one sight record of possible nesting and a sighting of immature young in the Starkville area, and waxwings are known to breed in northern Alabama, Tennessee, and Kentucky. Their range extends from Alaska and Canada south into western Panama. The breeding range extends north into southeastern Alaska and the northern parts of the southern provinces of Canada east into Newfoundland, south into the mountains of northern Georgia and northern Alabama, and west into northwestern California and western Oregon.

Over a period of 13 consecutive years, a flock of waxwings in late winter roosted in a southern red oak tree over my driveway. The flock arrived around sunset and sat on the higher limbs, then suddenly they would all fly and perch in the brown leaf clusters that remained on the lowest limb. They occupied their roost posture well before dark and never seemed disturbed by a flashlight beam later at night.

Laniidae (Shrikes)

Loggerhead Shrike *Lanius ludovicianus*

"Catbird," "butcherbird," or "French mockingbird" are common names identifying this species. A conspicuous bird usually seen perched on wires or fence rows along roadsides, it is found commonly as a permanent resident throughout Mississippi. It can be mistaken momentarily for the Northern Mockingbird, which it resembles somewhat in general coloration. It differs, however, by its large head, black face mask, lighter gray color on the upperparts, short hooked beak, shorter tail, and contrasting black-and-white wing and tail marks. The young have slight vermiculations on the breast feathers. The shrike flies with wingbeats too fast to count and usually low to the ground until it rises abruptly to a perch.

The Loggerhead Shrike derives its name from the large size and shape of its head. It feeds mostly on insects including grasshoppers, crickets, and beetles, but will sometimes take larger animals such as mice, small birds, frogs, small snakes, and lizards. Larger prey is often carried and impaled on thorns of bushes or on barbed wire fences, hence the name "butcherbird." The small feet of the shrike

Loggerhead Shrike

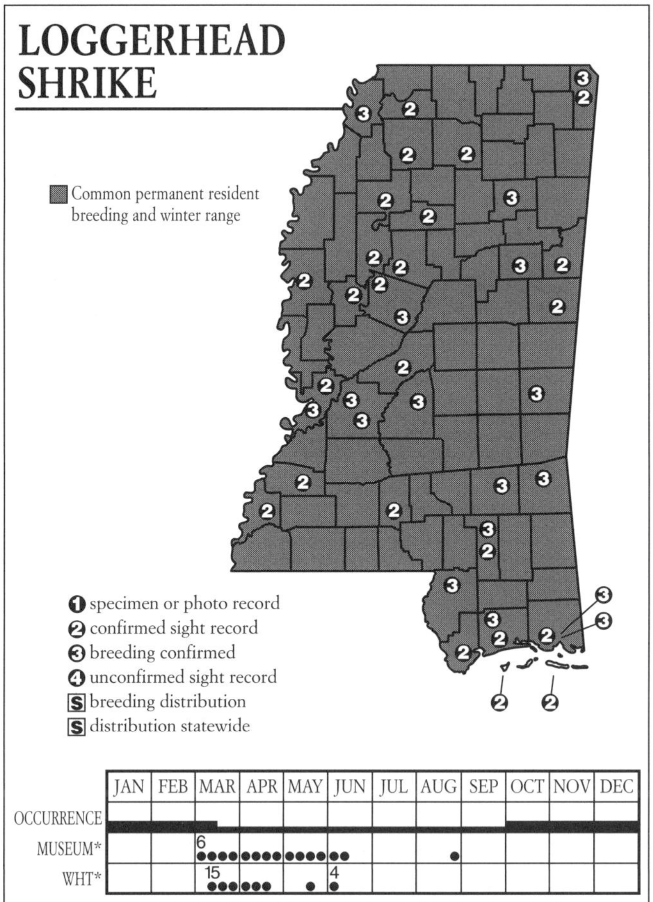

*Breeding confirmed by egg, sight, or photographic record.

are of no assistance in catching or holding prey. After impaling food, the shrike proceeds to tear it apart without the use of its feet.

The call of the Loggerhead Shrike is a series of harsh, unmusical shrieks. In spring and summer, males sing. The song consists of guttural, unmusical phrases interspersed with more musical notes that are not unpleasing.

I once made a recording of this shrike's song, and when played back in the presence of small birds, they immediately became quiet and went into hiding. The playback also called up another shrike that flitted about low to the ground, wings beating rapidly. The small birds remained absolutely quiet for a considerable time after the shrike had disappeared.

The Loggerhead Shrike is an early nester, beginning in March and April, with renesting occurring through June. Warriner recorded a nest with young in Alcorn County on July 2. Burleigh recorded an active nest near Saucier on March 6.

Its nest is built of tightly packed and woven coarse weed stalks, twigs, and grasses almost invariably lined with finer grasses, hair, string, cotton, wool, thistle down, feathers, or other soft materials. Preferred nesting sites are thorny or dense shrubs or vine-covered fence rows and trees around pastures or other open areas. The nest is usually from eight to 20 feet aboveground. The eggs are laid in sets of five or six, but sometimes only four. They are gray or buff in ground color, heavily and variously spotted or splotched with shades of yellowish brown to umber, and sometimes with blackish scrawls on the larger end.

Although the shrike occasionally kills small birds such as sparrows, kinglets, or warblers, its food habits are mostly beneficial. Shrikes are noted for perching on low bushes and wires along roadsides. From here they watch for insects and pounce to catch them on the ground, then fly to an elevated perch to eat. I once watched a shrike catch insects on my front lawn from a low perch on a tree limb. This bird made 10 round trips in 12 minutes to catch and feed insects to six young in a nearby nest.

Sturnidae (Starlings and Allies)

European Starling *Sturnus vulgaris*

The European Starling was introduced and established in this country when 100 birds were imported and deliberately released in New York City's Central Park during 1890 and 1891. From this release, the starling has spread and now has overrun this country.

This bird family is found throughout Eurasia, Asia, and Africa, and introductions have been made on Pacific islands

European Starling

EUROPEAN STARLING

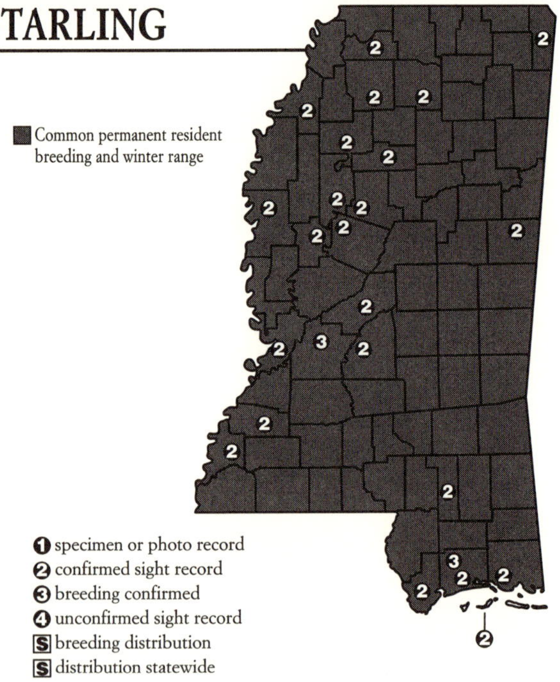

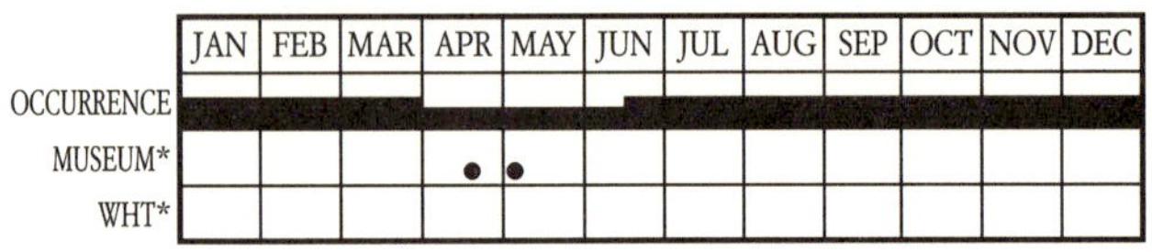

*Breeding confirmed by egg, sight, or photographic record.

and elsewhere. A related species, the Crested Myna, is established in British Columbia and individuals have appeared in Oregon and Washington. Common Myna that have escaped from captivity are established in southern Florida.

The species was first recorded in Mississippi by Townsend (1926) in the Vicksburg National Military Park on January 26, 1926. My first sighting of starlings was in the late 1920s when I was about 11 years old. A flock of 40 or more appeared during the winter while the ground was covered with snow and ice. They fed on the berries of cedar trees near our home in Clinton. The appearance of this exotic species helped to arouse my interest in birds, an interest that has continued to grow.

The starling is an interesting and attractive bird in appearance and behavior. Although it generally is regarded as a nuisance, its food habits are mostly beneficial to humans. On the positive side, the bird's food consists largely of insects and their larvae. It is a nuisance where large roosts congregate on buildings or in shade trees, where their droppings damage property. European Starlings compete with hole-nesting birds and appropriate their nesting cavities.

The starling is probably responsible for a decline in Northern Flicker and Red-headed Woodpecker populations in parts of their range by displacing them from their nest excavations. Starlings will sometimes destroy the nests and eggs of these and other cavity or box-nesting birds such as the Wood Duck, Great Crested Flycatcher, Purple Martin, and Eastern Bluebird. Along with hordes of blackbirds, starlings consume livestock feed and help deplete some of the natural food supplies of other more attractive birds.

Moreton (1943) observed starlings feeding on the backs of cattle near Brookhaven. Cottam (1944) commented on Moreton's observation that similar habits were seen in New Zealand, where starlings were also introduced. They ate the ticks and maggots on sheep. Probing for ox warbles in the backs of cattle on the Great Plains also was reported by Cottam.

The starling is stocky, somewhat like a meadowlark. Its flight is fast and direct. The wings are long, and the tail is short, giving the bird a triangular shape in flight, like a Purple Martin. The starling walks or runs instead of hopping.

In alternate plumage, both sexes appear to be black, but a close inspection reveals a gloss with iridescent purple and green. The bill is usually dark, but changes to a bright, lemon yellow during the breeding season. The legs are a dull, red color. The young are brownish gray until a complete postjuvenile molt occurs in late summer, and fall and winter adult, basic plumage is attained. The birds appear grayish, but actually they are heavily speckled with cinnamon or white spots edged with black. Wear and fading of the feathers cause the spots to disappear by late winter or early spring.

The call of the starling is a harsh *tseeer.* The song is a jumble of harsh, grating sounds interspersed with rattles, whistles, clicking noises, and mimicry. The singing bird usually displays itself and drops and flutters the wings. I have heard it mimic the bluebird, Eastern Meadowlark, bobwhite, and Killdeer. I have a tape recording of a starling's song with almost perfect imitations of the Eastern Bluebird's melodious warbling.

Although starlings are permanent residents, they do migrate. In winter, they gather into huge flocks and sometimes roost with blackbirds and cowbirds. Feeding flocks disperse over the countryside. W. Marvin Davis (pers. comm.) saw about 12,000 in a flock on September 6, 1987, in Washington County. Favorite feeding places are pasture sod and lawns, where they walk and probe for insects and their larvae.

Once in late winter, I watched a feeding flock probe a wet lawn amid great activity and saw them locate and consume large numbers of "grub worms" or ground beetle larvae, leaving their probe holes everywhere they went. I also have seen flocks take flight and pursue birds of prey as if in play, circling and wheeling about in unison to make a striking, ever-changing aerial display. In such displays, they fly in tight formation, (called "murmuring").

The starling now nests commonly throughout Mississippi except in large wooded areas. The nest is built in tree cavities or buildings, woodpecker holes, or nest boxes. Four or five pale blue eggs are laid in a nest, which is composed of green leaves, lichens, and all sorts of debris piled sufficiently high to almost fill the cavity and form a nest cup. Robins (1934) reported an early nesting record for the starling in a building cavity near Guntown. Starlings were nesting in Jackson in the late 1930s on the Old Asylum property and the Old Capitol Building. Burleigh (1945) recorded a nest with five fully fledged young at Lyman on April 7, 1943.

White-eyed Vireo

Vireonidae (Vireos)

Vireos are small, greenish olive- or gray-backed birds, which are generally drab in appearance and may or may not have wing bars. The bills of vireos are larger than warblers and slightly hooked. Otherwise, although less trim, vireos resemble some of the wood warblers (Parulinae). In proportion to body size, the head is also larger than the warblers'. Vireos live in wooded areas, but some prefer brushy locations. Of the nine vireo species recorded in Mississippi, four are known breeding birds. Vireos build pendent nests in trees or bushes suspended from the fork of twigs.

The Philadelphia Vireo is less often seen in the spring, but occurs as a regular fall transient in September and early October. Bell's Vireo occurs rarely in Mississippi, with only two specimen records and a few sight records. The Blue-headed Vireo is infrequently seen as a fall and winter resident. It departs in April or early May for its northern breeding grounds.

White-eyed Vireo *Vireo griseus*

This vireo is commonly known as "swamp-bird," and it is an inhabitant of undergrowth and brushy thickets. It is more often heard than seen, and is frequently found in stream bottoms and openings in uplands having brushy thickets. The White-eyed Vireo is small, olive backed with yellowish sides, and has two conspicuous white wing bars, a white throat, and yellow "spectacles" about the eyes. The latter two marks help confirm identification of this species. The iris of adults is white, but young birds have dark eyes.

The White-eyed Vireo is a common, summer-resident, breeding bird and rarely winters inland and on the Gulf Coast. It arrives in spring around mid-March and departs for its wintering grounds by late October. On the coast, this bird sometimes appears in waves when landfall occurs

WHITE-EYED VIREO

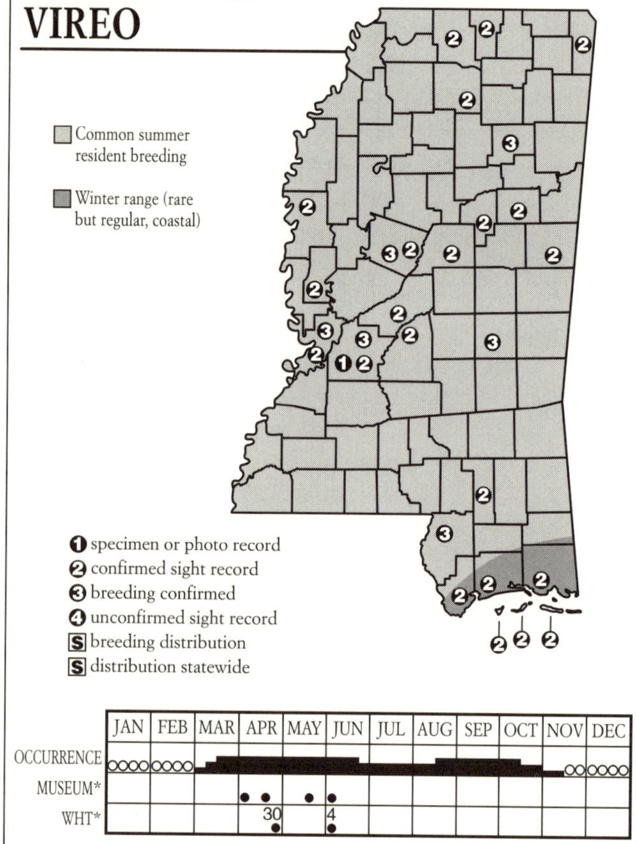

*Breeding confirmed by egg, sight, or photographic record.

in unfavorable weather. The northward passage of these birds on the way to more northern breeding territories occurs before the end of April.

The song is loud for so small a bird. Roger T. Peterson (1980) describes the song as "an emphatic *chic'-a-perweeoo-chick'*," but I have noted many variations by individual birds. The first note is always an emphatic spitting sound, and the last one is nearly always similar to the first.

The White-eyed Vireo has a reputation for mimicking other bird calls, but I have never detected this in its songs. It is very active for a vireo, but its song and call notes are unmistakable once they are learned. I look forward to hearing its familiar voice during the last week in March when we go hunting for morel mushrooms. The redbud is past its glory and the dogwood is beginning to show white when this bird usually arrives.

The nest is a pendent or semipendent structure, loosely but neatly made and held together with spiderweb. It is composed of thin, light-colored strips of bark, dried leaves, dried grass, cane leaves, dried moss, and decayed wood. The edge of the cup is nearly always decorated with bits of dried green moss, and decayed wood is used for decoration. The nest is lined with dried grass or plant fibers.

Nesting occurs from early April through June. Three or four eggs constitute a clutch. They are white and sparsely speckled with brown or blackish spots or scrawls about the large end. The nest is usually suspended about waist high between a terminal forked twig of a bush in or near a dense thicket. Brooding birds are very tame on the nest.

The White-eyed Vireo is one of the more site-specific vireos in its nesting habits. In 1993, David L. Watts with the Department of Wildlife, Fisheries and Parks banded 13 of these birds as part of the Monitoring Avian Productivity and Survivorship (MAPS) program. Of the birds banded, four White-eyed Vireos were caught again by Watts in 1994, almost all within the same mist nets as the year before and in the same habitat.

The MAPS banding project is part of a nationwide effort called Partners in Flight (PIF) that is attempting to understand what's behind the decline in populations of many species of Neotropical migratory birds. According to analysis of breeding bird survey data, the White-eyed Vireo is declining in many parts of its range in the Southeast and is a species of concern among PIF biologists.

Bell's Vireo *Vireo bellii*

This vireo is little known or extremely rare in Mississippi. Only two collection records and a few sight records for this species exist. Burleigh (1945) collected a specimen on September 18, 1939, at Deer Island in Harrison County. The other specimen was taken in Washington County by Ralph Caston on May 11, 1973, according to a record on file in the MMNS.

Ben B. Coffey Jr. saw one on July 30, 1940, along U.S. 90 between Ocean Springs and Fountainebleau in Jackson County. W. Marvin Davis (pers. comm.) identified a singing male at the same location in Tunica County on June 6, 1971, and June 27, 1972. Larry Gates reported seeing a Bell's Vireo at Hattiesburg on August 11, 1979 (Jackson and Schardien 1980a). Gene and Shannon Knight identified a singing bird south of Oxford on August 29, 1987, as a Bell's Vireo.

Bell's Vireo is the western counterpart of the White-eyed Vireo, and the ranges of these species overlap in the Midwest. Both prefer dense thickets, preferably along stream bottoms. Its warbling song with rising and falling inflections, *cheedle-weedle-wee; cheedle-weedle-woo,* as if asking and answering a question, is distinctly different from the song of the White-eyed Vireo.

The Bell's Vireo always has *black eyes,* but only the young of the White-eyed Vireo have dark eyes. The Bell's wears faint *whitish "spectacles"* compared to the yellow ones of the White-eyed Vireo. The *sides are faintly washed with yellow.* The White-eyed Vireo has bright, yellowish sides. Both have white wing bars.

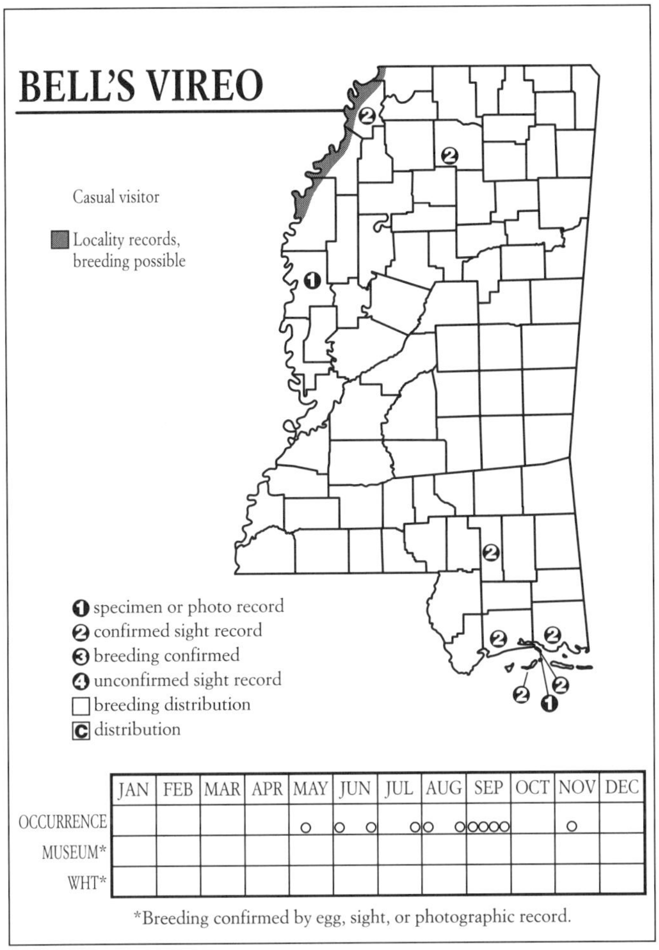

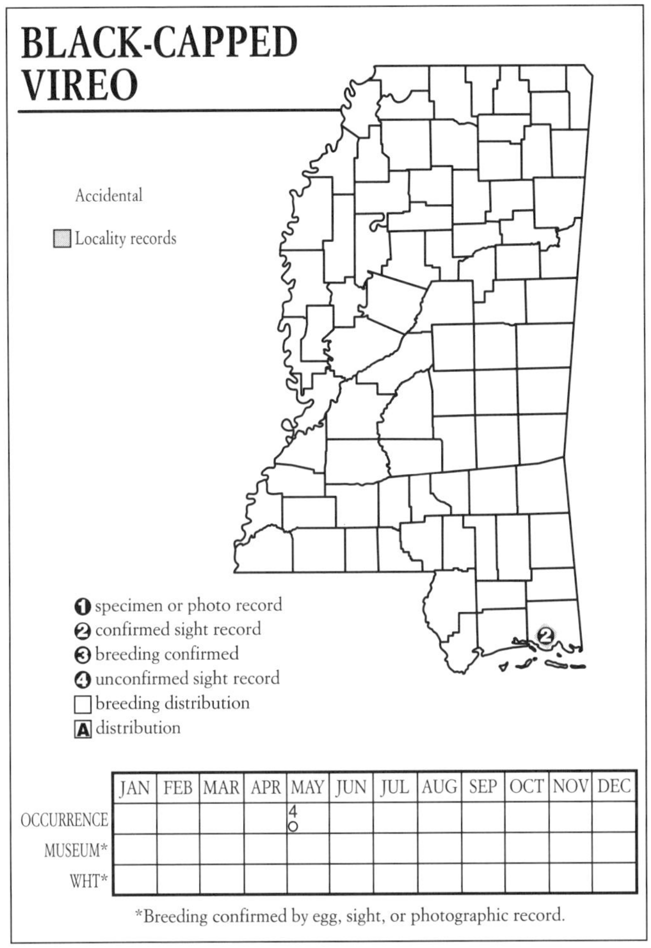

[Black-capped Vireo] *Vireo atricapillus*

This vireo was recorded at Bellefontaine Beach near Ocean Springs on May 4, 1978. Larry Gates and Judith A. Toups identified a male and a female in scrubby growth following rainy weather with strong, westerly winds (Imhof 1978; Jackson and Cooley 1978). Occurrence in Mississippi as an accidental visitor is possible during migration, most likely during inclement weather with prevailing westerly winds.

This small vireo was locally common as a breeding bird in west-central Texas and southwestern Oklahoma. Recently, it has been listed as endangered due to habitat loss and cowbird parasitism. It occurs in thickets of cedar-oak and scrub oak, and is hard to locate except by its song.

The adult male has a shiny, *black cap* and contrasting *white eye ring* and lores. The female's small size and dark gray head with white lores and eye ring are distinctive. The juvenile is more brownish above, but otherwise resembles the female. Upperparts of adult plumage are olive. Underparts are white below with yellowish flanks. The wing bars have a yellowish wash.

Blue-headed Vireo *Vireo solitarius*

This vireo occurs in Mississippi in fall, winter, and spring. It is a northern species, common as a summer resident in northern mixed hardwood and coniferous forests. The Blue-headed Vireo appears in Mississippi in early October. In the southernmost part of the state, it is a fairly common winter resident. In northern Mississippi, it occurs uncommonly in almost all wooded sections in winter. It is sometimes found with Pine Warblers, Yellow-rumped Warblers, Carolina Chickadees, Tufted Titmice, and other small insect eaters, but is rarely seen with others of its kind while wintering here. The latest occurrence date is May 18, recorded by Vaiden (1947) in Bolivar County.

The Blue-headed Vireo, once called the Solitary Vireo, is easily identified by the blue gray head and greenish or grayish back, yellow flanks, and white "spectacles," wing bars, throat, and belly. Though usually silent, it sometimes sings during warm winter and early spring days. The song is similar to the Red-eyed Vireo, although slower and higher pitched. The Blue-headed has scolding call notes that, with the bird's slow and deliberate movements, help locate and identify it in the field.

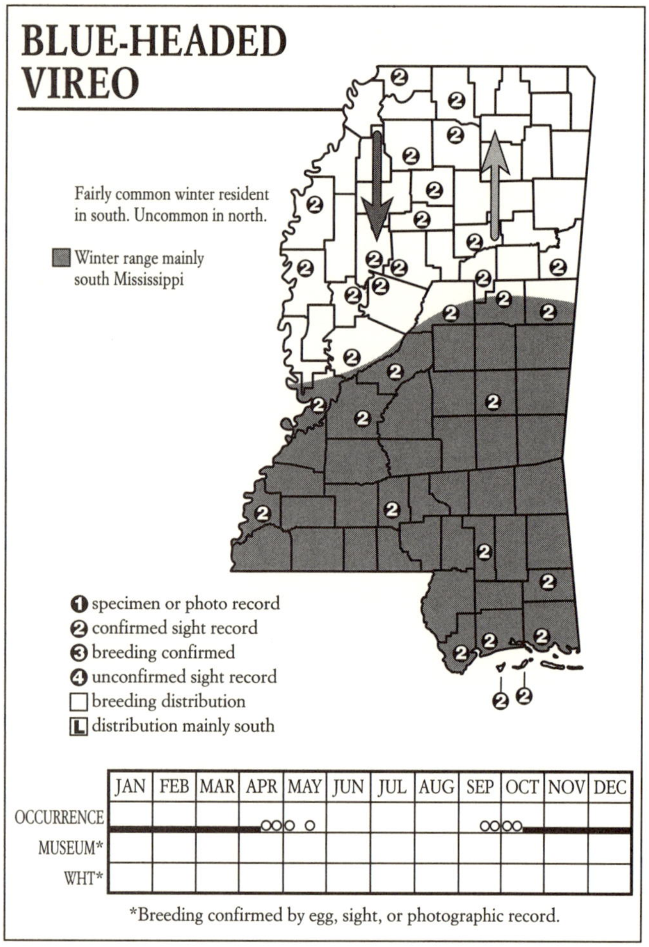

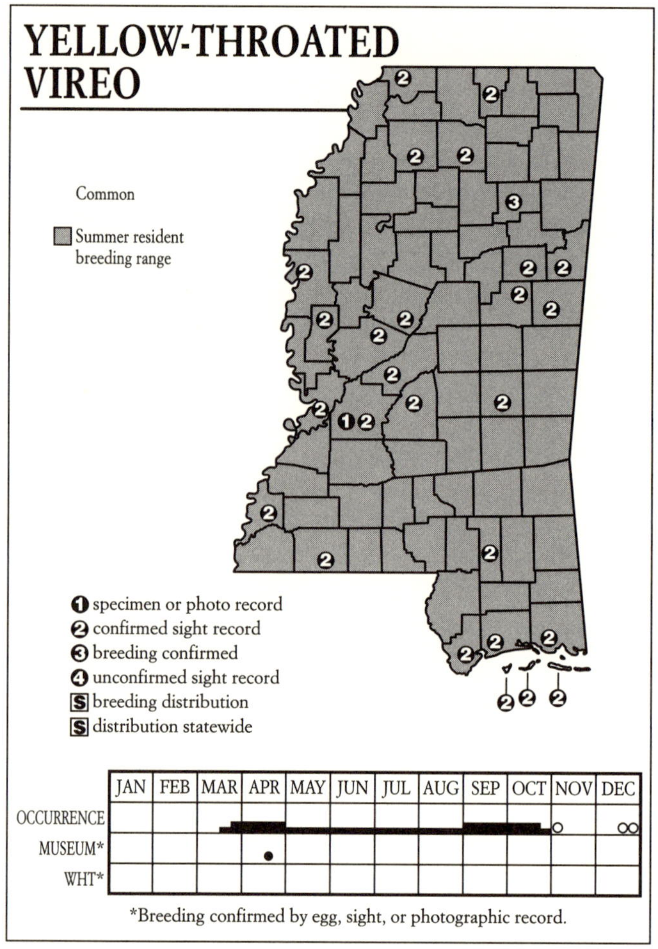

Yellow-throated Vireo *Vireo flavifrons*

Identifying marks of this vireo are bright yellow throat and breast, greenish back and head with yellow "spectacles," gray tail, and wings with two white bars. Its song is distinctive, though similar to the Red-eyed Vireo. The song of the Yellow-throated Vireo is louder and punctuated with longer pauses between the slurred musical phrases that are repeated over and over again in a regular order. Lowery Jr. (1974) describes the song phrase as *sweetie, come here!*

The Yellow-throated Vireo is common throughout the state from mid-March or early April through October and is frequently encountered as a summer resident in woodlands. Near the Gulf Coast, it is found uncommonly and locally as a summer resident. A coastal winter sighting was recorded on December 17 in Jackson County (Toups and Jackson 1987). Terrie Fairley saw one bird at Hattiesburg on December 28 and 30, 1979 (Jackson and Schardien 1980a).

This vireo is usually heard before it is seen as it is a bird of the top canopy in drier upland stands of oaks or mixed pine and hardwoods. It is common on the ridgetops of the Loess Bluff forests.

Although this vireo nests here, its breeding in Mississippi was not confirmed by collection or photograph for many years. I have seen two inactive nests of this vireo near Clinton. The nests were on the outer ends of post oak limbs about 25 feet aboveground, partially suspended between forked twigs and identifiably ornamented on the outside with bits of lichens held in place by cobwebs. The eggs of this species are creamy white and variously spotted on the larger end with shades of brown.

On April 19, 1962, I saw a pair of Yellow-throated Vireos completing a typical nest 30 feet high on a limb of a sweet gum tree (Turcotte 1962b). This observation was made in Chickasaw County near Davis Lake east of Houlka.

Warbling Vireo *Vireo gilvus*

This plain-colored vireo without wing bars is difficult to identify because it *lacks* any prominent field mark. The *absence* of a black line, but *presence of a white line,* above the eye, its greenish gray upperparts, and white throat and underparts are its distinguishing characteristics. The best clue to this bird's identity is its warbling song, which is not broken into phrases. The song is unlike other vireos and is

Warbling Vireos are fairly common summer resident breeding birds in cottonwoods and willows around oxbow lakes and the batture lands between the mainline levees along the Mississippi River.

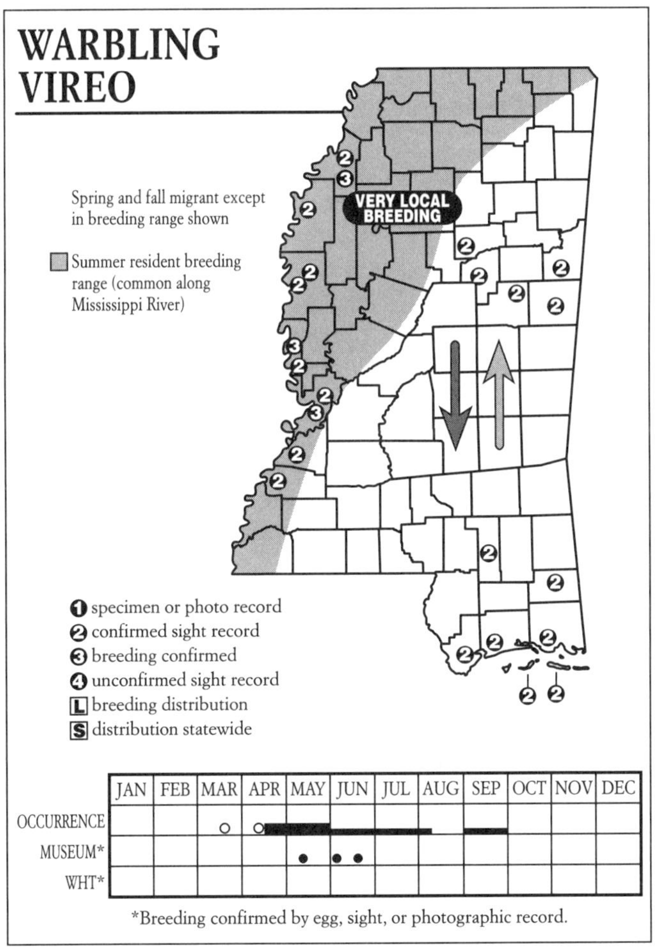

similar to the Orchard Oriole. The warbling notes are in ascending continuous phrases repeated over and over without variation or pause. This vireo is noted for singing while incubating on the nest.

The favored habitat is in large cottonwood and willow trees around the edges of large bodies of water. In Mississippi, the Warbling Vireo is infrequently seen except in the vicinity of the Mississippi River. I have found it to be a fairly common summer resident around Eagle Lake, Chotard Lake, and on Tennessee Bar in Warren and Issaquena Counties, and have found two nests. It is most frequently heard and seen in large cottonwood and willow groves in the batture between the levees, along borrow pits, and beside the Mississippi River and its oxbow lakes.

This species arrives mostly in April and nests in May and June in cottonwood, hackberry, or other trees. It is a fairly common nesting species. The nest is a compact, pendent structure suspended in the fork of twigs located from 20 to 50 feet aboveground. The eggs are white and lightly spotted with brown.

M. G. Vaiden collected a male specimen in Bolivar County on May 27, 1937, near its nest. Two sets of eggs in the MMNS were taken on May 21 and June 16, 1940, both in the Sherard area of Coahoma County. The bird departs soon after the nesting season. The latest sight record was September 23 (Toups and Jackson 1987).

Philadelphia Vireo *Vireo philadelphicus*

This species was named and described by John Cassin in 1851 from a specimen taken in a woodland near Philadelphia, Pennsylvania. In Mississippi, it apparently occurs only as a rare spring transient and a fairly common autumn migrant. It usually frequents the middle and upperparts of hardwoods, and because it is difficult to identify, it probably is more common than records indicate.

Based upon collection and sight records in the MMNS, the Philadelphia Vireo occurs as a fall transient during late September and the first three weeks in October. Spring records date from late April and May. My experience with this species is limited to several fall sightings. On the morning of October 2, 1965, I collected 10 specimens at the base of the WJTV and WLBT television towers near Raymond in Hinds County (Turcotte 1966b). A heavy fallout of birds had occurred the previous night, and 222 dead birds were picked up and identified, totaling 39 species, and including 19 species of warblers and four species of vireos.

This vireo is greenish gray above, has a faint eye stripe, is without wing bars, and has *pale yellowish underparts.* The Warbling Vireo and Red-eyed Vireo also lack wing bars, but they have no yellow on the breast, as does the

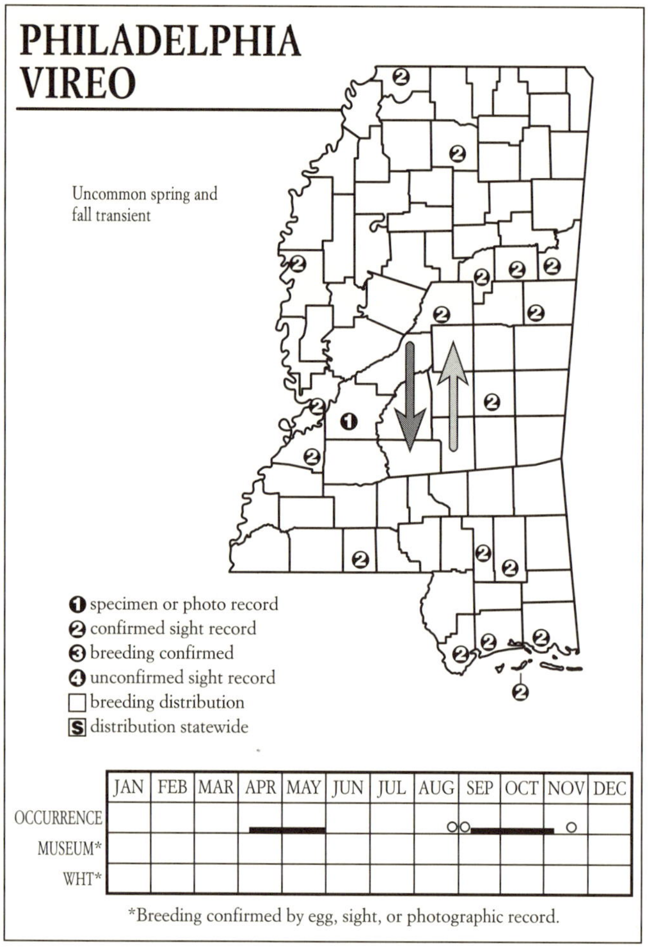

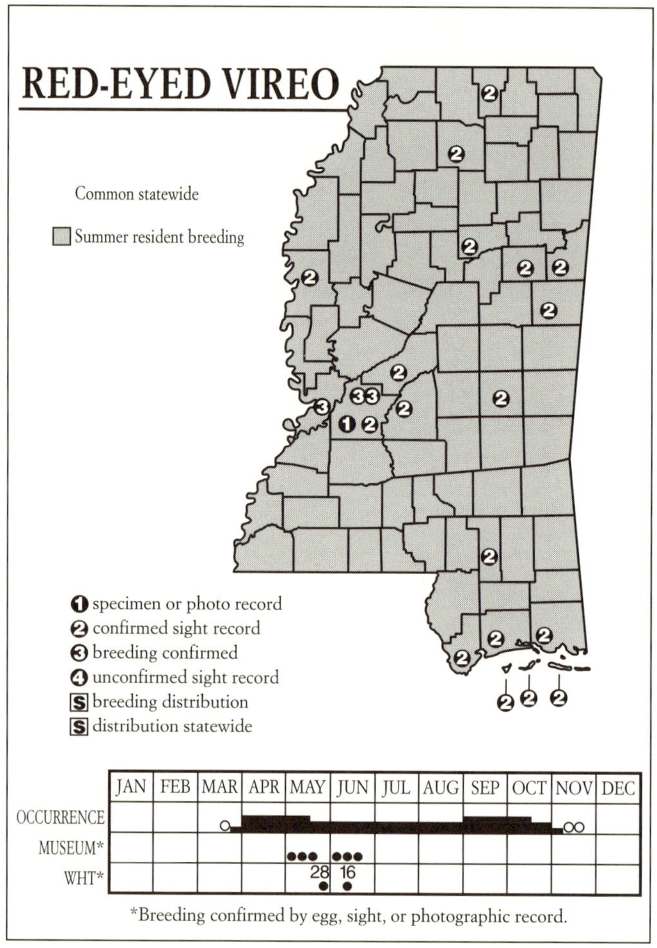

Philadelphia Vireo. The Yellow-throated Vireo has prominent wing bars, prominent yellow "spectacles," and very bright yellow on the throat and breast.

During the fall migration, the Philadelphia Vireo often feeds on fruit. On October 9, 1971, I observed six birds at the Grand Gulf Military Park in Claiborne County busily feeding upon the ripened white fruits of the swamp dogwood. One or two at a time would fly down to the small dogwood tree to feed, then return to the higher branches of surrounding trees.

Red-eyed Vireo *Vireo olivaceus*

This vireo is said to be the most abundant bird in eastern deciduous forests. It is commonly called "preacher-bird" because of the long duration of its persistent singing interrupted only by short pauses between phrases. Except for a blue gray cap, it is olive green above with no wing bars. It has white eye stripes bordered with heavy black lines. The iris is bright red and the underparts are white.

The Red-eyed Vireo lives in the upperstory of bottomland and upland hardwoods. This bird is often difficult to see while it is singing on a perch or as it feeds in foliage. It is a summer resident throughout most of the state except in pine forests. Spring migrants appear mostly after mid-March and continue until mid-May. Fall migrants occur from August to late October.

The Red-eyed Vireo builds a semipensile nest made of flexible strands of bark fibers and grasses, usually placed on the outer end of a horizontal branch of a hardwood tree or sapling. It is held together between forked twigs by caterpillar silk or spiderwebs. Most nests are ornamented on the outside and underneath with the white egg cocoons and webs of spiders.

Three or four white eggs, which are spotted with brown about the larger end, constitute a clutch. The dates for nine egg records for the Red-eyed Vireo deposited in the MMNS extend from May 6 through June 20.

The Red-eyed Vireo's song is robinlike in phrases each lasting about one second with frequent variations. Pauses between phrases are very short and not nearly as deliberate as in the song of the Yellow-throated Vireo. Probably no other bird sings as long and monotonously throughout the day as does the Red-eyed Vireo on its breeding territory.

[Black-whiskered Vireo] *Vireo altiloquus*

This vireo is a subtropical species, fairly common in southern Florida, mainly along both coasts and in the Everglades and Florida Keys. It breeds in mangrove swamps and hammocks and occurs as a casual visitor to inland Florida. Along the northern Gulf Coast to Louisiana, it occurs as an accidental spring visitor.

The Black-whiskered Vireo is similar to the Red-eyed Vireo except that it has a *larger bill* and *black whisker stripe*. The song is deliberate in phrases like the Red-eyed, but hoarser and more robinlike.

The first Mississippi sight record was by Larry and Terrie Gates, Judith Toups, and Joe Magee on April 9, 1982, in a yaupon thicket and a nearby live oak at close range at Bellefontaine Beach in Jackson County (Gates and Izral 1982). Larry Gates saw the first bird in a yaupon thicket on a sand dune. The next day, John Izral identified another Black-whiskered Vireo in woods about a mile farther, without prior knowledge of the first sighting. Peggy and Jack Smith reported a third sighting near the first location. On April 11, 1982, Margaret Halstead saw one at her yard in Ocean Springs near the beach.

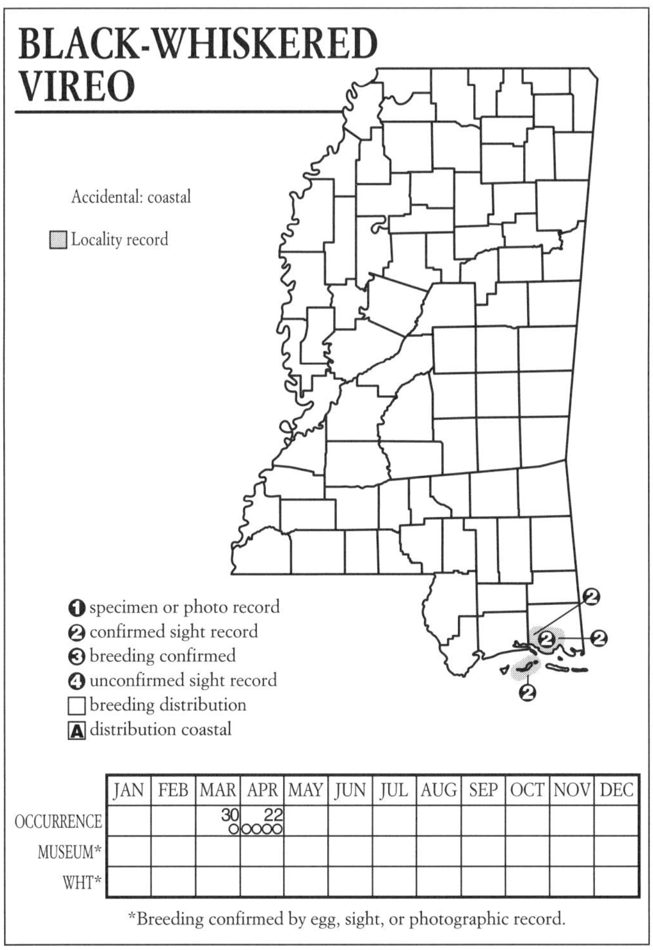

Other Black-whiskered Vireos were seen by Tom Butra and Ted Simmons in early April 1986 on East Ship Island. On March 30, 1987, Chita Cassibry and James Spence saw another at Davis Bayou in Jackson County (Toups and Jackson 1987).

Numerous other spring records have been made along the Gulf Coast of Alabama, Florida, and Louisiana. This species should occur on the coast during spring migration when strong northeasterly or southeasterly winds and bad weather may precipitate fall-outs.

American Redstart

Emberizidae (Warblers, Sparrows, and Allies)

This large and diverse group includes tanagers, grosbeaks, buntings, sparrows, orioles, and blackbirds. They are genetically related species, but they differ greatly in color, behavior, and habits. The American sparrows and wood warblers are unique to the New World.

Wood warblers (Parulinae) are small, active, brightly colored, and have distinctive song patterns. Most are smaller than sparrows and have some yellow mark. Identification in fall plumage is difficult, but easier for spring males on breeding territories by the distinctive calls and songs, head marks, and presence or absence of wing bars. Females usually have marks resembling spring males. Bills are thin, sharp, straight, and slender. All wood warblers are almost entirely insectivorous.

Most members of this family are Neotropical migrants and summer residents that breed in and remain close to their selective nesting habitats. Many warblers, such as the Bachman's, Swainson's, Prothonotary, Cerulean, Prairie, Blue-winged, Hooded, Black-and-white, Kentucky, Worm-eating, and Yellow-throated, and the Northern Parula, Ovenbird, and Louisiana Waterthrush are species of concern to biologists and scientists working in the Neotropical Migratory Bird Conservation Program, called Partners in Flight. These species and others are experiencing population declines due to habitat fragmentation on the breeding grounds, destruction of tropical rain forest wintering habitat, nest predation by Brown-headed Cowbirds, and other factors.

Bachman's Warbler *Vermivora bachmanii*

This species is probably the least observed of all North American songbirds. It was discovered by Rev. John Bachman near Charleston, South Carolina, in 1833. John James Audubon described the two specimens taken by Bachman and named them in his honor. Almost 50 years passed before this warbler was seen again. Charles S. Galbraith, while collecting small birds for the millinery trade, took over 30 specimens between 1886 and 1888 near Lake Ponchartrain in Louisiana, most during March (Bent 1953).

About 60 years after the discovery of this bird, the first nests and eggs were found. In 1897 Otto Widmann found Bachman's Warblers breeding in the St. Francis River bottoms of Arkansas and Missouri. Arthur T. Wayne discovered nests in heavily timbered overflow lands in South Carolina near Charleston in 1906. The nests were in low, aquatic bushes, canes, and vines. George C. Embody found this warbler nesting in Logan County Kentucky in 1906. In 1920 Ernest G. Holt found it breeding in Autauga County, Alabama (Bent 1953; Hamel 1986).

Bachman's Warbler is an extremely rare, local, and erratic summer resident in a restricted part of the southeastern states from South Carolina into western Kentucky and southeastern Missouri (Hamel 1986). It is listed as an endangered species in several states and by the federal gov-

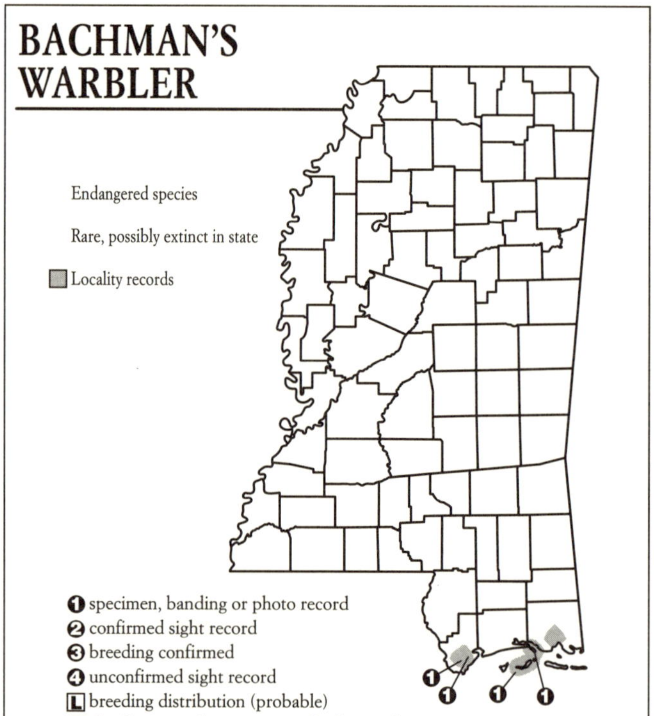

❶ specimen, banding or photo record
❷ confirmed sight record
❸ breeding confirmed
❹ unconfirmed sight record
[L] breeding distribution (probable)
[E] distribution unknown – records all coastal migrants

	JAN	FEB	MAR	APR	MAY	JUN	JUL	AUG	SEP	OCT	NOV	DEC
OCCURRENCE		28 ○	○○ 26				4 ○					
MUSEUM*												
WHT*												

*Breeding confirmed by egg, sight, or photographic record.

ernment. It breeds in river bottoms and heavily wooded swamps with openings, where it nests in canes, low bushes, and briers within a few feet of the ground.

The nest is made of leaves and grasses lined with plant fibers. The three or four eggs are white. There is no evidence of this species breeding in Mississippi, but it may nest in swampy woods in the northeastern part of our state or in large tracts of hardwoods with canebrakes along the Mississippi River.

There are few occurrence records of the Bachman's Warbler in Alabama. Breeding records are below the fall line, a ridge bordering the coastal plain on the south that crosses from the east-central to the northwestern part of that state. Less than a dozen recent records have been reported in Louisiana.

Only four coastal specimen records exist in Mississippi. Andrew Allison (1906a) collected two specimens at Bay St. Louis, one on March 26, 1902, and another on July 4, 1906. Thomas D. Burleigh (1945) collected a single specimen on Deer Island on March 21, 1941. The last Mississippi record is a specimen shot February 28, 1949, on Ship Island during work on a study of encephalitis (Sciple 1950).

There are good reasons for this warbler's scarcity. In its remote swamp habitat, it usually stays in the higher branches. And because of its small size and usually inconspicuous habits, it can be overlooked easily. The song is a buzzy, monotonous trill much like the song of the Northern Parula, but rendered in the same pitch. Few birders would recognize the song.

The male Bachman's Warbler is a small bird with a yellow face, eye ring, chin, and belly. The crown is gray with the front part blending into black. The upperparts are olive green (without wing bars), and there is a broad, black bib across the throat and upper breast. The female lacks the black throat patch, and the crown is blue gray with no black on the front portion.

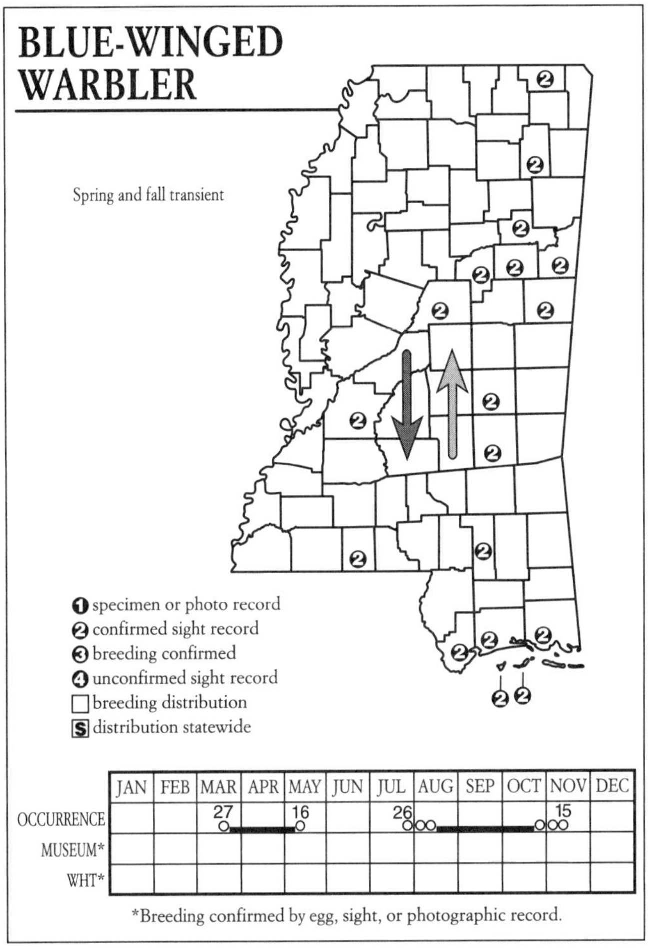

Blue-winged Warbler *Vermivora pinus*

This species has yellow underparts and yellow on the top of the head and face. The upperparts, except for the top of the head, are olive yellow. A narrow black line through the eye and prominent white bars on the bluish wings are diagnostic. The song is a two-noted buzzing, with the second note usually lower in pitch than the first.

The Blue-winged Warbler is an irregular spring transient, uncommon to fairly common in most of the state. It is fairly common as a fall transient. Extreme dates of occurrence in the spring migration are March 27 in Pike County and May 16 in Bolivar County. Extreme fall migration dates are July 26 in Lauderdale County and November 15 on the Mississippi Coast. This warbler is not known to breed in Mississippi, although it is uncommon to fairly common as a local summer resident in the Tennessee Valley of northern Alabama and Georgia.

This species hybridizes with the Golden-winged Warbler (see next account). A single sight record of a rare hybrid, the Lawrence's Warbler, was made by Sandra Davis at Oxford on May 19, 1969. One sighting of the other dominant hybrid, Brewster's Warbler, was recorded by Larry Gates (Jackson and Weber 1976) at Hattiesburg on October 7, 1976. Two sightings by Sandra Davis, on May 4, 1967, and May 4, 1974, were made at Oxford.

Golden-winged Warbler *Vermivora chrysoptera*

The Golden-winged Warbler is a fairly common spring and fall transient. It is handsome with its pearl gray upperparts, yellow forehead, white underparts, golden yellow wing bars, and black throat and cheeks. Except for the yellow forehead patch and wing bars, the male resembles a chickadee. The female and immatures have gray instead of black cheeks and throats.

Spring migration extreme dates are from April 8 to May 8, and fall migration extremes are from July 28 to November 3.

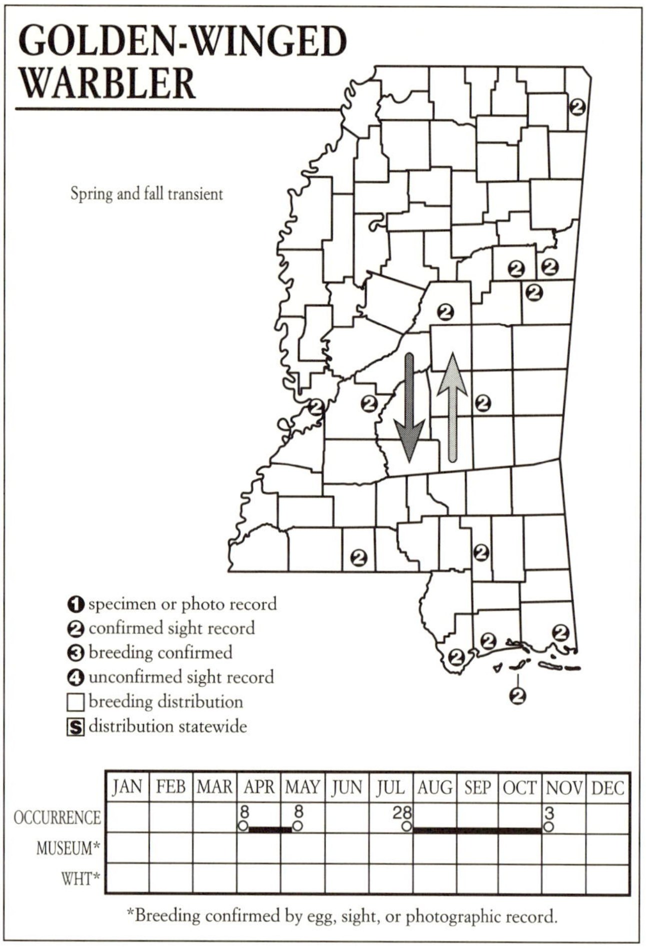

The Golden-winged Warbler breeds mainly in the south-central provinces of Canada, the upper Mississippi Valley eastward into the New England states, and in the mountains south to northern Georgia. Where the breeding ranges of the Golden-winged and the Blue-winged Warbler overlap, fertile hybrids occur. The dominant hybrid, known as the Brewster's Warbler, resembles the Blue-winged Warbler, but has a yellow wing patch and *white* underparts instead of yellow. The Lawrence's Warbler, a rarer recessive hybrid, resembles the Golden-winged Warbler with white wing bars, yellow underparts, and black bib and cheeks.

The song of the Golden-winged Warbler is buzzy. The first note is longer and higher, followed by three or four at a lower pitch.

Tennessee Warbler *Vermivora peregrina*

In spring, this warbler is a common transient from about mid-April to mid-May. It is conspicuous during spring migration because it sings frequently, and the song is a distinctive loud series of evenly spaced chips that become more rapid at the end, like the sound of a sewing machine. It usually forages high in treetops. This species is often the most abundant of fall migrant warblers, occurring from early September to mid-November. Extremes of recorded spring migration are March 27 and May 20, and in fall from September to November.

The Tennessee Warbler has completely white underparts in spring. The male has a conspicuous white stripe over the eye and a gray head. In spring, the female is less gray on the head with a yellowish wash on the underparts. The back of both sexes is bright greenish. In fall, the eye stripe is yellowish but conspicuous, undertail coverts are white, and the breast is yellowish. Those features in combination with a single, yellowish wing bar are diagnostic for both adults and immatures in fall plumage.

In the fall this species resembles the Philadelphia Vireo, but the thin warbler bill and more active behavior separate it from vireos. It also resembles the Orange-crowned Warbler. The Orange-crowned has faint streakings on the breast that are lacking in the Tennessee, and the Tennessee Warbler has white undertail coverts and a faint yellow wing bar.

In Mississippi, this warbler is found only as a spring and fall migrant. It breeds in aspen and spruce woods of Canada, extending to the far north and into the northern

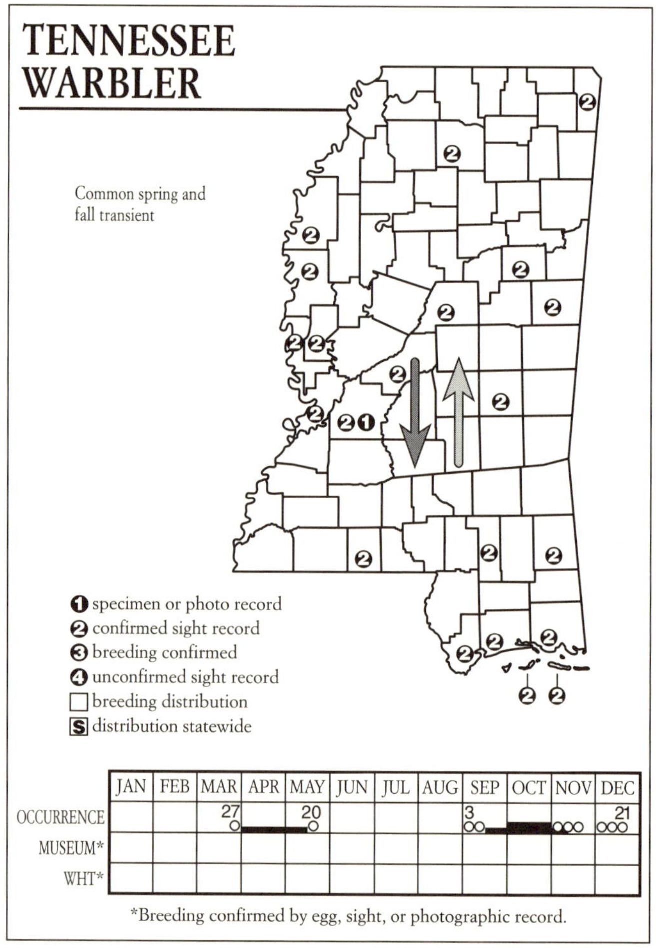

parts of Minnesota, Wisconsin, Michigan, New York, Vermont, New Hampshire, and Maine. The nest is built on the ground of fine grasses, hair, and plant fibers and is usually concealed in a clump of moss. The species winters in Mexico and south into northern South America.

Orange-crowned Warbler *Vermivora celata*

In winter this small, dark green or grayish green warbler is usually seen in brushy thickets of low woodlands. It has a decided preference for this habitat along streams and water areas, particularly wooded swamps.

This species is nondescript, having no distinct field marks such as wing bars or other marks that characterize most warblers. The best field marks for identifying this bird are its uniform appearance, solitary habits, and lack of distinctive marks. It is totally plain greenish or grayish above, dingy grayish green below with faint streakings on the sides, and the underparts lack white. A patch of brownish orange in the crown is concealed by the outer green tips of these feathers.

It is a fairly common winter resident along the coast. Elsewhere in the state, it is regular in occurrence but uncommon to rare in winter in the central and northern counties. The Orange-crowned Warbler arrives here usually after mid-September and remains until late April. May 2 is a late date of spring departure, substantiated by a specimen collected in Tishomingo County by H. L. Owens. A late spring sighting on the coast was April 26.

Nashville Warbler *Vermivora ruficapilla*

Alexander Wilson (1832) named and described this warbler after collecting several specimens near Nashville. During the early history of the Nashville Warbler, ornithologists regarded it as a rare species. On the coast and in the southern counties of Mississippi, it occurs rarely and only in the fall. Nearly all occurrence and collection records for this bird were made in northern Mississippi. These records indicate that in spring and fall this warbler migrates eastward or westward across northern Mississippi. It is found elsewhere only as an uncommon fall transient.

Lowery Jr. (1974) records the Nashville Warbler as a "fairly regular and moderately common spring and fall transient" in Louisiana. He observes, however, that it is "seldom observed in spring anywhere in the eastern half of

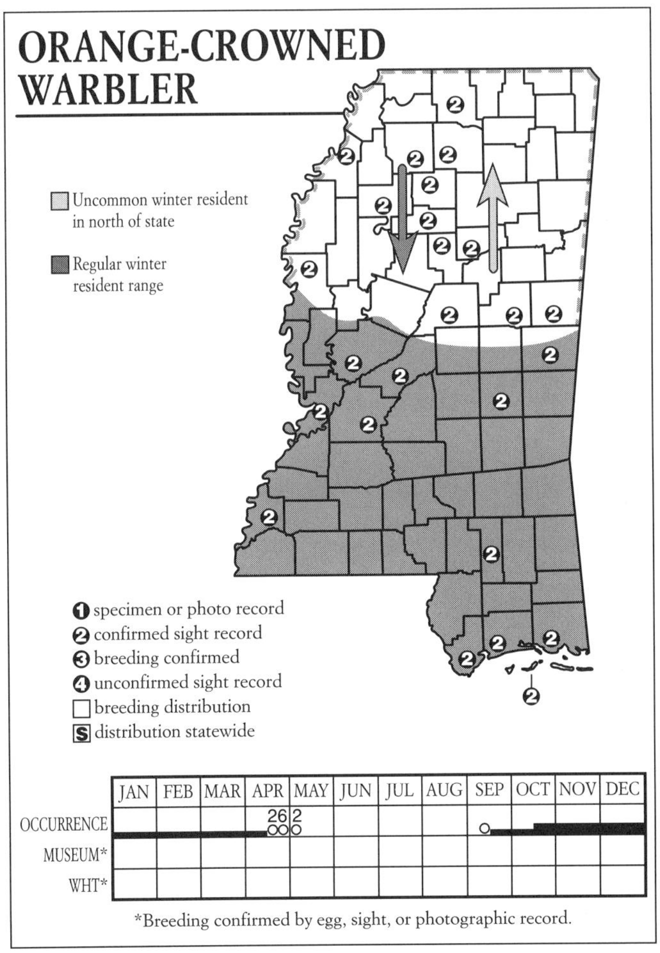

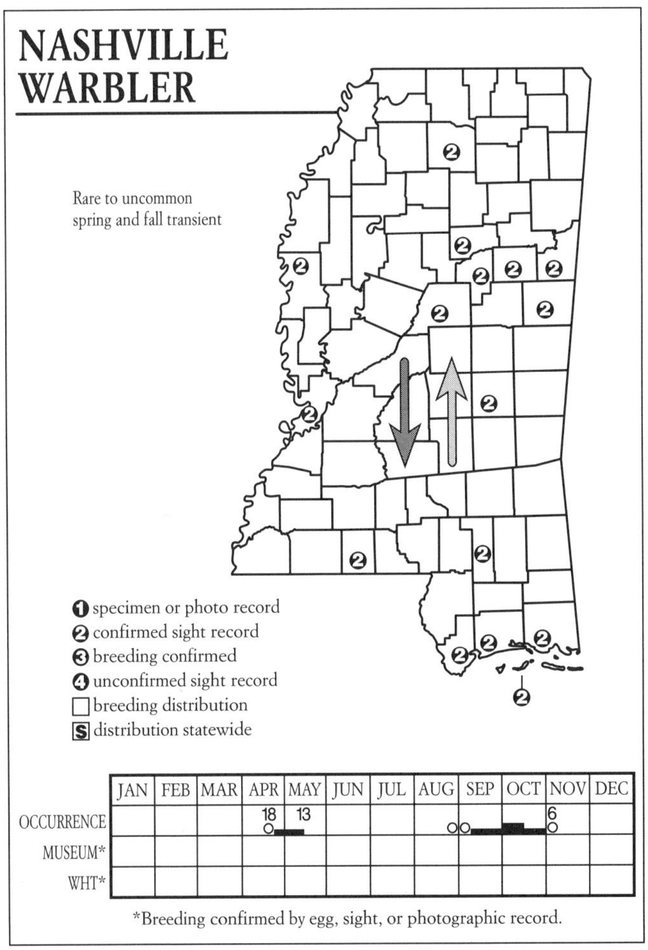

the state." In his Alabama bird book, Imhof (1976) describes this species as occurring in spring only north of the fall line (in northern Alabama) and on the Gulf Coast, where it is rare. Spring migration records in Mississippi extend from April 18 to May 13, and fall records from late August to November 6.

The Nashville Warbler is plain olive green on the back, wings, and tail. The underparts and throat are bright yellow. The head is bluish gray with a concealed, reddish brown crown patch. A white eye ring combined with the gray head and yellow throat are diagnostic field marks.

Northern Parula *Parula americana*

The parula is one of the smallest of our warblers. Its distinctive, ascending, buzzy trill with an abrupt drop at the end is a familiar sound during spring and summer. This warbler occurs commonly in Mississippi as a breeding bird wherever large trees are draped with Spanish moss, which is where this species builds its nest. In northern areas the nest is built in beard moss, *Usnea,* a lichen resembling Spanish moss.

The nest is made of fine grass and black inner moss fibers woven into a small cup, and usually lined with moss flowers and fibers. The nest is neatly concealed in the hanging moss from a few feet to 75 feet or more aboveground. Three to five eggs with reddish brown marks constitute a clutch. Breeding occurs in Mississippi from early April through June.

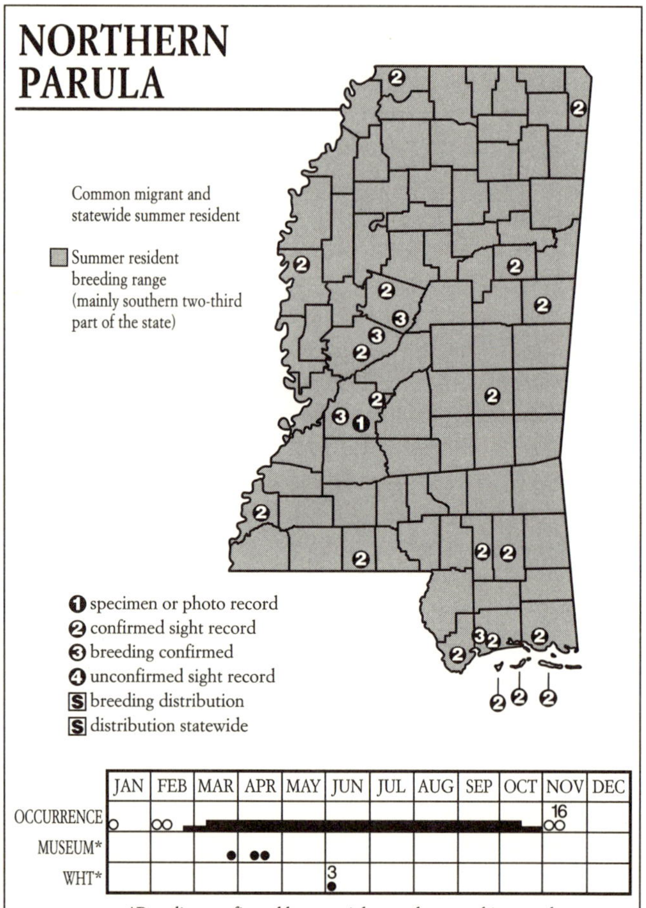

*Breeding confirmed by egg, sight, or photographic record.

This warbler is one of the first migrants to arrive in the spring. It appears on the Gulf Coast in late February and early March, and is one of the most common spring migrants from mid-March until early May. Southward migration for this species begins in late July or early August and continues into October with a few remaining until early November.

The Northern Parula is abundant as a summer resident, especially in river swamps and hardwood forests. It also is a breeding bird on upland sites where Spanish moss is abundant and in the moss-draped live oaks along the Gulf Coast. The name "northern" is given to this warbler to separate it from a close relative, the Tropical Parula, which occurs in southern Texas, Central America, and South America.

The Northern Parula is bluish gray above except for a patch of greenish yellow on the back. The throat and breast of both sexes and the immatures are yellow. The male has a narrow, dusky, chestnut-bordered band separating the yellow of the throat and breast. The lower belly, undertail coverts, and tips of the outer-tail feathers are white. There are two wide, white wing bars, and the eyelids are white in the adults. Immatures are yellowish green above and resemble the adult female.

Yellow Warbler *Dendroica petechia*

This warbler is entirely yellow in appearance and has bright yellow spots near the tip of the tail. These spots are brighter yellow than the rest of the plumage and are useful in identifying this species. The sexes are similar in the spring, but the male is bright yellow with reddish brown streaks on the breast. The female is less brightly colored, and the breast is only sparingly streaked. Fall immatures are sometimes dull in appearance, but can be separated from the Wilson's and Hooded Warblers by the bright yellow tail spots.

The Yellow Warbler is a common spring and fall migrant. It has been noted from April 8 to June 4, on July 1, and from July 20 through November. No known breeding records exist for Mississippi, although it is fairly common as a summer-resident, breeding bird in parts of northern Alabama and the Tennessee River Valley.

During migration, the Yellow Warbler usually inhabits small trees and shrubs in fairly open habitats. It seems fond of lakes and streams where willows are growing in thickets.

This warbler's song consists of seven or eight loud and sweetly delivered notes. The first four or five notes are evenly spaced and on the same pitch, followed by two or

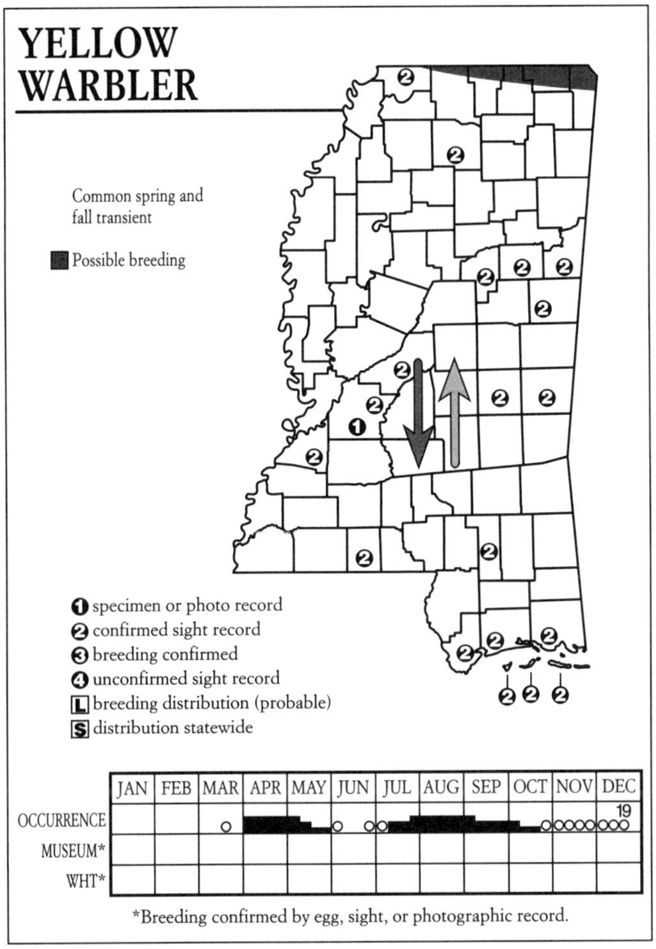

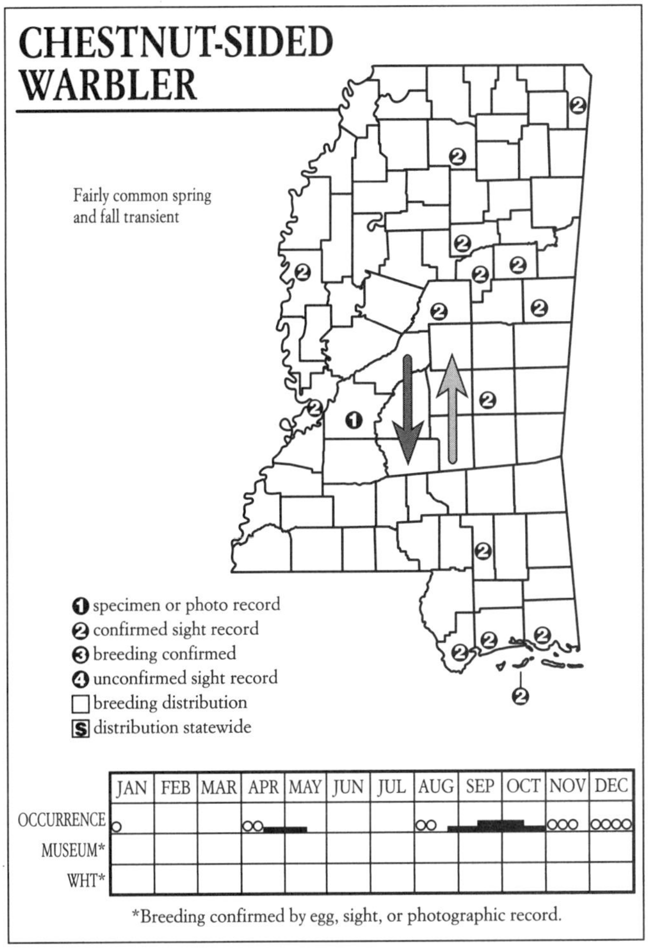

three notes on a lower pitch more rapidly delivered, and ending with one or two notes at the original timing and pitch. The song was interpreted by Francis H. Allen as *wee see wee see wiss wiss'u.*

Chestnut-sided Warbler *Dendroica pensylvanica*

In spring, the adults of this species are marked distinctively with a lemon yellow crown and chestnut sides. The underparts are immaculate white, and the back is lemon green streaked with black. Adults in fall are lemon green above, white below, with a white eye ring and two pale, lemon yellow wing bars. They usually have some chestnut side marks. The Bay-breasted Warbler has chestnut on its sides and also on the throat, upper breast, and crown. Immature Chestnut-sided Warblers are plain grayish white below with light green upperparts, which are sharply defined where they meet, and two yellowish wing bars.

This warbler is a late spring transient, irregular on the Gulf Coast and fairly common in northern Mississippi. It arrives late in April and has departed usually by the third week of May. In autumn, it is a regular and common transient from mid-September to mid-October. Extremes for arrival are April 4 to May 19, and August 2 to December 1 for the fall migration. Burleigh (1945) collected two specimens of this warbler at Deer Island on January 6 and December 1, 1942, but wintering here should be considered a casual occurrence.

This warbler breeds in the northern states and across Canada from central Saskatchewan east into Nova Scotia and south in the mountains to northern Georgia. It nests near the ground in shrubs, small trees, or in brush sprouts during the early stages of forest regeneration or abandonment of farm or pasture land. The winter range is in Central America.

The song is loud, clear, and musical in quality, consisting of four to six rhythmic notes followed by a louder, higher-pitched next-to-last note, with the last note slurred downward. The song has been appropriately described as *I wish, I wish to see Miss Bee'-cher.*

Magnolia Warbler *Dendroica magnolia*

Alexander Wilson (1832) named this beautiful little warbler in the early 1800s after collecting one among magnolia trees in Wilkinson County near Fort Adams. He called it the "black-and-yellow warbler" and gave it the scientific name *Sylvia magnolia* before it became the Magnolia Warbler.

Although scarce and irregular on the coast, this warbler is a fairly common spring migrant through most of the state. The bulk of the spring passage occurs from the last week of April until about mid-May. The extreme dates of recorded spring migration are March 1 and June 2.

This species is a common fall transient, occurring regularly from mid-September until mid-October. Extremes of recorded fall migration in Mississippi are August 14 and November 18. There are two winter records by Burleigh (1945) for this warbler on the Mississippi Coast, specimens taken in 1942 near Gulfport on January 11 and near Biloxi on December 23. Two other recent sightings in Jackson and Hancock Counties were on December 18 and 29.

The Magnolia Warbler is mostly bright yellow below and dark gray above, with broad white patches on the wings and *rectangular white patches on the black tail* midway between the tip and base. The yellow underparts are heavily streaked with black on the breast and flanks, and there is a yellow rump patch. The top of the head is gray and cheek patches are black. Females and immatures have less streaking on the sides. The yellow throat combined with the broad, white, rectangular tail patches on the outer-tail feathers are distinctive field marks.

Cape May Warbler *Dendroica tigrina*

This species has been recorded in Mississippi mostly as a spring transient. It is known to winter in the West Indies. The Cape May Warbler migrates through Florida and along the Atlantic Coast to and from breeding grounds in spruce and fir forests of the northern states and the Canadian provinces west into northeastern New Brunswick. It is rarely seen during spring migration this far west.

Allison (1907) collected the first Mississippi specimen in Tishomingo County on May 4, 1904. Thomas D. Burleigh (1945) collected two Cape May Warblers and observed another on May 1, 1940, on Ship Island, the only known early records for the coast. M. G. Vaiden collected a specimen in Bolivar County on May 9, 1945. Spring records are by Coffey Jr. (1941a) in DeSoto County on April 27, 1941, and Warriner (1944) near Corinth in Alcorn County on May 6, 1944.

Fall sightings of Cape May Warblers extend from September 17 to November 23. An individual was seen by

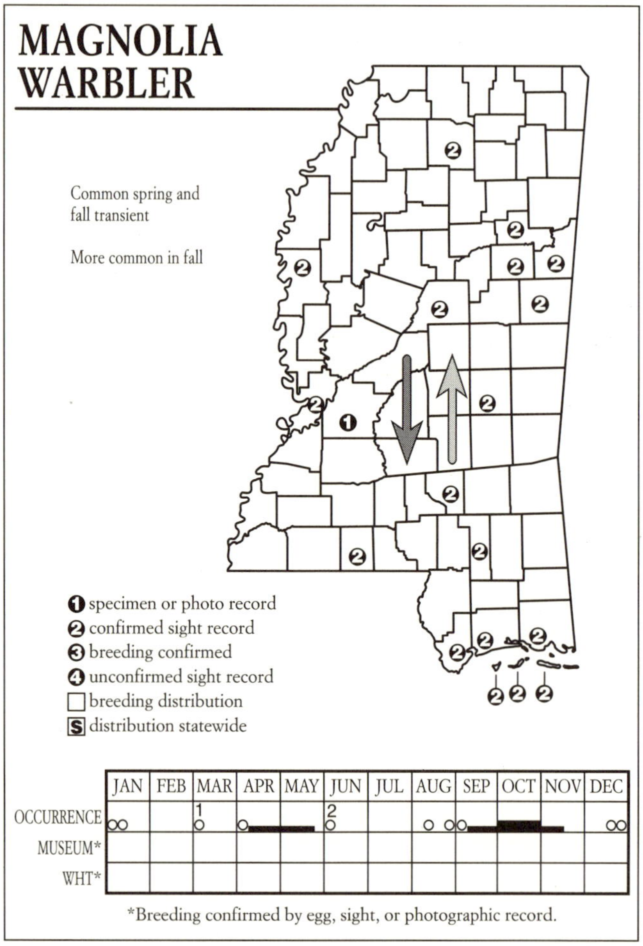

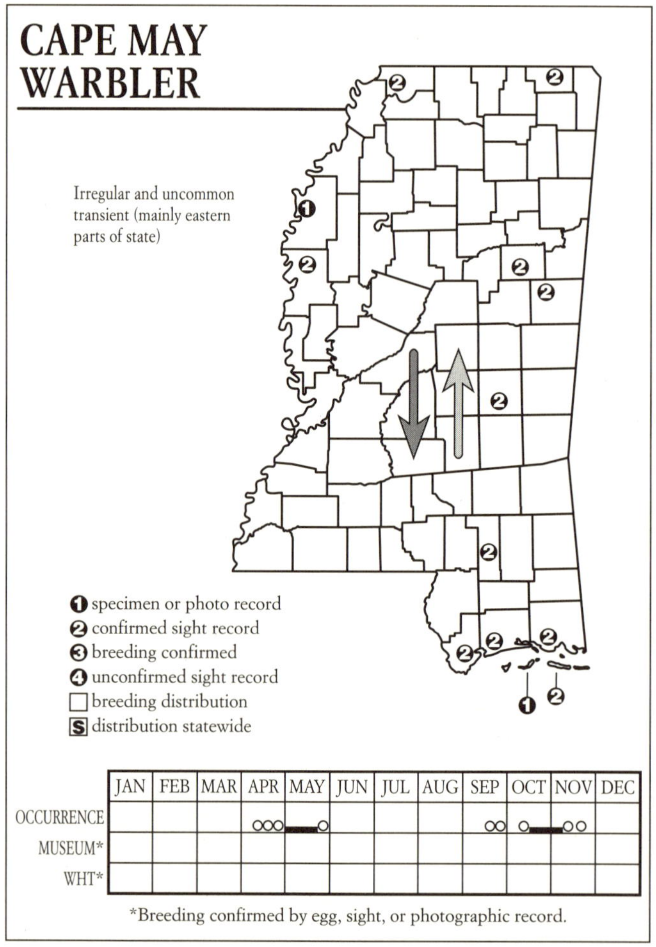

Marvin and Sandra Davis (pers. comm.) at Oxford in Lafayette County on November 23, 1975, and another on October 10, 1976. A record 25 birds were seen by MOS members at Waveland following the passage of Hurricane Juan on November 2, 1985. This storm hovered off the coasts of Mississippi and Louisiana, then turned eastward to make landfall in Alabama. Migrants and some western species piled up along the coast in record numbers until the storm passed.

In spring, the male Cape May Warbler is readily identified by its yellow rump, large white wing patch, chestnut-colored cheeks, and yellow breast, which is heavily streaked with black. Females and immatures are duller and much less yellow below, have a patch of yellow behind the ear, and a yellow rump. This species in any plumage can be identified by the heavily streaked underparts, yellow rump, and yellow neck patch. In the fall, use caution in identifying this species in the field because of its similarities with the Blackburnian Warbler.

BLACK-THROATED BLUE WARBLER

Irregular, rare

Transient

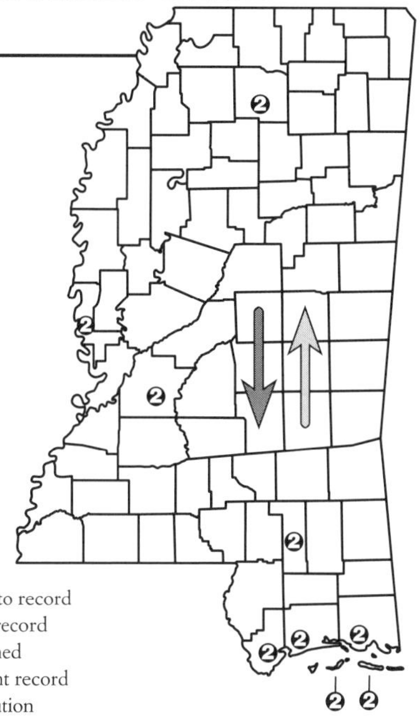

❶ specimen or photo record
❷ confirmed sight record
❸ breeding confirmed
❹ unconfirmed sight record
□ breeding distribution
S distribution statewide (mainly eastern part of state)

	JAN	FEB	MAR	APR	MAY	JUN	JUL	AUG	SEP	OCT	NOV	DEC
OCCURRENCE		o		ooo	o o				ooo	oooo	o	
MUSEUM*												
WHT*												

*Breeding confirmed by egg, sight, or photographic record.

Black-throated Blue Warbler *Dendroica caerulescens*

Like the Cape May Warbler, the Black-throated Blue Warbler migrates along a route through Florida and the Atlantic Coast states in the Southeast. Few Mississippi records exist, since it appears here rarely during spring or fall migration. Burleigh (1945) collected specimens on Deer and Ship Islands on April 10 and 30, May 1, and September 20.

Two specimens in the MMNS were collected by Eugene Patton in Lee County on September 26 and October 1. Vaiden (1952a) obtained a specimen in Bolivar County on October 21. Sight records have been recorded by Ethel Floyd and others in the Jackson area on April 25, by Burleigh on Deer Island on October 12, and by Allison (1907) in Tishomingo County on April 29. On the basis of these records the Black-throated Blue Warbler can be expected to occur rarely throughout the state in early April into early May, and again in the fall in the latter part of September until November.

The breeding range is in the north-central and northeastern states and south into the Appalachians to northern Georgia. The breeding range in Canada extends from western Ontario eastward through southern Quebec and Nova Scotia. The usual winter range is in the West Indies and casually north into extreme southern Florida.

In all seasons, the male is blue gray above with a black face, throat, and sides. The lower breast, belly, and a patch in the wing at the base of the primary wing feathers are white. The female and immatures are dark olive brown on the upperparts and the cheeks. The underparts are yellowish buff. A whitish line over the eye, a white patch in the wings, unstreaked dark coloration, dark cheeks, and white undertail coverts are field marks that help identify the female and immatures. The song is a slow, wheezy, ascending buzz.

Yellow-rumped Warbler *Dendroica coronata*

Until recently this species was called the Myrtle Warbler. A similar, yellow-throated form, previously known as Audubon's Warbler and found in the western states, was described as a separate species until the American Ornithologists' Union combined the two as one species with the name Yellow-rumped Warbler. The eastern and western forms were found to interbreed, which led to their being considered as geographical variations of one species.

This warbler is a common winter resident throughout Mississippi, but it is especially abundant during migration and on the coast. It occupies all kinds of habitat and frequently occurs in flocks. At times, it prefers trees and shrubs over water, where it can be seen hawking after aquatic insects much like a flycatcher. It is by far the most numerous winter-resident warbler and one of our most conspicuous winter birds. It arrives in numbers in early

YELLOW-RUMPED WARBLER

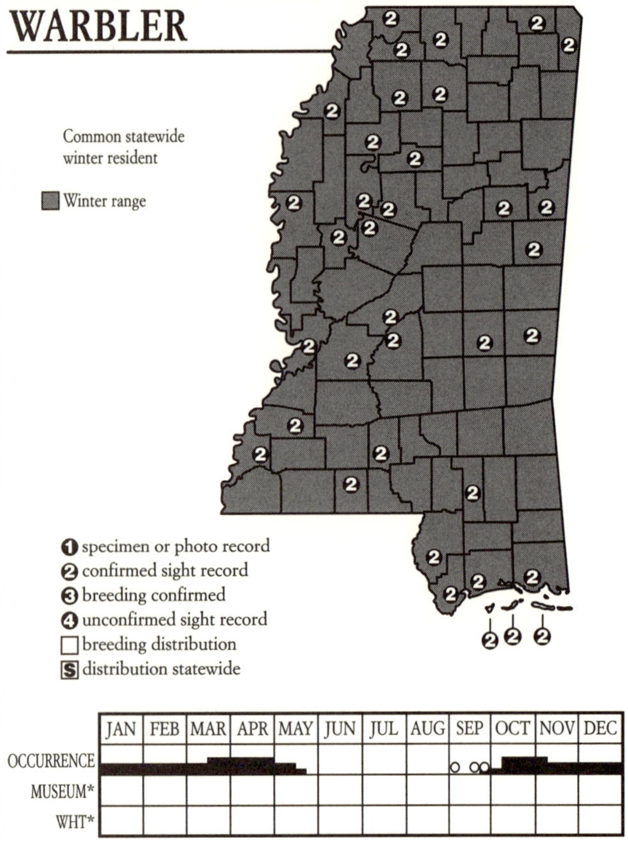

*Breeding confirmed by egg, sight, or photographic record.

October and remains through April or early May. Extreme dates of arrival and departure are September 7 and May 23.

One of the largest of the wood warblers, this species is easily recognized by a single loud *check* note. The song is a low, soft, irregular warble, usually heard in late spring during or after the molt into alternate plumage.

In fall and winter basic plumage, the Yellow-rumped Warbler is brownish above, dull white below, and streaked with a dark brownish color. The throat is white, and in all plumages the base of the tail is bright yellow. There is a wash of yellow on the sides at the front of each wing and a yellow crown patch that may be concealed in first-winter plumage of immatures.

The male in alternate spring plumage is blue gray above, white below, white throated, black across the chest spreading to streaks along the sides, and *bright yellow* on the rump, crown, and sides at the point of the wings. The cheeks of the spring male are black. The female in spring is brownish gray wherever the male is black and dark gray.

Insects are the main food of this warbler, but in winter it subsists on a variety of seeds and berries. In early spring it feeds by "flycatching" insects. The fruits of wax myrtle and poison ivy are commonly eaten. The ability to subsist on fruits and seeds probably enables large numbers of this warbler to winter farther north than most other warblers. It will sometimes utilize feeders, where it eats bread crumbs, suet, and peanut butter.

[Black-throated Gray Warbler]
Dendroica nigrescens

There are few Mississippi records for this casual western winter visitor. Amy Tolman reported the first sighting in Pearl River County near Picayune on April 21, 1949. R. Demett Smith Jr. (1957), Ben and Lula Coffey Jr., and Alice Smith carefully observed and identified a male at Natchez in Adams County, on December 30, 1956. This bird was first seen with a group of Pine Warblers by R. Demett Smith Jr. in the top of an oak tree, and was watched for 10 minutes as it moved about feeding from one tree to another.

Haberyan (1960) recorded a male at Gulfport in Harrison County, on September 26, 1960. This bird was observed by Haberyan and Ethel Floyd the following day and studied carefully at close range. All plumage characteristics, even the yellow spots anterior to the eyes, were readily seen. It was noted the following morning at the same loca-

BLACK-THROATED GRAY WARBLER

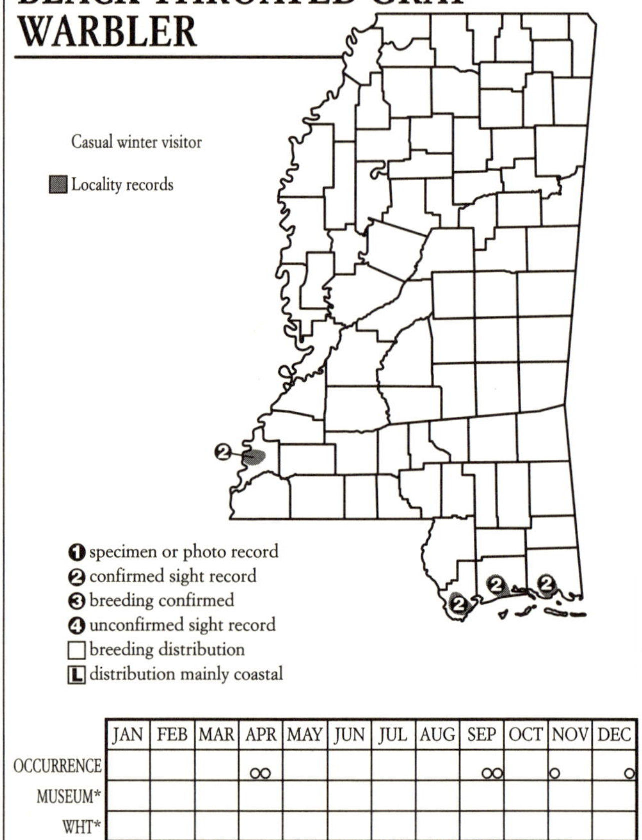

*Breeding confirmed by egg, sight, or photographic record.

tion in slash pines, but left during the day and was not seen again. Judith A. Toups recorded an adult male at Bellefontaine Beach in Jackson County on April 14, 1983 (Imhof 1983). Terrie and Larry Gates reported one adult female at Logtown in Hancock County on November 2, 1985 (Purrington 1986).

The male Black-throated Gray Warbler has a faintly streaked, gray back and white underparts with black streaks on the sides. The crown, cheeks, and throat are black. The female is similar, but lacks the black throat and the crown is less black. Both sexes have two prominent, white wing bars.

The only other all black-and-white warblers are the Blackpoll and Black-and-white Warbler. The male Blackpoll Warbler has a *white throat and cheeks,* the Black-and-white Warbler has a *striped* crown and its back streaked with white, while the Black-throated Gray Warbler has black crown and black cheeks separated by white.

[Townsend's Warbler] *Dendroica townsendi*

This species, whose breeding range is restricted to the Pacific Northwest, can be included here on the basis of a single female specimen collected by Burleigh (1945) at Gulfport on September 17, 1939. That record, along with a sighting of one male by Sandra Davis (pers. comm.) at Oxford on May 23, 1967, and one on December 19, 1992, on the Jackson County Christmas Bird Count (Imhof 1993), are the only state records for this accidental visitor. Lowery Jr. (1974) lists no record for Louisiana. It occurs as a migrant west of the Pecos River and as a rare migrant in the Texas Panhandle.

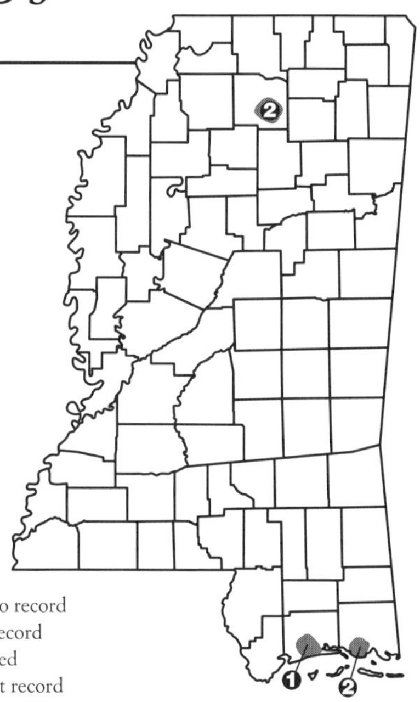

	JAN	FEB	MAR	APR	MAY	JUN	JUL	AUG	SEP	OCT	NOV	DEC
OCCURRENCE					23 o				17 o			19 o
MUSEUM*												
WHT*												

*Breeding confirmed by egg, sight, or photographic record.

Townsend's Warbler is similar to the Black-throated Gray Warbler, except the Townsend's has *yellow* on the face, breast, and sides instead of white. The *dark cheek patch* outlined by the yellow face distinguishes this species in all plumages. The Black-throated Green Warbler in fall plumage is similar to the Townsend's, but has only a slightly dark cheek patch, and the throat is white or pale yellow instead of bright yellow like the Townsend's. The female or immature can be confused with the fall Blackburnian female and immature. Careful viewing of all field marks is necessary for certain identification.

This species breeds in the fir forests of the Northwest north into the southern Yukon of Alaska. It winters along the coastal region of California and south into Nicaragua.

Black-throated Green Warbler *Dendroica virens*

This handsome warbler occurs in Mississippi as a spring and fall transient and as a casual winter resident on the Gulf Coast. In the spring, it is erratic and scarce on the coast, except when cold fronts ground concentrations of returning migrants. Farther inland, it is a fairly common spring transient. In the fall, it is often abundant as a transient throughout the state.

Migration usually extends from late March to mid-May and from about mid-August to late October. Extremes of recorded spring and fall migration are March 10 to May 24, and July 30 to November 25. Two winter sightings in Hancock County occurred on December 16 and 18, 1985.

The Black-throated Green Warbler breeds in northern evergreen and oak forests from western Alberta east into Nova Scotia and south to central Minnesota, southern Michigan, and northern New Jersey. In the eastern mountains, the breeding range extends to north-central Alabama, northern Georgia, and along the coast of the Carolinas and Virginia. The winter range extends from southern Texas and Florida southward to the Bahamas, Cuba, and Panama. It is also a casual winter resident south of New Orleans.

The spring male is strikingly colored with its black throat and sides, olive green crown and back, and white underparts and wing bars. The sides of the head are yellow, framed by the olive green crown and black throat. The female is duller and has less black on the throat. Immatures

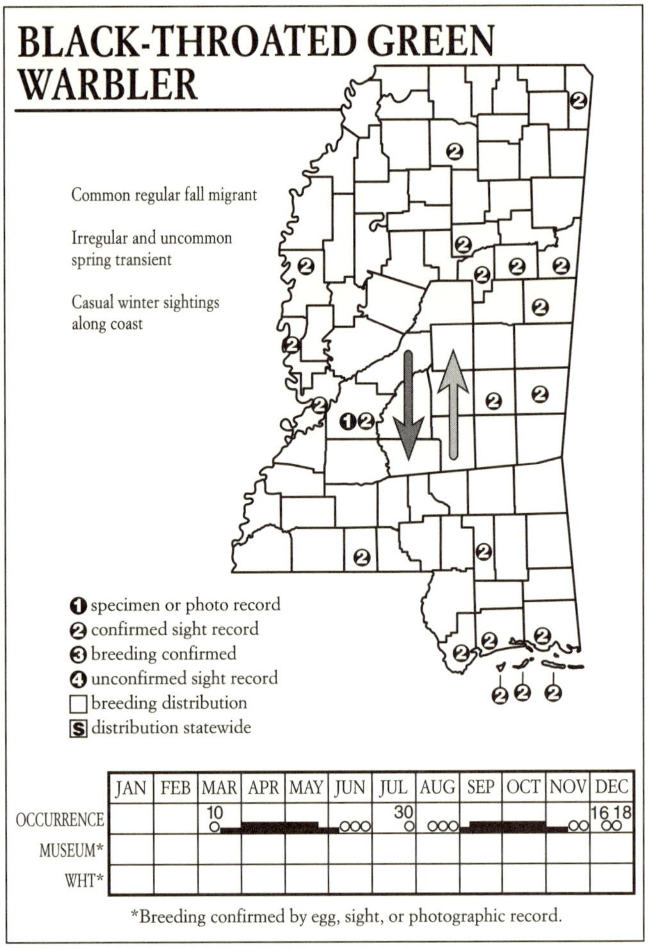

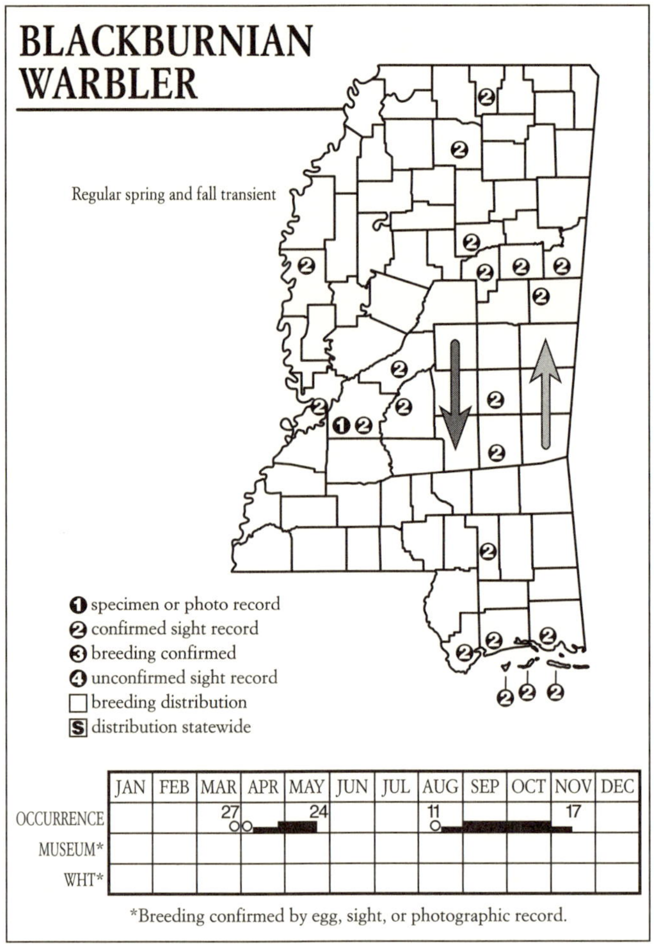

are whitish on the throat, but the throat is dusky along the sides. In all plumages the olive green back and bold yellow cheeks are distinctive field marks.

Blackburnian Warbler *Dendroica fusca*

Like the Black-throated Green Warbler, the Blackburnian is a treetop warbler. It is also a transient, most frequently observed in spring after the first week of April until mid-May. In fall, migration occurs mostly during September and early October. Extremes of recorded migration are March 27 to May 24, and August 11 to November 17.

The bright, fiery orange throat and head marks of the spring male Blackburnian Warbler are distinctive. The female and immatures are similarly marked with an orange or yellowish throat, with paler marks on the head and body like the pattern of the male. The underparts are white with black streaks on the sides of the breast, black-and-white stripes on the back, and white wing bars. A dark ear patch, yellow throat, and light stripes on the back are helpful in identifying this species in fall plumages. The song is high pitched and almost inaudible, and has four or five high, thin notes on the same pitch with a slurred ending.

This warbler breeds in the fir forests of the Northern states and eastern Canada, and south into the eastern mountains to northern Georgia. Its winter range is in Central America and northern South America.

Yellow-throated Warbler *Dendroica dominica*

This warbler is one of the first migrants to arrive in the spring, making its appearance on the Mississippi Coast in early March. There, it is a very common spring transient until mid-April. Elsewhere in the state and along the lower Pearl River in Hancock County, it is a common summer resident in wooded bottomland swamps.

In most of Mississippi, its preferred nesting habitat is old cypress-tupelo swamps and cypress-bordered oxbow lakes. Also, it frequents and nests in open stands of tall pines, both in upland sites and those bordering streams or water areas. A treetop warbler, this species is often seen foraging for insects while creeping about on the trunks and branches of trees.

There are records for this warbler in every month, however, it rarely winters in our coastal counties. There are sight records on December 23 in Hancock County and

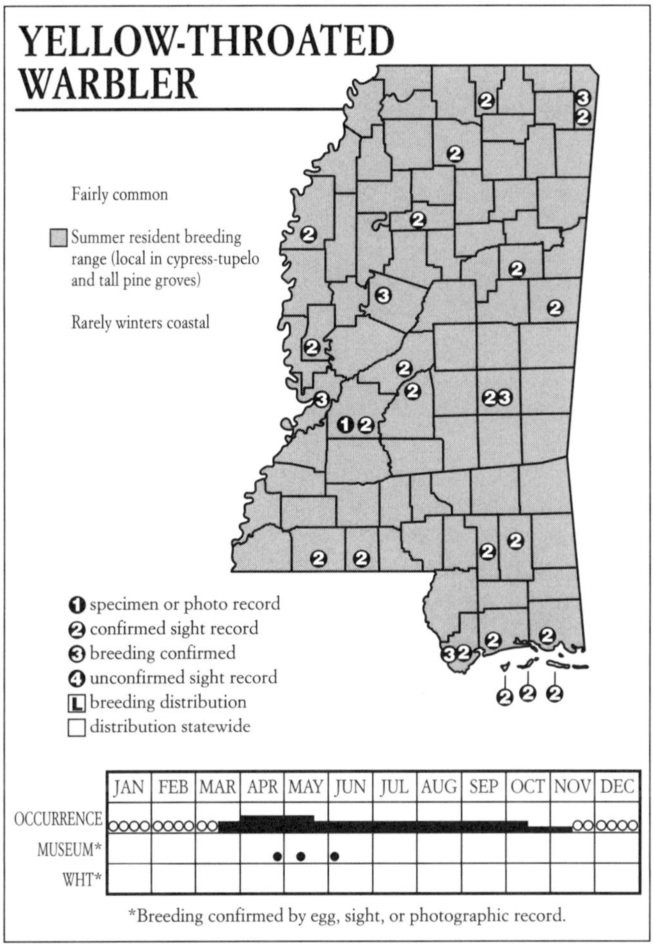

January 12 in Jackson County. Extreme dates of spring arrival and fall departure are February 27 and October 18. Most spring migrants arriving on the coast are seen during the latter half of March. Fall departure begins in late July and continues through early October.

Field marks of the Yellow-throated Warbler make it easily distinguishable. Look for a solid gray back, a bright yellow bib covering throat and breast, a prominent white stripe over the eye, two white wing bars, striped sides, and white underparts.

The warbler's distinctive song announces its presence. The male sings incessantly from its arrival on the breeding grounds until late June. The loud, clear song, delivered high in the trees, consists of several notes slurred downward, with the last notes becoming fainter and ending with a weak trill. The song is similar to that of the Louisiana Waterthrush. The Yellow-throated Warbler responds to a playback of its song on its breeding territory, and in response will often descend to lower branches.

The nest of the Yellow-throated Warbler is sometimes built in a clump of Spanish moss, and is similar to the Pine Warbler's (Turcotte 1957c). It is a compact cup of grass, weed stems, strips of bark, plant fibers, and spider or caterpillar silk lined with plant down, feathers, or hair. The eggs are usually four to a set, grayish white, and wreathed around the larger end with brown, lavender, and gray. The one nest I have found was situated 40 feet aboveground atop a limb in a pine, which was in an open pine grove beside Bear Creek in Tishomingo State Park on April 27, 1957 (Turcotte 1957c).

Pine Warbler *Dendroica pinus*

This warbler could not be better named, for it is usually found closely associated with mature pines. It feeds actively among pine branches and needle clusters, where it searches for insects, much like the Brown-headed Nuthatch. During winter, it often feeds on the ground, and I have seen flocks of Pine Warblers feeding in this manner with juncos and sparrows in open pine-grove pasture land. Also, Pine Warblers flock together in winter and often travel and feed in roving bands with kinglets, chickadees, titmice, nuthatches, Brown Creepers, and Downy Woodpeckers.

In winter, the resident population is augmented by migrants from the north. At this time, Pine Warblers occur in unlikely places such as hardwood bottomlands in the

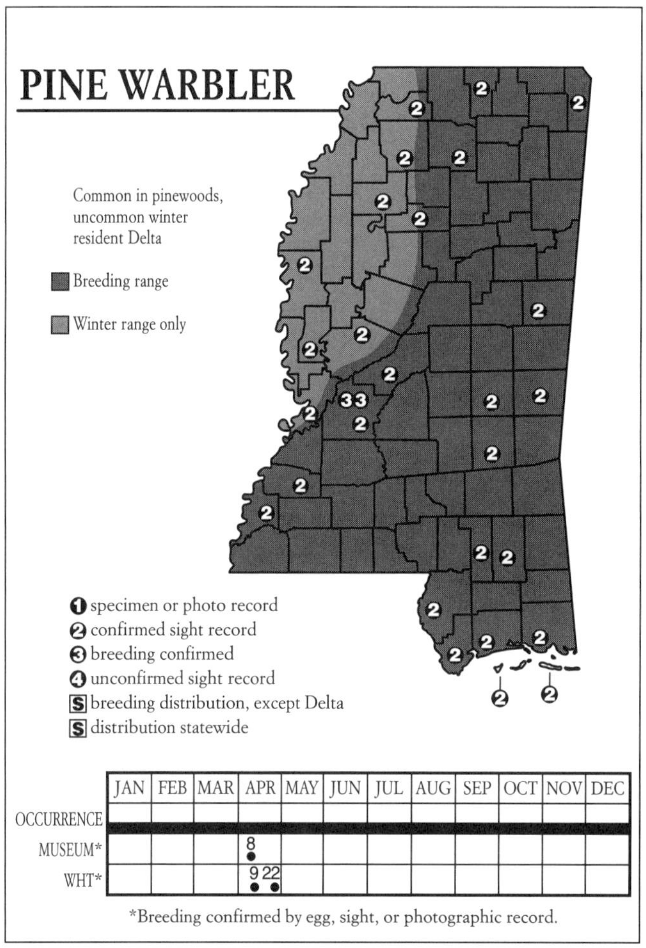

Yazoo Delta region. During the breeding season, it has not been recorded in the Yazoo Delta or in the northwestern part of the state, except where pines occur or have been planted.

The Pine Warbler is an abundant, permanent resident throughout the pineland sections of the state. It begins nest-building in late March or early April. The nest is compactly made of weed stems, bark, grass, and soft materials compressed into a firm cup, which is held together with cobwebs and lined with hair, fine grasses, and a few feathers. The nest may be placed on a pine limb or in a cluster of pine cones or needles and may be from 20 to 50 feet aboveground.

The eggs are grayish white, and marked with shades of brown and gray in a wreath around the large end. Nest records confirmed by egg collection (MMNS) are April 9 and 22, 1940, in Hinds County and April 8, 1940, in Jones County. Each of these nests contained four fresh eggs.

The Pine Warbler often sings during late winter, but is most vocal during the breeding season. The song is a pleasant, musical trill with considerable variation either up or down in pitch. This variation in pitch helps distinguish its slower song from that of the Chipping Sparrow's simple trill, which is all on the same pitch.

The adult male Pine Warbler resembles the Yellow-throated Vireo except for the bill shape, the faint streaks on the sides, and in *lacking the yellow "spectacles"* of the vireo. Field marks to look for in all plumages are a plain, unstreaked back; gray wings with two prominent, white wing bars; *white outer-tail spots;* white belly; and a faint eye stripe. Fall and winter specimens are highly variable in the amount of yellow on the underparts. The immatures are dingy gray or brownish with no streaking on the upperparts, dull white on the underparts with a slight wash of dinginess across the breast, and have two prominent white wing bars, and *white spots on the outer-tail feathers.*

This warbler ranges north into southeastern Canada and south through the Gulf States to east-central Texas, and to the West Indies. It winters in the southern part of its breeding range. Insects are its main source of food, but it eats wild fruits and seeds in winter and will visit feeders for tidbits.

Prairie Warbler *Dendroica discolor*

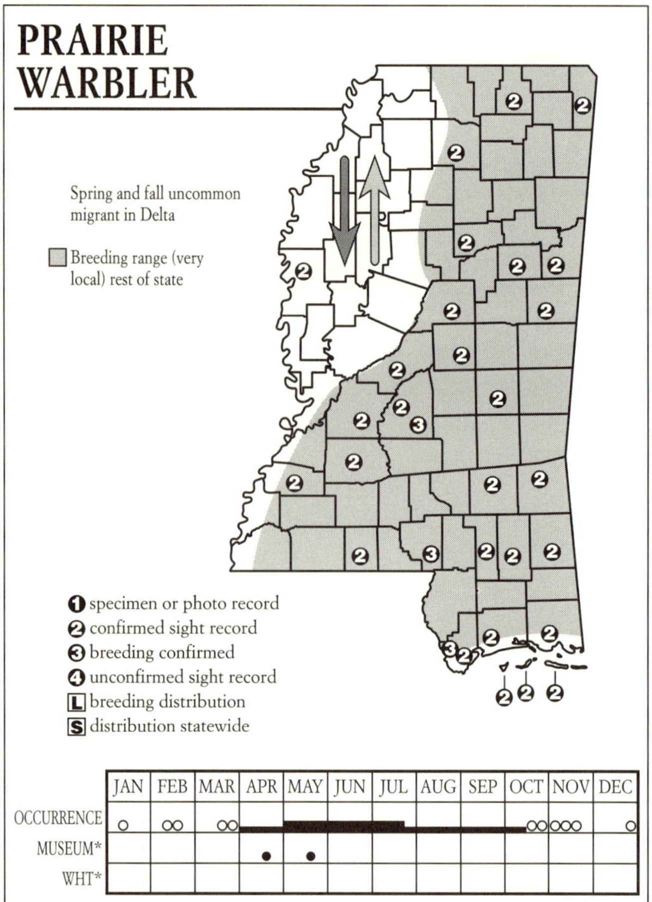

*Breeding confirmed by egg, sight, or photographic record.

The Prairie Warbler is not, as its name implies, a bird of open prairies. Its habitat is dry, upland, forested areas that have been heavily cut or burned over and are growing back in bushes, young trees, and stump sprouts (Gandy 1965b). Steep hillsides or dry ridges with open, mixed stands of hardwoods and pine, and understory shrubs of blueberry, huckleberry, yaupon, wax myrtle, and hardwood sprouts are preferred locations for this warbler. The Prairie Warbler's distribution as a breeding bird is spotty because of the variable nature of its habitats, which in the absence of fire or other disturbance factors soon become unsuitable. It occurs locally as a summer-resident, breeding bird in suitable nesting habitat throughout Mississippi, except in the Yazoo Delta and rarely in the Loess Bluff region.

The Prairie Warbler arrives around mid-March and its migration continues through April. Extreme dates of spring migration are March 18 and May 1. Fall migration begins as early as July 22, when arrivals have been recorded on the Gulf Coast, and is virtually completed by the end of September. In the coastal counties and offshore islands, this species may remain in scrubby growths until late October. Fall migration records are few for this warbler in the Yazoo Delta. Individual winter records have been reported by Judith Toups in Hancock, Perry, and Jackson Counties on January 12, and February 14 and 19.

Singing begins as soon as males arrive on the breeding grounds. The small, cup-shaped nest is made of fine grasses, weed stems, and plant down, and lined with hair, rootlets, and feathers. It is placed near the ground in low bushes or saplings. I have found nests in myrtle, blueberry, and huckleberry bushes, and in sweet gum and oak sprouts, all within two or three feet of the ground. Usually four white eggs, which are finely spotted with reddish brown, are laid.

The distinctive song is by far the best clue to locating the Prairie Warbler. The song is a series of short, buzzy notes ascending the scale and ending on a very high pitch.

The adult male Prairie Warbler has yellow underparts finely striped with black only on the sides. The back is olive green with chestnut streaks. The face is yellow with black marks through and below the eye converging to a V-shape in front of the eye. The outer-tail feathers are white, and the two wing bars are yellowish. The female is similar to the male but paler and with less extensive streaking. Immatures in fall plumage have faint, dusky marks instead of the black of the adult, and are gray and white around the eye, face, and throat instead of yellow. The habit of constantly twitching the tail from side to side is characteristic and, in combination with the bright yellow underparts and dusky mark on the neck, identifies this bird in the field.

The breeding range of the Prairie Warbler extends north into central Ontario, east to central New England, and south to the Gulf Coast. The winter range is from southern Florida south to Nicaragua, with casual winter records on the Mississippi Coast and in Perry County, southern Alabama, southern Louisiana, and coastal South Carolina.

I have found both active and abandoned nests of this warbler on the coastal terrace in Jackson County, and an active nest in Marion County on April 28, 1967 (Turcotte and Phares 1967). A nestling photographed by Judith Toups near Kiln in Hancock County substantiates a coastal breeding record. June breeding bird surveys conducted by Judith Toups further indicate that singing males are common, with 34 singing males recorded on May 28, 1986. Nests are built in April and May, as confirmed by nest and egg records extending from April 28 to May 28 (MMNS).

Palm Warbler *Dendroica palmarum*

The Palm Warbler is an uncommon spring and fall migrant in northern Mississippi and is rarely found as a winter resident in the central and northern counties. In the coastal counties, this species is a regular and moderately common winter resident, although it can be overlooked if it is not sought in the brushy habitat of open pine and scrub oak woods or in weedy fields and pastures. In winter, it is somewhat gregarious and gathers in small flocks, often with Pine Warblers and sparrows. This species feeds mostly on or near the ground and seems to prefer recently burned-over areas.

The adult male Palm Warbler is mostly dark brown above with a reddish brown crown. Its *tail coverts are olive above and yellow below,* and it is finely streaked with brown on the breast and sides. The color of the breast and belly varies from yellow to dirty white. The tail coverts combined with almost constant *tail-bobbing* separate the Palm Warbler from the Prairie Warbler in any plumage.

The paler western population of this species is more common as a transient than as a winter resident. The eastern population, which has more yellow on the breast and belly, winters more commonly on the Mississippi Coast. Burleigh (1945) collected specimens representing both populations in the coastal area, observing that the eastern population arrived later and departed earlier than the western birds. Extreme dates of arrival and departure for Mississippi are September 5 and May 27. The northward migration occurs largely after March 20 and extends through April, rarely later.

The Palm Warbler winters in the southern United States, particularly in the coastal regions and Florida, and the West Indies. It breeds across Canada from southern Newfoundland and Quebec to northern Manitoba and southern Mackenzie. The breeding range extends south to northeastern British Columbia, central Saskatchewan, northern Minnesota, northern Michigan, and Maine.

Nests of plant fibers and fine grass lined with feathers or soft plant materials are placed on or near the ground,

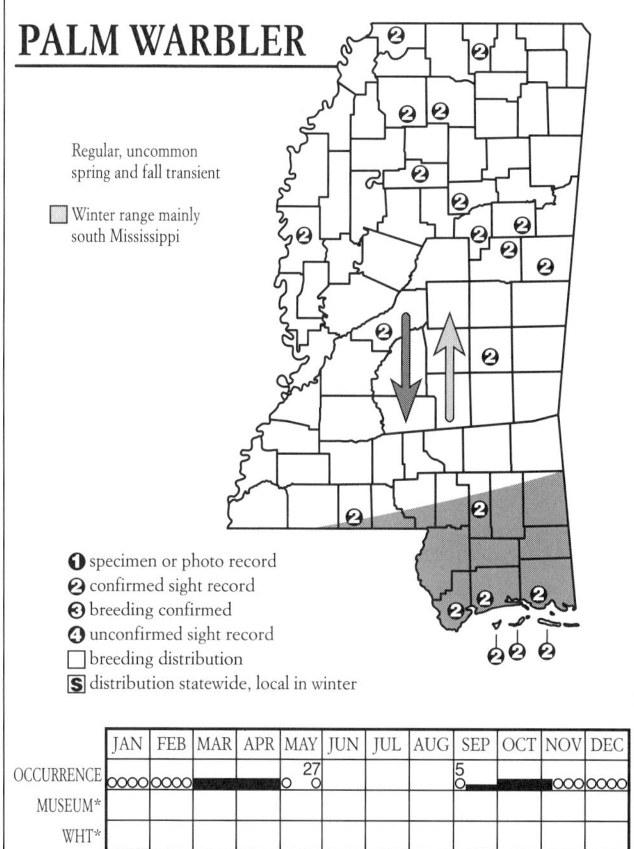

*Breeding confirmed by egg, sight, or photographic record.

concealed in a low spruce, moss, or other ground vegetation in or near bogs or muskeg. Four or five eggs marked with brown and gray make up a clutch. The song of the Palm Warbler is a weak, slightly musical trill similar to that of the Chipping Sparrow.

Bay-breasted Warbler *Dendroica castanea*

The chestnut crown, uppper breast, throat, and sides, and a buff-colored patch on each side of the neck are diagnostic for the male Bay-breasted Warbler in spring. Females are similar, but much duller. In the fall, adults and immatures are olive green above and buffy below with two white wing bars, and adults may have some chestnut on the flanks.

In autumn, the Blackpoll Warbler is similar to the Bay-breasted. In this plumage, the Blackpoll has light breast streaks and white undertail coverts. The breast and undertail coverts of the fall Bay-breasted are buffy. The Blackpoll has yellow legs and feet, while those of the Bay-breasted are black. The Blackpoll is unlikely to occur here in fall migration. The song of the Bay-breasted is high and thin, much like the Black-and-white Warbler's song and rendered *tee'si, tee'si, tee'si.*

Like most other late spring transients, this warbler is irregular in its appearance on the coast, except during bad weather. In northern Mississippi, it occurs more regularly during the spring migration, a period from the last 10 days of April to mid-May.

Extreme records of spring passage for this bird are March 19 and May 29. In the fall, this species is a regular transient in late September and October. Extreme dates of fall arrival and departure recorded in Mississippi are August 18 (Toups and Jackson 1987) and November 25.

The breeding range of the Bay-breasted Warbler extends eastward from central Manitoba into Nova Scotia and southward in the coniferous forests from northern Wisconsin to northern New England. The winter range is south of the canal zone in central Panama, south to Venezuela and Colombia.

Blackpoll Warbler *Dendroica striata*

The Blackpoll Warbler is a fairly common, late spring transient, except on the Gulf Coast where its appearance is erratic. Extreme dates of arrival and departure are April 16 and May 29.

Blackpoll Warbler breeding grounds are in the extensive northern coniferous forests from Alaska and Labrador,

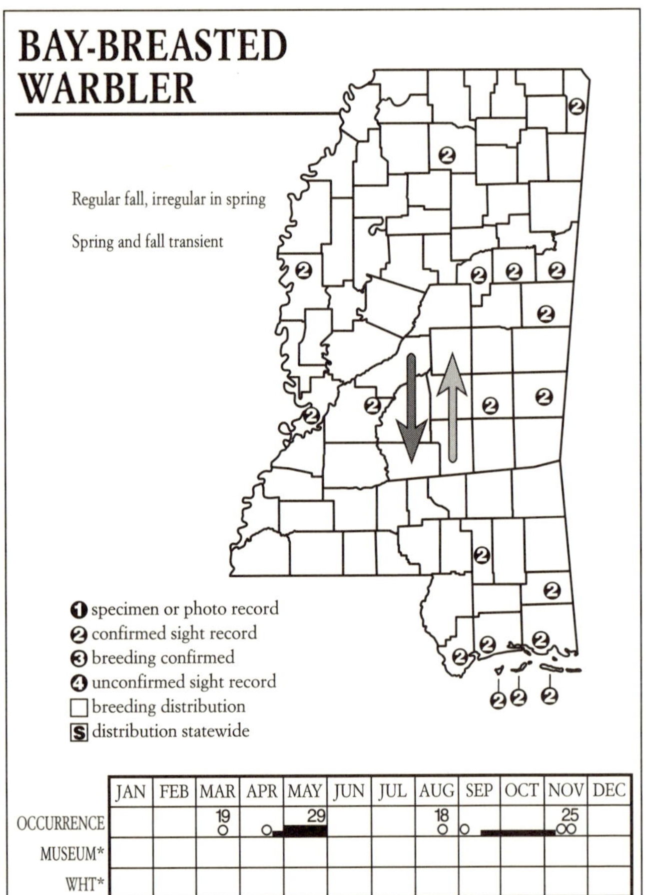

*Breeding confirmed by egg, sight, or photographic record.

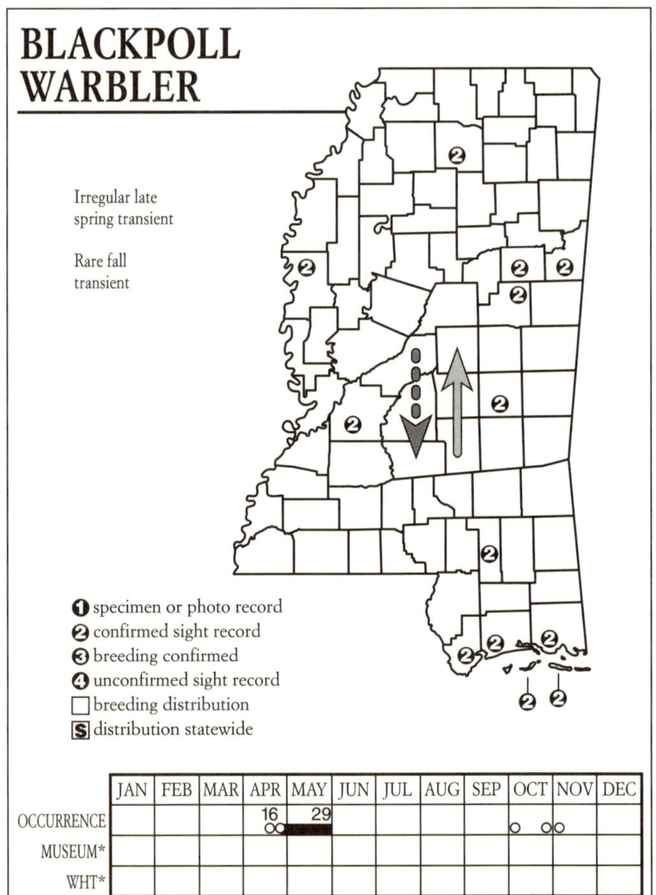

*Breeding confirmed by egg, sight, or photographic record.

and south into Maine, New Hampshire, and northern parts of New York and Massachusetts. It returns southward in the fall mainly along a migration route from Atlantic Coast states down through Florida and the West Indies. A few sight records of the Blackpoll Warbler exist for October and November (Schardien and Jackson 1983; Toups and Jackson 1987).

The nest is usually built in small spruce trees not far above the ground or occasionally on the ground. It is a bulky structure of weed stems, bark, grasses, and soft materials lined with rootlets, hair, plant fibers, and feathers. Three to five white or cream-colored eggs speckled or wreathed with shades of brown make up a set.

In spring the male Blackpoll can be identified by its solid black crown, white throat and cheeks, black malar streak, two white wing bars, white underparts, and black-streaked sides and back. The adult female is drab olive on the back and wings, with less black streaking on the back and sides, and lacks the black cap of the spring male.

Fall birds are greenish olive above with lightly streaked back and sides. They closely resemble the fall Bay-breasted Warblers, but have *yellowish buff* feet and legs and *white* undertail coverts. In autumn the Bay-breasted Warbler has *black* feet and legs, and its undertail coverts are buffy. The Blackpoll's song is a thin, high-pitched series of notes all on the same pitch, which is louder in the middle and diminishes at the end.

CERULEAN WARBLER

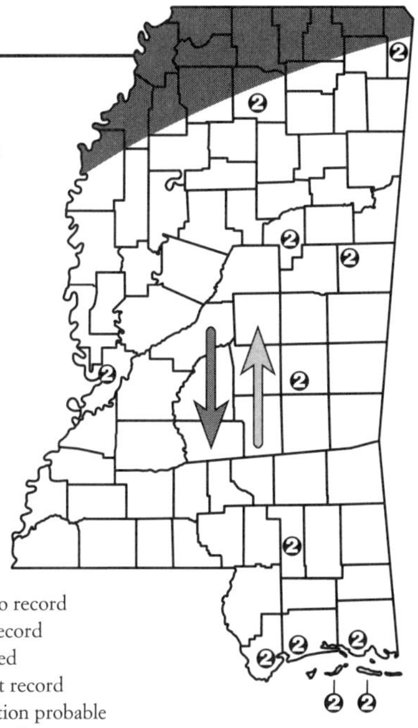

Spring and fall migrant

Probable breeding

❶ specimen or photo record
❷ confirmed sight record
❸ breeding confirmed
❹ unconfirmed sight record
[L] breeding distribution probable
[S] distribution statewide

	JAN	FEB	MAR	APR	MAY	JUN	JUL	AUG	SEP	OCT	NOV	DEC
OCCURRENCE				5	13		26		30			
MUSEUM*												
WHT*												

*Breeding confirmed by egg, sight, or photographic record.

Cerulean Warbler *Dendroica cerulea*

In spring, the male Cerulean Warbler is a beautiful shade of pale blue on the upperparts and lightly streaked with gray on the back and sides of the breast and flanks. Males are white below with a narrow blackish band across the breast. Both adults and immatures have two white wing bars.

The female and young are dull blue gray on the crown, olive green on the back with a yellowish tinge on their plain underparts. Tennessee Warbler females and immatures are similar to female and immature Ceruleans, but have no white wing bars. The song of the Cerulean Warbler suggests a Northern Parula. It is a buzzing trill of four or five notes that rises to a higher pitch at the end.

This warbler is a spring and fall transient, and there are no established records of its breeding in Mississippi. There are several records during late May and June in extreme northeast Mississippi and the northern Yazoo Delta, and it might be found breeding in those parts of our state. Extremes of recorded spring and fall migration are April 5 to May 13, and July 26 to September 30.

The Cerulean is a treetop warbler, and where I have seen it during spring migration, it was in the tops of tall, deciduous trees in bottomlands. Its habits make this warbler hard to see. Those I have observed in the spring were singing incessantly, and they were in groups of a half dozen or more.

Black-and-white Warbler *Mniotilta varia*

The Black-and-white Warbler is a small bird heavily streaked with black-and-white above and below, except on its white belly. The mature male has black cheeks and throat. Females and immatures lack the black cheeks. The underparts of the female are mostly white with light streaking on the sides. The crown of both sexes and immatures is streaked.

The song, a high-pitched whistling, consists of a series of double notes, the first one a higher pitch and louder than the one following. The song suggests *we'see* repeated about six or seven times in rapid succession.

This warbler feeds by creeping about like a nuthatch, feeding consistently on the trunks and limbs of trees. The Black-and-white Warbler is a common migrant, a casual winter resident, and a rare and local breeder in hardwoods or mixed woods in central and northern Mississippi.

One of the first migrants to arrive in spring, it appears sometimes as early as the second week in March and becomes

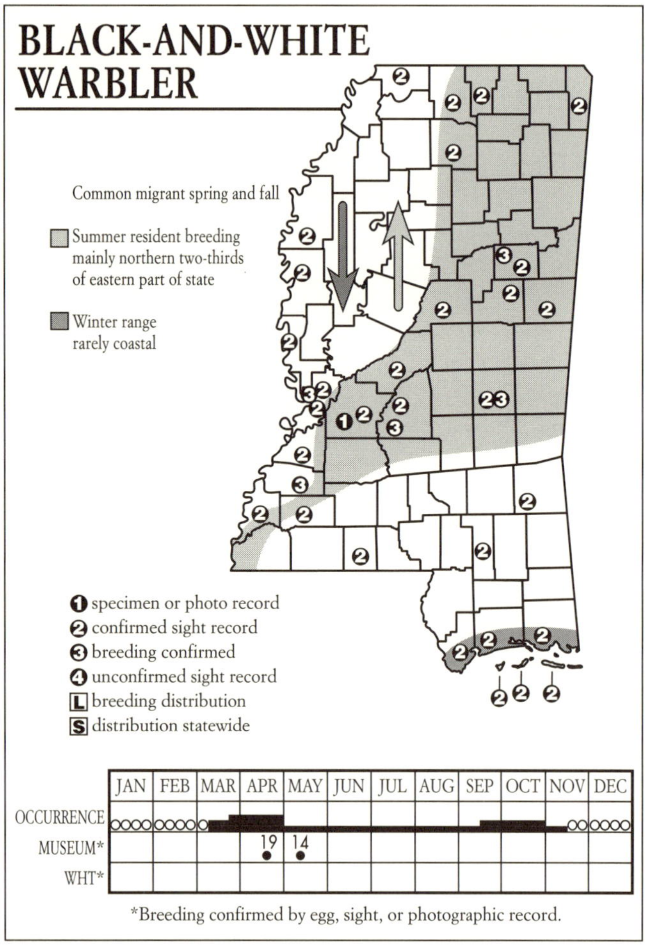

plentiful by late March and early April. Migrants are some of the first to reappear in the fall, arriving around mid-July and becoming most plentiful in August and September. Except for a few late stragglers, the fall migration is virtually complete by mid-November.

The Black-and-white Warbler builds a cup nest of leaves, grasses, bark, and pine needles that is well lined with fine grass, rootlets, or hair. The nest is placed on the ground in dry woodlands, well concealed from above by overhanging leaves or pine needles. The four or five white eggs are heavily spotted with brown.

Although numerous occurrence records of this species exist during the breeding season, there are few substantiated nesting records. I collected a fledgling out of the nest for a museum specimen on May 14, 1942, south of Star in Rankin County. A nest with six eggs atop a ridge in the Loess Bluff Experimental Forest in Warren County was photographed by C. E. Grissom (Grissom et al. 1963) and R. D. Caldwell. They furnished a color slide of the nest and eggs taken on April 19, 1963 (MMNS).

American Redstart *Setophaga ruticilla*

The adult male American Redstart is unmistakable in his flashy garb of jet black on the head, breast, and upperparts; salmon red wing, tail, and shoulders; and a white belly. The female is similarly marked, but has grayish or olive green where the adult male is black, and yellow flash-patches on the wings, tail, and shoulders. The immature male is similar to the female, but yellow marks often are tinged with orange.

Redstarts are active birds and usually frequent the upperparts of deciduous trees. They have flat, flycatcher-like bills and habits similar to flycatchers. They often can be seen nervously flitting about in pursuit of flying insects, sometimes making long swoops after them. Their wings characteristically spread downward against their body. The very long tail is narrow at the base and broader at the end. It is fanned out frequently to reveal the red or yellow rectangular tail patches at the base of the outer feathers.

A common migrant in spring and abundant in the fall in all woodlands except pinelands, this species is a widespread summer resident in hardwood bottomlands and in beech-magnolia ravines of the Loess Bluffs of western Missis-

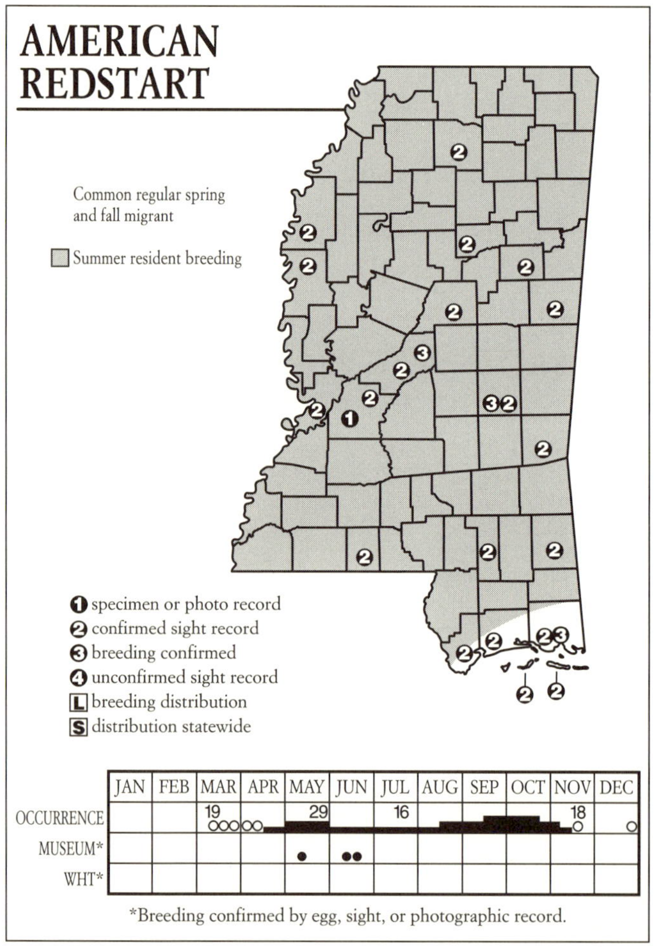

sippi. Late May and June collection and sight records indicate that American Redstarts breed in various parts of the state, in the larger stream bottoms and extensive deciduous woodlands, except in the immediate vicinity of the coast.

I have observed adults feeding young out of the nest in the Pearl River swamp near Jackson. John H. Phares and I found a pair building a nest in a winged elm tree in the Pearl River bottom near the old Meek's Ferry bridge in Madison County on May 10, 1958 (Turcotte 1958c). The completed nest was abandoned when rechecked on June 1. It was compactly made of shredded plant bark, fibers, rootlets, and grass stems held together by cobwebs and lined with fine grasses and rootlets. The nest was fastened to two upright shoots from the top of a limb near the trunk and was about 20 feet aboveground. The American Redstart lays three or four white eggs that are marked reddish brown and gray around the larger end.

On the Mississippi Coast, the American Redstart appears in early April and continues arriving into the second week of May. On the coast, fall migrants appear the last of July and become plentiful during their southward passage until late October. Extreme dates for spring and fall migration on the Mississippi Coast are March 19 to May 29, and July 16 to November 18.

The breeding range extends from southeastern Alaska across Canada into central Quebec and Newfoundland, south into Oregon, Utah, northeastern Texas, and from southern Louisiana into northwestern Florida. The winter range is Puerto Rico, Cuba, and central Mexico south into northern South America. It has been reported as a casual winter resident in southern Louisiana by Lowery Jr. (1974).

The song of the American Redstart is a series of four or five thin, high-pitched single or double notes, the last ending in the same pitch. There are several song variations, usually sung alternately, and rendered as *tsee-tsee-tsee-tseet* or *teetsa, teetsa, teetsa, tseet, tsee-tsee-tsee-tset.*

Prothonotary Warbler *Protonotaria citrea*

Except along the Gulf Coast where it occurs only in migration, the Prothonotary Warbler is a common to abundant spring and summer resident. It appears in the spring shortly after mid-March, and by April the species is plentiful in wooded swamps, and ravines of the Loess Bluff. Fall migration for this bird begins in late July and August and extends to the end of September, when departure is mostly complete. Occasional stragglers may remain through October.

It is nearly always found close to water or watercourses, especially oxbow lakes, sloughs, and bayous bordered by cypress, tupelo gum, and willow trees. In these locations, it usually nests in tree stump cavities. Sometimes it nests in gourds, boxes, or cans around houses or hunter camps near water. David Watts reports finding a Prothonotary Warbler nest with two eggs in the sidewall of a pickup truck in April 1993 at the Turcotte Field Station on Ross Barnett Reservoir north of Jackson. The nest was later abandoned and the eggs taken to the MMNS. In 1994 at the same field station, Watts and John Skains observed in the tongue of a boat trailer a nest that had fledged five young.

Cypress and tupelo trees occupy the lowest parts of valuable bottomland hardwoods. This is the preferred nesting habitat for Prothonotary and Yellow-throated warblers.

The Prothonotary Warbler nest is composed of bits of leaves and green moss, which nearly fill the nest cavity, and is lined with rootlets, grasses, hair, and fine leaf stems. The three to six eggs are pinkish, and liberally blotched or spotted with shades of brown, gray, and lavender. The nesting period extends from April through June.

The Prothonotary Warbler is one of the most eye-catching and attractive of the wood warblers. The male has a golden yellow head and underparts. The wings are plain blue gray without bars. The tail is blue gray above, with white underneath and in the outer-tail feathers. The back is yellowish green. The female is similar to the male, though considerably duller in coloration. Both sexes have a long, straight, dark bill. The immature plumage and the basic plumage of both sexes are somewhat dusky above and light yellow below.

The song is loud and clear and consists of five or six notes on the same pitch described as: *sweet, sweet, sweet, sweet, sweet.*

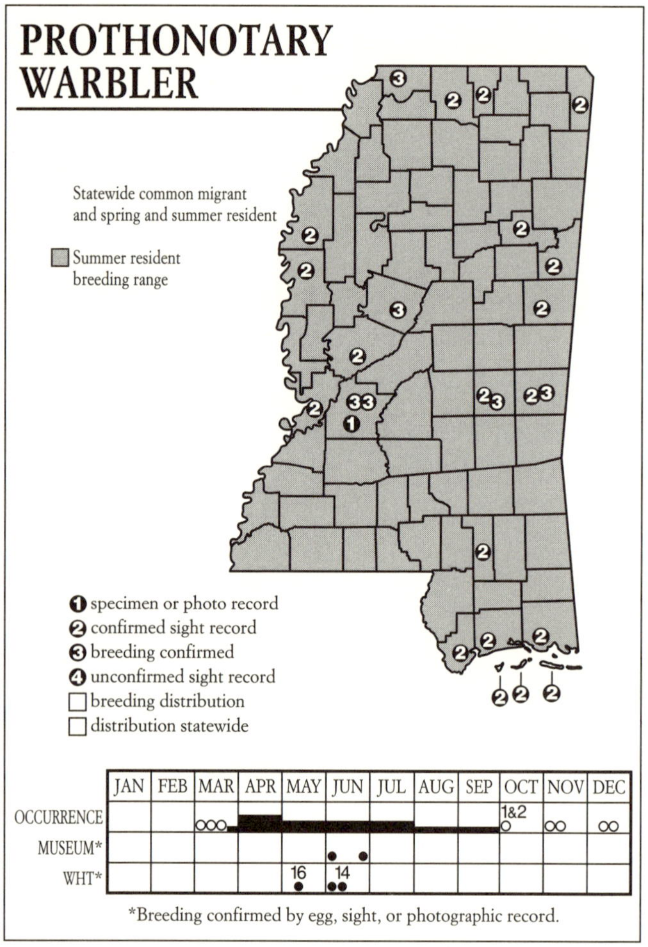

Almost impossible to spot in the ground and leaf litter is the nest of a Worm-eating Warbler. It was discovered after watching an adult bird return to the young. It was located on a beech-magnolia bluff amid the Loess Bluff hills north of Bovina in Warren County on May 29, 1972.

Worm-eating Warbler *Helmitheros vermivorus*

The Worm-eating Warbler is a fairly common spring and fall transient, and is extremely local as a summer resident in Mississippi. R. M. Freeman recorded juvenile Worm-eating Warblers being fed by an adult bird in Jones County near Indian Springs on July 14, 1939. He also reported finding two adults feeding three flying young near Woodville in Wilkinson County on August 1, 1939. While working with Freeman, B. A. Bloodsworth recorded in his field notes another observation in Wilkinson County on August 2, 1939, of both parents feeding fledged young.

On numerous occasions since 1963, I have observed singing males and feeding adults during May and June. They occurred in wooded ravines bordered by beech bluffs north of Bovina in Warren County. On May 25, 1963, I saw adults feeding a fledgling just out of the nest in a ravine at the headwaters of Clear Creek, about seven miles north of Bovina (Turcotte 1963d, 1972f). On May 25, 1968, I saw adults feeding a flying juvenile on the opposite side of the same ravine. Over a period of eight years, I searched this ravine for nests numerous times without success.

Then on May 20, 1972, while on a field trip with members of the Jackson Audubon Chapter, we observed a Worm-eating Warbler carrying nest material to a partly completed nest on the slope of a beech bluff. This nest, which was completed on May 25, was situated under the overhanging fronds of a Christmas fern and had a lining of the coarse, reddish brown flower or fruit pedicels of red maple.

Also on May 25, 1972, while with John Phares and Wendell Neal, I found in the same ravine a second nest with an adult and four newly hatched young. This nest, with the adults feeding young, was photographed during return visits on May 29 and 30 (Turcotte 1972f). The basal structures of both nests were made entirely of dried and skeletonized beech leaves arranged clockwise in spiral fashion.

The nests were built in a horizontal plane against the slope of a ridge, supported and partly concealed by dead leaves and other vegetation. The lining of the second nest consisted of fine, dried grass, and the blackish terminal rachises and pinnae of the maidenhair fern, *Adiatum pedatum.* The first nest was abandoned, probably because of egg predation, since shell fragments were found in the bottom of the nest.

The nests just described are typical of the Worm-eating Warbler on the beech-magnolia hillsides bordering deep-gullied ravines of the Loess Bluff region. The eggs number four or five in a set. The white ground color is speckled with brown or reddish brown.

The Worm-eating Warbler is plain, dull olive on the back and has wings with rich, buffy underparts. The head is buff

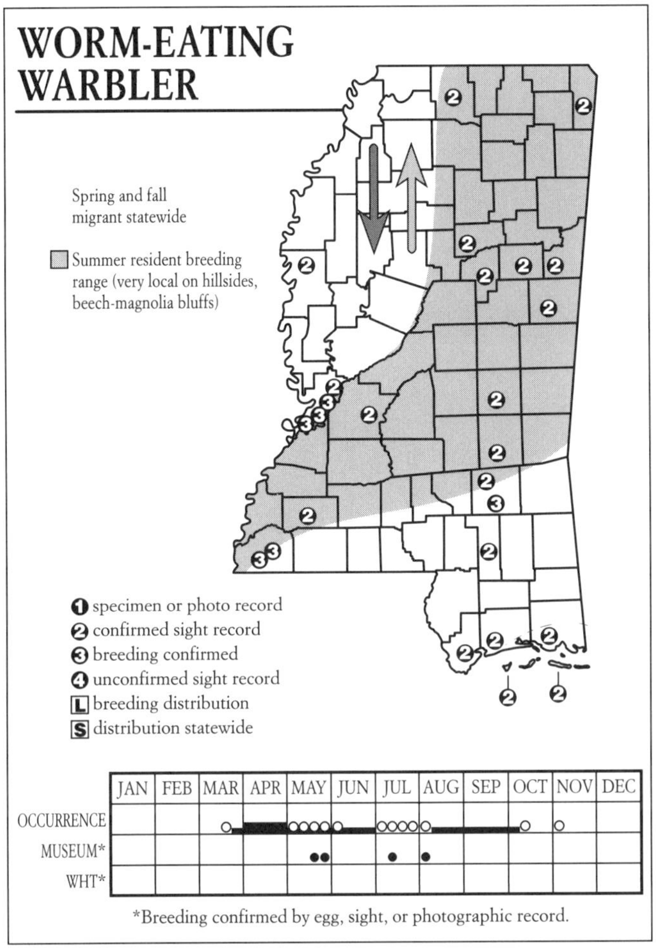

colored and prominently marked with four black stripes. Two of the stripes are on top of the head and the others pass through each eye and extend from the bill to the nape. The sexes are alike in appearance. The song is a thin buzzing much like the Chipping Sparrow, but slightly higher and more rapid.

This warbler arrives in late March and is most numerous during April. Fall migration begins in late July, becomes the heaviest in September, and ends in early October.

This species is unique in its selection of steep, hillside microhabitats for its nests. The nests I found were on slopes too steep to walk up without following a contour and holding onto a bush or sapling. The selection of naturally curved elements of certain plants growing in the habitat for lining the nest is also unique.

This species feeds on insect larvae in the midstory of trees. I noticed most feeding in beech trees and observed adults feeding young in and out of the nest on brown and green inchworms.

Swainson's Warbler *Limnothlypis swainsonii*

Discovery of the Swainson's Warbler was first reported by John Bachman about 1832 when he collected specimens along the Edisto River in South Carolina. John James Audubon, a good friend of Bachman, described the new bird and named it after another friend, the English ornithologist William Swainson.

For the next 50 years, the species went unrecorded. In 1884 William Brewster and Arthur T. Wayne made significant studies and collections near Charleston, South Carolina. Wayne reported the first Swainson's Warbler nest in 1885 near Charleston. After the early part of the twentieth century, it again almost became a lost species. Ornithologists began to rediscover it after about 1930. More recently, much has been learned about this bird's distribution and habits (Meanley 1971; Turcotte 1972d).

The Swainson's secretive habits and the character of its usual, deep swamp and river bottom haunts make it difficult to find. It is one of the least known of southern songbirds and is often overlooked by most bird-watchers.

In Mississippi, this warbler is a fairly common, widely distributed, spring- and summer-resident, breeding bird (Turcotte 1972d). Its breeding range is mainly north of the coastal counties. Typical breeding habitats are alluvial stream bottoms and the wood ravines of the Loess Bluffs bordering the Yazoo Delta and Mississippi River.

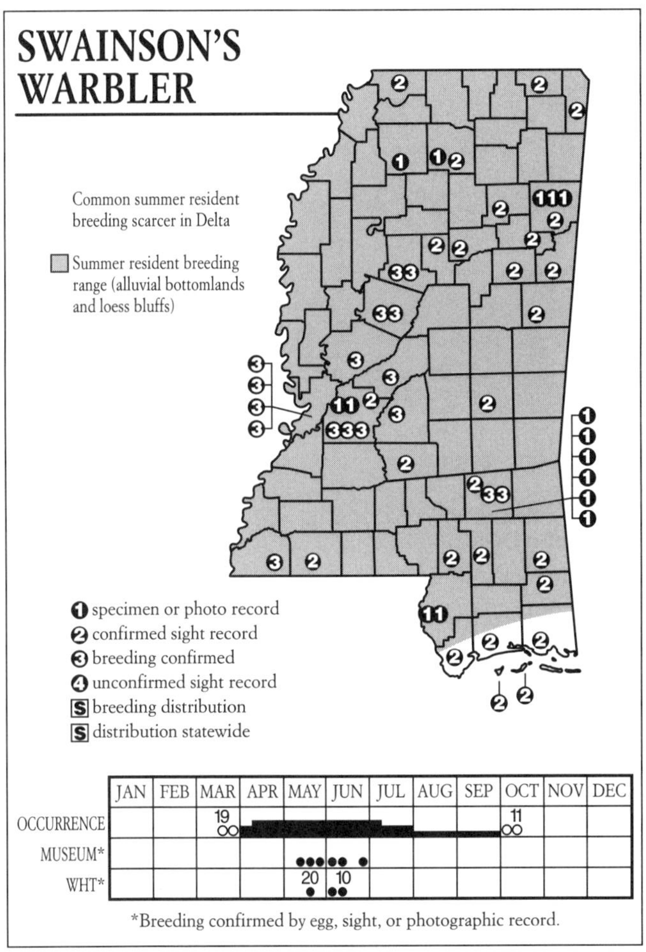

The basic requirements of breeding habitat for the Swainson's Warbler are proximity to water; an understory of tree, shrub, and vine tangles; a scattering of dead leaves and decaying vegetation; ground cover of shade-tolerant plants; and a nearly closed canopy of hardwoods or mixed stands of pine and hardwood trees. Cane thickets are preferred nesting habitat. The axils of cane stalks, greenbrier vines, and vine-covered shrubs are used for nest support.

The nest is a bulky cup built of loosely compressed leaves, small twigs, and vine tendrils lined with finer materials such as dead grass or weed stems, rootlets, fine strips of bark, small cypress twigs and needles, pine needles, moss fibers, flower stalks, or hair. Nests resemble a bunch of dead leaves lodged by high water. The nest height is usually from two to six feet, averaging about four feet. Three or four white eggs make up a clutch.

The Swainson's Warbler appears to be short and rather stockily built for a warbler. The sexes are alike in appearance. Upperparts are olive brown with a solid brown crown. Underparts are plain buffy white or very faintly yellowish. There is a conspicuous white stripe above the eye. The brownish back, brown cap, and plain underparts are diagnostic.

The song of the Swainson's Warbler is a series of loud, clear, musical whistles. It consists of two or three separate, introductory, slurred whistles followed by a phrase of four or five slurred, rapidly uttered syllables. The best description of the song, which may vary among individuals, is *whee, whee, whee, whit-tzee-wee'-o*. Both sexes have loud alarm *chips* and softer *chip* or *zeep* notes, which resemble a waterthrush or the Kentucky Warbler.

Spring arrival dates for this species recorded on the Gulf Coast extend from March 19 to April 19. North of the coastal counties, arrival dates extend from March 25 to April 30 (average date is April 21). Fall migration and departure dates south of Hattiesburg extend from August 1 to October 11.

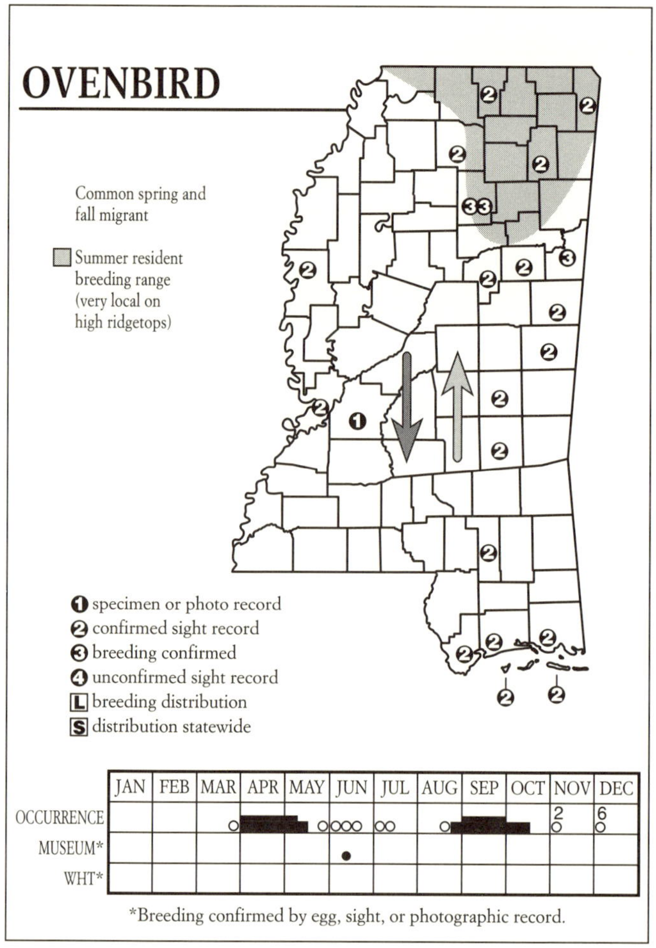

Ovenbird *Seiurus aurocapillus*

The Ovenbird is a common, spring and fall migrant throughout Mississippi. In northern and northeastern Mississippi, it occurs locally as a summer-resident, breeding bird, usually at higher elevations in deciduous woodlands. It was first recorded nesting in Lowndes County by Stockard (1905), who described a typical oven-shaped nest on the ground in vines and grass in a wooded valley. The nest contained five fresh eggs on May 26, 1895. Hanson (1958) reported an Ovenbird nesting in Calhoun County in June 1954 and June 1958. Specimens of the Ovenbird in the MMNS taken on June 22 and July 10, 1939, by H. L. Owens in Tishomingo County were probably breeding in that area.

This warbler dwells mainly on or near the ground in shady, secluded, dense places strewn with leaves on the forest floor. Its distinctive territorial song is loud and clear, described as *tea-cher* repeated rapidly about 10 times and becoming louder and louder toward the end. The male also has a flight song that is delivered during courtship or in the evening or night.

The Ovenbird is a regular spring migrant arriving during April and departing by mid-May. Extremes of recorded spring arrival and departure dates for Mississippi are March 31 and May 21. Fall migration through Mississippi occurs mainly between September 15 and October 15. Extremes of fall migration are August 22 and November 2, with one anomalous December 6 record on the coast.

This warbler builds a nest on the ground, usually in a forest opening covered with leaf litter. The bird first makes a slight depression in the ground, and then adds a cup of leaves, grass, fibers, and straw. Finally, the new nest is roofed over with similar material and an opening created on one side to form an oven-shaped structure. It is lined with hair or fine, fibrous plant materials before the bird lays its four to six white eggs, which are speckled with shades of gray and reddish brown. The Ovenbird's nest is difficult to find because it is almost completely concealed from view.

At first glance, this bird has the appearance of a small thrush with its olive brown back; brown-streaked, white underparts; and pinkish legs. Black stripes over the eye on each side of a dull, *central, orange stripe on the crown and a white eye ring* distinguish it from similar waterthrushes, which have a light eye stripe instead of an eye ring. The Ovenbird *walks,* rather than hops, and teeters and bobs its tail. However, so do waterthrushes.

The Ovenbird breeds north into southern Canada and south into Colorado, Oklahoma, northern Arkansas, northern Mississippi, northern Alabama, and northern Georgia. In winter, this species ranges casually north to southern Louisiana, southern Georgia, southern South Carolina, and Florida. It winters regularly in the West Indies, Mexico, Central America, and northern South America.

Northern Waterthrush *Seiurus noveboracensis*

Ovenbirds and Northern and Louisiana Waterthrushes are very similar in appearance and habits. All three are "tail-bobbers." They teeter and walk with the body held in a horizontal posture instead of hopping.

The Northern Waterthrush is dark olive brown above, with a prominent yellowish stripe over the eye and heavily striped underparts strongly tinged with yellow or buff. The Northern Waterthrush can be separated from the Louisiana Waterthrush by the former's *spotted* throat, *yellowish* or *buffy* eye stripe (not always a reliable field identification mark), *small* bill, and *more yellowish underparts.* The Louisiana Waterthrush always has a *wider* and *longer,* pure white eye stripe; a large bill; a white throat without spots; and is darker above and whiter below than the Northern Waterthrush.

This warbler is an irregular spring transient that apparently is never common during its northward passage through Mississippi. There are only two spring collection records among 11 specimens of this bird in the MMNS. These were taken on April 28 and May 14. Burleigh (1945) collected a series of 44 Northern Waterthrushes on the Mississippi Gulf Coast, and only nine were spring records, birds taken between April 19 and May 17.

The spring passage of this migrant occurs mainly after mid-April to May 15. It is regular and common in the fall migration. Extreme dates for its occurrence in Mississippi during fall are August 13 and October 24, with most records occurring during September and the first week in October. In migration, this species is usually found in thickets along stream courses or lakes.

The breeding range extends from north-central Alaska across Canada to Labrador, south to northern Idaho, along the northern edge of the United States to southern New England, and locally in mountainous regions of West Virginia, western Virginia, and western North Carolina. The winter range is mainly in the West Indies, Mexico, Central America, and northern South America.

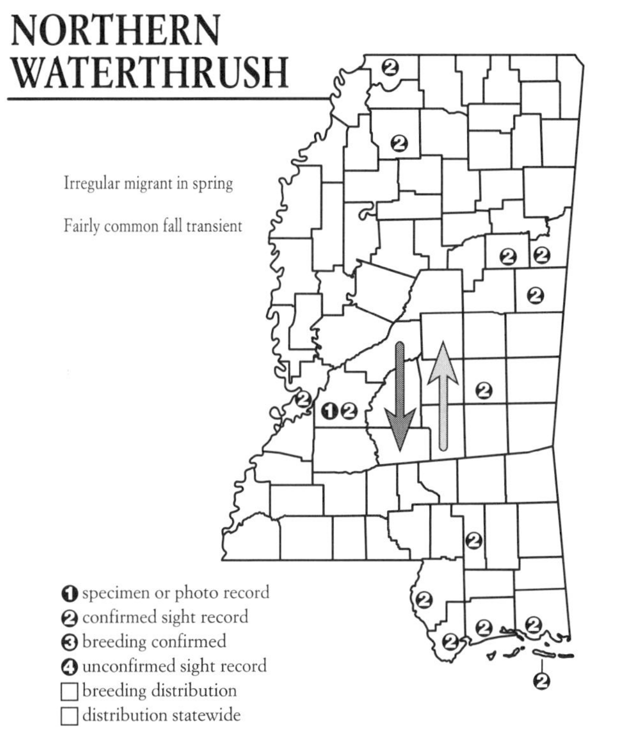

	JAN	FEB	MAR	APR	MAY	JUN	JUL	AUG	SEP	OCT	NOV	DEC
OCCURRENCE			○	○○○○	15 ○○○			13 ○○○	○○○○	24 ○○○○		
MUSEUM*												
WHT*												

*Breeding confirmed by egg, sight, or photographic record.

The well-concealed nest of the Northern Waterthrush is usually near water, under overhanging banks or tree roots, in upturned roots of blown-down trees, or in log cavities or stumps. Made of leaves, green moss, twigs, and shreds of bark, the nest is lined with moss, hair, or rootlets. The four or five eggs are creamy white and spotted or blotched with shades of brown and gray.

The song, loud and ringing, is described by Roger T. Peterson as *twit, twit, twit, twee, twee, twee, chew, chew, chew,* dropping in pitch and accelerating at the end. In my experience, the Louisiana Waterthrush song is distinctly different from the transient Northern Waterthrush.

Louisiana Waterthrush *Seiurus motacilla*

The Louisiana Waterthrush is a locally common, summer-resident, breeding bird in stream bottoms throughout most of Mississippi, except on the coast. It is an erratic, early spring transient from the coast northward for about 50 miles. In mid-March, breeding birds begin arriving, with the passage of migrants of this species mostly complete by mid-April. Extreme dates of recorded spring migration on the coast are March 8 and April 26. This species begins its southward migration early, according to records kept by Thomas D. Burleigh. Fall migration records extend from July 9 to October 29, with most birds in passage during late July and August.

Distinguishing field marks for the two waterthrushes are described in the preceding species accounts. The call note of the Louisiana Waterthrush is a sharp *chink*. The song is three shrill, slurred notes followed by jumbled twitterings on a descending scale. It can be confused with the song of the Swainson's Warbler when heard at a distance.

Resident breeding males are actively singing as soon as they arrive on their nesting territories. I found a newly completed nest on March 29, 1973, concealed in a roadside bank near a stream north of Bovina in Warren County. A nest found near the same place under roots in a stream bank on April 29, 1967, contained four newly hatched young.

Other nests containing eggs have been recorded on May 2 in Wayne County (three eggs collected by V. E. Trigg), and on May 16 in Jones County (four eggs collected by B. A. Bloodsworth; MMNS). I collected a set of four fresh eggs

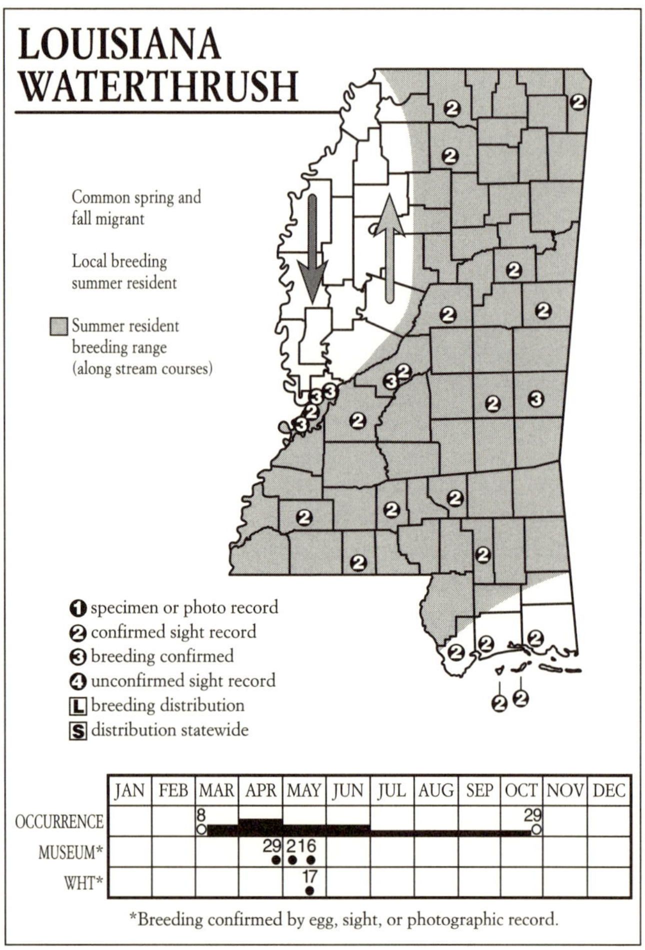

on May 17, 1940, from a typical, well-concealed nest under an overhanging ditch bank at Gin Creek near Center Hill in Lauderdale County. The bulky nest was made of leaves and green moss and was lined with fine grass. The white eggs of the Louisiana Waterthrush are boldly blotched or variously spotted with shades of brown and gray.

I had a unique experience with this warbler while on two trips to the Bovina hills in Warren County. As I was walking along a wooded ravine on a turkey hunt in that area on March 26, 1984, I heard a singing male Louisiana Waterthrush. When approached, the bird flew from a stream course and continued its territorial singing. I assumed the bird would remain at this potential nesting site, so I returned the next morning at daybreak with equipment for recording the song.

The bird appeared and sang at the site, and I set up the recorder, tripod, and parabolic reflector. After about 30 minutes, I got a *prized* recording and decided to walk farther down the stream to listen for a wild gobbler.

I crossed the stream on a foot bridge, and walked about a half mile and back, but went past the bridge. So, I decided to walk a log across the stream. Something told me not to try it, but while holding onto a sapling I took two steps, then one too many. The log cracked, and I fell six or seven feet before the butt end of the log caught my shin and cracked the small bone above the left ankle. I managed to pull myself from the stream bed, find a stout oak limb for a crutch, and then discovered my bifocals were missing.

After recovering my glasses from the stream bed and getting back to my equipment, I decided to go the rest of the distance without it. I had to crawl on hands and knees up a steep bank to get to the car. Fortunately, some nearby pulpwood cutters retrieved my equipment for the price of a six-pack. I made it to the hospital emergency room before reporting the mishap, and was rescued and later cared for by my wife, Dorothy.

This prized recording cost about $1100 in medical bills. Your forbearance for this hard-luck story, please. It was worth all the effort, and I have since given up walking logs.

Kentucky Warbler *Oporornis formosus*

The Kentucky Warbler is a common, summer-resident, breeding bird throughout Mississippi. It arrives in late March and early April, and migration continues through early May. On the Mississippi Coast, fall migration begins as early as July 31 and continues through August and September. The latest recorded departure date is October 9.

The breeding habitat is moist, shady, deciduous woodlands with a dense understory of shrubs, ferns, and other shade-tolerant plants in stream bottoms, the bottoms of wooded ravines, and swamp edges. The nest is built on top of the ground in concealing vegetation, usually beside a

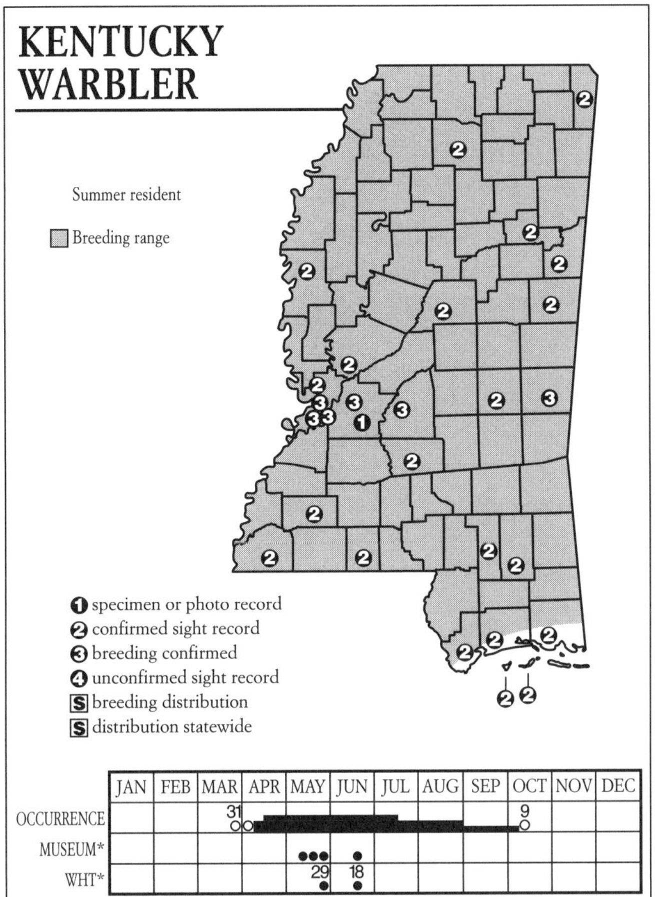

*Breeding confirmed by egg, sight, or photographic record.

small sapling and near a small opening. It is bulky and loosely constructed of leaves and coarse grass and lined with hair and fine rootlets. When available, dead cane leaves are preferred material to build the basal part of the nest. The four or five eggs are creamy white and speckled with reddish brown and shades of gray.

Most of the nests I have seen were found accidentally while walking near them, flushing the female from the nest. When flushed, the incubating or brooding bird runs rapidly along the ground, dragging the wings and feigning injury. Egg records for this species extend from May 3 to June 20.

For four years David L. Watts operated a bird banding station on the edge of a swamp near the Pearl River north of Jackson. The study was part of the national Monitoring Avian Productivity and Survivorship (MAPS) program to capture passerine land birds, take certain data, band, and release them. Each year the study extended from mid-May through early August.

Of the more than 15 species Watts worked with, the Kentucky Warbler was the species captured the most. One male Kentucky Warbler was caught in his mist nets every year of the study, an indication of this species' fidelity to a nesting habitat.

The Kentucky Warbler spends most of its time on the ground or in the dense understory. The male usually mounts to a midstory elevation, where he moves about very actively while singing. The song is distinctive and should be learned, for it usually serves to indicate the bird's presence before it can be seen. The song is a two-syllable chant best described as *tur-dle, tur-dle, tur-dle, tur-dle.* It strongly resembles the Carolina Wren's song in tone and cadence, but the wren's song is louder, more variable, and usually three syllables. The call notes are loud, sharp *chips* resembling those of the Swainson's and Hooded Warblers and also the Eastern Chipmunk's alarm call.

This warbler is easily recognized by its plain, olive green upperparts, bright yellow underparts, yellow "spectacles," black forehead, and "sideburns" under the eye and alongside the neck. The feet and legs are flesh colored. The male Common Yellowthroat has a broad, black mask running through the eye, and its belly is dull white. The Kentucky Warbler has no white in the tail and no wing bars. The adult fall female and immature plumages are duller than that of the summer male.

The breeding range of the Kentucky Warbler extends north into southeastern Nebraska, eastern Iowa, southern Wisconsin, northeastern Illinois, east into New Jersey, south to northwestern Florida, and along the northern Gulf Coast westward to central Texas, eastern Oklahoma, and eastern Kansas. The winter range is southern Mexico, Central America, northern Colombia, and Venezuela.

[Connecticut Warbler] *Oporornis agilis*

This warbler's fall migration route is mainly eastward along and east of the Appalachian Mountains. During spring migration, the return route is north and eastward from Mississippi. There are few Mississippi records because of this migration pattern.

The Connecticut Warbler breeds in damp woodlands and spruce bogs of the lower, central Canadian provinces and into northern parts of Minnesota, Wisconsin, and upper Michigan. It is local and uncommon in the breeding range and difficult to detect in the brushy cover it inhabits while migrating.

Except for males in breeding plumage, warblers *without* black head marks, striping, and wing bars are not easily identified. Mourning, Connecticut, and Nashville Warblers, and female and immature Common Yellowthroats can be confusing to identify under most field conditions, especially in fall.

The male Connecticut Warbler in breeding dress has a bluish gray hood, yellow underparts, greenish olive tail and upperparts, yellow undertail coverts extending *nearly to the end of the tail,* and a *complete, white eye ring.* Females and fall immatures are duller, but have a suggestion of a

CONNECTICUT WARBLER

Accidental spring and fall transient

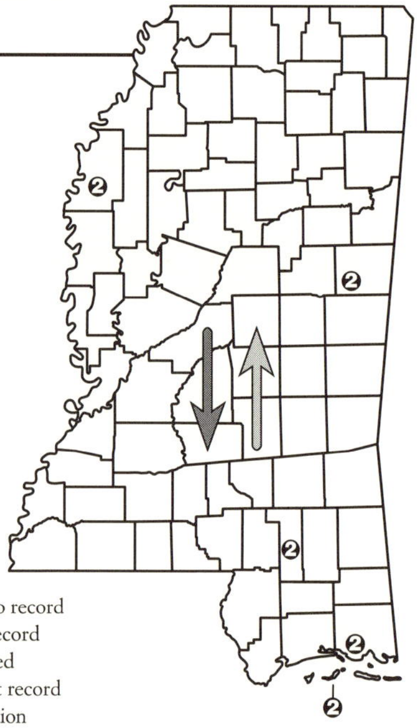

❶ specimen or photo record
❷ confirmed sight record
❸ breeding confirmed
❹ unconfirmed sight record
☐ breeding distribution
🅂 distribution statewide

	JAN	FEB	MAR	APR	MAY	JUN	JUL	AUG	SEP	OCT	NOV	DEC
OCCURRENCE					3-10 ○○					5-7 ○○	5 ○	
MUSEUM*												
WHT*												

*Breeding confirmed by egg, sight, or photographic record.

dull gray hood extending to the upper breast. A *white eye ring* is present on females and immatures. These warblers habitually *walk* and feed on the ground or on low limbs, usually in thick undergrowth or in dense, brushy places during migration.

Only two spring and three fall sightings of Connecticut Warblers have been reported. Henry D. Haberyan (Gandy, pers. comm.) reported the first sight record of an individual at Gulfport on October 7, 1962. A second sighting was by Judith A. Toups and other observers, who saw one walking on the ground in underbrush on Bellefontaine Beach in Jackson County on November 5, 1977 (Weber and Jackson 1978). Malcolm F. Hodges Jr. saw another at the same location on May 10, 1978 (Jackson and Cooley 1978).

Larry Gates recorded an individual sighting on October 6, 1978, at Hattiesburg, and C. Dwight Cooley saw a singing male on May 3, 1978, at Noxubee National Wildlife Refuge (Jackson and Cooley 1978). Sandra Davis saw one Connecticut Warbler on October 5, 1981, at Oxford (pers. comm.). This species should recur in spring as an accidental migrant visitor when prevailing weather conditions and easterly winds direct its movements westward along the northern Gulf Coast. This warbler should be regarded as casual in fall migration.

Mourning Warbler *Oporornis philadelphia*

The Mourning Warbler is a rare, late spring transient and an uncommon fall transient in Mississippi. There are no spring records on the coast. I can find only two spring collection records for this species, one taken in Lee County on June 5, 1940, by Eugene Patton, and another taken by Vaiden (1947) in Bolivar County on May 19, 1945. Two spring sight records have been reported, one by Stevenson (1945) on May 10, 1944, at Abbeville in Lafayette County, and another by Floy Barefield on April 15, 1951, in DeSoto County at Lakeview. Fall migration records for this warbler extend from September 1 to October 29.

The four specimens in the MMNS were taken by H. L. Owens at Gunnison in Bolivar County on September 5; by Eugene Patton in Lee County on September 9; and two specimens by W. H. Turcotte at Raymond in Hinds County on October 2. Burleigh (1945) collected four fall specimens on the coast on September 11, 12, and 13 (two specimens). Vaiden (1947) recorded specimens taken in Bolivar County on September 1, 4, 6, 7, and 14, 1946. A late fall record exists; two immatures were seen at Oxford on October 29, 1983, by W. Marvin Davis.

MOURNING WARBLER

Uncommon spring and fall transient

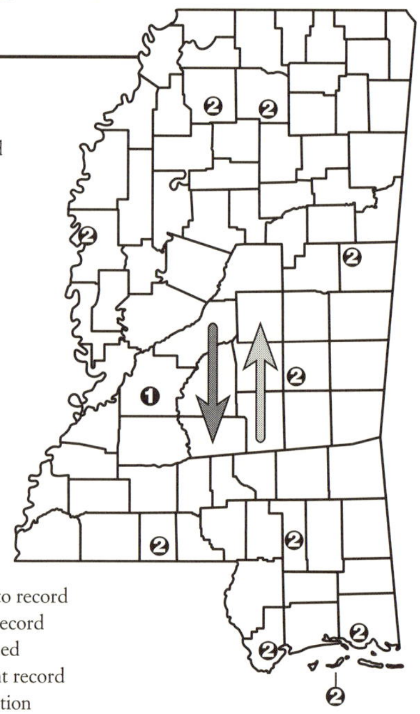

❶ specimen or photo record
❷ confirmed sight record
❸ breeding confirmed
❹ unconfirmed sight record
☐ breeding distribution
🅂 distribution statewide

	JAN	FEB	MAR	APR	MAY	JUN	JUL	AUG	SEP	OCT	NOV	DEC
OCCURRENCE				15 ○○		5 ○	31 ○		1 ○	29 ○○		
MUSEUM*												
WHT*												

*Breeding confirmed by egg, sight, or photographic record.

In alternate plumage, this warbler is olive green above with *no wing bars*. It has bright yellow underparts, a bluish gray hood, and *no eye ring*. The male in spring has a blackish throat and a black band across the breast, where the hood joins yellow underparts. Fall females and immatures may have an *incomplete eye ring* broken in front of the eye. The Connecticut Warbler, a larger but similar species for which there are few definite Mississippi records, has an *unbroken* white eye ring and yellow undertail coverts, which extend almost to the end of the tail. Tail coverts of the Mourning Warbler extend about half the length of its tail.

This species inhabits heavy underbrush and patches of shrubs or rank, weedy growths, where it skulks about and remains well hidden. It nests on or near the ground in tangled growths of briers, weeds, and grass bordering bogs or marshland in the northern tier of states from North Dakota into southern New England, south in the mountains of Maryland and West Virginia, and in Canada from northeastern British Columbia into Newfoundland. The winter range is from southern Nicaragua south into Venezuela, Ecuador, and Colombia.

The song of the Mourning Warbler is described as *chirry, chirry, chorry, chorry.* It is in three or four two-note phrases similar to the Kentucky Warbler's, but with a falling inflection at the end. I have heard and recorded this bird's song in northern Minnesota. My personal experience with this bird in hand is limited to finding two specimens among 19 species of warblers killed the night of October 1, 1965, when they struck television towers near Raymond in Hinds County.

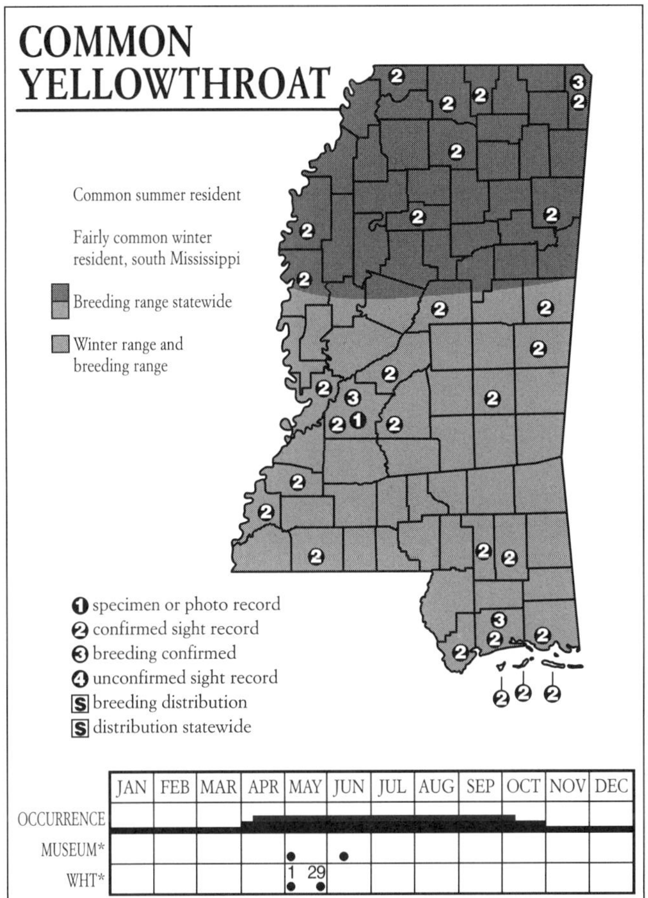

*Breeding confirmed by egg, sight, or photographic record.

Common Yellowthroat *Geothlypis trichas*

This warbler is appropriately named, for it occurs as a breeding bird in all states except Hawaii. Its summer range extends from southeastern Alaska into Newfoundland and southward to southern Florida and central Mexico. The winter range is the southern United States south into Panama.

In Mississippi, the Common Yellowthroat is a common, statewide summer resident, an uncommon winter resident in northern parts of the state, and a fairly common winter resident in southern Mississippi and along the coast. It is common to abundant as a spring and fall transient. During most breeding bird surveys conducted annually during the month of June over randomly selected Mississippi routes, it consistently has ranked among the 20 most commonly seen or heard birds.

This small, wrenlike warbler inhabits moist, sunlit, grassy, or shrubby areas. It is particularly fond of weedy, brushy openings with rank grasses and brier patches like those along streams, railroad tracks, and marshy areas. In winter, this species usually is found near wet places where stands of thick shrubs, vines, dead grasses, cattails, or other dense vegetation provide protection from the weather. It is secretive in winter and during most of the summer, but during the breeding period, the male often mounts a wire or sits atop a small tree to sing.

The territorial song is usually several high-pitched, clear, three-note phrases, but there are variations with more or fewer notes. It is best described as *witch'ity-witchity-witchity*, or *witch'ity-witchity-wit*. As soon as the males arrive on their breeding territories, they are in full song. The male has a "flight song" given as it rises to a height of about 20 feet. This song is an outburst of bubbling, stuttering notes mixed with some of the *witch'ity* phrases of the ordinary song.

The yellowthroat is so well concealed by the vegetation of its usual haunts that it is sometimes difficult to see. It is curious, however, and readily excited by intruders, so that nearly always it will give its distinctive, sharp *tchep* call. A squeaking noise made by pressing the lips against the back of the hand while sucking air into the mouth will bring one of these birds into plain view.

The male Common Yellowthroat is readily identified by its black, rectangular mask, which goes across the front of the head, through the eyes, across the face, and along the sides of the neck. This mask is bordered above by a grayish white line separating the plain olive green crown and upperparts. The throat and breast are rich yellow, the belly is dull white, and the tail coverts are mostly yellow. Females have a brownish crown, paler yellow throat, light-colored eye ring, flanks and sides washed with brown, and a *white belly.*

Similar warblers with greenish olive upperparts and yellow underparts usually are all yellow underneath or have other identifying field marks. Female and immature yellowthroats lack the black face mask. Immatures are very nondescript, generally olive brown to greenish olive above. Their throat is dull yellow to buffy, with a white belly and yellow undertail coverts. They are best identified in the field by the distinctive, single call note.

The Common Yellowthroat nest is made of coarse grass, leaves, and weed stems forming the bulk of the nest, and is lined with finer grasses, plant fibers, and hair. It is well hidden by supporting vegetation on or very near the ground. Nesting sites are selected in clumps of goldenrod, vigorous grasses, briers, and other herbaceous growth offering complete concealment. The three to five white eggs are speckled or scrawled with brown, umber, or black, mostly around the large end.

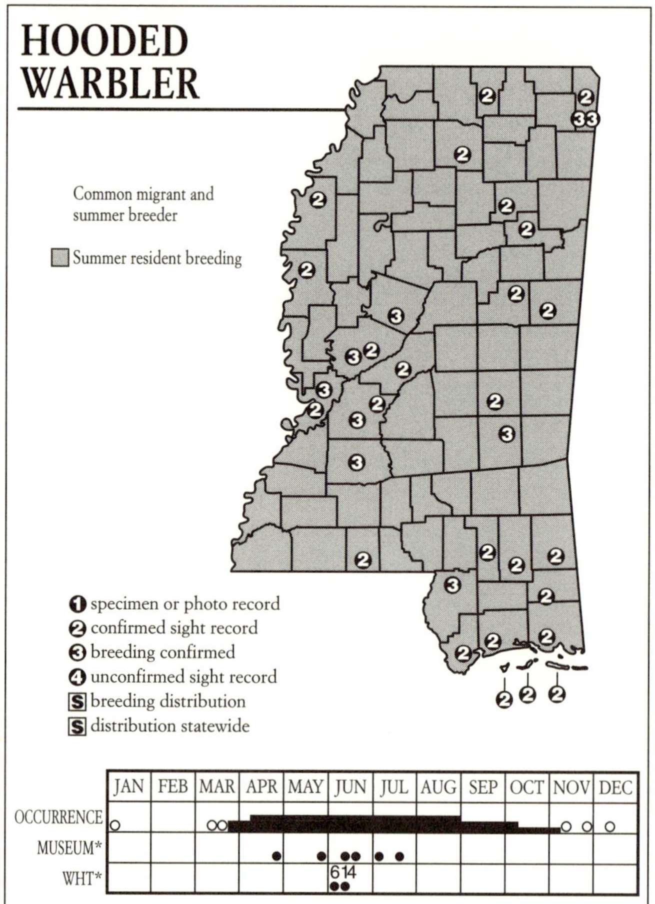

*Breeding confirmed by egg, sight, or photographic record.

Hooded Warbler *Wilsonia citrina*

This common summer resident breeds in nearly every stream bottom in Mississippi. It occurs in mixed hardwood uplands, particularly in moist, shady ravines of the Loess Bluff region in the western part of our state. The nesting habitat of the Hooded Warbler is a dense, shrubby understory, where it builds a nest two to four feet aboveground in the fork of a shrub, cane, or hardwood sapling. The nest is usually hidden in the middle of a thicket.

The small, well-made nest, constructed of dead leaves, plant fibers, and bark strips, is loosely made at the bottom, but neatly compressed and bound together at the top and rim with spider or caterpillar silk. The lining is made of fine bark shreds, grasses, and hair or black moss fibers. The eggs are creamy white, marked at the large end with reddish brown, and number three or four to a set. Egg records at the MMNS extend from April 29 to July 23.

The Hooded Warbler dwells mainly in understory vegetation, where it tends to be elusive when approached. The singing male often ascends to a midstory or higher perch to sing, and does not remain long in one place. From the time it arrives in spring until mid-July, the song is one of the most consistently heard in river and creek bottom woodlands. Andrew Allison described the song as *whee, whee, whe'e-a-whe'e.* It is distinctive, but might be confused with songs of the Louisiana Waterthrush or Swainson's Warbler. The call note used by both sexes is a sharp *chip.*

Adult males are easily identified by the yellow face and forehead, which is entirely surrounded by a black hood covering the crown, neck, throat, and upperpart of the breast. The back, wings, and upperpart of the tail are plain olive green. In all plumages, the underparts are bright yellow, and the outer-tail feathers when spread display a large amount of white. The adult female is very similar to the male without the black hood, although some individuals have a considerable amount of black on the crown and throat. Immatures and females are best recognized by their bright yellow face, forehead pattern, and the white tail spots that are visible when the tail is spread.

The Hooded Warbler begins arriving on the coast soon after mid-March, with migration continuing statewide throughout April and early May. Extreme dates of spring and fall arrival on coastal islands recorded by Burleigh (1945) are March 14 and July 30. Fall migration extends through August, September, and into early October. A few later fall migration records extend to November 12. One winter collection record is available, a specimen collected by M. G. Vaiden (1939) in Leflore County on January 1, 1937. A December 15, 1980, record of one male in Forrest County is an anomalous winter record.

Wilson's Warbler *Wilsonia pusilla*

This species is a summer resident northward into the northern tree line of Alaska and Canada. In the eastern United States, the breeding range extends to Maine and northern parts of New Hampshire, Vermont, Michigan, and Minnesota. In the West, the summer range reaches south to the mountains of western Texas, north-central New Mexico, and southern California.

In Mississippi, the Wilson's Warbler is a regular spring transient, an uncommon fall migrant, and in some years a casual winter resident in southern Mississippi. Fall records extend from September 5 to November 3.

Amy Tolman recorded a Wilson's Warbler at Bay St. Louis in Hancock County on December 26, 1952; January 19 and February 10, 1953; and again on February 6, 1954. She recorded the bird near Picayune in Pearl River County on January 15 and 25, and on February 7, 1957. The bird's winter range is normally from northern Mexico to Panama, only casually in the Rio Grande Valley and southern Texas Coast, southern Louisiana, and Florida.

I have seen the Wilson's Warbler on its northern breeding grounds but on only one occasion in Mississippi, a male in full song in a brushy thicket on the bank of Bear Creek in Tishomingo State Park on May 12, 1973. John A. Izral located the bird, and it was a first spring sighting for most of the party of MOS members present during their annual spring field trip. I was impressed by the brightness of the overall yellow coloring, the contrasting shiny black eyes and cap, and spirited actions as it flitted about feeding in the low shrubs. The song was a distinctive, long, clear series of chattering notes dropping in pitch near the end.

The male Wilson's Warbler is plain olive above with no wing bars. The underparts, face, and forehead are *bright* yellow. The glossy black cap is distinctive. The immature female lacks the black cap. Older females have beady black eyes on a yellow face and a smaller cap than the males. Females and immatures of the Hooded Warbler are similar to the Wilson's Warbler, but have white tail spots. The Yellow Warbler has yellow tail spots, while the Wilson's Warbler is smaller with *no white* in the tail.

Canada Warbler *Wilsonia canadensis*

Occurrence records for this late spring and early fall transient in Mississippi extend from April 25 to June 5, and

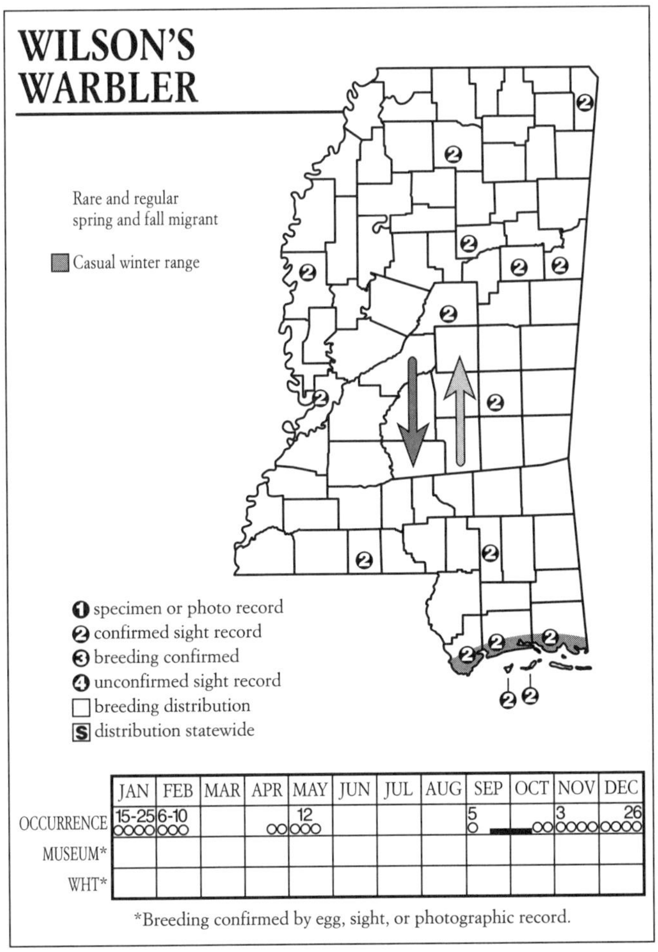

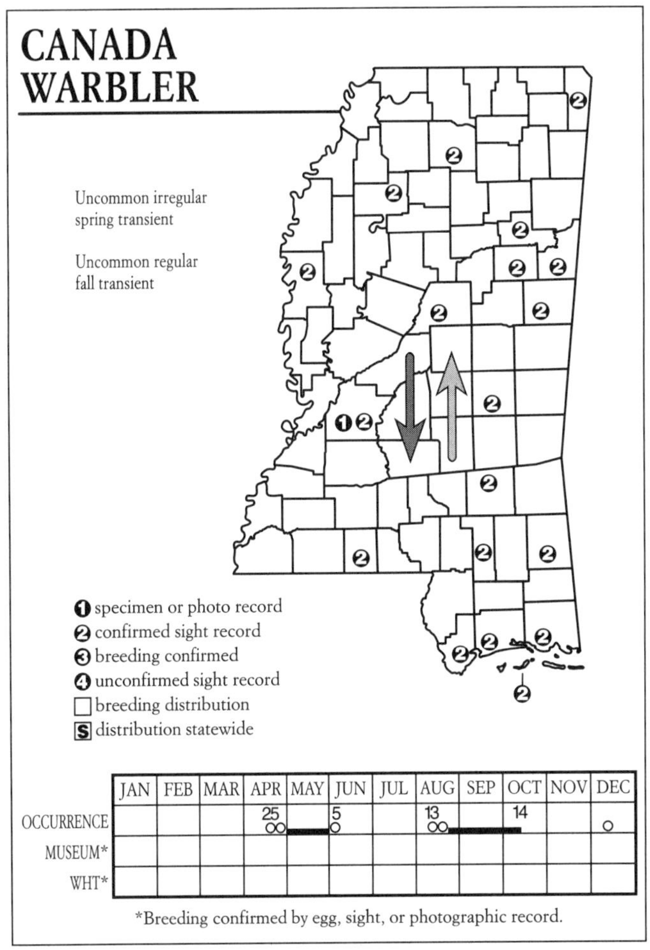

August 13 to October 14. On the coast it is scarce in spring, although regular but uncommon in most areas during the fall. Over the remainder of the state, it is uncommon and irregular during the spring passage and fairly common in fall from late August through September.

The Canada Warbler is plain, bluish gray above and yellow below with yellow "spectacles" and a distinctive "necklace" of black spots extending across the breast. These marks are faint on the female in fall, and faint or absent on immatures. The absence of white in the wings and tail helps to confirm identification in all plumages.

All of my sightings of this species have been in thick, shaded undergrowth in bottomland or upland hardwoods not more than 10 feet aboveground. Once on a May morning in the bottom woods of a small creek north of Jackson, I saw six Canada Warblers. All were in the shrub layer and never rose above it.

The breeding range of this attractive warbler is in southern Canada from northern Alberta to Newfoundland, and from northern Minnesota across northern parts of Wisconsin, Michigan, Ohio, New York, New Jersey, and south into the mountains to western North Carolina, northeastern Georgia, and eastern Tennessee. The nest is made on or near the ground in moss or other concealing vegetation, on fallen logs, in stump and bank cavities, or among exposed roots of fallen trees. Leaves, bark, grasses, and plant fibers are used to form the bulky nest structure, which is lined with rootlets, hair, and plant fibers. The three to five white eggs are variously marked with shades of brown and gray.

This warbler migrates through Central America and winters in northern Venezuela, western Colombia, and south through Ecuador to central Peru.

[Painted Redstart] *Myioborus pictus*

An unmistakable, first sight record of this Mexican warbler occurred at Waveland in Hancock County on October 5, 1987. Judith A. Toups and Chita Cassibry first saw the bird, an adult in full plumage. It was feeding and flycatching in typical redstart fashion. Others in the party who saw the bird were Robert Jeffrey, Albert Jenkins, and Lydia Schultz (Toups et al. 1987). Four of these observers had recent experience identifying this species in the United States and two had seen it in Mexico. The bird appeared after cool and windy frontal movements had brought in transient landbirds, including warblers and other western species.

The Painted Redstart has a black head and upperparts, a black throat bordering a *red breast and upper belly*, white lower belly and tail coverts, outer-tail feathers that are white to the tip and often fanned, and a *bold, white wing patch*. The sexes and fall immatures are alike.

PAINTED REDSTART

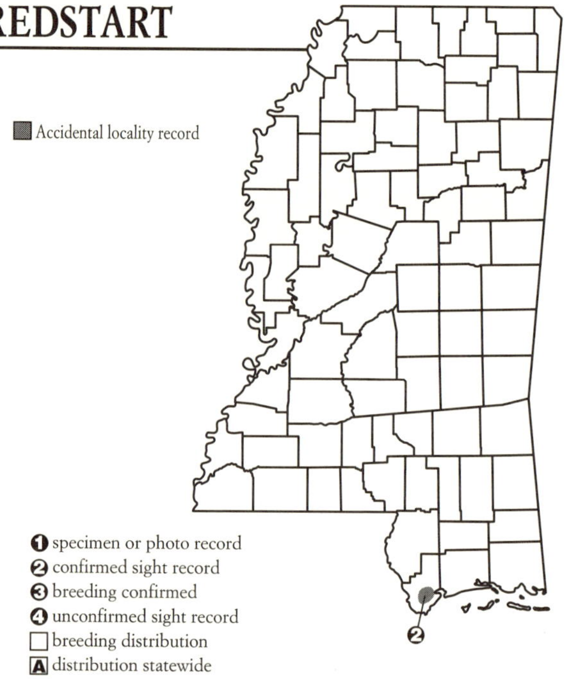

	JAN	FEB	MAR	APR	MAY	JUN	JUL	AUG	SEP	OCT	NOV	DEC
OCCURRENCE										5 ●		
MUSEUM*												
WHT*												

*Breeding confirmed by egg, sight, or photographic record.

This species is resident to northern Mexico and breeds in pine-oak canyons and piñon-juniper forests in Arizona, New Mexico, and the mountains of southwestern Texas. The song is a soft, rich, and deliberate warbling, similar to that of the Yellow-rumped Warbler.

Yellow-breasted Chat *Icteria virens*

The Yellow-breasted Chat is our largest member of the wood warbler subfamily. Bigger than a House Sparrow and almost as large as an Eastern Towhee, this species is noted for its ludicrous actions, comical flight songs, and raucous repertoire of catcalls, whistles, grunts, chuckles, chatterings, cackles, and squeals. These various indescribable sounds that constitute its song are delivered in irregular order at intervals of various lengths. The alarm call is a softer mewing sound not usually heard while the chat is singing.

The flight song of the male is something comical to behold. The chat usually works his way up to the top of a bush or tree, then suddenly flips upward with wings slowly flopping up and down and noisily popping together behind his back. The tail and legs are left dangling and the flight is jerky, labored, and so slow as to appear to barely sustain the weight of the bird in the air. The song pours out until the flight has reached its zenith, and the singer drops to his perch in another tree or descends into a thicket. Here, he continues to sing, bowing and twisting about, with tail pointing downward and throat puckered out. It is no wonder that the chat is known as "the clown of the brier patch."

The chat is elusive and sometimes hard to see. It is bright yellow below with a white belly and undertail coverts. A white line runs over and underneath the eye. A dark band extends from the large, black bill back through the eye and beneath the lower white eye line, giving the appearance of a comic mask. The eyes and inside of the mouth are black.

Dense tangles of low shrubs, brier patches, vine tangles, and scattered growths of young trees bordering woodlands, poorly tended pastures, burned or cut-over areas, and grown-up and abandoned fields make ideal habitat for this unwarbler-like bird. It nests from three to five feet aboveground in a small tree, shrub clump, vine tangle, or brier thicket. Coarse grasses, leaves, weed stems, and vine tendrils form the loosely made base of the nest cup, which is lined with finer grasses and plant stems. The four slightly glossy white eggs are blotched or speckled with shades of light brown, reddish brown, and a drab color. The young are completely naked when hatched.

The chat is a common, summer-resident, breeding bird statewide except in the immediate vicinity of the coast, where it is local and scarce. It has not been recorded breeding on the islands in Mississippi Sound. During spring and fall migration, it is sometimes locally abundant.

Extreme dates of spring arrival and fall departure are April 11 and October 29. Spring arrival is usually after about mid-April. Out-of-season records are March 7, 1938, a specimen collected at Meridian in Lauderdale County by K. L. Thomas, and February 24, 1971, one individual caught in a mist net at Landon in Harrison County by Jacob H. Miller. Twenty egg collection dates on record at the MMNS extend from May 3 to June 17. Most sets collected contained four eggs, except three that contained three eggs.

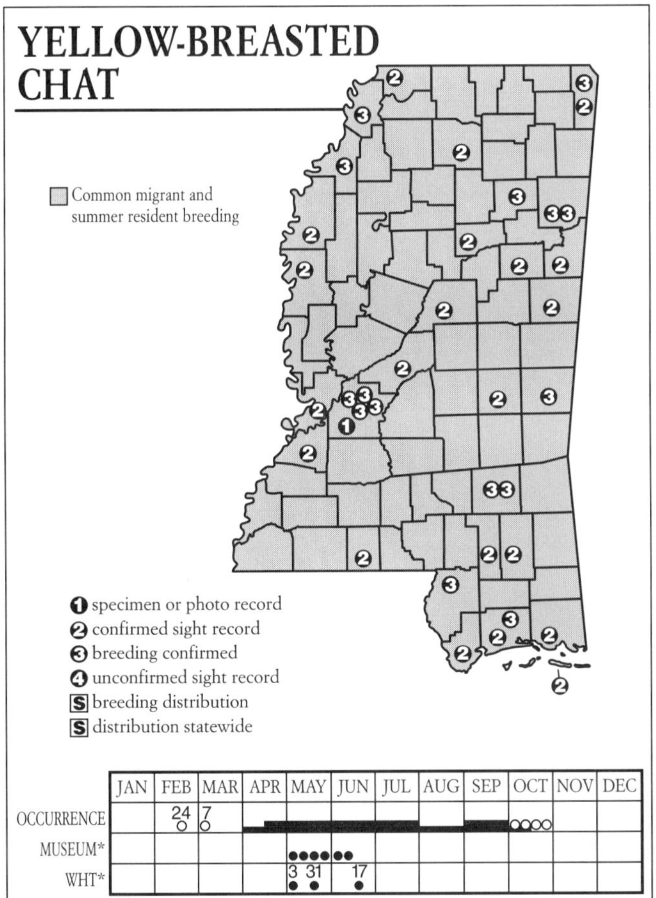

*Breeding confirmed by egg, sight, or photographic record.

Summer Tanager

Thraupinae (Tanagers)

Tanagers are thrush-sized, tree-dwelling, brilliantly colored birds of tropical origin. Only four species are native to North America, and all have robinlike songs delivered in short phrases. Adult male tanagers have large amounts of red in their plumage during the breeding season. Females and immatures are greenish or olive above with yellow underparts. The Western Tanager is the only United States species that has wing bars, and all have large, thick, or "swollen" bills. The juveniles and females resemble yellow orioles, though orioles are more active and have straighter, sharply pointed bills.

Tanagers build shallow, cup-shaped nests. These nests are rather small and frail for their size, but are delicately made, neatly held together, and usually situated on the outer branch of a horizontal tree limb. There are numerous other species of tanagers in the tropical and subtropical regions of the world.

Summer Tanager *Piranga rubra*

The "summer redbird" is one of our most colorful songbirds. The adult male is rose red all over without any semblance of wing bars, and he retains this plumage year-round. The female is olive above and orange yellow below with a yellowish bill. The adult male has a lighter, horn-colored bill. Immatures resemble the female in fall. Juveniles are darker than the female and lightly streaked on the breast, throat, and sides with dusky brown. First-year males in prenuptial dress show a great variation in plumage. They are more orange in the fall than the females. In the spring they may not become fully red, showing a patchy mixture of red and greenish yellow feathers in their plumage.

The Summer Tanager is a common, summer-resident, breeding bird throughout the state except in the immediate vicinity of the coast, where it rarely nests. It is common in mature pine-oak woods and usually nests in open groves of pines, oaks, and mixtures of oak and hickory. This tanager has a peculiar preference for placing its nests over a road or open ground.

The nest is a small, frail, shallow cup made of weed stems and lined with green grass stems that later turn golden yellow. Nests are placed on the outer end of a horizontal limb from 10 to 30 feet aboveground. Most of the nests I have seen were in pine or post oak trees, but other hardwoods are also used.

The three or four eggs have very thin shells. They are bluish green and heavily spotted with reddish brown or cinnamon brown. Egg records extend from May 8 to June 30. The latest nesting record is July 17, 1977, when fledglings were reported ready to leave the nest.

The song is robinlike, more musical, and not as raspy as the Scarlet Tanager song. Call notes of the Summer Tanager are a distinctive *chick-a-tuck-tuck*.

Arrival and departure occurs from mid-March to the end of October. Some Summer Tanagers overwinter rarely in Mississippi and are usually observed at feeders. Imma-

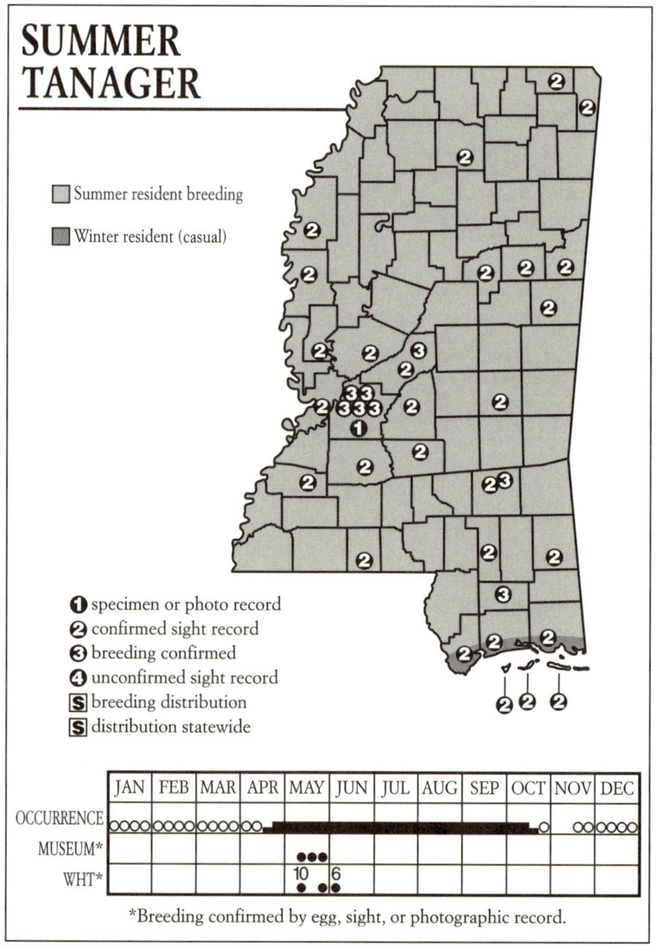

*Breeding confirmed by egg, sight, or photographic record.

tures and females are separated from the immature Western Tanager by the *conspicuous* yellow wing bars on the Western, with none on the Summer Tanager.

Scarlet Tanager *Piranga olivacea*

In his bright scarlet head and body plumage accented by jet black wings and tail, the adult Scarlet Tanager is a thing of eye-catching splendor. Females have yellow green plumage and dark green wings. Immatures in fall look much like females, but the immature male in his first fall plumage has black wing coverts.

The adult male loses his red plumage after the breeding season by gradual replacement with greenish feathers, but his wings remain black. In early spring, a prealternate molt occurs, and the males attain the red alternate plumage. Males in first breeding plumage are paler (or slightly more orange colored) than older males. Adult males in molt have a patchy, red-and-green appearance.

In northern Mississippi, this tanager is an uncommon summer resident, breeding locally in the oak-hickory woods, usually at the higher elevations. R. M. Freeman collected one of three fledglings that were just out of the nest and being fed by both adults at State Line in Tishomingo County on July 12, 1939. This specimen is in the MMNS and substantiates the first state breeding record of known origin. Henry L. Owens collected a flying juvenile with breast streaking and black wing coverts on July 11, 1939, at the same location, but its origin in the state could be questioned.

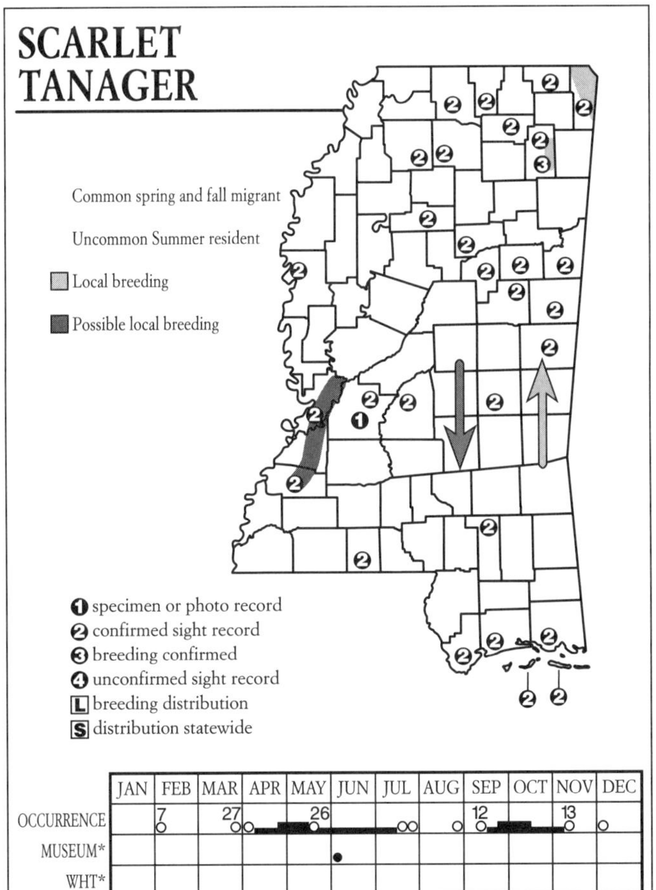

*Breeding confirmed by egg, sight, or photographic record.

Merritt G. Vaiden recorded the Scarlet Tanager breeding near Rosedale in Bolivar County, where he observed a pair with two half-grown young on June 21, 1965. Howell (1976) reported another breeding record one mile west of Guntown in Lee County, where Mrs. W. E. Wesson saw two or three fledglings just out of the nest and accompanied by an adult male on June 8, 1974.

The Scarlet Tanager is a fairly common spring and fall transient on the Gulf Coast. It is a fairly common spring migrant in northern Mississippi, but is observed less frequently in the central and southern portions. In fall migration, this species is not frequently seen or reported, probably because of its inconspicuous fall plumage. Extremes of reported spring migration are March 27 at Rosedale in Bolivar County by M. G. Vaiden, and May 26, 1977, at Jackson in Hinds County. Fall migration records extend from September 12 to November 13. A male Scarlet Tanager seen near Bluff Lake at Noxubee National Wildlife Refuge on February 7, 1971, is a winter record reported by Webster (1971).

The Scarlet Tanager builds a frail, shallow, cup-shaped nest of weed stems, small twigs, and grasses, which is lined with rootlets, weed stems, and grasses. It is usually placed well out from the trunk on a limb of a hardwood or pine. The three to five eggs are greenish blue and speckled with shades of brown.

The song of the Scarlet Tanager consists of four or five phrases, delivered like a robin, but rather hoarse and burry in comparison with the Summer Tanager, which is louder and with more musical quality. The call is a low *chip-churr.*

Western Tanager *Piranga ludoviciana*

This distinctly marked Rocky Mountain and far western visitor was first recorded in Mississippi by Burleigh (1945). He collected a female specimen at Gulfport on October 25, 1940. I collected an immature specimen (with yellow wing bars, but of indeterminate sex) on March 7, 1958, in Hinds County west of Jackson, the only inland specimen record (Turcotte 1958b).

The fully adult male has a bright yellow body, black wings and tail, yellow wing bars, and a red head or face. In fall and winter dress, the male loses most of the red on its head. Females and young can be separated from other North American tanagers by their yellow wing bars.

WESTERN TANAGER

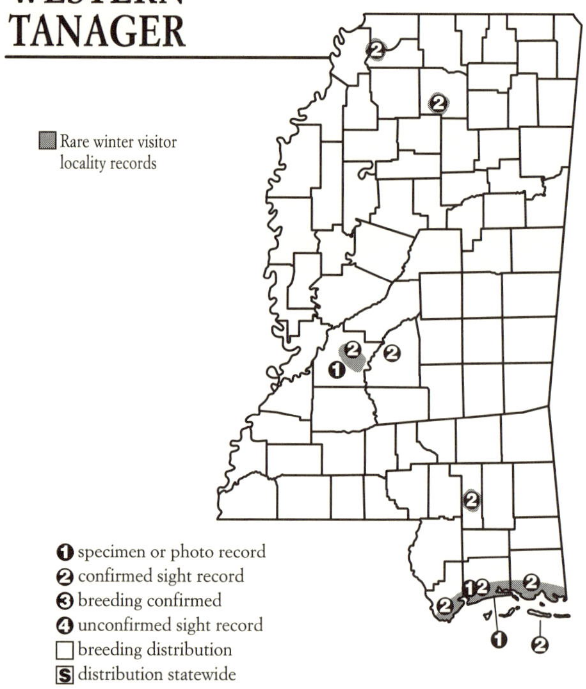

	JAN	FEB	MAR	APR	MAY	JUN	JUL	AUG	SEP	OCT	NOV	DEC
OCCURRENCE	o o	o o	o o	oo	oo			o	o o	o o	o	o
MUSEUM*												
WHT*												

*Breeding confirmed by egg, sight, or photographic record.

The Western Tanager is a fairly common inhabitant of fir, spruce, or pine forests of southern Alaska, western Canada, and southward across the western states and Rocky Mountains into Texas. It normally winters from Mexico southward to Costa Rica. It is a casual spring or fall migrant and occasional winter resident along the northern Gulf Coast from Florida to eastern Texas. It is rarely found inland in the southeastern Gulf states.

There are five more recent sight records from the Mississippi Coast (May 8, 1962; April 12, 1969; December 19, 1979; September 8, 1982; and April 14, 1987) in all three coastal counties (Toups and Jackson 1987).

Recent inland sight records occurred during the Arkabutla Lake Christmas Bird Count on December 27, 1992 (Imhof 1993), and in Brandon in Rankin County at a feeder from February 28 to March 1, 1993 (B. E. Gandy and multiple observers).

Blue Grosbeak

Cardinalinae (Grosbeaks, Buntings, and Sparrows)

These birds are widespread and at home in a wide variety of habitats. Buntings and grosbeaks are colorful songsters. All have conical beaks adapted for cracking and eating seeds, but insects are also important in their diets.

Buntings and sparrows have proportionally smaller bills than grosbeaks. Most sparrows are brown colored, heavily streaked on the upperparts, with many species having some breast streaking. Male and female sparrows of most species have similar plumage. Most immature sparrows having black or reddish brown crowns are duller as juveniles and immatures.

Sparrows are found mostly on the ground or in grass, or stay hidden except in the spring breeding season when males sing from conspicuous perches. They nest in a wide variety of shrubs, trees, grasses, weeds, and on the ground.

Of the 35 species of this subfamily recorded in Mississippi, 11 have nested here. These include the Northern Cardinal, Blue Grosbeak, Painted and Indigo Buntings, Dickcissel, Eastern Towhee, and five sparrows. The Grasshopper Sparrow probably breeds in northern Mississippi, but confirmation is needed.

Northern Cardinal *Cardinalis cardinalis*

The Northern Cardinal is commonly called "redbird" by most Mississippians. It is an abundant, statewide, permanent resident. The adult male is instantly recognized by the overall bright red color, black face, prominent crest, and large red bill. The female is grayish brown with yellowish brown underparts, red bill, and dark red accents on the wings, tail, and crest. Immatures resemble the female, but have little or no red in the plumage, and the bill is almost black.

The cardinal lives in any kind of habitat having tangles and thickets near open spaces such as woodland borders, stream banks, open wooded swamps, field edges, parks, and residential areas. It is nonmigratory, but individuals may wander over considerable distances. In winter, it gathers in loose flocks of a dozen or more birds.

Seeds and fruits of wild plants make up most of their diet, supplemented by many kinds of insects. At feeding stations, sunflower and melon seeds are especially attractive to these birds, but they also like scratch grain.

Cardinals are highly territorial during their breeding season. The males start territorial singing very early in March and continue throughout the breeding period. The male mounts to a high perch while singing. The song is a loud and musical series of whistled notes in short, slurred phrases. Some common interpretations of the song are *what-cheer, what-cheer; sweet, sweet, sweet; rit, ma-rit, ma-rit, ma-teer; purty, purty, purty.*

NORTHERN CARDINAL

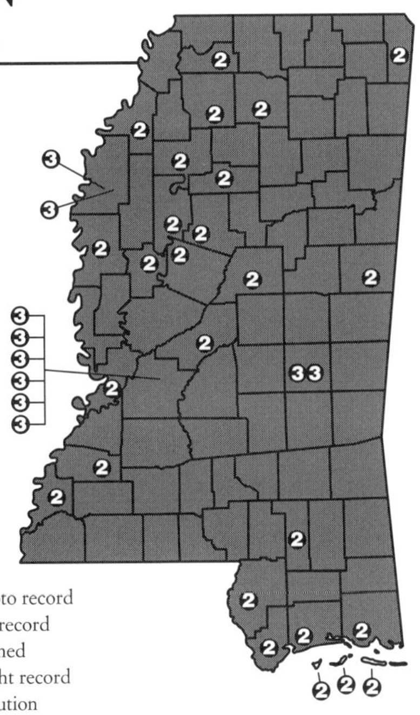

■ Common permanent resident breeding

❶ specimen or photo record
❷ confirmed sight record
❸ breeding confirmed
❹ unconfirmed sight record
[S] breeding distribution
[S] distribution statewide

	JAN	FEB	MAR	APR	MAY	JUN	JUL	AUG	SEP	OCT	NOV	DEC
OCCURRENCE												
MUSEUM*									●			
WHT*				13 ●●	14 ●●							

*Breeding confirmed by egg, sight, or photographic record.

The songs are highly variable among individual birds, and individuals often can be heard singing several song variations while on the same perch. Females are also capable singers, but sing less frequently than males. The call note is a high, sharp *tsink*.

Cardinals build a loose, cup nest of weed stems, strips of bark, and leaves, which is lined with grass stems. It is usually less than six feet from the ground in a shrub, vine, or low limb in or near dense cover. The three or four eggs are white or bluish white, boldly splotched with shades of brown. Nesting extends from late March to July, with two broods usually produced in a season.

Rose-breasted Grosbeak
Pheucticus ludovicianus

This handsome spring and fall transient occurs regularly and frequently travels in small flocks while migrating through Mississippi. Usually it is found in the upper or middle levels of deciduous woodlands. In northern Mississippi, it is a common spring and fall migrant and is fairly common in passage on the Gulf Coast. The spring migration occurs mostly after mid-April and extends to mid-May. Fall passage occurs mainly from late September through October. Extremes of recorded spring and fall migration are April 1 to May 25, and September 1 to November 17.

The male Rose-breasted Grosbeak in full adult alternate plumage is unmistakable. The head and upperparts are mostly black. The underparts are white, except for the distinctive, heart-shaped, rose-colored bib and wing linings. The large conical bill is white, and the wings and tail have prominent white spots.

The female is streaked with grayish brown and white and has wide, brown head stripes separated by a bold, white stripe above the eye, a buffy stripe in the center of the crown, two white wing bars, and *orange yellow* wing linings sometimes conspicuous in flight. The similar female Black-headed Grosbeak is browner on the breast with streaking only on the sides and bright *lemon yellow* wing linings. Fall males resemble females but show rose red on the breast and wing linings. Immatures look much like females but are buffier.

This grosbeak is usually silent during migration, but its robinlike, whistling song may be heard occasionally in the spring. Its call note, a loud, sharp, metallic *peenk*, is similar to the call note of the Northern Cardinal, but not as high pitched. The call notes of this grosbeak often reveal its presence before it can be seen.

Its breeding range extends east of the Rocky Mountains from northeastern British Columbia to central Manitoba, southern Quebec, and Nova Scotia, south to eastern Kansas, Missouri, central Ohio, and central New Jersey,

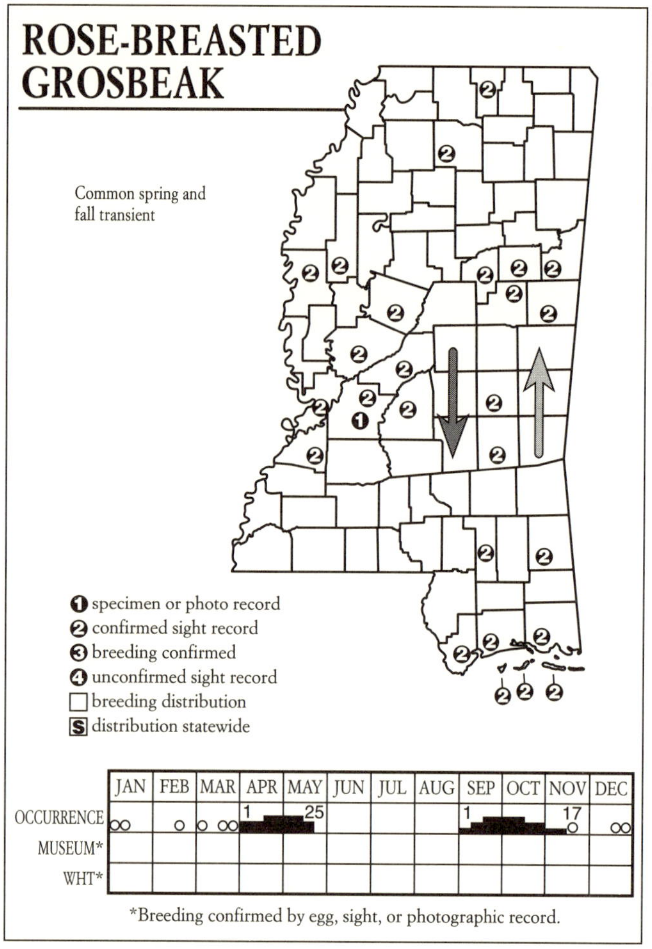

and south in the eastern mountains to northern Georgia. The Rose-breasted Grosbeak winters from southern Mexico southward into Venezuela and Ecuador. Lowery Jr. (1974) reported 11 winter records for this grosbeak in southern Louisiana.

My introduction to this bird in its breeding haunts occurred at a small lake in Minnesota, where I was trying to record the voices of a pair of Common Loons and their young. This required a lot of waiting on my part because the loons seldom called. During all of this, I heard what I first took to be a tanager song across the lake.

The next day I set up the recording equipment on the opposite side of the lake and heard the same song again in the distance behind me. I turned the parabolic reflector toward the bird song and recorded part of it. The bird responded to a playback and came closer and sang loud enough to show a level reading on the meter. When I played the tape back, a beautiful male Rose-breasted Grosbeak came and sat in a shrub about 20 feet in front of me, singing at the top of his voice and bouncing the level meter at low recording level for a good song tape. Needless to say, I was pleased with the entire performance.

Black-headed Grosbeak
Pheucticus melanocephalus

This casual winter visitor from the Rocky Mountains and far western states might have escaped notice in Mississippi if there had been no bird banding and feeding stations. The first sighting was reported by Amy Tolman at her feeding station near Picayune in Pearl River County, where a single male was seen on January 9, 1962. It visited the feeder daily until the bird was collected on January 19, 1962, by Clawson (1962). This first specimen is in the MMNS in Jackson.

On January 16, 1963, Henry D. Haberyan (Turcotte 1963b) recorded a male at Bellefontaine Beach in Jackson County, and he collected it on January 20 for the second MMNS specimen record. Amy Tolman reported another occurrence at her feeder on January 2, 1964.

This species then went unrecorded until March 20 and 21, 1969, when Ethel Floyd banded a male at Mississippi City in Harrison County. Sanders (1977) recorded and photographed a male Black-headed Grosbeak at his home near Kosciusko in Attala County. It appeared on January 10, 1977, and was last seen on February 8. It fed with cardinals and sparrows on chopped corn tossed onto the roof of an outbuilding.

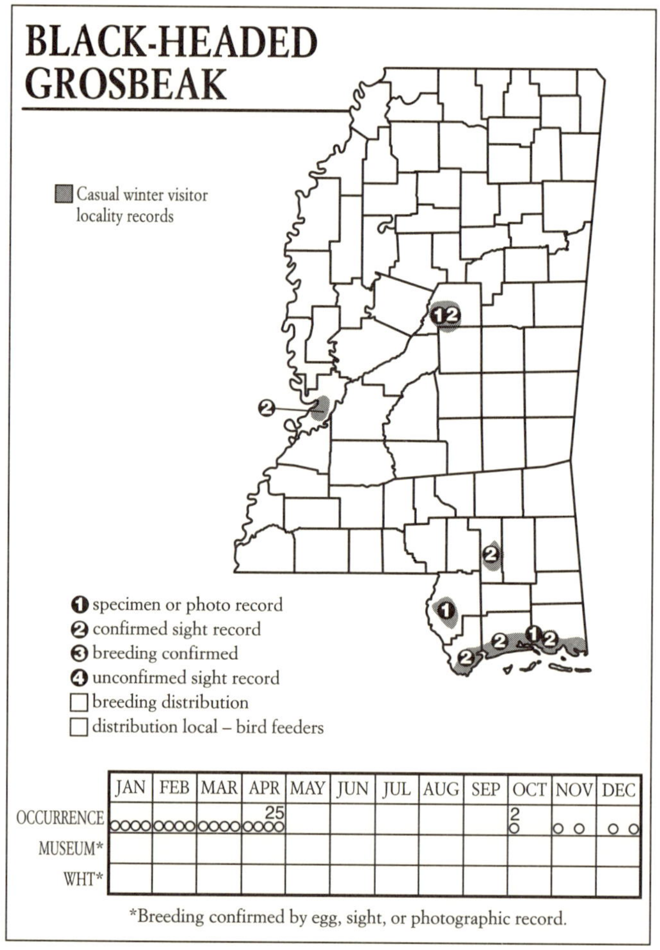

H. B. Simmons recorded a male Black-headed Grosbeak that visited a sunflower seed feeder at his home at Vicksburg in Warren County. It was there almost daily over a period of about two months from January 1, 1977, until last seen on March 1. Subsequent records at Hattiesburg (February 13, 1980), on the coast at Ansley (October 2, 1980), at Ocean Springs (January 15, 1980), and at Vicksburg from February 24 to April 25, 1989, indicate this species may be a regular winter visitor.

The male Black-headed Grosbeak can be recognized easily by its rusty orange breast, yellow belly, black head, and bold white marks on the black wings and tail. In flight, the wing linings show lemon yellow, not orange yellow as in the female and immature Rose-breasted Grosbeak. The back is streaked with brown and the rump is cinnamon colored.

Adult females are similar to the female Rose-breasted Grosbeak, but with no streaking on the *rusty brown* breast, light streaking only on the sides, and lemon yellow wing linings. Immatures in their first winter resemble immature Rose-breasted Grosbeaks, and are best identified by the faint streakings on the sides and the lemon yellow wing linings.

The breeding range extends from western Canada through the western states southward to central Mexico. It winters in Mexico and casually to coastal and central Texas, Louisiana, and eastward rarely as a casual winter visitor on the coastal plain.

My first sighting of this species was a "car-stopper" on the road leading to the basin in the Chisos Mountains of Big Bend National Park in western Texas. A brightly colored male was singing atop a bush beside the road. The song was like the Rose-breasted Grosbeak, with which it hybridizes, but seemed to lack some of the quality or clarity of the Rose-breasted Grosbeak songs that I have heard in the northern and eastern states.

Blue Grosbeak *Guiraca caerulea*

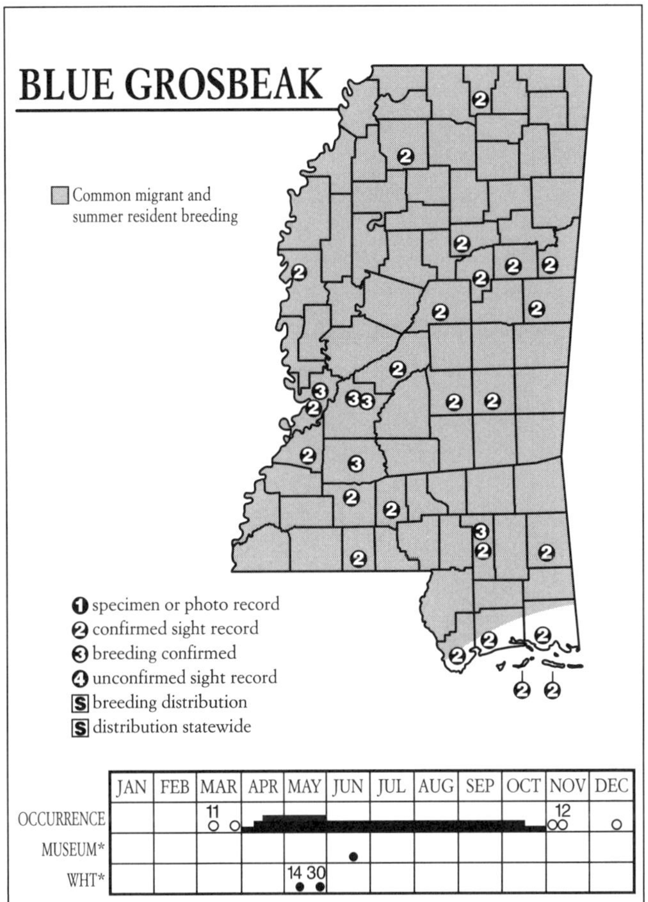

*Breeding confirmed by egg, sight, or photographic record.

This handsome summer resident, about the size of a cowbird, is a common migrant and locally common breeding bird in central and northern Mississippi. In summer, it i nhabits brushy fields and borders or openings in mixed pine-oak woodlands that offer an abundance of briers and low shrubs or bushes. In fall, the bird is usually found in open country containing brier thickets, tall weeds, grasses, and brushy places such as roadsides, hedgerows, and field borders.

In summer this grosbeak commonly sits on roadside utility wires, and during spring migration is often abundant along roadsides and near fields of grain and legumes, often in the company of Indigo Buntings and Orchard Orioles. The spring migration begins in early April and continues until about mid-May. Fall migration occurs from mid-August to the end of October, rarely later. Extremes of recorded spring arrival and fall departure are March 11 and November 12.

The Blue Grosbeak nests in low bushes, seldom more than five feet aboveground. Most of the nests I have found were well concealed in thick oak or sweet gum bushes in old fields or idle ground growing up in tall grass, weeds, and hardwood sprouts or bushes.

The first nest I found near Clinton in Hinds County on May 14, 1931, contained four pale blue, unmarked eggs. I described it this way: "The nest was about three feet from the ground in a water oak bush and made of leaves, weed stems, grass, and lined with fine grasses. It was compactly pressed together and ornamented on the outside with snakeskin and spiderwebs. The female was seen to fly off the nest." Sometimes nests contain paper, cellophane, rags, or cotton when snakeskin is unavailable. Three or four pale blue eggs are laid. Egg records extend from May 9 to June 17. Cowbirds had parasitized some of the nests I have checked.

The male in full alternate plumage is dark violet blue with two prominent brown and tan wing bars. Females and immatures have light brown underparts and are darker brown on the wings, tail and back, with two buffy wing bars. Adult males in winter and in incomplete alternate plumage have mixtures of brown in the otherwise blue coloring of the feathers. These birds sometimes flip their tails, especially when alarmed near the nest.

The song of the Blue Grosbeak is a pleasant warbling, throaty and rich in quality, with rising and falling phrases varying in pitch and loudness. The call is a sharp, nasal *pink*.

[Lazuli Bunting] *Passerina amoena*

Mississippi has only one record for this accidental visitor, the western counterpart of our Indigo Bunting. A first-spring male appeared at a feeder in Oxford on March 18, 1988. Gene and Shannon Knight, Benton Brewer, Jean Young, and the feeder owners, Mr. and Mrs. Farris E. Dendy, observed the bird after it was reported by Mrs. Dendy to Gene and Shannon Knight. This record with all supporting details was reported by Mrs. Dendy (1993). The Lazuli Bunting was last seen at feeders on March 28.

The adult male Lazuli Bunting is turquoise blue on the head, neck, back, and rump, with pale cinnamon on the breast and sides. The belly and undertail coverts are white. Two *prominent white bars* on the wings are distinctive. The female is unstreaked brown above and a paler unstreaked brown below with noticeable, pale wing bars and traces of blue in the wings and tail feathers. Hybrids between Lazuli and Indigo Buntings occur where their ranges overlap in the northern Great Plains.

My first and only acquaintance with the Lazuli Bunting was on June 21, 1985, at the Theodore Roosevelt National Memorial Grasslands Unit northwest of Medora, North Dakota. My wife and I had just experienced the excitement of having a herd of 100 or more American bison surround our car. A short time later we stopped to watch for a Rock Wren seen diving headlong down a roadside cliff.

As I watched for the wren to reappear, a somewhat familiar bird song from a clump of conifers attracted my attention. When the Rock Wren failed to show, I crossed the road to investigate the songster. It was a beautiful *turquoise blue,* male Lazuli Bunting that flew from a dense conifer in full sunlight and disappeared from view on a brushy hillside.

LAZULI BUNTING

❶ specimen or photo record
❷ confirmed sight record
❸ breeding confirmed
❹ unconfirmed sight record
☐ breeding distribution
[A] distribution statewide, local and coastal

	JAN	FEB	MAR	APR	MAY	JUN	JUL	AUG	SEP	OCT	NOV	DEC
OCCURRENCE			18 28 ○○○									
MUSEUM*												
WHT*												

*Breeding confirmed by egg, sight, or photographic record.

Indigo Bunting *Passerina cyanea*

This little finch is slightly larger than a Chipping Sparrow. The adult breeding male is bright blue and darker on the crown. The female is plain brown above with no wing bars, and pale brown and dingy white below with faint streakings. The young have faint wing bars, and immatures resemble the female.

The lack of streaking on the back separates females and immatures from all sparrows. Both females and juveniles may show faint tinges of blue on the wings and tail. Males in fall, winter, and early spring plumage are rusty brown with blue in the wings, tail, and elsewhere, but without streaks or wing bars.

During migration, Indigo Buntings often travel in flocks. In the spring, they attract immediate attention when flocks flush from roadsides and fields and flit away excitedly in the bright sunlight. During the breeding season, singing males often perch on roadside utility wires or in the tops of bushes and trees.

In direct light, the male's iridescent blue is striking, but in indirect light or shadow he sometimes appears almost black. The blue color is due to refraction of blue light and the absorption of other colors by structures in the feather barbs, so that we see only reflected blue light. This seems strange, but there is no blue pigment in their feathers, only physical structures that absorb specific wavelengths. The shade of blue we see depends on the angle and intensity of the reflected light and the physical structure of the feathers. I have taken some color photographs of this bird in shadow and they appear almost black.

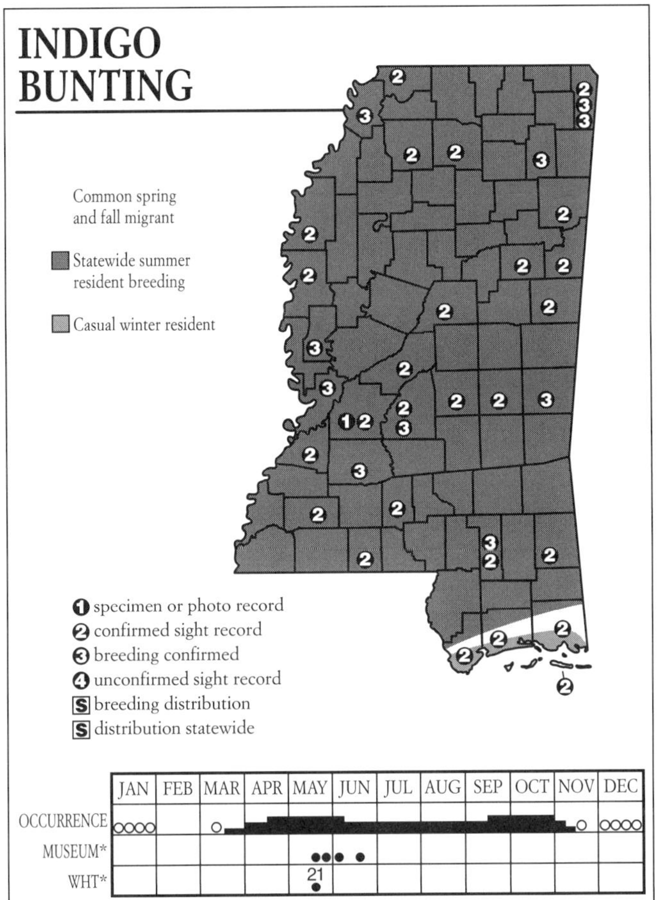

*Breeding confirmed by egg, sight, or photographic record.

The Indigo Bunting begins arriving on our Gulf Coast in late March, but its main spring passage occurs in late April and early May. Fall migration occurs in late September and October. Extremes of recorded spring arrival and fall departure are March 16 and November 18.

One winter sight record on December 13, 1932, was reported by Burleigh (1945) near Gulfport in Harrison County. David L. Watts reported seeing an Indigo Bunting still in alternate plumage on December 28, 1985, in a brushy area beside Ross Barnett Reservoir north of Jackson during the Christmas Bird Count. Winter records on the coast extend from December 13 to January 24.

This bird is locally common as a breeding bird in all but the southernmost counties. There are no nesting records for the coastal counties, although it probably breeds there. Preferred breeding habitats are brushy places and edges or openings in woods, stream bottoms, bushy clearings, and edges of deciduous woods.

Nests are placed in low bushes, coarse weeds, canes, or vines in or near dense cover. The nest is a compactly woven cup of stems, bark, leaves, and coarse grasses held together with cobwebs and lined with fine grass, usually within four feet of the ground. The usual clutch is three or four pale blue, unmarked eggs. The nests of this bunting are commonly victimized by the parasitic Brown-headed Cowbird. Egg record dates for the Indigo Bunting extend from May 6 to June 20. Vaiden (1952b) reported a pair building a nest in a cotton plant in Bolivar County on July 17, 1952.

The call note is a sharp *tseet.* The lively, long, high-pitched song is delivered from a wire or treetop perch and consists of thin, strident, paired notes in measured phrases alternating between high and low pitch, becoming weaker toward the end. The male is a persistent singer through most of the breeding season and sings actively during midday.

Painted Bunting *Passerina ciris*

Without exception, the male Painted Bunting is our most gaudily colored bird. In Louisiana, this bird is appropriately known as "nonpareil," meaning "no equal" or "nothing like it." In full adult plumage, he has a red eye ring and underparts, an indigo blue head, chartreuse back, and dark green and red on the wings. Charles R. Stockard reported that in Louisiana when caged birds were legally kept, for unknown reasons this bird was called "pop" (Lowery 1974). The female is plain, bright green above and below, shading to greenish yellow on the belly. Immatures are quite similar to the female. The male retains the adult plumage year-round.

Painted Buntings occur on the Gulf Coast as fairly common spring and fall transients, and a few regularly remain as very local, breeding summer residents. In the eastern half of our state, this species is rarely seen during migration. In counties bordering the Mississippi River, in the Yazoo Delta, and in bordering hill counties, it is a common transient and locally common, summer-resident, breeding bird.

The spring arrival begins in early April. During migration, small flocks are locally common in the western part of the state. This species often migrates with Indigo Buntings and Blue Grosbeaks.

Even when locally common, the Painted Bunting is difficult to see because it usually remains hidden in thickets. It is easily located only by its song or when the bright and colorful male exposes himself to sing from a utility wire or treetop. The female is shy and elusive and seen most often only momentarily before she dives into the nearest cover. Even the singing male prefers concealment in the foliage of a tree or in the shade of the cross arm on a power pole as he sits and sings on the support bar below.

This bunting inhabits the edges of woods, hedgerows, and streams having an abundance of low thickets of briers, brush, and tall weeds or grasses. Dense hedges of multiflora rose make particularly attractive habitat. Vacant lots, ditch banks, railroad rights-of-way, and other grown-up, idle plots of ground often support breeding pairs.

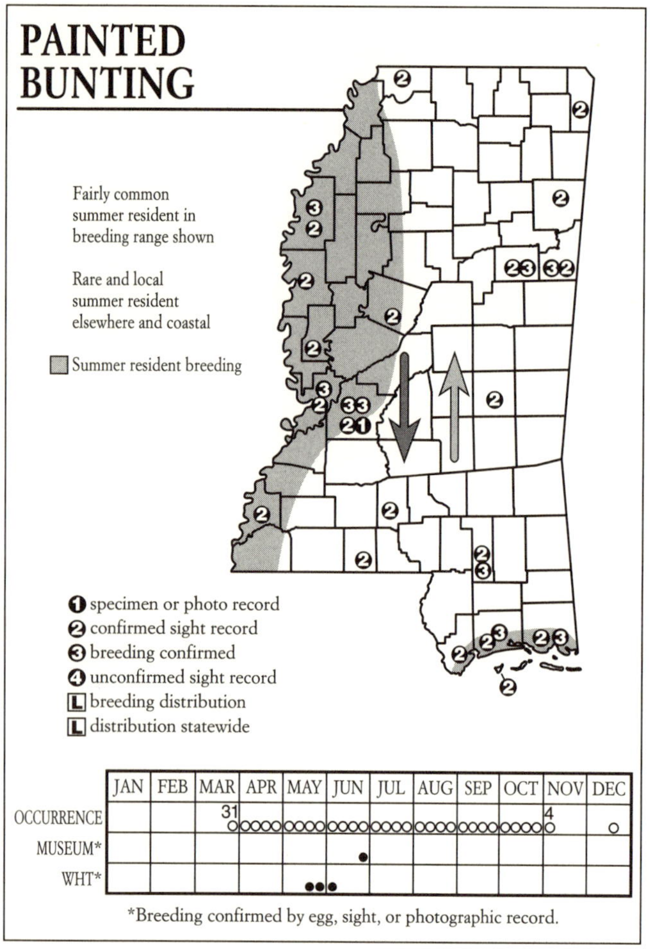

The nest is built in low vegetation, bushes, briers, or shrubbery within several feet of the ground. Nests I have found in Hinds and Warren Counties were in low bushes, on a drooping blackberry cane, in a clump of blooming vetch bordering a shrubby fence row, and in a privet shrub growing beside a house within one foot of the doorway. This species also has been recorded nesting in Bolivar County, and in Biloxi and Pass Christian.

The nest is well hidden and compactly woven of weed and grass stems, weed bark, and leaves or bits of paper. It is held together and bound to supporting vegetation by cobwebs, and lined with fine grasses, hair, and other fine materials. The three or four eggs are white and marked with reddish and grayish brown spots. Nests of the Painted Bunting are often parasitized by cowbirds.

The Painted Bunting's song is a bright, pleasant, soft warble beginning with two notes on about the same pitch, then alternating lower and higher paired notes, and trailing off at the end. Once learned, the song often will reveal the bird's presence when it otherwise might escape notice. The singing male readily responds to a tape recording of its song and will show aggressive behavior by puffing out the feathers, spreading the tail, and rapidly vibrating its wings. I have had them approach within several feet and sing lustily in response to a recorded playback of their song.

The fall migration of Painted Buntings begins in late August and extends through October. Extremes of recorded spring arrival and fall departure are March 31 and November 4.

Dickcissel *Spiza americana*

The Dickcissel is a locally common, variably breeding summer resident in the Yazoo Delta and Black Belt counties of northeastern Mississippi. It also occurs irregularly as a breeding bird in the west-central and north-central hill counties, where it is highly local and variable from year to year.

During the nesting season it frequents the field edges of small grains, patches of tall weeds, vetch, low bushes, vines, and tall grasses growing along highways, ditch banks, field borders, levees, and railroads. In southern Mississippi, it has been recorded only as an uncommon spring and fall transient and rare winter resident.

Spring migration seldom begins before mid-April and goes to mid-May, usually coinciding with the passage of Bobolinks. The fall migration of Dickcissels goes unnoticed inland. First arrivals appear on the coast in late August and September.

Egg record dates extend from May 9 to June 19. Stockard (1905) recorded nesting in an unspecified locality from May 9 to 23, 1900, when he collected 14 sets of eggs from a vetch field. The nests were placed in vetch tangles a few inches from the ground, and each contained four or five eggs. Warriner (1935) recorded Dickcissels nesting in Alcorn County, three miles west of Corinth on May 20, 1935, and also several years prior.

This nest and eggs of the Dickcissel were found and photographed by the author in a stand of goldenrod at the Raymond Airport on May 16, 1978.

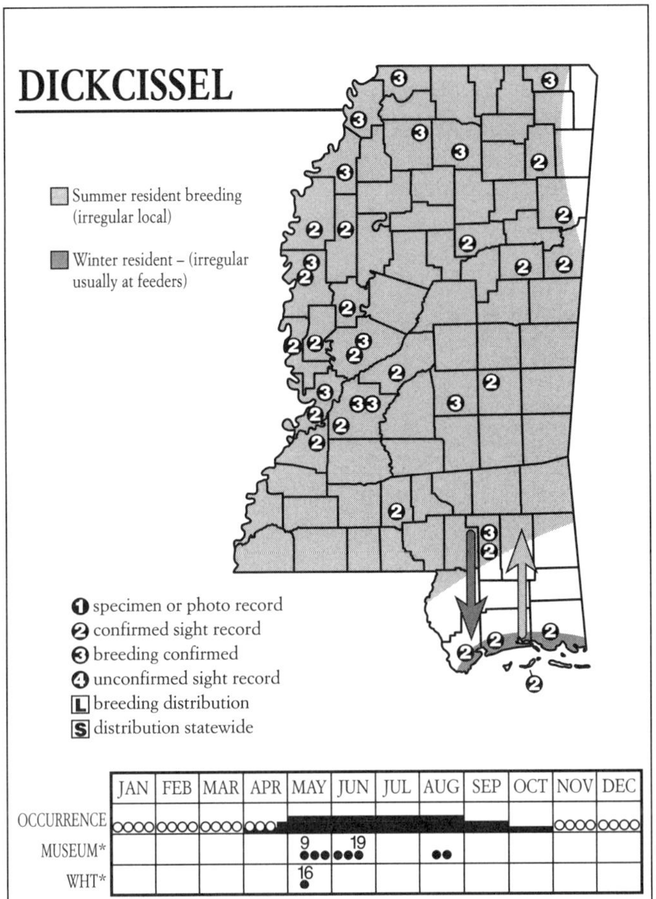

*Breeding confirmed by egg, sight, or photographic record.

Egg records in the MMNS substantiate nesting in Coahoma, Lafayette, Panola, and Washington Counties. I located and photographed a nest containing four eggs on the perimeter of the Raymond airport in Hinds County on May 16, 1978 (Turcotte 1978). Specimen and sight records between May 10 and June 20 further substantiate occurrence of this species during the breeding period in Bolivar, Hinds, Lee, Madison, Sunflower, Warren, and Yazoo Counties.

The Dickcissel nest is a woven cup of coarse grasses lined with finer grass, hair, and rootlets, and placed on or close to the ground in grass, weeds, low vines, briers, or bushes. The three to five eggs (usually four or five) are light blue and unmarked.

The Dickcissel is a conspicuous bird. Males perch and sing incessantly on convenient wires, fences, or tall weeds, proclaiming their breeding territories with a raspy, distinctive song suggestive of its name: one or two *dicks* followed by a staccato *ciss, ciss, ciss*. The male in alternate plumage has a white chin, black throat bib, a yellow breast, and a stripe over the eye and behind the angle of the jaw. The top of its head and cheeks are dark gray, and the nape and sides have a grayish wash. Upperparts are brown, streaked with black. A conspicuous chestnut shoulder patch is present on both sexes and immatures. The female resembles a female House Sparrow, but has a whiter line over the eye, is more heavily streaked on the back with a narrow, dark streak at the side of the throat, a trace of yellow on the breast, and a rufous shoulder patch.

In winter, adults and immatures resemble fall Bobolinks or the female House Sparrow. A rusty shoulder patch, a narrow streak at the sides of the throat, and traces of yellow aid in separating them. Wintering Dickcissels have been recorded by Frances Wills Jr. in Jackson from December 31 to March 10; by Amy Tolman and Ethel Floyd in Gulfport from February 1 to 18; by Frances Wills Jr. and Christine Berry in Madison County on January 21; and by Larry and Terrie Gates at Petal in Forrest County from January 19 to February 29.

In late June after their breeding season, Dickcissels become inconspicuous and are rarely seen during the normal fall migration. The few fall records available on the Gulf Coast are in September, October, November, and December. Apparently, the species migrates early to the wintering grounds in South America, traveling at night and somehow avoiding detection.

[Green-tailed Towhee] *Pipilo chlorurus*

The Green-tailed Towhee has been sighted and reported on only three occasions in Mississippi. There are no photographs or specimens to confirm identification. Two were seen and recorded at Bellefontaine Beach in Jackson County by John Izral and Steve Peterson during the Christmas Bird Count on December 18, 1976 (Jackson and Weber 1977). Both are competent observers, and all field marks were noted.

Another sighting was reported by Bobby Merritt (pers. comm.), who described all identifying field marks of a Green-tailed Towhee on the last weekend of December 1976. The bird was in brush bordering Old Fitler Lake in Issaquena County, and was watched at close range from a duck blind at the water's edge as it leisurely fed. Merritt recognized it as an unusual bird and carefully noted the rufous crown, greenish gray upperparts, white throat, and white and gray undersides.

On October 20, 1983, a Green-tailed Towhee in adult plumage was observed by Judith A. Toups, Michael Baker, and Dalton King at Pearlington in Hancock County. The bird was observed at 10 feet in good light with all field marks noted and described in detail for a confirmed state record (Toups et al. 1984).

This western, ground-dwelling finch breeds from southeastern Washington and southern Montana southward into southern California and west-central Texas. The winter

GREEN-TAILED TOWHEE

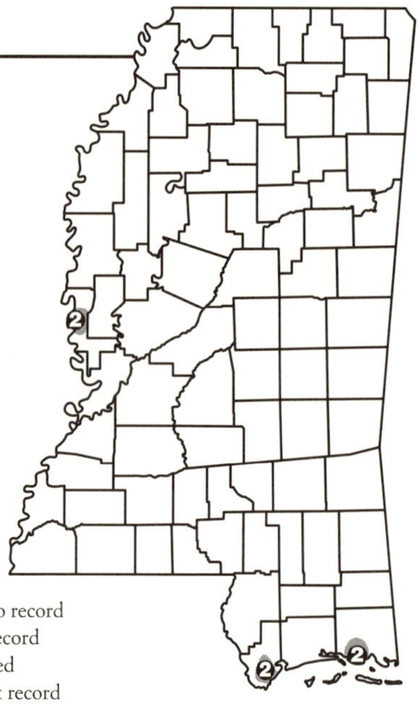

Accidental

■ Locality records

❶ specimen or photo record
❷ confirmed sight record
❸ breeding confirmed
❹ unconfirmed sight record
□ breeding distribution
🄰 distribution statewide

	JAN	FEB	MAR	APR	MAY	JUN	JUL	AUG	SEP	OCT	NOV	DEC
OCCURRENCE										20 ○		18 ○○
MUSEUM*												
WHT*												

*Breeding confirmed by egg, sight, or photographic record.

range is normally from western Texas and southern California southward to central Mexico. It has occurred in the Southeast only as a casual winter visitor. This towhee has occurred in Alabama and Louisiana and has strayed to other eastern states in late fall and winter.

Eastern Towhee *Pipilo erythrophthalmus*

This large and attractive ground-dwelling finch is abundant in winter, and is a common, statewide, summer-resident, breeding bird where brush and thickets provide nesting habitat. The Eastern Towhee is known widely by the names "chewink" and "joree," which allude to its loud call. The name "ground robin" is sometimes used locally because of its habit of feeding mostly on the ground and bearing a vague resemblance to the American Robin.

The male is entirely black on the head and upperparts. The sides are rufous, the belly white, and undertail coverts buffy. The long, rounded tail has an extensive amount of white in outer feathers, which shows in flight and when the bird flicks its tail. There is a small, white patch at the base of the outer primary wing feathers, but this usually is concealed by the rufous feathers on the sides.

The female has identical marks, except the black is replaced by brown. The juvenile is rich brown above, like the female, and buffy below and streaked with darker brown. The juvenile plumage changes to adult by early fall. Juveniles have brown eyes that change to red or reddish orange in the adult.

The Eastern Towhee calls attention to itself by its call, a loud *chewink'* or *shrink* and by vigorous scratching and scattering about dead leaves. Both feet are thrown forward and quickly withdrawn to kick backwards the leaves, straw, and forest debris to reach the rich humus below, which harbors insect food and seeds. I have watched towhees almost bury themselves while scratching in leaf litter.

The Eastern Towhee is essentially a bird of dense thickets and brushy cover found at the edge of woods or fields and in forest openings. It is usually seen flitting through underbrush, where it soon disappears. In spring, however, the male mounts to a high perch in a tree where he sings a loud *drink-your-tee-e-e-e.* The song begins with a high note followed by a note on a lower pitch and ends in a wavering trill. The song varies among the geographical distribution of individual birds.

EASTERN TOWHEE

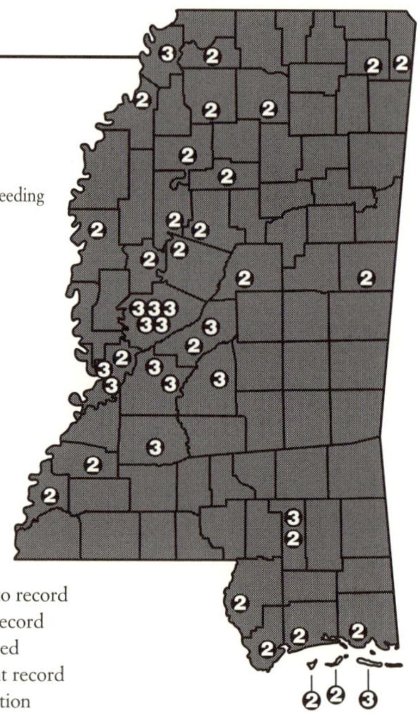

Common statewide

■ Permanent resident breeding

❶ specimen or photo record
❷ confirmed sight record
❸ breeding confirmed
❹ unconfirmed sight record
🅂 breeding distribution
🅂 distribution statewide

	JAN	FEB	MAR	APR	MAY	JUN	JUL	AUG	SEP	OCT	NOV	DEC
OCCURRENCE	■	■	■	■	■	■	■	■	■	■	■	■
MUSEUM*			•	• •	••		•	•				
WHT*				28 •	•••	4 •						

*Breeding confirmed by egg, sight, or photographic record.

In winter there is an influx of Eastern Towhees from northern and eastern populations. These wintering birds have white margins on the edges of the primaries forming a white spot. Our permanent-resident Eastern Towhees have very little or no white mark.

The Eastern Towhee builds a substantial cup-shaped nest of dead leaves, grass stems, grass blades, and bark strips with a lining of fine grasses. It is usually within two or three feet of the ground and concealed in a thick bush or vines. Cedar (juniper) bushes, leafy vines, and briers near the ground are preferred locations. Nests are sometimes placed on the ground, though I have found only one such nest. It was placed beside a low bush and sedge grass clump in a brushy clearing in open woods.

I found one nest in a cluster of climbing hydrangea vines growing on a sapling and situated seven feet aboveground under a closed deciduous forest canopy. The three or four eggs are white or pinkish white and finely sprinkled with reddish brown over the entire surface.

I observed the nesting cycle of a pair found building a nest in a shrub in my yard. On May 24 when I found the nest, the basal structure of leaves was complete. On May 26 the nest was finished, and eggs were laid on May 27, 28, and 29. Incubation began May 30, and the three young hatched on June 10. The three fledglings left the nest on June 19 and remained in nearby shrubbery until the following day. I removed two Brown-headed Cowbird eggs from the nest during the egg-laying period.

Towhees respond to feeding. Place mixed bird seed on the ground under shrubbery. They prefer to scratch for their food, but will sometimes use elevated feeders.

Bachman's Sparrow *Aimophila aestivalis*

This species was discovered by John Bachman around 1830. His friend, John James Audubon, described and named it between 1833 and 1834 after its discoverer. Bachman took the first specimens at Parker's Ferry, South Carolina. Later it was known as the "pine-woods sparrow" because of its preferred habitat of open pine or pine-oak forest.

The Bachman's Sparrow is one of our most elusive birds and would otherwise escape detection by most observers were it not for the ethereal, ringing song, which is by far the most varied and beautiful of all the sparrows. Although a fairly common winter resident, especially in southern Mississippi, it is so secretive and difficult to flush that it is often overlooked. It occurs uncommonly and locally as a permanent-resident breeding bird east of the Loess Bluff and is rare or absent, except in migration, in counties bordering the Mississippi River and the Delta counties. Resident populations are supplemented by northern birds wintering mostly in southern Mississippi.

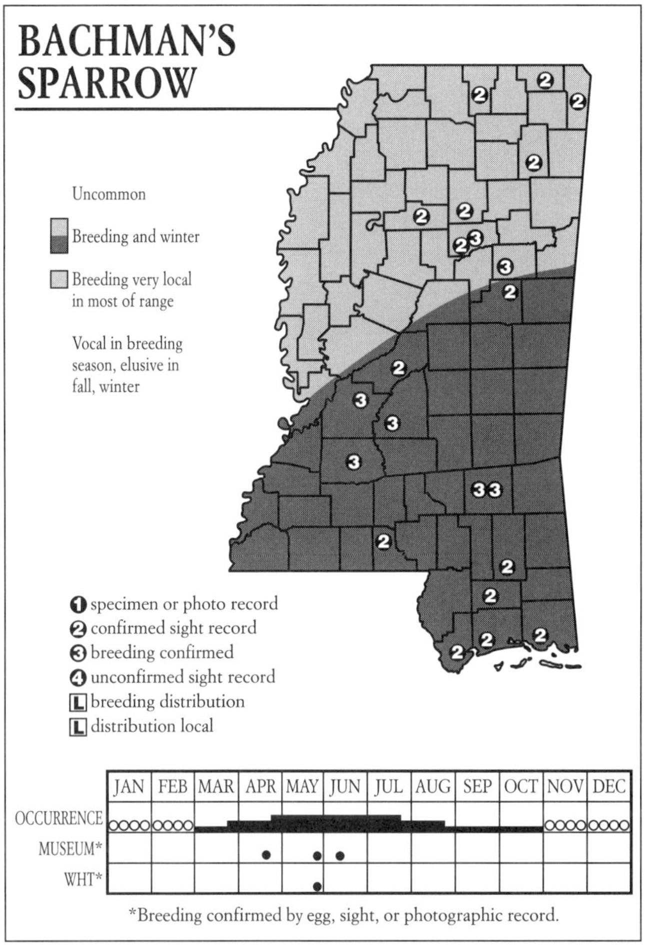

This shy sparrow always nests on the ground. The nest is composed of coarse grass lined with fine grass stems. The rim is slightly arched over to partly conceal the three or four unmarked white eggs. The nest is placed in or beside concealing grass or other vegetation. It is one of the most difficult nests to find—the only two I have found were discovered by glimpsing the white eggs on their open sides. Egg records for this species extend from April 24 to June 17. Breeding has been confirmed by collection records in Harrison, Hinds, Jones, and Rankin Counties.

The Bachman's Sparrow may be declining in numbers. It requires dry, open, pine or pine-oak woods interspersed with grassy openings growing up in scattered patches of scrub oak, blackberry briers, and low bushes. In the absence of fire, pinelands tend to grow up thick and brushy within a few years and soon develop a closed canopy, suppressing cover needed by this sparrow for nesting. Many old fields and forest openings have been closed into dense forest or have been reclaimed for cultivation or pasture. Land use for pasture, crops, and trees has eliminated favorable habitat for this sparrow over wide areas.

The lovely, plaintive, liquid songs of this sparrow are heard best in the morning and late afternoon. The song consists of highly variable phrases usually starting with a long note of exceptional sweetness, followed by trills, and then a series of fast notes of different pitch. A dozen or more song variations may sometimes be heard from the same individual. Words cannot adequately describe the beauty of this sparrow's song, which is often given from a favorite perch on a lower dead limb in or near pine woods.

Field marks of this sparrow are not distinctive. It is reluctant to flush and quick to hide. It is streaked above with reddish brown and gray, giving the back a purplish look. The underparts are *unstreaked, dingy buff.* The *large, dark bill* and flat head are reminiscent of the Grasshopper Sparrow, but the Bachman's Sparrow has a *long, dark tail.* It can be distinguished from the pink-billed Field Sparrow by the less rusty appearance, yellow at the bend of the wing, dark upper mandible, and darker crown. Immatures are streaked across the buffy breast.

American Tree Sparrow *Spizella arborea*

This sparrow rarely winters south of the central United States. It is likely to occur in the Gulf states only in very cold weather with large amounts of ice and snow.

Few published records and two collected specimens substantiate this bird's occurrence in Mississippi. The first, a sight record by Warriner (1936), was in a mixed flock of sparrows about three miles southeast of Corinth in Alcorn County on December 30, 1935. This bird was seen following extremely cold weather with three to four inches of snow and ice on the ground. Vaiden (1939) collected a specimen in Bolivar County on April 1, 1938, the second occurrence record and also the latest occurrence date for this species.

A specimen in the MMNS was taken by H. L. Owens on February 1, 1940, on Chookatonchee Creek in Chickasaw County following the ice, snowstorms, and extreme cold. This record almost coincides with another sighting recorded by George Lowery Jr. (1974) at a roadside near Lottie, Louisiana, on January 27, 1940.

Other sight records are: Noxubee Refuge (January 2, 1973), Grenada (December 27, 1973), Natchez (January 3, 1976), Hattiesburg (October 28, November 1 and 4; Moore et al. 1980), single birds seen in Jackson County (December 20, 1980), in Hancock County (December 27, 1980) by Terrie Gates, and three and six birds, respectively, in Lafayette County near the southern shore of Sardis Lake by W. Marvin Davis (January 15–22, 1977, and February 10, 1979). All distinctive field marks were carefully observed and noted on these sightings.

A solid gray breast with a *central black spot, rufous brown cap and line behind the eye,* gray stripe above the eye, *dark upper and yellow lower mandibles,* dark legs, and two prominent, white wing bars are identifying field marks. The

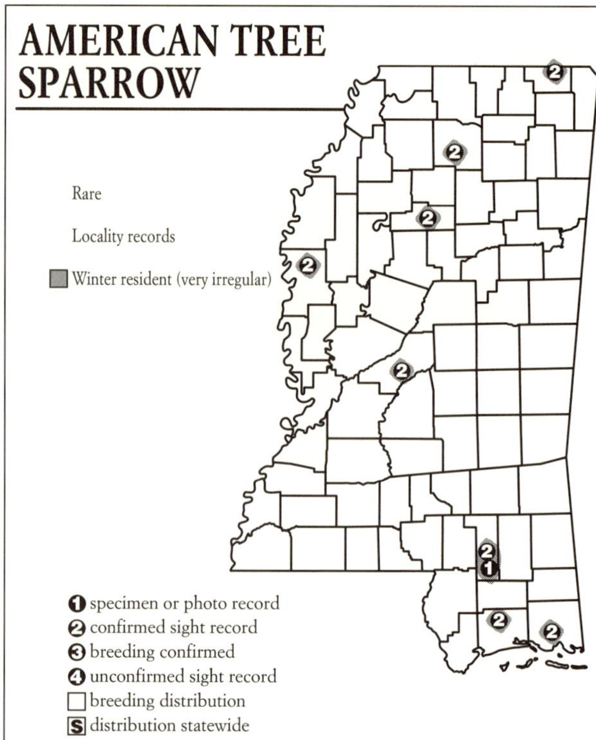

	JAN	FEB	MAR	APR	MAY	JUN	JUL	AUG	SEP	OCT	NOV	DEC
OCCURRENCE	oo	o		o						o	o	oo
MUSEUM*												
WHT*												

*Breeding confirmed by egg, sight, or photographic record.

Field Sparrow is similar but smaller, lacks the black breast spot, and has a pink bill and pinkish legs. The Chipping Sparrow is much smaller, has a *white* line over the eye and a *black line through the eye.* These three rusty-capped sparrows are similar in general appearance, but the central breast spot, two-toned bill, and larger size distinguish the American Tree Sparrow. The Swamp Sparrow also has a rusty cap, but lacks the breast spot and two prominent, white wing bars.

Chipping Sparrow *Spizella passerina*

This small sparrow is a permanent, statewide resident found breeding locally in dry, open, pine-oak groves in open, short-grass areas such as parks, golf courses, pastures, lawns, and the edges of fields or orchards. An influx of wintering birds begins in late October. The species is common in southern Mississippi during migration, and in winter large flocks occur in suitable, open-ground habitat.

"Chippies" often travel in mixed flocks with Pine Warblers, juncos, and other sparrows. When large feeding flocks are approached, they move restlessly ahead and often take flight from tree to tree before descending to the ground. They are primarily ground feeders, but sing from elevated perches.

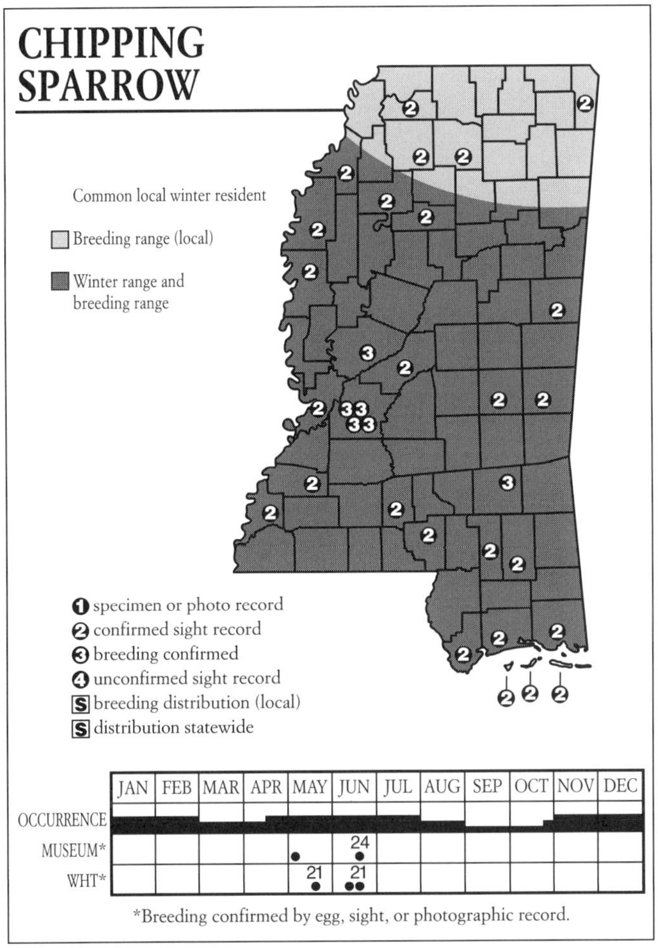

The song is a continuous series of rapid, monotonous, trilling notes all on the same pitch. The call is a simple *tsip*.

Chipping Sparrows are not common wintering birds in central and northern Mississippi. Frequently, they are not recorded on Christmas Bird Counts in the central, northern, and Delta counties. They are rare and local breeding birds in the coastal counties and rare or absent in the Delta. In the remainder of the state, they breed locally, sometimes in small colonies.

I remember a nesting colony near Clinton in Hinds County around a small pond with open groves of loblolly pine and oaks, where the surrounding pasture was heavily grazed. I found several nests at a time on the outer branches of pine and oak limbs in trees bordering the pond. Chippies will nest in other trees and bushes, but prefer to build in loblolly pine.

The small, neat, cup-shaped nest made of fine grass and weed stems is lined with fine grasses and hair. The three or four eggs are greenish blue and marked sparingly around the large end with blackish brown and purplish. Egg record dates extend from May 1 to June 24.

The Chipping Sparrow is identified by its small size, bright chestnut brown cap, a black line through the eye, and a white line over the eye. The black bill and grayish white underparts are distinctive. Young in summer can be recognized by their small size and fine streaking on the underparts. Immatures in winter are buffier than the adults and have a striped crown.

Clay-colored Sparrow *Spizella pallida*

This small, western, pale-colored sparrow is a rare transient or winter resident on the Gulf Coast. Burleigh (1945) collected a specimen at Saucier in Harrison County on October 26, 1938. There are few occurrence records for this bird in Mississippi. Five coastal records in Hancock County by Judith Toups, Terrie and Larry Gates (photograph), W. Marvin Davis, Gene Knight, and Robert Chapel extend from September 22 to December 31.

The Clay-colored Sparrow is identified by its clear breast, small size, brown ear patch bordered by dark brown lines, a light stripe through the center of the crown, and buffy brown rump. The similar sized, clear-breasted Chipping Sparrow does not have the ear patch outlined above and below with dark brown lines, and the rump is gray instead of buffy brown.

Field identification of the Clay-colored Sparrow is difficult without a careful view of the brownish rump; dark-outlined,

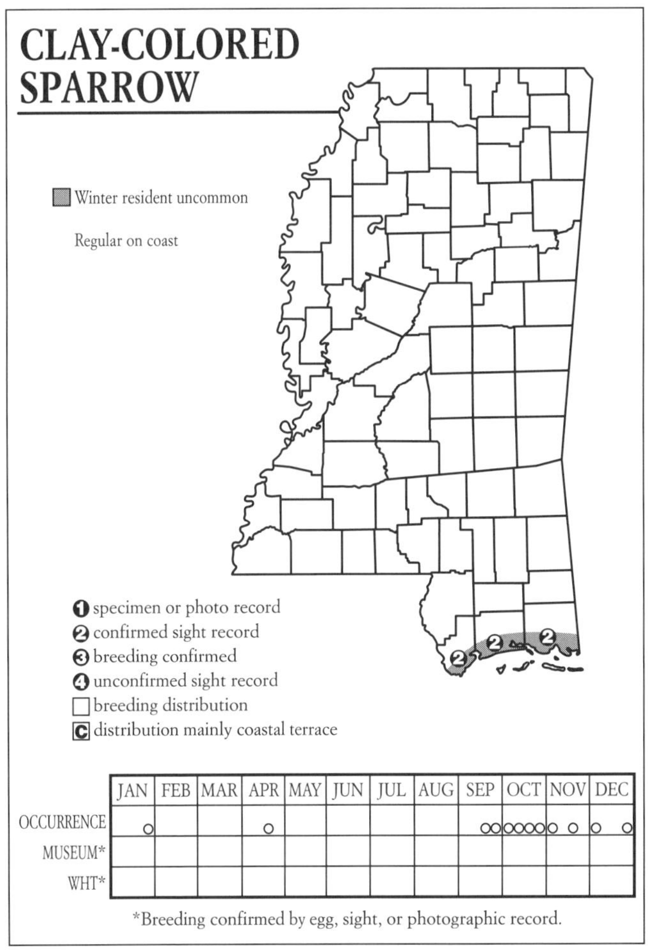

brown cheek patch; and a median, light-colored crown stripe. Immature Clay-colored and Chipping Sparrows are difficult to separate in fall and winter unless the buffy brown rump of the Clay-colored is seen plainly. All Chipping Sparrows have a gray rump.

This species winters north along the Gulf Coast from eastern to southwestern Texas and into Mexico. It breeds on the brushy prairies of the midwestern states and western and central Canadian provinces. The song is unusual for a bird, consisting of three or four low buzzy notes spaced equally apart and sounding like a hoarse insect. I found this sparrow to be rather common on brushy, short-grass prairie and recorded the song on the Lostwood National Wildlife Refuge near Kenmare, North Dakota.

Field Sparrow *Spizella pusilla*

The Field Sparrow is a fairly common, permanent-resident, breeding bird, except in the Yazoo Delta and in the longleaf pine country near the coast, where it is an uncommon breeder. In late October, wintering flocks arrive in Mississippi from northern areas and remain until late March or early April. In winter, Field Sparrows are common to abundant in brushy fields, particularly those with broomsedge. It also inhabits woodland and field edges grown up in weeds, briers, and bushes.

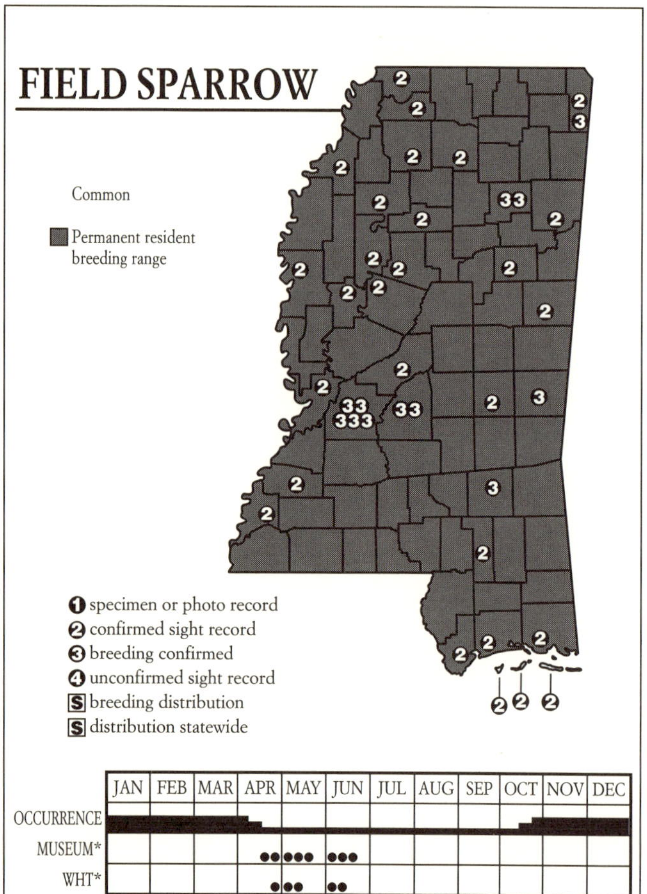

*Breeding confirmed by egg, sight, or photographic record.

The Field Sparrow is *plain breasted* and *rusty capped* with reddish brown upperparts, a *pink bill,* and noticeable *white eye ring.* The young have fine streaks below and pink bills.

Field Sparrows nest in open, abandoned fields and in pastures or burned-over open land growing back in briers, weeds, grass, and low bushes. Weedy pastures with scattered clumps of dog fennel, brier patches, broomsedge, and low bushes are preferred nesting habitat.

Breeding activity begins in early April when fruit trees bloom. The clear, sweet, melancholy song of the male can be heard at that time and throughout the breeding season. The first several long, sweet, and plaintive notes are slurred downward, followed by an ascending or descending trill. There is much variation in the songs of different individuals, but little variation in successive songs of individual birds.

Nesting begins about mid-April and extends through June. Egg record dates extend from April 14 to June 17. The small but substantially built nest is made of fine grass and weed stems lined with finer grasses and hair. Nests may be placed on the ground in a clump of broomsedge, dog fennel, or other concealing vegetation, but more often are built in low bushes or blackberry and smilax briers not more than two or three feet aboveground. The three or four bluish white eggs are blotched and speckled with rufous, mostly around the large end.

In winter this sparrow feeds mostly on the ground on grass seeds. Summer foods consist of insects with some seeds and fruits. In winter, I have often watched them alight on broomsedge stems and vigorously extract the long, narrow seeds of this plant, which seems to me an ever-present part of their winter habitat.

Vesper Sparrow *Pooecetes gramineus*

The ground-dwelling Vesper Sparrow is a fairly common to common, statewide winter resident in open fields, burnt-over ground, open roadsides, and pastures. It prefers fallow or recently cultivated fields with bare ground, sparse grass, and cover, such as cotton and corn fields afford through the winter when the stalks are not plowed under.

The Vesper looks somewhat like a grayish Song Sparrow in size and general appearance until it flies and shows the dark tail with *white outer feathers* flashing conspicuously and without the pumping action of the tail so characteristic of the Song Sparrow's flight. The Vesper Sparrow has a soft, grayish or olivaceous brown appearance, and

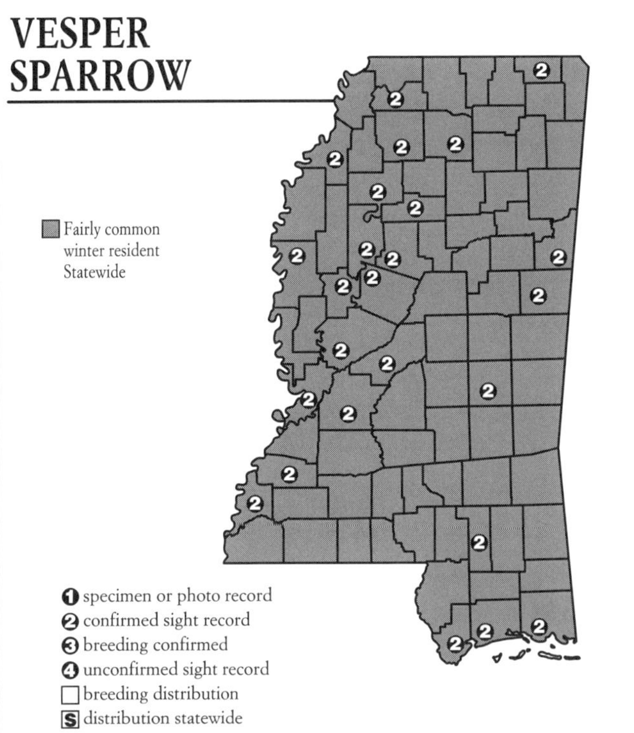

	JAN	FEB	MAR	APR	MAY	JUN	JUL	AUG	SEP	OCT	NOV	DEC
OCCURRENCE				17		15				6		
MUSEUM*												
WHT*												

*Breeding confirmed by egg, sight, or photographic record.

the streaking on the center of the breast does not run together to form a spot, as on most Song and Savannah Sparrows. Reddish brown shoulder patches, a light eye ring, white belly, and notched tail are field marks to look for when the Vesper can be seen at rest. Juncos have white outer-tail feathers, but are mostly slate gray. The Lark Sparrow, unlikely seen in winter, has large, white spots at the corner of the rounded tail.

This sparrow occurs in flocks arriving in late October or early November and remains until early April. Extremes of arrival and departure are October 6 and April 17. An out-of-season specimen in the MMNS was taken in Sunflower County by Sammy Ray on June 15, 1940.

I have found these birds many times in small flocks along the borders of cotton fields. The standing stalks provided perfect escape cover into which the birds usually flew; then they ran along the ground between the cotton rows. A studied view of this sparrow shows a pleasing mixture of earth colors on the upperparts and pale buff on the sides with brown streaking. The earth colors remind me of the American Pipit and Horned Lark. I think this species is one of the prettiest of our winter sparrows.

Lark Sparrow *Chondestes grammacus*

This species is a rare, *local,* summer-resident, breeding bird in western Hinds County, in the black belt and hill counties of northeastern Mississippi, and possibly in the northernmost counties bordering Tennessee, where it has occurred during the breeding season. It is apparently absent during summer in southern Mississippi. Elsewhere in our state as available records show, it occurs rarely in winter, casually in late summer as a transient, and early in spring as a migrant during April.

Spring arrival and departure dates extend from April 6 to 30. Fall departure begins late in July and extends until about mid-September. Extremes of spring arrival and fall departure are April 6 and November 3.

Few winter records have been reported. Andrew Allison (1906) reported, "We found this species (February 13 to 16, 1904 in Hancock County) in the pine clearings, about equally common with the Vesper Sparrow, and in song. Up to this time we found it only very rarely." Thomas D. Burleigh (1945) never recorded the Lark Sparrow wintering on the Gulf Coast during eight years of intensive field work there. Recent records indicate that the Lark Sparrow is a regular but uncommon winter resident in the Gulf Coast counties.

This large, handsome, white-breasted sparrow has a black breast spot; a black, rounded, white-tipped tail; prominent chestnut ear patch; chestnut and white crown stripes; and a black streak along the jaw line and sides of the throat. Immatures have a streaked, upper breast without the spot, a dull face pattern, and a rounded tail with white in the corners.

I first observed Lark Sparrows on May 28, 1935, when I found a pair nesting on the ground in an overgrazed pasture near Clinton in Hinds County. There was a small colony of nesting birds that remained until 1942, after the pasture had been made into a little-used, nine-hole golf

Nest and eggs of Lark Sparrow

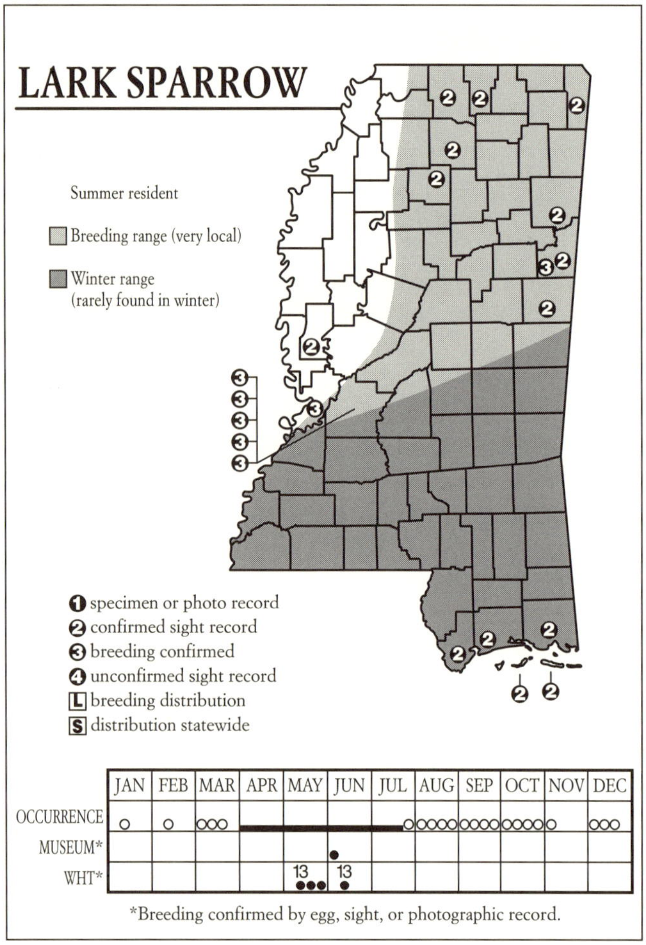

course. Open pine and post oak groves interspersed and surrounded the open pasture, which had occasional low bushes, clumps of low-growing Cherokee rose, milkweeds, thin or overgrazed grass patches, and barren spots of ground in gullies where cows had trampled the vegetation.

I found at least six nests, all except one built in a slight hollow in the ground. They were made from weed stems and grasses to form an open cup and lined with fine grasses, rootlets, or hair. One nest was found on the lower, horizontal limb of a pine tree about 10 feet aboveground at the edge of open pasture.

These nests contained three to five white eggs, prettily blotched and scrawled with black, mostly at the larger end. Other nests with young and adults feeding fledglings also were seen. Nests on the ground were placed in or beside low vegetation, such as a weed or grass clump, small bush, dead limb, or low Cherokee rose trailing on the ground. Most nests were not well concealed by vegetation.

Egg dates recorded extend from May 13 to June 13. Young have been recorded in or out of the nest from May 28 to July 13. On the Utica breeding bird survey route, I recorded one sighting of adults feeding young out of the nest on June 1, 1968, in a pasture south of Dry Grove in Hinds County. Eugene Patton collected two fledged young on June 13, 1940, in Lee County, the only other substantiated Mississippi breeding record (MMNS).

The Lark Sparrow's distinctive song is usually given while perched on a low bush, tree, fence post, or wire. It is a broken sequence of melodious, throaty notes interspersed with high trills, low unmusical buzzes, and churring sounds. The call note is a weak *tsip*.

The Lark Sparrow seems to have a breeding distribution in Mississippi somewhat similar to the Grasshopper Sparrow, Bewick's Wren, and Dickcissel. Look for it locally north of a diagonal line from southwestern Hinds County to the black belt of northeastern Mississippi. There are few records from the intervening hill counties.

[Lark Bunting] *Calamospiza melanocorys*

This western sparrow breeds in the dry prairies, plains, and Rocky Mountain valleys, especially where sagebrush is extensive. Males in black alternate plumage are conspicuous along roadside fences and while engaged in song flight, which is similar to that of the Bobolink. The bird's winter range extends westward from central Texas into

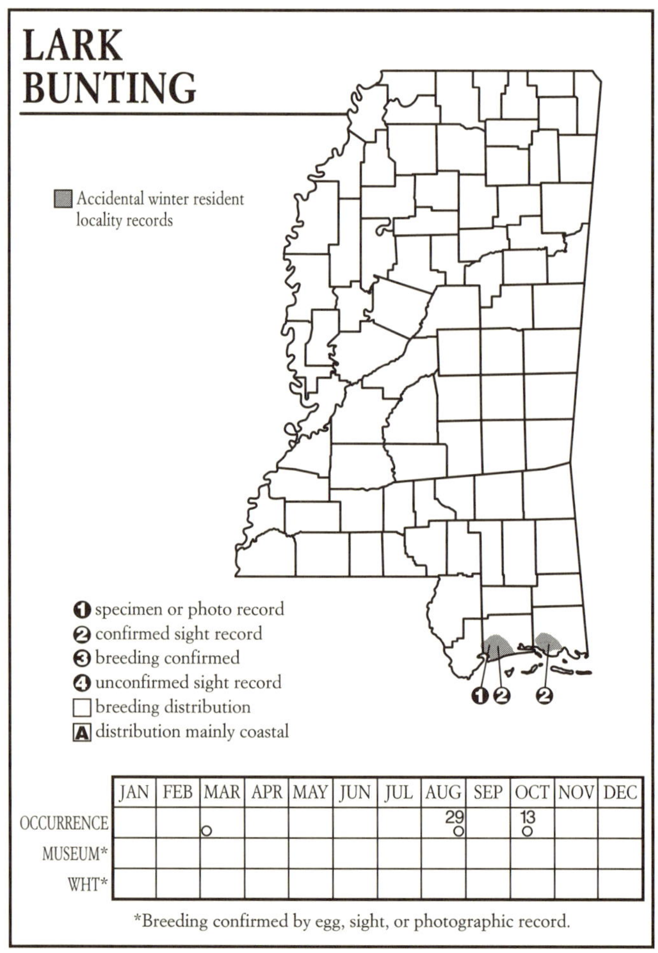

southern New Mexico. Lark Buntings are gregarious in winter feeding flocks, postbreeding, and migration periods. They are irregular near the margins of their range and casual or accidental east of central Texas.

My first encounter with Lark Buntings was during the winter of 1942–1943. Large feeding flocks were numerous in cultivated fields and open pastures between San Antonio and Hondo, Texas, where I was stationed briefly during World War II. These birds were recognized in their dusky, heavily streaked plumage with some having whitish wing patches. In later years, during the summer months while traveling through the prairies, plains, mountains, and desert country from southern New Mexico to eastern Montana, these birds were locally conspicuous. I spent a rather frustrating hour or more in windy Montana grasslands recording the flight song of a single male. Finally, I got a good recording of the song by facing the microphone into the wind, which reduced the wind noise to an acceptable level.

The adult breeding male is black with a bluish gray bill; a conspicuous, large, white patch on the upperwings; and a contrasting white patch under the tip of the tail. Winter males are streaked gray and brown with a black chin patch. Females and immatures resemble the female Purple Finch, but show wide whitish wing bars. They are browner than the darker gray brown of the winter male. In winter plumage, Lark Buntings have a stocky, short-tailed appearance.

The song is a long series of varied single notes, whistles, and trills, given either from a conspicuous perch or frequently in flight.

Two occurrence records for the coast have been reported. At Bellefontaine Beach in Jackson County on October 13, 1979, a female or immature was found feeding with sparrows in brush along a roadside (Gates et al. 1980). The second record was a female at a feeding station at Gulfport on August 29, 1980. The bird was photographed feeding on the ground with other feeder birds (Toups and Hodges 1981b).

Savannah Sparrow *Passerculus sandwichensis*

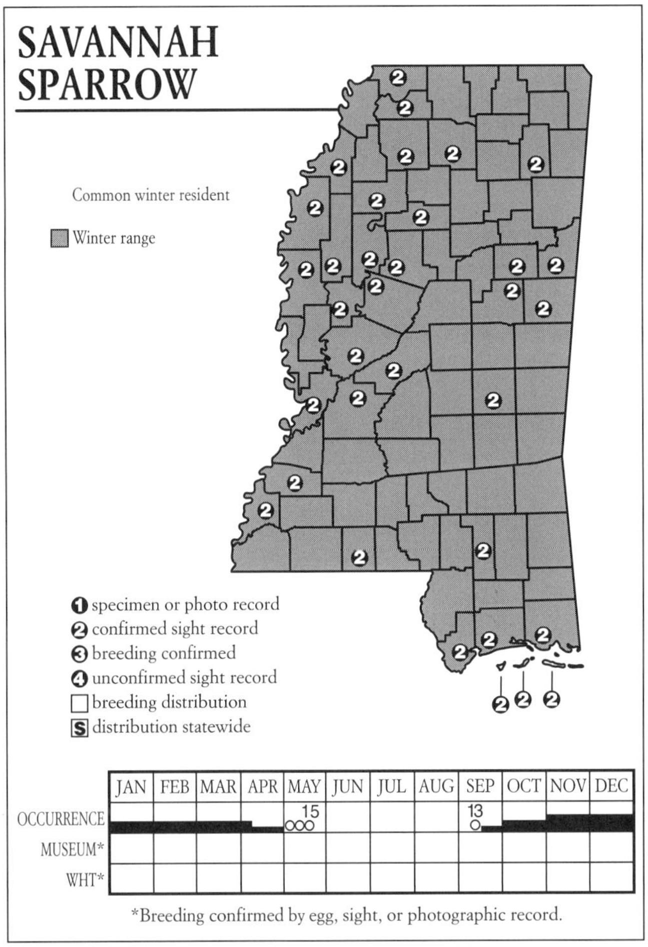

This is the most common of our winter-resident sparrows of open country. The Savannah Sparrow occurs throughout Mississippi and is often locally abundant. Early arrivals appear the first week in October, and they become common by early November. Departure begins around mid-April and continues until about mid-May. Extremes of recorded fall arrival and spring departure are September 13 and May 15.

This sparrow spends most of its time on the ground, feeding largely on grass and weed seeds, and occasionally perching on wires or fences in or near the usual habitat. When flushed, it flies a short distance with a bounding flight before dropping down and scurrying into the nearest cover. Airports, wet and weedy pastures, fallow fields with low moist areas, roadsides, open shorelines, and marshy edges are its favorite haunts.

The breeding range of this bird extends from northern Labrador and northern Alaska, southward into New Jersey, Missouri, northern New Mexico, northwestern Mexico, southern California, and Baja California.

The Savannah Sparrow is heavily streaked with brown above, and it has a white breast with fine brown streaks. The streaks tend to concentrate at the center of the breast to form a fine spot. In this respect, it is similar to the Song Sparrow, but the Savannah has a central pale stripe through the crown, usually a yellow or yellowish spot in front of the eye and at the bend of the wing, a slightly notched tail, and pink legs. The Song Sparrow has a long, rounded tail that it pumps up and down in flight.

The song of the Savannah Sparrow consists of two to six identical short notes, followed by two lisping, insectlike, buzzy trills, with the second trill on a lower pitch: *tzip-tzip-tzip, seeeee, tzaaaaa.*

On its breeding grounds, this species is a "wire-sitter" and singer from utility lines along roadsides in open country. It is a common species around hay fields and on short-grass prairies in the northern states and Canadian provinces. On the prairies, it sings from the tops of low bushes and is one of the most common summer-resident, breeding birds.

The cup nest, placed in a depression on the ground in dense vegetation, is made of plant stems lined with finer material. The four or five eggs are bluish green, and usually heavily blotched or dotted with reddish brown.

Grasshopper Sparrow
Ammodramus savannarum

Small sparrows that inhabit grasslands, variously known as "grassbirds," "stinkbirds," or "grass sparrows," are difficult to see well and identify. The Savannah, Grasshopper, Henslow's, and Le Conte's Sparrows fall into this category. Quail hunters know them as "stinkbirds" because even well-trained bird dogs will point them or be temporarily distracted by their scent.

The Grasshopper, Henslow's, and Le Conte's Sparrows usually are found in dense growths of broomsedge, or in grassy flats of open pine woods in southern Mississippi. These birds are seldom seen except when flushed out of their grassy cover, only to fly a short distance and pitch down

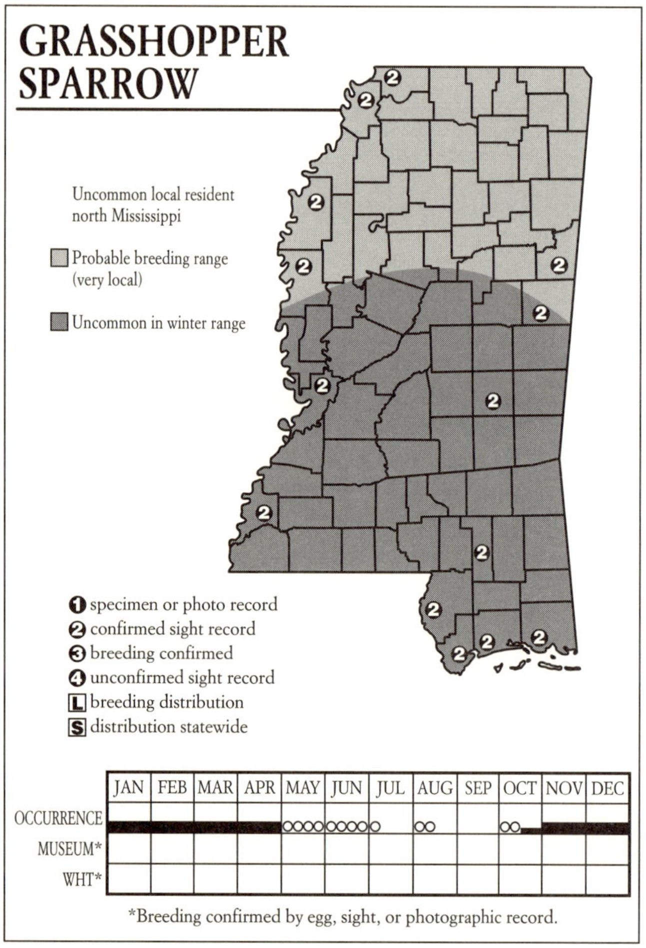

into the grass again. Repeated pursuit and flushing will sometimes cause these elusive sparrows to perch on a grass or weed stem for a few seconds of viewing with binoculars.

The Grasshopper Sparrow is an uncommon winter resident in southern Mississippi, where it is found locally in broomsedge fields. Arriving in late October, this winter-resident species usually departs by late April. There are only a few summer records for this species. This sparrow probably breeds rarely and locally in the Black Belt Prairie and parts of northwestern Mississippi.

An MMNS specimen collected on June 19 in Lee County, and others observed in May, June, and early August near Lakeview in DeSoto County, indicate possible breeding in those areas. W. Marvin Davis recorded four in 1970 on the Aberdeen breeding bird route, and a total of 90 in Tunica County on the Dundee survey route in June from 1970 through 1973. These birds were in pastureland bordering the Mississippi River levee. Ben B. Coffey Jr. recorded this species in 1974 and 1975 in June on the Corinth breeding bird survey route. Actual nesting of the Grasshopper Sparrow in Mississippi has not been confirmed. Possible nesting in the Northeast Prairie and suitable habitat elsewhere in northwestern Mississippi needs further investigation.

This small, short-tailed sparrow has a plain, buff-colored breast; a short, narrow, bristly tail; black and chestnut-striped back; a buffy, median crown stripe; a flat-headed appearance; and disproportionately large head and neck. Its song begins with two or three short ticks and ends with a grasshopper-like trill. The nest is an arched-over, grassy cup sunken into the ground and well concealed in grass. The four or five eggs are white, specked with reddish brown.

On a field trip to the Yazoo National Wildlife Refuge in Washington County in early May with a party of other birders, I came upon a number of Grasshopper Sparrows in migration. They were seen in a harvested soybean field grown up in dockweed, trumpet vines, and an early spring flowering and seeding plant of the mustard family. Horned Larks also were feeding in an adjacent field across the road.

The larks and sparrows evidently were feeding on the shattered seeds of a wild mustard. The tiny pods with their silvery inner lining gave the whole field a whitish appearance. Several Grasshopper Sparrows were singing from the tips of dockweed plants or clumps of trumpet vines. Their thin and buzzy song, barely audible from a distance, reminded me of an insect's trilling.

I met these sparrows again on the short-grass prairie at Lostwood National Wildlife Refuge in North Dakota in the summer of 1985. I recorded their song with Baird's Sparrows singing in the background. A singing male Grasshopper Sparrow responded to a playback of his song and circled close around me, singing from the tops of small clumps of wild roses dotting the prairie grasslands. I found this bird difficult to locate solely by hearing its song. I would be looking ahead at times when the bird had circled and was singing behind me.

Henslow's Sparrow *Ammodramus henslowii*

This small, short-tailed, winter-resident sparrow with a flat-headed appearance occupies broomsedge and wire grass (*Aristida* spp.) fields and associated weedy or shrubby areas, particularly in wet or boggy sites in the pine barrens of southern Mississippi. These birds are so difficult to flush from cover that field identification is often impossible. They run and hide in the grass and will sometimes remain motionless and invisible until almost stepped upon.

It is possible that Henslow's Sparrow may be more common than available records indicate because they are so difficult to flush and identify. There are more specimen and sight records south of Hattiesburg, indicating that it is more common in suitable habitat near the coast. In spite of its elusive habits, this sparrow can sometimes be observed with binoculars by flushing and intently following its movements as the bird flies a short distance, then chasing and flushing it until it finally perches. Specimen and sight records extend through every month from October 8 to May 22.

Look for the *olive green* head, neck, and face tones; reddish brown wings; two black streaks on the side of the throat; a finely streaked necklace; and narrowly streaked sides. The low, erratic flight is accompanied by a peculiar twisting motion of the tail. The song is described as a short *flee-sik*.

Henslow's Sparrow is uncommon and declining over much of its breeding range. It nests in wet meadows and shrubby fields of the north-central and midwestern states, eastward into New England, and southward into northern Kentucky and Virginia.

Le Conte's Sparrow *Ammodramus leconteii*

A small, sharp-tailed winter resident, the Le Conte's Sparrow occurs in broomsedge and wire grass (*Aristida* spp.) fields. The bird usually is found in dry, upland fields on rolling hills instead of the wetter broomsedge, weed, and shrub bottoms preferred on inland sites by other sparrow species. The Henslow's, Le Conte's, Sharp-tailed, and Seaside Sparrows have narrow and sharp-pointed tail feathers that, when closed, give the whole tail a narrow, pointed appearance.

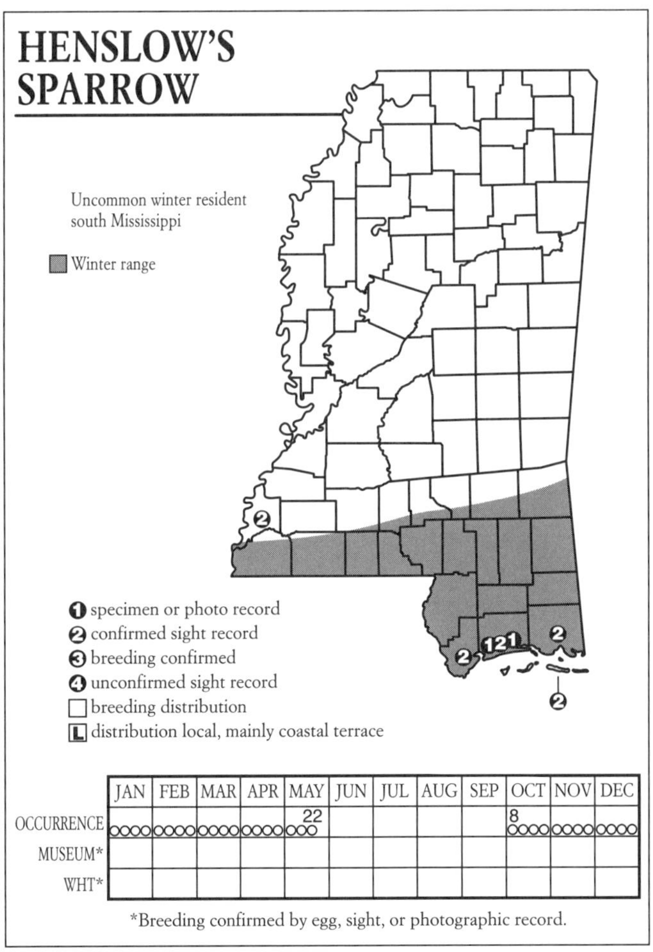

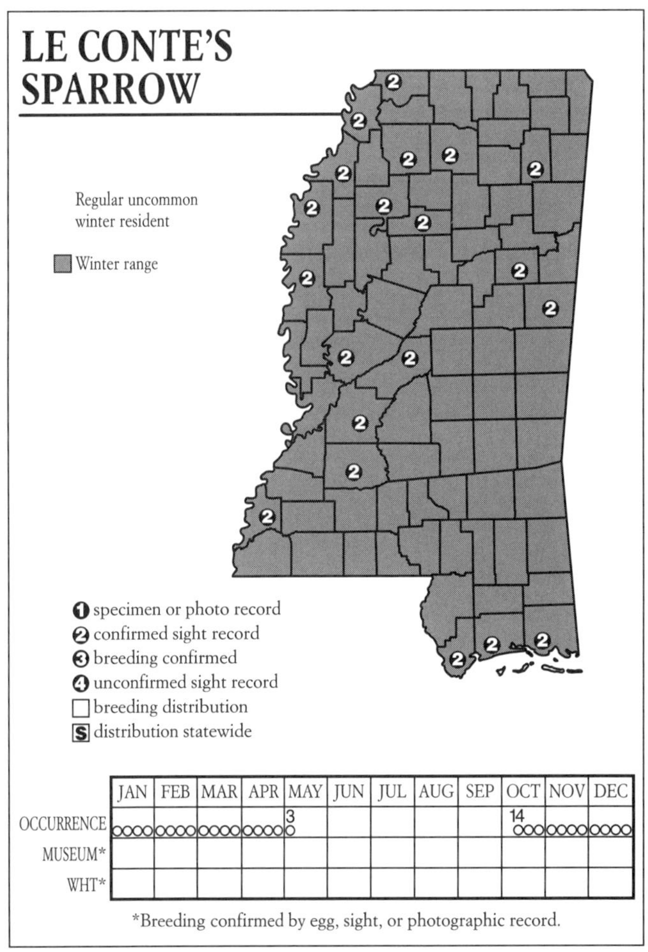

Le Conte's has the lightest appearance of the four sharp-tailed sparrows. The back is strongly striped, and underparts are buffy ocher and finely streaked from the neck down along the sides. Distinctive field marks are the ocher breast; a white stripe through the crown; a broad, buff, orange buff, or grayish line over the eye; and a broad collar of pinkish brown specks around the nape. The song is a thin and insectlike buzz of two syllables not likely to be heard except on the breeding grounds, where it nests around weedy, grassy places and marshes.

The Le Conte's Sparrow is difficult to find because it rarely flushes from its dense ground cover until very closely approached. When flushed, it flies low over the grass with a jerky, twisting motion for a short distance before dropping down again. Quail hunting dogs will point this "stinkbird" or "stinkpot." This sparrow often runs along the ground when pursued and will flush again some distance from where it was last seen. Repeated flushing toward brushy field edges will sometimes allow viewing when it perches in a bush.

This sparrow is a statewide, uncommon winter resident. Extremes of fall arrival and spring departure dates are October 14 and May 3. These birds are usually encountered singly, but occasionally they may be found scattered in loose flocks of a dozen or more. Their winter range is the Gulf states. The breeding range of the Le Conte's Sparrow is in south-central Canada and the prairies of the north-central United States.

SHARP-TAILED SPARROW

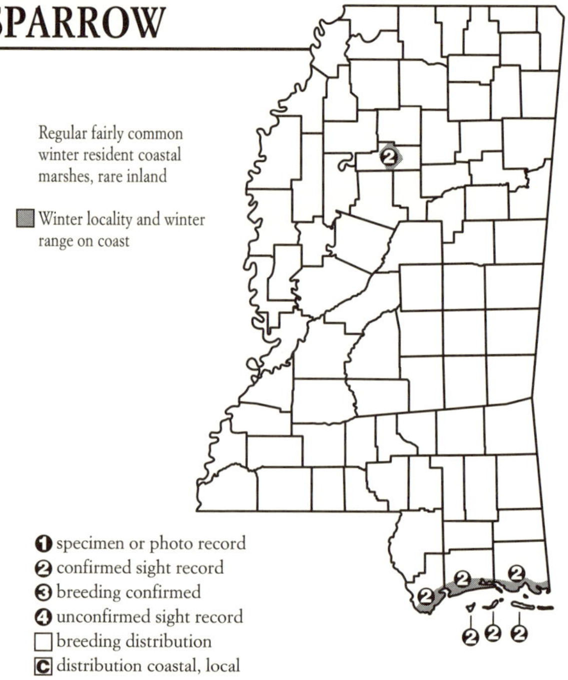

*Breeding confirmed by egg, sight, or photographic record.

Sharp-tailed Sparrow
Ammodramus caudacutus

This is a marsh sparrow, and its occurrence has been mainly in the salt marshes of the Gulf Coast and on the coastal islands. There, it is a regular resident throughout the winter. The earliest arrival date is September 15, and the latest occurrence record is a MMNS specimen collected on May 12, 1962, by Lovett E. Williams Jr. at Spanish Point near Pascagoula in Jackson County.

This sparrow breeds in freshwater and salt marshes of the northern United States and most of southern Canada. It has been recorded inland during migration in Louisiana and Alabama, but only rarely. Evidently, this sparrow overflies most of inland areas during migrations, but it should be searched for around inland lakes having cattails and aquatic plants. A recent sighting of one individual on Grenada Lake on November 3, 1984, by Judith Toups (Hodges and Jackson 1984) is one of a few inland records.

The Sharp-tailed Sparrow is fairly common in the salt marshes, both on the mainland and the barrier islands of Mississippi Sound. This sparrow is a skulker and must be sought out. When it flushes, it gives little chance for an observer to see field marks. It is inquisitive, however, and a squeaking noise will sometimes cause a bird to show itself in the open for viewing.

Distinguishing field marks are a gray ear patch, completely surrounded by a patch of triangular orange buff, which forms a line over the eye and covers the malar region and the side of the neck. The crown is dark gray and unstreaked. The breast is buffy, devoid of streaks, or sometimes more or less sharply streaked. Except for the triangular, orangish face marks, this sparrow resembles the Le Conte's Sparrow, but lacks the Le Conte's reddish collar and white stripe through the center of the crown.

I have never seen the Sharp-tailed Sparrow on any inland area of Mississippi. The best chance I had to view one at leisure was on a field trip with Robert E. Noble to a marsh in Cameron Parish, Louisiana. One sat on an open perch long enough for us to observe all comparative field marks. Noble was familiar with the species and identified it before calling the bird to my attention. A few other sightings on the Mississippi Gulf Coast have been too fleeting to permit a study of field marks, and my experience spent observing the marsh sparrows on the coast has been limited.

After an unsuccessful effort to locate and record the songs of this species and the Le Conte's Sparrow on the Agassiz National Wildlife Refuge in Minnesota, I had about given up on finding either. Later, at Lostwood National Wildlife Refuge in North Dakota, I was directed to a small, isolated, freshwater marsh. After failing to locate the site, I was taken there by Robert Murphy, a refuge biologist.

He pointed out the peculiar song, and at first I had difficulty recognizing it because of the constant wind. The bird would sing spasmodically from the middle of the marsh, and I succeeded in getting several songs on tape, but they were spoiled by the overriding wind noise. I spent several hours trying to get a good recording, hoping the wind would subside. Finally, I gave up without ever seeing the bird, which sang only in concealment of marsh vegetation.

The song of this Sharp-tailed Sparrow sounded as if the bird was being strangled. It made several quick gasps for breath and then gave a short, wheezy *tsh-e-e-e-e,* but it was so short that I wondered afterward if I had heard anything, much less a bird's song. According to my experience, anyone seeking this bird on its northern breeding grounds will need advance knowledge of the bird's location or local guidance. Also, I was told the same applies in locating the Le Conte's Sparrow on its nesting territory.

Seaside Sparrow

Seaside Sparrow *Ammodramus martimus*

The Seaside Sparrow is a fairly common, permanent-resident, breeding bird in saltwater marshes bordering the bays and estuaries of the Mississippi Gulf Coast. Here, it inhabits matted needlegrass *(Juncus roemerianus)* and sedges that grow above high tide. Like the Sharp-tailed Sparrow, it is secretive and skulks in the grasses. But it can be called into view by making a squeaking noise so that distinctive field marks can be noted.

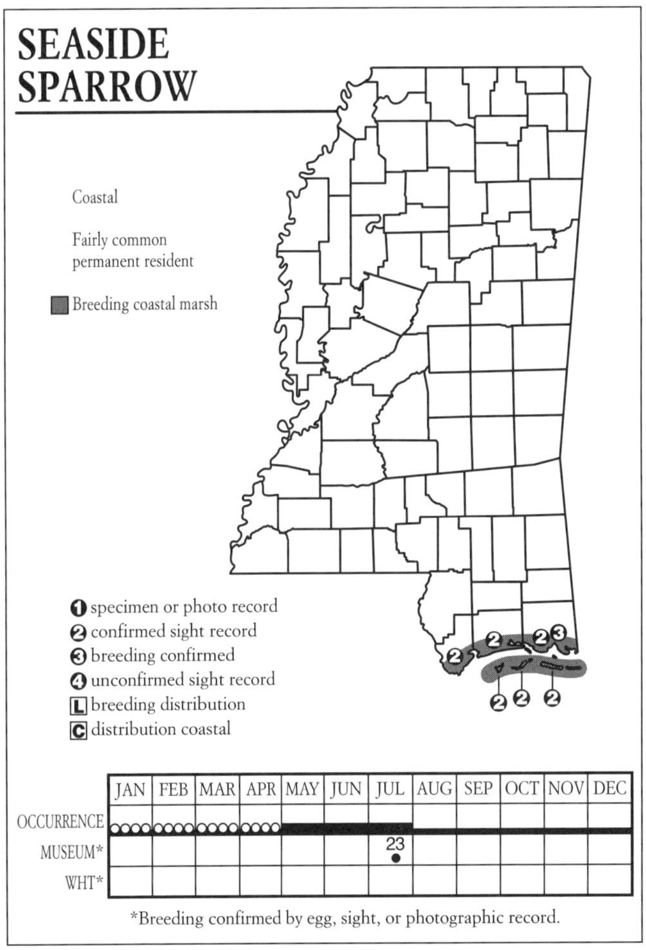

The Seaside Sparrow is dark gray and dingy above and below with a white throat, a white stripe at the jaw bordered below by a black "whisker" mark, a yellow patch in front of the eye, a whitish jaw streak, and a bit of yellow at the bend of the wing. The bill is conical, but very long for a sparrow. The tail is short, narrow, and pointed like other sharp-tailed sparrows.

These sparrows feed largely on insects, crustaceans, and other small animal life found on the ground or in debris brought to the shore by waves.

This sparrow's song is a weak, raspy, and husky rendition similar to the Red-winged Blackbird's, described by Roger T. Peterson as *cutcut, zhe'-eeeeeee.* The call note is a low *chack,* also similar to the Red-wing Blackbird's.

The nest is a cup of coarse grass, which is situated in marsh grass or a low bush near shore over water. The four to six eggs are white and densely speckled with reddish brown or purplish brown. The Seaside Sparrow has been found nesting in Jackson County in the Pascagoula River delta by Williams Jr. (1962b). Also, Henry D. Haberyan found two nests on May 6 and 7, 1961, and another on June 23, 1962. Hundreds of these birds were singing and breeding where these nests were found. Burleigh (1945) noted breeding colonies in marshes at the mouth of the Pascagoula River and Graveline Bayou in Jackson County, and on all the islands in Mississippi Sound.

Fox Sparrow *Passerella iliaca*

This large, handsome sparrow has the colors of the red fox. The rich rusty red, gray, and white combine to give it an exceedingly attractive appearance. It is the largest of our eastern sparrows and next in size to the Harris' Sparrow, a casual western winter visitor here.

The orange brown rump and tail, gray upperparts, white underparts heavily streaked with reddish brown, and a central breast spot readily identify the Fox Sparrow. The bill is horn colored above and slightly yellowish below and slightly swollen. At first glance the Fox Sparrow in flight may be confused with the Hermit Thrush. Both have reddish brown tails. But a glance at the thin bill, spotted breast, and tail-wagging of the thrush compared with the heavy streaking of this sparrow readily distinguishes them. The Hermit Thrush and Fox Sparrow often occupy the same wintering habitat in stream bottom woodland thickets.

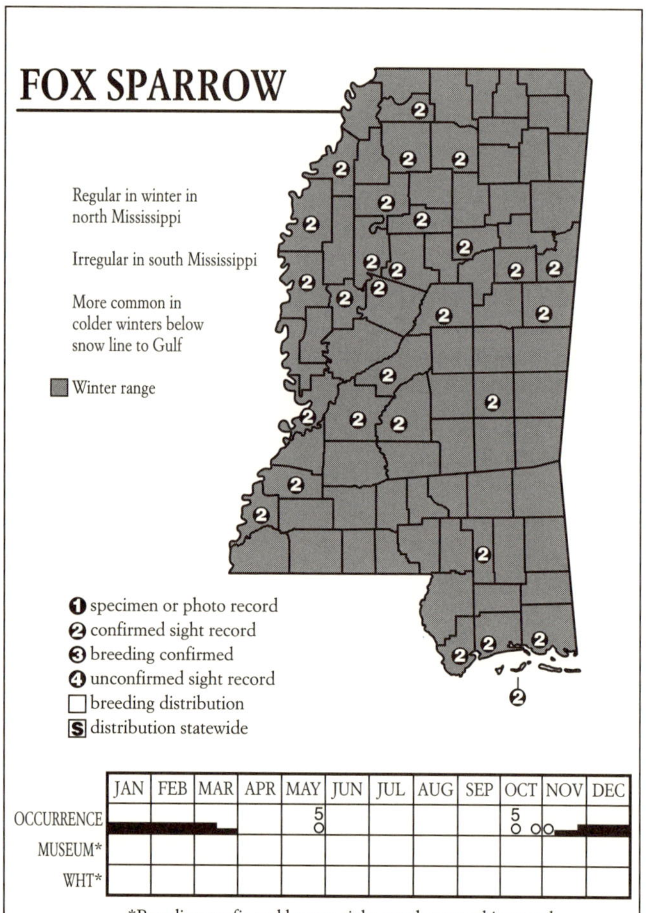

*Breeding confirmed by egg, sight, or photographic record.

The Fox Sparrow usually occurs in small flocks of less than a dozen birds. They prefer wet bottomland thickets and are shy and sometimes difficult to approach. They often mingle with White-throated Sparrows in dense woods. Fox Sparrows are mostly ground feeders, and, like the White-throat, scratch vigorously with both feet among the leaves on the forest floor, where they find seeds, some fruits, insects, and other small invertebrates.

This sparrow is a regular, fairly common winter resident in northern Mississippi, but it becomes scarce south of Jackson and Meridian. On January 24, 1940, a severe snowstorm followed by freezing rain, sleet, and extended subfreezing temperatures caused large numbers of these sparrows to pile up on the ice-free Gulf Coast, where they were common over a period of three weeks.

Fox Sparrows arrive later than most winter-resident sparrows. They seldom appear in numbers before late October in northern Mississippi. A gradual increase in numbers occurs with colder weather. Spring departure begins in late February and few remain after the end of March. Extremes of recorded arrival and departure dates are October 5 and April 30, a bird banded at Starkville by Nellie Hughes.

To hear the ethereal song of the Fox Sparrow is a rare treat. I first recognized it many years ago while resting on a creek bank near Clinton after a winter afternoon quail hunt. I had just seen Hermit Thrushes in the swamp thickets and had read about the sweetness of their song. My first thought was, "a Hermit Thrush singing?" But the singer was one of a small company of Fox Sparrows moving across the creek to roost in heavier cover. Since then I have observed this sparrow singing on warm winter days in early morning and near sundown. The rich, clear, flute-like, whistled song begins softly, rises in volume and pitch, and ends lower in pitch and softness.

Song Sparrow *Melospiza melodia*

Song Sparrows are common, statewide winter residents, but none have been found breeding in Mississippi, although the species breeds locally in Tennessee. They begin arriving early in October and are plentiful by November. Their ranks thin during March, and by mid-April most have departed to widespread breeding grounds in western and northern states and lower Canadian provinces.

The Song Sparrow is an abundant and conspicuous songbird around farms; towns; developed areas; and open,

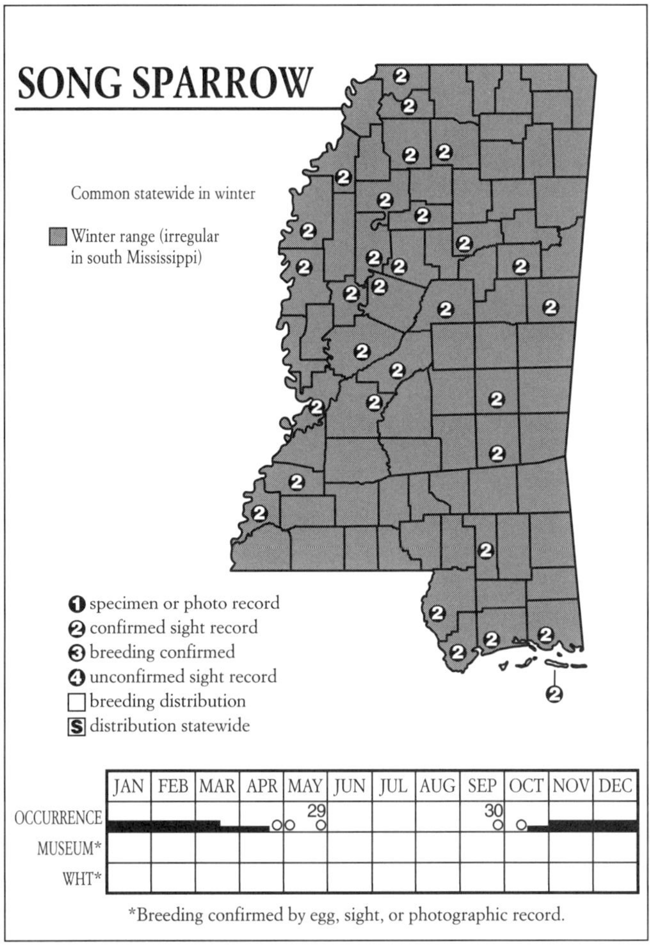

sunlit, shrubby, weedy places. It nests on or near the ground. Grass, weed stems, bark, and leaves form the nest, which is lined with fine grass or hair. The greenish white eggs are variously splotched with shades of brown.

When these sparrows arrive on the wintering grounds in the Southeast, they stay away from developed areas. They are shy and secretive and occupy hedgerows, streamside brier thickets, dense stands of weeds, tall grasses, or cattails, often but not always in wet places near water. Extremes of occurrence recorded in Mississippi are September 30 and May 29.

The medium-sized Song Sparrow is easily recognized by the heavy, reddish brown streaking of its underparts that converges to a conspicuous central breast spot. It can be separated from the Savannah Sparrow, which also has streaked underparts and a less conspicuous central breast spot, by the long, rounded tail and jerky flight with a pumping motion of the tail. The Savannah has a short, notched tail. The uncommon Lincoln's Sparrow has a wide, buffy breast band and much finer breast streaks without a central spot.

Occasionally on warm, late winter days the song can be heard. Several similar short notes are followed by lively, varied musical and buzzy notes, ending with a trill. The call is a distinctive nasal *tchunk* or a softer *tseet.*

Lincoln's Sparrow *Melospiza lincolnii*

Lincoln's Sparrow is an uncommon statewide migrant and rare winter resident. Mississippi records indicate passage in April and May of northbound migrants, during which time this sparrow may be encountered in *brush piles,* wood margins, and streamside thickets. It is nearly always found singly, and I have never seen more than one at a time anywhere.

Lincoln's Sparrow resembles grass and marsh sparrows, but it has a longer, rounded tail. It is much like a Song Sparrow, but lacks the heavy breast streaking and large central breast spot. The Lincoln's is best recognized by the *broad, buffy band* across the breast and *fine dark streaking* on the breast and sides. It is also much trimmer than the Song Sparrow. The olive brown and gray streaked upperparts, finely streaked brown crown, narrow eye ring, and gray face further confirm identification.

This sparrow is a skulker and prefers to hide in brush piles, tangled thickets along streamsides, or wet places with shrubby margins. It usually stays out of sight near the ground. Squeaking noises made by an observer usually will bring one into view, but not for long.

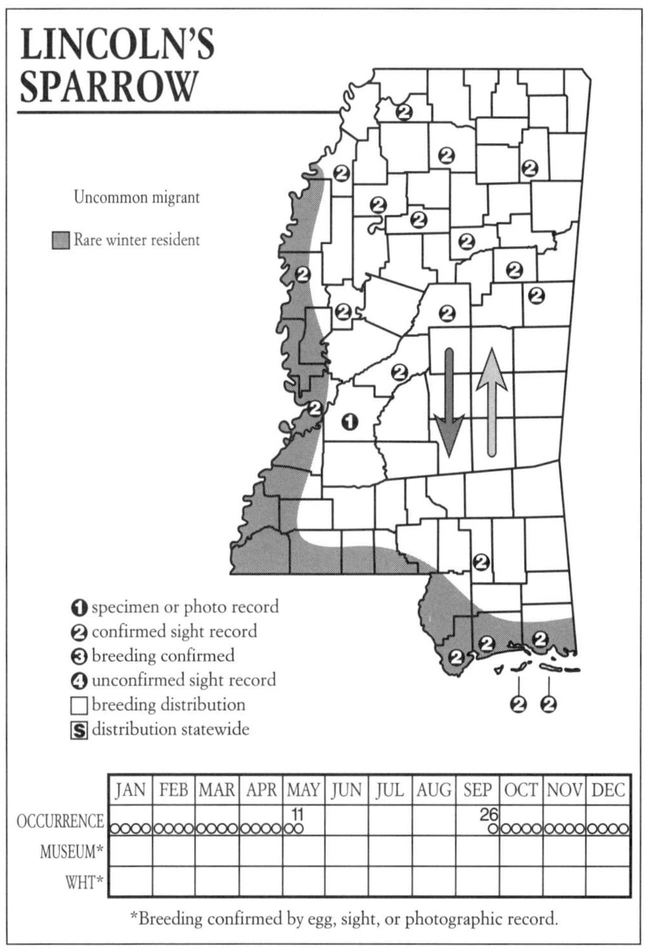

Locating and identifying one of these shy and uncommon birds among the large numbers of other wintering sparrows is a challenge to observers. This species will not appear on many birder's lists of winter birds. Extremes of arrival and departure are September 26 and May 11 (Lafayette County).

Swamp Sparrow *Melospiza georgiana*

This common, statewide winter resident is often abundant and limited only by the extent of marshy places or wet, weedy, shrubby, broomsedge, and brier-grown fields near water. It avoids heavily wooded swamps in preference of more open wetlands.

This gray-breasted, gray-cheeked, white-throated sparrow, with reddish wings, cap, and tail has heavy black streaks on the back. Immatures lack reddish brown and gray cheeks and have blurry streaks on the breast instead of the clear-cut breast streaks of the Lincoln's Sparrow.

The Swamp Sparrow arrives in early October and soon becomes abundant. It remains throughout the winter before beginning departure in late March. Only a few remain by the end of April. First arrival and latest departure records are September 27 and May 18.

The song of the Swamp Sparrow is a trill like the Chipping Sparrow's, but somewhat more musical, slower, and lower in pitch. It is seldom heard while wintering in Mississippi. The call, a sharp, metallic *chink,* often announces its presence in a thicket of cattails before it can be seen. When disturbed, it usually makes a short flight before hiding again. The best way to observe this species is to sit or stand still and watch for them to appear.

White-throated Sparrow *Zonotrichia albicollis*

The White-throated Sparrow is an abundant, statewide winter resident found in dense undergrowth and brushy thickets. It seldom ventures far from cover, and is usually found in flocks of about a dozen or more. Most of its feeding is done on the ground, where it scratches vigorously with both feet like the Eastern Towhee and Fox Sparrow.

The well-defined white throat is diagnostic. The striped crown, a yellow spot in front of the eye, and grayish underparts confirm identification. Fall immatures have more obscure head marks and faint breast streaks. The head marks of fall adults are less distinct than in spring, when the yellow lores, white throat, and head stripes are much brighter.

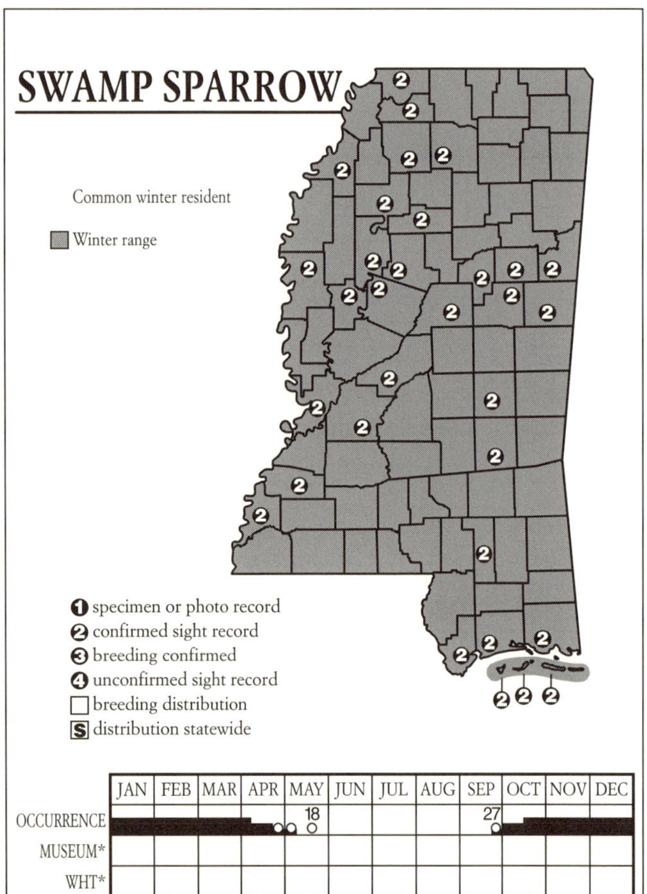

*Breeding confirmed by egg, sight, or photographic record.

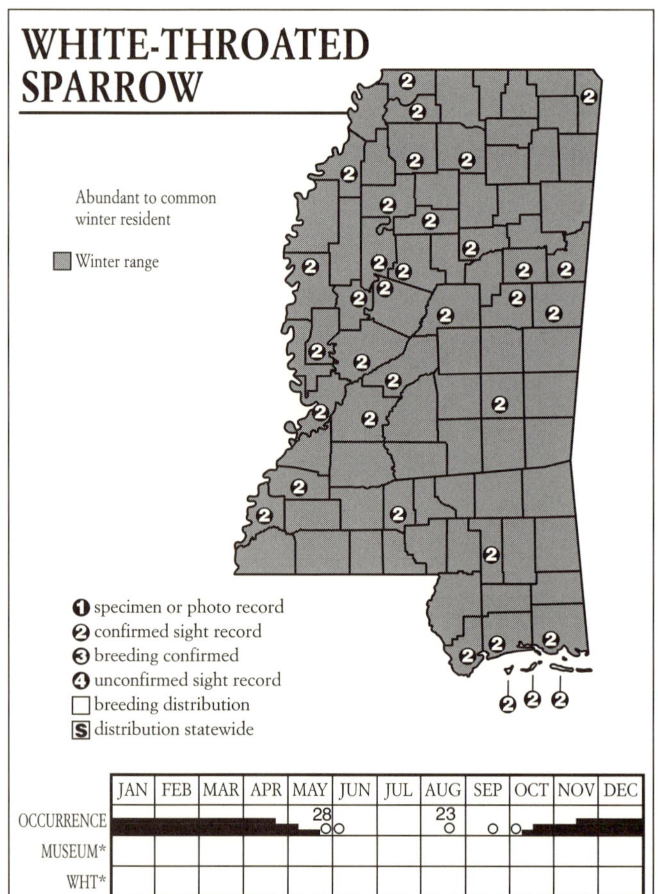

*Breeding confirmed by egg, sight, or photographic record.

The dark bill, white throat, and short-necked posture distinguish the White-throat from the White-crown, which has a pink bill and holds itself erect.

This species begins arriving in early October and gradually increases until early November, when it becomes common throughout the state in thickets, hedges, and undergrowth. Departure begins in March, and their ranks thin during April, though a few may remain until mid-May. Late records on May 28 at Gulfport, on June 2 at Oxford, and on August 23 at Rosedale are anomalous.

The sweet, clear, whistled song of this sparrow is one of the most delightful sounds. It can be heard in winter, but the song is best shortly before spring departure. The song consists of two or three clear, plaintive whistles, followed by several quavering phrases on a lower pitch and likened to *Old Sam Peabody, Peabody, Peabody.* The second note has the highest pitch. The call note is a thin, high *tseet.* Sharp *chink* notes and a variety of chipping or twittering sounds can be heard when White-throats are going to roost at nightfall.

This sparrow feeds largely on grass and weed seeds, fruits, waste grains, and insects. In spring, they mount to the higher branches of trees to feed on buds and the early maturing seeds of elm trees.

White-crowned Sparrow *Zonotrichia leucophrys*

The White-crowned Sparrow is a local winter resident throughout the Yazoo Delta and open bottomlands of counties bordering the Mississippi River below Vicksburg. It is very local and uncommon in the open lands of the Loess Bluff hills and the bordering brown loam belt. In Mississippi's northern counties and the Black Belt Prairie, it is locally fairly common.

This sparrow usually gathers in wintering flocks of up to 20 birds. After taking up winter residence in a suitable place, a flock will usually remain through the winter near the same spot and return to the same thicket to roost. Flocks apparently return to the same location each winter until changes in land use make it unsuitable. Extremes of fall arrivals and spring departure dates are October 8 and May 11 (Lafayette County).

The White-crowned Sparrow is slightly larger than the abundant, winter-resident White-throated Sparrow. Unlike the White-throat, which occurs commonly throughout the state in brushy and weedy cover, the White-crown is found in open country with adjacent hedgerows, low thickets, or patches of tall weeds. Adults are easily recognized by the clear, gray breast and throat, a dignified posture, a black-and-white striped and slightly raised crown, and a pink bill. Immatures are buffier and have reddish brown and buff crown stripes. Immatures frequently outnumber adults in wintering flocks.

WHITE-CROWNED SPARROW

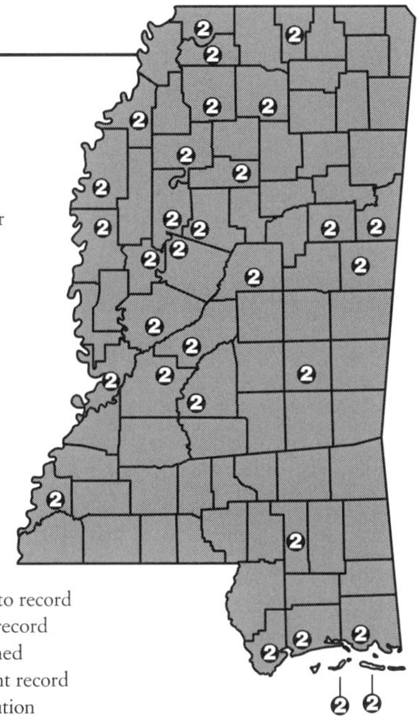

Local and irregular winter resident

■ Winter range (irregular in south Mississippi)

❶ specimen or photo record
❷ confirmed sight record
❸ breeding confirmed
❹ unconfirmed sight record
☐ breeding distribution
S distribution statewide

	JAN	FEB	MAR	APR	MAY	JUN	JUL	AUG	SEP	OCT	NOV	DEC
OCCURRENCE					11					8		
MUSEUM*												
WHT*												

*Breeding confirmed by egg, sight, or photographic record.

White-crowned Sparrows are absent or rarely found in southern and eastern Mississippi below the black belt. On the coast, they have occurred mostly as rare, early fall transients. Burleigh (1945) noted the species only four times in eight years and collected four specimens in Harrison County. Two of these birds were identified as a western subspecies formerly known as Gambel's White-crown, which has the white stripe extending from the bill backward through the eye, instead of backward from the eye.

The song starts with one or two clear, pleasant whistles, followed by descending, burry trills of lower volume. While resting and just before roosting, flocks frequently sing in pleasing choruses during winter and spring.

Harris' Sparrow *Zonotrichia querula*

This largest of our sparrows, almost the size of an Eastern Towhee, has as distinctive field marks a pink bill, black or scaly blotched crown and bib, and streaked sides. Immature birds have a buffy face; a scaly, buff and black crown; and a patch of dark breast spots below the white throat. The throat of second-winter birds is black and separated from the black breast patch by lighter blotches or a band. The sexes are alike.

HARRIS' SPARROW

Casual winter resident

■ Winter locality records

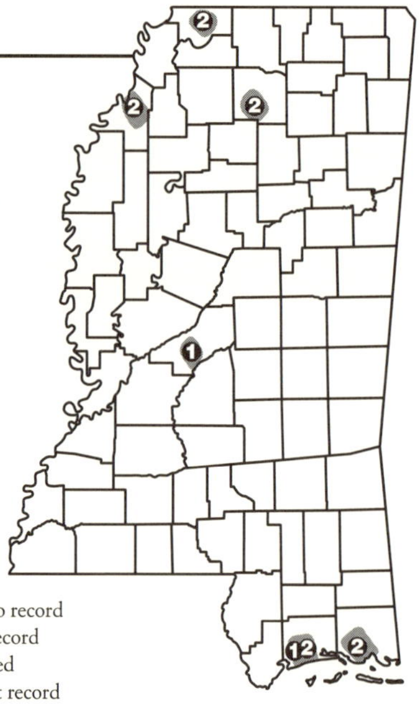

❶ specimen or photo record
❷ confirmed sight record
❸ breeding confirmed
❹ unconfirmed sight record
□ breeding distribution
[S] distribution casual

	JAN	FEB	MAR	APR	MAY	JUN	JUL	AUG	SEP	OCT	NOV	DEC
OCCURRENCE	oo o	oo		20 o							3 o o	ooo
MUSEUM*												
WHT*												

*Breeding confirmed by egg, sight, or photographic record.

The Harris' Sparrow is a casual winter visitor to Mississippi and prefers wintering habitat similar to that of White-crowned and White-throated Sparrows. It breeds in north-central Canada at timberline and winters mainly in the Great Plains and Midwest into northern and central Texas, and occasionally into eastern Texas, western Louisiana, western Tennessee, and northwestern Mississippi.

Four specimen records substantiate its occurrence in Mississippi. The first bird was taken by Burleigh (1945) on February 17, 1942, at Gulfport in Harrison County. Vaiden (1953a) took two specimens from a flock of five birds at Rosedale in Bolivar County on April 18 and 19, 1953. On January 1, 1966, while I was with Ben and Lula Coffey Jr. on a rural road south of Canton in Madison County, I collected an immature specimen for the MMNS (Turcotte 1966a). Two coastal records are December 16, 1978 (Gates 1979), and November 7, 1981 (Toups and Jackson 1987). Published records of eight separate sightings by Coffey Jr. (1956a) near Hernando and Lake View in DeSoto County extend from November 3 to April 20, the earliest and latest available arrival and departure dates.

Dark-eyed Junco *Junco hyemalis*

Until recently this slate-colored sparrow with pinkish bill and legs, white belly, and white outer-tail feathers was called Slate-colored Junco. The name change occurred after the Slate-colored and Oregon Juncos were found to hybridize where their ranges overlapped in the high plains and western mountain regions. The enlarged species was given the new common name by the American Ornithologists' Union, and the specific name, *J. hyemalis,* was retained due to its priority over *J. oreganus*.

These birds are commonly called "snowbirds" because of their apparent tendency to move ahead of ice and snow conditions. They appear to be most abundant during extremely cold weather, especially in southern Mississippi where juncos are not common as winter residents until ice or snow storms drive them farther south. They feed mostly on the ground, and must move south when snow covers the ground for extended periods. They often feed on bare ground or road shoulders, where snow melts faster.

Juncos arrive from mid-October to mid-November, about when White-throated Sparrows appear, and they remain until early April. They are abundant winter resi-

DARK-EYED JUNCO

Common winter resident
irregular on coast

■ Winter range

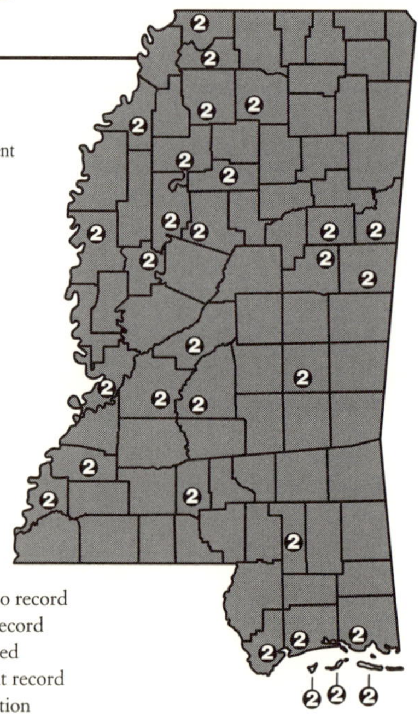

❶ specimen or photo record
❷ confirmed sight record
❸ breeding confirmed
❹ unconfirmed sight record
□ breeding distribution
[S] distribution statewide

	JAN	FEB	MAR	APR	MAY	JUN	JUL	AUG	SEP	OCT	NOV	DEC
OCCURRENCE				oo	22 o					10 oo		
MUSEUM*												
WHT*												

*Breeding confirmed by egg, sight, or photographic record.

dents in northern Mississippi and regular but more scarce on the Gulf Coast, except in periods of severe cold. Juncos usually are seen in small flocks, often in the company of other sparrows. They utilize mixed bird seed at feeders, but prefer to feed from the ground.

Extremes of recorded fall arrival and spring departure are October 10 and May 22 (an unusually late record). Spring departure usually occurs before the second week of April.

The song is a trill more musical than, but suggestive of, the Chipping Sparrow's. The juncos' calls consist of high-pitched twittering notes usually heard when these birds take flight.

I have seen the Oregon variant, *hyemalis*, on Mount Rainer and Mount Hood in Washington and Oregon, and other variants of this species in mountain regions. It is difficult for me to understand the name change from Slate-colored Junco to Dark-eyed Junco. I suppose it is because all juncos have dark eyes, except the adult Mexican Junco, *J. phaeonotus*, now called the Yellow-eyed Junco. The Mexican species is confined to a small part of southern Arizona and southwestern New Mexico, and the immatures also have dark eyes.

All juncos have various degrees of gray or slate coloring, white outer-tail feathers, and white bellies. The western forms have varying shades of brown on the back and rusty or pinkish brown on the sides. All eastern adult juncos are dark gray on the head, upperparts and sides, and the females are similarly marked with slate brown.

Only one reported sighting of the Oregon Junco in Mississippi exists. One junco among three seen at Shepard State Park near Gautier in Jackson County was identified as this race on December 4, 1980, by Judith Toups and Margaret Hamilton. This and one other western race have been reported in Louisiana (Lowery 1974). Imhof (1976) reported seven records in northern Alabama near Birmingham. Observers looking for the Oregon Junco should watch for the adult form, which has a *black head and neck* with *red brown back* and *rusty sides*. Females and immatures of this race can be confusing when mixed with flocks of the common, dark-eyed form.

Lapland Longspur *Calcarius lapponicus*

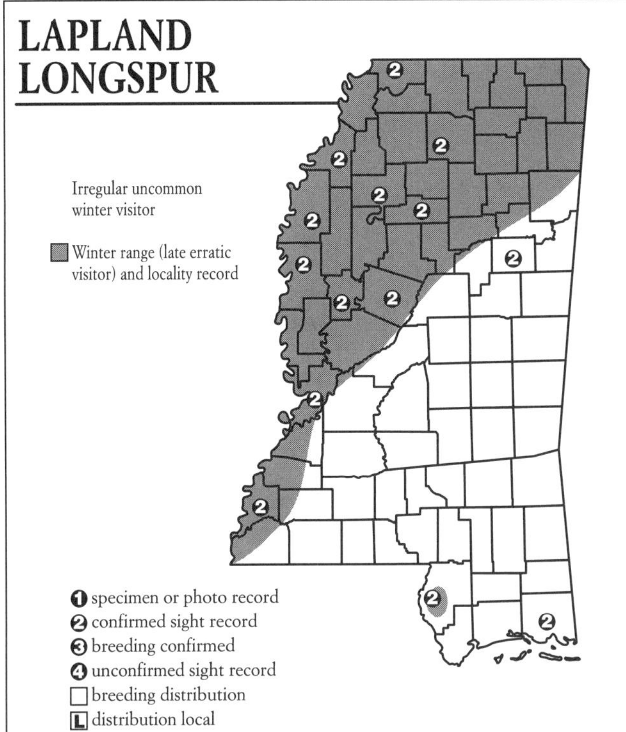

	JAN	FEB	MAR	APR	MAY	JUN	JUL	AUG	SEP	OCT	NOV	DEC
OCCURRENCE	31 ○○○○										2 ○ ○○	○○○○○
MUSEUM*												
WHT*												

*Breeding confirmed by egg, sight, or photographic record.

Lapland Longspurs are uncommon, late winter visitors from the lower parts of the Arctic barren grounds. The Lapland is encountered where Horned Larks and pipits are likely to be seen, such as clipped cotton fields, plowed ground, airports, short grass, windswept pastures, levees, and open dunes. They seldom venture farther south than the Yazoo Delta and Northeast Prairie counties unless heavy snows to the north completely cover the ground.

In late January 1940, this species appeared in Forrest County during extreme ice and snow conditions, and six museum specimens were collected near Hattiesburg by D. C. Weddle. H. L. Owens also collected four specimens the same week in Chickasaw County. Tolman (1958) observed three Lapland Longspurs feeding in a small pasture near Picayune in Pearl River County on January 9, 10, and 17, 1958. A sight record of an individual was recorded on the Jackson County Christmas Bird Count, December 19, 1982 (Gates 1982). Other state records are from the northern Delta and northern Mississippi counties. Occurrence dates extend from November 2 to January 31.

Lapland Longspurs usually occur in flocks of a few to several hundred or more. Coffey Jr. (*in* Jackson 1981a) reported a surprising 6000 in a single flock observed at Fletcher Field near Clarksdale in Coahoma County on December 31, 1955. Most of the time this longspur is a winter visitor to the northern third of Mississippi. To find them is mostly a matter of diligence, good fortune, and selecting the right time to visit airports; large, open, short-grass areas; and cultivated fields in midwinter.

Two species of longspurs have been recorded in Mississippi, the Lapland Longspur being the more common. In winter basic plumage, as they occur in Mississippi, both sexes are duller, and their size and general appearance is vaguely similar to a House Sparrow. The male has a *chestnut collar,* two white wing bars, and a *black smudge on the breast* partially concealed by lighter feather edges. The underparts are white with black streaks on the sides and flanks. A small amount of white shows in the outer-tail feathers, much less than in the Smith's Longspur. The female is whiter on the belly and prominently streaked, not buffy like the Smith's. The call is a dry rattle of four notes given in flight.

Smith's Longspur *Calcarius pictus*

This longspur is a rare, local winter visitor to northern Mississippi. All available records are of small flocks from five localities on short-grass areas on or near airports. Coffey Jr. (1961a), Lula Coffey Jr., George Peyton Jr., and Harry Landis Jr. made the first sightings of 11 birds at Sanders Field near Walls in DeSoto County on November 29, 1953. Eight birds were present on March 6, 1954, at the same location, and a specimen was collected for the Louisiana State University Museum of Zoology.

At the Tupelo airport in Lee County on December 6, 1953, Ben Coffey Jr. observed six birds, and two more were found at this location on March 4, 1956, by Lula Coffey Jr. and Alice Smith. Lula Coffey Jr. found three birds at the old Oxford airport near the Yocona River in Lafayette County on January 23, 1955. The fourth locality record was at Bruce Campbell Field in Madison County, where one bird was seen on January 3, 1954, and 13 observed on January 2, 1956. W. Marvin Davis (1971a) saw and heard three at the Grenada airport on January 24, 1970.

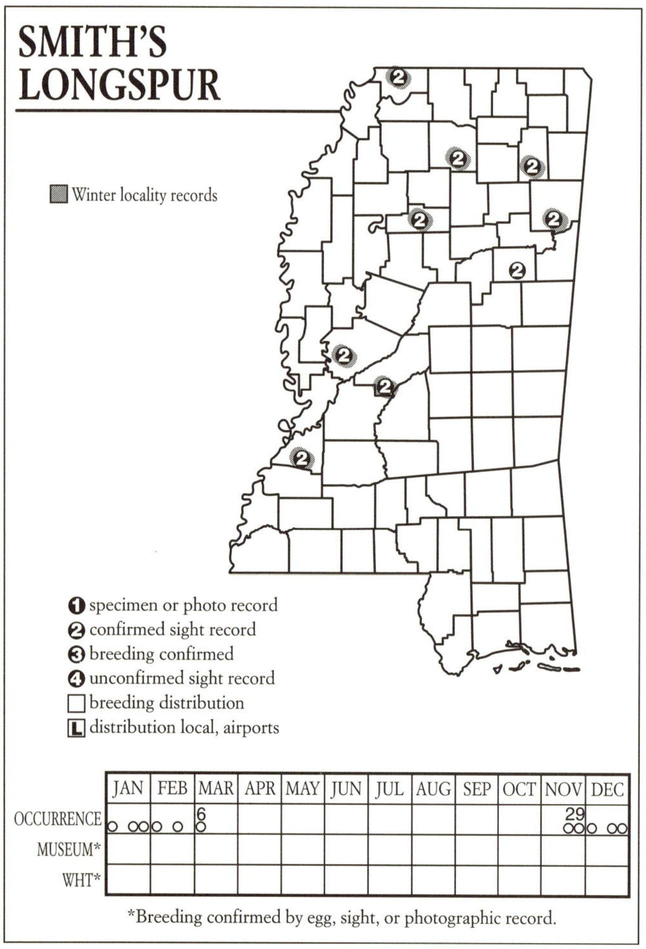

Ben B. Coffey Jr. (1961a) described the habitat where Smith's Longspur and Sprague's Pipit occur. The Smith's Longspur occurs in small flocks (occasionally down to singles) in restricted localities. Flocks favor the part of the field where the grass *Aristida* spp. is present. This has been true for all records—four localities in Mississippi—though many more fields with *Aristida* have been worked unsuccessfully. The species apparently shuns the heavier stands, and is found only where the grass is sparse to moderate. At Walls, this grass was identified by Mrs. Coffey as *Aristida oligantha.* It has long, needle-like, three-awned seeds that somehow give sustenance to this longspur.

Ben B. Coffey Jr. (1961a) further described the field identification marks, behavior, and calls. The more common Lapland Longspur and the Smith's Longspur both have white outer-tail feathers. One does not notice this white on the Lapland as it flies up ahead, only when it is overhead. Looking down, as the Smith's flushes, the white is conspicuous. In the air, a short white arc is noted at the front of the wing on some; the underparts are buffy.

The rattle of the Smith's is softer than the Lapland and has been compared to the *winding of a cheap watch.* The Smith's also gives a weak, sparrowlike note.

The two species do not associate. The Lapland occurs in more varied fields, old cotton fields, plowed ground, and levees. It is easy to stalk and study a flock of the Lapland Longspur. However, one will not know the Smith's are present until the field is walked. The Smith's flush only at 20 to 50 feet, and without walking them up, they may remain undetected. Those in the air circle, sometimes widely; all assemble and eventually drop back into the grass elsewhere.

[Snow Bunting] *Plectrophenax nivalis*

Snow Buntings breed commonly on the Arctic tundra from northern Alaska into Greenland, and winter in southern Canada and the northern United States. They are rare winter visitors farther south.

The basis for my inclusion of this species is a sighting, a photograph, and a banding record of a single bird that appeared on November 14, 1977, in the parking lot at the Mississippi State University biology building (Weber and Jackson 1978). It remained in the area until November 19, and was seen by numerous students and other observers. It ate bird seed at the parking lot and later took seed off the

SNOW BUNTING

Accidental winter visitor

■ Winter locality record

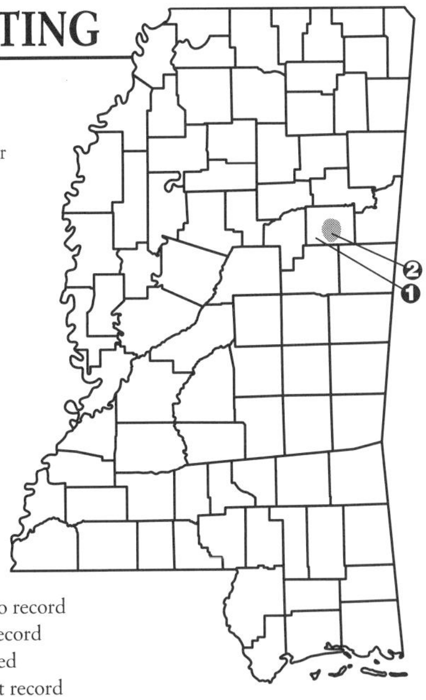

❶ specimen or photo record
❷ confirmed sight record
❸ breeding confirmed
❹ unconfirmed sight record
□ breeding distribution
🅰 distribution statewide

	JAN	FEB	MAR	APR	MAY	JUN	JUL	AUG	SEP	OCT	NOV	DEC
OCCURRENCE											14–19 OO	
MUSEUM*												
WHT*												

*Breeding confirmed by egg, sight, or photographic record.

biology building roof, where it was trapped, banded, and photographed by Jerome A. Jackson. The bird was in good plumage. Its appearance here in our state was soon after blizzards in the north-central states.

In winter, the Snow Bunting has a pink bill and patches of reddish brown on the head, cheeks, breast, and sides. The upperparts are streaked with reddish brown and dusky with much white on the head and body. The wings and tail are mostly white, except for dusky tips and inner parts of some feathers. The call is a single- or double-noted whistle sometimes followed by a descending trill.

The Snow Bunting often associates with longspurs and Horned Larks. In winter, it is found on windswept grasslands, shoreline beaches, and dune areas, where it feeds on grass and weed seeds. It can be regarded only as accidental in Mississippi.

Eastern Meadowlark

Icterinae (Meadowlarks, Blackbirds, and Orioles)

Twelve species of this subfamily have been recorded in Mississippi. They are medium to large birds having heavy, conical, sharp-pointed bills with the upper ridge parting the feathers of the forehead. Some members of this group breed in loose colonies, and many have strong flocking habits. Most are predominantly black with strong accents of orange, yellow, or red plumage.

Meadowlarks dwell mostly on the ground and conceal their domed nests in grasses on the ground. Blackbirds are sometimes exceedingly numerous on winter roosts and feeding grounds. Their roosts can be a nuisance, and depredation on grain crops and livestock feeders causes economic loss to farmers. Orioles are brightly colored and are fine singers. They build deep, woven, sometimes pendulous nests.

Bobolink *Dolichonyx oryzivorus*

The Bobolink, also called "ricebird" in the Carolinas and Louisiana, is a common spring transient, and locally abundant at times. The regularity of this bird's spring passage during the last few days of April and the first two weeks in May is astounding. Records indicate this is the peak of spring migration with extreme dates of April 17 and May 23.

Bobolinks migrate in small flocks and often hundreds will congregate in uncut fields of hay, oats, wheat, or winter legumes. At the usual time of migration, common vetch is blooming along roadsides and in fields. I look for Bobolinks in spring while the purple flowers of this vetch are noticeable.

Fall records for Mississippi are: September 29, 1984, at Waveland in Hancock County; December 11, 1982, at Pascagoula River marsh in Jackson County; and seven sightings between August 23 and October 6, 1980, in Oktibbeha County.

This species breeds in southern Canada and the northern United States. It migrates in fall mostly through Atlantic Coast states and the West Indies. A few pass through the Mississippi Valley, but sightings are *very rare.* Wintering grounds are in central South America from north-central Argentina north into Bolivia and Brazil.

The spring migration returns mostly through the West Indies and enters along the northern Gulf Coast from Florida into eastern Texas. The song of the Bobolink is a long series of indescribable, melodious, tinkling, and bubbling *ink-ink-ink* notes, usually heard in concert with others in a flock during the migration through Mississippi.

Male Bobolinks are unmistakable in their spring plumage of black head and underparts, with a pale yellow nape and prominent white patches across the wings and on the lower back and tail. The female, immature, and fall male are similar, being plain, buffy and sparrowlike, striped with black above, and with prominent buffy crown stripes. The tail feathers are narrow and pointed in all plumages.

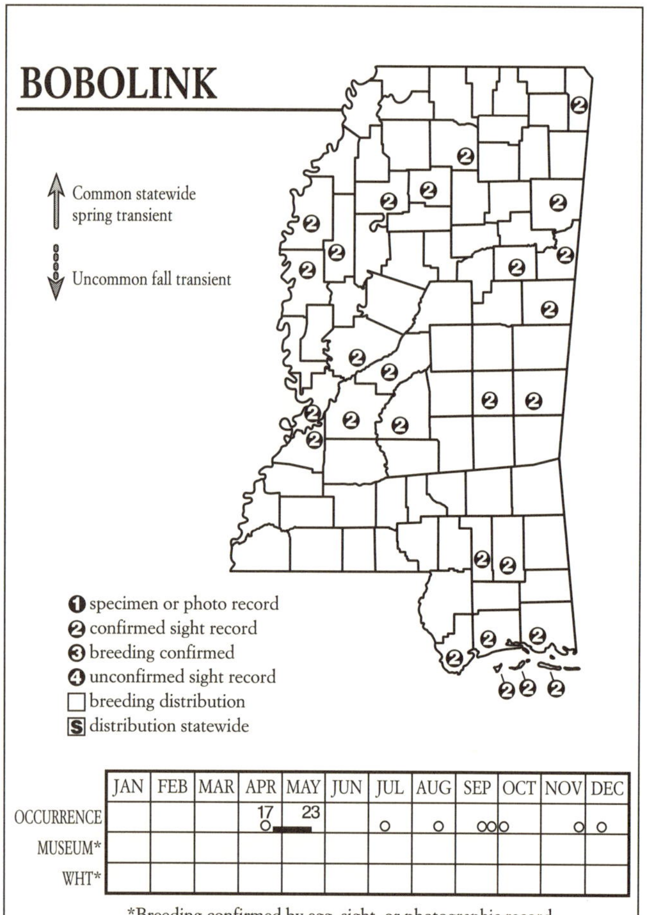

*Breeding confirmed by egg, sight, or photographic record.

On the breeding grounds in the northern states and lower Canada, the male Bobolink is a conspicuous occupant in the short-grass prairie of the high plains and grassy, wet meadowlands and hay fields. The bubbly flight song is loud and carries a considerable distance as the male rises and hovers while singing, then descends on quivering wings as if at the height of ecstacy.

The nest cup of weed stems and grasses, formed in a depression in the ground, is lined with finer grasses and well concealed by taller grass in open fields. Four to seven eggs are laid. The ground color varies from bluish gray to brownish and is variously blotched with darker brown, dark purple, and lavender.

The Lark Bunting of the western prairies, high plains, and some mountain valleys has a flight song similar to the Bobolink. It has black-and-white marks confined to the wings, whereas the Bobolink has a yellow nape and prominent white on the back and tail.

I had a unique experience with a flock of Bobolinks in my backyard one May morning. I was playing a tape recording of the Eastern Meadowlark song to entice a singing male, when the tape ran over into the tinkling flock calls of migrating Bobolinks. Suddenly a flock of a dozen or more Bobolinks appeared from nowhere and lit in a pine tree in the yard. They had heard and responded to the unintentional playing of their recorded calls.

Red-winged Blackbird *Agelaius phoeniceus*

The adult male "redwing" is unmistakable in his cloak of jet black and scarlet shoulder patches edged with dull yellow. The young and females are dark brown above and heavily streaked with brownish black. Underparts are dull white with well-defined, brownish black stripes, and the throat and shoulders often are tinged with reddish buff. The immature male is dull brown with some red on the shoulders.

The Red-winged Blackbird is one of our most common and conspicuous, summer-resident, breeding birds. It breeds throughout the state in open areas such as marshes, lowlands, and weedy fields, even along roadways and ditch banks, wherever tall grasses, weeds, and bushes near water grow. During the winter and early spring, large numbers of migrant redwings from northern and western areas join our resident populations to fly, feed, and roost together in huge flocks.

Winter roosts may number in the millions of blackbirds, grackles, cowbirds, starlings, and sometimes robins. Dense stands of young pines, red cedars, willows, or swampy woods are used for roosts. When roost sites are large and near human habitations, they become a nuisance because of noise and accumulations of droppings beneath and

RED-WINGED BLACKBIRD

Common statewide

■ Permanent resident breeding

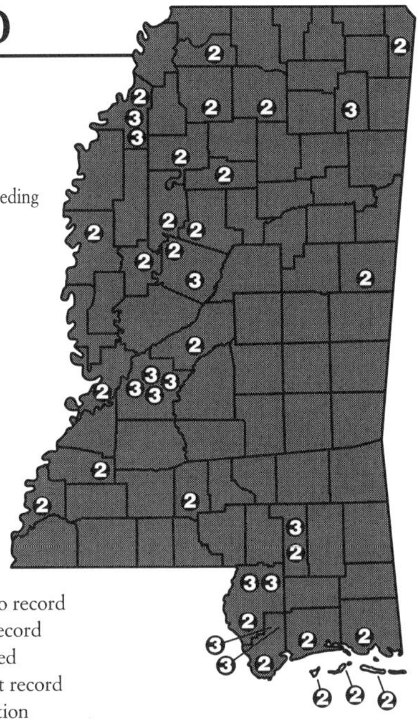

❶ specimen or photo record
❷ confirmed sight record
❸ breeding confirmed
❹ unconfirmed sight record
[S] breeding distribution
[S] distribution statewide

	JAN	FEB	MAR	APR	MAY	JUN	JUL	AUG	SEP	OCT	NOV	DEC
OCCURRENCE	▬	▬	▬	▬	▬	▬	▬	▬	▬	▬	▬	▬
MUSEUM*				●	●● ●	15 ●●						
WHT*				20 ●	22 ●	1 ●						

*Breeding confirmed by egg, sight, or photographic record.

around the roost. Wintering hordes of blackbirds foraging in every direction from large roosts may cause economic loss when they raid livestock feeders, though this is offset by the good in helping to control insects.

In early spring, adult male Red-winged Blackbirds begin establishing territories. At this time, the females and young of the past year are still in separate flocks. The adult male selects a suitable spot and remains perched on some post or bush and sings his gurgling *king-ler-ee'ee!* Each time he sings, he flashes the scarlet wing patches and quickly drives intruders away from his sharply defined territory. The call note is a loud *chack*. The alarm note, is a sharp, high-pitched, slurred *tee-err* and is given when a nest site is approached.

Nest-building starts in late April after the females arrive on the territory established by the male. Coarse grasses and other fibers are loosely woven around cattails, weed stalks, tall grasses, or limbs of bushes and small trees to form a suspended, cup-shaped nest lined with finer grass or roots. Most nests are near the ground, occasionally in loose colonies, and often over water in marshy places or water edges. Sometimes nests are put in higher places, especially in willows growing at the water's edge.

Usually four pale bluish green eggs, scrawled and splotched with purplish brown and black, are laid. Egg records in the MMNS extend from April 20 to June 15, with the height of nesting occurring in May.

Eastern Meadowlark *Sturnella magna*

The Eastern Meadowlark, or "field lark," is a bird of open, grassy country and most commonly seen on the ground or perched on posts, roadside wires, and fences. In flight, it appears quite chunky and brownish above, with a conspicuous patch of white feathers on each side of the tail. The flight is jerky with alternate flapping of wings and sailing. When perched on a fence post or on open ground, the bright yellow throat and underparts with a V-shaped black band across the breast are distinctive field marks.

The meadowlark is a common permanent resident throughout the state. It occurs in loose flocks during the fall and winter. In early spring pair bonds are formed and nesting follows during April, May, and June. The males tend to sing from fence posts, wires, and the tops of small trees or bushes in open, grassy fields and along roadsides.

EASTERN MEADOWLARK

■ Common permanent resident breeding

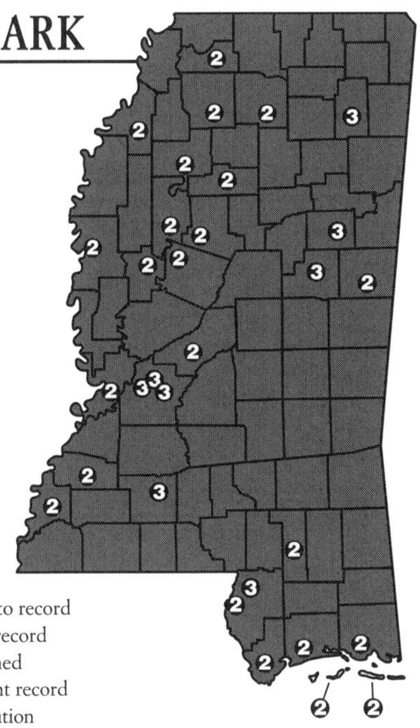

❶ specimen or photo record
❷ confirmed sight record
❸ breeding confirmed
❹ unconfirmed sight record
[S] breeding distribution
[S] distribution statewide

	JAN	FEB	MAR	APR	MAY	JUN	JUL	AUG	SEP	OCT	NOV	DEC
OCCURRENCE	▬	▬	▬	▬	▬	▬	▬	▬	▬	▬	▬	▬
MUSEUM*				●	●●●●	●●●						
WHT*					5 ●	4 ●						

*Breeding confirmed by egg, sight, or photographic record.

The song is a clear and cheerful whistle slurred downward at the end and rather variable, described by George H. Lowery Jr. as *laziness-will-kill'-you*. It is surprising that I first heard this same interpretation of the song from my brother-in-law, who heard it from either his forebears or their tenant farmers. The call is a sharp note often followed by guttural chatterings.

Meadowlarks build nests on the ground partly or completely domed and composed entirely of grasses. They are concealed in a slight depression among grasses, weeds, sedge grass clumps, or other grassland vegetation. Nests are difficult to find and usually contains five eggs, which are pure white and heavily speckled or blotched over the surface with reddish brown and purplish, but never obscuring the ground color.

Western Meadowlark *Sturnella neglecta*

Few people are aware that two species of meadowlarks occur in Mississippi. There is little difference in the general appearance of the birds, and although their breeding ranges overlap, there is apparently no intergrading of the two species.

The western species can be detected and identified positively in the field by its song, which is entirely different from the Eastern Meadowlark. Its song is longer than the Eastern's and has eight to 10 double notes that are gurgling and flutelike in quality, something akin to the notes of the Baltimore Oriole. Great Plains people interpret the song as *time-to-plant-your-wheat*. The four clear, slurred, whistled notes of the Eastern Meadowlark are distinctly different. Field identification is virtually impossible without hearing the song.

Compared with the Eastern, the Western Meadowlark is paler in appearance, and more grayish than brownish on the back. Another recognizable difference with the bird in hand is that the yellow on the throat of the Western Meadowlark nearly extends to the cheek and almost covers the malar region. Close examination of the tail, rump, and innerwing feathers shows that the dark barrings of the Western Meadowlark extend across the feather shaft, but are not connected along the shaft. The same feathers on the Eastern Meadowlark have the bars connected along the shaft, giving them a much darker overall appearance.

The Western Meadowlark is an uncommon winter resident in northwestern Mississippi and along the Gulf Coast. Vaiden (1953b) collected a series of seven specimens during the winter of 1952–1953 from "many fine flocks" at different dates and localities in the vicinity of Rosedale in Bolivar County. He noted that these birds showed a "preference for row-plowed land without a particle of growing grass."

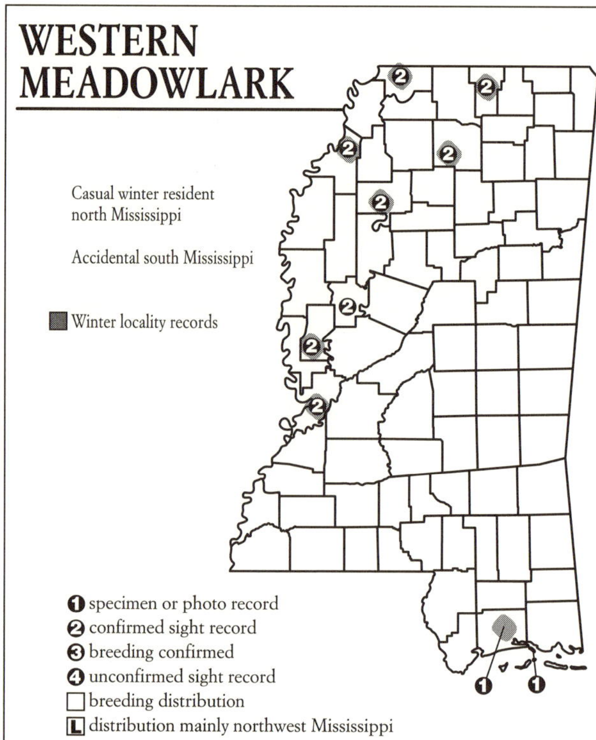

	JAN	FEB	MAR	APR	MAY	JUN	JUL	AUG	SEP	OCT	NOV	DEC
OCCURRENCE	o	oooo	oo	oo 26 o				o		2 oo	oo o	oooo
MUSEUM*												
WHT*												

*Breeding confirmed by egg, sight, or photographic record.

The Mississippi collection and sight records for the Yazoo Delta and Gulf Coast regions extend from October 2 to April 26. A male specimen taken by Vaiden (1952b) on April 26, 1952, had sex organs fully developed, but nesting was not substantiated. Other sight records have been reported as follows: one near Lakeview in DeSoto County on August 24, 1940, by A. Burdick and others; one at Hickory Flat in Benton County on December 25, 1955, by Ben B. Coffey Jr.; four at the same location on February 19, 1956, by Lula Coffey Jr. and Mrs. Yancey; and one at Holly Springs Experiment Station in Marshall County on March 4, 1956, by Ben B. Coffey Jr. The series of 48 meadowlark skins in the MMNS contains no specimens of the Western Meadowlark.

The western species is found in Mississippi (most likely in the Yazoo Delta) as an uncommon, local winter resident. The habits of the two meadowlarks are similar in most respects. The breeding range of the western species is mainly in the Great Plains from British Columbia to southwestern Ontario, southward into northern Mexico, and eastward to Wisconsin, Illinois, east-central Missouri, and casually into southwestern Tennessee, northwestern Arkansas, northwestern Louisiana, and central Texas.

The nest, eggs, food habits, and behavior of both species are alike. They roost on the ground in grassy places and travel together in loose flocks, except during the breeding season. They may occur in mixed flocks, but the western birds in winter are seen most often in separate flocks. In my travels across western prairies and plains, I enjoyed the pleasant, gurgling song of the Western Meadowlark at nearly every rest stop. Across those broad, bare expanses of open country, it was usually the first and only bird song I heard.

Yellow-headed Blackbird *Xanthocephalus xanthocephalus*

This casual visitor from the marshes of the Great Plains and the western United States and Canada has been recorded in Mississippi as a rare, irregular, mostly fall and winter visitor. The first sighting at Moss Point in Jackson County was reported by Mrs. H. N. Tait (Turcotte 1966c). An almost mature male was first seen by Mrs. Tait at a ground feeding station in her backyard on April 9, 1965. The bird was seen almost daily by her and a neighbor, Vard Cannon, at another feeder until last seen by Mrs. Tait on April 26.

Jackson (1975) collected an immature male on the southern farm at Mississippi State University in Oktibbeha County on March 26, 1973. This specimen, now in the MSU collection, is the first collection record in Mississippi. Recent sight records occurred in June, July, November, March, and April in Forrest, Hancock, Lafayette, Oktibbeha, and all coastal counties.

The adult male, nearly the size of a Common Grackle, presents a striking appearance with its yellow head and breast, black body, and white wing patches. The female and immature male are brownish, with yellow mostly confined to the throat and breast. Females have part of the lower breast streaked with white. Immature males and females do not have white wing patches.

The breeding range of the Yellow-headed Blackbird covers a wide area of the western states and western Canada east into northern Texas, northwestern Oklahoma, northeastern Missouri, northeastern Illinois, north-central Wisconsin, and northern Minnesota. This blackbird nests in colonies among reeds and other tall vegetation growing in marshes. The nest is woven into the supporting vegetation, and consists of strips of dead leaves, grasses, and roots placed from six inches to three feet above water. The three to five eggs are grayish to greenish white, and speckled with shades of brown and gray.

The winter range is in Mexico and parts of bordering states to southwestern Texas. The species occurs as a casual spring and fall migrant along the Atlantic seaboard. Look for it in flocks of other blackbird species foraging in open fields and pastures.

YELLOW-HEADED BLACKBIRD

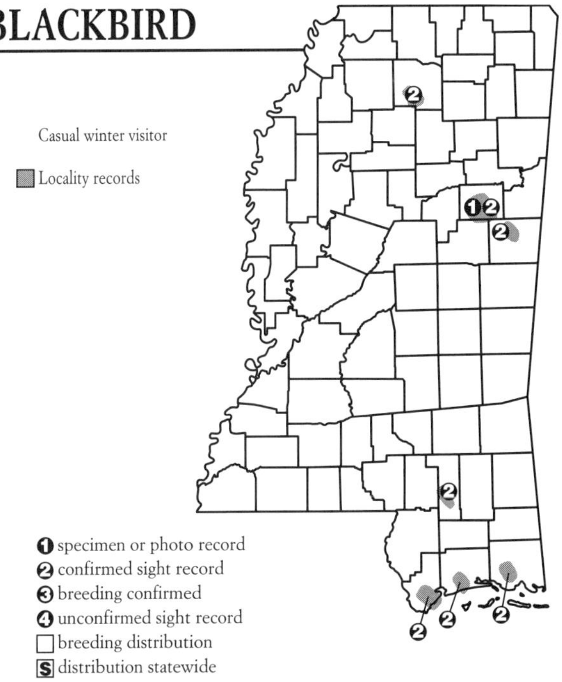

	JAN	FEB	MAR	APR	MAY	JUN	JUL	AUG	SEP	OCT	NOV	DEC
OCCURRENCE	oooo	oooo	oooo	oooo	o	o	oo		ooo	ooo	oooo	oooo
MUSEUM*												
WHT*												

*Breeding confirmed by egg, sight, or photographic record.

The song of the Yellow-headed Blackbird consists of low rasping notes ending with a harsh descending buzzing sound, which is long and drawn out at the end. The call note is a low raucous croak.

Rusty Blackbird *Euphagus carolinus*

The Rusty Blackbird is a winter visitor in Mississippi. Extreme dates of occurrence are October 27 and May 18. It is a regular winter resident in most of the state from the first week in November until the second week in April, but rarely later. On the Mississippi Gulf Coast, it appears erratically and uncommonly. Elsewhere, it is fairly common to locally abundant. This blackbird shows a decided preference for open swampy woodlands, but feeds in fields, wooded pastures, and orchards in large or small flocks. The feeding Rusty is noted for flipping leaves in search of food in wet woodlands and pastures. It sometimes mixes with flocks of other blackbirds and grackles.

This species breeds to the tree line in Alaska, through most of Canada, and to northern parts of the New England states. It builds a bulky nest of grass, sticks, mud, leaves, and moss, lined with green grasses, and placed in thick

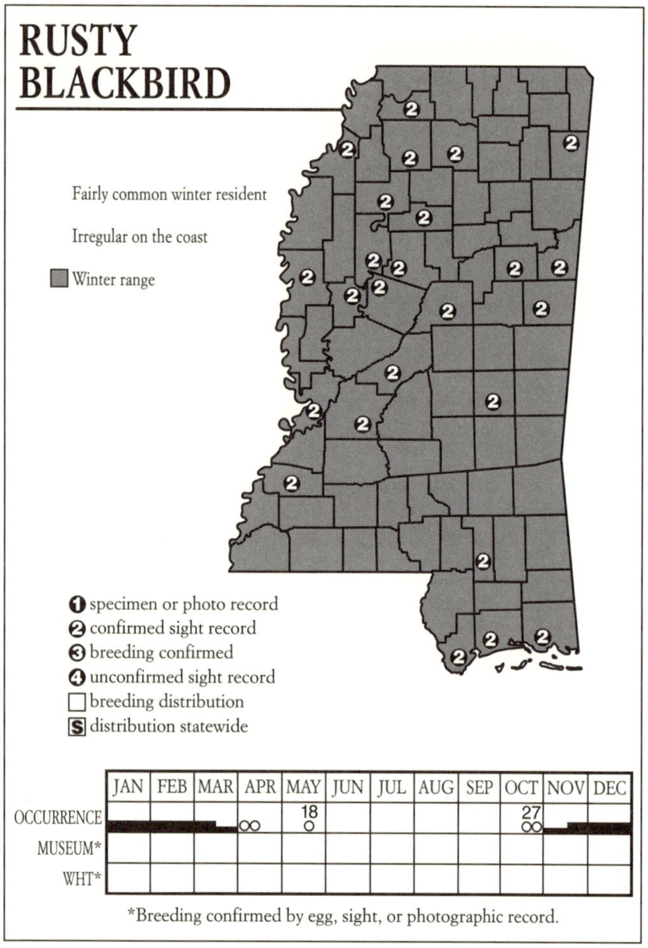

evergreens, willows, or shrubs. Look for the nest close to the ground over or near water. Most winter in the southeastern states and westward to central Texas.

The Rusty Blackbird is about the size and shape of the Red-winged Blackbird, but it has a more slender bill and a longer tail. Adults and young look rusty in the fall and winter due to the brown edges of the feathers. These edges wear off by late spring, when the male becomes black glossed over with a dull greenish color, while the female becomes slate colored with *yellow* (not dark) eyes. In fall and winter, adults and young appear rusty brown with a distinct, closely barred pattern on the underparts and back when viewed at close range.

In late winter, male Rusty and Brewer's Blackbirds look similar. In spring, the male Rusty Blackbird almost lacks iridescence. The male Brewer's Blackbird has a purplish iridescence on the head, and greenish on the body. Females can be separated by eye color, the Rusty having whitish eyes and the female Brewer's having dark brown eyes.

The song of the Rusty Blackbird is a series of musical, gurgling sounds punctuated by high-pitched squeaky notes. The call is a coarse *cack* or *kuk*. The flight is more direct and less undulating than that of the Red-winged Blackbird, but less direct than the almost level flight of the Common Grackle.

Brewer's Blackbird *Euphagus cyanocephalus*

This species is the western counterpart of the Rusty Blackbird. Its breeding range extends through the Great Plains into southwestern Canada, westward to the Pacific Coast, and south to northern Mexico. In Mississippi, it is a regular and fairly common winter resident on and near the coast, where it exceeds the Rusty Blackbird in numbers. Winter flocks containing up to 600 Brewer's Blackbirds have been recorded by Judith A. Toups and others in Hancock County.

In central Mississippi, this blackbird is a regular but uncommon to locally common winter resident, but is greatly outnumbered by the Rusty Blackbird. In extreme northern Mississippi, it is rarely seen in winter. Unlike the Rusty Blackbird, this species prefers open pastures, cultivated fields, orchards, and burned-over areas. It particularly likes freshly plowed fields or areas where cattle are grazing. Extremes of occurrence in Mississippi are November 6 and April 12.

The Brewer's Blackbird nests in loose colonies or in single pairs. Nesting sites are variable and may be on the ground in thick vegetation or in bushes and trees at various heights aboveground. Lake or stream margins, meadows, marshes,

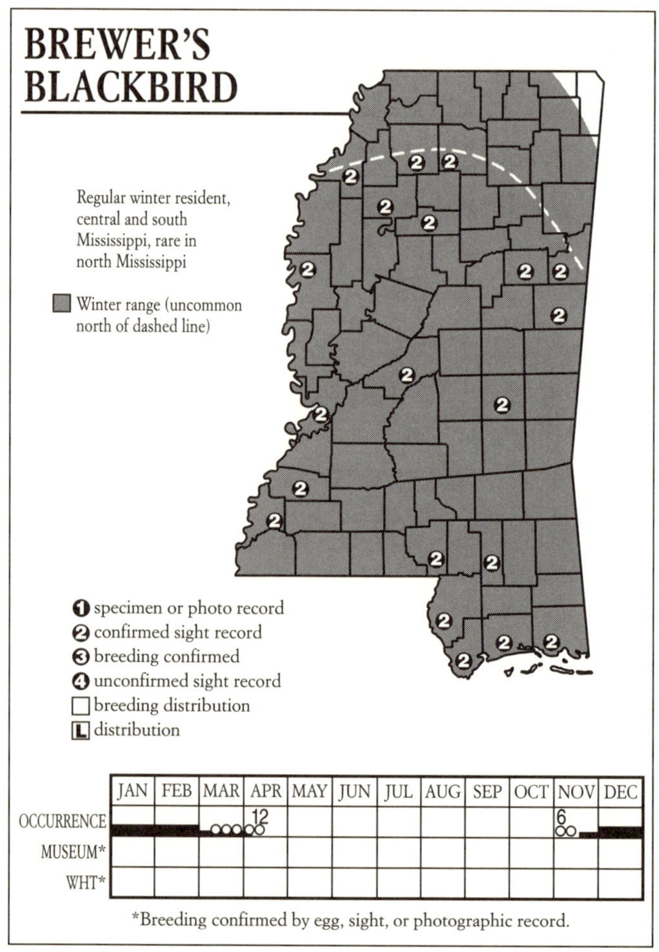

dense evergreens, ornamental trees and shrubs, windbreaks, and brushy roadsides are used as nesting habitat.

The nest is built of grass and twigs, often held together by mud or manure, and lined with fine grasses, moss, rootlets, or hair. The three to seven eggs are dull white to greenish gray, blotched and clouded with brownish drab, and streaked with black.

Field marks of the male are a *purplish* iridescence on the head and a *greenish* sheen on the body in favorable light. By contrast, the male Rusty Blackbird shows dull greenish on the head, while the iridescent sheen on the body is almost lacking. The eyes of the male Brewer's are white while the Rusty's are yellow. Female Brewer's have dark brown eyes and Rusty's have whitish eyes. These two blackbirds should not be confused with the larger Common Grackle, which has a long, rounded, keel-shaped tail that is broad at the end. In good light the grackle has much brighter iridescence on the head and body.

The call note of the Brewer's Blackbird is a harsh *check* similar to the Rusty Blackbird's. The song is squeaky and ascending at the end.

Boat-tailed Grackle *Quiscalus major*

BOAT-TAILED GRACKLE

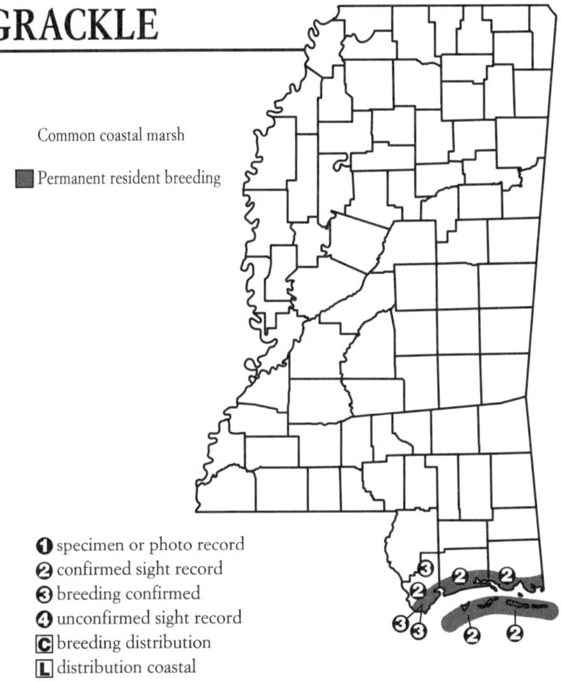

	JAN	FEB	MAR	APR	MAY	JUN	JUL	AUG	SEP	OCT	NOV	DEC
OCCURRENCE												
MUSEUM*				22 •		5 •						
WHT*				•								

*Breeding confirmed by egg, sight, or photographic record.

The Boat-tailed Grackle is the largest blackbird in Mississippi. Its habitat is in or near the salt or brackish coastal marshes and on islands off the Gulf Coast, from which it seldom strays inland for more than a short distance. On the coast, it is a permanent-resident, breeding bird. In winter, this grackle gathers in small flocks and becomes less conspicuous.

In the spring and summer, this species concentrates around marsh areas to nest in small colonies. "This large grackle," Thomas D. Burleigh (1945) wrote, "is a common breeding bird on the Mississippi Coast, but since it occurs only about the larger stretches of open salt marsh, it is rather local in its distribution during the summer months. It is one of the few species that is more numerous on the islands than on the mainland."

The large, deep nest is made of coarse grasses and other marsh vegetation woven around supporting vegetation, strengthened with mud, and lined with finer grasses. The nest is built in reeds or bushes usually over or near water and from two to four feet above the water or ground. The eggs are bluish gray to bluish green, usually three in number, and prettily scrawled, blotched, clouded, and irregularly marked with black, purplish brown, and gray. They are similar to, but larger than, eggs of Common Grackles.

The Boat-tailed Grackle in Mississippi has brown eyes. The Atlantic coastline ecotypes have yellow eyes. In Cameron and Calcasieu Parishes of southwest Louisiana and westward into the coastal and inland parts of Texas, the similar Great-tailed Grackle, recognized now as a separate species *(Q. mexicanus),* also has bright yellow eyes.

This species gets its name from the long and wide V-shaped or keel-like tail of the male, which widens at the end. The overall length of the male is about 16 inches, slightly exceeding the length of a Fish Crow. The female is smaller and averages about 12 inches long.

The male Boat-tail is glossy, iridescent black on the head, back, and underparts, and less glossy on the wings and tail. The female is brownish on the head and body with dark brown wings and tail, separable in the field from the female Common Grackle by the paler and browner plumage. Also, the Common Grackle is not common around salt water, where the Boat-tail usually occurs. The male Boat-tail attains its full breeding plumage only after the second fall molting.

In late February and March, breeding territories are established. The courtship antics of this grackle are interesting to observe. While nesting is in progress, the males put on a great show of posturing and display of their attractive plumage with its metallic blue, purple, and green color reflections.

Courtship displays are performed on any elevated perch or on the ground. The wings droop downward, the tail is fanned and held rigid, while the head and neck are stretched upward with the feathers fluffed out and the long bill pointing straight up. This display is carried on in the presence of other males or females and also at times when no other birds are in sight.

The song or voice of the male is a long series of loud, noisy, harsh, guttural, rasping, and rattling or rolling sounds. The song is very impressive to a casual observer. The noisy vocalizations of the male attract more attention to this already conspicuous bird. Boat-tailed Grackles are polygamous, and the male does not assist in nest-building, incubation, or rearing young, all of which are left to the females.

The Boat-tail breeds in small colonies locally in the coastal marshlands, and it has been recorded commonly on the barrier islands of Mississippi Sound during the breeding season. Egg record dates from collection records in Hancock County extend from April 23 to June 5. I collected two sets of three eggs in a marsh near the mouth of the Pearl River in Hancock County on April 23, 1941. The two nests were close together and about two feet above water in reeds bordering the river bank at the edge of a marsh.

E. J. Giering collected a set of two eggs from a nest in willows and marsh grass over water in Hancock County on June 5, 1940. Lovett E. Williams Jr. and Sterling G. Clawson reported sighting an incubating Boat-tail on a nest near Lakeshore in Hancock County, on April 22, 1962.

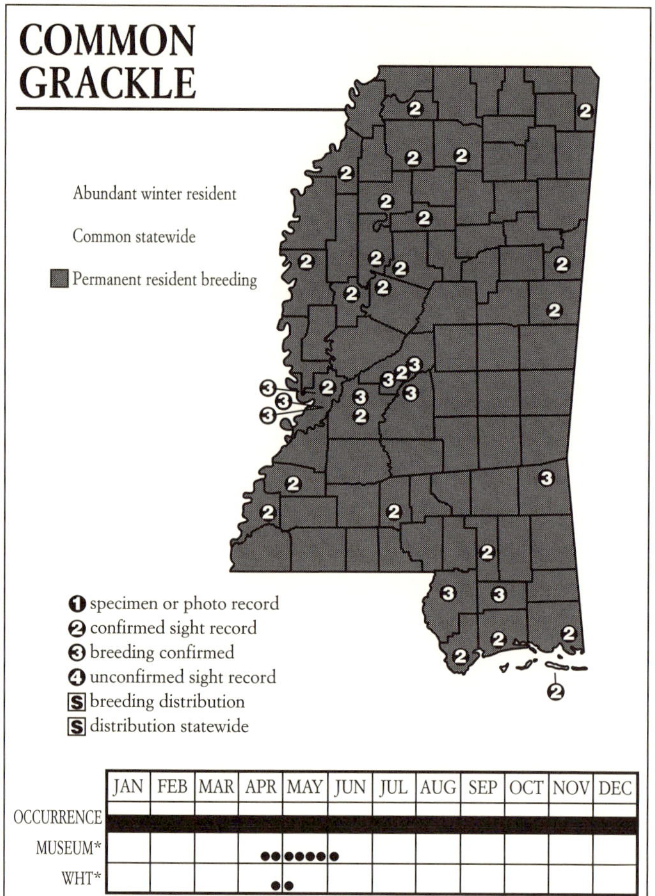

*Breeding confirmed by egg, sight, or photographic record.

Common Grackle *Quiscalus quiscula*

This large, abundant blackbird is a statewide permanent resident, except on the barrier islands where it occurs only occasionally. It breeds in small colonies throughout the state, except in the coastal marshes and islands, where it is replaced by the larger Boat-tailed Grackle.

At a distance this species appears all black. In direct sunlight at close range, the head and neck feathers refract metallic blues and greens with mostly metallic bronze reflections on the back and sides. Some populations east of the Appalachian Mountains have more purple on the head, with parts of the wings and back showing iridescent bars. Because interbreeding occurs among the "bronze" and "purple" grackles, they are regarded as variants of the same species.

The Common Grackle ranges from western and southern Canada east of the Rocky Mountains to the Atlantic and Gulf Coasts. It is partially migratory throughout most of its range. In Mississippi great numbers spend the winter. These wintering grackles roost with aggregations of other blackbirds, cowbirds, and starlings.

Winter roosts sometimes number into thousands or even millions of birds. Individual flocks, sometimes numbering several thousand, forage out from the roosts in all directions for 20 miles or more. In late evening, flocks assemble into wavy bands as they approach their roosts. Thickets of young pines, cedars, willows, hardwoods, cane, and bamboo often are used for roosts. Large roosts in or near towns or cities frequently become nuisances, and nearby residents complain about the noise and accumulation of droppings. Sometimes these roosts can be moved by harassment with aerial bombs or amplified recordings of distress calls played as the birds come to roost.

The Common Grackle nests in trees near water, usually in open groves or viney thickets of willow, pine, cottonwood, water locust, sweet gum, and oak. The nests are placed at various heights from a few feet aboveground in shrub swamps to 40 or 50 feet high in large trees. Nests are usually placed near the trunk of trees and often in honeysuckle or other tree-climbing vines that afford concealment.

The large, bulky, and deeply cupped nest is made of coarse grass plastered inside with mud or fresh cow manure and lined with finer grass. The four or five eggs are dull greenish white and splashed, blotched, and spotted with shades of brown, gray, and black in an endless variety of marks. Egg record dates extend from April 20 to June 6.

Nesting colonies of these grackles are sometimes located in towns or cities. The species adapts to nesting in a variety of places such as streamside thickets, cypress and willow brakes, shrub swamps, orchards and groves, or large shade trees on farmlands and ranches.

The Common Grackle can be recognized in flight by the long, keel-like tail shaped like a V. Its flight is straight and level with regular wingbeats, quite unlike the undulating flight of the Red-winged and other blackbirds. The call is a hoarse *chock,* and the song is a raspy note followed by an ascending squeak.

During courtship, several males often pursue a single female. The male displays by puffing out his feathers, spreading the tail, drooping the wings, and with neck outstretched the head and bill are pointed straight up. He sings the squeaky song intermittently while posturing before the brownish female, which has much less iridescence on the head and body.

This species is often regarded as a nuisance around bird feeders. Livestock farmers also regard it as an economic pest at their feedlots. These grackles feed largely on the ground and take a large variety of insects and other animal foods as well as small grains, weed seeds, nuts, and fruits.

At times, they may eat baby birds and eggs, but I have never observed predation. In the lower Yazoo Delta, I have found many Mourning Dove nests with eggs and young that went unmolested in the same locust trees where a colony of grackles nested. During an outbreak of forest tent caterpillars in that region in May 1990, I saw these birds feeding on larvae, pupae in cocoons, and adults of this moth, which defoliated an estimated 50 percent of the canopy trees in the Delta National Forest. A more serious outbreak did not occur the following year. This grackle surely helped control the reproductive success of this moth.

[Shiny Cowbird] *Molothorus bonariensis*

SHINY COWBIRD

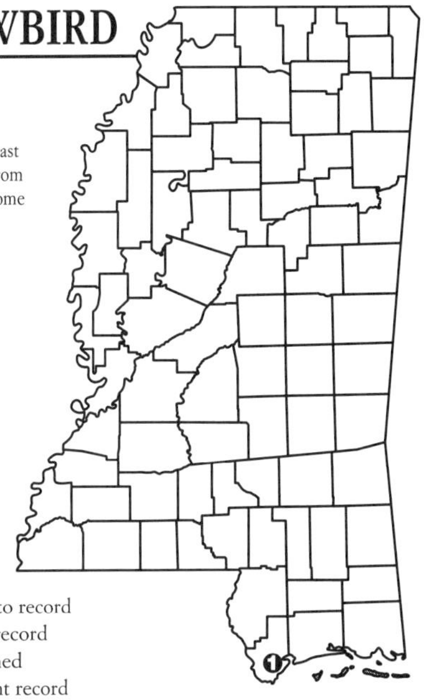

Accidental on Gulf Coast of recent occurrence from Caribbean. Could become alien resident species.

❶ specimen or photo record
❷ confirmed sight record
❸ breeding confirmed
❹ unconfirmed sight record
☐ breeding distribution
☐ distribution: statewide and local

	JAN	FEB	MAR	APR	MAY	JUN	JUL	AUG	SEP	OCT	NOV	DEC
OCCURRENCE						12 •						
MUSEUM*												
WHT*												

*Breeding confirmed by egg, sight, or photographic record.

The Shiny Cowbird, a native of tropical and subtropical South America east of the Andes and eastern Panama, has extended its range northward. It reached the Florida Keys in 1985. It occurred in the Florida Everglades in 1987 and spread across Florida to the Florida Panhandle between 1988 and 1989 (Smith and Sprunt 1987).

This species appeared in the coastal zones of Georgia, North and South Carolina, and Louisiana in 1989. It was recorded at Fort Morgan, Alabama, on April 25, 1990, and at Fort Hood, Texas, on May 23, 1990. On June 12, 1990, a single male specimen was caught in a cowbird trap at Wichita Mountains National Wildlife Refuge in Oklahoma (Grzybowski and Fazio 1991).

The first Mississippi record documented by a photograph of a single male was identified by Judith A. Toups and Lydia Schultz on June 12, 1991, at a feeding shelf in Waveland in Hancock County (Purrington 1991). It was feeding with Brown-headed Cowbirds, Mourning Doves, starlings, and grackles when it was photographed by Ray Russell (1991).

The male Shiny Cowbird is glossy black to bluish black overall with a black face mask. It is similar in size to the Brown-headed Cowbird and often feeds with its tail elevated like that species.

The impact of parasitism on the nests of passerine birds by the Shiny Cowbird is unknown. Whether it will compete with or hybridize with the Brown-headed Cowbird, only the future will tell.

[Bronzed Cowbird] *Molothrus aeneus*

The Bronzed Cowbird is a recent interloper from the Southwest. It has been extending its winter range eastward into Texas and Louisiana. Lowery Jr. (1974) recorded the first sighting in Cameron Parish on December 31, 1961. Since then, it has been noted breeding by numerous observers in southern Louisiana and parasitizing the Orchard Oriole (T. A. Imhof, pers. comm.). Like other cowbirds, it lays its eggs in other birds' nests.

The Bronzed Cowbird is distinguishable from the Brown-headed Cowbird by the *hunch-backed appearance* of the *neck ruff, red eyes,* larger and longer bill, uniform dark appearance of male and female, and *absence* of the contrasty brown head of the male Brown-headed Cowbird. Immatures are dark brown. Adult females are dull black and lack the bronze glossiness of the male. Both sexes are noticeably larger than the Brown-headed Cowbird.

This cowbird made its first recorded appearance near the Pascagoula River port on January 6, 1979 (Hodges and Toups 1979), and from then until February 25, as many as 15 Bronzed Cowbirds were identified at the same place (Hamilton 1979). A single bird was seen by Stephen W. Peterson in December 1979. In Hancock County on June 17, 1986, James L. Spence and Russ Hackman identified a male and female Bronzed Cowbird just east of Pearl River in southern Hancock County. On a subsequent visit, Spence and Toups (Jackson and Hodges 1986) obtained confirming photographs. A male was seen there in courtship display with two females by Gerry Morgan and Mickey Baker.

Considering the large number of wintering and resident blackbirds in flocks for much of the year, this southwestern and Mexican species can easily escape notice. Especially in southern Mississippi, birders should keep a weather eye open for hunch-backed, red-eyed birds among flocks of Brown-headed Cowbirds and Brewer's and Rusty Blackbirds in pastures and around livestock feeders. Observations of this species during the breeding period are needed to confirm probable breeding.

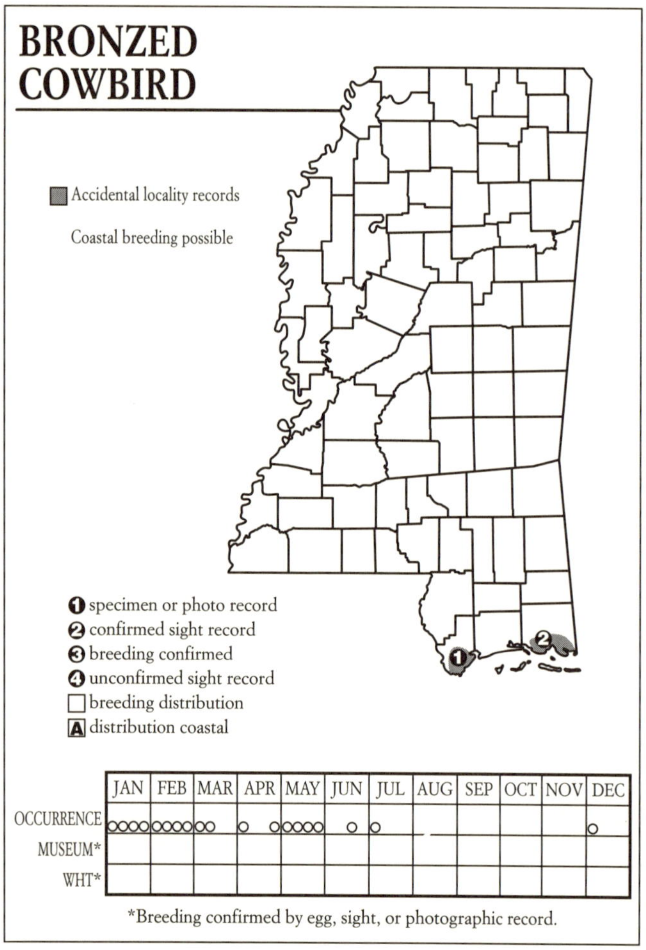

Brown-headed Cowbird *Molothrus ater*

This small, glossy black blackbird with a short, conical bill and dark brown head is a statewide permanent resident. The female cowbird is mouse gray, except for a lighter colored throat. Immatures of both sexes are dark olive brown above with light buff edging to the feathers, and the underparts are dirty white or buff colored on the throat, breast, and sides with dark brown streaking.

Cowbirds often flock with other blackbirds and can be recognized by their smaller size; heavy, conical, sparrow-like bill; and a tendency to walk with the wings dropped downward and short tail tilted upward. They frequently associate with cattle and feed upon insects, grass and weed seeds, and waste grain, some undoubtedly from animal droppings. The cowbird's association with domestic livestock has given it an appropriate common name. In earlier times, it was called "buffalo-bird."

The cowbird is best known, however, for its habit of laying eggs in the nests of smaller birds. Cowbirds build no nests and rely entirely on other species to rear their young. Egg record dates in the MMNS extend from April 21 to June 21. These records are all of one cowbird egg each found in the nests of White-eyed Vireo, Red-eyed Vireo, Kentucky Warbler, Hooded Warbler, Indigo Bunting, Orchard Oriole, Summer Tanager, Common Yellowthroat, and Northern Cardinal. I have also found single cowbird eggs in the nests of the Eastern Towhee, Painted Bunting, and Blue Grosbeak.

Cowbird eggs are white or grayish white, evenly speckled and blotched over the surface with shades of dark brown. Hatching requires about 11 days and the young fledge from the nest in only eight to 10 days. The rapid development and larger size of the young cowbird allow it to dominate the young of the smaller host species and obtain all of the food it needs. The victimized host species continues to feed the young cowbird until it is fully developed. The young of the host may be starved and crowded out of the nest. I have observed a White-eyed Vireo feeding two flying cowbird young of different ages, a fledgling and a fully developed juvenile (Turcotte 1981).

The Brown-headed Cowbird is promiscuous, and during the breeding season it is not uncommon to see a female accompanied by several males. The female is an expert at finding nests of the species it parasitizes. She stealthily locates the nest and lays an egg while the owner is absent, usually before the host begins incubation.

BROWN-HEADED COWBIRD

Common winter resident statewide

■ Permanent resident breeding

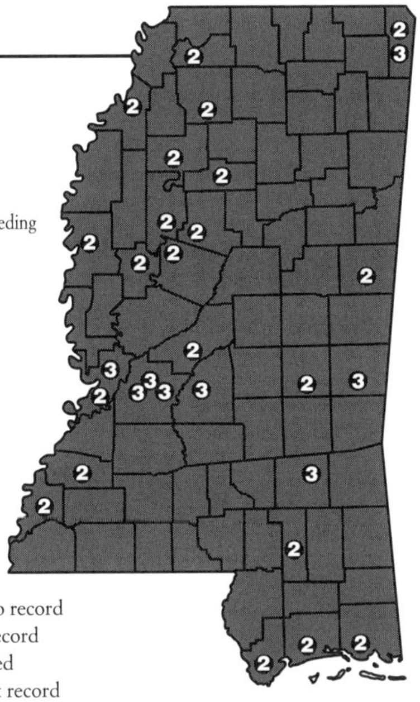

❶ specimen or photo record
❷ confirmed sight record
❸ breeding confirmed
❹ unconfirmed sight record
□ breeding distribution
[S] distribution statewide

	JAN	FEB	MAR	APR	MAY	JUN	JUL	AUG	SEP	OCT	NOV	DEC
OCCURRENCE	▬	▬	▬	▬	▬	▬	▬	▬	▬	▬	▬	▬
MUSEUM*					●●●●		● ●					
WHT*						2 ●						

*Breeding confirmed by egg, sight, or photographic record.

Often one or more host eggs is removed and may be eaten by the parasitic cowbird. Usually only one cowbird egg is laid, but sometimes two or more may be found in a nest. The host species may abandon a cowbird-victimized nest or cover it and build a new nest on top of it.

The Brown-headed Cowbird is an abundant winter resident, and large flocks can be seen from late November through March. It often flocks and roosts with other blackbirds and starlings. Its song is a low, liquid gurgling accompanied by a very high, thin, squeaky note at the end. The call note is a short *chuck*.

The male performs a courtship display usually in a treetop. He ruffles the neck feathers, spreads the wings and tail, and points the head and bill upward. During the display, he sings the short, low, bubbly song ending with a very shrill whistled note while bowing downward.

Orchard Oriole *Icterus spurius*

Only two species of orioles have been recorded in Mississippi, the Orchard Oriole and the Baltimore Oriole. The smaller and less brilliantly colored is the Orchard Oriole, an abundant, statewide summer resident. It nests commonly throughout the state and on the barrier islands. Its basketlike nest is woven of green grasses and lined with thistle down or other soft plant down. By the time the young fledge, the nest grasses have turned golden yellow.

Nests are usually placed in the upper or outermost fork of a sapling, tall shrub, orchard, or shade tree in groves, pastures, fence rows, roadsides, or idle lands reverting to trees. Sweet gum, elm, and pecan trees are favored sites. Occasionally, nests are built in strands of Spanish moss hanging from large trees or partly suspended between twigs or branches. Most nests are 10 to 20 feet high, though I have found two nests seven feet high and one in a bush only four feet aboveground. Nests are substantially woven around supporting branches. Three to five bluish white eggs spotted, scrawled, and splashed with shades of brown and lavender are laid mostly during May, with some renesting extending through June.

The male Orchard Oriole is one of my favorites of the common, summer-resident songbirds. Its song is a joyous, variable, musical, and hurried burst of clearly whistled notes, immediately recognizable and heard from the time of its arrival until nesting ends in early July. Often the bird sings while making short flights from tree to tree. The call is a *chack*

ORCHARD ORIOLE

■ Casual wintering on coasr

□ Common summer resident breeding

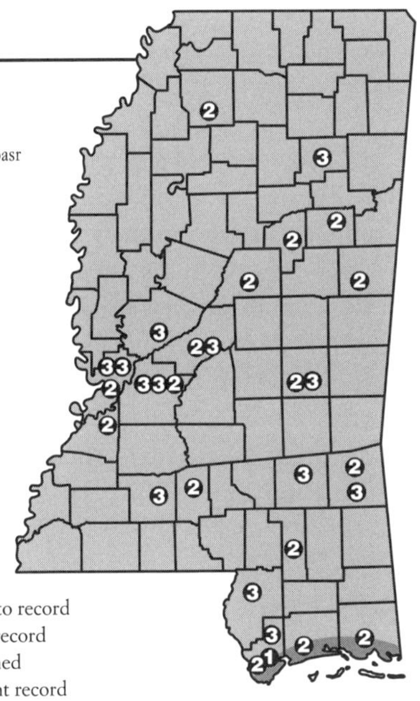

❶ specimen or photo record
❷ confirmed sight record
❸ breeding confirmed
❹ unconfirmed sight record
[S] breeding distribution
[S] distribution statewide

	JAN	FEB	MAR	APR	MAY	JUN	JUL	AUG	SEP	OCT	NOV	DEC
OCCURRENCE			3 ○○	▬	▬	▬	▬	▬	10 ○			
MUSEUM*					●●●●	●●●●●						
WHT*					●●●							

*Breeding confirmed by egg, sight, or photographic record.

similar to that of the Red-winged Blackbird. An alarm call frequently given around the nest site is *che'-lick*. A squeaky chattering is sometimes interspersed with its song or call notes.

The adult breeding male is entirely black on the head, back, tail, and most of the wings. Underparts, rump, and shoulders are brick red, giving an overall dark appearance. This plumage is acquired by the second breeding season. The female and young are olive or greenish yellow above with white wing bars and greenish yellow underneath. Orchard Orioles are about twice the size of any yellow warbler of similar appearance. The first-year male is more greenish above than the female, and has two white wing bars and a black bib.

This oriole feeds almost entirely on insects, but is fond of wild fruits, particularly mulberries. Sometimes cultivated fruits are eaten, especially figs and muscadines, but not enough to be of any economic importance.

I have noticed this bird and the Baltimore Oriole eat nectar of the tubular flowers of woodbine, or coral honeysuckle *(Lonicera sempervirens)*, and a domesticated strain of trumpet vine *(Campsis radicans)*. I have cultivated these flowering vines in my yard for many years, and orioles come annually to feed on them. With their sharp beaks they split the tubular flowers at the base and suck out the nectar. I have observed this repeatedly, usually in early morning from a distance of eight to 10 feet from a trumpet vine growing just outside a bedroom window. Although I have not actually seen orioles feeding on woodbine nectar, I have seen the red tubular flowers of this vine punctured at the base in the same manner as trumpet vine.

The Orchard Oriole arrives on the Mississippi Gulf Coast during late March. It is often locally abundant during spring migration in late April and early May, when it occurs in loose flocks along roadsides. Departure occurs early in the fall, and most of birds have left by late September. Extreme dates of arrival and departure are March 3 (Jones County) and September 10 (Harrison County). I can find only three August records and no winter records. This species can be expected to occur as a casual winter resident on the Mississippi Coast. Lowery Jr. (1974) has reported a dozen or more winter sightings in and below New Orleans.

Baltimore Oriole *Icterus galbula*

It is always a bit startling to behold the fiery orange and black plumaged Baltimore Oriole. The fully adult male is attired as brilliantly as any tropical species. The entire head and most of the back, wings, and tail are black. The underparts, shoulders, lower back, rump, and outer parts of the tail feathers are bright orange. The greater wing coverts, secondaries, and primaries are white on the outer edges.

The female and young are olive brown above and yellow below, with two white wing bars. There is enough orange tint on the underparts to plainly separate them from the smaller females and immatures of the Orchard Oriole, which are yellow or greenish yellow below. Female tanagers (except the Western Tanager) lack wing bars and have unusually stout and swollen beaks unlike the slender, sharp, pointed beaks of orioles.

On the Gulf Coast in spring, this oriole is a scarce transient and begins arriving in early April. Northward migration continues until early May. Spring males are in full song as soon as they arrive on the breeding grounds. Some nesting activity begins by late April, but is usually not in full swing until late May and early June.

In the southern and eastern halves of the state, this species is uncommon and local as a summer-resident, breeding bird. In the brown loam soil areas extending eastward from the Loess Bluffs north of Lincoln County, the Baltimore Oriole is a local and common breeding bird in pecan groves and shade trees around cities, towns, and countryside homes.

Along the Mississippi River and in the Loess Bluff and Yazoo Delta regions, this species is a common to abundant breeder in open groves, shade trees, and edges of woodlands. In the edges of open woodlands, and in cottonwood

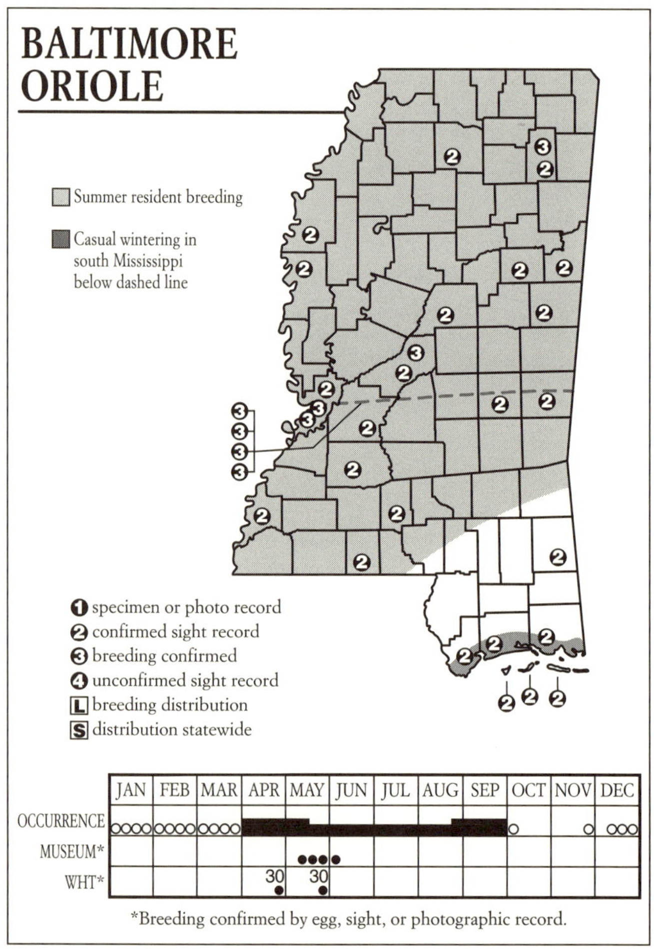

and pecan groves of Mississippi River batture areas and oxbows, this oriole is as plentiful as the Orchard Oriole and nests commonly wherever suitable trees are found.

The nest is a deep pouch up to 10 inches long woven of grass, string, horse hair, plant bark, or fibers, and lined with thistle or plant down. It is swung from two or more terminal twigs of an outer tree limb, usually 10 to 30 feet aboveground. The four to six white eggs are beautifully scrawled and blotched around the large end with dark brown, black, and gray.

The male's song is a series of loud, clear, whistled notes in two-note phrases combined with single notes and short or long pauses. I have tape recorded the songs of many of these birds and no two individuals sound alike, but there is a similarity in fullness of the voice. It is like a pretty, exclamatory sentence punctuated with pauses and ending abruptly. The songs are often interspersed with low chatterings, and the call notes sound like *hew'-lick*.

A similar western species breeds from southwestern Canada through the Great Plains and western states. It is considered a separate species known as Bullock's Oriole *(I. bullockii)*. The Bullock's Oriole has only the top of the head, lores, and bib black. The sides of the head are yellowish orange, the shoulder patches are larger and white instead of orange, and the orange in the outer-tail feathers extends outward from the base of the tail for about two-thirds of its total length.

The Bullock's and Baltimore variants of this oriole interbreed where their ranges overlap. They were formerly considered the same species under the name Northern Oriole. The Bullock's Oriole has been reported in Mississippi. It is fairly regular during winter in western and southern Louisiana and has been recorded in southern Alabama during the winter months. Look for this bird here during the winter or early spring months. Sight records are one each on October 25, 1981, at Escatawpa and August 28, 1983, at Hattiesburg by Terrie and Larry Gates and Judith Toups, and April 23, 1983, by Edward Alexander Jr. at Greenville.

The Baltimore Oriole has been recorded wintering at Yazoo National Wildlife Refuge in Washington County, Vicksburg, Jackson, Richland, and Picayune. By late September, fall migration from the state is complete except for the few individuals that may overwinter. I find few October or November records for Mississippi, but the Baltimore Oriole has been recorded every other month in the year from December 10 to September 27.

Orioles will respond readily to sugar water or hummingbird feeders upon arriving from their wintering grounds. Feeder use is sporadic during the nesting season with little use afterward. Feeders can be made by hanging a small jar on a limb.

American Goldfinch

Fringillidae (Finches)

The finches are seedeaters. And, except for the American Goldfinch and the relative newcomer, the House Finch, most species breed farther north. They appear here in numbers mainly during winter. Their populations can be cyclic.

Many nest in the far north or high mountain regions and seldom come as far south as the northern Gulf states. Those that do are erratic casual or accidental winter visitors, like the Evening Grosbeak and the Red Crossbill. The latter is an erratic breeder outside its normal breeding range when food supplies fall short. Previously at least one or more pairs have remained to nest in Mississippi.

Finches have *undulating flight,* perhaps because of their short tails. The Purple Finch and Pine Siskin are regular winter visitors, but their numbers vary annually.

Purple Finch *Carpodacus purpureus*

This attractive winter resident sometimes shows up in large numbers with the arrival of severe cold weather, but may be scarce during mild winters. The first arrivals appear around mid-November with most departing in late March. Extremes of recorded arrival and departure dates are October 18 and May 4. Purple Finches usually travel in small flocks of up to 30 or more.

In late winter they are sometimes common at feeding stations and show a preference for sunflower seeds. They often strip the berries of Japanese privet and then descend to feed on those fallen to the ground. They regularly eat tree buds and the seeds of elms in the early spring.

A Purple Finch is the size of a House Sparrow. The female and immature are boldly streaked above and below with dark brown, with broad white lines behind and beneath the eye, and *prominent dark cheeks and malar stripes*. The fully adult male is rose red on the head, throat, breast, and rump, streaked on the back withduller reddish brown, and with white on the sides and belly. The tail is deeply notched, and the bill is larger and stouter than any sparrow's. The flight is distinctly undulating.

The double-noted, metallic, *tick-tick* call is distinctive and often announces this bird's presence before it is seen. The song is a pleasing sequence of liquid warbling heard on rare occasions during the winter and occasionally before spring departure.

The Purple Finch breeds in northern coniferous forests, where it usually nests in an evergreen tree or bush. After the nesting season, these birds wander in flocks, but occur erratically, so that in some years they appear to be abundant in one area and rare in others. Females and immatures in winter flocks nearly always outnumber the colorful and easily identifiable males.

This finch occurs regularly in most of Mississippi except on the coast, where it is seen at intervals and in smaller numbers. It avoids dense woodlands or stands of pure pine, preferring open woods or woodland edges, where it feeds on winter fruits, seeds, buds, and insects.

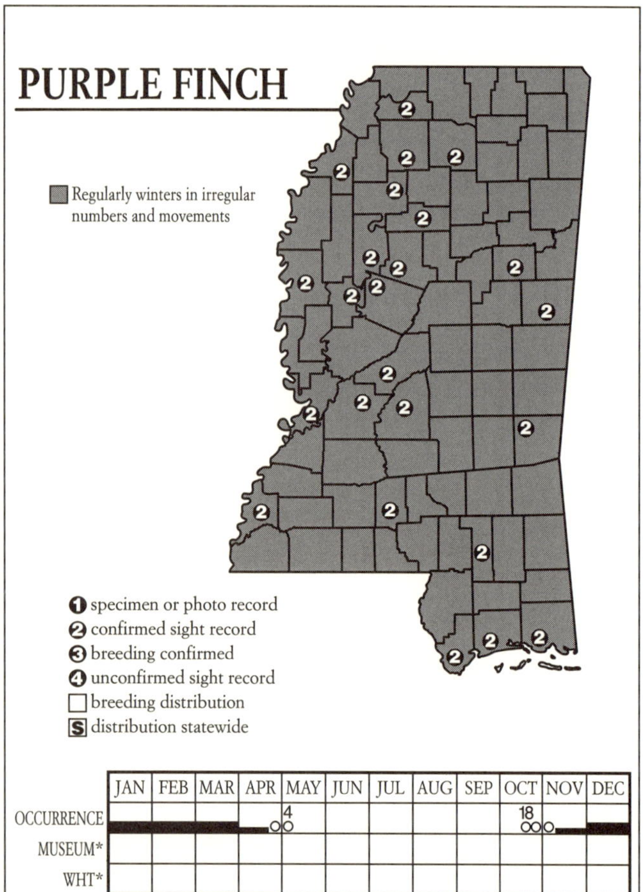

*Breeding confirmed by egg, sight, or photographic record.

House Finch *Carpodacus mexicanus*

This finch is a relative newcomer to Mississippi and the eastern United States. It is an abundant resident of all western states to the high plains and into west-central Texas, where it inhabits brushy lowlands up to 5000 feet and commonly occurs in urban areas. In the 1940s, it was introduced into the New York City area, and since the 1960s it has spread explosively across the states east of the Mississippi River. It has expanded rapidly westward into Louisiana, Arkansas, and Missouri. In Mississippi, it has become a fairly common winter resident, usually noted at feeding stations in towns and cities. In some places it is a permanent resident.

The House Finch was first sighted in Mississippi by Margaret Copeland and Elsie Croft at the Copeland residence feeding station in Starkville on January 11, 1980 (Jackson 1981d). At Starkville, during the winter until April 5, about 14 House Finches were present, and some were banded and photographed by Jerome A. Jackson.

A male was seen by Terrie Fairley and David Hamilton on February 9, 1980, at a feeding station in Petal in Forrest County. The first coastal and earliest fall record, a female or immature, was seen at the Port Bienville Industrial Park in Hancock County, on November 18, 1980 (Toups and Hodges 1981a). In the winter of 1989–1990, sightings of three to 24 birds occurred at feeders at eight localities in the Jackson metropolitan area.

Breeding was first confirmed at Starkville on July 11, 1986, by Jerome A. Jackson and Nancy Jamison (Jackson and Hodges 1986; Jackson et al. 1986). An adult male and female were seen feeding a fledgling at two locations, presumably from the same nest. The first summer record for this species in central Mississippi was a single male seen and photographed at a feeder by Vic Duvic (pers. comm.) in Jackson on July 14, 1984. This bird occasionally was seen through August 20, 1984. Male and female House Finches also appeared in the summer of 1985 in Starkville. They were seen by multiple observers from July 22 through August 6.

Typically the adult male has a deep red throat and bib distinctly set apart from *brown-streaked underparts*. The crown and sides of the head are brown bordered by a wide band of red *above* the eye and *across* the forehead. The brown streaked back, red rump patch, and squarish tail confirm identification. Adult male variants may appear reddish orange or yellowish.

Females are striped gray brown above and below, with

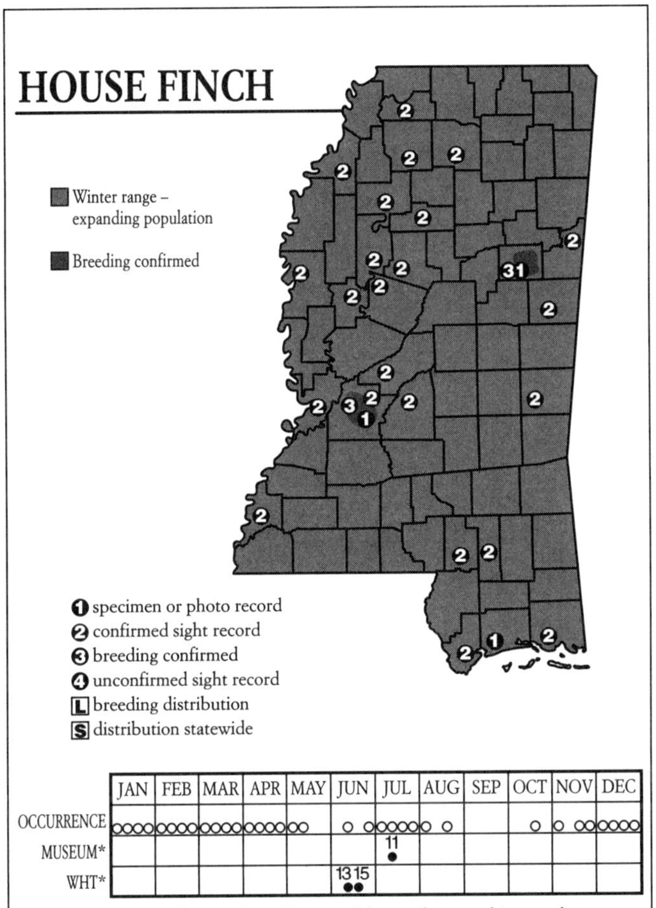

*Breeding confirmed by egg, sight, or photographic record.

a plain, grayish brown head *without* the dark brown mustache marks and cheek patches of the female Purple Finch. Immatures resemble the female.

House Finches and Purple Finches often associate at feeding trays. Casual observers easily might mistake this newcomer for the Purple Finch. However, I have noticed a distinct difference in appearance and behavior. The House Finch is slimmer and smaller, compared with the stocky Purple Finch, and more active when feeding. The notched tail and frequently raised crown feathers of the Purple Finch help distinguish the two species.

Nesting by the House Finch has been confirmed in Alabama, central Tennessee, and Arkansas. It seems destined to become an abundant winter-resident and permanent-resident breeding bird in most southeastern states. On June 15, 1991, breeding was confirmed by photographs of nestlings in downtown Jackson (Turcotte and Hutto 1991). The three nests held four young, one held one egg, and one was under construction. All nests were in wire mesh covers over ceiling light fixtures on the open top floor of a parking garage. Adult pairs were seen at all nests. Nesting in hanging fern baskets has occurred in residential parts of the city. Three or four faintly spotted, pale blue eggs are laid in a cup-shaped nest.

[Red Crossbill] *Loxia curvirostra*

The Red Crossbill is an unpredictable wanderer. It breeds in northern evergreen forests and mountainous regions, and usually winters throughout its breeding range. The seeds of conifers are its main winter food. When pines in their normal range have a poor seed crop and more southern areas experience a bountiful season, these birds range more widely and sometimes nest outside their normal breeding range.

In the winter of 1972–1973, Red Crossbills made their first known appearance in Mississippi. On October 29, 1972, Jackson (1973) found a freshly killed specimen on a gravel road near the Noxubee National Wildlife Refuge headquarters. Later that winter on February 24, 1973, a female and a singing male were sighted near the same place by Jim and Gloria Maender. The second seasonal appearance in Mississippi occurred during the fall and winter of 1975–1976, when sightings were made on Noxubee Refuge. Two birds were observed by Robbie Howell on the Homochitto National Forest in Franklin County on March 7, 1976.

On February 25, 1976, Warren (Warren et al. 1977) found a pair of Red Crossbills nesting in a loblolly pine

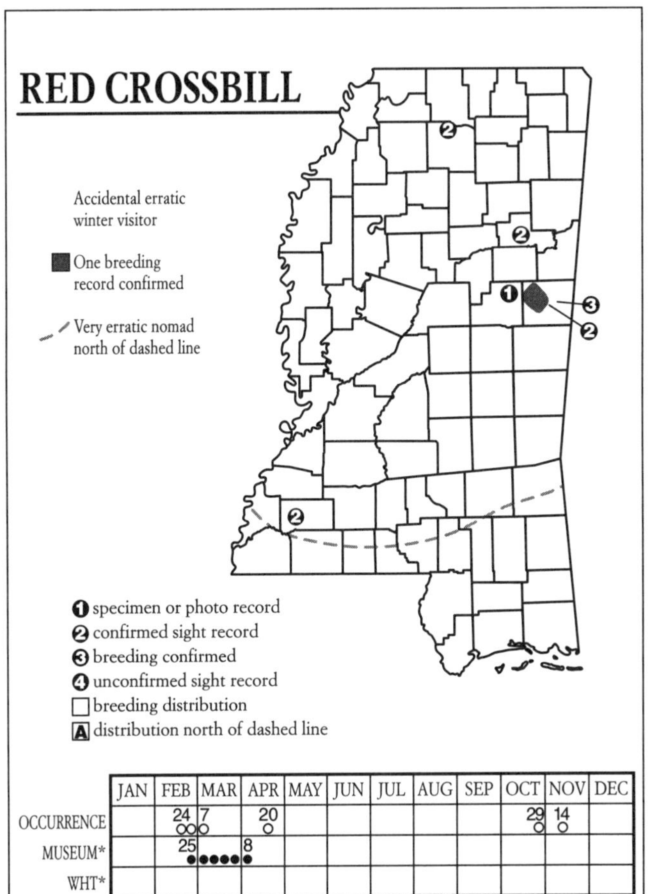

*Breeding confirmed by egg, sight, or photographic record.

on Noxubee Refuge in Winston County. The nest-building, hatching, and rearing of three young was observed until they fledged on April 8. Red Crossbills in flocks numbering up to 11 were seen nearby, but no additional nests were found. Dead shortleaf pine twigs were used in the nest construction and a lining was added. The nest was placed 47 feet aboveground on a terminal branch of the pine. The male fed the female throughout the incubation period and both parents fed the young.

As many as 15 Red Crossbills were seen November 14, 1990, at Oxford by Gene and Shannon Knight (Jackson 1991). On April 20, 1991, a flock of six Red Crossbills was seen by Terence Schiefer in Clay County (Stedman 1991).

As the name implies, the mandibles of this bird cross each other at the tips. This gives the bird an amazing ability to open pine cones and extract the seeds. Crossbills feed like parrots, dangling by their feet and bills as they clamber around on limbs and pine cones.

The adult male is brick red with dusky wings and tail. The immature male is a mixture of dull red, green, and yellow, giving the appearance of orange red. Females are greenish yellow with blackish wings and tail and a yellow rump. The call is a two- or three-noted shrill, *pip-pip-pip*, similar to that of a baby chicken. The song is a finchlike warbling followed by a trill.

Pine Siskin *Carduelis pinus*

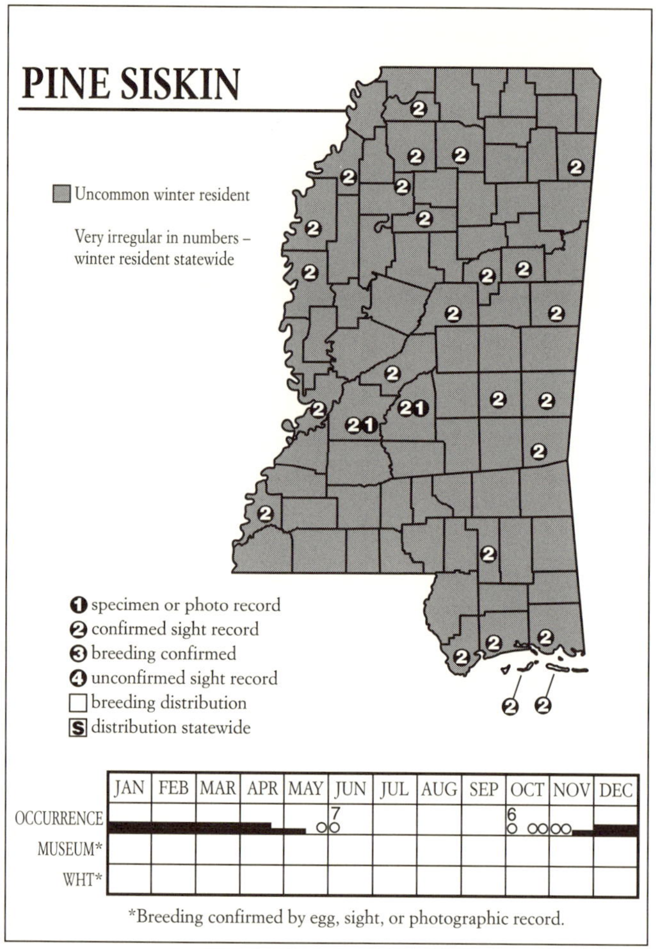

Almost every year a few Pine Siskins are recorded in Mississippi. They are usually scarce winter visitors to the northern half of the state. Very rarely do they occur in numbers as far south as the coastal counties. They have appeared erratically in fairly large numbers over most of the state in recent years. They commonly are seen in company with American Goldfinches feeding on seeds of sweet gum, alder, dandelion, sunflower, and various weeds or grasses. They frequently appear on lawns and feeding stations in flocks or mixed with goldfinches.

Stevenson (1945) recorded a flock of 16 at Oxford in Lafayette County on October 30, the earliest arrival date at the time for this species. Gene Knight recorded early arrivals at Oxford on October 6, 24, and 25. M. G. Vaiden recorded a late departure date for this bird at Rosedale in Bolivar County on May 12. One bird remained at our feeder in Richland until the first week in June.

The Pine Siskin is slightly smaller than the American Goldfinch and is uniformly streaked above and below with brown. The diminutive size; deeply notched tail; wing bars; concealed yellow patches on the wings and tail; and conical, but slender, sharply pointed bill are distinctive field marks. The call, a buzzy and husky, penetrating *zree-e-e-e* note, rises in pitch at the end. The call is huskier in quality than the similar note of the American Goldfinch.

The winter of 1972–1973 was an invasion year for Pine Siskins when they were recorded in numbers at Hattiesburg, Natchez, Jackson, Meridian, Kosciusko, and Grenada. They were seen and reported mostly at feeders. The Meridian Christmas Bird Count on December 31, 1972, recorded 50 Pine Siskins, and the Natchez count recorded 20 birds on December 23, 1972. A flock of 16 birds was seen in Jackson on February 19 and 20, 1973, and others appeared at feeders in northeast Jackson. Walter V. Davis (1972) observed a flock of 25 feeding on crushed pecans in a parking lot in Kosciusko, and he continued feeding them on cracked pecans for several weeks until February 12, 1972, when a Red-tailed Hawk swooped down and captured one.

The Pine Siskin breeds in northern evergreen forests of Canada and the mountains of the northeastern and western states. The nest is a shallow cup built of bark, grass, and moss lined with plant down, fur, and feathers. It is usually concealed in foliage of a conifer near the end of a branch, 10 to 20 feet aboveground. The three to five eggs are pale blue green and dotted with brown and black.

American Goldfinch *Carduelis tristis*

In spring and summer plumage, the male American Goldfinch is bright canary yellow with black wings, tail, and forehead. The tail coverts and wing bars are white. The summer female is unstreaked, grayish, and olive green above and dull olive yellow below with a whitish rump and two white bars on the blackish wings. In winter plumage, the male and immatures resemble the summer female. In all plumages, the deeply *undulating flight,* stubby finch bill, and the high-pitched *per-chick-o-ree* or *swee* call notes with upward inflections are distinctive. The song is a long series of lively, high, sweet, canary-like notes.

The goldfinch, often called "wild canary," is known by its fondness for seeds of sweet gum, thistle, wild lettuce, dandelion, sunflower and other composites, ragweed, common chickweed, and various grasses. It is a common winter resident throughout Mississippi. It frequents weedy field borders, open woods, and woodland edges, and commonly uses feeders where sunflower, thistle, and other seeds are available.

Flocks usually are small, but infrequently 50 or more may be encountered in spring when they congregate to feed in an urban park or on a neighborhood lawn. They are especially noticeable in their bright breeding plumage.

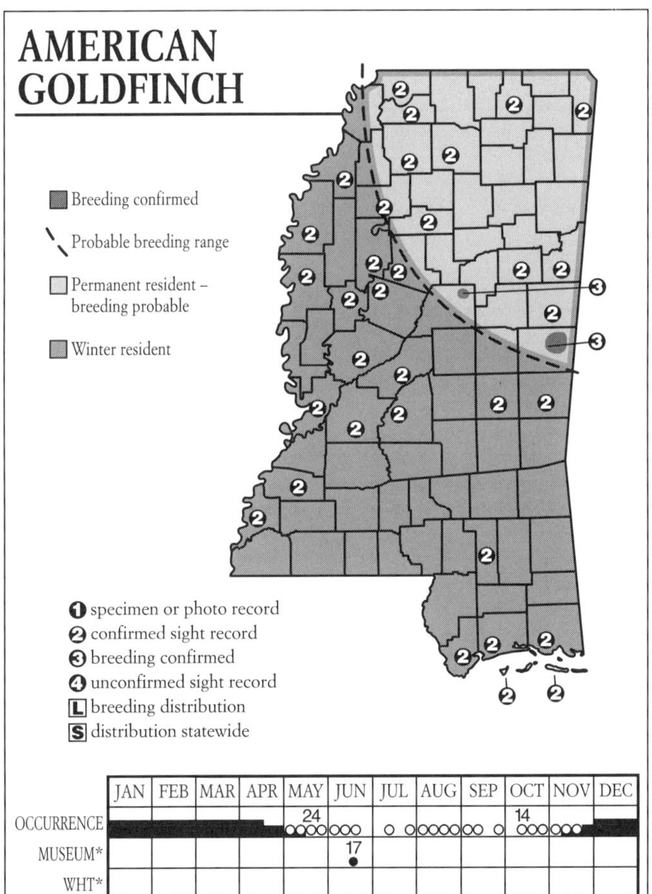

*Breeding confirmed by egg, sight, or photographic record.

The American Goldfinch arrives in late November and occurs regularly throughout the winter. It is most numerous during the northward spring migration from late March to early May. Extremes of fall arrival and spring departure are October 14 and May 24.

A typical nest containing three eggs, discovered by Randall C. Warren (Warren and Hurst 1979) on June 17, 1976, in Kemper County, is proof of breeding. The nest was about 3.5 feet aboveground in the fork of a willow oak bush in a five-year-old pine plantation. It was lined with thistle down from plants common in the immediate vicinity.

Summer sight records indicate that nesting may occur locally in northern Mississippi. July and August collection and sight records in Grenada, Lafayette, Lauderdale, and Tishomingo Counties probably were breeding birds. Since the American Goldfinch is noted for being a late nester, sightings during late May or even June do not positively indicate nesting activity.

In Alabama, nesting has been recorded in the Tennessee Valley, upper coastal plain, and mountains. This goldfinch can be expected to breed in the northern and northeastern portions of Mississippi. The nest is a substantial, open cup made of grasses, plant bark, and stems, which is thickly lined with thistle down and bound together with cobwebs. The nest usually is built in the fork of a low bush or briers, but may be placed on the outer limb of a pine. The normal set is five pale blue eggs.

Evening Grosbeak *Coccothraustes vespertinus*

The short tail, chunky body, and oversized bill that varies from chalky white to pale green, along with the yellow, black, and white plumage make this large cardinal-sized finch unmistakable. The male has a yellow body and yellow on the forehead with a line over the eye. The top of the head, tail, and wings are black, except for white secondaries and coverts. The remainder of the head, upper back, and breast are olive brown.

The female Evening Grosbeak is silvery gray on the head and body with a slight yellow wash on the nape and sides. The white throat is bordered by thin malar stripes. The wings and tail are black except on secondary coverts. The inner primaries and tips of the tail and uppertail coverts are white. Immatures show less yellow than the female, but are otherwise similar. The strident, loud calls are *cle-ip* or *cleer.*

The Evening Grosbeak breeds in the boreal forests of Canada, the northern edge of the northeastern United States, and the western mountains southward into Mexico. In winter, it seldom migrates far from its breeding grounds, for it is capable of enduring harsh, cold weather. In winter, it is irregular but sometimes common in the southern part of the breeding range. However, it seldom migrates as far south as the Gulf Coast.

The first record of this species in Mississippi was reported by Barry O. Freeman, a sighting of a male and female in his yard at Oxford in Lafayette County on March 20, 1960 (Turcotte 1960a). They were seen again in the same tree on March 26. The species appeared again in Franklin County where Edward G. Sullivan (1962) observed and reported eight in a flock seen from December 17 to 19, 1961.

The first specimen of record was taken by Gandy (1962a) from a small flock at Jackson in Hinds County. It was first seen by Mrs. John S. Winbigler on January 29 and collected on February 22, 1962. Sightings were subsequently reported in Jackson by Gandy (1962b) until May 2, 1962. As many as 10 were counted at one time at the feeder of E. H. Magruder, who took special delight in seeing them feeding on sunflower seeds. At one time a flock was seen feeding on seeds of box elder trees near Magruder's home. Epple (1973) described and analyzed the 1961–1963 grosbeak invasion after a survey of the eastern United States.

Evening Grosbeaks were not recorded again in Mississippi until late February 1966, when small flocks appeared at Jackson, Kosciusko, and Raleigh. The following two winters they were not seen.

In the winter of 1968–1969 a spectacular invasion of these northern visitors occurred between December 15, 1968, and April 26, 1969. Flocks numbering up to 200 birds were recorded in Natchez, and other flocks were at feeders in Amory, Starkville, Okolona, Edwards, Kosciusko, Brandon, Canton, Hattiesburg, and Ocean Springs. From January to April 10, 1970, small flocks appeared in Jackson, Natchez, Kosciusko, Hickory Flat, and at Noxubee National Wildlife Refuge.

In the winter of 1971–1972, Evening Grosbeaks first appeared on December 19 at Noxubee National Wildlife Refuge, and others were recorded in Hinds, Oktibbeha, Benton, and Scott Counties in flocks of 15 to 50. Some remained in Jackson until April 20, 1972.

The winter of 1972–1973 brought the greatest invasion of Evening Grosbeaks (Turcotte 1973). First appearing near Starkville on November 23, 1972, they were recorded by Donald Lewis on November 24 in Marion County and last seen at a feeder in Oktibbeha County on May 10, 1973. Jackson (1974) conducted a survey to document the distribution of birds and the magnitude of this invasion. MOS members and other respondents recorded the occurrence of these grosbeaks in 21 counties, reported by 42 observers. The grosbeaks appeared in all sections of the state, but few were seen in the Yazoo Delta. Observers during that winter reported grosbeaks eating buds and tree seeds, but most sightings were at sunflower-seed feeders.

EVENING GROSBEAK

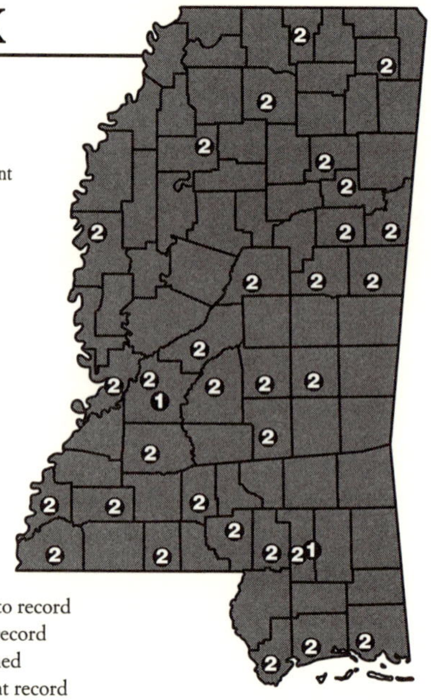

Uncommon and very irregular winter resident since 1960

1 specimen or photo record
2 confirmed sight record
3 breeding confirmed
4 unconfirmed sight record
□ breeding distribution
S distribution statewide, mainly at feeders

	JAN	FEB	MAR	APR	MAY	JUN	JUL	AUG	SEP	OCT	NOV	DEC
OCCURRENCE					28						23	
MUSEUM*												
WHT*												

*Breeding confirmed by egg, sight, or photographic record.

In the winter of 1973–1974, Evening Grosbeaks were conspicuously absent from the state and did not return until January 1975, when one female appeared at a feeder in Jackson and two at a feeder in Vicksburg. In the winter of 1975–1976, a flock of 12 Evening Grosbeaks was sighted in Madison County on the Jackson Christmas Bird Count on December 27, 1975. Jerome A. Jackson reported flocks numbering from two to 80 at Sturgis, Kosciusko, and Starkville from January 1976 to April 16, 1976. They have become irregular in appearance and total numbers in recent years. Imprinting on this environment may have caused them to return to wintering grounds in the Deep South.

The sporadic appearance of this northern visitor may be due to conditions favoring increased brood production, failure of natural food supplies in usual wintering areas, and increased use of sunflower seeds to attract and encourage the return of wintering flocks. Whatever the cause, these attractive birds are welcome visitors in the southland.

Passeridae (Weaver Finches)

The weavers are a large, Old World family not related to our native sparrows. They are widespread over Europe, Asia, and Africa. These birds build large, domed nests with entrance holes on the side.

Two species of sparrow-weavers have been introduced to North America: the common House Sparrow, or English Sparrow, and the European Tree Sparrow *(Passer montanus)*. The latter was introduced from Germany to a park in St. Louis, Missouri, in 1870. It now occurs only in the vicinity of St. Louis and in southeastern Illinois. Later, House Sparrows became established in St. Louis, and the European Tree Sparrow apparently could not compete with them in spreading to other areas. Both species are nonmigratory. The House Sparrow nests in all kinds of crevices around buildings that offer a place for its bulky nest. This species is regarded as a nuisance and an economic pest.

House Sparrow *Passer domesticus*

Imported from England, the House Sparrow was first introduced in New York City around 1850. Since then, it has occupied all suitable habitats in North America. It has passed the highest level of abundance and may be declining, or at least is at a stable population level. In towns, cities, and around farmhouses, it is probably the most numerous bird species. In Mississippi, it has ranked among the 10 most commonly seen or heard birds on randomly selected June breeding bird survey routes from 1966 to 1970. Numerically, it was consistently outranked during that five-year period only by the Red-winged Blackbird, Common Grackle, and surprisingly by the Northern Bobwhite (Turcotte 1971b).

This is a bird familiar to everyone because of its abundance and adaptability on farms, in the suburbs, and in cities. It has the distinction, along with the European Starling, of being an unprotected species. Nests of this sparrow clutter buildings, and its noisy, dirty roosts soil walkways. A redeeming feature of this bird is that some, but not all, of its food habits are beneficial. When nestlings are present and at times when insect plagues occur, it helps destroy harmful garden insects.

To me, the House Sparrow's voice is a monotonous chirping or chattering. Occasionally twittering notes can be heard that resemble a song.

In towns and cities, the House Sparrow is often so dingy or sooty that its true colors escape notice. Many people, who hardly give so common a bird a second glance, cannot adequately describe the adult male. When clean, the bird is attractive. The top of the head is blue gray, the nape is chestnut, the throat and bill are black, the cheeks are white, and the underparts are dull white. The back is chestnut and brown streaked with black, and the feathers around the rump are brownish gray. Wing-covert feathers are chestnut with white tips on the middle and buffy tips on the greater coverts.

On a Christmas Bird Count in rural Madison County, I saw a House Sparrow that was really pretty. One bright-plumaged male in a multiflora rose hedgerow stood out among a small group of sparrows. The breast of the bird was immaculate white with bright chestnut coloring and contrasting black throat.

The House Sparrow molts once a year in late summer. Part of the new plumage has gray tips to the feathers, which conceal some of the color. As the gray tips wear off, the colors become brighter and are best seen in spring. The female and young are similar, being brownish above with a buffy eye line and dingy white below. The bills of the female are horn colored to pinkish instead of black.

Nests of the House Sparrow are composed of coarse grasses, leaves, string, cloth, paper, cotton, and various kinds of trash. The nest is usually stuffed into a building cavity, bird box, woodpecker hole, or tree cavity and lined with feathers near the top center. Sometimes colony nesting occurs in ivy or other climbing vines on buildings. Tree

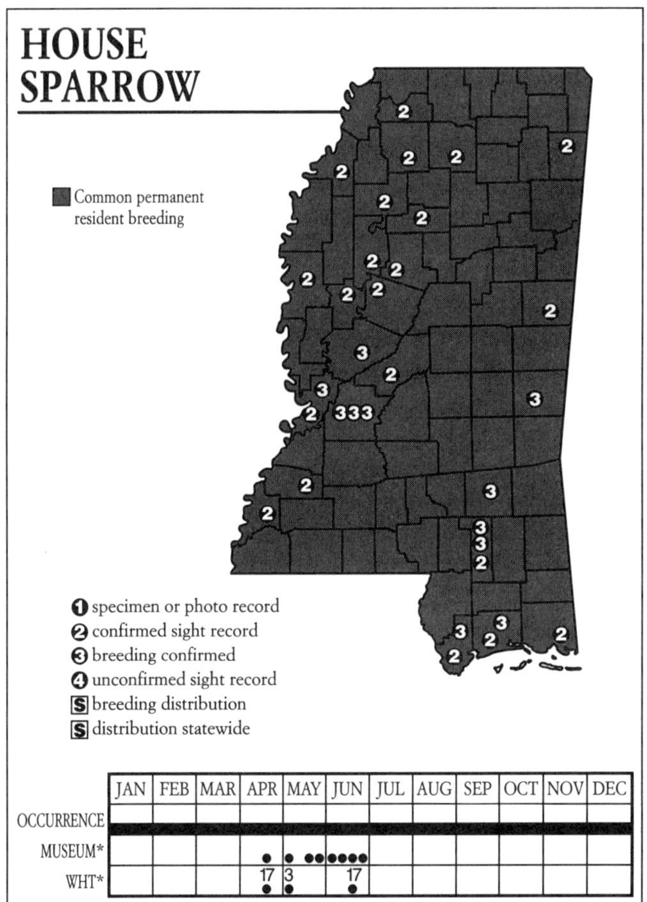

*Breeding confirmed by egg, sight, or photographic record.

nests are less common, but sometimes colony nesting occurs in thick trees like live oaks. Nests built in trees are globular in shape, well roofed, with an entrance hole on the side. Data on 13 sets of House Sparrow eggs in the MMNS describe the nests as "trash" in crevices of houses, in barns, cotton gins, a martin house, and other buildings.

Nesting begins in March, sometimes earlier, and several broods may be produced in a season. The five to seven eggs are white and heavily marked with black and shades of gray over the entire surface. When not nesting, these birds often roost in colonies in leafy trees, inside buildings and cavities, or crevices offering protection and concealment.

One cannot help but admire this pesky alien for its cheerfulness, ingenuity, resourcefulness, and ability to survive in spite of its enemies, including man. Regardless of its citizenship status, the House Sparrow is destined to remain here as a permanent resident. By now it is obvious that it can be neither destroyed nor deported.

The Breeding Birds of Mississippi

Arranged in checklist sequence, the breeding bird records that follow are substantiated by specimens, photographs, published records, or written details in the MMNS records file. Species name, county, date of collection, photograph, source of record, and other details are given. One or more records are cited for each species. (Other records may be cited in the species account.) Earliest state records are shown in most, but not all, instances. This appendix is for convenience in locating sources of additional documentation found elsewhere and not included in this book under the species accounts.

Pied-billed Grebe, Washington Co., April 29, 1940, 6 eggs.

Double-crested Cormorant, Tunica Co., May 18, 1952, 12 nests with young, B. B. Coffey Jr.

Anhinga, Holmes Co., April 29, 1934, 5 eggs.

Least Bittern, Washington Co., April 29, 1940, 4 eggs.

Great Blue Heron, Washington Co., April 29, 1940, 4 eggs.

Great Egret, Holmes Co., April 29, 1934, 4 eggs.

Snowy Egret, Jackson Co., Petit Bois Island, June 30, 1963, 4 flightless young, H. D. Haberyan.

Little Blue Heron, Holmes Co., April 29, 1934, 5 eggs.

Tricolored Heron, Jackson Co., Petit Bois Island, May 27, 1963, 4 flightless young banded, H. D. Haberyan.

Cattle Egret, Washington Co., May 1967, 4000 in Yazoo National Wildlife Refuge nesting colony, eggs and young, E. Cunningham; Madison Co., south of Canton, July 1, 1993, 10,000 in nesting colony with young at Pearl River Wildlife Refuge on Ross Barnett Reservoir, D. L. Watts (pers. comm.).

Green Heron, Hinds Co., May 1, 1932, 4 eggs.

Yellow-crowned Night-Heron, Holmes Co., April 29, 1934, 4 eggs.

White Ibis, Warren Co., May 25 to July 15, 1975, nests, eggs, and young in colony of 200 adults, photographs, H. Moore and W. H. Turcotte.

Canada Goose, Madison Co., Pearl River Waterfowl Refuge, May to July, 1988, 70 goslings with adults.

Wood Duck, Warren Co., May 27, 1937, 5 eggs.

Mottled Duck, Hancock Co., Lakeshore, 1962, nest photo and 6 eggs, L. E. Williams Jr. and S. G. Clawson.

Blue-winged Teal, Jackson Co., Pascagoula marsh, July 9, 1979, adult and 6 half-grown young, J. A. Toups and P. V. Donaldson.

Hooded Merganser, Hinds Co., May 8, 1960, brood of 5 half-grown young, W. H. Turcotte; Lowndes Co., Madison Co., and Montgomery Co., 1972, 45 nests in boxes, 19 nest-starts as early as March 19, L. Strong Jr.

Black Vulture, Hinds Co., Clinton area, March 13, 1933, 2 eggs.

Turkey Vulture, Hinds Co., north of Clinton, April 1, 1934, 2 eggs.

Osprey, Jackson Co., Horn Island, adults at active nests on May 29, 1963; April 15, 1979, aerial survey, active nests, 3 on Round Island, 10 on Horn Island, 6 on Ship Island, and 15 along Escatawpa River bottom, J. A. Jackson and B. J. Schardien (1979).

Swallow-tailed Kite, Jackson Co., Bluff Creek area, June 20, 1982, active nest in tall pine, J. A. Izral (1982).

White-tailed Kite, Hancock Co., April 17, 1983, 2 eggs in nest, J. A. Jackson; Hancock Co., May 16, 1984, 3 fledglings in nest, J. A. Toups and W. C. Weber.

Mississippi Kite, Issaquena Co., July 24, 1960, 1 large fledgling in nest in cottonwood at base of main levee, W. H. Turcotte.

Bald Eagle, Harrison Co., April 10, 1940, small young and parent birds near nest on Ship Island, T. D. Burleigh (1945).

Cooper's Hawk, Hinds Co., Baker's Creek near Clinton, April 21, 1934, 4 eggs.

Red-shouldered Hawk, Hinds Co., near Clinton, February 28, 1932, 3 eggs.

Broad-winged Hawk, Yazoo Co., near Phoenix, May 10, 1940, 3 eggs, B. Hamberlin.

Red-tailed Hawk, Chickasaw Co., near Okolona, March 31, 1939, 2 eggs, H. L. Owens.

American Kestrel, Holmes Co., near Lexington, May 2, 1940, 5 eggs; Chickasaw Co., near Okolona, May 24, 1940, 4 eggs, H. L. Owens.

Wild Turkey, Stone Co., near Black Creek, April 26, 1961, 11 eggs in deserted nest by roadside, W. H. Turcotte.

Northern Bobwhite, Hinds Co., near Clinton, May 21, 1932, 6 eggs.

Clapper Rail, Hancock Co., May 28, 1940, 6 eggs, E. J. Giering and C. D. Turnipseed.

King Rail, Hancock Co., May 28, 1940, 2 eggs, E. J. Giering; Hinds Co., near Clinton, April 22, 1961, 8 downy black chicks with adult at marshy pond, A. M. Gill.

Purple Gallinule, Washington Co., May 31, 1937, 7 eggs, F. Stribling.

Common Moorhen, Hancock Co., May 6, 1962, 2 eggs; Madison Co., August 30, 1986, brood of 4 on Pearl River Wildlife Area, F. Wills Jr., R. Downey, and E. Tackett.

American Coot, Noxubee Co., Bluff Lake, May 28, 1983, adult with 3 half-grown young, J. A. Jackson and J. R. Watson; Hancock Co., Jackson marsh, July 26, 1985, 20 adults with many immatures, J. A. Toups, D. King, and M. F. Hodges Jr.

Mississippi Sandhill Crane, Jackson Co., Fountainbleau, May 9, 1941, 2 eggs; Ben Williams Pond, May 9, 1941, 2 newly hatched young in nest, photograph, R. M. Freeman and W. H. Turcotte.

Snowy Plover, Harrison Co., beach at Mississippi City, May 3, 1978, photograph of nest and 3 eggs, M. B. Hays (1978).

Wilson's Plover, Jackson Co., Pascagoula marsh landfill, June 18, 1961, 4 eggs, W. H. Turcotte.

Killdeer, Hinds Co., near Clinton, May 4, 1931, 4 eggs.

Black-necked Stilt, Jackson Co., Pascagoula River dredge-filled marsh, July 6, 1977, nest, eggs broken, in MSU collection, W. C. Weber et al. (1978); July 22, 1977, nest with 3 eggs; August 12, 14, 19, 21, 1977, juveniles; Bolivar Co., drained catfish ponds near Shaw, summer 1990, 1 nest destroyed by mower, adult and 4 young, adult and 1 young, N. Herbert.

Willet, Harrison Co., Deer Island, May 29, 1936, 4 eggs, T. D. Burleigh (1945); Jackson Co., Pascagoula River marsh, June 11, 1978, adults and 1 three-fourths grown downy juvenile, J. A. Jackson and C. D. Cooley (1978).

American Woodcock, Pontotoc Co., March 1937, 4 eggs; Lincoln Co., February 25, 1958, adult and 4 downy chicks, S. E. Moreton; Oktibbeha Co., experimental forest, February 25, 1972, photograph, in MSU collection, nest and 4 eggs, G. A. Hurst (1972).

Laughing Gull, Jackson Co., Petit Bois Island, June 30, 1962, eggs collected; June 24, 1962, 3000 pairs with eggs and young, L. E. Williams Jr. (1962b).

Gull-billed Tern, Jackson Co., Bayou Casotte, June 4, 1962, 2 eggs.

Caspian Tern, Jackson Co., Petit Bois Island, 1967 and 1968, small numbers nesting in up to 15 nests, J. W. Portnoy (1977).

Royal Tern, Jackson Co., Petit Bois Island, June 30, 1962, 3 eggs; June 24 and 30, 1962, 500 pairs with eggs and young, L. E. Williams Jr. (1962b).

Sandwich Tern, Jackson Co., Petit Bois Island, June 30, 1962, 2 eggs; June 24 and 30, 1962, 2500 nests and young, 1400 banded in summer, L. E. Williams Jr. (1962b).

Common Tern, Jackson Co., Spanish Point, 1 mile west of Pascagoula, July 14, 1962, nest photograph, 2 eggs, MMNS, L. E. Williams Jr. (1962b) and S. G. Clawson.

Least Tern, Warren Co., June 1, 1937, 2 eggs; Harrison Co., Cat Island, May 15, 1938, 2 eggs; Jackson Co., Pascagoula landfill, May 13, 1962, 2 eggs, colony of 400 pairs.

Black Skimmer, Jackson Co., Pascagoula marsh landfill, June 4, 1962, 2 eggs, colony of 150 pairs; Petit Bois Island, July 18, 1962, 50 pairs, L. E. Williams Jr. (1962b).

Rock Dove, Hinds Co., Clinton, July 12, 1931, 2 eggs.

Mourning Dove, Hinds Co., Clinton, June 14, 1930, 2 eggs; Rankin Co., Brandon, March 24, 1993, nest and 2 young, D. L. Watts (pers. comm.).

Common Ground-Dove, George Co., June 18–28, 1995, nest with 2 young fledglings, photograph.

Yellow-billed Cuckoo, Hinds Co., Clinton, June 9, 1932, 4 eggs.

Barn Owl, Hinds Co., Baker's Creek, 2 miles south of Clinton, April 2, 1942, 5 eggs.

Eastern Screech-Owl, Hinds Co., Clinton, April 11, 1933, 3 eggs.

Great Horned Owl, Hinds Co., Bogue Chitto Creek north of Clinton, January 25, 1942, 2 eggs.

Barred Owl, Hinds Co., Bogue Chitto Creek north of Clinton, February 16, 1941, 2 eggs; February 20, 1942, 3 eggs.

Common Nighthawk, Hinds Co., Clinton, May 21, 1932, 2 eggs.

Chuck-will's-widow, Hinds Co., May 31, 1933, 2 eggs; May 5, 1946, 2 eggs.

Whip-poor-will, Oktibbeha Co., June 22, 1992, photograph of small downy chick by D. McEwen (Muth 1992).

Chimney Swift, Hinds Co., Clinton, June 1, 1933, 5 eggs.

Ruby-throated Hummingbird, Hinds Co., near Clinton, June 11, 1933, 2 eggs.

Belted Kingfisher, Hinds Co., Clinton, April 17, 1934, 5 eggs; Warren Co., Lake Centennial, May 23, 1938, 5 eggs.

Red-headed Woodpecker, Hinds Co., Clinton, June 22, 1930, 5 eggs.

Red-bellied Woodpecker, Hinds Co., Clinton, May 22, 1931, 5 eggs.

Downy Woodpecker, Jones Co., Bogue Homa, May 28, 1941, 5 eggs.

Hairy Woodpecker, Hinds Co., near Clinton, April 22, 1940, 3 eggs.

Red-cockaded Woodpecker, Rankin Co., Pisgah area, May 23, 1940, 1 egg, D. H. Joyner.

Northern Flicker, Hinds Co., Clinton, May 18, 1930, 18 eggs taken daily from nest, 7 more laid and hatched; Rankin Co., Richland, June 14, 1993, 5 young in nest box, W. H. Turcotte.

Pileated Woodpecker, Tishomingo Co., May 2, 1940, 3 eggs, H. L. Owens.

Eastern Wood-Pewee, Hinds Co., near Clinton, July 5, 1932, 3 eggs.

Acadian Flycatcher, Hinds Co., Caney Creek, south Jackson, May 30, 1941, 3 eggs.

Willow Flycatcher, Tallahatchie Co., June 21 to July 27, 1996, nest with 1 young and 1 Brown-headed Cowbird, both young fledged and flying on August 10, G. and S. Knight and multiple observers.

Eastern Phoebe, Tishomingo Co., April 28, 1957, 4 eggs, W. H. Turcotte.

Great Crested Flycatcher, Hinds Co., Clinton, June 18, 1932, 5 eggs; Rankin Co., Richland, June 14, 1993, nest and 2 young, D. L. Watts (pers. comm.).

Eastern Kingbird, Hinds Co., Clinton, May 20, 1930, 5 eggs; May 26, 1933, 4 eggs.

Scissor-tailed Flycatcher, Lee Co., near Tupelo, July 5–6, 1975, 3 fledged young from nest discovered by W. T. Watson (Jackson and Werschkul 1977); Newton Co., Lawrence, June 20, 1977, female incubating on inaccessible nest, W. H. Turcotte (1977).

Horned Lark, Yazoo Co., Holly Bluff, April 13, 1961, 4 eggs, W. H. Turcotte.

Purple Martin, Hinds Co., Clinton, June 1, 1931, 4 eggs.

Tree Swallow, Lafayette Co., Sardis Lake, May 27 to July 7, 1995, nest and young fledged, photograph, W. M. Davis (1995).

Northern Rough-winged Swallow, Washington Co., near Glen Allen on Lake Washington, April 17, 1940, 7 eggs.

Cliff Swallow, Grenada Co., Grenada Lake, Graysport Crossing, 2 pairs nesting, W. C. Weber (1979b); Hinds Co., Natchez Trace Parkway in agricultural underpass, August 4, 1975, active nest and adults, photograph, W. H. Turcotte (1975a); Hancock Co., Pearlington, drawbridge spanning East Pearl River, June 10, 1986, photograph, 30 pairs nesting, J. L. Spence and J. A. Toups (1986).

Barn Swallow, Rankin Co., Whitfield, June 15, 1961, 5 eggs, 6 eggs in 2 nests under bridge; Claiborne Co., August 4, 1975, 34 nests in Natchez Trace culvert, 2 with eggs, 3 with young, W. H. Turcotte; Wilkinson Co., at Pond community southwest of Woodville, June 8, 1993, nest and 2 young, D. L. Watts (pers. comm.).

Blue Jay, Hinds Co., Clinton, April 14, 1934, 4 eggs.

American Crow, Hinds Co., near Clinton, March 15, 1934, 5 eggs.

Fish Crow, Harrison Co., Pass Christian, May 12, 1962, 12 active inaccessible nests; Jackson Co., Bayou Casotte, June 4, 1962, 1 active nest, L. E. Williams Jr. (1962b).

Carolina Chickadee, Hinds Co., Clinton, April 11, 1931, 4 eggs; Tishomingo Co., May 14, 1993, nest and 5 young, D. L. Watts (pers. comm.).

Tufted Titmouse, Hinds Co., west Jackson, May 31, 1965, pair feeding young in nest box, W. H. Turcotte (1966d); Hinds Co., southwest Jackson, May 7, 1993, nest and 5 eggs, D. L. Watts (pers. comm.); Tishomingo Co., south of Iuka, May 14, 1993, nest and 5 eggs, D. L. Watts (pers. comm.).

White-breasted Nuthatch, Hinds Co., Mayes Lake in north Jackson, April 1–7, 1962, adults feeding young in natural cavity of oak, C. Berry and F. Wills Jr. (1962).

Brown-headed Nuthatch, Leake Co., west of Carthage, April 7, 1941, 5 eggs; 9 miles northeast of Carthage, April 3, 1941, 6 eggs.

Carolina Wren, Hinds Co., Clinton, May 24, 1933, 5 eggs.

Bewick's Wren, Hinds Co., Clinton, May 7, 1940, 7 eggs in open cup nest in can in open shed; Chickasaw Co., northwest of Okolona, 4 eggs.

Marsh Wren, Jackson Co., west of Pascagoula, May 12, 1962, 1 egg; June 3, 1962, 4 eggs, L. E. Williams Jr. (1962b).

Blue-gray Gnatcatcher, Hinds Co., Clinton, May 31, 1933, 5 eggs.

Eastern Bluebird, Hinds Co., Clinton, May 24, 1930, 4 eggs.

Wood Thrush, Hinds Co., Clinton, June 3, 1930, 4 eggs.

American Robin, Hinds Co., Clinton, April 12, 1933, 3 eggs; Hinds Co., Bolton, May 8, 1993, nest and 3 young, D. L. Watts (pers. comm.).

Gray Catbird, Hinds Co., Clinton, May 17, 1930, 4 eggs.

Northern Mockingbird, Hinds Co., Clinton, April 14, 1930, 4 eggs.

Brown Thrasher, Hinds Co., Clinton, May 27, 1930, 4 eggs; Hinds Co., Richland, May 29, 1993, nest and 2 young, D. L. Watts (pers. comm.).

Cedar Waxwing, Oktibbeha Co., summer 1990, 2 localities, nest-building, adult feeding recently fledged young, T. Schiefer (1991).

Loggerhead Shrike, Hinds Co., Clinton, April 3, 1932, 5 eggs.

European Starling, Lee Co., Guntown, 1934, nest in building cavity, J. A. Robins (1934); Harrison Co., Lyman, April 7, 1943, 5 young, T. D. Burleigh (1945).

White-eyed Vireo, Hinds Co., near Clinton in creek swamp, May 28, 1933, 4 eggs.

Yellow-throated Vireo, Chickasaw Co., east of Houlka, April 19, 1962, adult completing nest, W. H. Turcotte (1962b).

Warbling Vireo, Coahoma Co., Sherard area, May 21 and June 16, 1940, 2 sets of eggs.

Red-eyed Vireo, Hinds Co., Hanging Moss Creek north of Jackson, April 30, 1941, 4 eggs.

Northern Parula, Hinds Co., north of Clinton, June 3, 1941, 3 eggs.

Yellow-throated Warbler, Tishomingo Co., Tishomingo State Park on Bear Creek, April 27, 1957, nest-building in tall pine, W. H. Turcotte (1957c).

Pine Warbler, Hinds Co., Clinton, April 9, 1940, 4 eggs.

Prairie Warbler, Marion County Wildlife Area, April 28, 1967, female finishing nest in sweet gum sprout, W. H. Turcotte and J. H. Phares (1967); Hancock Co., May 22, 1986, nestling photograph, J. A. Toups and D. King.

Black-and-white Warbler, Warren Co., April 19, 1963, color slide in MMNS, nest and 6 eggs; Rankin Co., 2 miles south of Star, May 14, 1942, preserved nestling specimen, MMNS.

American Redstart, Rankin Co., Meek's Ferry Bridge, May 10, 1958, pair at completed nest in elm tree, W. H. Turcotte (1958c).

Prothonotary Warbler, Lauderdale Co., Okatibbee Creek, May 16, 1940, 4 eggs; Hinds Co., Pearl River in Jackson, June 8, 1940, 5 eggs; Madison Co., south of Canton, June 1993, nest and 2 eggs, D. L. Watts (pers. comm.); Hinds Co., southeast of Raymond, May 26, 1993, nest and 4 young, D. L. Watts (pers. comm.).

Worm-eating Warbler, Warren Co., Spring Creek bluffs, May 20, 1963, adult feeding fledgling; May 25, 1972, photograph, nest and 4 newly hatched young, W. H. Turcotte (1972f).

Swainson's Warbler, Holmes Co., east of Goodman in Big Black River swamp, June 3, 1940, 3 eggs, W. H. Turcotte (1972d).

Ovenbird, Lowndes Co., May 26, 1895, nest and 5 eggs, C. R. Stockard (1905); Calhoun Co., June 1954 and 1958, 2 nests, N. F. Hanson (1958).

Louisiana Waterthrush, Lauderdale Co., Gin Creek, May 17, 1940, 4 eggs.

Kentucky Warbler, Hinds Co., Clinton, June 18, 1933, 3 eggs.

Common Yellowthroat, Rankin Co., south of Star, May 29, 1940, 5 eggs.

Hooded Warbler, Hinds Co., Jackson, Riverside Drive, June 14, 1940, 3 eggs.

Yellow-breasted Chat, Lauderdale Co., Loper Creek, May 21, 1940, 4 eggs.

Summer Tanager, Hinds Co., near Clinton, May 31, 1932, 4 eggs.

Scarlet Tanager, Lee Co., Guntown, June 8, 1974, adult and fledglings out of nest, R. Howell (1976).

Northern Cardinal, Hinds Co., Clinton, May 4, 1930, 3 eggs.

Blue Grosbeak, Hinds Co., Clinton, May 14, 1931, 4 eggs.

Painted Bunting, Hinds Co., Clinton, May 17, 1933, 2 eggs and 1 egg of Brown-headed Cowbird.

Dickcissel, Hinds Co., Raymond airport, May 16, 1978, nest and 4 eggs, color slide, W. H. Turcotte (1978).

Eastern Towhee, Hinds Co., Clinton, June 4, 1930, 4 eggs.

Bachman's Sparrow, Hinds Co., near Clinton, May 31, 1933, 4 eggs.

Chipping Sparrow, Hinds Co., near Clinton, May 13, 1939, 4 eggs.

Field Sparrow, Hinds Co., near Clinton, June 3, 1931, 3 eggs.

Lark Sparrow, Hinds Co., near Clinton, May 28, 1935, young in nest; May 13, 1936, 4 eggs; May 21, 1942, 5 eggs; Lee Co., June 13, 1940, 2 young out of nest, E. Patton.

Seaside Sparrow, Jackson Co., near Pascagoula marsh, June 23, 1962, nest and 1 egg, L. E. Williams Jr. (1962b).

Red-winged Blackbird, Hinds Co., near Clinton, May 22, 1931, 4 eggs.

Eastern Meadowlark, Hinds Co., near Clinton, May 5, 1933, 5 eggs.

Boat-tailed Grackle, Hancock Co., near mouth of Pearl River, April 23, 1941, 2 nests, 3 eggs each, W. H. Turcotte.

Common Grackle, Hinds Co., Jackson area, April 19, 1941, 5 eggs.

Brown-headed Cowbird, Hinds Co., near Clinton, June 2, 1933, 1 egg from nest of Common Yellowthroat; May 17, 1933, 1 egg and 2 eggs of Painted Bunting.

Orchard Oriole, Hinds Co., near Clinton, June 2, 1932, 4 eggs.

Baltimore Oriole, Hinds Co., near Clinton, May 28, 1933, 5 eggs.

House Finch, Oktibbeha Co., Starkville, July 11, 1986, adults feeding a fledgling at 2 nearby locations, J. A. Jackson and M. F. Hodges Jr. (1986); June 13, 1989, nest and 3 young, M. F. Hodges Jr. (Muth 1989); Hinds Co., downtown Jackson, June 15, 1991, nest and 4 young, nest and 1 egg, female on nest, photographs, W. H. Turcotte and M. Hutto (1991).

Red Crossbill, Winston Co., Noxubee National Wildlife Refuge, February 25, 1976, nest; April 8, 1976, nest-building, hatching, and fledging of young, R. C. Warren et al. (1977).

American Goldfinch, Kemper Co., near Wahalak, June 17, 1976, 3 eggs, eggs taken by predator, nest in MSU collection, R. C. Warren and G. A. Hurst (1979).

House Sparrow, Hinds Co., April 27, 1941, 5 eggs.

Bibliography

Bird Song Records and Cassettes

Borror, D. J., and W. W. H. Gunn. 1985. Songs of the warblers of North America. Three-disk, two-cassette album, 37 species, 37 pp. Ithaca, N.Y.: The Cornell Laboratory of Ornithology, Library of Natural Sounds and the Federation of Ontario Naturalists.

Mississippi Department of Wildlife, Fisheries and Parks. 1985. A guide to Mississippi bird songs. Two 60-minute cassettes, 115 species. Jackson: Mississippi Wildlife Heritage Program.

National Geographic Society. 1983. Bird sounds. Four-disk album, 174 species. Ithaca, N.Y.: The Cornell Laboratory of Ornithology.

Peterson, R. T., ed. 1990. Field guide to bird songs. Two-disk, two-cassette album, 300 species. Boston, Mass.: Houghton Mifflin.

Checklists

Gulf Coast Audubon Society. 1975. Mississippi Coast birds: Field checklist. Available by writing to: J. Dubisson, Treasurer, 22410 Glad Acres, Pass Christian, MS 39571.

Mississippi Ornithological Society. 1991. Birds of Mississippi: Field checklist, 380 species. Available by writing to: Mississippi Museum of Natural Science, 111 N. Jefferson St., Jackson, MS 39202.

Articles and Books

Aldrich, J. 1972. A new subspecies of Sandhill Crane from Mississippi. *Proc. Biol. Soc. Wash.* 85:63–70.

Alexander, G. E. 1973. Cinnamon Teal reported. *MOS Newsletter* 18(4):13.

Alexander, G. E. 1976. Observations of the Vermilion Flycatcher: Washington County, Mississippi. *Miss. Kite* 6(1):2–4.

Allison, A. 1899. The sparrows of Mississippi. *Auk* 16:266–270.

Allison, A. 1900. Louisiana and Mississippi bird notes. *Auk* 17:297.

Allison, A. 1906a. Notes from Hancock County, Mississippi. *Auk* 23:232–233.

Allison, A. 1906b. Notes on the winter birds of Hancock County, Mississippi. *Auk* 23:44–47.

Allison, A. 1907. Notes on the spring birds of Tishomingo County, Mississippi. *Auk* 24:12–25.

Austin, L., M. Powell, J. Spence, and H. Wessel. 1984. Another Great Cormorant on the Mississippi Gulf Coast. *Miss. Kite* 14(2):10–11.

Banko, W. E. 1960. The Trumpeter Swan: Its history, habits, and population in the United States. *North American Fauna.* No. 63.

Battalio, J. 1987. 1986 fall hawk migration over Vicksburg, Mississippi. *Miss. Kite* 17(2):17–22.

Bellrose, F. C. 1976. *Ducks, geese, and swans of North America.* Harrisburg, Pa.: Stackpole Books.

Bent, A. C. 1919. Life histories of North American diving birds. *U.S. Natl. Mus. Bull.* No. 107.

Bent, A. C. 1921. Life histories of North American gulls and terns. *U.S. Natl. Mus. Bull.* No. 113.

Bent, A. C. 1922. Life histories of North American petrels and pelicans and their allies. *U.S. Natl. Mus. Bull.* No. 121.

Bent, A. C. 1923–1925. Life histories of North American wild fowl. *U.S. Natl. Mus. Bull.* Nos. 126 and 130.

Bent, A. C. 1926. Life histories of North American marsh birds. *U.S. Natl. Mus. Bull.* No. 135.

Bent, A. C. 1927–1929. Life histories of North American shore birds. *U.S. Natl. Mus. Bull.* Nos. 142 and 146.

Bent, A. C. 1932. Life histories of North American gallinaceous birds. *U.S. Natl. Mus. Bull.* No. 162.

Bent, A. C. 1937–1938. Life histories of North American birds of prey. *U.S. Natl. Mus. Bull.* Nos. 167 and 170.

Bent, A. C. 1939. Life histories of North American woodpeckers. *U.S. Natl. Mus. Bull.* No. 174.

Bent, A. C. 1940. Life histories of North American cuckoos, goatsuckers, hummingbirds, and their allies. *U.S. Natl. Mus. Bull.* No. 176.

Bent, A. C. 1942. Life histories of North American flycatchers, larks, swallows, and their allies. *U.S. Natl. Mus. Bull.* No. 179.

Bent, A. C. 1946. Life histories of North American jays, crows, and titmice. *U.S. Natl. Mus. Bull.* No. 191.

Bent, A. C. 1948. Life histories of North American nuthatches, wrens, thrashers, and their allies. *U.S. Natl. Mus. Bull.* No. 195.

Bent, A. C. 1949. Life histories of North American thrushes, kinglets, and their allies. *U.S. Natl. Mus. Bull.* No. 196.

Bent, A. C. 1950. Life histories of North American wagtails, shrikes, vireos, and their allies. *U.S. Natl. Mus. Bull.* No. 197.

Bent, A. C. 1953. Life histories of North American wood warblers. *U.S. Natl. Mus. Bull.* No. 203.

Bent, A. C. 1958. Life histories of North American blackbirds, orioles, tanagers, and allies. *U.S. Natl. Mus. Bull.* No. 211.

Bent, A. C. 1968. Life histories of North American cardinals, grosbeaks, buntings, towhees, finches, sparrows, and allies. *U.S. Natl. Mus. Bull.* No. 237.

Berry, C., and F. Wills. 1962. White-breasted Nuthatch nesting. *MOS Newsletter* 7(3):15.

Blockstein, D. E., and H. B. Tordoff. 1985. Gone forever: A contemporary look at the extinction of the Passenger Pigeon. *Am. Birds* 39:845–851.

Boise, C. M. 1979. Lesser Sandhill Crane banding program on the Yukon-Kuskokwim Delta, Alaska. In *Proceedings of the 1978 crane workshop (Rockport, Texas),* ed. J. C. Lewis, 229–236. Fort Collins: Colorado State University Printing Service.

Brown, A. J. 1964. *History of Newton County, Mississippi, from 1834 to 1894.* Decatur, Miss.: Melvin Tingle.

Burleigh, T. D. 1945. *The bird life of the Gulf Coast region of Mississippi.* Jackson: Mississippi Game and Fish Commission. Reprinted from *LSU Mus. Zool. Occas. Papers* No. 20, 1944.

Caylor, R. L. 1936. A north Mississippi heronry. *Migrant* 7:44–45.

Clark, W. S., and B. K. Wheeler. 1987. *A field guide to hawks of North America.* Boston, Mass.: Houghton Mifflin.

Clawson, S. G. 1961. Late note—Noddy found at Gulfport. *MOS Newsletter* 6(5):9.

Clawson, S. G. 1962. Black-headed Grosbeak specimen collected. *MOS Newsletter* 7(2):10.

Clawson, S. G., and L. E. Williams. 1962. Gray Kingbird. *MOS Newsletter* 7(3):12.

Coffey, B. B. 1931. Snowy Owl visitors. *Migrant* 2(1):7.

Coffey, B. B. 1936. A preliminary list of the birds of Mississippi. Unpublished manuscript. Jackson: Mississippi Museum of Natural Science Library.

Coffey, B. B. 1940. Prairie Horned Lark notes (Miss.-Tenn.). *Migrant* 11:78–79.

Coffey, B. B. 1941a. The season: Memphis area. *Migrant* 12:35–36.

Coffey, B. B. 1941b. Heron banding. *Migrant* 12:26.

Coffey, B. B. 1951. Swallow-tailed Kite at Lakeview, Mississippi. *Migrant* 22:41.

Coffey, B. B. 1952. Double-crested Cormorants nesting in Mississippi. *Migrant* 23:31–32.

Coffey, B. B. 1953. American Rough-legged Hawk near Walls, Mississippi. *Mid-South Bird Notes* 2(5):12.

Coffey, B. B. 1956a. Harris' Sparrow in the Mid-south. *Migrant* 27:37–39.

Coffey, B. B. 1956b. The season. *Migrant* 27:16–17.

Coffey, B. B. 1957. Natchez Christmas count and enroute. *MOS Newsletter* 2(1):2.

Coffey, B. B. 1961a. The Sprague's Pipit and Smith's Longspur in Mississippi. *MOS Newsletter* 6(2):1–4.

Coffey, B. B. 1961b. Andrew Allison. Obituary. *MOS Newsletter* 6(3):1–3.

Coffey, B. B. 1970. Summer Whip-poor-wills in Mississippi. *MOS Newsletter* 15(1):6.

Coffey, B. B. 1971. Summer Whip-poor-wills: 1970. *MOS Newsletter* 16(1):2.

Coffey, B. B. 1976. The Eastern Phoebe as a summer resident in Mississippi. *Miss. Kite* 6(2):38–41.

Coffey, B. B., and L. Coffey, comps. 1965. 374. Moon Lake (Lula), Mississippi. *Audubon Field Notes* 19:220.

Coffey, B. B., and L. Coffey. 1971. Whip-poor-will counts, 1971. *MOS Newsletter* 16(3):4–5.

Coleman, E. W. 1961. Woodcock nest—Bolivar County. *MOS Newsletter* 6(3):5.

Commer, M. 1987. *The history of Mississippi's wildlife monarch, the Wild Turkey.* Edgefield, S.C.: National Wild Turkey Federation, Mississippi Chapter.

Committee on Rare and Endangered Species. 1975. *Preliminary list of rare and threatened vertebrates of Mississippi.* Jackson: Mississippi Game and Fish Commission.

Cook, F. A. 1945a. Game birds in Mississippi. Survey bulletin. Jackson: Mississippi State Game and Fish Commission.
Cook, F. A. 1945b. Fur resources of Mississippi. Survey bulletin. Jackson: Mississippi State Game and Fish Commission.
Cook, F. A. 1956. Trip to the Pelican rookery on North Island. *MOS Newsletter* 1(2):4–5.
Cooley, C. D., J. A. Jackson, and D. K. Cavin. 1979a. Blue-faced Booby near Horn Island, Mississippi. *Miss. Kite* 9(2):42.
Cooley, C. D., J. A. Jackson, B. J. Schardien, and F. Swan. 1979b. Band-tailed Pigeon: First state record for Mississippi. *Miss. Kite* 9(1):5–6.
Corrington, J. D. 1922. The winter birds of the Biloxi, Mississippi, region. *Auk* 39:530–556.
Cottam, C. 1944. Starlings feeding on the backs of cattle. *Migrant* 15:24–25.
Covington, M., J. McGee, and J. A. Toups. 1985. Great Black-backed Gull: First Mississippi records. *Miss. Kite* 15(1):9–10.
Cross, R. D., R. W. Wales, and C. T. Traylor. 1974. *Atlas of Mississippi.* Jackson: University Press of Mississippi.
Danna, S. 1963. Scissor-tailed Flycatcher. *MOS Newsletter* 8(1):5.
Davis, W. M. 1970. Inland records and first specimen of Black-legged Kittiwake from Mississippi. *Auk* 87:804.
Davis, W. M. 1971a. Field notes. *MOS Newsletter* 16(1):3–4.
Davis, W. M. 1971b. A specimen of the Little Gull from northern Mississippi. *Auk* 88:437–438.
Davis, W. M., comp. 1973. 501. Grenada, Mississippi. *Am. Birds* 27:347.
Davis, W. M., comp. 1976. 562. Sardis Lake, Mississippi. *Am. Birds* 30:403.
Davis, W. M. 1985. First north Mississippi record of the Red Phalarope. *Miss. Kite* 15(1):2–4.
Davis, W. M. 1986a. North Mississippi records of Black-legged Kittiwake, Little Gull, and Common Black-headed Gull. *Miss. Kite* 16(1):13–16.
Davis, W. M. 1986b. Laughing Gull and Franklin's Gull records from north Mississippi. *Miss. Kite* 16(1):22–23.
Davis, W. M. 1990. A Ruddy Shelduck shot in Panola County, Mississippi. *Miss. Kite* 20(1):2–3.
Davis, W. M. 1992. A guide to birding in the Oxford, Mississippi, area. *Miss. Kite* 22(1):2–10.
Davis, W. M. 1995. Tree Swallows: First documented nesting in Mississippi. *Miss. Kite* 25(2):16–18.
Davis, W. M., and G. Knight. 1989. First Mississippi record of the Mountain Plover. *Miss. Kite* 19(1):2–3.
Davis, W. M., J. T. Fulton, and G. E. Alexander. 1987. Habitat choice of Vermilion Flycatchers wintering in Mississippi. *Miss. Kite* 17(2):14–16.
Davis, W. M., G. Knight, and J. R. Wilson. 1991. Photographic documentation and new sites for the Common Black-headed Gull in Mississippi. *Miss. Kite* 21(2):33–34.
Davis, W. M., G. Knight, S. Knight, and R. Briscoe. 1992. Prairie Falcon: First documented record in Mississippi. *Miss. Kite* 22(2):17–19.
Davis, W. V. 1972. Pine Siskins in Kosciusko. *MOS Newsletter* 17(2):8–9.
Dendy, Mrs. Farris E. 1993. Lazuli Bunting in Oxford, Mississippi. *Miss. Kite* 23(1):12.
Donaldson, P. V. 1978. Hudsonian Godwits at Pascagoula, Mississippi. *Miss. Kite* 8(2):41.
Doren, M. V., ed. 1928. *Travels of William Bartram.* New York, N.Y.: Dover Publications.
Downey, R., E. Tackett, and F. Wills. 1981. Observation of a Franklin's Gull at Ross Barnett Reservoir, Jackson, Mississippi. *Miss. Kite* 11(2):50.
Dunbar, W. 1930. *Life, letters, and papers of William Dunbar of Elgin, Morayshire, Scotland, and Natchez, Mississippi: Pioneer scientist of the southern United States.* Jackson: Press of the Mississippi Historical Society.
Dunne, P., and D. Sibley. 1988. *Hawks in flight: The flight identification of North American migrant raptors.* Boston, Mass.: Houghton Mifflin.
Epple, A. C. 1973. The Evening Grosbeak invasion of 1961–63. *Passenger Pigeon* 24:110–124.
Feduccia, A. 1974. Photograph of Horned Lark nest. *Miss. Kite* 4(1):frontispiece.
Floyd, E. 1964. Gray Kingbird. *MOS Newsletter* 9(1):2.
Freeman, B. O. 1961. Nighthawk concentration. *MOS Newsletter* 6(5):8.
Fulton, J. 1987. Ross' Goose in Mississippi. *Miss. Kite* 17(1):2–4.
Gandy, B. E. 1962a. Evening Grosbeak specimen collected. *MOS Newsletter* 7(2):10.
Gandy, B. E. 1962b. Evening Grosbeaks in Jackson until May 2, 1962. *MOS Newsletter* 7(3):16.
Gandy, B. E. 1962c. Glossy Ibis records for Hancock County, Mississippi, confirmed. *MOS Newsletter* 7(4):21.
Gandy, B. E. 1962d. King Eider collected at Pascagoula, Mississippi. *MOS Newsletter* 7(4):20.
Gandy, B. E. 1963. Charts showing seasonal occurrence of Mississippi birds. Unpublished manuscript. Jackson: Mississippi Museum of Natural Science Library.
Gandy, B. E. 1965a. In memoriam: Miss Fannye Cook. *Miss. Kite* 1(1):8–10.
Gandy, B. E. 1965b. The Prairie Warbler. *Miss. Kite* 1(1):16–17.
Gandy, B. E. 1969. *A preliminary check list of the vertebrates of Mississippi.* 2d rev. ed. Jackson, Miss.: State Wildlife Museum.
Gandy, B. E., and W. H. Turcotte. 1970. *Catalog of Mississippi bird records.* Vol. 1, *Loons through flycatchers.* Jackson, Miss.: State Wildlife Museum.
Ganier, A. F. 1902. The Mississippi Kite *(Ictinia mississippiensis). The Osprey* 6:85–90.
Ganier, A. F. 1963. Mississippi Kite nests. *MOS Newsletter* 8(1):10.
Ganier, A. F. 1973. Mississippi Kites at home. *Miss. Kite* 3(1):frontispiece.
Gates, L. 1975a. King Eider record in Hattiesburg area. *MOS Newsletter* 20(1):2–3.

Gates, L. 1975b. Spring bird records for Hattiesburg, Mississippi (1975). *MOS Newsletter* 20(3):19–20.

Gates, L. 1976. Northern Phalarope in Hattiesburg, Mississippi. *Miss. Kite* 6(2):37.

Gates, L., comp. 1979. 599. Jackson County, Mississippi. *Am. Birds* 33:508.

Gates, L., comp. 1980. 628. Jackson County, Mississippi. *Am. Birds* 34:508–509.

Gates, L., comp. 1982. 687. Jackson County, Mississippi. *Am. Birds* 36:580.

Gates, L., comp. 1987. JC MS. Jackson County, Mississippi. *Am. Birds* 42:850.

Gates, L., and T. Fairley. 1979. Bridled Tern: First observation of a live bird in Mississippi. *Miss. Kite* 9(2):40–41.

Gates, L., and T. Gates, comps. 1985. 722. Jackson County, Mississippi. *Am. Birds* 39:613–614.

Gates, L., and J. Izral. 1982. Observations of a Black-whiskered Vireo on the Mississippi Coast. *Miss. Kite* 12(1):5.

Gates, L., and J. R. Moore. 1978. A Red-necked Grebe in Hattiesburg, Mississippi. *Miss. Kite* 8(2):40.

Gates, L., and J. Runzo. 1978. A Red Phalarope in Hattiesburg, Mississippi. *Miss. Kite* 8(1):2.

Gates, L., M. Hamilton, D. Hamilton, and T. Fairley. 1980. Lark Buntings in Mississippi. *Miss. Kite* 10(1):5–6.

Grant, P. J. 1982. *Gulls: A guide to identification.* Staffordshire, England: T. & A. D. Poyser, Calton, Waterhouses.

Greene, E. R. 1946. Great White Heron in Mississippi. *Auk* 63:104–105.

Grissom, C. E., J. E. Ballew, R. D. Caldwell, and R. E. Bell. 1963. A checklist of the birds of the loess hills of Warren County, Mississippi. Unpublished manuscript. Excerpted in *MOS Newsletter* 8(3):18–19.

Gruber, K. 1987. *Encyclopedia of associations. National organizations of the United States.* Vol. 1. Detroit, Mich.: Gale Research.

Grzybowski, J. A., and V. W. Fazio. 1991. Shiny Cowbird reaches Oklahoma. *Am. Birds* 45:50–52.

Gunter, G. 1972. Peculiar mass movements of Blue Jays along the Alabama, Mississippi, and Louisiana coasts in October 1972. *MOS Newsletter* 17(5):21–22.

Gunter, G. 1975. Further information on mass movements of Blue Jays on the Alabama, Mississippi, and Louisiana coasts in October 1972. *Miss. Kite* 5(1):4–7.

Gunter, G., and W. D. Burke. 1977. Notes on the status of the Gannet *(Morus bassanus)* in the Gulf of Mexico, with a record from Mississippi. *Gulf Res. Ref.* 6:83–86.

Haberyan, H. D. 1960. Black-throated Gray Warbler. *MOS Newsletter* 5(5):5–6.

Haberyan, H. D. 1961. Gulf Coast notes. *MOS Newsletter* 6(3):4–5.

Haberyan, H. D. 1962a. Bird and bird banding notes—Gulfport area. *MOS Newsletter* 7(1):4–5.

Haberyan, H. D. 1962b. Gulf Coast notes. *MOS Newsletter* 7(3):13–14.

Haberyan, H. D. 1963a. Fall and winter Gulf Coast notes. *MOS Newsletter* 8(1):6–7.

Haberyan, H. D. 1963b. Four hours on Horn Island—23 May 1963. *MOS Newsletter* 8(3):13–15.

Hahn, P. 1963. *Where is that vanished bird?* Toronto: Royal Ontario Museum and the University of Toronto Press.

Hamel, P. B. 1986. *Bachman's Warbler, a species in peril.* Washington, D.C.: Smithsonian Institution Press.

Hamilton, R. B. 1979. Central southern region. *Am. Birds* 33:287–290.

Hamilton, R. B. 1980. Central southern region. *Am. Birds* 34:279–282.

Hamilton, R. B. 1981. Central southern region. *Am. Birds* 35:307–309.

Hanson, N. F. 1958. Ovenbird nesting. *MOS Newsletter* 3(3):4.

Hayman, P., J. Marchant, and T. Prater. 1986. *Shorebirds: An identification guide to waders of the world.* Boston, Mass.: Houghton Mifflin.

Hays, M. B. 1978. Snowy Plovers nesting on the mainland in Mississippi. *Miss. Kite* 8(2):34–36.

Hays, M. B. 1979. First record of the Bridled Tern in Mississippi. *Miss. Kite* 9(2):39.

Hays, M. B. 1980. Breeding biology of the Least Tern, *Sterna albifrons,* on the Gulf Coast of Mississippi. Master's thesis, Mississippi State University.

Headstrom, R. 1949. *Birds' nests: A field guide.* New York, N.Y.: Ives Washburn.

Herbert, N., and D. R. Simons. 1991. Trumpeter Swan in Bolivar County, Mississippi. *Miss. Kite* 21(2):29–32.

Hewitt, O. H., ed. 1967. *The Wild Turkey and its management.* Washington, D.C.: The Wildlife Society.

Hodges, M. F., comp. 1985. Birds around the state: December 1984–November 1985. *Miss. Kite* 15(2):24–38.

Hodges, M. F. 1986. First sighting of the Sooty Shearwater in Mississippi. *Miss. Kite* 16(2):42–43.

Hodges, M. F., comp. 1987. Birds around the state: December 1986–November 1987. *Miss. Kite* 17(2):27–46.

Hodges, M. F, comp. 1988. Birds around the state: December 1987–November 1988. *Miss. Kite* 18(2):11–37.

Hodges, M. F. 1989. Aqua incognita: Birding catfish farms in northwest Mississippi. *Birding* 21:288–292.

Hodges, M. F., and J. A. Jackson, comps. 1984. Birds around the state: December 1983–November 1984. *Miss. Kite* 14(2):12–25.

Hodges, M. F., and J. A. Toups. 1979. Bronzed Cowbird: First Mississippi records. *Miss. Kite* 9(1):2–4.

Hodges, M. F., and J. A. Toups. 1981. A flock of Franklin's Gulls in Bay St. Louis, Mississippi. *Miss. Kite* 11(1):17.

Hodges, M. F., and J. A. Toups. 1986. Broad-winged Hawk: Confirmation of nesting on the Mississippi Coast. *Miss. Kite* 16(2):45.

Hoover, E. B. 1971. Observation on Leach's Petrel. *MOS Newsletter* 16(1):4–5.

Howell, R. 1976. Scarlet Tanager breeding in Lee County. *Miss. Kite* 6(1):4–5.

Hurst, G. A. 1972. Woodcock nest recorded. *MOS Newsletter* 17(3):14.

Imhof, T. A., comp. 1962. Central southern region. *Audubon Field Notes* 16:43–47.

Imhof, T. A. 1976. *Alabama birds.* 2d ed. Tuscaloosa: University of Alabama Press.

Imhof, T. A. 1978. Central southern region. *Am. Birds* 32:1017–1021.

Imhof, T. A., ed. 1980. Tennessee, Alabama, Mississippi. *Am. Birds* 34:342–343.

Imhof, T. A., ed. 1983. Central southern region. *Am. Birds* 37:878–882.

Imhof, T. A., ed. 1984. Tennessee, Alabama, Mississippi. *Am. Birds* 38:417–418.

Imhof, T. A., ed. 1989. Tennessee, Alabama, Mississippi. *Am. Birds* 43:585–586.

Imhof, T. A. 1993. Tennessee, Alabama, Mississippi. *Am. Birds* 47:503–504.

Izral, J. A. 1982. First Mississippi nesting record for the Swallow-tailed Kite. *Miss. Kite* 12(1):8.

Jackson, G. D. 1991. Central southern region. *Am. Birds* 45:113–114.

Jackson, J. A. 1973. First record of the Red Crossbill in Mississippi. *Miss. Kite* 3(1):3–4.

Jackson, J. A. 1974. The Evening Grosbeak in Mississippi. *Miss. Kite* 4(1):2–8.

Jackson, J. A. 1975. The Yellow-headed Blackbird in Mississippi. *Miss. Kite* 5(1):7–8.

Jackson, J. A., comp. 1976a. Birds around the state. *Miss. Kite* 6(1):14–19.

Jackson, J. A. 1976b. Some aspects of the nesting ecology of Least Terns on the Mississippi Gulf Coast. *Miss. Kite* 6(2):25–35.

Jackson, J. A., comp. 1979. Birds around the state: June and July 1979. *Miss. Kite* 9(2):43–45.

Jackson, J. A., ed. 1981a. The "Mid-south bird notes" of Ben B. Coffey Jr. *Special Publ. Mississippi Ornithological Society* No. 1.

Jackson, J. A., ed. 1981b. In memoriam: Burton S. Webster. *Miss. Kite* 11(1):35.

Jackson, J. A., comp. 1981c. Birds around the state: June 1980–May 1981. *Miss. Kite* 11(1):18–34.

Jackson, J. A. 1981d. The House Finch, a new species in Mississippi. *Miss. Kite* 11(1):7–9.

Jackson, J. A., comp. 1982. Birds around the state: January–December 1982. *Miss. Kite* 12(2):14–31.

Jackson, J. A. 1986. Great Cormorant at the Pascagoula River marsh, Mississippi. *Miss. Kite* 16(2):49.

Jackson, J. A. 1988. The history of Ivory-billed Woodpeckers in Mississippi. *Miss. Kite* 18(1):3–10.

Jackson, J. A. 1989. Past history, habitats, and present status of the Ivory-billed Woodpecker *(Campephilus principalis)* in North America. Final report. Atlanta, Ga.: U.S. Fish and Wildlife Service.

Jackson, J. A. 1990. 10-volume index to the Mississippi Kite, 1981–1990. *Miss. Kite* 20:32–62.

Jackson, J. A., and C. D. Cooley, comps. 1978. Birds around the state: December 1977–November 1978. *Miss. Kite* 8(2):48–62.

Jackson, J. A., and C. D. Cooley. 1980. A Noddy Tern from Horn Island, Mississippi. *Miss. Kite* 10(1):4–5.

Jackson, J. A., and M. F. Hodges, comps. 1986. Birds around the state: June–November 1986. *Miss. Kite* 16(2):50–60.

Jackson, J. A., and B. J. S. Jackson. 1985. Status, dispersion, and population changes of the Least Tern in coastal Mississippi. *Colonial Waterbirds* 8:54–62.

Jackson, J. A., and B. Schardien, comps. 1979. Birds around the state: December 1978–May 1979. *Miss. Kite* 9(1):16–26.

Jackson, J. A., and B. Schardien, comps. 1980a. Birds around the state: August 1979–May 1980. *Miss. Kite* 10(1):10–20.

Jackson, J. A., and B. J. Schardien. 1980b. The Red-breasted Merganser as a summer bird on the Mississippi Coast. *Miss. Kite* 10(1):8–9.

Jackson, J. A., and J. R. Watson. 1983. Nesting of the American Coot at Noxubee National Wildlife Refuge, Mississippi. *Miss. Kite* 13(1):4–5.

Jackson, J. A., and W. C. Weber, comps. 1976. Birds around the state. *Miss. Kite* 6(2):47–54.

Jackson, J. A., and W. C. Weber, comps. 1977. Birds around the state: Winter 1976–77. *Miss. Kite* 7(1):27–30.

Jackson, J. A., and D. Werschkul. 1977. Recent records of the Scissor-tailed Flycatcher in Mississippi. *Miss. Kite* 7(2):34–35.

Jackson, J. A., M. W. Roberts, and J. E. Wright. 1972. The winter roosts and food habits of Marsh Hawks in east central Mississippi. *Miss. Kite* 2(2):25–32.

Jackson, J. A., D. Werschkul, R. Howell, and T. Darden. 1976. Extension of the known breeding range of the Eastern Phoebe in Mississippi. *Miss. Kite* 6(1):6.

Jackson, J. A., C. D. Cooley, and B. J. Schardien. 1978. Sooty Terns on Horn Island, Mississippi. *Miss. Kite* 8(2):42.

Jackson, J. A., B. J. Schardien, and C. D. Cooley. 1979. Dispersion, phenology, and population sizes of nesting colonial seabirds on the Mississippi Gulf Coast. Proceedings of the 1979 conference. *Colonial Waterbird Group* 3:145–155.

Jackson, J. A., B. J. S. Jackson, and M. F. Hodges. 1986. First breeding of the House Finch in Mississippi. *Miss. Kite* 16(1):10–12.

James, F. C., comp. 1960. Central southern region. *Audubon Field Notes* 14:314–318.

James, F. C., comp. 1965. Central southern region. *Audubon Field Notes* 19:385–388.

Jenkins, W. 1933. *Wildlife of Mississippi.* Natchez, Miss.: Reporter Printing Co.

Johnson, B. C., and J. H. Phares. 1959. Ground Doves. *MOS Newsletter* 4(3):3.

Kaufman, K. 1990. *A field guide to advanced birding: Birding challenges and how to approach them.* Boston, Mass.: Houghton Mifflin.

King, D. S. 1985. Brown Noddy sighted in Gulfport, Mississippi. *Miss. Kite* 15(2):18–19.
King, D. S., J. A. Toups, and M. F. Hodges. 1985a. 1985 Sooty Tern sightings along the Mississippi Coast. *Miss. Kite* 15(2):14–15.
King, D. S., J. A. Toups, and M. F. Hodges. 1985b. First sightings of Wilson's Storm-Petrel on the Mississippi Gulf Coast. *Miss. Kite* 15(2):22–23.
Leopold, A. 1929. Report on a game survey of Mississippi submitted to the Game Restoration Committee, Sporting Arms and Ammunition Manufacturers' Institute. Unpublished manuscript. Jackson: Mississippi Museum of Natural Science Library.
Lincecum, G. 1874a. Personal reminiscences of an octogenarian. *The American Sportsman* 4(April–October):374.
Lincecum, G. 1874b. The nesting of Wild Pigeons. *The American Sportsman* 4(April–October):194–195.
Lowery, G. H. 1974. *Louisiana birds.* Baton Rouge: Louisiana State University Press.
Mackler, D. G., and R. A. Hall. 1986. First Mississippi record of the Cave Swallow. *Miss. Kite* 16(2):44.
Madge, S., and H. Burn. 1987. *Wildfowl: An identification guide to the ducks, geese, and swans of the world.* London: Christopher Helm.
Hayman, P., J. Marchant, and T. Prater. 1986. *Shorebirds: An identification guide.* Boston, Mass.: Houghton Mifflin.
McGee, J. M. 1986. A sight record of Townsend's Solitaire in Newton County, Mississippi. *Miss. Kite* 16(1):26–27.
McGraw, K. A., M. R. Smith, W. D. Burke, and G. Gunter. 1973. Mass migration of Blue Jays along offshore Mississippi and Louisiana islands. *Miss. Kite* 3(1):2–3.
McIlhenny, E. A. 1938. Florida Crane, a resident of Mississippi. *Auk* 55:598–602.
McKinley, D. 1981. The Carolina Parakeet in Mississippi: An historical review. *Miss. Kite* 11(1):2–6.
Meanley, B. 1971. Natural history of the Swainson's Warbler. *North American Fauna* No. 69.
Mississippi Game and Fish Commission. 1978. Mississippi statewide wildlife habitat and population inventory. Jackson: Mississippi Game and Fish Commission.
Monette, J. W. 1824–1851. Drafts of chapters of a projected six-volume work to be called "The valley of the Mississippi." Ann Arbor: University of Michigan, Clements Library, Division of Manuscripts.
Moore, H. 1988. Nesting of White Ibis in Warren County, Mississippi. *Miss. Kite* 18(1):1–2.
Moore, H. 1989. Lewis Patrick Cashman Jr. 1916–1988. *Miss. Kite* 19(1):12.
Moore, J. R., T. Fairley, and P. S. Rodriguez. 1980. An October record for the Tree Sparrow in Hattiesburg, Mississippi. *Miss. Kite* 10(1):7.
Moore, J. R., T. Fairley, D. Hamilton, and P. Rodriguez. 1981. Observations on a Red Phalarope in Hattiesburg, Mississippi. *Miss. Kite* 11(1):15–17.
Moreton, S. E. 1943. Starlings remove larvae from backs of cattle. *Migrant* 14:54–55.
Muth, D. P. 1985. Central southern region. *Am. Birds* 39:175–179.
Muth, D. P. 1989. Central southern region. *Am. Birds* 43:323–328.
Muth, D. P. 1991. Central southern region. *Am. Birds* 45:455–460.
Muth, D. P. 1992. Central southern region. *Am. Birds* 46:1144–1146.
Myers, B. M. 1960. Red-throated Loon. *MOS Newsletter* 5(4):6.
National Geographic Society. 1987. *Field guide to the birds of North America.* 2d ed. Washington, D.C.: National Geographic Society.
Newman, R. J. 1955. Central southern region. *Audubon Field Notes* 9:31–34.
Newman, R. J. 1956. Central southern region. *Audubon Field Notes* 10:387–390.
Newman, R. J. 1957. Central southern region. *Audubon Field Notes* 11:350–357.
Noble, R. E. 1967. An investigation of the status of the Sandhill Crane in Mississippi. Report of the Pittman-Robertson Project 98-R. Jackson: Mississippi Game and Fish Commission.
Noble, R. E. 1971. Woodcock. *MOS Newsletter* 16(3):5.
Peterson, R. T. 1980. *A field guide to the birds: A completely new guide to all the birds of eastern and central North America.* 4th ed. Boston, Mass.: Houghton Mifflin.
Peterson, R. T. 1984. Least Terns find sandy salvation on man-made beach. *Smithsonian* 15(1):68–74.
Peterson, R. T. 1988. My greatest birding moment. *Audubon* (Suppl.) 90(2):64.
Peterson, R. T., G. Mountfort, and P. A. D. Hollom. 1967. *A field guide to the birds of Britain and Europe.* 2d rev. ed. Boston, Mass.: Houghton Mifflin.
Peterson, S., and W. H. Turcotte, comps. 1990. JA MS. Jackson, Mississippi. *Am. Birds* 44:771.
Peterson, S. W. 1975. First record of a Saw-whet Owl in Mississippi. *MOS Newsletter* 20(2):8.
Pettingill, O. S. 1970. *Ornithology in laboratory and field.* 4th ed. Minneapolis, Minn.: Burgess Publishing Co.
Pettingill, O. S. 1977. *A guide to bird finding east of the Mississippi.* New York, N.Y.: Oxford University Press.
Phares, J. H. 1958. Long-eared Owls. *MOS Newsletter* 3(4):4.
Phares, J. H. 1970. Camille victims. *MOS Newsletter* 15(1):4.
Phares, J. H. 1975. Cliff Swallows nesting—Itawamba County. *MOS Newsletter* 20(3):21.
Phares, J. H., and S. C. Thompson. 1958. Man-o'-war-birds blown inland by storm. *MOS Newsletter* 3(1):1.
Phares, J. H., and A. B. Tolman. 1958. Vermilion Flycatcher. *MOS Newsletter* 3(4):3.
Portnoy, J. W. 1977. Nesting colonies of seabirds and wading birds: Coastal Louisiana, Mississippi, and Alabama. U.S. Fish and Wildlife Service, Biological Services Program, FWS/OBS-77-07.
Purrington, R. D. 1979. Central southern region. *Am. Birds* 33:185–188.

Purrington, R. D. 1983. Central southern region. *Am. Birds* 37:189–192.
Purrington, R. D. 1984. Central southern region. *Am. Birds* 38:211–214.
Purrington, R. D. 1986. Central southern region. *Am. Birds* 40:124–130.
Purrington, R. D. 1990. Central southern region. *Am. Birds* 44:1143–1147.
Purrington, R. D. 1991. Central southern region. *Am. Birds* 45:1124–1128.
Purrington, R. D. 1995. Central southern region. *Nat. Aud. Soc. Field Notes* 49:937–941.
Reed, C. A. 1965. *North American bird eggs*. Rev. ed. New York, N.Y.: Dover Publications.
Riley, F. L. 1906. Life and literary services of Dr. John W. Monette. *Publications of the Mississippi Historical Society* 9:199–237.
Robbins, C. S., B. Bruun, and H. S. Zim. 1966. *Birds of North America: A guide to field identification.* New York, N.Y.: Golden Press.
Robbins, C. S., J. R. Sauer, R. Greenberg, and S. Droege. 1989. Population declines in North American birds that migrate to the Neotropics. *Proc. Nat. Acad. Sci.* 86:7658–7662.
Robins, J. A. 1934. Starlings westward. *Migrant* 5:42.
Rowland, D. 1907. *Mississippi: Comprising sketches of counties, towns, events, institutions, and persons, arranged in cyclopedic form.* Vol. 2. Atlanta, Ga.: Southern Historical Publishing Association.
Russell, R. 1991. Pictorial highlights: Summer 1991. *Am. Birds* 45:1179–1181.
Sanders, J. A. 1976. A Northern Phalarope in Attala County, Mississippi. *Miss. Kite* 6(2):36.
Sanders, J. A. 1977. A Black-headed Grosbeak in Attala County, Mississippi. *Miss. Kite* 7(1):18–19.
Sanderson, G. C., ed. 1977. *Management of migratory shore and upland game birds in North America.* Washington, D.C.: International Association of Fish and Wildlife Agencies.
Schardien, B. J., and J. A. Jackson, comps. 1983. Birds around the state: January–December 1983. *Miss. Kite* 13(2):15–28.
Schiefer, T. L., comp. 1990. Birds around the state: December 1988–December 1989. *Miss. Kite* 20(1):8–30.
Schiefer, T. L., comp. 1991. Birds around the state: January–December 1990. *Miss. Kite* 21(1):7–27.
Schiefer, T. L., comp. 1992. Birds around the state: January–December 1991. *Miss. Kite* 22(2):20–42.
Schiefer, T. L., and M. F. Hodges. 1987. Baird's Sandpipers in Oktibbeha County, with a review of previous records for the state. *Miss. Kite* 17(1):8–10.
Schiefer, T. L., and M. F. Hodges. 1990. First inland sighting of Gull-billed Tern in Mississippi. *Miss. Kite* 20(1):6–7.
Schueler, D. G. 1980. *Preserving the Pascagoula.* Jackson: University Press of Mississippi.
Schultz, L. 1988. The hummers of summer. *Mississippi Outdoors* 51(4):7–10.
Sciple, G. W. 1950. Recent record of Bachman's Warbler, *Vermivora bachmanii,* from Gulf Coast of Mississippi. *Auk* 67:520.
Smith, D. 1957. The season: Memphis. *Migrant* 28:6–8.
Smith, P. W., and A. Sprunt. 1987. The Shiny Cowbird reaches the United States. *Am. Birds* 41:370–371.
Sorenson, M. F., and S. M. Carney. 1972. Species, age and sex of ducks bagged in the 1971 hunting season in comparison to prior years. *Bur. Sport Fish. and Wildl. Adm. Rep.* 218.
Spence, J. L., and J. A. Toups. 1986. First nesting of the Cliff Swallow on the Mississippi Coast. *Miss. Kite* 16(1):20–21.
Stedman, S. J. 1991. Central southern region. *Am. Birds* 45:282–286.
Stedman, S. J. 1992. Central southern region. *Am. Birds* 46:274–279.
Stedman, S. J. 1996. Central southern region. *Nat. Aud. Soc. Field Notes* 50:179–182.
Stevenson, H. M. 1945. Notes on the birds of north Mississippi. *Migrant* 16:41–44.
Stewart, J. R., comp. 1964. Central southern region. *Audubon Field Notes* 18:512–515.
Stockard, C. R. 1904. Nesting habits of the woodpeckers and the vultures in Mississippi. *Auk* 21:463–471.
Stockard, C. R. 1905. Nesting habits of birds in Mississippi. *Auk* 22:146–158; 273–288.
Strong, L. 1972. Utilization of artificial nesting structures by Hooded Mergansers in Mississippi. *Miss. Kite* 2(2):23–24.
Sullivan, E. G. 1962. Evening Grosbeaks in Franklin County. *MOS Newsletter* 7(2):9.
Sullivan, J. 1992. Sinking in the Shawnee. *Living Bird* 11(4):14–19.
Sunby, P. 1986. Sight record of a Purple Sandpiper in coastal Mississippi. *Miss. Kite* 16(2):48.
Tabor, A. R. 1958. Kites and Ospreys. *MOS Newsletter* 3(3):2–3.
Tanner, J. T. 1942. The Ivory-billed Woodpecker. *National Audubon Society Research Report* No. 1.
Theobald, V., and W. M. Davis. 1986. North Mississippi sighting of a Vermilion Flycatcher. *Miss. Kite* 16(1):19.
Tolman, M. 1958. Lapland Longspurs in Pearl River County. *MOS Newsletter* 3(2):2.
Tolman, M. 1959. Fourth annual meeting. *MOS Newsletter* 4(2):1–2.
Toups, J. A. 1976. A brief history of efforts to protect the Least Tern on the Mississippi Coast. *Miss. Kite* 6(2):22–24.
Toups, J. A., comp. 1978. 597. Southern Hancock County, Mississippi. *Am. Birds* 32:665–666.
Toups, J. A. 1980a. 10-volume index to the Mississippi Kite, 1965–1980. *Miss. Kite* 10:26–52.
Toups, J. A., comp. 1980b. 633. Southern Hancock County, Mississippi. *Am. Birds* 34:510.
Toups, J. A. 1985. First Mississippi records of Lesser Black-backed Gull. *Miss. Kite* 15(1):7–8.
Toups, J. A., and P. V. Donaldson. 1979. First Mississippi breeding record of Blue-winged Teal. *Miss. Kite* 9(1):14–15.

Toups, J. A., and M. F. Hodges. 1980. Olivaceous Cormorant: First Mississippi record. *Miss. Kite* 10(1):2–3.

Toups, J. A., and M. F. Hodges. 1981a. House Finch on the Mississippi Coast. *Miss. Kite* 11(1):10–11.

Toups, J. A., and M. F. Hodges. 1981b. Lark Bunting in Mississippi: Photographic documentation. *Miss. Kite* 11(1):11–13.

Toups, J. A., and M. F. Hodges. 1985. Mississippi Jaeger sightings: Fall 1985. *Miss. Kite* 15(2):20–21.

Toups, J. A., and M. F. Hodges. 1986. Notes on a heronry in mainland Harrison County, Mississippi. *Miss. Kite* 16(2):46–47.

Toups, J. A., and J. A. Jackson. 1987. *Birds and birding on the Mississippi Coast.* Jackson: University Press of Mississippi.

Toups, J. A., and C. Roemer. 1982. A Ruff at Pascagoula: First Mississippi record. *Miss. Kite* 12(1):2–4.

Toups, J. A., M. F. Hodges, and P. V. Donaldson. 1979. Northern Phalarope at Pascagoula: First photographic record. *Miss. Kite* 9(1):9–10.

Toups, J. A., M. A. Baker, and D. King. 1984. Green-tailed Towhee sight record from Hancock County, Mississippi. *Miss. Kite* 14(1):7–8.

Toups, J. A., M. F. Hodges, and D. S. King. 1985a. Bridled Terns along the Mississippi Coast. *Miss. Kite* 15(2):16–17.

Toups, J. A., J. A. Jackson, and E. Johnson. 1985b. Black-shouldered Kite: Range expansion into Mississippi. *Am. Birds* 39:865–867.

Toups, J. A., C. Cassibry, R. Jeffrey, A. M. Jenkins, and L. Schultz. 1987. Observations of a Painted Redstart in Hancock County: First state record. *Miss. Kite* 17(2):24–26.

Townsend, C. W. 1926. The European Starling in Mississippi and in Florida. *Auk* 43:371.

Turcotte, W. H. 1948. The fox situation. *Mississippi Game and Fish* 11(8):3–7.

Turcotte, W. H., ed. 1956. Account of first annual meeting of MOS. *MOS Newsletter* 1(1):1–2.

Turcotte, W. H. 1957a. Long-eared Owl. *MOS Newsletter* 2(1):3.

Turcotte, W. H., ed. 1957b. Man-o'-war-bird or Frigatebird. *MOS Newsletter* 2(2):2.

Turcotte, W. H. 1957c. Tishomingo County trip. *MOS Newsletter* 2(2):1–2.

Turcotte, W. H., ed. 1958a. Early woodcock nesting record. *MOS Newsletter* 3(1):3–4.

Turcotte, W. H., ed. 1958b. Western Tanager. *MOS Newsletter* 3(1):3.

Turcotte, W. H. 1958c. Redstart nesting. *MOS Newsletter* 3(2):3.

Turcotte, W. H. 1958d. Bird islands off the Mississippi Gulf Coast. *Mississippi Game and Fish* 21(12):4–5, 8.

Turcotte, W. H., ed. 1960a. Evening Grosbeaks. *MOS Newsletter* 5(3):2.

Turcotte, W. H. 1960b. Hooded Merganser breeding record. *MOS Newsletter* 5(4):6.

Turcotte, W. H., ed. 1960c. Red-throated Loon and Western Kingbird. *MOS Newsletter* 5(5):8.

Turcotte, W. H. 1961a. Further extension of Barn Swallow breeding range. *MOS Newsletter* 6(5):9.

Turcotte, W. H., ed. 1961b. Glaucous Gull collected near Pascagoula. *MOS Newsletter* 6(1):7.

Turcotte, W. H. 1961c. Horned Lark breeding record established in Yazoo County. *MOS Newsletter* 6(4):5.

Turcotte, W. H., ed. 1961d. Letter to the editor. *MOS Newsletter* 6(5):3–4.

Turcotte, W. H., ed. 1961e. New state record: Black-necked Stilt. *MOS Newsletter* 6(1):7.

Turcotte, W. H. 1961f. Sandhill Crane colony in Jackson County may be threatened by superhighway routing. *MOS Newsletter* 6(5):1–2.

Turcotte, W. H., ed. 1961g. White-fronted Goose. *MOS Newsletter* 6(1):7.

Turcotte, W. H. 1962a. Mist-netting for birds. *Mississippi Game and Fish* 24(11):8–9.

Turcotte, W. H. 1962b. Yellow-throated Vireo nesting. *MOS Newsletter* 7(3):15.

Turcotte, W. H., ed. 1963a. In memoriam: Sterling Gene Clawson. *MOS Newsletter* 8(1):1.

Turcotte, W. H., ed. 1963b. Fall and winter Gulf Coast notes. *MOS Newsletter* 8(1):6–7.

Turcotte, W. H. 1963c. Spring migrant plovers. *MOS Newsletter* 8(2):11–12.

Turcotte, W. H. 1963d. Worm-eating Warbler breeding record. *MOS Newsletter* 8(3):15–16.

Turcotte, W. H. 1964. Short-eared Owls. *MOS Newsletter* 9(1):1.

Turcotte, W. H. 1965a. Brown Pelicans extirpated on Gulf Coast? *MOS Newsletter* 10(1):2–4.

Turcotte, W. H., ed. 1965b. Banding work on the coast and Gulf Coast notes. *MOS Newsletter* 10(1):4–5.

Turcotte, W. H. 1965c. MOS field notes. *Miss. Kite* 1(1):13–15.

Turcotte, W. H. 1966a. Christmas count—Jackson area. *MOS Newsletter* 11(1):4.

Turcotte, W. H. 1966b. T.V. tower bird fallout: October 1–2, 1965. *MOS Newsletter* 11(1):1–2.

Turcotte, W. H., ed. 1966c. Yellow-headed Blackbird: Coast record. *MOS Newsletter* 11(1):2.

Turcotte, W. H. 1966d. Last spring nesting records. *MOS Newsletter* 11(1):5.

Turcotte, W. H., ed. 1967a. Spring field trip. *MOS Newsletter* 12(2):2.

Turcotte, W. H. 1967b. Surf Scoters recorded on Ross Barnett Reservoir. *MOS Newsletter* 12(1):3.

Turcotte, W. H., ed. 1968a. Cattle Egrets nesting. *MOS Newsletter* 13(3):7–8.

Turcotte, W. H., ed. 1968b. Roseate Spoonbills at Noxubee Refuge. *MOS Newsletter* 13(1):2.

Turcotte, W. H., ed. 1971a. Anhinga. *MOS Newsletter* 16(3):6–7.

Turcotte, W. H. 1971b. June breeding bird surveys, 1966–1970. *MOS Newsletter* 16(3):5, appendix 1.

Turcotte, W. H. 1971c. A large hawk migration. *MOS Newsletter* 16(4):1–2.
Turcotte, W. H. 1971d. The Mississippi Sandhill Crane. *Mississippi Game and Fish* 34(4):3–6.
Turcotte, W. H. 1972a. Sandhill Cranes recent visitors in Delta. *MOS Newsletter* 17(1):2.
Turcotte, W. H. 1972b. A Scissor-tailed Flycatcher record. *Miss. Kite* 2(2):32.
Turcotte, W. H. 1972c. Western Grebe sight record. *MOS Newsletter* 17(5):25.
Turcotte, W. H. 1972d. The breeding biology and distribution of the Swainson's Warbler in Mississippi. *Miss. Kite* 2(1):2–13.
Turcotte, W. H., ed. 1972e. Ani on Gulf Coast, Harrison County. *MOS Newsletter* 17(3):13.
Turcotte, W. H. 1972f. Nesting record of the Worm-eating Warbler in Mississippi. *Miss. Kite* 2(2):33–39.
Turcotte, W. H., ed. 1973. Evening Grosbeak incursion. *MOS Newsletter* 18(1):2.
Turcotte, W. H. 1974a. On the behavior of the Horned Lark. *Miss. Kite* 4(1):12–13.
Turcotte, W. H. 1974b. Crane endangered: Mississippi Sandhill Crane. *Miss. Kite* 4(1):14.
Turcotte, W. H. 1975a. Breeding range extension of the Cliff Swallow. *MOS Newsletter* 20(3):21–22.
Turcotte, W. H. 1975b. White Ibis rookery—Warren County. *MOS Newsletter* 20(3):18.
Turcotte, W. H. 1975c. Successful eagle nesting on Mississippi Coast. *Miss. Kite* 5(1):14–15.
Turcotte, W. H. 1977. A second locality nesting record of the Scissor-tailed Flycatcher in Mississippi. *Miss. Kite* 7(2):33.
Turcotte, W. H. 1978. Nesting of the Dickcissel in Hinds County. *Miss. Kite* 8(2):37–39.
Turcotte, W. H. 1981. A White-eyed Vireo feeding Brown-headed Cowbird young of different ages. *Miss. Kite* 11(1):14.
Turcotte, W. H., and M. Hutto. 1991. Nesting of the House Finch in downtown Jackson, Mississippi. *Miss. Kite* 21(2):36–38.
Turcotte, W. H., and J. H. Phares. 1967. Some miscellaneous spring notes. *MOS Newsletter* 12(2):3.
Vaiden, M. G. 1939. Notes on birds of Mississippi. *Migrant* 10:44–46.
Vaiden, M. G. 1940. Further notes on Mississippi birds. *Migrant* 11:35–37.
Vaiden, M. G. 1943. Notes on Mississippi birds. *Migrant* 14:50–52.
Vaiden, M. G. 1947. Some Bolivar County, Mississippi, birds. *Migrant* 18:33–38.
Vaiden, M. G. 1948. Additional records of birds from Bolivar County, Mississippi. *Migrant* 19:61–64.
Vaiden, M. G. 1952a. Some birds of the Yazoo-Mississippi Delta. *Migrant* 23:1–4.
Vaiden, M. G. 1952b. Additional birds of the Yazoo-Mississippi Delta. *Migrant* 23:66–67.
Vaiden, M. G. 1953a. Interesting Bolivar County, Mississippi, birds. *Migrant* 24:74–76.
Vaiden, M. G. 1953b. Notes on Bolivar County, Mississippi, birds. *Migrant* 24:8–10.
Vaiden, M. G. 1960. Additional birds of the Yazoo-Mississippi Delta. *Mississippi Delta Naturalist's Club, Occasional Papers* 1(2).
Valentine, J. M. 1963. The status of the Florida Sandhill Crane in Jackson County, Mississippi. Atlanta, Ga: U.S. Bureau of Sport Fisheries and Wildlife.
Valentine, J. M. 1971. Field observations: Yellow Rails. *MOS Newsletter* 16(2):2–3.
Valentine, J. M. 1984. Recovery plan for the Mississippi Sandhill Crane, *Grus canadensis pulla*. Rev. ed. Atlanta, Ga.: U.S. Fish and Wildlife Service.
Valentine, J. M., and R. E. Noble. 1970. A colony of Sandhill Cranes in Mississippi. *J. Wildl. Manage.* 34:761–768.
Wailes, B. L. C. 1854. Aves, or birds. In *Report on the agriculture and geology of Mississippi*, 317–327. Jackson, Miss.: State Printer.
Walkinshaw, L. H. 1949. The Sandhill Cranes. *Cranbrook Inst. Sci. Bull.* No. 29.
Walkinshaw, L. H. 1960. Some Mississippi Crane notes. *Migrant* 31:41–43.
Warren, R. C., and G. A. Hurst. 1979. A nest record for the American Goldfinch in Mississippi. *Miss. Kite* 9(2):35.
Warren, R. C., J. A. Jackson, and T. L. Darden. 1977. Nesting of the Red Crossbill in Mississippi. *Am. Birds* 31:1100.
Warriner, B. R. 1935. Notes from Corinth, Mississippi. *Migrant* 6:35.
Warriner, B. R. 1936. Tree Sparrow at Corinth, Mississippi. *Migrant* 7:12,21.
Warriner, B. R. 1944. Notes from Corinth, Mississippi. *Migrant* 15:29.
Warriner, B. R. 1945. Prairie Horned Larks at Corinth, Mississippi. *Migrant* 16:45.
Warriner, B. R. 1962. Limpkin at Corinth, Mississippi. *Migrant* 33:20.
Weber, W. C., comp. 1977. Summary of Mississippi Christmas bird counts, 1976–77. *Miss. Kite* 7(1):24–27.
Weber, W. C., comp. 1978a. Summary of Mississippi Christmas bird counts, 1977–78. *Miss. Kite* 8(1):14–17.
Weber, W. C. 1978b. Red-throated Loon sightings on Ship and Horn islands, Mississippi. *Miss. Kite* 8(1):10–11.
Weber, W. C. 1979a. A Brant on East Ship Island: First record for Mississippi. *Miss. Kite* 9(1):10–11.
Weber, W. C. 1979b. Recent notes on the Cliff Swallow in Mississippi. *Miss. Kite* 9(1):7–9.
Weber, W. C. 1979c. Bird species of casual or accidental occurrence in Mississippi: Partial list of records. Unpublished manuscript. Jackson: Mississippi Museum of Natural Science Library.
Weber, W. C. 1979d. Summary of Mississippi Christmas bird counts, 1978–79. *MOS Newsletter* 24(1):1–3.

Weber, W. C. 1983. A comparison of mainland and island pine-forest bird communities in coastal Mississippi. Ph.D. diss., Mississippi State University.

Weber, W. C., and J. A. Jackson. 1977a. First nesting record of Gray Kingbirds in Mississippi. *Miss. Kite* 7(1):10–12.

Weber, W. C., and J. A. Jackson, comps. 1977b. Birds around the state: Spring migration and breeding season, 1977. *Miss. Kite* 7(2):42–53.

Weber, W. C., and J. A. Jackson, comps. 1978. Birds around the state: Fall migration, 1977. *Miss. Kite* 8(1):19–27.

Weber, W. C., L. J. Gates, R. P. Russell, and J. A. Toups. 1978. Black-necked Stilt: A new breeding species for Mississippi. *Miss. Kite* 8(1):2–6.

Weber, W. C., L. J. Gates, J. A. Toups, and G. Neubauer. 1979. Western Wood-Pewee at Bellefontaine Beach, Mississippi. *Miss. Kite* 9(1):12–13.

Webster, B. S. 1971. Scarlet Tanager. *MOS Newsletter* 16(1):6.

Whittington, R. L. 1980. Mountain Bluebird near Grenada, Mississippi. *Miss. Kite* 10(1):6–7.

Williams, L. E. 1962a. Eared Grebe and Black-legged Kittiwake at Pascagoula, Mississippi. *MOS Newsletter* 7(3):14.

Williams, L. E. 1962b. Notes on nesting of certain coastal birds in Mississippi. *MOS Newsletter* 7(4):17–20.

Williams, L. E. 1962c. An offshore boat trip in Mississippi waters (Gannets and Parasitic Jaegers observed and specimens collected). *MOS Newsletter* 7(2):8–9.

Williams, L. E. 1962d. White-fronted Goose and Franklin Gull in Mississippi. *MOS Newsletter* 7(2):8.

Williams, L. E. 1965. Banding work on the coast and Gulf Coast notes. *MOS Newsletter* 10(1):4.

Williams, L. E., and S. G. Clawson. 1960. Summer notes from the Gulf Coast. *MOS Newsletter* 5(5):1–5.

Williams, L. E., and S. G. Clawson. 1963. First specimens of ten species of birds for Mississippi. *Auk* 80:199–201.

Wilson, A. 1832. *American ornithology.* London: Cassell, Petter and Galpin.

Woodson, S. A., and S. M. McClellan. 1981. Audubon's Caracara: First Mississippi record. *Miss. Kite* 11(1):13–14.

Index

Inclusive page numbers are given for orders, families, and subfamilies at the scientific name. Page references for species accounts appear at scientific and common name entries; those for other in-text mentions appear only at the common name entry. References to illustrations are printed in boldface type.

Names formerly used on a wide scale are given in parentheses after the common name. Colloquial names, given in quotation marks, are usually followed by the common name and all pertinent page references; those requiring separate listings are followed by *See* references.